East Africa

Mary Fitzpatrick
Tom Parkinson, Nick Ray

MURCHISON FALLS (p541)
The world's most powerful waterfall, with hippos, crocodiles and elephants nearby

SOURCE OF THE NILE (p493)
Top-notch white-water rafting, kayaking, bungee jumping and quad biking at East Africa's adrenaline centre

KAKAMEGA FR (p406)
A sublime slab of the once mighty Guineo-Congolian tropical rainforest

MT KENYA (p376)
Tremendous trekking past equatorial glaciers and jagged peaks

LAMU ARCHIPELAGO (p341)
The ultimate Swahili immersion experience, from Lamu's winding streets to the empty beaches of Kiwayu

MT KILIMANJARO (p175)
Challenging trekking on East Africa's highest peak

PARC NATIONAL DES VOLCANS (p583)
The original *Gorillas in the Mist* backdrop spread across the wild slopes of the Virunga volcanoes

LAKE BUNYONI (p528)
A breathtakingly beautiful lake, surrounded by stunning landscapes and ideal for relaxing

**SERENGETI NP (p193) &
MASAI MARA NR (p393)**
Unmatched wildlife and the world's
most fascinating traffic jam –
the annual wildebeest migration

USAMBARA MOUNTAINS (p165)
Village-to-village hiking along
shaded forest footpaths

ZANZIBAR ARCHIPELAGO (p128)
Picture-perfect beaches and
exotic Stone Town

SOUTHEASTERN TANZANIA (p236)
A palm-fringed coastline and centuries of
Swahili history and culture

NGORONGORO CRATER (p199)
Ethereal blue-green vistas and
wildlife galore

INDIAN

OCEAN

MOMBASA

DAR ES SALAAM

DODOMA

TANZANIA

BURUNDI

DEMOCRATIC
REPUBLIC OF
THE CONGO

ZAMBIA

MALAWI

ELEVATION

3000m
2000m
1000m
500m
250m
0

LEGEND

FR   Forest Reserve
GR   Game Reserve
NP   National Park
NR   Nature Reserve

Primary
Secondary
Tertiary
Unsealed

150 km
90 miles

Destination East Africa

Stampeding wildebeest, a snow-capped mountain on the equator, paradisiacal beaches and an amazing array of tribal cultures – all this and more await you in East Africa, one of the continent's most enticing corners.

Here you'll find the exotic offshore archipelagos of Zanzibar (Tanzania) and Lamu (Kenya), with their long Swahili roots; mountain gorillas cavorting beneath misty inland peaks in the Virunga highlands (Rwanda and DR Congo); seething white-waters at the source of the Nile (Uganda); idyllic lakeshore panoramas (Burundi); and a stellar collection of national parks. Amid all this natural magnificence is the everyday beauty and vibrancy of African life: swerving Kenyan *matatus* (minibuses) filled to bursting and careening through the streets of Nairobi; street hawkers peddling their wares; the Lake Tanganyika steamer chugging along the shoreline, its decks lively with people and produce.

Then there are the many contrasts: humble thatched huts shadowed by luxurious safari lodges; red-cloaked Maasai warriors sitting beside office workers in Western dress; bustling, cosmopolitan cities fringed by dusty villages where the nearest primary school is two hours' walk away.

Somewhere amidst all this diversity and contradiction is the 'real' East Africa, with something on offer for almost every interest and budget. Major towns offer a wide range of accommodation and dining options, the transport infrastructure is reasonable, international flight connections are good, and there's the advantage that you can make your way in most areas speaking English. Best of all – thanks in part to centuries of history during which outsiders have arrived and been assimilated – is the warmth of East Africa's welcome, with its people and cultures likely to continue beckoning long after you've completed your travels.

GREG EL

Highlights

Enjoy the vibrant colours of the Maasai women's traditional dress, Masai Mara National Reserve (p393), Kenya

DAVID WALL

Recreate your own *Gorillas in the Mist* experience, Democratic Republic of the Congo (p559)

OTHER HIGHLIGHTS

- Check out Murchison Falls (p541) – the world's most powerful waterfalls – on a wildlife-watching bonanza on a boat up the Victoria Nile, Uganda
- Learn more about the horrors of Rwanda's past at Kigali Memorial Centre (p576) – a haunting genocide memorial in the capital, Rwanda

ARIADNE VAN ZANDBERGEN

Be amazed by the volume of wildlife in Serengeti National Park (p193), Tanzania

DAVID W

Make an appointment with a witch doctor from Kikuyu tribe (p50), Kenya

Scale Miziyagembi Peak and hike village-to-village through the Usambara Mountains (p165), Tanzania

DAVID ELSE

MITCH REARDON

Chill out with the vultures while the sun sets in Masai Mara National Reserve (p393), Kenya

Click away at the unparalleled concentrations of wildlife in Ngorongoro Crater (p199), Tanzania

MASON FLORENCE

OTHER HIGHLIGHTS

- Get down to some monkey business in the towering Parc National Nyungwe Forest (p591) with a visit to the huge troops of colobus, Rwanda
- Hit the best inland beaches in Africa for some fun in the sun at Saga Beach (p612), Burundi

JOHN HAY

Get close to a flock of stunning greater flamingos, Ngorongoro Crater (p199), Tanzania

Spy on elephants taking a drink in Queen Elizabeth National Park (p520), Uganda

DAVID WALL

DENNIS JOHN

Relive centuries of trade on a dhow in Zanzibar (p130), Tanzania

Come face to face with the 'king of the jungle' (p62), Kenya

ALEX DISSANAYAKE

Experience Swahili culture at its best at Lamu (p341), a World Heritage site, Kenya

ARIADNE VAN ZANDBERGEN

Contents

Regional Map Contents

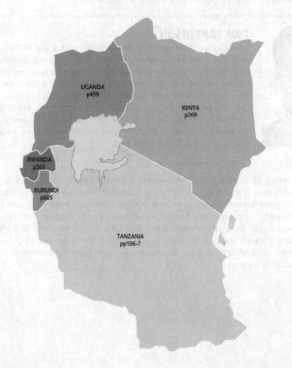

UGANDA
p459

KENYA
p268

RWANDA
p566

BURUNDI
p605

TANZANIA
pp106–7

The Authors

MARY FITZPATRICK   Coordinating Author, Tanzania

Originally from Washington, DC, Mary set off after graduate studies for several years in Europe. Her fascination with languages and cultures soon led her further south to sub-Saharan Africa, where she has spent much of the past decade living and working, including extended periods in Tanzania. She has authored and coauthored numerous guidebooks on East Africa and elsewhere on the continent, speaks Swahili and is convinced she holds an unofficial record for kilometres travelled in buses along East Africa's roads. Mary works as a full-time travel writer from her home base in Cairo, from where she continues to journey frequently to the land of Kilimanjaro.

Life on the Road

When on assignment in East Africa, life tends to revolve around transport. Travelling from Lindi to Mtwara one afternoon, all the buses had left for the day. After finding a pick-up truck and willing driver, we set off, rattling past the sunbaked palm- and baobab-studded landscapes so typical of this part of the continent. About 30km before Mtwara, the petrol tank ran dry. The driver, seeking to maximise his profit from our arrangement, hadn't wanted to splurge on an extra litre. A man pedalled past on his bicycle, and I was soon perched behind him, moving slowly closer to Mtwara. About 10km onwards – and happily for all concerned – I managed to find a lift, sent someone to bring petrol to the still-stranded driver and another day's travel in East Africa came to an end.

TOM PARKINSON   Kenya

Tom's association with East Africa began with a trip to Tanzania in his student days, and he has returned regularly as an author, handling two successive editions of *Kenya*. For his latest adventure he swapped the safari interior for the somewhat different delights of Nairobi and the coast, and also took time out to work on the Zanzibar International Film Festival, mixing literary debates and cultural appreciation with some hefty beach parties. Having worked extensively in North and Central Africa for Lonely Planet, Tom is no stranger to the myriad rhythms of African life, but finds Kenya keeps giving him reasons to come back.

Life on the Road

Thanks to the openness of its people and the diversity of its landscapes, Kenya has a habit of throwing up surprising experiences – at some point in my various trips here I've been stranded in the desert near Lake Turkana, gone tuxedo shopping at local markets, run away from elephants in bamboo forests, chatted with Swahili ex-professional footballers on quiet islands, dodged potholes and punctures on 10,000km of roads and danced the night away with Lamu's civil servants. Of all the things that made an impression, though, the one I'll never forget is seeing the moon rise bright orange over Mt Kenya as the glaciers cracked and groaned 50ft away: awesome, unearthly, and even with an altitude headache, a memory to treasure.

NICK RAY   Burundi, Rwanda, Uganda & Detour: Democratic Republic of the Congo

A Londoner of sorts, Nick comes from Watford, the sort of town that makes you want to travel. Nick has travelled through many countries in Africa over the years – including the southern stunner that is Mozambique, and Morocco with all its northern mystique – but it is Uganda and Rwanda that he finds to be small but perfectly formed. He relished the chance to return for another round of towering volcanoes, plentiful primates and blessed beers from Kampala to Kigali. He also managed some hit and runs on Burundi and DR Congo, fascinating countries emerging from their tortured pasts. Nick currently lives in Phnom Penh, Cambodia and has worked on more than 20 titles for Lonely Planet.

Life on the Road

Hitting the DR Congo for a couple of days was one hell of a trip. I barely scraped the surface, as you could easily fit 100 or more Rwandas into this vast heart of Africa, but I what I saw gave me cause for hope. The gorillas, the jungle, the volcanoes, the people and their music – the rest of the world doesn't realise what it has been missing. The beaches in Burundi are blissful and I had a fine afternoon watching locals try their luck on surfboards. Rwanda is hauntingly beautiful and easy to explore, but most people associate it with death and suffering. Memories of the genocide are everywhere, but none more poignant or better expressed than the Kigali Memorial Centre. And Uganda, what a place! The best of Africa packed into one little country. Track gorillas and chimps, chill out in Bunyoni, up the adrenaline in Jinja and join the Kampala nightshift for one of the best rumbles outside the jungle.

CONTRIBUTING AUTHOR

Dr Caroline Evans wrote the Health chapter. Caroline studied medicine at the University of London, and completed General Practice training in Cambridge. She is the medical adviser to Nomad Travel Clinic, a private travel health clinic in London, and is also a GP specialising in travel medicine. She has been an expedition doctor for Raleigh International and Coral Cay expeditions.

LONELY PLANET AUTHORS

Why is our travel information the best in the world? It's simple: our authors are independent, dedicated travellers. They don't research using just the Internet or phone, and they don't take freebies in exchange for positive coverage. They travel widely, to all the popular spots and off the beaten track. They personally visit thousands of hotels, restaurants, cafés, bars, galleries, palaces, museums and more – and they take pride in getting all the details right, and telling it how it is. For more, see the authors section on www.lonelyplanet.com.

Getting Started

East Africa has a wide selection of hotels and restaurants in tourist areas and major towns, plus some of Africa's most elite safari lodges and luxury tented camps. If you're on a midrange or top-end budget, travel here is Africa made easy, with just enough adventure to keep things satisfying.

If you're travelling on a shoestring, things get more rugged. Expect to stay in basic guesthouses, and to put in time bumping over rough roads on crowded buses. The rewards: getting into the pulse of East Africa, and seeing how most locals live.

Whatever your style, there's plenty to keep you busy – mountain trekking, wildlife safaris, up-close encounters with our primate relatives, moss-covered ruins, palm-fringed beaches and much more. Costs range from high, for people staying in upscale safari lodges (especially in Tanzania, which is generally the most expensive destination in the region), to modest, for those living local style.

If you don't have time pressures it's quite easy to set your itinerary as you go, but, especially for safaris and treks, you'll get better quality and prices by doing some advance planning. When charting your route, remember that East Africa is large; it's much better to concentrate on one or two areas, than to try and cover too much distance in one visit. Major destinations are connected by reasonably good air connections and reliable (albeit often gruelling) bus routes, but you'll need plenty of time to cover the often long distances.

WHEN TO GO

See p622 for climate charts

The main tourist seasons are the hotter, drier months of mid-December through January, and the cool, dry months from June to August, although the region can be visited at any time of year. For more information on climate in the region see p621, and check individual country chapters for more detailed Climate and When to Go sections.

During the long rains (roughly March through May), things are much quieter: there are few tourists, accommodation prices come down, and some places close completely. While main routes in most areas remain

---

DON'T LEAVE HOME WITHOUT...

You can buy almost anything you'll need in Nairobi, Dar es Salaam and Kampala, except specialist trekking and sporting equipment, and certain toiletries such as contact lens solution. However, especially outside of Nairobi, choice is limited and prices high. Some things to bring from home:

- binoculars for wildlife watching
- torch (flashlight)
- mosquito repellent and net (p644)
- zoom lens for wildlife shots (p627)
- light, rubber-soled shoes for beach walking
- sleeping bag and waterproof gear for trekking
- sturdy water bottle
- travel insurance (p625)
- wind- and waterproof jacket, especially for highland areas.

CUTTING COSTS

Whatever your budget, the following are some tips if you're trying to cut costs while travelling in East Africa.

■ Travel in the low season.

■ Always ask about children's discounts.

■ Travel in a group (four is ideal) for organised treks and safaris.

■ Keep your schedule flexible to take advantage of last minute deals.

■ Carry a tent, and camp whenever possible.

■ Focus on easily accessed parks and reserves to minimise transportation costs.

■ Use public transport.

■ Eat local food.

■ Stock up on food and drink in major towns to avoid expensive hotel fare and pricey shops in tourist areas and national parks.

■ Offer to pay in cash – sometimes this may result in a discount if you ask.

passable, secondary roads are often closed, especially in parts of Uganda and Tanzania. You can expect to get drenched for at least a few hours each day, and it will be too muddy in many areas for hiking, but everything will be beautifully green.

Particularly in Kenya and Tanzania, watch out for peak-season hotel prices around the Christmas-New Year holidays, and during the July-August high season.

COSTS & MONEY

Travel in East Africa is considerably more expensive than in Asia or India and you'll need to work to stick to a shoestring budget. That said, it's quite possible to get by on limited funds, and in so doing you'll be able to immerse yourself more fully into local life. At the other end of the spectrum, East Africa has some of the most expensive lodges and hotels to be found anywhere, with all the corresponding comforts. Tanzania is the most expensive country in the region for travel, followed by Rwanda, Kenya and Uganda. Burundi's delicate political situation gives it a special status, and accommodation is generally expensive, thanks in part to the large UN presence in the country.

At the budget level throughout the region, plan on spending from about US$20 to US$25 per day – that's staying at budget guesthouses, eating mostly local food, travelling primarily with local transport and excluding safaris and other organised activities. For midrange hotels, Western-style meals and more travel comfort, a realistic budget would start at around US$60 per day, excluding 'extras' such as park entrance fees, visa fees, the price of vehicle rentals or safaris, plus any airfares. Top-end luxury lodge travel costs anywhere from US$150 to US$400 or more per person per day, with prices at the upper end of this spectrum usually for all-inclusive safari packages.

For more money issues, including how to access and carry it, see p625.

READING UP
Books

Peter Matthiessen's *The Tree Where Man Was Born* offers a timeless portrayal of life on the East African plains.

The classic *Out of Africa* by Karen Blixen is one European's nostalgic perspective on life in colonial-era Kenya. For a more recent and realistic take, look for David Bennun's *Tick Bite Fever*.

Green Hills of Africa by Ernest Hemingway and *Death in the Long Grass* by Peter Hathaway Capstick chronicle the days of African big game hunting. Another title by Hemingway – *The Snows of Kilimanjaro* – deals with some of the larger questions of life in an East African setting.

Among the many beautiful coffee table books that will whet your appetite for travels in the region are *Africa Adorned* by Angela Fisher and *Africa's Great Rift Valley* by Nigel Pavitt.

The Ukimwi Road: From Kenya to Zimbabwe by inimitable Dervla Murphy is a sobering though highly readable chronicle of the author's bicycle journey through the ever-present reality of AIDS in East and southern Africa.

Websites

Afrol.com (www.afrol.com) African news and current affairs.

ArtMatters (www.artmatters.info) Focuses on Kenyan arts, but also has excellent regional cultural links.

East Africa Living Encyclopedia (www.africa.upenn.edu/NEH/neh.html) Part of the University of Pennsylvania's African Studies Center, with country information and lots of links.

Integrated Regional Information Network (www.irinnews.org) Regional news and humanitarian issues.

Kamusi Project (www.yale.edu/swahili/) A 'living' online Swahili dictionary, plus East Africa links.

Lonely Planet (www.lonelyplanet.com) Travel tips, the Thorn Tree bulletin board and helpful links to other sites.

Pambazuka (www.pambazuka.org) Articles on regional and continent-wide social and humanitarian issues.

MUST-SEE MOVIES

East Africa's stunning panoramas and turbulent human history have featured in many films. There are quite a few to look for before setting off.

Hotel Rwanda (2004) is the real-life story of a Rwandan Hutu who sheltered hundreds of refugees in his four-star hotel during the outbreak of the Rwandan genocide; see p571 for more about this film.

FAVOURITE FESTIVALS & EVENTS

The best festivals and events are often the unannounced ones, such as a small-town wedding, a rite of passage celebration, or local market day. Larger-scale happenings include the following.

- The Serengeti–Masai Mara wildebeest migration – one of Earth's greatest natural spectacles (see p193).

- Zanzibar International Film Festival – taking place in Zanzibar around July, and part of the Festival of the Dhow Countries, this is East Africa's major cultural gathering (see p253).

- Sauti za Busara Swahili Music Festival – a celebration of all things Swahili, held around February in Zanzibar, and featuring artists from throughout East Africa (see p253).

- Maulid – marking the birthday of the Prophet Mohammed, best seen on Lamu in Kenya (see p353).

- Eid al-Fitr – the end of Ramadan fasting, and especially colourful on Zanzibar and elsewhere along the coast (see p624).

- Kenya Music Festival – Kenya's longest-running music festival, held in Nairobi over 10 days in August (see p286).

CONDUCT IN EAST AFRICA

East Africa comfortably mixes a generally conservative outlook on life with a great deal of tolerance and openness towards foreigners, and meeting locals is one of the highlights of regional travel. The following are a few tips to smooth the way.

- While most East Africans will probably be too polite to tell you so directly, they'll be privately shaking their head about travellers doing things like not wearing enough clothing or sporting tatty clothes. Especially along the Muslim coast, cover up the shoulders and legs, and avoid plunging necklines, skin-tight fits and the like.

- Pleasantries count! Even if you're just asking for directions, take time to greet the other person. Handshake etiquette is also worth learning, and best picked up by observation. In many areas, East Africans often continue holding hands for several minutes after meeting, or even throughout an entire conversation.

- Don't eat or pass things with the left hand.

- Respect authority; losing your patience or undermining an official's authority will get you nowhere, while deference and a good-natured demeanour will see you through most situations.

- Avoid criticising the government of your host country, and avoid offending locals with public nudity, open anger and displays of affection (between people of the same or opposite sex).

- When visiting a rural area, seek out the chief or local elders to announce your presence, and ask permission before setting up a tent or wandering through a village – it will rarely be refused.

- Receive gifts with both hands, or with the right hand while touching the left hand to your right elbow. When giving a gift, don't be surprised if the appreciation isn't expressed verbally.

Showcasing magnificent footage of the cycle of life on the Serengeti plains, *Africa – The Serengeti* (1994) features the annual wildebeest migration.

Kilimanjaro: To the Roof of Africa (2002) is a gripping preview of what is to come if you're contemplating climbing the mountain (p175), and a good armchair adventure if you're not.

The film version of Karen Blixen's classic book (see p17), *Out of Africa* (1985) is notable primarily for its evocative locational footage of Kenya. Another classic, *Born Free* (1966), is a family-friendly film, set in Kenya and focused around hand-rearing a lion cub, that still forms many Westerners' first ideas about East Africa.

Nowhere in Africa (2002) is the absorbing tale of a Jewish family who flee Nazi Germany to settle in colonial-era Kenya and *Keepers of Memory* (2004) is a moving look at the Rwandan genocide through the eyes of survivors; see p567 for more on this subject.

Maasai: The Rain Warriors (2005) is a somewhat contrived but intriguing look at a group of Maasai as they walk across Kenya to track down a legendary lion and thus break a drought.

RESPONSIBLE TRAVEL

Tourism is big business in East Africa, especially in Tanzania and Kenya. The following are a few guidelines for minimising strain on the local environment. For tips on etiquette, see above, and for more on deforestation and other environmental problems where tourist behaviour can have an impact, see p80.

- Support local enterprise.
- Buy souvenirs directly from those who make them.
- Choose safari and trekking operators that treat local communities as equal partners, and that are committed to protecting local ecosystems.

'Always ask permission before photographing people'

- For cultural attractions, try to pay fees directly to the locals involved, rather than to tour company guides or other middlemen.
- Always ask permission before photographing people.
- Avoid indiscriminate gift giving; donations to recognised projects are more sustainable and have a better chance of reaching those who need them most.
- Don't buy items made from ivory, skin, shells, etc.
- Save natural resources, especially water and wood, and don't take hot showers if the water is heated by firewood. To wash yourself or your clothing, fill a container with water and carry it elsewhere to avoid polluting the source.
- Respect local culture and customs.
- Don't litter! On treks, in parks or when camping, carry out all your litter, and leave trails, parks and campsites cleaner than you found them.
- A major danger in parks, especially in Kenya, is land degradation resulting from too many vehicles crisscrossing the countryside. Keep to the tracks when on safari (or encourage your driver to do so).

Itineraries
CLASSIC ROUTES

BEACH & BUSH
Two to Three Weeks

This classic beach and bush combination mixes wildlife watching *par excellence* with postcard-perfect beaches and the allure of Swahili culture, plus the chance for detours in between. You can squeeze in the essential destinations in as little as a week (albeit very pressed), but two to three weeks will allow you to explore at a more leisurely pace and to include some detours. Fly into **Nairobi** (p278), from where you can head off for a safari in either the **Masai Mara National Reserve** (p393) or **Amboseli National Park** (p300). Alternatively, make your way overland from Nairobi to **Arusha** (p178) for a safari in **Serengeti National Park** (p193) and **Ngorongoro Crater** (p199).

After getting a taste of the wildlife, head eastwards to the coast. In Kenya, not-to-miss destinations include **Lamu** (p341) and the ruins at **Gede** (p334). In Tanzania, the **Zanzibar Archipelago** (p128) is the highlight, and an ideal base for diving, snorkelling and relaxing, plus taking in the charm and historical attractions of Zanzibar's old **Stone Town** (p133). When your time is up, fly out of **Dar es Salaam** (p114), Nairobi or Zanzibar, whichever is most convenient. With extra time in either Kenya or Tanzania, it's possible to take in a few more highlights en route between bush and beach, including hiking in Tanzania's cool, green Usambara Mountains around **Lushoto** (p166), trekking on **Mt Kilimanjaro** (p175) or – with a bit more detouring – visiting some of Kenya's Rift Valley lakes. Highlights here include **Lake Nakuru** (p364), **Lake Bogoria** (p366), **Lake Baringo** (p368) and the starkly beautiful and otherworldly **Lake Turkana** (p427), though you'll need several extra days for this.

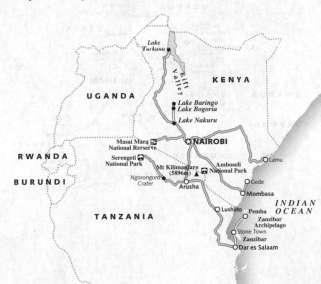

Wildlife and beaches have long been East Africa's top draws. This classic itinerary combines the best of both, and can be easily trimmed or extended, depending on the time at hand. Distance covered by this route is about 700km at a minimum, though it could be considerably lengthened to take advantage of all that's on offer.

EAST AFRICA OVERLAND   Three Months

For those with a bit of wanderlust, plenty of time, a tolerance for rugged travel and a desire to immerse themselves in local life, East Africa is an ideal destination for exploring on a classic overland route, either on a shoestring budget, or more upscale.

One possibility is to start off in Uganda, where – in addition to visiting as many national parks as you possibly can and going **gorilla tracking** (p100) – you can spend time in laid-back **Kampala** (p470), on the relaxing **Ssese Islands** (p537) or white-water rafting the **source of the Nile** (p495) close to **Jinja** (p491). Once you've had your fill, make your way via **Bukoba** (p207) and **Mwanza** (p202) on Lake Victoria to view wildlife galore at **Serengeti National Park** (p193) and then on to **Arusha** (p178). From Arusha, head south towards **Dodoma** (p220) and then eastwards to **Dar es Salaam** (p114) and the beautiful **Zanzibar Archipelago** (p128). From here, turn north to explore **Mombasa** (p309), with its fascinating Old Town, and the **Kenyan coast** (p309) with Malindi and Gede.

Once you've had enough of the sand and the sea, make your way inland until your time runs out, enjoying highlights such as a trek on Africa's second-highest mountain, **Mt Kenya** (p376), and the beautiful **Kakamega Forest Reserve** (p406), or detouring north for a **Lake Turkana** (p424) safari, including stops at **Maralal** (p425), **South Horr** (p427), **Loyangalani** (p428) and perhaps even **Marsabit** (p422). Depending where in Kenya fortune finds you when you've finished your travels, you can continue either to Kampala or **Nairobi** (p278) for a flight home. This itinerary can also be started in Nairobi, or done in reverse from Kampala – both alternatives are good options for those wanting more time in Kenya.

Whether you're a Gap-year traveller or a mid-life adventurer, following this classic overland route is one of the best ways to get into East Africa's pulse. You can make things as rough or luxurious as you wish. The main requirement for covering this approximately 3500km loop is time.

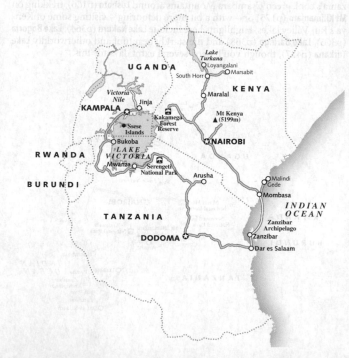

ROADS LESS TRAVELLED

RWANDA & BURUNDI SAMPLER   Two to Three Weeks

Rwanda and Burundi, although war-scarred, are topographically magnificent and culturally fascinating, and make rewarding destinations for intrepid and savvy travellers. If you're lucky enough to make it to these countries, a good first stop is **Kigali** (p572), with its lush, mountainous setting, resurgent nightlife and peppy atmosphere. Next, head southwest via **Butare** (p589) to **Parc National Nyungwe Forest** (p591), with its abundance of chimpanzees and other primates, and then via **Cyangugu** (p592) to the scenic inland beaches on Lake Kivu around **Kibuye** (p593) and **Gisenyi** (p586). From here, it's just a short hop on to **Ruhengeri** (p581) and the mountain gorillas of **Parc National des Volcans** (p583), and then back to Kigali. Alternatively (and security situation permitting) adventure over to **Parc National des Virungas** in Democratic Republic of the Congo (DR Congo; p561) for some gorilla tracking on the wild side. In Burundi, apart from **Bujumbura** (p607) – which makes an agreeable enough introduction to the country – the impressive **Chutes de la Kagera** (p612), near Rutana, are well worth a visit, as is **Gitega** (p612), Burundi's second-largest town. More rewarding destinations – only possible once the security situation stabilises – include **Parc National de la Rurubu** (p607), with its beautiful views, **Parc National de la Rusizi** (p607) near Bujumbura and **Parc National de la Kibira** (p607), with patches of rainforest. With time remaining, head from Burundi into Tanzania, or from Rwanda into Uganda, both of which have plenty to keep you busy.

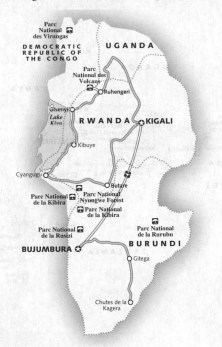

Long off the trodden trail, the lush, mountainous panoramas and vibrant cultures of these two East African gems will captivate anyone who ventures their way. Although it covers barely 400km, allow as much time as possible for this journey into the heart of Africa.

CONNOISSEUR'S CHOICE   One Month

If East Africa is your dreamed-of trip of a lifetime, and if the budget isn't too tight, here's an itinerary that will surely please the most discerning traveller. Fly first into **Nairobi** (p278), and after a night in a comfortable hotel acclimatising, head off on safari to **Masai Mara National Reserve** (p393), where one magnificent morning can be spent floating over the savanna, with your own bird's eye view of the giraffes from a **hot air balloon** (p393). Then head north to the central **Rift Valley lakes** (p356) – Baringo, Bogoria and Nakuru – where you can pamper yourself around **Lake Naivasha National Park** (p360) or stretch your legs in **Hell's Gate National Park** (p360). From here, journey westwards to Uganda to take in some of the parks before visiting the mountain gorillas in **Bwindi Impenetrable National Park** (p523) or, better still, across the border in Rwanda's **Parc National des Volcans** (p583). From here, make your way to **Arusha** (p178) in Tanzania, either overland via Lake Victoria or an easy flight from **Kigali** (p572). After catching your breath at one of the upscale lodges nearby, head off to explore some of Tanzania's national parks – **Arusha** (p188) and (in the dry season) **Tarangire National Parks** (p192) are both excellent choices if you don't have time for the **Serengeti** (p193). Other possibilities include a few days relaxing on the shores of **Lake Eyasi** (p201), or a couple of nights spent in one of the cosy highland lodges around **Karatu** (p199). To finish things up, head to the coast. In addition to the obvious destination – the **Zanzibar Archipelago** (p128) – consider spending time at the laid-back **Saadani Game Reserve** (p160), or relaxing either on the beaches around **Ushongo** (p162) or at one of the wonderful lodges overlooking **Mafia Island's Chole Bay** (p241).

Travelling in East Africa doesn't have to be rough. With purse strings that aren't too tight, a generous allotment of time and discerning taste, you can explore the region while indulging yourself in a series of classic safari camps and luxurious coastal lodges, many of which are destinations in themselves. The full circuit is about 2500km.

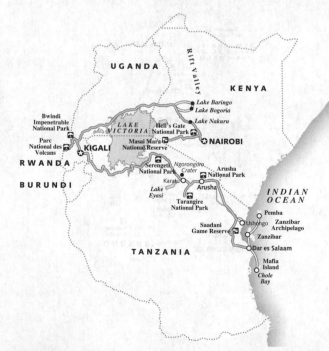

TAILORED TRIPS

SWAHILI SPECIAL

East Africa's Swahili heritage fuses influences past and present, African and Arabian, Indian, Asian and European, and delving in brings you on a fascinating journey through the continents and the centuries. The narrow streets of **Lamu** (p341) are an ideal place to start, followed by jaunts to **Paté** and nearby islands (p356). **Mombasa** (p309) with its fascinating old town; the mystery-shrouded ruins at **Gede** (p334); and the equally intriguing **Mnarani ruins** (p331) at Kilifi are other essential stops. **Zanzibar** (p130) and **Pemba** (p151) are worth as much time as you can spare, although to immerse yourself in things Swahili, you'll need to get away from the resorts and into the villages. Across the Zanzibar Channel is **Dar es Salaam** (p114), where modern-day urbanity is only a thin veneer over long Swahili roots. From here, it's an easy detour to **Bagamoyo** (p158) or **Pangani** (p161), both once major coastal ports. Alternatively, continue south to the ruins at **Kilwa Kisiwani** (p243) – silent witnesses to the days when this part of the coast was the centre of far-flung trading networks. Further south are pretty, palm-fringed **Lindi** (p244) and tiny **Mikindani** (p247), a charming Swahili village. Time remaining? Follow old trade caravan routes inland to **Tabora** (p211), and to **Ujiji** (p216), with its Swahili-style houses and flourishing tradition of dhow building.

WORLD HERITAGE SITES

For an unforgettable sampling of East Africa's wildlife, culture and history, plan a trip focused on Unesco World Heritage sites. In Tanzania, move from the snowy heights of **Mt Kilimanjaro** (p175) to the plains of the **Serengeti** (p193) and the varied expanses of the **Ngorongoro Conservation Area** (p197), before heading into the wilds of **Selous Game Reserve** (p236) and on to the coast. Here, the ruins at **Kilwa Kisiwani** (p244) and **Songo Mnara** (p244) carry you back into the centuries, while the winding, cobbled alleyways of Zanzibar's **Stone Town** (p133) draw you deeper into history with every turn.

In Kenya, divide your time between fascinating **Lamu Old Town** (p341), with its well-preserved Swahili lifestyle and time-warp atmosphere; the glacier-clad summit and forested slopes of **Mt Kenya National Park** (p376); and the remote Lake Turkana national parks in the far north – consisting of **South Island National Park** (p428) and **Central Island National Park** (p433), and **Sibiloi National Park** (p429), with its wealth of ancient archaeological finds.

Uganda rounds out East Africa's Unesco trio with the rugged, snow-dusted heights of **Rwenzori Mountains National Park** (p516); the misty **Bwindi Impenetrable National Park** (p523); and the mystery-shrouded **Kasubi tombs** (p475) in Kampala, which are at the spiritual heart of traditional Uganda.

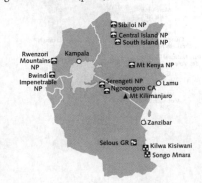

FOR FITNESS FANATICS

Want to stay fit while travelling? For the ultimate challenge, trek to the top of Africa in **Mt Kilimanjaro National Park** (p175), make the rigorous climb up to **Mt Kenya's** (p376) snowy peak, or watch the mists roll back from the summit of Mt Stanley in Uganda's **Rwenzori Mountains National Park** (p516) – or try combining all three. Tanzania's **Mt Meru** (p190) and the rugged expanses of the **Ngorongoro Conservation Area** (p197) offer off-beat but highly satisfying alternatives. Less dramatic but equally enjoyable is the easy, rolling terrain around **Lushoto** (p166), where the cool climate, winding paths and picturesque villages will keep you walking for days. In Kenya's **Cherangani Hills** (p410), you can travel overnight from alpine meadows to searing desert, while **Aberdare National Park** (p373) in the Kenyan Central Highlands treats you to panorama after panorama of unspoiled mountain wilderness. If you still have energy, head for Uganda's **Mt Elgon National Park** (p503), with trekking that is just as rewarding as in the Rwenzoris but at only a fraction of the price; or to the picturesque **crater lakes** (p512) near Fort Portal, with village-to-village walking. Finish up with white-water rafting at the **source of the Nile** (p495) near Jinja; diving around the **Zanzibar Archipelago** (p128), **Malindi** (p336) or **Watamu** (p331); or cycling or microlight flying near Tanzania's **Lake Manyara National Park** (p191).

WILD WANDERINGS

East Africa boasts one of the world's best collections of national parks and reserves. For a few weeks wandering on the wild side, start with the magnificent **Serengeti–Masai Mara** (p193 and p393) ecosystem, famed for the annual wildebeest migration. Nearby are Tanzania's wildlife-packed **Ngorongoro Crater** (p199) and **Tarangire National Park** (p192), with its baobabs and elephants. **Ruaha National Park** (p229) provides the chance for a serene wilderness experience, while **Katavi National Park** (p218) is one of Africa's last great frontier areas. For communing with the chimps, make your way to **Mahale Mountains** (p217) or world-renowned **Gombe Stream** (p216) National Parks. In Kenya, don't miss the lush **Kakamega Forest** (p406), with its plethora of birds; **Amboseli National Park** (p300) with elephants, giraffes and more wandering around against the backdrop of Mt Kilimanjaro; **Lake Nakuru National Park** (p364), with birds, rhinos and hippos; and the vast **Tsavo National Park** (p303), with its sweeping plains and the 'Big Five'. Rwanda's highlight is **Parc National des Volcans** (p583) with its gorillas, while often-overlooked Uganda's offerings include **Kibale Forest National Park** (p511) with its chimps; the Nile's thundering falls at **Murchison Falls National Park** (p541); **Queen Elizabeth National Park** (p520), with antelopes, buffaloes and hippos; and **Budongo Central Forest Reserve** (p545) with its chimps and dense forest.

Snapshot

East Africa defies all attempts at neat classification. On the one hand, the region seems to be striding towards a better future. Peace is solidifying in Rwanda and slowly taking root in Burundi – helped along by a US$290 million per year United Nations (UN) presence. Tanzania is enjoying an economic upswing, thanks in part to shrewd fiscal policies, and in part to a positively booming tourism industry. Kenya – long a regional powerhouse – has announced its intent to bid to host the 2016 Olympics, and has been a major contributor in international attempts to stabilise neighbouring Somalia. Uganda's President Yoweri Museveni has spearheaded one of the continent's highest profile AIDS campaigns, and the country's once-soaring HIV/AIDS infection rate has dropped significantly in recent years. After years of stalling and delays, Kenya, Tanzania and Uganda have joined hands in a customs union – paving the way for a full revival of the long-defunct East African Community. East Africa's music and woodcarvings are being exported around the world, its films regularly gain critical acclaim, and the vibrancy of the region's tribal traditions – together with its unparalleled network of national parks – unfailingly impress visitors from all corners of the globe.

Yet, there's another, more sombre side of the picture. Kenya, which held one of its most peaceful political transitions on record in 2002, is now overshadowed by a massive government corruption scandal. Kenya has also fallen 20 places on the UN Human Development Index (HDI) over the past three years, and all five of the countries covered in this book are ranked in the bottom third globally on the HDI. Northern Uganda continues to host what the UN Undersecretary General for Humanitarian Affairs & Emergency Relief recently referred to as the 'biggest neglected humanitarian emergency in the world', with thousands of children being kidnapped and brutalised by the Lord's Resistance Army. In Rwanda, although more than a decade has passed since the outbreak of the genocide, deep scars remain, while across the border in neighbouring Burundi, many wounds are still open. Malaria – a scourge throughout sub-Saharan Africa – continues to claim the lives of East Africans daily, while HIV/AIDS ravages the younger generation, and has left over two million children orphans.

So, what is the bottom line? For most East Africans there is no clear answer, with life, politics and culture revolving around a fusion of all these realities. Things *are* looking up for the most part, while at the same time, daily life *is* often a struggle. The rough and tumble of urban streets – with overflowing *matatus* (minibuses) careening past fruit vendors, sidewalk hawkers and modern highrises – contrasts sharply – or does it? – with the serenity of a night on the East African plains under a velvet-black sky, or the primeval majesty of one of the Rift Valley lakes at dawn. If there's any thread uniting all the apparent contradictions and tying together the region's diverse peoples and cultures, it's the conviction that the path forward must be according to East Africa's ways, with East Africans setting the beat and with East Africans calling the final shots.

'... the region's tribal traditions – together with its unparalleled network of national parks – unfailingly impress visitors from all corners of the globe'

History

CRADLE OF HUMANITY

East Africa, with its valleys, plains and highlands, has one of the longest documented human histories of any region in the world. Ancient hominid (humanlike) skulls and footprints, some over three million years old, have been found at various sites, including at Olduvai Gorge in Tanzania and Lake Turkana in Kenya. Although similarly ancient traces have also been found elsewhere on the continent, the East African section of the Rift Valley is popularly considered the 'cradle of humanity'.

By about one million years ago, these early ancestors had come to resemble modern humans, and had spread well beyond East Africa, as far as Europe and Asia. Roughly 100,000 years ago, possibly earlier, *homo sapiens* – or modern man – arrived on the scene.

See www.pbs.org/wgbh /evolution/humans /humankind/d.html for an overview of human evolution in East Africa.

The earliest evidence of modern-day East Africans dates to about 10,000 years ago, when much of the region was home to Khoisan-speaking hunter-gatherer communities. On the western fringes of East Africa, including parts of the area that is now Rwanda and Burundi, there were also small populations of various so-called Pygmy groups.

THE RELATIVES ARRIVE

Beginning between 3000 and 5000 years ago, a series of migrations began that were to indelibly shape the face of East Africa. Cushitic- and Nilotic-speaking peoples from the north and Bantu-speakers from the west converged on the Khoisan and other peoples already in the area, eventually creating the rich tribal mosaic that is East Africa today.

The first to arrive were Cushitic-speaking farmers and cattle herders who made their way to the region from present-day Ethiopia, and settled both inland and along the coast. They moved mostly in small family groups, and brought with them traditions that are still practiced by their descendents, including the Iraqw around Tanzania's Lake Manyara, and the Gabbra and Rendille in northern Kenya.

Africa – A Biography of the Continent by John Reader takes you on a sweeping journey through Africa from its earliest days, and includes some fascinating text on East Africa.

The next major influx began around 1000 BC, when Bantu-speaking peoples from West Africa's Niger Delta area began moving eastwards, arriving in East Africa around the 1st century BC. Thanks to their advanced agricultural skills, and knowledge of ironwork and steel production, these Bantu-speakers were able to absorb many of the Cushitic- and Khoisan-speakers who were already in the region, as well as the Pygmy populations around the Great Lakes. Soon they became East Africa's most populous ethno-linguistic family – a status which they continue to hold today.

A final wave of migration began somewhat later, when smaller groups of Nilotic peoples began to arrive in East Africa from what is now southern Sudan. This influx continued through to the 18th century, but the main movements took place in the 15th and 16th centuries. Most of these Nilotic peoples – whose descendants include the present-day Maasai and Turkana – were pastoralists, and many settled in the less fertile areas of southern Kenya and northern Tanzania where their large herds would have sufficient grazing space.

TIMELINE	c 3.5 million years ago	c 100 BC
	Hominid (humanlike) creatures wander around the East African plains	Bantu-speakers arrive in the region

Today the population diversity resulting from these migrations is one of the most fascinating aspects of travel in East Africa.

MONSOON WINDS

As these migrations were taking place in the interior, coastal areas were being shaped by far different influences. Azania, as the East African coast was known to the ancient Greeks, was an important trading post as early as 400 BC, and had probably been inhabited even before then by small groups of Cushitic peoples, and by Bantu-speakers. The *Periplus of the Erythraean Sea*, a navigator's guide written in the 1st century AD, mentions a place called Raphta as the southernmost trading port of the region. Although Raphta's location remains a mystery, it is believed to have been somewhere along the Kenyan or Tanzanian coast, possibly on the mainland opposite Manda or Paté Islands (north of Lamu), or further south near the Pangani or Rufiji estuaries.

'....Two days' sail beyond, there lies the very last market-town of the continent of Azania, which is called Rhapta... in which there is ivory in great quantity, and tortoise-shell....' (*Periplus of the Erythraean Sea*)

Trade seems to have grown steadily throughout the early part of the first millennium. Permanent settlements were established as traders, first from the Mediterranean and later from Arabia and Persia, came ashore on the winds of the monsoon and began to intermix with the indigenous peoples, gradually giving rise to Swahili language and culture. The traders from Arabia also brought Islam, which by the 11th century had become entrenched.

Chinese porcelain fragments have been discovered at Gede and elsewhere along the East African coast – testaments to old trade routes between Africa and the Orient.

Between the 13th and 15th centuries, these coastal settlements flourished. Ports including Shanga (on Paté Island), Gede, Lamu and Mombasa (all in present-day Kenya) and those on the Zanzibar Archipelago and at Kilwa Kisiwani (both in Tanzania) traded in ivory, gold and other goods with places as far away as India and China.

THE FIRST EUROPEANS

The first European to reach East Africa was the intrepid Portuguese explorer Vasco da Gama, who arrived in 1498, en route to the Orient. Within three decades, the Portuguese had disrupted the old trading networks and subdued the entire coast, building forts at various places, including Kilwa and Mombasa. Portuguese control lasted until the early 18th century, when they were displaced by Arabs from Oman.

SWAHILI

The word 'Swahili' ('of the coast', from the Arabic word *sāhil*) refers both to the Swahili language, as well as to the Islamic culture of the various people inhabiting the East African coast from Mogadishu (Somalia) in the north down to Mozambique in the south. Both language and culture are a rich mixture of Bantu, Arabic, Persian and Asian influences.

Although Swahili culture began to develop in the early part of the 1st millennium AD, it was not until the 18th century, with the ascendancy of the Omani Arabs on Zanzibar, that it came into its own. Swahili's role as a lingua franca was solidified as it spread throughout East and Central Africa along the great trade caravan routes. European missionaries and explorers soon adopted the language as their main means of communicating with locals. In the second half of the 19th century, missionaries, notably the German Johan Ludwig Krapf, also began applying the Roman alphabet. Prior to this, Swahili had been written exclusively in Arabic script.

---

c 750 AD	1498
Islam reaches the East African coast; Swahili civilisation begins to prosper	Vasco da Gama arrives in East Africa

As the Omani Arabs solidified their foothold, they began to turn their sights westwards, developing powerful trade routes that stretched inland as far as Lake Tanganyika and Central Africa. Commerce grew at such a pace that in the 1840s, the Sultan of Oman moved his capital from Muscat to Zanzibar.

The slave trade also grew rapidly during this period, driven in part by demand from European plantation holders on the Indian Ocean islands of Réunion and Mauritius. Soon slave traders, including the notorious Tippu Tip, had established stations at Tabora (Tanzania) and other inland towns. By the mid-19th century, the Zanzibar Archipelago had become the largest slave entrepôt along the East African coast, with nearly 50,000 slaves – abducted from as far away as Lake Tanganyika – passing through Zanzibar's market each year.

Portuguese influence is still seen in architecture, customs and language of the area – the Swahili gereza (jail), from Portuguese igreja (church), dates to the days when Portuguese forts contained both in the same compound.

COLONIAL CONTROL

Tales of both the horrors of the slave trade and of the attractions of East Africa soon made their way back to Europe, and Western interests were piqued. In 1890 Germany and Great Britain signed an agreement defining 'spheres of influence' for themselves, which formally established a British

---

THE SLAVE TRADE

Slavery has been practised in Africa throughout recorded history, but its greatest expansion in East Africa came with the rise of Islam, which prohibits the enslavement of Muslims. Demands of European plantation holders on the islands of Réunion and Mauritius were another major catalyst, particularly during the second half of the 18th century.

At the outset slaves were taken from coastal regions and shipped to Arabia, Persia and the Indian Ocean islands. Kilwa Kisiwani, off the southern Tanzanian coast, was one of the major export gateways. As demand increased, traders made their way further inland, so that during the 18th and 19th centuries slaves were being brought from as far away as Malawi and the Congo. By the 19th century, with the rise of the Omani Arabs, Zanzibar had eclipsed Kilwa Kisiwani as East Africa's major slave-trading depot. According to some estimates, by the 1860s between 10,000 and as many as 50,000 slaves were passing through Zanzibar's market each year. Overall, close to 600,000 slaves were sold through Zanzibar between 1830 and 1873, when a treaty with Britain paved the way for the trade's ultimate halt in the region by the early 20th century.

As well as the human horrors, the slave trade caused major social upheavals on the mainland. In the sparsely populated south of present-day Tanzania it fanned up interclan warfare in the politically decentralised area, as ruthless entrepreneurs raided neighbouring tribes for slaves. In other places, the slave trade promoted increased social stratification and altered settlement patterns. Some tribes, for example, began to build fortified settlements encircled by trenches, while others concentrated their populations in towns as self-defence. Another fundamental societal change was the gradual shift in the nature of chieftaincy, from being religiously based to becoming a position resting on military power or wealth – both among the 'gains' of trade in slaves and commodities.

The slave trade also served as an impetus for European missionary activity in East Africa, prompting the establishment of the first Christian stations and missionaries' penetration of the interior. One of the most tireless campaigners against the horrors of slavery was the Scottish missionary-explorer David Livingstone (1813–74), whose efforts, combined with the attention attracted by his funeral, were the decisive factors mobilising British initiatives to end human trafficking.

1850–1870	1890
Zanzibar's slave market becomes the largest along the East African coast	Britain and Germany establish footholds in East Africa

protectorate over the Zanzibar Archipelago. Most of what is now mainland Tanzania, as well as Rwanda and Burundi, came under German control, and was known as German East Africa (later Tanganyika), while the British took Kenya and Uganda.

The 19th century was also the era of European explorers, including Gustav Fischer (a German whose party was virtually annihilated by the Maasai at Hell's Gate on Lake Naivasha in 1882), Joseph Thomson (a Scot who reached Lake Victoria via the Rift Valley lakes and the Aberdare Ranges in 1883) and Count Teleki von Szek (an Austrian who explored the Lake Turkana region and Mt Kenya in 1887). Anglican bishop James Hannington set out in 1885 to establish a diocese in Uganda, but was killed when he reached the Nile. Other explorers included Burton and Speke, who were sent to Lake Tanganyika in 1858 by the Royal Geographical Society, and the famous Henry Morton Stanley and David Livingstone.

By the turn of the 20th century, Europeans had firmly established a presence in East Africa. Both the British and German colonial administrations were busy building railways and roads to open their colonies to commerce, establishing hospitals and schools, and encouraging the influx of Christian missionaries. Kenya's fertile and climatically favourable highlands proved suitable for European farmers to colonise. In Tanganyika, by contrast, large areas were unable to support agriculture and were plagued by the tsetse fly, which made cattle grazing and dairy farming impossible.

INDEPENDENCE

As the European presence in Africa solidified, discontent with colonial rule grew and nationalist demands for independence became insistent. In the 1950s and early 1960s, the various nationalist movements coalesced and gained strength across East Africa, culminating in the granting of independence to Tanzania (1961), Uganda, Rwanda and Burundi (all in 1962), and Kenya (1963). Independence and postindependence trajectories varied from country to country. In Kenya, the path leading to independence was violent and protracted; in Tanzania and Uganda the immediate pre-independence years were relatively peaceful, while in Rwanda and Burundi, long-existing tribal rivalries were a major impediment.

In Kenya, the European influx increased rapidly during the first half of the 20th century, so that by the 1950s there were about 80,000 settlers in the country. Much of the land expropriated for their farms came from the homelands of the Kikuyu people. The Kikuyu responded by forming an opposition political association in 1920, and they instigated the Mau Mau rebellion in the 1950s, something which marked a major turning point in Kenyan politics.

In Tanganyika, the unpopular German administration continued until the end of WWI, when the League of Nations mandated the area to the British, and Rwanda and Burundi to the Belgians. British rule was equally unpopular, however, with the Brits neglecting development of Tanganyika in favour of the more lucrative and fertile options available in Kenya and Uganda. Political consciousness soon began to coalesce in the form of farmers' unions and cooperatives, through which popular demands were expressed. By the mid-20th century, there were over 400 such cooperatives, which soon joined to form the Tanganyika Africa

For an intriguing glimpse at life in precolonial Kenya, look for a copy of Khadambi Asalache's *A Calabash of Life*.

The Lunatic Express by Charles Miller is a very readable recounting of the expansion of East Africa's rail network and other colonial interventions.

Zamani – A Survey of East African History, edited by renowned Kenyan historian BA Ogot with JA Kieran, is one of the best introductions to the region's precolonial and colonial history from an African perspective.

1961-1963	1984
The countries of East Africa gain independence	Kenya reports its first AIDS case

Association (TAA), a lobbying group for the nationalist cause based in Dar es Salaam.

In Uganda, the British tended to favour the recruitment of the powerful Buganda people for the civil service. Members of other tribes, unable to acquire responsible jobs in the colonial administration or to make inroads into the Buganda-dominated commercial sector, were forced to seek other ways of joining the mainstream. The Acholi and Lango, for example, chose the army and became the tribal majority in the military. As resentment grew, the seeds were planted for the intertribal conflicts that were to tear Uganda apart following independence.

In Rwanda and Burundi, the period of colonial rule was characterised by the increasing power and privilege of the Tutsi. The Belgian administrators found it convenient to rule indirectly through Tutsi chiefs and their princes, and the Tutsi had a monopoly on the missionary-run educational system. As a result long-existing tensions between the Tutsi and Hutu were exacerbated, igniting the spark that was later to explode in the 1994 Rwanda genocide.

For more about the independence movements, and the history of each country since independence, see the country chapters.

Shake Hands With the Devil by Roméo Dallaire is a searing account of the Rwandan genocide by the head of the UN peacekeeping mission to Rwanda.

INTO THE FUTURE

Take a stroll through East Africa today, and you'll see all these threads of history come to life: from Olduvai Gorge, with its fascinating fossil finds, to the winding lanes and ornate lintels of old Swahili settlements such as Lamu and Zanzibar's Stone Town, to bustling coastal dhow ports, Portuguese-era garrisons and the more recent colonial architecture lining Dar es Salaam's waterfront. Interspersed with all this is East Africa's more modern face – glitzy high-rise office blocks, elegant luxury lodges, crass Western-style resorts – and tying it all together are the rich tribal heritages that are the region's lifeblood.

Browse www.nationmedia.com/eastafrican/current/index.htm to keep up with what's happening in East Africa today.

The next decades are going to involve a continual reconciling of all these threads – traditional and modern, foreign and local. Yet, in many ways, East Africa has never been better positioned to do this. Peace has gained a foothold in the previous trouble spots of Rwanda and Uganda, and is slowly progressing in Burundi. Tourism is more than holding its own as a burgeoning regional industry, while the local cultural scene continues to be as vibrant as ever. Whatever the future holds, it's likely that East Africa's move into the next chapter of its history won't be fast, but it will certainly be fascinating.

1994	2002
Rwandan genocide unleashed	Peaceful and fair elections in Kenya

The Culture

DAILY LIFE

Despite East Africa's size and diversity, daily life follows remarkably similar patterns throughout much of the region. In general, rural rhythms set the beat: life is centred around tending small farm plots, and money – especially for paying school fees or building a house – is a constant concern. Women always work, either outside the home or tending to the family and garden, and many students don't have the opportunity to finish secondary school. Throughout the region tourism provides employment opportunities, though good positions are for the lucky few, and both unemployment and underemployment are rife. At the other end of the spectrum are the small cadres of wealthy in Nairobi and other capital cities who drive fancy 4WDs, live in Western-style houses in posh residential areas and send their children to university in London or elsewhere. Most East Africans fall somewhere in between these scenarios, although far more are closer to the former than the latter.

Throughout East Africa, family life is central, with weddings, funerals and other events holding centre stage, and celebrations being grand affairs – often aimed at demonstrating status.

Family ties are strong, and it is expected that those who have jobs will share what they have with the extended family. The extended family also forms an essential support network in the absence of government social security systems. Given that average per capita income in the region ranges between about US$150 in Burundi and US$400 in Kenya (compared with about US$24,000 in the UK), the system works remarkably well, with surprisingly few destitute people on the streets in most areas.

Invisible social hierarchies lend life a sense of order, with men ruling the roost in the working world and, at least symbolically, in the family as well. Although women arguably form the backbone of the economy

I Laugh So I Won't Cry: Kenya's Women Tell the Stories of Their Lives, edited by Helena Halperin, offers a fascinating glimpse into the lives of East African women. Also look for *Three Swahili Women: Life Histories from Mombasa, Kenya* by Sarah Mirza and Margaret Strobel.

AIDS IN EAST AFRICA

Together with malaria, AIDS is now the leading cause of death in sub-Saharan Africa, and East Africa is no exception. In Uganda alone, there are almost one million AIDS orphans under 15 years of age – one of the highest figures in the world – and an estimated 53,000 children 14 years old or younger living with HIV/AIDS. The figures elsewhere in the region are just as sobering. Kenya has close to 550,000 AIDS orphans, and an estimated 78,000 children living with HIV/AIDS. Women are particularly hard hit. In Burundi, for example, where an estimated 20% of urban dwellers and 6% of rural dwellers are HIV positive, infection rates in girls aged 15 to 19 years old are four times greater than those for similarly aged boys.

On the positive side, East African governments now discuss the situation openly, and you'll notice AIDS-related billboards in Dar es Salaam, Nairobi and elsewhere in the region. Ugandan president Yoweri Museveni is often cited for his outspokenness and leadership in combating the scourge, and thanks to vigorous public awareness campaigns and other government efforts Uganda's AIDS rates have dropped over the past decade. Yet, at the grass-roots level in many areas of the region, the stigma remains. AIDS-related deaths are often kept quiet, with 'tuberculosis' used euphemistically as a socially acceptable catch-all diagnosis. Also, many of the AIDS clinics and counselling centres that exist still operate anonymously; if a sign were hung out, many victims wouldn't enter for fear of recognition. In one study in Kenya, over half of the women surveyed who had acquired HIV hadn't told their partners because they feared being beaten or abandoned.

In coastal areas, watch for henna painting – intricate designs on the hands and feet made with a paste from leaves of the henna plant, and traditionally applied only to brides and married women.

throughout the region – with most juggling child-rearing plus work on the family farm or in an office – they are frequently marginalised when it comes to education and politics. Exceptions include Kenya, which is notable for its abundance of nongovernmental organisations, many headed by women, and Uganda, where women play prominent roles in educational and literary circles.

With the exception of Tanzania, where local chieftaincies were abolished following independence, tribal identity and tribal structures are generally strong – sometimes with disastrous consequences, as seen in the Rwandan genocide. Otherwise, clashes between traditional and modern lifestyles are generally fairly low profile, with outside indications often limited to nothing more than the occasional disparaging remark about the neighbours.

The spectre of AIDS looms on the horizon throughout East Africa (see p33). While there has been some high profile public awareness campaigns, East African societies in general are conservative, and away from urban centres real discussion remains limited.

ECONOMY

Take a look at East Africa's economy, and you'll find a mixed picture. On the one hand, inflation is at low to moderate levels, economies are growing and tourism – despite several hard blows in recent years – is a major and increasingly important money earner. Yet all of the five countries covered in this book are ranked in the bottom third of the global United Nations' Human Development Index, which measures the overall achievements of a country according to factors such as income, life

FEMALE GENITAL MUTILATION

Female genital mutilation (FGM) – often euphemistically referred to as 'female circumcision' – is the partial or total removal of the female external genitalia. In Kenya, an estimated 50% of women – most in the northeast, near Somalia – have undergone FGM. In Tanzania, the figures are estimated at between 10% and 18%, while in Uganda, it's about 5%.

FGM is usually carried out for reasons of cultural or gender identity, and is entrenched in tribal life in some areas. Long-standing traditional beliefs about hygiene, aesthetics and health also play a role in the continuance of FGM. Yet among the very real risks of the procedure are infection, shock and haemorrhage, as well as lifelong complications and pain with menstruation, urination, intercourse and childbirth. For women who have had infibulation – in which all or part of the external genitalia are removed, and the vaginal opening then narrowed and stitched together – unassisted childbirth is impossible, and many women and children die as a consequence.

Since the mid-1990s there have been major efforts to reduce the incidence of the practice, and while concrete successes have been limited, the very fact that FGM can now be openly discussed is a major step forward.

In Kenya, government hospitals have been instructed by the Ministry of Health to stop the practice, and several nongovernmental women's organisations have taken a leading role in bringing FGM to the forefront of media discussion. There is also a growing movement towards alternative rites that offer the chance to maintain traditions while minimising the health complications, such as ntanira na mugambo or 'circumcision through words'.

In Uganda, FGM has been declared illegal and condemned by the government. While the practice continues in the northeast, support is waning and local community leaders have declared that they want to eradicate it completely within the next decade.

In Tanzania, although the overall prevalence of FGM is significantly lower than in neighbouring Kenya, progress in reducing its incidence has been slower. In 1998 FGM was declared illegal for girls under 18 years old, but there have been few if any prosecutions, and mass 'circumcisions' continue in some areas.

expectancy and education standards. And annual per capita income levels are just a fraction of what they are in most western countries.

These figures are tempered by the extensive informal economy that exists throughout the region, as well as by wide variations between rural and urban areas. There are also significant income disparities; for example Kenya, one of the world's poorest countries, also registers one of the largest gaps between rich and poor.

In human terms the statistics mean that daily life is a struggle for most East Africans. Life expectancy averages around 45 years for the region as a whole, and at birth an average East African has between a 30% and 50% statistical probability of not surviving to the age of 40. Reliable banking services and savings accounts remain inaccessible for most people, especially rural dwellers, and it's a common scenario for those few students who make it through secondary school to be faced with only meagre job prospects upon graduation.

While all this can be rather discouraging, it's worth keeping in mind that East Africa is not a historically cohesive area where sweeping generalities can easily be made, whether the topic is economic development or politics. It's only relatively recently that the region has been packaged into the neatly bordered national entities that we take for granted today, and just 200 years ago the main forces were relatively small, community-based tribal groupings. This means that, as a traveller, the most encouraging aspects of the East African economic picture that you're likely to see are those at the village or community level – a sustainable microlending scheme, for example, or a profitable women's cooperative. While successes at this level are no excuse for neglecting the bigger picture, they at least help to put some of the statistics into a more balanced perspective, and serve as proof that the efforts of one or several individuals can make a difference.

The very readable *African Voices, African Lives: Personal Narratives from a Swahili Village* by Patricia Caplan takes an inside look at local culture and customs on Tanzania's Mafia Island.

The Worlds of a Maasai Warrior: An Autobiography by Tepilit Ole Saitoti presents an intriguing perspective on the juxtaposition of traditional and modern in East Africa.

GOVERNMENT & POLITICS

East Africa has made headlines in recent years, during the Kenyan elections (for more see p270) and with the slow but steady steps towards the reactivation of a modified version of the old East African Community (EAC) customs union. Until 1977 Kenya, Uganda and Tanzania were members of the EAC, an economic union which linked the currencies of the three countries and provided for freedom of movement and shared telecommunications and postal facilities. In 1996, following the EAC's break-up and a decade of regional disputes, the presidents of Tanzania, Kenya and Uganda established the Tripartite Commission for East African Cooperation, which laid the groundwork for re-establishing the old economic and customs union in 2000. It is this new East African Community which today serves as the main intragovernmental organisation in the region. A common passport was adopted in 1997, and in early 2005 a customs union came into effect with the ultimate goal of duty-free trade between the three countries. Next on the agenda is a common currency, and a loose political federation, although a realisation of these is probably still well in the future.

Former Kenyan president Jomo Kenyatta once argued that FGM was such an integral part of initiation rites and Kikuyu identity that its abolition would destroy the tribal system.

MULTICULTURALISM

Almost since the dawn of humankind, outsiders have been arriving in East Africa to be assimilated into its seething, simmering and endlessly fascinating cultural melting pot. From the Bantu-, Nilotic- and Cushitic-speaking groups that made their way to the region during the early migrations (see p28), to Arab and Asian traders and colonial-era Europeans, a long stream of migrants have left their footprints here. Today the region's modern face reflects this rich fusion of influences, with over 300 tribal groups, plus small but economically significant numbers of Asians, Arabs and Europeans – most well-integrated linguistically – all rubbing shoulders.

Coastal East Africa's rich cultural melting pot is surveyed on www.pbs .org/wonders/fr_e2.htm.

While national identities have become entrenched over the past half-century of independence, tribal loyalties also remain strong in many areas. The highest profile conflicts resulting from intertribal clashes have been in Rwanda – where in 1994 long-standing tensions exploded into brutal genocidal violence, the effects of which have scarred the nation – and in Burundi, where intertribal conflicts culminated in a long civil war that still casts shadows over the country.

At the other end of the spectrum is Tanzania, which has earned itself a name for its remarkably harmonious society, and its success in forging tolerance and unity out of diversity.

There are dozens of beautiful photojournal books documenting East Africa's diverse cultures, including *Turkana: Kenya's Nomads of the Jade Sea* by Nigel Pavitt, and *African Warriors* by Thomasin Magor.

While intrareligious frictions do exist (primarily between Christians and Muslims) they are at a generally low level, and not a major factor in contemporary East African politics.

SPORT

Football (soccer) dominates sporting headlines throughout the region and throughout the year, and matches always draw large and enthusiastic crowds. Kenya's team, the Harambee Stars, regularly participate in pan-African competitions and World Cup qualifiers, and there are also occasional appearances by Uganda's Kobs and Rwanda's Amavubi (Wasps).

More low-key than football at home, but surpassing it on the international sports stage, is running, where Kenya dominates in long-distance competitions throughout the world.

THE GENDER GAP

The good news on the East African educational scene is that at primary school level, the 'gender gap' (the difference between the percentage of boys versus the percentage of girls enrolled in school) is gradually lessening, and in some cases has been completely eliminated. In Tanzania and Kenya, for example, initial primary school enrolment is roughly evenly divided between boys and girls. In Uganda, which has the highest level of overall primary school enrolment in the region, the gender gap is about 9%, in favour of boys, but less than it was a decade ago. However, the rest of the picture is less rosy. In Tanzania, only 5% of girls obtain a secondary level education, while in Uganda and Kenya the figures are 9% and 22% respectively.

Comparatively low initial enrolment numbers and high drop-out rates among girls at the secondary level are due in part to cultural attitudes, with traditional preferences for sons diminishing the value of girls' education. Early marriage and early pregnancies are another factor. In Uganda – which has the dubious distinction of having the highest rate of adolescent pregnancy in sub-Saharan Africa – 43% of girls are either pregnant or have given birth by age 17, and 70% by age 19. HIV/AIDS is also a major contributor. As the number of AIDS orphans in the region rises, girls are required to stay home to take care of ill family members or younger siblings. Among East Africa's nomadic and pastoralist communities, such as those in parts of northeastern Kenya, the demands of a migratory lifestyle often cause families to remove girls from school. Sexual harassment both in and out of school also leads to nonattendance and drop out.

Several countries in the region have signed on to a continentwide African Girls' Education Initiative, although there has been little measurable progress thus far. A few countries, including Kenya, have also adopted re-entry policies for school-aged girls who give birth, although these remain largely ineffectual. There are a handful of private girls' schools around the region which have registered some impressive gains, and steady progress is also being made at the grass-roots level in increasing awareness of the value of education for all children, including girls. However, especially in rural areas, attitudes are slow to change and there's still a long way to go.

> **BAO**
>
> It's not exactly sport, but *bao* (also known as *kombe*, *mweso* and by various other names) is one of East Africa's favourite pastimes. It's played throughout the region, and is especially popular on the Zanzibar Archipelago and elsewhere along the coast, where you'll see men in their *kanzus* (white robe-like outer garment worn by men) and *kofia* (a cap, usually of embroidered white linen, worn by men) huddled around a board watching two opponents play. The rules vary somewhat from place to place, but the game always involves trying to capture the pebbles or seeds of your opponent, which are set out on a board with rows of small hollows. Anything can substitute for a board, from finely carved wood to a flattened area of sand on the beach, and playing well is something of a patiently acquired art form. For more on the intricacies of *bao* see the comprehensive www.gamecabinet.com/rules/Bao.html or www.driedger.ca/mankala/Man-1.html.

The East African Safari Rally is another attention-getter. This rugged 3000-km rally – which has been held annually since 1953 – passes along public roadways through Kenya, Uganda and Tanzania, and attracts an international collection of drivers with their vintage (pre-1971) automobiles.

Also likely to get increasing regional press coverage in the near future is Kenya's recent surprise announcement of its intention to bid for the 2016 Olympic Games.

See www.eastafricansafari rally.com for the latest news about the region's most famous road race.

RELIGION

Africans in general are profoundly spiritual in their outlook on life, and East Africans are no exception. The major religions are Christianity and Islam, with Islam especially prevalent in coastal areas. A sizable number of people also observe traditional religions, and there are small communities of Hindus, Sikhs and Jains.

Christianity

The first Christian missionaries reached East Africa in the mid-19th century. Since then the region has been the site of extensive missionary activity, and today most of the major denominations are represented, including Lutherans, Catholics, Seventh-Day Adventists and Baptists. In many areas, mission stations have been the major, and in some cases the only, channels for development assistance. This is particularly so with health care and education, with missions still sometimes providing the only schools and medical facilities in remote areas.

In addition to the main denominations, there is also an increasing number of home-grown African sects, especially in Kenya. Factors that are often cited for the growth of such local Christian sects include cultural resurgence, an ongoing struggle against neocolonialism, and the alienation felt by many job-seekers who migrate to urban centres far from their homes.

Church services throughout East Africa are invariably beautifully vibrant and colourful. Even if you can't understand the language, you'll certainly be captivated by the unaccompanied choral singing, which only Africans can do with such beauty and precision.

We Wish to Inform You That Tomorrow We Will be Killed With Our Families: Stories from Rwanda by Philip Gourevitch is a compelling account of the Rwandan genocide and its aftermath, as told by survivors.

Islam

Islam was founded in the early 7th century by the Prophet Mohammed. By the time of his death, the new religion had begun to spread throughout the Arabian peninsula, from where it was then carried in all directions over the subsequent centuries, including along the East African coast.

The five pillars of Islam that guide Muslims in their daily lives include the following:

Haj (pilgrimage) It is the duty of every Muslim, who is fit and can afford it, to make the pilgrimage to Mecca at least once.

Sala (prayer, sometimes written *salat*) This is the obligation of prayer, done five times daily when muezzins call the faithful to pray, facing Mecca and ideally in a mosque.

Sawm (fasting) Ramadan commemorates the revelation of the Qur'an to Mohammed, and is the month when Muslims fast from dawn to dusk.

Shahada (the profession of faith) 'There is no God but Allah, and Mohammed is his Prophet' is the fundamental tenet of Islam.

Zakat (alms) Giving to the poor is an essential part of Islamic social teaching.

Most East African Muslims are Sunnis, with a small minority of Shiites, primarily among the Asian community. The most influential of the various Shiite sects represented are the Ismailis, followers of the Aga Khan.

Traditional Religions

East Africa's traditional religions are animist, centring on ancestor worship, the land and various ritual objects. Most acknowledge the existence of a supreme deity with whom communication is possible through the intercession of ancestors. Ancestors thus play a strong role in many areas, with their principal function to protect the tribe or family. Some groups also recognise lesser gods in addition to the supreme deity, while among the Maasai and several other tribes, there is no tradition of ancestor worship; the supreme deity is the sole focus of devotion.

> Traditional medicine in East Africa is closely intertwined with traditional religion, with practitioners using divining implements, prayers, chanting and dance to facilitate communication with the spirit world.

ARTS
Architecture

East Africa is an architectural treasure-trove, with its colonial-era buildings and religious architecture, including both churches and mosques. The real highlights, however, are the old town areas of Zanzibar, Lamu (both Unesco World Heritage sites) and Mombasa, all of which display mesmerising combinations of Indian, Arabic, European and African characteristics in their buildings and street layouts.

In Lamu, Paté and elsewhere along the coast you'll see examples of Swahili architecture. At the simplest level, Swahili dwellings are plain rectangular mud and thatch constructions, set in clusters and divided by small, sandy paths. More elaborate stone houses are traditionally constructed of coral and wood along a north–south axis, with flat roofs and a small open courtyard in the centre, which serves as the main source of light.

The various quarters or neighbourhoods in Swahili towns are symbolically united by a central mosque, usually referred to as the *msikiti wa Ijumaa* or 'Friday mosque'. In a sharp break with Islamic architectural custom elsewhere, traditional Swahili mosques don't have minarets; the muezzin gives the call to prayer from inside the mosque, generally with the help of a loudspeaker.

Cinema

> The ZIFF website (www.ziff.org) is the best jumping-off point into the world of East African cinema.

East Africa's long-languishing, and traditionally underfunded, film industry received a major boost with the opening of the Zanzibar International Film Festival (ZIFF, p253), which has been held annually on Zanzibar since 1998, and is now one of the region's premier cultural events. The festival serves as a venue for artists from the Indian Ocean basin and beyond, and has had several local prize-winners, including *Maangamizi – The Ancient One,* co-directed by Tanzanian Martin M'hando and shot in

Tanzania. M'hando is also known for his film *Mama Tumaini* (Women of Hope).

Rwandan Eric Kabera is known worldwide for his *Keepers of Memory, 100 Days* (produced together with Nick Hughes) and *Through My Eyes* – all documenting the Rwandan genocide and its aftermath, and also ZIFF award-winners.

Another notable East African cinematographer is Tanzanian Flora M'mbugu-Schelling, who won acclaim for *These Hands,* a short but powerful documentary focusing on the life of Mozambican women refugees working crushing rocks in a quarry near Dar es Salaam.

For more on films from the region, see the country chapters.

Literature

East Africa's first known Swahili manuscript is an epic poem dating from 1728 and written in Arabic script. However, it wasn't until the second half of the 20th century – once Swahili had become established as a regional language – that Swahili prose began to develop. One of the best known authors from this period is Tanzanian Shaaban Robert (see p110).

In more recent years there has been a flowering of English-language titles by East African writers, including *Weep Not, Child* and *Detained: A Prison Writer's Diary,* both by Kenyan Ngugi wa Thiong'o; *Song of Lawino* by Ugandan Okot p'Bitek; and *Abyssinian Chronicles* by Ugandan Moses Isegawa. See the country chapters for more on these and other authors.

There is also a rich but often overlooked body of English-language literature by East African women, particularly in Uganda, where female writers have organised as Femrite, the Ugandan Women Writers' Association. Some names to watch for include Mary Karooro Okurut, whose *A Woman's Voice: An Anthology of Short Stories by Ugandan Women* provides a good overview, and the internationally recognised Kenyan writer Grace Ogot, known in particular for *The Promised Land.*

> Swahili prose got a relatively late start, but Swahili oral poetry traditions have long roots. See www.humnet.ucla.edu/humnet/aflang/swahili/SwahiliPoetry/index.htm for an excellent overview and anthology.

Music & Dance

The single greatest influence on the modern East African music scene has been the Congolese bands that began playing in Dar es Salaam and Nairobi in the early 1960s, and which brought the styles of rumba and *soukous* (Congolese dance music) into the East African context. Among the best known is the Orchestre Super Matimila, which was propelled to fame by the renowned Congolese-born and Dar es Salaam-based Remmy Ongala ('Dr Remmy'). Many of his songs (most are in Swahili) are commentaries on contemporary themes such as AIDS, poverty and hunger, and Ongala has been a major force in popularising music from the region beyond Africa's borders. Another of the Congolese bands is Samba Mapangala's Orchestra Virunga. Mapangala, a Congolese vocalist, first gained a footing in Uganda in the mid-1970s with a group known as Les Kinois before moving to Nairobi and forming Orchestra Virunga.

As Swahili lyrics replaced the original vocals, a distinct East African rumba style was born. Its proponents include Simba Wanyika (together with offshoot Les Wanyika), which had its roots in Tanzania, but gained fame in the nightclubs of Nairobi.

> For an overview of the East African music scene check out http://members.aol.com/dpaterson/eamusic.htm.

In the 1970s Kenyan *benga* music rose to prominence on the regional music scene. It originated among the Luo of western Kenya and is characterised by its clear electric guitar licks and bounding bass rhythms. Its ethnic roots were maintained, however, with the guitar taking the place of the traditional *nyatiti* (folk lyre), and the bass guitar replacing the drum, which originally was played by the *nyatiti* player with a toe ring. One of the best-known proponents of *benga* has been DO Misiani, whose group Shirati Jazz has been popular since the 1960s.

On Zanzibar and along the coast, the music scene has long been dominated by *taarab* (Zanzibari music combining African, Arabic and Indian influences), which has experienced a major resurgence in recent years, and which gets airplay in other parts of the region as well (for more, see p142).

Throughout East Africa, dance plays a vital role in community life, although masked dance is not as common in most parts of the region as it is in West Africa. A wide variety of drums and rhythms are used, depending on the occasion, with many dances serving as expressions of thanks and praise, or as a means of communicating with the ancestors or telling a story. East Africa's most famous dance group is the globally acclaimed Les Tambourinaires du Burundi.

> A good starting point for learning more about *taarab* music is the Dhow Countries Music Academy (www.zanzibarmusic.org).

Textiles & Handicrafts

The brightly coloured lengths of printed cotton cloth seen throughout the region – typically with Swahili sayings printed along the edge – are known as *kanga* in Kenya, Tanzania and parts of Uganda. Many of the sayings are social commentary or messages – often indirectly worded, or containing puns and double meanings – that are communicated by the woman wearing the *kanga,* generally to other women. Others are simply a local form of advertising, such as those bearing the logo of political parties.

In coastal areas, you'll see the *kikoi*, which is made of a thicker textured cotton, usually featuring striped or plaid patterns, and traditionally worn by men. Also common are beautiful batik-print cottons depicting everyday scenes, animal motifs or geometrical patterns.

> Kanga sayings range from amorous outpourings to pointed humour. For a sampling of what's being said around you, see www.glcom.com/hassan /kanga.html.

Basketry and woven items – all of which have highly functional roles in local society – have also become popular as tourist souvenirs, particularly in Nairobi.

Jewellery, especially beaded jewellery, is another local art form, notably among the Maasai and Turkana. It is used in ceremonies as well as in everyday life, and often indicates the wearer's wealth and marital status.

Visual Arts

PAINTING

In comparison with woodcarving, painting has a fairly low profile in East Africa. One of the most popular styles is Tanzania's Tingatinga painting (for more, see p111).

SCULPTURE & WOODCARVING

East Africa is renowned for its exceptional figurative art, especially that of Tanzania's Makonde, who are acclaimed throughout the region for their skill at bringing blocks of hard African blackwood (*Dalbergia melanoxylon* or, in Swahili, *mpingo*) to life in often highly fanciful depictions. Among the most common carvings are those with *ujamaa* motifs, and those known as *shetani,* which embody images from the spirit world. *Ujamaa* carvings are designed as a totem pole or 'tree of life' and contain interlaced human and animal figures around a common ancestor. Each generation is connected to those that preceded it, and gives support to those that follow. Tree of life carvings often reach several metres in height, and are almost always made from a single piece of wood. *Shetani* carvings are much more abstract, even grotesque, with the emphasis on challenging viewers to new interpretations while giving the carver's imagination free reign.

> *African Art* by Frank Willet surveys the entire continent, and is a good introduction if you're interested in East African sculpture and woodcarving.

FOOD & DRINK

Imagine dining under the stars with your feet in the sand, sitting down in the shade of palm trees to a plate of freshly grilled fish, or relishing five-star cuisine at one of East Africa's luxurious safari camps. While it's not all like this – it would be easy to come away from East Africa thinking that the region subsists almost entirely on rice or *ugali* (thick, porridgelike maize- or cassava-based staple) and sauce – there are some surprising treats to be found. In general, the best cuisine is found along the coast, where savoury seafood dishes cooked with coconut milk, coriander and other spices are the speciality. Elsewhere, meals centre around a staple with beans or sauce, with the best part of the dining experience the surrounding ambience and friendly local company, rather than the food itself.

Staples & Specialities

Throughout the region, you'll find East Africans sitting down to piping hot plates of *ugali*. While beloved by many locals, it's somewhat of an acquired taste for most foreigners. Rice – best on the coast, where it is frequently flavoured with coconut milk – and *matoke* (cooked plantains) are other common staples, while chips, potatoes and chapati are ubiquitous in larger towns.

Most visitors have more of an affinity for *nyama choma* (seasoned, roasted meat), *sambusas* (deep-fried pastry triangles stuffed with spiced mince meat – be sure they haven't been sitting around too long) and *mandazi* (semisweet doughnutlike products). *Chipsi mayai* is another local favourite – basically a puffy omelette with chips mixed in. On almost every street corner you'll find vendors selling corncobs roasted on a wire grill over a bed of hot coals. Another popular street-corner snack is deep-fried yam, eaten hot with a squeeze of lemon juice and a sprinkling of chilli powder. Along the coast, the offerings are rounded out by an abundance of delectable seafood dishes, often grilled, or cooked in coconut milk or in a curry style.

Three meals a day is the norm, with the main meal eaten at midday, and breakfast frequently nothing more than coffee or tea and bread. In out-of-the-way areas, many places are closed in the evening and the only option may be street food.

According to local belief, lurking inside many carvings are the spirits they represent, thus giving them supernatural powers.

Drinks

Sodas (soft drinks) – especially Coca Cola and Fanta – are found almost everywhere, even where bottled water isn't. Fresh juices, including pineapple, sugar cane and orange are widely available and a treat, although check first to see whether they have been mixed with unsafe water. Another delicious variant is the milkshake – fresh juice, chilled milk and syrup. Most refreshing of all, though, and never a worry hygienically, is the juice of the *dafu* (young coconut), which you'll find along the coast. Western-style supermarkets sell imported fruit juices.

Although East Africa exports high-quality coffee and tea, what you'll usually find locally is far inferior, with instant coffee the norm. Both tea and coffee are generally drunk with lots of milk and sugar.

East Africa has several local beers, and a good selection of imports. Among the most common are Kenya's Tusker Lager and South Africa's Castle Lager, which is also produced locally. Especially in Kenya, many locals prefer their beer warm, so getting a cold beer can be a task.

Kenya and Tanzania have small and very fledgling wine industries, although it is doubtful either will be putting wine importers out of business anytime soon.

Although cash is becoming an increasingly common replacement, cattle are still a coveted bride price in many parts of East Africa.

Locally produced home-brews – commonly fermented mixtures made with bananas or millet and sugar – are widely available. However, avoid anything distilled – in addition to being illegal, it's also often lethal.

Where to Eat & Drink

For dining local style, nothing beats taking a seat in a small local eatery – known as *hoteli* in Swahili-speaking areas – and watching life pass by. Many *hoteli* will have the day's menu – rarely costing more than US$1 – written on a chalkboard, and often a TV in the corner broadcasting the latest football match. Rivalling *hoteli* for local atmosphere are the bustling night markets that you'll find in some areas, where vendors set up grills along the roadside and sell *nyama choma* and other street food.

For something more formal, or for Western-style meals, stick to cities or main towns, where you'll find a reasonable array of restaurants, most moderately priced compared with their European equivalents. There's at least one Chinese restaurant (often somewhat East-Africanised) in every capital. Especially in coastal areas, there's usually also a good selection of Indian cuisine, found both at inexpensive eateries serving up good Indian snacks, and in pricier restaurants. Most main towns have at least one supermarket selling imported products such as canned meat, fish and cheese.

Vegetarians & Vegans

While there isn't much in East Africa that is specifically billed as 'vegetarian', there are many veggie options, and you can find *wali* (cooked rice) and *maharagwe* (beans) almost everywhere. The main challenges away

---

DINING EAST AFRICAN STYLE

If you're lucky enough to be invited to share a meal with East Africans, you'll find that some customs are different from what you may be used to.

Before eating, a bowl and a pitcher of water are often passed around for washing hands. If the bowl is brought to you first as the guest, and you aren't sure what to do, indicate that it should be taken to the head of the family, then do what they do. The usual procedure is to hold your hands over the bowl while your hostess pours water over them. Sometimes soap is provided, and a towel for drying off.

The centre of the meal is usually *ugali* (thick, porridgelike maize- or cassava-based staple) or similar, which is normally taken with the right hand from a communal pot, rolled into a small ball with the fingers, dipped into some sort of sauce, and eaten. Eating with your hand is a bit of an art and may seem awkward at first, but after a few tries it will start to feel more natural. Food is never handled or eaten with the left hand, and in some areas it is even considered impolite to give someone something with the left hand, as this is normally reserved for toiletries.

The underlying element in all meal invitations is solidarity between the hosts and the guests, and the various customs, such as eating out of a communal dish, are simply expressions of this. If you receive an invitation to eat but aren't hungry, it's OK to explain that you have just eaten. However, you should still share a few bites of the meal in order to demonstrate your solidarity with the hosts, and to express your appreciation.

At the end of the meal, don't be worried if you can't finish what is on your plate, as this shows your hosts that you have been satisfied. However, do try to avoid being the one who takes the last handful from the communal bowl, as this may leave your hosts worrying they haven't provided enough.

Other than fruit, desserts are generally not served. Following the meal, the water and wash basin are brought around again so that you can clean your hand. Saying 'chakula kizuri' (delicious food!) in Swahili-speaking areas, or whatever the local equivalent is, lets your host know that the food was appreciated.

from major towns will be keeping some variety and balance in your diet, and getting enough protein, especially if you don't eat eggs or seafood. In larger towns, Indian restaurants are the best places to try for vegetarian meals. Elsewhere, try asking Indian shop owners if they have any suggestions; many will also be able to help you find good yogurt. Peanuts (*karanga* in Swahili-speaking areas) are widely sold on the streets, and fresh fruits and vegetables are abundant throughout most of the region. If you eat seafood, you'll have no problems along the coast or near any of the lakes, and even in inland areas good fish is often available from rivers and streams. Most tour operators are willing to cater to special dietary requests – such as vegetarian, kosher or halal – as long as they have advance notice.

Eating With Kids

East Africans are generally quite family-friendly, and dining out with children is no problem. Hotel restaurants in tourist areas often have highchairs, and staff do their best to be sure that everyone stays happy. While special children's meals aren't common, it's easy enough to find menu items that are suitable for young diners. The main things to avoid are curries and other spicy dishes, uncooked or unpeeled fruits and vegetables, meat from street vendors (as it's sometimes undercooked) and unpurified water. Child-size boxes of fresh juice are sold at supermarkets in major towns and make good snacks, as do fresh fruits (tangerines, bananas and more), which are widely available. For more on travelling with children, see p621.

Habits & Customs

Meals connected with any sort of social occasion are usually drawn out affairs for which the women of the household will have spent several days preparing. Typical East African style is to eat with the (right) hand from communal dishes in the centre of the table. There will always be somewhere to wash your hands, either a basin and pitcher of water that are passed around or a sink in the corner of the room. Although food is shared, it's not customary to share drinks, and children generally eat separately.

For East Africa's Maasai and other Nilotic peoples, milk – sometimes curdled – is a dietary mainstay, often mixed together with blood drawn from living cows' jugular veins.

Street snacks and meals-on-the-run are common. European-style restaurant dining – while readily available in major cities – is not an entrenched part of local culture. Much more common are large gatherings at home, or perhaps at a rented hall, to celebrate special occasions, with the meal as the focal point.

Throughout East Africa, lunch is served between about noon and 2.30pm, and dinner from around 6.30pm to about 10pm. The smaller the town, the earlier its dining establishments are likely to close; after about 7pm in rural areas it can be difficult to find anything other than street food. During Ramadan many restaurants in coastal areas close completely during daylight fasting hours.

Eat Your Words

Want to know *mkate* from *maandazi*, and *ndizi* from *nyama*? Conquer the cuisine scene by getting to know the language. The following Swahili words and phrases will help in Kenya, Tanzania and some parts of Uganda, and occasionally in Rwanda and Burundi as well. For pronunciation guidelines see p649.

USEFUL PHRASES

I'm a vegetarian.	*Nakula mbaga tu.*
I don't eat meat.	*Mimi sili nyama.*

Always boil or purify water, and be wary of ice and fruit juices diluted with unpurified water. With fruits and vegetables, it's best to follow the adage: 'Cook it, peel it, boil it or forget it.' For more on water safety see p648.

Is there a restaurant near here?	*Je, kuna hoteli ya chakula hapo jirani?*
Do you serve food here?	*Mnauza chakula hapa?*
I'd like...	*Ninataka/Ninaomba ...*
Without hot pepper, please.	*Bila pilipili, tafadhali.*
Please bring me the bill.	*Nipe bili/risiti tafadhali.*

MENU DECODER

biryani	casserole of spices and rice with meat or seafood
maandazi	semisweet, flat doughnuts
matoke	cooked plantains
mchuzi	sauce, sometimes with bits of beef and very well-cooked vegetables
mishikaki	kebab
mochomo	barbecued meat
ndizi	banana
nyama choma	roasted meat
pilau	spiced rice, cooked in broth with seafood or meat and vegetables
supu	soup – usually somewhat greasy, and served with a piece of beef, pork or meat fat in it.
ugali	thick, porridgelike maize- or cassava-based staple, available almost everywhere, and known as *posho* in Uganda.
wali na...	cooked white rice with...
kuku	chicken
nyama	meat
maharagwe	beans
samaki	fish

FOOD GLOSSARY

Basics

baridi	cold
kijiko	spoon
kikombe	cup
kisu	knife
kitambaa cha mikono	napkin
sahani	plate
tamu	sweet
uma	fork
ya moto	hot

Staples

chipsi	chips
maharagwe	beans
matoke	plantains (when cooked and mashed)
mkate	bread
ndizi	plantains
viazi	potatoes
wali	rice (cooked)

Other Dishes & Condiments

asali	honey
chumvi	salt
mayai (ya kuchemsha)	eggs (boiled)
mgando, mtindi, maziwalala	yogurt
sukari	sugar

Meat & Seafood

kaa	crab
kuku	chicken
nyama mbuzi	goat
nyama ya ng'ombe	beef
nyama ya nguruwe	pork
pweza	octopus (usually served grilled, at street markets)
samaki	fish

Fruits & Vegetables

chungwa	orange
dafu	coconut (green)
embe	mango
matunda	fruit
mboga	vegetables
nanasi	pineapple
nazi	coconut (ripe)
ndizi	banana
nyana	tomatoes
papai	papaya
sukuma wiki	spinach (boiled)
viazi	potatoes
vitunguu	onions

Drinks

bia (baridi)	beer (cold)
jusi ya machungwa	orange juice
maji (ya kuchemsha/ya kunywa/safi)	water (boiled/drinking/mineral)
waragi	millet-based alcohol
soda	soda

Along the coast, look for *chai masala* (spiced tea), or buy your coffee from vendors strolling the streets with a freshly brewed pot in one hand, cups and spoons in the other.

The Peoples of East Africa

East Africa has a rich mosaic of tribal cultures, with over 300 different groups packed into an area roughly a quarter the size of Australia. The vitality of their traditions is expressed in everything from splendid ceremonial attire to pulsating dance rhythms, refined artistry and highly organised community structure. Experiencing and witnessing all this is likely to be a highlight of your travels.

AKAMBA

The heartland of the Bantu-speaking Akamba people is in the area east of Nairobi. Relative newcomers to East Africa, the Akamba first migrated here from the south about 200 years ago in search of food. Because their own low-altitude land was poor, they were forced to barter to obtain food stocks from the neighbouring Maasai and Kikuyu. Soon, they acquired a reputation as great traders, with business dealings extending from the coast as far inland as Lake Victoria and north to Lake Turkana.

Renowned for their martial prowess, many Akamba were drafted into Britain's WWI army; today, they're still well-represented among Kenyan defence and law enforcement brigades.

The recent history of the Akamba illustrates the tensions that have marked so many encounters between East Africa's traditional cultures and Western 'values'. In the 1930s, during the height of the colonial era, the British administration settled large numbers of white farmers on traditional Akamba lands, and tried to limit the number of cattle the Akamba could own by confiscating them. In protest, the Akamba formed the Ukamba Members Association, which marched en masse to Nairobi and squatted peacefully at Kariokor Market until their cattle were returned. Large numbers of Akamba were subsequently dispossessed to make way for Tsavo National Park.

All Akamba go through initiation rites at about the age of 12, and have the same age-set groups common to many of the region's peoples (see below). Young parents are known as 'junior elders' (*mwanake* for men, *mwiitu* for women) and are responsible for the maintenance and upkeep of the village. They later become 'medium elders' (*nthele*), and then 'full elders' (*atumia ma kivalo*), with responsibility for death cere-

---

AGE SETS

The great significance of age among many of East Africa's traditional cultures is seen in the widespread use of age-based groups. In these, all youths of the same age belong to an age-set, and pass through the various stages of life and their associated rituals together. Each group has its own leader and community responsibilities, and definition of the age-sets is often highly refined. Among the Sukuma, for example, who live in the area south of Lake Victoria, each age-based group traditionally had its own system for counting from one to 10, with the system understood by others within the group, but not by members of any other group. Among the Maasai, who have one of the most highly stratified age group systems in the region, males are organised into age-sets and further into subsets, with interset rivalries and relationships being one of the defining features of daily life. Although the importance of age-sets among some tribes has diminished in recent times, they continue to play an important role in many areas.

monies and administering the law. The last stage of a person's life is that of 'senior elder' *(atumia ma kisuka)*, with responsibility for holy places.

BUGANDA

The Bantu-speaking Buganda are Uganda's largest tribal group, comprising about 17% of the population. Their traditional lands are in the areas north and northwest of Lake Victoria, including Kampala, although today you will meet Buganda throughout the country. Due to significant missionary activity most Buganda are Christian, although animist traditions do survive.

The Buganda are the source of Uganda's name, which means Land of the Buganda.

Historically, the Buganda, together with the neighbouring Haya, were known as one of East Africa's most highly organised tribes. Their political system was based around the absolute power of the *kabaka* (king), who ruled through district chiefs. This system reached its zenith during the 19th century, when the Buganda came to dominate various neighbouring groups, including the Nilotic Iteso people (who now comprise about 8% of Uganda's population; see p466). Buganda influence was solidified during the colonial era, with the British favouring their recruitment to the civil service. During the chaotic Obote/Amin years of the late 1960s and early 1970s, the Bugandan monarchy was abolished, to be restored in 1993, although with no political power.

EL MOLO

The Cushitic-speaking El-Molo are one of East Africa's smallest tribes, numbering less than 4000. Historically the El-Molo were one of the region's more culturally distinct groups, but in recent times they have been forced to adapt or relinquish many of their old customs in order to survive, and intermarriage with members of other tribes is now common.

The El-Molo traditionally subsisted on fish, supplemented by the occasional crocodile, turtle, hippopotamus or bird.

The ancestral home of the El-Molo is on two small islands in the middle of Lake Turkana in Kenya. Over the years an ill-balanced diet and the effects of too much fluoride began to take their toll. The El-Molo became increasingly susceptible to disease and, thus weakened, to attacks from stronger tribes, and their numbers plummeted.

Women of the El-Molo tribe (left) from Lake Turkana, Kenya
PHOTO BY TOM COCKREM

TRADITION, MODERNITY & THE FORESTS

East African society is full of contrasts, but nowhere is the clash between the traditional and the Western way of life more apparent than among the region's hunter-gatherer and forest-dwelling peoples. These include the Twa, who live primarily in the western forests of Rwanda and Burundi, where they comprise less than 1% of the overall population, and the Hadzabe, whose traditional lands are in north-central Tanzania around Lake Eyasi. Typically, these communities are among the most marginalised in East African society, lacking political influence and discriminated against by more prominent groups.

For the Twa, the Hadzabe and other communities, loss of land and forest means loss of the only resource base that they have. Over the past decades, the rise of commercial logging, the ongoing clearing of forests in favour of agricultural land, and the establishment of parks and conservation areas have combined to dramatically decrease the forest resources and wildlife on which these people depend for their existence. Additional pressures come from hunting and poaching, and from nomadic pastoralists – many of whom in turn have been evicted from their own traditional areas – seeking grazing lands for their cattle. The Hadzabe say that the once plentiful wildlife in their traditional hunting areas is now gone, and that many days they return empty-handed from their daily search for meat. Others lament the fact that once-prized skills such as animal tracking and knowledge of local plants are being relegated to irrelevance.

Although some Hadzabe have turned to tourism and craft-making for subsistence, the benefits of this are sporadic and limited in scope. Some now only hunt for the benefit of the increasing numbers of tourists who come to their lands, and a few have given up their traditional lifestyle completely. In Rwanda, the Twa have begun mobilising to gain increased political influence and greater access to health care and education, but the government response has thus far been negligible. Throughout the region, it's likely to be at least several decades before these people are given their voice, and the chance to define their own role in East African society.

Today, while the El-Molo have managed to temporarily stabilise their population, they face an uncertain future. While some continue to eke out a living from the lake, others have turned to cattle herding or work in the tourism industry. Commercial fishing supplements their traditional subsistence, and larger, more permanent settlements in Loyangalani, on Lake Turkana's southeastern shores, have replaced the El-Molo's traditional dome-shaped island homes of sticks covered with thatch and animal skins.

HAYA

The Haya, who live west of Lake Victoria around Bukoba, have both Bantu and Nilotic roots, and are one of the largest tribes in Tanzania.

While they're not the most colourful of the groups you'll encounter during your travels, the Haya have an exceptionally rich history, and in the precolonial era boasted one of the most highly developed early societies on the continent.

At the heart of traditional Haya society were eight different states or kingdoms, each headed by a powerful and often despotic *mukama*, who ruled in part by divine right. Order was maintained through a system of appointed chiefs and officials, assisted by an age group–based army. With the rise of European influence in the region, this era of Haya history came to an end. The various groups began to splinter, and many chiefs were replaced by persons considered more malleable and sympathetic to colonial interests.

Resentment of these propped-up leaders was strong, spurring the Haya to regroup and form the Bukoba Bahaya Union in 1924. This association was initially directed towards local political reform but soon

The Haya are renowned dancers and singers, and count East African pop stars Saida Karoli and Maua among their number.

Man of the Hadzabe tribe
(opposite), Tanzania
PHOTO BY ARIADNE VAN
ZANDBERGEN

developed into the more influential and broad-based African Association. Together with similar groups established elsewhere in Tanzania it constituted one of the country's earliest political movements and was an important force in the drive towards independence.

HUTU

The Hutu are the original Bantu-speaking farmers who inhabited the area that is now Rwanda and Burundi. Their origins are unclear, although it is thought that they were settled in the region by the 11th century, and had possibly begun arriving as early as the 5th century. From around the 14th century, the Hutu were joined by the Tutsi, who over the years were able to wrest control of significant political and economic power. Gradually the Hutu lost ownership of their land, with many living under Tutsi domination in a feudalistic client-patron relationship known as *ubuhake* in which land and cattle (and thus power) became further concentrated in the hands of the Tutsi minority.

The resentment engendered by the inequities of this system was given full vent in the 1994 genocide in Rwanda, with which the Hutu are inextricably linked – although large numbers of Hutu have also been massacred in neighbouring Burundi over the years. Reconciliation between the two groups has made gradual progress in Rwanda, but in Burundi the Hutu remain outside the political spectrum, and extremist elements continue to be an ongoing force for instability in the region (see p56 for more).

Under the *ubuhake* system, many Hutu were forced to indenture themselves to Tutsi overlords, leading to almost total Hutu disenfranchisement.

KALENJIN

The Kalenjin people are one of the largest groups in Kenya and – together with the Kikuyu, Luo, Luyha and Kamba – account for 70% of the country's population. Although viewed as a single ethnic entity, the term 'Kalenjin' was actually coined in the 1950s to refer to a loose collection of several different Nilotic groups, including the Kipsigi, Nandi, Marakwet, Pokot and Tugen (Former Kenyan president Daniel arap Moi's people). These groups speak different dialects of the same language (Nandi), but otherwise have distinct traditions and lifestyles. Thanks to the influence of arap Moi, the Kalenjin have amassed considerable political power in Kenya.

The Kalenjin are known for their female herbalist doctors, and for their many world-class runners, including Paul Tergat and Tecla Lorupe.

The traditional homeland of the various Kalenjin peoples is along the western edge of the central Rift Valley area, including Kericho, Eldoret, Kitale, Baringo and the land surrounding Mt Elgon. Originally pastoralists, Kalenjin today are known primarily as farmers. An exception to this are the cattle-loving Kipsigi, whose cattle rustling continues to cause friction between them and neighbouring tribes.

The Nandi, who are the second largest of the Kalenjin communities and comprise about one-third of all Kalenjin, settled in the Nandi Hills between the 16th and 17th centuries, where they prospered after learning agricultural techniques from the Luo and Luyha. They had a formidable military reputation and, in the late 19th century, managed to delay construction of the Uganda railway for more than a decade until Koitalel, their chief, was killed.

As with many tribes, the Kalenjin have age-sets into which a man is initiated after circumcision. Administration of the law is carried out at the *kok,* an informal court led by the clan's elders.

KARAMOJONG

When cattle are grazed in dry-season camps away from the family homestead, the Karamojong warriors tending them live on blood from live cattle, milk and sometimes meat.

The marginalised Karamojong – at home in Karamoja, in northeastern Uganda – are one of East Africa's most insulated, beleaguered and colourful tribes. As with the Samburu, Maasai and other Nilotic pastoralist peoples, life for the Karamojong centres around cattle, which are kept at night in the centre of the family living compound and grazed by day on the surrounding plains. Cattle are the main measure of wealth, ownership is a mark of adulthood, and cattle raiding and warfare are central parts of the culture. In times of scarcity, protection of the herd is considered so important that milk is reserved for calves and children.

Long the subject of often heavy-handed government pressure to abandon their pastoralist lifestyle, the Karamojong's plight has been exacerbated by periodic famines, and by the loss of traditional dry-season grazing areas with the formation of Kidepo Valley National Park in the 1960s. While current Ugandan president Yoweri Museveni has permitted the Karamojong to keep arms to protect themselves against raids from other groups, including the Turkana in neighbouring Kenya, government expeditions targeted at halting cattle raiding continue. These factors, combined with easy access to weapons from neighbouring Sudan and a breakdown of law and order, have made the Karamoja area off limits to outsiders in recent years.

KIKUYU

The Kikuyu god, *Ngai,* is believed to reside on Mt Kenya, and many Kikuyu homes are still oriented to face the sacred peak.

The heartland of the Kikuyu, who comprise about 20% of Kenya's population and are the country's largest ethnic group, surrounds Mt Kenya. They are Bantu people, who are believed to have migrated into the area from the east and northeast from around the 16th century onwards, and to have undergone several periods of intermarriage and splintering. According to the rich oral traditions of the Kikuyu, there are nine original *mwaki* (clans), all of which trace their origins back to male and female progenitors known as Kikuyu and Mumbi. The administration of these clans, each of which is made up of many *nyumba* (family groups) was originally overseen by a council of elders, with great significance placed on the roles of the witch doctor, medicine man and blacksmith.

Initiation rites consist of ritual circumcision for boys and clitoridectomy for girls, though the latter is becoming less common. The practice of clitoridectomy was a source of particular conflict between the Kikuyu and Western missionaries during the late 19th and early 20th centuries.

Kikuyu witch doctor
(left) and his assistant,
Kenya.
PHOTO BY ANDERS BLOMQVIST

The issue eventually became linked with the independence struggle, and the establishment of independent Kikuyu schools.

The Kikuyu are also known for the opposition association they formed in the 1920s to protest against the European seizure of large areas of their lands, and for their subsequent instigation of the Mau Mau rebellion in the 1950s. Due to the influence of Jomo Kenyatta, Kenya's first president, the Kikuyu today are disproportionately represented in government and business. This has proved to be a source of ongoing friction with other groups, and a persistent stumbling block on Kenya's path to national integration.

LUO

The northeastern shores of Lake Victoria are home to the Nilotic Luo people, who began their migration to the area from Sudan around the 15th century. Although their numbers are relatively small in Tanzania, in Kenya they comprise about 12% of the population and are the country's third-largest group.

During the independence struggle, many of Kenya's leading politicians and trade unionists were Luo – including Tom Mboya (assassinated in 1969) and the former vice president of Kenya, Jaramogi Oginga Odinga – and they continue to form the backbone of the Kenyan political opposition.

The Luo have also had a decisive influence on the East African musical scene. They are notable in particular for their contribution of the highly popular *benga* style (characterised by its electric guitar licks and bounding bass rhythms), which has since been adopted by musicians from many other tribes.

The Luo were originally cattle herders, but the devastating effects of rinderpest (an acute contagious viral disease of cattle) in the 1890s forced them to adopt fishing and subsistence agriculture, which continue to be the main sources of livelihood for most Luo today. Luo family groups consist of the man, his wife or wives, and their sons and daughters-in-law. The family unit is part of a larger grouping of families or *dhoot* (clan), several of which in turn make up an *ogandi* (a group of geographically

Instead of circumcision,
the Luo traditionally
extracted four to six teeth
at initiation.

Luo village children
(p401), Mfangano Island,
Kenya
PHOTO BY DAVE LEWIS

related people), each led by a *ruoth* (chief). Traditional Luo living compounds, which you'll still see when travelling around Lake Victoria, are enclosed by fences, and include separate huts for the man and for each wife and son. The Luo view age, wealth and respect as converging, with the result that elders control family resources and represent the family to the outside world.

MAASAI

Although comprising less than 5% of the population in Kenya and Tanzania, it is the Maasai, more than any other tribe, who have become for many the definitive symbol of 'tribal' East Africa. With a reputation (often quite exaggerated) as fierce warriors, and a proud demeanour, the Maasai have insisted on maintaining their ethnic identity and traditional lifestyle, often in the face of great government opposition. Today the life of the Maasai continues to be inextricably bound with that of their large herds of cattle, which they graze along the Tanzania–Kenya border.

The Maasai are Nilotic people who first migrated to the region from Sudan about 1000 years ago. They eventually came to dominate a large area of what is now central Kenya until, in the late 19th century, their numbers were decimated by famine and disease, and their cattle herds routed by rinderpest.

During the colonial era in Kenya, it was largely Maasai land that was taken for European colonisation through two controversial treaties. The creation of Serengeti National Park in Tanzania and the continuing colonial annexation of Maasai territory put much of the remaining traditional grazing lands of the Maasai off limits. During subsequent years, as the populations of both the Maasai and their cattle increased, pressure for land became intense and conflict with the authorities was constant. Government-sponsored resettlement programs have met with only limited success, as Maasai traditions scorn agriculture and land ownership.

The Maasai leave drums and other instruments behind in their famous dancing, which is accompanied only by chants and vigorous leaping.

One consequence of this competition for land is that many Maasai ceremonial traditions can no longer be fulfilled. Part of the ceremony where a man becomes a *moran* (warrior) involves a group of young men around the age of 14 going out and building a small livestock camp after their circumcision ceremony. They then live alone there for up to eight years before returning to the village to marry. Today though, while the tradition and the will to keep it up survive, the land is often unavailable.

The Maasai have vibrant artistic traditions that are most vividly seen in the striking body decoration and beaded ornaments worn by both men and women. Women in particular are famous for their magnificent beaded platelike necklaces, while men typically wear the red-checked *shuka* (blanket) and carry a distinctive balled club.

While tourism provides an income to an increasing number of Maasai, the benefits are not widespread. In recent years many Maasai have moved to the cities or coastal resorts, becoming guards for restaurants and hotels.

The Samburu people who live directly north of Mt Kenya are closely related to the Maasai linguistically and culturally.

MAKONDE

Although they have their home in one of the most isolated areas of East Africa, the Makonde have gained fame throughout the region and beyond for their beautiful and highly refined ebony woodcarvings.

The tribe has its origins in northern Mozambique, where many Makonde still live – though in recent years a subtle split has begun to develop between the group's Tanzanian and Mozambican branches. Today most Tanzanian Makonde live in southeastern Tanzania, on the waterless Makonde plateau, although many members of the carving community have since migrated to Dar es Salaam.

Like many of their southern neighbours, the Makonde are matrilineal. Although customs are gradually changing, children and inheritances normally belong to the woman, and it's still common for husbands to move to the villages of their wives after marriage. Makonde settlements are widely scattered – possibly a remnant of the days when they sought to evade slave raids – and there is no tradition of a unified political system. Despite this, a healthy sense of tribal identity has managed to survive. Makonde villages are typically governed by a hereditary chief and a council of elders.

Because of their remote location, the Makonde have succeeded in remaining largely insulated from colonial and postcolonial influences. They are known in particular for their steady resistance to Islam. Today most Makonde continue to adhere to traditional religions, with the complex spirit world given its fullest expression in their well-known carvings.

The Makonde traditionally practised body scarring. Many elders still sport facial markings and (the women) wooden lip plugs.

PARE

The Bantu-speaking Pare people inhabit the Pare Mountains in north-eastern Tanzania, where they migrated several centuries ago from the Taita Hills area of southern Kenya.

The Pare people are one of Tanzania's most educated groups and, despite their small numbers, have been highly influential in shaping the country's recent history. In the 1940s, they formed the Wapare Union, which played an extremely important role in Tanzania's drive for independence.

Among the patrilineal Pare, a deceased male's ghost influences all male descendants for as long as the ghost's name is remembered.

The Pare are also known for their rich oral traditions, and for their elaborate rituals centring on the dead. Near most villages are sacred areas in which skulls of tribal chiefs are kept. When people die, they are believed to inhabit a netherworld between the land of the living and the spirit world. If they are allowed to remain in this state, ill fate will befall their descendants. As a result, rituals allowing the deceased to pass into the world of the ancestors hold great significance. Traditional Pare beliefs also hold that when an adult male dies, others in his lineage will die as well until the cause of his death has been found and 'appeased'. Many of the possible reasons for death have to do with disturbances in moral relations within the lineage or in the village, or with sorcery.

SUKUMA

The Sukuma, who live in the southern Lake Victoria region, comprise almost 15% of Tanzania's total population, although it is only relatively recently that they have come to view themselves as a single entity. Bantu-speakers, they are closely related to the Nyamwezi, who are Tanzania's second-largest tribal group and based around Tabora.

The Sukuma are renowned for their sophisticated drumming, and for their skilled and energetic dancing. Among the focal points of tribal life are lively meetings between the two competing dance societies, the Bagika and the Bagulu.

The Sukuma are also known for their highly structured form of village organisation, in which each settlement is subdivided into chiefdoms ruled by a *ntemi* (chief) in collaboration with a council of elders. Divisions of land and labour are made by village committees consisting of similarly aged members from each family in the village. These age-based groups perform numerous roles, ranging from assisting with the building of new houses to farming and other community-oriented work. As a result of this system – which gives most families at least a representational role in many village activities – Sukuma often view houses and land as communal property.

SWAHILI

East Africa's coast is home to the Swahili (People of the Coast), descendants of Bantu-Arab traders who share a common language and traditions. Although they are generally not regarded as a single ethnic group, the Swahili have for centuries had their own distinct societal structures, and consider themselves to be a single civilisation.

Swahili culture first began to take on a defined form around the 11th century, with the rise of Islam. Today almost all Swahili are adherents of Islam, although it's generally a more liberal version than that practised in the Middle East. Thanks to this Islamic identity, the Swahili have traditionally considered themselves to be historically and morally distinct from peoples in the interior, and believe they have links northeastwards to the rest of the Muslim world.

Swahili festivals follow the Islamic calendar. The year begins with Eid al-Fitr, a celebration of feasting and almsgiving to mark the end of Ramadan fasting. The old Persian New Year's purification ritual of *Nauroz* (or *Mwaka*) was also traditionally celebrated, with the parading of a bull counterclockwise through town followed by its slaughter and several days of exuberant dancing and feasting, though in many areas *Nauroz* has now become merged with Eid al-Fitr and is no longer observed. The festival of Maulid (marking the birth of the Prophet) is another major Swahili festival, marked by decorated mosques and colourful street processions.

The Sukuma are renowned for their daring hyena, snake and porcupine dances, though dancers (and often animals, too) are usually treated with traditional medicines beforehand – as protection for the dancers, and to calm the animals.

Swahili is now spoken in more countries and by more people than any other language in sub-Saharan Africa.

Arabic Swahili (opposite) henna design being made, Kenya.
PHOTO BY ARIADNE VAN ZANDBERGEN

TURKANA

The Turkana, one of East Africa's most colourful tribes, are a Nilotic people who live in the harsh desert country of northwestern Kenya, where they migrated to from southern Sudan and northeastern Uganda. Although the Turkana only emerged as a distinct ethnic group during the early to mid-19th century, they are notable today for their very strong sense of tribal identification. The Turkana people are closely related both linguistically and culturally to Uganda's Karamojong people (see p50).

Like the Samburu and the Maasai (with whom they are also linguistically linked), the Turkana are primarily cattle herders, although in recent years increasing numbers have turned to fishing and subsistence farming. Some also earn a livelihood through basket weaving and producing other crafts for the tourism industry. Personal relationships based on the exchange of cattle, and built up by each herd owner during the course of a lifetime, are of critical importance in Turkana society and function as a social security net during times of need.

The Turkana are famous for their striking appearance and traditional garb. Turkana men cover part of their hair with mud, which is then painted blue and decorated with ostrich and other feathers. Despite the intense heat of the Turkana lands, the main garment is a woollen blanket, often with garish checks. Turkana accessories include a stool carved out of a single piece of wood, a wooden fighting staff and a wrist knife. Tattooing is another hallmark of Turkana life. Witch doctors and prophets are held in high regard, and scars on the lower stomach are usually a sign of a witch doctor's attempt to cast out an undesirable spirit.

In addition to personal adornment, other important forms of artistic expression include finely crafted carvings and refined a cappella singing. Ceremonies play a less significant role among the Turkana people than among many of their neighbours, and they do not practice circumcision or clitoridectomy.

Turkana men were traditionally tattooed on the shoulder and upper arm for killing an enemy – the right shoulder for killing a man, the left for a woman.

TUTSI

The tall, warriorlike Tutsi people are thought to have migrated to present-day Rwanda and Burundi from Ethiopia or southern Sudan between the 14th and 17th centuries. Through their ownership of cattle and advanced combat skills, they were soon able to establish economic and political control over the local Hutu, and this dominance continues to the present day. At the top of the Tutsi-Hutu feudal relationship (see p49) was the Tutsi king, or *mwami*, who was believed to be of divine origin.

While thousands of Tutsi were massacred during the Rwandan genocide of 1994, in Burundi the Tutsi-dominated regime has also been responsible for the deaths of many Hutu in the period since independence. Relations between the Tutsi and neighbouring tribes remain fraught with mistrust.

The Watusi – popular in the USA in the 1960s – is a Westernised version of a traditional Tutsi dance.

Wildlife Guide

East Africa is teeming with wildlife. From the vast wildebeest herds that stampede across the plains of Serengeti National Park and Masai Mara National Reserve, to chimpanzee bands frolicking in the rainforests of southwestern Uganda, the region is one of the continent's premier safari destinations. In few other places on earth can you find such an impressive collection of large animals and such a diversity of environmental and climatic conditions within a similarly sized geographical area. Best of all, much of this natural wealth is readily accessible to visitors, thanks to enlightened conservation policies and an unparalleled collection of national parks and reserves. The East African safari experience is made all the more alluring as the habitats favoured by early humans – mosaics of riverine forest, savanna and lake shore – remain much as they did a million years ago, when our ancestors shared the plains with many of the animal species that still roam around today.

Wherever you head in the region, and whatever type of safari you choose, it's worth remembering that watching wildlife is about far more than just 'seeing' the animals and ticking them off on checklists. It's much more about experiencing East Africa untamed, getting a glimpse into nature's magnificent synchrony and understanding how the rhythms of the wild can be best protected for future generations. Doing all this takes time – time to loiter for hours at a watering hole, to sit in one spot at dawn while the morning rises around you, or to learn about the animals' habits and migration patterns, and the myriad factors affecting them. It also often takes money as well, although it's possible with some planning to keep things at a reasonable level. The more understanding you can accumulate about the animals and their environment, the more satisfied you'll be that your East African safari has been time and money well spent.

Lions drinking, Ruaha National Park, Tanzania
PHOTO BY ARIADNE VAN ZANDBERGEN

PRIMATES

Greater bushbabies are named for their plaintive wailing calls (the calls of lesser bushbabies are rarely noticed).
PHOTO BY MITCH REARDON

BUSHBABY
Greater or thick-tailed bushbaby (*Otolemur crassicaudatus*, pictured); East African lesser bushbaby *(Galago senegalensis)*; Zanzibar lesser bushbaby *(Galagoides zanibaricus)*

A primitive primate, bushbabies have heightened night vision and extremely sensitive hearing, making them ideally adapted to their nocturnal way of life. Fruit and tree-sap are the mainstay of their diet, supplemented by insects and, in the case of the greater bushbaby, lizards, nestlings and eggs. Locally very common, they are difficult to see because they are strictly nocturnal.
Size: Greater bushbaby length 80cm, including 45cm tail; weight up to 1.5kg. Lesser bushbaby length 40cm; weight 150g to 200g. **Distribution**: Lightly wooded savanna to thickly forested areas; greater and lesser bushbabies occur throughout the region. **Status**: Common, but strictly nocturnal.

The male vervet monkey has a distinctive bright-blue scrotum, an important signal of status in the troop.
PHOTO BY ARIADNE VAN ZANDBERGEN

VERVET MONKEY
Cercopithecus aethiops

Conspicuous inhabitants of the woodland-savanna, vervet monkeys are easily recognised by their grizzled grey hair and black face fringed with white. Troops may number up to 30. Vervet monkeys have a sophisticated vocal repertoire, with, for example, different calls for different predators. They are diurnal, and forage for fruits, seeds, leaves, flowers, invertebrates and the occasional lizard or nestling. They rapidly learn where easy pickings can be found around lodges and camp sites, but become pests when they are accustomed to being fed.
Size: Length up to 1.3m, including 65cm tail; weight 3kg to 9kg; male larger than female.
Distribution: All savanna and woodland habitats. **Status**: Very common and easy to see.

The blue monkey's social group may be as large as 30 but generally number between four and 12.
PHOTO BY ANDERS BLOMQVIST

BLUE (SAMANGO) MONKEY
Cercopithecus mitis

Similar to vervet monkeys, but slightly larger and much darker, blue monkeys have a grey to black face, black shoulders, limbs and tail, and a reddish-brown or olive-brown back. They are more arboreal than vervet monkeys, and generally prefer dense forest and woodland rather than savanna. They feed largely on fruit, bark, gum and leaves. Social groups usually consist of related females and their young, and a single adult male. Their broad diet allows them to occupy relatively small home ranges.
Size: Length 1.4m, including 80cm tail; weight normally up to 15kg, but as much as 23kg; male larger than female. **Distribution**: Throughout most evergreen forests and forest patches. **Status**: Locally common; active by day; often difficult to see in foliage. Easy to see in Uganda's Kibale Forest.

BABOON
Papio cynocephalus

Baboons are unmistakable. The yellow baboon *(P. c. cynocephalus)* and the olive baboon *(P. c. anubis;* pictured) are named for their differing hair colour. Baboons live in troops of between eight and 200; contrary to popular belief, there is no single dominant male. Social interactions are complex, with males accessing only certain females, males forming alliances to dominate other males, and males caring for unrelated juveniles. Baboons forage in woodland-savanna for grasses, tubers, fruits, invertebrates and occasionally small vertebrates.

Size: Shoulder height 75cm; length 1.6m, including 70cm tail; weight up to 45kg; male larger than female, and twice as heavy. **Distribution**: Throughout the region. **Status**: Abundant.

Ever opportunistic, baboons often visit camp sites and may become (dangerous) pests.
PHOTO BY JASON EDWARDS

CHIMPANZEE
Pan troglodytes

The chimpanzee is our closest living relative and behaves like it, engaging in cooperative hunting, tool manufacture and use, and war. They are highly sociable, living in communities numbering up to 120; however, all individuals in a social group rarely congregate and the typical group size is much smaller. Individuals may also spend considerable time alone. Primarily vegetarians consuming fruit, bark, stems and leaves, chimps also eat insects, nestling birds, eggs and larger prey, including monkeys.

Size: Up to 1.7m when standing; weight 25kg to 55kg, male larger than female. **Distribution**: Equatorial forest in western Tanzania, Rwanda, Burundi and western Uganda; best seen in Gombe Stream and Mahale Mountains National Parks. **Status**: Threatened by habitat destruction and hunting (ie illegal chimp trafficking), chimpanzees are endangered and occur in small isolated populations.

Though requiring a rich year-round food supply and preferring productive, moist forests, the chimpanzee is adaptable and is found in a wide range of habitats.
PHOTO BY ARIADNE VAN ZANDBERGEN

GORILLA
Gorilla gorilla

Two races occur in the region: eastern lowland gorillas *(G. g. graueri)*, numbering 4000 in eastern Democratic Republic of the Congo and Rwanda; and mountain gorillas *(G. g. beringei*; pictured), of which there are only 600 to 700 left in the DR Congo/Rwanda/Uganda border region. Gorillas inhabit humid equatorial rainforest up to 4000m. Groups number between two and 20, usually with a single adult male (silverback), though large groups of the eastern race may contain up to four silverbacks. They are vegetarians.

Size: Height up to 1.8m; mass up to 210kg (males), 70kg to 100kg (females). **Distribution**: Equatorial forest in western Tanzania, Rwanda, Burundi and southwestern Uganda. **Status**: Threatened by poaching, habitat destruction and civil unrest; highly endangered.

Male gorillas make all decisions regarding movements, foraging, and where and when to rest.
PHOTO BY DOUG MCKINLAY

CARNIVORES

GENET
Small-spotted genet (*Genetta genetta,* pictured); large-spotted genet *(G. tigrina)*

Relatives of mongooses, genets resemble long, slender domestic cats, with foxlike faces. The two species in the region can be differentiated by the tail tips – white in the small-spotted, black in the large-spotted. The former has a crest along the spine, which it raises when threatened. All-black individuals of both species may occur, particularly in mountainous regions. They feed on rodents, birds, reptiles, eggs, insects and fruits.
Size: Shoulder height 18cm; length 85cm to 1.1m, including 45cm tail; weight up to 3kg.
Distribution: Widely distributed throughout the region. **Status**: Very common, but strictly nocturnal; often the most common small carnivore seen at night.

MONGOOSE

Many of the small animals that dash in front of cars in Africa are mongooses. A few species, such as the dwarf mongoose (*Helogale parvula;* pictured) and the banded mongoose *(Mungos mungo)* are intensely social, keeping contact with twittering calls while foraging. Others, such as the slender mongoose (*Galerella sanguinea)* – with a black-tipped tail that it holds aloft when running – and the white-tailed mongoose *(Ichneumia albicauda),* are usually solitary. Family groups are better at spotting danger and raising kittens. Invertebrates are their most important prey.
Size: Ranges from the dwarf mongoose at 40cm in length and up to 400g in weight, to the white-tailed mongoose at 1.2m and up to 5.5kg. **Distribution**: Widely distributed. They prefer open areas. **Status**: Common; sociable species are diurnal, while solitary species are generally nocturnal.

AARDWOLF
Proteles cristatus

The smallest of the hyena family, aardwolves subsist almost entirely on harvester termites (which are generally ignored by other termite eaters because they are so noxious), licking more than 200,000 from the ground each night. Unlike other hyaenids, they don't form clans; instead they forage alone and mates form only loose associations with each other. The male assists the female in raising the cubs, mostly by babysitting at the den while the mother forages. Aardwolves are persecuted in the mistaken belief that they kill stock.
Size: Shoulder height 40cm to 50cm; length 80cm to 1m, including tail of up to 25cm; weight 8kg to 12kg. **Distribution**: Widespread in savanna and woodland habitats from central Tanzania into the arid north of Kenya. **Status**: Uncommon; nocturnal but occasionally seen at dawn and dusk.

STRIPED HYENA
Hyaena hyaena

Hyenas are lean, long-legged animals whose overall appearance is of more robust animals due to their long, shaggy manes and 'capes' along their backs. Striped hyenas subsist largely by scavenging from the kills of other predators and carrying off large parts to cache. They also catch insects and small vertebrates, but are poor hunters of larger prey.

Size: Shoulder height 65cm to 80cm; mass 25kg to 45kg. **Distribution**: Central Tanzania into arid zones of northern Kenya. **Status**: Uncommon; strictly nocturnal.

Striped hyenas forage alone, but groups of up to seven may congregate on large carcasses.

PHOTO BY D MASON/ WINDRUSH PHOTOS

SPOTTED HYENA
Crocuta crocuta

Widely reviled as scavengers, spotted hyenas are highly efficient predators with a fascinating social system. Females are larger than, and dominant to, males and have male physical characteristics, including an erectile clitoris that renders the sexes virtually indistinguishable at a distance. Spotted hyenas are massively built and appear distinctly canine, but they are more closely related to cats than dogs. They can run at a speed of 60km/h, and a pack can easily dispatch adult wildebeests and zebras. Their 'ooo-oop' call is one of the most distinctive East African night sounds.

Size: Shoulder height 85cm; length up to 1.8m, including tail of up to 30cm; weight up to 80kg. **Distribution**: Throughout the region, increasingly restricted to conservation areas. **Status**: Common where there is suitable food and often the most common large predator in protected areas; mainly nocturnal but also seen during the day.

Spotted hyena clans, which can contain dozens of individuals, are led by females.

PHOTO BY ARIADNE VAN ZANDBERGEN

CHEETAH
Acinonyx jubatus

The world's fastest land mammal, cheetahs can reach speeds of over 105km/h, but become exhausted after a few hundred metres and therefore usually stalk prey to within 60m before unleashing their tremendous acceleration. Cheetahs prey on antelopes weighing up to 60kg as well as hares and young wildebeests and zebras. Litters may be as large as nine, but in open savanna habitats most cubs are killed by other predators, particularly lions. Young cheetahs disperse from the mother when aged around 18 months. The males form coalitions; females remain solitary for life.

Size: Shoulder height 85cm; length up to 2.2m, including tail up to 70cm; weight up to 65kg. **Distribution**: Largely restricted to protected areas or the regions surrounding them; shuns densely forested areas. **Status**: Uncommon, with individuals moving over large areas; frequently seen in national parks.

Three out of every four hunts fail for cheetahs.

PHOTO BY ALEX DISSANAYAKE

Leopards are heard more often than seen; their rasping territorial call sounds very much like a saw cutting through wood.
PHOTO BY MITCH REARDON

LEOPARD
Panthera pardus

Supreme ambush hunters, leopards stalk close to their prey before attacking in an explosive rush. They eat everything from insects to zebras, but antelopes are their primary prey. Leopards are highly agile and climb well, spending more time in trees than other big cats – they hoist their kills into trees to avoid losing them to lions and hyenas. They are solitary animals, except when a male and female remain in close association for the female's week-long oestrus.

Size: Shoulder height 50cm to 75cm; length 1.6m to 2.1m, including 70cm to 1.1m tail; weight up to 90kg; male larger than female. **Distribution**: Widely spread throughout the region, they also persist in human-altered habitat due to their great adaptability. **Status**: Common but, being mainly nocturnal, they are very difficult to see.

Young male lions are ousted from the pride at the age of two or three, becoming nomadic until around five years old, when they are able to take over their own pride.
PHOTO BY ALEX DISSANAYAKE

LION
Panthera leo

Lions spend nights hunting, patrolling territories (of 50 to 400 sq km) and playing. They live in prides of up to about 30, comprising four to 12 related females, which remain in the pride for life, and a coalition of unrelated males, which defend females from foreign males. Lions hunt – certainly as a group, perhaps cooperatively – virtually anything, but wildebeests, zebras and buffaloes are their main targets.

Size: Shoulder height 1.2m; length 2.5m to 3m, including tail up to 1m; weight up to 260kg (male), 180kg (female). **Distribution**: Largely confined to protected areas and present in all savanna and woodland parks in the region. **Status**: Common where they occur; mainly nocturnal but easy to see during the day.

Caracals' long back legs power prodigious leaps – they even take birds in flight.
PHOTO BY DAVID WALL

CARACAL
Felis caracal

Sometimes called African lynxes due to their long, tufted ears, caracals are robust, powerful cats that prey mostly on small antelopes, birds and rodents but also take prey much larger than themselves. Caracals are largely solitary and, although male-female pairs may associate more than most other cats, females raise their one to three kittens alone. The sandy body colour is excellent camouflage, but the ears and face are strikingly patterned in black and white and are highly mobile and expressive – features are used for visual signalling.

Size: Shoulder height 40cm to 50cm; length 95cm to 1.2m, including tail up to 30cm; weight 7kg to 18kg; male slightly larger than female. **Distribution**: Throughout the region. **Status**: Fairly common, but largely nocturnal and difficult to see.

AFRICAN WILD CAT
Felis lybica

The progenitor of the household tabby, African wild cats were originally domesticated by the Egyptians. They differ from domestic cats in having reddish backs to their ears, proportionally longer legs and a generally leaner appearance. African wild cats cross freely with domestic cats close to human habitation where the two meet, and this is probably the greatest threat to the integrity of the wild species. They are solitary, except when females have kittens.

African wild cats subsist mainly on small rodents, but also prey on birds and insects, and species up to the size of hares.

PHOTO BY ABI

Size: Shoulder height 35cm; length 85cm to 1m; mass up to 6kg. **Distribution**: Throughout the region. **Status**: Common; nocturnal, although sometimes spotted at dawn and dusk.

SERVAL
Felis serval

The first impression one gains of servals – tall, slender, long-legged cats – is that they look quite like small cheetahs. Their tawny to russet yellow coat has large black spots, forming long bars and blotches on the neck and shoulders. All-black individuals also occasionally occur particularly in Kenya's mountainous regions. Other distinguishing features of the serval include large upright ears, a long neck and a relatively short tail. Servals are associated with vegetation near water, and are most common in flood-plain savanna, wetlands and woodlands near streams. Birds, small reptiles and occasionally the young of small antelopes are also taken.

Servals are rodent specialists, feeding on mice, rats and spring-hares.

PHOTO BY MITCH REARDON

Size: Shoulder height 60cm; length up to 1.3m, including tail up to 30cm; weight up to 16kg. **Distribution**: Well-watered habitats throughout the region. **Status**: Relatively common, but mainly nocturnal, sometimes seen in the early morning and late afternoon.

BAT-EARED FOX
Otocyon megalotis

These little foxes eat mainly insects, especially termites, but also wild fruit and small vertebrates. They are monogamous, and are often seen in groups comprising a mated pair and offspring. Natural enemies include large birds of prey, spotted hyenas, caracals and larger cats. They will bravely attempt to rescue a family member caught by a predator by using distraction techniques and harassment, which extends to nipping larger enemies on the ankles.

The huge ears of bat-eared foxes detect the faint sounds of invertebrates below ground, before they unearth them in a burst of frantic digging.

PHOTO BY ARIADNE VAN ZANDBERGEN

Size: Shoulder height 35cm; length 75cm to 90cm, including 30cm tail; weight 3kg to 5kg. **Distribution**: Throughout the region. **Status**: Common, especially in national parks; mainly nocturnal but often seen in the late afternoon and early morning.

Jackals scavenge from the kills of larger predators, but are also efficient hunters.
PHOTO BY DENNIS JONES

JACKAL
Golden jackal *(Canis aureus)*; black-backed jackal (C. *mesomelas,* pictured); side-striped jackal *(C. adustus)*

Golden jackals are often the most numerous carnivores in open savanna and are very active by day. Black-backed jackals have a mantle of silver-grey hair and black-tipped tails; they are the most common night scavengers. Side-striped jackals are the least common. They're grey with a light stripe along each side and a white-tipped tail. All have a similar social and feeding behaviour. Pairs are long-lasting and defend small territories.

Size: Shoulder height 38cm to 50cm; length 95cm to 1.2m, including 25cm to 40cm tail (shortest in the golden jackal); weight up to 15kg. **Distribution**: Widespread with a wide habitat tolerance, preferring open plains and woodlands; side-striped jackal most abundant in well-watered wooded areas. **Status**: Abundant in parks and settled areas.

Wild dogs are endurance hunters; the pack chases prey until exhaustion, then cooperates to pull it down.
PHOTO BY ARIADNE VAN ZANDBERGEN

WILD DOG
Lycaon pictus

Wild dogs' blotched black, yellow and white coat, and their large, round ears, are unmistakable. They live in packs of up to 40, though usually 12 to 20. They are widely reviled for eating their prey alive, but this is probably as fast as 'cleaner' methods used by other carnivores. Mid-sized antelopes are their preferred prey, but wild dogs can take animals as large as buffaloes. They require enormous areas of habitat and they are among the most endangered carnivores in Africa.

Size: Shoulder height 65cm to 80cm; length 1m to 1.5m, including 35cm tail; weight 20kg to 35kg. **Distribution**: Much reduced, now restricted to the largest protected areas in the region. **Status**: Highly threatened: numbers reduced by persecution, disease and habitat loss.

The honey badger's thick, loose skin is an excellent defence against predators, bee stings and snake bites.
PHOTO BY LORNA STANTON/ABPL

HONEY BADGER (RATEL)
Mellivora capensis

Pugnacious and astonishingly powerful for their size, honey badgers have a fascinating relationship with honey guide birds. Honey guides lead them to bees' nests, which honey badgers rip open for honey, and in doing so provide honey guides access to their favoured food – beeswax. Honey badgers are omnivorous, feeding on small animals, carrion, berries, roots, eggs, honey, and social insects (ants, termites and bees) and their larvae. Honey badgers are best viewed in parks, where they sometimes scavenge from bins.

Size: Shoulder height 30cm; length 95cm, including 20cm tail; weight up to 15kg. **Distribution**: Widespread in the region, in most habitats. **Status**: Generally occurs in low densities, but populations are sustainable; apparently active by day in parks but nocturnal in areas of human habitation.

UNGULATES

AFRICAN ELEPHANT
Loxodonta africana

Elephants usually live in groups of 10 to 20 females and their young, congregating in larger herds at common water and food resources. Vocalisations include a deep rumble felt as a low vibration, and a high-pitched trumpeting given in threat or when frightened. Consuming

Bull elephants live alone or in bachelor groups, joining herds when females are in season.
PHOTO BY ARIADNE VAN ZANDBERGEN

250kg of vegetation daily, elephants can decimate woodlands, but this may be part of the savanna's natural cycle. They live for up to 100 years.
Size: Shoulder height up to 4m (male), 3.5m (female); weight 5 to 6.5 tonnes (male), 3 to 3.5 tonnes (female). **Distribution:** Widely distributed in the region, though large populations only occur in protected areas. **Status:** Very common in most of the larger national parks.

HYRAX
Rock hyrax (*Procavia capensis*, pictured); tree hyrax (*Dendrohyrax arboreus*); yellow-spotted or bush hyrax (*Heterohyrax brucei*)

Although hyraxes resemble large, robust guinea-pigs, they are most closely related to elephants. Three species occur, the most common being the rock hyrax found on

If accustomed to humans, hyraxes are often approachable but will dash off if alarmed, uttering shrill screams.
PHOTO BY ARIADNE VAN ZANDBERGEN

mountains or rocky outcrops. They form colonies of up to 60, often with the yellow-spotted hyrax, which is slightly smaller with distinctive white underparts. Kopjes (rock outcrops) in the Serengeti are excellent sites for observing the two species. The tree hyrax prefers forest rather than rocks.
Size: Length 60cm; mass up to 5.5kg. **Distribution**: Bush and rock species very widely distributed; tree hyraxes restricted to lowland rainforest and best seen in forest reserves, such as Aberdare, Mt Kenya and the Rwenzoris. **Status**: Common; a regular inhabitant of lodges, where they become tame.

BLACK (HOOK-LIPPED) RHINOCEROS
Diceros bicornis

In many countries rhinos have been exterminated and the white rhino (*Ceratotherium simum*) is now very rare in East Africa (it remains numerous in southern Africa). The smaller of the two species, black rhinos are more unpredictable and prone to charging when alarmed or

Poaching for horns has made the rhinoceros Africa's most endangered large mammal.
PHOTO BY JASON EDWARDS

uncertain about a possible threat. They use their pointed, prehensile upper lip to feed selectively on branches and foliage. Black rhinos are solitary and aggressively territorial, usually only socialising during the mating season; however, they may form temporary associations.
Size: Shoulder height 1.6m; length 3m to 4m; weight 800kg to 1.4 tonnes; front horn up to 1.3m long. **Distribution**: Restricted to relict populations in a few reserves. **Status**: Highly endangered in the region, but seen in protected areas.

ZEBRA
Common or Burchell's zebra (*Equus burchelli*, pictured); Grevy's zebra (*Equus grevyi*)

Two species occur in the region, the most common being Burchell's zebra, famous for its huge migrating herds. Burchell's zebras are marked with broad alternating black-and-white stripes, interspersed with faint 'shadow stripes'. Grevy's zebras are marked all over with much finer stripes and lack shadow stripes. Both species are grazers, but occasionally browse on leaves and scrub. The social system centres around small groups of related mares over which stallions fight fiercely.

Size: Shoulder height 1.4m (Burchell's zebras), 1.6m (Grevy's). Mass up to 360kg (Burchell's), up to 390kg (Grevy's). **Distribution**: Burchell's zebras occur throughout the region. Grevy's zebras restricted to northern Kenya. **Status**: Burchell's zebras common. Grevy's zebras only common in Kenya's northern frontier district.

WARTHOG
Phacochoerus aethiopicus

Warthogs are abundant in all savanna and woodland habitats in East Africa. They grow two sets of tusks: their upper tusks grow as long as 60cm, and their lower tusks are usually less than 15cm long. Sociality varies, but groups usually consist of one to three sows and their young. Males form bachelor groups or are solitary, only associating with females during oestrus. Warthogs feed mainly on grass, but also on fruit and bark. In hard times they grub for roots and bulbs. They den in abandoned burrows or excavate their own burrows.

Size: Shoulder height 70cm; weight up to more than 100kg, but averages 50kg to 60kg; male larger than female. **Distribution**: Throughout the region. **Status**: Common, diurnal and easy to see.

HIPPOPOTAMUS
Hippopotamus amphibius

Hippos are found close to fresh water, spending most of the day submerged and emerging at night to graze on land. They can consume about 40kg of vegetation each evening. They live in large herds, tolerating close contact in the water but foraging alone when on land. The scars found on bulls resulting from conflicts are often a convenient indicator of the sex of hippos. Cows with calves are aggressive towards other individuals. Hippos are extremely dangerous when on land and kill many people each year, usually when someone inadvertently blocks the animal's retreat to the water.

Size: Shoulder height 1.5m; weight 1 to 2 tonnes. **Distribution**: Occur widely, usually found near large areas of fresh water. **Status**: Common in major water courses and easy to see.

GIRAFFE
Giraffa camelopardalis

A giraffe's neck has seven cervical vertebrae – the same as all mammals.
PHOTO BY MATT FLETCHER

There are several distinctly patterned subspecies of giraffe, including reticulated giraffes and Masai giraffes, which are more common. The 'horns' (knobs of skin-covered bone) of males have bald tips; females' are covered in hair. Giraffes form loose, ever-changing groups of up to 50; females are rarely seen alone, while males are more solitary. Browsers, giraffes exploit foliage out of reach of most herbivores – males usually feed from a higher level than females. Juveniles are prone to predation and lions even take adults; giraffes are most vulnerable when drinking.

Size: Height 4m to 5.5m (male); 3.5m to 4.5m (female); weight 900kg to 1.4 tonnes (male), 700kg to 1 tonne (female). **Distribution**: Reticulated giraffe occurs in northern Kenya; Masai giraffe is widespread southwest of Nairobi extending into Tanzania; Rothschild's giraffe is restricted to Uganda and western Kenya near Lake Baringo. **Status**: Relatively common and easy to see.

KLIPSPRINGER
Oreotragus oreotragus

When disturbed, a pair of klipspringers often gives a duet of trumpetlike alarm calls.
PHOTO BY ARIADNE VAN ZANDBERGEN

Small, sturdy antelopes, klipspringers are easily recognised by their curious tip-toe stance – their hooves are adapted for balance and grip on rocky surfaces, enabling them to bound up impossibly rough and steep rockfaces. Klipspringers normally inhabit rocky outcrops; they also sometimes venture into adjacent grasslands, but always retreat to the rocks when alarmed. Klipspringers form long-lasting pair bonds and the pair occupies a territory, nearly always remaining within a couple of metres of each other.

Size: Shoulder height 55cm; weight 9kg to 15kg; horns up to 15cm; female larger than male. **Distribution**: Rocky outcrops and mountainous areas throughout the region. **Status**: Common, but wary; often seen standing on high vantage points.

KIRK'S DIK-DIK
Madoqua kirkii

A dik-dik's territory is marked by up to a dozen large piles of dung placed around the boundary.
PHOTO BY ARIADNE VAN ZANDBERGEN

Dik-diks are identified by their miniature size, the pointed flexible snout and a tuft of hair on the forehead; only the males have horns. Dik-diks are monogamous and pairs are territorial. If one is seen, its mate is usually nearby, as well as that year's young. Both members of the pair, and their young, use dung piles to mark their territory, placing their deposits as part of an elaborate ceremony. Dik-diks feed by browsing on foliage and, being well adapted to their dry environments, don't drink.

Size: Shoulder height 35cm to 45cm; weight 4kg to 7kg; horns up to 12cm. **Distribution**: Throughout the region. **Status**: Common, but wary and easy to miss; active day and night.

If a predator approaches, steenboks lie flat with neck outstretched, zigzagging away only at the last moment.
PHOTO BY MITCH REARDON

STEENBOK
Raphicerus campestris

Steenboks are pretty and slender antelopes; their back and hindquarters range from light reddish-brown to dark brown with pale underpart markings. The nose bears a black, wedge-shaped stripe. Males have small, straight and widely separated horns. Although usually seen alone, it's likely that steenboks share a small territory with a mate, but only occasionally does the pair come together. Steenboks are active in the morning and afternoon and by night; they may become more nocturnal where frequently disturbed.

Size: Shoulder height 50cm; weight up to 16kg; horns up to 19cm; female a little larger than male. **Distribution**: Restricted to central and northern Kenya into Tanzania. **Status**: Relatively common, but easily overlooked.

Often dismissed by tourists because they are so abundant, impalas are unique antelopes with no close relatives.
PHOTO BY DENNIS JONES

IMPALA
Aepyceros melampus

Male impalas have long, lyre-shaped horns averaging 75cm in length. They are gregarious animals, forming resident herds of up to 100 or so. Males defend female herds during the oestrus, but outside the breeding season they congregate in bachelor groups. Impalas are known for their speed and ability to leap – they can spring as far as 10m in one bound, or 3m into the air. They are the common prey of lions, leopards, cheetahs, wild dogs and spotted hyenas.

Size: Shoulder height 85cm; weight 40kg to 80kg; horns up to 90cm; male larger than female. **Distribution**: Savanna regions from central Kenya extending south into Tanzania. **Status**: Very common and easy to see.

Gazelles are often the main prey of predators – so they are very fleet of foot and wary of attack.
PHOTO BY ARIADNE VAN ZANDBERGEN

GAZELLE
Gerenuk (*Litocranius walleri*); Grant's gazelle (*Gazella granti*); Thomson's gazelle (*G. thomsonii*, pictured)

Often the most common medium-sized antelope where they occur, gazelles form the main prey item of many predators in East Africa. Three species are common in the region. Thomson's gazelle is the smallest. It is often found in with the impala-sized Grant's gazelle, which lacks the 'Thommy's' black side stripe. The gerenuk has uniquely long limbs and neck, allowing it to reach otherwise inaccessible parts of trees. All three species are sociable, but the gerenuk forms small herds rarely numbering more than 12.

Size: Shoulder height 90cm (Grant's), 70cm (Thomson's), 1.05m (gerenuk). Mass 65kg (Grant's), 29kg (Thomson's), 45kg (gerenuk). **Distribution**: Grant's/Thomson's common in savanna and woodland; gerenuks from northwestern Tanzania through central Kenya. **Status**: Grant's/Thomson's common; gerenuk less so.

BLUE WILDEBEEST
Connochaetes taurinus

Blue wildebeests are gregarious, and in some areas form herds of up to tens of thousands.
PHOTO BY ANDREW VAN SMEERDIJK

Blue wildebeests often form herds in association with zebras and other herbivores. Wildebeests are grazers, and move constantly in search of good pasture and water, preferring to drink daily – this gives rise to the famous mass migration in the Serengeti–Masai Mara ecosystem. Elsewhere, especially where food and water are more permanent, groups of up to 30 are more usual, with larger congregations being less frequent. In both situations, males are territorial and attempt to herd groups of females into their territory.

Size: Shoulder height 1.4m; weight 200kg to 300kg (males), 140kg to 230kg (females); horns up to 85cm; male larger than female. **Distribution**. Widely distributed. **Status**: Very common; 1.5 million occur in the Serengeti–Masai Mara ecosystem.

HARTEBEEST
Alcelaphus buselaphus

Hartebeests prefer grassy plains but are also found in sparsely forested savannas and hills.
PHOTO BY ARIADNE VAN ZANDBERGEN

Hartebeests are red to tan in colour, medium-sized, and easily recognised by their long, narrow face and short horns. In both sexes, the distinctively angular and heavily ridged horns form a heart shape, hence their name, which comes from Afrikaans. Dominant males defend territories, which herds of females and their young pass through; other males move in bachelor groups. Herds typically number up to about a dozen (male herds are generally smaller), but aggregations of hundreds and (in the past) thousands also occur.

Size: Shoulder height 1.2m; weight 130kg to 170kg (males), 115kg to 150kg (females); horns up to 85cm. **Distribution**: Wide ranging; Coke's hartebeest, also known as 'Kongoni', is common in southern Kenya and northern Tanzania; Jackson's hartebeest is confined to areas near Lake Victoria. **Status**: Common.

TOPI
Damaliscus lunatus

Topis' horns, carried by both sexes, curve gently up, out and back.
PHOTO BY TONY WHEELER

Topis are reddish brown, with glossy violet patches on the legs and face. Their social system is highly variable. In grassy woodlands, males hold territories with harems of up to 10 females. On floodplains with dense populations, nomadic herds of thousands may form, males establishing temporary territories whenever the herd halts. Elsewhere, males gather on breeding-season display grounds; females visit these 'leks' to select their mates. Both sexes often stand on high vantage points (commonly termite mounds) to view their surroundings and as territorial advertisement.

Size: Shoulder height 1.2m; weight 110kg to 150kg (male), 75kg to 130kg (female); horns up to 45cm. **Distribution**: Widespread throughout medium-length grasslands, abundant in the Serengeti ecosystem. **Status**: Common.

The sable is a fierce fighter and there are occasional records of males killing lions when attacked.

PHOTO BY ARIADNE VAN ZANDBERGEN

SABLE ANTELOPE
Hippotragus niger
Sables are often considered the most magnificent of Africa's antelopes. Their colouring is dark-brown to black, with white bellies and face markings; the males' coats are a rich glossy black when adult. Both sexes have long sweeping horns, but those of the male are longer and more curved. Sables feed mainly on grass, but foliage accounts for around 10% of their diet. Females and the young live in herds, while males are territorial or form bachelor groups. Other predators include leopards, hyenas and wild dogs.

Size: Shoulder height 1.35m; mass up to 270kg. **Distribution**: In East Africa, restricted to southeastern Kenya and Tanzania. **Status**: Uncommon; in Kenya, they occur only in Shimba Hills National Reserve. They are more widely distributed in Tanzania.

To conserve water, oryxes let their body temperature rise to levels that would kill most mammals.

PHOTO BY MATT FLETCHER

ORYX
Oryx gazella
Adapted for arid zones, oryxes can tolerate areas uninhabitable for most antelopes. Two races occur in the region: beisa oryxes *(O. g. beisa)* of northern Kenya; and the slightly smaller fringe-eared oryxes *(O. g callotis)* of southern Kenya and northern Tanzania. Oryxes are solid and powerful animals with long, straight horns, which are present in both sexes. Oryxes are principally grazers but also browse on thorny shrubs unpalatable to many species. They can survive for long periods without water. Herds vary from five to 40 individuals.

Size: Shoulder height 1.5m; mass up to 300kg. **Distribution**: Northern Kenya (beisa oryxes); southern Kenya and northern Tanzania (fringe-eared oryxes). **Status**: Relatively common where they occur, and easy to see. They are, however, often shy, and flee from humans at great distances.

Strong jumpers, kudus flee with frequent leaping, clearing obstacles more than 2m high.

PHOTO BY MITCH REARDON

KUDU
Greater kudu (*Tragelaphus strepsiceros,* pictured); lesser kudu *(T. imberbis)*
Greater kudus are Africa's second-tallest antelope; males carry massive spiralling horns (the largest of any antelope). They are light grey in colour, with six to 12 white stripes down the sides. Lesser kudus have 11 to 15 stripes; males are blue-grey and females are a bright rust colour. In both species, one to three females and their young form groups, and are joined by males during the breeding season. Kudus are browsers, finding their diet in woodland-savanna with fairly dense bush cover.

Size: Greater kudu shoulder height 1.2m to 1.5m; weight 190kg to 320kg. Lesser kudu shoulder height 95cm to 1.1m; weight 90kg to 110kg. Males larger than females. **Distribution**: Greater kudus can be found throughout the region, except in the driest areas; lesser kudus prefer the arid regions of Tanzania and northern Kenya. **Status**: Greater kudus scattered; lesser kudus common.

ELAND
Taurotragus oryx

Africa's largest antelope, elands are massive. The horns of both sexes average 65cm, spiralling at the base then sweeping straight back. The male has a distinctive hairy tuft on the head, and stouter horns. Herds consist of adults, or adults and young, or sometimes just young – group membership and composi-

Aggregations up to 1000 elands form where new grass is growing.
PHOTO BY MITCH REARDON

tion change often. The most common large groups consist of 10 to 60 females and young. Males are less gregarious, coming together more sporadically and in smaller numbers, but one or more often join female-and-young herds.

Size: Shoulder height 1.5m to 1.8m (male), 1.25m to 1.5m (female); weight 450kg to 950kg (male), 300kg to 500kg (female); horns up to 100cm long. **Distribution**: Patchy distribution in arid zones; best seen in Nairobi and Tsavo National Parks. **Status**: Low density, but relatively common and easy to see.

WATERBUCK
Kobus ellipsiprymnus

Waterbucks have a shaggy brown coat and white rump, face and throat markings; only males have horns. Females have overlapping ranges, coming and going to form loose associations of normally up to a dozen animals. Young, non-territorial males behave similarly. Mature males hold territories, onto

The waterbuck's oily hair has a strong, musky odour, potent enough for humans to smell.
PHOTO BY ANDERS BLOMQVIST

which females wander (nonterritorial males are also often allowed access). These essentially independent movements sometimes produce herds of 50 to 70. They always stay near water and are good swimmers, readily entering water to escape predators.

Size: Shoulder height 1.3m; weight 200kg to 300kg (males), 150kg to 200kg (females); horns up to 1m. **Distribution**: Wet areas throughout the region. **Status**: Common and easily seen.

AFRICAN BUFFALO
Syncerus caffer

Both sexes of African buffaloes have distinctive curving horns that broaden at the base to meet over the forehead in a massive 'boss' – the female's are usually smaller. Local populations of buffaloes inhabit large home ranges and at times herds of thousands form, but the population's social organisation

Male buffaloes associate with the females during breeding, and at other times they form male herds or are solitary.
PHOTO BY DAVID WALL

is fluid: groups of related females and their young coalesce and separate into larger or smaller herds. Although generally docile, buffaloes can be dangerous – especially lone bulls, and females protecting their young.

Size: Shoulder height 1.6m; weight 400kg to 900kg; horns up to 1.25m long; female somewhat smaller than male. **Distribution**: Widespread, but large populations only occur in parks. **Status**: Common and may be approachable where protected.

The aardvark digs deep, complex burrows for shelter, which are also used by many other animals, such as warthogs and mongooses.
PHOTO BY ANTHONY BANNISTER/ABPL

AARDVARK
Orycteropus afer

Vaguely piglike (its Afrikaans name translates as 'earth-pig') with a long tubular snout, powerful kangaroo-like tail and large rabbitlike ears, the aardvark is unique and has no close relatives. Protected by thick wrinkled pink-grey skin, aardvarks forage at night by sniffing for termite and ant nests, which they rip open with their astonishingly powerful front legs and large spadelike nails. Normally nocturnal, they occasionally spend cold winter mornings basking in the sun before retiring underground.

Size: Shoulder height 60cm; length 1.4m to 1.8m, including a 55cm tail; weight 40kg to 80kg.
Distribution: Widely distributed throughout nearly the entire region. **Status**: Uncommon; nocturnal and rarely seen.

RODENTS

If attacked, a porcupine drives its rump into the predator – the quills are easily detached from their owner, but can remain embedded in the victim, causing serious injury or death.
PHOTO BY DAVE HAMMAN

PORCUPINE
Hystrix africaeaustralis

The Cape porcupine is the largest rodent native to Southern Africa. Its spread of long black-and-white banded quills from the shoulders to the tail makes it unmistakable. For shelter, it either occupies caves or excavates its own burrows. The porcupine's diet consists mainly of bark, tubers, seeds, and a variety of plant and ground-level foliage. The young are born during the hot summer months, in litters of between one and four.

Size: Length 70cm to 1m, including a 15cm tail; weight 10kg to 25kg. **Distribution**: Throughout the region. **Status**: Nocturnal but occasionally active on cooler days; difficult to see.

Although swift and able to leap several metres in a single bound, the springhare is preyed upon by everything from jackals to lions.
PHOTO BY ANTHONY BANNISTER/ABPL

SPRINGHARE
Pedetes capensis

In spite of its name and large ears, the springhare is not a hare but a very unusual rodent with no close relatives. With its powerful, outsized hind feet and small forelegs, it most resembles a small kangaroo and shares a similar energy-efficient hopping motion. The springhare digs extensive burrows, from which it emerges at night to feed on grass and grass roots. Reflections of spotlights in its large, bright eyes often give it away on night safaris.

Size: Length 80cm, including a 40cm tail; weight 3kg to 4kg. **Distribution**: Widespread in Kenya southwards into mid-Tanzania; favours grassland habitats with sandy soils. **Status**: Common, but strictly nocturnal.

Environment

THE LAND

Straddling the equator, edged to the east by turquoise Indian Ocean tides and to the west by a long chain of Rift Valley lakes, is East Africa – a region that is as diverse geographically and environmentally as it is culturally.

One of the most inviting zones is the coast, with its coral reefs, sultry white-sand beaches, river deltas teeming with life, littoral forest and – most famously – the Lamu and Zanzibar Archipelagos. This low-lying coastal belt stretches inland for between 15km and 65km before starting to rise, steeply at times, to a vast central plateau averaging between 1000m and 2000m above sea level and extending westwards beyond Rwanda and Burundi. The plateau is punctuated by escarpments, ravines, mountain ranges and lakes, and spliced by the East African rift system (see p74), which – in addition to accounting for most of the region's lakes – also gives rise to its highest mountains: glacier-capped Mt Kilimanjaro (5896m) and Mt Kenya (5199m). The Rwenzori Mountains on the Uganda–Democratic Republic of the Congo (DR Congo) border are also a result of rift-system geology, formed where uplift occurred between parallel geological fault lines. Other major mountain ranges include the Eastern Arc chain (in southern Kenya and northeastern Tanzania) and the Aberdare Range (Kenya).

Rimming East Africa's central plateau to the northeast, and extending from central Kenya to the borders of Somalia and Ethiopia, is a vast, trackless area of bushland, scrub and desert, where rainfall is sparse and the land is suitable only for cattle grazing.

> It's estimated that Mt Kilimanjaro's glaciers will disappear completely by 2020.

WILDLIFE

East Africa's primeval natural splendour and untamed rawness are among the region's major drawcards. Experiencing this magnificence – whether gazing across vast plains trammelled by thousands of wildebeest, or surrounded by moist, dripping rainforest echoing with the calls of mountain gorillas – is likely to be a highlight of any visit.

> East Africa boasts the continent's highest and lowest points (Mt Kilimanjaro and Lake Tanganyika's floor), and its largest and deepest lakes (Lakes Victoria and Tanganyika).

Animals

East Africa's plains, forests, rivers and lakes are home to an unparalleled number and diversity of wildlife, including an exceptionally high concentration of large animals. While it's the 'Big Five' (lions, buffaloes, elephants, leopards and rhinos) that get most of the attention, there are many more animals to be seen. Zebras, wildebeests, hippos, giraffes, antelopes, elands,

---

DON'T FEED THE ELEPHANTS!

One of East Africa's major attractions is the chance to get 'up close and personal' with the wildlife. Remember, however, that the region's animals are not tame and their actions are often unpredictable. Heed the warnings of guides and rangers when on safari, and seek the advice of knowledgeable locals before venturing off on your own. Never get between a mother and her calves or cubs, and if you want good photos, invest in a telephoto lens instead of approaching an animal at close range. Be particularly aware of the dangers posed by crocodiles and hippos – a quick dip in an isolated waterhole or a beckoning river can have more consequences than you'd bargained for.

THE GREAT RIFT VALLEY

The Great Rift Valley is part of the East African rift system – a massive geological fault slicing its way almost 6500km across the African continent, from the Dead Sea in the north to Beira (Mozambique) in the south. The rift system was formed more than 30 million years ago when the tectonic plates that comprise the African and Eurasian landmasses collided and then diverged again. As the plates moved apart, massive tablets of the earth's crust collapsed between them, resulting over the millennia in the escarpments, ravines, flatlands and lakes that mark much of East Africa today.

The rift system is especially famous for its calderas and volcanoes (including Mt Kilimanjaro, Mt Meru and the calderas of the Crater Highlands) and for its lakes. Some of these lakes – including Lakes Tanganyika and Nyasa – are very deep, with floors plunging well below sea level, although their surfaces may be several hundred metres above sea level.

The East African section of the Rift Valley consists of two branches formed where the main rift system divides north of Kenya's Lake Turkana. The western branch, or Western Rift Valley, makes its way past Lake Albert in Uganda through Rwanda and Burundi down to Lake Tanganyika, after which it meanders southeast to Lake Nyasa. Seismic and volcanic disturbances still occur throughout the western branch. The eastern branch, known as the Eastern or Gregory Rift, runs south from Lake Turkana past Lakes Natron and Manyara in Tanzania before joining again with the Western Rift in northern Malawi. The lakes of the Eastern Rift are smaller and shallower than those in the western branch, with some of them only waterless salt beds.

Places where the escarpments of the Rift Valley are particularly impressive include Kenya's Rift Valley Province, the Nkuruman Escarpment east of Kenya's Masai Mara National Reserve, and the terrain around Ngorongoro Conservation Area and Lake Manyara National Park in Tanzania.

kudus, gazelles and dik-diks are all commonly seen, and there are many predatory animals prowling around in addition to those already mentioned, including hyenas and wild dogs. East Africa is also renowned for its primates, including chimpanzees (especially in Tanzania's Gombe Stream and Mahale Mountains National Parks) and gorillas (in southwestern Uganda and in Rwanda). See the Wildlife Guide (p57) and the Mountain Gorillas chapter (p97) for more details.

Despite all the attention East Africa's wildlife has received over the decades, new species are still being discovered. See www.kipunji.org for the story behind the discovery of the region's newest monkey.

Keeping all of these company are over 60,000 insect species, including the malaria-carrying anopheles mosquito and the bothersome tsetse fly; several dozen types of reptiles and amphibians; and many species of snake.

In addition to the rich coastal marine life found in East Africa's Indian Ocean waters, Lake Tanganyika and Lake Nyasa are notable for having among the highest fish diversities of any lakes in the world, with an exceptionally large number of colourful cichlid species.

Fluttering around and above all this terrestrial wealth are close to 1500 different types of birds, including colourful kingfishers, raucous hornbills, stately fish eagles, ostriches and enough flamingos to turn many lakes into a haze of pink. There are also many rare birds, including the elusive shoebill stork. Uganda alone – which many ornithologists consider to be one of the continent's premier bird-watching destinations – hosts over 1000 bird species within its 236,000 sq km.

ENDANGERED SPECIES

Black rhinos have gained one of the highest profiles among East Africa's endangered species, as they struggle against the ravages of poaching, trying to keep their horns from being used for traditional medicines in Asia and for dagger handles in Yemen. Thanks to major conservation efforts, black rhino numbers are again on the rise, although there are still very few in the wild. Rhino sanctuaries and breeding areas include those in Mkomazi Game Reserve, Tsavo and Lake Nakuru National Parks. Otherwise, Tanzania's Ngorongoro Crater is one of the best places for trying to spot one.

Other species fighting for survival include East Africa's famed mountain gorillas (see p97); wild dogs (most likely spotted in Tanzania's Selous Game Reserve); hawksbill, green, olive ridley and leatherback turtles; dugongs; red colobus monkeys (best seen in Zanzibar's Jozani Forest, p150); and Pemba flying fox bats.

Rare or endangered bird species include Uganda's shoebill stork; Uluguru bush shrikes; Usambara weavers; Amani sunbirds; and roseate terns.

For more on endangered sea turtles, and how they're being helped in parts of East Africa, see http://news.bbc.co.uk/2 /hi/africa/4371363.stm.

Plants

East Africa is bursting with plant life that is just as diverse and intriguing as its wildlife. This ranges from cool, dark patches of moist tropical forest to the dusty, acacia-studded bushlands and thickets so typical of the East African savanna. While much of the region's original forest cover has been cleared for agriculture, small but significant areas remain. The rainforests of southwestern Uganda and in bordering areas of Rwanda are the most extensive. There are also small but highly biodiverse areas of tropical rainforest in northeastern Tanzania. Montane forests exist throughout the highlands of Kenya and in western Uganda, and high-altitude heather and moorlands are found above the tree line in these areas. Along the coast are stands of coconut palms and extensive mangrove forests.

Another tree that you're likely to see is the baobab, the rootlike branches of which make it look as if it were standing on its head. You'll also undoubtedly see various species of acacia, including the distinctive flat-topped acacia trees that are among the first impressions of East Africa for many visitors.

Gorillas in the Mist by Dian Fossey offers an intriguing look at the complexities of halting poaching while recounting the author's life among Rwanda's mountain gorillas.

NATIONAL PARKS

East Africa has one of the world's most impressive collections of national parks, all of which are worth as much time as you are able to spare.

Parks (the term is used loosely here to refer to national parks, wildlife reserves and conservation areas) notable for their high concentrations of wildlife include Serengeti National Park (p193) and Ngorongoro Conservation Area (p197) in Tanzania, and Masai Mara National Reserve (p393) and Amboseli National Park (p300) in Kenya. Other parks are famous

---

THE DOS & DON'TS OF PARK VISITING

Whichever of East Africa's parks you visit, help out the animals and the environment by following these guidelines:

- Don't camp away from official sites.
- Don't drive off the tracks.
- Don't honk your car horn.
- Don't drive within park borders outside the officially permitted hours.
- Don't litter, and be especially careful about discarding burning cigarette butts and matches.
- Don't pick flowers or remove or destroy any vegetation.
- Don't exceed the speed limits (in most parks, between 30km/h and 50km/h).

EAST AFRICA'S TOP PARKS & RESERVES

Park	Features	Activities	Best Time to Visit	Page
Burundi				
PN de la Rusizi	wetlands	hippo viewing	year-round	p607
Democratic Republic of the Congo (DR Congo)				
PN des Virungas	chain of volcanoes; mountain gorillas	gorilla tracking	May-Sep	p561
Kenya				
Aberdare NP	dramatic highlands, waterfalls & rainforest; elephants, black rhinos, bongo antelopes, black leopards	trekking, fishing, gliding	year-round	p373
Amboseli NP	dry plains & scrub forest; elephants, buffaloes, lions, antelopes	wildlife drives	Jun-Oct	p300
Arabuko Sokoke FR	coastal forest; Sokoke scops owls, Clarke's weavers, elephant shrews, butterflies, elephants	bird tours, walking, running, cycling	year-round	p334
Hell's Gate NP	dramatic rocky outcrops & gorges; lammergeyers, eland, giraffes, lions	cycling, walking	year-round	p360
Kakamega FR	virgin tropical rainforest; red-tailed monkeys, flying squirrels, 330 bird species	walking, bird-watching	year-round	p406
Lake Bogoria NR	scenic soda lake; flamingos, greater kudu, leopards	bird-watching, walking, hot springs	year-round	p366
Lake Nakuru NP	hilly grassland & alkaline lakeland; flamingos, black rhinos, lions, warthogs, birds	wildlife drives	year-round	p364
Malindi MNP & Watamu MNP	clear waters & coral reefs; tropical fish, turtles	diving, snorkelling	Oct-Mar	p338/ p332
Masai Mara NR	savanna & grassland; Big Five, antelopes, cheetahs, hyenas	wildlife drives, ballooning	wildebeest migration, Jul-Oct	p393
Meru NP	rainforest, swamplands & grasslands; white rhinos, elephants, lions, cheetahs, lesser kudu	wildlife drives, fishing	year-round	p387

Key

CA – Conservation Area	FR – Forest Reserve	GR – Game Reserve	MNP – Marine National Park
NP – National Park	NR – National Reserve	PN – Parc National	

Park	Features	Activities	Best Time to Visit	Page
Mt Elgon NP	extinct volcano & rainforest; elephants	walking, trekking, fishing	Dec-Feb	p413
Mt Kenya NP	rainforest, moorland & glacial mountain; elephants, buffaloes, mountain flora	trekking, climbing	Jan-Feb, Aug-Sep	p376
Nairobi NP	open plains with urban backdrop; black rhinos, birdlife, rare antelopes	wildlife drives, walking	year-round	p294
Saiwa Swamp NP	swamplands & riverine forest; sitatunga antelopes, crown cranes, otters, colobus monkeys	walking, bird-watching	year-round	p412
Samburu, Buffalo Springs & Shaba NRs	semiarid open savanna; elephants, leopards, crocodiles	wildlife drives	year-round	p421
Shimba Hills NR	densely forested hills; elephants, sable antelopes, leopards	walking, forest tours	year-round	p321
Tsavo NP	sweeping plains & ancient volcanic cones; Big Five	wildlife drives, rock climbing, walking	year-round	p303
Rwanda				
PN des Volcans	towering volcanoes; mountain gorillas	gorilla tracking, volcano climbing	May-Sep	p583
PN Nyungwe Forest	dense tropical forest; chimpanzees & huge troops of Angolan colobus monkeys	chimp tracking, waterfalls	May-Sep	p591
Tanzania				
Arusha NP	Mt Meru, lakes & crater; zebras, giraffes, elephants	trekking & vehicle safaris, walking	year-round	p188
Gombe Stream NP	lakeshore, forest; chimpanzees	chimp tracking	year-round	p216
Katavi NP	floodplains, lakes & woodland; buffaloes, hippos, antelopes	vehicle & walking safaris	Jun-Oct	p218
Lake Manyara NP	Lake Manyara; hippos, water birds, elephants	canoe & vehicle safaris	Jun-Feb	p191
Mikumi NP	Mkata floodplains; lions, giraffes, elephants	vehicle safaris	year-round	p225
Ngorongoro CA	Ngorongoro Crater; black rhinos, lions, elephants, zebras, flamingos	vehicle safaris	Jun-Feb	p197

EAST AFRICA'S TOP PARKS & RESERVES (CONTINUED)

Park	Features	Activities	Best Time to Visit	Page
Rubondo Island NP	Lake Victoria; birdlife, sitatungas, chimpanzees	walks, chimp tracking, boating, fishing	Jun-Nov	p206
Saadani GR	Wami River, beach; birds, hippos, crocodiles	boat trips, wildlife drives & walks	Jun-Feb	p160
Selous GR	Rufiji River, lakes, woodland; elephants, hippos, wild dogs, black rhinos, birds	boat, walking & vehicle safaris	Jun-Oct, Jan-Feb	p236
Serengeti NP	plains & grasslands, Grumeti River; wildebeests, zebras, lions, cheetahs, giraffes	vehicle & balloon safaris	year-round	p193
Tarangire NP	Tarangire River, woodland, baobabs; elephants, zebras, wildebeests, birds	vehicle safaris	Jun-Oct	p192
Uganda				
Budongo Central FR	dense tropical forest; packed full of primates	chimp tracking, forest walks, bird viewing	May-Aug	p545
Bwindi Impenetrable NP	primeval tropical forest; mountain gorillas	gorilla tracking, bird-watching	May-Sep	p523
Kibale Forest NP	lush forest; highest density of primates in Africa	chimp tracking, forest elephant viewing	May-Aug	p511
Lake Mburo NP	savanna & lakes; zebra, impalas, eland & topi	wildlife walks, boat trips	year-round	p535
Mgahinga Gorilla NP	volcanoes; mountain gorillas	gorilla tracking, pygmy villages, bird-watching	Jun-Sep	p531
Mt Elgon NP	extinct volcano; duikers, buffalos, lammergier vultures	trekking	Dec-Feb & Jun-Aug	p502
Murchison Falls NP	thundering falls & the Victoria Nile; elephants, hippos, crocodiles, shoebill storks	launch trip, wildlife drives	year-round	p541
Queen Elizabeth NP	lakes, gorges & savanna; hippos, birds, chimpanzees	launch trip, chimp tracking	year-round	p520
Rwenzori Mountains NP	Africa's highest mountain range; blue monkeys, chimpanzees, hyraxes	rugged trekking, mountain climbing	Jun-Aug	p516

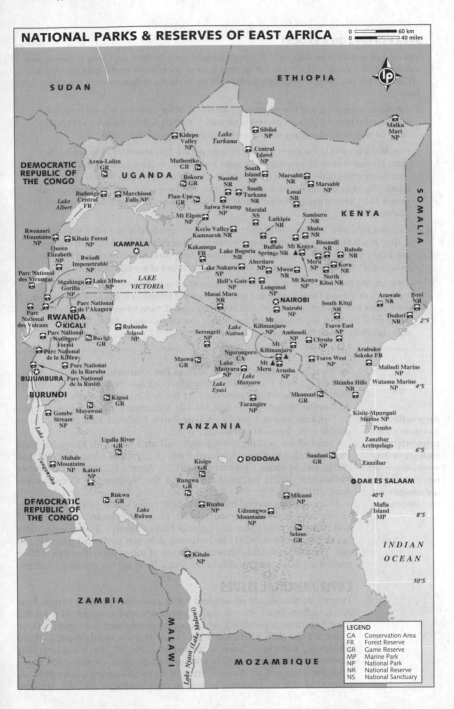

NATIONAL PARKS & RESERVES OF EAST AFRICA

0 — 60 km
0 — 40 miles

SUDAN

ETHIOPIA

SOMALIA

DEMOCRATIC REPUBLIC OF THE CONGO

UGANDA

KENYA

Kidepo Valley NP
Lake Turkana
Sibiloi NP
Malka Mari NP
Aswa-Lolim GR
Matheniko GR
Central Island NP
Bokora GR
Nasolot NR
South Island NP
Marsabit NR
Marsabit NP
Budongo Central FR
Murchison Falls NP
Pian-Upe GR
South Turkana NR
Losai NR
Lake Albert
Mt Elgon NP
Saiwa Swamp NP
Maralal NS
Laikipia NR
Samburu NR
Shaba NR
Bisanadi NR
Rahole NR
Rwenzori Mountains NP
Kibale Forest NP
Kerio Valley NR
Kamnarok NR
Buffalo Springs NR
Mt Kenya NP
Meru NP
Kora NR
Queen Elizabeth NP
Bwindi Impenetrable NP
KAMPALA
Kakamega FR
Lake Bogoria NR
Aberdare NP
Mwea NR
Mt Kenya NP
North Kitui NR
Parc National des Virungas
Mgahinga Gorilla NP
Lake Mburo NP
LAKE VICTORIA
Lake Nakuru NP
Hell's Gate NP
Longonot NP
Parc National des Volcans
Masai Mara NR
NAIROBI
Nairobi NP
Arawale NR
Boni NR
Parc National de l'Akagera
RWANDA
KIGALI
Rubondo Island NP
Mt Kilimanjaro NP
South Kitui NR
Dodori NR
Parc National Nyungwe Forest
Burigi GR
Serengeti NP
Lake Natron
Amboseli NP
Chyulu NP
Tsavo East NP
Parc National de la Kibira
Maswa GR
Ngorongoro CA
Mt Kilimanjaro NP
Arusha NP
Tsavo West NP
Arabuko Sokoke FR
BUJUMBURA
Parc National de la Rurubu
Lake Manyara NP
Mt Meru
Malindi Marine NP
Parc National de la Rusizi
Lake Eyasi
Lake Manyara
Shimba Hills NR
Watamu Marine NP
BURUNDI
Kigosi GR
Mkomazi GR
Kisite-Mpunguti Marine NP
Gombe Stream NP
Moyowosi GR
Tarangire NP
Pemba
Ugalla River GR
TANZANIA
Zanzibar Archipelago
Mahale Mountains NP
Katavi NP
Kisigo GR
DODOMA
Saadani GR
Zanzibar
Rukwa GR
Rungwa GR
DAR ES SALAAM
DEMOCRATIC REPUBLIC OF THE CONGO
Ruaha NP
Mikumi NP
Mafia Island MP
Udzungwa Mountains NP
Lake Rukwa
Selous GR
INDIAN OCEAN
Kitulo NP
ZAMBIA
MALAWI
Lake Nyasa (Lake Malawi)
MOZAMBIQUE

2°S
4°S
6°S
8°S
10°S
40°E

LEGEND
CA	Conservation Area
FR	Forest Reserve
GR	Game Reserve
MP	Marine Park
NP	National Park
NR	National Reserve
NS	National Sanctuary

PARK HOPPING ON A BUDGET

Visiting East Africa's parks can be a challenge if you're on a budget. Park fees, transport and accommodation costs, and the costs of getting around once you're in the park, quickly add up, and before you know it, your daily budget will be in shreds. Following are a few things to consider.

- For maximum savings, visit parks with lower entry fees. While daily fees at most parks are between US$15 and US$50 per day, there are a few – notably Gombe Stream and Mahale Mountains in Tanzania – where fees have been set higher to moderate visitor use.

- Fees at many parks in the region cover a 24-hour period. This means you can get the best value for your money by entering about noon and getting in good evening and morning wildlife-watching hours before leaving or having to pay again at noon the next day. A few parks – Ngorongoro Conservation Area is the main one here – regulate entry times, which means you'll have to pay significantly more for the same amount of time watching the wildlife.

- Camping is possible in or near most parks, and can save considerably on costs compared with staying in a lodge or luxury tented camp. Remember, though, to stick to public or 'ordinary' campsites, since 'special' campsites cost much more. Most parks have a mixture of both, but in Tanzania's Kilimanjaro, for example, all camping is charged at 'special' campsite rates.

- Parks located near a convenient access town are usually a good bet, as there will be public transport, or transport organised with a tour operator will be relatively inexpensive. However, once at the park you'll then have the costs of getting around. Parks where you can take public transport to the gate, and then get around on your own steam – eg by hiking or organising a walking safari – will be the cheapest.

Mangroves play an essential role in coastal ecosystems by controlling erosion, enriching surrounding waters with nutrients and providing local communities with insect-resistant wood.

for a particular type of animal, such as Parc National des Volcans (p583) in Rwanda and Bwindi Impenetrable National Park (p523) in Uganda (both set aside for the protection of the endangered mountain gorillas). At Gombe Stream (p216) and Mahale Mountains (p216) National Parks in Tanzania, and at Uganda's Kibale Forest National Park (p511), chimpanzees are the main attraction.

Places where trekking is a highlight include Kenya's Mt Kenya National Park (p376), Mt Elgon National Park (Kenya and Uganda, p502 and p503), and Tanzania's Kilimanjaro (p175), Arusha (p188) and Udzungwa Mountains (p226) National Parks and the Ngorongoro Conservation Area (p197).

There are also several marine national parks where you can go diving or snorkelling on an underwater safari. The main ones are Malindi (p338) and Watamu (p332) Marine National Parks in Kenya. There's also Mafia Island Marine Park (p241) in Tanzania, although most diving here is top end. The following table gives an overview of major parks. For more information on these, and on others not listed here, see the country chapters.

ENVIRONMENTAL ISSUES

Despite its abundance of national parks and other protected areas, East Africa suffers from several major environmental scourges. One of the most notorious is poaching, which occurs throughout the region. In one sense, it's not difficult to see why: 1kg of ivory is worth about US$300 wholesale, and rhino horn is valued at US$2000 per kilogram. This amounts to as much as US$30,000 for a single horn, or about 100 times what the average East African earns in a year. Poaching is also difficult to control due to resource and personnel shortages and the vastness and inaccessibility of many areas. Entrenched interests are also a major contributing factor, with everyone from the poachers themselves (often local villagers struggling to earn some money) to ivory dealers, embassies and government officials at the highest levels trying to get a piece of the pie.

In 1990, following a vigorous campaign by conservation groups, the Convention on International Trade in Endangered Species (Cites) implemented a ban on ivory import and export. Although this worldwide ban was subsequently downgraded in some areas to permit limited trade in ivory, it allowed dwindling elephant populations in East and southern Africa to make marked recoveries. Whether these gains will be lasting remains to be seen. The now partially reopened ivory trade seems to have resulted in an increase in poaching across the continent, although this connection is disputed by those who note that funds from legal ivory sales can be used towards conservation.

Just as worrisome as poaching is deforestation, with East Africa's forest areas today representing only a fraction of the region's original forest cover. On the Zanzibar Archipelago, for example, only about 5% of the dense tropical forest that once blanketed the islands still remains. In sections of the long Eastern Arc mountain chain, which sweeps in an arc from southern Kenya down towards central Tanzania, forest depletion has caused such serious erosion that entire villages have had to be shifted to lower areas. In densely populated Rwanda and Burundi, many previously forested areas have been completely cleared to make way for agriculture.

Deforestation brings with it soil erosion, shrinking water catchment and cultivable areas, and decreased availability of traditional building materials, foodstuffs and medicines. It also means that many birds and animals lose their habitats, and that local human populations risk losing their lifeblood. While the creation of forest reserves, especially in Kenya and Tanzania, has been a start in addressing the problem, tree-felling prohibitions are often not enforced.

Unregulated tourism and development also pose serious threats to East Africa's ecosystems. On the northern tip of Zanzibar, for example, new hotels are being built at a rapid rate, without sufficient provision for waste disposal and maintenance of environmental equilibrium. Inappropriate visitor use is another aspect of the issue: the tyre tracks crisscrossing off-road areas of Kenya's Masai Mara, the litter found along some popular trekking routes on Mt Kilimanjaro, and the often rampant use of firewood by visitors and tour operators alike are prime examples.

The Solutions?

For years, the conservation 'establishment' regarded human populations as a negative factor in environmental protection, and local inhabitants were often excluded from national parks or other protected areas because it was assumed that they damaged natural resources. A classic example is that of the Maasai, who were forced from parts of their traditional grazing lands around Serengeti National Park for the sake of conservation and tourism.

Fortunately, the tide has begun to turn, and it's now recognised that steps taken in the name of conservation will ultimately backfire if not done with the cooperation and involvement of local communities. Community-based conservation has become a critical concept as tour operators, funding organisations and others recognise that East Africa's protected areas are unlikely to succeed in the long term unless local

In Battle for the Elephants, *Iain and Oria Douglas-Hamilton describe with harsh clarity the ongoing political battles over elephants and the ivory trade in Africa.*

No Man's Land *by George Monbiot is a fascinating albeit controversial account of how the Maasai were forced from their traditional grazing lands in the name of conservation.*

The Green Belt Movement *by Wangari Maathai makes for dry reading, but the story is inspiring – chronicling East Africa's first female Nobel Peace Prize winner as she launches a highly successful grass-roots initiative.*

See www.esok.org for an introduction to regional ecotourism initiatives.

people can obtain real benefits. If there are tangible benefits for local inhabitants – benefits such as increased local income from visitors to wilderness areas – then natural environments have a much better chance of evading destruction.

Much of this new awareness is taking place at the grass-roots level, with a sprouting of activities such as Kenya's Green Belt Movement and community-level erosion control projects. It also helps when visitors become more aware of the issues; see p19 for some tips on what you can do.

Safaris

The hoof beats of thousands of wildebeests echoing across the Serengeti Plains; vast, open vistas broken only by the occasional stand of acacia thorn trees; a pink haze of flamingos wading in the shallows – these are likely to be among the most indelible images that you will take back from an East African safari. The chance to observe wildlife in its natural surroundings is one of the region's top attractions, and the safari industry here is highly developed.

Because the industry has become so competitive, especially in Tanzania and Kenya, it's worth putting extra time into planning. This is especially so at the budget level, where there's often only a fine line between operators running no-frills but reliable safaris and those that are either dishonest, or who have cut things so close that problems are bound to arise. At the higher end of the price spectrum, ambience, safari style and the operator's overall focus are important considerations.

This chapter provides an overview of factors to consider when planning a safari; many apply in equal measure to organised treks. See p89 for a few things to keep in mind if you're arranging things on your own.

PLANNING A SAFARI
Booking
If you're on a shoestring budget, or don't want to be pinned down with specific dates, the best thing to do is to wait until you get to East Africa, shop around at various operators to see what's on offer and then arrange things on the spot. This gives you the advantages of being able to hunt for lower walk-in rates, maintain flexibility, and meet up with other travellers to form a group and thereby lower costs. Being on-site also gives you a better feel for what you'll be getting. One of the disadvantages is that during the high season you may need to wait around several days before an opening arises or vehicles become free. During the low season, it can take a while to find a large enough group; four is the minimum for many budget companies. Another disadvantage is having to deal with safari touts. Although they're not all bad, many are quite aggressive, and the whole experience can be rather intimidating. If you wait until arriving in East Africa to book, keep your schedule flexible, allow some extra days to arrange things, and don't rush into any deals.

The other option is to book your safari or trek directly through the operator before arriving in the region. These days most midrange and top-end safaris are prebooked, as are some budget safaris. The main drawback of prebooking is that it decreases flexibility, especially if you're doing your safari as part of longer travels in the region. It also can be more expensive, although if you shop around and can take advantage of last-minute offers, it's possible to find some good deals, and many operators now offer prebooked trips at around the same price as walk-ins. Among the advantages of prebooking are that you won't need to spend time on the ground shopping around for an operator (which takes at least a day), it minimises the amount of cash or travellers cheques that you'll need to carry and you'll have someone to sort out the logistics for you. If you're travelling on your own and hoping to find other travellers to join, you can still consider prebooking, as some companies will permit you to adjust your booking on arrival, though you should confirm this in advance.

For an armchair preview of East Africa's major parks, check out www.tanzaniaparks.com (Tanzania), www.kws.org (Kenya) and www.uwa.or.ug/parks.html (Uganda).

In addition to prebooking with locally based companies such as most of those listed in this chapter, you can prebook through tour operators in Europe, the USA, Australia and elsewhere; a small sampling is listed on p635. This, however, will be considerably more expensive as most will sub-contract to local operators. It's almost always cheaper to deal directly with the operating company; if all or part of your itinerary is subcontracted, the commissions will be reflected in the prices you pay.

If you're going to prebook, the general rule is to do so as far in advance as possible, especially if you'll be travelling in popular areas during the July/August and December/January high seasons.

Costs

There are essentially two types of organised safaris: those where you camp, and those where you stay in lodges or luxury tented camps. (For explanations of tented and fly camps, see p618.) Camping safaris are the least expensive option. Most cater to shoestring travellers, the young (or young at heart) and those who are prepared to put up with a little discomfort and who don't mind helping to pitch the tents and set up camp. But, if you plan things right, they offer the chance for an authentic adventure in the African bush, often with nothing between you and the animals at night except a sheet of canvas and the embers of a dying fire.

East Africa boasts an impressive collection of Unesco biosphere reserves, modelling the successful fusion of conservation, development and research initiatives. See www .unesco.org/mab /brlistAfr.htm for a full listing.

Safaris based in lodges or luxury tented camps cost more than camping safaris, with the price usually directly proportional to the quality of the accommodation and staff, and the amount of individualised attention you'll get. Some upscale lodges and tented camps quote 'all-inclusive' prices, which in addition to accommodation, full board and occasionally park fees as well, normally include two 'activities' (usually wildlife drives, or sometimes one wildlife drive and one walk per day, each lasting about two to three hours). A few quote accommodation-only prices, which means you'll need to pay extra to go out from the lodge and actually look for wildlife.

When comparing prices, check to see what's included. Relevant items here are park entrance fees, camping fees and accommodation costs, transport and fuel, number of meals per day, tent rental, and wildlife drives or walks. Drinks are almost always excluded, except at the highest price level. Budget safari prices also normally exclude sleeping-bag rental, which costs anywhere from US$5 per day to US$15 per trip.

If you're booking a group safari, find out how many people will be sharing the vehicle with you (the larger your group, the cheaper the per person cost), and how many people per tent or room. The norm is two, and most operators charge a supplement for single occupancy ranging from 20% to 50% of the shared-occupancy rate. Prices quoted in this chapter are based on the cost per person for shared occupancy.

You'll also need to factor in tips, which are commonly given to drivers, guides and porters assuming service has been good. You can use 10% of the overall cost of your safari as a rough guide. Depending on where you are, for camping safaris this averages from about US$8 to US$10 per day per group for the driver-guide/cook, more for upscale safaris, large groups or an especially good job. Another way to calculate things is to give an additional day's wage for every five days worked, with a similar proportion for a shorter trip, and a higher than average tip for exceptional service. Wages in East Africa are low, and if someone has made a special effort to make your trip memorable, you should be generous.

Kenya is the cheapest place in the region for safaris. In Uganda, most companies rely heavily on pricier lodge and hotel accommodation, and even where camping is involved it's usually the luxury tented variety.

BUDGET

The goal of keeping costs to a minimum on budget safaris is achieved by camping or staying in basic guesthouses, working with comparatively large group sizes to minimise per-head transport costs, and keeping to a no-frills setup with basic meals and minimal staff. In some areas the camp sites may be outside park boundaries to save on park entry fees and comparatively high fees for park camping grounds – though this means you'll lose time in prime morning and evening wildlife-viewing hours shuttling to and from the park. Also, for most safaris at the budget level as well as for many in the midrange, there are kilometre limits placed on how far the vehicle drives each day, though operators seldom publicise this.

The bare minimum for a budget camping safari in Kenya is about US$65 to US$80 per person per day. In Tanzania, expect to pay from US$85 to US$100. Genuine budget camping safaris are few and far between in Uganda. Throughout the region, it's often possible to find discounts during the low season.

Check out www.eawildlife.org for an excellent introduction to conservation efforts in East Africa.

MIDRANGE

Most midrange safaris use lodges, where you'll have a comfortable room and eat in a restaurant. In general, you can expect reliability and reasonably good value in this category. A disadvantage is that the safaris may have a package-tour atmosphere, although this can be minimised by carefully selecting a safari company and accommodation, and giving attention to who and how many other people you travel with. In both Kenya and Tanzania, expect to pay from a minimum of about US$130 to US$140 per person per day for a midrange lodge safari, although most will start at about US$160 or higher. Particularly in Tanzania, good deals are available at some of the lodges during the low season, so it's always worth asking about these. In Uganda, plan on anywhere from US$150 to US$250 per day.

TOP END

Top-end safaris use private lodges or luxury tented camps, and sometimes private fly camps. For the price you will pay – from US$200 up to

---

TANZANIA VS KENYA

If you're heading to East Africa to see wildlife, and are trying to decide whether to go on safari in Kenya or in Tanzania, the best answer is to do both and compare things for yourself. Assuming this isn't possible, it depends what you're after. Budget camping safaris are almost always cheaper in Kenya than in Tanzania, although for midrange safaris you can often find good deals in Tanzania. Kenya also tends to be somewhat less expensive generally, as a travel destination.

Apart from that, each country has its fans. Many connoisseurs say that the scenery and abundance of wildlife is better in Tanzania, while old Kenya hands would argue these points vehemently. Another difference is that in Tanzania, you're required to stick to designated roadways in most areas, which isn't the case in Kenya, much to the detriment of local ecosystems. If you're not a fan of large urban areas, another consideration may be that for an organised safari in Kenya, you'll likely need to at least spend a day in Nairobi (enough to send some people running for Tanzania). In Kenya, however, the road network and infrastructure are better, and getting acclimatised is somewhat easier, making it perhaps a 'softer' introduction if it's your first time in Africa.

The list of comparisons could go on, but in the end, it's all beautiful. The animals don't know which country they're in, and having a reliable, competent operator, a good guide and enjoyable travelling companions are just as important to your overall experience as the destination. And, if you can't decide between the two, there's always Uganda, where you'll have striking surroundings and many areas to yourself.

US$500 or more per person per day – expect a full range of amenities. Even in remote settings you can enjoy hot bush-style showers, comfortable beds and fine dining. Also expect a high level of personalised attention, expert guides, an often intimate atmosphere (many places at this level have fewer than 20 beds), and emphasis on achieving an 'authentic' bush experience.

When to Go

Throughout East Africa, getting around is easier in the dry season from late June to October, and in many parks this is when animals are easier to find around water holes and rivers. Foliage is also less dense, making it easier to spot wildlife. However, as the dry season corresponds in part with the high-travel season, lodges and camps get crowded and accommodation prices are often at a premium.

The Kingdon Field Guide to African Mammals by Jonathan Kingdon makes a wonderful safari companion, with a wealth of information on East African wildlife. *Field Guide to the Birds of East Africa* by Terry Stevenson and John Fanshawe is similar for birding.

Apart from these general considerations, the ideal time to make a safari very much depends on which parks and reserves you want to visit and what you want to see and do. If it's birding you're interested in, for example, the wet season is the best time in many areas. However, some lowland parks may be completely inaccessible during the rains. Wildlife concentrations also vary markedly, depending on the season. Tanzania's Tarangire National Park is best visited during the dry season when animal concentrations there are highest. In Serengeti National Park, there are comparatively fewer animals during the dry season, although overall numbers continue to be high and you'll probably see wildlife there at any time of year. The dry season is also best for the park's famous lions and other predators.

If you're timing your safari around specific events, such as the wildebeest migration in Serengeti National Park and Masai Mara National Reserve, remember that there are no guarantees, as seasons vary from year to year and are difficult to accurately predict in advance. More details on the individual parks are given in the country chapters.

What to Bring

Useful items include binoculars; field guides; a good quality sleeping bag, especially if you'll be doing any trekking; mosquito repellent; rain gear and waterproofing for wet-season travel, especially for camping safaris or treks; sunglasses; camera and film; extra contact-lens solution and your prescription glasses as the dust can be irritating; and a good book for the downtime in the middle of the day between wildlife drives or walks. Top-end lodges and tented camps usually have mosquito nets, but it can't hurt to bring one along, and you'll need one for budget guesthouses. For walking safaris bring lightweight, long-sleeved/-legged clothing in subdued colours, a head covering and sturdy, comfortable shoes. For budget safaris, it's a good idea to bring extra food and snacks and a roll of toilet paper. In and near most parks, there's little available except hotel meals and perhaps a few basics, so if you're on a tight budget stock up on mineral water and supplies in the nearest major town.

Tsetse flies can be unwelcome safari companions in some areas. To minimise the nuisance, wear thick, long-sleeved shirts and trousers in khaki or other drab shades, and avoid bright, contrasting and very dark clothing.

TYPES OF SAFARI
Organised Vehicle Safaris

The options here range from two days up to several weeks, with five to seven days ideal. At least one full day will normally be taken up with travel, and after seven, you may well feel like a rest. If you pack too much distance or too many parks into a short period, chances are that you'll feel as if you've spent your whole time in transit, shuttling from place to place, rather than enjoying the destination.

SAFARI STYLE

While price can be a major determining factor in safari planning, there are other considerations that are just as important:

■ Ambience – will you be staying in or near the park? (If you stay well outside the park, you'll miss the good early morning and evening wildlife-viewing hours.) Are the surroundings atmospheric? Will you be in a large lodge or an intimate private camp?

■ Equipment – mediocre vehicles and equipment can significantly detract from the overall experience (and on mountain treks, inadequate equipment can mean the difference between reaching the summit or not, or worse).

■ Access and Activities – if you don't relish the idea of hours in a 4WD on bumpy roads, consider parks and lodges where you can fly in. Parks and reserves where walking and boat safaris are possible are the best bet for getting out of the vehicle and into the bush.

■ Guides – a good driver or guide (often the same person) can make or break your safari. Staff at reputable companies are usually knowledgeable and competent. With borderline operators trying to cut corners, chances are that staff are unfairly paid, and will likely not be particularly knowledgeable or motivated.

■ Setting the agenda – some drivers feel that they have to whisk you from one good 'sighting' to the next. If your preference is to stay in one strategic place for a while to simply experience the environment and see what comes by, don't hesitate to discuss this with your driver. Going off in wild pursuit of the 'Big Five' means you'll miss the more subtle aspects of the surrounding nature.

■ Extracurriculars – in some areas, it's common for drivers to stop at souvenir shops en route. While this gives the driver an often much-needed break from the wheel, most shops pay drivers commissions to bring clients, which means you may find yourself spending a lot more time souvenir shopping than you'd bargained for. If you're not interested in this, discuss it with your driver at the outset of your safari, ideally while you're still at the safari company's offices.

■ Less is more – if you'll be teaming up with others to make a group, find out how many people will be in your vehicle, and try to meet your travelling companions before setting off.

■ Special interests – if bird-watching or other special interests are important, arrange a private safari with a specialised operator.

Minivans are the most common option throughout Kenya and northern Tanzania, but if you have a choice, go for a good Land Rover–style 4WD instead. Apart from aesthetics, minivans accommodate too many people for a good experience, the rooftop opening is usually only large enough for a few passengers to use at once, and at least some passengers will get stuck in middle seats with poor views.

Whatever type of vehicle you're in, you should try to avoid crowding. Sitting uncomfortably scrunched together for several hours over bumpy roads, or squeezed into a middle seat, detracts significantly from the safari ambience. Most prices you will be quoted are based on groups of three to four passengers, which is about the maximum for comfort for most vehicles. Some companies put five or six passengers in a standard 4WD, but the minimal savings don't compensate for the extra discomfort.

Other Safaris

If you're the type that gets antsy sitting cooped up in a vehicle for several days on end, there is an increasing number of options for walking, cycling and other more energetic pursuits, sometimes on their own, and sometimes in combination with a vehicle safari.

In addition to the safaris listed here, see p26 for more ideas on ways to get out and moving.

WALKING, HIKING & CYCLING SAFARIS

At many national parks you can arrange relatively short walks of two to three hours in the early morning or late afternoon. The focus is on watching animals rather than covering distance, and walks like these are often included in organised vehicle-safari packages, especially at the top end of the scale.

For keen walkers, and those who want to minimise their time in safari minibuses, there are an increasing number of more vigorous options, usually involving point-to-point walks or longer circuits. Kenya in particular has a wide array of organised safaris combining walking, hiking and cycling, with side trips by vehicle into the parks to see wildlife. Popular areas include Mt Kenya, Mt Elgon, the Cherangani Hills and around the Rift Valley lakes. In Tanzania, activity-oriented safaris are getting into full swing, so expect lots of new developments within the next few years. For now the best areas include the Ngorongoro Conservation Area, and Mt Kilimanjaro and Arusha National Parks, all with highly rewarding hiking. Longer walks can also be arranged in areas bordering the Serengeti, in Ruaha National Park and in Selous Game Reserve. Uganda also offers some excellent opportunities – everything from tracking gorillas and chimpanzees to birding walks in Bwindi Impenetrable and Kibali Forest National Parks, to climbing Mt Elgon or trekking in the Rwenzori Mountains.

BOAT & CANOE SAFARIS

Serengeti: Natural Order on the African Plain and In the Lion's Den – both by Mitsuaki Iwago – are superb photographic documentaries of the majestic rhythms of nature on the East African plains.

Like walking safaris, boat safaris are an excellent way to experience the East African wilderness, and offer a welcome break from dusty, bumpy roads. They're also the only way to fully explore riverine environments, and they'll give you new perspectives on the terrestrial scene as you approach hippos or crocodiles at close range, float by a sandbank covered with birds, or observe animals on shore from a river vantage point.

Good places for boat safaris include along the Rufiji River in Tanzania's Selous Game Reserve; and in Uganda, Queen Elizabeth National Park, or the launch trip up the Victoria Nile to the base of Murchison Falls. In Tanzania's Arusha National Park, you can take canoe safaris on the Momela Lakes (p188). Also see p549.

CAMEL SAFARIS

Camel safaris offer the chance to get off the beaten track and into areas where vehicle safaris don't or can't go. Most take place in Kenya's Samburu and Turkana tribal areas between Isiolo and Lake Turkana. Camel safaris can also be arranged at Mkuru, Tanzania (see p187). Although you may well see wildlife along the way, the main attractions are the journey itself, and the chance to immerse yourself in nomadic life and to mingle with the indigenous people. You have the choice of riding the camels or walking alongside them. Most travelling is done in the cooler parts of the day, and a camp site is established around noon. In Kenya, camel safaris are quite straightforward, with operators doing the organising and most providing camping equipment and ablution facilities. In Tanzania, however, you will need to be self-sufficient and sort out most of the logistics yourself.

BALLOON SAFARIS

Drifting over the Serengeti Plains or along a riverbed in a hot-air balloon is a superb way to experience East African nature if you have the funds. While everything depends on wind and weather conditions, and wildlife can't be guaranteed, the captains try to stay between 500m and 1000m above ground, which means that if animals are there you'll be able to see them. The main places for balloon safaris are Kenya's Masai Mara National Reserve and Tanzania's Serengeti National Park. For more information, see p435 and p194.

For beautiful photos, especially of the Masai Mara, look for *Mara-Serengeti: A Photographer's Paradise* by Jonathan and Angela Scott.

HORSEBACK-RIDING SAFARIS

Horseback-riding safaris are gaining in popularity, particularly in Tanzania; most require previous riding experience. See p250.

DO-IT-YOURSELF SAFARIS

If you're lucky enough to have your own vehicle, or have a group to split rental costs, it's relatively easy to organise your own safari, though less commonly done than in southern Africa. Doing things yourself offers the great advantages of flexibility and being able to choose who you travel with. Just remember to bring enough extra petrol (as it's not available in most parks), and some mechanical knowledge and spares; many park areas are quite remote, and if you break down, you'll be on your own. The main additional cost – apart from accommodation, park fees, petrol and other standard items – is likely to be the vehicle fees charged by many parks. For most areas, you'll need a 4WD. Apart from costs, the main disadvantages of organising your own safari are breakdown and security concerns, finding your way (if you're unfamiliar with the area), and the fact that whoever is driving is going to be too busy concentrating on the road to notice much of the wildlife.

As for organising a safari via public transport: while it's possible to reach many parks with public transport, you'll then need to arrange a vehicle to get around once you get to the park gates. With the exception of Ngorongoro Crater and Katavi National Park, both in Tanzania, and a handful of other areas, there's no vehicle hire at most parks or reserves, and hiring a car specifically for safari usually works out at least as expensively as going through a tour operator, unless you are in a group. Hitching a lift isn't usually a realistic option either, especially in Uganda, where there's very little traffic into the national parks, and in Tanzania, where it's not permitted in most parks.

In addition to the 'Big Five' (elephants, lions, leopards, buffaloes and rhinos), there's also a 'Little Five' (elephant shrews, ant lions, leopard tortoises, buffalo weavers and rhino beetles).

For hiking or other safaris where you don't need a vehicle to get around once you're at the park, doing things yourself via public transport is much easier, with the main considerations being time, sorting things out with park fees, guides and other logistics, and finding some travelling companions. Allow up to a full day at the access town or trail head to organise food, equipment and guides.

CHOOSING AN OPERATOR

Competition among safari companies is fierce these days, and corners are often cut, especially at the budget level. Some companies enter wildlife parks through side entrances to avoid park fees, while others use glorified *matatu* (Kenyan minibus) or *daladala* (pick-up truck or minibus) drivers as guides, offer substandard food and poorly maintained vehicles, or underpay and otherwise poorly treat their staff. There are also many high-quality companies who have excellent track records. Companies recommended in this chapter enjoyed a good reputation at the time of research, as do many others that couldn't be listed due to space considerations. However, we can't emphasise enough the need to check on the current situation with all of the listed companies and any others you may hear about. Following are some things to keep in mind when looking for an operator:

■ Do some legwork (the Internet is a good start) before coming to East Africa. Get personal recommendations, and once in the region, talk with as many people as you can who have recently returned from a safari or trek with the company you're considering.

■ Be sceptical of price quotes that sound too good to be true, and don't rush into any deals, no matter how good they sound.

■ Don't fall for it if a tout tries to convince you that a safari or trek is leaving 'tomorrow' and that you can be the final person in the group. Take the time to shop around at reliable outfits to get a feel for what's on offer, and if others have supposedly registered, ask to speak with them.

■ In Tanzania and Kenya, check with Tanzanian Association of Tour Operators (TATO) or Kenyan Association of Tour Operators (KATO), and in Uganda with the Uganda Tourist Board, to find out whether the operator you're considering is licensed. (See below for contact details.)

■ Don't give money to anyone who doesn't work out of an office, and don't arrange any safari deals at the bus stand or with touts who follow you to your hotel room. Also be wary of sham operators trading under the same names as companies listed in this or other guidebooks. Don't let business cards fool you; they're easy to print up and are no proof of legitimacy.

■ Go with a company that has its own vehicles and equipment. If you have any doubts, don't pay a deposit until you've seen the vehicle that you'll be using. (Also be aware that it's not unknown for an operator to show you one vehicle, but then on the actual safari day, arrive in an inferior one.)

■ Especially at the budget level, there's a lot of client swapping between companies that have full vehicles and those that don't. You could easily find yourself on safari with a company that isn't the one you booked with, especially if you're booking from abroad. Reputable companies will inform you if they're going to do this. Although getting swapped

---

KATO & TATO

Kenya and Tanzania have tour-operator associations that serve as local regulatory bodies, and with whom reputable safari companies will be registered members. While they're not always the most powerful of entities, going on safari with one of their members will give you at least some recourse to appeal in case of conflict or problems. They're also good sources of information on whether a company is reputable or not, and it's well worth checking in with them before finalising your plans. Their contacts are as follows:

Kenyan Association of Tour Operators (KATO; ☎ 020-713348; www.katokenya.org)
Tanzanian Association of Tour Operators (TATO; ☎ 027-250 4188; www.tatotz.org)

In Tanzania, TATO publishes a list of registered operators on its website. Other good sources of information on tour operators:

Kenya Professional Safari Guides Association (☎ 020-609355; www.safariguides.org)
Tanzania Tourist Board Tourist Information Centre (Map pp180–1; ☎ 027-250 3843; www.tanzania -web.com; Boma Rd, Arusha)
Uganda Tourist Board (Map p472; ☎ 041-342196; www.visituganda.com; 13/15 Kimathi Ave, Kampala)

into another company's safari isn't necessarily a bad thing, be sure that
the safari you booked and paid for is what you get, and try to meet the
people you'll be travelling with before setting off.

▪ Unless you speak the local language, be sure your driver can speak
English.

▪ Go through the itinerary in detail and confirm what is expected/
planned for each stage of the trip. Be sure that the number of wildlife
drives per day and all other specifics appear in the written contract, as
well as the starting and ending dates and approximate times. Normally,
major problems such as complete vehicle breakdown are compensated
for by adding additional time onto your safari. If this isn't possible
(for example, if you have an onward flight), reliable operators may
compensate you for a portion of the time lost. However don't expect
a refund for 'minor' problems such as punctured tyres or lesser breakdowns. Also note that park fees are nonrefundable.

TANZANIA

ITINERARIES
Northern Circuit

Arusha National Park is the best bet for a day trip, while Tarangire and
Lake Manyara National Parks are each easily accessed as overnight trips
from Arusha, although all these parks deserve more time to do them
justice. For a half-week itinerary, try any of the northern parks alone
(although for the Serengeti, it's worth flying at least one way, since it's a
full day's drive from Arusha), or Ngorongoro Crater together with either
Lake Manyara or Tarangire. With a week, you'll have just enough time
for the classic combination of Lake Manyara, Tarangire, Ngorongoro and
the Serengeti, but it's better to focus on just two or three of these. Many
operators offer a standard three-day tour of Lake Manyara, Tarangire
and Ngorongoro (or a four- to five-day version including the Serengeti).
However, distances to Ngorongoro and the Serengeti are long, and the
trip is likely to leave you feeling that you've spent too much time rushing from park to park and not enough time settling in and experiencing
the actual environments. If you're serious about a safari in the north,
especially if you want to visit Serengeti National Park, allow a minimum
of five days from Arusha.

In addition to these more conventional itineraries, there are countless
other possibilities combining wildlife viewing with visits to other areas.
For example, a vehicle safari in the Ngorongoro Crater followed by a climb
of Oldoinyo Lengai, trekking elsewhere in Ngorongoro Conservation
Area, or visiting Lake Eyasi.

The Serengeti is Tanzania's
largest park (14,763 sq
km), and home to the
greatest concentration
of large mammals in
the world. About half
of the park is pristine
wilderness, without even
a road.

Southern Circuit

Mikumi National Park and Saadani Game Reserve are both good destinations if you have only one or (better) two nights. With three to four days,
try Selous Game Reserve, or Ruaha National Park if you fly. With a bit
longer, you could combine the Selous and Ruaha, Ruaha and Katavi (in
the west) or – for a safari and hiking – Mikumi and Udzungwa Mountains
National Parks.

Western Parks

Trips to Katavi, Mahale Mountains or Gombe Stream National Parks will
require a bit more planning, and unless you have lots of time, will involve

some flights. For Katavi, a minimum of three days would be ideal, given the effort it takes to reach the park. For Gombe Stream, budget at least two days, and for Mahale, a bit longer to revel in the remoteness.

OPERATORS

Africa Travel Resource (www.intotanzania.com) A Web-based safari broker that matches your safari ideas with an operator, and helps you plan and book customised itineraries. All budgets.

Akaro Tours Tanzania (Map p172; ☎ 027-275 2986; www.akarotours.com; Ground fl, NSFF House, Old Moshi Rd, Moshi) No-frills Kilimanjaro treks, day hikes on Kilimanjaro's lower slopes and a range of cultural tours. Budget.

Coastal Travels (Map p118; ☎ 022-211 7959/60; safari@coastal.cc; Upanga Rd, Dar es Salaam) A long-established outfit with its own fleet of planes and safari camps and lodges in Ruaha National Park, the Selous Game Reserve and on Mafia Island. They often have good-value 'last-minute' flight-accommodation deals. Midrange.

East African Safari & Touring Company (Map pp180-1; ☎ 0744-741354; www.eastafrican safari.info; Goliondoi Rd, Arusha) Customised itineraries for individuals and small groups, with focus on the ecosystems around Tarangire National Park, where they operate a camp. Midrange to top end.

Foxes African Safaris (☎ 0744-237422; www.tanzaniasafaris.info) A family-run company with lodges and camps in Mikumi, Ruaha and Katavi National Parks, on the coast near Bagamoyo and in the Southern Highlands. Offers combination itineraries to these destinations via plane, road and their own private luxury train. Midrange to top end.

George Mavroudis Safaris (☎ 027-254 8840; gmsafaris@gmsafaris.com) Exclusive, customised mobile safaris in off-beat areas of the northern circuit, done in vintage style. Also offers combination Tanzania-Rwanda itineraries. Top end.

Green Footprint Adventures (☎ 027-250 2664; www.greenfootprint.co.tz) One of the best contacts if you're interested in anything action-oriented in the northern circuit (though they also cater to those with more sedentary tastes as well). All safaris are individually tailored and highly personalised. Activities generally range from a few hours to a half day, and include canoe safaris in Arusha National Park, mountain biking and walking around Lake Manyara, short hikes in the Crater Highlands and bush guide courses. Upper midrange to top end.

Hippotours & Safaris (Map p118; ☎ 022-212 8662/3; www.hippotours.com; Nyumba ya Sanaa, Ohio St, Dar es Salaam) Southern-circuit itineraries, especially in Selous Game Reserve and on Mafia Island. Midrange to top end.

Hoopoe Safaris (Map pp180-1; ☎ 027-250 7011; www.hoopoe.com; India St, Arusha) One of the best companies in the industry, with top-quality luxury camping and lodge safaris, plus a range of treks. Hoopoe has its own tented camps in the border areas of Lake Manyara and Serengeti National Parks and elsewhere in the northern circuit, where they have formed partnerships with the surrounding communities. They also arrange trekking and safari itineraries combining Tanzania, Kenya and Rwanda. Upper midrange and top end.

IntoAfrica (www.intoafrica.co.uk) A small company offering fair-traded cultural safaris and treks in northern Tanzania and Kenya, and earning consistently high marks from readers. It supports local communities in the areas where it works, and is a fine choice if your interest is more in gaining insight into local life and culture than in experiencing the luxury-lodge atmosphere. Itineraries include treks on Mts Kilimanjaro and Meru, plus a seven-day wildlife-cultural safari in Maasai and Chagga areas. Midrange.

Kahembe's Trekking & Cultural Safaris (☎ 027-253 1088, 027-253 1377; www.authentic culture.org; Babati) A small outfit offering Mt Hanang treks and a range of no-frills cultural safaris around Babati; a good choice for experiencing Tanzania from a local perspective. Budget.

Key's Hotel (☎ 275 2250; www.keys-hotels.com; Uru Rd, Moshi) A long-established place offering reliable Kilimanjaro packages. Midrange.

Moshi Expeditions & Mountaineering (Map p172; ☎ 027-275 4234; www.memtours.com; Kaunda St, Moshi) Kilimanjaro treks and northern-circuit safaris at competitive prices. Budget to midrange.

Nature Beauties (Map pp180-1; ☎ 027-254 8224; nature.beauties@habari.co.tz; Old Moshi Rd, Arusha) Kilimanjaro treks and northern-circuit safaris. Budget.

Bernhard Grzimek's 1959 film *The Serengeti Shall Not Die* was one of the most influential wildlife films ever made, drawing world attention not just to the Serengeti but to conservation throughout the continent.

Nature Discovery (☎ 027-254 4063; info@naturediscovery.com) Environmentally responsible northern-circuit safaris, and treks on Kilimanjaro, Meru and in the Crater Highlands. Midrange.

Roy Safaris (Map pp180-1; ☎ 027-250 2115, 027-250 8010; www.roysafaris.com; Serengeti Rd, Arusha) A highly regarded family-run company offering budget and semiluxury camping safaris in the northern circuit, plus luxury-lodge safaris and treks on Mt Kilimanjaro, Mt Meru and in the Crater Highlands. Their vehicle fleet is the cream of the crop, and safaris and treks are consistently good value for money. All budgets.

Safari Makers (Map pp180-1; ☎ 027-254 4446; www.safarimakers.com; India St, Arusha) Reliable no-frills northern-circuit camping and lodge safaris and treks at very reasonable prices, some of which also incorporate Cultural Tourism Program tours. Budget.

Shah Tours (Map p172; ☎ 027-275 2370, 027-275 2998; www.kilimanjaro-shah.com; Mawenzi Rd, Moshi) Quality Kilimanjaro and Meru treks at reasonable prices. Midrange.

Sunny Safaris (Map pp180-1; ☎ 027-250 8184, 027-250 7145; www.sunnysafaris.com; Colonel Middleton Rd, Arusha) A wide selection of no-frills camping and lodge safaris at reasonable prices, as well as Kilimanjaro and Meru treks, and day walks in the area around Arusha. Budget.

Tropical Trails (☎ 027-250 0358, 027-254 8299; www.tropicaltrails.com; Masai Camp, Old Moshi Rd, Arusha) A long-standing company offering high-quality treks and walking safaris on Kilimanjaro, Meru, in the Crater Highlands and in the Monduli Mountains. Kosher treks, photographic camping safaris and other special-interest tours can be arranged, and a portion of the company's profits goes towards supporting education projects in Maasai schools. Upper midrange.

Zara Tanzania Adventures (Map p172; ☎ 027-275 0011; www.zaratravel.com; Rindi Lane, Moshi) An efficient outfit that does a brisk business with Kilimanjaro treks, plus some northern-circuit safaris. Budget to midrange.

> An essential safari companion is Lonely Planet's *Watching Wildlife East Africa*, which is full of tips on spotting wildlife, maps of East Africa's parks and background information on animal behaviour and ecology.

Most hotels in Marangu also organise Kilimanjaro treks at price levels roughly corresponding with their accommodation rates. For listings, see p175. Marangu Hotel, in addition to fully catered treks, also offers a no-frills 'hard way' option: for US$170 plus park fees for a five-day Marangu climb, the hotel will take care of hut reservations and provide a guide with porter; you must provide all food and equipment.

KENYA

ITINERARIES

Whether you take a camping safari or a lodge safari, there's a plethora of options available ranging from two days to 15 days and, in some cases, up to six weeks.

Most shorter itineraries of half a week or less concentrate on Masai Mara National Reserve and Lake Nakuru National Park, while short Amboseli and Tsavo National Parks safaris are also common. You'll need a little more time to head north to the popular Samburu and Buffalo Springs National Reserves, while a week will give you time to tag on visits to Lakes Nakuru, Bogoria and Baringo to either a Masai Mara, Amboseli or northern parks itinerary. With a week and a half you could take in two or more of the Rift Valley lakes plus Masai Mara, Amboseli and Tsavo, or Samburu and Buffalo Springs, Meru, Lake Nakuru and Masai Mara.

Most of the safari companies cover the standard routes described in the previous paragraph, but some also specialise in different routes designed to take you off the beaten track. Meru, Mt Elgon, Saiwa Swamp and the Aberdare National Parks are all possible. Also popular are itineraries combining wildlife safaris with visits to Lake Turkana; for example, visiting either or both of Samburu and Buffalo Springs and either Meru National Park or Shaba National Reserve and then heading up to Marsabit National Park before crossing the Chalbi Desert to Lake Turkana.

In the high season many companies have daily or every second day departures to the most popular national parks – Amboseli, Masai Mara and Tsavo. They generally leave only once or twice per week for the less frequented parks such as Samburu and Buffalo Springs, Shaba and Meru. In addition, most companies will leave for any of the most popular national parks at any time so long as you have a minimum number of people wanting to go – usually four. If you are on your own you may have to wait around for a while to be put together with a larger group, which means it makes sense to book ahead or get a group together yourself rather than just turning up and expecting to leave the next morning.

OPERATORS

Basecamp Explorer (☎ 020-577490; www.basecampexplorer.com; Ole Odume Rd, Hurlingham, Nairobi) An excellent Scandinavian-owned ecotourism operator offering a nine-day camping itinerary to Samburu, Lake Nakuru and the Masai Mara, with walking at Mt Kenya, Lake Bogoria and Lake Baringo. The firm also runs plenty of conservation-based safaris, including trips to Lamu, Tanzania, Mt Kenya and Kilimanjaro. Top end.

Best Camping Tours (Map pp282-3; ☎ 020-229667; www.bestcampingkenya.com; I&M Towers, Kenyatta Ave, Nairobi) This company offers camping safaris on all the main routes including Amboseli or Masai Mara (three to four days) and Amboseli and Tsavo West (four days). Budget.

Bike Treks (☎ 020-446371; www.biketreks.co.ke; Kabete Gardens, Westlands, Nairobi) This company offers walking and cycling as well as combined walking/cycling safaris. Its shortest safari is a three-day Masai Mara trip, and there are also six-day walking or cycling trips to the Maasai land west and south of Narok. Midrange.

Bushbuck Adventures (☎ 020-7121505; www.bushbuckadventures.com; Peponi Rd, Westlands, Nairobi) Bushbuck is a small company specialising in personalised safaris. It's relatively expensive, but some company profits are put into conservation projects. The company is also strong on walking safaris. Midrange.

Eastern & Southern Safaris (Map pp282-3; ☎ 020-242828; www.essafari.co.ke; Finance House, Loita St, Nairobi) A classy and reliable outfit. Safaris in Tanzania and Uganda are also available, and departures are guaranteed with just two people for some itineraries. Midrange to top end.

Gametrackers (Map pp282-3; ☎ 020-338927; www.gametrackersafaris.com; Nginyo Towers, cnr Koinange & Moktar Daddah Sts, Nairobi) Long established and usually reliable, this company offers a full range of camping and lodge safaris around Kenya. There are also short excursions, walking, Mt Kenya treks and numerous long-haul trips to Tanzania, Uganda and further afield. Budget and midrange.

IntoAfrica (www.intoafrica.co.uk) This environmentally and culturally sensitive company gets more praise from readers than just about any other, placing an emphasis on fair trade. Trips on offer include a variety of routes up Mt Kenya as well as cultural treks with Maasai people. Midrange.

Ketty Tours (ketty@africaonline.co.ke) Diani Beach (☎ 040-203582; Diani shopping centre, Diani Beach); Mombasa (Map p314; ☎ 041-2315178; Ketty Plaza, Moi Ave, Mombasa) This company specialises in short tours of the coastal region and into Tsavo East or West. However, it also offers camping safaris to all the usual parks from two to 10 days. Budget and midrange.

Let's Go Travel (Map pp282-3; ☎ 020-340331; www.letsgosafari.com; Caxton House, Standard St, Nairobi) This excellent travel agent runs its own safaris and excursions and also sells on an amazing range of trips from other companies, covering Tanzania, Uganda, Ethiopia and even the Seychelles. Prices are on the high side for camping, but it's also a good port of call for unusual lodge safaris and car hire. Midrange.

Ontdek Kenya (☎ 061-2030326; www.ontdekkenya.com; PO Box 2352, Nyeri) This small operator has been recommended by several readers and offers walking trips catered to women, vegetarians and bird-watchers. Destinations include the Rift Valley lakes and Mt Kenya. Budget.

Origins Safaris (Map pp282-3; ☎ 020-312137; www.originsafaris.info; Fedha Towers, Standard St, Nairobi) Origins offer tailored bird-watching trips and a superb range of exclusive cultural safaris around the country, including such rare sights as Samburu circumcision ceremonies and tribal initiation rites in southern Ethiopia. Top end.

About 8000 elephants roam Tsavo's expanses – one-third of Kenya's overall total, but a huge drop from the 40,000-plus elephants at home here before poaching took its toll.

Safari Seekers (www.safari-seekerskenya.net) Mombasa (Map p314; ☎ 041-220122; Diamond Trust Arcade, Moi Ave, Mombasa); Nairobi (Map pp282-3; ☎ 020-652317; Jubilee Insurance Exchange Bldg, Kaunda St, Nairobi) Has its own permanent camp sites in Amboseli, Samburu and Masai Mara, and runs camping and lodge safaris both in Kenya and Tanzania, plus trips into Uganda. Budget and midrange.

Saferide Safaris (Map pp282-3; ☎ 020-253129; www.saferidesafaris.com; Avenue House, Kenyatta Ave, Nairobi) A relatively new operator consistently recommended by readers for its camping excursions. Budget.

Sana Highlands Trekking Expeditions (Map pp282-3; ☎ 020-227820; www.sanatrekking kenya.com; Contrust House, Moi Ave, Nairobi) Another of the big budget players and a regular stop on the tout circuit. However, they have had a reasonable reputation in the past for walking safaris as well as the usual camping and lodge itineraries. Budget.

Somak Travel (www.somak-nairobi.com) Mombasa (Map p328; ☎ 041-487349; Somak House, Nyerere Ave, PO Box 90738); Nairobi (☎ 020-535508; Somak House, Mombasa Rd, Nairobi) Runs the usual range of lodge safaris and other options such as luxury camel treks. Top end.

Southern Cross Safaris (www.southerncrosssafaris.com) Malindi (Map p337; ☎ 042-30547; Malindi Complex, Lamu Rd); Mombasa (Map p312; ☎ 041-475074; Kanstan Centre, Nyali Bridge, Malindi Rd, Mombasa); Nairobi (☎ 020-884712; Symbion House, Karen Rd, Nairobi) A long-standing operator and travel agent with an excellent reputation around the country. Top end.

UGANDA

ITINERARIES

Uganda is a compact country in comparison with some of its neighbours, and most safari itineraries are relatively short, averaging from one to three weeks. Some include a detour to neighbouring Rwanda. Shorter trips to view the mountain gorillas or Murchison Falls are also popular with travellers combining Uganda with visits to Kenya or Tanzania.

The shortest safaris, taking a week or less, focus on the southwest, usually combining a gorilla visit in Uganda or Rwanda with Queen Elizabeth and Lake Mburo National Parks or Kibale Forest National Park. With 10 to 12 days, you'll be able to cover most of Uganda's highlights, following a loop from Kampala south via Lake Mburo to Bwindi Impenetrable National Park or Parc National des Volcans in Rwanda, before heading north through Queen Elizabeth National Park and Kibale Forest National Park on to Murchison Falls National Park. With two or more weeks, you'll also be able to include other parks in the west such as Semliki National Park or Semliki Valley Game Reserve and even consider a flying visit to remote Kidepo Valley in the northeast. This time frame will also allow more time to relax en route, and for other activities such as guided bird-watching or white-water rafting.

Uganda's Murchison Falls National Park is one of the few places in the world for spotting the rare shoebill stork, though sightings are far from guaranteed.

OPERATORS

Afri Tours & Travel (Map p472; ☎ 041-233596; www.afritourstravel.com; Daisy's Arcade, 13 Buganda Rd, Kampala) One of the better all-round safari companies in Uganda, offering safaris at prices for every pocket. It operates the Sambiya River Lodge in Murchison and promotes some excellent-value short safaris to what is arguably Uganda's best national park, as well as offering full safari itineraries throughout the country. All budgets.

African Pearl Safaris (Map p472; ☎ 041-233566; www.africanpearlsafaris.com; Impala House, 13 Kimathi Ave, Kampala) Offers a wide range of shorter safaris around Uganda with a focus on Bwindi Impenetrable National Park where it operates the Buhoma Homestead. Midrange.

Great Lakes Safaris (☎ 041-267153; www.safari-uganda.com; Suzie House, Gaba Rd, Kampala) One of the newer safari companies in Uganda, the team has been generating rave reviews for friendly service and flexibility. They cover all the major national parks in Uganda. All budgets.

Mantana African Safaris (☎ 041-321552; www.kimbla-mantana.com; 17 Nambi Rd, Entebbe) Known throughout East Africa for its luxury lodges and tented camps, Mantana offers a limited range of safaris around Uganda. Most of its trips combine stays at one or several of their camps at Lake Mburo, Bwindi and Kibale Forest, plus visits to Queen Elizabeth and the crater lakes. Midrange to top end.

Uganda Safari Company (Map p471; ☎ 041-251182; www.safariuganda.com; Emin Pasha Hotel, Aki Bua Rd, Kampala) Formerly Semliki Safaris, this is a specialist operator offering all-inclusive safaris throughout Uganda for around US$300 per day, including Semliki Valley Game Reserve, Queen Elizabeth, Murchison Falls and the mountain gorillas. As well as offering tailored trips for bird-watchers, fishers and other special-interest groups, it runs the luxurious Semliki Lodge in western Uganda and Apoka Lodge at beautiful Kidepo Valley. Top end.

Volcanoes Safaris Kampala (Map p471; ☎ 041-346464; www.volcanoessafaris.com; 27 Lumumba Ave, Kampala); UK office (☎ 0870-870 8480; salesuk@volcanoessafaris.com) An extensive choice covering the highlights of Uganda, with a particular focus on the mountain gorillas here and in Rwanda. The organisation also operates upmarket camps at Mgahinga, Bwindi and Sipi Falls. It's also possible to make enquiries or bookings through its UK office. Midrange to top end.

RWANDA

ITINERARIES

The few organised safaris that include Rwanda are generally short – most less than a week – yet expensive due to the lack of competition. All concentrate on trips to Parc National des Volcans.

OPERATORS

In addition to the following companies, it's worth checking with the national tourism office in Kigali (see p575) for an updated listing of operators working in Rwanda.

Jane Goodall's classic, In the Shadow of Man, is essential and fascinating reading for anyone planning to go chimpanzee tracking in East Africa.

Primate Safaris (Map p574; ☎ 503428; www.primatesafaris-rwanda.com; Ave de la Paix, Kigali) Offers a range of short safaris to Ngungwe Forest National Park and Parc National des Volcans; in addition, the owners have years of experience in the Kenyan safari business.

Thousand Hills (Map p574; ☎ 505151; www.thousandhills.rw; Hotel des Milles Collines, Kigali) New operator with a very experienced team who have worked all over the world. Gorilla visits, national park visits and an emphasis on local culture. Their motto is 'paradise needs to be shared'.

Volcanoes Safaris (Map p574; ☎ 576530; salesrw@volcanoessafaris.com; Hotel des Milles Collines, Kigali) The Rwandan branch office for Volcanoes Safaris of Uganda; see p95 for more information.

Mountain Gorillas

Coming face to face with mountain gorillas is the ultimate wildlife experience in Africa. No bars, no windows – you are a humble guest in their domain. Tracking through dense vegetation, nothing quite prepares you for the moment when you come upon a gorilla family in the wild; the first glimpse of black as a juvenile jumps off a nearby branch, a toddler clinging to the back of its mother, and the shiver of fear as a giant silverback slowly crosses your path. This is one of life's great experiences and is not to be missed when travelling through East Africa.

There are thought to be fewer than 700 mountain gorillas *(Gorilla gorilla beringei)* left in the world today, all found in a small area of East Africa straddling the borders of Uganda, Rwanda and the Democratic Republic of the Congo (DR Congo). This makes them a critically endangered species.

Relations between humans and gorillas have not always been fraternal. For centuries gorillas were considered fearsome and aggressive – with portrayals like King Kong hardly helping their image – and it was only last century that we finally learned that they are gentle and vegetarian. In reality chimpanzees are far more aggressive than the relatively docile gorillas.

The first European to encounter the mountain gorillas was Oscar von Beringe, in 1902. He shot two on the slopes of Mt Sabinyo and the 'new' subspecies was named after him. Hunting the gorillas was a popular pastime until one hunter, Carl Akeley, decided that something must be done to preserve the population of these magnificent creatures. In 1925 he persuaded the Belgian government to create Africa's first protected area, Albert National Park, which is now Parc National des Virungas in DR Congo. Sadly, over the years agriculture and administrative division reduced the size of this protected area, and poaching further reduced the number of gorillas.

The first scientific study of the mountain gorillas in the Virunga volcanoes area was undertaken by George Schaller in 1959. His work was continued by Dian Fossey from 1967 and her story has been made the subject of a film, *Gorillas in the Mist*. Fossey's confrontational, uncompromising stance on poaching most likely led to her murder in 1985.

GORILLA TOURISM

By the late 1960s gorilla tracking had already become quite popular in DR Congo, and from 1978 gorilla tourism was also being promoted in Rwanda, with tremendous results for the local economy. During the 1980s gorilla tourism was an important source of income for Rwanda, and the animals became a symbol of national pride. Uganda was slow to realise the potential of promoting its primates, but, due to political instability in neighbouring Rwanda and DR Congo, by the late 1990s it was Uganda which had established itself as the most popular country for encountering gorillas.

Gorilla tourism today stands at a crossroads. All three countries where the remaining gorillas live have a history of instability that makes it hard for international conservation organisations to operate with any certainty. The International Gorilla Conservation Programme (IGCP) and the Dian Fossey Gorilla Fund (DFGF) have tried to promote sustainable agricultural and tourism practices, and to encourage the active participation of local communities in conservation, and this has played a large part in ensuring the gorillas' survival during turbulent times. However, many of the local communities around these protected areas remain bitter, as they're aware

Gorilla: Struggle for Survival in the Virungas (1996) is coauthored by George Schaller, the primatologist who pioneered the study of mountain gorillas in the Virungas. This is a biography of these gentle creatures and the efforts undertaken to protect them in a hostile environment.

In 1978 Bill Weber and Amy Vedder began studying mountain gorillas with Dian Fossey in Rwanda. *In the Kingdom of Gorillas: Fragile Species in a Dangerous Land* tells how they established the Mountain Gorilla Project and encouraged the ecotourism which may save these majestic creatures from extinction.

of the vast sums of money flowing in from visitors, and very little of it reaches them.

The Ugandan authorities pioneered a program to give 10% of gorilla revenue to the local communities around Bwindi Impenetrable and Mgahinga Gorilla National Parks. However, after the initial fanfare, the amount was quietly trimmed back to 10% of park entrance fees, not 10% of gorilla-tracking fees – which is the difference between US$2 and US$36 per visitor or more than US$1000 per day! Unless the local communities have more of an incentive to protect these beautiful creatures, the future of the gorillas will never be secure.

Currently Bwindi, in Uganda, and Rwanda's Parc National des Volcans are the two most popular places to track the mountain gorillas. Mgahinga in Uganda used to be popular with independent travellers, as permits were available at short notice; however, the solitary family once resident there has been on an extended vacation on the Rwanda side of the border, and may not return. The good news for visitors to the region is that Parc National des Virungas in DR Congo is once again open for gorilla tracking and there are 36 permits a day available at Djomba and Bukima. This is currently the easiest place to pick up a permit at short notice.

The most important development for the future of gorilla tourism could be a long-term plan, currently under discussion, to create a tri-national protected area under a single administration, which would market the gorillas internationally. However, with relations between the governments of Uganda, Rwanda and DR Congo frosty to say the least, this will remain a conservationist's dream rather than a geographic reality for several years to come.

THE GORILLAS

Gorillas are the largest of the great apes and share an astonishing 97% of their biological make-up with human beings. Gorillas used to inhabit a swathe of land that cut right across central Africa, but the ice age diminished the forests and divided them into three groups: the western lowland gorilla, the eastern lowland gorilla and the mountain gorilla. Mountain gorillas are now found only in two small populations of about 330 or so each in the forests of Bwindi, and on the slopes of the Virunga volcanoes, encompassing Rwanda's Parc National des Volcans and Dr Congo's Parc National de Virungas. There is no doubt that mountain gorillas are a very rare species – there is just one for every 10 million people on earth.

Mountain gorillas are distinguished from their lowland relatives by longer hair, a broader chest and a wider jaw. The most obvious thing that sets apart the gorillas in Bwindi from those of the Virunga volcanoes is that they are less shaggy, most likely due to the lower altitude of Bwindi compared with the volcanoes. More recently, DNA tests have suggested that the Bwindi gorilla is a distinct subspecies from the mountain gorilla, although that's of more concern to scientists than the average tourist.

Daily Life

Gorillas spend 30% of their day feeding, 30% moving and foraging, and the remainder resting. They spend most of their time on the ground, moving around on all fours, but stand up to reach for food. Gorillas are vegetarians and their diet consists mainly of bamboo shoots, giant thistles and wild celery, all of which contain water and allow the gorillas to survive without drinking for long periods of time. Insects are a popular source of protein.

The group's dominant silverback, also known as the alpha male, dictates movements for the day, and at night each gorilla makes its own nest.

Dian Fossey spent most of her life fighting to protect the mountain gorillas and the Dian Fossey Gorilla Fund (www.gorillafund .org) continues her work through antipoaching measures, monitoring, research, education and supporting local communities.

The International Gorilla Conservation Project (IGCP; www.mountain gorillas.org) is a unique partnership between the African Wildlife Foundation (AWF), Fauna & Flora International (FFI) and the World Wide Fund for Nature (WWF). Their goal is the protection of mountain gorillas and their forest habitat in Rwanda, Uganda and the DR Congo.

Nests are only used once and the age of a nest is usually determinable by the dung left there. Gorillas will usually only travel about 1km a day, unless they have encountered another group in which case they may move further.

Families

Gorillas generally live in family groups of varying sizes, usually including one or two older silverback males, younger black-back males, females and infants. Most groups contain between 10 and 15 gorillas but in Rwanda and DR Congo there are groups of 30 or more.

There are strong bonds between family individuals and status is usually linked to age. Silverbacks are at the top of the hierarchy, then females with infants or ties to the silverbacks, then black-backs and other females.

Most gorillas leave the group when they reach maturity, which helps prevent interbreeding among such a small population.

Conflict

Gorillas are relatively placid primates and serious confrontations are rare, although violence can flare if there is a challenge for supremacy between silverbacks. Conflicts are mostly kept to shows of strength and vocal disputes.

Conflict between groups is also uncommon, as gorillas are not territorial. However, ranges can often overlap and if two groups meet, there is usually a lot of display and bravado on the part of silverbacks, including mock charges. Often the whole group joins in and it is at this point that young adult females may choose to switch allegiance.

If gorillas do fight, injuries can be very serious as these animals have long canine teeth. If a dominant male is driven from a group by another silverback, it is likely the new leader will kill all the young infants to establish his mating rights.

For a better understanding of how intelligent gorillas are, take a look at www.koko.org, dedicated to Koko the gorilla at San Francisco Zoo, who can understand more than 1000 words.

Communication

Gorillas communicate in a variety of ways, including facial expressions, gestures and calls. Adult males use barks and roars during confrontations or to coordinate the movement of their groups to a different area. Postures and gestures form an important element of intimidation and it is possible for a clash to be diffused by a display of teeth-baring, stiff-legging and charging. And if all this fails, a terrifying scream is enough to deter most outsiders.

Friendly communication is an important part of group bonding and includes grunts of pleasure, particularly associated with food and foraging. Upon finding food, gorillas will grunt or bark to alert other members of the group. Grooming, however, is not as common as among other primates.

The heaviest gorilla on record was an eastern lowland gorilla, weighing a whopping 210kg or more than 460lbs.

Biology

Gorillas are the largest primates in the world and adult males weigh as much as 200kg (440lbs). Females are about half this size. Mountain gorillas are the largest of the three gorilla species, although the largest gorilla ever recorded was an eastern lowland male.

Males reach maturity between eight and 15 years – their backs turning silver as they enter their teens – while females enter adulthood at the earlier age of eight. Conception is possible for about three days each month and once a female has conceived for the first time, she spends most of her life pregnant or nursing.

The duration of pregnancy is about 8½ months. Newborn infants are highly dependent on adults, and a young infant will rarely leave its mother's arms during its first six months. Initially the infant clings to the front of its mother, but gradually it spends more time on her back.

In its second year, a young gorilla begins to interact with other members of the group and starts to feed itself. Infant gorillas and silverbacks often form a bond and it is not uncommon for a silverback to adopt an infant if its mother dies. This distinguishes gorillas from other primates, where child-rearing duties are left to females.

From about three years, young gorillas become quite independent, and build their own nests. However, 30% of gorillas die before the age of six.

WHERE TO TRACK THE GORILLAS

For many visitors to East Africa, a gorilla visit is the single largest expenditure they'll make in the region. It is worth putting some thought into where to visit these incredible creatures, not only to get the most out of the experience, but to ensure a safe visit as well.

In the last few years the choice really came down to Bwindi National Park in Uganda or Parc National des Volcans in Rwanda, as the Mgahinga gorillas aren't always in Uganda and DR Congo was closed. However, with DR Congo welcoming visitors once more, it's easier to get a permit than it used to be. Rwanda offers 40 permits a day to visit five habituated families, DR Congo offers 36 permits a day, also to visit five habituated families, while Uganda offers 32 permits daily to visit four families. The towering Virunga volcanoes are a majestic backdrop, making Rwanda and DR Congo the more evocative settings in which to track the gorillas.

During peak season it can be very difficult to get gorilla permits in Uganda and Rwanda, so book ahead if you are planning to visit in December and January or July and August. Flexible travellers who don't want to fix a date in advance should consider DR Congo, as the waiting time is much shorter than in Rwanda and Uganda.

Bwindi Impenetrable National Park, Uganda

Since the middle of the 1990s, Bwindi has been the number-one place to track the mountain gorillas – although Parc National des Volcans in Rwanda is almost as popular these days. Its popularity and reputation took a plunge after the murder of eight tourists here in March 1999, but security has since been considerably beefed up and it is once again regularly booked out.

As the name suggests, this is a dense forest with steep slopes, so tracking the gorillas can be quite hard work. Visibility is often poor, and fast film or push processing is necessary for good photographic results.

The trip to Bwindi can be done in a car, but a 4WD is preferable. Public transport dries up within 17km of the park. See p523 for more information.

> No mountain gorillas have ever been successfully reared in captivity, contributing to the precarious nature of their existence.

> Gorilla-tracking permits generate vast sums of money for the countries involved. Rwanda can make US$15,000 a day when all the permits are sold, Uganda stands to make US$11,520 and DR Congo US$9000.

ILLEGAL GORILLA VISITS

We hear occasional reports of illegal gorilla visits in the region. Usually this takes the form of tourists bribing rangers into taking them into the mountains to view the gorillas, but it is not unknown for rangers to approach tourists – particularly if business is booming and there are simply no gorilla permits available.

Illegal gorilla visits can increase the animals' stress levels, which in turn reduces immunity to disease. The threat of increased stress levels should not be underestimated, considering three out of 10 gorillas die before adulthood. Although seeing gorillas may be the highlight of your trip, the only way illegal visits can be stopped is if visitors play by the rules.

RULES FOR GORILLA TRACKING

Before meeting the mountain dwellers of East Africa, all visitors must observe the following rules of gorilla etiquette.

■ Anyone with an illness cannot track the gorillas. Shared biology means shared illness.

■ Eating and smoking near the gorillas is prohibited – they might want to join in.

■ Flash photography is banned; turn off the autoflash or you will be mighty unpopular with both rangers and gorillas.

■ Speak quietly and don't point at the gorillas – they might get paranoid.

■ Leave *nothing* in the park; take out everything you bring in.

■ Stay very close to your guide. Keep a few metres back from the gorillas.

■ Hard as it seems to stand still when faced by 200kg of charging silverback, never ever run away…crouch down until he cools off.

ARRANGING PERMITS

It can be very difficult to get permits for Bwindi. Numbers have increased to 32 per day, but local and international tour operators tend to book the bulk of them months in advance and there is no effective stand-by system in place. There are three mountain gorilla groups habituated to human contact which can be visited from the Buhoma sector of the park, and one family that can be tracked from the newer Nkuringo sector. A gorilla permit costs US$360 including park entry fee and must be paid for in US dollars cash at the **Uganda Wildlife Authority** (UWA; ☎ 346287; uwa@uwa.or.ug; 7 Kira Rd) headquarters in Kampala. Alternatively, try and book ahead through a Ugandan tour operator (see p95).

For more on mountain gorillas in Uganda, see the Uganda Wildlife Authority website at www.uwa.or.ug.

Mgahinga Gorilla National Park, Uganda

Mgahinga encompasses part of the Virunga volcanoes, which span the borders of Uganda, Rwanda and DR Congo. This park used to be popular with independent travellers as advance bookings were not possible due to the gorillas' tendency to duck over the border into Rwanda or DR Congo. That was the good news, the bad news is that they seem to have decided to stay in Rwanda for the time being, and that means eight fewer permits a day in Uganda. Mgahinga is more accessible by public transport than Bwindi (see p531 for more information).

ARRANGING PERMITS

Assuming the gorillas return to Mgahinga some day, the procedure for arranging permits is the same as at Bwindi (see opposite).

Parc National des Volcans, Rwanda

This was *the* place to view the mountain gorillas during the 1980s, but the security situation kept it off the travel map for much of the 1990s. However, the park reopened to visitors in 1999 and has regained its reputation as the best place to see the gorillas.

This park is where Dian Fossey was based and where the film about her work was made. If you want the most authentic gorilla experience, this may be the place to come, as the towering volcanoes form a breathtaking backdrop.

Security here is very tight, and an elite military unit guards the park. Access is quite straightforward from Kigali or southwestern Uganda. The park is about 13km from Ruhengeri in northwest Rwanda (for more information, see p583).

ARRANGING PERMITS

For more on mountain gorillas in Rwanda, see the ORTPN website at www.rwandatourism.com.

As tourism in Rwanda takes off again, it is getting more difficult to get a permit during the peak seasons of July and August, and December to January. There are 40 gorilla permits available each day and the cost is US$375, including the park entry fee. You can book a permit with the **ORTPN** (☎ 576514; www.rwandatourism.com; 1 Blvd de la Revolution; ☼ 7am-5pm Mon-Fri, 8am-2pm weekends) in Kigali (see p575) or through Rwandan tour operators (see p96).

Parc National des Virungas, DR Congo

This is where gorilla tourism began, back in the 1960s, and now it is back in business at long last. The park closed in 1998 following the kidnapping of some tourists, but reopened again in 2004. It is currently the easiest place to pick up a permit in the region, as most tour operators are steering clear for the time being.

For more on mountain gorillas in DR Congo, see the Institut Congolais pour le Conservation de la Nature (ICCN) at www.iccnrdc.cd.

There are two places to track the gorillas, one at Djomba near the Uganda border and the other at Bukima 40km north of Goma. Djomba is currently more popular, but Bukima offers more permits. Both are stunning locations with a string of volcanoes behind.

Security at the park looks reasonable, but given recent events in DR Congo, it is probably fair to say that things are less organised than in Rwanda and Uganda. However, the Congolese are trying their best to attract visitors and deserve support as long as the security situation remains stable.

ARRANGING PERMITS

Parc National des Virungas is the easiest place to arrange a permit at the time of writing. There are 36 gorilla permits available each day and the cost is US$250, including the park entry fee. There are eight permits available at the Djomba sector and 28 permits available at Bukima. Permits can be arranged through **Backpackers Hostel** (☎ 256-41-274767; www.backpackers .co.ug) in Kampala, the official Uganda representative for gorilla visits in DR Congo. Coordinator **Alex Mujyambere** (☎ 256-71-626194; mujaalex@yahoo .co.uk) journeys up and down to Congo every week. This situation might change as the DR Congo re-establishes itself as a tourist destination; see p559 for more details.

Tanzania

Few areas of the continent captivate the imagination as does Tanzania. Snowcapped Mt Kilimanjaro towers majestically over the horizon, flamingos stand sentinel in the salt pans of Ngorongoro Crater, and the hoof beats of thousands of wildebeest echo over the Serengeti Plains. In many ways, this is the Africa of legend, where hot, dusty afternoons end abruptly in glorious blazes of sunset and velvet-black star-studded skies enfold the hills, where Indian Ocean breezes caress white sands and moss-covered ruins of ancient Swahili city-states dot the shoreline.

Despite all this, Tanzania is remarkably unassuming and low-key, and thus far has remained enviably untouched by the tribal rivalries and political upheavals that plague many of its neighbours. While it's ideal for exploring in combination with the other countries covered in this book, it also has more than enough attractions to be a journey on its own.

The most popular areas – the northern safari circuit around Arusha and the Zanzibar Archipelago – have scaled main roads and an array of hotels and restaurants, and are easily incorporated into a larger East African loop. With more time, and for more adventure, head south and west, where you'll soon find yourself well off the beaten path, surrounded by a Tanzania that is far removed from Western development and amenities.

Wherever you visit, the highlight inevitably winds up being Tanzanians themselves, with their characteristic warmth, politeness and dignity. Chances are that you'll want to come back for more, to which most Tanzanians will say '*karibu tena*' (welcome again).

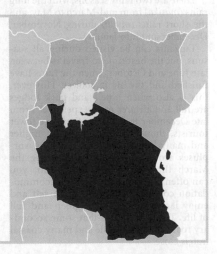

FAST FACTS

- **Area** 943,000 sq km
- **Birthplace of** Freddie Mercury; humankind
- **Capital** Dodoma
- **Country code** 255
- **Famous for** Serengeti; Mt Kilimanjaro; Zanzibar; Julius Nyerere; cloves; chimpanzees
- **Languages** Swahili and English
- **Money** Tanzanian Shilling (TSh); US$1 = TSh1176; €1 = TSh1424
- **Population** 34.5 million

HIGHLIGHTS

- **Wildlife Safaris** (p91) From world-famous Serengeti to remote Katavi, immerse yourself in the sounds, scents and rhythms of life in the wild.
- **Exotic Islands** (p249) Follow the monsoon winds back through the centuries on Zanzibar, Mafia or Kilwa Kisiwani.
- **Majestic Mountains** (p250) Scale Mts Kilimanjaro and Meru or amble past picturesque villages in the Usambara range.
- **Picture-perfect Beaches** (p249) Take your pick of beach – from idyllic offshore islands, the palm-fringed mainland coast or serene inland lakes.
- **Chimpanzees** (p250) Meet the chimpanzees at Mahale Mountains or Gombe Stream National Parks.

CLIMATE & WHEN TO GO

Throughout the country, the coolest months are from June to October and the warmest from December to March, but there are marked regional differences. Along the coast, conditions are tropical, with high humidity and temperatures averaging between 25°C and 29°C. On the central highland plateau, temperatures range from 20°C to 27°C between June and August, sometimes dropping lower in more elevated areas such as Njombe, Mbeya and Arusha. Between December and March they can soar above 30°C. See p621 for climate charts for major towns.

There are two rainy seasons, with the long rains (*masika*) from mid-March to May, and the short rains (*mvuli*) during November, December and into January.

Tanzania can be visited during all seasons, but the best time to travel is between late June and October, when the rains have finished and the air is coolest. However, this is also when hotels and park lodges are full and airfares most expensive. From late December to February there are fewer tourists, though temperatures are higher and many hotels charge high-season surpluses around the holidays. During the March through May rainy season, you can often save substantially on accommodation costs, have things to yourself and enjoy landscapes that are green and full of life. The downside is that some secondary roads are impassable and many coastal hotels close.

HOW MUCH?

- **Midrange safari** US$200 per person per day
- **Plate of ugali** TSh500
- **Serengeti National Park entry** US$50 per person per entry
- **Papaya** TSh300
- **Short taxi ride** TSh1500

LONELY PLANET INDEX

- **Litre of petrol** TSh1040
- **Litre of bottled water** TSh500
- **Safari Lager** TSh500
- **Souvenir T-shirt** TSh10,000
- **Street snack (mishikaki)** TSh200

HISTORY

Tanzania's history begins with the dawn of humankind. Hominid (humanlike) footprints unearthed near Olduvai Gorge (p200), together with archaeological finds from Kenya and Ethiopia, show that our earliest ancestors may have been roaming the Tanzanian plains and surrounding areas over three million years ago. For more on these and subsequent millennia, and an overview of colonial-era developments, see p28.

The Struggle for Independence

The earliest seeds of Tanzanian independence can be traced to the Maji Maji rebellion of 1905 (see p235). During the following decades, the nationalist movement in Tanganyika – as mainland Tanzania was then known – gradually solidified. Farmers' cooperatives began to play an increasingly important political role, and soon Tanganyika's fledgling political scene was dominated by the Tanganyika Africa Association (TAA), which served as a channel for grass-roots resentment against colonial policies.

In 1953 the TAA elected a teacher named Julius Nyerere as its president. Under his leadership, the TAA was quickly transformed into an effective political organisation. A new internal constitution was introduced on 7 July 1954 (an anniversary now celebrated as Saba Saba Day) and the TAA became the Tanganyika African National Union (TANU), with the rallying cry of *'uhuru na umoja'* (freedom and unity).

One of the first items on TANU's agenda was independence. In 1958 and 1959, TANU-supported candidates decisively won general legislative elections, and in 1959 Britain agreed to the establishment of internal self-government, requesting Nyerere to be chief minister. On 9 December 1961 Tanganyika became independent and on 9 December 1962 it was established as a republic, with Nyerere as president.

On the Zanzibar Archipelago, which had been a British protectorate since 1890, the main push for independence came from the radical Afro-Shirazi Party (ASP). Opposing the ASP were two minority parties, the Zanzibar & Pemba People's Party (ZPPP) and the sultanate-oriented Zanzibar Nationalist Party (ZNP), both of which were favoured by the British. As a result, at Zanzibari independence in December 1963, it was the two minority parties that formed the first government.

This government did not last long. Within a month, a Ugandan immigrant named John Okello initiated a violent revolution against the ruling ZPPP-ZNP coalition, leading to the toppling of the government and the sultan, and the massacre or expulsion of most of the islands' Arab population. The sultan was replaced by an entity known as the Zanzibar Revolutionary Council, which was comprised of ASP members and headed by Abeid Karume.

On 26 April 1964 Nyerere signed an act of union with Karume, creating the United Republic of Tanganyika (renamed the United Republic of Tanzania the following October).

Formation of the union, which was resented by many Zanzibaris from the outset, was motivated in part by the then prevailing spirit of pan-Africanism, and in part as a cold war response to the ASP's socialist program.

Karume's government lasted until 1972, when he was assassinated and succeeded by Aboud Jumbe. Shortly thereafter, in an effort to subdue the ongoing unrest resulting from the merger of the islands with the mainland, Nyerere authorised formation of a one-party state and combined TANU and the ASP into a new party known as Chama Cha Mapinduzi (CCM; Party of the Revolution). This merger, which was ratified in a new union constitution on 27 April 1977, marked the beginning of the CCM's dominance of Tanzanian politics, which endures to this day.

TANZANIA TRAVELS

Getting around Tanzania takes time, so it's best to choose one or two regions and concentrate on exploring them well, rather than trying to fit too much into one visit. Here are a few suggestions.

One Week

Arriving in Dar es Salaam, spend a day there getting oriented, a couple of nights at Saadani Game Reserve or Mikumi National Park and the remainder of the week on Zanzibar. For a week starting in Arusha, divide your time between a couple of the northern-circuit parks; split it between a wildlife safari and a few days hiking near Lushoto; or spend a day or two in or near Arusha and the rest of the week in and around the Ngorongoro Conservation Area.

Two Weeks

For the classic bush-and-beach itinerary, spend a week on the northern-safari circuit or climbing Kilimanjaro, followed by a week chilling out on Zanzibar. Alternatively, you can expand on the itineraries suggested under 'One Week': stay longer on Zanzibar; go to Pemba; relax on the beaches around Pangani en route to/from the Usambaras.

One Month

With a month, combine any of the above itineraries; travel between Lake Victoria and northern or northeastern Tanzania via the western Serengeti; make your way southwest between Morogoro and Mbeya with stops en route at Mikumi and Ruaha National Parks; or follow the coast south, with stops in Kilwa, Lindi, Mikindani and Mtwara.

TANZANIA

TANZANIA

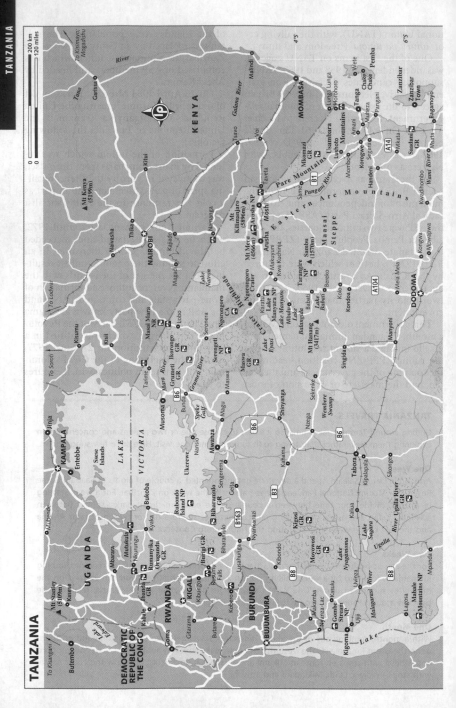

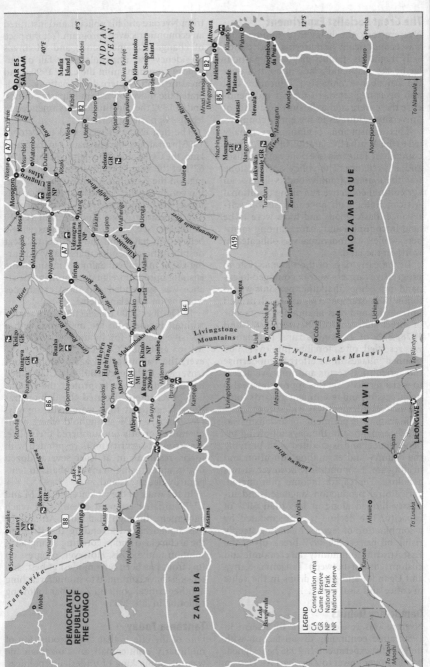

LEGEND
CA   Conservation Area
GR   Game Reserve
NP   National Park
NR   National Reserve

The Great Socialist Experiment

Nyerere took the helm of a country that was economically foundering and politically fragile, its stability plagued in particular by the mainland's lack of control over the Zanzibar Archipelago. Education had also been neglected, so that at independence there were said to be only a handful of university graduates in the entire country.

This inauspicious beginning eventually led to the Arusha Declaration of 1967, which committed Tanzania to a policy of socialism and self-reliance. The policy's cornerstone was the *ujamaa* (familyhood) village – an agricultural collective run along traditional African lines, with an emphasis on self-reliance. Basic goods and tools were to be held in common and shared among members, while each individual was obligated to work on the land.

In the early days of the *ujamaa* system, progressive farmers were encouraged to expand in the hope that other peasants would follow their example. This approach proved unrealistic, and was abandoned in favour of direct state control. Between 1973 and 1978, 85% of Tanzania's rural population was resettled, often forcibly, into over 7000 planned villages in an effort to modernise the agricultural sector and improve access to social services. Yet this approach was also unsuccessful, and resentment towards compulsory resettlement was widespread.

Tanzania's experiment in socialism was widely acclaimed in the days following independence, and is credited with unifying the country and expanding education and health care. Economically, however, it was a failure. Per capita income plummeted, agricultural production stagnated and industry limped along at less than 50% of capacity. The decline was precipitated by a combination of factors, including steeply rising oil prices, the 1977 break-up of the East African Community (an economic and customs union between Tanzania, Kenya and Uganda) and sharp drops in the value of coffee and sisal exports.

Democracy Debuts

Nyerere was re-elected to a fifth term in 1980, amid continuing dissatisfaction with the socialist experiment. In 1985 he resigned, handing over power to Zanzibari Ali Hassan Mwinyi. Mwinyi tried to distance himself from Nyerere and his policies, and instituted an economic recovery program. Yet the pace of change remained slow, and Mwinyi's presidency was unpopular. The fall of European communism in the early 1990s, and pressure from Western donor nations, accelerated the move towards multiparty politics, and in 1992 the constitution was amended to legalise opposition parties.

The first elections were held in October 1995 in an atmosphere of chaos. On the mainland, the CCM, under Benjamin Mkapa, won 62% of the vote in relatively smooth balloting. On the Zanzibar Archipelago, however, the voting for the Zanzibari presidency was universally denounced for its dishonesty. The opposition Civic United Front (CUF) candidate, Seif Shariff Hamad, was widely believed to have won the presidential seat despite official results marginally favouring CCM incumbent Salmin Amour. In the ensuing uproar, foreign development assistance was suspended and most expatriates working on the islands left.

In October 2000 the elections proceeded without incident on the mainland, with a decisive victory for incumbent president Mkapa and the CCM. On Zanzibar, however, the balloting was again highly controversial. In January 2001 the CUF called for demonstrations to protest the results. The government declared the demonstrations illegal, but they were held anyway. On Pemba, a CUF stronghold where demonstrators greatly outnumbered the police, government security units responded with force, resulting in at least several dozen deaths and causing many Pembans to temporarily flee the island.

In the wake of the violence, the CCM and CUF initiated renewed attempts to reach agreement through dialogue. An accord was signed aimed at ending the strife on the archipelago and negotiating a long-term solution to the crisis. However, progress on this front has been only modest at best, and tensions have continued to simmer, reaching another critical point on Zanzibar following balloting in late 2005.

Tanzania Today

One of the effects that the introduction of multiparty politics had on Tanzanian life was the unmasking of underlying political, economic and religious frictions, both on the mainland and between the mainland and the Zanzibar Archipelago. The tensions involving the archipelago are perhaps the most visible example. Yet – the Zanzibar situation notwithstanding – Tanzania as a whole remains reasonably well integrated, with comparatively high levels of religious and ethnic tolerance, particularly on the mainland. Tanzanians have earned a name for themselves in the region for their moderation and balance, and most observers consider it highly unlikely that the country would disintegrate into the tribal conflicts that have plagued some of its neighbours.

On the political front, President Mkapa was constitutionally prevented from seeking another term in the 2005 presidential elections, which were won in a landslide by CCM's Jakaya Kikwete, the former Foreign Minister. Perhaps more significant is the future of multiparty politics in Tanzania. If anything, this seems to have taken several steps backwards in recent years with entrenchment of the CCM and splintering of the opposition. Progressing beyond this situation may result in some growing pains in the short term. However, chances are high that Tanzania will continue to move forward, maintaining the stable and moderate outlook that has characterised its development since independence.

THE CULTURE
The National Psyche

It takes a lot to ruffle a Tanzanian, and it's to this fact that the country's remarkably harmonious and understated demeanour is attributable. In contrast to Kenya and other neighbours, tribal rivalries are almost nonexistent. It's rare for a Tanzanian to identify themselves at the outset according to tribe; primary identification is always as a Tanzanian, and the *ujamaa* ideals of Julius Nyerere permeate society. Religious frictions are also minimal, with Christians and Muslims living side by side in a relatively easy coexistence. Although political differences flare up – look at recent events on the Zanzibar Archipelago (opposite) – they rarely come to the forefront in interpersonal dealings.

The workings of society are oiled by a subtle but strong social code. Tanzanians place a premium on politeness and courtesy. Greetings are essential, and you'll probably be given a gentle reminder should you for-

---

GOVERNMENTAL AFFAIRS

In Tanzania's fledgling multiparty democracy, executive power rests with the president and the ruling Chama Cha Mapinduzi (CCM; Party of the Revolution). The president and members of the unicameral 295-seat National Assembly are elected by direct popular vote for five-year terms. The major opposition party is the Civic United Front (CUF).

The union government has jurisdiction over foreign and monetary policy, postal and telecommunications systems and defence, while the Zanzibar government is responsible for education, infrastructure and other nonunion matters on the islands of the Zanzibar Archipelago.

Although no serious politicians are currently calling for a completely independent Zanzibar, most Zanzibaris would be happy with a bit more autonomy and a larger share of the pie than they now have. In early 2005 the archipelago even began flying its own flag.

---

get this and launch straight into a question without first enquiring as to the wellbeing of your listener and his or her family. Tanzanian children are trained to greet their elders with a respectful *shikamoo* (literally, 'I hold your feet'), often accompanied in rural areas by a slight curtsey, and strangers are frequently addressed as *dada* (sister); *mama*, in the case of an older woman; *kaka* (brother); or *ndugu* (relative or comrade).

Daily Life

Want to take a peek inside a Tanzanian home? First call out *'hodi'*, then wait for the inevitable *'karibu'* (welcome), and step inside. Although you'll see some impressive, Western-style houses in posh residential areas of Dar es Salaam, home for most Tanzanians is of cinderblock or mudbrick, with roofing of corrugated tin or thatch, a latrine outside and water drawn from a nearby pump or river. Mealtimes typically centre around a pot of *ugali* (the stiff and doughy maize- and/or cassava-based national dish) or a similar staple served with sauce, and rural rhythms set the beat, with women and children spending much of their day working a small *shamba* (farm plot).

As elsewhere in the region, family life plays a central role, although it's sometimes hard to know where the family ends and the community begins. Doors are always open, helping out others in the *jamaa* (clan, community) is assumed, and celebrations involve everyone. Child-raising is the expected occupation for women, and breadwinning for men. Village administrators (known as *shehe* on Zanzibar) oversee things, and make important decisions in consultation with other senior community members. Tribal structures, however, range from weak to nonexistent – a legacy of Nyerere's abolishment of local chieftaincies following independence.

While Tanzania's 8% adult HIV/AIDS infection rate has prompted a spate of billboards and public awareness campaigns, real public discussion is limited, and AIDS deaths are commonly explained away as tuberculosis, or with silence.

Population

Tanzania's heart pulses with the blood of close to 120 tribal groups, plus Asians, Arabs, Europeans and more. Despite the diversity, most tribes are very small, with almost 100 of them combined accounting for only one-third of the total population.

The vast majority of Tanzanians are of Bantu origin, the largest groups including the Sukuma (who live around Mwanza and southern Lake Victoria), the Makonde (southeastern Tanzania), the Haya (around Bukoba) and the Chagga (around Mt Kilimanjaro). The Maasai and several smaller groups (all in northern Tanzania) are of Nilo-Hamitic or Nilotic origin. The Iraqw, who live in the area around Karatu and northwest of Lake Manyara, are Cushitic, as are the tiny northern-central tribes of Gorowa and Burungi, while the Sandawe and, more distantly, the Hadzabe (around Lake Eyasi), belong to the Khoisan ethnolinguistic family.

About 3% of Tanzania's total population, or about one million people, live on the Zanzibar Archipelago, with about one-third of these on Pemba. Members of the non-African population consider themselves descendants of immigrants from Shiraz in Persia (Iran). Filling out Tanzania's melting pot are small but economically significant Asian (primarily from the Indian subcontinent) and Arabic populations, concen-

AFRICA'S MELTING POT

Tanzania is the only African country boasting indigenous inhabitants from all of the continent's main ethnolinguistic families (Bantu, Nilo-Hamitic, Cushitic, Khoisan). They live in closest proximity around Lakes Eyasi and Babati, in north-central Tanzania.

trated in major cities and along the coast, plus a small European community.

Tanzania is one of the least urbanised countries in sub-Saharan Africa, with urban dwellers constituting only about one-third of the total population. However, the number of city dwellers is steadily growing, at about 4.9% per year in Dar es Salaam. Average population density is 39 people per square kilometre, although this varies radically from one area to the next. Among the most densely populated areas are Dar es Salaam and the surrounding coast, the Usambara and Pare Mountains, the slopes of Mt Kilimanjaro, the Mwanza region, and the Zanzibar Archipelago.

RELIGION

About 35% to 40% of Tanzanians are Muslim and between 40% and 45% are Christian. The remainder follow traditional religions. There are also small communities of Hindus, Sikhs and Ismailis. Muslims are traditionally found along the coast and in the inland towns that line the old caravan routes. One of the areas of highest Christian concentration is in the northeast around Moshi, which has been a centre of missionary activity since the mid-19th century.

The population of the Zanzibar Archipelago is almost exclusively Sunni Muslim, with tiny Christian and Hindu communities.

ARTS
Literature

Tanzania's literary scene is dominated by renowned poet and writer Shaaban Robert (1909–62). Robert, who was born near Tanga, is considered the country's national poet, and was almost single-handedly responsible for the development of a modern Swahili prose style. Among his best-known works are the autobiographical *Maisha yangu* (My Life), and several collections of folk tales.

Almost as well-known as Robert is Zanzibari Muhammed Said Abdulla, who gained fame with his *Mzimu wa watu wa kale* (Graveyard of the Ancestors), and is considered the founder of Swahili popular literature. Other notable authors of Swahili-language works include Zanzibari novelist Shafi Adam Shafi, short-story writer Joseph Mbele and dramatist Ebrahim Hussein.

One of Tanzania's most widely acclaimed contemporary writers is Abdulrazak Gurnah, who was born on Zanzibar in 1948. His novel *Paradise*, which is set in East Africa during WWI, made the short list for the UK's Booker Prize in 1994.

Other contemporary Tanzanian authors of English-language works include Peter Palangyo, who wrote the novel *Dying in the Sun*; William Kamera (known for his poetry and for *Tales of the Wairaqw of Tanzania*); and Tolowa Marti Mollel, who has authored many short stories, including *The Orphan Boy*, a retelling of a local Maasai legend. May Balisidya, who authored the novel *Shida* (Hardships) as well as several plays and children's books, was one of the few first-generation women writers of Swahili literature.

Music & Dance
One of the most common traditional musical instruments is the *kayamba* (a shaker made with grain kernels that's frequently used by church choirs and other groups to accompany singing). Others include the *mbira* (a type of thumb piano with metal strips of varying lengths), the *marimba* (xylophone) and, of course, *ngoma* (drums). Drums are found in a wide variety of shapes and sizes, with most corresponding to particular tribes or dances.

Thanks to state subsidies, Tanzania's music scene has traditionally been one of the most dynamic in the region, with many bands that start here later going on to play at nightclubs in Nairobi and elsewhere. One of the country's most famous musicians is Remmy Ongala ('Dr Remmy'); for more on Ongala and his Orchestre Super Matimila, see p39. Other well-known groups include Mlimani Park and its offshoot International Orchestra Safari Sound (IOSS). A popular figure from the 1970s was Patrick Balisidya. In addition to his Afro 70 band, Balisidya, who died in 2004, was known for his song 'Harusi', which is still a staple at Tanzanian weddings.

See p39 for more on local music. See p142 for more on *taarab* music.

The main place for masked dance is in the southeast, where it plays an important role in the initiation ceremonies of the Makonde (who are famous for their *mapiko* masks) and the Makua.

Painting
Tanzania's best-known school of painting is Tingatinga, which takes its name from the self-taught artist Edward Saidi Tingatinga, who began it in the 1960s in response to demand from the European market. Tingatinga paintings are traditionally composed in a square format, and feature brightly coloured animal motifs set against a monochrome background. One of the most distinctive characteristics of the style is its use of undiluted and often unmixed enamel and

---

BACK TO BASICS

Tanzania has one of the lowest rates of secondary-school enrolment in the world, with less than 7% of students enrolled. Yet, despite this rather shocking statistic, literacy rates in Tanzania (which average about 70% for adults) are somewhat higher than those in many neighbouring countries. This is due in large part to the legacy of Julius Nyerere, who was convinced that the key to success for his philosophy of socialism and self-reliance lay in having an educated populace. During the early years of his presidency he set aside 14% of the national budget for education, offered government assistance to villages to build their own schools and made primary education free and compulsory. By the late 1980s Tanzania's literacy rate was one of the highest in Africa, although much of this initial momentum has since been lost.

Today Tanzania's educational system is loosely modelled on that of Britain. There are seven years of primary school, which are free and – in theory – compulsory, plus four years of secondary school with an additional two years required for university entrance. Primary-school instruction is in Swahili, while secondary-level and university instruction is in English.

high-gloss paints, which give the paintings their characteristic shiny appearance.

The best place to buy Tingatinga paintings is at the Tingatinga Arts Cooperative Society (p124) near Morogoro Stores in Dar es Salaam. Other good spots include Msasani Slipway (p124), also in Dar es Salaam, and the vendors along Hurumzi St in Zanzibar's Stone Town.

Mawazo Art Gallery (p123) and **Wasanii Art Centre** (Msasani Slipway, Dar es Salaam) are among the best places to get acquainted with the contemporary Tanzanian art scene. Nyumba ya Sanaa (p124) also hosts exhibitions by contemporary Tanzanian artists.

Cinema

Despite its miniscule size, Tanzania's indigenous film industry holds its own with those of other countries in the region. See p38 for more.

In addition to the Tanzanian-produced titles mentioned in that section, films shot at least in part in Tanzania include the 1951 classic The African Queen, starring Katharine Hepburn and Humphrey Bogart; and Mogambo (1953), with Clark Gable, Ava Gardner and Grace Kelly.

Numerous documentaries about Tanzania's wildlife have been filmed on location, including Africa: The Serengeti (1994), which was shot in both Tanzania and Kenya, and focuses on the annual wildebeest migration.

Sculpture & Woodcarving

Tanzania's Makonde are known throughout East Africa for their beautiful and highly stylised ebony woodcarvings; see p40. The country's major centres of Makonde carving are in the southeast on the Makonde Plateau and in Dar es Salaam.

ENVIRONMENT
The Land

Tanzania – East Africa's largest country – is over 943,000 sq km, or almost four times the size of the UK. It's bordered to the east by the Indian Ocean, and to the west by the deep lakes of the Western Rift Valley. Much of the mainland consists of a central highland plateau, averaging between 900m and 1800m in altitude, and nestled between the eastern and western branches of the geological fault known as the Great Rift Valley. Edging this is a narrow, low-lying coastal strip, and in the northwest is the enormous, shallow Lake Victoria basin. Tanzania's mountain ranges are grouped into a sharply rising northeastern section (the Eastern Arc), and an open, rolling central and southern section (the Southern Highlands or Southern Arc). There is also a range of volcanoes, known as the Crater Highlands, that rises from the side of the Great Rift Valley in northern Tanzania.

The largest river is the Rufiji, which drains the Southern Highlands region. Other major waterways include the Ruvu, the Wami, the Pangani and the Ruvuma (forming the border with Mozambique).

Wildlife
ANIMALS

Among Tanzania's more than four million wild animals are representatives of 430 species and subspecies, including all the 'classic' African animals mentioned under Wildlife on p73. Tanzania is particularly notable for its elephant population, which is one of the largest on the continent, and for its large cats, especially lions, which are routinely seen in Serengeti National Park (p193) and Ngorongoro Crater (p199). The country is also known for the large herds of wildebeest and zebras found especially in its northern parks, and for its buffalo herds. Katavi and Ruaha National Parks host populations of both roan and sable antelopes.

Complementing this terrestrial wealth are over 1000 species of birds, including various types of kingfisher, hornbills (around Amani), bee-eaters (along the Rufiji and Wami rivers), fish eagles (Lake Victoria) and flamingos (Lake Magadi in the Ngorongoro Crater, and Lake Natron, among other places). Species unique to Tanzania include the Udzungwa forest partridge, the Pemba green pigeon and the Usambara weaver. For more on endangered species, see p74.

PLANTS

If you're interested in plants, few places on the continent surpass Tanzania's Eastern Arc range, where small patches of tropical rainforest provide home to a rich assortment of plants, many of which are found nowhere else in the world. South and west of the Eastern Arc range are impressive stands of baobab. Kitulo National Park – bursting with over 50 orchid species – is another highlight.

Away from the mountain ranges, much of the country is covered by *miombo* or 'moist' woodland, where the main vegetation is various types of *Brachystegia* tree. Much of the dry central plateau is covered with savanna, bushland and thickets, while grasslands cover the Serengeti Plain and other areas that lack good drainage.

National Parks & Reserves

Tanzania's unrivalled collection of protected areas includes 14 national parks, 13 wildlife reserves, the Ngorongoro Conservation Area (NCA), two marine parks and several protected marine reserves.

Until recently, development and tourism have focused almost exclusively on the so-called northern circuit: Serengeti, Lake Manyara, Tarangire, Arusha and Kilimanjaro National Parks and the NCA. As a result, all of these places are easily accessible, well equipped with facilities and heavily visited. In addition to the natural beauty, the northern circuit's main attractions are the high concentration, diversity and accessibility of its wildlife.

The 'southern circuit' – Ruaha, Mikumi and Udzungwa Mountains National Parks and the Selous Game Reserve – has been receiving increasing attention, although it still doesn't see close to the number of visitors that the north does. Most areas tend to have more of a wilderness feel and the wildlife is just as impressive, although it's often spread over larger areas.

In western Tanzania are Mahale Mountains and Gombe Stream National Parks, where the main drawcards are the chimpanzees, and remote Katavi National Park, with its large herds of wildlife. Rubondo Island National Park in Lake Victoria is of particular interest to bird-watchers. Saadani Game Reserve lets you mix beach and bush.

For an overview of the major parks and reserves, see p76.

NATIONAL PARKS

All parks are managed by the **Tanzania National Parks Authority** (Tanapa; ☎ 027-250 3471, 027-250 4082; www.tanzaniaparks.com). Entry fees – see individual park listings for details – must be paid in hard currency, preferably US dollars cash. For accommodation and guide fees, see the following table. Guide and vehicle fees for Ngorongoro Crater and Saadani and

Selous Game Reserves are given in those sections. For general information on park accommodation, see p249.

Accommodation	US$ (16 yrs +)	US$ (5-15 yrs)
Ordinary camp site	30	5
Special camp site	50	10
Hostel	10	-
Resthouse (Serengeti, Arusha, Ruaha, Katavi)	30 (Gombe Stream 20)	-
Banda or Hut	20 (Mt Kilimanjaro 50)	-

Other costs include guide fees of US$10 per day (US$15 for overnight and US$20 for walking safaris) and vehicle fees of US$40 per day for a foreign-registered car (TSh10,000 for a Tanzania-registered car).

WILDLIFE RESERVES

With the exception of Saadani, which is a national park in everything but name, and is managed by Tanapa, wildlife reserves are administered by the **Wildlife Division of the Ministry of Natural Resources & Tourism** (☎ 022-286 6376, 022-286 6064; cnr Nyerere & Changombe Rds, Dar es Salaam). Fees – see individual listings for details – should be paid in US dollars cash. Saadani and Selous are the only reserves with tourist infrastructure. Large areas of many others have been leased as hunting concessions.

MARINE PARKS & RESERVES

The Ministry of Natural Resources & Tourism's **Marine Parks & Reserves Unit** (☎ 022-215 0420, 022-215 0621; marineparks@raha.com; Olympio St, Upanga, Dar es Salaam) oversees marine parks and reserves. For information on Tanzania's marine parks, see p240 and p247.

Environmental Issues

Although Tanzania has one of the highest proportions of protected land of any African country (about 39% is protected in some form, including several Unesco World Heritage sites, see p25), limited resources hamper conservation efforts, and erosion, soil degradation, desertification and deforestation continue to whittle away at the natural wealth. According to some estimates, Tanzania loses 3500 sq km of forest land annually as a result of agricultural and commercial clearing. In the national parks, poaching and inappropriate visitor use – especially in the northern circuit – threaten wildlife and ecosystems. Deforestation is also a problem on the offshore islands, with about 95% of the tropical high forest that once covered Zanzibar and Pemba now gone. Dynamite fishing has also been a serious threat, both on the archipelago and in mainland coastal areas, although significant progress has been made in halting this practice.

On the positive side, great progress has been made in recent years to involve communities directly in conservation, and local communities are now stakeholders in several lodges and other tourist developments.

The best local contact on environmental issues is the **Wildlife Conservation Society of Tanzania** Arusha (www.wcstarusha.org; Boma St); Dar es Salaam (☎ 022-211 2518; wcst@africaonline.co.tz; Garden Ave). For more on what you can do to help, see p19.

FOOD & DRINK

Tanzania's unofficial national dish is *ugali*. For more on this and other local cuisine see p41. Other favourites – most more appealing to foreign palates than *ugali* – include *mishikaki*, *mtindi* and *mgando*. *Mishikaki* (marinated meat kebabs) are found almost everywhere, grilled over the coals at street stalls. Refreshing *mtindi* and *mgando*, cultured milk products similar to yogurt, are usually drunk with a straw out of plastic bags. Many Tanzanians start their day with *uji*, a thin, sweet porridge made from bean, millet or other flour. Watch for ladies stirring bubbling pots of it on the street corners if you are out in the early morning. *Vitambua* – small rice cakes vaguely resembling tiny, thick pancakes – are another morning treat, especially in the southeast. On Zanzibar, look for *mkate wa kumimina*, a bread made from a batter similar to that used for making *vitambua*.

In major towns, there's a good selection of places to eat, ranging from local food stalls to Western-style restaurants. In smaller towns you're likely to just find *hoteli* (small, informal restaurants) serving chicken, beef or fish with rice or another staple. The main meal is at noon; in rural areas, many places are closed in the evening, and often the only option is street food.

Bottled water and soft drinks are widely sold; tap water should be avoided. Tanzania's array of beers includes the local Safari and Kilimanjaro labels, plus Castle Lager and various Kenyan and German beers. Finding a beer is usually no problem, but – as elsewhere in the region – finding one cold can be a challenge.

DAR ES SALAAM

☎ 022

With a population of nearly three million and an area of more than 1350 sq km, Dar es Salaam is Tanzania's major city, and capital in everything but name. Yet, despite its size, Dar es Salaam is a down-to-earth, manageable place, with a picturesque seaport, an intriguing mix of African, Arabic and Indian influences, and close ties to its Swahili roots. While there's not too much to actually do, there are enough historic buildings, shops and good restaurants to keep most visitors busy for at least several days.

For a break from the bustle, try the easily accessed beaches north and south of town (see p126), or head to Zanzibar – just a short ferry ride away.

HISTORY

Until the mid-19th century, what is now Dar es Salaam was just a humble fishing village, one of many along the East African coast. In the 1860s Sultan Sayyid Majid of Zanzibar decided to develop the area's inland harbour into a port and trading centre, and named the site Dar es Salaam (Haven of Peace). No sooner had development of the harbour begun, than the sultan died and the town sunk again into anonymity, overshadowed by Bagamoyo, an important dhow port to the north. It wasn't until the 1880s that Dar es Salaam assumed new significance, first as a station for Christian missionaries making their way from Zanzibar to the interior, and then as a seat for the German colonial government, which viewed Dar es Salaam's protected harbour as a better alternative for steamships than the dhow port in Bagamoyo. In 1891 the colonial administration was officially moved from Bagamoyo to Dar es Salaam. Since then the city has remained Tanzania's undisputed political and economic capital, although the legislature was transferred to Dodoma in 1973.

ORIENTATION

The congested centre, with banks, forex bureaus, shops and street vendors, runs along Samora Ave from the clock tower to the Askari monument. The area northwest of Samora Ave, around India and Jamhuri Sts, is chock-a-block with Indian traders and scents from the subcontinent. West of Mnazi Mmoja Park are the rougher but colourful neighbourhoods of Kariakoo and Ilala.

On the other side of town, northeast of Askari monument, are shady, tree-lined streets with the National Museum, Botanical Gardens and State House. Proceeding north from here along the coast, you first reach the upper-middle class section of Upanga and then, after crossing Selander Bridge, the fast-developing diplomatic and upmarket residential areas of Oyster Bay and Msasani.

The city's main stretch of sand is at Coco Beach, near Oyster Bay, but much better beaches to the south and north are only a short jaunt away.

Maps

The *Dar es Salaam City Map & Guide*, put out by the **Surveys & Mapping Division Map Sales Office** (Map p118; cnr Kivukoni Front & Luthuli St; ☾ 8am-2pm Mon-Fri), is widely available and gives a good overview of the street layout, though it's unwieldy to manage while walking around.

For something smaller, try one of the free maps at the tourist information centre.

INFORMATION

Bookshops

A Novel Idea (☎ 260 1088; www.anovelidea-africa.com) Msasani Slipway (Map p116; Msasani Slipway, Msasani Peninsula); Sea Cliff Village (Map p116; Sea Cliff Village, next to Sea Cliff Hotel, Msasani Peninsula); Steers (Map p118; cnr Ohio St & Samora Ave) Dar's best bookshop, with classics, modern fiction, travel guides, Africa titles, maps and more.

Cultural Centres

Alliance Française (Map p116; ☎ 213 1406; afdar@ africaonline.co.tz; Ali Hassan Mwinyi Rd)
British Council (Map p118; ☎ 211 6574/5; www .britishcouncil.org/tanzania; cnr Ohio St & Samora Ave)
Nyumba ya Sanaa (Mwalimu Julius K Nyerere Cultural Centre; Map p118; Ohio St)

Emergency

Central police station (Map p118; ☎ 211 5507; Sokoine Dr) Near the Central Line Railway Station.
Flying Doctors/Amref (Map p118; ☎ 211 6610, Nairobi emergency ☎ 254-20-315454, 254-20-602492; www.amref.org; Ali Hassan Mwinyi Rd, Upanga) For emergency evacuations; see p625 for membership details.
Oyster Bay police station (Map p118; ☎ 266 7332; Toure Dr) North of Coco Beach; for Msasani Peninsula.
Traffic police (Map p118; ☎ 211 1747; Sokoine Dr) Near the Central Line Railway Station.

SKIP DAR ES SALAAM?

It's quite easy these days to bypass Dar es Salaam entirely by using Kilimanjaro International Airport (KIA), or by flying into Entebbe (Uganda) or Nairobi (Kenya), and then entering Tanzania overland. Even if you're combining the northern circuit parks with Zanzibar, it's not usually necessary to overnight in Dar es Salaam thanks to frequent flights and ferry connections. If you do find yourself here for the night and are unhappy about the prospect, the beaches north and south of the city (p126) are easily accessed, and have plenty of accommodation possibilities.

Yet, while you'll find few people raving about the city, it's really not that bad, especially compared with other African urban areas. Many long-term visitors would – albeit grudgingly – even admit to a certain affection for it. Away from the congestion, noise and some moderately aggressive moneychangers in the central area, 'Dar' is a laid-back place at heart, with a notably slower pace and softer edge than nearby Nairobi. Dar es Salaam also merits a visit if you're interested in understanding Tanzania, as it's the country's political and economic hub. On a practical level, it's a good place to stock up and get things done if you've been on the road for a while.

The central area is dominated by concrete and an ever-increasing number of glitzy high-rise buildings, although everything's still relatively small-scale and manageable, even on foot. In the outlying neighbourhoods to the south and west the mood changes, with unassuming Swahili-style houses lining unpaved roadways, small markets, patches of coconut palms in the areas near the coast, and a generally languid atmosphere. To the north, on Msasani Peninsula, you'll be treated to sea breezes and glimpses of the water, and it's easy to forget you're in one of East Africa's major metropolises.

DAR ES SALAAM

0 ——————— 2 km
0 ——————— 1 mile

INFORMATION
A Novel Idea............................(see 29)
A Novel Idea............................(see 30)
Aga Khan Health Clinic...........(see 30)
Alliance Française....................(see 3)
Barclays ATM..........................(see 29)
Belgian Embassy...........................**1** C5
Burundian Embassy...................(see 7)
Democratic Republic of the
  Congo Embassy........................**2** C5
French Embassy.............................**3** B4
Indian High Commission.............**4** B4
Irish Embassy...............................**5** B2
IST Medical Clinic & International
  School.....................................**6** B2

INFORMATION (cont)
Italian Embassy..............................**7** B5
Kearsley Travel..........................(see 30)
Kenyan High Commission............**8** A3
Oyster Bay Police Station.............**9** A3
Rwandan Embassy......................**10** C5
Seaside Forex Bureau...............(see 30)
Standard Chartered ATM...........(see 27)
Ugandan High Commission........**11** B3
US Embassy.................................**12** A3

SIGHTS & ACTIVITIES
Kariakoo Market.........................**13** B6

SLEEPING
Akana Lodge................................**14** A3
Courtyard....................................**15** A3
Hotel Karibu................................**16** B3
Msasani Slipway Apartments....(see 29)
Msimbazi Centre Hostel.............**17** A6
Oyster Bay Hotel.........................**18** B3
Palm Beach Hotel.......................**19** B5
Protea Dar es Salaam
  Apartments..............................**20** B3
Sea Cliff Hotel............................**21** C1
Souk..(see 29)
Swiss Garden Hotel....................**22** B5

EATING
Addis in Dar................................**23** A3
Garden Bistro..............................**24** B1
La Trattoria Jan...........................**25** B3
Saverio's.....................................**26** A3
Shopper's Plaza & Shopper's
  Supermarket............................**27** A3
Shoprite....................................(see 29)
Sweet Eazy................................(see 18)
Turquoise..................................(see 30)

ENTERTAINMENT
California Dreamers.....................**28** B4
New Msasani Club.....................(see 12)

SHOPPING
Msasani Slipway..........................**29** B2
Seacliff Village.............................**30** B1
Tingatinga Centre & Morogoro
  Stores......................................**31** B3

TRANSPORT
Daladala Junction & Taxi Stands.**32** B3
Daladalas to Kisarawe.................**33** B6
Evergreen Car Rentals.................**34** B6
Scandinavian Bus Terminal.........**35** B6

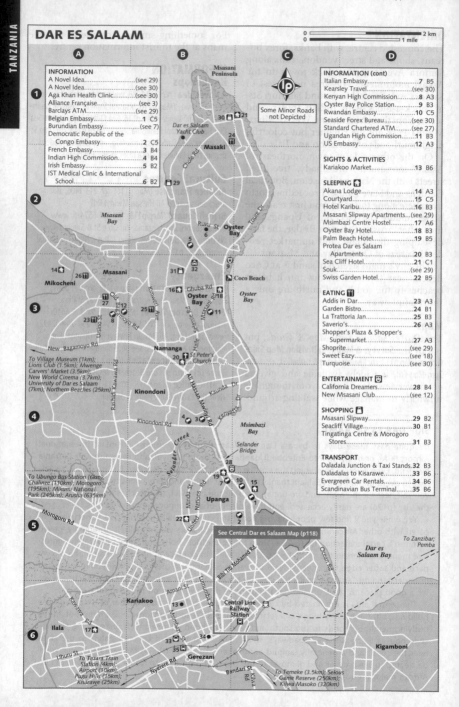

Some Minor Roads
not Depicted

Msasani
Peninsula

Dar es Salaam
Yacht Club

Masaki

Msasani
Bay

Ruvu St

Oyster
Bay

Coco Beach

Msasani

Mikocheni

Chuba Rd

Oyster
Bay

Oyster
Bay

New Bagamoyo Rd

Namanga

St Peter's
Church

To Village Museum (1km);
Lions Club (1.5km); Mwenge
Carvers' Market (3.5km);
New World Cinema (3.7km);
University of Dar es Salaam
(7km); Northern Beaches (25km)

Kinondoni

Kinondoni Rd

Msimbazi
Bay

Selander
Bridge

To Ubungo Bus Station (6km);
Chalinze (110km); Morogoro
(195km); Mikumi National
Park (245km); Arusha (635km)

Morogoro Rd

Upanga

See Central Dar es Salaam Map (p118)

To Zanzibar;
Pemba

Dar es
Salaam Bay

Kariakoo

Central Line
Railway
Station

Kigamboni

Ilala

Gerezani

Uhuru St

To Tazara Train
Station (4km);
Airport (10km);
Pugu Hills (15km);
Kisarawe (25km)

Nyerere Rd

Bandari St

To Temeke (3.5km); Selous
Game Reserve (250km);
Kilwa Masoko (320km)

Immigration Office
Wizara ya mambo ya ndani (Map p118; ☎ 211 8640/3; cnr Ghana Ave & Ohio St; ☽ 8am-1pm Mon-Fri for visa applications, until 3pm for visa collection)

Internet Access
Alpha Internet Café (Map p118; Garden Ave; per hr TSh500; ☽ 8.30am-6pm Mon-Sat)
Hotspot Internet Café (Map p118; Ground fl, JM Mall, Samora Ave; per hr TSh1000; ☽ 8am-7pm Mon-Fri, 9am-7pm Sat, 9.30am-2pm Sun)
Kool Surfing (Map p118; per hr TSh500; ☽ 8am-10pm Mon-Sat, 9am-10pm Sun) Just off Jamhuri St.
Mealz Internet Café (Map p118; cnr Pamba Rd & Sokoine Dr; per hr TSh1000; ☽ 8am-9pm Mon-Sat, 10am-6pm Sun)

Media
International newspapers and magazines are available from top-end hotels, and sometimes at newsstands downtown.

Medical Services
All listings here provide 24-hour emergency service
Aga Khan Health Clinic (Map p116; ☎ 260 1484, 24hr 0748-911111; Seacliff Village, Msasani Peninsula; ☽ 8am-12.30pm & 2-4.30pm Mon-Fri, or by appointment) Western doctors on call.
IST Medical Clinic (Map p116; ☎ 260 1307/8, 24hr 0744-783393; istclinic@istafrica.com; Ruvu St; ☽ 8am-6pm Mon-Fri, 9am-noon Sat) A Western-run clinic found on the Masaki campus of the International School of Tanganyika.
Regency Medical Centre (Map p118; ☎ 215 0500, 215 2966; Allykhan St) In Upanga, just off Bibi Titi Mohammed Rd.

Money
Forex bureaus give the fastest service and best rates for exchange; there are many scattered around the centre of town on or near Samora Ave.
American Express (Map p118; ☎ 211 0960, 211 4094; amex@intafrica.com; Upanga Rd) At Rickshaw Travels, next to Citibank; no cash advances and no replacement of stolen checks, but issues US-dollar travellers cheques up to US$1500 against an Amex card.
Coastal Travels' Local Currency Outlet (Map p118; Upanga Rd; ☽ 9am-4pm Mon-Fri, to noon Sat) Withdraw Tanzanian shillings (or dollars, for an additional 6% commission) using Visa or MasterCard. Up to US$500 per transaction; higher amounts available with advance notice.
Galaxy Forex Bureau (International Arrivals Area, Airport; ☽ open for all flights) Cash and travellers cheques; to the right as you exit customs.

Jamani Forex Bureau (International Arrivals Area, Airport; ☽ open for all flights) Straight ahead as you exit customs; cash and travellers cheques.
National Bank of Commerce (NBC; Map p118; cnr Azikiwe St & Sokoine Dr) Changes cash and travellers cheque, and has an ATM.
Royal Palm Forex Bureau (Map p118; Mövenpick Royal Palm Hotel, Ohio St; ☽ 8am-8pm Mon-Sat, 10am-1pm Sun & holidays) Cash and travellers cheques.
Seaside Forex Bureau (Map p116; Seacliff Village; ☽ 11.30am-6pm) Cash and travellers cheques.

ATMS
All ATMs give shillings on a Visa card, to a limit of TSh400,000 per day at Barclays, TSh1,000,000 per week at Standard Chartered and TSh300,000 per day at NBC.
Barclays Opposite Mövenpick Royal Palm Hotel and at Msasani Slipway.
NBC ATMs at all branches, including at headquarters (cnr Azikiwe St & Sokoine Dr) and next to Ubungo Bus Terminal.
Standard Chartered At NIC Life House (cnr Ohio St & Sokoine Dr); Shoppers' Plaza; JM Mall (Samora Ave); and next to Holiday Inn (Garden Ave).

Post
Main post office (Map p118; Maktaba St; ☽ 8am-4.30pm Mon-Fri, 9am-noon Sat) Stamps, letters and poste restante.

Telephone
Cardphones are everywhere, including in front of Extelecoms House and the main post office. Cards are sold during business hours at nearby shops.
Extelecoms House (Map p118; cnr Bridge St & Samora Ave; ☽ 7.30am-6pm Mon-Fri, 9am-3pm Sat) Operator placed calls from US$2.50 per minute to USA, Europe and Australia.

Tourist Information
What's Happening in Dar es Salaam is a free monthly magazine with tide tables, airline schedules etc; available from travel agencies and the tourist information centre. The *Dar es Salaam Guide* has more of the same.
Tanzania Tourist Board Information Centre (Map p118; ☎ 212 0373, 213 1555; www.tanzania-web.com; Samora Ave; ☽ 8am-4pm Mon-Fri, 8.30am-12.30pm Sat) Just west of Zanaki St, with free tourist maps and brochures and city information.

Travel Agencies
For information on safari and trek operators, see p92.

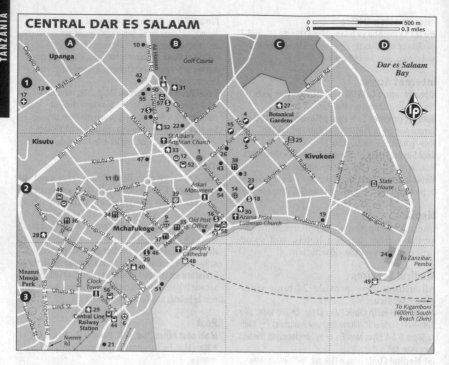

CENTRAL DAR ES SALAAM

Afri-Roots (☎ 0744-459887; www.afriroots.co.tz) Budget cycling, hiking and camping in and around Dar es Salaam.
Coastal Travels (Map p118; ☎ 211 7959, 211 7960; safari@coastal.cc; Upanga Rd) Flights around the country; especially recommended for travel to Zanzibar, and to northern and southern safari circuit destinations.
Kearsley Travel (www.kearsleys.com) Holiday Inn (Map p118; ☎ 211 5026, Garden Ave); Seacliff Village (Map p116; ☎ 260 0538, 260 0467)
Rickshaw Travels Mövenpick Royal Palm Hotel (Map p118; Ohio St); Upanga St (Map p118; ☎ 211 0960, 211 4094; ricksales@intafrica.com) Amex agent.

DANGERS & ANNOYANCES

Dar es Salaam is considered to be safer than many other big cities in the region, notably Nairobi, though it has its share of muggings and thefts. During the day, watch out for pickpocketing, particularly at crowded markets and bus and train stations, and for bag snatching through vehicle windows. Take the usual precautions, try to avoid carrying bags or cameras, and, if possible, leave your valuables in a reliable hotel safe. At night take a taxi, rather than taking a *daladala* (minibus) or walking, and avoid

walking alone along the path paralleling Ocean Rd, and on Coco Beach (which is only safe on weekend afternoons, when it's packed with locals).

SIGHTS & ACTIVITIES

Dar es Salaam's craft stands and markets are great for browsing (see p124), and its otherwise modest selection of attractions should be enough to keep you busy until you can escape to the beach (the closest swimming beaches are those just south and north of the city, p126) or points further afield.

National Museum

The **National Museum** (Map p118; ☎ 212 2030, 211 7508; Shaaban Robert St; adult/child/student US$3/1.50/2; ⏰ 9.30am-6pm) is home to the famous fossil discoveries of *Zinjanthropus* (nutcracker man) from Olduvai Gorge (p200), plus scattered displays on various other topics, including the Shirazi civilisation of Kilwa, the Zanzibar slave trade, and the German and British colonial periods. It's near the Botanical Gardens, between Samora Ave and Sokoine Dr.

Village Museum

The centrepiece of the open-air **Village Museum** (☎ 2700437; www.homestead.com/villagemuseum/; cnr New Bagamoyo Rd & Makaburi St; adult/child/student US$3/1.50/2, camera/video US$3/20; ☼ 9.30am-6pm) is a collection of authentically constructed dwellings meant to show traditional life in various parts of Tanzania. The best time to come is in the afternoon, when there are often traditional music and dance performances (see p123).

The museum is 10km north of the city centre; take the Mwenge *daladala* from New Posta transport stand and get off at the museum (TSh200, 30 minutes) or take a taxi (TSh5000).

Markets

For a gentle initiation into Dar es Salaam's markets, head to the **fish market** (Map p118; Ocean Rd), near Kivukoni Front. It's fairly calm as urban markets go, and you can watch fish auctions or browse past rows of Indian Ocean delicacies. For more excitement, get a reliable taxi driver or Tanzanian friend to take you to the huge, sprawling **Kariakoo Market** (Map p116; cnr Msimbazi & Mkunguni Sts), Tanzania's largest; don't bring valuables, and watch out for pickpockets. For Western-style shopping, try **Msasani Slipway** or **Seacliff Village** (both at the northern end of Msasani Peninsula), both with a good assortment of shops.

Bird Walks

Dar es Salaam boasts a surprisingly rich variety of birdlife, especially once you make it outside the centre of town. The best introduction is on one of the Wildlife Conservation Society of Tanzania's (p113) bird walks (free, duration is from two to three hours), which depart from their office at 7.30am

SCAMS

Like any big city, Dar es Salaam has its complement of hustlers and con artists. Some to watch out for:

- Men who want to strike up a conversation and try to sell you marijuana (*bangi* or *ganja*). Before you've had a chance to shake them loose, policemen (sometimes legitimate, sometimes not) suddenly appear and insist that you pay a huge fine for being involved in the purchase of illegal drugs. Once they've arrived, there's often little you can do, other than instantly hightailing it in the opposite direction if you smell this scam coming. If you're caught, insist on going to the nearest police station before paying anything, and whittle the bribe down as low as you can. Initial demands may be as high as US$300, but if you're savvy, you should be able to get away with under US$50.

- Anyone who tries to sell you Zanzibar ferry tickets at discounted resident prices, or who tries to persuade you to come into town with them – or to anywhere other than the real (and well-signed) ticket offices with promises of discounted tickets. Unless you have a resident permit, there's no such thing as a discounted ticket, and you'll just get caught later on.

- Anyone who tries to sell you a yellow-fever vaccination card (no longer required to enter Tanzania or Zanzibar).

- Anyone (especially around the port area) who starts regaling you with their tale of woe – usually involving being a refugee from somewhere – and showing you a list of all the people who have signed on to help them with donations. Your money has a better chance of reaching those most in need when channeled through registered charities or churches.

on the first and the last Saturday of each month.

DAR ES SALAAM FOR CHILDREN

With young ones in tow, good diversions include the beaches north of the city, especially their water parks (see p127); the supervised **play area** at Sea Cliff Village, next to Sea Cliff Hotel (p122), where you can leave your child with a nanny while you head off shopping; and Msasani Slipway (p124), with ice-cream cones and a small playground.

SLEEPING

If you're relying on public transport, it's cheaper and more convenient to stay in the city centre, which is where most budget lodging is anyway. If you don't mind paying for taxis, or travelling the distance from the airport (about 20km), the hotels on Msasani Peninsula are a break from the urban crush. To avoid the city entirely, head for the beaches south or north of Dar es Salaam (p126). All top-end hotels accept credit cards.

The closest places for camping are at Pugu Hills (p128), and at the beaches north and south of town.

City Centre
BUDGET

Most budget lodging is clustered around the busy Kisutu area or the equally busy area around the main post office.

YWCA (Map p118; ☎ 212 2439; Maktaba St; s/d with shared bathroom TSh9000/12,000) Just up from the post office, and a good budget deal. Rooms are clean, with net, fan and sink, and the convenient central location makes up for the street noise. Rooms around the inner courtyard are quieter. Men and women are accepted, and food is available.

YMCA (Map p118; ☎ 213 5457; Upanga Rd; s/d with shared bathroom US$10/13) Around the corner from the YWCA, and marginally quieter. Rooms have mosquito nets, and there's a canteen. Men and women are accepted.

Safari Inn (Map p118; ☎ 211 9104; safari-inn@lycos .com; s/d TSh10,000/16,500, d with air-con TSh26,500; ⊠ ⬚) A popular travellers' haunt in Kisutu, on the western edge of the city centre. Rooms have fans, and are sprayed each evening. It's off Libya St.

Jambo Inn (Map p118; ☎ 211 4293, 211 0686; jambo innhotel@yahoo.com; Libya St; s/d TSh12,000/16,000, d with air-con TSh24,000; ⊠) Around the corner from the Safari Inn, and also popular, Jambo Inn has fans, flyscreens in the windows, erratic hot-water supplies and a small restaurant.

Luther House Centre Hostel (Map p118; ☎ 212 6247; luther@simbanet.net; Sokoine Dr; s/tw US$20/25; ❄) Centrally located, about two blocks southeast of the post office. Rooms have fan, nets and air-con, and breakfast is available (at extra charge) at Dar Shanghai Restaurant (p123), downstairs.

Kibodya Hotel (Map p118; ☎ 211 7856; Nkrumah St; d 1Sh9600) Large, no-frills rooms with fans. It's in a busy area off the southwestern end of Samora Ave near the clock tower; there's no food.

Msimbazi Centre Hostel (Map p116; ☎ 286 3508, 286 3204; Kawawa Rd; s/d TSh8500/12,000) Tiny, stuffy singles with fan and net, breezier doubles with two rooms sharing bathroom facilities, and a canteen, all run by the Archdiocese of Dar es Salaam. It's noisy, especially on weekends, but otherwise is reasonable value. It's about 2km southwest of the city centre; take the Buguruni *daladala* from the Old Posta transport stand and ask to be dropped off (TSh2500 in a taxi).

MIDRANGE & TOP END

Mövenpick Royal Palm Hotel (Map p118; ☎ 211 2416; www.movenpick-daressalaam.com; Ohio St; s/d from US$185/210; ❄ 🖳 🏊) This five-star establishment is Dar es Salaam's classiest, with plush rooms and top-notch service. In addition to the pool (TSh10,000 for nonguests), there are fitness and business centres, restaurants and a café-patisserie. It's centrally located in attractive grounds near the golf course.

Harbour View Suites (Map p118; ☎ 212 4040; www .harbourview-suites.com; Samora Ave; ste US$90-140; ❄ 🖳) New and very nice business travellers' studio apartments with views over the city or the harbour, kitchenette, broadband connections and a business centre. Rooms are spotless and good value; below is JM Mall, with an ATM, supermarket and forex bureau. Breakfast is extra.

Holiday Inn (Map p118; ☎ 213 7575; www.holiday -inn.com; Garden Ave; s/d US$144/160; ❄ 🖳) A pleasant and popular place, with modern rooms and the standard amenities, including a business centre. It's on a quiet side street near the National Museum and next to Standard Chartered Bank.

Msasani Peninsula & Upanga
MIDRANGE

Swiss Garden Hotel (Map p116; ☎ 215 3219; swiss garden@bluewin.ch; Mindu St; s/d from US$50/70; 🖳) A cosy B&B in a quiet, leafy neighbourhood, with small, spotless rooms and helpful hosts. It's in Upanga, just off United Nations Rd.

Palm Beach Hotel (Map p116; ☎ 212 2931, 213 0985; www.pbhtz.com; Ali Hassan Mwinyi Rd; s/d/tr US$55/80/90; ❄ 🖳) This Dar es Salaam institution has been completely renovated, and now offers spartan but spacious rooms with TV, wireless Internet access and a restaurant.

Hotel Karibu (Map p116; ☎ 260 2946; www.hotel karibu.com; Haile Selassie Rd; s/d US$80/90; ❄ 🏊) A quirky place in Oyster Bay with reasonable rooms (ask for one that has been refurbished) and a large free-form pool that's usually a hit with children.

TANZANIA'S STREET CHILDREN

In Tanzania, as in so many other places in the world, there are distressingly high numbers of children and youths – particularly boys – on the streets. Some are orphans, often due to AIDS. Others are fleeing violence or stressful living situations at home, lack access to education, or have dropped out of school and turned to the street as an alternative.

While there are few statistics, the scope of the problem is hinted at by the large numbers of children who seek help at outreach programs. These programs generally seek community reintegration for those children who have families, or foster care or adoption for those who don't, in the meanwhile offering services such as residential, health and counselling programs, plus basic education. Some also do advocacy work on various issues, including popularising the United Nations Convention on the Rights of the Child, seeking to end corporal punishment and the practice of expelling pregnant girls in schools, formulating fair employment standards for Tanzania's youth and simply raising awareness. If you're interested in learning more or in getting involved, good initial contacts include **Dogo Dogo Centre for Street Children** (dogodogo@cats-net .com; Dar es Salaam), **Boona Baana Centre** (www.boonabaana.org; Dar es Salaam) and **Mkombazi** (www .mkombozi.org; Moshi).

Msasani Slipway Apartments (Map p116; ☎ 260 0893; slipway@coastal.cc; apt US$80, day use US$60; 🖾) Slick, modern apartments in a good location at the Msasani Slipway. All have a hotplate, sink and refrigerator, and some have views over the bay. Discounted long-term rates are available.

Souk (Map p116; ☎ 260 0893; slipway@coastal.cc; r US$80, day r US$60; 🖾) The same management also has hotel-style rooms (without kitchenette) at this adjoining establishment in the centre of the shopping area. For meals, you have all the Slipway restaurants at your doorstep.

Akana Lodge (Map p116; ☎ 270 0122, 277 5261; www.akanalodge.com; s/d US$50/70; 🖾) Spacious rooms in a private home, with a few smaller ones next door in an annexe, and local-style meals available on request. It's about 7km north of the city centre: go north on Old Bagamoyo Rd past Shopper's Plaza, then left at the Akana signpost.

TOP END

Sea Cliff Hotel (Map p116; ☎ 260 0380/7; www.hotel seacliff.com; Toure Dr; s/d with/without sea view US$180/160; 🖾 🖳 🖭) Sea Cliff has an excellent, breezy setting overlooking the ocean at the northern tip of Msasani Peninsula, plus a small fitness centre and several restaurants. Avoid the less appealing, viewless rooms in the neighbouring annex.

Courtyard (Map p116; ☎ 213 0130; info@thecourtyard -dar.com; Ocean Rd; s/d from US$109/129; 🖾 🖳 🖭) Dark and heavily furnished but comfortable rooms around a small courtyard, with the better (brighter) ones on the upper level. It's 1km south of Selander Bridge. If you don't like air-con, note that the windows don't have flyscreens.

Protea Dar es Salaam Apartments (Map p116; ☎ 266 6665; proteadar@bol.co.tz; cnr Haile Selassie & Ali Hassan Mwinyi Rds; fully serviced apt from US$100; 🖾 🖳 🖭) Modern apartments in a secure compound just north of Selander Bridge. All come with kitchenette, TV and access to the fitness and business centres; short- and long-term rentals are possible.

Oyster Bay Hotel (Map p116; ☎ 260 0352/4; ob hotel@acexnet.com; Toure Dr; s/d US$100/120; 🖾 🖳) The location of this place – across the road from the seafront – and its collection of shops and eateries compensate somewhat for the seemingly permanent scaffolding around the grounds. Although the hotel is

often overlooked for the more modern and better value places in this price range, some of the rooms are surprisingly OK (take a look at several, as they vary considerably).

EATING

Dar es Salaam has a good selection of moderately priced restaurants scattered around the city centre and on the Msasani Peninsula. Most places in the centre are closed on Sunday. For self-catering, try **Shoprite** City Centre (JM Mall, Samora Ave & Mission St); Msasani Peninsula (Msasani Slipway); and **Shopper's Supermarket** (Shopper's Plaza, Old Bagamoyo Rd) in the Namanga area, about 5km north of the city centre.

City Centre

BUDGET

For inexpensive Indian food and takeaways and lots of local atmosphere, head to the area around Zanaki and Jamhuri Sts, where a good place to start is the tiny **Al-Mahdi Tea House** (Map p118; Zanaki St; snacks from TSh200; 🕙 8am-8pm Mon-Fri, 8am-2pm Sat).

Chef's Pride (Map p118; Chagga St; meals from TSh2000; 🕙 lunch & dinner, closed during Ramadan) A long-standing and popular local eatery within easy walking distance of the Kisutu budget hotels. The large menu features standard fare, plus pizzas, Indian and veg dishes, and Chinese cuisine.

Nyumba ya Sanaa (Map p118; Ohio St; meals from TSh3000; 🕙 lunch & dinner) A small, informal eatery in the Nyumba ya Sanaa crafts and cultural centre, serving up plates of chicken and chips, and other local fare. See also p124.

Steers (Map p118; cnr Samora Ave & Ohio St; meals from TSh2000; 🕙 8am until late) A branch of the popular South African chain, with burgers and fast food.

MIDRANGE & TOP END

Cynics Café & Wine Bar (Map p118; ☎ 213 8422; sandwiches & salads TSh3500-6000; ☾ 10am-6pm Mon-Thu, to 9pm Fri) A great little place tucked in next to Barclay's bank, between Ohio and Upanga Sts, with sandwiches and salads, plus good juices and coffees, yogurt and cakes.

Dar Shanghai Restaurant (Map p118; ☎ 213 4397; Luther House Centre Hostel, Sokoine Dr; meals from TSh3500; ☾ breakfast, lunch & dinner, closed Sun lunch) The best bet for Chinese food, with a wide menu selection, reasonable prices and friendly staff. It's behind Swiss Airlines in the Luther House Centre Hostel building.

Kibo Bar (Map p118; ☎ 211 2416; Mövenpick Royal Palm Hotel, Ohio St; ☾ until 11.30pm) Features a good-value lunch special on weekdays for around TSh6000 to TSh10,000, with design-your-own pasta, sandwich, omelette and salad stations.

Serengeti Restaurant (Map p118; ☎ 211 2416; Ohio St; buffet TSh17,000-22,000; ☾ breakfast, lunch & dinner) Next door to the Mövenpick, this eatery has a full-course buffet and á la carte dining.

Baraza (Map p118; ☎ 213 7575; Holiday Inn Hotel, Garden Ave; meals from TSh6000; ☾ breakfast, lunch & dinner) A popular place with a small luncheon buffet, and á la carte dining featuring seafood grills and Swahili cuisine.

Alcove (Map p118; ☎ 213 7444; Samora Ave; meals from TSh6000; ☾ lunch & dinner, closed Sun lunch) Dark, heavy décor and tasty Indian and Chinese cuisine, including a decent selection of vegetarian dishes.

Msasani Peninsula

Sweet Eazy (Map p116; ☎ 0745-754074; Oyster Bay Shops; Toure Drive) The Dar es Salaam branch of this Zanzibar restaurant features Thai and Swahili cuisine, relaxing outdoor terrace seating, and music on Thursday and Saturday evenings.

Addis in Dar (Map p116; ☎ 0741-266299; 35 Ursino St; meals from TSh5000; ☾ lunch & dinner Mon-Sat) One of Dar es Salaam's insider tips if you like Ethiopian food, with *doro wat* (chicken accompanied by a hard-boiled egg served in a hot sauce of butter, onion, chilli, cardamom and *berbere*) and other delicacies, and a good range of vegetarian dishes. It's signposted off Mgombani St. Advance reservations recommended.

Saverio's (Map p116; ☎ 270 0393; Old Bagamoyo Rd; meals from TSh3500; ☾ lunch & dinner Tue-Sun) Good pizzas, grills and seafood.

Garden Bistro (Map p116; ☎ 260 0800; Haile Selassie Rd; dinner daily, lunch Sat & Sun) Indian and continental dishes and grills served in nice garden *bandas* (thatched-roof huts).

La Trattoria Jan (Map p116; ☎ 255 7640, 266 8739; Kimweri Ave; meals from TSh4000; ☾ lunch & dinner) A homy, long-standing place that attracts a loyal group of regulars with its good pizzas and Italian dishes.

There's a good selection of eateries at **Seacliff Village** (Map p116; Toure Dr; ☾ all day), including **Turquoise** (Map p116; ☎ 260 0979; meals from TSh5000) for delicious Turkish cuisine. **Msasani Slipway** (Map p116; Msasani Slipway; ☾ all day) is also good, with everything from burgers to sushi, plus an ice-cream shop and a waterside setting.

DRINKING

Neither the café nor the pub scene have made their way into local Dar es Salaam life, but there are nevertheless a few good spots to quench your thirst.

Cynics Café & Wine Bar (Map p118; ☎ 213 8422; ☾ 10am-6pm Mon-Thu, to 9pm Fri) Live music on some Friday evenings.

Garden Bistro (Map p116; ☎ 260 0800; Haile Selassie Rd) A popular spot for a drink, with live music on weekends.

Sweet Eazy (Map p116; Oyster Bay Shopping Centre) A well-stocked bar, and music on Thursday and Saturday evenings.

Mawazo Art Gallery & Café (Map p118; ☎ 0748-782770; Upanga Rd; ☾ 10am-5.30pm Mon-Sat, until 8.30pm Wed) A small, bright art gallery-café in the YMCA grounds.

Épid'Or (Map p118; ☎ 213 6006; Samora Ave; ☾ 7am-7pm Mon-Sat; ☒) Good coffee and juices, and a great place for a midday break.

Kibo Bar (Map p118; Mövenpick Royal Palm Hotel, Ohio St) Upmarket sports bar at the hotel.

ENTERTAINMENT

For the latest on what's going on around town, check the listings magazines (p117), the bulletin board at Nyumba ya Sanaa (p124) and www.naomba.com.

Nightclubs

Dar es Salaam holds its own in the East African music scene, though it takes time to discover all it has to offer. Most nightspots only get going after 11pm. Admission averages TSh5000 on weekends.

California Dreamers (Map p116; Ali Hassan Mwinyi Rd) Upmarket Western-style disco.

Club Bilicanas (Map p118; Mkwepu St) More of the same.

Lions Club (Sheikilango Rd) Lots of local flavour, best on Friday and Saturday; in Sinza, just off New Bagamoyo Rd.

New Msasani Club (Map p116; Old Bagamoyo Rd) Near the US embassy, and with a moderately upmarket clientele; Friday, Saturday and Sunday.

Cinemas

British Council (Map p118; ☎ 211 6574/5; Sokoine Dr) Occasional free cultural films. See also p115.

Msasani Slipway (Map p116; Msasani Peninsula) Movies Friday, Saturday and Sunday evenings.

New World Cinema (www.darcinemas.com; New Bagamoyo Rd, Mwenge) Daily screenings of Indian and Western films.

Traditional Music & Dance

Mwalimu Julius K Nyerere Cultural Centre (Map p118; Nyumba ya Sanaa, Ohio St) This centre has traditional dance performances at 7pm on Fridays, and is the best place to find out about other traditional dance events around town.

Village Museum (☎ 270 0437; www.homestead .com/villagemuseum/; cnr New Bagamoyo Rd & Makaburi St) The museum hosts *ngoma* performances for TSh2500 from 2pm to 6pm on weekends and most weekdays as well, and also has occasional special programs highlighting the dances of individual tribes.

SHOPPING

For souvenirs, try the **Msasani Slipway Weekend Craft Market** (Map p116; Msasani Slipway, Msasani Peninsula; ⏰ Sat & Sun). Prices are higher here than elsewhere in town, but quality is good and the atmosphere calm. It's on the western side of Msasani Peninsula, just off Chole Rd. For high-quality paintings, woodcarvings and more, a good place to start is Mawazo Art Gallery & Café (p123).

The best place for Tingatinga paintings is the bustling **Tingatinga Centre** (Map p116; Morogoro Stores, Haile Selassie Rd, Oyster Bay; ⏰ 8.30am-5pm), where you can watch the artists at work and stroll among their wares. For woodcarvings, head to the **Mwenge Carvers' Market** (Sam Nujoma Rd; ⏰ 8am-6pm), near the Village Museum off New Bagamoyo Rd. It's packed with vendors, and you'll be able to see how some of the carving is done. Take the Mwenge *dala-dala* from New Posta to the end, from where it's five minutes on foot to the left, down Sam Nujoma Rd. Closer to town, **Nyumba ya Sanaa** (Map p118; Ohio St, next to Mövenpick Royal Palm Hotel; ⏰ daily) is a local artists' cooperative

that sells textiles and crafts from various parts of the country; you can also watch some of the artists at work.

If you save your craft shopping until the last minute, several shops in the international departures lounge at the airport have good selections.

GETTING THERE & AWAY
Air

Dar es Salaam International Airport is Tanzania's international and domestic flight hub. Most domestic flights and all international flights depart from Terminal Two (the 'new' terminal, and the first one you reach coming from town). Many flights on small planes (including most Zanzibar flights) and most charters depart from Terminal One ('old' terminal), about 700m further down the road.

AIRLINE OFFICES

Air India (Map p118; ☎ 215 2642; cnr Ali Hassan Mwinyi & Bibi Titi Mohamed Rds)

Air Tanzania Airport (☎ 284 4239; Terminal Two; ⏰ 6am-midnight); City Centre (Map p118; ☎ 211 8411, 284 4239; ATC Building, Ohio St)

British Airways (Map p118; ☎ 211 3820, 284 4082; Mövenpick Royal Palm Hotel, Ohio St)

Coastal Aviation Airport (☎ 284 3293; Terminal One); City Centre (Map p118; ☎ 211 7959/60; aviation@coastal .cc; Upanga Rd)

EgyptAir (Map p118; ☎ 211 0333; Samora Ave)

Emirates Airlines (Map p118; ☎ 211 6100; Haidery Plaza, cnr Kisutu & India Sts)

Ethiopian Airlines (Map p118; ☎ 211 7063; Ohio St) Opposite Mövenpick Royal Palm Hotel.

Kenya Airways (Map p118; ☎ 211 3666, 211 9376/7; Upanga Rd, cnr Ali Hassan Mwinyi & Bibi Titi Mohamed Rds)

KLM (Map p118; ☎ 213 9790/1; Upanga Rd) Together with Kenya Airways.

Linhas Aéreas de Moçambique (Map p118; ☎ 213 4600; Ground fl, JM Mall, Samora Ave) At Fast-Track Travel, www.fasttracktanzania.com.

Oman Air (Map p118; ☎ 213 5660; omanair@cats-net .com; Ground Fl, JM Mall, Samora Ave)

Precision Air Airport (☎ 284 3547; Terminal Two); City Centre (Map p118; ☎ 212 1718; cnr Samora Ave & Pamba Rd)

South African Airways (☎ 211 7044; Raha Towers, cnr Bibi Titi Mohamed & Ali Hassan Mwinyi Rds)

Swiss International Airlines (Map p118; ☎ 211 8870; Luther House, Sokoine Dr)

Yemenia Yemen Airways (Map p118; ☎ 212 6036; Ohio St) Opposite Mövenpick Royal Palm Hotel.

ZanAir (☎ 284 3297; www.zanair.com; Terminal One, Airport)

Boat

The main passenger routes are between Dar es Salaam, Zanzibar and Pemba; and Dar es Salaam and Mtwara.

MTWARA

The only connection is on the ailing MV *Safari*, which departs at 8am Saturday from Dar es Salaam, and at 2pm Tuesday from Mtwara (US$25 including port tax, 25 to 30 hours). Tickets are sold at the **MV Safari office** (Map p118; ☎ 212 4504/6; Sokoine Drive) at the port, just down from the Zanzibar ferry terminal, and opposite the back of JM Mall.

ZANZIBAR & PEMBA

There are four 'fast' ferry trips (on *Sea Star*, *Sea Express* or *Sea Bus*) daily from Dar es Salaam to Zanzibar, departing daily at 7.30am (*Sea Express*), 10.30am (*Sea Star*), 2pm (*Sea Bus*) and 4pm (*Sea Bus*). All take 1½ hours and cost US$35/40 regular/VIP (VIP gets you a seat in the air-con hold, but isn't worth the extra money). There's also one slow ferry called the *Flying Horse*, which takes almost four hours. It departs daily at 12.30pm and costs US$20 one way. The ticket windows for all ferries are opposite St Joseph's Cathedral.

Travelling in the other direction, departures from Zanzibar are daily at 7am (*Sea Star*), 10am (*Sea Bus*), 1pm (*Sea Bus*), 4pm (*Sea Express*) and 10pm (*Flying Horse*, arriving before dawn the next day).

Only buy your tickets at the ticket windows, and don't fall for touts at the harbour trying to collect extra fees for 'doctors' certificates', departure taxes and the like. The only fee is the ticket price (which includes the US$5 port tax). Also, avoid touts who try to steer you to fake booking offices in the port area, who want to take you into town to buy 'cheaper' ferry tickets, or who offer to purchase ferry tickets for you at less-expensive resident rates. Although it's easy enough to get resident-rate tickets and get on the boat with them, you're likely to have problems later when the tout or his buddies come around to collect payment for the favour.

For information on ferry connections to Pemba, see p154 and p157.

Bus

All buses except Scandinavian Express depart from and arrive at the main bus station at Ubungo, about 8km west of town

on Morogoro Rd. It's a sprawling place with the usual bus-station hustle, so keep an eye on your luggage and your wallet, and try to avoid arriving at night. *Dala-dalas* to Ubungo (TSh200) leave from New Posta and Old Posta local transport stands. Taxis from the city centre cost TSh8000 to TSh10,000. Arriving at Dar es Salaam, you can sometimes stay on the bus past Ubungo until the bus line's town office – which is worth doing, as it will be less chaotic and you'll have a cheaper taxi fare to your hotel. For departures, book tickets at the bus-line offices (listed following), most of which are in Kisutu, near the Libya St post office. Only buy tickets inside the bus office itself.

Dar Express (Map p118; Libya St) runs daily buses to Arusha departing at 6am (TSh12,000), 7am, 8am and 9am (all TSh14,000), while **Royal Coach** (Map p118; ☎ 212 4073; Libya St) runs daily departures to Arusha at 9am.

Scandinavian Express (Map p116; ☎ 218 4833/4; www.scandinaviagroup.com; cnr Msimbazi St & Nyerere Rd) has its own terminal for arrivals, departures and ticket bookings, which is much calmer than Ubungo, and closer to the city centre. All Scandinavian buses also pass by Ubungo.

Destination	Price (TSh)	Frequency (per day)
Arusha	15,000–24,000	2
Dodoma	7500–10,000	3
Iringa	8500–10,000	3
Kampala	50,000	1
Kyela	18,000–20,000	2
Mbeya	18,000–20,000	3
Mombasa	19,000	1
Mwanza	44,000	1
Nairobi	38,000	1
Songea	17,000–19,000	1
Tanga	7500	1
Tunduma	17,000	1

Transport to Kilwa Masoko also departs from Temeke bus stand, about 5km southwest of the city centre, just off Nelson Mandela Rd.

For information about buses between Dar es Salaam and Kenya, Uganda, Zambia and Malawi, see p256.

Train

For information about the Tazara line between Dar es Salaam, Mbeya and Kapiri

Mposhi (Zambia), see p265. For more on Central Line trains between Dar es Salaam, Kigoma and Mwanza, see p265.

The **Tazara station** (☎ 286 5187; www.tazara.co .tz; cnr Nyerere & Nelson Mandela Rds) is about 6km southwest from the city centre (TSh5000 in a taxi). *Daladalas* depart from the New and Old Posta transport stands, and are marked Vigunguti, U/Ndege or Buguruni.

Tanzanian Railways Corporation (Central Line) station (Map p118; ☎ 211 7833; www.trctz.com; cnr Railway St & Sokoine Dr) is in the city centre just southwest of the ferry terminal.

GETTING AROUND
To/From the Airport
Dar es Salaam International Airport is 12km from the city centre. *Daladalas* (marked U/ Ndege) depart from New Posta transport stand. In traffic the trip can take over an hour. Much better are taxis, which cost TSh8000 to TSh10,000, depending on your bargaining abilities.

Car & Motorcycle
Most of the rental agencies listed on p263 offer special business packages within Dar es Salaam.

Public Transport
Daladalas are invariably packed to overflowing and are difficult to board with luggage. First and last stops are shown in the front window, but routes vary, so confirm that the driver is really going to your destination. Rides cost TSh100 to TSh200. Main stops:

New Posta (Map p118; Maktaba St) In front of the main post office.

Old Posta (Map p118; Sokoine Dr) Just down from the Azania Front Lutheran Church.

Stesheni (Map p118; Algeria St) Off Samora Ave near the Central Line Railway Station. *Daladalas* to Temeke bus stand also leave from here; ask for 'Temeke *mwisho'*.

Taxi
Taxis charge TSh1000 to TSh2000 per short trip within the centre. Fares to Msasani Peninsula start at TSh2500 (TSh5000 to Sea Cliff Village).

Taxi ranks include those opposite Mövenpick Royal Palm Hotel, on the corner of Azikiwe St and Sokoine Dr (opposite the Azania Front Lutheran Church) and on the Msasani Peninsula on the corner of Msasani and Haile Selassie Rds.

AROUND DAR ES SALAAM

SOUTHERN BEACHES
The coastline south of Dar es Salaam gets more attractive, tropical and rural the further south you go, and makes an easy getaway. The budget places begin south of Kigamboni, which is opposite Kivukoni Front and reached in a few minutes by ferry. About 25km south are a few exclusive resorts.

Kigamboni
☎ 022
The beach south of Kigamboni is the closest spot to Dar es Salaam for camping. It's also an easy day trip if you're staying in town and want some sand and surf.

SLEEPING & EATING
Kipepeo Village (☎ 282 0877, 0744-276178; www .kipepeovillage.com; s/d/tr banda US$50/65/95) Raised cottages lined up about 200m in from the beach, all with balconies and mosquito nets. Breakfast is not included.

Kipepeo Campsite (☎ 282 0877; www.kipepeocamp .com; camping US$4, s/d banda US$13/20) This camp site is on the beach. It has a restaurant-bar, a grill and simple beachside *bandas*. On weekends, there's a TSh3000 fee for day use of the beach. Kipepeo is 8km south of the ferry dock.

Gendayeka Beach Village (camping TSh5000, r per person with shared bathroom TSh10,000) A simple place on the beach 700m south of Kipepeo Campsite. No-frills bungalows with shared facilities. Women in particular should note that a padlock is required as most bungalows are not secured. Make bookings through Chef's Pride restaurant (p122).

GETTING THERE & AWAY
The Kigamboni ferry (per person/vehicle TSh100/800, five minutes) runs throughout the day between the eastern end of Kivukoni Front and Kigamboni village. Once on the other side, *daladalas* head south from Kigamboni; ask the driver to drop you off. Taxis from Kigamboni charge about TSh2000 to Kipepeo and Gendayeka.

Gezaulole
Gezaulole village, 13km south of Kigamboni on the beach, has a Cultural Tourism

Program (CTP), which introduces you to the life of the local Zaramo people and sails out to nearby Sinda Island. The starting point is at **Akida's Garden** (☎ 0744-505725; camping TSh2500, bandas per person with shared bathroom TSh7000), signposted about 1km off the main road. There's also **camping** (TSh2000) under the palms on the sublime Kim Beach, nearby. With an early start, it's possible to visit as a day trip from Dar es Salaam on public transport. CTP fees are about TSh7000 per person per half day, and Sinda Island trips cost TSh5000.

Take a *daladala* from the Kigamboni ferry dock towards Kimbiji or Gezaulole, and ask the driver to drop you at the turn-off for Akida's Garden (TSh400). Taxis from Kigamboni charge about TSh7000.

Ras Kutani

This cape about 30km south of Dar es Salaam boasts secluded tropical surroundings and good fishing. Both lodges requiring advance bookings.

Ras Kutani (www.selous.com; s/d full board US$308/410) is an intimate retreat set between the sea and a small lagoon, and comes about as close as you can get to a tropical island getaway without leaving the mainland. Accommodation is in barefoot-luxury-style bungalows and bird-watching and other activities can be arranged.

For more of a resort atmosphere, head just south and around the bend from Ras Kutani bungalows to the exclusive **Amani Beach Club** (☎ 0744-410033; www.proteahotels.com; s/d full board US$140/240; ✗ ▯ ♋), spread across large, manicured lawns overlooking the sea. It has spacious luxury cottages and a full array of excursions and water sports.

NORTHERN BEACHES

☎ 022

The beaches about 25km north of central Dar es Salaam and east of New Bagamoyo Rd are lined with resorts and are popular weekend getaways. While they lack the exotic ambience of Zanzibar's beaches, they make a relaxing break from the city. They're also close enough that you can visit for the day, or use them as a base if you want to avoid Dar es Salaam entirely.

Activities

Diving around Bongoyo and Mbudya Islands can be arranged at **Sea Breeze Marine**

Dive Centre (www.seabreezemarine.org) at White Sands Hotel (below).

There are several water parks, with pools, water slides and other Disney-style amusements. **Kunduchi Wet 'n' Wild** (☎ 265 0326, 265 0332; wetnwild@raha.com; adult/child TSh4000/3800; ☒ 9am-6pm, Tue women only) is the largest, with pools, water slides, bumper cars, video arcades and more. Take a *daladala* to Mwenge and then a taxi.

Sleeping & Eating

Jangwani Sea Breeze Lodge (☎ 264 7215, 0741-320875; www.jangwani.com; s/d from US$90/115; ☒ ▯ ♋) A tidy establishment with comfortable if somewhat over-furnished rooms (all across the road from the beach), a bougainvillea-draped courtyard, and a restaurant with weekend buffets.

White Sands Hotel (☎ 264 7621, 211 3678; www.hotelwhitesands.com; s/d US$105/120, weekend discounts; ☒ ▯ ♋) A sprawling hotel on the beach. Rooms have TV, minifridge and small balconies. Windsurfing, deep-sea fishing and excursions can be arranged. There's a disco on weekend evenings.

Silver Sands Beach Hotel (☎ 265 0567/8; camping US$3, per vehicle US$2, dm US$9, ordinary/deluxe r US$30/45; ☒) The best budget choice, with camping facilities with hot water, and dorm beds that come with mosquito nets and breakfast. There are also rooms set around a small lawn, and a restaurant.

Getting There & Away

Jangwani Sea Breeze Lodge and White Sands Hotel are reached via the same signposted turn-off from the Bagamoyo road. About 3km further north along the Bagamoyo road is the signposted turn-off for Silver Sands.

Take a *daladala* from Dar es Salaam's New Posta to Mwenge. For Jangwani and White Sands, continue via *daladala* from Mwenge towards Tegeta and disembark at Africana Junction, from where you can find a taxi to the hotels (from TSh2000). For Silver Sands, stay on until the Kunduchi Junction stop, where you'll need to look for a taxi for the remaining 2km or so (about TSh1500). Don't walk though, as there have been several muggings along this stretch of road.

Taxis from the city centre/airport cost about TSh15,000/25,000.

PUGU HILLS

The Pugu Hills area begins about 15km southwest of Dar es Salaam and extends past Kisarawe. It's lightly wooded, with several small forest reserves, and offers a break from urban noise and bustle. Despite its proximity to the city, many communities here have remained quite traditional and conservative. Pugu is also of interest from a historical perspective, as the site of Pugu Secondary School, where Julius Nyerere worked as a teacher before entering politics full time. There's a military base nearby, so use caution when taking photos.

Pugu Hills (☎ 0744-565498, 0744-394875; www.pugu hills.com; entry TSh2000, camping TSh6000, 4-6 person bandas US$50) is a good, breezy place set on a hillside backing onto a forest reserve. There's camping, four spacious en suite *bandas* and a restaurant with vegetarian dishes and other meals (meals TSh7000). Large groups and overland trucks cannot be accommodated. The compound is open for visiting at any time, but you'll need to make a booking in advance by phone or email. Pick-ups from the airport (about 20 minutes away) can be arranged.

Getting There & Away

Daladalas to Kisarawe leave from Msimbazi St in Kariakoo (Dar es Salaam), and from Nyerere Rd at the airport turn-off. For Pugu Hills camping ground and restaurant, ask the driver to drop you at the old Agip station (about 7km before Kisarawe, and about 7km past the airport). From here, continue along the Kisarawe road for about 200m, to the end of a tiny group of shops on your left, where there is a dirt path leading up to Pugu Hills (about 15 minutes further on foot); ask for Bwana Kiki's place. By vehicle, from the old Agip station follow the sealed road to the left, continue 1.2km, then turn right at a dirt path about 50m before the railroad tracks. Continue 2km uphill to Pugu Hills.

OFFSHORE ISLANDS

The islands of Bongoyo, Mbudya, Pangavini and Fungu Yasini, just off the coast of Dar es Salaam, were gazetted in 1975 as part of the Dar es Salaam Marine Reserve system. They boast pristine patches of sand, a decent array of fish and enjoyable diving and snorkelling. The TSh1000 per person

reserve entry fee is usually included in the price of excursions.

About 7km north of Dar es Salaam is **Bongoyo Island Marine Reserve** (admission TSh1000), the most popular of the islands, with a quiet (except on holiday weekends) stretch of beach and some short walking trails. You can arrange a seafood meal with locals on the beach; bring your own drinks. Swimming here is not tide dependent. There's no accommodation.

A boat to Bongoyo departs Msasani Slipway daily at 9.30am, 11.30am and 1.30pm, returning at 10.30am, 12.30pm and either 2.30pm or 4.30pm (US$10 return, minimum four people, including entry fees and lunch).

ZANZIBAR ARCHIPELAGO

The lure of the 'spice islands' is legendary. From exotic Stone Town with its fascinating labyrinth of narrow streets, to palm-fringed beaches and pristine coral reefs, the archipelago is a complete change of pace from the mainland with which it is linked as part of the United Republic of Tanzania.

While Zanzibar gets most of the attention, the archipelago is also made up of Pemba to the north, plus numerous smaller islands and islets offshore. Each of the main islands has its own distinct character. Zanzibar's main attraction is Stone Town, with its whitewashed, coral-rag houses, quaint shops, bazaars, mosques, courtyards and squares. Another draw card is its spectacular turquoise sea, abounding in marine life and striking coral formations and edged by fine, white-sand beaches. Although many places have become very developed, there are still some quiet and relatively unspoiled spots left.

The island of Pemba, in contrast, is seldom visited and very laid-back. In addition to its attractive, hilly terrain, the island offers an intriguing, largely undiscovered culture, some attractive offshore islands and challenging diving.

History

The archipelago's history stretches back at least to the start of the first millennium, when Bantu-speaking peoples from the mainland first made the trip across the

Zanzibar and Pemba channels. The islands had likely been visited at an even earlier date by traders and sailors from Arabia. *The Periplus of the Erythraean Sea,* an early mariner's guide, documents small Arabic trading settlements along the coast that were already well established by the 1st century, and makes reference to the island of Menouthias, which many historians believe to be Zanzibar. From around the 8th century Shirazi traders from Persia also began to make their way to East Africa, where they established settlements on Pemba and probably also at Zanzibar's Unguja Ukuu.

Between the 12th and 15th centuries the archipelago came into its own, as trade links with Arabia and the Persian Gulf blossomed. Zanzibar became a powerful city-state, supplying slaves, gold, ivory and wood to places as distant as India and Asia, while importing spices, glassware and textiles. Along with the trade from the east came Islam and the Arabic architecture that still characterises the archipelago today.

The arrival of the Portuguese in the early 16th century temporarily interrupted this golden age, as Zanzibar and then Pemba fell under Portuguese control. Yet Portuguese dominance didn't last long. It was challenged first by the British, who found Zanzibar an amenable rest stop on the long journey to India, and then by Omani Arabs, who, in the mid-16th century, gave the Portuguese the routing that they probably deserved. By the early 19th century Oman had gained the upper hand on Zanzibar, and trade on the island again flourished, centred on slaves, ivory and cloves. Caravans set out for the interior, and trade reached such a point that in the 1840s the Sultan of Oman relocated his court here from the Persian Gulf.

From the mid-19th century, with increasing European interest in East Africa and the end of the slave trade, Omani rule over Zanzibar began to weaken, and in 1862 the sultanate was formally partitioned. Zanzibar became independent from Oman, with Omani sultans ruling under a British protectorate. This arrangement lasted until 10 December 1963, when Zanzibar gained its independence. Just one month later, in January 1964, the sultans were overthrown in a bloody revolution instigated by the ASP, which then assumed power. On 12 April 1964 Abeid Karume, president of the ASP,

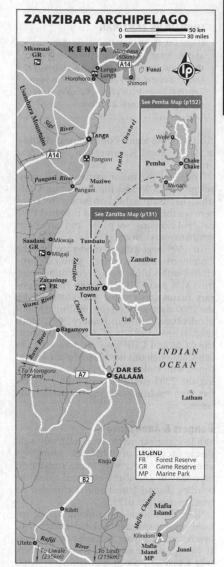

ZANZIBAR ARCHIPELAGO

signed a declaration of unity with Tanganyika (mainland Tanzania) and the union, fragile from the outset, became known as the United Republic of Tanzania.

Karume was assassinated in 1972, and Aboud Jumbe assumed the presidency of Zanzibar until resigning in 1984. A succession of leaders followed, culminating in

TANZANIA

UNGUJA VS ZANZIBAR

Unguja is the Swahili name for Zanzibar, and is often used locally to distinguish the island from the Zanzibar Archipelago (which also includes Pemba), as well as from Zanzibar Town. In this book, for ease of recognition, we've used Zanzibar.

2000 with the highly controversial election of Aman Abeid Karume, son of the first president.

Today the two major parties in the archipelago are CCM and the opposition CUF, which has its stronghold on Pemba. Tensions between the two peaked in the disputed 1995 national elections (see p108), and have been simmering ever since.

In 1999 negotiations moderated by the Commonwealth secretary general concluded with a brokered agreement between the CCM and CUF. However, the temporary hiatus this created was shattered by the 2000 elections, and the resulting violent incidents on Pemba in January 2001. Since then, renewed efforts at dialogue between the CCM and CUF have restored a fragile calm, although this has been broken several times, with violence leading up to and during the 2005 elections, and little progress has been made at resolving the underlying issues.

Dangers & Annoyances

While Zanzibar remains a relatively safe place, incidents of robberies, muggings and the like occur with some frequency, especially in Zanzibar Town and along the beaches. *Papasi* (street touts) can also be troublesome; see p133.

Take the normal precautions: avoid isolated areas, especially isolated stretches of beach, and keep your valuables out of view. If you go out at night in Zanzibar Town, take a taxi or walk in a group. Also avoid walking alone in Stone Town during the predawn and dawn hours. As a rule, it's best to leave valuables in your hotel safe, preferably sealed or locked.

If you've hired a bicycle or motorcycle, avoid isolated stretches of road, including the section between Jambiani and Makunduchi, on the southeast coast, and don't stop if you're flagged down in isolated areas.

Given the ongoing history of political tensions on Zanzibar and Pemba, it's a good idea to check your government's travel advisory site (see p624) before planning your travels.

ZANZIBAR

☎ 024

Step off the boat (or plane) from the mainland onto Zanzibar, and you'll find yourself transported thousands of miles: to the ancient kingdom of Persia, to the Oman of bygone days with its caliphs and sultans, to the west coast of India, with its sensual rhythms and heavily laden scents. While this reverie likely won't last too long – hassles from the island's ever-present street touts will pull you quickly back to reality – Zanzibar has an undeniable allure that will continue to captivate long after you've finished your visit.

Most people who visit arrive first at Zanzibar Town, the island's main population centre and commercial hub. At the heart of Zanzibar Town is the old Stone Town, with its labyrinthine alleyways and fascinating architecture. Just beyond here, and within easy reach, is an unsurpassed collection of beaches where the sand is powdery white and the sea ethereal shades of turquoise.

Getting There & Around

Getting to Zanzibar is very easy, with daily flights plus several daily ferries between Dar es Salaam and Zanzibar Town. There are also daily flights between Zanzibar Town, Pemba and Tanga, and boat connections several times weekly between Zanzibar and Pemba. Once on Zanzibar, taxi and motorbike hire is quite affordable, and there's a network of cheap, slow and crowded *daladalas,* or faster private minivans, that will take you wherever you want to go.

A Tanzanian visa (see p255) is required to visit Zanzibar; there are no separate visa requirements for the archipelago.

Orientation

Zanzibar Town, on the western side of the island, is the heart of the archipelago, and the first stop for most travellers. The best-known section by far is the old Stone Town, surrounded on three sides by the sea and bordered to the east by Creek Rd. Directly east of Stone Town is the bustling but much less atmospheric section of Ng'ambo, which

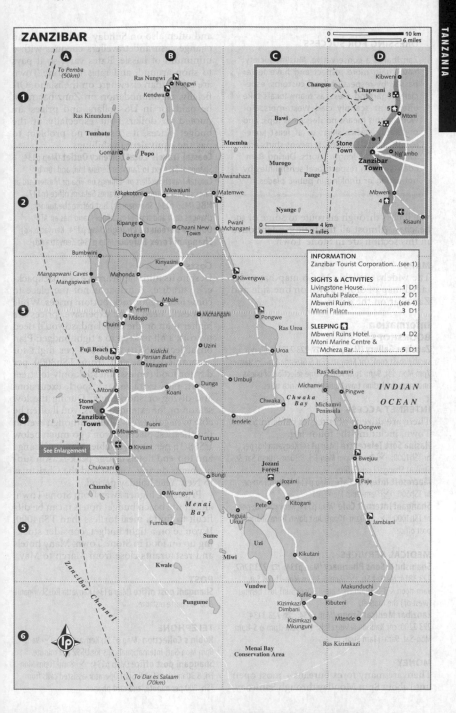

ZANZIBAR

0 — 10 km
0 — 6 miles

INFORMATION
Zanzibar Tourist Corporation...(see 1)

SIGHTS & ACTIVITIES
Livingstone House....................1 D1
Maruhubi Palace.....................2 D1
Mbweni Ruins........................(see 4)
Mtoni Palace........................3 D1

SLEEPING
Mbweni Ruins Hotel..................4 D2
Mtoni Marine Centre &
  Mcheza Bar........................5 D1

TANZANIA

DRESSING FOR SUCCESS

Zanzibar is a conservative, Muslim society. You'll gain more respect and have fewer hassles by respecting local customs, especially regarding dress, as many locals take offence at scantily clad Westerners. For women, this means no sleeveless tops, and preferably slacks, skirts or at least knee-length shorts. For men, it means shirts and slacks or knee-length shorts. During Ramadan, you can respect local sensibilities by not eating or drinking in public places.

---

you'll pass through en route to some of the beaches. Almost all the listings mentioned in this section are in Stone Town.

MAPS

The widely available MaCo map has a detailed map of Stone Town on one side and Zanzibar on the other.

Information

BOOKSHOPS

Zanzibar Gallery (Map p134; ☎ 223 2721; gallery@ swahilicoast.com; cnr Kenyatta Rd & Gizenga St; ⏱ 9am-7pm Mon-Sat, 9am-1pm Sun) A large selection of books and maps, including travel guides and Africa titles.

INTERNET ACCESS

There are dozens of Internet cafés in Stone Town, including the following:

Hasina Soft Telecentre (Map p134; Kenyatta Rd; per hr TSh1000; ⏱ 8am-10pm Mon-Fri, 8.30am-10pm Sat & Sun) At Shangani post office.

Macrosoft Internet Café (Map p134; Hurumzi St; per hr TSh500; ⏱ 9am-9pm Mon-Sat)

Shangani Internet Café (Map p134; Kenyatta Rd; per hr TSh1000; ⏱ 8.30am-10pm) Just down from Shangani post office.

MEDICAL SERVICES

Shamshu & Sons Pharmacy (Map p134; ☎ 223 1262, 223 3814; Market St; ⏱ 9am-8.30pm Mon-Thu & Sat, 9am-noon & 3-8.30pm Fri, 9am-1.30pm Sun) Just behind (west of) the market.

Zanzibar Medical Group (Map p134; ☎ 223 3134, 223 2200; cnr Kaunda & Vuga Rds; ⏱ 9am-1pm & 5-8pm Mon-Sat, 9am-11am Sun)

MONEY

There are many forex bureaus – most open until about 8pm Monday through Saturday,

and often also on Sunday – where you can change cash and travellers cheques with a minimum of hassle. Rates vary, so it pays to shop around, and rates in Stone Town are better than elsewhere on the island. Officially, accommodation on Zanzibar must be paid for in US dollars, and prices are quoted in dollars, but especially at the budget places, it's usually no problem to pay the equivalent in shillings.

Coastal Travels' Local Currency Outlet (Map p134; Shangani St) Next to Zanzibar Serena Inn, and run by Coastal Travels; dollars or shillings on Visa or MasterCard at rates similar to those in the Dar es Salaam office (p117).

NBC (Map p134; Shangani St) Just before the tunnel; changes cash and travellers cheques, and has an ATM.

Queens Bureau de Change (Map p134; Kenyatta Rd)

Shangani Forex Bureau (Map p134; Kenyatta Rd)

Costs

Despite its initial appearance as a backpacker's paradise, Zanzibar is not the place to come looking for rock-bottom prices. While it doesn't need to be expensive, prices are higher than on the mainland, so you'll need to work a bit to keep to a tight budget. Plan on at least US$10 to US$15 per night for accommodation, and from TSh8000 per day for food (unless you stick only to street food), plus extra for transport, excursions and diving or snorkelling. During the low season or for extended stays, you'll often be able to negotiate discounts, although even at the cheapest places it won't go much below US$8/16 per single/double. Many midrange and top-end hotels charge peak-season supplements during August and the Christmas to New Year holiday period.

Prices are higher away from Stone Town, and at the beach budget hotels it can be difficult to find a meal for less than TSh4000. If you're on a tight budget, consider stocking up on food in Stone Town. Many hotels and restaurants close from March to May.

POST

Shangani post office (Map p134; Kenyatta Rd, Shangani) Also has poste restante.

TELEPHONE

Robin's Collection (Map p134; Kenyatta Rd; ⏱ 9am-8pm Mon-Sat) International calls for US$2 per minute.

Shangani post office (Map p134; ⏱ 8am-10pm Mon-Fri, 8.30am-9pm Sat & Sun) Operator-assisted calls from TSh1800 per minute, and card phones.

TOURIST INFORMATION

The free quarterly *Recommended in Zanzibar* has information on cultural events, transport schedules, tide tables etc.

Zanzibar Tourist Corporation (Map p134; ☎ 223 8630; ztc@zanzinet.com; Bububu rd) Headquarters in Livingstone House.

TRAVEL AGENCIES

For excursions around the island, and plane and ferry tickets, agencies to try include the following. (Only make bookings and payments inside the offices, and not with anyone outside claiming to be staff.)

Eco + Culture Tours (Map p134; ☎ 223 0366; www .ecoculture-zanzibar.org; Hurumzi St) Opposite Emerson & Green hotel.

Fernandes Tours & Safaris (Map p134; ☎ 223 0666; fts@zanlink.com; Vuga St)

Madeira Tours & Safaris (Map p134; ☎ 223 0406; madeira@zanzinet.com) Just off Kenyatta Rd, opposite Baghani House Hotel; all price ranges.

Sama Tours (Map p134; ☎ 223 3543; samatours@zitec .org; Hurumzi St)

Suna Tours (Map p134; ☎ 223 7344) At the southwestern edge of Forodhani Gardens.

Tropical Tours (Map p134; ☎ 223 0868, 0747-413454; tropicalts@hotmail.com; Kenyatta Rd) Opposite Mazsons Hotel; budget.

Zan Tours (Map p134; ☎ 223 3042, 223 3116; www .zantours.com) A wide range of high-quality upmarket tours on the archipelago and beyond. It's off Malindi St.

Sights

If Zanzibar Town is the archipelago's heart, Stone Town is its soul, with a magical jumble of cobbled alleyways where it's easy to spend days wandering around and getting lost – although you can't get lost for long because, sooner or later, you'll end up on either the seafront or on Creek Rd. Nevertheless, each twist and turn of the narrow streets brings something new, be it a school full of children chanting verses from the Quran, a beautiful old mansion with overhanging verandas, a coffee vendor with his long-spouted pot fastened over coals, clacking cups to attract custom, or a group of women in *bui-bui* (garments worn by Islamic women) sharing a joke and local gossip. Along the way, watch the island's rich cultural melange come to life: Arabic-style

---

PAPASI

In Zanzibar Town, you'll undoubtedly come into contact with street touts, known in Swahili as *papasi* (ticks). They are not registered guides, although they may carry (false) identification cards, and while a few can be helpful, others can be aggressive and irritating. Many of the more annoying ones are involved with Zanzibar's drug trade, and are desperate for money for their next fix, which means you are just asking for trouble if you arrange anything with them.

If you do decide to use the services of a tout (and they're hard to avoid if you're arriving at the ferry dock for the first time and don't know your way around), tell them where you want to go or what you are looking for, and your price range. You shouldn't have to pay anything additional, as many hotels pay commissions. If they tell you your hotel of choice no longer exists or is full, take it with a grain of salt, as it could well be that they just want to take you somewhere where they know they'll get a better commission.

Another strategy is to make your way out of the port arrivals area and head straight for a taxi. This will cost you more, and taxi drivers look for hotel commissions as well, but most are legitimate, and once you are 'spoken for', hassles from touts usually diminish.

One other thing about using *papasi*: most are hoping that your stay on the island will mean ongoing work for them as your guide, so if you do use one to help you find a hotel, he'll invariably be outside waiting for you later. If you're not interested in this, explain so (politely) once you've arrived at your hotel. If you want a guide to show you around Stone Town, it's better to arrange one with your hotel or a travel agency. For any dealings with the *papasi*, if you're being hassled, a polite but firm approach usually works best – yelling or showing irritation, although quite tempting at times, won't get you anywhere. Another thing to remember is that you have a better chance of getting a discount on your hotel room if you arrive alone, since the hotel can then give you the discount that would have been paid to the touts as commission.

When arranging tours and excursions, never make payments on the street – be sure you're paying at a legitimate office, and get a receipt.

TANZANIA

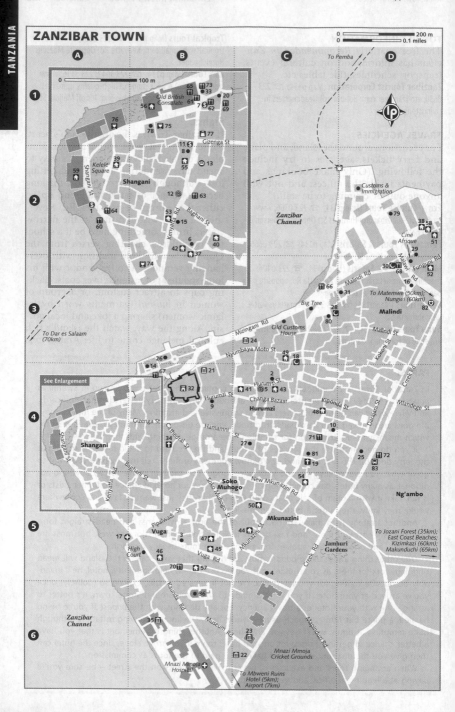

houses with their recessed inner courtyards rub shoulders with Indian influenced buildings boasting ornate balconies and latticework, and bustling oriental bazaars alternate with lively street-side vending stalls.

While the best part of Stone Town is simply letting it unfold before you, it's worth putting in an effort to see its major features.

BEIT EL-AJAIB (HOUSE OF WONDERS)

Beit el-Ajaib – home to the **Zanzibar National Museum of History & Culture** (Map p134; ☎ 223 0873; Mizingani Rd; admission US$3; ⏰ 9am-6pm Mon-Fri, to 3pm Sat & Sun) – is one of the largest structures in Zanzibar. It was built in 1883 by Sultan Barghash (r 1870–88) as a ceremonial palace. In 1896 it was the target of a British naval bombardment, the object of which was to force Khalid bin Barghash, who had tried to seize the throne after the

death of Sultan Hamad (r 1893–96), to abdicate in favour of a British nominee. After it was rebuilt, Sultan Hamoud (r 1902–11) used the upper floor as a residential palace until his death. Inside are exhibits on the dhow culture of the Indian Ocean, Swahili civilisation and 19th-century Zanzibar, plus smaller displays on *kangas* (printed cotton wraparound, incorporating a Swahili proverb, worn by women) and the history of Stone Town. There's also a life-sized *mtepe* (a traditional Swahili sailing vessel made without nails, the planks held together only with coconut fibres and wooden pegs).

BEIT EL-SAHEL (PALACE MUSEUM)

Just north of the Beit el-Ajaib, is **Beit el-Sahel** (Map p134; Mizingani Rd; admission US$3; ⏰ 9am-6pm Mon-Fri, to 3pm Sat & Sun). This palace served as the sultan's residence until 1964 when the dynasty was overthrown. Now it's a museum devoted to the era of the Zanzibar sultanate.

The ground floor displays details of the formative period of the sultanate from 1828 to 1870. There is also memorabilia of Princess Salme, a Zanzibari princess who eloped with a German to Europe, and later wrote an autobiography. The exhibits on the 2nd floor focus on the period of affluence from 1870 to 1896, during which modern amenities such as piped water and electricity were introduced to Zanzibar under Sultan Barghash. The 3rd floor consists of the modest living quarters of the last sultan, Khalifa bin Haroub (r 1911–60), and his two wives, each of whom clearly had very different tastes in furniture. Outside is the Makusurani graveyard, where some of the sultans are buried.

OLD FORT

Just south of the Beit el-Ajaib is the Old Fort (Map p134), a massive, bastioned structure originally built around 1700 on the site of a Portuguese chapel by Omani Arabs as a defence against the Portuguese. In recent years it has been partially renovated to house the **Zanzibar Cultural Centre**, and the offices of the Zanzibar International Film Festival (ZIFF). Inside is an open-air theatre for music and dance performances.

ANGLICAN CATHEDRAL & OLD SLAVE MARKET

Constructed in the 1870s by the Universities' Mission to Central Africa (UMCA), the **Anglican cathedral** (Map p134; admission TSh1000; ⊙ 8am-6pm Mon-Sat) was the first Anglican cathedral in East Africa. It was built on the site of the old slave market alongside Creek Rd, although nothing remains of the slave market today other than some holding cells under St Monica's Hostel next door. Services are still held at the cathedral on Sundays; the entrance is next to St Monica's Hostel.

ST JOSEPH'S CATHEDRAL

The spires of **St Joseph's Roman Catholic cathedral** (Map p134; Cathedral St) are one of the first sights travellers see when arriving at Zanzibar by ferry. Yet the church is deceptively difficult to find in the narrow confines of the adjacent streets. (Follow Kenyatta Rd to Gizenga St, then take the first right to the back gate of the church, which is usually open, even when the front entrance is closed.) The

cathedral, which was designed by French architect Beranger, celebrated its centenary in 1998, and is still in active use.

MOSQUES

The oldest of Stone Town's mosques is **Msikiti wa Balnara** (Malindi Minaret Mosque; Map p134), originally built in 1831, enlarged in 1841 and extended again by Seyyid Ali bin Said in 1890. Others include the **Aga Khan Mosque** (Map p134) and the impressive **Ijumaa Mosque** (Map p134). It's not permitted to enter many of the mosques, as they're all in active use, although exceptions may be made if you are appropriately dressed.

HAMAMNI PERSIAN BATHS

Built by Sultan Barghash in the late 19th century, these **baths** (Map p134; Hamamni St; admission TSh500), which are no longer functioning, were the first public baths on Zanzibar. To get in, ask the caretaker across the alley to unlock the gate.

BEIT EL-AMANI
(PEACE MEMORIAL MUSEUM)

The larger of the two buildings that make up **Beit el-Amani** (Map p134; cnr Kaunda & Creek Rds) previously contained a history of the island from its early days until independence, while the smaller building across the road housed a decaying natural history collection. Both are in the process of being merged with the Zanzibar National Museum of History & Culture at Beit el-Ajaib (p135), and are currently closed.

LIVINGSTONE HOUSE

About 2km north of town, **Livingstone House** (Map p131; Bububu Rd) was built around 1860 and used as a base by many European missionaries and explorers before they started their journeys to the mainland. David Livingstone also stayed here before setting off on his last expedition. The building now houses the Zanzibar Tourist Corporation. You can walk from town, or take a 'B' *daladala*.

OLD DISPENSARY

Near the port, the **Old Dispensary** (Map p134; Mizingani Rd) was built at the turn of the 20th century by a wealthy Indian merchant. It has been renovated by the Aga Khan Charitable Trust, and now houses boutiques and shops, and small displays of local artists' work.

FORODHANI GARDENS

One of the best ways to ease into life on the island is to stop by **Forodhani Gardens** (Jamituri Gardens; Map p134) in the evening, when the grassy plaza comes alive with dozens of vendors serving up such delicacies as grilled *pweza* (octopus), plates of goat meat, Zanzibari pizza (rolled-up, omelette-filled chapati), a thick, delicious local version of *naan*, plus piles of chips, samosas and more. The gardens are also a social meeting point, with women sitting on the grass chatting about the events of the day, children playing and men strolling along the waterfront. The gardens are along the seafront opposite the Old Fort.

DARAJANI MARKET

The dark, narrow passageways of chaotic Darajani market (Map p134) assault the senses, with occasional whiffs of spices mixing with the stench of fish, the clamour of vendors hawking their wares, brightly coloured piles of fruits and vegetables, and dozens of small shops selling everything from plastic tubs to auto spares. It's just off Creek Rd, and at its best in the morning, before the heat and the crowds, and when everything is still fresh.

VICTORIA HALL & GARDENS

The imposing Victoria Hall, which is diagonally across from Mnazi Mmoja hospital on Kaunda Rd, housed the legislative council during the British era. Today it's closed to the public, as is the State House, opposite.

Activities

DIVING & SNORKELLING

For more on diving around the archipelago, see p138. Most of the archipelago's dive operators also offer snorkelling. Equipment hire costs from US$5 to US$15; when you're selecting it, pay particular attention to getting a good mask. Most snorkelling sites are only accessible by boat. Trips average US$20 to US$50 per half day, often including a snack or lunch. Recommended operators include the following:

    Bahari Divers (Map p134; ☎ 0748-245786, 0747-415011; www.zanzibar-diving.com) is a small, family-friendly outfit that primarily organises dives around the islands offshore from Stone Town. The office is near NBC bank. They also have a base opposite Sharouk Guest

House (p156) in Wete for diving around Pemba.

    One Ocean/The Zanzibar Dive Centre (Map p134; ☎ 223 8374, 0748-750161; www.zanzibaroneocean.com) is a PADI five-star centre with more than a decade of experience on Zanzibar. They have several branches, including at Matemwe Beach Village (p146), and organise dives along the east coast, as well as around Stone Town. The main office – just down from the tunnel and NBC bank – hires underwater cameras, prescription masks and Suunto computers.

SPICE TOURS

While spices no longer dominate Zanzibar's economy as they once did, plantations still dot the centre of the island. It's possible to visit them – learning about what cloves, vanilla and other spices look like in the wild – on 'spice tours'. These half-day excursions take in some plantations, as well as ruins and other sights of historical interest.

    To organise things, try **Mr Mitu's office** (☎ 223 4636), signposted off Malawi Rd near Ciné Afrique. Tours cost US$10 per person in a group of 15, and include a lunch of local food seasoned with some of the spices you've just seen. They depart about 9.30am and return by about 2.30pm (later, if a stop at Mangapwani Beach is included). It's best to book a day in advance, though it's usually no trouble to just show up in the morning.

Festivals & Events

Muslim holidays are celebrated in a big way on Zanzibar; see p624. Other festivals include Mwaka Kogwa, the ZIFF and Sauti za Busara; for more information see p253.

Sleeping

BUDGET

Mkunazini

The following places are on the eastern edge of town near the Anglican cathedral:

    St Monica's Hostel (Map p134; ☎ 223 0773; monicas zanzibar@hotmail.com; s/d/tr with shared bathroom US$12/24/36, s/d with private bathroom US$28/32) An old, rambling place next to the Anglican cathedral, with spacious rooms, including some with a small veranda, and an inexpensive restaurant next door.

    Flamingo Guest House (Map p134; ☎ 223 2850; flamingoguesthouse@hotmail.com; Mkunazini St; s/d

TANZANIA

DIVING THE ZANZIBAR ARCHIPELAGO

The archipelago's turquoise waters are just as amazing below the surface as they are from above, with a magnificent array of hard and soft corals, and a diverse collection of sea creatures, including shadowy manta rays, hawksbill and green turtles, barracudas and sharks. Other draws include the possibility of wall dives, especially off Pemba; the fascinating cultural backdrop; and the opportunity to combine wildlife safaris with underwater exploration. On the down side, visibility isn't as reliable as in some areas of the world, although sometimes you'll be treated to ranges of 25m to 30m. Another thing to consider, if you're a serious diver and coming to the archipelago exclusively for diving, is that unless you do a live-aboard arrangement, you'll need to travel – often for up to an hour – to many of the dive sites. And prices are considerably higher than in places like the Red Sea or Thailand.

Seasons

Diving is possible year-round, although conditions vary dramatically. Late March until mid-June is generally the least favourable time because of erratic weather patterns and frequent storms. However, even during this period you can have some good days, particularly in March when water temperatures are also warmer. July or August through to February or March tend to be the best overall, although again, conditions vary and wind is an important factor. On Pemba, for example, the southeastern seas can be rough around June and July when the wind is blowing from the south, but calm and clear as glass from around November to late February when the monsoon winds blow from the north. On both islands, the calmest time is generally from around September to November during the lull between the annual monsoons.

Water temperatures range from lows of about 22°C in July and August to highs of about 29°C in February and March, with the average about 26°C. Throughout, 3mm wetsuits are standard; 4mm suits are recommended for some areas during the July to September winter months, and 2mm are fine from around December to March or April.

Costs, Courses & Planning

Costs are somewhat cheaper on Zanzibar than on Pemba. Expect to pay from US$350 for a four-day Professional Association of Dive Instructors (PADI) open-water course, about US$45/75 for a single-/double-dive package, and from about US$50 for a night dive. Most places discount about 10% if you have your own equipment, and for groups. In addition to open-water certification, many operators also offer other courses, including Advanced Open Water, Medic First Aid, Rescue Diver, and speciality courses including underwater photography and navigation.

As for deciding where to dive: very generally speaking, Zanzibar is known for the corals and shipwrecks offshore from Stone Town, and for fairly reliable visibility, high fish diversity and the chance to see pelagics to the north and northeast. While some sites are challenging, there are many easily accessed sites for beginner and midrange divers.

Unlike Zanzibar, which is a continental island, Pemba is an oceanic island located in a deep channel with a steeply dropping shelf. Because of this, diving tends to be more challenging, with an emphasis on wall and drift dives, though there are some sheltered areas for beginners, especially around Misali Island. Most dives are to the west around Misali, and to the north around the Njao Gap.

For more on diving, see p619. Dive operators are listed by location elsewhere in this chapter.

---

with shared bathroom US$8/16, with private bathroom US$10/20) No-frills but fine, with straightforward rooms and a TV. They're often willing to negotiate on prices.

Jambo Guest House (Map p134; ☎ 223 3779; jambo guest@hotmail.com; s/d/tr with shared bathroom US$15/20/30; ☒) Just around the corner from Fla-

mingo Guest House, Jambo has free tea and coffee, clean rooms and an Iternet café opposite.

Soko Muhogo

South of Mkunazini, off Soko Muhogo St, are a few more good places:

Haven Guest House (Map p134; ☎ 223 5677/8; s/d US$15/25) Clean rooms, a travellers' bulletin board, free coffee and tea and a small kitchenette.

Manch Lodge (Map p134; ☎ 223 1918; moddybest@yahoo.com; r per person US$10) Around the corner from Haven Guest House, and similar, though without the kitchenette; some rooms have bathroom.

Vuga

Near the southern edge of Stone Town, around Vuga Rd:

Florida Guest House (Map p134; ☎ 0747-421421, 0747-411335; floridaznz@yahoo.com; Vuga Rd; r per person US$15) Small, clean rooms (check out a few as they're all different) – many with bathroom – and solicitous proprietors. It's next to Culture Musical Club, and there are discounts for stays of over two days.

Garden Lodge (Map p134; ☎ 223 3298; gardenlodge@zanlink.com; Kaunda Rd; s/d/tr downstairs US$15/25/35, upstairs US$25/40/50) Friendly, family-run and somewhat pricier than others in this category, but the location – diagonally across from the High Court – is convenient and the upstairs rooms are spacious and good value.

Victoria House (Map p134; ☎ 223 2861; r per person with shared bathroom US$10) Dilapidated but spacious rooms, including a quad with its own shower, and an agreeably green location just off Kaunda Rd.

Malindi

On the northern side of town, and about a five-minute walk from the port, is another clutch of lodges:

Malindi Guest House (Map p134; ☎ 223 0165; malindi@zanzinet.com; s/d with shared bathroom US$20/30, with private bathroom US$25/40; ✷) Whitewashed walls and atmospheric rooms.

Warere Town House (Map p134; ☎ 223 3835; www.wareretownhouse.com; s/d US$20/40) Good-value rooms – some with small balconies and all with hot water and fan – plus a rooftop terrace. It's just minutes from the port, around the corner from Bandari Lodge.

Bandari Lodge (Map p134; ☎ 223 7969, 0747-423638; r per person US$12) Straightforward rooms, plus a common kitchen and fridge. Turn right as you exit the port; it's just two minutes ahead.

Malindi Lodge (Map p134; ☎ 223 2350; sunset bungalows@hotmail.com; Funguni Rd; s/d US$15/25; ✷)

Clean and nicely decorated, and with hot water and cheaper annex rooms nearby; it's just around the corner from Malindi Guest House.

Hotel Kiponda (Map p134; ☎ 223 3052; hotel kiponda@email.com; Nyumba ya Moto St; s/d/tr with shared bathroom US$18/35/45, d/tr with private bathroom US$45/55) Spotless rooms in a convenient location, tucked away in a small lane near the waterfront. There's also a restaurant.

MIDRANGE
Shangani

Most midrange places are in or near Shangani.

Baghani House Hotel (Map p134; ☎ 223 5654; baghani@zanzinet.com; s US$40, d US$50-60) This atmospheric hotel has characterful rooms – most on the upper level, reached via a steep staircase – dark wood and Zanzibari furnishings. Advance bookings and reconfirmations are recommended. It's just off Kenyatta Rd.

Chavda Hotel (Map p134; ☎ 223 2115; chavda@zanzinet.com, Baghani St; s/d US$70/90) Chavda is a quiet, reliable hotel with some period décor, a range of bland, carpeted rooms with TV, telephone and minibar, and a rooftop bar and restaurant (high season only). It's just around the corner from Baghani House Hotel.

Mazsons Hotel (Map p134; ☎ 223 3694; mazsons@zanlink.com; Kenyatta Rd; s/d US$60/80; ✷) The long-standing Mazsons has impressively restored lobby woodwork and a convenient location that go some way to compensating for its soulless rooms.

Shangani Hotel (Map p134; ☎ 223 3688, 223 6363; shanganihotel@hotmail.com; Kenyatta Rd; s/d US$65/80) An unpretentious place opposite Shangani post office with cluttered but comfortable rooms, most with TV, fridge and fan. It also has a restaurant.

Elsewhere in Stone Town

Outside the Shangani area are several more choices.

Clove Hotel (Map p134; ☎ 0747-484567; www.zanzibarhotel.nl; Hurumzi St; s/d US$30/45, family r US$55) Painted in pleasing shades of lavender and peach, Clove has good-value rooms with nets and fan. The family rooms also have small balconies with views down onto the small square below. On the rooftop is a terrace for breakfast, drinks and views.

Hotel International (Map p134; ☎ 223 3182; hotel inter@zanlink.com; s/d US$45/60; ✷) This cavernous, multistorey place is just off Kiponda St, with a forex bureau, a restaurant and rather soulless rooms, though some aren't bad. Check a few, and avoid those on the lower floor. Most have TV, fridge and small balcony, and there's a rooftop terrace.

TOP END

Shangani

Zanzibar Serena Inn (Map p134; ☎ 223 3587; zserena@zanzinet.com; Kelele Sq; s/d from US$210/265; ❄ 🏊) The Zanzibar Serena, in the refurbished Ex-telecoms House, is Zanzibar Town's most upmarket accommodation, with a beautiful setting on the water, plush rooms with all the amenities, and a business centre.

Beyt al-Chai (Map p134; ☎ 0747-444111; www.stonetowninn.com; Kelele Sq; s US$75-200, d US$100-225) A good new place opposite Zanzibar Serena Inn, with six rooms, each individually designed, and all with period décor. For a splurge, try one of the Sultan suites, with views to the sea in the distance, and raised Jacuzzi-style baths.

Tembo House Hotel (Map p134; ☎ 223 3005; www.tembohotel.com; s/d from US$85/95; ❄ 🏊) This attractively restored building has a waterfront location, and modern rooms – some with sea views – in new and old wings. Most have a TV and fridge. The hotel also has a restaurant and a buffet breakfast. No alcohol is served; the hotel is a favourite with tour groups.

Dhow Palace (Map p134; ☎ 223 3012; dhowpalace@zanlink.com; s/d US$60/90; 🕑 Jun-Mar; 🏊) This is another classic place with old Zanzibari décor, a fountain in the tastefully restored lobby and small but well-appointed rooms. It's just off Kenyatta Rd.

Hurumzi

Emerson & Green (Map p134; ☎ 0747-423266; www.emerson-green.com; Hurumzi St; r US$165-200) Emerson & Green – in two adjacent historic buildings that have been completely restored – is full of character and has become a Zanzibar institution. Each room is unique – one even has its own private rooftop teahouse – and all are decadently decorated to give you an idea of what Zanzibar must have been like in its heyday. It's several winding blocks east of the Old Fort.

Outside Stone Town

Just outside Stone Town are a few more options that make agreeable bases if you want proximity to the town as well as greenery and relaxing surroundings.

Mbweni Ruins Hotel (Map p131; ☎ 223 5478/9; www.mbweni.com; s/d US$100/180; ❄ 🏊) Mbweni is a quiet, genteel establishment set in wonderful, lushly vegetated gardens about 5km from town, and several kilometres off the airport road. In addition to well-appointed rooms and a relaxing ambience, it has stands of mangroves for bird-watching and a very good restaurant, and is well worth a splurge. The property was formerly the site of the UMCA mission school for the children of freed slaves.

Mtoni Marine Centre (Map p131; ☎ 225 0140; mtoni@zanzibar.cc; s/d US$60/80, deluxe s/d US$80/120, 4-/6-person bungalows US$60/90; ❄ 💻 🏊) This family-friendly establishment has a range of rooms plus some older cottages set around pleasant gardens. It has a nice beach, a popular waterside bar and good dining in the main restaurant. It's about 3km north of town along the Bububu road.

Eating

Note that during the low season and Ramadan many restaurants close or operate for reduced hours.

RESTAURANTS

La Fenice (Map p134; ☎ 0747-411868; Shangani St; meals about TSh8000; 🕑 lunch & dinner) A breezy little patch of Italy on the waterfront, with outdoor tables where you can enjoy your pasta while gazing out at the turquoise sea in front of you. For dessert, try a scoop of homemade ice cream.

Amore Mio (Map p134; Shangani St; 🕑 high season) Across the road from La Fenice. This has delectable ice cream as well as light meals, cappuccino and other coffees, served against a wonderful seaside backdrop.

Monsoon Restaurant (Map p134; ☎ 0747-411362, 0747-410410; meals TSh4000-12,000; 🕑 noon-midnight) The impeccably decorated Monsoon offers traditional dining on floor cushions, and Swahili cuisine served to a backdrop of *taarab* music, *ngoma* or *kidumbak*. It's at the southwestern edge of Forodhani Gardens.

Archipelago Café-Restaurant (Map p134; ☎ 223 5668; mains from TSh3500-6000; 🕑 lunch & dinner) This new place has a breezy location on a 1st-floor terrace overlooking the water just opposite NBC bank in Shangani, and has a menu featuring such delicacies as vegetable coconut curry, and orange and ginger snapper, plus an array of homemade cakes and sweets. There's no bar, but you can bring your own alcohol.

Sweet Eazy (Map p134; ☎ 0745-768433; meals TSh5000-10,000; ☉ noon-midnight) With its relaxing ambience, good Thai and African cuisine, and varied entertainment offerings, this place is one of Stone Town's more popular evening destinations. It's also one of the few spots in town where you can get food late at night. It's on the waterfront near NBC bank.

Emerson's & Green Tower Top Restaurant (Map p134; ☎ 0747-423266; www.emerson-green.com; Hurumzi St; meals US$25-30; ☉ dinner) Dinner at this rooftop restaurant has become a Zanzibari institution, and while its popularity means that it is no longer the intimate dining experience it once was, it still makes an enjoyable evening out. The menu is fixed, and reservations are essential. On Friday, Saturday and Sunday, meals are served to a backdrop of traditional music and dance.

Mtoni Marine Centre (Map p131; ☎ 225 0140; mtoni@zanzinet.cc; meals TSh8000-TSh20,000; ☉ dinner) The main restaurant here offers a range of seafood and meat grills, and waterside barbecues (TSh17,500) on Tuesday and Saturday, with a backdrop of *taarab* or other traditional music.

Mercury's (☎ 223 3076; meals about TSh5000; ☉ 10am-midnight) Named in honour of Queen vocalist Freddie Mercury (who was born just a few blocks away), this is one of Stone Town's main waterside hang-outs. On offer are seafood grills and pizzas, a well-stocked bar and a terrace that's a prime location for sipping sundowners.

Radha Food House (☎ 223 4808; thalis TSh4500) This great little place is tucked away on the small side street just before the Shangani tunnel. The menu – strictly vegetarian – has *thalis, lassis,* homemade yogurt and other dishes from the subcontinent.

Sambusa Two Tables Restaurant (☎ 223 1979; meals TSh10,000; ☉ dinner) For sampling authentic Zanzibari dishes, it's hard to beat this small, family-run restaurant off Kaunda Rd, where the proprietors bring out course after course of delicious local delicacies. Advance reservations are required.

China Plate Restaurant (☎ 0744-490796; meals TSh3000-6000; ☉ lunch & dinner) Tasty Chinese food served on a breezy 1st-floor terrace overlooking the water. It's just next to NBC.

Zanzibar Serena Inn (☎ 223 2306, 223 3587; zserena@zanzinet.com; meals TSh9000; ☉ lunch & dinner) Fine dining overlooking the sea, with a Swahili buffet (US$25) on Wednesday evening.

Livingstone Beach Restaurant (☎ 0748-694803; meals TSh7000-10,000) A new place in the old British Consulate Building, and opposite Sweet Eazy, about to open when we passed through, with beachside seating and seafood and other dishes.

QUICK EATS
Forodhani Gardens (meals TSh500; ☉ dinner) These waterside gardens (p137) feature vendors selling piles of grilled fish and meat, chips and snacks, served up on a paper plate or rolled into a piece of newspaper, and eaten while sitting on benches or the lawn, soaking up the atmosphere and enjoying the passing scene. Locals advise against eating fish and meat during the height of the low season (when food turnover is slower), but countless travellers come here, and we've never heard of any problems. Watch for overcharging.

For a much more subdued version of Forodhani, without the sea views, head to Creek Rd opposite Darajani market, where a small collection of vendors serve up equally good street food at rock-bottom prices.

There are also plenty of local-style places where you can eat well for under TSh3000:

Passing Show (Map p134; Malawi Rd; meals from TSh500) A Zanzibar institution, with piping hot bowls of beans and rice, spicy biriyani and similar fare.

Fany's Green Restaurant (Map p134; ☎ 223 3918; ☉ 7.30am-10pm; meals TSh3500) More tourist-oriented. Near Shangani post office.

Shamshuddin's Cash & Carry (Map p134; Soko St) Behind Darajani market. The best bet for self-caterers.

Drinking & Entertainment
Stone Town isn't known for its nightlife, but there are a few popular spots.

BARS & NIGHTCLUBS
Africa House Hotel (Map p134; Shangani St) Sundowners daily from the upstairs terrace bar overlooking the sea.

Sweet Eazy (Map p134; ☎ 0745-768433; znz@sweet eazy.com) Live music Friday and Saturday evenings, daily happy hour and sundowners overlooking the water. See also left.

Mercury's (Map p134; ☎ 223 3076) Waterside sundowners, and live music many nights. See also left.

Garage Club (Map p134; Shangani St; ☺ from 10pm Wed-Mon) Stone Town's main disco. Diagonally across from Tembo House Hotel; taxis wait outside.

Dharma Lounge (Shangani St; ☺ 5pm-late Wed-Mon; ☒) Zanzibar's first and only cocktail lounge, with a good selection of music. It's next to the Garage Club.

Mcheza Bar (Map p131; Mtoni Marine Centre) A sports bar that draws a mainly expat crowd. See also p140.

Starehe Club (Shangani St) Very laid-back (sometimes it doesn't happen at all), with occasional reggae nights.

TRADITIONAL MUSIC & DANCE
On Tuesday, Thursday and Saturday evenings from 7pm to 10pm, there are traditional *ngoma* performances at the Old Fort (TSh5000, with dinner TSh10,000), although be prepared for rather flat tourist displays.

Shopping
Stone Town has wonderfully atmospheric craft shopping, and if you can sort your way through some of the kitsch, there are some excellent buys to be found. The best place to start is Gizenga St, which is lined with small shops and craft dealers.

Zanzibar Gallery (Map p134; ☎ 223 2721; gallery@swahilicoast.com; cnr Kenyatta Rd & Gizenga St; ☺ 9am-7pm Mon-Sat, to 1pm Sun) Has a large collection of

souvenirs, textiles, woodcarvings, antiques and more, in addition to its books.

Memories of Zanzibar (☎ 223 9376; memories@zanzinet.com; Kenyatta Rd) Just down the road, with a selection of jewellery, textiles and curios.

Getting There & Away
AIR
Daily flights with Coastal Aviation and ZanAir connect Zanzibar with Dar es Salaam (US$55), Arusha (US$140 to US$175), Pemba (US$70), Selous Game Reserve (US$130) and the northern parks. Coastal Aviation also goes daily to/from Tanga via Pemba (US$80). Air Tanzania flies daily between Zanzibar and Dar es Salaam, with connections to Nairobi, and Precision Air/Kenya Airways have direct flights between Zanzibar, Dar es Salaam, Nairobi and Mombasa.

There are direct international connections from Zanzibar on Oman Air via Muscat.

Airline offices in Zanzibar Town include the following:

Air Tanzania (Map p134; ☎ 223 0213; Shangani St) Diagonally across from Tembo Hotel.

Coastal Aviation (Map p134; ☎ 223 3112, 0747-334582) Next to Zanzibar Serena Inn, and at the airport.

Kenya Airways (Map p134; ☎ 223 4521; Kenyatta Rd) Together with Precision Air.

Oman Air (Map p134; ☎ 223 8308; Mizingani Rd) Just southeast of the Big Tree.

TAARAB MUSIC

No visit to Zanzibar would be complete without spending an evening listening to the evocative strains of *taarab*, the archipelago's most famous musical export, combining African, Arabic and Indian influences.

Taarab-style music was played in Zanzibar as early as the 1820s at the sultan's palace, where it had been introduced from Arabia. However, it wasn't until the 1900s, when Sultan Seyyid Hamoud bin Muhammed encouraged formation of the first *taarab* clubs, that it became more formalised. The performances themselves are quite an event, and audience participation is key. There is also always a singer involved, with themes centring around love, and many puns and double meanings intertwined.

Famous *taarab* singers include Siti Binti Saad, who was the first *taarab* singer on the archipelago, and Bi Kidude, the first lady of *taarab* music, who helped popularise *taarab* clubs. Today most Zanzibaris distinguish between 'old *taarab*', which is played by an orchestra using primarily traditional instruments, and 'modern *taarab*', which expands *taarab*'s traditional base with keyboards, guitars and synthesised sound.

For an introduction to *taarab* music you can stop by the Zanzibar Serena Inn (p140), where a group called the Twinkling Stars plays from about 6pm to 7.30pm on Tuesday and Friday. For something livelier, head to the **Culture Musical Club** (Map p134; Vuga Rd; admission TSh1000, sometimes free; ☺ Tue-Sat), with rehearsals from about 7.30pm Monday to Friday. An excellent time to see *taarab* performances is during the Festival of the Dhow Countries (p253) in July.

Precision Air (Map p134; ☎ 223 4521; Kenyatta Rd) Next to Mazsons Hotel.

ZanAir (Map p134; ☎ 223 3670) Just off Malindi Rd, opposite Ciné Afrique.

BOAT

For ferry connections between Zanzibar and Dar es Salaam, see p125. For ferry connections between Zanzibar and Pemba, see p154 and p157. You can get tickets at the port or through a travel agent. If you leave Zanzibar on the *Flying Horse* night ferry, take care with your valuables, especially when the boat docks in Dar es Salaam in the early morning hours.

Foreigners are not permitted on dhows between Dar es Salaam and Zanzibar. For other routes, ask around at the beach behind Tembo House Hotel (p140), though captains are generally unwilling to take tourists. Allow from 10 to 48 hours or more to reach the mainland. Also see p261.

TRAIN

Riverman Hotel (Map p134), near the Anglican Cathedral, makes bookings for the Tazara line for a TSh1000 fee; you pay for the ticket at the Tazara station in Dar es Salaam.

Getting Around

TO/FROM THE AIRPORT

The airport is about 7km southeast of Zanzibar Town and it costs TSh6000 to TSh10,000 to travel between them in a taxi, depending on your negotiating skills. The No 505 bus line also does this route, departing from the corner opposite Mnazi Mmoja hospital. Many Stone Town hotels offer free airport pick-ups for confirmed bookings, though some charge. Hotels elsewhere on the island charge about US$30, depending on location.

CAR & MOTORCYCLE

It's easy to arrange car, moped or motorcycle hire. Prices are reasonable, although breakdowns are fairly common, as are moped accidents. Considering how small the island is, it's often more straightforward and not that much more expensive just to work out a good deal with a taxi driver.

You'll need either an international driving licence, a licence from Kenya, Uganda or South Africa, or a Zanzibar permit. Zanzibar permits can be obtained on the spot at the **traffic police office** (Malindi, cnr Malawi & Creek Rds) for TSh6000, or through any tour company.

Daily hire rates average about US$25 for a moped, US$30 for a motorcycle, and from US$50 to US$70 for a Suzuki 4WD. You can hire through any of the tour companies; through **Asko Tours & Travel** (Map p134; ☎ 0747-422841; askotour@hotmail.com; Kenyatta Rd), next to Shangani post office; or by asking around in front of the market, near the bus stand. If you're not mechanically minded, bring someone along who can check that the motorbike or vehicle you're hiring is in reasonable condition, and take a test drive. Full payment is usually required at the time of delivery, but don't pay any advance deposits.

DALADALAS

Open-sided pick-ups (*daladalas*) packed with people and produce link all major towns on the island, leaving from Creek Rd opposite Darajani market. For most destinations, including all the main beaches, there are several vehicles daily, with the last ones back to Stone Town departing by about 3pm or 4pm. None of the routes cost more than TSh1000, and all take plenty of time (eg about three hours from Zanzibar Town to Jambiani). Commonly used routes:

Route	Destination
101	Mkokotoni
116	Nungwi
117	Kiwengwa
118	Matemwe
121	Donge
206	Chwaka
214	Uroa
308	Unguja Ukuu
309	Jambiani
310	Makunduchi
324	Bwejuu
326	Kizimkazi
501	Amani
502	Bububu
504	Fuoni
505	Airport (marked 'U/Ndege')
509	Chukwani
510	Mtoni/Kidatu

PRIVATE MINIVAN

Private minivans run daily to Nungwi and to Paje, Bwejuu and Jambiani on the east

TANZANIA

coast, although stiff competition and hassles with touts mean that a splurge on a taxi isn't a bad idea. Book through any travel agency the day before you want to travel, and the vans will pick you up at your hotel in Stone Town between 8am and 9am. Travel takes 1½ to two hours to any of the destinations, and costs a negotiable TSh3000 per person. Don't believe anything about a hotel's status until you see it yourself, and insist on being taken to the destination you'd originally agreed on. Also, don't pay for the return trip in advance, as you may see neither the driver nor your money again.

TAXI
Taxis don't have meters, so agree on a price with the driver before getting into the car. Town trips cost TSh1000 to TSh2000.

AROUND ZANZIBAR
Ruins
There are a number of historical sites around Zanzibar Town, many of which are included in spice tours (see p137).

MBWENI
Mbweni, around 5km south of Zanzibar Town, was the site of a 19th-century UMCA mission station that was used as a settlement for freed slaves. In addition to the small and still functioning St John's Anglican church, dating to the 1880s, you can see the atmospheric ruins of the UMCA's St Mary's School for Girls, set amid lush gardens in the grounds of the Mbweni Ruins Hotel.

MARUHUBI PALACE
The once-imposing Maruhubi palace, about 4km north of Zanzibar Town, was built by Sultan Barghash in 1882 to house his large harem. In 1899 it was destroyed by fire, although the remaining ruins – primarily columns that once supported an upper terrace, an overhead aqueduct and small reservoirs covered with water lilies – hint at its previous scale. The ruins are just west of the Bububu road and are signposted.

MTONI PALACE
The ruins of Mtoni palace, built by Sultan Seyyid Said as his residence in the early 19th century, are just northeast of Maruhubi. In its heyday the palace was a beautiful building with a balconied exterior, an observation turret and a mosque. By the mid-1880s it had been abandoned, and today nothing remains of Mtoni's grandeur other than a few walls, although you can get an idea of how it once must have looked by reading Emily Said-Reute's Memoirs of an Arabian Princess. Continue north past the Maruhubi palace turn-off for about 2km, from where the ruins are signposted to the west.

KIDICHI PERSIAN BATHS
The Persian Baths, northeast of Zanzibar Town, are another construction of Sultan Seyyid, built in 1850 for his Persian wife at the island's highest point. Like the other nearby ruins, they're rather unremarkable now, but with a bit of imagination, you can see the Sultan's lavishly garbed coterie disrobing to test the waters. Take a 502 daladala to the Bububu junction, from where it's about a 3km walk east down an unpaved road.

Mangapwani Caves
The Mangapwani caves are located about 20km north of Zanzibar Town along the coast. There are actually two locations. The first is a large **natural cave** with a freshwater pool, supposedly used in connection with the slave trade. North of here is the sobering **slave cave**, a dank, dark cell that was used as a holding pen to hide slaves after the legal trade was abolished in the late 19th century.

Follow the main road north past Bububu to Chuini, from where you head left down a dirt road for about 8km towards Mangapwani village. Continue towards the sea until you see a small sign for the slave cave. Daladalas also run between Stone Town and Mangapwani village.

Beaches
Zanzibar has superb beaches, with the best along the island's east coast and to the north. Although some have become overcrowded and built-up, all offer a wonderful respite from bumping along dusty roads on the mainland. The east coast beaches are protected by coral reefs offshore and have fine, white coral sand. Depending on the season, they may also have lots of seaweed (most abundant from December to February).

Everyone has a favourite, and which beach you choose is a matter of preference. For meeting other travellers, enjoying some nightlife, and staying at relatively inexpensive accommodation, the best choices are Nungwi in the north, followed by Paje on the east coast. Bwejuu and Jambiani on the east coast are also popular – and among the finest stretches of palm-fringed sand you'll look anywhere – but everything is more spread out and quieter than in the north. For a much quieter atmosphere, try Matemwe, Pongwe or the northern end of Kiwengwa. If you're seeking the large resort scene, the main area is the beach north of Kiwengwa towards Pwani Mchangani. Except for Nungwi (and nearby Kendwa Beach), where you can take a dip at any time, swimming at all of the beaches is tide dependent.

BUBUBU (FUJI BEACH)
This modest stretch of sand, 10km north of town in Bububu, is the closest place to Zanzibar Town for swimming. It's accessed via the dirt track heading west from just north of the Bububu police station.

Bububu Beach Guest House (☎ 225 0110; www .bububu-zanzibar.com; s/d US$15/30) is a budget haunt that has airy no-frills rooms near the beach and meals on request. It's at the end of the dirt track heading west from the Bububu police station; you can arrange free transport from the airport or Stone Town.

NUNGWI
This big village, at Zanzibar's northernmost tip, is a dhow-building centre and one of the island's major tourist destinations. It's also where traditional and modern knock against each other with full force. On the beautiful white-sand beach, fishermen sit in the shade repairing their nets while the morning's catch dries on neat wooden racks nearby. Yet take a few steps back from the sand and enter into another world, with blaring music, a motley collection of guesthouses, and a definite party atmosphere. For some travellers it's the only place to be on the island; others will likely want to give it a wide berth. Most hotels, the better beaches, and the centre of all the action are just north and west of Nungwi village, where it can get quite crowded. The eastern side of the peninsula is much quieter, with a few hotels set on low cliffs overlooking the water and small patches of beach.

Information
There's Internet access at Amaan Bungalows and at Nungwi Inn Hotel, and a forex bureau

at Amaan Bungalows that changes cash and travellers cheques at bad rates.

Diving
For more on diving around Zanzibar, see p138. Locally based operators include the following:

Ras Nungwi Beach Hotel (☎ 223 3767; www.ras nungwi.com) A PADI five-star centre based at Ras Nungwi Beach Hotel.

Scuba Do (☎ 0748-415179; www.scuba-do-zanzibar) Kendwa's only PADI dive centre; just north of Kendwa Rocks.

Sleeping & Eating – Budget
All the beach places are within a few minutes walk of each other.

Cholo's (camping US$5; bandas per person with shared bathroom US$10) Very chilled out, and the only spot to pitch a tent; it also has some basic *bandas*, plus Nungwi's best bar.

Jambo Brothers (s/d with shared bathroom US$15/25) Low key, with clean, no-frills rooms on the sand, and meals (order early). It's just next to Cholo's.

Union Beach Bungalows (s/d with shared bathroom US$15/25) Next to Jambo Brothers, and another agreeable shoestring option.

Amaan Bungalows (☎ 224 0026; www.amaan bungalows.com; standard s US$25-40, d US$30-60, s/d with sea views US$50/75; 🖳) At the centre of activity, and the biggest place, with various levels of accommodation, including nicer sea-view rooms, plus several restaurants (meals around TSh5000).

Baraka Beach Bungalows (☎ 0747 415569; baraka bungalow@hotmail.com; s/d US$20/40) Small and friendly, just around the bend from Amaan Bungalows.

Sleeping & Eating – Midrange & Top End
Most places in this category are on Nungwi's eastern side.

Mnarani Beach Cottages (☎ 224 0494; www.light housezanzibar.com; s/d US$60/84, d/q family cottage US$104/177) This small lodge is the first place you come to on the placid eastern side of Nungwi. It's set on a small outcrop overlooking the sea, with a dozen unassuming cottages, some with sea views, plus a few larger sea-facing family cottages with minifridge, and a honeymoon chalet.

Ras Nungwi Beach Hotel (☎ 223 3767; www.ras nungwi.com; s/d full board US$195/270, with sea view from US$235/350; 🌓 Jun-Mar) The most upmarket hotel at Nungwi, with a low-key ambience, airy chalets nestled on a hillside overlooking the sea, and less expensive 'garden view' rooms in the main lodge. It's about 1km south of Mnarani Beach Cottages.

Flame Tree Cottages (☎ 224 0100; www.flametree cottages.com; s/d/tr/70/90/105; ☾ Jun-Mar; ✷) A good midrange choice for quiet and relaxation, with spotless, comfortable bungalows, all with nets, small porches and kitchenette use (US$10 per day extra). It's on the eastern edge of central Nungwi.

Baobab Beach Bungalows (www.baobabbeach bungalows.com; s US$50-90, d US$60-130) At the northwestern end of Nungwi, after the crush of budget places, and a bit quieter, with standard bungalows plus some nice 'deluxe' rooms that are closer to the beach, and worth the splurge.

Smiles Beach Hotel (☎ 224 0472; smilesbeachhotel@ zanzinet.com; s/d US$65/85; ✷) Smiles – on the eastern edge of Nungwi centre – has two-storey cottages overlooking a manicured lawn and the beach, with more space and quiet than at the other central Nungwi hotels.

Getting There & Away

Bus 116 runs daily between Nungwi and Zanzibar Town (TSh700), but most travellers go via private minivan (p143).

KENDWA

To the southwest of Nungwi is Kendwa, a long, wide stretch of sand known among other things for its laid-back atmosphere and its full-moon parties. Apart from the full-moon parties, when it's loud until the wee hours, the beach is quieter than at Nungwi, and more spread out, without Nungwi's crush of activity and accommodation. Offshore are some reefs for snorkelling, and at high tide you still have some beach – unlike at Nungwi, where it essentially disappears.

Sleeping & Eating

White Sands (☎ 0747-480987; www.zanzibar-white -sands-hotel.com; d US$40-70) One of Kendwa's best, with cheery, good-value en suite cottages on a small cliff above the beach – all have bathroom and fan, and all but the cheapest have hot water – and a great beach-side bar and restaurant.

La Rosa dei Venti (☎ 0747-411314; www.rosazanzibar .com; 2-3 person bungalow US$75, s/d US$30/45, club s/d US$35/55) Friendly and family-run, this small guesthouse is set just behind a grove of palm

trees leading down to the beach, with a few simple but spacious bungalows, or smaller rooms in the main family house.

Kendwa Rocks (☎ 0747-415475; www.kendwarocks .com; bandas per person US$12, s/d from US$30/45) A Kendwa classic, with beach *bandas*, simple wooden bungalows on the sand, some cooler stone and thatch versions nearby and the biggest full-moon parties.

Sunset Bungalows (☎ 223 2350; sunsetbungalows@ hotmail.com; d cottages US$35-45, beachfront with air-con US$55; ✷) Straightforward cottages on a small cliff overlooking the beach, plus some pricier ones closer to the water and a beach-side bar-restaurant.

Amaan Kendwa Beach Resort (☎ 0747 492552; amaankendwa@hotmail.com; s/d US$40/60, with sea view US$50/75) Huge and sprawling, with three rows of rooms on a hillside sloping down to the beach. Most face the garden (or the back of the row in front), but a few have sea views. There's a waterside restaurant.

Getting There & Away

You can walk to Kendwa from Nungwi at low tide in about 25 to 30 minutes, but take care as there have been some muggings. Alternatively, inexpensive boats go from near Amaan Bungalows a few times daily depending on demand. From Stone Town, have the 116 *daladala* drop you at the sign for Kendwa Rocks (a few kilometres south of Nungwi), from where it's about a 2km walk to the beach.

MATEMWE

The long, idyllic beach at Matemwe has some of the finest sand on Zanzibar. It's also the best base for diving and snorkelling around Mnemba, which lies just offshore.

Sleeping & Eating

Matemwe Beach Village (☎ 223 8374, 0747-413656; www.matemwebeach.com; s/d from US$65/100, ste half board US$200-350; ☾ Jun–mid Apr; ✷) This recommended beachfront place has a seaside setting, an agreeably low-key ambience and cosy bungalows with small verandas. There's also a plush honeymoon suite with its own plunge pool, plus several very nice two-storey 'shamba suites'. One Ocean/The Zanzibar Dive Centre (see p137) has a branch here, which means if you dive with it in Stone Town, you can get in some east-coast diving as well. In Stone Town, book through One Ocean, which can also help with transport arrangements.

Matemwe Bungalows (☎ 027-250 2799; www .matemwe.com; s/d full board US$250/400; ☒ mid-Jun–Easter; ☒) Matemwe Bungalows, about 1km north of Matemwe Beach Village, is a relaxing, upmarket place with spacious bungalows lined up along the sea – all with their own veranda and hammock – a genteel, pampered atmosphere and consistently rave reviews. There are also more luxurious suites, including one for honeymooners.

Matemwe Baharini Villas (☎ 0747-417768; www .matemwevillas.com; s/d villa US$30/50, s/d bungalow US$40/70) On the beach between Matemwe Beach Village and Matemwe Bungalows, with a choice of rooms; all have been recently renovated. There's a restaurant.

There are also several shoestring places, including **Mohammed's Place** (☎ 0747-431881; r per person with shared bathroom US$10), with three very simple rooms in a local house set away from the beach in Matemwe village.

Getting There & Away

Daladalas travel here daily from Stone Town (two hours), passing the Matemwe Beach Village hotel on the way, and stopping within about 2km of Matemwe Bungalows.

KIWENGWA

Kiwengwa village is spread out along a fine, wide beach, much of which is occupied by large, Italian-run resort hotels, although there are some quieter stretches to the north and south.

The cosy and intimate **Shooting Star Lodge** (☎ 0747-414166; www.zanzibar.org/star; d garden lodge/ sea view from US$110/205; ☒) is an excellent choice, with tastefully decorated stone-and-thatch cottages on a small cliff overlooking the sea, plus some equally nice 'lodge rooms' set around a garden, as well as superb cuisine and a good stretch of beach. The overall ambience is tranquil, and the lodge is an ideal place to relax. It's at the far northern end of Kiwengwa.

Reef View (☎ 0747-413294, 414030; banda per person with shared bathroom US$15, d US$50) is the only budget option, with *makuti* (palm leaf–thatched) *bandas* sharing facilities, plus an en suite double, a restaurant and a book exchange. It's on the beach about 20 minutes walk south of Kiwengwa centre (along the beach at low tide). Alternatively, you can

pay the 117 bus driver about TSh1000 extra to be taken there.

Bluebay Beach Resort (☎ 2240240/1; www.bluebay zanzibar.com; d half board US$240-510; ☒ ☒ ☒) One of the nicer Kiwengwa resorts, with expansive grounds and a quieter, more subdued atmosphere than those of its neighbours.

PONGWE

This quiet arc of beach, about 5km south of Kiwengwa, is dotted with palm trees and backed by dense vegetation, and is about as close to the quintessential tropical paradise as you can get.

The attractive, intimate and unassuming **Pongwe Beach Hotel** (☎ 0748-336181; www.pongwe .com; s/d US$70/110) has just 10 bungalows (including one honeymoon bungalow with a large Zanzibari bed), nestled among the palms on the best section of beach. All are sea-facing, spacious and breezy, the cuisine is good, and when you tire of the turquoise panoramas at your doorstep, you can amuse yourself with such pursuits as game fishing and deep-sea fishing or excursions to Stone Town.

Santa Maria Coral Park (☎ 0747-432655; www .santamaria-zanzibar.com; s US$25-35, d US$35-50) is a laid-back budget haunt on a lovely stretch of sand just south of Pongwe Beach Hotel and Pongwe village. There are a handful of simple *makuti bandas*, a restaurant and a beachside bar with evening bonfires.

UROA

This centreless village lies on an attractive and seldom-visited stretch of beach that's of similar appeal to that at nearby Chwaka (p148), just to the south.

Tamarind Beach Hotel (☎ 223 7154, 0747-411191; www.tamarind.nu; s/d US$40/60) is one of the oldest hotels on the east coast, and an ideal choice for families. Accommodation is in good-value bungalows within just a few metres of a placid pine-fringed beach, all with sea views, a small porch and a pleasing, homy ambience. There's a restaurant, and staff can organise excursions to Michamvi or Stone Town.

The 214 *daladala* runs between Zanzibar Town and Uroa several times daily. Sometimes you can get this at Darajani market, but usually you need to take bus 501 (Amani Stadium) to Mwembe Radu junction (just ask the *daladala* driver), where you can pick up the 214. Alternatively, bus 206 (Chwaka) sometimes continues northwards as far as Uroa. The last departure from Uroa back to Stone Town is about 4pm.

CHWAKA

Chwaka, a small fishing village on Chwaka Bay, due east of Zanzibar Town, doesn't receive too many visitors these days, and as a consequence has a sleepy charm. The modest beach is below average compared with others on Zanzibar's east coast.

Chwaka Bay Resort (☎ 224 0289; s/d with fan US$45/60, with air-con US$55/72; ▨ ▣) has simple bungalows set on a small hillside in from the beach, and nicer two-storey cottages with sea views and balconies.

Bus 206 runs several times daily to/from Zanzibar Town.

PAJE

Paje is a wide, white beach at the end of the Tarmac where the coastal road north to Bwejuu and south to Jambiani joins with the road from Zanzibar Town. There's a cluster of places here, and somewhat of a party atmosphere, though it's quieter than in Nungwi. Many hotels in Paje organise dolphin trips to Kizimkazi for about TSh15,000 per person in a group.

Kinazi Upepo (☎ 0748-655038; www.kinaziupepo .com; banda with shared bathroom US$20-25, bungalow US$35-50) Good vibes and good value are the main attractions at this place nestled amid the palms and coastal pines on a nice section of beach. You can sleep in simple *makuti bandas* on low stilts, or in large bungalows with Zanzibari beds. There's a well-stocked bar, and Saturday evenings currently feature an all-night East Coast Beach Party.

Other recommendations:

Arabian Nights Guesthouse (☎ 224 0190/1; www .pajedivecentre.com/arabiannights; s/d US$70/80, with sea view US$80/90) Comfortable, tastefully furnished cottages on the beach, plus a restaurant and a dive centre.

Paradise Beach Bungalows (☎ 223 1387; www .geocities.jp/paradisebeachbungalows/; s/d from US$25/ 35) A low-key place hidden among the palms on the beach at the northern edge of Paje, with sushi and other Japanese cuisine available with advance order.

Kitete Guest House (☎ 224 0226; www.kitetebeach .com; s/d from US$25/40) A small guesthouse right on the beach.

Paje by Night (☎ 0747-460710; www.pajebynight.net; standard s/d US$35/40, large d with hot water US$60,

2-/4-person 'jungle bungalow' US$70/100) A fairly raucous place known for its bar, with straightforward rooms around a courtyard set in from the beach, *makuti*-roofed 'jungle bungalows' and a restaurant with a pizza oven.

Getting There & Away

Bus 324 runs several times daily between Paje and Stone Town en route to/from Bwejuu, with the last departure from Paje leaving at about 3pm.

BWEJUU

The large village of Bwejuu lies about 3km north of Paje on a long, palm-shaded beach. It's very spread out, quieter than Paje, and much less crowded than Nungwi, with a mellow atmosphere and nothing much more to do other than wander along the sand and listen to the breezes rustling the palm trees.

Sleeping & Eating

Mustapha's Nest (☎ 224 0069; www.fatfishfish.co.uk /mustaphas/; r per person with shared bathroom US$10-15, with private bathroom US$20-25) This chilled-out, welcoming place has a laid-back Rasta atmosphere and a variety of simple, creatively decorated rooms, some with their own bathroom and all with their own theme. Meals are taken family style, and Mustapha and family are helpful in sorting out things like bike hire, drumming lessons and other diversions. It's south of Bwejuu village, and just across the road from the beach.

Robinson's Place (☎ 0747-413479; www.robinsons place.net; s/d from US$25/40) A Robinson Crusoe–style getaway, it has a small collection of appealingly designed rooms nestled amid the palms directly on the beach. The two-storey Robinson House has a wonderful upstairs tree house double, open to the sea and the palms. Downstairs is a tidy single, and there are a few more rooms in a separate house, some with private bathroom. Eddy, the Zanzibari owner, cooks up great breakfasts and dinners (for guests only) served in a seaside *banda*. It's at the northern end of Bwejuu; just keep heading up the sandy track until you see the sign.

Other recommendations:

Sunrise Hotel & Restaurant (☎ 224 0170; www .sunrise-zanzibar.com; s/d r US$65/75, s/d bungalow with sea view US$80/90; ▣) The Belgian-run Sunrise has rooms and bungalows set around a small garden area, and a highly regarded restaurant. The beach-facing bungalows are worth the extra money, and are much nicer than the rooms, which are dark. It's on the beach about 3km north of Bwejuu village.

Evergreen Bwejuu (☎ 224 0273; www.evergree -bungalows.com; r with shared bathroom from US$30, with private bathroom from US$40) Pricey but nice two-storey bungalows. Some have a bathroom, and the upper-level rooms have their own balcony.

Twisted Palm (☎ 0747-438121; s/d from US$15/25) OK bungalows (the ones closest to the water are better), a beachside bar and a raised restaurant overlooking the water.

Getting There & Away

Bus 324 goes daily between Stone Town and Bwejuu village, and private minivans come here as well.

MICHAMVI PENINSULA

Beginning about 4km north of Bwejuu, budget accommodation disappears, with a few upmarket retreats the only options. Once past Bwejuu, there's no public transport. Local boats cross from Michamvi village (on the northwestern side of the peninsula opposite Karafuu Hotel) to Chwaka, usually departing Michamvi in the early morning (TSh1000), or you can arrange to hire one at any time of day (about TSh15,000 return). In Michamvi, there are a few simple *bandas* where you can arrange grilled fish or other local fare.

Breezes Beach Club (☎ 0747-440883; www.breezes -zanzibar.com; s/d half-board from US$155/250; 🗶 🖳 🖳) is a plush resort, with a full range of amenities and activities, and a minimum of the hectic, homogenised atmosphere found at some of the other east-coast places.

JAMBIANI

Jambiani Beach stretches several kilometres down the coast. There's a good selection of budget accommodation, and you could do worse than spend a few days here gazing out at turquoise seas.

Sleeping & Eating

Oasis Beach Inn (☎ 224 0259; d US$25, s/d with shared bathroom US$8/16) One of the cheapest places, the beachside Oasis has simple but decent rooms with shared bathroom.

Blue Oyster Hotel (☎ 224 0163; www.zanzibar.de; s/d with shared bathroom US$20/30, with private bathroom US$45/50) This German-run place has pleasant, spotless rooms, a breezy terrace restaurant, and a convenient setting at the northern end of the beach.

Kimte Beach Inn (☎ 224 0212; www.kimte.com; dm US$10, d with shared bathroom US$25, with private bathroom US$30) At the southern end of Jambiani, this friendly and laid-back Rasta-run place has rooms on the land side of the road, about half a minute's walk from the beach, a good vibe, and a beachside bar with music and evening bonfires.

Gomani Bungalows (☎ 224 0154; gomanibunga lows@yahoo.com; s/d US$15/30) This spiffy beach-side place is at the southern end of Jambi-ani just after Kimte Beach Inn. Rooms are around a garden on a tiny cliff overlooking the sea, and there's a restaurant.

Mt Zion Long Beach (☎ 0747-439001, 439034; www .mountzion-zanzibar.com; s/d/tr US$25/50/65) Another Rasta-run place with nicely decorated, spot-less stone-and-thatch bungalows set around large, lush gardens just up from the beach. They also have a couple of less expensive no-frills *makuti bandas* directly on the sand, plus a bar built around polished drift-wood, and tasty food. It's about 1.5km north of Jambiani village.

Hakuna Majiwe (☎ 0747-454505; www.hakuna majiwe.net; s/d US$100/140; 🗶 🖳 🖳) A pleasing fusion of Zanzibar and Italy with nicely decorated attached cottages, all with shady porches and Zanzibari beds, and most large enough to accommodate extra beds for children. It's at the far northern end of Jambiani, near Mt Zion Long Beach.

Shehe Bungalows (☎ 224 0149; r per person US$15) Simple rooms at the southern end of Jambi-ani. Most have bathroom and some have a minifridge. There's a seaside restaurant.

Getting There & Away

Jambiani Beach is reached by bus 309 from Stone Town (1½ hours).

KIZIMKAZI

This small village actually consists of two adjoining settlements: Kizimkazi Dimbani to the north and Kizimkazi Mkunguni to the south. It's known mainly for the dol-phins that favour the nearby waters. Trips can be organised through tour operators in Stone Town from about US$20 per person, depending on group size. Some of the ho-tels at Paje and Jambiani also organise tours from TSh15,000 per person, as does Kizidi Bungalows (p150) for TSh40,000 per boat with up to eight people, plus TSh2500 per person for hire of poor-quality snorkelling equipment. While the dolphins are beautiful, the tours are often quite unpleasant, due to the hunt-and-chase tactics used by many of the tour boats, and they can't be recommended. If you do go out, the best time is early morning when the water is calmer and the sun is cooler. Late afternoon is also good, although winds may be stronger (and if it's too windy, it's difficult to get in and out of the boats to snorkel).

Kizidi Restaurant & Bungalows (☎ 223 0081; s/d/tr US$30/40/50) is a large place on the northern end of the beach in Kizimkazi Dimbani. Accommodation is in no-frills cottages overlooking the water, with net, hot water and twin or double beds. There's a large restaurant.

Getting There & Away
To get here from Stone Town, take bus 326 (Kizimkazi) direct, or take 310 (Makunduchi) as far as Kufile junction, where you'll need to get out and wait for another vehicle heading towards Kizimkazi, or walk (about 5km). As you approach Kizimkazi, you'll come to another fork; Dimbani is to the right and Mkunguni to the left.

Jozani Forest
Cool and lush **Jozani Forest** (adult/child US$8/4; ☺ 7.30am-5.30pm) is the largest area of mature forest left on Zanzibar, and is known in particular for its populations of the rare red colobus monkey.

The best times to see the red colobus are in the early morning and late evening. It's important not to get too close – park staff recommend no closer than 3m – both for your safety and the safety of the animals. If the monkeys were to catch a human illness, it could spread, endangering the already threatened population.

Jozani is about 35km southeast of Zanzibar Town off the road to Paje. It can be reached via bus 9 or 10, via chartered taxi or with an organised tour from Zanzibar Town. Many Kizimkazi dolphin tours stop at Jozani, although the Jozani entry fee isn't normally included in the price.

Menai Bay & Unguja Ukuu
Tranquil Menai Bay, fringed by the sleepy villages of Fumba to the west and Unguja Ukuu to the east, is home to an impressive assortment of corals, fish and mangrove

---

WATCHING THE DOLPHINS
Unfortunately for Kizimkazi's dolphins, things have gotten out of hand these days, and it's not uncommon to see a group of beleaguered dolphins being chased by several boats of tourists. If you want to watch the dolphins, heed the advice posted on the wall of the WWF office in Zanzibar Town: as with other animals, viewing the dolphins in their natural environs requires time and patience, and sightings can't be guaranteed. Shouting and waving won't encourage them to approach your boat. Rather than forcing the boat operator to chase the dolphins or approach at close range, be satisfied with passive observation, especially when they are resting. If you decide to swim with them, get into the water quietly and without splashing. Remember that the dolphins are wild and their whereabouts cannot be predicted. It is they who choose to interact with people, not the other way around...

---

forests, some idyllic sandbanks and deserted islets, and a sea-turtle breeding area. It's protected as part of the **Menai Bay Conservation Area** (admission US$3), and offers a relaxing getaway, plus the chance to sail around the islets and sandbanks offshore, and sometimes to see dolphins. Unguja Ukuu was the site of Zanzibar's earliest settlement, dating to at least the 8th century.

Menai Bay Beach Bungalows (☎ 0747-413915; www.menaibaybungalows.com; s/d US$30/50) has pleasant cottages scattered around leafy grounds just in from the beach, a nice stretch of sand, and a restaurant.

Fumba Beach Lodge (☎ 0747-860504; info@fumba beachlodge.co.tz; s/d US$177/284) has more nice cottages well-spaced near the water, plus a placid beach and the chance for diving, snorkelling or sailing on a dhow.

Offshore Islands
CHANGUU
Also known as Prison Island, **Changuu** (admission US$5, payable in US$ only) lies about 5km and an easy boat ride northwest of Zanzibar Town. It was originally used to detain 'recalcitrant' slaves and later as a quarantine station. Today the island is pushed as a day excursion, although it's a bit overrated. Nearby

is a reef offering some novice snorkelling; you'll need your own gear. Changuu is also known for its large family of imported giant tortoises.

Zanzibar Town tour operators can arrange an excursion. Alternatively, you can hire a fishing boat from the beach near Tembo House Hotel for about TSh15,000 for a return day trip.

BAWI

Tiny Bawi, about 7km west of Zanzibar Town and several kilometres southwest of Changuu, offers a beautiful beach and snorkelling. There's nothing else, however, so you'll need to bring food, drinks and snorkelling equipment with you. Fishing boats from the beach near Tembo House Hotel charge from TSh15,000; the trip takes about 40 minutes. Various tour operators run day trips to Bawi with a stop en route at Changuu from about TSh15,000, usually including lunch.

CHAPWANI

This tiny, privately owned island (also known as Grave Island, thanks to its small cemetery and tombs of colonial-era British seamen) is about 4km north of Zanzibar Town. It's surrounded by crystal waters, and makes an agreeable getaway from Stone Town.

Chapwani Island Lodge (www.chapwaniisland.com; s/d full board US$245/300; Jun-Mar) has cosy bungalows along the sand, and provides transfers from Stone Town.

TUMBATU

The large island of Tumbatu is situated off Zanzibar's northwestern coast and is populated by the Tumbatu people. There's no accommodation, but the island can be easily visited as a day trip from Kendwa or Nungwi, where the hotels can help you organise a boat (from US$35 to US$50 per boat). Alternatively, local boats sail throughout the day between Tumbatu and **Mkokotoni** village, which lies just across the channel on Zanzibar, and which is known for its bustling fish market. Before visiting, it's best to get permission first from the police station in Mkokotoni, or from the *shehe* (village chief) in Nungwi, who will probably request a modest fee. There's at least one bus daily between Mkokotoni and Stone Town. Camping isn't permitted.

MNEMBA

Tiny Mnemba, just northeast of Matemwe, is the ultimate tropical paradise for those who have the money to enjoy it. While the island itself is privately owned, the surrounding coral reef can be visited by anyone. It's one of Zanzibar's best diving and snorkelling sites, with a huge array of fish, including tuna, barracuda, moray eels, reef sharks and lots of colourful smaller species.

The exclusive **Mnemba Island Lodge** (www.ccafrica.com; per person all-inclusive from US$585; Jun-Mar) is a playground for the rich and famous, and is often rented out in its entirety.

CHUMBE

This uninhabited island, 12km south of Zanzibar Town, has an exceptional shallow-water coral reef along its western shore that is in close to pristine condition and abounding with fish life. Since 1994, when the reef was gazetted as Zanzibar's first marine sanctuary, the island has gained widespread acclaim, including from the United Nations, as the site of an impressive ecotourism initiative centred around an ecolodge and local environmental education programs. It's now run as Chumbe Island Coral Park, a private, nonprofit nature reserve.

In addition to nearly 200 species of coral, the island's surrounding waters host about 370 species of fish, groups of dolphins, and hawksbill turtles.

Chumbe Island can be visited as a day trip, although staying overnight in one of the seven wonderfully rustic **eco-bungalows** (223 1040; www.chumbeisland.com; s/d all-inclusive US$230/400) is highly recommended. Advance bookings are essential. Day visits (also by advance arrangement only) cost US$70 per person, including transfers and food.

PEMBA
024

About 50km north of Zanzibar across the deep, dark waters of the Pemba channel lies hilly, verdant Pemba – the archipelago's 'other' island, seldom visited and long overshadowed by Zanzibar, its larger, more visible and more politically powerful neighbour to the south. Yet those tourists who venture across the channel for a visit are seldom disappointed.

Unlike flat, sandy Zanzibar, Pemba's terrain is hilly, fertile and heavily vegetated.

Dense mangrove swamps line its coast, opening only occasionally onto stunning white-sand coves, while inland, a patchwork of neat farm plots covers the hillsides. In the days of the Arab traders it was even referred to as *al Khuthera* or 'the Green Island'. Throughout much of the period when the sultans of Zanzibar held sway over the East African coast, it was Pemba, with its extensive clove plantations and agricultural base, that provided the economic foundation for the archipelago's dominance.

Pemba has also been long renowned for its voodoo and traditional healers, and people still make their way here from elsewhere in East Africa seeking cures or to learn the skills of the trade.

Thanks to the mangroves lining much of the coast, Pemba is not a beach destination. However, there are a few good stretches of sand and some idyllic offshore islets, and the surrounding waters offer rewarding diving.

Tourism on Pemba is still in its infancy, and infrastructure is for the most part fairly basic, although this is slowly changing. Much of the island is relatively 'undiscovered' and you'll still have things more or less to yourself, which is a big part of Pemba's charm. The main requirement for travelling around independently is time, as there's little transport off main routes.

History

Pemba is geologically much older than Zanzibar and is believed to have been settled at an earlier date, although little is known about its original inhabitants. It's likely that they migrated from the mainland, perhaps as early as several thousand years ago. The Shirazi presence on Pemba is believed to date from at least the 9th or 10th century.

The Portuguese attacked Pemba in the early 16th century and sought to subjugate its inhabitants by ravaging towns and demanding tributes. As a result, many Pembans fled to Mombasa. By the late 17th century the Busaidi family of Omani Arabs had taken over the island and driven away the remaining Portuguese. Before long, however, the Mazrui, a rival group of Omanis based in Mombasa, gained the upper hand and governed until 1822. In 1890 Pemba, together with Zanzibar, became a British protectorate.

Following the Zanzibar revolution in 1964, President Karume closed Pemba to

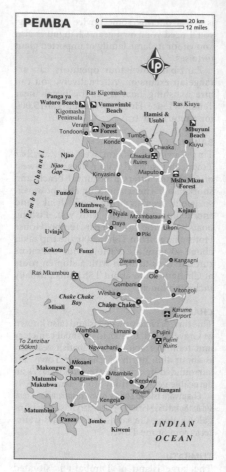

foreigners in an effort to contain strong antigovernment sentiment. The island remained closed until the 1980s, although the situation continued to be strained. Tensions peaked during the 1995 elections, and relations deteriorated thereafter, with Pembans feeling increasingly marginalised and frustrated. This was hardly surprising, considering that illiteracy rates are as high as 95% in some areas and roads and other infrastructure badly neglected. In January 2001, in the wake of the October 2000 elections, tensions again peaked, resulting in at least several dozen deaths and causing many people to flee the island (see p108). Since then, most have returned, and daily life is back to normal.

Orientation

Chake Chake, in the centre of the island on the western coast, is Pemba's main town. The only other towns of any size are Wete in the north, and Mkoani in the south, where most of the ferries arrive.

MAPS

A map (1:100,000) put out by the Commission for Lands & Environment is available from the Bureau of Lands & Environment just outside Chake Chake in Machomane. Head north from the town centre for 1km and take the first right; the bureau is 100m down in a two-storey white building.

Information

There's no accommodation outside main towns except for a few tourist resorts. Away from hotels and guesthouses, the main eating venues are Pemba's lively night markets – found in all the major towns, but best in Chake Chake – which sell *mishikaki* (skewered meat), grilled *pweza* (octopus) and other delicacies. Other than hotel bars and local brew there's little alcohol available on the island.

Most businesses operate from 8am to 4pm, and almost everywhere shuts down for prayers from about 4pm or 4.30pm, and at midday on Friday.

There is a Chinese-run government hospital in Mkoani, but it's better to get yourself to the mainland or to Nairobi.

Chake Chake is the only place to change money, and even here facilities are limited, so come prepared and bring enough cash US dollars. You'll need to pay cash for all diving and accommodation listed here except as noted.

Activities

DIVING

Other than exploring the island, diving is Pemba's main activity. Given the distances from main towns to most of the dive sites, live-aboard arrangements are an appealing option, and most of the following operators can arrange these, as well as **sailing charters**. As currents are often strong, and conditions challenging, most diving around Pemba is best suited for experienced divers.

Fundu Lagoon (☎ 223 2926; www.fundulagoon.com) 'Fully catered' diving in five-star conditions; based at Fundu Lagoon (p154), and mainly for hotel guests.

Manta Reef Lodge (☎ 0747-424637, 423930; www .mantareeflodge.com) Diving at a range of sites around the island, and live-aboard arrangements on the schooner *SY Jambo;* based at Manta Reef Lodge (p157). There's a booking office in Chake Chake (Map p155).

Pemba Afloat (www.pembaisland.com) An excellent outfit based aboard the yachts *Karibu* and *Sitra*, which are moored in Njao Gap, northwest of Wete.

Wimbi Nyota (www.zanzibarsail.com) The *Wimbi Nyota* offers sailing and live-aboard arrangements around Pemba and northern Zanzibar, together with its sister ship, the catamaran *Julia*.

Getting There & Around

Mkoani is Pemba's main ferry port, and there are also weekly ferry connections from the mainland to Wete. All flights arrive at the island's only airport near Chake Chake. Once on Pemba, getting around is easy but slow. A plodding local bus network connects the three main towns and several smaller ones. To reach destinations off these routes, take one of the buses to the nearest intersection, from where you'll either have to walk, rely on sporadic pick-ups, or negotiate an additional fee with the bus driver. There are no regular taxis as there are on Zanzibar or the mainland, but there are plenty of pick-up trucks that you can charter – best arranged in Chake Chake. The main roads between Mkoani and Wete are Tarmac in various stages of repair; no secondary routes are paved.

Pemba is small, and cycling is an excellent way to get around the island, although you'll need to bring your own (mountain) bike and spares, unless you're content with one of the single-speed bicycles available locally. Distances are relatively short and roads are only lightly travelled.

Mkoani

Although it is Pemba's major port, Mkoani has managed to fight off all attempts at development and remains a very small and boring town. However, its good budget guesthouse goes a long way to redeeming it, and it makes a reasonable base for exploring the southern and central parts of the island.

INFORMATION

The government hospital is on the main road, and is best avoided except in dire emergencies.

The immigration officer usually meets all boat arrivals. Otherwise, if you're coming from anywhere other than Zanzibar, you'll need to go to the immigration office and get stamped in. It's 500m up the main road from the port in a small brown building with a flag.

SLEEPING & EATING

Jondeni Guest House (☎ 245 6042; jondeniguest@hot mail.com; dm US$10, s/d with shared bathroom US$15/20, s/d with private bathroom US$25/30) The only choice at the moment is this good backpackers' guest-house, with clean, no-frills rooms and good meals (TSh6000). Staff have lots of information on Pemba, and can help you arrange excursions elsewhere on the island. To get here, head left when exiting the port, and walk about 800m up to the top of the hill.

Floating Beach Resort (www.floatingbeach.com; s/d full board US$88/176) Fifteen rooms on a comfortable boat moored off the coast of Pemba, north of Mkoani. Rates include excursions to nearby beaches.

Apart from Jondeni Guest House, which has Mkoani's best cuisine, it can be difficult to find meals, although there is decent street food in the evenings by the port.

GETTING THERE & AWAY

Boat

The fitful **MS Sepideh** (☎ 0741-414343, 0747-420243) sails in theory on Monday, Thursday and Saturday in both directions between Dar es Salaam and Mkoani via Zanzibar, departing Dar es Salaam at 7.30am and Zanzibar by 10am. In the other direction, the boat departs Mkoani at 12.30pm, reaching Zanzibar at 3pm, and then to Dar es Salaam at 4pm. The *Sepideh* is good when it runs, but service is sporadic. The fare is US$45/55 in economy class between Pemba and Zanzibar/Dar es Salaam, including port tax.

The much less comfortable and marginally more reliable *Serengeti* also sails three times weekly between Zanzibar and Mkoani, departing Mkoani at 10am Tuesday, Thursday and Saturday, reaching Zanzibar between 4pm and 5pm (US$25, six to seven hours). Departures from Zanzibar are at 10pm, reaching Pemba the next morning at about 6am. If you take the night run, try to get to the port early to get one of their '1st class' couches; there's no extra charge, but it's more comfortable than the other

seating, although 'comfortable' is an overstatement. Both boats have their main booking offices at the port in Mkoani. You can also arrange tickets through travel agencies in Chake Chake, and with Sharouk Guest House in Wete.

Bus

Bus No 303 runs throughout the day to/ from Chake Chake (TSh700, two hours). The bus station is about 200m east of the port, up the hill and just off the main road. For Wete, you'll need to change vehicles in Chake Chake.

Kiweni

Kiweni (Shamiani on some maps) is an island that lies just off Pemba's southeastern coast. It's home to five of Pemba's six endemic bird species, and a nesting ground for some sea-turtle colonies. There's nowhere to stay, but a five-star resort is planned.

Take any bus along the Mkoani–Chake Chake road to Mtambile junction. From Mtambile, you can find pick-ups to Kengeja, from where you'll have to walk a few kilometres to the water and then take a boat over to Kiweni (about TSh2000).

Wambaa

The main reason to come to Wambaa is to luxuriate at **Fundu Lagoon** (☎ 223 2926; www .fundulagoon.com; s/d full board from US$475/670; ☾ mid-Jun–mid-Apr), Pemba's only five-star resort, with all the usual amenities plus a dive team.

Chake Chake

Lively Chake Chake, set on a ridge overlooking Chake Chake Bay, is Pemba's main town. Although it has been occupied for centuries, there is little architectural evidence of its past other than the ruins of an 18th-century fort near the hospital, and some ruins at nearby Ras Mkumbuu.

INFORMATION

Adult Computer Centre (connection fee TSh1000, plus per minute TSh300; ☾ 8am-8pm) On the main Mkoani–Wete road, opposite the telecom building; you can also place/receive international calls here.

Partnership Travel & Tours (☎ 245 2278) Ferry tickets and island excursions; at the main junction.

Pemba Island Reasonable Tours & Safaris (☎ 0747-435266) Next door, and more of the same.

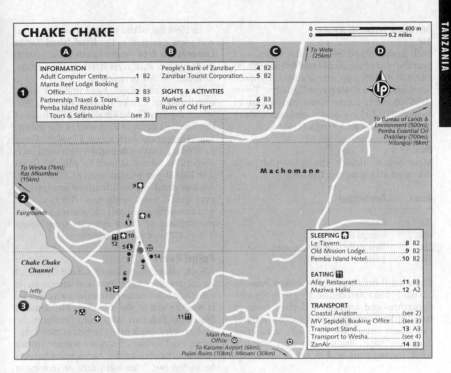

CHAKE CHAKE

0 — 400 m
0 — 0.2 miles

INFORMATION	People's Bank of Zanzibar............1 B2
Adult Computer Centre...............1 B2	Zanzibar Tourist Corporation......5 B2
Manta Reef Lodge Booking	
Office.....................................2 B3	**SIGHTS & ACTIVITIES**
Partnership Travel & Tours........3 B3	Market....................................6 B3
Pemba Island Reasonable	Ruins of Old Fort....................7 A3
Tours & Safaris...................(see 3)	

To Wete
(25km)

To Bureau of Lands &
Environment (500m);
Pemba Essential Oil
Distillery (700m);
Vitongoji (6km)

To Wesha (7km);
Ras Mkumbuu
(15km)

Machomane

Fairgrounds

Chake Chake
Channel

Jetty

Main Post
Office
To Karume:Airport (6km);
Pujini Ruins (10km); Mkoani (30km)

SLEEPING	
Le Tavern..................................8 B2
Old Mission Lodge......................9 B2
Pemba Island Hotel..................10 B2
EATING	
Afay Restaurant.......................11 B3
Maziwa Halisi...........................12 A2
TRANSPORT	
Coastal Aviation......................(see 2)
MV Sepideh Booking Office.......(see 3)
Transport Stand.......................13 A3
Transport to Wesha................(see 4)
ZanAir....................................14 B3

People's Bank of Zanzibar Changes cash and travellers cheques to a daily limit of US$200. At the main junction.

Zanzibar Tourist Corporation Come here for tourist information. It's at the main junction, on the 2nd floor of the building with the flag.

SIGHTS & ACTIVITIES

An easy bike ride away, about 6km east of town past the sleepy **Pemba Essential Oil Distillery** (admission TSh1500; 7.30am-3.30pm Mon-Fri), are some tiny, baobab-dotted **beaches** near Vitongoji.

SLEEPING & EATING

Pemba Island Hotel (245 2215, 0747-435266; reasonabletourspemba@hotmail.com; s/d/tw US$20/35/50;) New and spotless, this hotel is good budget value, with small rooms with nets, TV, minifridge and hot water, a rooftop terrace restaurant and a 10% price discount for longer stays. It's on the Wesha road, about 100m downhill from the bank. The owners also run a cheaper annex nearby.

Old Mission Lodge (245 2786; www.swahilidivers .com; dm/d US$23/68, r with shared bathroom US$53-82;) This lodge is in a restored Quaker mis-

sion house in the centre of Chake Chake, with spacious, rustic and somewhat over-priced rooms complete with creaky wooden floors, tiny shared bathrooms and high ceilings. It's primarily a dive base, but plenty of nondivers stay here as well. It's on the main road in the town centre, about 200m north of the bank. No travellers cheques accepted; credit cards plus 10%. Lunch is available for US$6 and dinner for US$12.

Le Tavern (245 2660; s/d with air-con US$25/30;) A reliable but slightly tatty establishment on the main road north of Old Mission Lodge, with clean, no-frills rooms with nets. Included in the price is an early morning wake-up call from the mosque next door. Meals (TSh4000) can be arranged.

Afay Restaurant (meals TSh2000; lunch & dinner) This homy local haunt offers good rice and fish and other standard fare.

There's also a lively night market around the main junction, where you can get grilled *pweza* (octopus), *maandazi* (doughnuts) and other local delicacies at rock-bottom prices.

Maziwa Halisi, downhill from the bank and after Pemba Island Hotel, sells yogurt.

TANZANIA

GETTING THERE & AWAY

Air

Both **ZanAir** (☎ 245 2990), on the main road near the post office, and **Coastal Aviation** (☎ 245 2162, 0747-418343), opposite ZanAir, fly daily between Chake Chake and Zanzibar Town (US$70), with connections on to Dar es Salaam (US$85). Coastal also goes daily between Pemba and Tanga (US$55).

Bus

Main routes include the following (with prices on all averaging TSh700):

Route	Destination
303	Mkoani
306	Wete via the 'old' road
334	Wete via the 'new' (eastern) road
335	Konde

There's a shuttle bus from Chake Chake to Mkoani (TSh1000) connecting with *Sepideh* departures and arrivals. It departs from in front of Partnership Travel & Tours about two hours before the *Sepideh*'s scheduled departure time. Book a place in advance when buying your boat ticket.

GETTING AROUND

To/From the Airport

Karume Airport, about 6km east of town, is Pemba's only airfield. There's no public transport to and from the airport, but at least one vehicle meets incoming flights (TSh5000 to Chake Chake centre).

Car & Motorcycle

Cars and motorbikes can be hired in Chake Chake through the Old Mission Lodge or either of the travel agencies. Some sample prices: US$15 between Mkoani and Chake Chake; US$10 one way between Chake Chake and Wete; and US$25 to US$30 return between Chake Chake and Ras Kigomasha, including stops at Vumawimbi Beach and Ngezi.

Misali

This little patch of paradise lies offshore from Chake Chake, surrounded by crystal waters and stunning coral reefs. On the northeast of the island is **Mbuyuni Beach**, with fine, white sands and a small visitor centre, and to the southeast are some mangroves.

In 1998 the island and surrounding coral reef were gazetted as the **Misali Island Marine Conservation Area** (adults/students US$5/3), with underwater and terrestrial nature trails. Camping is not permitted.

To get to the island, head first to Wesha, northwest of Chake Chake, via bus 305, which departs Chake Chake from in front of the People's Bank of Zanzibar in the morning. Hiring a car costs about TSh6000. Once in Wesha, you can negotiate with local boat owners to take you over to Misali (about TSh40,000 per person return). There's no food or drink on the island, so bring whatever you'll need with you. Alternatively, you can arrange Misali excursions through guesthouses or travel agencies from about TSh45,000 per person return.

Pujini Ruins

About 10km southeast of Chake Chake at Pujini are the overgrown and atmospheric ruins of a town dating from the 14th century. It was the seat of the infamous Mohammed bin Abdul Rahman, who ruled Pemba in the 15th century, prior to the arrival of the Portuguese. For Pembans, his name is synonymous with cruelty due to the harsh punishments he meted out. The main area of interest is framed by what were once the ramparts surrounding Rahman's palace – now little more than a mound of earth in many places.

The best way to get here is by bicycle, following the road southeast past farm plots, small villages and mangroves. Car hire from Chake Chake costs TSh10,000 return.

Wete

The lively port- and market-town of Wete makes an agreeable base from which to explore northern Pemba. The road leading from Chake Chake to Wete via Ziwani is pretty, with hills, villages and lots of banana trees.

INFORMATION

The best place for arranging excursions to Vumawimbi Beach, Ngezi forest and elsewhere is Sharouk Guest House, which can also help with booking ferry tickets. **Bahari Divers** (☎ 0747-417333) has a base just opposite for diving; see p137.

SLEEPING & EATING

Sharouk Guest House (☎ 245 4386; s/d with shared bathroom US$10/20, with private bathroom US$20/40) This welcoming guesthouse, just off the main road at the western end of town, has simple, clean rooms with net and fan, and the best meals in town (meals TSh4000).

Bomani Guest House (☎ 245 4384; s/d with shared bathroom US$15/20, with private bathroom s/d US$25) In the unlikely event that Sharouk's is full, try this place diagonally opposite.

GETTING THERE & AWAY

The small *Takrima* sails roughly weekly on a constantly changing schedule between Wete and Tanga (on the mainland). It currently departs Wete at 10am Wednesday and Tanga at 10am Sunday (US$25, five hours). The scruffy *Aziza* sails weekly between Zanzibar and Wete, departing Zanzibar at 10pm Friday, and departing Wete at 8am on Wednesday (US$20, eight hours). Sharouk Guest House is the best place for updated information on both.

The main bus routes are 306 (Wete to Chake Chake along the 'old' road via Ziwani), 334 (Wete to Chake Chake along the 'new' road via Ole) and 324 (Wete to Konde).

A shuttle bus from Wete to Mkoani (TSh1000) connects with *Sepideh* departures and arrivals, departing from Raha Tours & Travel, off the main road near the Wete post office, about three hours before the *Sepideh*'s scheduled departure time.

Tumbe

The large village of Tumbe lies on a sandy cove, and is the site of Pemba's largest **fish market**. There's nowhere to stay or eat, but if you're in the area, it's worth a stop, especially in the mornings when the day's catch is brought in.

About 2km southeast from Tumbe at Chwaka are some overgrown **ruins**, primarily at the signposted 'Haruni' site, east of the main road. Harun was the son of Mohammed bin Adbul Rahmin (see opposite), and reputedly just as cruel as his father.

Take the 335 bus and ask the driver to drop you at the junction, from where Tumbe is an easy walk.

Ngezi

The small, dense forest at Ngezi is part of the much larger natural forest that once covered wide swathes of Pemba. It is notable for resembling the highland rainforests of East Africa more than the lowland forests found on Zanzibar, as well as for being the home of the Pemba flying fox – a bat unique to the island. The forest is now a protected **reserve** (admission TSh4000; ☻ 8am-4pm) with a short nature trail that winds its way beneath the shady forest canopy.

Ngezi is along the main road between Konde and Tondooni. Via public transport, take the bus to Konde, from where it's a 3km to 4km walk. Bus drivers are sometimes willing to drop you at the information centre for an additional TSh1000 to TSh2000. Better is to combine Ngezi with a visit to Vumawimbi Beach (below).

Kigomasha Peninsula

The main reason to come to the Kigomasha Peninsula in Pemba's northwestern corner is to relax on beautiful **Vumawimbi Beach** on the peninsula's eastern side. Other than a small fishing village, there's nothing here, so bring whatever food and drink you'll need with you.

The best way to get to Vumawimbi is on bicycle from Konde, or via hire car from Chake Chake. Alternatively, try to negotiate a lift with one of the Konde bus drivers. Hitching is slow going.

On the northwestern end of the Kigomasha peninsula are **Panga ya Watoro Beach** and the superbly situated **Manta Reef Lodge** (☎ 0747-424637, 423930; www.mantareeflodge.com; s/d full board US$170/240; ☻ mid-Jun–mid-Apr), on a windy cliff top with spectacular views over the open ocean. Accommodation is in comfortably rustic sea-facing cabins, and the lodge can help you organise diving. To get here, stop by Manta Reef's booking office on the main street in Chake Chake, opposite ZanAir. Otherwise, there's at least one pick-up daily in the morning from Konde to Makangale village, about 4km or 5km south of Manta Reef, from where you'll need to walk or pay the driver extra to bring you all the way up.

NORTHEASTERN TANZANIA

Northeastern Tanzania is located between Tanzania's most popular attractions – the northern safari circuit and the Zanzibar Archipelago – but it's still quite low-key as far as tourism is concerned. It's a rewarding area to explore if you're looking for something more off-the-beaten-track than the standard tourist loop but don't have time to venture further afield. Most places are easily accessed from both Dar es Salaam and Arusha, and it's quite possible to combine coastal attractions – Saadani Game Reserve and the beaches north or south of Pangani – with inland mountain areas such as Amani and the western Usambaras within a reasonable time frame and budget.

BAGAMOYO
☎ 023

Sleepy Bagamoyo was once one of the most important dhow ports along the East African coast and was the terminus of the trade caravan route linking Lake Tanganyika with the sea. Later it served as a way station for missionaries travelling from Zanzibar to the interior, and many of the European explorers, including Burton, Stanley and Livingstone, began and ended their trips here. From 1887 to 1891 Bagamoyo was the capital of German East Africa, and in 1888 it was the site of the first major uprising against the colonial government. In 1891 the capital was transferred to Dar es Salaam, sending Bagamoyo into a slow decline from which it is only now beginning to recover, spurred along by completion of a good Tarmac road from Dar es Salaam. While most buildings are in an advanced stage of decay, Bagamoyo's long history, sleepy charm and nearby beaches make it an agreeable day or weekend excursion from Dar es Salaam.

Information
There's a card phone at the telecom building at the town entrance. The National Microfinance Bank, next door, changes cash. For Internet, try **4MSK** (per hr TSh2000; ☻ 9am-6pm) at the Catholic mission.

The small tourist information office at the main junction at the entrance to town can help with guides and excursions.

Sights & Activities
With its crumbling German-era colonial buildings and narrow streets dotted with Zanzibar-style carved doors, **central Bagamoyo** is well worth a leisurely stroll, especially the area along Ocean Rd. Nearby on the beach is the colourful **port**, where you

can watch boat builders at work, or visit the **fish market**.

About 2km north of town and reached via a mango-shaded avenue is the **Holy Ghost Catholic Mission**, with an excellent **museum** (☎ 244 0010; admission free, donations appreciated; ☻ 10am-5pm). Nearby is the chapel where Livingstone's body was laid before being taken to Zanzibar Town en route to Westminster Abbey.

About 500m south of Bagamoyo along the road to Dar es Salaam is **Chuo cha Sanaa** (College of Arts; www.college-of-arts.org), home of the national dance company and site of occasional traditional dancing and drumming performances.

Further south along the beach are the overgrown but intriguing **Kaole ruins** (admission TSh1500). These include the remains of a 13th-century mosque (one of the oldest on mainland Tanzania), and some gravestones from the 15th century. To get here, head south along the beach for about 5km past Kaole village into the mangrove swamps. Where the beach apparently ends, go a few hundred metres inland and look for the stone pillars. There's an easier, slightly longer route along the road running past Chuo cha Sanaa. Both routes, and especially the beach route, have a reputation for muggings, so it's best to walk in a group and with a guide, and not carry valuables.

Sleeping & Eating
BUDGET

Mary Nice Place (☎ 0744-024015; maryniceplace@yahoo.co.uk; r from TSh10,000-20,000) Simple and homy, this is the best budget bet – a converted house with a small garden, clean, no-frills rooms with fan, and the possibility of meals. It's just in from the road to the left, a few minutes on foot after passing Chuo Cha Sanaa, and is unsignposted. Anyone should be able to point you in the right direction. Look for the thatched entry gate covered with bougainvillea blossoms.

MIDRANGE

Travellers Lodge (☎ 244 0077; www.travellers-lodge.com; camping with shower TSh5000, s/d garden cottage TSh35,000/45,000, s/d beach cottage TSh45,000/55,000) This is one of the better-value beach places, with cottages scattered around expansive grounds and a restaurant. It's on the road running parallel to the beach, just south of the entrance to the Catholic mission.

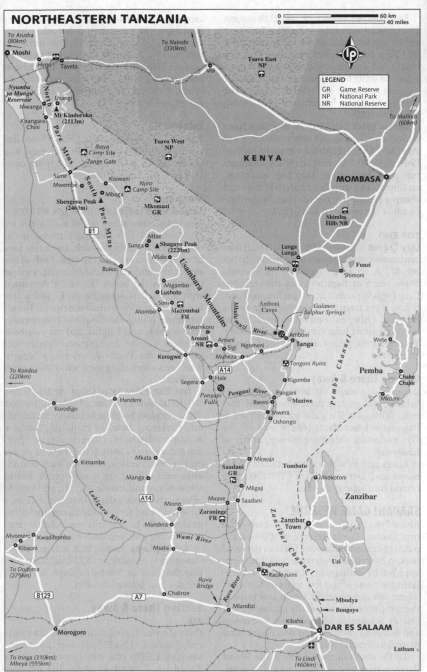

NORTHEASTERN TANZANIA

0		60 km
0		40 miles

LEGEND
GR   Game Reserve
NP   National Park
NR   National Reserve

To Arusha (80km)

Moshi

To Nairobi (330km)

Tsavo East NP

Himo

Taveta

Voi

Nyumba ya Mungu Reservoir

Mwanga

Usangi

Mt Kindoroko (2113m)

Kisangara Chini

North Pare Mtns

Ibaya Camp Site

Zange Gate

Tsavo West NP

KENYA

MOMBASA

Same

Mwembe

Kisiwani

Mbaga

Njiro Camp Site

Mkomazi GR

Shengena Peak (2463m)

South Pare Mtns

B1

Shimba Hills NR

Mtae

Shagayu Peak (2220m)

Sunga

Mlalo

Lunga Lunga

Funzi

Shimoni

Buiko

Usambara Mountains

Horohoro

Migambo

Lushoto

Soni

Amboni Caves

Galanos Sulphur Springs

Mombo

Mazumbai FR

Kwamkoro

Wete

Amani NR

Amani

Sigi

Ngomeni

Amboni

Tanga

Pemba Channel

Pemba

Korogwe

Muheza

A14

Hale

Tongoni Ruins

Kigombe

Chake Chake

To Kondoa (220km)

Segera

Pangani Falls

Pangani River

Pangani

Bweni

Maziwe

Mkoani

Handeni

Korodigo

Mwera

Ushongo

Kimamba

Mkata

Mkwaja

Saadani GR

Tumbatu

Mkokotoni

Manga

Mligaji

Zanzibar

A14

Miono

Mvave

Saadani

Lukigura River

Mandera

Zaraninge FR

Wami River

Zanzibar Town

Uzi

Mvomero

Kwadihombo

Kibaoni

Msata

To Dodoma (275km)

B129

A7

Ruvu Bridge

Ruvu River

Bagamoyo

Kaole ruins

Mbudya

Bongoyo

Chalinze

Morogoro

Mlandizi

Kibaha

DAR ES SALAAM

To Iringa (310km); Mbeya (555km)

To Lindi (460km)

Latham

To Malindi (60km)

Bagamoyo Beach Resort (☎ 2440083; bbr@baganet .com; bandas per person with shared bathroom TSh9000, s/d with fan TSh26,000/32,000, with air-con TSh34,000/42,000; ❄) Fine and friendly, with rooms in two blocks (ask for the one closer to the water), a few no-frills beach *bandas* and a seaside location just north of Travellers Lodge. The cuisine is vaguely French, and tasty (meals from TSh4000).

Badeco Beach Hotel (☎ 244 0018; www.badeco beachhotel.com; camping with showers TSh3000, d with shared bathroom TSh12,000, d/tr with private bathroom TSh24,000/30,000) This long-standing German-run place has a large, thatched restaurant, en suite rooms with Zanzibar-style beds and cheaper rooms sharing facilities. It's on the beach at the southern end of town.

TOP END

Lazy Lagoon (☎ 0748-237422, 0744-237422; www .tanzaniasafaris.info; s/d full board & boat transfers US$160/ 240; ☒) A relaxing, upmarket place about 10km south of Bagamoyo on the secluded Lazy Lagoon peninsula. To get here by road, follow signs from the main highway to the Mbegani Fisheries compound, from where it's just a short boat ride over to the lodge. You can leave your vehicle in the fisheries compound.

Getting There & Away

Bagamoyo is about 70km north of Dar es Salaam, and an easy drive along good Tarmac. With a 4WD it's also possible to reach Bagamoyo from Msata (65km west on the Dar es Salaam–Arusha highway, north of Chalinze).

Buses and minibuses ply between Bagamoyo and Dar es Salaam (TSh1000, 1½ hours) throughout the day.

SAADANI GAME RESERVE

About 70km up the coast from Bagamoyo is tiny Saadani Game Reserve, a 1000-sq-km patch of coastal wilderness that is a national park in everything but name (awaiting final approval by Parliament). Laid-back and relaxing, it's one of the few spots in Tanzania where you can enjoy the beach and bush at the same time. It's also easily accessed from Dar es Salaam as an overnight excursion and is a good choice if you don't have time to explore further afield.

To the south of the reserve is the Wami River, where you're likely to see hippos,

crocodiles and many birds, including lesser flamingos (in the delta), fish eagles, hammerkops and kingfishers. Giraffes are commonly seen, and with some effort you may also see elephants, Lichtenstein's hartebeest and (rarely) lions. The main activities are boat trips along the Wami River and wildlife drives and walks.

Information

Entry to the reserve costs US$20/5 per day per adult/child aged five to 15 years, and guides cost US$10 per day. Camping costs US$20/5 per adult/child.

Sleeping

Saadani Safari Lodge (☎ 022-277 3294, 0741-555678; www.saadanisafarilodge.com; s/d full board & park fees US$290/500; ☒) This beachside retreat is the only lodging within the park, and a fine base from which to explore the area. Each of the nine cosy and comfortable cottages is set directly on the beach. There's a restaurant with a raised sundowner deck, and a tree house overlooking a small waterhole. The atmosphere is unpretentious and comfortable, staff friendly and helpful, and the cuisine is excellent. Leisure-time pursuits include boat safaris on the Wami River, vehicle safaris, walks and snorkelling excursions to a nearby sandbank.

Tent With a View Safari Lodge (☎ 022-211 0507, 0741-323318; www.saadani.com; s/d full board US$255/350) This secluded, tropical hideaway makes another relaxing base for exploring Saadani. Accommodation is in luxurious raised *bandas* hidden away among the coconut groves on the beach just outside the park boundaries, and everything is very plush, but in a low-key, comfortable way. In addition to vehicle and boat safaris, there's the chance for excursions around the camp, including guided walks to a nearby green-turtle nesting site. No children under eight years old.

Warthog Camp (camping US$8, tent rental US$10), Camping is possible at this basic camp outside the park in Saadani village. It has pit latrines and bucket showers.

Getting There & Away
AIR

Daily ZanAir flights connect Dar, Zanzibar and Saadani (US$50 one way Zanzibar–Saadani, US$75 one way Dar–Saadani, via Zanzibar). Coastal Aviation flies between

Saadani and Selous Game Reserve (US$130 one way, minimum two passengers).

ROAD

Both lodges provide road transport to/from Dar es Salaam for about US$200 per vehicle, one way (about four hours).

From Dar es Salaam, the route is via Chalinze on the Morogoro road, and then 50km north to Mandera village along the Arusha highway. It's easy to get to Mandera by bus, but there's no public transport for the remaining 60km from there to Saadani.

To reach Saadani from Pangani, you need to first cross the Pangani River by ferry, then continue south along a rough road (4WD only) to the reserve's northern gate at Mligaji. Tent With A View Safari Lodge and the Tides (p162) provide transfers for US$100 per vehicle each way (about one hour). There's also a daily bus between Tanga and Mkwaja (TSh5000, five hours), from where you could be collected by the lodges.

PANGANI

☏ 027

About 55km south of Tanga is the small and charmingly dilapidated Swahili outpost of Pangani. It rose from obscure beginnings as just one of many coastal dhow ports to become a terminus of the caravan route from Lake Tanganyika, a major export point for slaves and ivory, and one of the largest ports between Bagamoyo and Mombasa. By the end of the 19th century, focus had shifted to Tanga and Dar es Salaam, and Pangani again faded into anonymity.

The most interesting area of town is near the river, where there are some carved doorways, buildings from the German colonial era, and old houses of Indian traders. About 10km offshore is **Maziwe Marine Reserve** (admission TSh1000), a small sand island where you can snorkel. The island can only be visited at low tide, and there's no food or drink.

Information

The closest banks are in Tanga. The sporadically functioning **Pangani Cultural Tourism Program office** (☉ 8am-5pm Mon-Fri, to noon Sat) on the riverfront can help organise town tours, river cruises and excursions to Maziwe Island, as can any of the hotels.

It's not safe to walk along the beaches close to town.

Sleeping & Eating

The best place to base yourself is on one of the beaches running north and south of town.

PANGANI & NORTH

Few travellers stay in town, most preferring the beaches to the north of the main junction (where the road from Muheza joins the coastal road), or those on the southern side of the river around Ushongo.

Peponi Holiday Resort (☏ 0748-202962, 0741-540139; www.peponiresort.com; camping US$4, d banda US$40, discounted family & backpacker rates) A relaxing and traveller-friendly place set in expansive grounds on a long, good beach about 19km north of Pangani. In addition to simple, breezy double *bandas*, there are several larger five-person chalets, a camping ground and ablution blocks. Tasty cuisine and a nearby reef for snorkelling complete the picture. The proprietors are helpful with information about excursions and onward connections, and the camp has its own *mashua* (motorised dhow) for sails. If you're camping, bring supplies with you, and if you'll be staying in the *bandas*, book in advance if possible. Take any bus running along the Pangani–Tanga coastal route and ask the driver to drop you near Kigombe village at the Peponi turn-off (TSh500 from Pangani, TSh800 from Tanga), from where it's just a short walk. Taxis from Tanga cost TSh20,000 to TSh25,000, depending on road conditions and your bargaining abilities.

Argovia Tented Lodge (☏ 263 0000, 0748-783613; argovia@kaributanga.com; camping US$5, s/d bandas US$30/40, s luxury tents US$51-60, d luxury tents US$60-84) This good-value establishment is the only upmarket accommodation along the northern coast. Most accommodation is in raised luxury tents of the sort you find in upscale safari camps. There are also some small stone *bandas*, a good restaurant and a range of excursions. It's on a low cliff overlooking the sea, and is signposted about 3km north of the main junction.

Tinga Tinga Resort (☏ 263 0022; camping TSh4000, s/d/tr US$25/35/45) The friendly and low-key Tinga Tinga is a reasonable choice, though the other beach places are better value. Accommodation is in large, faded twin-bedded bungalows set inland, and just north of the main junction. Five minutes' walk away is a

TANZANIA

restaurant-bar gazebo (meals about TSh4000) overlooking the water.

New River View Inn Restaurant & Lodge (Jamhuri St; s/d with shared bathroom TSh2500/4000) This is the cheapest place, with no-frills rooms sharing facilities. It's on the waterfront road, just east of the Customs House. There's no food, but try Pangani's lively night markets in the surrounding streets.

SOUTH OF PANGANI

The long, palm-fringed beach about 15km south of Pangani around Ushongo makes a wonderful coastal getaway. Swimming isn't tide dependent, and apart from the area in the immediate vicinity of Ushongo village, you'll have most spots to yourself.

Tides (☎ 0748-225812; www.thetideslodge.com; s/d half board US$110/150) This unpretentious place mixes an intimate seaside location with spacious, breezy bungalows and excellent cuisine. The seven bungalows – lined up amid the coconut palms along the beach – are wonderful, with huge beds surrounded by billowing mosquito nets, and large bathrooms. There's a beachside bar, and staff can sort out excursions, including to Maziwe island. For a honeymoon location, or beachside retreat, it's hard to beat the value here. Pick-ups from Pangani can be arranged, as can transfers to/from Saadani Game Reserve, and to/from Segera, where there are connections to the Scandinavian Express bus between Dar es Salaam and Arusha.

Emayani Beach Lodge (☎ 250 1741; www.emayani lodge.com; s/d/tr US$63/79/100) Emayani, on the beach about 2km north of the Tides, has a row of agreeably rustic bungalows strung out along the sand, and a restaurant, and is about as laid-back as it gets. The bungalows are made entirely of *makuti*, and are very open and natural. Staff can arrange sails on a *ngalawa* (outrigger canoe) and other excursions. Pick-ups from Pangani cost US$20 return.

Coco Beach Resort (☎ 0741-333449; camping US$6, s/d with shared bathroom US$18/36, s/d/tr with private bathroom US$21/42/60) Small, serviceable cottages just in from the beach south of Emayani Beach Lodge.

Getting There & Away
AIR
There's an airstrip within about 1km of Ushongo for charter flights. ZanAir and

Coastal Aviation are the best lines to check with, as both have scheduled flights to nearby destinations (ZanAir to Saadani and Coastal to Saadani and Tanga).

BOAT
Dhows sail regularly between Pangani and Mkokotoni, on the northwestern coast of Zanzibar.

ROAD
The best connections between Pangani and Tanga are via the rehabilitated coastal road, with about five buses daily (TSh1500, 1½ hours), except during the height of the rainy season. The first departs Pangani at about 6.30am so you can connect with a Tanga–Arusha bus. It's also possible to reach Pangani from Muheza (TSh1000), from where there are connections to Tanga or Korogwe, but the road is worse and connections infrequent.

To Ushongo and the beaches south of Pangani, all the hotels do pick-ups. Alternatively, there's a bus that runs between Tanga and Mkwaja (at the edge of Saadani Game Reserve) that passes Mwera village (6km from Ushongo) daily about 7am going north, and about 3.30pm going south.

Another possibility is to hire a bike in Pangani and cycle down to Ushongo.

The vehicle ferry over the Pangani River runs in theory between 6.30am and 6.30pm daily (TSh100/4000 per person/vehicle), and there are small passenger boats (large enough to take a motorcycle) throughout the day (TSh200).

TANGA
☎ 027
One of Tanzania's major industrial towns until the collapse of the sisal market, and still an important seaport, Tanga has a sleepy, semicolonial atmosphere and faded charm. There's little reason to make a special detour to visit, although it makes a convenient stop en route to and from Mombasa.

Information
Kaributanga.com (Sokoine St; per hr TSh500; ◷ 9am-9pm) Come here for Internet access.

MD Pharmacy (☎ 264 4067; cnr Sokoine St & Mkwakwani Rd; ◷ 8am-12.45pm & 2-6pm Mon-Fri, 8am-12.15pm Sat & Sun) Opposite the market.

NBC (cnr Bank & Sokoine Sts) Just west of the market; changes cash and travellers cheques, and has an ATM.

Tourcare Tanzania (☎ 264 4111; Mkwakwani Rd; 🕑 8am-5pm Mon-Sat) Just down from Patwas restaurant; helpful with information on nearby attractions, and with arranging guides for excursions (TSh10,000 per group per day).

Sleeping
BUDGET
Kiboko Restaurant, Bar & Campsite (☎ 264 4929; jda -kiboko@bluemail.ch; Amboni Rd; camping US$4) Good, secure camping in a large yard, spotless ablutions, power points, a well-stocked bar and a nice garden restaurant. Management are helpful with excursions and information on Tanga. The turn-off from Hospital Rd is signposted about 500m before Inn by the Sea.

Inn by the Sea (☎ 264 4614; Hospital Rd; r with fan/ air-con TSh7000/10,000; 🔁) Inn by the Sea has a pleasant waterside setting on the southwestern edge of Ras Kazone, and very run-down rooms, although they're fair enough value for the price. Meals can be arranged; allow about two hours.

Other recommendations:

Ocean Breeze Hotel (☎ 264 4445; cnr Tower & Sokoine Sts; r with fan/air-con TSh7000/12,000; 🔁) Rooms here are on the scruffy side, but OK, and many have nets. It's just east of the market, and one of the better budget choices in the town centre.

Asad Hotel (☎ 264 4711, 264 6801; d TSh12,500; 🔁) Functional rooms with views over the bus stand; it's in a multistorey building just off Taifa Rd in the Ngamiani area.

MIDRANGE
Panori Hotel (☎ 264 6044; panori@africaonline.co.tz; Ras Kazone; s/d in new wing TSh25,000/30,000, in old renovated wing TSh18,000/22,000, in old wing TSh15,000/18,000; 🔁) If you don't mind the location, in a residential area about 3km from the centre (no public transport), this is one of the better midrange choices. There are clean, modern rooms in the new wing, all with nets and fan, and an outdoor restaurant with slow service and tasty meals. Take Hospital Rd east to Ras Kazone, and follow the signposts.

Hotel Kola Prieto (☎ 264 4206; India St; r TSh25, 500; 🔁) This centrally located high-rise hotel has good modern rooms (no nets or screens), efficient service and, despite the bland

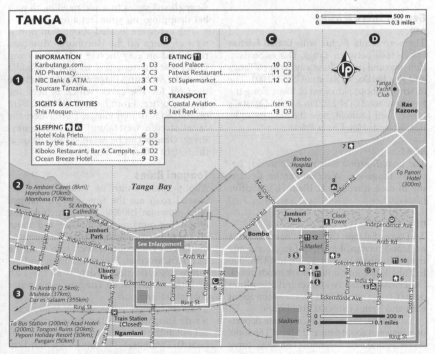

TANGA

INFORMATION	
Kaributanga.com	1 D3
MD Pharmacy	2 C3
NBC Bank & ATM	3 C3
Tourcare Tanzania	4 C3

SIGHTS & ACTIVITIES	
Shia Mosque	5 B3

SLEEPING	
Hotel Kola Prieto	6 D3
Inn by the Sea	7 D2
Kiboko Restaurant, Bar & Campsite	8 D2
Ocean Breeze Hotel	9 D3

EATING	
Food Palace	10 D3
Patwas Restaurant	11 C3
SD Supermarket	12 C2

TRANSPORT	
Coastal Aviation	(see 5)
Taxi Rank	13 D3

Tanga Yacht Club
Ras Kazone
Bombo Hospital
To Panori Hotel (300m)
Tanga Bay
To Amboni Caves (8km); Horohoro (70km); Mombasa (170km)
St Anthony's Cathedral
Mombasa Rd
Jamhuri Park
Port Rd
Independence Ave
Sokoine (Market) St.
Uhuru Park
Chumbageni
Goan St
Kilimanjaro Rd
Eckernförde Ave
Usambara St
Guinea Rd
Custom St
Swahili St
Ring St
Railway St
To Airstrip (2.5km); Muheza (37km); Dar es Salaam (355km)
Ring Rd
Train Station (Closed)
To Bus Station (200m); Asad Hotel (200m); Tongoni Ruins (20km); Peponi Holiday Resort (30km); Pangani (50km)
Taifa Rd
Mkwakwani Rd
Ngamiani
See Enlargement
Arab Rd
Makorora Rd
Hospital Rd
Bombo
Amboni Rd
Jamhuri Park
Clock Tower
Independence Ave
Market
Bank St
Tower Rd
Sokoine (Market) St.
India St
Guinea Rd
Usambara St
Eckernförde Ave
Custom St
Mkwakwani Rd
Stadium
Ring St
0　500 m
0　0.3 miles
0　200 m
0　0.1 miles

ambience, does a good job of fulfilling the promise of its business card to provide you with the 'finest hospitality sensation'.

Eating

Tanga compensates for its dearth of good accommodation with a few culinary gems:

Patwas Restaurant (Mkwakwani Rd; meals from TSh1500; 8am-8pm Mon-Sat) An unassuming place, and the best restaurant in Tanga, with *lassis*, fresh juices, tasty, good-value meals and helpful owners. It's just south of the market.

Food Palace (264 6816; Sokoine St; lunch Mon, breakfast, lunch & dinner Tue-Sun) Another good choice, this place has an array of tasty Indian snacks and meals, including some vegetarian selections.

Kiboko Restaurant & Bar (meals from TSh3000) Garden seating, a well-stocked bar and a huge menu featuring *kiboko*- (hippo-) sized portions of such delicacies as prawns with green pepper-sauce, kingfish curry, sandwiches and *mishikaki*. See also p163.

For self-catering try **SD Supermarket** (Bank St), behind the market.

Getting There & Away

AIR

There are daily flights with **Coastal Aviation** (264 6548) between Tanga, Dar es Salaam, Zanzibar and Pemba (one way between Tanga and Pemba/Dar es Salaam US$55/100). The airstrip is about 3km west of town along the Korogwe road (TSh2500 in a taxi). Coastal's office is off India St, near the Shia mosque, not far from Hotel Kola Prieto.

BOAT

The boat *Takrima* sails roughly weekly between Tanga and Wete on Pemba, departing in each direction at 10am (US$25, five hours).

BUS

To Dar es Salaam, the fastest connection is on Scandinavian, departing Tanga (en route from Mombasa) about 12.30pm (TSh7000 to TSh10,000, four hours; book in advance). Otherwise, Raha Leo and several other lines depart Tanga every few hours between about 8am and 3pm (TSh6000, five hours).

To Arusha, there are at least three departures between about 6am and 11am (TSh9000, seven hours). To Lushoto (TSh4000, three

to four hours), there are a couple of direct buses departing by 7am, or you can take any Arusha bus and transfer at Mombo.

To Pangani (TSh1500, 1½ hours), there are small buses throughout the day along the coastal road.

For Mombasa, see p257; the Scandinavian bus from Dar to Mombasa passes Tanga about noon.

AROUND TANGA
Amboni Caves

Long the subject of local legend, these **limestone caves** (admission TSh2000) make an intriguing, off-beat excursion for anyone with an interest in spelunking, although it's not all it's made out to be in the Tanga tourist brochures.

The caves were originally thought to extend up to 200km or more, and are said to have been used by the Kenyan Mau Mau during the 1950s as a hide-out from the British. Although a 1994 survey concluded that their extent was much smaller, rumours of them reaching all the way to Mombasa persist. If you visit, bring along a torch, and wear closed shoes to avoid needing to pick bat droppings off your feet afterwards.

The caves are located about 8km northwest of Tanga off the Horohoro–Mombasa road, and an easy bicycle ride from town. Otherwise charter a taxi, or take a *daladala* towards Amboni village and get out at the turn-off for the caves, which is near the forestry office. From here, it's about 2.5km on foot to Kiomoni village, from where the caves stretch west along the Mkulumuzi River. Guides can be arranged locally or at the tourist office in Tanga.

Tongoni Ruins

About 20km south of Tanga along the coastal road are the time-ravaged **Tongoni ruins** (admission TSh2000). They include the crumbling remains of a mosque and about 20 overgrown Shirazi pillar-style tombs – the largest collection of such tombs on the East African coast. Both the mosque and the tombs are estimated to date from the 14th or 15th century, when Tongoni was a major coastal trading port.

To get here, take any vehicle heading towards Pangani along the coastal road and get out at the turn-off (look for a rusty signboard). From here, the ruins are about 1km east on foot. Get an early start, as finding a lift back in the afternoon can be difficult.

MUHEZA
☎ 027

Muheza is a scrappy junction town where the roads to Amani Nature Reserve and to Pangani branch off the main Tanga highway. There are a few guesthouses in town, including the grubby **Hotel Ambassador** (s/d with shared bathroom TSh2500/3500) on the main road towards Tanga.

There's a Scandinavian Express bus booking office next to Hotel Ambassador (for buses between Dar es Salaam and Mombasa via Muheza and Tanga). Buses to Amani Nature Reserve leave from the main junction along the road leading towards the market.

KOROGWE
☎ 027

Korogwe is of little interest other than as a transport junction. In the western part of town, known as 'new' Korogwe, are the bus stand and several guesthouses. To the east is 'old' Korogwe with the train station (no passenger service).

Motel White Parrot (☎ 264 1068; s/d TSh30,000/ 40,000; ☒) is a large roadside rest stop with a restaurant (meals TSh4000), and with spiffy rooms that have TV and minifridge. It's on the main highway and is unmissable.

For something cheaper, try **Travellers Inn** (d TSh7500), opposite the bus stand.

USAMBARA MOUNTAINS

With their wide vistas, cool climate, winding paths and picturesque villages, the Usambaras are one of northeastern Tanzania's highlights. It's easily possible to spend at least a week here hiking from village to village, or relaxing in one spot and doing your exploring as a series of day walks.

The mountains, which are part of the ancient Eastern Arc chain, are divided into two ranges separated by a 4km-wide valley. The western Usambaras are the most accessible and have the better road network, while the eastern Usambaras, around Amani, are less developed. Both ranges are densely populated, with the main tribes the Sambaa, the Kilindi, the Zigua and the Mbugu.

While the climate is comfortable year-round, paths get very muddy during the rainy season.

Amani Nature Reserve

This often overlooked nature reserve is located west of Tanga in the heart of the eastern Usambara mountains. It's a peaceful place with some pleasant walks along shady forest paths, and a worthwhile detour for the ornithologically or botanically inclined.

INFORMATION

At Sigi, there is a good **information centre** (☯ 8am-6pm) at the old Station Master's House, with information about the area's plants and animals, history, local medicinal plants and more.

The main **reserve office** (☎ 027-264 0313; entry fee per person US$30, per vehicle US$5) is at Amani. Entry and guide fees (US$20 per group per day) can be paid here, or at the Sigi information centre.

Most trails take between one and three hours. They are detailed in the booklet, *A Guide to Trails and Drive Routes in Amani Nature Reserve,* on sale at the information centre at Sigi, and at the reserve office in Amani.

SLEEPING & EATING

The **Amani Conservation Centre** (☎ 027 264 0313) runs two guesthouses: the **Amani Conservation Centre Rest House** (r with shared bathroom TSh5000) at Amani and the **Sigi Rest House** (r TSh5000) at Sigi. Both are good, with hot water for bathing, and filtered water for drinking. The rooms at Sigi have bathrooms and are marginally more comfortable, while the setting and rustic atmosphere are better at Amani. Meals (breakfast TSh2500, lunch and dinner TSh5000) are available at both, though it's a good idea to bring fruit and snacks as a supplement. The Sigi Rest House is opposite the Sigi information centre. To reach the Amani Conservation Centre Rest House, once in Amani, continue straight past the main fork, ignoring the 'resthouse' signpost, to the reserve office. The Rest House is next to the office.

Camping (US$5) is possible at both Sigi and Amani with your own tent and supplies.

GETTING THERE & AWAY

Amani is 32km northwest of Muheza along a dirt road that is in fair condition except for the final seven kilometres, which are in bad shape (4WD only). There's at least one truck or bus daily from Muheza to

Sigi, sometimes continuing on to Amani (TSh1500) and Kwamkoro, about 9km beyond Amani, and usually departing Muheza between noon and 2pm. Going in the other direction, transport usually passes Amani about 6.30am. If you're driving from Muheza, the route is straightforward until the final junction, where you'll see Bulwa signposted to the right; Amani is about 2km further along to the left (staying on the main road).

Lushoto
☎ 027

Lushoto is a leafy highland town nestled in a fertile valley at about 1200m, and surrounded by pines and eucalyptus mixed with banana plants and other tropical foliage. It's the centre of the western Usambaras and makes an excellent base for hikes into the surrounding hills.

During the German era, Lushoto (or Wilhelmstal, as it was then known) was a favoured vacation spot for colonial administrators, and was even slated at one point to become the colonial capital.

INFORMATION
ELCT Office (per hr TSh2000; ☺ 8am-8pm Mon-Sat) Internet access; on the main road, next to Tumaini Restaurant.
National Microfinance Bank (☺ 8am-3pm Mon-Fri) On the main road; changes cash and travellers cheques (minimum US$40 commission for travellers cheques).
Tourist Information Centre (☎ 264 0132) Just down the small road running next to the bank, and a good spot for arranging hikes. If would-be guides approach you on the street, check here first to verify that they are official before starting out.

ACTIVITIES
The hills surrounding Lushoto offer some wonderful walking along well-worn footpaths that weave past villages, cornfields and banana plantations, and range from a few hours to several days.

An easy starter hike is to **Irente viewpoint** (about 1½ hours return), which begins on the road running southwest from the Anglican church and offers wide views down to the plains below; camping is possible. En route and shortly before the viewpoint is Irente Farm, where you can buy fresh cheese, yogurt and bread.

There's also a good three- to four-day hike through villages and forests from Lushoto to

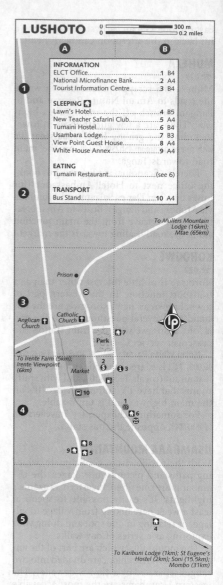

LUSHOTO

0 — 300 m
0 — 0.2 miles

INFORMATION
ELCT Office..................................1 B4
National Microfinance Bank............2 A4
Tourist Information Centre..............3 B4

SLEEPING
Lawn's Hotel................................4 B5
New Teacher Safarini Club..............5 A4
Tumaini Hostel.............................6 B4
Usambara Lodge..........................7 B3
View Point Guest House.................8 A4
White House Annex.......................9 A4

EATING
Tumaini Restaurant...................(see 6)

TRANSPORT
Bus Stand..................................10 A4

To Mullers Mountain Lodge (16km); Mtae (65km)

Prison

Anglican Church
Catholic Church

Park

To Irente Farm (5km); Irente Viewpoint (6km)
Market

To Karibuni Lodge (1km); St Eugene's Hostel (2km); Soni (15.5km); Mombo (31km)

Mtae, a small village north of Lushoto with a beautiful cliff-top setting. The tourist office can offer suggestions for other routes. Rates vary depending on the hike, but expect to pay about TSh25,000 per person per day (less in a group) on multiday hikes, including camping or accommodation in basic guesthouses, guide and village-development fees, but excluding food. It gets chilly and wet in Lushoto, so bring a jacket and warm, waterproof clothes.

SLEEPING & EATING
Budget
Karibuni Lodge (www.karibunilodge.com; camping US$3, dm US$6, s/d from US$12/16) This small backpackers' house, surrounded by a small patch of forest, has a cosy, woodsy feel, large rooms (some with bathroom), a book swap, tasty meals and a crackling hearth. It's about 1.5km south of the town centre near the district hospital and is signposted; ask the bus to drop you at the hospital.

Tumaini Hostel (☎ 264 0094; tumaini@elct.org; s/d TSh10,000/17,000) Functionality is the theme here, with a few long hallways of reasonable-value rooms in a two-storey compound on the main road near the telecom building.

Tumaini Restaurant (☎ 264 0027; meals from TSh1500; ☯ breakfast, lunch & dinner) This is just next door, and has inexpensive meals.

Lawn's Hotel (☎ 264 0005/66; www.lawnshotel .com; camping with hot shower TSh4500, s/d with shared bathroom TSh14,000/18,000, with private bathroom TSh30,000/35,000) This Lushoto institution at the entrance to town has rooms that are quite faded these days, but still retains vestiges of rustic charm. It's ideal for camping, however, with large lawns, hot showers and lots of space.

White House Annex (d with shared bathroom TSh6000, s/d with private bathroom Sh7000/8000) No-frills rooms with hot water, and meals on order. It's five minutes' walk from the bus stand: head over the small bridge, turn left and go up the hill.

Usambara Lodge (s/d with shared bathroom 3500/6000) More no-frills rooms, and a good location near the park, away from the clutch of budget hotels near the bus stand.

At Irente Viewpoint, there's camping at **Irente Viewpoint Campsite** (camping TSh2500), on the edge of the escarpment, and at the nearby **Irente Farm** (☎ 264 000; camping TSh2000, r with shared bathroom TSh6000).

There are lots of basic guesthouses near the market, all with serviceable, grubby rooms and bucket showers, including **View Point Guest House** (☎ 264 0031; r with shared bathroom TSh5000), diagonally across from and just before White House Annex, and **New Teacher Safarini Club** (r with shared bathroom TSh3500), directly opposite White House Annex.

Midrange
St Eugene's Hostel (☎ 264 0055; s/d/ste TSh18,000/ 30,000/40,000) This quiet place has spotless, comfortable rooms, all with good, hot showers and balconies with views over the hills, and is the best accommodation in this range close to the town centre. It's run by an order of sisters and profits go to support their work with local children. Meals are available (TSh5000), and homemade cheese and jam are sold on the premises. St Eugene's is along the main road about 3km before Lushoto; ask the bus to drop you at the Montessori Centre.

About 15km outside Lushoto near Migambo village are several more places, all well situated for walking, and reasonable options if you have your own transport. The main one is **Mullers Mountain Lodge** (☎ 264 0204; mullers mountainlodge@yahoo.com; camping TSh3500, s/d/tr/q TSh30,000/40,000/50,000/70,000), a sprawling family homestead with rooms in the main house or in nearby cottages. There are also a few less appealing cement huts with shared bathroom, and a camping area.

GETTING THERE & AWAY
Daily buses travel between Lushoto and Tanga (TSh4000, three to four hours), Dar es Salaam (TSh8000, seven to nine hours) and Arusha (TSh7000 to TSh8000, six hours), all departing in the morning, and there are *daladalas* throughout the day between Lushoto and Mombo (TSh1000, one hour). If you're going from Lushoto to either Dar es Salaam, Moshi or Arusha, you can take a direct bus from Lushoto or (often faster) get a bus to Mombo, the junction town on the main highway, and then get one of the larger express buses to Dar es Salaam. The place to wait is at New Liverpool Hotel, on the main road about 1km west of the Mombo junction, where all the Dar–Arusha buses stop for a rest break, beginning from about 10am.

For the lodges near Migambo, take the road heading uphill and northeast of town to Magamba, turn right at the signposted junction and continue for about 7km to Migambo, where all three lodges are signposted. Swiss Farm Cottage is the first one you'll reach, about 1km off the main road to the left. Mullers is about 1km further down the Migambo road. There's a daily bus to/from Tanga that goes to within around 2kms of the lodges, departing Tanga at about 9am or 10am and reaching the Migambo area at around 2pm.

Soni

☎ 027

Tiny Soni, about halfway along the Mombo–Lushoto road, lacks Lushoto's infrastructure, but makes a good change of pace if you'll be staying a while in the Usambaras. It's known for nearby **Kwa Mungu** hill, about 30 minutes away on foot, and is home to some attractive butterflies. Hikes to these and other destinations can be arranged at Maweni Farm or at the tourist office in Lushoto.

Maweni Farm (☎ 264 0426, 0748-608313; www .maneno.net; camping per tent US$10, s/d full board with shared bathroom US$35/70, with private bathroom US$45/90) This atmospheric old farmhouse is set in rambling grounds about 3km from the main junction. Rooms are no-frills and spacious, although overpriced. There are also some tented *bandas*, plus meals and guides for organising walks. Coming from Lushoto, take the dirt road branching left at the main Soni junction and follow it for about 2km.

Soni is about halfway along the road between Mombo and Lushoto, and is easy to reach via *daladala* from either destination; Maweni Farm provides free pick-ups if you're staying in their rooms.

Mombo

☎ 027

Mombo is the junction town at the foot of the Usambara Mountains where the road to Lushoto branches off the main Dar es Salaam–Arusha highway.

Tembo Lodge & Campsite (☎ 264 1539, 0748-663205; tembo.lodges@iwayafrica.com; camping per tent US$4, s/d US$14/18; 🏊) This place, at the foot of the mountains about 15km west of town, has camping, rooms, food, a bar and a swimming pool, and will come collect you for free from Mombo. It's about 1km off the main highway and is signposted.

PARE MOUNTAINS

The Pare Mountains, northwest of the Usambaras, are also part of the Eastern Arc chain, and like the Usambaras they are divided into two ranges: north and south. The main tribal group in this region is the Pare (Asu).

Although the Pare Mountains are not as accessible or developed for tourism as the Usambaras, they offer rewarding hiking, although you will need to be self-sufficient and arrange things yourself. The best way to explore is to spend a night at Mwanga (for the north Pares) or Same (for the south Pares) getting organised, and then head up to either Usangi or Mbaga, from where you can access the best hikes.

Lodging and food in the Pare Mountains are for the most part very basic. With the exception of Hill-Top Tona Lodge in Mbaga, most accommodation is with villagers, or camping.

Organised hiking is done in the framework of the CTP, which charges TSh25,000 for two people per day, including a guide, camping fees and meals. For the South Pares, the CTP is based in Same, 105km south of Moshi on the Arusha–Dar highway. For the North Pares, the CTP is at Usangi, reached via Mwanga along the same highway.

The Pares can be visited comfortably at any time of year, except during the March to May long rains, when paths become too muddy.

Same

☎ 027

Same (*sah*-may) is the main town in the South Pares. There's little tourist infrastructure, and the town is more suitable as a starting point for excursions into the Pares than as a base. The CTP information office is in the Padeco Building, diagonally across from the bus stand. If it's closed, ask at Elephant Motel, or head directly to Hill-Top Tona Lodge, where there's a knowledgeable English-speaking guide for arranging treks.

SLEEPING & EATING

Elephant Motel (☎ 275 8193; www.elephantmotel.com; s/d TSh15,000/20,000) Same's most 'upmarket' accommodation, with faded but reasonable rooms, a cavernous restaurant serving up good meals, and a TV. It's on the main highway about 1km southeast of town.

Amani Lutheran Centre (☎ 275 8107; s/d with shared bathroom TSh3500/5000) Simple rooms around a quiet compound, and a restaurant.

GETTING THERE & AWAY

Most buses on the Dar es Salaam–Arusha highway stop at Same on request. Otherwise, minibuses travel daily between Same, Dar es Salaam and Moshi, leaving Same in the morning. There is a direct bus between Arusha and Same, departing Arusha at around 8am (TSh4000, 2½ hours). To Mbaga, transport leaves Same most days between about 11am and 2pm.

Mbaga

Mbaga, about 30km southeast of Same near Mkomazi Game Reserve, offers hikes to the surrounding hills and villages, and to the top of 2463m Shengena Peak (two or three days), the highest in the Pare Mountains.

The rustic former mission house of **Hill-Top Tona Lodge** (☎ 0744-852010; tona_lodge@hotmail .com; camping US$5, r per person with shared bathroom US$10) is one of the best bases in the Pares, with good views, helpful staff, simple cottages and reasonable hiking prices (guides cost US$6 per group of up to three people; village-development fee US$2 per person per day). Meals are available for TSh2500.

There are one or two vehicles daily between Same and Mbaga, with the last one departing Same by about 2pm (TSh2500, two to three hours). From Moshi, you'll need to get a bus by 8am in order to get to Mbaga the same day. Coming from Dar es Salaam, you'll probably need to overnight in Same. Hiring a vehicle up to Mbaga costs about TSh40,000 one way; ask at Safari Grill, near the Same bus stand.

Mwanga

Mwanga is about 50km north of Same on the Dar es Salaam–Arusha highway. The main reason to come here is to change vehicles to get to Usangi, the starting point for excursions in the northern Pares. For overnight accommodation, try the clean but noisy **Angela Guesthouse** (d TSh8500), about 1km in from the main highway near the new market.

Usangi

Usangi, in the hills east of Mwanga, is the centre of the north Pares and is the best base for hiking in this area.

The main point of interest as far as hiking is concerned is **Lomwe Secondary School**, which is the CTP base, where you'll find guides and accommodation. There's a camping ground here with water, and the school serves as a **hostel** (camping & dm per person TSh3000) when classes are not in session. Otherwise,

there's a simple **guesthouse** (r with shared bathroom TSh4000) near the main mosque.

Several pick-ups go daily between Mwanga and Usangi. From Arusha and Moshi, there's a direct bus, departing in the morning (TSh5000; four hours from Arusha). Ask the driver to drop you at Lomwe Secondary School.

Mkomazi Game Reserve

The completely undeveloped Mkomazi Game Reserve spreads along the Kenyan border in the shadow of the Pare Mountains, its dry savanna lands contrasting sharply with the moist forests of the Pares. The reserve, which is contiguous with Kenya's Tsavo West National Park, is known for its black rhinos, which were introduced into the area from South Africa for breeding. Other animals include elephants, giraffes, zebras and antelopes, although it takes luck and effort to see these. If you're in the area and want to get off the beaten track, Mkomazi can make an interesting albeit very off-beat safari destination – appealing primarily for the chance it offers for wilderness walking, rather than for wildlife watching, which can't compare with the northern parks.

Reserve entry costs US$20 per day. Visits to the black rhino breeding area at Kisima can be arranged with park staff at Zange Gate (the main entrance to the reserve, about 5km east of Same). Walking tours are the reserve's main attraction. You'll need to be accompanied by an armed ranger, which can be arranged at reserve headquarters at Zange Gate. For overnighting, there are several basic **camping grounds** (camping US$20), including at Ibaya, about 15km from Zange Gate. For all, you'll need to be completely self-sufficient. A more upscale development is planned to open soon.

Daladalas between Same and Mbaga can drop you at Zange Gate, from where you can begin a walking safari.

NORTHERN TANZANIA

With features including the snowcapped peaks of Mt Kilimanjaro, the wildlife-packed Ngorongoro Crater and the vast plains of the Serengeti, northern Tanzania embodies what is for many quintessential

TANZANIA

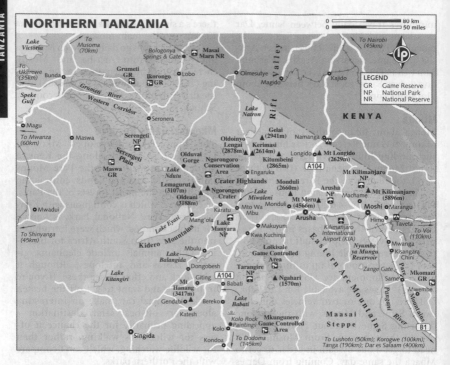

Africa. The main draw is of course the wildlife watching, which is among the finest to be found anywhere.

Yet there's much more. Haunting calls of waterbirds fill the air at serene Lake Eyasi; stately Mt Meru beckons with unforgettable sunrise panoramas from its summit; and the barren landscapes of the Crater Highlands offer rugged but satisfying hiking for everyone.

Exploring northern Tanzania is relatively easy. The tourist infrastructure is good, with plenty of accommodation and dining options in many if the major towns. There's also direct air access from Europe and elsewhere in East Africa via Kilimanjaro International Airport (KIA), which is becoming an increasingly important hub. The main caveat is price – the north is Tanzania's most costly region, and for safaris, you'll need to plan on at least a midrange budget. If you don't mind roughing things a bit, there are some inexpensive alternatives, including Cultural Tourism Programs (p264), the seldom-visited Mt Hanang, and intriguing rock art.

MOSHI
☎ 027

Moshi, a bustling town at the foot of Mt Kilimanjaro, is home of the Chagga people and centre of one of Tanzania's major coffee-growing regions. Most visitors use the town as a starting point for climbing Mt Kilimanjaro, although it's a pleasant place in its own right to relax for a couple of days. It also tends to be less expensive than Arusha.

Information
For trekking operators, see p92.

Executive Bureau de Change (Boma Rd) Cash and travellers cheques.

Fahari Cyber Café (Hill St; per hr TSh800; ⏰ 8.30am-8pm Mon-Sat, 10.30am-8pm Sun) Also does CD burning for digital photos.

Immigration Office (Boma Rd; ⏰ 7.30am-3.30pm Mon-Fri)

Kicheko.com (Mawenzi Rd; per hr TSh1000; ⏰ 8.30am-8pm) Internet access.

Kilimani Pharmacy (☎ 275 1100; Hill St; ⏰ 8am-8pm Mon-Sat, 9am-1pm Sun)

NBC (clock tower roundabout) Changes cash and travellers cheques and has an ATM.

Shanty Town Dispensary (☎ 275 1601, 275 1418; Lema Rd; ◷ 9am-5pm Mon & Wed-Fri, to 12.30pm Sat, 4-5pm Tue) Head here if you're ill.

Standard Chartered bank (Rindi Lane) ATM.

TTCL building (cnr Boma & Mawenzi Rds) Local and international calls; near the clock tower.

Sights & Activities

Central Moshi is full of activity and atmosphere, and makes an interesting walk, especially the area around the market and Mawenzi Rd, which has a vaguely Asian flavour, with a Hindu temple, several mosques and many Indian traders.

A dip in the 25m **pool** (adult/child TSh3000/1500; ◷ 9am-6pm Mon-Sat, to 4.30pm Sun) at the YMCA (right) is a good way to beat the heat.

The area outside Moshi is beautiful, and Machame and other towns above Moshi on Kilimanjaro's lower slopes are all linked by easy-to-follow footpaths. Staff at the Coffee Shop (p173) can help you find a guide.

Another option is the **Machame Cultural Tourism Program** (☎ 027-275 7033), based in Kyalia village about 14km north of the main Moshi–Arusha highway near Kilimanjaro's Machame trailhead. Everything is very basic, and you will need to be self-sufficient with food and water; call in advance to be sure someone will be around. Alternatively, base yourself out of town at Kilemakyaro or Protea Hotel Aishi Machame (p173), both of which organise hikes for their guests.

Makoa Safaris (☎ 0744-312896; www.makoa-farm .com) has horseback riding safaris based out of a farm, which is set amid coffee plantations 16km west of Moshi off the Machame road. Rides (which require a minimum of two persons) range from half a day (US$75) to 11 days (about US$1700 all-inclusive), with days spent in the bush and nights in a rustic farmhouse setting or camping.

Sleeping
BUDGET

Buffalo Hotel (☎ 275 2775; buffalocompany2000@ yahoo.com; New St; r with shared bathroom TSh8000, s/d/ tr with private bathroom TSh10,000/15,000/20,000) The long-standing and popular Buffalo Hotel has straightforward rooms with fan, net and hot water, and a good restaurant. The entrance is on a small street off Mawenzi Rd, directly behind Hotel New Castle.

Kindoroko Hotel (☎ 275 4054; kindoroko@yahoo .com; Mawenzi Rd; s/d from US$15/30; ▣) Kindoroko's

spotless, good-value rooms, rooftop bar and central location make it a justifiably popular choice. Other services include a forex bureau and a restaurant.

Honey Badger Cultural Centre (☎ 275 4608, 275 3365; honeybadger@africamail.com; camping TSh5000; s/d TSh20,000/30,000) Enclosed grassy grounds for camping, rooms in a large family house or in a separate block nearby, and meals (about TSh4000) on order. Overlanders and groups are welcome. It's about 5km from town off the Marangu road; take a Kiboroloni *dala-dala* from the town centre and asked to get dropped off at the turn-off.

Golden Shower Restaurant (☎ 275 1990; Taifa Rd; camping US$3) This inauspiciously named place is conveniently located, with a small, shaded area to pitch your tent, grubby showers and a restaurant-bar. It's about 1.5km northeast of the centre along the Marangu road.

Other recommendations:

A&A Hill St Accommodation (☎ 275 3455; sajjad _omar@hotmail.com; Hill St; s/d/tr TSh7000/10,000/ 12,000) Six clean rooms with fan in a convenient location near the bus stand, with an inexpensive restaurant just below. There's no breakfast.

Hotel Da Costa (☎ 275 5159; hoteldacosta@yahoo.com; Mawenzi Rd; s/d with shared bathroom TSh4800/9600) Small, clean rooms, plus a bar and restaurant and a convenient central location. Under the same management as Kindoroko Hotel.

Lutheran Umoja Hostel (☎ 275 0902; uhuru@elct.org; cnr Market & Liwali Sts; s/d with shared bathroom TSh5000/8000, with private bathroom TSh10,000/12,000) Clean, no-frills rooms around a small courtyard.

YMCA (☎ 275 1754; Taifa Rd; s/d with shared bathroom US$10/13; ▨) Spartan, noisy rooms, some with views over Kilimanjaro. It's north of the clock tower on the roundabout between Kibo and Taifa Rds.

MIDRANGE

Lutheran Uhuru Hostel (☎ 275 4084; www.uhuru hostel.org; Sekou Toure Rd; s/d US$16/22, in newer wing US$35/45, in annexe with shared bathroom US$14/19; ▣) This place has spotless good-value rooms in leafy, expansive grounds – the ones in the new wing have balconies – and a good restaurant. Across the street are some budget rooms in a rustic annexe with shared facilities and a kitchen. It's about 3km northwest of the town centre on the Arusha road (TSh2000 in a taxi).

Bristol Cottages (☎ 275 5083, 275 2833; briscot@ kilionline.com; Rindi Lane; s/d cottage US$54/67, s/d r US$41/54; ▧) Bristol has spotless, modern

MOSHI

0 .... 400 m
0 .... 0.2 miles

INFORMATION
Executive Bureau de Change.............1 C3
Fahari Cyber Café.....................(see 15)
Immigration Office.....................2 B3
Kicheko.com...........................3 C4
Kilimani Pharmacy.....................4 B4
Kilimanjaro Porter Assistance
Project Office......................(see 18)
NBC Bank & ATM......................5 D3
Standard Chartered Bank & ATM......6 C4
TTCL..................................7 C4

SIGHTS & ACTIVITIES
Akaro Tours Tanzania..................8 D3
Clock Tower...........................9 C3
Hindu Temple.........................10 C5
Moshi Expeditions &
Mountaineering....................11 D4
Mosque..............................12 C4
Shah Tours..........................13 C4
Zara Tanzania Adventures............14 C3

SLEEPING
A&A Hill St Accommodation...........15 C5
Bristol Cottages......................16 C4
Buffalo Hotel.........................17 C5
Hotel Da Costa.......................18 B5
Kilimanjaro Crane Hotel..............19 D3
Kindoroko Hotel......................20 C5
Lutheran Umoja Hostel...............21 B5
Philip Hotel..........................22 C3
YMCA................................23 D2

EATING
Chrisburger..........................24 C3
Coffee Shop..........................25 C5
Hill St Food Snacks & Takeaway.....(see 15)
Hole in the Wall Supermarket.........26 C5
Indotaliano Restaurant................27 C5
Safari Supermarket...................28 B5
Salzburger Café......................29 B5

DRINKING
Pub Alberto..........................(see 24)

SHOPPING
Our Heritage.........................30 C5
Shah Industries......................31 C6

TRANSPORT
Air Tanzania.........................32 C3
Akamba Bus Office...................33 C5
Central Bus Station..................34 C4
Dar Express Bus Office...............35 D3
Davanu Shuttle......................36 C4
Impala Shuttle.......................37 C3
Precision Air.........................38 D3
Riverside Shuttle....................39 C3
Royal Coach Bus Office..............40 C4
Scandinavian Express Bus Office.....41 C5
Taxi Stand...........................42 C4
Taxi Stand...........................43 C3

To Key's Hotel
(400m)

To Golden Shower Restaurant
& Camping (1.5km); Honey
Badger Cultural Centre (5km);
Marangu (40km);
Dar es Salaam (555km)

To Kilemakyaro
Lodge (7.5km);
Kibosho (12km)

Catholic
Cathedral

To Lutheran Uhuru Hostel (700m);
Shanty Town Dispensary (1.5km);
Impala Hotel (1.5km);

To Umbwe (14km);
Makoa Farm (15km);
Protea Hotel Aishi Machame (16km);
Kyalia (21km);
Machame (26km);
KIA Lodge (45km);
Kilimanjaro International Airport (45km);
Arusha (80km)

Train Station
(Closed)

Market

Market

To Moshi
Airport (3km)

Kilimanjaro
Rd

Uru Rd
Marangu Rd
Kibo Rd
Old Moshi Rd
Rindi Ln
Kaunda St
Sekou Toure Rd
Taifa Rd
Horombo Rd
Rengua Rd
Boma Rd
Rindi St
Aga Khan Rd
Mawenzi Rd
Arusha Rd
Hill St
Kenyatta St
Kawawa St
Selous St
Chagga St
Liwali St
Market St
Makinga St
Nehru Rd
Chagga St
Chalis St
Riadha Rd
Liwali St

attached cottages – some with air-con and others with fans – in quiet grounds just next to Standard Chartered bank. There are also newer rooms in a two-storey block, and a small restaurant serving snacks, and dinner with advance notice.

Key's Hotel (☎ 275 2250; keys-hotel@africaonline.co .tz; Uru Rd; r US$50, air-con plus US$10; 🕮 🛎) Key's, about 1km northeast of the clock tower on a quiet side street, has been popular with travellers for years. Rooms in the main building are spacious and high-ceilinged, and there are discounts for guests who book a Kilimanjaro trek with the hotel. There are also smaller rondavels (circular African buildings) for the same price, plus a restaurant and a bar.

Kilimanjaro Crane Hotel (☎ 2751114; www.kiliman jarocranehotels.com; Kaunda St; s/d US$30/40, d with air-con US$60; 🕮) Good-value rooms, with fans, nets, TV and large beds. Downstairs is a restaurant. It's on a small side street running parallel to and just east of Old Moshi Rd.

Other recommendations:

Philip Hotel (☎ 275 4746/8; philipht@africaonline.co.tz; cnr Rindi Lane & Horombo Rd; s/d US$30/40) A central location, but the twin-bedded rooms with TV, fan and net are soulless.

KIA Lodge (☎ 255 4194; www.kialodge.com, s/d US$100/136; 🛎) This is located at Kilimanjaro airport. The thatched, upmarket bungalows make an agreeable spot to relax if you have a night flight or early arrival; day rooms are available.

TOP END

Impala Hotel (☎ 275 3443/4; impala@kilinet.co.tz; Lema Rd; s/d US$72/83; 🛎) Central Moshi's only upmarket option offers well-appointed rooms in prim and tranquil grounds, plus a good restaurant. It's about 4km from the clock tower roundabout in Shantytown.

Kilemakyaro Lodge (☎ 275 4925; www.kilimanjaro safari.com; s/d US$65/110) Rooms here – in en suite stone rondavels with TV – are fine, though undistinguished, but the beautiful hilltop setting with views of Kilimanjaro in the distance compensates. It's about 6km from town off the Kibosho road (TSh6000 in a taxi).

Protea Hotel Aishi Machame (☎ 275 6948, 275 6941; proteaaishi@africaonline.co.tz; s/d US$115/145; 🛎) The Aishi Machame is the classiest hotel in the area, with beautiful, lush surroundings just below Kilimanjaro's Machame trailhead, well-appointed rooms, walking

in the surrounding area, and horseback riding nearby.

Makoa Farm (☎ 0744-312896; www.makoa-farm.com; d US$96-132, day d US$60) This scenic place is just down the road from Protea Hotel Aishi Machame and is in equally beautiful surroundings. It's primarily a base for doing horseback riding safaris (see p171), but also has a few lovely, rustic guest cottages and rooms where you can arrange a farm stay.

Eating & Drinking

Salzburger Café (☎ 275 0681; Kenyatta St; meals TSh3000-6000; 🕐 7am-midnight) The Alps meet Africa at this place, which comes complete with waitresses sporting faux-leopard-skin vests, Austrian bar décor on the walls and a selection of good, cheap dishes.

Coffee Shop (☎ 275 2707; Hill St; snacks & meals from TSh1000; 🕐 8am-8pm Mon-Fri, to 4.30pm Sat) Good coffee, plus a delectable assortment of homemade breads, cakes, yogurt, breakfast and light meals. Proceeds go to a church project.

Indotaliano Restaurant (☎ 275 2195; New St; meals about TSh3000, 🕐 10am-11pm) This homey restaurant, opposite Buffalo Hotel, has chequered tablecloths and a good mix of Indian and Italian cuisine.

Also recommended:

Hill Street Food Snacks & Take Away (Hill St) Cheap plates of local fast food.

Chrisburger (☎ 275 0419; Kibo Rd; 🕐 8am-5pm Mon-Fri, 8am-2pm Sat) Good burgers and snacks.

Pub Alberto (🕐 6pm until dawn Tue-Sun) Next door to Chrisburger; Moshi's most popular bar.

Hole in the Wall Supermarket (Solanki's; New St) For self-caterers.

Safari Supermarket (Riadha St) Ditto.

Shopping

Some places to try for crafts:

Our Heritage (Hill St) A good selection of carvings and other crafts.

Shah Industries Just south of town over the railway tracks; it also offers tours of its leather workshop.

Getting There & Away

AIR

Almost all flights to Moshi land at Kilimanjaro International Airport (KIA), about 50km west of town off the main highway. There's also the small Moshi airport about 3km southwest of the town centre along the extension of Market St, which handles occasional charters. There are daily flights connecting KIA with Dar es Salaam (US$130), Zanzibar (US$135) and Entebbe on **Air Tanzania** (☎ 275 5205; Rengua Rd), which has an office near the clock tower. **Precision Air** (☎ 275 3495; Old Moshi Rd) has daily flights connecting KIA with Dar es Salaam, Mwanza (via Shinyanga, US$140 to Mwanza) and Nairobi (US$209).

BUS

Buses and minibuses run throughout the day to Arusha (TSh1000, one to 1½ hours) and Marangu (TSh700, one hour).

To Dar es Salaam, the best lines are Royal Coach (TSh17,000) departing Moshi at 10.15am, and Scandinavian Express, departing at 8.30am (TSh17,000), at 10am (TSh15,000 for ordinary bus and TSh24,000 for luxury bus) and at 1pm (TSh24,000). All start in Arusha, except the 1pm Scandinavian bus, which comes from Nairobi and is often fully booked. If you're trying to get to Dar es Salaam in time for the afternoon ferry to Zanzibar, Dar Express has a bus departing Moshi at 6.30am (TSh12,000) that usually arrives in time, as well as later departures at 7.30am (TSh14,000) and 9am.

To Nairobi (TSh8000 to TSh17,000) and Mwanza (TSh22,000 to TSh32,000), the best lines are Scandinavian and Akamba, both of which go daily, and should be booked in advance. The other option to Nairobi is one of the shuttle buses, though you'll need to wait an hour in Arusha in transit; see p257. **Davanu shuttle** (cnr Old Moshi & Mawenzi Rds) is in Kahawa House near the clock tower roundabout; **Riverside shuttle** (Boma Rd) is just opposite, in the THB building, and **Impala shuttle** (☎ 275 1786; Kibo Rd) is just north of the clock tower. Departures from Moshi are at 6.30am and 11.30am.

Except for the lines listed following, all transport leaves from the main bus station in the town centre between Market St and Mawenzi Rd. The station is chaotic and full of touts and disreputable types wanting to take advantage of new arrivals, and it can be quite intimidating getting off the bus (which is a good reason to take Scandinavian or one of the other lines that let you disembark at their offices). To minimise hassles, watch for the area of the station where the taxis are gathered before disembarking and head

straight over and look for a driver there, rather than getting caught in the fray by the bus door. Even if your hotel is close enough to walk, it's worth paying the TSh1000 for a taxi, just to get away from the station. When leaving Moshi, go to the station the day before without your luggage and book your ticket, so that the next morning you can just arrive and board.

Bus offices include the following:

Akamba (☎ 275 3908; cnr New & Makinga Sts) Just around the corner from Buffalo Hotel.

Dar Express (Old Moshi Rd) Opposite KCNU Hotel, off the clock tower roundabout.

Royal Coach (cnr Aga Khan Rd & Kaunda St) Opposite the bus stand and just down from the mosque.

Scandinavian Express (☎ 275 1387; Mawenzi Rd) South of the bus stand, opposite the Hindu temple.

Getting Around

TO/FROM THE AIRPORT

Air Tanzania and Precision Air have transport to/from KIA for most of their flights, departing from their offices two hours before flight time (TSh2000). Riverside and Impala have a shuttle to/from KIA (US$10), departing from their Moshi offices at 6pm daily and coordinated with KLM flight departures. They also wait to meet arriving passengers on KLM.

TAXI & DALADALA

There are taxi stands near the clock tower, and at the bus station. *Daladalas* depart from the bus station.

MARANGU

☎ 027

Marangu is a small town on the slopes of Mt Kilimanjaro about 40km northeast of Moshi, and is a convenient overnight stop if you're trekking on the Marangu route. It's also a pleasant place in its own right, with an agreeable highland atmosphere, cool, leafy surroundings and some hiking possibilities on the mountain's lower slopes.

Information

Most Marangu hotels organise Kilimanjaro treks, and can also help you find guides for shorter cultural walks to experience local Chagga life and see nearby waterfalls (about US$15 per person per day, with lunch). You can do a day hike in Kilimanjaro National Park from Marangu Gate as far as Mandara

Hut (about two hours up, one hour down; US$60 per person for park fees, plus US$10 per guide, arranged at the park gate).

At the main junction, behind the post office is the **Marangu Internet Café** (per hr TSh2000; ☼ 8am-6pm).

Sleeping & Eating

BUDGET

Coffee Tree Campsite (☎ 275 6513, 275 6604; kilimanjaro@iwayafrica.com; camping US$8, per person per day fireplace use fee TSh500, rondavel per person US$10, chalet per person US$12) Prices are high for camping, but the grounds are green and well maintained, and there are hot-water showers, tents for hire, and a few four- to six-person rondavels and chalets. It's about 700m east of the main road down a steep hill and signposted near Capricorn Hotel.

Babylon Lodge (☎ 275 1315; www.babylonlodge.com; camping US$5, s/d/tr US$25/40/60) The Babylon – a budget hotel at heart, masquerading behind midrange prices – has a row of small, no-frills rooms clustered around a small enclosed green area about 700m east of the main junction.

Bismarck Hut Lodge (☎ 0744-318338; r per person with shared bathroom US$10) This is one of the few shoestring places in Marangu, but rooms are quite run-down these days. It's along the road to the park gate, shortly before the turnoff to Capricorn Hotel.

MIDRANGE

Marangu Hotel (☎ 275 6591/4; www.maranguhotel.com; camping with hot showers US$3, s/d half board US$70/100; ▣) This long-standing place is the first hotel you reach coming from Moshi, with expansive grounds and inviting rooms. Accommodation discounts are available if you join one of the hotel's fully equipped climbs.

Kibo Hotel (☎ 275 1308; www.kibohotel.com; camping US$5, s/d US$32/52) The rustic Kibo has wooden flooring, large old-fashioned windows, spacious rooms and a restaurant. It's about 1.5km west of the main junction.

Nakara Hotel (☎ 275 6571; www.nakara-hotels.com; r per person US$50) A reliable midrange establishment with reasonable rooms and a restaurant. It's just off the main road, and is signposted near Capricorn Hotel.

Capricorn Hotel (☎ 275 1309; s/d US$85/120) The Capricorn is probably the most upmarket of the Marangu hotels, at least on the surface, with a slightly pretentious feel, spacious

rooms that are OK but don't quite seem worth the price, and a restaurant. It's about 3km north of the main junction.

Banana Jungle Lodge (☎ 275 6565, 0744-270947; www.yellowpages.co.tz/jungle/index.htm; camping US$5, s/d US$20/40) Banana Jungle is a private home, where you can sleep in modernised 'Chagga huts', eat local food (meals US$4 to US$6) and arrange cultural walks in the area. It's set amid pleasant gardens about 4km east of Marangu, more or less en route to the Rongai route trailhead. Head right at the main junction, go about 2km to the Mamba Lutheran church, stay left at the fork, and continue another 2.5km.

Getting There & Away

Minibuses run throughout the day between Marangu and Moshi (TSh800). In Marangu they drop you at the main junction. From here, there are sporadic pick-ups to the park gate (TSh300). Otherwise, you'll need to walk (5km).

TREKKING ON MT KILIMANJARO

At 5896m, Mt Kilimanjaro is the highest peak in Africa and one of the continent's most magnificent sights. From cultivated farmlands on the lower levels, the mountain rises through lush rainforest, alpine meadows and a barren lunar landscape to the twin summits of Kibo and Mawenzi.

A trek up 'Kili' lures hundreds of trekkers each year, and is even more attractive because, with the right preparation, you can walk all the way to the summit without the need of ropes or technical climbing experience. Yet the climb is a serious (as well as expensive) undertaking, and only worth doing with the right preparation. For more details about trekking on the mountain, check out Lonely Planet's *Trekking in East Africa*.

Information

Park entry fees are US$60/10 per adult/child per day, and must be paid in US dollars, cash or travellers cheques. Huts (Marangu route) cost US$50 per person per night, and there is a US$20 rescue fee per person per trip for treks on the mountain. Camping costs US$50 per person per night on the Marangu route, and US$40 per person per night for all other camping. Guide and porter fees (but not tips) are handled directly by the trekking companies.

Kilimanjaro National Park Headquarters (☎ 275 6605/2) is located at the **park gate** (◷ 8am-6pm) in Marangu.

It's not permitted to climb Kilimanjaro independently, and you'll need a guide and at least one porter (for the guide). See p92 for trekking company listings. Most trekking companies allow two to three porters per trekker depending on the length of the trek.

Weather conditions on the mountain are frequently very cold and wet, no matter what the time of year it is, so waterproof your gear and bring a full range of waterproof cold-weather clothing and equipment. While you can hire sleeping bags and some cold-weather gear at the Marangu park gate, quality and availability can't be counted on.

ROUTES

There are at least 10 trekking routes that begin on the lower slopes, but only three continue to the summit. You'll need to camp on all except the Marangu route, which has a series of three 'huts' (bunkhouses) spaced a day's walk apart. (You can also camp on the Marangu route, but still need to pay the hut fees.)

The **Marangu route**, which is the most popular, is usually sold as a five-day, four-night return package, although at least one extra night is highly recommended to help acclimatisation. Other routes usually take six or seven days. The increasingly popular and challenging **Machame route** has a gradual ascent before approaching the summit. The **Umbwe route** is much steeper, with a more direct way to the summit. The top, very steep section (up the Western Breach) is often covered in ice or snow, and the route should only be considered if you are experienced and properly equipped, and going with a reputable operator. Also beware of operators who try to sell a 'short' or 'economy' version of the Machame route, which switches near the top to the final section of the Umbwe route and summits via the Western Breach. Other possibilities include the **Rongai route** and the attractive **Shira Plateau route** (or Londorosi route).

Trekkers on the Machame, Umbwe and Shira Plateau routes descend via the Mweka route. Treks on the Rongai route use the Marangu route for descent. The Marangu route is briefly described later.

COSTS

Standard five-day four-night treks up the Marangu route start at about US$750 including park fees. For budget treks of six to seven days on the Machame route expect to pay from around US$800. Better-quality trips on the Marangu/Machame routes start at about US$950. The Umbwe route is often sold by budget operators for about the same price as Marangu, and billed as a quick and comparatively inexpensive way to reach the top. Don't fall for this – the route should only be done by experienced trekkers, and should have an extra day for acclimatisation built in.

Whatever you pay for your trek, remember that US$520 goes to park fees for a five-day Marangu route climb, more for longer treks. If you cut things too close, expect barely adequate meals, mediocre guides and problems with hut bookings and park fees.

GUIDES & PORTERS

Guides and at least one porter (for the guide) are compulsory and are provided by the trekking company. Guides are required to be registered with the national park authorities, and should have permits showing this, though 'sharing' of permits among guides working for some of the less reputable companies is fairly common. Porters will carry bags weighing up to 15kg (not including their own food and clothing); your bags will be weighed before you set off.

Most guides and porters receive only minimal wages from the trekking companies, and depend on tips as their major source of income. As a guideline, plan on tipping about 10% of the total amount you've paid for the trek, divided among the guides and porters. For the Marangu route, tips are commonly from US$40 to US$60 for the guide, and US$15 each for the porters. Plan on more for the longer routes, or if the guide and porters have been particularly good.

Marangu Route
STAGE 1: MARANGU GATE TO MANDARA HUT
(7km, 4-5hr, 700m ascent)
The path begins at 1980m and ascends through a section of forest. From Mandara Hut (2700m) you can visit nearby Maundi Crater (two hours return) for good views to the main peaks of Kibo and Mawenzi.

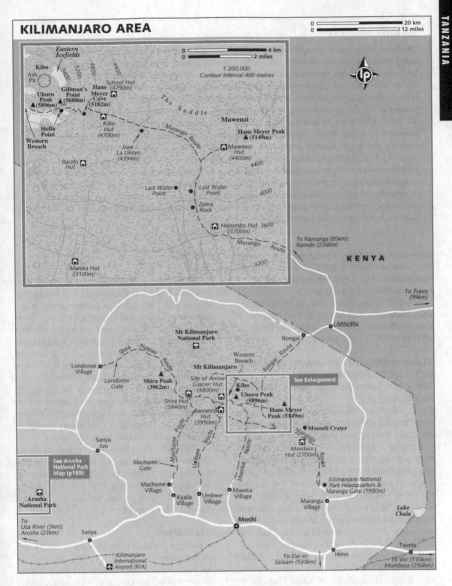

KILIMANJARO AREA

STAGE 2: MANDARA HUT TO HOROMBO HUT
(11km, 5-7hr, 1000m ascent)

Two roughly parallel paths run through the forest and then a zone of giant heather, meeting near the start of open moorland. The terrain is undulating and steep in places, but the paths are easy to follow to Horombo

Hut (3700m), a good place to spend an extra acclimatisation night.

STAGE 3: HOROMBO HUT TO KIBO HUT
(10 km, 5-7hr, 1000m ascent)

The path divides after Horombo, with the more popular one to the west. After passing the landmark Last Water Point and

TANZANIA

SERIOUS BUSINESS

Whatever route you choose, remember that climbing Kilimanjaro is a serious undertaking. While many hundreds of trekkers reach Uhuru Peak without major difficulty, many more don't make it because they ascend too quickly and suffer from altitude sickness. And every year a few trekkers die on the mountain. Come prepared with appropriate footwear and clothing, and most importantly, allow yourself enough time. If you're interested in reaching the top, seriously consider adding at least one extra day onto the 'standard' climb itinerary, no matter which route you do. Although paying an additional US$150 or so per extra day may seem like a lot when you're planning your trip, it will seem a relatively insignificant saving later on if you've gone to the expense and effort to start a trek and then need to come down without having reached the top. And don't feel badly about insisting on an extra day with the trekking companies: standard medical advice is to increase sleeping altitude by only 300m per day once above 3000m – which is about one-third of the daily altitude gains above 3000m on the standard Kilimanjaro climb routes offered by most operators. Another perspective on it all: Uhuru Peak is several hundred metres higher than Everest Base Camp in the Nepal Himalaya, which trekkers often take at least two weeks to reach from Kathmandu.

crossing the Saddle, it joins with the steeper and rougher eastern path at Jiwe La Ukoyo (pointed rocks), from where it's one to 1½ hours to Kibo Hut (4700m).

Kibo Hut is more basic than Horombo and Mandara, and lacks a reliable supply of water (which must be carried from Horombo or one of the Last Water Points).

STAGE 4: KIBO HUT TO UHURU PEAK & DESCENT TO HOROMBO HUT

(4km, 7-8½hr, 1200m ascent; plus 14km, 4½-7hr, 2200m descent)

From Kibo Hut the path zigzags up a scree slope to Hans Meyer Cave (5182m), where it becomes steeper and decidedly a slog. From Gillman's Point (5680m), with spectacular views, it's another two to 2½ hours along the edge of the crater rim to Uhuru Peak, Africa's highest point. It's usual to start this stage – the most strenuous – just after midnight so as to see the sunrise from the crater rim, and because the scree slope up to Gillman's Point and the snow on the path to Uhuru Peak will still be frozen, making the walking safer.

The return from Uhuru to Gillman's takes about one to 1½ hours, and it's another easy two hours from there to Kibo Hut. From Kibo to Horombo is two to three hours.

STAGE 5: HOROMBO HUT TO MARANGU GATE

(18km, 5-7hr, 1900m descent)

The final day retraces the route to Marangu gate, with Mandara Hut at about the halfway point.

ARUSHA

☎ 027

Arusha is one of Tanzania's most developed and fastest-growing towns. It was headquarters of the East African Community when Tanzania, Kenya and Uganda were members of this economic and customs union. Today, it's the seat of the Tripartite Commission for East African Cooperation – a revived attempt at regional collaboration – and the site of the Rwanda genocide tribunal.

Arusha is also the gateway to Serengeti, Lake Manyara, Tarangire and Arusha National Parks, and to the Ngorongoro Conservation Area. As such, it's the safari capital of Tanzania and a major tourism centre.

The town sits in lush countryside at about 1300m in altitude at the foot of Mt Meru, and enjoys a temperate climate throughout the year. Surrounding it are many coffee, wheat and maize estates tended by the Arusha and Meru people.

Orientation

Arusha is divided into two sections by the small Naura River valley. To the east of the valley are most hotels, the post office, immigration, government buildings, safari companies, airline offices and craft shops. To the west are the commercial and industrial areas, the market, some budget hotels and the bus stations.

MAPS

MaCo puts out a good, widely available map of Arusha (TSh5000). Old photocopied town maps are available free from the TTB Tourist Information Centre.

Information
IMMIGRATION OFFICE
Immigration Office (7.30am-3.30pm Mon-Fri; Simeon Rd)

INTERNET ACCESS
Impala Hotel (250 2398, 250 8448/51; www.impala hotel.com; cnr Moshi & Old Moshi Rds; per hr TSh5000; 8am-11pm)
KamNet (per hr TSh1000; 8am-7pm) Just off Boma Rd, opposite Coastal Aviation.
New Safari Hotel (250 3261; www.newsafarihotel .co.tz; Boma Rd; per hr TSh1000; 24hr)
Patisserie (Sokoine Rd; per hr TSh1000; 7.30am-7.30pm Mon-Sat, 8.30am-2pm Sun)

MEDICAL SERVICES & EMERGENCIES
Accident Air Rescue (AAR; 250 8020; Haile Selassie Rd, Plot 54) Just off Old Moshi Rd; lab tests and a doctor on call 24 hours.

Moona's Pharmacy (250 9800, 0741-510590; Sokoine Rd; 8.45am-5.30pm Mon-Fri, to 2pm Sat)

MONEY
Impala Hotel (250 2398, 250 8448/51; www.impala hotel.com; cnr Moshi & Old Moshi Rds; 8am-midnight) Cash shillings and dollars on credit cards at poor rates.
Kibo Palace Bureau de Change (Joel Maeda St; 8am-5pm Mon-Sat, 9am-2pm Sun)
Rickshaw Travels (250 6655; reservation2@ rickshaw.africaonline.co.tz; Sokoine Rd) The Amex representative, but doesn't issue travellers cheques.

There are several ATMs:
Barclays (Sopa Lodges Bldg, Serengeti Rd) Visa and MasterCard.
NBC (Sokoine Rd) Visa; also changes travellers cheques.
Standard Chartered (Goliondoi Rd) Takes Visa.

TELEPHONE
TTCL (Boma Rd; 8am-8pm Mon-Sat, 9am-8pm Sun & holidays) Domestic and international calls, and card phones.

FAIR PLAY
Kilimanjaro guides and porters have a reputation for being aggressive and demanding when it comes to tips, and higher tips are expected here than elsewhere in the region. Yet there's another side, too, with porter abuse and exploitation becoming a serious concern.

Most of the porters who work on Kilimanjaro are local residents who work freelance, usually with no guarantees of a salary beyond the present job. The work is hard, rates are low and it's safe to say that even the best-paid porters earn only a pittance in comparison with the salaries of many of the trekkers whose bags they are carrying. Due to stiff job competition, it's common for porters to agree to back-to-back treks without sufficient rest in between. It's also common for porters to work without proper shoes or equipment, and without adequate protection at night from the mountain's often cold and wet conditions. (This said, it's common practice among some of the more enterprising porters to take good-quality clothing and equipment that they have been given by clients at the end of a trek, sell it and then continue climbing the mountain in threadbare clothing.) Equally concerning are cases where unscrupulous guides bribe the rangers who weigh porters' loads, so that the porter is faced with the choice of carrying an overly heavy load or not getting the job at all.

Porters depend on tourism on the mountain for their livelihood, but as a trekker you can help ensure that they aren't exploited and that working conditions are fair. When selecting a trekking operator, tell them this is a concern. Be aware of what goes on around you during your trek, and if you see exploitative treatment, tell the tour operator when you get back. Also get in touch with the UK-based **Tourism Concern** (www.tourismconcern.org.uk), which has mounted a worldwide campaign to improve conditions for porters. Another good contact is the **International Mountain Explorers Connection** (IMEC; www.mountainexplorers.org), which runs the **Kilimanjaro Porter Assistance Project** (info@mountainexplorers.org), a nonprofit group that channels trekking clothing donations to porters, arranges informal English language training opportunities and lobbies local tour operators to establish a code of conduct on porter pay and conditions. See their guidelines at www.hec.org/club/properporter.htm#guidelines, or visit their **office** (Mawenzi Rd) next to Hotel Da Costa in Moshi. Both they, as well as Tourism Concern, keep lists of trek operators who promote fair treatment of their staff.

TANZANIA

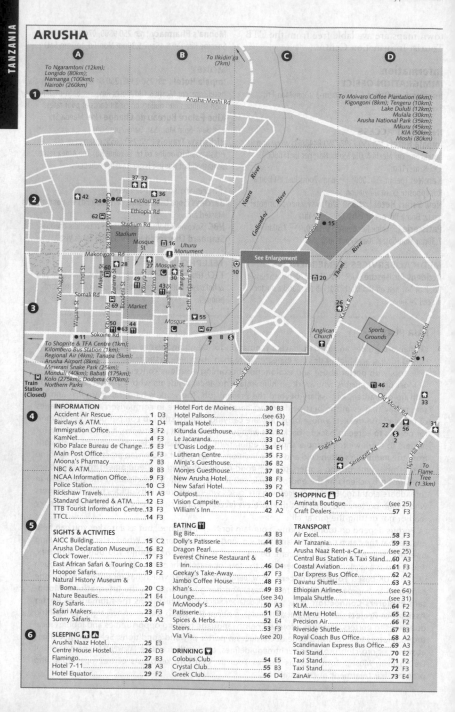

ARUSHA

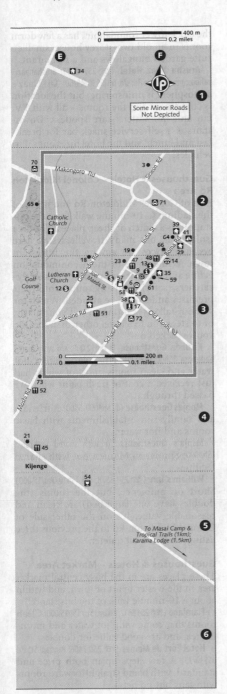

TOURIST INFORMATION

There are travellers bulletin boards at the Patisserie (p184) and the Tourist Information Centre, which are also good spots to look for safari companions.

Ngorongoro Conservation Area Authority (NCAA) Information Office (☎ 254 4625; www.ngornogoro -crater-africa.org; Boma Rd; ☒ 8am-1pm & 2-5pm Mon-Fri, to 1pm Sat) Just down from the TTB tourist office.

Tanzania National Parks Headquarters (Tanapa; ☎ 250 3471, 250 4082, 250 8216; www.tanzaniaparks .com) About 5km west of town along the Dodoma road.

Tanzania Tourist Board (TTB) Tourist Information Centre (☎ 250 3843; ttb-info@habari.co.tz; Boma Rd; ☒ 8am-4pm Mon-Fri, 8.30am-1pm Sat) Just up from the post office; it has information on Arusha, the northern parks and local Cultural Tourism Programs. There are also copies of a 'blacklist' of tour operators as well as a list of registered tour companies.

TRAVEL AGENCIES

For listings of safari and trekking operators, see p92.

Coastal Aviation (☎ 250 0087; Boma Rd) For northern and southern circuit itineraries, Zanzibar and flight charters.

Rickshaw Travels (☎ 250 6655; reservation2@rickshaw .africaonline.co.tz; Sokoine Rd) For domestic and international flight bookings.

Dangers & Annoyances

Arusha is the worst place in Tanzania for street touts and slick tour operators who prey on the gullibility of newly arrived travellers by offering them safaris and treks at ridiculously low prices. Their main haunts include along Boma and Goliondoi Rds, at the bus station and near the budget hotels at the northern and western ends of town. If you're booking on arrival, be sure that any tour company you sign up with is properly registered; get recommendations from other travellers, and check the current 'blacklist' at the TTB Tourist Information Centre on Boma Rd.

At night, take a taxi if you go out. It's not safe to walk, especially over the bridge on Old Moshi Rd near the clock tower, and in the area between the Mt Meru Hotel and the Arusha International Conference Centre (AICC) building.

Sights & Activities

The **Arusha Declaration Museum** (☎ 250 7800; Makongoro Rd; adult/student US$2/1; ☒ 9am-6pm) has a display on postcolonial Tanzanian history, while the **Natural History Museum** (☎ 250 7540; Boma Rd; adult/student US$2/1; ✆ 9.30am-5.30pm), in the old German *boma* (government administrative office or fort), has a few fossils. Other diversions include the **markets** at Ngaramtoni (Thursday and Sunday), about 12km north of town off the Nairobi road, and at Tengeru (Saturday), about 10km east of town on the Moshi road; and the **swimming pool** at the Impala Hotel.

It's possible to observe the proceedings of the United Nations International Criminal Tribunal for Rwanda at the AICC building, which take place Monday through Thursday; admission is free, but you'll need your passport.

Sleeping
BUDGET
Guesthouses & Hotels – Clock Tower Roundabout Area

All the following places are in the green eastern part of town, within easy access of the post office and many safari operator offices.

Centre House Hostel (☎ 250 2313, 250 3027; aid suhai@linux.net; Kanisa Rd; r per person with shared bathroom TSh6000) Run by the Catholic diocese, this no-frills place has spacious rooms – a quad, a triple and several doubles – with shared facilities, and meals on order. The compound gates shut at 10pm unless you've made previous arrangements. It's about 300m in from Old Moshi Rd.

Lutheran Centre (☎ 250 8857; elcthq@elct.or.tz; Boma Rd; r per person with shared bathroom TSh5000) If the drab, institutional atmosphere doesn't put you off, rooms here are good value. There's no food, and unless you've made prior arrangements, check-in and checkout are during regular business hours Monday to Friday only. It's diagonally across from the post office in a multistorey building.

Everest Chinese Restaurant & Inn (☎ 250 8419; everesttzus@yahoo.com; Old Moshi Rd; s/d/tw/tr US$30/40/40/50) Clean, good-value rooms behind Everest Chinese restaurant. There's a triple in the main house, and twins and doubles in a small block building in the garden behind, all with nets and bathroom. It's about 500m southeast of the clock tower roundabout, and signposted along Old Moshi Rd.

Outpost (☎ 254 8405; www.outposttanzania.com; Serengeti Rd; dm/s/d US$18/38/49; ✆) The Outpost, in a leafy residential area about 500m off Old Moshi Rd and about 1km southeast of the clock tower roundabout, has a few dorm rooms in an old two-storey house, small en suite garden bungalows and a restaurant.

Arusha Naaz Hotel (☎ 257 2087; arushanaaz@yahoo.com; Sokoine Rd; s/d/tr US$30/45/60; ✆) Naaz's atmosphere is uninspiring, but the location is convenient and the rooms – all with TV, fan and hot water – are spotless. Downstairs is a self-service snack bar for breakfast and lunch, and the hotel hires out safari vehicles.

Guesthouses & Hotels – Colonel Middleton Rd Area

East of Colonel Middleton Rd and north of the stadium (a 10-minute walk from the bus station) is a clutch of cheap places. The area isn't great, but many travellers stay here because prices are among the lowest in town. While some of the accommodation is fine and quite decent value, others let fly-catchers (safari company touts) onto their premises and should be avoided. Watch for smooth talkers wanting to sell you safaris, or to steer you to a hotel other than the one you've picked out.

Kitunda Guesthouse (r TSh12,000, s/d with shared bathroom TSh6000/8000) This place offers hot water and clean rooms, most of which had just received a coat of fresh paint when we passed through.

Monjes Guesthouse (d TSh4000-5500) A friendly and family-run establishment, with basic rooms and hot water.

Minja's Guesthouse (r with shared bathroom TSh4000) Similar to Monjes, but with shared facilities.

William's Inn (☎ 250 3578; s/d TSh10,000/15,000) Short on ambience, but the rooms (the doubles have one large bed) are clean and reasonable value. It's on the other side of Colonel Middleton Rd to the previous three listings, and is a bit quieter.

Guesthouses & Hotels – Market Area

These places are in the busy central market area in the western part of town, and within about a 10-minute walk of the bus stand.

Flamingo (☎ 254 8812; Kikuyu St; r TSh15,000) Clean rooms that come with hot water and morning tea, and are good value for doubles.

Hotel Fort de Moines (☎ 250 7406; Pangani St; s/d US$30/35) A few steps up in both price and standard, with bland straightforward rooms with fans but no nets.

Hotel 7-11 (☎ 250 1261; Zaramo St; s/d US$25/30) At the central bus station (look for the white multistorey building directly opposite), with clean, noisy rooms. The doubles are decent value.

Camping

Masai Camp (☎ 250 0358; www.masaicamp.com; camping US$3, banda per person with shared bathroom US$5, r per person with shared bathroom US$7; 🖳) Masai Camp is a long-time favourite, and is popular with overlanders, with hot showers, pool tables, satellite TV, a restaurant featuring pizzas, burgers, Mexican dishes and more (meals from TSh3000), plus a bar and a children's play area. Tents and sleeping bags can be hired, and there are a few no-frills rooms and a dorm-style *banda*. It's about 3km southeast of the town centre off Old Moshi Rd, and also the base for Tropical Trails (p93).

Meserani Snake Park (☎ 253 8282; www.feinc.net /SnakePark; camping first night incl admission to the snake park TSh3000, per night thereafter TSh2000) Popular with overlanders, with hot showers, a restaurant and a couple of emergency rooms if you're ill. It's about 25km west of Arusha, just off the Dodoma road.

Vision Campsite (camping US$3) Small, shaded and very basic, this is the only place to pitch a tent in the town centre.

MIDRANGE

L'Oasis Lodge (☎ 250 7089; www.loasislodge.com; backpackers r per person with shared bathroom US$15, s/d/tr US$65/75/94; 🖳 🖳) This good place has a mix of cosy African-style rondavels and airy stilt houses set around nice gardens, plus a few 'corporate rooms' with their own telephone/ Internet connection, and the Lounge, an excellent restaurant (see p184). There are also rustic 'backpacker' doubles with shared facilities, including hot water, in a separate building nearby. Full breakfast is included in room prices, and volunteer discounts are available for the nonbackpacker rooms. It's about 2km from the clock tower, and about 1km off the main Moshi to Nairobi road; the turn-off is diagonally across from Mt Meru Hotel.

Le Jacaranda (☎ 254 4624; jacaranda@tz2000.com; s/d/tr US$45/50/65) Pleasantly faded rooms and a restaurant in a large house just off Old Moshi Rd.

New Safari Hotel (☎ 250 3261; www.newsafarihotel .co.tz; Boma Rd; s/d US$70/95; 🔀 🖳) Completely renovated and recently reopened, this hotel has spiffy rooms in a central location, a restaurant, secure parking and 24-hour Internet access.

Hotel Equator (☎ 250 8409, 250 3727; reservations@ newarusha.com; Boma Rd; s/d US$60/70; 🔀) Also recently renovated, though not to the same standards as the New Safari Hotel. The rooms with garden views are much nicer.

TOP END

Impala Hotel (☎ 250 7398, 250 8448/51; www.impala hotel.com; cnr Moshi & Old Moshi Rds; s/d US$72/83; 🔀 🖳 🖳) Large, reliable and centrally located, this establishment is good value, with efficient staff, a forex bureau, several restaurants, a small garden area, and good, hot showers in rooms in the new wing.

Karama Lodge (☎ 250 0359, 0744-475188; www .karama-lodge.com; s/d US$79/107, day r US$40) Karama is nestled under the trees on a forested hillside in the Suye Hill area just south of town, and is a good choice if you want proximity to nature close to the town centre. Accommodation is in 12 rustic bungalows, each raised on stilts with verandas looking towards Kilimanjaro and Meru. There's also a restaurant. Follow Old Moshi Rd south about 2km from the edge of town to the signpost; turn left and continue 1.5km further.

Moivaro Coffee Plantation (☎ 255 3242/3; www .moivaro.com; s/d US$100/136; 🖳 🖳) Set amid the coffee plantations about 6km east of Arusha, this is an ideal spot to spend a few days recovering from jet lag or relaxing after a Kilimanjaro climb. Accommodation is in cosy cottages, each with its own fireplace, and there are surrounding gardens. It's about 2km south of the Arusha–Moshi highway and signposted.

Kigongoni (☎ 250 2799; www.kigongoni.net; s/d/tr US$140/180/210; 🖳) Kigongoni has a tranquil hilltop perch about 8km outside Arusha, a cosy common area with fireplaces and reading nooks, a restaurant and spacious cottages, all with porches, wonderful large bathtubs and views. Birding and village walks are possible in the surrounding area. Follow the Moshi road east for about 8km to the signposted turn-off, from where it's another 1km.

New Arusha Hotel (☎ 250 7777, 250 8870; reservations@newarusha.com; s/d from US$140/160; 🖳) Directly on the clock tower roundabout, the New Arusha has been completely renovated, and is now the most upmarket option in the town centre. Rooms are of a high standard, and there's a restaurant and expansive gardens out back.

Eating

Lounge (☎ 250 7089; meals TSh5500-6500; ☯ 10am-late) This low-key place has the best cuisine in Arusha, featuring homemade tagliatelle, gourmet wraps, crispy salads, a good selection of meat and seafood grills, plus pizzas and 'Kilimanjaro nachos'; everything freshly made and excellently seasoned, and served in generously large portions against a relaxed backdrop of comfortable lounge seating and music. It's at L'Oasis Lodge (p183), on the northern edge of town.

Big Bite (cnr Somali Rd & Swahili St; meals from TSh6500; ☯ closed Tue) Delicious Indian food, including numerous vegetarian dishes, in a no-frills setting.

Flame Tree (☎ 0744-370474; Njiro Hill; meals from TSh8000; ☯ closed Sun evenings) This popular place about 1.5km south of the Impala Hotel roundabout has cosy seating – both indoors or outdoors overlooking the lush gardens – and tasty mostly continental cuisine.

Jambo Coffee House (Boma Rd; meals TSh4000-6000; ☯ until 10pm) European café chic in a Tanzanian setting. There's an á la carte menu, and a good-value plate of the day for about TSh4500.

Via Via (meals from TSh3500; ☯ 10am-10pm Mon-Sat) Via Via is set in the gardens behind the Natural History Museum. The cuisine and atmosphere – a mixture of local and European – are agreeable, and it's a good spot to meet people.

Spices & Herbs (☎ 250 2279, Moshi Rd; meals from TSh4000; ☯ lunch & dinner) The place to come for Ethiopian cuisine, just in case you've had your fill of Tanzanian fare.

There's stiff competition among Arusha's Chinese restaurants; they're all good, with meals from TSh5000 to TSh10,000. Two to try are **Everest Chinese Restaurant & Inn** (☎ 250 8419; Old Moshi Rd) and the **Dragon Pearl** (☎ 254 4107; Old Moshi Rd), both with pleasant garden seating areas.

There are dozens of places for burgers, pizza and other Western-style fast food for between TSh1500 and TSh4000. Popular ones include the **Patisserie** (Sokoine Rd; snacks & meals from TSh1000; ☯ 7am-6pm), which also has soup, light meals, baked goods and an Internet café; the similar **Dolly's Patisserie** (Sokoine

Rd; ☯ 8am-8pm Mon-Sat, 9am-4pm Sun); **McMoody's** (Sokoine Rd; ☯ 11am-10pm Tue-Sun), with mostly burgers; and a branch of the South African chain, **Steers** (Joel Maeda St).

For more local flavour, try **Geekay's Take-Away** (India St; meals from TSh1000; ☯ 7.30am-6pm Mon-Sat), with plates of rice, *ugali* and sauce; or **Khan's** (Mosque St; mixed grill TSh4500; ☯ from 5.30pm), an auto-spares store by day and a popular barbecue by night, with a huge spread of grilled, skewered meat, and salads.

Just out of town next to Shoprite is **TFA Centre** (Dodoma rd), a shopping mall with everything to satisfy cravings for things Western, including gelato and gourmet coffee.

Self-caterers should head to **Shoprite** (Dodoma rd; ☯ 9am-7pm Mon-Fri, 8am-5pm Sat, 9am-1pm Sun), about 2km west of town at TFA Centre.

Drinking & Entertainment

Via Via (Boma Rd) is one of the best spots for a drink, and to find out about upcoming music and traditional dance events; it's in the grounds of the Natural History Museum.

Greek Club (cnr Old Moshi & Serengeti Rds; ☯ closed Mon & Thu) A popular expat hang-out, especially on weekend evenings; free movies on Sunday afternoon, pizza, and a lively sports bar.

Colobus Club (Old Moshi Rd; admission TSh3000; ☯ 10pm-dawn Fri-Sat) Arusha's loudest and brashest nightclub.

Crystal Club (Seth Benjamin Rd; ☯ from 11pm Fri & Sat) Dancing until late.

Shopping

The small alley just off Joel Maeda St is full of craft dealers. Hard bargaining is required. There are several large craft stores west of town, signposted along the Dodoma road. **Aminata Boutique** (Sokoine Rd), in the entryway to Arusha Naaz Hotel, has textiles.

Colourful local markets include the **Ngaramtoni market** (☯ Thu & Sun), about 12km north of town off the Nairobi road, and the **Tengeru market** (☯ Sat), about 10km east of town along the Moshi road.

Getting There & Away

AIR

There are daily flights to Dar es Salaam and Zanzibar (ZanAir, Coastal Aviation, Precision Air, Air Tanzania), Nairobi (Precision Air), Seronera and other airstrips in Serengeti National Park (Coastal Aviation, Air Excel, Regional Air). There are also daily flights to Mwanza (Precision Air, via Shinyanga), and Lake Manyara and Tarangire National Parks (Coastal Aviation, Air Excel, Regional Air). Some flights use Kilimanjaro International Airport, about halfway between Moshi and Arusha off the main highway, while others use Arusha airport, 8km from town along the Dodoma road; verify the departure point when buying your ticket. International airlines flying into KIA include KLM and Ethiopian Air. Sample prices: Arusha–Dar es Salaam (US$130), Arusha–Mwanza (US$140) and Arusha–Seronera (US$150).

Airline offices include the following:

Air Excel (☎ 254 8429, 250 1597; reservations@airexcel online.com; Gollondoi Rd)

Air Tanzania (☎ 250 3201/3; www.airtanzania.com; Boma Rd)

Coastal Aviation (☎ 250 0087; arusha@coastal.cc; Boma Rd)

Ethiopian Airlines (☎ 250 6167, 250 7512; tsm-a@ ethair.co.tz; Boma Rd)

KLM (☎ 250 8062/3; reservations.arusha@klm.com; Boma Rd)

Precision Air (☎ 250 2818, 250 2836; www.precision airtz.com; Boma Rd) Also handles Kenya Airways bookings.

Regional Air (☎ 250 4477, 250 2541; www.airkenya .com; Nairobi Rd)

ZanAir (☎ 024-223 3670; www.zanair.com; Moshi Rd) In Bushbuck Safaris building.

BUS

Arusha has two main bus stations: the central bus station near the market, for buses to Dar es Salaam, Tanga, Nairobi, Mombasa and other points north and east; and the Kilombero bus station, about 2km west of town along the Dodoma road, opposite Shoprite, for buses to Mwanza, Babati and other points west and south. Both, especially the central bus station, are chaotic and popular haunts for flycatchers and touts. Watch your luggage, and don't negotiate any safari deals at the stations. If you're arriving for the first time, head straight for a taxi, or – if arriving at the central station – duck into the lobby of Hotel 7-11 across the street to get your bearings.

If you're arriving at the central bus station (and unless you're staying in the budget-hotel area downtown, in which case it makes sense to stay on the bus), you can avoid the bus station altogether by asking the driver to drop you in front of the Mt

Meru Hotel. All buses coming from Dar es Salaam and Moshi pass by here. There are taxis at the hotel (fares to town shouldn't be more than TSh2000) and across the street, and the scene is much less hectic than at the station. When departing Arusha, the best thing to do is book your ticket the day before, so that in the morning when you arrive with your luggage you can get straight on your bus. For predawn departures, take a taxi to the station and ask the driver to drop you directly at your bus. Despite what you may hear, there are no luggage fees (unless you have an extraordinarily large pack).

Babati, Kolo, Kondoa & Dodoma

Mtei line buses run three to four times daily between Arusha and Babati (TSh4000, four to six hours), departing between 6.30am and 1pm. There are occasional direct buses from Arusha to Kolo, Kondoa and on to Dodoma (about 10 hours), but usually you'll need to change vehicles at Babati, as most transport to Dodoma uses the longer Tarmac route via Chalinze.

Dar es Salaam

The main lines to/from Dar es Salaam all depart from and arrive at their own offices, thereby avoiding the main bus stations completely. The main lines include the following:

Dar Express (☎ 0744-946155; Colonel Middleton Rd) Buses depart Arusha at 6am (luxury TSh14,000) and, with luck, arrive in Dar es Salaam in time to catch the 4pm ferry to Zanzibar. If you're trying to do this, stay on the bus past Ubungo bus station in Dar es Salaam until the bus terminates at its offices in the city centre near Kisutu. From here, it's TSh1500 and about 10 minutes in a taxi to the ferry docks. There are also buses at 7.30am, 8.15am and 9am (ordinary TSh12,000). The Arusha office is diagonally across from Golden Rose Hotel.

Royal Coach (☎ 250 7959, 0744-366121; Colonel Middleton Rd) Departures at 9am (TSh17,000) from the Royal Coach booking office behind Golden Rose Hotel.

Scandinavian Express (☎ 250 0153; cnr Somali St & Kituoni Rd) Departures at 7am (coming from Kampala or Mwanza, luxury TSh24,000), 8.30am (ordinary/luxury TSh15,000/24,000) and 11am (luxury TSh24,000).

Kampala (Uganda)

Scandinavian Express goes daily between Arusha and Kampala (TSh35,000, 17 hours); see also p259.

Lushoto
Fasaha departs daily at 6.30am (TSh8000, six hours). It's faster but more expensive to take an express bus heading for Dar as far as Mombo, and then get local transport from there to Lushoto.

Mbeya
Hood line runs a daily bus to Mbeya, departing Arusha at 5.30am (TSh27,500, 16 hours).

Musoma & Mwanza
Scandinavian Express buses go to Mwanza via Nairobi and Musoma (TSh32,000 plus US$20 for a Kenyan transit visa, 20 hours), departing Arusha about 3.30pm.

The other option is to go via Singida and Shinyanga in a large and very rugged southwestern loop, but the road is in bad shape, and the trip can take several days.

Moshi
Buses and minibuses run throughout the day between Arusha and Moshi (about TSh1500, one hour). It's pricier, more comfortable and safer to take one of the Arusha–Nairobi shuttles (p257, TSh4000 between Moshi and Arusha).

Nairobi (Kenya)
For more on this route see p257.

Tanga
Tashriff departs Arusha daily for Tanga at 8.30am and 11.30am (TSh9000, seven hours). Otherwise, take any Dar es Salaam bus and transfer at Segera junction.

Getting Around
TO/FROM KILIMANJARO INTERNATIONAL AIRPORT
Both Air Tanzania and Precision Air have shuttles to both airports for their passengers, departing from their offices about two hours before scheduled flight departure. In the other direction, look for the airlines' buses in the airport arrivals area.

Riverside and Impala shuttles have a daily bus to KIA coordinated with KLM departures and arrivals. They cost US$10, and depart at 6pm from the Mt Meru and Impala Hotels respectively. They also wait for arriving passengers.

Taxis from town to KIA charge about TSh30,000, more at night.

TO/FROM ARUSHA AIRPORT
Any *daladala* heading out along the Dodoma road can drop you at the junction, from where you'll have to walk about 1.5km to the airstrip. Taxis from town charge TSh10,000.

Precision Air sometimes runs a shuttle from its office at the AICC building to Arusha airport, departing AICC about 1½ hours before scheduled fight departures.

CAR HIRE
Arusha Naaz Rent-a-Car (☎ 250 2087; arushanaaz@ yahoo.com; Sokoine Rd) Based at Arusha Naaz Hotel; rates (from US$80 to $120 per day for 4WD) include 120 free kilometres per day.

TAXI
There are taxi stands around the central bus station, opposite Mt Meru Hotel, on the southern side of the clock tower roundabout near New Arusha Hotel, and at the eastern end of Makongoro Rd. Town rides cost TSh1000 to TSh2000.

AROUND ARUSHA
Cultural Tourism Programs
Several villages outside Arusha have organised Cultural Tourism Programs that provide an opportunity to experience local culture. All can be booked through the TTB Tourist Information Office (p181), which can also tell you the best transport connections. Book a day in advance for the more distant ones; for Ng'iresi and other programs close to town, guides usually wait at the TTB office on stand-by each morning. (Check with the TTB to be sure the one you go with is authorised.) Tours average about TSh15,000/25,000 per person for a half-/full-day program with lunch (less for two or more people), and include the following:

Ilkiding'a Come here for walking (from half-day strolls to a three-day 'cultural hike'), and the chance to experience the traditional culture of the Arusha people around Ilkiding'a, 7km north of Arusha.

Lake Duluti This small and tranquil crater lake lies about 11km east of Arusha, just off the main road near the village of Tengeru (known for its colourful Saturday market). It's part of a forest reserve, and there's an ecotourism program of sorts here, where you can arrange to go canoeing (per person US$20) or take guided nature walks around the lake. The best contact for this is Green Footprint Adventures (p92).

Longido Hike to the top of Mt Longido (2629m; eight to 10 hours return from the main road), and visit a Maasai cattle market at Longido, about 80km north of Arusha.

Mkuru A camel camp near Arusha National Park's Momela Gate, where you can take camel safaris ranging from a half day to several days, or climb nearby Mt Ol Doinyo Landaree (about two hours to the summit). Bring everything with you, including drinking water, and allow extra time to organise things.

Mulala About 30km northeast of Arusha, and implemented completely by women. It involves visits to a local women's cooperative, and some short walks.

Ng'iresi A village about 7km north of Arusha where you can visit local irrigation projects, see Maasai houses and enjoy some walking.

Via public transport, have any bus or *dala-dala* along the Moshi–Arusha highway drop you at the Tengeru junction, from where it's about a 1.5km walk to the lake.

Usa River

☎ 027

This tiny, nondescript town along the Moshi–Arusha highway, about 20km east of Arusha, is of interest for its proximity to Arusha National Park, and for its handful of atmospheric, upmarket lodges.

Rivertrees Country Inn (☎ 255 3894; www.rivertrees.com; s/d US$125/150, river cottage US$240; ▢) has genteel old-world ambience, impeccable service, hearty family-style cuisine and comfortably rustic rooms either in a beautifully renovated colonial-era farmhouse or in the gardens. There are also two private 'river cottages', each with their own fireplaces and one with wheelchair access. It's in shaded grounds running along the Usa River, and signposted off the main highway.

Mt Hanang & Babati

☎ 027

Volcanic Mt Hanang (3417m) rises steeply from the plains about 200km southwest of Arusha. It's Tanzania's fourth-highest mountain and, while time-consuming to reach, makes a rewarding trek that can be done at a fraction of the cost of Mt Kilimanjaro or Mt Meru. The surrounding area is home to numerous tribes, including the Barabaig, who still follow a seminomadic traditional lifestyle. The jumping-off point for climbs is the lively market town of Babati, which is set in fertile countryside about 175km southwest of Arusha. Flanking Babati to the southwest is the tranquil Lake Babati, fringed by tall reeds and home to hippos and water birds.

There are several routes to Hanang's summit. The most popular and logistically the easiest is the Jorodom route, which starts near Katesh village on the mountain's southern side. It's described in more detail in Lonely Planet's *Trekking in East Africa*. While it's possible to climb Hanang independently, most travellers organise climbs through Kahembe's Trekking & Cultural Safaris (p92), based in Babati, and charging about US$40 per person per day for a three-day Hanang climb from Arusha, including a guide, simple meals and accommodation in a basic guesthouse in Katesh before and after the trek. If you're organising things on the spot, just ask for Kahembe's Guest House when you arrive in Babati and you'll be pointed in the right direction. Watch out for touts and fake guides in both Babati and Katesh, or touts pretending to be from Kahembe's. In Babati, only go with a guide after you've checked in with Kahembe's Guest House or office. In Katesh, Kabwogi's Restaurant near the Lutheran Mission in the centre of town can help you find a reliable guide.

Guesthouses in Babati include **Kahembe's Modern Guest House** (☎ 253 1088, 253 1377; kahembeculture@yahoo.com; s/d TSh12,000/15,000), with self-contained rooms and hot water; **Motel Paa-Paa** (☎ 253 1111; s with shared bathroom TSh3000, d with private bathroom TSh4000), near the old bus stand; and **Dodoma Transport Hotel** (☎ 253 1089; r TSh10,000), on the main road opposite the petrol station. In Katesh, 75km southwest of Babati and the main village near the mountain, try **Colt Guest House** (☎ 253 0030; s/d with shared bathroom TSh2000/3000, d with private bathroom TSh5000) or the more basic **Hanang View** (s/d TSh2000/3000).

Kolo Rock Paintings

The tiny village of Kolo lies at the centre of one of the most impressive and most overlooked collections of ancient rock art on the African continent. The history of most of the paintings remains shrouded in mystery, with little known about either their artists or their age. One theory maintains they were made by the Sandawe, who are distantly related linguistically to South Africa's San, a group also renowned for its rock art. Others say the paintings, particularly some of the more recent ones, were done by various Bantu-speaking peoples, who moved into the area at a later date. While some of the paintings date back more than 3000 years, others are much more recent, probably not more than a few hundred years old.

To visit, you'll first need to arrange a guide and a permit (TSh4000) with the Department of Antiquities in Kolo. You'll then need to walk about two to 2½ hours from Kolo to reach the paintings. With your own vehicle (4WD), you can drive to within a few kilometres of the first sites.

You can also organise trips to Kolo through Arusha-based tour operators, and (for budget excursions) through Kahembe's Trekking & Cultural Safaris (p92) in Babati (US$60 per day plus transport costs).

There's a basic **camping ground** (camping TSh2000) near Kolo, for which you'll need to be fully equipped. Otherwise, the closest overnight base is Kondoa, 20km south, where there are numerous guesthouses, the best of which is **New Planet** (r TSh6500), near the bus stand.

Kolo is about 100km south of Babati and 275km southwest of Arusha. The best bus connections are from Babati, from where there are several small buses daily to Kolo and on to Kondoa (20km further). Alternatively, there's at least one direct bus daily between Arusha and Kondoa via Kolo, departing Arusha about 6am or 7am, and reaching Kolo about six hours later. Going in the other direction, there are several daily buses from Kondoa to Arusha, departing between about 6am and 10am. Kolo can also be reached from Dodoma, 180km to the south.

ARUSHA NATIONAL PARK
☎ 027

Although it's one of Tanzania's smallest parks, Arusha National Park is one of its most beautiful and topographically varied. Its main features are Ngurdoto Crater, the Momela Lakes and Mt Meru. The park has a variety of vegetation zones supporting many animal species, and wildlife viewing is usually quite rewarding, though on a smaller scale than in the other northern parks. You'll probably see zebras, giraffes, elephants, klipspringers and buffaloes. There are no lions, however, and no rhinos due to poaching.

The **Momela Lakes** are particularly good for bird-watching. Like many in the Rift Valley, they are shallow and alkaline and attract a wide variety of wader birds. The lakes are fed by underground streams; due to their varying mineral content, each lake supports a different type of algal growth, which gives them different colours. Birdlife also varies quite distinctly from one lake to another, even where they are only separated by a narrow strip of land.

While you can see much of the park in a day, it's better to allow a night or two to appreciate the wildlife and do a walking safari.

Information
Entry fees are US$35/10 per adult/child per day. For camping fees see p113. There's a US$20 rescue fee per person per trip for treks on Mt Meru. Armed rangers (required for all walks) cost US$15 per day, and the huts on Mt Meru cost US$20.

The main entrance is at Ngongongare Gate, about 10km from the main road. **Park headquarters** (☎ 255 3995; ⏲ 6.30am-6.30pm) – the main contact for making camp-site or resthouse reservations, and for arranging guides and porters to climb Mt Meru – is about 14km further in near Momela Gate. There is another entrance at Ngurdoto Gate, on the southeastern edge of the park. Walking is permitted on the Mt Meru side of the park, and there is a walking trail along part of the Ngurdoto Crater rim (though it's not permitted to descend to the crater floor). Green Footprint Adventures (p92) does **canoe safaris** (per person US$40, plus transfer from Tengeru US$10, plus park fees, plus per person park canoeing fee cash only adult/child US$20/5) on the Momela Lakes.

There's nowhere in the park to buy food or petrol.

Sleeping
The park has four ordinary camp sites, three near Momela Gate (including one with a shower), and one near Ngurdoto Gate. There are also two resthouses near park headquarters with kitchen facilities.

Hatari Lodge (☎ 255 3456/7; www.hatarilodge.com; r per person full board plus safaris US$295) Hatari has an upscale ambience, creative 'modern retro' room décor, a wonderful location on large lawns frequented by giraffes, and views that take in both Meru and Kilimanjaro on clear days. It's on the edge of the park about 1.5km north of Momela Gate.

Momella Wildlife Lodge (☎ 250 6423/6; www.lions -safari-intl.com/momella.html; s/d/tr half board US$68/98/ 128) This long-standing establishment is just

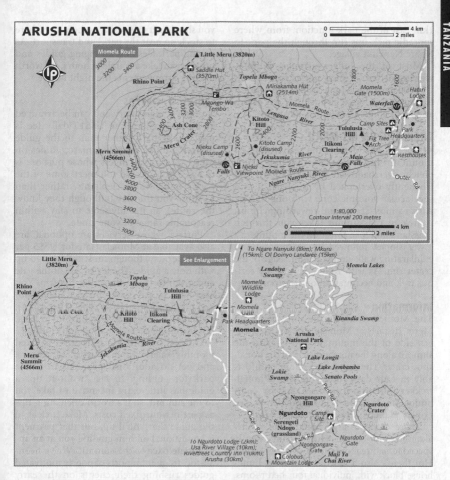

ARUSHA NATIONAL PARK

north of Hatari Lodge, and about 1.5km off the road from Momela Gate. Small, serviceable cottages are set around modest gardens, and the lodge can provide a vehicle and driver for visiting the park for US$30/60 per half/full day.

Other recommendations:

Ngurdoto Lodge (☎ 255 3701; ngurdoto-lodge@ habari.co.tz; r per person full board US$150) An upmarket lodge with attentive hosts and five spacious double bungalows set on a large lawn with views of Kilimanjaro and Meru. It's about 7km north of the main highway along the road to Ngongongare Gate.

Colobus Mountain Lodge (☎ 255 3632; camping US$5, s/d US$35/50) A two-minute walk from Ngongongare Gate, with bougainvillea-dotted grounds, a camping area, reasonable budget-style rooms and a restaurant.

Getting There & Around

The gate to Arusha National Park is about 35km from Arusha. Take the main road between Arusha and Moshi until you reach the national park signboard, where you turn left. From here, it's about 10km to Ngongongare Gate, where you pay your fees. This is also where the road divides, with both forks joining up again at Momela Gate.

Via public transport, there's a daily bus between Arusha and Ngare Nanyuki (10km north of Momela Gate), departing Arusha at 1pm and Ngare Nanyuki at 7am, that can drop you at the park gate (TSh2000, 1½ hours from Arusha to Ngongongare Gate). Otherwise, take any bus between Arusha and Moshi, and get off at Usa River village,

1km east of the park junction, from where sporadic pick-ups run through the park to Ngare Nanyuki village.

Most of the lodges arrange wildlife-viewing drives for their guests from about US$100 per vehicle for a drop at the gate, up to double this for an all-inclusive day safari, and from about US$50 for a day safari.

TREKKING ON MT MERU

At 4566m, Mt Meru is the second-highest mountain in Tanzania. Although completely overshadowed by Kilimanjaro and frequently overlooked by trekkers, it is a spectacular volcanic cone with one of East Africa's most scenic and rewarding climbs. A trek to the summit takes you through grassland and lush forest on the mountain's lower slopes, followed by a dramatic and exhilarating walk along the knife edge of the crater rim. As with Kilimanjaro, it's a serious trek and acclimatisation is important.

Information

The Momela route is the only route up Meru. It starts at Momela gate on the eastern side of the mountain and goes to the summit along the northern arm of the horseshoe crater. The route can be done comfortably in four days (three nights), although trekkers often do it in three days by combining Stages 3 and 4. For more details, see Lonely Planet's *Trekking in East Africa*.

There are two large bunkhouses (Miriakamba and Saddle Huts), conveniently spaced for a three- or four-day trek. At Saddle Hut there's also a newly constructed bunkhouse block with individual four-bed rooms. However, all the bunkhouses operate on a first-come, first-served basis, and during the high season often fill up. For this reason, it's a good idea to carry a tent, though even if you camp, whether by choice or necessity, you'll still need to pay hut fees.

COSTS

Most companies that organise Kilimanjaro treks also organise treks on Mt Meru. See p92 for listings. Rates for a four-day trip range from about US$500 to US$650.

Organised treks are not obligatory, and you can do things quite easily on your own. The main costs for an independent trek are park-entrance, hut and guide fees (see p188). Also add in the costs of food (which

you should get in Arusha, as there's nowhere to stock up near the park) and transport. As paying park fees and arranging guides and porters can take a couple of hours, it's worth making arrangements the night before.

GUIDES & PORTERS

A guide is mandatory and can be arranged at Momela Gate. The US$15 daily fee is paid to the park rather than to the guide himself. Unlike on Kilimanjaro, guides on Meru are armed rangers whose purpose is to assist you in case you meet some of the park's buffaloes or elephants, rather than to show you the way (although they know the route), so it's advisable to stay within reasonable range of your guide.

Porters, whose services are optional, are also available at Momela Gate for US$5 per porter per day, though most trekkers go up with only a guide. The fee is paid at the gate and given to the porters after the trip. You also have to pay park-entrance (TSh1500) and hut fees for porters (TSh800 per night). Porters will carry packs weighing up to 15kg, not including their own food and clothing.

Guides on Mt Meru receive a fixed monthly salary for their work as rangers, and get no additional payment from the park for guiding. In fact, without tips a guide has little extra incentive to take you to the summit, so it's worth calculating tips as part of your fixed costs. Make it clear to the guide that you'll tip, but that payment is conditional on him guiding you at an appropriate pace to the summit. We've heard all-too-frequent reports of poorly motivated guides rushing their clients on the early stages of the climb, with the result that the trekkers themselves are forced to bail out before reaching the top. As a guideline, for a good guide who has gone with you to the summit, plan on about TSh10,000 per day per group. Porter tips for a standard trek average about TSh5000 per porter.

Momela Route

STAGE 1: MOMELA GATE TO MIRIAKAMBA HUT
(10km, 4-5hr, 1000m ascent)

There's a choice of two routes from Momela Gate. The more interesting one is a track going through the forest towards the crater floor and then steeply up to Miriakamba Hut (2514m). The second, shorter option climbs gradually through the grassland to Miriakamba, and makes a good descent route. Some guides prefer to go up and down the shorter route, and it may require some persuading to take the forest route.

STAGE 2: MIRIAKAMBA HUT TO SADDLE HUT
(4km, 2-3hr, 1050m ascent)

From Miriakamba the path climbs steeply up through pleasant glades between the trees to reach Topela Mbogo (Buffalo Swamp) and Mgongo Wa Tembo (Elephant Ridge), from where there are good views into the crater and up to the cliffs below the summit. It continues through some open grassy clearings and over several stream beds (usually dry) to Saddle Hut (3570m). There are side trips from Saddle Hut to Little Meru (3820m) and to Rhino Point, both of which offer impressive views of Meru's Ash Cone.

STAGE 3: SADDLE HUT TO MERU SUMMIT & DESCENT
(5km, 4-5hr, 1000m ascent; 5km, 2-3hr, 1000m descent)

This stage, along a very narrow ridge between the outer slopes of the mountain and the sheer cliffs of the inner crater, is one of the most dramatic and exhilarating sections of trekking anywhere in East Africa. During the rainy season, ice and snow can occur on this section of the route, so take care.

From Saddle Hut, the path goes across a flat area, then steeply up through bushes before giving way to bare rock and ash. Rhino Point is marked by a cairn and a pile of bones. From Rhino Point the path drops slightly then rises again to climb steeply around the edge of the rim over ash scree and bare rock patches. Continue for three to four hours to reach Meru summit.

If the sunrise is your main interest but you're not keen on attempting this section in the dark, the views at dawn are just as impressive from Rhino Point, about an hour from Saddle Hut.

STAGE 4: SADDLE HUT TO MOMELA GATE
(9km, 3-5½hr, 2000m descent)

From Saddle Hut, retrace the Stage 2 route to Miriakamba (1½ to 2½ hours). From Miriakamba, you can either return through the forest (2½ to three hours), or take a shorter route down the ridge directly to Momela Gate (1½ to 2½ hours).

LAKE MANYARA NATIONAL PARK
☎ 027

Among the attractions of the often underrated Lake Manyara National Park are its superb birdlife, its elusive tree-climbing lions and its abundance of hippos, which you can observe at closer range here than at most other places. There's also the park's striking setting, bordered to the west by the dramatic western escarpment of the Rift Valley. Finally, there's the chance to do night drives, go microlight flying above the lake and the magnificent Rift Valley escarpment, or cycle in park border areas.

Information

Entry fees are US$35/10 per adult/child per day. For camping fees see p113. The park gate and **park headquarters** (☎ 253 9112/45) are at the northern tip of the park near Mto Wa Mbu village.

Green Footprint Adventures (p92) organises village walks, mountain biking and forest hikes, as well as night drives inside the park (Manyara is the only northern park where you can do this) for US$130 per person plus park fees, including a predrive bush dinner under the stars. Prices decrease with two or more people. Budget cultural walks outside the park can be organised through the Mto Wa Mbu Cultural Tourism Program (see p192). You can also arrange microlight flying (US$125/255 for 20 minutes/one hour) through them, or directly at the microlight base, on the escarpment along the road leading to the park gate.

Up-close wildlife-viewing opportunities are scarce at Manyara in comparison with the other northern parks, so bring binoculars.

Sleeping

The park has two ordinary camp sites, about 10 double *bandas* with bathroom (US$20 per person), and a student hostel, all near the main gate. There are also three special camp sites in the park. The *bandas* have bedding, a cooking area and, with luck, hot water.

Basic foodstuffs are available at the market in Mto Wa Mbu; otherwise you'll need to stock up in Arusha.

LODGES & TENTED CAMPS
Kirurumu Luxury Tented Camp (☎ 250 7011, 250 7541; www.kirurumu.com; s/d full board US$165/250) A genteel, low-key ambience, closeness to the natural

surroundings and memorable cuisine are the hallmarks at this highly regarded camp. It's set on the escarpment about 12km from the park gate and 6km from the main road, with views of Lake Manyara in the distance. The 20 double tents are hidden away in the vegetation, and well spaced for privacy, and there are several larger 'family suite' tents.

Lake Manyara Serena Lodge (☎ 250 4158/3; www.serenahotels.com; s/d full board US$285/420; 🔊) Serena is large and not the least bit intimate, but the views are great, and accommodation – in two-storey conical bungalows – is comfortable, with all the amenities. It's southwest of Kirurumu on the escarpment overlooking the Rift Valley, and about 2km from the main road.

E Unoto Retreat (☎ 0744-360908; www.maasai village.com; s/d full board US$224/408) A classy lodge with Maasai overtones and spacious luxury bungalows nestled at the base of the Rift Valley escarpment near Lake Miwaleni. There's birding in the area, as well as cycling and cultural walks. E Unoto is 10km north of Mto Wa Mbu, off the road to Lake Natron.

Lake Manyara Tree Lodge (www.ccafrica.com; per person all-inclusive US$490-630; 📅 Jun-Mar; 🔊) Lake Manyara's most exclusive lodge, and the only one within the park boundaries, with 10 intimate 'tree house suites' set in the forest at the southern end of the park.

Mto Wa Mbu

☎ 027
The touristy village of Mto Wa Mbu (River of Mosquitoes) is redeemed from scruffiness by its lively market, and by its beautiful vegetation – a profusion of palms, baobabs and acacia trees framed by the backdrop of the Rift Valley escarpment. There are cultural walks in the surrounding area, best organised through the **Cultural Tourism Program office** (☎ 253 9393; mtoculturalprogramme@ hotmail.com) at the Red Banana Café on the main road opposite the post office. Rates average TSh25,000 per person per day, plus TSh4000 per day for bicycle hire.

SLEEPING & EATING

There are several inexpensive guesthouses in town, all with basic rooms from about TSh2500 (shared facilities) to TSh6000 (with bathroom), including Sayari Lodge behind the market, and Sunlight Lodge, along the main road.

Lake Manyara Tented Camp (☎ 255 3242; www .moivaro.com; per person half board US$107/133) The main attraction of this unassuming place – formerly Migunga Forest Camp – is its setting, in a grove of fever trees that echoes with bird calls. The tents are rustic but adequate, and safaris to Lake Manyara National Park and Ngorongoro Crater can be arranged. It's about 2km south of the main road and signposted.

Twiga Campsite & Lodge (☎ 253 9101; twiga campsite@habari.co.tz; camping US$5, d/tr with shared bathroom US$30/45; 🔊) A large compound along the main road with ablution blocks with hot and cold water, cooking facilities and a restaurant. Car hire to visit Lake Manyara and Ngorongoro Conservation Area costs US$140 per day including petrol and driver.

GETTING THERE & AWAY

Coastal Aviation, Air Excel and Regional Air offer scheduled daily, or near-daily, services between Arusha and Lake Manyara for about US$65 one way. The airstrip is at the northwestern edge of the park.

By public transport, the best connections are on the Ngorongoro Crater bus (p199), which passes Mto Wa Mbu about 12.30pm coming from Arusha, and about 10.30am in the other direction.

While it's easy to reach Mto Wa Mbu with public transport, once there you'll need to hire a vehicle to explore the park, which can be arranged through the places listed under Sleeping, and will cost from about US$140 per day. There's no vehicle hire at the park itself. Petrol is available in Mto Wa Mbu.

TARANGIRE NATIONAL PARK

☎ 027
Baobab-studded Tarangire National Park stretches southeast of Lake Manyara around the Tarangire River. Like nearby Lake Manyara National Park, it's often assigned no more than a day visit as part of a larger northern-circuit safari, although it's well worth longer exploration. The park is a classic dry-season destination, particularly between August and October, when it has one of the highest concentrations of wildlife of any of the country's parks. Large herds of zebras, wildebeest, hartebeest and – in particular – elephants can be found here

until October when the short wet season allows them to move on to new grasslands. The park is also good for bird-watching, especially between October and May, with over 300 different species recorded.

Tarangire is part of an extended ecosystem through which animals roam freely, and it's possible to do walks and night drives in the border areas.

Information

Entry fees are US$35/10 per adult/child per day. For bookings, contact the **senior park warden** (☎ 253 1280/1, 250 8642). The entry gate is at the northwestern tip of the park.

Sleeping

There's an ordinary camp site near park headquarters and about 12 special camp sites. There's nowhere to stock up near the park, so bring what you need from Arusha.

Tarangire Safari Lodge (☎ 2544752; www.tarangire safarilodge.com; s/d full board US$125/200; ⊠) This large lodge is good value, with a prime location on a bluff overlooking the Tarangire River, about 10km inside the park gate, and accommodation in tents or thatched bungalows.

Oliver's Camp (☎ 250 2799; www.asilialodges.com; s/d all-inclusive US$350/600; ⊗ Jul-Feb) A fine, intimate camp, with six tents set on a ridge overlooking the swamplands of southeastern Tarangire in one of the park's wildest sections. You can also do walking safaris.

Tamarind Camp Tarangire (☎ 250 7011, 250 7541; www.kirurumu.com; s/d full board US$165/250; ⊗ Jun-Mar) Intimate and rustic, this comfortable camp is a good base if you're interested in doing nature or wildlife walks together with your safari. Night drives are also possible. It's about 20 minutes' drive from the park gate and signposted off the Makuyuni road.

Other recommendations:

Tarangire Treetops Lodge (☎ 250 0630/9; info@ elewana.com; s/d full board incl wildlife drives US$385/ 770; ⊗ Jun-Mar) Pampered and upmarket, with spacious bungalows set on low stilts, or built tree house–style around the baobabs. It's outside Tarangire's northeastern border.

Tarangire Swala (☎ 250 9816; www.sanctuarylodges .com; s/d all-inclusive US$505/810) Tarangire's most exclusive option, nestled in a grove of acacia trees and overlooking the Gurusi wetlands in the southwestern part of the park.

Naitolia Camp (☎ 0744-470447, 275451; info@tarangire conservation.com; per person all-inclusive US$175) A low-key lodge with three rustic tented cabins, all with attached

bathroom and open-air shower, and a tree house. It's just outside the park's northern border (about 45 minutes by vehicle to the gate), with the chance for walks and night drives.

Kikoti (☎ 250 8090; www.tzphotosafaris.com; s/d full board plus bush walk US$295/440) On a rise just east of the park boundaries, this camp has spacious, well-appointed luxury tents and the chance for walks and night drives.

Getting There & Away

Coastal Aviation, Air Excel and Regional Air all stop at Tarangire on request on their flights between Arusha and Lake Manyara (approximately US$60 per seat).

There's nowhere in or near Tarangire to hire vehicles. The closest place to buy petrol is in Makuyuni.

SERENGETI NATIONAL PARK

Serengeti National Park, which covers 14,763 sq km and is contiguous with Masai Mara National Reserve in Kenya, is Tanzania's largest and most famous national park. On its vast, treeless plains tens of thousands of hoofed animals are constantly on the move in search of fresh grassland. The wildebeest, of which there are over one million, are the chief herbivores and also the main prey of large carnivores such as lions and hyenas, and their annual migration is the Serengeti's biggest drawcard.

During the rainy season between December and May the herds are widely scattered over the southern section of the Serengeti and the Ngorongoro Conservation Area (NCA). As these areas have few large rivers and streams, they dry out quickly when the rains cease. When this happens, the wildebeest concentrate on the few remaining green areas, and form large herds that migrate north and west in search of food. The wildebeest then spend the dry season, from about July to October, outside the Serengeti and in the Masai Mara, before they again start moving south in anticipation of the rains. Around February, the calving season, over 8000 wildebeest calves are born per day, although about 40% of these will die before they are four months old.

The Serengeti is also famous for its lions, as well as cheetahs, zebras (of which there are about 200,000) and large herds of giraffes. You're also likely to see Thomson's and Grant's gazelles, elands, impalas, klipspringers and warthogs, as well as diverse birdlife.

The Serengeti offers unparalleled safari opportunities, and the beauty and synchrony of nature can be appreciated here as in few other places. If you're able to visit, it's a chance not to be missed. Try to set aside as much time as possible to explore the park's varied zones and appreciate its vastness.

Information

Entry fees are US$50/10 per adult/child per day. Bookings for camp sites, resthouses and the hostel should be made through the **Tourism Warden** (☎ 028-262 0091, 028-262 1515/04; www .serengeti.org). Park headquarters are at Fort Ikoma, just outside the park, while the tourism division is at Seronera.

There's is an excellent Visitors Information Centre at Seronera, and a small shop selling maps and sometimes film, among other items.

WHEN TO GO

The concentration of wildlife in the Serengeti is greatest between about December and June, although the park can be visited rewardingly at any time of year. If you are primarily interested in the wildebeest, the best base from about December to April is at one of the camps near Seronera or in the southeastern part of the park. The famous crossing of the Grumeti River, which runs through the park's Western Corridor, usually takes place between May and July, although the actual viewing window can be quite short. In particularly dry years, the herds tend to move northwards sooner, avoiding or only skirting the Western Corridor. The northern Serengeti, around Lobo and Klein's Gate, is a good base during the dry season, particularly between August and October.

Activities

An expensive but enjoyable way to experience the Serengeti is via balloon safari. This costs US$449 per person for about an hour floating over the plains at dawn, followed by a full English champagne breakfast in the bush under the acacia trees, complete with linen tablecloths. The flight route varies depending on the winds, but often follows a stretch of the Grumeti River. Bookings can be made in Arusha through **Serengeti Balloon Safaris** (☎ 027-250 8578; www .balloonsafaris.com), or through any of the central Serengeti lodges.

Walking in the Serengeti isn't permitted, though it's easily arranged in areas that border the park, especially in the north around Loliondo, and in the adjoining NCA.

Sleeping

There are about nine ordinary camp sites in the park, including six around Seronera, one at Lobo, one at Kirawira in the Western Corridor and one near Ndabaka Gate in the far west along the Mwanza–Musoma road. Several have pit toilets and at least one has a shower, though for most you'll need to be self-sufficient, including with water. There are also several rustic but comfortable resthouses at Seronera with bathrooms and bedding, and a large hostel. You can also buy simple meals and basic foodstuffs at Seronera.

There are at least two dozen special camp sites, including at Seronera, Lobo and Naabi Hill Gate. There are also a number of lodges and tented camps in the park, as detailed following.

CENTRAL SERENGETI

The main lodge area is at Seronera, in the centre of the park. While it's Serengeti's most crowded area, it's also a reliable 'fall-back' for most of the year, with relatively easy access to most of the park's other zones if you don't have the time or interest to explore further afield.

Seronera Wildlife Lodge (☎ 027-254 4595, 027-254 4795; www.hotelsandlodges-tanzania.com; r per person full board US$180) This is the best overall value, with a good location convenient to prime wildlife-viewing areas, modest but pleasant rooms and a lively end-of-the-day safari atmosphere at the evening buffet.

Serengeti Serena Lodge (☎ 027-250 4158, 027-250 4153; www.serenahotels.com; s/d full board US$285/420; 🖭) About 20km northwest of Seronera airstrip, and not as favourably located as Seronera Wildlife Lodge, but otherwise a good choice, and very comfortable. Accommodation is in two-storey 'Maasai bungalows' with all the amenities.

Serengeti Sopa Lodge (☎ 027-250 0630/39; info@ sopalodges.com; s/d full board US$175/280; 🖭) Ponderous and architecturally unappealing, but rooms – all spacious, with small sitting rooms and two double beds – have all the comforts, and facilities are on a par with those at the other Sopa lodges.

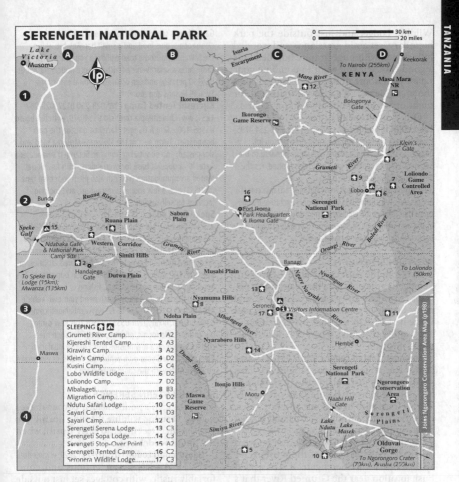

SERENGETI NATIONAL PARK

0 ——— 30 km
0 ——— 20 miles

SLEEPING 🏠 ⛺
Grumeti River Camp.................1 A2
Kijereshi Tented Camp.............2 A3
Kirawira Camp.........................3 A2
Klein's Camp............................4 D2
Kusini Camp.............................5 C4
Lobo Wildlife Lodge.................6 D2
Loliondo Camp.........................7 D2
Mbalageti..................................8 B3
Migration Camp.......................9 D2
Ndutu Safari Lodge.................10 C4
Sayari Camp.............................11 D3
Sayari Camp.............................12 C1
Serengeti Serena Lodge.........13 C3
Serengeti Sopa Lodge............14 C3
Serengeti Stop-Over Point.....15 A2
Serengeti Tented Camp..........16 C2
Seronera Wildlife Lodge.........17 C3

NORTHERN SERENGETI

The north has an excellent collection of camps and makes a fine base between August and October. The area bordering this part of the park, to the east, is also ideal for combining a safari with walks (including multiday walks) and cultural activities focusing on the local Maasai; Loliondo Camp and Sayari Camp are good contacts for this.

Migration Camp (☎ 027-250 0630/39; www.elewana.com; s/d full board incl wildlife drives US$385/770; 🏊) A luxurious camp, recently completely rebuilt, with an intimate bush atmosphere, and views over the Grumeti River in a good wildlife-viewing area.

Klein's Camp (www.ccafrica.com; per person all-inclusive US$560; 🏊) Exclusive and strikingly situated

just outside the northeasternmost park boundary, with eight luxurious cottages, and the chance to do night wildlife drives.

Sayari Camp (☎ 027-250 2799; www.asilialodges.com; s/d all-inclusive US$350/600) This excellent eight-tent seasonal camp follows the Serengeti migration, so that it's at the heart of the action. From mid-June through November, it's in a particularly beautiful setting on the Mara River, while from mid-December through March, it's just outside the Serengeti's southeastern border, with access to the herds of wildebeest in the Ndutu area, and the chance for cultural activities and walking.

Loliondo Camp (☎ 027-250 7011, 027-250 7541; www.kirurumu.com; s/d all-inclusive US$620/840; 🌙 Oct–Mar) An intimate five-tent camp east of Lobo

Wildlife Lodge, and just outside the park boundary, set amid grasslands and wooded hills dotted with huge granite boulders. It's a good choice if you want to combine your safari with some cultural interaction with the local Maasai. It's also well situated for night drives and multiday walking safaris.

Other recommendations:

Lobo Wildlife Lodge (☎ 027-254 4595, 027-254 4795; www.hotelsandlodges-tanzania.com; r per person full board US$180) Well located and similar in standard to the Seronera Wildlife Lodge. If your budget is limited, it's the best value in this part of the park.

Serengeti Safari Camp (www.nomad-tanzania.com; per person all-inclusive US$480) A highly exclusive mobile camp that follows the wildebeest migration, with some of the best guides in the Serengeti. The camp can only be booked through upmarket travel agents.

WESTERN SERENGETI

Apart from the park camp sites, the western Serengeti is the only area that has budget options (all outside the park). It also has several of the Serengeti's most upmarket lodges, and is the best base in the park between around May and early July, when the wildebeest move through.

Serengeti Tented Camp (☎ 027-255 3242; www .moivaro.com; per person full board US$160/213) This small camp is just outside the park boundary and 3km from Ikoma Gate. It has 12 simple tents with bathrooms and hot water, plus the chance for night drives and guided walks in the surrounding area.

Grumeti River Camp (www.ccafrica.com; per person all-inclusive US$630; 🏊) One of the most exclusive camps in the Serengeti. It's in a wild bush location near the Grumeti River that's especially prime around June–July when the wildebeest are often around. Accommodation is in 10 spacious luxury tents with all the amenities.

Kirawira Camp (☎ 027-250 4158/3, 028-262 1518; www.serenahotels.com; s/d all-inclusive US$870/1340; 🏊) Kirawira, set on a small rise about 90km west of Seronera, is more open and somewhat tamer in feel than Grumeti, with luxurious tents in what its advertising describes as an ambience of 'colonial opulence'.

Other recommendations:

Serengeti Stop Over Point (☎ 0748-406996; www .serengetistopover.com; camping US$5, tent rental per person US$10, s/d US$20/30) A camping ground along the Mwanza–Musoma highway about 1km from Ndabaka

Gate. There's space to pitch a tent and a few simple, clean rooms, plus food and a small bar. Any bus along the Mwanza–Musoma road will drop you nearby. The camp hires a safari vehicle (with advance notice) for about US$150 per day, and can organise cultural excursions, Swahili lessons and more.

Kijereshi Tented Camp (☎ 028-250 0127, 028-262 1231; www.hoteltilapia.com; s/d US$40/70, with full board US$65/100; 🏊) A budget place just outside the park boundaries, 18km east of the Mwanza–Musoma road and signposted, and about 2km from the Serengeti's Handajega Gate. It's a popular base for overlanders, with functional tented accommodation (you can also pitch your own tent for US$5) plus a few rooms, a restaurant, and cooking facilities for self-caterers.

Speke Bay Lodge (☎ 028-262 1236; spekebay@ africaonline.co.tz; s/d tents with shared bathroom US$31/44, s/d bungalows US$80/100) On Lake Victoria about 15km southwest of Ndabaka Gate and 125km north of Mwanza. Accommodation is in simple tents with shared facilities, or in spotless, if soulless, en suite four-person bungalows. The hotel can help you organise boat, fishing or birding excursions on the lake; for safaris, you'll need your own vehicle.

Mbalageti (☎ 027-254 8632; www.mbalageti.com; d full board r/luxury tent US$310/550) This new camp has comfortable rooms, plus two-dozen luxury tented chalets set out on a low hillside north of the Mbalageti River. You'll need your own vehicle for safaris, or else make arrangements with the camp in advance.

SOUTHEASTERN SERENGETI

The Serengeti's southeastern corner makes a good base for wildlife viewing during the wet season (December to early April), when it's full of wildebeest.

Ndutu Safari Lodge (☎ 027-250 2829; www.ndutu .com; s/d US$156/210) Unpretentious and comfortably rustic, with cottages set just outside the Serengeti in the far western part of NCA. It's especially well situated for observing the enormous herds of wildebeest in this area between about December and April, and makes a good stop if you're en route between Ngorongoro Crater and central or western Serengeti. Walking safaris are possible in the surrounding NCA. In addition to NCA fees, you'll need to pay Serengeti fees any time that you cross into the park.

SOUTHWESTERN SERENGETI

Kusini Camp (☎ 027-250 9816; www.sanctuarylodges .com; s/d all-inclusive US$485/770) Laid-back luxury in a good wet-season setting amid rocky outcrops in the very remote southwestern Serengeti.

Getting There & Away

Coastal Aviation, Air Excel and Regional Air all have daily flights from Arusha to several of the Serengeti airstrips for between US$145 and US$170 per person one way. Some of Coastal's flights continue on to Mwanza and Rubondo Island National Park on demand.

Most travellers visit the Serengeti with an organised safari or with their own vehicle. For shoestring travellers the only other option for trying to get a glimpse of the animals is to take a bus travelling between Arusha and Mwanza or Musoma via the Western Corridor (see p205), although you won't be able to stop to observe the wildlife. You will need to pay park fees and, if you get out at Seronera, you'll have the considerable problem of getting onward transport, as hitching is not permitted in the park.

The main access gates are **Naabi Hill Gate** (🕐 6am-6pm), 50km from Seronera at the southeastern edge of the park, and **Ndabaka Gate** (🕐 6am-4pm), about 140km northeast of Mwanza along the Mwanza–Musoma road. Bologonya Gate, 5km from the Kenyan border, is en route to/from Kenya's Masai Mara National Reserve, but the border is open only to East African residents or citizens. There are other entry points at Handajega (Western Corridor) and in the north near Klein's Camp. Driving is not permitted in the park after 7pm.

Petrol points en route from Arusha include Makuyuni, Mto Wa Mbu and Karatu. Petrol is also usually available at Ngorongoro Crater (Park Village) and at the Seronera Wildlife Lodge. It's not available anywhere else in the park, so if you are in your own vehicle, come prepared with sufficient supplies. Coming from the west, the most reliable petrol points are Mwanza, Musoma and usually Bunda.

NGORONGORO CONSERVATION AREA

☎ 027

The world-renowned Ngorongoro Crater is just one part of a much larger area of interrelated ecosystems consisting of the beautiful Crater Highlands together with vast stretches of plains, bush and woodland. The entire NCA covers about 8300 sq km and encompasses Olduvai (Oldupai) Gorge, the alkaline Lakes Ndutu and Masek (although Ndutu is actually just over the border in the

Serengeti) and a long string of volcanoes and collapsed volcanoes (often referred to as calderas), most of which are inactive. Just outside the NCA's eastern boundary is the archaeologically important Engaruka, and to the south is Lake Eyasi. To the northeast of the NCA on the Kenyan border is the alkaline Lake Natron.

Information

The NCA is under the jurisdiction of the **Ngorongoro Conservation Area Authority** (NCAA; ☎ 253 9108, 253 7019, 253 7060; ncaa_hq@habari. co.tz). Its headquarters is at Park Village at Ngorongoro Crater, with a tourist information office in Arusha.

Entry fees – which you'll need to pay to visit Ngorongoro Crater and for all activities within the NCA – are US$30 per person per day (discounted for children). Guides cost US$15 per day, and US$20 for walking safaris. To drive into Ngorongoro Crater, there's an additional US$100 vehicle fee per entry, valid for six hours, although this limit is not currently being enforced. Camping fees are US$20/40 per person in an ordinary/special campsite.

The two entry points to the NCA are **Lodoare Gate** (🕐 6.30am-6pm), just to the south of Ngorongoro Crater, and **Naabi Hill Gate** (🕐 6am-6pm), on the border with Serengeti National Park.

Crater Highlands

The ruggedly beautiful Crater Highlands consist of an elevated range of volcanoes and collapsed volcanoes that rises up from the side of the Great Rift Valley and runs along the eastern edge of the NCA. The peaks include Oldeani (3216m), Makarot (Lemagurut, 3132m), Olmoti (3100m), Loolmalasin (3648m), Empakaai (3262m, also spelled Embagai), the still-active Ol Doinyo Lengai (2878m, 'Mountain of God' in Maasai) and of course, Ngorongoro (2200m). The main residents of the area are the Maasai, who have grazed cattle here for hundreds of years.

TREKKING IN THE CRATER HIGHLANDS

Apart from Ngorongoro Crater, much of the Crater Highlands area is remote and seldom visited, although it offers some of Tanzania's most unusual scenery, as well as good trekking. For all routes, you'll need to

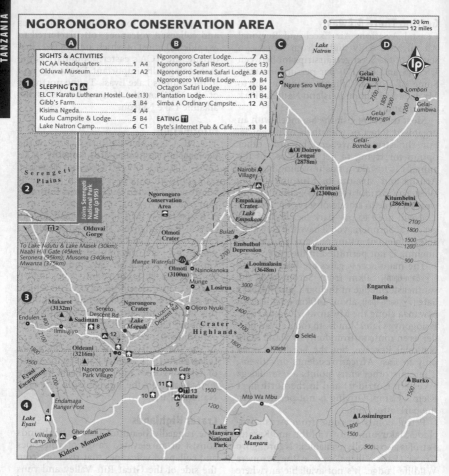

NGORONGORO CONSERVATION AREA

be accompanied by a guide, and for anything except day hikes you'll need donkeys or vehicle support to carry supplies.

Most visitors arrange treks through a tour company; expect to pay from at least US$150 per person per day, including NCA entry fees. Alternatively, you can organise things directly with the NCAA, although you'll need to give at least one month's notice for overnight hikes, as well as provide all camping equipment and supplies yourself, including water, plus hire a vehicle (essential for accessing all treks). The NCAA takes care of arranging the camp sites, guides and donkeys. Everything is usually based from designated Maasai 'cultural *bomas*', each of which has a TSh5000 entry fee. By the

time you sort everything out, in the end it works out about the same to go through a tour operator.

There are no set routes. One popular option is to start just north of Ngorongoro Crater and cross the highlands to finish at Ngare Sero near Lake Natron. This takes four days, but can be cut to three by starting at Nainokanoka, or extended one more day to climb Ol Doinyo Lengai. For something shorter and less expensive, try hiking at Makarot or Oldeani, or at Empakaai or Olmoti Craters. All can easily be done in a day from a base at Ngorongoro Crater and, apart from transport costs, involve only the NCA entry and guide fees. There are no camps apart from the facilities at Ngorongoro Crater.

Ngorongoro Crater

With its blue-green vistas, close-range viewing opportunities and unparalleled concentrations of wildlife, Ngorongoro is one of East Africa's most visited destinations. At about 20km wide it's also one of the largest calderas in the world. Within its walls is an astounding variety of animals and vegetation, including grasslands, swamps, forests, saltpans, a freshwater lake and rich birdlife. You are likely to see lions, elephants, buffaloes and many of the plains herbivores such as wildebeest, Thomson's gazelles, zebras and reedbucks, as well as hundreds of flamingos wading in the shallows of Lake Magadi, the soda lake at the crater's base. Chances are good that you'll also see a black rhino or two.

Despite the crater's steepness, there's considerable movement of animals in and out, thanks to the permanent water and grassland on the crater floor. Wildlife shares the crater with local Maasai, who have grazing rights, and you may come across them tending their cattle.

For fee information, see p197. Ngorongoro can be visited at any time of the year, but during April and May it can be wet and difficult to negotiate, and access to the crater floor is sometimes restricted.

The gates down to the crater floor open at 7am, and close (for descent) at 4pm; all vehicles must be out of the crater area before 6pm.

It can get quite chilly and raw on the crater rim, so bring a jacket and come prepared, especially if you're camping.

SLEEPING

The only ordinary camp site is Simba A, which has basic facilities (toilets and cold showers) and isn't that clean, but it has good views over the crater if you're lucky enough to be there when there's no cloud cover. It's along the road from Lodoare Gate, and not far from NCAA headquarters. There are also numerous special camp sites, including a cluster of sites near Lakes Ndutu and Masek, and one near Empakaai. Bring all your supplies from either Karatu or Arusha.

There are several lodges on or near the crater rim – ideally positioned to minimise travel time down to the crater floor. They include the following:

Ngorongoro Wildlife Lodge (☎ 254 4595, 254 4795, or direct ☎ 253 7058/73; www.hotelsandlodges-tanzania .com; r per person full board US$180) Straightforward rooms and a beautiful setting on the southern rim of the crater.

Ngorongoro Crater Lodge (www.ccafrica.com; per person all-inclusive US$630) This lodge – actually three separate camps – is the most interesting in terms of design, with an eclectic collection of styles and décor. Service and amenities are ultra-top-end, and prices include your own butler. It's on the southwestern rim of the crater.

Ngorongoro Serena Safari Lodge (☎ 250 4158/3; www.serenahotels.com; s/d full board US$285/420) The attractive and perennially popular Serena is in a good location on the southwestern rim of the crater, past Ngorongoro Crater Lodge and near the main crater descent route. Green Footprint Adventures (p92) organises short hikes from the lodge, including nature walks and day hikes to Olmoti.

GETTING THERE & AWAY

The large, white Ngorongoro Crater bus trundles daily between Arusha's central bus station and NCAA headquarters (TSh4000, seven hours), departing Arusha at 10am and Park Village (where vehicles can be hired) at 7am. It's also possible to get the bus in Karatu and Mto Wa Mbu.

GETTING AROUND

You can arrange guides and vehicle hire at NCAA headquarters for US$100/140 for a half/full day; vehicle hire should be booked in advance. You can also hire vehicles in Karatu for about the same price. The only petrol between Karatu and Seronera (in the Serengeti) is at NCAA headquarters, near the Ngorongoro Crater.

Only 4WDs are allowed down into the crater, except at certain times during the dry season when the authorities *may* allow 2WD vehicles to enter. All roads into the crater, except the road from Sopa Lodge on the eastern side, are steep, so if you're driving your own vehicle, make sure it can handle them.

Karatu

☎ 027

This small, scruffy town about 15km east of Lodoare Gate is surrounded by some beautiful countryside, and makes a convenient base for visiting Ngorongoro.

There is a post office, an NBC branch that exchanges cash and travellers cheques and has an ATM, and **Bytes Internet Café** (per hr TSh2000; ☻ 8am-11pm), which is also good for food.

SLEEPING & EATING
Budget

In addition to the following listings, there are several basic guesthouses in the centre of town, all of about the same standard, and all with rooms for about TSh3000.

Ngorongoro Safari Resort (☎ 253 4059, 253 4287; safariresort@yahoo.com; camping US$5, s/d US$65/80) Good, though crowded, camping facilities, hot showers, overpriced rooms and meals from TSh2500. It's on the main road in the town centre. Car hire to Ngorongoro or Lake Manyara costs from US$110/120 per half/full day.

ELCT Karatu Lutheran Hostel (☎ 253 4230; s/d/tr TSh16,000/22,000/32,000) The Lutheran Hostel has simple, clean rooms with hot water, and good meals. It's on the main road at the western end of town.

Kudu Campsite & Lodge (☎ 253 4055; kuducamp@ habari.co.tz; camping US$6, s/d/tr bungalows US$95/100/110) Kudu, at the western end of town, and just south of the main road, has a large lawn to pitch your tent, hot-water showers, bungalows and a bar. Meals can be arranged.

Bytes Internet Pub & Café (☎ 253 4488; bytes@ afsat.com; meals from TSh4000; ☻ 8am-11pm) Freshly squeezed juices, cappuccino and gourmet-style meals are the attraction here. They also do takeaway picnic lunches (three days advance notice). It's along the main road behind the Crater Highlands petrol station.

For self-catering, there are several small supermarkets along the main road, including Olduvai Supermarket and Karatu Mini-Market.

SLEEPING & EATING
Midrange & Top End

Gibb's Farm (☎ 253 4040; www.gibbsfarm.net; s/d half board US$147/208) The long-established Gibb's Farm has a rustic atmosphere, a wonderful setting with wide views over the nearby coffee plantations and cosy garden bungalows, and gets consistently good reviews, as does the cuisine. It's about 5km north of the main road and signposted.

Plantation Lodge (☎ 253 4364/5; www.plantation -lodge.de; s/d half board US$135/187; ☒) A genteel place, with spacious, well-appointed cottages set in green and expansive grounds, large verandas with views over the hills, a crackling fireplace and a cosy, highland ambiance. It's about 2km north of the main road.

Octagon Safari Lodge (☎ 253 4525; www.octagon lodge.com; r per person full board US$100) A good, new place just off the main road, with airy cottages set in attractive grounds, a restaurant and a cosy pub.

GETTING THERE & AWAY

In Karatu, the bus stand is at the western end of town, behind the Total petrol station.

Olduvai Gorge

Olduvai Gorge is a canyon about 50km long and up to 90m deep running to the north-west of Ngorongoro Crater. Thanks to its unique geological history, in which layer upon layer of volcanic deposits were laid down in orderly sequence over a period of almost two million years, it provides remarkable documentation of ancient life.

The most famous of Olduvai's fossils is the 1.8-million-year-old apelike skull known as *Australopithecus boisei*, which was discovered by Mary Leakey in 1959 and which gave rise to a heated debate about human evolution. The skull is also often referred to as *Zinjanthropus,* which means 'nutcracker man', referring to its large molars. In 1972 hominid (humanlike) footprints estimated to be 3.7 million years old were discovered at Laetoli, about 45km south of Olduvai Gorge. Other lesser-known but significant fossils excavated from the upper layers of Olduvai provide some of the oldest evidence of *Homo sapiens* in the area.

There's a small **museum** (☻ 8am-3pm) here just off the road to Serengeti. It's possible to go down into the gorge, accompanied by a guide, which can be arranged at the museum.

As well as the standard fees applying to the NCA, there's an additional US$2 per person per day fee to visit Olduvai Gorge, including the museum.

Engaruka

Engaruka, on the eastern edge of the NCA, is a small village known for its ruins of a complex and mysterious irrigation system with terraced stone housing sites estimated to be at least 500 years old. There's speculation

TANZANIA

about the origin of the ruins; some say they were built by ancestors of the Iraqw (Mbulu) people who live in the area today, while others suggest that the site was built by the Sonjo, a Bantu-speaking people.

The local Cultural Tourism Program offers tours of the ruins, a two-day hike to Mt Ol Doinyo Lengai or a day climb of Mt Kerimasi (2614m). Contact the program guides through the tourist information office in Arusha, or at Jerusalem Campsite in Engaruka.

There are several camping grounds, including one in Engaruka village, and the nicer Jerusalem Campsite just after the river, on the left near the Engaruka Juu primary school.

Pick-ups go sporadically to Engaruka, usually departing Mto Wa Mbu in the late afternoon and Engaruka around dawn. It's possible to hike in from Empakaai Crater, but you'll need a guide from the NCAA.

Lake Natron

Lake Natron, on the Kenyan border, is an alkaline lake known for the huge flocks of flamingos that gather here at the end of the rainy season. The surrounding area is remote, with a desolate, otherworldly beauty, and offers a rewarding – albeit very hot – off-the-beaten track excursion. It's also a good base for climbing the challenging Mt Ol Doinyo Lengai, 25km south. During much of the year, the swampy marshes around the lake's banks make access difficult, and at any time, you'll need 4WD. There have been security problems here in the past, so ask locally for an update.

There's a basic camping ground, as well as **Lake Natron Camp** (☎ 027-255 3242; www.moivaro .com; per person half board US$140/187), with straightforward en suite tents, and an adjoining camping ground. The camp is the best contact for organising treks up Ol Doinyo Lengai, and can also help with arranging hikes in the Crater Highlands. Advance bookings are required.

Lake Natron Camp can organise transfers to the lake from Mto Wa Mbu and Arusha; there's no public transport.

Lake Eyasi

Starkly beautiful Lake Eyasi lies between the Eyasi Escarpment in the north and the Kidero Mountains in the south. It's a hot, dry area, around which live the Hadzabe (also known as Hadzapi or Tindiga) people, who are believed to have lived here for nearly 10,000 years and who continue to follow hunting-and-gathering traditions. Also in the area are the Iraqw (Mbulu), a people of Cushitic origin who arrived about 2000 years ago, as well as the Maasai and various Bantu groups. The area is Tanzania's main onion-growing centre, and there are impressive irrigation systems along the Chemchem River near the village camping ground. The main village is Ghorofani, at the lake's northeastern end.

Although visitor numbers are relatively small, Eyasi is gaining in popularity as a detour on a Ngorongoro trip. Guides can be easily arranged if you're interested in visiting nearby Hadzabe communities; plan on paying about TSh15,000 per small group.

Near the Chemchem River and 2km from Ghorofani is a **village camping ground** (TSh3500), with a small spring. About 5km further on, in a sublime setting on the lakeshore with doum palms in the background, is **Kisima Ngeda** (☎ 027-253 4128, 027-254 8840; kisima@ habari.co.tz; camping US$5, s/d luxury tented bungalow full board US$170/270), with luxury tented bungalows overlooking the lake, and several camping grounds. For camping, stock up in Karatu. Land Rovers go daily between Karatu and Ghorofani (TSh2500, two hours), from where you'll need to walk to the camping grounds or pay extra to have the driver drop you. Alternatively, hitch a lift with one of the onion trucks.

LAKE VICTORIA

If it were it not Africa's largest lake, and the second-largest freshwater lake in the world, it would be easy to overlook Lake Victoria. The Tanzanian part of this enormous patch of blue sees only a trickle of tourists; lakeshore towns, apart from a sleepy waterside charm, have little to hold passing visitors, and infrastructure lags behind that in many other parts of the country. Yet, if you find yourself passing through, and have a bent for the offbeat, the surrounding region holds a surprising number of attractions, including the Bujora Cultural Centre near Mwanza; Bukoba, the heartland of the Haya people; and Rubondo Island National Park, for bird-watching and just relaxing about.

TANZANIA

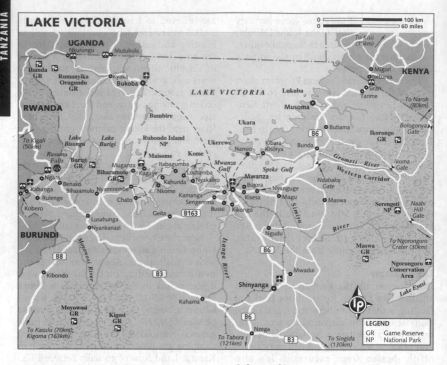

LAKE VICTORIA

LEGEND
GR Game Reserve
NP National Park

The best way to explore the region is as part of a larger East African loop combining Uganda and/or Kenya with Tanzania's northern circuit via the western Serengeti. As many lakeshore areas are infested with bilharzia (p645), swimming from the coastline isn't recommended.

MWANZA
☎ 028

Mwanza, one of Tanzania's largest towns, is the economic centre of the lake region. The surrounding area – characterised by hills strewn with enormous boulders – is home to the Sukuma, Tanzania's largest tribe.

At first glance, the town may put you off, with its layers of dust in the dry season, mud during the rains and a notable lack of things to 'do'. But it's a down-to-earth place with a low-key atmosphere, and most people who spend time here come to like it. It's also the best base for visiting Rubondo Island National Park. In the dry season Mwanza is a possible starting or finishing point for a safari through the western Serengeti, though don't expect many budget deals.

Orientation

The central part of town can be easily covered on foot. To the west, and a short walk from the clock tower, are the passenger-ferry docks and several banks and shops. East of the clock tower area are more shops, guesthouses and mosques; further east are the market and bus stand. In the southwestern corner of town, about five minutes on foot from the clock tower, is the train station. Just beyond here is Capri Point, a small peninsula with lake views and an upmarket hotel.

Information

INTERNET ACCESS

Barmedas.com (Nkrumah St; per hr TSh1000; ☷ 8am-8.30pm) Internet access. One block north of Nyerere Rd.
Karibu Internet Café (cnr Post St & Kenyatta Rd; per hr TSh1000; ☷ 8am-8.30pm Mon-Fri, 8am-6pm Sat, 9am-5pm Sun) Internet access.

MEDICAL SERVICES

Aga Khan Medical Centre (☎ 250 2474; Mitimrefu St; ☷ 24hr) Southeast of the bus station, behind the Ismaili mosque and before Bugando Hospital.

FDS Pharmacy (☎ 250 3284; Post St; ☺ 8am-11pm Mon-Sat, 9am-11pm Sun) At New Mwanza Hotel.

MONEY
DBK Bureau de Change (Post St) At Serengeti Services & Tours, and the easiest place to change cash or travellers cheques.
NBC (Liberty St) NBC changes travellers cheques.
Standard Chartered (Makongoro Rd) This bank is near the clock tower, and has ATMs.

TELEPHONE
TTCL (Post St; ☺ 7am-8pm) Operator-assisted calls.

TRAVEL AGENCIES
In Mwanza you can book flights and trips to Rubondo Island and Serengeti National Parks, and hire a car. For a two day, one-night return trip to Seronera in Serengeti National Park, transport only, expect to pay from US$350 per vehicle (four to six persons) including petrol. It's not that easy to meet other travellers in Mwanza, so organising a Serengeti safari here works best if you're already in a group.
Dolphin Tours & Safaris (☎ 250 0096, 250 0128; www.auricair.com; cnr Post St & Kenyatta Rd)
Fourways Travel Service (☎ 250 2620, 250 2273; www .fourwaystravel.net; Station Rd) Long-established agency offering Rubondo and Serengeti safaris and vehicle hire.
Serengeti Services & Tours (☎ 250 0061, 250 0754; www.serengetiservices.com; Post St) Rubondo and Serengeti safaris, vehicle hire and general travel assistance.

Sleeping
BUDGET
The closest places for camping are Bujora Cultural Centre (p206), or near the Serengeti's Ndabaka Gate (p196).

There are many inexpensive guesthouses in the town centre with serviceable singles/doubles for about TSh2500/3500 with shared facilities, though most make their living from business by the hour. Try the **Kishamapanda Guest House** (☎ 42523; cnr Uhuru & Kishamapanda Sts).

Christmas Tree Hotel (☎ 250 2001; r TSh13,500) Good-value rooms, each with a small double bed, hot water and TV. Some have nets, and there's a restaurant. It's in the town centre just off Karuta St.

Hotel La-Kairo (☎ 250 0343/5; s/d TSh20,000/24,000) Friendly and family-run, this place is another good option. It has a restaurant, and spotless rooms with fan. It's found on a small, leafy street around 4km out of

town, just off the airport road and signposted.

St Dominic's (Makongoro) Hostel (☎ 250 0830; s/d with shared bathroom TSh4000/6000, with private bathroom TSh12,000/15,000) Staid and spartan, this church-run hostel has rooms with shared bathroom (no hot water), plus newer en suite ones (with hot water). Breakfast is breakfast TSh1000. It's about five minutes' walk north of the clock tower roundabout, off Balewa Rd.

Lake Hotel (☎ 250 0658; Station Rd; ground floor s/d TSh7200/8400, upstairs d TSh15,000) Lake Hotel is ageing and tatty, but its shortcomings are easy to overlook if you've just disembarked from a 40-hour haul on the Central Line train. Upstairs rooms – complete with trickling hot-water shower, fan and net – are best, and management let three people sleep in them for no additional charge.

MIDRANGE & TOP END
Hotel Tilapia (☎ 250 0517, 250 0617; www.hoteltilaplia .com, Capri Point, d/ste from US$00/100; ☒ ▢ ▣) Central Mwanza's best hotel is in a breezy setting overlooking the water on the eastern side of Capri Point. It has a lakeside terrace, a business centre, several restaurants and your choice of rooms or bungalow-style suites. A buffet breakfast is included in the price, and credit cards are accepted (5% surcharge).

Tunza Lodge (☎ 256 2215; enquiries@rcnair.com; s/tw/d US$45/55/60) An agreeable anglers' lodge, with cottages scattered over an expansive lawn sloping down to the lake, and a restaurant (meals from TSh4000). It's about 8km from town and 2km from the airport. From town, take a *daladala* to Ilemela, from where it's a 2.5km walk (left) to the lake.

New Mwanza Hotel (☎ 250 1070/1; www.new mwanzahotel.com; cnr Post St & Kenyatta Rd; s/d TSh50,000/60,000; ☒) This three-star place with five-star aspirations is the only 'proper' hotel in the town centre. The bland rooms have TV, and there's also a terrace-level restaurant.

Wag Hill Lodge (☎ 250 2445, 0744-917974; www .waghill.com; per person full board & transfers to/from Mwanza US$250; ☒) A good splurge for a getaway or if you're an angling aficionado. Its three bungalows are nestled into a forested hillside on a peninsula jutting into the lake. The price includes fishing and boat transfers.

TANZANIA

MWANZA

0 — 300 m
0 — 0.2 miles

INFORMATION
Aga Khan Medical Centre..............1 D5
Barmedas.com.................................2 C4
DBK Bureau de Change...............(see 8)
Dolphin Tours & Safaris..................3 B4
FDS Pharmacy............................(see 16)
Fourways Travel Service...................4 B4
Karibu Internet Café.........................5 B4
NBC Bank & ATM..............................6 D4
Post Office................................(see 10)
Saa Nane Game Reserve Office......7 A6
Serengeti Services & Tours..............8 B4
Standard Chartered Bank & ATM......9 B4
TTCL..10 B4

SIGHTS & ACTIVITIES
Clock Tower...................................11 B4

SLEEPING 🏠
Christmas Tree Hotel......................12 C5
Hotel Tilapia...................................13 A6
Kishamapanda Guest House..........14 B3
Lake Hotel.....................................15 B5
New Mwanza Hotel........................16 B4
St Dominic's (Makongoro) Hostel.....17 C2

EATING 🍴
Imalaseko.................................(see 9)
Kuleana Pizzeria............................18 B4
Salma Cone...................................19 C4
Street Food...................................20 A4

Street Food...................................21 B4
Street Food...................................22 B5
Szechuan Mahal.............................23 B4

TRANSPORT
Air Tanzania..................................24 B4
Akamba Bus Office.........................25 C4
Auric Air Charters.......................(see 3)
Bus Stand.....................................26 D5
Kamanga Ferry Terminal................27 A4
Local Transport Stand....................28 C5
Local Transport Stand (Airport &
   Ilemela)....................................29 B4
Mwanza North Port & Lake Ferries
   Terminal...................................30 A3
Precision Air..................................31 B4
Scandinavian Bus Office.................32 C5

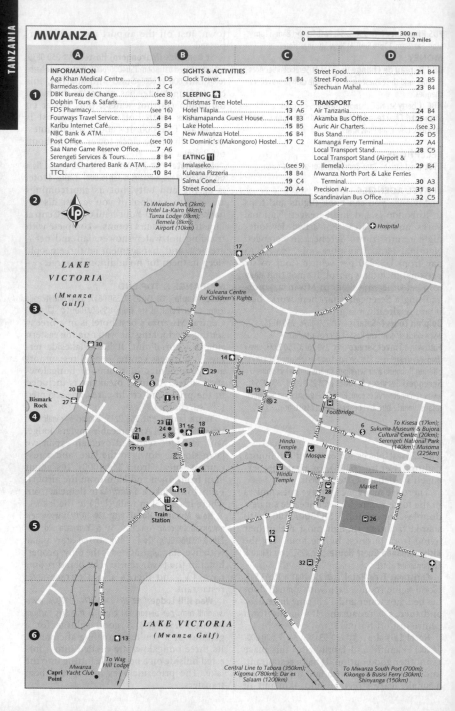

To Mwaloni Port (2km);
Hotel La-Kairo (4km);
Tunza Lodge (8km);
Ilemela (8km);
Airport (10km)

🕀 Hospital

LAKE
VICTORIA

(Mwanza
Gulf)

Kuleana Centre
for Children's Rights

Bismark
Rock

Footbridge

To Kisesa (17km);
Sukuma Museum & Bujora
Cultural Centre (20km);
Serengeti National Park
(140km); Musoma
(225km)

Hindu
Temple

Mosque

Hindu
Temple

Market

Train
Station

Central Line to Tabora (350km);
Kigoma (780km); Dar es
Salaam (1200km)

To Mwanza South Port (700m);
Kikongo & Busisi Ferry (30km);
Shinyanga (150km)

LAKE VICTORIA
(Mwanza Gulf)

Mwanza
Yacht Club

To Wag
Hill Lodge

Capri
Point

Eating

For street food, try the stalls opposite the post office, or the area along the train tracks near the ferry terminals.

Salma Cone (Bantu St; ☪ until 10pm) On hot days locals head here for soft-serve ice cream and fast food.

Kuleana Pizzeria (☎ 256 0566; Post St; meals TSh2000; ☪ 9am-9pm) Good food (pizzas, sandwiches, yogurt, desserts, fresh-squeezed juices and more) and good vibes are the features here. Profits go to support the nearby Kuleana Centre for Children's Rights. It's near New Mwanza Hotel.

Szechuan Mahal (☎ 40339; Kenyatta Rd; meals from TSh6000; ☪ dinner) If the drab exterior doesn't put you off, the delicately seasoned Chinese food here is some of Mwanza's best cuisine.

Hotel Tilapia (☎ 250 0517, 250 0617; www.hotel tilaplia.com; Capri Point; buffet TSh4000, meals from TSh4000; ☪ lunch & dinner) The Tilapia's popular weekend lunchtime barbecue is an ideal excuse to while away an afternoon sipping a cold drink. Downstairs are several other restaurants with pricier á la carte dining.

Imalaseko (Makongoro Rd) For self-catering, come here. It's in the CCM building near the clock tower.

Getting There & Away

AIR

There are daily flights to/from Dar es Salaam on **Air Tanzania** (☎ 250 0046; Kenyatta Rd) and to/from Dar es Salaam and Bukoba on **Precision Air** (☎ 250 0819; pwmwz@africaonline.co .tz; Kenyatta Rd). **Coastal Aviation** (☎ 256 0443/1; coastalmwanza@coastal.cc; Airport) flies twice weekly between Mwanza and Rubondo (US$70).

BOAT

Passenger ferries connect Mwanza with Bukoba and with several islands in Lake Victoria, including Ukerewe and Maisome (for Rubondo Island). For schedule and fare information see p262. A speedboat service between Mwanza and Bukoba is planned to start soon; check at North Port for an update.

Ferries to Bukoba use Mwanza North Port, near the clock tower. For Ukerewe, most departures are from North Port, with sporadic smaller boats leaving from Mwaloni, about 2.5km north of the town centre off the airport road. Cargo boats to Port Bell (Uganda) and Kenya depart from Mwanza

South Port, about 1.5km southeast of the centre; see p260.

To go by road from Mwanza anywhere west or southwest, you'll need to cross the Mwanza Gulf between Mwanza and Sengerema. There are two ferries. The northernmost and more reliable Kamanga ferry docks just south of the passenger ferry terminal at Mwanza North Port, and departs Mwanza daily at 8.30am, 10.30am, 12.30am, 2.30pm (except Sunday), 4.30pm and 6.30pm (TSh300/3600 per person/vehicle, 20 minutes). Departures from Kamanga are every two hours from 8am until 6pm, except there's no 2pm ferry on Sunday.

The more southerly Busisi ferry operates in theory until 10pm. Its eastern terminus is at Kikongo, about 25km south of Mwanza.

BUS

All departures are from the main bus stand near the market, except for Scandinavian Express, which departs from the **Scandinavian office** (☎ 250 3315; Rwagasore St) just south of the market; and Akamba buses, which depart from the **Akamba office** (☎ 250 0272), off Mtakuja St near Majukano Hotel.

To Musoma, buses go throughout the day from 6am until about 2pm (TSh4000, four hours); some continue to the Kenyan border.

To Geita, there's a daily bus, usually continuing to Biharamulo (TSh6500), from where there are connections to Bukoba, Lusahunga and on to Benako and Ngara for the Rwanda and Burundi borders. To Benako and Ngara, it's just as fast to go via Shinyanga and Kahama (TSh6000, eight hours between Kahama and Benako). There are also weekly buses direct from Mwanza to Ngara (TSh10,500). To Muganza (for Rubondo Island), there are several direct buses weekly (TSh6000, eight hours).

To Bukoba, it's best to do the trip in stages via Biharamulo. The road journey is long and rough (until you get to Biharamulo, where it gets smoother), and almost everyone takes the ferry or flies.

To Tabora, Mohammed Trans goes daily via Shinyanga (TSh8000, seven hours), departing in each direction at 6.30am.

To Arusha and Moshi (TSh32,000 plus US$20 for a Kenyan transit visa) and Dar es Salaam (TSh44,000 to TSh58,000 plus Kenyan transit visa costs, about 30 hours), the best route is via Nairobi (TSh23,000 to TSh28,000 plus Kenyan visa costs), and the best line is Scandinavian. Akamba also does the route. Alternatively, you can try the long and gruelling loop via Singida (TSh30,000, two days), traversed by Tawfiq, or – for a fleeting safari – go on Coast Line, which travels twice weekly between Mwanza and Arusha via the Serengeti (TSh23,000, plus entry fees for Serengeti National Park and Ngorongoro Conservation Area, 15 hours). Departures are currently at 5am Tuesday and Friday from Arusha, and at 6am on Monday and Thursday from Mwanza.

To Kigoma, there are three buses weekly, mostly via Biharamulo, with at least one weekly via Kahama and Shinyanga. Buses depart at about 5am and arrive the next day if you're lucky.

See p257 and p259 for buses to Kenya and Uganda.

TRAIN

Mwanza is the terminus of a branch of the Central Line from Dar es Salaam. See p265.

Getting Around
TO/FROM THE AIRPORT

Mwanza's airport is 10km north of town (TSh5000 in a taxi). *Daladalas* (TSh150) leave from near the clock tower.

LOCAL TRANSPORT

Daladalas for destinations along the Musoma road, including Kisesa and Igoma (for Bujora), depart from the Bugando Hill stand, southeast of the market, while those running along the airport road depart from near the clock tower.

AROUND MWANZA
Bujora Cultural Centre
(Sukuma Museum)

If you're interested in learning about Sukuma culture, the **Sukuma Museum & Bujora Cultural Centre** (http://photo.net/sukuma; admission TSh3000; ☉ 8am-6pm Mon-Sat, 1-6pm Sun) makes a worthwhile day trip from Mwanza. Among other things, you'll see traditional Sukuma dwellings, the house of a traditional healer and the royal drum pavilion, built in the shape of the stool used by Sukuma kings. The church in the centre of the grounds was built in 1969 by David Fumbuka Clement, the Quebecois missionary priest who

founded the museum. An English-speaking guide is available.

There's **camping** (TSh2500) on the grounds of the centre, and no-frills **rooms** (r per person with shared bathroom TSh3000) with bucket showers; meals can be arranged with advance notice.

Bujora is about 20km east of Mwanza off the Musoma road. Take a *daladala* to Igoma (TSh250), from where you can get a pick-up to Kisesa. Once in Kisesa, walk a short way along the main road until you see the sign for Bujora Primary School (*Shule ya Msingi Bujora*). Turn left and follow the dirt road for 2km to 3km to the cultural centre.

Ukerewe
☎ 028

Ukerewe Island lies in Lake Victoria, well away from Mwanza's dust, and well off the beaten track. It's known for its traditional healers and birdlife, and is agreeable for wandering around and learning about local life.

Gallu Beach Hotel (☎ 251 5094; www.gallu.net; camping TSh1500; r TSh5600) is the best place to stay, with simple rooms and meals. It's located in Ukerewe's main town, Nansio, and is an easy walk from the ferry. Staff can help you organise excursions.

Ferries sail twice daily between Nansio and Mwanza's North Port (TSh3500/2000 in 2nd/3rd class, three hours).

It's also possible to reach Nansio from Bunda, about 30km north of the Serengeti's Ndabaka Gate on the Mwanza–Musoma road, which means that you can go from Mwanza to Ukerewe and then on towards Musoma or the Serengeti – or vice versa – without backtracking. Via public transport, take any vehicle between Mwanza and Musoma and disembark at Bunda. From Bunda, you can get transport to Kibara-Kisorya, from where it's a short boat ride to Ukerewe. Both the Mwanza–Nansio and Kibara-Kisorya–Ukerewe ferries take vehicles; the Kibara-Kisoria ferry runs throughout the day between 8am and 6pm.

RUBONDO ISLAND NATIONAL PARK

Rubondo Island National Park, in Lake Victoria's southwestern corner, is known for its lovely tranquil atmosphere and its excellent birding. Close to 400 species have been identified here including the fish eagle, heron, stork, ibis, kingfisher and cormorant. Keeping them company are chimpanzees, hippos, crocodiles and even elephants (which were introduced several decades ago), as well as sitatungas, 'amphibious' antelopes that like to hide among the marshes and reeds along the shoreline.

Information

Park entry fees are US$20/5 per adult/child per day. For camping fees, see p113. There's a US$50 per week sport-fishing fee. Camp-site bookings are best done via radio, arranged through any Mwanza travel agency.

Both the park and Rubondo Island Camp organise chimpanzee tracking. However, if your primary interest is chimps, the chances of sightings and close-up observation are much better in Gombe Stream or Mahale Mountains National Parks.

Sleeping

The park has an ordinary camp site and some nice double *bandas* on the lakeshore just south of park headquarters (at Kagaye). There's a tiny shop selling a few basics, but it's better to bring all essentials with you.

Rubondo Island Camp (☎ 027 254 4109; www .flycat.com; s/d full board US$175/280, s/d all-inclusive except fishing US$265/460; ☒) This intimate luxury camp has a lakeside setting, cosy en suite tents, tasty cuisine and a relaxing ambience. Excursions include guided walks, boat trips and fishing. Ask about low-season discounts.

Getting There & Away
AIR

Air charters can be arranged through **Auric Air Charters** (☎ 250 0096, 250 0128; www.auricair.com; cnr Post St & Kenyatta Rd), **RenAir** (☎ 028 256 2069, 256 2215; www.renair.com; Mwanza Airport) or Coastal Aviation (p205), all in Mwanza, or through any Mwanza travel agency. Costs are about US$300/450 one way from Mwanza for a three-/five-seater plane. Coastal Aviation also has twice-weekly flights connecting Rubondo with Arusha and Serengeti National Park.

BOAT

The cheapest way to reach the park is to travel by ferry or bus to one of the villages on the lakeshore opposite Rubondo, from where you can arrange a boat pick up with park headquarters. The main villages for doing this are Muganza (on the mainland southwest of Rubondo), Nkome (southeast of Rubondo), and Maisome (on Maisome

Island, just east of Rubondo). For Muganza, there are several direct buses weekly from Mwanza along a rough but reasonable road. If you get stuck here for the night, there are a few basic guesthouses. For both Nkome and Maisome, there are occasional ferry connections; see p262. Nkome can also be reached by bus via a rough road (allow a full day from Mwanza); if you're driving, you can leave your vehicle at the ranger post there.

You'll need to radio park headquarters in advance to let them know you'll be arriving this way; in Mwanza, travel agencies or the Saa Nane Game Reserve office near Hotel Tilapia can help you call, and there's also a radio at the police station in Muganza. Plan on paying about TSh40,000 per boat from Muganza, and up to double this from Nkome or Maisome, although with some negotiating you may be able to get it for less. Local fishing boats don't generally enter Rubondo, though if you sort out the permissions in advance with park headquarters, the captains will give you a better deal (eg about TSh10,000 from Maisome to Rubondo).

BUKOBA
☎ 028

Bukoba, home of the Haya people, is Tanzania's second-largest port on Lake Victoria. It's a small but bustling place with an attractive waterside setting and a typical African small-town feel, and makes an agreeable stop en route to/from Uganda.

Information

Bukoba Cybercafé (cnr Jamhuri & Kashozi Rds; per hr TSh2000; ☒ 8.30am-10pm) Internet access.

Kiroyera Tours (☎ 222 0203; www.kiroyeratours.com; Sokoine St) A keyed-in place opposite the market, and an essential stop if you're in Bukoba. They have information on nearby attractions, and can organise cultural and historical outings in and around town.

Main post office Opposite the library on the southeastern edge of town; has a fast Internet connection for TSh600 per hour.

NBC (Jamhuri Rd) Changes cash and travellers cheques and has an ATM.

TTCL (☒ 7.30am-9pm Mon-Fri, 8am-5pm Sat) For operator-assisted calls.

Sights

Along the lakeshore are some **colonial-era buildings**, now housing the university and government offices. At the eastern edge of

TANZANIA

BUKOBA

0 _____ 300 m
0 _____ 0.2 miles

INFORMATION
Bukoba Cybercafé.....................1 B1
Kiroyera Tours..........................2 B2
Main Post Office & Internet........3 B2
NBC.......................................4 B2
TTCL......................................5 B2

SIGHTS & ACTIVITIES
Colonial-Era Buildings..............(see 7)
Lake Hotel..............................6 D3
University of Bukoba.................7 C3

SLEEPING
ELCT Conference & Training Centre..8 D3
Walkgard Annex........................9 B3

EATING
Cosmopolitan Supermarket.........10 B2
Fido Dido Supermarket...............11 B2
New Rose Café.........................12 B2

TRANSPORT
Air Tanzania...........................13 B2
Bus Station............................14 A2
Precision Air...........................15 B2

LAKE VICTORIA

town near the lake is the old **Lake Hotel** –
functioning in name only – where Ava
Gardner and Frank Sinatra reportedly enjoyed a drink or two when filming *Mogambo* in the area northwest of the Kagera
River near the Uganda border.

Sleeping
BUDGET
ELCT Conference & Training Centre (☎ 222 3121;
elct-hotel@bukobaonline.com; Aerodrome Rd; d/tr with
shared bathroom US$12/18, large s/d with private bath-
room US$20/30) A good, long-standing place
with clean, comfortable rooms and pleasant
grounds along the airport road near the
lake. Breakfast costs extra.

Spice Beach Motel (☎ 222 0142; s/d TSh8000/
12,000) This small guesthouse is at the southeastern edge of town near the port. It has
one single with shared facilities, several
small en suite doubles – ask for one facing
the lake – and a restaurant.

MIDRANGE
Yassila Hotel (☎ 222 1251; s/d TSh20,000/30,000; 🔀)
A popular hotel near the port. Rooms have

TV, minifridge and air-con, and the restaurant serves up good *tilapia* (Nile perch)
grills and other dishes.

Walkgard Hotel (☎ 222 0935; www.walkgard.com;
s/d/ste US$30/40/60; 🔀 🖳 🛜) This three-star
place is Bukoba's top of the line, targeted
primarily at local business clientele and
conferences. Check out a few rooms, as they
vary, though all come with full breakfast,
TV and telephone. The hotel is inconven-
iently located about 3km from the town
centre in the Kashura area (TSh2500 in a
taxi).

Walkgard Annex (☎ 2220935; s/d TSh20,000/25,000)
Run by the same management that runs
Walkgard Hotel, this is in the town centre.
Its rooms come with fan, net and TV. It's
about 300m southeast of the telecom build-
ing on the western side of town.

Kolping Bukoba Hotel (☎ 222 0199; hotel@
kolpingtz.com; s/d/ste TSh25,000/30,000/40,000) This
hotel is just next to Walkgard Hotel, and
gives it stiff competition. Rooms here are
similar value to those at the Walkgard,
although often noisier, and meals can be
arranged.

Eating

New Rose Café (Jamhuri Rd) A local institution, with inexpensive meals and snacks.

The restaurant at Yassila Hotel is the town's main gathering spot, and why not, with lake views and tasty pepper steak, grilled *tilapia* and other dishes. Spice Beach Hotel is also a good choice, with an equally nice setting and slow service. In town, try the restaurant at Walkgard Annex (meals from TSh3500).

For self-catering, there's **Fido Dido** (Jamhuri Rd) or **Cosmopolitan** (Jamhuri Rd) nearby.

Getting There & Away

AIR

There are daily flights to/from Mwanza (TSh87,000) on **Precision Air** (☎ 222 0861; Bukoba Machinery Bldg; Kawawa Rd). **Air Tanzania** (☎ 0748-737259; Global Travel, Jamhuri Rd) has a representative in Bukoba, although currently no Bukoba flights.

BOAT

There is passenger-ferry service between Bukoba and Mwanza on the MV *Victoria*; see p262.

BUS

Bukoba's roads are getting a face-lift, and you can now go on good Tarmac roads all the way to Kampala in Uganda. Heading south, the road is Tarmac as far as Biharamulo. All the bus companies and their ticket offices are based at or near the **bus station** (Tupendame St).

Buses go daily to Biharamulo (TSh7000), from where you can catch onward transport to Lusahunga, and from there on to Ngara or Benako and the Burundi and Rwanda borders.

To Kigoma, there's a weekly direct bus via Biharamulo and Kasulu, departing Fridays at 6am (TSh13,500, at least 12 hours), but it's faster to go to Biharamulo and catch onward transport from there. Depending on the security situation, you may or may not be accompanied by an armed convoy between Lusahunga and Kigoma; for more see p257.

To Mwanza, you can try making your way in stages via Biharamulo, but it's better to take the ferry or fly.

To Kampala (Uganda), the best connections are on Jaguar/Dolphin; see p259.

MUSOMA

☎ 028

Quiet Musoma, on the eastern shores of Lake Victoria, is capital of the Mara region and an agreeable stopping point en route between Mwanza and Kenya. The surrounding countryside is a melting pot of cultures, with the Kuria, Jita, Luo, Taturu and many more all rubbing shoulders.

The local NBC branch, four blocks south of the main street, changes cash and travellers cheques, and both NBC and the nearby CRDB have ATMs. For Internet, try **Musoma Communications Centre** (🕑 daily), just up from CRDB.

Sights

The **Mwalimu Julius K Nyerere Museum** (adult/child/student US$3/1/2; 🕑 9.30am-6pm), about 45km southeast of Musoma in Butiama, is highly recommended for anyone interested in the statesman's life and in Tanzanian history. It contains memorabilia from Tanzania's early postindependence days, Nyerere's personal effects and a large collection of photographs. Nearby are the Nyerere family home and the graves of Nyerere and his parents.

Take a minibus to Nyasho (TSh1000), from where you can get transport to Butiama (TSh1000). Taxis charge about TSh20,000 return, including waiting time.

Sleeping & Eating

Tembo Beach Hotel (☎ 262 2887; d with shared bathroom TSh11,000, with private bathroom TSh16,500) Rooms here are reasonably clean, there's a small strip of sand out front, and the setting is ideal, with views of sunrise and sunset. It's also the main stop in town for overland trucks. The hotel is set on a narrow peninsula about 1.5km north of town; follow the road from the CRDB bank north along the edge of the lake.

Hotel Orange Tree (☎ 262 2651; Kawawa St; s/d 6500/8500) A modest establishment on the eastern edge of town with basic but clean rooms and a restaurant (meals from TSh2000).

Afrilux Hotel (☎ 262 0031; s/d TSh15,000/20,000; 🍴) This slightly garish, modern hotel is in a multistorey building about halfway between the lake and the bus stand in the town centre. Rooms are good value, and there's a restaurant (meals from TSh3500).

Peninsula Hotel (☎ 264 0119, 264 2526; Makoko rd; s/d/ste TSh25,000/33,000/60,000; 💢 🖳) The Peninsula, which hovers between two and three stars, is the main upmarket option in the town centre. Rooms are faded but plush in a 1970s sort of way, and there's a restaurant (meals TSh5000). It's about 1km from the town centre on the Makoko road.

Lukuba Island Lodge (☎ 0744-090100, 027-254 8840; www.lukubaisland.com; per person full board plus transfers to/from Musoma US$230) If Robinson Crusoe were a moneyed angler, this exclusive retreat in the middle of Lake Victoria is undoubtedly where he would choose to spend his days. It makes an excellent getaway, with wonderfully rustic bungalows, and the chance for hiking, birding, boating and fully equipped fishing. Advance reservations are required.

Mara Dishes Frys (meals from TSh1000) This local favourite, around the corner from the NBC, is good for plantains or chicken and chips.

For self-catering, try Kotra in the town centre.

Getting There & Away

Frequent buses and minibuses connect Musoma and Mwanza, departing between about 6am and 2pm daily (TSh3500, four hours). There are minibuses throughout the day to Sirari on the Kenyan border, where you can change to Kenyan transport. **Scandinavian Express** (☎ 262 0006), with its office near Mara Dishes Frys, stops at Musoma on its Mwanza–Nairobi–Dar es Salaam route (TSh42,000/56,000 for semiluxury/luxury between Musoma and Dar es Salaam, both departing Musoma at 2pm).

Daladalas run throughout the day between the town centre and the Makoko section of Musoma. The *daladala* stand is along the road between town and the airfield.

BUNDA
☎ 028

Bunda is a minor transport hub that you'll probably pass through if you're heading to/ from Kenya or Ukerewe Island, or coming from the western Serengeti. The bus stand is along the main Mwanza–Musoma highway.

CN Motel (☎ 262 1064; small/large s TSh6000/9000) is at the northern edge of town along the main highway, and has meals and clean rooms.

SHINYANGA
☎ 028

Shinyanga would likely be relegated to complete anonymity were it not the site of one of the world's largest diamond pipes (about 45km northeast of town near Mwadui, and now operating at only a fraction of its former capacity) and a regional transport hub. It has an NBC bank with an ATM, and an Internet café, both on the main road.

Places to stay include **Mwoleka Hotel** (☎ 276 2249, 276 3004; s/d TSh10,000/15,000, s/d ste TSh25,000/ 35,000), near the bus stand, and the similar but slightly less pretentious **Shinyanga Motel** (☎ 276 2458; r with fan TSh15,000, with air-con & TV from TSh20,000; 💢), near the train station. For something less expensive try **Shellatone Hotel** (d TSh7000), near the bus station.

Shita's (meals from TSh2000) has inexpensive, piping-hot plates of rice and sauce and other local fare.

Precision Air flies five times weekly between Dar es Salaam and Shinyanga (US$140 one way). Mohammed Trans goes daily to Tabora (TSh6500, six hours, departing by 7am, book in advance) and to Mwanza (TSh3500, three hours, several departures between 6am and 8.30am).

SINGIDA
☎ 026

Pretty Singida is well away from Lake Victoria, but it's likely you'll pass through it if you're travelling between Mwanza and Arusha via the rugged southwestern loop. It's also a possible detour from Babati and Mt Hanang.

The surrounding area is dotted with huge granite boulders and two lakes – Lake Singidani (just north of town), and the smaller Lake Kindai (to the south) – both of which attract flamingos, pelicans and many other water birds.

An **Internet café** (per hr TSh2000) is just north of the market, and an NBC bank, near the post office, is on the northern side of town.

Sleeping & Eating

Legho Singida Motel (☎ 250 2526; r TSh11,500) Quieter than the Stanley Hotel, and one of the better places to stay. It's on the northern edge of town, with a nice garden and a restaurant.

Stanley Hotel (☎ 250 2351; s/d with shared bathroom TSh6000/8000, d with private bathroom TSh12,000)

A reliable place near the bus stand with no-frills rooms and a restaurant.

Social Training Centre (☎ 250 3464; s with shared bathroom TSh3500, with private bathroom TSh10,000) A clean, simple place run by the local Catholic diocese. It's behind the TTCL building, and near the NSSF compound; meals can be arranged.

Shana Resort, just west of the market, has good juices and local dishes, while Florida has the usual assortment of snacks, chicken and fries.

Getting There & Away

There are at least two daily buses along the mostly unpaved route between Singida and Arusha (eight to 10 hours), but it's better to break the trip at Babati or Katesh (for Mt Hanang). Daily buses also run between Singida and Dodoma (eight to 12 hours), but it's better to take the train (see p265). There's also a daily direct bus between Singida and Dar es Salaam via Dodoma, departing in both directions about 6am (14 to 20 hours).

WESTERN TANZANIA

The west is Tanzania's rough, remote frontier land, with few tourists, minimal infrastructure, vast trackless expanses crossed only by the aging Central Line train and little to draw you here – unless you're interested in chimpanzees. For this, and for watching wildlife in one of Tanzania's most pristine settings, it's among the best spots on the continent.

Highlights include Jane Goodall's world-renowned chimpanzee research station at Gombe Stream National Park, the isolated and beautiful Mahale Mountains National Park, wild Katavi National Park and Lake Tanganyika itself, which is the world's longest and second-deepest freshwater lake. Wherever you go, expect minimal tourist facilities and rough, rugged travel, with train, boat and truck often the only transport choices.

TABORA
☎ 026

Tabora – a sleepy town basking in the shade of mango and flame trees – was once a major trading centre along the old caravan route connecting Lake Tanganyika

with Bagamoyo and the sea. Known in its early days as Kazeh, it was the domain of famed Nyamwezi king Mirambo, as well as the headquarters of infamous slave trader Tippu Tib. A string of European explorers passed through its portals, most notably Stanley and Livingstone, and Burton and Speke. After the Central Line railway was constructed, Tabora became the largest town in German East Africa.

Today it's a useful transport junction where the Central line branches for Mwanza and Kigoma; if you're travelling by train, you'll probably need to spend at least a day here.

NBC Bank (Market St) changes cash and travellers cheques, and has an ATM. For Internet, try **MI Internet Café** (Lumumba St), just east of the bus stand.

Sights

About 6km southwest of town in Kwihara is **Livingstone's tembe** (flat-roofed Arabic-style house; admission TSh1500), where he stayed in 1072 after being found by Stanley in Ujiji. Now a museum, it houses a diary and other Livingstone memorabilia. Take any *daladala* heading towards Kipalapala and have them drop you at the turn-off, from where it's about 2km further on foot. Taxis from town charge about TSh7000 return.

Sleeping & Eating

Orion Tabora Hotel (☎ 260 4369; cnr Boma & Station Rds; s/d TSh30,000/40,000) The old railway hotel has been nicely restored, and is now the best place in town. Rooms have TV and nets, and there's a restaurant-bar (meals from TSh3500). Staff are accommodating if you're travelling by train, and there is someone around to let you in for predawn train arrivals.

Hotel Wilca (☎ 5397; Boma Rd; s/d TSh7200/8500) Clean, quiet rooms (all with nets) and a good restaurant. It's at the northeastern edge of town along Boma Rd.

Moravian Hostel (☎ 260 4710; Mwanza Rd; tw with shared bathroom TSh3000, s/tw with private bathroom TSh5000/6000) A good shoestring deal, with spartan twin-bedded rooms with nets. Breakfast costs TSh1000. It's northwest of the centre and about 2.5km from the train station. Head along Lumumba St and turn right just behind the market. The hostel is about 300m down on the right, next to the church.

TANZANIA

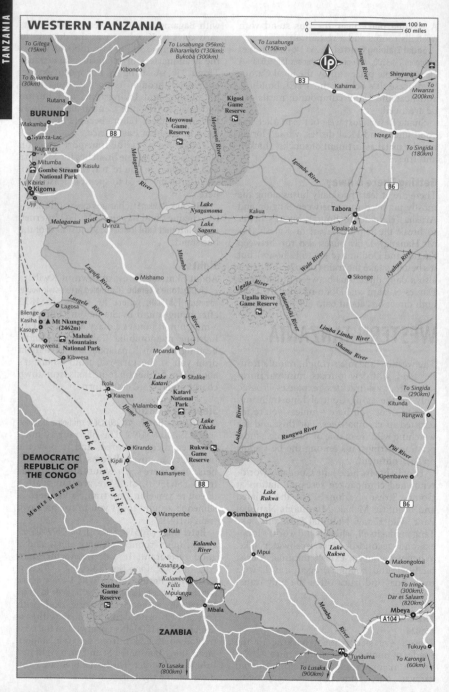

WESTERN TANZANIA

0 ────── 100 km
0 ────── 60 miles

To Gitega (15km)
To Lusahunga (95km); Biharamulo (130km); Bukoba (300km)
To Lusahunga (150km)
Iyanga River
Shinyanga
To Bujumbura (30km)
Kibondo
B3
Kahama
To Mwanza (200km)
Rutana
Kigosi Game Reserve
BURUNDI
Makamba
Moyowosi Game Reserve
Nzega
Nyanza-Lac
B8
Moyowosi River
To Singida (180km)
Kagunga
Mitumba
Igombe River
Kasulu
Gombe Stream National Park
Lake Nyagamoma
B6
Kibirizi
Kigoma
Kaliua
Tabora
Ujiji
Lake Sagara
Kipalapala
Malagarasi River
Uvinza
Mtambo
Mishamo
Wala River
Nyahua River
Lugufu River
Sikonge
Ugalla River
Ugalla River Game Reserve
Luegele River
Lagosa
Kaumbuki River
Bilenge
Kasiha
Mt Nkungwe (2462m)
River
Limba Limba River
Kasoge
Mahale Mountains National Park
Shama River
Kangwena
Kibwesa
Mpanda
Ikola
Lake Katavi
Sitalike
To Singida (290km)
Karema
Katavi National Park
Kitunda
Malambo
Rungwa
DEMOCRATIC REPUBLIC OF THE CONGO
Ifume River
Lake Chada
Lukima River
Rungwa River
Piti River
Kirando
Kipili
Rukwa Game Reserve
Kipembawe
Monts Marungu
Namanyere
B8
Lake Tanganyika
Lake Rukwa
B6
Wampembe
Sumbawanga
Kala
Lake Rukwa
Kalambo River
Mpui
Makongolosi
Kasanga
Chunya
To Iringa (300km); Dar es Salaam (820km)
Sumbu Game Reserve
Kalambo Falls
Mpulungu
Mbeya
A104
Mbala
Momba River
ZAMBIA
Tukuyu
To Lusaka (800km)
To Lusaka (900km)
Tunduma
To Karonga (60km)

Golden Eagle (☎ 260 4623; Jamhuri St; s/d without bathroom TSh8000/9000, d with TV from TSh15,000) Run-down but reasonable rooms with fan, food, and a convenient location near the bus stand.

Aposele Guesthouse (☎ 260 4510; d with shared bathroom TSh4000, s/d with private bathroom TSh4000/6000) Large, no-frills rooms on a small side street off Station Rd, just a few minutes walk from the train station.

Mayor's Restaurant & Ice Cream Parlour (cnr Market & School Sts; snacks from TSh500, meals TSh1000; ⊗ breakfast, lunch & dinner) A great stop for snacks, including fresh pineapple juice and soft-serve ice cream, plus samosas and light meals.

For self-catering, try **Cash & Carry Supermarket** (☎ 260 4327; Jamhuri St).

Getting There & Away
AIR
Precision Air (☎ 260 4818; Lumumba St) stops at Tabora five times weekly on its flights between Dar es Salaam and Kigoma. Their office is near the market. The airport is about 5km south of town.

BUS
Mohammed Trans runs between Tabora and Mwanza, departing daily in each direction at 6.30am (TSh8000, 7½ hours). Heading east, you can disembark at Nzega (which is also serviced by daily Land Rovers), and then catch a bus on to Singida, though this means an overnight in Nzega. It's possible to drive between Tabora and Mbeya (4WD only), but it's a long slog, and the route is serviced by three to four buses weekly during the dry season. To Kigoma, the only option is the train.

TRAIN
Tabora is the main Central Line junction for trains north to Mwanza, west to Kigoma and south to Mpanda; see p265. Trains from Mpanda reach Tabora about 3am, trains from Kigoma and Mwanza arrive by about 5am, and trains from Dar es Salaam reach Tabora by about 9pm. Travelling between Kigoma and Mwanza, you'll need to spend the day in Tabora, and to reconfirm your onward reservation. If you arrive in the middle of the night, ask the taxi driver to

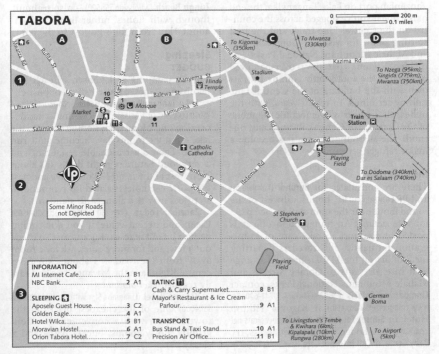

TABORA

0 ___ 200 m
0 ___ 0.1 miles

To Kigoma (350km)

To Mwanza (330km)

Kazima Rd

To Nzega (95km); Singida (275km); Mwanza (350km)

Mnama Rd
Rufita St
Congoni St
Boma Rd
Coronation Rd

Stadium

Manyema St
Hindu Temple
Balewa St
Lumumba St
Ujiji Rd
Market St
Uhuru St
Salamini St
Ngambo St

Market

Mosque

Train Station

Station Rd

Playing Field

Catholic Cathedral

Itetemia Rd

Jamhuri St
School St

To Dodoma (340km); Dar es Salaam (740km)

St Stephen's Church

Findikira Rd
Hill Rd
Kilimatinde Rd

Some Minor Roads not Depicted

Playing Field

German Boma

INFORMATION	
MI Internet Cafe................1 B1	
NBC Bank................2 A1	

EATING	
Cash & Carry Supermarket................8 B1	
Mayor's Restaurant & Ice Cream Parlour................9 A1	

SLEEPING	
Aposele Guest House................3 C2	
Golden Eagle................4 A1	
Hotel Wilca................5 B1	
Moravian Hostel................6 A1	
Orion Tabora Hotel................7 C2	

TRANSPORT	
Bus Stand & Taxi Stand................10 A1	
Precision Air Office................11 B1	

To Livingstone's Tembe & Kwihara (6km); Kipalapala (10km); Rungwa (280km)

To Airport (5km)

wait until you're sure that there's someone around at your hotel to let you in.

UVINZA

Salt production has kept Uvinza on the map for at least several centuries, and the town is still one of Tanzania's major salt-producing areas. To visit the Uvinza salt factory, you'll need to arrange a permit at the entry gate. For lodging try **Sibuondo Guest House** (r with shared bathroom TSh5000) in the town centre.

Uvinza is about two hours southeast of Kigoma via the Central Line train. There's no regular public transport to/from the town; expect to pay about TSh2500 for a lift with a lorry from Uvinza to Kasulu, from where there are daily minibuses to Kigoma (TSh2500). Trucks also run between Uvinza and Mpanda (about TSh5000, one day); stock up before setting off.

KIGOMA

☎ 028

The scrappy but agreeable town of Kigoma sprawls along the lakeshore in a green and tropical waterside setting. It's the major Tanzanian port on Lake Tanganyika, the end of the line if you've slogged across the country on the Central Line train, and the best starting point for visits to Gombe Stream and Mahale Mountains National Parks. For much of Kigoma's past it was overshadowed by Ujiji to the south, only coming into its own with the building of the Central Line railway terminus. In recent years, with the upheavals in nearby Democratic Republic of the Congo (DR Congo), Rwanda and Burundi, the surrounding area has become a major refugee centre.

Information

There are consulates for **Burundi** (Kakolwa St) and **DR Congo** (Kaya Rd), both southwest of the roundabout near the train station. See p252 for visa details. An immigration officer is posted at the port to take care of immigration formalities for travellers departing for Zambia on the MV *Liemba*. To arrange boat hire, or visits to Gombe Stream and Mahale Mountains National Parks, contact **Chimpanzee Safaris** (☎ 280 4435/7, 0741-620154; www.chimpanzeesafaris.com) at Kigoma Hilltop Hotel, or **Sunset Tours** (☎ 280 2408; aqua@cats-net .com) at Aqua Lodge. For Internet access, try **Baby Come 'n' Call Internet Café** (Lumumba St; per hr

TSh3000; ☷ 8am-8pm Mon-Sat) just up from the train station. **Baptist Mission Hospital** (☎ 280 2241) is near the airport, and **NBC** (Lumumba St) changes cash and travellers cheques, and has an ATM.

Sights & Activities

Kigoma's lively **market** abounds with produce and is worth a stroll, as is the colourful fishing village of **Kibirizi**, which is 2km north of town and best visited in the early morning when the fishing boats pull in. In town, watch for the stately German-built **train station** at the base of Lumumba St.

Several kilometres southwest of town on the lake is the tiny but attractive **Jakobsen's Beach** (admission TSh3000), reached via steps down a vegetated hillside. The beach is private, but nonmembers can use it for a daily fee of TSh2000, and the lake here is reportedly bilharzia-free. To get here, take a Katonga *daladala* from the train station roundabout and ask the driver to drop you at a signpost reading 'Zungu Beach'; head uphill for about 2.5km to the fork; Jakobsen's is about 1.5km further to the right. **Zungu Beach** (admission TSh500) – also tranquil, though with stones, rather than sand – is about 1km from the signpost to the left.

Sleeping

BUDGET

There's camping at Jakobsen's Beach (see Jakobsen's Guest House listing, opposite).

Lake Tanganyika Beach Hotel (☎ 280 4894; s/d TSh10,000/15,000) This hotel's setting is ideal – overlooking a long lawn sloping down to the lake – but the rooms have become quite run down. There's a reasonable restaurant and a very loud Saturday night disco. It's about 1km west of town, off Kakolwa Ave and past the port. The hotel is slated for renovations, so prices may rise along with standards.

Zanzibar Lodge (☎ 280 3306; r TSh3500-9500) Clean and decent value, if you don't mind being a bit out of town. Rooms vary so check out a few, and for more quiet, ask for a room away from the road. It's about 2km from central Kigoma in the Mwanga area and easily reached via *daladala*.

Kigoma Hotel (Lumumba St; r with shared bathroom TSh4000) One of the cheapest places in the town centre, with a convenient location, grubby, noisy rooms, bucket baths and a sleazy bar.

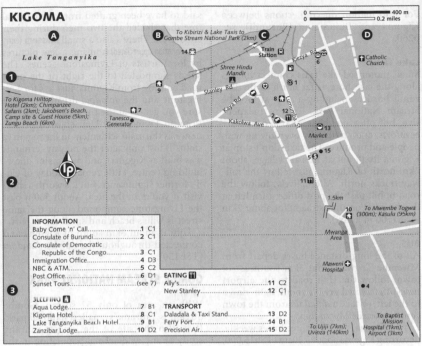

KIGOMA

0 ——— 400 m
0 ——— 0.2 miles

Lake Tanganyika

To Kibirizi & Lake Taxis to
Gombe Stream National Park (2km)

14

Train
Station

Kigeza Rd

6

Catholic
Church

9

Shree Hindu
Mandir

Stanley Rd

@ 1

To Kigoma Hilltop
Hotel (2km); Chimpanzee
Safaris (2km); Jakobsen's Beach,
Camp site & Guest House (5km);
Zungu Beach (6km)

7

Tanesco
Generator

Kaya Rd

3

8

2

12

Kakolwa Ave

13

Market

5

15

11

1.5km

10

To Mwembe Togwa
(300m); Kasulu (95km)

Mwanga
Area

Maweni
Hospital

4

To Ujiji (7km);
Uvinza (140km)

To Baptist
Mission
Hospital (1km);
Airport (3km)

INFORMATION	
Baby Come 'n' Call	1 C1
Consulate of Burundi	2 C1
Consulate of Democratic Republic of the Congo	3 C1
Immigration Office	4 D3
NBC & ATM	5 C2
Post Office	6 D1
Sunset Tours	(see 7)

SLEEPING	
Aqua Lodge	7 B1
Kigoma Hotel	8 C1
Lake Tanganyika Beach Hotel	9 B1
Zanzibar Lodge	10 D2

EATING	
Ally's	11 C2
New Stanley	12 C1

TRANSPORT	
Daladala & Taxi Stand	13 D2
Ferry Port	14 B1
Precision Air	15 D2

MIDRANGE & TOP END

Kigoma Hilltop Hotel (☎ 280 4435/6/7; www.kigoma
.com; s/d full-board & airport pick-up from US$90/140;
) Kigoma's best hotel, with a prime
setting on an escarpment overlooking the
lake, comfortable cottages with minifridge
and TV, and a restaurant.

Aqua Lodge (☎ 280 2408; aqua@cats-net.com; s/d
TSh15,000/18,000) A long-standing place with
good-value rooms (breakfast costs extra) and
a restaurant. It's at the western edge of town,
opposite the Tanesco generator.

Jakobsen's Guest House (☎ 0741-534141; ferie
land@hotmail.com; accommodation per family for first/
succeeding nights TSh45,000/30,000 plus extra charge per
additional adult TSh10,000, electricity per hour TSh2500)
This is a private guesthouse located well
out of town near Jakobsen's Beach (see
opposite), and generally rented out in its
entirety. At the nearby beach, the same
owners run a small camping ground
(camping per adult per night TSh6000)
with ablutions, a grill, lanterns and a water
supply. For both camping and the guesthouse, you'll need to bring along your own
food from town.

Eating

New Stanley (Kakolwa Ave; meals TSh2500; lunch &
dinner) This is several steps up from Ally's in
price and ambience, with reasonable grilled
chicken/fish and other staples, plus a popular
disco for postmeal entertainment.

Ally's (Lumumba St; meals TSh1000) A local favourite, with piping hot *wali maharagwe* (rice
and beans), or *ugali* and sauce.

Getting There & Away
AIR

There are five flights weekly between Dar es
Salaam and Kigoma, usually via Tabora, on
Precision Air (☎ 280 4720, 280 3166). Chimpanzee
Safaris (opposite) has several charter flights
weekly connecting Kigoma with Arusha, and
with Mahale Mountains and Katavi National
Parks, as well as regular charters between
Kigoma and Kigali (Rwanda). The airport is
about 5km southeast of the town centre.

BOAT
Lake Ferries

The venerable MV *Liemba* plies between
Kigoma and Mpulungu (Zambia); see p260.

For information on connections between Kigoma and Bujumbura (Burundi), see p260.

Lake Taxis

Small, motorised lake 'taxis' connect villages along the lakeshore as far north as the Burundi border, including a stop at Gombe Stream National Park. They're inexpensive, but offer no shade or other creature comforts, and are usually overflowing with people and produce. The taxis don't stop at Kigoma itself, but at Kibirizi village, about 2km north of Kigoma; just follow the railway tracks north. Alternatively, follow the road uphill past the post office, turn left at the top and continue straight for about 2km (TSh1500 in a taxi).

BUS

All of the long-distance buses depart from Mwembe Togwa, about 3km southeast of town; follow the Ujiji road to the airport turn-off, from where it's about 500m down to the left, or take a *daladala* from the town centre towards Mwandigo.

To Mwanza, there are three buses weekly, departing Kigoma about 5.30am (TSh15,000, at least 20 hours). Most go via Lusahunga and Biharamulo, though there's usually one weekly going via Kahama and Shinyanga.

To Bukoba, there are several buses weekly, departing at 5.30am (TSh13,500, 10 hours).

The road to Mpanda is quite feasible during the dry season (and sometimes during the rains as well), though there's no direct public transport apart from the occasional lorry.

TRAIN

The classic way to reach Kigoma (apart from sailing in on the MV *Liemba*) is with the ageing Central Line train from Dar es Salaam, Mwanza or Tabora. See p265.

UJIJI

Tiny Ujiji, one of Africa's oldest market villages, earned its place in travel lore as the spot where explorer-journalist Henry Morton Stanley uttered his famously casual 'Dr Livingstone, I presume?' The site where Stanley's encounter with Livingstone allegedly occurred is commemorated by a plaque set in a walled compound near a small garden. Nearby are two mango trees, which are said to have been grafted from the original tree that shaded the two men during their encounter. There's also a small **museum** (entry free, donation appreciated) housing a few pictures by local artists of Livingstone scenes. The site is signposted to the right of the main road coming from Kigoma; just ask for Livingstone and the *daladala* driver will make sure you get off at the right place.

Prior to Livingstone, Ujiji enjoyed prominence as the main settlement in the region (a status it lost only after the railway terminus was built at Kigoma), and as a major dhow-building centre. Little remains today of Ujiji's former significance, but it's worth a short visit if you're in the area. About 500m past the Livingstone compound along the same street is Ujiji's beach and small dhow port.

Ujiji is about 8km south of Kigoma and connected throughout the day by *daladala* (TSh150).

GOMBE STREAM NATIONAL PARK
☎ 028

With an area of only 52 sq km, Gombe Stream is Tanzania's smallest national park. It is also the site of the longest-running study of any wild animal population in the world and, for those interested in primates, a fascinating place.

The Gombe Stream area was gazetted as a wildlife reserve in 1943. In 1960 British researcher Jane Goodall arrived to begin a study of wild chimpanzees, and in 1968 Gombe was declared a national park. Goodall's study is now in its fifth decade.

Gombe's approximately 150 chimps are well habituated, which means that sightings are almost guaranteed, and you can sometimes get to within 5m of the them. Other animals you may see include colobus and vervet monkeys, bushbucks, baboons and bush pigs. If you're serious about chimps, allow at least two days for a visit.

Information

Entry fees are US$100/20 per adult/child per day. Guides cost US$20 per group per day. Children aged under seven are not permitted in the park. Bookings for the hostel and resthouse can be made through Kigoma travel agencies, or directly through the **senior park warden** (☎ 280 2586). All tourism activities are south of here at Kasekela, on the beach near the centre of the park, which is where you'll need to disembark. Bring high-speed film for use in the forest, as flashes aren't permitted.

Sleeping

There is a **hostel** (per person US$10) and a somewhat nicer **resthouse** (per person US$20), which has nets; both are on the beach at Kasekela. You can also **camp** (camping US$20) on the beach, although park staff don't recommend it because of the danger from baboons, and you'll need to have a metal container for storing food. A small shop at park headquarters, north of Kasekela, sells drinks and a few basics, and it's sometimes possible to arrange inexpensive grilled fish meals with staff. Otherwise, bring whatever you'll need from Kigoma.

    Gombe Luxury Tented Camp (☎ 280 4435/6/7; www.chimpanzeesafaris.com; s/d all-inclusive US$500/800) This relaxing camp is on the beach at Mitumba in the northern part of the park, and makes a good splurge if you want some comforts at the end of a hard, sweaty day tracking the chimps. It's run by Kigoma Hilltop Hotel in Kigoma, and they have transport-accommodation deals.

Getting There & Away

The only way to reach Gombe is by charter boat or lake taxi. Lake taxis depart from Kibirizi (opposite) between about noon and 3pm Monday to Saturday (TSh1000, three to four hours). Returning to Kibirizi, they pass Gombe around 8am (which means you'll need to spend two nights at the park if travelling by public transport).

    Alternatively, you can arrange with local fishermen to charter a boat – and you'll be besieged with offers to do so – although this will be expensive. For a return trip, you may have to pay an advance for petrol (which should not be more than one-third of the total price), but don't pay the full amount until you have arrived back in Kigoma. It's common practice for local boat owners to try to convince you that there are no lake taxis, in an effort to get business.

    Fast boats can be organised through Sunset Tours (US$200 return per boat for up to 15 passengers, plus a US$80 per night stopover fee) and Kigoma Hilltop Hotel (US$400 return per boat for up to 20 passengers, plus a US$50 per night stopover fee from the second night onwards), both in Kigoma.

MAHALE MOUNTAINS NATIONAL PARK

Clear, blue waters, white-sand beaches backed by lushly forested mountains, challenging wildlife watching and unrivalled remoteness are the draws at Mahale – Tanzania's most isolated park. Like Gombe Stream to the north, Mahale is primarily a chimpanzee sanctuary, with a population of about 700 chimps, plus roan antelopes, buffaloes, zebras and even some lions (although the lions are seldom seen).

    While the communities that have been focal points of research are well habituated, they're not as accessible as those at Gombe, although almost everyone who spends at least a few days here comes away rewarded.

Information

Entry fees are US$80/30 per adult/child per day. For camping fees see p113. Children under seven aren't permitted in Mahale. Camping and park *bandas* can be booked through the **senior park warden** (PO Box 1374, Kigoma), or through Kigoma Hilltop Hotel (p215) in Kigoma, which can also help you contact park headquarters if you'll be arriving independently. Guide fees are US$20 per group; fishing permits cost US$50 per person per day.

    Park headquarters, where fees are paid, are at Bilenge in the park's northwestern corner. About 10km south of here are Kasiha (site of the park camp site and *bandas*) and Kangwena Beach (with two upscale camps). Bring high-speed film for use in the forest; flashes aren't permitted.

Sleeping

There is a park **camp site** (US$20) and a cluster of quite nice double **bandas** (US$20) at Kasiha. For both, bring everything from Kigoma, as there's nothing available in the park.

    Mahale Camp (www.nomad-tanzania.com; per person all-inclusive US$505; ☣ mid-May–mid-Mar) This exclusive camp on Kangwena Beach offers what is probably the ultimate getaway, if for no other reason than that it's so remote. Accommodation is in six rustic thatched tented *bandas* without electricity or running water, although solar power and bush showers mean you still have all the comforts. The camp can only be booked through upmarket travel agencies. Children under 12 years are not permitted on chimpanzee-tracking walks.

Nkungwe Luxury Tented Camp (☎ 028-280 4435/ 6/7; www.chimpanzeesafaris.com; s/d all-inclusive US$500/ 800) Nkungwe camp, run by Kigoma Hilltop Hotel in Kigoma, is on the beach north of Kangwena and about 1km north of Mahale Camp. It has six comfortable double tents, and makes a good-value alternative to Mahale Camp.

Getting There & Away

Mahale is on the lake about 130km south of Kigoma, and is reachable by plane or boat.

AIR

Kigoma Hilltop Hotel runs twice-weekly charter flights connecting Mahale with Kigoma, Arusha and Katavi National Park.

BOAT

The MV *Liemba* stops at Lagosa (also called Mugambo), to the north of the park (US$25/ 20/15 in 1st/2nd/3rd class, about 10 hours from Kigoma). From Lagosa, it's possible to continue with small local boats to park headquarters, about two hours further south, but not advisable as the *Liemba* reaches Lagosa about 2am or 3am. It's better to radio park headquarters in advance from Kigoma and arrange a pick-up. Kigoma Hilltop Hotel and the *Liemba* office in Kigoma can help with the radio call. The park boat costs US$50 per boat (for up to about 15 people, one way), although if the park is sending a boat up anyway, you may be able to negotiate something better. Coming from Mpulungu (Zambia), the *Liemba* passes Lagosa sometime between late Saturday evening and early Sunday morning around 3am or 4am.

Boat charters from Kigoma (arranged through Kigoma Hilltop Hotel or Sunset Tours in Kigoma) cost from about US$1200 to US$2000 per boat return, including two to three days at the park.

MPANDA

☎ 025

Mpanda is of interest mainly as a starting point for visits to Katavi National Park.

Super City Hotel (☎ 282 0459; s/d TSh3500/5000) has clean rooms with nets, and a slow restaurant. It's along the Sumbawanga road at the southern edge of town; from the train station, follow the tracks to the end, then take the first left and look for the multistorey building. Slightly cheaper, but less conven-

iently located, is **Moravian Hostel** (☎ 282 0187; s/d with shared bathroom TSh2500/3000), just northeast of the centre, with no-frills rooms, meals and bucket baths.

Getting There & Away

BUS

Land Rovers to Katavi National Park and Sumbawanga depart in the mornings from in front of Super City Hotel. Sumry bus line departs Mpanda for Sumbawanga (TSh7500, seven hours) by noon on Tuesday, Thursday and Saturday, after waiting for the train.

Trucks ply the route towards Uvinza and Kigoma fairly regularly, especially during the dry season; allow at least 12 hours. Train is the best option to Kigoma.

From Mpanda southwest to Karema and Ikola (the main Lake Tanganyika ports in this area), there are occasional lorries, which are usually timed to coincide with arrivals of the *Liemba* ferry.

TRAIN

A branch of the Central Line connects Mpanda with Tabora via Kaliua; see p265. If you're heading to Kigoma or Mwanza from Mpanda, you can use Kaliua as the transfer junction, but as there are few guesthouses and little to do, most travellers continue on to Tabora and wait there.

KATAVI NATIONAL PARK

Katavi, 35km southwest of Mpanda, is Tanzania's third-largest park and one of its most unspoiled wilderness areas. Its predominant feature is an enormous flood plain, the vast, grassy expanses of which cover much of the park's northern section, and the seasonal lakes of which support large populations of hippos, crocodiles and birds. The park comes to life in the dry, when the river and lakes dry up and huge herds of buffaloes, elephants, lions, zebras, giraffes make their way to the remaining pools in search of water.

Because of its remote location and completely underpublicised attractions, Katavi receives very few visitors. You'll probably have the place to yourself, and are almost guaranteed to see animals.

Information

Entry fees are US$20/5 per adult/child per day. For camping fees see p113. **Park headquarters** (ktnp@afsat.com), for hut bookings and entry-fee payments, is just off the main road, about 1.5km south of Sitalike, on the park's northern edge. Park vehicles can be hired, if they aren't being used by staff, at a rate of US$1 per kilometre (minimum charge US$100) plus guide fees. Walking safaris are permitted with an armed ranger. For any visit, bring along thick, long-sleeved shirts and trousers, preferably in khaki or other drab shades (avoid anything bright, very contrasting or very dark), as protection against tsetse fly bites.

Sleeping

There are several ordinary camp sites, including the well-situated Chada Campsite near Lake Chada and Lake Katavi Campsite, just west of the Sumbawanga–Mpanda road, and the six-bed Chief Nsalamba Resthouse, about 2km from park headquarters. Bring all provisions with you.

Chada Katavi Camp (www.nomad-tanzania.com; per person all-inclusive US$445; ☉ Jun-Oct & mid-Dec–mid-Mar) An absolute must for the well-heeled, ruggedly inclined safari connoisseur, with just seven double tents and an unbeatably rustic atmosphere. It can only be booked through upscale travel agencies.

Katavi Wildlife Camp (☎ 0748-237422, 0744-237422; www.tanzaniasafaris.info; s/d all-inclusive US$410/700) A comfortable, rustic camp in a prime setting near Ikuu ranger post.

Katavi Hippo Garden Hotel (r per person US$30) In Sitalike village, just outside the park gate.

Getting There & Away

There are airstrips for charter flights in Mpanda, Sitalike and at Ikuu ranger post near Lake Chada. Chimpanzee Safaris (p214) runs twice-weekly charter flights connecting Katavi with Kigoma, Arusha and Mahale Mountains National Park.

Buses between Mpanda and Sumbawanga will drop you at the gate, where vehicle hire can be arranged (best done in advance). Hitching is not permitted in the park. If you are driving, the closest petrol stations are in Mpanda and Sumbawanga.

SUMBAWANGA

☎ 025

The peppy capital of the Rukwa region is set on the fertile Ufipa Plateau at about 1800m altitude in the far southwestern corner of the country, and makes a useful stopping point if you're travelling between Zambia or Mbeya and Katavi National Park. East of Sumbawanga, below the escarpment, is the vast, shallow Lake Rukwa (p232), which becomes two lakes during the dry season.

Sleeping & Eating

Moravian Conference Centre (☎ 280 2853/4; confcen@ atma.co.tz; Nyerere Rd; standard s/d TSh5000/10,000, executive s/d TSh10,000/20,000) Clean, good-value rooms and inexpensive meals. It's about 1km from the town centre along the road to the Regional Block area.

Upendo View Hotel (☎ 280 2242; Kiwelu Rd; d TSh6500) Clean and centrally located, just southeast of the bus stand. The main disadvantage (if you want to sleep) is that it doubles as Sumbawanga's main nightspot.

Forestway Country Club (☎ 280 2800; Nyerere Rd; r TSh20,000) Sumbawanga's only proper hotel also has a good restaurant. It's 2km from town on Nyerere Rd in the Regional Block area, past the Moravian Conference Centre (TSh1500 in a taxi from the bus stand).

Sim's Restaurant (Kiwelu Rd; meals TSh1000) Cheap meals just opposite Upendo View Hotel.

Getting There & Away

Sumry line buses run daily between Mbeya and Sumbawanga via Tunduma (for Zambia), departing in each direction between 6am and 7am (TSh8000, six hours, book in advance). To Mpanda, Sumry has buses departing Sumbawanga at 1pm on Monday, Wednesday and Friday (TSh7500, seven hours). There are also daily Land Rovers departing from the petrol station on the main road starting about 7am (TSh8500). The road passes through Katavi National Park, though it's not necessary to pay park fees if you are just in transit.

KASANGA & KALAMBO FALLS

The 250m Kalambo Falls, southwest of Sumbawanga on the Zambian border, is the second-highest single-drop waterfall in Africa. Several significant Stone Age archaeological finds have been made in the surrounding area. It's possible to reach the falls from Kasanga; you'll need to look for a lift towards the falls, and then walk for about four hours in each direction.

There's a very basic **guesthouse** (r with shared bathroom about TSh2000) in the Muzei section of Kasanga.

Trucks go sporadically between Sumbawanga and Kasanga, and a bus meets the *Liemba* arrivals. These are anywhere between midnight and 6am, although the boat often remains at the dock until dawn. You're allowed to stay on board, but the boat pulls out without much warning so ask staff to wake you in time to disembark.

THE SOUTHERN HIGHLANDS

Officially, the Southern Highlands begin at Makambako Gap, about halfway between Iringa and Mbeya, and extend southwards into Malawi. In this book the term is used to designate the entire region along the mountainous chain running between Morogoro in the east and Lake Nyasa and the Zambian border in the west. It's a very scenic area, with wide, rolling panoramas, good hiking, a temperate climate and a profusion of wildflowers on the hillsides during the rains. While many travellers pass through en route to or from Malawi or Zambia, few stop along the way, although there's much of interest.

DODOMA
☎ 026

Dodoma, in the centre of the country, has been Tanzania's capital and headquarters of the ruling CCM party since 1973. According to the original plan – long since abandoned – the government was supposed to move here by the mid-1980s. This proved unrealistic due in part to insufficient water supplies and an inadequate economic base, and Dar es Salaam remains the unquestioned political and economic centre of the country.

There's little reason to come to Dodoma. However, if you find yourself here, it's not a bad place to spend a day or two. With its grandiose street layout and the imposing architecture of many church and government buildings – all sharply contrasting with the slow-paced reality of daily life – it's easy to get the feeling that the town is dressed in clothes that are several sizes too big.

Information
From the bus stand, the main (Dar es Salaam) road heads west into the centre of town where it meets Kuu St at a large roundabout. Just south of here are the railway tracks, after which everything turns into small dusty lanes. To the north, a warren of small avenues run off Kuu St into the busiest part of town, with the market and lots of shops. Because of Dodoma's many government buildings, photography is prohibited in most areas of town.

Aga Khan Hospital (☎ 232 1789; Sixth St; ☼ 8am-8pm Mon-Sat, 9am-noon Sun) On a small side street just northeast of Food Junction.

Aladdin's Cave Internet Café (per hr TSh1000; ☼ 9.30am-1pm & 3.30-8.30pm Tue-Sun, 9.30am-1pm Mon) One block east of Kuu St, and about three blocks north of the Ismaili mosque.

NBC (Kuu St) Changes cash and travellers cheques, and has an ATM.

RAL Internet Café (Kuu St; per 60min TSh1000; ☼ 8am-9pm Mon-Sat, 2-9pm Sun) Just north of the main roundabout.

Sights & Activities
The **Museum of Geosciences** (Nyumba ya Mayonyesho ya Madini; adult/child TSh500/100; ☼ 8am-3.30pm Mon-Fri) contains rock samples and geological information on the entire country. It's behind New Dodoma Hotel.

The **Parliament** (*Bunge*) is housed in a modern complex on the eastern edge of town just off the Dar es Salaam road. It's possible to observe when they're in session; bring your passport along.

Dodoma is also a good springboard to Kolo (180km north) and its centuries-old rock art (p187).

Sleeping
Water supplies are erratic, so expect bucket baths at the cheaper hotels. Also, hotels fill up whenever parliament is in session, so don't be surprised if you need to try several before finding a room.

BUDGET
Christian Council of Tanzania (CCT; ☎ 232 1682; s/d TSh4500/9000, r with shared bathroom TSh4500) The most convenient budget lodging, with a central location (at the main roundabout, next to the Anglican church), tatty rooms with mosquito nets, and bucket baths. Breakfast costs extra.

Kibo Peak Guest House (☎ 232 2902; s TSh7000, with TV TSh10,000) Clean rooms with fan and net, and an almost exclusively male clientele.

THE SOUTHERN HIGHLANDS

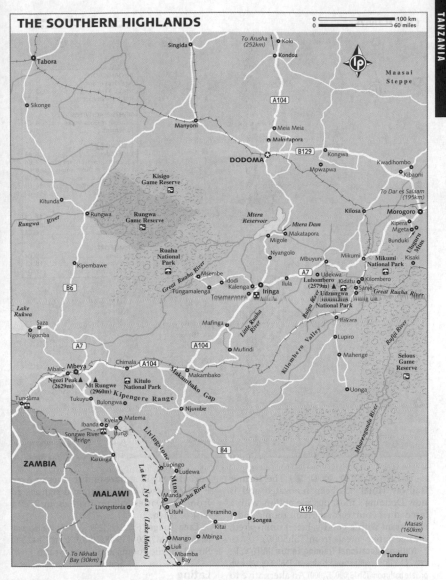

It's about 1km north of the main roundabout off Mpwapwa Rd (reached via Kuu St).

Dodoma Blue Guest House (☎ 234 2085; Mpwapwa Rd; d TSh10,000) Just around the corner from Kibo Peak, and of similar standard. Rooms have nets and small double beds.

Yarabi Salama (r with shared bathroom TSh2500) The cheapest recommendable option near the bus station. It's about a 10-minute walk west of the bus station, and two blocks east of Kuu St.

MIDRANGE & TOP END

New Dodoma Hotel (Dodoma Rock Hotel; ☎ 232 1641; reservation_newdodomahotel@yahoo.com; Railway St; s/d with fan TSh45,000/55,000, deluxe s/d with

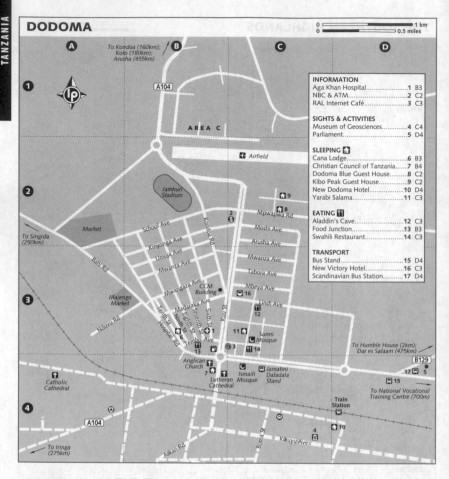

DODOMA

INFORMATION	
Aga Khan Hospital.....................1	B3
NBC & ATM..............................2	C2
RAL Internet Café.....................3	C3

SIGHTS & ACTIVITIES	
Museum of Geosciences..........4	C4
Parliament.............................5	D4

SLEEPING ⌂	
Cana Lodge............................6	B3
Christian Council of Tanzania....7	B4
Dodoma Blue Guest House.......8	C2
Kibo Peak Guest House............9	C2
New Dodoma Hotel................10	D4
Yarabi Salama.......................11	C3

EATING ⋔	
Aladdin's Cave......................12	C3
Food Junction.......................13	B3
Swahili Restaurant.................14	C3

TRANSPORT	
Bus Stand............................15	D4
New Victory Hotel.................16	C3
Scandinavian Bus Station........17	D4

air-con TSh60,000/70,000; ✗ ▢ ▣) The former Railway Hotel has been renovated and is now Dodoma's most upscale option, with a large inner courtyard, pleasant rooms and a restaurant with a good-value, if uninspired, dinner buffet (meals from TSh5000).

National Vocational Training Centre (NVTC; VETA; ☎ 232 2181; s with shared bathroom TSh8500, s/d with private bathroom TSh13,000/17,000) An alternative to the standard hotel scene, with simple, clean rooms, professional staff and a restaurant (meals from TSh4000). It's about 2km east of the centre off the Dar es Salaam road.

Humble House (☎ 235 2261; Area E; s/d TSh12,000/ 14,000; ▢) A B&B-style place with spotless rooms and a small garden. It's mainly an option if you have your own transport; it's buried away in a maze of dirt lanes in Area E (also known as Ipagala), and signposted from the Dar es Salaam road about 2.5km east of town.

Cana Lodge (☎ 232 1199; costerki@yahoo.com; Ninth St; s TSh12,000, d TSh18,000-20,000; ste TSh40,000) Small, sterile rooms and a restaurant.

Eating

Aladdin's Cave (snacks TSh500-1500; ☯ 9.30am-1pm Mon, 9.30am-1pm & 3.30-8.30pm Tue-Sun) Milkshakes, soft-serve ice cream and other snacks (no fresh ice cream on Monday). It's one block east of Kuu St, north of the Ismaili mosque.

Swahili Restaurant (meals from TSh1500; ☯ lunch & dinner) Indian snacks and standard fare, including yogurt and a few vegetarian dishes.

It's near the roundabout, and one block north of the Dar es Salaam road.

Food Junction (Tembo Ave; meals from TSh1000; ⊗ 8.30am-3.30pm & 6.45-10pm Mon-Sat) A popular spot for budget meals, with chicken and rice, and various Indian snacks. It's near the main roundabout, west of Kuu St.

Getting There & Away
BUS
Scandinavian Express has daily departures in each direction at 9.15am (luxury) and 11am (ordinary), costing TSh7500/10,000 ordinary/luxury and taking six hours, from their terminal about 1km east of town along the Dar es Salaam road.

To Iringa, there's a daily bus via Makatapora; see p228.

To Kondoa and Kolo (TSh5500), there's a bus departing from New Victory Hotel off Kuu St at 6am Monday, Wednesday and Saturday. In the other direction, departures from Kolo are on Sunday, Tuesday and Thursday at 3.30am. Alternatively, Satellite Coach line has buses from Dodoma's main bus stand departing daily about noon for Kondoa (TSh4000, four to five hours), from where you can get onward transport to Kolo.

To Singida, it's best to take the train (see p265). Otherwise, there are through buses (TSh5000, at least eight hours) coming from Dar es Salaam that pass Dodoma's main bus station about noon, although they are often full.

TRAIN
Dodoma lies on the Central Line railway connecting Dar es Salaam with Kigoma and Mwanza. Trains from Dodoma westwards depart at about 8am, and eastwards depart at about 6pm. There's also a spur line between Dodoma and Singida; see p265.

MOROGORO
☎ 023
Bustling Morogoro would otherwise be a fairly scruffy town were it not for its verdant setting at the foot of the Uluguru Mountains, which brood over the landscape from the southeast. While there's no real reason to come here, it's an agreeable place, with some easily arranged hiking just outside town.

Information
NBC (Old Dar es Salaam Rd) Changes cash and travellers cheques, and has an ATM.
Wats Internet Café (Mahenge St; per hr TSh1000; ⊗ 8.30am-9pm) Diagonally across from Princess Lodge.

Sleeping
BUDGET
Princess Lodge (☎ 0744-319159; Mahenge St; d from TSh10,000, r with shared bathroom TSh7000) The best shoestring option, with clean, small rooms, most with double bed, fan and net, and a restaurant downstairs. It's one block in from the main road in the town centre.

Sofia Hotel (☎ 260 4848; Mahenge St; s/d with shared bathroom TSh6000/7000, with private bathroom

---

HIKING IN THE ULUGURU MOUNTAINS

The Uluguru Mountains southeast of Morogoro contain some of the oldest original forest in Africa, and while it is much depleted these days, the range is green and scenic, and offers enjoyable hiking.

From Morogoro the most popular route is to **Morningside**, an old German mountain hut to the south of town at about 1000m (about two to three hours on foot). The path starts at the Regional Administration buildings about 3km south of the town centre at the end of Boma Rd. From here, a track leads uphill and then curves to the right through small farm plots and degraded forest before reaching more heavily vegetated highland areas and the Morningside building. It's possible to camp here with your own tent and supplies; there's a small waterfall nearby. Another possibility from town is the hike to **Lupanga Peak** (2147m), the highest point in the immediate vicinity (about five hours return).

The Wildlife Conservation Society of Tanzania (WCST), together with the Uluguru Mountains Biodiversity Conservation Project, publishes the helpful *Tourist Information for the Uluguru Mountains*, with detailed route descriptions and accommodation info for these and other routes. It's for sale at the **WCST office** (☎ 023-261 3122; 1st fl, Bodi ya Pamba Bldg, Old Dar es Salaam Rd) in the centre of Morogoro, or can be downloaded for free (www.africanconservation.com/uluguru; click on Contents, then on Section 4). The WCST office is the best place to arrange a guide.

TANZANIA

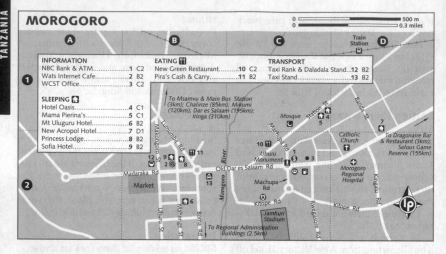

MOROGORO

INFORMATION		EATING 🍴		TRANSPORT	
NBC Bank & ATM	1 C2	New Green Restaurant	10 C2	Taxi Rank & Daladala Stand	12 B2
Wats Internet Cafe	2 B2	Pira's Cash & Carry	11 B2	Taxi Stand	13 B2
WCST Office	3 C2				

SLEEPING 🛏	
Hotel Oasis	4 C1
Mama Pierina's	5 C1
Mt Uluguru Hotel	6 B2
New Acropol Hotel	7 D1
Princess Lodge	8 B2
Sofia Hotel	9 B2

TSh12,000/15,000) A long-standing place with small rooms, and a restaurant. It's diagonally across from Princess Lodge.

Mt Uluguru Hotel (☎ 260 4153, 260 3489; d TSh15,000) This nondescript multistorey hotel is conveniently located and has reasonable rooms (ask for one with a view) and an inexpensive restaurant. It's south of the main road, and just off Mahenge St.

Mama Pierina's (Station St; d TSh9000) Tatty rooms set around a tiny garden, all with fan and nets. Attached is a restaurant serving large portions of unexciting food.

MIDRANGE & TOP END

Hotel Oasis (☎ 261 4178, 261 3535; www.hoteloasistz .com; Station Rd; r from US$40; 🍴 🏊) The Oasis has good-value rooms – all with fan, air-con, TV and small fridge – plus grassy grounds, efficient staff and a restaurant. Room prices include a breakfast buffet.

New Acropol Hotel (☎ 261 3403, 0744-309410; www .newacropolhotel.biz; s/d TSh45,000/55,000; 🍴 🖥) This upscale B&B-style hotel is popular with expats, with a handful of spacious rooms (all with TV and large double bed) and a restaurant. It's about 300m east of the centre on Old Dar es Salaam Rd.

Eating

Princess Lodge (☎ 0744-319159; Mahenge St; meals TSh2000; 🕑 breakfast, lunch & dinner) Bright and friendly, and the best bet for local dishes, with efficient service and meals promised in '30 minutes or less'.

New Green Restaurant (☎ 261 4021; Station Rd; meals from TSh3000; 🕑 lunch & dinner, closed Sun dinner) A long-standing establishment with Indian dishes, grilled chicken and a few vegetarian choices.

Dragonaire Bar & Restaurant (☎ 0748-470713; 🕑 lunch & dinner, also breakfast Sat & Sun) Green grounds, a good mix of locals and expats, and pizzas on weekends. It's signposted about 2.5km east of town, and about 700m off the Old Dar es Salaam Rd.

For self-catering, try **Pira's Cash & Carry** (Lumumba Rd), just north of the main road.

Getting There & Away
BUS
The bus station is 3km north of town in Msamvu, on the main Dar es Salaam road (TSh2000 in a taxi, and TSh150 in a *daladala*).

Scandinavian Express goes daily to Dodoma, Mikumi, Iringa, Mbeya and Dar es Salaam, but as no buses originate in Morogoro it's best to book in advance; the office is at the bus station. To Dar es Salaam, there are also many local buses, running from 5.45am until about 4pm (TSh2500, 3½ hours).

To Tanga, there is a direct bus daily (TSh4500, five hours), departing by 8am.

The main *daladala* stand is out in front of the market, where there's also a taxi rank. There's another taxi rank a couple of blocks further east on Old Dar es Salaam Rd.

TRAIN

Morogoro is on the Central Line (p265), but to Dar es Salaam, it's faster to travel by bus.

MIKUMI NATIONAL PARK

☎ 023

Mikumi National Park is easily accessible from Dar es Salaam and is a good destination if you don't have much time but want to see wildlife. Within its 3230 sq km, set between the Uluguru Mountains to the north and the Lumango Mountains to the southeast, the park hosts populations of buffaloes, giraffes, elephants, lions, zebras, leopards, crocodiles and more. The best and most reliable viewing is around the Mkata floodplains, to the northwest of the main road. Among other attractions here are the **Hippo Pools**, where you can watch these lumbering behemoths at close range, plus do some fine birding.

Mikumi is contiguous with Selous Game Reserve to the south (though there's currently no official road linking the two), and is close enough to Udzungwa Mountains National Park to easily combine the two.

Information

Entry fees are US$20/5 per adult/child per day. For camping fees see p113. The park is best visited in the dry season. For campsite bookings, contact the **senior park warden** (☎ 262 0498). Foxes African Safaris, which runs two lodges in the park, has safari vehicles for its guests. Otherwise, you'll need to either have your own vehicle to visit the park, or arrange an organised tour. Guided walking safaris can be arranged at the park entrance.

Sleeping

The park has four ordinary camp sites, and a special camp site near Choga Wale in the north.

Fox's Safari Camp (☎ 0748-237422, 0744-237422; www.tanzaniasafaris.info; s/d all-inclusive US$280/470; 🏊) This camp, operated by the same family that operates Ruaha River Lodge (p229), is set well away from the road on a rocky outcrop in a good wildlife-viewing area in Mikumi's far north. Access is via a signposted turn-off about 25km northeast of the main park gate. Walks and fly camping can be arranged.

Kikoboga (☎ 022-260 0352/4; obhotel@acexnet .com; s/d full board US$130/220; 🏊) Kikoboga, about

500m northeast of the park gate, has nice stone cottages spread out on a grassy field frequented by grazing zebras and gazelles. Given its proximity to the highway, it's not a wilderness experience, but the animals don't seem to mind, and you'll likely see plenty from your front porch.

Vuma Tented Camp (☎ 0748-237422, 0744-237422; www.tanzaniasafaris.info; s/d all-inclusive US$280/470; 🏊) An easily accessed camp set on a rise about 7km south of the main road, and under the same management as Fox's Safari Camp. The turn-off is diagonally across from the park entry gate.

Also see sleeping options in Mikumi town (p226), 23km west.

Getting There & Away

ROAD

Although getting to the gate of Mikumi is easy via public transport (take any of the buses running along the Morogoro–Iringa highway and ask the driver to drop you off), there is no vehicle hire at the park, so you'll need your own car unless you've arranged otherwise with one of the lodges. The best budget way to visit the park is on one of the frequent special deals offered by Coastal Travels (p118) and other Dar es Salaam-based tour operators, or to take the bus to Mikumi town and organise transport to the park through Genesis Motel (p226).

The park gate is about a four-hour drive from Dar es Salaam; speed limits on the highway inside the park are controlled (70km/h daytime and 50km/h at night). Some roads in Mikumi's northern section are accessible with a 2WD during the dry season, but in general 4WD is best.

TRAIN

For a splurge, take the private luxury train run by Foxes African Safaris between Dar es Salaam and Kidatu (about 40km south of Mikumi town); see p239.

MIKUMI

☎ 023

Mikumi is the last of the lowland towns along the Dar es Salaam–Mbeya highway before it starts its climb up into the hills and mountains of the Southern Highlands, and is of interest primarily as a starting point for visits to Mikumi or Udzungwa Mountains National Parks.

TANZANIA

Sleeping & Eating

Genesis Motel (☎ 262 0461; camping with shower TSh3000, r per person TSh15,000) On the edge of Mikumi town, directly on the main highway and about 2.5km east of the Ifakara junction. The setting is noisy and a bit too close to the truck stops to be enjoyable, but staff are helpful and there's a decent restaurant (Mikumi's best). It's a good place to organise budget safaris to Mikumi National Park (US$100 per vehicle per day, transport only).

Getting There & Away

Minibuses towards Udzungwa Mountains National Park leave throughout the day from the Ifakara junction just south of the highway (about TSh2000, two hours). Through buses on the Dar es Salaam–Mbeya route stop just east of the Ifakara junction. Few buses originate in Mikumi, so you'll need to stand on the roadside and wait until one comes by with space.

Going west, the best bet is Scandinavian Express from Dar es Salaam, which passes Mikumi daily on its routes to Iringa, Mbeya and Songea, beginning about 9.30am. There is also a direct bus from Kilombero to Iringa, passing Mikumi about 5.30am. Going east, buses to Dar es Salaam start to pass Mikumi from 8.30am.

UDZUNGWA MOUNTAINS NATIONAL PARK

☎ 023

Towering steeply over the Kilombero Plains about 350km southwest of Dar es Salaam are the wild, lushly forested slopes of the Udzungwa Mountains, portions of which are protected as part of Udzungwa Mountains National Park. In addition to an abundance of unique plants, the park is home to a healthy population of primates (10 species – more than in any of Tanzania's other parks) and makes an intriguing off-beat destination for anyone botanically inclined or interested in hiking well away from the crowds.

Information

Entry fees are US$20/5 per adult/child per day. For camping fees, see p113. Porter fees range from TSh3000 to TSh6000 per day, depending on the trail. For all hikes, you'll need to be accompanied by a guide (US$15 per day, or US$25 for the armed ranger guide necessary for longer hikes). For over-

night hikes, allow an extra day at Mang'ula to organise things, and time to get from park headquarters to the trailheads. For all hikes on the eastern side of the park, there are plenty of streams to fill up your water bottle, but you'll need a filter or purifying tablets.

The entrance gate, **park headquarters** (☎ 262 0224; www.udzungwa.org) and the senior park warden's office are located in Mang'ula, 60km south of Mikumi town along the Ifakara road. An entry post at Udekwa village, on the western side of the park, is scheduled to open soon, which will be useful if you are coming from Iringa.

There's a tiny market in town, but stock up on major items in Dar es Salaam or Morogoro.

Hiking

There are no roads in Udzungwa; instead, there are about five major and several lesser hiking trails. Popular routes include a short but steep half-day circuit through the forest to **Sanje Falls**, and a two-night, three-day hike up to **Mwanihana Peak**, at 2080m, the park's second-highest point. For all except the easy Sanje Falls route, the going can be tough in parts: trails are often muddy, steep, humid and densely overgrown; infrastructure is rudimentary; and you'll need to have your own tent and do your hiking accompanied by a guide. Check with park headquarters about the challenging four- to five-day trail from Mang'ula to **Luhombero Peak** (2579m, and the park's highest point), which is currently being cleared, as well as about the six-day **Lumemo Trail**.

Sleeping

The three camp sites near park headquarters are rarely used, as they're pricier (per person US$20) than the local guesthouses. Camp sites along the trails are charged at the same rate.

Udzungwa Mountain View Hotel (☎ 262 0260; camping TSh2000, r per person TSh15,000) Under the same management as Genesis Motel in Mikumi, with basic but clean rooms and a restaurant (meals about TSh4500). It's about 500m south of the park entrance, along the road.

Twiga Hotel (☎ 262 0239; r with shared bathroom TSh4000, with private bathroom TSh5000) Basic rooms that are several notches down from those at Udzungwa Mountain View, though they are arguably better shoestring value. Meals can be arranged. It's just outside the park gate, about 200m off the road and signposted.

Getting There & Away
BUS
Minibuses run daily between Mikumi town and Kilombero, where you'll need to wait for onward transport towards Mang'ula. It's usually faster to wait for one of the larger through buses coming from either Dar es Salaam or Morogoro to Ifakara, which pass Mikumi between about 8.30am and 2pm (TSh3000 between Mang'ula and Mikumi).

From Dar and Morogoro there are buses to Ifakara and Mahenge via Mang'ula departing from 6.30am (TSh6000, seven to eight hours from Dar to Mang'ula).

From Iringa, there's a daily bus to Kilombero, departing around noon.

Between the Mang'ula park gate and Sanje (the main trailhead, 10km north), there are sporadic minibuses (TSh500, 30 minutes) and the occasional lorry. Alternatively you can try your luck arranging a lift with park vehicles (TSh10,000 one way).

TRAIN
Tazara line ordinary trains stop at Mang'ula station, about 3km from park headquarters. Express trains stop only at Ifakara, about 50km further south, and two hours by bus to Mang'ula. The other option is the private luxury train operated by Foxes African Safaris, which follows the Tazara line along the northern border of the Selous to Kidatu (US$120/150 one way/return Dar es Salaam–Kidatu, seven hours), about 25km north of the park gate; see p239.

IRINGA
☎ 026
With its bluff-top setting, jacaranda-lined streets and highland feel, Iringa is a likeable place, and one of the most agreeable stops along the Dar es Salaam–Mbeya highway. The town, which is perched at a cool 1600m on a cliffside overlooking the valley of the Little Ruaha River, was initially built up by the Germans at the turn of the century as a bastion against the local Hehe people.

Information
Aga Khan Health Centre (Jamat St; ☺ 8am-6pm Mon-Fri, to 2pm Sat & Sun) Next to the Lutheran cathedral.

JM Business Consulting (Uhuru Ave; per hr TSh500; ☺ 8am-9.30pm Mon-Sat, 10am-9.30pm Sun) Internet access & international calls.

MR Hotel (Mkwawa Rd; per hr TSh1000; ☺ 7.30am-9.30pm) Internet access.

NBC (Uhuru Ave) Opposite the Catholic cathedral; changes cash and travellers cheques, and has an ATM.

Top Internet Café (Uhuru Ave; per 70min TSh1000; ☺ 8.30am-9pm)

Sights
Just northeast of town is **Gangilonga Rock**, where the famous Hehe chief Mkwawa used to go to meditate, and where he learned that the Germans were after him. It's just a few minutes' walk to the top for views over town.

Sleeping
BUDGET
Riverside Campsite (☎ 272 5280/2; phillips@africa online.co.tz; camping TSh2500, tent rental TSh2000) A camping ground, 13km northeast of Iringa along the main road, with a lovely setting on the banks of the Little Ruaha River, hot showers and cold drinks; bring your own food. Take a *daladala* towards Ilula and ask the driver to drop you off (TSh500); it's about 1.5km off the main road.

Iringa Lutheran Centre (☎ 270 2489; Kawawa Rd; s/d with shared bathroom TSh2500/3500, d with private bathroom TSh5000) A good shoestring option, with relatively clean rooms, and meals on request. Breakfast costs TSh500. It's on the northeastern edge of town, about 700m from the main road.

Annex of Staff Inn (☎ 270 0165; Uhuru Ave; r TSh7500-15,000) A local favourite along the main road near the bus stand with no-frills rooms and meals.

MIDRANGE & TOP END
MR Hotel (☎ 270 2006, 270 2779; www.mrhotel.co.tz; Mkwawa Rd; s/d/ste US$25/32/37; ☒ ▯) A good multistorey hotel next to the bus station, with efficient staff, modern rooms and a restaurant. They also organise car hire, Ruaha safaris and other excursions.

Huruma Baptist Conference Centre (☎ 270 1532, 270 0182; camping with shower TSh2500, s/d TSh10,000/20,000) This place is set on large grounds 3km from the town centre down Mkwawa Rd, near the Danish School, with simple rooms and inexpensive meals. It's about a 25-minute walk from the town centre; *daladalas* run nearby.

TANZANIA

IRINGA

INFORMATION
Aga Khan Health Centre............1 C3
JM Business Consulting............2 C3
NBC & ATM.............................3 A3
Post Office.........................(see 5)
Top Internet Café....................4 C2
TTCL...................................5 C3

SLEEPING
Annex of Staff Inn...................6 B3
Iringa Lutheran Centre..............7 D2

Isimila Hotel.........................8 D1
MR Hotel..............................9 C3

EATING
Hasty Tasty Too.....................10 C2
Lulu's...............................11 D2
Premji's Cash & Carry...............12 B3
Saju's Home Cooking.................13 D2

TRANSPORT
Daladalas to Ipogoro...............14 C3
Scandinavian Bus Booking
Office...............................15 C3
Town Bus Station....................16 B3

Some Minor Roads
not Depicted

Isimila Hotel (☎ 270 1194; Uhuru Ave; s/d/ste TSh9000/11,500/18,000) Reasonable-value rooms and a restaurant, at the northern end of town.

Eating

Hasty Tasty Too (☎ 270 2061; Uhuru Ave; snacks & meals from TSh500; ☼ 7.30am-8pm) One of Iringa's highlights, with good breakfasts, yogurt, shakes and reasonably priced main dishes. The owner is helpful with arranging budget safaris to Ruaha, and can also organise food if you're planning to camp in the park.

Saju's Home Cooking (Haile Selassie St; snacks & meals from TSh500; ☼ 7am-11pm) This homy family-run eatery makes a good stop for cheap local food. It's at the northern end of town, on a small lane running parallel to the main road.

Lulu's (☎ 270 2122; snacks & meals from TSh500; ☼ 8.30am-3pm & 6.30-9pm Mon-Sat) Quiet and friendly, with light meals, soft-serve ice cream and an outdoor seating area. It's one block southeast of the main road, just off Kawawa Rd.

For self-catering, try **Premji's Cash & Carry** (☎ 270 2296; Jamat St).

Getting There & Away

To catch any bus not originating in Iringa, you'll need to go to the main bus station at Ipogoro, about 3km southeast of town below the escarpment (TSh1000 in a taxi to town), where the Morogoro to Mbeya highway bypasses Iringa. This is also where you'll get dropped off if you're arriving on a bus continuing towards Morogoro or Mbeya. *Daladalas* to Ipogoro leave from the edge of Uhuru Park in town. All buses originating in Iringa start at the bus station in town, stopping also at Ipogoro.

Scandinavian Express has three buses to Dar es Salaam, leaving at 6.30am, 9am and 10.30am daily (TSh9000/10,000, ordinary/semiluxury, 7½ hours); book in advance at its office, opposite the town bus station.

To Mbeya, there's a bus departing daily about 6am (TSh6500, four to five hours). Alternatively, book a seat on the Scandinavian bus from Dar es Salaam, passing Iringa (Ipogoro) about 1pm.

To Njombe, there's one bus daily departing in the morning from the town bus station. For Songea, change in Njombe, though for both Njombe and Songea, it's faster to wait for the Scandinavian bus from Dar es Salaam.

To Dodoma, there's a daily bus departing about 8am in each direction (TSh7000, 10 to 12 hours), going via Nyangolo and Makatapora. Otherwise, all transport is via Morogoro. If you're driving to Dodoma via Makatapora, allow five to six hours.

AROUND IRINGA

Isimila Stone-Age Site

About 15km outside Iringa, off the Mbeya road, is **Isimila** (admission TSh500), where in the late 1950s archaeologists unearthed one of the most significant Stone-Age finds ever identified. The tools found at the site are estimated to be between 60,000 and 100,000 years old. The display itself isn't exciting, but the surrounding area is worth the journey, with bizarrely eroded sandstone pillars.

Isimila is an easy bicycle ride from Iringa. Otherwise, take a *daladala* towards Tosamaganga (TSh500) and ask to be dropped off at the turn-off, from where it's about a 20-minute walk. Taxis from town cost about TSh5000 return.

Kalenga

The former Hehe capital of Kalenga is 15km from Iringa on the road to Ruaha National Park. It was here that Chief Mkwawa – one of German colonialism's most vociferous resistors – had his administration until Kalenga fell to the Germans in the 1890s, and it was here that he committed suicide rather than succumb to the German forces.

The small **Kalenga Historical Museum** (admission TSh1500) contains Mkwawa's skull and a few other relics from the era. It's just off the park road and is signposted.

RUAHA NATIONAL PARK

Ruaha National Park forms the core of a wild and extended ecosystem covering about 40,000 sq km, and providing home to one of Tanzania's largest elephant populations. Other residents include large herds of buffaloes, as well as greater and lesser kudus, Grant's gazelles, wild dogs, ostriches, cheetahs, roan and sable antelopes, and more than 400 different types of birds. The Great Ruaha River winds through the eastern side of the park, and is home to hippos, crocodiles and many water birds.

Ruaha is notable for its wild and striking topography: undulating plateau with occasional rocky outcrops, and low mountains in the south and west. Running through the park are several 'sand' rivers, most of which dry up completely during the dry season, when they are used by wildlife as corridors to reach areas where water remains.

Information

Entry fees are US$20/5 per adult/child per day. For accommodation fees, see p113.

The main gate is about 8km inside the eastern park boundary. **Park headquarters** (kudu@bushlink.co.tz) is nearby at Msembe.

Except for the February to May wet season, lodges organise walks, as does the park for those staying in the camp sites or *bandas*.

Sleeping

There are two ordinary camp sites about 9km northwest of park headquarters, and about five special camp sites; none have water.

The park maintains several *bandas* about 2km from headquarters, and a resthouse. Water is available for showers and the park sells a few basics, but otherwise you'll need your own supplies. For all park accommodation, book in advance during the high season. In Iringa, the antipoaching office on the edge of town can help you radio the park to make bookings. Head west out of town on the Ruaha road. Take the first right after the roundabout at the edge of town, and then the first left. The antipoaching unit is about 200m down on the left opposite the mosque.

Ruaha River Lodge (☎ 0748-237422, 0744-237422; www.tanzaniasafaris.info; s/d all-inclusive US$280/470) This classy but unpretentious lodge is directly on the river about 15km inside the park gate, with cosy stone *bandas* and views over the water. Fly camping can be arranged, and there are reasonable drive-in rates available.

Mwagusi Safari Camp (in UK ☎ 020-8846 9363; www.ruaha.org; s/d all-inclusive US$450/780; ☼ Jun-Mar) Mwagusi is an exclusive and highly regarded luxury tented camp in a top-notch wildlife-viewing location on the Mwagusi Sand River about 20km inside the park gate. The atmosphere is intimate, with just 16 beds, and guiding is excellent.

Other recommendations:

Mdonya Old River Camp (☎ 022-211 7959/60; safari@coastal.cc; s/d all-inclusive US$290/480; ☼ Jul-Easter) Rustic and comfortable, this camp is in the western part of the park, about 1½ hours' drive from Msembe. While not as luxurious or as well-located as some of the other camps, if you take advantage of Coastal Aviation's 'last minute' deals, Mdonya offers very good value.

Jongomero Camp (www.selous.com; s/d all-inclusive US$495/660; ☺ Jun-Mar; ☒) This wonderfully exclusive camp is set off on its own in the remote southwestern part of the park, about 60km from Msembe. It has just eight tents – all very luxurious and superbly furnished – and you're unlikely to see any other visitors.

With your own transport, it's also possible to stay outside the park boundaries.

Tandala Tented Camp (☎ 026-270 3425, 023-260 1569; tandala@iwayafrica.com; per person full-board US$110) Just outside the park boundary along the Tungamalenga road, and about 12km from the park gate. Accommodation is in raised tents, and the camp can help you arrange vehicle hire to Ruaha (US$50 per person for a full-day safari) and transport from Iringa.

Tungamalenga Camp (☎ 026-278 2198/6; tung camp@yahoo.com; camping US$5, r per person with break-fast/full board US$20/40) In Tungamalenga village, about 35km from the park gate, with simple en suite *bandas* around a tiny garden (where you can pitch a tent) and a restaurant. The camp has a vehicle that you can hire (US$100 per day to the main gate area).

Getting There & Away

Coastal Aviation flies from both Dar es Salaam and Zanzibar to Ruaha via Selous Game Reserve (US$300 one way from Dar es Salaam or Zanzibar, US$270 from Selous Game Reserve), and sometimes between Ruaha and Arusha. Foxes African Safaris (p92) has a plane based in Ruaha for flights to Katavi (US$400), Dar es Salaam (US$300), Arusha (US$300), Selous (US$270), Mikumi and other destinations on request.

A bus goes daily between Iringa and Tungamalenga, departing Iringa at 1pm and Tungamalenga at 3am (TSh2500, 3½ to five hours). From Tungamalenga, there is only the occasional park vehicle, though you can hire a vehicle from Tungamalenga Camp.

Hasty Tasty Too (p228) in Iringa organises transport from US$130 per vehicle per day, five persons maximum, for two days and one night, and, if you're travelling alone or in a small group, can sometimes put you in touch with other travellers who are interested in visiting the park.

The closest petrol is in Iringa.

IRINGA TO MAKAMBAKO

From Iringa, the Tanzam highway continues southwest, winding its way gradually up, past dense stands of pine, before reaching the junction town of Makambako. About 40km southwest of Iringa, and about 1km off the main road, is **Kisolanza – The Old Farm House** (www.kisolanza.com; camping with hot showers US$3, self-catering chalets per chalet US$15-25, cottages per adult/child half board US$50/12), a farm homestead with camping, chalets and cottages, plus a shop selling fresh produce and other items. Scandinavian Express and other buses will drop you at the turn-off.

Makambako itself is a windy, dusty junction town where the road from Songea meets the Dar es Salaam–Mbeya highway. If you get stuck here overnight, your only choices are the basic **Lutheran Centre Hotel & Guest House** (☎ 026-273 0047; s/d with shared bath-room TSh2000/3000), opposite the train station, or the more expensive **Uplands Hotel** (☎ 026-273 0201; r about TSh10,000), also on the main road, about 500m west of the junction. Buses from Makambako to Mbeya cost TSh3000.

MBEYA
☎ 025

Mbeya lies in a gap between the verdant Mbeya Range to the north and the Poroto Mountains to the southeast. It was founded in 1927 as a supply centre for the gold rush at Lupa, to the north. Today Mbeya is a bustling regional capital, the major town in southwestern Tanzania and an important transit point en route to/from Zambia and Malawi. Thanks to its altitude of about 1800m, the climate is pleasantly cool year-round.

There's not much to the town itself, but it's a good place for stocking up, and the surrounding area is scenic, with some hiking possibilities.

Information

Aga Khan Medical Centre (☎ 250 2043; ☺ 8am-8pm Mon-Sat, to 1pm Sun) Just north of the market.
Nane Information Centre (per hr TSh500; ☺ 8am-10pm) Internet access; on the western side of the market square.
NBC (cnr Karume & Kaunda Aves) Changes travellers cheques with purchase receipts, and has an ATM.

Dangers & Annoyances

Mbeya attracts many transients, particularly in the area around the bus station.

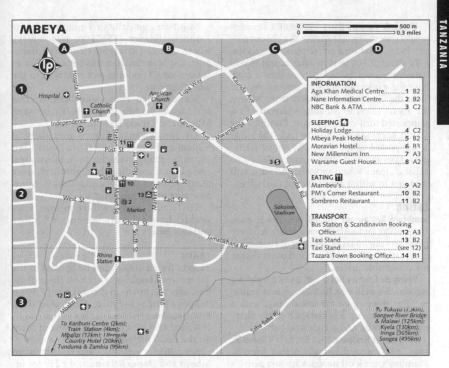

MBEYA

0   500 m
0   0.3 miles

INFORMATION
Aga Khan Medical Centre..............1 B2
Nane Information Centre..............2 B2
NBC Bank & ATM..............3 C2

SLEEPING
Holiday Lodge..............4 C2
Mbeya Peak Hotel..............5 B2
Moravian Hostel..............6 B3
New Millennium Inn..............7 A3
Warsame Guest House..............8 A2

EATING
Mambeu's..............9 A2
PM's Corner Restaurant..............10 B2
Sombrero Restaurant..............11 B2

TRANSPORT
Bus Station & Scandinavian Booking
Office..............12 A3
Taxi Stand..............13 B2
Taxi Stand..............(see 12)
Tazara Town Booking Office..............14 B1

To Karibuni Centre (2km);
Train Station (4km);
Mbalizi (12km); Utengule
Country Hotel (20km);
Tunduma & Zambia (95km)

To Tukuyu (75km),
Songwe River Bridge
& Malawi (125km);
Kyela (130km);
Iringa (365km);
Songea (495km)

Watch your luggage and your pockets, and avoid walking alone through the small valley behind the station. Also watch out for *faux* guides, and don't make any arrangements with anyone loitering around the bus or train stations.

Sleeping

BUDGET

Karibuni Centre (☎ 250 3035; mec@atma.co.tz; camping per double tent TSh2000 plus per person additional TSh1000, d/tr/q TSh10,000/12,000/14,000) A clean, quiet mission-run place in an enclosed compound where you can also pitch a tent. There's also a restaurant (meals from TSh3000; open 7am-9pm Monday to Friday, lunch Saturday). It's 3km southwest of the town centre, and about 10 minutes on foot from the *dala-dala* stop for transport into town. Watch for the signpost along the north side of the main highway, and about 500m west of the first junction coming from Dar es Salaam. From the turn-off, head through what looks like an empty lot for about 300m to the place.

Holiday Lodge (☎ 250 2821; Jamatikhana Rd; s/d TSh6000/7500) A whitewashed local guesthouse

with clean rooms – some with bathroom – and a restaurant. It's just off the main road behind the large Rift Valley Hotel, about a 10-minute walk from the market area, and about 15 minutes on foot from the bus stand.

Other recommendations:

Moravian Hostel (☎ 250 2643, 250 3676; Jacaranda Rd; s TSh6500, d with shared bathroom TSh4200) No-frills rooms (breakfast costs extra). Meals are sometimes available on order. It's about 800m south of the market, and not safe to walk to, especially at night (TSh1000 in a taxi from town).

Warsame Guest House (Sisimba St; s/d with shared bathroom TSh2500/3500) Grubby shared facilities and a central location just northwest of the market.

New Millennium Inn (☎ 250 0599; Mbalizi Rd; s with shared bathroom TSh5000, with private bathroom TSh6500) Directly opposite the bus station and noisy, but convenient if you have an early bus.

MIDRANGE & TOP END

Mbeya Peak Hotel (☎ 250 3473; Acacia St; s/d/ste TSh12,000/15,000/30,000) A central, sunny setting and decent rooms, some with views over the hills. It's on a small side street just east of the market. There's also a restaurant.

Utengule Country Hotel (☎ 256 0100; utengule@
iwayafrica.com; s/tw/ste US$45/80/120; ⊠) This attrac-
tive lodge is set on a coffee plantation in the
hills about 20km west of Mbeya, and if you
have your own transport, it makes a cosy
base for exploring the surrounding region.
Take the Tunduma road west from Mbeya
for about 12km to Mbalizi, where there's a
signposted turn-off to the right. Continue for
8.5km, keeping left at the first fork. The lodge
is signposted to the right. Via public transport, take any Tunduma-bound *daladala* to
Mbalizi, from where sporadic pick-ups will
take you to within about 2km of the lodge.

Eating

Sombrero Restaurant (☎ 250 3636; Post St, mains
TSh2500-3500; ☉ breakfast, lunch & dinner) A lively
place serving up large portions of vegetarian
curry, spaghetti bolognaise and other dishes
for reasonable prices.

Utengule Country Hotel (☎ 256 0100; utengule@
iwayafrica.com; meals about TSh10,000; ☉ lunch and dinner) The place to go for fine dining, with a
daily set menu or à la carte, a Sunday afternoon barbecue and a convivial bar.

PM's Corner Restaurant (cnr Sisimba St & Market Sq;
meals TSh1000) and, diagonally across from it,
Mambeu's, are local staples, with inexpensive
ugali, chips, chicken and the like.

For self-catering, try the small shops
around the market area, most of which have
reasonable selections of boxed juices, tinned
cheese and the like.

Getting There & Away

BUS

Scandinavian Express has two buses daily
to Dar es Salaam (TSh15,000 to TSh17,000,
12 hours); book in advance at their office at
the bus station.

Super Feo has daily morning departures
to Njombe (TSh6000, four hours) and Songea (TSh11,000, eight hours).

Daladalas go several times daily from
Mbeya to Tukuyu (TSh700), Kyela (TSh1500)
and Malawi. For Itungi, change vehicles in
Kyela. There is also daily transport between
Mbeya and the Malawi border, where you
can pick up Malawian transport heading to
Karonga and beyond. To Lilongwe, there's
a bus several times weekly, departing Dar
at 5am, reaching Mbeya between 3pm and
4pm, and then continuing to Lilongwe. See
also p258.

Minibuses go daily to Tunduma, on the
Zambian border (TSh2500, two hours),
where you can change to Zambian transport; the Scandinavian bus between Dar es
Salaam and Tunduma passes Mbeya in the
late afternoon.

Scandinavian runs daily between Dar
and Lusaka via Mbeya (TSh36,000 between
Mbeya and Lusaka); see p259.

To Sumbawanga, Sumry goes daily at
5.30am and 7am (TSh8000, six hours). For
Mpanda, change vehicles in Sumbawanga,
and plan on spending the night there, since
most vehicles to Mpanda depart Sumbawanga in the morning.

To Tabora, there are three to four buses
weekly during the dry season via Chunya
and Rungwa.

TRAIN

Tickets for all classes can be booked at the
Tazara town booking office near the post office, which is open (in theory) from 7.30am
to 3pm Monday to Friday. Otherwise, book
at the **station** (☉ 7.30am-12.30pm & 2-5pm Mon-Fri,
10.40am-12.40pm & 2-4pm Sat), 4km west of town
on the main highway.

See p265 for schedules and fares between
Mbeya and Dar es Salaam, and p259 for information about connections with Zambia.

Getting Around

There are taxi stands at the bus station, and
near the market. *Daladalas* to Tazara and
Mbalizi depart from the road in front of New
Millennium hotel.

AROUND MBEYA

Mbeya Peak

Mbeya Peak (2818m), the highest peak
in the Mbeya range, can be climbed as a
day hike from Mbeya. The most common
route goes from Mbalizi junction, 12km
west of town on the Tunduma road. Take a
daladala to Mbalizi, get out at the sign for
Utengule Country Hotel, head right, and
follow the dirt road for 900m to a sign for St
Mary's Seminary. Turn right and follow the
road up past the seminary to Lunji Farm,
and then on to the peak (about four to five
hours return).

Lake Rukwa

Remote Lake Rukwa is a large salt lake notable for its many water birds and its crocodile

population. The northern section is part of Rukwa Game Reserve, which is contiguous with Katavi National Park. As the lake has no outlet, its water level varies significantly between the wet and dry seasons. Visits are only practical with a 4WD. The main approaches are from Sumbawanga, or from Mbeya via Chunya and Saza to Ngomba, on the lakeshore. There are no facilities.

TUKUYU
☎ 025

Tukuyu is an agreeable town set among rolling hills and orchards near Lake Nyasa. The area holds the potential for some good hiking, but tourist facilities are minimal and there's no infrastructure, so for anything you undertake you'll be on your own. NBC, in the centre of town, changes cash and travellers cheques and has an ATM, and you can get online at **Siaki Internet Café** (per hr TSh1000), diagonally across from the bank.

Activities
HIKING
One possibility is the summit of the 2960m **Mt Rungwe**, to the east of the main road between Tukuyu and Mbeya; allow about 10 hours. The climb starts from Rungwe Secondary School, where you can arrange a guide; it's signposted off the Mbeya road about 15km north of Tukuyu.

Further north and about 7km west of the main road is the volcanic **Ngozi Peak** (2629m), which has an impressive crater lake that is the subject of local legends. Take any *dala-dala* travelling between Mbeya and Tukuyu and ask to be dropped off. Once at the turn-off, you'll be approached by local guides if you haven't already come with one; the going rate is TSh1000.

Sleeping & Eating
Landmark Hotel (☎ 255 2400; s/d/ste TSh25,000/30,000/50,000) Modern rooms, all with TV and hot water, and a restaurant. It's the unmissable two-storey building at the main junction.

Langboss Lodge (☎ 255 2080; s/d with shared bathroom TSh2000/3000, d with private bathroom TSh4000) The main shoestring option, with basic rooms and cold water. It's about 1km east of the town centre; from the small roundabout at the top of town, head straight and then right.

Lutengano Moravian Centre (camping TSh2000 plus per small/large car per night TSh1000/2500, tr TSh3500, s with shared bathroom TSh2500) This no-frills place off the main road north of Tukuyu has a handful of simple rooms with nets, plus large grounds where you can pitch a tent, and is sometimes used by overland trucks. Head north from Tukuyu for about 3km to the signposted turn-off on the western side of the road, from where it's 7km further down a dirt road. Occasional pick-ups run to/from town.

Getting There & Away
Minibuses run several times daily between Tukuyu and both Mbeya (TSh1000, one to 1½ hours along a scenic, Tarmac road) and Kyela (TSh1000, one hour).

KITULO PLATEAU
Nestled at about 2600m in the highlands northeast of Tukuyu is this flower-clad plateau, part of which is protected as **Kitulo National Park**. During the rainy season from about November until April, it explodes in a profusion of colour, with terrestrial orchids (over 50 species have been identified thus far), irises, aloes, geraniums and many more flowers carpeting its grassy expanses. The best months for seeing the orchids – the plateau's most renowned resident – are December through March, which is also when hiking is at its muddiest. The park also offers excellent birding.

The best access is via Chimala, about 80km east of Mbeya along the main highway. From here, turn south at the park signpost on the western edge of town and continue another 42km on a rough road that climbs over a seemingly endless series of hairpin turns to the sizeable settlement of Matamba (current park headquarters), the park's Mwakipembo Gate and Kitulo Farm (site of future park headquarters). Pick-ups go at least twice daily as far as Matamba, where there are a couple of basic guesthouses. From here, you'll need to walk or have your own transport; allow about six to seven hours on foot between Matamba and Kitulo Farm.

Park fees (US$20 per day) are now being collected at the park offices in Matamba. There's currently only the most rudimentary infrastructure. For any hiking, you'll need to be self-sufficient with food and

TANZANIA

water, and carry a GPS. Camping is possible at Kitulo Farm.

LAKE NYASA

Lake Nyasa (known to many non-Tanzanians as Lake Malawi) is Africa's third-largest lake after Lake Victoria and Lake Tanganyika, and hosts close to one-third of the earth's known cichlid (freshwater fish) species. The Livingstone Mountains to the east form a stunning backdrop. Places of interest around the Tanzanian side of the lake include the following (listed by location from north to south).

Kyela
☎ 025

There's no reason to come here unless your boat arrives late at Itungi and you need somewhere to stay overnight. Photography is prohibited in most areas of town.

Makete Half London Guest House (☎ 254 0459; s TSh4500) has clean, basic rooms with net. It's in the town centre, opposite the Scandinavian Express bus office.

Pattaya Hotel (☎ 254 0015; s/d TSh5000/6000) is on the same road as Makete, and is similar.

Scandinavian departs for Dar es Salaam at 6am daily (TSh17,000, 15 hours). To Tukuyu and Mbeya (TSh1500), you can take the Scandinavian bus, or a minibus from the stand about two blocks north of Pattaya Hotel. Pick-ups run daily between Kyela and Itungi, in rough coordination with boat arrivals and departures.

Itungi

Itungi, 11km south of Kyela, is the main Tanzanian port for the Lake Nyasa ferry. There's no accommodation, and photography is forbidden. For ferry information, see p261.

Matema

Quiet and pretty Matema is the only spot on northern Lake Nyasa with any sort of tourist infrastructure, and it makes an ideal spot to relax. You can arrange rides in local canoes or take excursions down the coast. Nearby are some small waterfalls and caves, and on Saturdays there's a lively pottery market at Lyulilo village, 1.5km down the coast. There's nowhere to change money.

SLEEPING & EATING
Matema Lake Shore Resort (☎ 025-250 4178; mec@ atma.co.tz; camping with shower TSh3000, 3-/4-/5-bed

r US$15-30 per room, d with shared bathroom US$8, with private bathroom US$25) A good place on the beach about 300m past the Lutheran Guest House, with en suite cottages and chalets. There's no restaurant, but there's a grill, or you can arrange meals with staff. You can also make bookings through Karibuni Centre in Mbeya.

Lutheran Guest House (☎ 0744-606225, 025-255 2597/8; tr/quad with shared bathroom TSh6200/13,200, d with private bathroom TSh8400) This charmingly dilapidated beachside place has simple rooms, and meals with advance notice. Check with the Lutheran mission in Tukuyu (just downhill from the NBC bank) to be sure space is available. You can also make bookings through the Lutheran mission in Tukuyu.

GETTING THERE & AWAY
Boat

The MV *Iringa* (p261) stops at Matema on its way from Itungi Port down the eastern lakeshore, arriving at Matema in the mid-afternoon. Note that the MV *Songea* (p260) doesn't stop here, which means you'll need to head back to Itungi Port if you're going to Malawi.

Road

From Tukuyu, pick-ups to Ipinda depart around 8am from the roundabout by the NBC bank (TSh2000, two hours). You'll then need to wait around Ipinda until about 2pm, when there's usually a pick-up to Matema (TSh1500, 35km). Departures from Matema back to Ipinda are around 6.30am. Chances are better on weekends for finding a lift between Matema and Ipinda with a private vehicle. If you get stuck in Ipinda, there are several basic guesthouses.

There are also sporadic pick-ups from Kyela to Ipinda (TSh1500), a few of which continue on to Matema, and from Kyela, it's easy to hire a vehicle to drop you off.

The Lutheran mission in Tukuyu can arrange transport between Tukuyu and Matema for about US$65 per vehicle one way.

Ikombe

The tiny village of Ikombe is notable for its clay pots, which are sold at markets in Mbeya and elsewhere in the region. It's reached via dugout canoe from Matema. There's nowhere to stay.

Mbamba Bay

This relaxing outpost is the southernmost Tanzanian port on Lake Nyasa. With its low-key ambience and attractive palm-fringed beach, it makes an agreeable place to spend a day or two.

Neema Lodge (Mama Simba's; ☎ Mbamba Bay 3; r with shared bathroom TSh5000) is the best value place to stay, with basic rooms and meals. To get here turn left just before the bridge as you enter town.

Another place to stay is **Nyasa View** (d with shared bathroom TSh6000), though the rooms here aren't worth the extra compared with Neema Lodge. Continue straight through town after the bridge, heading towards the beach.

There are occasional direct vehicles from Songea, usually coordinated with ferry arrivals, but you'll generally need to change vehicles at Mbinga (at least TSh2500 for each of the two legs).

For details of ferry services between Mbamba Bay and Itungi port, see p261. For ferry connections with Nkhata Bay (Malawi), see p260.

Northbound, there are occasional 4WDs to Liuli mission station. Entering or leaving Tanzania via Mbamba Bay, you'll need to stop at the immigration post/police station near the boat landing for passport formalities; it's possible to buy Tanzanian visas here.

NJOMBE

☎ 026

Njombe is a workaday town that would be completely unmemorable but for its highly scenic setting on the eastern edge of the Kipengere mountain range at almost 2000m, surrounded by hills that roll into the horizon. There's no tourist infrastructure, so any hiking will need to be under your own steam and with a GPS. For a few route suggestions, look for *A Guide to the Southern Highlands of Tanzania*, available at some hotels.

Chani Motel (☎ 278 2357; s/d TSh8500/10,500) is Njombe's best, with running water (usually hot) and meals. It's about 2km north of town, and about 500m off the main road, signposted to the west.

Lutheran Centre Guest House (☎ 278 2403; s/d with shared bathroom TSh2000/3500) is about 700m south of the bus stand along the main road, in the Lutheran church compound.

Minibuses go daily between Njombe and Songea (TSh5000, three to four hours) and to Makambako, where you can get transport to Mbeya, and there's also at least one direct bus to Mbeya. Scandinavian charges between TSh14,000 and TSh17,500 to Dar es Salaam, and TSh5000 to/from Songea.

SONGEA

☎ 025

Songea is a bustling regional capital that will look like a major metropolis if you've just

---

THE MAJI MAJI REBELLION

The Maji Maji rebellion was the strongest local revolt against the colonial government in German East Africa. It began about the turn of the 20th century when colonial administrators set about establishing enormous cotton plantations near the southeastern coast and along the railway line running from Dar es Salaam towards Morogoro. These plantations required large numbers of workers, many of whom were recruited as forced labour and required to work under miserable conditions. Before long anger at this harsh treatment and long-simmering resentment of the colonial government combined to ignite a powerful rebellion. The first outbreak was in 1905 in the area around Kilwa, on the coast. Soon all of southern Tanzania was involved, from Kilwa and Lindi in the southeast to Songea in the southwest. Thousands died, both on the battlefield and due to the famine precipitated by the Germans' 'scorched-earth' tactics, in which fields and grain silos were set on fire. Fatalities were exacerbated by a belief among the Africans that enemy bullets would turn to water before killing them, and that their warriors would therefore not be harmed – hence the name Maji Maji (*maji* means water in Swahili).

By 1907, when the rebellion was finally suppressed, close to 100,000 people had lost their lives, large areas of the south were left devastated, and malnutrition was widespread.

The uprising resulted in the temporary liberalisation of colonial rule. More significantly, it promoted development of a national identity among many ethnic groups and intensified anti-colonial sentiment, kindling the movement towards independence.

come from Tunduru or Mbamba Bay. The main ethnic group here is the Ngoni, who migrated into the area from South Africa during the 19th century. Songea takes its name from one of their greatest chiefs, who was killed following the Maji Maji rebellion (p235), and is buried about 1km from town near the Maji Maji museum.

NBC, behind the market, changes cash and travellers cheques, and has an ATM. For Internet, try **Valongo Internet Café** (per hr TSh2000; ⓨ 9am-6pm), nearby.

Sleeping & Eating

Angoni Arms Hotel (☎ 260 2279, 0745-512373; r TSh15,000) The only choice approaching mid-range, with clean en suite rooms, hot water and a restaurant. It's about 1km from the market, along the Tunduru road.

Anglican Church Hostel (☎ 260 0693; s/d with shared bathroom TSh2000/2500, with private bathroom TSh3000/3500) Clean rooms with mosquito nets, just northwest of the main road. Next door is a small restaurant. Head uphill from the bus stand past the market to the Tanesco building. Go left and wind your way back about 400m to the Anglican church compound.

Don Bosco Hostel (d with shared bathroom TSh4000) Spartan rooms just off the main road, behind the Catholic church and near the bus stand.

Getting There & Away

Scandinavian departs daily at 6am (ordinary) and 6.15am (luxury) for Dar es Salaam (TSh17,000/19,000 ordinary/luxury, 12 to 13 hours); it's best to book in advance.

To Mbeya, Super Feo departs at 6am daily in each direction (TSh10,000, eight hours).

To Njombe, minibuses and pick-ups go daily in the morning, or take Scandinavian or Super Feo and have them drop you off.

For Mbamba Bay, transport goes daily in the mornings to Mbinga (TSh3500, four hours), from where you can get onward transport to Mbamba Bay (TSh3000).

TUNDURU

Dusty Tunduru, halfway between Songea and Masasi, is in the centre of an important gemstone-mining region and has a bit of a Wild West feel to it. You'll need to spend a night here if you're travelling between Songea and Masasi. The better guesthouses are at the western end of town. There are

plenty to chose from, all around the same standard.

There's at least one bus daily between Tunduru and Masasi, departing from about 5am (seven to 10 hours). Between Tunduru and Songea, the main options are Land Rovers, which go daily (TSh17,000, eight to 11 hours, departing Tunduru between 3am and 7am), and usually one bus (TSh10,000, departing at 6am). If you are staying at a guesthouse near the Land Rover 'station', you can arrange for the driver to come and wake you before departure. Bring food and water with you.

SOUTHEASTERN TANZANIA

Tanzania's often forgotten southeastern corner is a vast, beautiful area of open savanna and long, white-sand beaches, though hardly anyone ventures this way to discover it. In addition to the Selous Game Reserve, there are two marine parks (at Mafia Island and Mnazi Bay); Kilwa Kisiwani, one of East Africa's most important archaeological sites; and old Swahili trading settlements, including Mikindani, Lindi and Kilwa Kivinje.

If you decide to visit, allow plenty of time and be ready to rough things, especially on the long, hard road journeys. The main exceptions to this are Mafia Island and the Selous Game Reserve, where a full range of amenities are available at five-star prices.

SELOUS GAME RESERVE

With an area of approximately 45,000 sq km (5% of Tanzania's total land area), the Selous Game Reserve is Africa's largest wildlife reserve and Tanzania's most extensive protected area. It provides shelter for large numbers of elephants, as well as populations of buffaloes, wild dogs, hippos and crocodiles, a rich variety of birdlife and some of Tanzania's last remaining black rhinos. One of the reserve's most striking features is the wide Rufiji River, which has one of the largest water-catchment areas in East Africa, and which offers excellent opportunities for boat safaris.

Only the section of the reserve from the Rufiji River northwards is open for tourism. Although overall wildlife density is lower

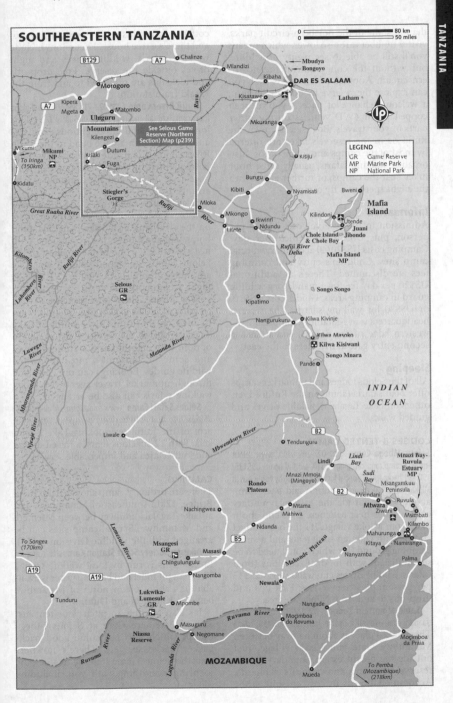

SOUTHEASTERN TANZANIA

0 — 80 km
0 — 50 miles

B129
A7
Chalinze
Mlandizi
Kibaha
Mbudya
Bongoyo
Kisarawe
DAR ES SALAAM
Morogoro
Kipera
Matombo
Mgeta
Uluguru
Mountains
Kilengezi
Dutumi
Kisaki
Fuga
Mikumi
Mikumi NP
To Iringa (150km)
Kidatu
Great Ruaha River
Stiegler's Gorge
See Selous Game Reserve (Northern Section) Map (p239)
Mkuranga
Kisiju
Bungu
Kibiti
Nyamisati
Bweni
Mafia Island
Mloka
Mkongo
Ikwiriri
Ndundu
Kilindoni
Utende
Juani
Jibondo
Chole Island & Chole Bay
Mafia Island MP
Rufiji River Delta
Latham

LEGEND
GR   Game Reserve
MP   Marine Park
NP   National Park

Rufiji River
Kilombero River
Lahombero River
Luwegu River
Mbarangandu River
Njesie River
Selous GR
Kipatimo
Nangurukuru
Kilwa Kivinje
Kilwa Masoko
Kilwa Kisiwani
Songo Mnara
Pande
Songo Songo

INDIAN OCEAN

Matandu River
Liwale
Mbwemkuru River
Tendunguru
B2
Lindi Bay
Mnazi Bay-Ruvula Estuary MP
Lindi
Mnazi Mmoja (Mingoyo)
Sudi Bay
Msangamkuu Peninsula
Rondo Plateau
B2
Mikindani
Mtwara
Ruvula
Ziwani
Msimbati
Nachingwea
Mtama
Mahiwa
Kilambo
Ndanda
B5
Mahurunga
Kitaya
Namiranga
Makonde Plateau
Nanyamba
Palma
Msangesi GR
Masasi
Chingulungulu
Nangomba
Newala
To Songea (170km)
A19
A19
Tunduru
Lukwika-Lumesule GR
Mpombe
Nangade
Moçimboa do Rovuma
Lumesule River
Masuguru
Negomane
Ruvuma River
Niassa Reserve
Lagenda River
Ruvuma River
Mueda
To Pemba (Mozambique) (218km)
Moçimboa da Praia

MOZAMBIQUE

than in some of the northern-circuit parks, visitor numbers are also lower, which means you'll still be able to see plenty of wildlife, but without the congestion of the northern circuit. Another advantage is that you can explore the reserve by boat or on foot; a welcome change of pace if you've been cooped up in 4WD vehicles during other parts of your travels. Boat safaris down the Rufiji or in the reserve's lakes are offered by most of the camps and lodges. Most also organise walking safaris, usually three-hour hikes near the camps, or further afield with the night spent at a fly camp.

Information

Admission to the reserve costs US$30 per person, plus US$30 per vehicle per day. Camping costs US$20/40 at ordinary/special camp sites. Children's entry and camping fees are discounted. There's an additional US$20 per day fee for a mandatory wildlife guard in camping areas. Guides cost US$10, or US$20 for walking safaris. The reserve headquarters is at Matambwe on the northwestern edge of the Selous, and there's a second entry gate at Mtemere to the east.

Sleeping

All of the Selous lodges and upmarket camps offer boat safaris (some on the Rufiji River, others on Lake Tagalala), wildlife drives and guided walks.

LODGES & TENTED CAMPS

Selous Mbega Camp (☎ 022-265 0250; www.selous -mbega-camp.com; camping US$10, s/d full board US$135/ 190, s/d 'backpackers' special for those arriving by public bus at Mloka US$70/100, excursions extra) A laid-back camp about 500m outside the eastern boundary of the Selous near Mtemere Gate and about 3km from Mloka village. It's the best budget choice, with eight en suite tents and a small camping ground (for which you'll need to be self-sufficient with food). Excursions (boat safaris, wildlife drives and walks) cost US$35 per person, plus reserve fees. Pick-ups and drop-offs to and from Mloka are free.

Sable Mountain Lodge (☎ 022-211 0507; www .saadani.com; s/d all-inclusive from US$340/450; ⚡) This relaxed place is about halfway between Matambwe Gate and Kisaki village, just outside the northwestern boundary of the reserve, in an area known for its elephants. Accommodation is in cosy en suite stone

cottages or in plusher honeymoon *bandas*, and there's a tree house. Excursions include walking safaris, wildlife drives and night drives outside the reserve. Free drop-offs and pick-ups are provided to and from the Kisaki train station.

Rufiji River Camp (☎ 022-212 8662/3; www.hippo tours.com; s/d all-inclusive US$310/500; ⚡) This long-standing and unpretentious camp has a fine location on a wide bend in the Rufiji River about 1km inside Mtemere Gate, and is frequented by pods of hippos. All tents have river views, and fly camping can be arranged.

Selous Impala Camp (☎ 022-211 7959/60; www .coastal.cc; s/d all-inclusive US$430/700) Attractively set on the riverbank near Lake Mzizimia amid borassus palms and other vegetation. With just six tents, it's one of the smallest of the Selous camps, and good value if you take advantage of some of Coastal Travels' (p118) flight-accommodation deals.

Sand Rivers Selous (www.nomad-tanzania.com; per person all-inclusive US$485) Set splendidly on its own on the Rufiji River south of Lake Tagalala, this is the Selous' most exclusive option, with eight luxurious stone cottages and some of Tanzania's most renowned wildlife guides. Bookings can only be made through upmarket travel agents. Multiday walking safaris can also be arranged.

Selous Safari Camp (www.selous.com; s/d all-inclusive US$525/700; ⚡) A luxurious camp set on a side arm of the Rufiji overlooking Lake Nzele-kela, with 12 spacious tents, a raised dining and lounge area and impeccable service.

CAMPING

There are ordinary camp sites at Beho Beho Bridge, 12km southeast of Matambwe, and at Lake Tagalala, midway between Mtemere and Matambwe. Special camp sites can be arranged with the Wildlife Division (p113).

Jukumu Society Scout Station Campsite (camping TSh5000) This is run by local wildlife scouts. There's a pit toilet and bathing water is available. It's about 60km north of Matambwe between Kilengezi and Dutumi.

It's also possible to pitch your tent just east of Mtemere Gate at Selous Mbega Camp, which also has some good backpacker deals; see left. There's nowhere near the Selous Game Reserve to stock up, so bring everything with you, including water.

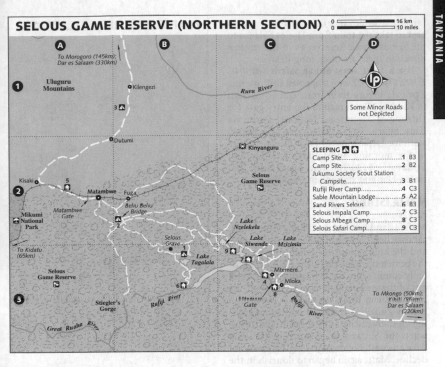

SELOUS GAME RESERVE (NORTHERN SECTION)

SLEEPING	
Camp Site...........................1	B3
Camp Site...........................2	B2
Jukumu Society Scout Station	
Campsite........................3	B1
Rufiji River Camp...................4	C3
Sable Mountain Lodge..........5	A2
Sand Rivers Selous	6 B3
Selous Impala Camp.............7	C3
Selous Mbega Camp.............8	C3
Selous Safari Camp...............9	C3

Getting There & Away

AIR

Coastal Aviation and ZanAir have daily flights linking Selous Game Reserve with Dar es Salaam (US$120 one way), Zanzibar (US$130) and Arusha (via Dar), with connections to northern-circuit airstrips. Coastal also has flights between the Selous and Mafia (US$120), plus three flights weekly between Selous and Ruaha National Park (US$270). Flights into the Selous are generally suspended during the March to May wet season. All lodges provide airfield transfers.

BUS

Akida and Mwera bus lines have buses daily between Dar es Salaam's Temeke bus stand (departing from the Sudan Market area) and Mloka village, about 10km east of Mtemere Gate (TSh5000, seven to nine hours). Departures in both directions are at 5am. From Mloka, arrange a pick-up with one of the camps in advance. There's no accommodation in Mloka, and hitching within the Selous isn't permitted.

CAR & MOTORCYCLE

There's no vehicle hire at the reserve, and motorcycles aren't permitted.

There are two road options. The first is from Dar es Salaam to Mkongo via Kibiti and then on to Mtemere (250km, about eight hours). Alternatively, you can go from Dar es Salaam to Kisaki via Morogoro and then on to Matambwe through the Uluguru Mountains (350km, at least nine hours). This route is sometimes impassable during the heavy rains.

From Dar es Salaam to Mtemere, the last petrol station is at Kibiti (about 100km northeast of Mtemere gate), and coming from the other direction, it's at Morogoro. There's no petrol available in the Selous.

TRAIN

All Tazara trains stop at Kisaki, which is about five to six hours from Dar es Salaam and the first stop for the express train. Ordinary trains stop at Kinyanguru and Fuga stations (both of which are closer to the central camps) and at Matambwe (near Matambwe Gate). All the lodges will do pick-ups (arranged in advance), see p265. It works best to take the train from Dar es Salaam to the Selous Game Reserve, as in the reverse direction there are often long delays.

For a treat, **Foxes African Safaris** (☎ 0748-237422, 0744-237422; www.safariexpress.info) operate a private luxury train from Dar es Salaam to Kidatu, 25km north of the entry gate for Udzungwa Mountains National Park, via Kinyanguru, Fuga, Matambwe and Kisaki stations. Departures in both directions are in the morning on Sunday, Tuesday and Friday (US$120/180 one way/return between Dar and stations in the Selous).

MAFIA ISLAND
☎ 023

Mafia Island lies about 120km off the coast, sandwiched between the Rufiji River delta and the high seas. After remaining well off the beaten track for years, the island is gradually coming into its own, although it's still out of the way enough to have escaped the mass tourism that's starting to overwhelm nearby Zanzibar. It was an important trading post from the 11th to 13th centuries, when the Shirazis ruled much of the East African coast. Following a lengthy period of decline, Mafia again began to flourish in the early 18th century as a trade centre linking Kilwa and Zanzibar.

Apart from its lack of hustle and bustle and the chance to experience slow-paced coastal life, Mafia's main attraction is its underwater environment, which hosts a vast number of aquatic species and diverse coral formations. To protect this, the southeastern part of the island, together with offshore islets and waters, have been gazetted as a national marine park. Mafia is also notable as a breeding ground for green and hawksbill turtles, which have nesting sites along the eastern shores of Mafia and on the nearby islands of Juani and Jibondo.

Information

Telephone calls can be made at New Lizu Hotel in Kilindoni. Pole Pole Resort's airport office doubles as a tourist information office.

Internet Café (per hr TSh1500; ☷ 9am-9pm) On Utende road, in the town centre.

National Microfinance Bank On the airport road, near the main junction; changes cash only (dollars, euros and pounds).

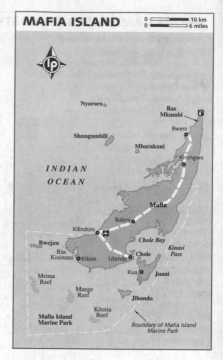

Sights & Activities

Most of the island is surrounded by mangroves, but if you're looking for beach, there are a few pristine sandbanks and small islets offshore. At **Ras Mkumbi**, Mafia's wild and windswept northernmost point, there's a **lighthouse** dating to 1892, as well as **Kanga Beach** and a forest that's home to monkeys and blue duikers, among others.

Most of the Chole Bay hotels organise diving and snorkelling, including certification courses.

Sleeping & Eating
BUDGET

Harbour View Resort (☎ 240 2692; s with shared bathroom & fan TSh7500, d with shared bathroom & air-con TSh12,000, with private bathroom & air-con TSh15,000; ☒) Clean, good-value budget rooms in a smart house overlooking the harbour; food can be arranged. Head down the hill in Kilindoni and go into the port area; turn left, and follow the waterside road for about 500m to Harbour View.

New Lizu Hotel (☎ 240 2683; s/d with shared bathroom TSh5000/10,000) Reasonable rooms (no frills,

---

MAFIA ISLAND MARINE PARK

Mafia Island Marine Park – the largest marine protected area in the Indian Ocean – shelters a unique complex of estuarine, mangrove, coral-reef and marine-channel ecosystems. These include the only natural forest on the island and close to 400 fish species. There are also about 10 villages within the park's boundaries, the inhabitants of which depend on its natural resources for their livelihoods. As a result, the park has been classified as a multi-use area, with the aim of assisting local communities to develop sustainable practices that will allow conservation and resource use to coexist.

The park isn't set up for tourism, especially at the budget level. The main way to explore it is to organise a diving excursion with one of the top-end hotels at Chole Bay. If you have your own gear, the park office may be able to help you out with snorkelling or set you up with a local fisherman to take you out.

Entry into the marine park area (payable by everyone, whether you dive or not) costs US$10/5 per adult/child per day. The fees are collected at a barrier gate across the main road about 1km before Utende, and can be paid in any major currency, cash. Save your receipt, as it's checked again when you leave. The **park office** (☎ 240 2690) is in Utende near Pole Pole Resort.

---

no nets), bucket baths, good cheap food and a convenient location at the main junction in Kilindoni, about a five-minute walk from the airfield.

Sunset Resort Camp (☎ 240 2522, ext 45, 0745-696067; carpho2003@yahoo.co.uk; camping US$5, bandas per person with shared bathroom US$12) Camping on a lawn set on a cliff above the water, and clean bucket showers. There are also a few simple twin-bedded *bandas* and meals on order. It's about 2km from Kilindoni's centre, behind the hospital (TSh2000 in a taxi).

MIDRANGE & TOP END

All the Chole Bay hotels are closed during the April–May rainy season. All are also within the marine park area, which means you'll also need to pay the US$10 daily park entry fee.

Mafia Island Lodge (☎ 022-211 7959/60; www .mafialodge.com; Utende; s/d from US$52/75; ✦ ◻) The former government hotel, this lodge on Chole Bay is a good choice if your budget or tastes don't stretch to a stay at one of its more upmarket neighbours. There's a mix of renovated and standard rooms, all about 300m in from the water, a restaurant and a resident dive instructor. Airport transfers are US$10 per person each way.

Pole Pole Resort (☎ 022-260 1530; www.polepole .com; s/d full board & airport transfers US$260/400) This beautiful place is set amid palm trees and tropical vegetation on a long hillside overlooking Chole Bay. The bungalows are constructed of local materials and have large, private verandas, meals are made primarily

with organic ingredients and are delicious, and there's an open-sided *duara* (gazebo) for relaxing. Excursions can be arranged.

Kinasi Lodge (☎ 022-284 2525, 0741-242977; www .mafiaisland.com; s/d full board & airport transfers from US$185/320; ✦) This is another top-notch choice, with 12 stone-and-thatch cottages set around a long, manicured hillside sloping down to Chole Bay, and a genteel, subdued ambience. There's an open lounge area with satellite TV, a small beach and windsurfer hire, plus a dive centre and excursions.

Chole Mjini (info@cholemjini.com; s/d all-inclusive US$210/360) If your idea of the ultimate getaway is sleeping in the treetops in a rustic but comfortable ambience, Chole Mjini is the place to stay. Accommodation is in six imaginatively designed tree houses (a couple of which are actually lower stilt houses), each set on its own with views over the bay, the mangroves or the Chole ruins, and each accommodating up to three people. There's no electricity, and the bathrooms are at ground level, where each tree house has its own outdoor shower garden. It's on Chole Island, offshore from Utende. Airport transfers cost extra.

Getting There & Away

Coastal Aviation has daily flights connecting Mafia with Dar es Salaam (US$90) and Kilwa Masoko (US$70), both with onward connections to Zanzibar, Selous Game Reserve and Arusha. Kinasi Lodge has its own aircraft for guests, with seats on a space-available basis for nonguests. All the Chole

Bay hotels arrange airfield transfers for their guests (included in the room price, except as noted).

Dhows go to the island from Kisiju, about 45km southeast of Mkuranga on the Dar es Salaam–Mtwara road. Take a *daladala* from Dar es Salaam to Mtoni-Mtongani (about 8km south of the city along the Kilwa road), from where several pick-ups daily go to Kisiju (TSh2000, two hours).

From Kisiju, dhows leave every day or two except Sunday for Mafia, and charge about TSh4000. Departures depend on the tides and are generally before dawn. The usual procedure is to arrive in Kisiju in the late afternoon, board the boat at about 9pm and sleep on it until departure. With good winds, you should arrive in Mafia by late afternoon, although the trip can take much longer. Going in the other direction, boats leave from the port at Kilindoni. The boarding procedure and departure times are the same as at Kisiju.

Getting Around

Daladalas to both Utende (TSh1500) and Bweni at about 1pm, returning from each destination about 7am. The Kilindoni *daladala* stop is along the road that goes down to the port. You can also hire pick-ups in Kilindoni to take you around the island; expect to pay about TSh15,000 return between Kilindoni and Utende.

Local boats can be chartered to Jibondo and the other islands, and there is also a sporadic local service. Expect to pay from TSh3000, depending on the destination.

KILWA KIVINJE

Kilwa Kivinje (Kilwa of the Casuarina Trees) owes its existence to Omani Arabs from Kilwa Kisiwani who set up a base here in the early 19th century following the fall of the Kilwa sultanate. By the mid-19th century the settlement had become the hub of the regional slave-trading network, and by the late 19th century, a German administrative centre. With the abolition of the slave trade, and German wartime defeats, Kilwa Kivinje's brief period in the spotlight came to an end. Today, it's a crumbling, moss-covered and highly atmospheric relic of the past with a Swahili small-town feel and an intriguing mixture of German-colonial and Omani-Arab architecture.

The best way to visit Kilwa Kivinje is as a day trip from Kilwa Masoko. Overnight options are limited to a clutch of nondescript guesthouses near the market, all with rooms for about TSh3000, and all rivalling each other in grubbiness. Among the better ones are King Wardo and Mziwanda near the market and New Sudi Guest House.

Pick-ups travel several times daily to/from Kilwa Masoko, and the bus between Dar es Salaam and Kilwa Masoko also stops at Kilwa Kivinje.

KILWA MASOKO

The town of Kilwa Masoko (Kilwa of the Market) is the springboard for visiting the ruins of the 15th-century Arab settlements at Kilwa Kisiwani and Songo Mnara, and as such, the gateway into one of the most significant eras of East African coastal history.

The National Microfinance Bank on the main road changes cash but not travellers cheques; there's no Internet connection.

On the eastern edge of town is Jimbizi Beach, an attractive, baobab-studded arc of sand.

Sleeping & Eating

New Mjaka Guest House & Hotel (Main Rd; s with shared bathroom TSh3000, s/d banda TSh5000/10,000) This hotel has no-frills rooms, nicer *bandas*, a reasonably reliable water supply and a restaurant.

Kilwa Seaview Resort (☎ 022-265 0250; www.kilwa .net; camping US$5, s/d/tr US$60/70/75) Spacious, breezy A-frame cottages perched along a small escarpment at the eastern end of Jimbizi Beach, a good restaurant (meals from TSh4500) and space to pitch a tent.

Kilwa Lodge (☎ 023-240 2397, 0748-205586; kilwa lodge@iwayafrica.com; Jimbizi Beach; per person full board standard/luxury chalet US$70/110; ✖ ⌨) An angling camp in the centre of Jimbizi Beach, with rustic en suite cabins set back from the water, a few beachside chalets, a restaurant and a popular beachside bar. In addition to fishing, sea kayaks and diving can also be arranged, as can excursions.

Roadside Classic Park (Main Rd; meals TSh1000) This place, diagonally across from New Mjaka, has local dishes, outdoor seating and a bar.

Kilwa's atmospheric night market, between the main street and the market, sells inexpensive fish and other snacks from dusk onwards.

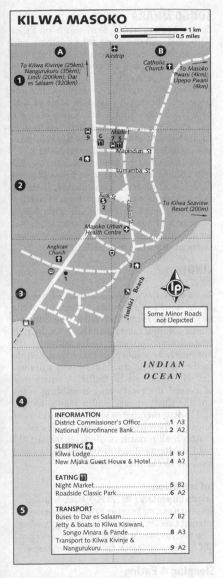

KILWA MASOKO

INFORMATION
District Commissioner's Office..............1 A3
National Microfinance Bank.................2 A2

SLEEPING
Kilwa Lodge..3 B3
New Mjaka Guest House & Hotel........4 A2

EATING
Night Market......................................5 B2
Roadside Classic Park.........................6 A2

TRANSPORT
Buses to Dar es Salaam.......................7 B2
Jetty & boats to Kilwa Kisiwani,
   Songo Mnara & Pande....................8 A3
Transport to Kilwa Kivinje &
   Nangurukuru..................................9 A2

Getting There & Away

Coastal Aviation has three flights weekly from Dar es Salaam to Kilwa via Mafia (US$110 one way Dar es Salaam to Kilwa, US$70 one way Mafia–Kilwa), and between Zanzibar and Kilwa (US$130 one way). The airstrip is about 2km north of town along the main road.

Rehabilitation work is underway on the road from the Rufiji River south to Kilwa Masoko, and it should soon be easily passable year-round.

To Nangurukuru (TSh1500, one hour) and Kilwa Kivinje (TSh1000, 45 minutes), pick-ups depart several times daily from the main road just up from the market.

To Dar es Salaam, a bus departs daily in each direction at about 5am (TSh6500, nine to 10 hours). Buses from Kilwa depart from the market, and should be booked in advance. Departures in Dar es Salaam are from the Temeke bus stand.

From Dar es Salaam it's also possible to get a bus heading to Lindi or Mtwara and get out at Nangurukuru junction, from where you can get local transport to Kilwa Kivinje (TSh500, 11km) or Kilwa Masoko (35km), but you'll generally need to pay the full Lindi or Mtwara fare.

Heading south, go first to Nangurukuru, from where there is a vehicle most mornings to Lindi.

KILWA KISIWANI

Kilwa Kisiwani ('Kilwa on the Island', historically known simply as Kilwa) was once East Africa's most important trading settlement – the seat of sultans and the centre of a vast trading network linking the gold fields of Zimbabwe with the Orient. Today the ruins of the settlement – together with the ruins of nearby Songo Mnara – are considered to be one of the most significant groups of Swahili buildings on the East African coast, and have been declared a Unesco World Heritage Site. Major rehabilitation work is underway, and the main sections of the ruins are more accessible than they have been in decades.

History

Although the coast near Kilwa Kisiwani has been inhabited for several thousand years, evidence of early settlements in the area dates back only to around the 9th century. In the early 13th century trade links developed with Sofala, 1500km to the south in present-day Mozambique. Ultimately, Kilwa came to control Sofala and dominate its lucrative gold trade, and it soon became the most powerful trade centre along the East African coast.

In the late 15th century Kilwa's fortunes began to turn. Sofala freed itself from the island's dominance, and in the early 16th century Kilwa came under the control of the Portuguese. It wasn't until 200 years later that Kilwa regained its independence and became a significant centre again – this time as a centre for the shipment of slaves to the islands of Mauritius, Réunion and Comoros. In the 1780s Kilwa came under the control of the sultan of Oman. By the mid-19th century the island town had completely declined and the local administration was relocated to Kilwa Kivinje.

Information
To visit the ruins, you will need to get a permit (TSh1500 per person) from the **district commissioner's office** (Halmashauri ya Wilaya ya Kilwa; ⏰ 7.30am-3.30pm Mon-Fri) in Kilwa Masoko, diagonally across from the post office. Go to Room 13, or ask for Ofisi ya Utamaduni (Antiquities Office). Guides (required to visit the island) can be arranged through the Antiquities Office, or through your hotel.

Ruins
The ruins are in two groups. When approaching Kilwa Kisiwani, the first building you'll find is the Arab **fort**, built in the early 19th century by Omani Arabs. To the southwest of the fort are the ruins of the now restored **Great Mosque**, some sections of which date to the late 13th century. Behind the Great Mosque is a smaller **mosque**, which dates from the early 15th century and is considered to be the best preserved of the buildings at Kilwa Kisiwani. To the west of the small mosque are the crumbling remains of the **Makutani**, a large walled enclosure in the centre of which lived some of the sultans of Kilwa Kisiwani.

About 1.5km from the fort along the coast is **Husuni Kubwa**, once a massive complex of buildings covering about 0.8 hectares and, together with the nearby **Husuni Ndogo**, the oldest of Kilwa Kisiwani's ruins, though now very overgrown. To get here, walk along the beach at low tide, or take the slightly longer inland route.

Getting There & Away
Local boats go from the port at Kilwa Masoko to Kilwa Kisiwani whenever there are passengers (one way TSh200). Chartering your own boat costs TSh1000 each way (TSh10,000 return for a boat with motor). There's also a TSh300 port fee.

SONGO MNARA
Songo Mnara, about 8km south of Kilwa Kisiwani, contains ruins at its northern end that are believed to date from the 14th and 15th centuries, and are considered in many respects to be more significant than those at Kilwa, although they're less visually impressive. The small island of **Sanje ya Kati**, between Songo Mnara and Kilwa Masoko, has some lesser ruins, also believed to date from the same era. The Kilwa Kisiwani permit includes the ruins at Songo Mnara.

You can charter a motorboat from the district commissioner's office in Kilwa Masoko (TSh35,000 return). Alternatively, there's a far cheaper motorised local dhow departing most mornings at about 6am from Kilwa Masoko for Pande that will stop on request at Songo Mnara. Returning to Kilwa Masoko, the boat departs Pande about 1pm.

LINDI
☎ 023
In its early days, Lindi was part of the sultan of Zanzibar's domain, a terminus of the slave caravan route from Lake Nyasa, the regional colonial capital and the main town in southeastern Tanzania. Today, although it's not nearly as atmospheric as Kilwa Kivinje further north, its small dhow port still bustles with local coastal traffic. A smattering of carved doorways and crumbling ruins line the dusty streets, and a Hindu temple and Indian merchants serve as reminders of once-prosperous trade routes to the east.

About 6km north of town off the airfield road is Mtema Beach, with soft drinks and food on weekends.

Information
Brigita Dispensary (☎ 220 2679; Makonde St) Near Gift Guest House; the best place for medical emergencies.
Internet Café (Amani St; per hr TSh2000; ⏰ 9am-7pm) A few blocks up from the harbour, near Muna's restaurant.
NBC (Lumumba St) Changes cash and travellers cheques.

Sleeping & Eating
Malaika (☎ 220 2880; Market St; s/d TSh7500/9000) One block east of the market with clean, no-frills rooms with net and fan. There's also a decent restaurant.
Gift Guest House (☎ 220 2462; cnr Market & Makonde Sts; r with shared bathroom TSh5000) Just down Market St from Malaika, and a decent, albeit more basic, alternative if Malaika is full.

TANZANIA

Adela Guest House (Ghana St; r with shared bathroom TSh4000) Another budget stand-by, with basic rooms with net and fan. It's just off the main road that goes towards Mtwara, near the Msinjaili primary school.

Muna's (Amani St; meals TSh2000) Just up from the harbour, Muna's has good, inexpensive meals.

Getting There & Away

Precision Air flies twice weekly between Dar es Salaam and Lindi, with onward connections to Nachingwea. The airfield is about 20km north of town.

Buses to Mtwara depart daily between about 5am and 10am.

To Masasi (TSh3000), there are several buses each morning.

For Dar es Salaam (TSh15,000, nine to 11 hours), there are direct buses daily, departing Lindi about 6am. There are no direct buses from Lindi to Kilwa Masoko or Kilwa Kivinje. To get to either of these places you'll need to catch the Dar es Salaam bus and get out at Nangurukuru (TSh6500, six to seven hours), from where you can get onward transport. Once the Tarmac road is completed between Lindi and Dar es Salaam – anticipated within the next several years – expect all this information to change.

MTWARA

☎ 023

Mtwara, southeastern Tanzania's major settlement, is a sprawling, friendly town on Mtwara Bay. It's well off most tourist itineraries and is easily overlooked, but it's a good staging point on the overland journey to/from Mozambique, and is a laid-back, likable place.

Mtwara was first developed after WWII by the British as part of their East African Groundnut Scheme, a project aimed at alleviating the postwar shortage of plant oils through the implementation of large-scale groundnut (peanut) production. Following the failure of the scheme, Mtwara's port continued to serve as a regional export channel, while development of the town came to a standstill.

Orientation

Mtwara is loosely centred around a business and banking area to the northwest,

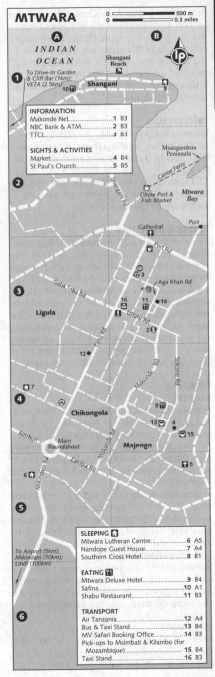

MTWARA

0 ─── 500 m
0 ─── 0.3 miles

INFORMATION
Makonde Net.....................1 B3
NBC Bank & ATM...............2 B3
TTCL..................................3 B3

SIGHTS & ACTIVITIES
Market................................4 B4
St Paul's Church.................5 B5

SLEEPING 🛏
Mtwara Lutheran Centre................6 A5
Nandope Guest House....................7 A4
Southern Cross Hotel......................8 B1

EATING 🍴
Mtwara Deluxe Hotel......................9 B4
Safina...10 A1
Shabu Restaurant............................11 B3

TRANSPORT
Air Tanzania....................................12 A4
Bus & Taxi Stand.............................13 B4
MV Safari Booking Office................14 B3
Pick-ups to Msimbati & Kilambo (for Mozambique)................................15 B4
Taxi Stand..16 B3

near Uhuru and Aga Khan Rds, and the market and bus stand about 1.5km away to the southeast, bordered by the lively neighbourhoods of Majengo and Chikongola. In the far northwest on the sea, and a good 30 minutes on foot from the bus stand, is the Shangani quarter, with a small beach and several guesthouses.

Information

Makonde Net (per hr TSh1000; ☑ 8.30am-6pm Mon-Sat, 9am-2pm Sun) Just off Aga Khan Rd in the town centre.
NBC (Uhuru Rd) Changes cash and travellers cheques, and has an ATM.
TTCL (Tanu Rd; ☑ 7.45am-12.45pm & 1.30-4.30pm Mon-Fri, 9am-12.30pm Sat) Operator-assisted domestic and international calls, and a card phone.

Sights & Activities

In town there's a lively **market** with a small traditional-medicine section next to the main building. Much of Mtwara's fish comes from Msangamkuu on the other side of Mtwara Bay, and the small **dhow port** and adjoining **fish market** are particularly colourful in the early morning and late afternoon. The **beach** in Shangani is popular for swimming on weekends (high tide only). For some impressive artwork, stop by **St Paul's church** in the Majengo area of town, south of the market.

Sleeping

BUDGET

Drive-In Garden & Cliff Bar (camping TSh2500) A shady, secure spot for camping, with an inexpensive restaurant and small bar. It's in Shangani: go left at the main junction and follow the road paralleling the beach for about 1.5km to the small signpost on your left.

Mtwara Lutheran Centre (☎ 233 3294; Mikindani Rd; dm TSh2500, d with shared bathroom TSh5000, s with private bathroom TSh 10,000) Decent rooms (most with nets), fairly reliable water and electricity supplies, and meals on request.

Nandope Guest House (☎ 233 4060; r with shared bathroom TSh3500) One of the cheapest options, with no-frills rooms, some with mosquito nets. It's about 400m west of Tanu Rd, down the unpaved road near the police station.

MIDRANGE

VETA (☎ 233 4094; s TSh15,000, ste TSh35,000; ☒) Good-value rooms, all with a large bed, TV and views over the water, plus a restaurant.

From the T-junction in Shangani, go left and continue for about 3km. It's about 200m in to the left (no swimming beach). There's no public transport; taxis charge TSh3000 from town.

Southern Cross Hotel (☎ 233 3206, 0741-506047; www.msemo.com; s/d US$30/50) This nice place directly overlooks the sea at the eastern end of Shangani Beach, with a relaxing and very tasty seaside restaurant, and a handful of spotless, good-value rooms. Profits from the hotel support primary healthcare services in the Mtwara region.

Eating

The fish market at the Msangamkuu boat dock is good for street food.

Of the restaurants mentioned under Sleeping, the ones at VETA and Southern Cross Hotel are the best. Other options include:

Shabu Restaurant (Aga Khan Rd; meals TSh1000; ☑ 8am-10pm Mon-Sat, to 1pm Sun) In the town centre, serving local fare, snacks and fresh yogurt.

Mtwara Deluxe Hotel (meals TSh2000; ☑ lunch & dinner) Near the bus stand, with Indian and other dishes.

Safina (Container Shop; ☑ 8am-9pm) For self-catering, at the main junction in Shangani. It has a good selection of basics, plus cold drinks.

Getting There & Away

There are daily flights between Mtwara and Dar es Salaam (TSh144,500, one hour) on **Air Tanzania** (☎ 233 3147; Tanu Rd; ☑ closed during flight arrivals and departures).

BUS

All long-distance buses depart from the main bus stand just off Sokoine Rd near the market; most departures are in the morning.

To Masasi (TSh3500, five to six hours), buses depart approximately hourly between about 6am and 2pm; once in Masasi you'll need to change vehicles for Tunduru and Songea.

To Lindi (TSh2000, three hours), there are two buses daily, departing Mtwara between about 9am and 11am. The post bus departs Mtwara at around noon daily except Tuesday. Departures in the other direction are in the mornings.

Buses to Newala (TSh5000, six to eight hours) use the southern route via Nanyamba, departing Mtwara between 6am and 8am daily. You can also reach Newala via Masasi, although this often entails an overnight stay in Masasi.

To Dar es Salaam, there are buses four times weekly (TSh17,000, about 20 hours), departing Mtwara anytime between morning and early afternoon, and from Dar es Salaam by 8am.

To Mozambique, there are several pickups daily to the Tanzanian immigration post at Kilambo (TSh3000), departing Mtwara between 8am and 11am. Departures are from the eastern side of the market in front of the Aaliyah Trading Company building. For more on crossing the Ruvuma River, see p260. The best places for information on the ferry are the Old Boma (right) and Ten Degrees South (right), in Mikindani.

BOAT

The MV *Safari* sails weekly between Dar es Salaam and Mtwara; see p125. The **booking office** (☎ 233 3591, 233 3550; Aga Khan St) is just up from Shabu Restaurant.

Getting Around

Taxis to or from the airport (6km southeast of the main roundabout) cost TSh5000. There are taxi ranks at the bus stand and near the corner of Uhuru and Tanu Rds. A few *daladalas* run along Tanu Rd to and from the bus stand.

MIKINDANI

☎ 023

Mikindani is a tiny Swahili town with an interesting history, lots of coconut groves and a picturesque bay. It's easily visited as a day trip from Mtwara, and also makes a good base in its own right.

The town gained prominence early on as a major dhow port and a terminus for trade caravans travelling from Lake Nyasa. In the 19th century Mikindani served as headquarters of the German colonial government and several buildings from the era remain, including the impressive *boma*, built in 1895.

Information

The closest banking facilities are in Mtwara. The Old Boma has a tourist information office, and is the best place for organising walking tours of town and excursions in the area.

Sleeping & Eating

Old Boma at Mikindani (☎ 233 3875, 0742-767642; www.mikindani.com; r half board with/without balcony US$120/100, ste US$180; ☒) This beautifully restored building offers spacious, high-ceilinged doubles and top-end standards, and is well worth a splurge. There's a 'sunset terrace' overlooking the bay, or you can climb the tower for views over town.

Ten Degrees South Lodge (☎ 0748-855833; www .eco2.com; r with shared bathroom US$15-25) A budget travellers' base, with simple rooms – all with large beds and nets – and a good restaurant-bar (meals from TSh4000) with a popular Saturday evening barbecue. Diving can be arranged through ECO2 (check out www .eco2.com), which is based at the hotel.

Getting There & Away

Mikindani is 10km from Mtwara along a sealed road, and an easy bike ride. Minibuses (TSh200) run between the two towns throughout the day.

MSANGAMKUU PENINSULA & MNAZI BAY–RUVUMA ESTUARY MARINE PARK

Msangamkuu Peninsula lies northeast of Mtwara and, together with Msimbati and Mnazi Bay to the south, has been gazetted as Tanzania's second marine park, protecting more than 400 marine species as well as coastal ecosystems. Everything's still very much in the initial stages, but it's hoped that ultimately the park will be the core of a conservation area extending as far as Pemba in Mozambique. Marine park entry fees are US$10 per day, and are collected at the marine park office near the entrance to Msimbati village. For diving, contact ECO2, based at Ten Degrees South Lodge (above) in Mikindani.

Msangamkuu Peninsula

The section of Msangamkuu Peninsula lying directly opposite Mtwara offers some decent beaches and snorkelling (bring your own equipment, and don't bring valuables). There's no accommodation.

Dhows and canoes go throughout the day to/from Shangani boat dock in Mtwara (one way TSh100).

Msimbati

The Msimbati Peninsula, about 42km from Mtwara on Mnazi Bay, boasts an excellent beach and a string of mostly unexplored offshore reefs. Most visitors head straight to the tiny settlement of **Ruvula**, which is about 7km beyond Msimbati village along a sandy track (or along the beach at low tide), and has the best stretch of sand in the area.

Ruvula Sea Safari (camping TSh5000, bandas per person with full board TSh35,000) in Ruvula has simple *bandas* near the sea and the beach at your doorstep. A few basics are available in Msimbati village, but if you're camping, stock up in Mtwara.

There's at least one pick-up daily in each direction between Mtwara and Msimbati (TSh2000, one hour), departing Mtwara by 11am from the eastern side of the market. Departures from Msimbati are at around 6am. On weekends it's easy enough to hitch. Between Msimbati and Ruvula the options are hitching, arranging a lift on a bicycle with locals or walking along the beach at low tide.

MAKONDE PLATEAU & AROUND

The seldom-visited Makonde Plateau, much of which lies between 700m and 900m above sea level, is home to the Makonde people, famed throughout East Africa for their carvings.

Newala
☎ 023
Dusty, bustling Newala is the major settlement on the plateau, with pleasantly cool temperatures and views over the Ruvuma Valley. There's an old German fort (now the police station) on the edge of the escarpment at the southern edge of town. Newala is near the Mozambican border, so it's a good idea to carry your passport when wandering around.

Country Lodge Bed & Breakfast (☎ 241 0355; s with shared bathroom TSh5000, s/d with private bathroom TSh7000/10,000) has simple rooms – most with nets – and a restaurant. It's about 600m from the centre of town along the Masasi road.

There are several less expensive guesthouses in the area around the market and the bus stand, with no-frills rooms sharing bathroom for about TSh3000.

Buses run daily between Newala and Mtwara (TSh5000, six to eight hours) and Newala and Masasi (TSh3500, three hours).

Ndanda
Ndanda, along the Mtwara–Tunduru road, about 40km northeast of Masasi, is notable for its large Benedictine monastery and the adjoining hospital that serves as the major health clinic for the region. About a 45-minute walk south of the monastery (uphill) is a small dam where you can swim.

Nuru Ndanda Hotel (r with shared bathroom TSh3500), diagonally across from the hospital at the bus stand, has basic rooms and a tiny restaurant.

Masasi
☎ 023
Masasi, a bustling district centre, stretches out along the main road off the edge of the Makonde Plateau against a backdrop of granite hills. It's an important transport hub for onward travel west towards Tunduru and north to Nachingwea and Liwale.

Better guesthouses include **Holiday Guest House** (r TSh6000), at the western end of town near the petrol station, and **Sayari Hotel** (☎ 251 0095; r TSh9400), at the eastern end of town near the post office, and with a restaurant.

GETTING THERE & AWAY
The bus stand is at the far western end of town on the Tunduru road. Coming from Mtwara, ask the driver to drop you at your hotel or at the petrol station to avoid the walk back to town. Buses leave for Mtwara approximately hourly between 6am and 2pm.

Land Rovers and (in the dry season) buses go to Tunduru daily, departing before dawn (12 hours, 200km).

TANZANIA DIRECTORY

This section covers information specific to Tanzania. For general information applicable to the region, see p617.

ACCOMMODATION
In this chapter, continental breakfast (coffee/tea, bread, jam and sometimes an egg) is included in accommodation prices unless noted. For safari lodges, quoted prices don't include wildlife drives or excursions except as stated. Inquire when booking, as these add significantly to the price. Many lodges and luxury camps in or near national parks quote all-inclusive prices, which means ac-

commodation plus excursions such as wildlife drives, short guided walks or boat safaris, and sometimes park entry fees and airport transfers.

From late June to August and again around the Christmas and New Year holidays, many hotels levy an additional 'peak-season' charge on top of regular high-season rates. During the March to early June low season you can often get discounts of up to 50% on room prices. A residents' permit also entitles you to some discounts.

Camping

It's a good idea to carry a tent if you're planning to travel in off-the-beaten-track areas, and it can save you some money in and around the northern parks (though camping in the parks themselves will cost at least $20 per person per night). Camping isn't permitted on Zanzibar.

NATIONAL PARKS

All of the parks have camp sites. 'Ordinary' camp sites have basic facilities; generally pit toilets and sometimes a water source. 'Special' camp sites are more remote, and have no facilities at all; the idea is that the area remain as close to pristine as possible. Unlike ordinary camp sites, special camp sites must be booked in advance, and you'll usually have them to yourself. For most national park camp sites, you'll need to bring everything in with you, including drinking water. Most parks also have simple huts or *bandas*, several have basic resthouses, and many northern circuit parks have hostels.

Homestays

Students spending extended periods in Tanzania studying Swahili frequently arrange to stay with local families. Costs are very reasonable, and you'll usually be expected to take your meals with the family.

Hostels, Guesthouses & Budget Hotels

Water can be a problem during the dry season, and many cheaper places don't have running or hot water, though all will arrange a bucket if you ask. Note that in Tanzanian Swahili, *hotel* (or *hoteli*) refers to food and drink, rather than accommodation. The more common term if you're looking for somewhere to sleep is *guesti* or 'guesthouse' or, more formally, *nyumba ya kulala wageni*.

Hotels, Lodges & Luxury Camps

In Tanzania, en suite rooms (ie with private bathroom) are widely referred to as 'self-contained' or 'self-container' rooms. In addition to a rapidly improving selection of midrange and top-end accommodation in major towns, the country also has some of East Africa's most beautiful luxury lodges on the safari circuits and on the coast, at correspondingly high prices – from US$70 to US$500 per person per night. Prices at the upper end of the spectrum are all-inclusive.

ACTIVITIES
Beachcombing & Island Hopping

Tanzania has a magnificent coastline, and it's easy to make a holiday out of exploring and relaxing on the beaches and nearby islands. Highlights include the Zanzibar Archipelago (p128); southeastern Tanzania (p236), with fine stretches of sand at Msimbati and elsewhere, plus Mafia and Kilwa Kisiwani islands; and the mainland coast around Pangani (p162).

Inland beaches and islands are equally alluring, including the languid Lake Nyasa shoreline (p234), the shoreline of Lake Tanganyika around Mahale Mountains National Park (p217) and the island habitats of Rubondo Island National Park (p206).

Bird-Watching

In addition to the national parks, top birding spots include Lake Victoria, Lake Eyasi and

TANZANIA

the eastern Usambara mountains. Useful websites include the **Tanzania Bird Atlas** (http://tanzaniabirdatlas.com/), the **Tanzania Bird Checklist** (www.tanzaniabirding.com/bird_checklists.htm) and the Tanzania Hotspots page on www.camacdonald.com/birding/africatanzania.htm.

Boating

Selous Game Reserve (p236) is the best place for boat safaris; there are also possibilities at Saadani Game Reserve (p160), and Arusha National Park (p188) has canoe safaris.

For upscale trips down the Rufiji River and to Mafia Island, contact Pole Pole Resort (p241) or Kinasi Lodge (p241).

Dar es Salaam, Tanga and Mikindani have yacht clubs, and there are several boats on the Zanzibar Archipelago that can be chartered for longer cruises; see p153.

Chimpanzee Tracking

Gombe Stream National Park (p216) and Mahale Mountains National Park (p217) are excellent destinations if you're interested in observing our primate cousins at close range. Gombe is the more easily accessible choice, and also has the advantage that the chimps are more readily spotted, with sightings almost guaranteed. Mahale has an unparalleled setting, and chances of sightings are also high, although you generally need to work a bit harder and climb more steeply to find them. There are also chimpanzees at Rubondo Island National Park (p206), but the chimp tracking here can't compare with that at the western parks.

Cycling & Mountain Biking

For general information see p636. Green Footprint Adventures (p92) organises short rides near Lake Manyara National Park. In Dar es Salaam, the best base for cyclists are the bicycle-friendly Pugu Hills, but there are no rentals here, so you'll need to bring your own bike. Alternatively, contact Afri-Roots (p118), which organises local cycling trips.

Diving & Snorkelling

The best diving is around the Zanzibar Archipelago (p138) and around Mafia Island. There's also diving in the largely unexplored waters of the Mnazi Bay–Ruvuma Estuary Marine Park (p247) and off the beaches north of Dar es Salaam (p127). Mnemba Atoll (p151) is a snorkelling highlight.

Fishing

Upscale hotels on Mafia, Pemba and Zanzibar can arrange deep-sea fishing charters. Other contacts include Ras Kutani (p127) and Kilwa Lodge (p242).

On Lake Victoria – renowned for its Nile perch – the best contacts are Lukuba Island Lodge (p210), Rubondo Island Camp (p207) and Wag Hill Lodge (p203).

Hiking & Trekking

Tanzania's main hiking areas are the Usambara and Pare Mountains in the northeast, Udzungwa Mountains National Park, the Uluguru Mountains near Morogoro, the lower slopes of Mt Kilimanjaro around Marangu and Machame, and the Crater Highlands. Other possibilities include Mt Hanang, and the areas around Mbeya, Tukuyu and the Kitulo Plateau in the southwest. Except in the western Usambaras around Lushoto (where there's an informal guide organisation and a network of guesthouses) and in the Crater Highlands (where most hiking is organised through operators), you'll need to organise things yourself. In most areas it is required or recommended to go with a guide, which, apart from adding to the cost, can feel quite constraining if you're used to just setting off on your own. When formalising your arrangements, be sure you and the guide agree on how much territory will be covered each day, as local expectations about suitable daily sections on standard routes in places like the Usambaras are often unsatisfyingly short if you're an experienced hiker.

The main trekking destinations are Mt Kilimanjaro (p175) and Mt Meru (p190). All trekking requires local guides and (usually) porters. Be aware of the dangers of Acute Mountain Sickness (AMS). In extreme cases it can be fatal. See p647 for more.

Horse Riding

In northern Tanzania, good contacts include Makoa Safaris (p171), near Moshi, and **Equestrian Safaris** (www.safaririding.com), based outside Arusha, which organises rides in west Kilimanjaro, in the Crater Highlands and around Lake Natron.

Wildlife Watching

This is one of Tanzania's top attractions. See p91 and the Wildlife special section (p57) for more information.

BOOKS

See p17 for titles to whet your appetite for East Africa. Lonely Planet's *Tanzania* covers the country in more depth. Some additional titles on Tanzania include the following.

An Ice-Cream War by William Boyd. A snapshot of what is now Tanzania during WWI.

Memoirs of an Arabian Princess by Emily Said-Ruete. The very readable autobiography of a Zanzibari princess who elopes with a German to Europe in the days of the sultans.

Sand Rivers by Peter Matthiessen. Go on safari with the author into the heart of Selous Game Reserve.

Through a Window by Jane Goodall. A vivid portrayal of the author's research and life with the chimpanzees of Gombe Stream National Park.

We Must Run While They Walk – A Portrait of Africa's Julius Nyerere by William E Smith. A good background on the statesman's life and philosophy.

Zanzibar Tales by George Bateman & Walter Bobbett. A translated collection of Swahili folk tales dating from the late 19th and early 20th centuries.

BUSINESS HOURS

In addition to regular banking hours, many forex bureaus remain open until 5pm Monday through Friday, and until noon on Saturday. Throughout the region, shops and offices often close for one to two hours between noon and 2pm, and – especially in coastal areas – on Friday afternoons for mosque services.

CHILDREN

See p621 for general information. All Tanzanian parks and reserves are free for children under five years of age, and entry and camping fees are discounted for those under 16 years of age. Children under seven years of age aren't permitted in Gombe Stream or Mahale Mountains National Parks. Hotel accommodation is usually discounted for those under 12 and free for those under two years old; extra children's beds added to double rooms usually cost about US$10. Some wildlife lodges, especially those in the national parks, are restricted for children, so inquire when booking. Always make sure you ask for children's discounts if booking a safari

through a tour operator, as otherwise they are often overlooked. Most upscale hotels have pools. Playgrounds are a rarity, though you'll find the occasional one in larger towns. Mosquito nets are best brought from home.

COURSES
Language

Tanzania is the best place in East Africa to learn Swahili. Schools (many of which can arrange home stays) include the following:

Institute of Swahili & Foreign Languages (Map p134; ☎ 024-223 0724, 223 3337; takiluki@zanlink.com; Vuga Rd, Zanzibar Town) Also see www.glcom .com/hassan/takiluki.html.

KIU Ltd (☎ 022-285 1509; www.swahilicourses.com) At various locations in Dar es Salaam.

Makoko Language School (☎ 028-264 2518; swahili musoma@juasun.net) On the outskirts of Musoma.

MS Training Centre for Development Cooperation (☎ 027-255 3837/8; www.mstcdc.or.tz) About 15km outside Arusha, near Usa River.

University of Dar es Salaam (☎ 022-241 0757; www .udsm.ac.tz/kiswahilicourses.html) In Dar es Salaam.

CUSTOMS

Exporting seashells, coral, ivory and turtle shell is illegal. You can export up to TSh2000 without declaration. There's no limit on importation of foreign currency; amounts over US$10,000 must be declared.

DANGERS & ANNOYANCES

Tanzania is in general a safe, hassle-free country, and can be a relief if you've recently been somewhere like Nairobi. That said, you do need to take the usual precautions. Avoid isolated areas, especially isolated stretches of beach, and in cities and tourist areas take a taxi at night. When using public transport, don't accept drinks or food from someone you don't know, and be sceptical of anyone who comes up to you on the street asking you whether you remember them from the airport, your hotel or wherever.

In tourist areas – especially Arusha, Moshi and Zanzibar – touts and flycatchers can be extremely aggressive, especially around bus stations and budget tourist hotels. Try to do everything you can to minimise the impression that you're a newly arrived tourist. Duck into a shop if you need to get your bearings, and don't walk around more than necessary with your luggage. While looking for a room, leave your bag with a friend or hotel rather than walking around town with it. Buy your bus tickets a day in advance (without your luggage), and when arriving in a new city, take a taxi from the bus station to your hotel. Be very wary of anyone who approaches you on the street, at the bus station or in your hotel offering safari deals, and never pay any money for a safari or trek in advance until you've thoroughly checked out the company. In western Tanzania, along the Burundi border, there are sporadic outbursts of banditry and political unrest. Get an update from your embassy if you plan on travelling there. Also see p120 and p622.

EMBASSIES & CONSULATES
Tanzanian Embassies & Consulates

Australia Sydney (☎ 02-9261 0911; www.tanzania consul.com; Level 3, 185 Liverpool St, Sydney, NSW 2000); Perth (☎ 08-9322 6222; legal@murcia.com.au; Level 25, QV1 Building, 250 St George's Terrace, Perth WA 6000) The Sydney office is for NSW, VIC, ACT and Tasmania; the Perth office for Perth, SA, NT and QLD.

Canada Ottawa (☎ 0613-232 1500; tzottawa@synapse .net; 50 Range Rd, Ottawa, Ontario KIN 8J4)

France Paris (☎ 01 53 70 63 70, 01 47 55 05 46; tanzanie@ infonie.fr; 13 Ave Raymond Poincare, 75116 Paris)

Germany Berlin (☎ 030-303 08 00; www.tanzania-gov .de; Eschenallee 11, 14050 Berlin-Charlottenburg)

Italy Rome (☎ 06-334 85 801; www.tanzania-gov.it; Viale Cortina d'Ampezzo 185, Rome)

Japan Tokyo (☎ 03-425 4531; tzrepjp@japan.co.jp; 21-9, Kamiyoga 4, Chome Setagaya-Ku, Tokyo 158)

Kenya Mombasa (tancon@users.africonline.co.ke; Palli House, Nyerere Ave); Nairobi (☎ 02-331056, 02-331104; tanzania@users.africaonline.co.ke; Reinsurance Plaza, 9th fl, between Tarifa Rd & Aga Khan Walk, Nairobi)

Mozambique Maputo (☎ 01-490110; Ujamaa House, 852 Ave Mártires de Machava, Maputo)

Netherlands (☎ 0180-32 09 39; Parallelweg Zuid 215, 2914 LE Nieuwerkerk aan den Ijssel)

Rwanda Kigali (tanzarep@rwandatell.rwandal.com; 15 Avenue Paul VI, Kigali)

South Africa Pretoria (☎ 012-342 4393; tanzania@cis .co.za; PO Box 56572, Arcadia 0007, Pretoria)

Uganda Kampala (☎ 41-256292, 41-256272; tzrepkla@ imul.com; 6 Kagera Rd, Kampala)

United Kingdom London (☎ 020-7499 8951; www .tanzania-online.gov.uk; 43 Hertford St, London W1Y 8DB)

USA New York (☎ 212-972 9160; 205 East 42nd St, New York, NY); Washington, DC (☎ 202-939 6125; www .tanzaniaembassy-us.org; 2139 R St, NW, Washington DC)

Zambia Lusaka (☎ 01-253320, 01-227698; tzreplsk@ zamnet.zm; Ujamaa House, 5200 United Nations Ave, Lusaka)

Tanzania also has diplomatic representation

in Belgium (Brussels), China (Beijing), DR Congo (Kinshasa), Egypt (Cairo), Ethiopia (Addis Ababa), India (New Delhi), Nigeria (Lagos), Sweden (Stockholm), Switzerland (Geneva) and Zimbabwe (Harare). There's no Tanzanian high commission in Malawi.

Embassies, Consulates & High Commissions in Tanzania

Australians can contact the Canadian embassy. Except as noted, most are open from around 8am to at least 3pm, often with a midday break. Visa information is given for Tanzania's neighbours; applications for all should be made in the morning. Diplomatic representations in Dar es Salaam (area code ☎ 022) include the following:

Belgium (Map p116; ☎ 211 4025, 211 2503; daressalaam@diplobel.org; 5 Ocean Rd, Upanga)

Burundi (Map p116; Lugalo St, Upanga; ☼ 8am-5pm Mon-Fri) One-month single-entry visas cost US$45 plus two photos and are issued within 24 hours. Burundi also has a consulate in Kigoma (p214).

Canada (Map p118; ☎ 211 2831; www.dfait-maeci.gc .ca/tanzania/menu-en.asp; 38 Mirambo St)

DR Congo (Map p116; Maliki Rd, Upanga; ☼ 8.30am-3pm Mon-Fri) One-month single-entry visas cost US$50, require two photos, and are available within three days. You'll need a letter from an employer, tour operator or embassy explaining your purpose. The consulate in Kigoma (p214) issues visas within 24 hours, and without a letter, but with lots of questions.

France (Map p116; ☎ 266 6021; www.ambafrance-tz .org; Ali Hassan Mwinyi Rd)

Germany (Map p118; ☎ 211 7409-15; www.german -embassy-daressalam.de; cnr Mirambo St & Garden Ave)

India (Map p116; ☎ 266 9040/2; www.hcindiatz.org; 82 Kinondoni Rd, Masaki)

Ireland (Map p116; ☎ 260 2355/6, 266 6211; iremb@ raha.com; 1131 Msasani Rd) Just off Haile Selassie Rd, near the International School.

Italy (Map p116; ☎ 211 5935; www.italdipldar.org; 316 Lugalo Rd, Upanga)

Kenya (Map p116; ☎ 270 1747; 14 Ursino, cnr Rashidi Kawawa & Old Bagamoyo Rds; ☼ 8am-2.30pm Mon-Fri) One-month single-entry visas cost TSh50,000 (no photos required), and are issued within 24 hours.

Malawi (Map p118; ☎ 0748-481740; 1st fl, Zambia House, cnr Ohio St & Sokoine Dr; ☼ 8am-3pm Mon-Fri) Many nationalities, including the USA and UK, don't require visas. For those that do, one-month single-entry visas cost US$70 plus two photos and are issued within 24 hours.

Mozambique (Map p118; ☎ 211 6502; 25 Garden Ave; ☼ 8am-3pm Mon-Fri) One-month single-entry visas cost US$40/35 for same-day/two-day service, plus two photos.

TANZANIA

Netherlands (Map p118; ☎ 211 0000; www.netherlands-embassy.go.tz; cnr Mirambo St & Garden Ave)

Rwanda (Map p116; ☎ 211 5889; 32 Ali Hassan Mwinyi Rd, Upanga; ☻ 8am-3.30pm Mon-Fri) One-month single-entry visas cost US$45 plus two photos, and are ready within three days.

Uganda (Map p116; ☎ 266 7009; 25 Msasani Rd; ☻ 8.30am-4.30pm Mon-Fri) Near Oyster Bay Primary School. Three-month single-entry visas cost US$30 plus two photos and are issued the same day.

UK (Map p118; ☎ 211 0101; bch.dar@fco.gov.uk; cnr Mirambo St & Garden Ave)

USA (Map p116; ☎ 266 8001; http://usembassy.state .gov/tanzania; cnr Old Bagamoyo & Rashidi Kawawa Rds)

Zambia (Map p118; ☎ 212 5529; Zambia House, cnr Ohio St & Sokoine Dr; ☻ visa applications 9-11am, visa pick-ups 2-3pm, Mon-Fri) Three-month single-entry visas cost TSh25,000 to TSh43,000 depending on nationality, and require two photos. They're processed the same day.

FESTIVALS & EVENTS

Sauti za Busara (☎ 024-223 2423; busara@zanlink.com) A three-day music and dance festival centred around all things Swahili; held in February on Zanzibar.

Kilimanjaro Marathon (www.kilimanjaromarathon .com) Something to do in the foothills around Moshi, just in case climbing to Kilimanjaro's summit isn't enough. Held in February or March.

Festival of the Dhow Countries (www.ziff.or.tz) A two-week extravaganza of dance, music, film and literature from Tanzania and other Indian Ocean countries; held in early July.

ZIFF This film festival is the centrepiece of the Festival of the Dhow Countries; held in early July.

Mwaka Kogwa A four-day festival held in late July to mark Nairuzim (the Shirazi New Year); festivities are best in Makunduchi, in Zanzibar's southeastern corner.

Bagamoyo Arts Festival (www.college-of-arts.org /index_festival.html) A week of traditional music, dance, acrobatics, poetry reading and more, featuring local and regional ensembles; held in late September.

HOLIDAYS

New Year's Day 1 January
Zanzibar Revolution Day 12 January
Easter (Good Friday, Holy Saturday and Easter Monday) March/April
Union Day 26 April
Labour Day 1 May
Saba Saba (Peasants' Day) 7 July
Nane Nane (Farmers' Day) 8 August
Nyerere Day 14 October
Independence Day 9 December
Christmas Day 25 December
Boxing Day 26 December

Major Islamic holidays are also celebrated as public holidays; see p624.

INTERNET RESOURCES

There's lots of information on Tanzania to be found on the Web. Following are a few sites to get you started:

Government of Tanzania (www.tanzania.go.tz) The government site – dry, but with visa info.

Tanzania News (www.tanzanianews.com) News clippings.

Tanzania Page (www.sas.upenn.edu/African_Studies /Country_Specific/Tanzania.html) Good links.

Tanzania Tourist Board (www.tanzaniatouristboard .com) TTB's official site.

Zanzibar Tourism (www.zanzibartourism.net) The Zanzibar Commission for Tourism's official site.

MAPS

Good country maps include those published by Nelles (1:1,500,000) and Harms-ic, both available in Tanzania. Harms-ic also publishes maps for Lake Manyara National Park and the Ngorongoro Conservation Area

An excellent series of colourful maps, hand-drawn by a man named Giovanni Tombazzi and marketed under the name MaCo, cover Zanzibar, Arusha and many northern Tanzania parks. They're widely available in Dar es Salaam, Arusha and Zanzibar Town.

MONEY

The currency in Tanzania is the Tanzanian shilling (TSh). There are bills of TSh10,000, TSh5000, TSh1000 and TSh500, and coins of TSh200, TSh100, TSh50, TSh20, TSh10, TSh5 and TSh1. For exchange rates, see p103. For more information on costs, see p17.

The best currency to bring is US dollars in a mixture of large and small denominations, plus some travellers cheques as emergency stand-by and a Visa card for withdrawing money from ATMs.

Travel in Tanzania is expensive, especially if you're doing an organised safari. While travelling on a modest or even a shoestring budget is quite possible, it will take some work, and you'll need to rough things. Whatever your budget, there are few real deals – comforts abound, but you'll need to pay. For some tips on cutting costs, see p17.

Tanzania has a 20% value-added tax (VAT) that's usually included in quoted prices.

ATMs

National Bank of Commerce (NBC) has ATMs that accept Visa at most of their branches (found in major towns countrywide). Standard Chartered (with branches in Dar es Salaam, Arusha, Moshi and Mwanza), Barclays (Dar and Arusha) and CRDB (in major towns) also have ATMs that allow you to withdraw shillings with a Visa card to a maximum of TSh400,000 per day. A few ATMs also accept MasterCard. All are open 24 hours in theory, though in practice they're often out of service.

Cash

Cash can be changed with a minimum of hassle at banks and foreign exchange (forex) bureaus in all larger towns; rates and commissions vary, so it pays to shop around. Forex bureaus are usually quicker, less bureaucratic and offer higher rates, although many smaller towns don't have them. The most useful bank for changing money is NBC, which has branches throughout the country. Note that US$50 and US$100 bills get better rates of exchange than smaller denominations. Old-style US bills are not accepted anywhere. Euros, British pounds and other major currencies are accepted in tourist areas and major towns.

In order to reconvert Tanzanian shillings to hard currency at the end of your trip, save at least some of your exchange receipts, though they are seldom checked. The easiest places to reconvert currency are at the airports in Dar es Salaam and Kilimanjaro.

In theory, it's required for foreigners to pay for accommodation, park fees, organised tours, upscale hotels and the Zanzibar ferries in dollars, though shillings are almost always accepted at the going rate.

Credit Cards

Some top-end hotels, tour operators and a few midrange establishments accept credit cards – most with a 5% to 10% commission – though their use isn't as common as in Kenya, or in the West.

You can get cash advances in dollars at poor rates against Visa or MasterCard in Dar es Salaam, Arusha and Zanzibar Town.

Tipping

For general guidelines on tipping, see p626. On treks and safaris in Tanzania, it's common practice to tip drivers, guides, porters and other staff if the service has been good. For guidelines on amounts see p84 (for safaris) and p176 and p190 (for treks).

Travellers Cheques

Travellers cheques can be changed in Dar es Salaam, Arusha, Zanzibar, Mwanza and other major centres – but not elsewhere in the country – at slightly lower rates than for cash. As with changing cash, forex bureaus are usually much quicker and less bureaucratic than banks. Wherever you change, you'll almost always be required to show your original purchase receipt before changing the cheques. Most banks (but not forex bureaus) also charge commissions ranging from 0.5% of the transaction amount (at NBC) to more than US$40 per transaction. Most hotels refuse to accept travellers cheques as direct payment.

PHOTOGRAPHY & VIDEO

Print film, including Kodak and Fuji, is sold in major towns and tourist areas (from about TSh3500 for a roll of 100ASA/36 exposures). Slide film (Kodak and Fuji, 100ASA) is available in Dar es Salaam (about TSh9000 for 36 exposures), Zanzibar and other tourist areas. Speeds above 200ASA are difficult to find.

CD-burning of digital images is possible at a handful of Internet cafés in major towns.

Region-wide restrictions on photographing anything connected with the government or military (see p627) are taken seriously, so if in doubt, don't take your camera out.

POST

Airmail postage to the USA/Australia/Europe costs from TSh600/800/500 and is reasonably reliable for letters. Package delivery is unreliable, so don't send any valuables.

There's poste restante service in all major towns, with a charge of TSh200 per received letter. Mail is held for at least one month.

TELEPHONE

You can make domestic (from about US$0.10 per minute) and international (from US$2 per minute) calls from Tanzania Telecom offices in all major towns, as well as from private communications shops. Occasionally you'll find places offering much cheaper Internet dialling, though it's officially not permitted. Calls to mobile phones cost

TSh500 per minute. There are card phones in major towns (buy cards during business hours at Tanzania Telecom or at shops near the phones), but for international calls, even with the most expensive card (TSh7500, 150 units), you'll only get a few minutes to talk. For the occasional one- or two-digit numbers still remaining, you'll need to place your call through the operator (☎ 900).

Mobile Phones

The rapidly expanding mobile network covers major towns in the country, plus a wide arc encompassing the north and northeast. In the south, west and centre, you often won't get a signal once you're away from the larger towns. Mobile phone numbers are six digits, preceded by (0)741 (Mobitel), (0)744 and (0)745 (Vodacom), (0)748 and (0)787 (Celtel), or (on Zanzibar) (0)747. To reach a mobile telephone number from outside Tanzania, dial the country code, then the mobile phone code without the initial 0, and then the six-digit number. From within, keep the initial 0 and don't use an area code.

All the companies sell prepaid starter packages, and top-up cards are on sale at shops throughout the country.

Phone Codes

Tanzania's country code is ☎ 255. To make an international call, dial ☎ 000, followed by the country code, local area code (without the initial '0') and telephone number.

Most telephone numbers are seven digits, although there are still a few four- and five-digit numbers around. Area codes (given at the start of town entries) must be used whenever you dial long distance.

TOURIST INFORMATION

The **Tanzania Tourist Board** (TTB; www.tanzania-web.com) has offices in Dar es Salaam (p117) and Arusha (p181). In the UK, the Tanzania Tourist Board is represented by the **Tanzania Trade Centre** (☎ 0207-407 0566; director@tanzatrade .co.uk; 80 Borough High St, London, SE1 1LL). In the USA, the TTB representative is the **Bradford Group** (☎ 212-447 0027; tanzania@bradfordmarketing .org; 347 Fifth Ave, Suite 610, New York, NY 10016).

VACCINATION CERTIFICATES

Tanzania no longer officially requires you to carry a certificate of yellow-fever vaccination unless you're arriving from an infected area (which includes Kenya, although arrivals aren't always checked). It's also a requirement in some neighbouring countries, including Rwanda, and thus is a good idea to carry. For more, see p646.

VISAS

Almost everyone needs a visa. A single-entry visa valid for up to three months costs between US$20 and US$50, depending on nationality. It's best to get the visa in advance (and necessary if you want multiple entry), though they're currently readily issued at Dar es Salaam and Kilimanjaro airports and at most border crossings (all nationalities US$50, US dollars cash only, single-entry only). Some embassies require you to show proof of an onward ticket before they'll issue a visa, though a flight itinerary will usually suffice. For extensions (free) within the usual three-month visa limit, there are immigration offices in all major towns. After three months, you'll usually need to leave the country and reapply for a new visa. For visas to neighbouring countries, see p252.

TRANSPORT IN TANZANIA

GETTING THERE & AWAY

For information on getting to East Africa from outside the region, see p631.

Entering Tanzania

Tanzania is straightforward to enter, whether at the airports or at overland borders. Visas are available at all major points of entry (see p629), and must be paid for in US dollars cash. You'll need proof of yellow-fever vaccination only if you're coming from a yellow-fever infected area (including Kenya), though it often isn't checked.

Passport

As long as you have complied with visa and entry permit requirements (see p629), there are no restrictions on any nationalities for entering Tanzania.

Air

Tanzania's major air hub is **Dar es Salaam International Airport** (code DAR; ☎ 022-284 2461, 284 4371, ext 2001). **Kilimanjaro International Airport** (code JRO; ☎ 027-255 4252, 255 4707; www.kilimanjaroairport.co.tz), midway between Arusha and Moshi, handles an increasing number of international flights and is the best option if you'll be concentrating on Arusha and the northern-safari circuit. It shouldn't be confused with the smaller **Arusha Airport** (code ARK), about 8km west of Arusha, which handles some domestic flights. There are also international flights to/from **Zanzibar International Airport** (code ZNZ). **Mwanza Airport** (code MWZ) and **Mtwara Airport** (code MYW) handle some regional flights.

Air Tanzania (airline code TC; ☎ 022-211 8411, 284 4239; www.airtanzania.com) is the national airline, with its hub at Dar es Salaam International Airport. It operates in partnership with South African Airways and is generally efficient and reliable. Regional and international routes include Nairobi to Dar es Salaam and Zanzibar, and Dar es Salaam to Moroni (Comores), Entebbe and Johannesburg. Credit cards are accepted at their Dar es Salaam office only.

The other major commercial carrier is **Precision Air** (airline code PW; ☎ 022-212 1718, 022-284 3547, in Arusha ☎ 027-250 2818, 027-250 6903, in Zanzibar ☎ 024-223 4520; www.precisionairtz.com; hub Dar es Salaam), which, in partnership with Kenya Airways, has flights from Nairobi to Dar es Salaam, Kilimanjaro and Zanzibar, and between Mombasa and Dar es Salaam via Zanzibar, plus numerous domestic routes. They are also about to start a flight between Kigoma and Bujumbura in partnership with Air Burundi.

Other regional and international carriers flying to/from Tanzania include the following (with useful flights between Tanzania and elsewhere in East Africa highlighted). All airlines service Dar es Salaam, except as noted.

Air Burundi (airline code 8Y; airbdi@cbinf.com;) Hub: Bujumbura. Bujumbura to Kigoma (to start soon).

Air India (airline code AI; ☎ 022-215 2642; www.airindia.com) Hub: Mumbai.

Air Kenya (airline code REG; ☎ 027-250 2541, in Nairobi ☎ 020-601727; www.airkenya.com) Hub: Nairobi. Nairobi to Kilimanjaro.

British Airways (airline code BA; ☎ 022-211 3820, 022-284 4082; www.britishairways.com) Hub: Heathrow Airport, London.

Egyptair (airline code MS; ☎ 022-211 0333; www.egyptair.com.eg) Hub: Cairo International Airport.

Emirates Airlines (airline code EK; ☎ 022-211 6100; www.emirates.com) Hub Dubai International Airport.

Ethiopian Airlines (airline code ET; ☎ 022-211 7063; www.flyethiopian.com) Hub: Addis Ababa. Also flies to Kilimanjaro International Airport (KIA).

Kenya Airways (airline code KQ; ☎ 022-211 9376/7; www.kenya-airways.com) Hub: Jomo Kenyatta International Airport, Nairobi. Nairobi and Mombasa to Dar es Salaam and Zanzibar.

KLM (airline code KL; ☎ 022-213 9790/1, in Arusha ☎ 027-250 8062/3; www.klm.com) Hub: Schiphol Airport, Amsterdam. Also serves Kilimanjaro International Airport.

Linhas Aéreas de Moçambique (airline code TM; ☎ 022-213 4600; www.lam.co.mz) Hub: Mavalane International Airport, Maputo.

Oman Air (airline code OMA; ☎ 024-223 8308; www.oman-air.com) Hub: Seeb International Airport. Also serves Zanzibar International Airport.

Rwandair Express (www.rwandair.com) Hub: Kigali. Kigali to Kilimanjaro International Airport.

South African Airways (airline code SA; ☎ 022-211 7044; www.flysaa.com) Hub: Johannesburg International Airport.

Swiss International Airlines (airline code LX; ☎ 022-211 8870; www.swiss.com) Hub: Kloten Airport, Zurich.

Yemenia Yemen Airways (airline code IY; ☎ 022-212 6036; www.yemenairways.net) Hub: Sana'a International Airport.

Chimpanzee Safaris (p214) run regularly scheduled charters between Kigoma (Tanzania) and Kigali (Rwanda) – useful if you're combining gorillas and chimpanzees.

Land
BUS
Buses cross the borders between Tanzania and Kenya, Malawi, Uganda and Zambia. Apart from sometimes lengthy waits at the border for passport checks, there are usually no hassles. At the border, you'll need to disembark on each side to take care of visa formalities, then reboard your bus and continue on. Visa fees are not included in bus-ticket prices for trans-border routes. It's also possible to travel to/from all of Tanzania's neighbours by minibus or (for Kenya) shared

---

DEPARTURE TAX

The departure tax for regional and international flights is US$30. It's included in the ticket price for departures from the mainland, but on Zanzibar is usually levied separately at the airport (payable in either US dollars or Tanzanian shillings).

taxis. Most main routes go direct, but sometimes you'll need to walk across the border and change vehicles on the other side.

CAR & MOTORCYCLE

If you're arriving via car or motorcycle, you'll need the vehicle's registration papers and your license (p263), plus pay for a temporary import permit at the border (TSh20,000 for one month), third-party insurance (TSh50,000 for one year) and a onetime fuel levy (TSh5000). You'll also need a *carnet de passage en douane*; see p638.

Most hire companies don't permit their vehicles to cross international borders; should you find one that does, arrange the necessary paperwork with them in advance.

For road rules, see p638. Most border posts don't have petrol stations or repair shops; head to the nearest large town.

TO/FROM BURUNDI

The main border crossing is at Kobero Bridge between Ngara and Muyinga (Burundi). Although the border is officially open, the security situation ebbs and flows, so get an update from your embassy first. The road between Kigoma and Lusahunga in particular is subject to occasional banditry, and it's sometimes necessary to travel in a convoy. There are also border crossings at Gisuru (east of Ruyigi) and further south at Mugina (near Makamba), but they are currently primarily for United Nations staff and others connected with refugee repatriation.

The trip is done in stages via Lusahunga, from where there are vehicles north towards Biharamulo and Lake Victoria and southeast via Kahama towards Nzega or Shinyanga. The road from Nzega to the Burundi border via Ngara is in fairly good condition. Time your travels so that if you need to overnight in Tanzania, it will be in either Biharamulo or Kahama, rather than in Lusahunga or other less safe points near the border.

TO/FROM KENYA
Border Crossings

The main route to/from Kenya is the sealed road connecting Arusha and Nairobi via the heavily travelled Namanga border post (open 24 hours). There are also border crossings at Horohoro, north of Tanga; at Taveta, east of Moshi; at Illassit, northeast of Moshi; at Bologonya in the northern Serengeti; and

---

BORDER HASSLES

At the Namanga border post between Kenya and Tanzania (en route between Nairobi and Arusha), watch out for touts – often claiming they work for the bus company – who tell you that it's necessary to change money, to pay a fee, or to come over to 'another building' to arrange the necessary payments to enter Tanzania/Kenya. Apart from your visa, there are no border fees, payments or exchange requirements for crossing, and the rates being offered for money exchange at the border are far below the norm.

---

at Isebania, northeast of Musoma. With the exception of the Serengeti–Masai Mara crossing, there is public transport across all Tanzania–Kenya border posts.

Kisii

Minibuses go daily between Musoma and the Sirari/Isebania border post, where you can change to Kenyan transport for Kisii, and then on to Kisumu or Nairobi. Scandinavian Express and Akamba also pass Kisii on their daily runs between Mwanza and Nairobi (TSh20,000 to TSh23,000, 12 to 14 hours between Mwanza and Nairobi), with some buses continuing on to Arusha and Dar.

Masai Mara

There's no public transport between the northern Serengeti and Kenya's Masai Mara Game Reserve, and only East African residents and citizens can cross here. If you're a resident and are exiting Tanzania, you should take care of immigration formalities in Seronera. Entering Tanzania from Masai Mara, park fees are payable at the Lobo ranger post, between the border and Seronera.

Mombasa

Scandinavian Express goes daily between Dar es Salaam and Mombasa, departing mornings in each direction (TSh19,000, 10 hours). Buses between Tanga and Mombasa depart daily in the morning (TSh5000 to TSh10,000, four to five hours).

Nairobi

Scandinavian Express goes between Dar es Salaam and Nairobi via Arusha, departing daily in each direction around 6.30am (TSh38,000, 13 hours). Scandinavian Express and Akamba bus line also have daily buses between Mwanza and Nairobi (TSh23,000 to TSh28,000 plus Kenyan visa costs, 12 to 14 hours).

Between Arusha or Moshi and Nairobi, the most popular option is one of the daily shuttle buses, which depart at 8am and 2pm in each direction (five hours). Main companies include the following:

Davanu Arusha (☎ 0744-400318, 0744-846160; Hotel Pallsons, Bondeni St, Arusha); Nairobi (☎ 254-20-222002, 254-20-217178; davanu@nbnet.co.ke; 4th fl, Windsor House, University Way, with a desk at the New Stanley Hotel)
Impala Arusha (☎ 027-250 7197; impala@cybernet.co .tz; Impala Hotel, cnr Moshi & Old Moshi Rds, Arusha); Nairobi (☎ 254-20-2717373; Silver Springs Hotel)
Riverside Arusha (☎ 027-250 2639, 027-250 3916; riverside_shuttle@hotmail.com; Sokoine Rd, Arusha, with a branch at Mt Meru Hotel); Nairobi (☎ 254-20-229618; Room 1, 3rd fl, Pan African Insurance House, Kenyatta Ave)

All charge US$25 one way, and with a little prodding, you can sometimes get the residents' price (US$10). In Arusha, all companies drop you at Mt Meru Hotel, as well as at their offices. In Nairobi, drop-offs are at centrally located hotels and at Jomo Kenyatta International Airport. When flying into Nairobi, shuttle representatives will meet your flight if you've booked in advance. Otherwise contact the shuttles through the tourist information desk in the international arrivals area. Confirm the drop-off point when booking, and insist on being dropped off as agreed. Also watch out for touts who may board the bus at the New Stanley Hotel (Nairobi) and insist that it's the end of the line to drum up business for waiting taxis.

Regular buses also link Arusha and Nairobi daily (TSh9000, six to seven hours), departing between 6.30am and 8am, and sometimes also in the afternoon about 2pm. Departures in Arusha are from the bus station; in Nairobi most are from Accra Rd.

Shared taxis go between the Arusha bus station and the Namanga border (TSh2500) throughout the day, beginning about 6am. Most are nine-seater sedans that do the journey at hair-raising speeds. At Namanga, you'll have to walk a few hundred metres across the border, and then catch one of the frequent *matatus* (Kenyan minivans) or shared taxis to Nairobi (about US$5). Com-

ing from Nairobi, the *matatu* and shared-taxi depots are on Ronald Ngala St, near the River Rd junction.

Voi
Minibuses go daily between Moshi and Voi, or the trip can be done in stages via Taveta on the border. There are also occasional direct buses between Moshi and Mombasa via Voi, although most reach Mombasa in the middle of the night.

TO/FROM MALAWI
The only border crossing is at **Songwe River bridge** (☯ 7.30am-6pm Tanzanian time, 6.30am to 5pm Malawi time), southeast of Mbeya.

Buses go three times weekly between Dar es Salaam and Lilongwe, departing Dar es Salaam about 5am (TSh47,000, 27 hours). It's better to take Scandinavian from Dar to Mbeya, and get onward transport there. From Mbeya, buses depart several times weekly in the afternoon, arriving in Lilongwe the next day (TSh29,000). There are also daily minibuses connecting both Mbeya and Kyela with the border; once at the border, there's about a 300m walk to the Malawian side, from where there are minibuses to Karonga. There's also at least one bus daily between the border and Mzuzu, departing the border by mid-afternoon and arriving by evening. Many vehicles and trucks ply between Mbeya and Karonga, so it's easy to find a lift.

Coming from Malawi, the best option is to take a minibus from the border to Mbeya, and then get an express bus onwards from there towards Dar es Salaam. This means overnighting in Mbeya, as buses to Dar es Salaam depart Mbeya between 6am and 7am.

TO/FROM MOZAMBIQUE
There are no bridges over the Ruvuma River (the border). The main crossing is at Kilambo (south of Mtwara), where there is a sometimes-operational ferry. It's also possible to get your passport stamped on the crossing between Newala and Moçimboa do Rovuma (Mozambique). If you travel by boat, there are border officials at Msimbati (Tanzania), and at Palma and Moçimboa da Praia (Mozambique). It's also reportedly possible to get stamped in at the crossing between Songea and Nova Madeira (Mozambique); otherwise, there's an immigration office in Songea.

Pick-ups depart Mtwara daily between 7am and 9am for the Kilambo border post (TSh3000, one hour), and on to the Rovuma, which is crossed via dugout canoe (TSh2000, 10 minutes to over an hour, depending on water levels; dangerous during heavy rains). On the Mozambique side, there are usually two pick-ups daily to the Mozambique border post (about 4km further) and on to Moçimboa da Praia (US$7, four hours), with the last one departing by about noon. If you get stuck at the Rovuma, there's a bedbug-ridden guesthouse on a sandbank in the middle of the river; camping on the Mozambique side is a better option.

The Rovuma crossing is notorious for pickpockets. Keep an eye on your belongings, especially when getting into and out of the boats, and keep up with the crowd when walking to/from the riverbank.

If you're travelling this route by private vehicle, there's a vehicle ferry at Kilambo that operates at high tide (TSh500/20,000 per person/large vehicle), though the captain has been known to skip off and leave vehicles waiting for several days. Get an update first at the Old Boma (p247) or Ten Degrees South (p247), or at **Russell's Place** (Cashew Camp; in Mozambique ☎ 082-686273; russellbott@yahoo .com) in Pemba (Mozambique).

The border crossing south of Newala is rarely used and entails long walks on both sides (up to 25km in Tanzania, and at least 10km in Mozambique). The main Mozambique town is Moçimboa do Rovuma, from where there's a daily vehicle to Mueda.

Further west, you can make your way from Songea to the Rovuma via sporadic public transport and on foot. Once in Mozambique, there's a truck every other day from the Rovuma to Lichinga via Nova Madeira and Macaloge.

TO/FROM RWANDA
The main border crossing is at Rusumu Falls, southwest of Bukoba. There have been no problems recently, but due to a long history of instability in this region, it's worth getting an update from your embassy or resident expatriates before setting off.

Daily pick-ups go between Benako (30km southwest of the border) and Rusumu Falls border post; see p205 for connections to Benako. At the border, walk across the bridge to the Rwandan border post, from where minibuses go to Kibungo and on to Kigali (US$5, three hours). There are also occasional direct buses between Mwanza and Kigali.

TO/FROM UGANDA
The main post is at Mutukula, northwest of Bukoba (although you actually get stamped in and out of Tanzania at Kyaka, about 30km south of the Mutukula border), with good Tarmac access routes on both sides. There's another crossing further west at Nkurungu, but the road is bad and sparsely travelled.

Scandinavian goes daily between Dar es Salaam and Kampala via Nairobi (TSh50,000, 27 hours) and Arusha, departing Dar in the morning, and Kampala at midday. Jaguar/ Dolphin (the best connection) and Tawfiq go daily between Bukoba and Kampala, departing Bukoba about 7am (TSh11,000, five to six hours). Departures from Kampala are at 7am and about 1.30pm. From Kampala, Tawfiq continues on to Nairobi and Dar (TSh40,000) plus transit visas for Uganda (US$15) and Kenya (US$20, 36 hours), though if you're headed to Nairobi it's better to sleep in Kampala and get another bus the next day as the Tawfiq bus arrives late at night.

From Mwanza, Akamba goes four times weekly to/from Kampala (TSh20,000, 19 hours).

TO/FROM ZAMBIA
The main border crossing is at **Tunduma** (🕙 7.30am-6pm Tanzania time, 6.30am-5pm Zambia time), southwest of Mbeya. There's also a crossing at Kasesha, between Sumbawanga and Mbala (Zambia).

Scandinavian goes daily between Dar es Salaam and Lusaka via Mbeya, departing at dawn from Dar es Salaam and in the evenings from Lusaka (TSh60,000, 24 hours). Otherwise, minibuses go frequently between Mbeya and Tunduma (TSh2500, two hours), where you walk across the border for Zambian transport to Lusaka (US$20, 18 hours).

The Tanzania–Zambia (Tazara) train line links Dar es Salaam with Kapiri Mposhi in Zambia (TSh55,000/39,100/31,500 in 1st/2nd/economy class, about 40 hours) twice weekly via Mbeya and Tunduma. From Kapiri Mposhi to Lusaka, you'll need to continue by bus. Tazara also has one slower 'ordinary' train weekly between Dar es Salaam and Mbeya (p265) and between

Kapiri Mposhi and Nakonde (on the Zambian side of the Zambia–Tanzania border, about 20 hours).

Sea & Lake

There's a US$5 port tax for all boats and ferries from Tanzanian ports.

TO/FROM BURUNDI

Ferry

The regular passenger-ferry service between Kigoma and Bujumbura is suspended. Previously there had been a weekly overnight service on the MV *Mwongozo* (US$30/25/20 in 1st/2nd/economy class, payment in US dollars cash only, 11 hours), which may resume as the political situation stabilises. Inquire at the port in Kigoma for an update.

Lake Taxi

Security situation permitting, you can take a lake taxi from Kibirizi (just north of Kigoma, p216) to just south of the Burundi border. Once there, walk a few kilometres to the border, from where there are minibuses to Nyanza Lac and Bujumbura.

TO/FROM DEMOCRATIC REPUBLIC OF THE CONGO

There's currently no passenger service to/from DR Congo.

TO/FROM KENYA

Dhow

Dhows sail sporadically between Pemba, Tanga and Mombasa; the journey can be long and rough. Ask at the ports in Tanga, or in Mkoani or Wete on Pemba for information on sailings. In Kenya, ask at the port in Mombasa, or at Shimoni.

Ferry

There's no passenger ferry service on Lake Victoria between Tanzania and Kenya. Occasional cargo boats depart Mwanza for Kenya that are sometimes willing to take passengers. Inquire at the Mwanza South Port about sailings.

TO/FROM MALAWI

Ferry

The MV *Songea* sails between Mbamba Bay and Nkhata Bay (Malawi), departing Mbamba Bay on Friday, and Nkhata Bay on Saturday (US$10/4 in 1st/economy class, four

to five hours). The schedule is highly variable and sometimes cancelled completely.

TO/FROM MOZAMBIQUE

Dhow

Dhows between Mozambique and Tanzania (12 to 30 hours) are best arranged at Msimbati or Moçimboa da Praia (Mozambique).

Ferry

The official route between southwestern Tanzania and Mozambique is via Malawi on the *Songea* ferry between Mbamba Bay and Nkhata Bay (see the preceding Malawi section), and then from Nkhata Bay on to Likoma Island (Malawi), Cóbuè and Metangula (both in Mozambique) on the *Ilala* ferry (in Malawi ☎ 01-587311; ilala@malawi .net). Unofficially, there are small boats that sail along the eastern shore of Lake Nyasa between Tanzania and Mozambique. However, Lake Nyasa is notorious for its severe and sudden squalls, and doing the journey this way is risky.

TO/FROM UGANDA

There's no passenger-ferry service, but it's relatively easy to arrange passage between Mwanza and Kampala's Port Bell on cargo ships (about 16 hours). On the Ugandan side, you'll need a letter of permission from the railway-station director (free). Ask for the managing director's office, on the 2nd floor of the building next to Kampala's railway station. In Mwanza, a letter isn't required, but you'll need to check in with the immigration officer at the South Port. Expect to pay about US$20, including port fees. Crew are often willing to rent out their cabins for a negotiable extra fee.

TO/FROM ZAMBIA

Ferry

The venerable MV *Liemba*, which has been plying the waters of Lake Tanganyika for the better part of a century, connects Kigoma with Mpulungu in Zambia weekly (US$55/45/40 in 1st/2nd/economy class, US dollars cash only; at least 40 hours). Stops en route include Lagosa (for Mahale Mountains National Park), Kalema (southwest of Mpanda) and Kasanga (southwest of Sumbawanga). Departures from Kigoma are on Wednesday afternoon, reaching Mpulungu Friday morning. Departures from Mpulungu

TANZANIA

are Friday afternoon. Food is available on board, but it's best to bring some supplements and drinking water. First class is relatively comfortable, with two reasonably clean bunks and a window. Second-class cabins (four bunks) and economy-class seating are both poorly ventilated and uncomfortable – better to find deck space than economy-class seating. Keep watch over your luggage, and book early if you want a cabin; Monday morning seems to be the best time.

There are docks at Kigoma and Kasanga, but at many smaller stops you'll need to disembark in the middle of the lake into small boats that take you to shore – a bit of an adventure (or nerve-racking, depending on your perspective) at night, if the lake is rough or you have a heavy pack.

Tours

Dozens of tour and safari companies organise package tours to Tanzania. While it's generally cheaper to organise your tour with a Tanzania-based company, this may be outweighed by the convenience of organising things in advance with a company at home. For tour operators covering Tanzania and elsewhere in East Africa, see p635. For safari and trekking operators, see p92.

GETTING AROUND
Air

The national airline, **Air Tanzania** (Map p118; Dar es Salaam ☎ 022-211 8411, 022-284 4293; www.air tanzania.com) has reliable flights connecting Dar es Salaam with Mwanza, Zanzibar, Kilimanjaro and Mtwara. Other airlines flying domestically include the following (all also do charters).

Air Excel (☎ 027-254 8429, 027-250 1597; reservations@ airexcelonline.com) Arusha, Serengeti, Lake Manyara, Dar es Salaam, Zanzibar.

Coastal Aviation (☎ 022-284 3293, 022-284 2877, 022-211 7959; www.coastal.cc) Arusha, Dar es Salaam, Kilwa Masoko, Lake Manyara National Park, Mafia, Mwanza, Pemba, Ruaha National Park, Rubondo Island National Park, Saadani Game Reserve, Selous Game Reserve, Serengeti National Park, Tanga, Tarangire National Park, Zanzibar.

Precision Air (☎ 022-212 1718, 022-213 0800, 027-250 2818; www.precisionairtz.com) Arusha, Bukoba, Dar es Salaam, Kigoma, Mwanza, Shinyanga, Tabora, Zanzibar.

Regional Air Services (☎ 027-250 4477, 027-250 2541; www.airkenya.com/docs/regair3.htm) Arusha, Kilimanjaro, Lake Manyara National Park, Serengeti National Park.

ZanAir (☎ 024-223 3670/8; www.zanair.com) Arusha, Dar es Salaam, Lake Manyara National Park, Mafia, Pemba, Selous Game Reserve, Serengeti National Park, Tarangire-National Park, Zanzibar.

Bicycle

As distances are long, often with little variation in topography in between, the most satisfactory cycling is often from a fixed base (eg the western Usambaras around Lushoto, or anywhere on Pemba). See p636 for general information.

In theory, bicycles can be transported on minibuses and buses, though many drivers are unwilling. For express buses, you'll need to make advance arrangements to stow your bike in the hold.

Boat
DHOW

Main routes include those connecting Zanzibar and Pemba with Dar es Salaam, Tanga, Bagamoyo and Mombasa; those connecting Kilwa Kivinje, Lindi, Mikindani and Mtwara with other coastal towns; and between Mafia and the mainland. Foreigners are officially prohibited on nonmotorised dhows, and on any dhows between Zanzibar and Dar es Salaam; captains are subject to heavy fines if they're caught, and may be unwilling to take you. See also p637.

FERRY

Ferries operate on Lake Victoria, Lake Tanganyika and Lake Nyasa, and between Dar es Salaam, Zanzibar and Pemba. There's a US$5 port tax per trip on all routes. For details of ferries between Dar es Salaam, Zanzibar and Pemba, see p125, p154 and p157.

Lake Nyasa

In theory, the MV *Songea* departs Itungi Port about 1pm on Thursday and makes its way down the coast via Lupingu, Manda, Mango and Liuli (but not via Matema) to Mbamba Bay (TSh14,000/8000 in 1st/economy class, 18 to 24 hours). It then continues across to Nkhata Bay in Malawi, before turning around and doing the return trip. This

---

DOMESTIC DEPARTURE TAX

Airport departure tax for domestic flights is TSh5000.

schedule is highly unreliable and frequently interrupted.

The smaller MV *Iringa* services lakeside villages between Itungi and Manda (about halfway down the Tanzanian lakeshore), departing Itungi about midday on Tuesday and stopping at Matema, Lupingu and several other ports en route before turning back again on Wednesday for the return trip. Schedules are very fluid and change often; the best places to get an update for both the *Iringa* and the *Songea* are with bus drivers along the Kyela route, or at one of the hotels in Matema (p234).

Lake Tanganyika

For the MV *Liemba* schedule between Kigoma and Mpulungu (Zambia), see p260. See p260 for information on connections between Kigoma and Bujumbura (Burundi).

Lake Victoria

The MV *Victoria* departs Mwanza for Bukoba at 10pm on Tuesday, Thursday and Sunday (TSh16,500/14,500/11,300/10,600 in 1st class/2nd-class sleeping/2nd-class sitting/3rd class plus port tax, nine hours). Departures from Bukoba are at 9.30pm Monday, Wednesday and Friday. First-class has two-bed cabins, and 2nd-class sleeping has six-bed cabins. Second-class sitting is uncomfortable, so if you can't get a spot in 1st-class or 2nd-class sleeping, the best bet is to buy a 3rd-class ticket. With luck, you may then be able to find a comfortable spot in the 1st-class lounge. First- and 2nd-class cabins fill up quickly in both directions, so book as soon as you know your plans. Food is available on board. A smaller, faster speedboat is expected to begin service imminently, which will at least halve the transit time.

The MV *Butiama* sails between Mwanza and Nkome (northwest of Geita, TSh6100/4300 in 2nd/3rd class) with numerous stops en route, including at Maisome Island. Departures from Mwanza are at 8.30am Saturday, arriving at Nkome about 6pm. Departures from Nkome are at 8am Sunday. At 8.30am Wednesday the *Butiama* departs Mwanza for Nyamirembe (northeast of Biharamulo) with a stop en route at Maisome Island (14 hours). Departures from Nyamirembe are around noon on Thursday.

For information on connections between Mwanza and Ukerewe Island, see p206.

Bus

Major long-distance routes have a choice of express and ordinary buses. Express buses make fewer stops, are less crowded than ordinary buses and depart on schedule. Some have air-con and toilets, and the nicest ones are called 'luxury' buses. On secondary routes, the only option is ordinary buses, which are often packed to overflowing, make many stops and run to a less rigorous schedule.

For popular routes, book your seat in advance, although you can sometimes get a place by arriving at the bus station an hour prior to departure. Scandinavian and Royal Coach fill up quickly on all routes, and should be booked at least one day in advance. Each bus line has its own booking office, usually at or near the bus station.

Most express buses have a compartment underneath for luggage. Otherwise, stow your pack under your seat or in the front of the bus, where there's usually space near the driver.

Prices are basically fixed, although overcharging isn't unheard of. Most bus stations are chaotic, and at the ones in tourist areas you'll be incessantly hounded by touts. Buy your tickets at the office, and not from the touts, and don't believe anyone who tries to tell you there's a luggage fee.

For short stretches along main routes, express buses will drop you off, though you'll often be required to pay the full fare to the next major destination.

Major bus companies and a sampling of their destinations:

Dar Express Arusha, Dar es Salaam.

Royal Coach Arusha, Dar es Salaam.

Scandinavian Express (www.scandinaviagroup.com) Arusha, Dar es Salaam, Dodoma, Iringa, Kampala (Uganda), Kyela, Mbeya, Mombasa (Kenya), Morogoro, Nairobi (Kenya), Njombe, Songea.

Other lines, none distinguished, include Takrim/Tawfiq (Arusha, Bukoba, Kampala, Mwanza, Nairobi, Singida), Sumry (Mbeya, Sumbawanga) and Jaguar (Bukoba, Kampala). You can book tickets online for Scandinavian Express routes, but need to collect (and pay for) your ticket at least three days prior to the journey date.

MINIBUS & SHARED TAXI

For shorter trips away from the main routes, the choice is often between 30-seater buses

('Coasters' or *thelathini*), and *daladalas*. Both options come complete with chickens on the roof, bags of produce wedged under the seats, and no leg room. Shared taxis are relatively rare, except in northern Tanzania near Arusha. Like ordinary buses, minibuses and shared taxis leave when full; they're probably the least safe of the various transport options.

Car & Motorcycle

Unless you have your own vehicle and are familiar with driving in East Africa, it's relatively unusual for travellers to tour mainland Tanzania by car. More common is to focus on one part of the country, and then arrange local transport through a tour or safari operator. On Zanzibar it's easy and economical to hire a car or motorcycle for touring. For information about bringing your own vehicle, see p638.

DRIVING LICENCE

On the mainland, you'll need your home driving licence or (preferably) an international driving licence. On Zanzibar, you'll need an international driving licence, or a licence from Zanzibar (see p143), Kenya, Uganda or South Africa.

FUEL & SPARE PARTS

Petrol costs about TSh1040 per litre (about TSh850 per litre for diesel). Filling and repair stations are readily available in major towns, but scarce elsewhere, so tank up whenever you can and carry basic spares. For travel in remote areas and in national parks, carry jerry cans with extra fuel.

HIRE

Dar es Salaam has a modest array of car-hire agencies. Daily rates for 2WD start about at US$40 excluding fuel, plus US$20 to US$30 for insurance and tax. Prices for 4WD range from US$70 to US$150 per day plus insurance (US$30 to US$40 per day), fuel and driver (US$15 to US$35 per day). There's also a 20% VAT.

For anything outside the city, most companies require 4WD. Also, most don't permit self-drive outside of Dar es Salaam, and none presently offer unlimited kilometres. Per kilometre charges average US$0.50 to US$1. Clarify what the company's policy is in the event of a breakdown.

Avis (Map p118; ☎ 022-211 5381; Skylink Travel & Tours, Ohio St, Dar es Salaam; avis@skylinktanzania.com) Opposite Mövenpick Royal Palm Hotel, with a branch in Arusha.

Evergreen Car Rentals (Map p116; ☎ 022-218 2107, 022-218 5419; evergreen@raha.com; cnr Nkrumah St & Nyerere Rd, Dar es Salaam)

Hertz (Map p118; ☎ 022-212 2130, 022-212 2363; hertz@cats-net.com; Mövenpick Royal Palm Hotel, Ohio St, Dar es Salaam)

Elsewhere in Tanzania, you can hire 4WD vehicles in Arusha, Mwanza and Zanzibar

---

PERILS OF THE ROAD

Road accidents are probably your biggest safety risk while travelling in Tanzania, with speeding buses being among the worst offenders. Road conditions are poor and driving standards leave a lot to be desired. Overtaking blind is a big problem, as are high speeds. Your bus driver may in fact be at the wheel of an ageing, rickety vehicle with a cracked windshield and marginal brakes on a winding, potholed road. However, he'll invariably be driving as if he were piloting a sleek racing machine on a straight road – nerve-racking to say the least. Impassioned pleas from passengers to slow down usually have little effect, and pretending you're sick often is counterproductive. Many vehicles have painted slogans such as *Mungu Atubariki* (God Bless Us) or 'In God we Trust' – probably in the hope that a bit of extra help from above will see the vehicle safely through the day's runs.

To maximise your chances of happy and uneventful travels, try to stick with more reputable bus companies such as Scandinavian Express and Royal Coach. Also, if you have a choice, it's usually better to go with a full-sized bus than a minibus or 30-seater bus.

Buses aren't permitted to drive at night in Tanzania, which is just as well, though at least in the dark you can't see the road swerving before you. On most routes, the last departure is generally timed so that the bus should reach its destination by evening (assuming that all goes well). For cross-border routes, departures are usually timed so that night driving will be done once outside Tanzania.

TANZANIA

Town and other centres through travel agencies, tour operators and hotels. Except on Zanzibar, most come with driver. Rates average US$70 to US$120 per day plus fuel, and less on Zanzibar (where it's also easy to hire motorcycles and minibikes, and arrange car hire privately). Clarify before setting out who bears responsibility for repairs.

ROAD CONDITIONS & HAZARDS
About 20% of Tanzania's road network is paved, including the roads from Dar es Salaam to Arusha via Chalinze, and from Dar es Salaam to Mbeya via Morogoro and Iringa. The road from Dar es Salaam to Mtwara is being paved. Secondary roads range from good to nearly impassable, depending on the season and on when they were last maintained. For most trips outside major towns, you'll need 4WD.

Hazards include vehicles overtaking on blind curves, pedestrians and animals in the road, and children running into the road.

ROAD RULES
In theory, driving is on the left, and traffic already in roundabouts has the right of way. Unless otherwise posted, the speed limit is 80km/h; on major routes, police have radar. Tanzania has a seatbelt law for drivers and front-seat passengers. The official traffic-fine penalty is TSh20,000.

Motorcycles aren't permitted in national parks, except for the section of the Dar es Salaam to Mbeya highway passing through Mikumi National Park, and on the road between Sumbawanga and Mpanda via Katavi National Park. Also see p638.

Hitching
Hitching in Tanzania is generally slow going. It's prohibited inside national parks, and is usually fruitless around them. That said, in remote areas, hitching a lift with truck drivers may be your only transport option, for which you'll need to pay. See also p638.

Local Transport
DALADALA
Local routes are serviced by *daladalas* and, in rural areas, pick-up trucks or old Land Rovers. Prices are fixed and inexpensive: from TSh100 for local town runs. The vehicles make many stops and are crowded. Accidents are frequent, particularly in minibuses. Many are caused when the drivers race each other to a station in order to collect new passengers. Destinations are either posted in the front window, or called out by the driver's assistant, who also collects fares.

TAXI
Taxis can be hired in all major towns. None have meters; the base rate for town trips is TSh1500.

Tours
For safari and trekking operators, see p92. For local tour operators, see listings in the regional chapters.

CULTURAL TOURISM PROGRAM

To see local life away from the organised safari scene, it's well worth trying a Cultural Tourism Program (CTP) tour. These are 'community-owned' ventures spread in various places around the country, including Ng'iresi, Ilkiding'a, Mulala, Mkuru and Longido (all accessed from Arusha), Machame (Moshi), Marangu, Engaruka and Mto Wa Mbu, Gezaulole (near Dar es Salaam), the Usambara Mountains (near Lushoto), the northern and southern Pare Mountains and Pangani. They range in length from a few hours to a few days, and usually centre around light hikes or other activities, with the focus on experiencing local cultures.

Some of the tours are a bit rough around the edges, but others are well organised, and they're great for getting to know Tanzania at the local level. Most have various 'modules' available, from half a day to several nights. Fees (listed in the regional chapters) are reasonable, and a portion of the income supports community projects such as school or well construction. Per person costs decrease with increasing group size. Payments should be made on site; always ask for a receipt.

Tours should be arranged directly with the local coordinator, although there's a CTP representative at the Tourist Information Office in Arusha (p181) who can help with those in the Arusha area and with general information.

TRAIN COSTS

Destination	1st class	2nd-class sleeping	2nd-class sitting	Economy
Dar es Salaam to Kigoma	TSh45,200	TSh33,100	–	TSh15,000
Dar es Salaam to Mwanza	TSh44,600	TSh32,600	TSh17,700	TSh18,800
Dar es Salaam to Tabora	TSh32,700	TSh24,200	TSh13,000	TSh11,000
Mwanza to Tabora	TSh17,600	TSh13,600	TSh7200	TSh6400
Tabora to Mpanda	TSh16,300	TSh12,600	–	TSh6000
Dodoma to Singida	–	–	TSh10,400	TSh6900

Train

Tanzania has two rail lines: **Tazara** (☎ 022-286 0340/4, 022-286 5339; www.tazara.co.tz; cnr Nyerere & Nelson Mandela Rds, Dar es Salaam) links Dar es Salaam with Kapiri Mposhi in Zambia via Mbeya and Tunduma; the Tanzanian Railway Corporation's **Central Line** (Map p118; ☎ 022-211 7833; www.trctz.com; cnr Railway St & Sokoine Dr, Dar es Salaam) links Dar es Salaam with Kigoma and Mwanza via Morogoro, Dodoma and Tabora. A branch of the Central Line links Tabora with Mpanda, there's also passenger service on the Dodoma–Singida spur.

Tazara is more comfortable and efficient, but on both lines, breakdowns and long delays are common.

CLASSES
There are three classes: 1st class (two- or four-bed compartments), 2nd-class sleeping (six-bed compartments); and economy class (benches, usually very crowded). Some trains also have a '2nd-class sitting section', with one seat per person. Men and women can only travel together in the sleeping sections by booking the entire compartment.

RESERVATIONS
Tickets for 1st and 2nd class should be reserved at least several days in advance, although occasionally you'll be able to get a seat on the day of travel. Economy-class tickets can be bought on the spot.

SCHEDULES & COSTS
Both lines are currently undergoing renovations and management changes, so you should probably expect schedule and price changes.

Central Line
Central Line trains depart Dar es Salaam three times weekly in the evening for both Kigoma and Mwanza (splitting at Tabora). In theory, both journeys take about 40 hours, though it's more often than not much longer. Trains from both Mwanza and Kigoma to Dar es Salaam also depart in the evenings.

Trains travelling between Tabora and Mpanda (about 14 hours) run three times weekly, departing Tabora in the evening and Mpanda around midday.

Trains run three times a week between Dodoma and Singida (taking around 11 hours), departing in each direction in the morning.

Tazara
Tazara runs three trains weekly: two 'express' trains between Dar es Salaam and Kapiri Mposhi in Zambia via Mbeya, and an 'ordinary' train between Dar es Salaam and Mbeya. Ordinary trains take about 24 hours between Dar and Mbeya, and cost TSh24,500/18,400/12,200 in 1st/2nd/ economy class.

KENYA

Kenya

For many people, Kenya is quite simply East Africa in microcosm. The region's premier tourist destination really does seem to have it all: wildlife and nightlife, cities and beaches, mountains and deserts, traditional cultures and modern arts, all couched in a range of landscapes as staggering in their diversity as they are stunning in their appearance. There are a million different reasons to come here, and picking just one is nigh on impossible.

The classic image of safari savanna is perhaps the single key selling point for Kenya's tourist industry, and with all the famous fauna no keen animal-spotter should go home disappointed. However, clued-up visitors face an infinite choice of alternative settings and activities, from trekking the glacial ridges of Mt Kenya to kitesurfing off the white sands of the Indian Ocean coast, and much more besides.

This sheer diversity is something to be relished, and is by no means limited to the natural surroundings. The people, too, represent a wide cross section of everything that is contemporary Africa, and everyday life brings together traditional tribes and urban families, ancient customs and modern sensibilities. Swapping the latest political gossip with the switched-on locals is just one more small pleasure that comes with the culture.

Finally, sooner or later on any trip here you'll look up at the starry skies and feel Africa all around you, living, breathing and fuelling a thousand dreams. Whatever your mental image of this region, and wherever you move on to afterwards, Kenya will provide a crucial part of the picture, and it's a microcosm not to be missed.

FAST FACTS

- **Area** 583,000 sq km
- **Birthplace of** Louis and Richard Leakey; Paul Tergat; Dennis Oliech
- **Capital** Nairobi
- **Country code** 254
- **Famous for** the Masai Mara; meat eating; marathon runners
- **Languages** Kiswahili, English, tribal languages
- **Money** Kenya Shilling (KSh); US$1 = KSh72; €1 = KSh88
- **Population** 31.6 million

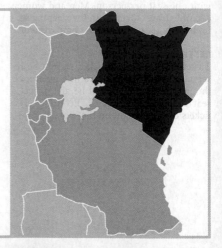

HIGHLIGHTS

- **Masai Mara National Reserve** (p393) Expansive savanna, unmatched wildlife and the world's most fascinating traffic jam – the annual wildebeest migration.
- **Mt Kenya** (p376) Equatorial glaciers, tremendous treks and jagged peaks that would make Mt Kilimanjaro blush with envy.
- **Lamu Archipelago** (p341) The ultimate Swahili immersion experience, from Lamu's winding coral streets to the empty beaches of Kiwayu.
- **Amboseli National Park** (p300) Elephants and Kilimanjaro, two big bulks combined in Kenya's most famous picture-postcard views.
- **Loyangalani** (p428) Home to harsh conditions, unforgettable tribes and the sublime jade waters of Lake Turkana.

HOW MUCH?

- **Local matatu (minibus transport) ride** KSh20
- **Plate of stew/biryani/pilau** KSh120
- **Large juice** KSh60
- **Pair of kangas** KSh350
- **Taxi home** KSh400

LONELY PLANET INDEX

- **Litre of petrol/gas** KSh72
- **Litre of bottled water** KSh55
- **Bottle of Tusker** KSh80
- **Souvenir T-shirt** KSh1000
- **Street snack (sambusa)** KSh10

CLIMATE & WHEN TO GO

There are a number of factors to take into account when considering what time of year to visit Kenya. The main tourist season is January and February, when the weather is generally considered to be the best – hot and dry, with high concentrations of wildlife. However, the parks can get crowded and rates for accommodation go through the roof. Avoid the Christmas and Easter holiday periods unless you want to pay a fortune.

June to October could be called the 'shoulder season' (see p433), as the weather is still dry. During this period the annual wildebeest migration takes place, with thousands of animals streaming into the Masai Mara National Reserve from the Serengeti in July and October.

During the long rains (from March to the end of May, the low season) things are much quieter, and you can get some good deals; this is also true during the short rains from October to December. The rains generally don't affect your ability to get around, it's just that you may get rained on, especially in the Central Highlands and western Kenya.

For more details see p621 and p438.

HISTORY

The early history of Kenya, from prehistory up until independence, is covered in the History chapter (p28).

Mau Mau Rebellion

Despite plenty of overt pressure on Kenya's colonial authorities, the real independence movement was underground. Tribal groups of Kikuyu, Maasai and Luo took secret oaths, which bound participants to kill Europeans and their African collaborators. The most famous of these movements was Mau Mau, formed in 1952 by disenchanted Kikuyu people, which aimed to drive the white settlers from Kenya forever.

The first blow was struck early in 1953 with the killing of a white farmer's entire herd of cattle, followed a few weeks later by the massacre of 21 Kikuyu loyal to the colonial government. The Mau Mau rebellion had started.

Within a month, Jomo Kenyatta and several other Kenyan African Movement (KAU) leaders were jailed on spurious evidence. The various Mau Mau sects came together under the umbrella of the Kenya Land Freedom Army, led by Dedan Kimathi, and staged frequent attacks against white farms and government outposts. By the time the rebels were defeated in 1956, the death toll stood at over 13,500 Africans (guerrillas, civilians and troops) and just over 100 Europeans.

Upon his release in 1959 Kenyatta resumed his campaign for independence. Soon even white Kenyans began to feel the winds of change, and in 1960 the British government officially announced their plan to transfer power to a democratically

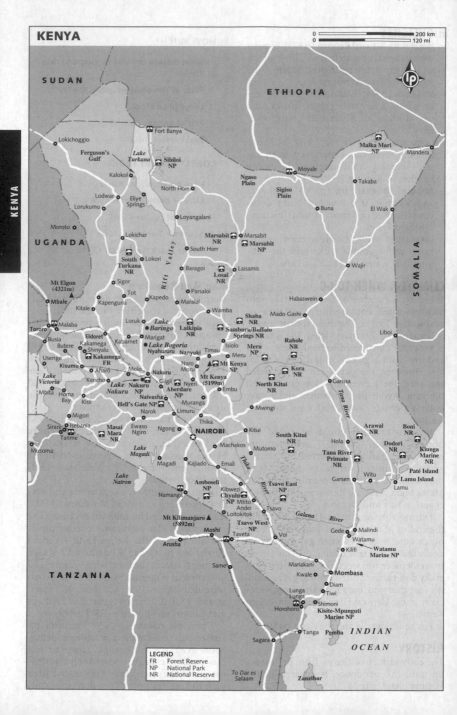

KENYA

0 _____ 200 km
0 _____ 120 mi

SUDAN

ETHIOPIA

KENYA

Lokichoggio

Ferguson's Gulf

Lake Turkana

Fort Banya

Sibiloi NP

Malka Mari NP

Mandera

Kalokol

Moyale

Lodwar

North Horr

Ngaso Plain

Sigiso Plain

Takaba

Lorukumu

Eliye Springs

Loyangalani

Buna

El Wak

Moroto

Lokichar

Marsabit NR

Marsabit

UGANDA

South Turkana NR

Lokori

South Horr

Marsabit NP

Mt Elgon (4321m)

Sigor

Baragoi

Losai NR

Laisamis

Wajir

Mbale

Kitale

Tot

Kapenguria

Kapedo

Parsaloi

Habaswein

SOMALIA

Tororo

Malaba

Loruk

Maralal

Wamba

Mado Gashi

Liboi

Busia

Eldoret

Kabarnet

Lake Baringo

Marigat

Laikipia NR

Shaba NR

Samburu/Buffalo Springs NR

Rahole NR

Butere

Kakamega

Shinyalu

Lake Bogoria

Nyahururu

Nanyuki

Timau

Isiolo

Meru NP

Usenge

Kakamega FR

Aharo

Molo

Naro Moru

Meru

Kora NR

Garissa

Kisumu

Kericho

Nakuru

Gilgil

Nyeri

Mt Kenya (5199m)

Mt Kenya NP

Embu

North Kitui NR

Lake Victoria

Lake Nakuru

Homa Bay

Kisii

Naivasha

Aberdare NP

Muranga

Mwingi

Mbita

Hell's Gate NP

Narok

Limuru

Migori

Isebania

Masai Mara NR

Ewaso Ngiro

Ngong

Thika

Kitui

Arawal NR

Boni NR

Sirare

Tarime

Lake Magadi

NAIROBI

South Kitui NR

Hola

Dodori NR

Musoma

Magadi

Kajiado

Machakos

Mutomo

Tana River Primate NR

Kiunga Marine NR

Lake Natron

Emali

Garsen

Witu

Paté Island

Lamu Island

Amboseli NP

Kibwezi

Chyulu NP

Tsavo East NP

Lamu

Namanga

Mtito Andei

Loitokitok

Tsavo

Galana *River*

Gede

Malindi

Mt Kilimanjaro (5892m)

Tsavo West NP

Watamu

Moshi

Taveta

Voi

Kilifi

Watamu Marine NP

Arusha

Mariakani

Mombasa

TANZANIA

Same

Kwale

Diam

Tiwi

Lunga Lunga

Shimoni

Horohoro

Kisite-Mpunguti Marine NP

Sagara

Tanga

Pemba

INDIAN OCEAN

To Dar es Salaam

Zanzibar

LEGEND
FR   Forest Reserve
NP   National Park
NR   National Reserve

elected African government. Independence was scheduled for December 1963, accompanied by grants and loans of US$100 million to enable the Kenyan assembly to buy out European farmers in the highlands and restore the land to the tribes.

Independence

With independence scheduled for 1963, the political handover began in earnest in 1962, with the centralist Kenya African National Union (KANU) and the federalist Kenya African Democratic Union (KADU) forming a coalition government.

The run-up to independence was surprisingly smooth, although the redistribution of land wasn't a great success; Kenyans regarded it as too little, too late, while white farmers feared the trickle would become a flood. The immediate effect was to cause a significant decline in agricultural production, from which Kenya has never recovered.

The coalition government was abandoned after the first elections in May 1963 and KANU's Kikuyu leader, Jomo Kenyatta (formerly of the KAU), became Kenya's first president on 12 December, ruling until his death in 1978. Under Kenyatta's presidency, Kenya developed into one of Africa's most stable and prosperous nations. The opposition KADU party was voluntarily dissolved in 1964.

While Kenyatta is still seen as one of the few success stories of Britain's withdrawal from empire, he wasn't without his faults. Biggest among these were his excessive bias in favour of his own tribe and escalating paranoia about dissent. Opponents of his regime who became too vocal for comfort frequently 'disappeared', and corruption soon became endemic at all levels of the power structure.

The 1980s

Kenyatta was succeeded in 1978 by his vice president, Daniel arap Moi. A Kalenjin, Moi was regarded by establishment power brokers as a suitable front man for their interests, as his tribe was relatively small and in thrall to the Kikuyu. Moi went on to become one of the most enduring 'Big Men' in Africa, ruling in virtual autocracy for nearly 25 years. In the process, he accrued an incredible personal fortune; today many believe him to be the richest man in Africa.

Although Moi's regime was stable compared to the desperate situation in many surrounding countries, it was also characterised by nepotism, corruption, arrests of dissidents, censorship, the disbanding of tribal societies and the closure of universities.

In 1982 the ruling KANU party publicly banned opposition parties, leading to a military coup by the air force, which was promptly quashed by pro-government forces. In the run-up to the 1987 election, Moi introduced a new voting system and jailed opposition leaders without trial, ensuring that the sole candidate from the sole political party in the country won the election – no prizes for guessing who that was!

After his 'win', Moi expanded the cabinet to fit in more of his cronies, and rushed through constitutional reforms allowing him to dismiss senior judges and public servants without any redress. When dissenting politicians were arrested, Christian church leaders took up the call for change, supported by another outspoken critic of government nepotism Professor Wangari Maathai, leader of the Green Belt Movement.

Sooner or later, something had to give.

The 1990s

With the collapse of communism and the break-up of the Soviet Union, it was no longer necessary for Western powers to prop up corrupt noncommunist regimes in Africa. Donors who had previously turned a blind eye to civil-rights misdemeanours began calling for multiparty elections if economic aid was to be maintained. The multiparty movement gained huge grassroots support in Kenya.

In response, KANU Youth was mobilised to disrupt pro-democracy rallies and harass opposition politicians. Things came to a head on 7 July 1990 when the military and police raided an opposition demonstration in Nairobi, killing 20 and arresting politicians, human-rights activists and journalists.

The rally, known thereafter as Saba Saba ('seven seven' in Swahili), was a pivotal event in the push for a multiparty Kenya. The following year the Forum for the Restoration of Democracy (FORD) party was formed, led by Jamagori Oginga Odinga, a powerful Luo politician who had been vice president under Jomo Kenyatta. FORD was initially banned and Odinga was arrested, but the resulting outcry led to his release and, finally, a change in the constitution that allowed opposition parties to register for the first time.

Faced with a foreign debt of nearly US$9 billion and blanket suspension of foreign aid, Moi was pressured into holding multiparty elections in early 1992, but independent observers reported a litany of electoral inconsistencies. Just as worrying, about 2000 people were killed during ethnic clashes in the Rift Valley, widely believed to have been triggered by KANU agitation. Nonetheless, Moi was overwhelmingly re-elected.

Following the elections, the KANU bowed to some Western demands for economic reforms, but agitation and harassment of opposition politicians continued unabated. The 1997 election, too, was accompanied by violence and rioting, particularly during the Saba Saba anniversary rally. Again mysterious provocateurs stirred up ethnic violence, this time on the coast. European and North American tour companies cancelled their bookings and around 60,000 Kenyans lost their jobs. Moi was able to set himself up as peacemaker, calming the warring factions and gaining 50.4% of the seats for KANU, compared to the 49.6% won by the divided opposition parties.

The scene was set for a confrontational parliament, but in a trademark Moi manoeuvre, the KANU immediately entered into a cooperative arrangement with the two biggest opposition parties, the Democratic Party (DP) and the National Development Party (NDP). Other seats were taken by FORD-Kenya and its various splinter groups.

While all this was going on, Kenya was lashed first by torrential El Niño rains and then by a desperate drought that continued right up to 2000, causing terrible hardship in rural areas.

Preoccupied with internal problems, Kenya was quite unprepared for the events of 7 August 1998. Early in the morning massive blasts simultaneously ripped apart the American embassies in Nairobi and Dar es Salaam in Tanzania, killing more than 200 people. The effect on Kenyan tourism, and the economy as a whole, was devastating. During the next four years, though, coastal businesses slowly moved to rebuild the tourist industry, helped in part by Italian tour operators, who filled the gap left by American, British and German companies.

Further terrorist activity shook the country on 28 November 2002, when suicide bombers slammed an explosives-laden car into the lobby of the Paradise Hotel at Kikambala, near Mombasa. Moments before missiles were fired at an Israeli passenger plane taking off from Mombasa's airport. Al-Qaeda subsequently claimed responsibility for both acts.

Despite a slump in tourism immediately after the attacks, the impact has been nowhere near as great as in 1998, and visitor numbers on the coast are now as healthy as ever. However, recent worldwide events have reawakened fears of terrorism, and there was widespread controversy when the press reported a shoot-to-kill order for terror suspects supposedly issued by National Security minister John Michuki. In a country with a significant Muslim population, it's no wonder that a jittery atmosphere prevails around these issues.

Kenya Today

In June 2001 the KANU entered into a formal coalition government with the NDP and DP, creating a formidable power base. However, with Moi's presidency due to end in 2002, many feared that Moi would alter the constitution again. This time, though, he announced his intention to retire – on a very generous benefits package – with elections to be held in December 2002.

Moi put his weight firmly behind Uhuru Kenyatta, the son of Jomo Kenyatta, as his successor. Meanwhile, 12 opposition parties – including the DP, FORD-Kenya, FORD-Asili, the National Party of Kenya and Saba Saba-Asili – and several religious groups united under the umbrella of the National Alliance Party of Kenya (NAK), later known as the National Rainbow Coalition (Narc). Presidential candidate Mwai Kibaki was the former head of the Democratic party.

Although initially dogged by infighting, within weeks the opposition transformed itself into a dynamic and unified political party. When the election came on 27 December 2002 it was peaceful and fair and the result was dramatic – a landslide two-thirds majority for Mwai Kibaki and Narc. Despite being injured in a car accident while campaigning, Kibaki was inaugurated as Kenya's third president on 30 December 2002.

Sadly the optimism that swept Narc into power faded fast, and the new regime has been plagued by a constant stream of party infighting, corruption and economic problems. Above all, the path to reform has been slower and more tortuous than many people had hoped. Most Kenyans still support the president himself, but there is a widespread perception that he is too much of a 'quiet man', unwilling to speak up on important issues while his government runs amok around him. Some progress has certainly been made, you only have to look at the new *matatu* (minibus transport) regulations and omnipresent anticorruption signs to see the efforts being made. However, security and corruption remain worrying issues, locals complain that the cost of living has virtually doubled, and Kenya has fallen 20 places on the UN Human Development Index since 2002.

Marking the halfway point in his term of office, 2005 was another uncomfortable year for Kibaki, who faced criticism over his handling of the national housing crisis, the Tom Cholmondeley murder case and the civil service strikes, where thousands of bureaucrats were sacked for taking strike action over pay and conditions. Even his wife had several high-profile brushes with the media!

The biggest setback came in November 2005, when the electorate voted against proposed constitutional changes. These were the first such reforms in Kenya for 40 years and a key part of the Narc election manifesto, having been thrashed out in committee after committee for nearly three years, but many claimed they would have handed the president more power, pushing the country back into shady political territory of earlier times. Kibaki, to his credit, accepted the public's decision gracefully and promptly dismissed his entire cabinet.

With elections due once again in 2007, an energetic Uhuru Kenyatta at the head of the newly regrouped KANU, and an ambitious bid for the 2016 Olympic Games attracting international attention, the next few years will be an interesting time in Kenyan politics, and Kibaki certainly has plenty of challenges still to come.

THE CULTURE
The National Psyche
It's fair to say that there is not a great sense of national consciousness in Kenya. Many residents of Kenya are more aware of their tribal affiliation than of being a 'Kenyan'; this is one of the more fascinating aspects of Kenyan life, but the lack of national cohesion undoubtedly holds the country back.

This focus on tribe, however, is generally accompanied by an admirable live-and-let-live attitude, such that only on rare occasions do tribal animosities or rivalries spill over into violence. In fact, Kenyans generally approach life with great exuberance. Be it on a crowded *matatu*, in a buzzing marketplace, or enjoying a drink in a bar, you cannot fail to notice that Kenyans are quick to laugh and are never reluctant to offer a smile.

This willingness to participate in life as it happens is perhaps a reflection of the African casual approach to time. You will be doing well to press a Kenyan into rushing anything. As is the case for many Africans, Kenyans tend to find that they have a lot of time on their hands so they don't see the need to do anything particularly urgently.

Education is of primary concern to Kenyans. Literacy rates are around 85% and are considerably higher than in any of her neighbours. Although education isn't compulsory, the motivation to learn is huge, particularly now that it's free, and you'll see children in school uniform everywhere in Kenya, even in the most impoverished rural communities.

Despite their often exuberant and casual approach, Kenyans are generally quite conservative, and are particularly concerned with modesty in dress. T-shirts and shorts are almost unheard of, though foreign men may *just* be able to pull it off. Shirts are an obsession for Kenyan men and almost everyone wears one, often with a sweater or blazer.

As Kenya undergoes a slow process of modernisation, tradition and modernity are locked in an almighty struggle, often resulting in the marginalisation of some elements of society. This is particularly the case as urbanisation happens apace. Kenya has its fair share of poverty, alienation and urban overcrowding, but even in the dustiest shanty towns life is lived to the full.

Daily Life
Tribe may be important in Kenya, but family is paramount. Particularly as the pace and demands of modern life grow, the role of the extended family has become even more

important. It is not unusual to encounter Kenyan children who are living with aunts, uncles or grandparents in a regional town while their parents are working a desk job in Nairobi or working at a resort in Watamu. Nonetheless, filial bonds remain strong, and the separation that brings about such circumstances in the first place is without exception a result of a parent's desire to further opportunities for their family and their children.

The strength of the family in Kenya is mirrored in the community. Life is generally played out in the streets and communal places. There is no such thing as daycare for young Kenyans; you will inevitably encounter the archetypical African scene where a range of children of different ages, usually with at least one older sister with a younger sibling on her hip, congregate and observe the hustle and bustle of daily life. This happens across Kenya, from coastal communities to villages in the Central Highlands to the shanty towns in Nairobi. And even as urbanisation happens and traditional community structures are fractured, street life remains lively. In any town of any size the afternoon rush hour is always a spectacle: it seems that all the world is afoot as they head home past street stalls and wandering pedlars and the dust rises gently into the coppery African twilight.

For all this, as Kenya gains a foothold in the 21st century it is grappling with increasing poverty. Once classed a middle-income country, Kenya has fallen to be a low-income country, with the standard of living dropping drastically from 2002 to 2005.

Population

Kenya's population in 2001 was estimated at 30,765,900. The population growth rate, currently at around 2.6%, has slowed in the last few years due to the soaring incidence of HIV/AIDS, which now infects 15% of adults.

According to 2001 UN figures, life expectancy in Kenya is 52 years, although some sources place it as low as 47, due to the effects of HIV/AIDS. Only 42% of the population has access to clean drinking water, but 87% are now thought to have access to adequate sanitation. The infant-mortality rate is 65 per 1000 births (a marked increase on the 1997 figure) and 51% of the population

is aged under 18. A sign of growing poverty in rural regions is migration to urban areas, where 33% of all Kenyans now live, many of them in squalid shanty towns.

Multiculturalism

Kenya's population is made up almost entirely of Africans, with small but influential minorities of Asians (about 80,000), Arabs (about 30,000) and Europeans (about 30,000).

AFRICANS

Kenya is home to more than 70 tribal groups; for detailed information see p46. The most important distinguishing feature between the tribes is language. The majority of Kenya's Africans fall into two major language groups: the Bantu and the Nilotic. The Bantu people arrived in East Africa in waves from West Africa after 500 BC, and include the Kikuyu, Meru, Gusii, Embu, Akamba and Luyha, as well as the Mijikenda, who preceded the Swahili in many parts of the coast.

Nilotic speakers migrated into the area from the Nile Valley some time later. This group includes the Maasai, Turkana, Samburu, Pokot, Luo and Kalenjin, which, together with the Bantu speakers, account for more than 90% of Kenya's African population. The Kikuyu and the Luo are by far the most numerous groups, and between them hold practically all the positions of power and influence in the country.

A third language grouping, and in fact the first migrants into the country, are the Cushitic speakers. They occupy the northeast of the country, and include such tribes as the El-Molo, Somali, Rendille and Galla.

On the coast, Swahili is the name given to the local people who, although they have various tribal ancestries, have intermarried with Arab settlers over the centuries and now have a predominantly Arabic culture.

ASIANS

India's connections with East Africa go back to the days of the spice trade, but the first permanent settlers from the Indian subcontinent were indentured workers, brought here from Gujarat and the Punjab by the British to build the Uganda Railway. After the railway was finished, the British allowed many workers to stay and start up businesses, and hundreds of *dukas* (small shops) were set up across the country.

Asian numbers were augmented after WWII and the Indian community came to control large sectors of the East African economy. However, few gave their active support to the black nationalist movements in the run-up to independence. This earned the distrust of the African community, who felt the Indians were simply there to exploit African labour.

Although Kenya escaped the anti-Asian pogroms that plagued Uganda during the rule of Idi Amin, thousands of shops owned by Asians were confiscated and Asians were forbidden to trade in rural areas. Fortunately, Kenya has learned from the lessons of the economic collapse in Uganda and calls for Asians to 'go home' have faded from the political agenda.

SPORT

Soccer is a big deal in Kenya. People are nuts about it, and even those who don't follow a local team will probably claim to support Arsenal or Manchester United. In the Kenyan Premiership, Harambee Stars, AFC Leopards and Mathare Utd vie for top slot, often drawing big crowds. The action is fast, furious and passionate, sometimes spilling onto the terraces. Tickets cost KSh300 to KSh600 and it's quite an experience.

Kenyan long-distance runners are among the best in the world, although much of their competitive running takes place outside the country. Even trials and national events in Kenya sometimes fail to attract these stars, despite being flagged in the press well in advance.

The annual **East African Safari Rally** (www.east africansafarirally.com) is a rugged 3000km rally that passes through Kenya, Uganda and Tanzania along public roadways, attracting an international collection of drivers with their vintage (pre-1971) automobiles.

RELIGION

It's probably true to say that most Kenyans outside the coastal and eastern provinces are Christians of one sort or another, while most of those on the coast and in the eastern part of the country are Muslim. Muslims make up some 30% of the population. In the more remote tribal areas you'll find a mixture of Muslims, Christians and those who follow their ancestral tribal beliefs, the latter are definitely a minority.

ARTS
Music

Although there is an indigenous Kenyan music scene, the overriding African musical influence here, as in the rest of East Africa, is Congolese *lingala* (dance music, also known as *soukous*). Kenyan bands produced some of the most popular songs in Africa in the 1960s, including Fadhili William's famous *Malaika* (Angel), and *Jambo Bwana*, Kenya's unofficial anthem, by the hugely influential Them Mushrooms.

Benga is the contemporary dance music of Kenya, characterised by electric guitar licks and bounding bass rhythms. It originated among the Luo people and became popular in the 1950s. Since then it has spread throughout the country, and been taken up by Akamba and Kikuyu musicians. Well-known exponents include DO Misiani and his group Shirati Jazz, who have been around since the 1960s. You should also look out for Globestyle, Victoria Kings and Ambira Boys.

Contemporary Kikuyu music often borrows from *benga*. Stars include Sam Chege, Francis Rugwati and Daniel 'Councillor' Kamau, popular in the 1970s and still going strong. Joseph Kamaru, the popular musician and notorious nightclub owner of the late 1960s, converted to Christianity in 1993 and now dominates the gospel-music scene.

Popular bands today are heavily influenced by *benga*, *soukous* and Western music, with lyrics often in Swahili. These include bands such as Them Mushrooms (now reinvented as Uyoya) and Safari Sound. For upbeat dance tunes, Nameless, Ogopa DJs and Deux Vultures are recommended acts.

The biggest thing in Kenya right now is American-influenced hip-hop, which has spawned both an avid listening public and an active subculture, particularly in Nairobi. Look out for local stars, like Necessary Noize, Nonini, Emmanuel Jal, the Homeboyz DJs and the Nairobi Yetu collective.

Literature

Two of Kenya's best authors are Ngugi wa Thiong'o and Meja Mwangi. Ngugi is uncompromisingly radical, and his harrowing

KENYA

criticism of the Kenyan establishment landed him in jail for a year (described in his *Detained – A Prison Writer's Diary*), lost him his job at Nairobi University and forced him into exile. Meja Mwangi sticks more to social issues and urban dislocation, but has a brilliant sense of humour that threads its way right through his books, including his latest, *The Mzungu Boy*.

Kenya's latest rising star is Binyavanga Wainaina, currently a writer for the South African *Sunday Times* newspaper, who won the Caine Prize for African Writing in July 2002. The award-winning short story *Discovering Home* is about a young Kenyan working in Cape Town who returns to his parents' village for a year.

Another interesting writer is Marjorie Oludhe Magoye, whose *The Present Moment* follows the life stories of a group of elderly women in a Christian refuge. For more writing by women in Africa try *Unwinding Threads*, a collection of short stories by many authors from all over the continent.

ENVIRONMENT
The Land

Kenya straddles the equator and covers an area of some 583,000 sq km, including around 13,600 sq km of Lake Victoria. It is bordered to the north by the arid bushlands of Ethiopia and Sudan, to the east by the Indian Ocean and the wastes of Somalia, to the west by Uganda and Lake Victoria, and to the south by Tanzania.

Kenya is dominated by the Rift Valley, a vast range of valleys that follows a 5000km-long crack in the earth's crust. Within the Rift are numerous 'swells' (raised escarpments) and 'troughs' (deep valleys, often containing lakes), and there are some huge volcanoes, including Mt Kenya, Mt Elgon and Mt Kilimanjaro (across the border in Tanzania).

The Rift Valley divides the flat plains of the coast from the hills along the lakeshore. Nairobi, the capital, sits in the Central Highlands, which are on the eastern edge of the Rift Valley. Kenya can roughly be divided into four zones: the coastal plains; the Rift Valley and Central Highlands; the lakeshore; and the wastelands of northern Kenya.

The main rivers in Kenya are the Athi/ Galana River, which empties into the Indian Ocean near Malindi, and the Tana River, which hits the coast midway between Malindi and Lamu. Aside from Lake Victoria, Kenya has numerous small volcanic lakes and mighty Lake Turkana, which straddles the Ethiopian border.

Within volcanic craters, and on the Rift Valley floor, are several soda lakes, rich in sodium bicarbonate, created by the filtering of water through mineral-rich volcanic rock and subsequent evaporation.

Wildlife
ANIMALS

There's such a dazzling array of animals in Kenya that viewing them in the national parks is one of the main reasons for visiting. The 'Big Five' – lion, buffalo, elephant, leopard and rhino – and a huge variety of other animals can be seen in at least two of the major parks. Some of the most interesting are described in the Wildlife Guide (p57), or in much more detail in Lonely Planet's *Watching Wildlife East Africa*.

The birdlife here is equally varied, and includes such interesting species as the ostrich, vulture and marabou stork. Around bodies of water you may see flamingos, cranes, storks and pelicans, while the forests are home to hornbills and rare species, such as the yellow weaver bird, sunbird and touraco. There are also dozens of other species of weaver bird, which make the distinctive baglike nests seen hanging from acacia trees.

Endangered Species

Many of Kenya's major predators and herbivores have become endangered because of the continuous destruction of their natural habitat and merciless poaching for ivory, skins, horn and bush meat.

The black rhino is probably Kenya's most endangered species, due to poaching for its horn. Faced with relentless poaching by heavily armed gangs in the 1980s, the wild rhino population plummeted from 20,000 in 1969 to just 458 today. **Rhino Ark** (☎ 020-604246; www.rhinoark.org) raises funds to create rhino sanctuaries in the parks, complete with electric fencing, and donations are always appreciated. There are currently sanctuaries in Tsavo and Lake Nakuru National Parks, while Aberdare National Park is in the process of being fenced.

While the elephant is not technically endangered, it is still the target of poachers, and a number are killed every year, especially in the area around Tsavo East. Current numbers are estimated at 28,000.

PLANTS

Kenya's flora is notably diverse because of the country's wide range of physiographic regions. The vast plains of the south are characterised by distinctive flat-topped acacia trees, interspersed with the equally recognisable baobab trees and savage whistling thorn bushes, which made early exploration of the continent such a tortuous process.

The savanna grassland of the Masai Mara supports a huge variety of animal life. The grass grows quickly after the rains, providing food for a huge range of herbivores and insects, which in turn feed a variety of predators. Trampling and grazing by herbivores promotes the growth of grasses, rather than broadleaf plants, which are more vulnerable to damage from grazing, drought and fire.

On the slopes of Mt Elgon and Mt Kenya the flora changes with altitude. Thick evergreen temperate forest grows between 1000m and 2000m, giving way to a belt of bamboo forest up to about 3000m. Above this height is mountain moorland, characterised by the amazing groundsel tree and giant lobelias. In the semidesert plains of the north and northeast the vegetation cover is thorny bush, which can seem to go on forever. In the northern coastal areas mangroves are prolific and there are still a few small pockets of coastal rainforest.

National Parks & Reserves

Around 10% of Kenya's land area is protected by law, and the national parks and reserves here rate among the best in Africa. Despite the ravages of human land exploitation and poaching, there is still an incredible variety of birds and mammals in the parks, and going on safari is an integral part of the Kenyan experience.

More popular parks, such as the Masai Mara National Reserve and Amboseli National Park, can become heavily overcrowded in the high season (January to February). Fortunately, the smaller and more remote parks, such as Saiwa Swamp National Park, see only a handful of visitors at any time of the year. A number of marine national parks have also been established, providing excellent diving and snorkelling.

Although all the parks provide the opportunity to get 'up close and personal' with wildlife, remember that these are wild animals and their actions can be unpredictable. Heed the warnings of guides and rangers while on safari, and seek local advice before venturing off alone into the wilds.

The most important national parks and reserves in Kenya are summarised on p76. Smaller parks include Mt Longonot National Park, a dormant volcano; Marsabit National Park, with large herbivores and dense forest; and Sibiloi and Central Island National Parks on Lake Turkana.

Entry fees to national parks are controlled by the KWS, while national reserves are administered by the relevant local council. See p276 for park categories and prices.

Environmental Issues
DEFORESTATION

More than half of Africa's forests have been destroyed over the last century, and forest destruction continues on a large scale in Kenya – less than 3% of the country's original forest cover remains. Land grabbing, illegal logging, charcoal burning and agricultural encroachment all take their toll. However, millions of Kenyans still rely on wood and charcoal for cooking fuel, so travellers will almost certainly contribute to this deforestation whether they like it or not.

The degazetting of protected forests is another contentious issue, sparking widespread protests and preservation campaigns. On the flip side, locals in forest areas can find themselves homeless if the government does enforce protection orders.

Despite these problems, some large areas of protected forest remain. The Mt Kenya, Mt Elgon and Aberdare National Parks, Kakamega Forest Reserve and Arabuko Sokoke Forest are all tremendous places to visit, packed with thousands of species of fauna and flora.

KENYA WILDLIFE SERVICE (KWS)

With a total ban on hunting imposed in 1977, the KWS was free to concentrate solely on conserving Kenya's wildlife. This came just in time, as the 1970s and '80s were marred by a shocking amount of poaching linked to the drought in Somalia, which drove hordes of poachers across the border into Kenya. A staggering number of Kenya's

KENYA

NATIONAL PARK FEES

Park entry fees in Kenya are slowly being converted to a 'smartcard' system. These cards must be charged with credit in advance and can only be topped up at certain locations; they remain the property of the Kenya Wildlife Service (KWS) and must be surrendered once they run out of credit. Any credit left once you finish your trip cannot be refunded.

At the time of research the smartcard system was in use at Nairobi, Lake Nakuru, Aberdare, Amboseli, Tsavo East and Tsavo West National Parks. Other parks still work on a cash system. You can purchase and charge smartcards at the KWS headquarters in Nairobi, at Aberdare headquarters, at Lake Nakuru main gate, at Voi gate in Tsavo East, and at the Malindi Marine National Park office.

Entry fees to the parks per person are as follows:

Parks (category)	Entry nonresident adult/child US$	Entry resident adult/child KSh	Camping nonresident adult/child US$	Camping resident adult/child US$
Aberdare, Amboseli, Lake Nakuru (A)	30/10	500/200	10/5	300/100
Meru, Tsavo East & West (B)	27/10	500/200	10/5	300/100
Nairobi, Shimba Hills (C)	23/10	500/200	10/5	300/100
all other parks (D)	15/5	500/200	8/5	200/100
marine parks	5/2	100/50	-	-

The land-based parks and reserves charge KSh200 for vehicles with fewer than six seats and KSh500 for vehicles seating six to 12. In addition to the public camping areas, special camp sites cost US$10 to US$15 per adult nonresident, plus a KSh5000 weekly reservation fee. Guides are available in most parks for KSh500 per day.

The Masai Mara, Samburu, Buffalo Springs and Shaba National Reserves have the same entry fees as category A national parks; entry to Mt Kenya National Park is US$15/8 per adult/child. Arabuko Sokoke and Kakamega Forest Reserves are joint KWS and Forestry Department projects and charge US$10/5 for an adult/child.

All fees cover visitors for a 24-hour period, but a recent change in regulations means that most parks will no longer allow you to leave and re-enter without paying twice.

rhinos and elephants were slaughtered, and many KWS officers worked in league with poachers until famous palaeontologist Dr Richard Leakey cleaned up the organisation in the 1980s and '90s. A core part of his policy was allowing KWS rangers to shoot poachers on sight, which seems to have dramatically reduced the problem.

However, there have been several new raids on elephants and rhinos since 2001. As a result, there is now open talk of abandoning some of the more remote parks and concentrating resources where they can achieve the best results and on the parks, that receive most visitors. At the same time community conservation projects are being encouraged, and many community-owned ranches are now being opened up as private

wildlife reserves, with the backing of the KWS and international donors.

PRIVATE CONSERVATION

It has been claimed that more than 75% of Kenya's wildlife lies outside the national parks and reserves, and an increasing number of important wildlife conservation areas now exist on private land. Lewa Wildlife Conservancy (p419), near Isiolo, is a prime example. Private wildlife reserves often have the resources to work intensively on specific conservation issues and it is no accident that some of the largest concentrations of rhinos are within these areas. Supporting these projects is a great way for visitors to contribute to Kenyan communities and assist wildlife preservation.

The **Laikipia Wildlife Forum** (☎ 062-31600; www .laikipia.org) is an umbrella organisation representing many lodges and conservation areas in Laikipia, the large slab of ranch land northwest of Mt Kenya. Ranches in this area are particularly active in wildlife conservation, and the forum is a good source of up-to-date information. Other private wildlife ranches and conservation areas can be found around Tsavo and Amboseli National Parks.

TOURISM

The tourist industry is the cause of serious environmental problems, most notably heavy use of firewood by tourist lodges and erosion caused by safari minibuses, which cut across and between trails and follow wildlife into the bush, creating virtual dustbowls in parks such as Amboseli, Samburu and Masai Mara.

The KWS now insists that every new lodge and camp must be designed in an ecofriendly manner. As a result, there are growing numbers of 'ecolodges' in Kenya, which keep their impact on the environment to a minimum through recycling, use of renewable energy resources, and strict controls on dumping of refuse and the types of fuel that are used.

As a visitor, the best way to help combat these problems is to be very selective about who you do business with. While you may end up paying more for an ecofriendly trip, in the long term you'll be investing in the preservation of Kenya's delicate environment.

FOOD & DRINK

The food in Kenya is essentially the same as you'll find in the rest of this region. *Nyama choma* is the one local speciality; this is technically barbecued meat, but bears little resemblance to any Western understanding of the term! You buy the meat (usually goat) by the kilogram, it's cooked over a charcoal pit and served in bite-sized pieces with a vegetable side dish. Sometimes it's surprisingly good, but often you'll require a large supply of toothpicks.

Despite the fact that Kenya grows some of the finest tea and coffee in the world, getting a decent cup of either can be difficult. *Chai* (tea) is drunk in large quantities, but the tea, milk and sugar are usually boiled together and stewed for ages, coming out milky and horrendously sweet. For tea

---

JIKO

One innovative idea to minimise firewood use is the *jiko* stove, based on a Thai design and modified to suit the Kenyan way of cooking. Easy and cheap to manufacture, the *jiko* consists of an hourglass-shaped metal casing and a ceramic insulator that delivers 25% to 40% of the heat from the fire to the pot, much more than open fires. After some uncertainty, Kenyans have embraced the *jiko* with enthusiasm and hundreds of open-air workshops now provide stoves for nearly a million households.

---

without milk ask for *chai kavu*. Coffee is also sweet and milky, with a bare minimum of instant granules. In Nairobi there are a handful of excellent coffee houses, and you can usually get a good filter coffee at any of the big hotels. With all the Italian tourists, you can get a decent cappuccino pretty much anywhere on the coast.

Soft drinks, such as Coke, Sprite and Fanta, are available everywhere under the generic term of sodas. The nation's favourite juice is passionfruit; pineapple, orange and mango juices also feature on most menus.

The local beers are Tusker, White Cap and Pilsner (all manufactured by Kenya Breweries), sold in 500ml bottles. Guinness is also available, but tastes nothing like the real thing – it's often drunk mixed with Coke! Castle (a South African beer) is also made under license by Kenya Breweries. Beers are cheapest from supermarkets (KSh45 for 500ml); bars charge KSh80 to KSh200. Other bottled drinks include Hardy's cider, Redd's and Kingfisher (fruity alcopops), and the ubiquitous Smirnoff Ice.

Kenya has a fledgling wine industry and the Lake Naivasha Colombard wines are said to be quite good, unlike local papaya wine, which tastes foul and smells worse. You can get cheap imported wine by the glass for around KSh150 in Nairobi restaurants. In the big supermarkets you'll pay anything from KSh500 to KSh1500 for a bottle of South African wine.

Although it is strictly illegal to brew or distil liquor, this still goes on. *Pombe* is the local beer, usually a fermented brew made with bananas or millet and sugar. It shouldn't do you any harm.

KENYA

NAIROBI

☎ 020 / pop 2.5 million

Who's afraid of big bad Nairobi? Well, quite a lot of people apparently – the city's reputation precedes it, so much so that most visitors arrive prepared to dive in and out in the shortest time possible. It's certainly true that Kenya's capital requires that bit more big-city common sense than most, and it's hard not to feel a little nervous once the streets empty after dark.

However, it's easy enough to sidestep the worst of the city's dangers, and there's absolutely no reason why a streetwise traveller can't survive and even enjoy a stay here. In terms of facilities, the city has more going for it than any other Kenyan conurbation: the cultural scene is thriving, the nightlife is unbridled and it's virtually the only place in the country where you can get a truly varied diet.

Even if the inner city does terrify you, it's easy to get out into the suburbs, where you can relax with the large local expat community, and make the most of even more top-rank amenities, award-winning restaurants and friendly bars.

HISTORY

As you might guess from all the tower blocks, Nairobi is a completely modern creation and almost everything here has been built in the last 100 years. Until the 1890s the whole area was just an isolated swamp, but as the rails of the East Africa railway fell into place, a depot was established on the edge of a small stream known to the Maasai as *uaso nairobi* (cold water). Nairobi quickly developed into the administrative nerve centre of the Uganda Railway, and in 1901 the capital of the British Protectorate was moved here from Mombasa.

Even when the first permanent buildings were constructed, Nairobi remained a real frontier town, with rhinos and lions freely roaming the streets, and lines of iron-roofed bungalows stretching across the plain. However, once the railway was up and running, wealth began to flow into the city. The colonial government built some grand hotels to accommodate the first tourists to Kenya – big game hunters, lured by the attraction of shooting the country's almost naively tame wildlife. Sadly almost all of the colonial-era buildings were replaced by bland modern office buildings following *uhuru* (independence) in 1963.

ORIENTATION

The compact city centre is in the area bounded by Uhuru Hwy, Haile Selassie Ave, Tom Mboya St and University Way. Kenyatta Ave divides this area in two; most of the important offices lie to the south, while there are hotels, the city market and more offices to the north. Most budget accommodation is northeast of the city centre, on the far side of Tom Mboya St and around Latema, Accra and River Rds. This area has a bad reputation for robbery.

North of the city centre are the University of Nairobi, the National Museum and the expat-dominated suburb of Westlands. Jomo Kenyatta International Airport is southeast of the central Nairobi; also south are Langata and Karen suburbs and Wilson airport.

Maps

For a rudimentary guide to the central area, a variety of free promotional maps are available. If you want more detailed coverage, the best option is the Survey of Kenya *City of Nairobi: Map & Guide*. Also adequate is the 1:15,000 *Map Guide of Nairobi City Centre* (KSh200) published by Interland Maps.

Much better, though bulkier, is *Nairobi AtoZ* (KSh510) by RW Moss, which covers the whole city in detail.

INFORMATION

Bookshops

Book Villa (Map pp282-3; ☎ 337890; Standard St) New, discounted and second-hand books.

Bookpoint (Map pp282-3; ☎ 211156; Moi Ave)

Bookstop (☎ 714547; Yaya Centre, Hurlingham)

Text Book Centre Kijabe St (Map pp280-1; ☎ 330340, Kijabe St); Westlands (Map p288; ☎ 3747405; Sarit Centre, Westlands) One of the best bookshops in East Africa.

Westland Sundries Bookshop Nairobi (Map pp282-3; ☎ 212776; New Stanley Hotel, Kenyatta Ave); Westlands (Map p288; ☎ 446406; Ring Rd Westlands, Westlands)

Cultural Centres

All the foreign cultural organisations have libraries open to the public.

Alliance Française (Map pp280-1; ☎ 340054; www .alliancefrnairobi.org; cnr Monrovia & Loita Sts; ☾ 8.30am-6.30pm Mon-Fri, 8.30am-5pm Sat) Has the best events program of all the cultural centres, showcasing Kenyan and African performing arts.

British Council (Map pp280-1; ☎ 334855; www .britishcouncil.org/kenya; Upper Hill Rd; ☾ 9.30am-5.30pm Mon-Fri, 9.30am-1pm Sat)

Goethe Institut (Map pp280-1; ☎ 224640; www .goethe.de/nairobi; Maendeleo House, cnr Monrovia & Loita Sts; ☾ 10am-12.30pm Thu-Tue, 2-5pm Mon-Fri)

Japan Information & Culture Centre (Map pp282-3; ☎ 340520; www.ke.emb-japan.go.jp; ICEA Bldg, Kenyatta Ave; ☾ 8.30am-5pm Mon-Fri) Free video shows and Japanese cinema screenings.

Nairobi Cultural Institute (Map pp280-1; ☎ 569205; Ngong Rd) Holds lectures and other functions of local cultural interest.

Emergency

AAR Health Services (Map pp280-1; ☎ 717376; Fourth Ngong Ave)

Aga Khan Hospital (Map pp280-1; ☎ 3662000; Third Parklands Ave)

Amref flying-doctor service (☎ 502699)

Emergency services (☎ 999) Fire, police and ambulance. Don't rely on their prompt arrival.

Police (☎ 240000) For less urgent police business.

Internet Access

There are literally hundreds of Internet cafés in central Nairobi, most of them tucked away in anonymous office buildings. Connection speed is usually pretty good.

AGX (Map pp280-1; Barclays Plaza, Loita St; per min KSh1; ☾ 8am-8pm Mon-Sat) Best connections in town.

Avant Garde e-centre (Map pp282-3; Fedha Towers, Kaunda St; per min KSh1.50; ☾ 7.30am-9pm Mon-Sat, 11am-6pm Sun) Enter via Standard St.

NAIROBI IN...

Two Days

While most people use Nairobi as a stopover, there's still plenty to do if you have a day or two to kill. Start at the **National Museum** (p284), then head to the city centre for **coffee** (p290), some **Chinese** (p289) and a **movie** (p291).

On the second day you can view the city from the **Kenyatta Conference Centre** (p285) and browse contemporary art at the **National Archives** (p285). In the evening **Carnivore** (p298) in Karen is a must, or you can dance dirty at **Simmers** (p291) and the infamous **New Florida** (p291).

Four Days

With another two days, you can also venture out towards the suburbs. Westlands has plenty of good eating spots between the shops at the **Sarit Centre** (p290) and Kenya's best Indian restaurant, **Haandi** (p289).

For your final 24 hours, breakfast at the **Pasara Café** (p289), do some **shopping** (p292), and finish at **Casablanca** (p291) for Moroccan food and drinks.

Capital Realtime (Map pp282-3; ☎ 247900; Lonhro House, Standard St; per min KSh2; ☾ 8.30am-7.30pm Mon-Fri, 10am-4pm Sat)

EasySurf (Map p288; ☎ 3745418; Sarit Centre, Westlands; per min KSh4; ☾ 9am-8pm Mon-Sat, 10am-2pm Sun)

Libraries

Kenya National Library (Map pp280-1; ☎ 2725550; www.knls.or.ke; Ngong Rd; ☾ 8am-6.30pm Mon-Thu, 8am-4pm Fri, 9am-5pm Sat) The main public library.

McMillan Memorial Library (Map pp282-3; ☎ 221844; Banda St; ☾ 9am-6pm Mon-Fri, 9.30am-4pm Sat) A smaller collection in a colonial-era building.

Medical Services

Avoid the Kenyatta National Hospital.

AAR Health Services Nairobi (Map pp280-1; ☎ 715319; Williamson House, Fourth Ngong Ave); Westlands (Map p288; ☎ 446201; Sarit Centre, Westlands)

Acacia Medical Centre (Map pp282-3; ☎ 212200; info@acaciamed.co.ke; ICEA Bldg, Kenyatta Ave; ☾ 7am-7pm Mon-Fri, 7am-2pm Sat)

Aga Khan Hospital (Map pp280-1; ☎ 740000; Third Parklands Ave; ☾ 24hr)

KENYA

NAIROBI

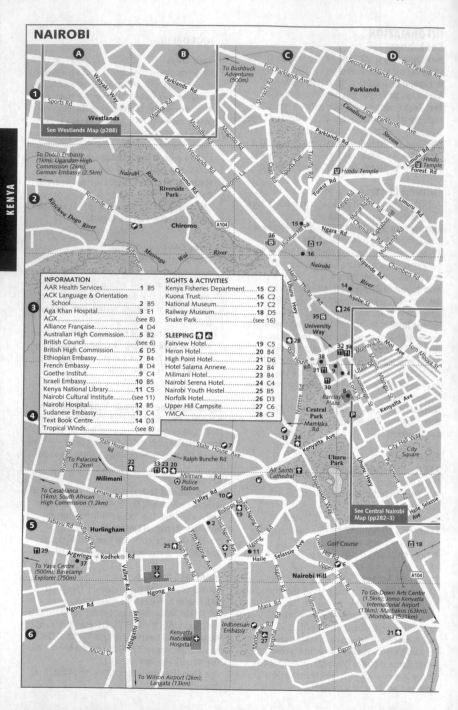

KENYA

INFORMATION
AAR Health Services.................**1** B5
ACK Language & Orientation
   School....................................**2** B5
Aga Khan Hospital.....................**3** E1
AGX...(see 8)
Alliance Française......................**4** D4
Australian High Commission.......**5** B2
British Council...........................(see 6)
British High Commission.............**6** D5
Ethiopian Embassy.....................**7** B4
French Embassy.........................**8** D4
Goethe Institut..........................**9** C4
Israeli Embassy........................**10** B5
Kenya National Library.............**11** C5
Nairobi Cultural Institute..........(see 11)
Nairobi Hospital......................**12** B5
Sudanese Embassy...................**13** C4
Text Book Centre.....................**14** D3
Tropical Winds.........................(see 8)

SIGHTS & ACTIVITIES
Kenya Fisheries Department.......**15** C2
Kuona Trust.............................**16** C2
National Museum......................**17** C2
Railway Museum......................**18** D5
Snake Park..............................(see 16)

SLEEPING
Fairview Hotel.........................**19** C5
Heron Hotel............................**20** B4
High Point Hotel......................**21** D6
Hotel Salama Annexe...............**22** B4
Milimani Hotel........................**23** B4
Nairobi Serena Hotel...............**24** C4
Nairobi Youth Hostel...............**25** B5
Norfolk Hotel..........................**26** D3
Upper Hill Campsite.................**27** C6
YMCA.....................................**28** C3

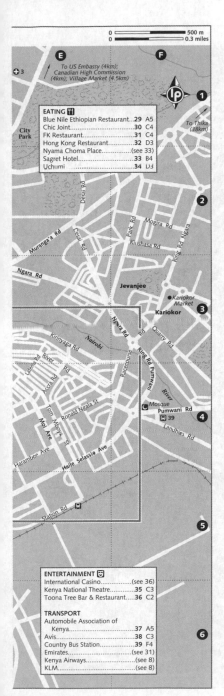

EATING 🍴
Blue Nile Ethiopian Restaurant...	29	A5
Chic Joint....................................	30	C4
FK Restaurant............................	31	C4
Hong Kong Restaurant..............	32	D3
Nyama Choma Place..................	(see 33)	
Sagret Hotel..............................	33	B4
Uchumi.....................................	34	D3

ENTERTAINMENT 🎭
International Casino..................	(see 36)	
Kenya National Theatre.............	35	C3
Toona Tree Bar & Restaurant.....	36	C2

TRANSPORT
Automobile Association of Kenya...................................	37	A5
Avis..	38	C3
Country Bus Station..................	39	F4
Emirates...................................	(see 31)	
Kenya Airways..........................	(see 8)	
KLM..	(see 8)	

KAM Pharmacy (Map pp282-3; ☎ 251700; Executive Tower, IPS Bldg, Kimathi St) Pharmacy, doctor's surgery and laboratory.

Medical Services Surgery (Map pp282-3; ☎ 317625; Bruce House, Standard St; ☼ 8.30am-4.30pm Mon-Fri)

Nairobi Hospital (Map pp280-1; ☎ 722160) Off Argwings Khodek Rd.

Money

In the centre of Nairobi, Barclays branches with guarded ATMs include those located on Muindi Mbingu St (Map pp282-3), Mama Ngina St (Map pp282-3), and on the corner of Kenyatta and Moi Aves (Map pp282-3). You will also find multiple branches in Westlands and Hurlingham. The other big bank in town is the Standard Chartered, which has numerous central branches.

Foreign-exchange bureaus offer slightly better rates for cash.

AmEx (Map pp282-3; ☎ 222906; Hilton Hotel, Mama Ngina St; ☼ 8.30am-4.30pm Mon-Fri) Handles travellers cheques and looks after mail for clients.

Cosmos Forex (Map pp282-3; ☎ 250582; Rehema House, Standard St)

Goldfield Forex (Map pp282-3; ☎ 244554; Fedha Towers, Kaunda St)

Mayfair Forex (Map pp282-3; ☎ 226212; Uganda House, Standard St)

Postbank (Map pp282-3; 13 Kenyatta Ave) For Western Union money transfers.

Travellers Forex Bureau (Map p288; ☎ 447204; The Mall, Westlands)

Post

The enormous **main post office** (Map pp282-3; ☎ 243434; Kenyatta Ave; ☼ 8am-6pm Mon-Fri, 9am-noon Sat) is a well-organised edifice close to Uhuru Park. There's a very basic poste-restante service in the same office as the parcel desk, where you'll need to bring your parcels so the contents can be examined. Bring a roll of parcel wrapping paper and parcel tape so you can seal the package once it's been inspected; you can buy these at **Seal Honey** (Map pp282-3; ☎ 216376; 27 Kenyatta Ave).

If you just want stamps, there are post offices on Moi Ave (Map pp282-3), Haile Selassie Ave (Map pp282-3) and Tom Mboya St (Map pp282-3). The Moi Ave office is a good place to send parcels; packing boxes are available to buy for KSh50 to KSh100.

KENYA

CENTRAL NAIROBI

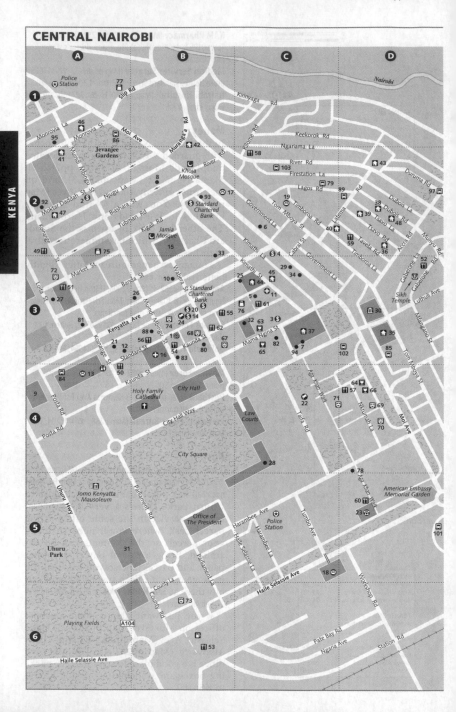

KENYA

EATING 🍴
Alan Bobbé's Bistro.................................49 A2
Beneve Coffee House.............................50 A4
Fiesta Restaurant & Bar..........................51 A3
Malindi Dishes......................................52 D3
Nyama Choma Stalls..............................53 B6
Panda Chinese Restaurant........................54 B3
Pasara Café...55 B3
Restaurant Akasaka................................56 B3
Seasons Restaurant................................57 D4
Supreme Restaurant...............................58 C2
Taj..59 D2
Tamarind Restaurant..............................60 D5
Tanager Bar & Restaurant........................61 C3
Thorn Tree Café.............................(see 44)
Trattoria...62 B3

DRINKING 🍷
Dormans Café.......................................63 C3
Green Corner Restaurant &
  Cactus Pub...64 D4
Kahawa..(see 54)
Nairobi Java House................................65 C3
Taco Bell...66 D4
Zanze Bar......................................(see 70)

ENTERTAINMENT 🎭
20th Century Cinema..............................67 B3
Club Soundd...68 B3
Florida 2000...69 D4
Kenya Cinema.......................................70 D4
Nairobi Cinema.....................................71 C4
New Florida..72 A3
Professional Centre................................73 B6
Simmers..74 B3

SHOPPING 🛍
City Market...75 A2
Gallery Watatu......................................76 C3
Maasai Market.......................................77 A1

TRANSPORT
Air India...78 D4
Airport Bus Departure Point............(see 102)
Akamba...79 C2
Akamba Booking Office...........................80 B3
Avenue Car Hire....................................81 A3
British Airways.......................................82 C3
Budget...83 B3
Bus & Matatu Stop (for
  Hurlingham & Milimani)......................84 A4
Bus Stop (for Langata, Karen &
  Airport)...85 D3
Bus Stop (for Westlands).........................86 A1
Buses to Kisii & Migori............................87 F3
Central Rent-a-car..................................88 B3
Coastline Safaris Office...........................89 D2
Crossland Services..................................90 F2
Easy Coach Office..................................91 E5
Ethiopian Airlines............................(see 16)
Gametrackers Ltd...................................92 A2
Glory Car Hire.......................................93 B2
Glory Car Hire.......................................94 C3
KBS Booking Office................................95 A1
KBS Bus Station.....................................96 F4
Main Bus & Matatu Area..........................97 D2
Matatus to Mtito Andei............................98 F3
Matatus to Naivasha &
  Namanga.....................................(see 99)
Matatus to Nyahururu & Nyeri...................99 F3
Matatus to Thika..................................100 F2
Matatus to Wilson Airport,
  Nairobi National Park,
  Langata & Karen..............................101 D5
Metro Shuttle Bus Stand........................102 D3
Scandinavia Express.............................103 C2

KAM Pharmacy.....................................11 C3
Let's Go Travel......................................12 A3
Main Post Office....................................13 A4
Mayfair Forex.......................................14 B3
McMillan Memorial Library.......................15 D2
Medical Services Surgery.........................16 B3
Post Office..17 B2
Post Office..18 C5
Post Office..19 C2
Postbank...20 B3
Seal Honey...21 A3
Spanish Embassy.............................(see 82)
Tanzanian High Commission....................22 C4
Telkom Kenya.......................................23 D5
Telkom Kenya.................................(see 13)
Ugandan High Commission
  (Consular Section)..............................24 B3
Westland Sundries Bookshop....................25 C3

SIGHTS & ACTIVITIES
Adventures Aloft............................(see 45)
Best Camping Tours................................26 B3
Eastern & Southern Safaris........................27 A3
Kenyatta Conference Centre......................28 C4
Mzizi Arts Centre...................................29 C3
National Archives...................................30 D3
Origins Safaris................................(see 54)
Parliament House...................................31 A5
Safari Seekers.......................................32 C3
Safaride Safaris.....................................33 B2
Sana Highlands Trekking
  Expeditions..34 C3

SLEEPING 🛏
Ambassadeur Hotel................................35 D3
Grand Holiday Hotel...............................36 D2
Hilton Hotel...37 C3
Hotel Africana......................................38 D2
Hotel Greton..39 D2
Iqbal Hotel...40 C2
Kenya Comfort Hotel..............................41 A2
Meridian Court Hotel..............................42 B1
New Kenya Lodge..................................43 D2
New Stanley Hotel..................................44 C3
Oakwood Hotel.....................................45 C3
Parkside Hotel.......................................46 A1
Terminal Hotel......................................47 A2
Wilton Gateway Hotel.............................48 D2

INFORMATION
Acacia Medical Centre.....................(see 10)
American Express.............................(see 37)
Avant Garde e-centre...............................1 B3
Barclays Bank..2 A2
Barclays Bank..3 C3
Barclays Bank..4 C2
Book Villa...5 C3
Bookpoint...6 C2
Bunson Travel..................................(see 55)
Capital Realtime...............................(see 55)
Cosmos Forex....................................(see 5)
Egypt Air..7 C3
Flight Centres..8 B2
Goldfield Forex.................................(see 54)
Immigration Office....................................9 A4
Italian Embassy................................(see 82)
Japan Information & Culture
  Centre...10 B3
Japanese Embassy............................(see 10)

Telephone

Public phones are common in Nairobi, but many just don't work.

Telkom Kenya (Map pp282-3; ☎ 232000; Haile Selassie Ave; ⏱ 8am-6pm Mon-Fri, 9am-noon Sat) Has dozens of payphones and you can buy phonecards. There's also a branch at the main post office.

Many stands in central Nairobi sell Telkom Kenya phonecards and top-up cards for pre-paid mobile phones. Alternatively, there are numerous private agencies in the city centre offering international telephone services. Typical charges are KSh150 to KSh200 per minute to almost anywhere in the world.

Tourist Information

Despite the many safari companies with signs saying 'Tourist Information', there is still no official tourist office in Nairobi. For events and other listings you'll have to check the local newspapers or glean what you can from a handful of magazines, which take a bit of effort to hunt down. *Go Places* (free) and the *Going Out Guide* (KSh150) are probably the most widespread, available from travel agents, airline offices and some hotels.

Travel Agencies

Bunson Travel (Map pp282-3; ☎ 221992; www.bunson kenya.com; Pan-African Insurance Bldg, Standard St) A good upmarket operator, with offices around Africa.

Flight Centres (Map pp282-3; ☎ 210024; Lakhamshi House, Biashara St) Discounted air tickets, camping safaris and overland trips.

Let's Go Travel (www.lets-go-travel.net) Central Nairobi (Map pp282-3; ☎ 340331; Caxton House, Standard St); Karen (Map p298; ☎ 882505; Karen shopping centre); Westlands ☎ 447151; ABC Place, Waiyaki Way, Westlands) Flights, safaris, car hire and pretty much anything else you might need. It publishes an excellent price list of accommodation in Kenya (also on its website), and acts as booking agent for many off-the-beaten-track options.

Tropical Winds (Map pp280-1; ☎ 341939; www .tropical-winds.com; Barclays Plaza, Loita St) Nairobi's STA Travel representative.

DANGERS & ANNOYANCES

Prospective visitors to Nairobi are usually understandably daunted by the city's un-enviable reputation – 'Nairobbery', as it is often called by residents, is commonly re-garded as the most dangerous city in Africa. Carjacking, robbery and violence are daily occurrences, and the underlying social ills behind them are unlikely to disappear in the near future.

However, the majority of problems happen in the slums, far from the main tourist zones. The central Nairobi area bound by Kenyatta Ave, Moi Ave, Haile Selassie Ave and Uhuru Hwy is comparatively trouble-free as long as you use a bit of common sense, and there are plenty of *askaris* (security guards) around at night. Stay alert and you should encounter nothing worse than a few persistent safari touts and the odd wannabe con artist.

Even around the city centre, though, there are places to watch out for: danger zones include the area around Latema and River Rds, a hotspot for petty theft, and Uhuru Park, which tends to attract all kinds of dodgy characters.

Once the shops have shut, the streets empty rapidly and the whole city takes on a slightly sinister air – mugging is a risk any-where after dark. Take a taxi, even if you're only going a few blocks. This will also keep you safe from the attentions of Nairobi's street prostitutes, who flood into town in force after sunset.

SIGHTS
National Museum

A grand alternative to the dozens of poky little local museums around the country, Kenya's **National Museum** (Map pp280-1; ☎ 742131; www.museums.or.ke; Museum Rd; adult/child KSh200/100; ⏱ 9.30am-6pm) is housed in an imposing building amid lush leafy grounds just out-side the city centre, and has a good range of cultural, geological and natural-history ex-hibits. Volunteer guides offer tours in Eng-lish, Dutch and French; it's worth booking them in advance. There's no charge for their services, but a donation is appropriate.

The 1st floor also contains the excellent **Gallery of Contemporary East African Art**, where local artists exhibit their work; as all the items are for sale the displays change regu-larly, and it's always an interesting cross sec-tion of the contemporary scene. For a look at the artists in action, the **Kuona Trust** (Map pp280–1), a nonprofit art studio where Ken-yan artists can gather and express them-selves, is just by the museum.

In the grounds, there's a recreated **Kikuyu homestead** and a **snake park** (adult/child KSh200/100; ⏱ 9.30am-6pm).

SCAMS

Nairobi's active handful of confidence tricksters seem to have relied on the same old stories for years. The usual tactic is to accost you in the street and strike up a conversation about current affairs in your country.

One local speciality is the Sudanese refugee scam, where your interlocutor has supposedly just won a scholarship to a university in your country and would love to have a chat with you about life there. Then at some point you'll get the confidential lowering of the voice and the Sudanese portion of the story kicks in with 'You know, I am not from here…', leading into an epic tale of woe.

Of course once you've shown due sympathy they'll come to the crux of the matter: all they need is KSh1700 to 'get to Dar es Salaam'. Giving money or anything else is likely to result in you being 'arrested' by fake policemen and forced to pay an exorbitant fine. In some cases these accomplices get so into their role that they beat up the original conman for the sake of authenticity!

As with all these type of scams, the best way of avoiding real trouble is to decline any offers or invitations made on the street. After a day or two in Nairobi you'll quickly learn to spot a budding 'refugee'.

National Archives

Right in the bustling heart of Nairobi is the distinctive **National Archives** (Map pp282-3; ☎ 749341; Moi Ave; admission free; ☒ 8.30am-5pm Mon-Fri, 8.30am-1pm Sat), an enormous collection of documents and reference material housed in the impressive former Bank of India building. The ground-floor atrium and gallery display an eclectic selection of contemporary art, historical photos of Nairobi, cultural artefacts, furniture and tribal objects, giving casual visitors a somewhat scatter-gun glimpse of East African heritage.

Railway Museum

You don't have to don an anorak to appreciate this interesting little **museum** (Map pp280-1; Station Rd; adult/child/student KSh200/20/100; ☒ 8.15am-4.45pm), which displays relics from the East African Railway. There are train and ship models, photographs, tableware and oddities from the history of the railway, such as the Engine Seat that allowed visiting dignitaries like Theodore Roosevelt to take pot shots at unsuspecting wildlife from the front of the train. In the grounds are dozens of fading locomotives in various states of disrepair, dating from the steam days to independence, including the steam train used in the movie *Out of Africa*.

The museum is reached by a long lane beside the train station, or you can cut across the vacant land next to the Shell petrol station on Haile Selassie Ave.

Parliament House

If you fancy a look at how democracy works in Kenya, it's possible to obtain a permit for a seat in the public gallery at **parliament house** (Map pp282-3; ☎ 221291; Parliament Rd) – just remember, applause is strictly forbidden! If parliament is out of session, you can tour the buildings by arrangement with the sergeant at arms.

Kenyatta Conference Centre

Towering over City Sq, Kenyatta Conference Centre (Map pp282-3), Nairobi's signature building, was designed as a fusion of modern and traditional African styles, though the distinctive saucer tower looks a little dated now. Staff will accompany you up to the rooftop **viewing platform** (adult/child KSh400/200) for wonderful views over Nairobi. The sight line goes all the way to the suburbs, and on clear days you can see aircraft coming in to land over the Nairobi National Park. You can take photographs from the viewing level but not elsewhere. Access may be restricted during events and conferences.

Arts Centres

The **Go-Down Arts Centre** (☎ 5552227; Dunga Rd), a converted warehouse in the Industrial Area in Nairobi's southeast, contains 10 separate art studios and is rapidly becoming a hub for Nairobi's burgeoning arts scene.

The **Mzizi Arts Centre** (Map pp282-3; ☎ 574372; Sonalux House, Moi Ave) is a good place to view

KENYA

contemporary Kenyan art, craft, dance, literature and performance art.

FESTIVALS & EVENTS

Kenya Fashion Week (☎ 0733-636300; Sarit Centre, Westlands) An expo-style fashion event held in June.

Tusker Safari Sevens (www.safarisevens.com; Impala Club, Ngong Rd, Karen) A high-profile international seven-a-side rugby tournament held every June. The Kenyan team has a strong record.

Kenya Music Festival (☎ 2712964; Kenyatta Conference Centre) Held over 10 days in August, the country's longest-running music festival was established almost 80 years ago by the colonial regime. African music now predominates, but Western musicians still take part.

SLEEPING
City Centre
BUDGET

Iqbal Hotel (Map pp282-3; ☎ 220914; Latema Rd; dm/s/d/tr KSh300/400/600/960) The Iqbal has been popular for years, and is still possibly the best place in the area to meet fellow budget-conscious travellers. It's secure and the *askari* can arrange taxis at reasonable prices.

New Kenya Lodge (Map pp282-3; ☎ 222202; www .nksafaris.com; River Rd; dm KSh300, r with shared bathroom KSh350, with private bathroom KSh650) A long-standing travellers' haunt, the New Kenya Lodge's staff are very friendly and there's a sociable lounge area. Hot water may be available in the evenings. The lodge also runs its own safaris, although we've had mixed reports.

THE AUTHOR'S CHOICE

Terminal Hotel (Map pp282-3; ☎ 228817; Moktar Daddah St; s/d/tr KSh1200/1500/1800) Sure, there are plenty of bigger, flashier and fancier places to stay in Nairobi, but for our money the Terminal is still one of the only hotels in town where the price actually feels right. The emphasis here is on doing the basics well, and it's an approach that works: staff are relaxed, tolerant and thoroughly amenable, the location's great, the water's hot, the beds are comfortable and most rooms are a decent size. There are a few downsides, but you could pay over twice as much even in Milimani for shoddier accommodation and impersonal service. For a reliable haven in fast-paced Nairobi you can't go wrong here.

Hotel Africana (Map pp282-3; ☎ 220654; Dubois Rd; s/d/tw/tr incl breakfast KSh600/800/1000/1500) The Africana has clean, bright rooms and is better looked after than many places in its class. The plain Coffee House restaurant specialises in Indian vegetarian food.

Wilton Gateway Hotel (Map pp282-3; ☎ 341664; Dubois Rd; s/d KSh600/900) A decent, comfortable hotel popular with Kenyan salesmen. The Gateway Pub below sells beer at 1990s prices, which explains the slight evening noise factor!

YMCA (Map pp280-1; ☎ 2724116; ymca@iconnect .co.ke; State House Rd; s/d with shared bathroom KSh690/1180, with private bathroom KSh940/1480) It might not convince the Village People, but this is an OK place with a range of passable rooms. Rates include the daily membership fee.

MIDRANGE

Kenya Comfort Hotel (Map pp282-3; ☎ 317606; www .kenyacomfort.com; cnr Muindi Mbingu & Monrovia Sts; s US$26-36, d US$32-42, tr US$42-45, q US52-55) An excellent addition to Nairobi's sleeping scene, this cheerily painted place is kept in top nick, offering a fine selection of modern tiled rooms. Breakfast in the popular 24-hour bar-restaurant costs an extra US$5 (US$4 if booked in advance).

Meridian Court Hotel (Map pp282-3; ☎ 313991; meridian@bidii.com; Muranga'a Rd; s/d/tr KSh2950/3650/4200; 🖥 🖳) The elaborate lobby is rather more prepossessing than the grey concrete blocks above it, but it's hardly worth complaining when you're essentially getting a suite for the price of a standard room. There's no great luxury involved but the facilities make it good value.

Parkside Hotel (Map ppp282-3; ☎ 333568; parkside@ insightkenya.com; Monrovia St; s/d/tr KSh1300/1700/2200) Just opposite Jevanjee Gardens, Parkside is modest but decent enough value. Breakfast in the rather nice downstairs restaurant will set you back KSh300 per person.

Ambassadeur Hotel (Map pp282-3; ☎ 246615; Tom Mboya St; s/d/tr US$35/45/65) Believe it or not this big hotel opposite the National Archives once belonged to the posh Sarova chain, and structurally not much has changed, though we suspect room standards were rather more exacting in those days. Breakfast costs US$10 per room.

Hotel Greton (Map pp282-3; ☎ 242891; greton@ wananchi.com; Tsavo Rd; s/d/tr incl breakfast KSh950/1200/1700) A big block hotel in the heart of the budget district, with a great balcony restaurant overlooking the street. Rooms are spacious and comfortable, there's a salon and gym, and the whole effect is more inviting than most of the cheap dives nearby.

Grand Holiday Hotel (Map pp282-3; ☎ 221244; grandholidaykenya@yahoo.com; Tsavo Rd; s & d KSh1050, tr/ste KSh2000/2200) White faces seem to be a bit of a novelty here, but Kenyan businessmen have latched onto it as a good deal, particularly the suites.

Oakwood Hotel (Map pp282-3; ☎ 218321; www .madahotels.com/oakwood.html; Kimathi St; s/d/tr US$60/75/85) It's questionable how it justifies these prices, but this very central hotel does at least offer a bit of character. The same chain runs several properties around Kenya and Uganda.

TOP END

Nairobi Serena Hotel (Map pp280-1; ☎ 2822000; nairobi@serena.co.ke; Central Park, Procession Way; s/d US$308/376, ste US$418-736; ☒ ☐) Consolidating its reputation as one of the best topflight chains in East Africa, this entry in the Serena canon displays a fine sense of individuality. Given the choice, opt for one of the amazing garden suites.

New Stanley Hotel (Map pp280-1; ☎ 316377; www .sarovahotels.com; cnr Kimathi St & Kenyatta Ave; s/d from US$225/250; ☒ ☐ ☒) A Nairobi classic: the original Stanley Hotel was established in 1902, but the current site has only been in use since 1912 and the latest version is a very smart modern construction, run by Sarova Hotels. Colonial décor still prevails inside, though, with lashings of green leather, chandeliers and old-fashioned fans. The various house eateries are all well regarded.

Norfolk Hotel (Map pp280-1; ☎ 216940; www .lonrhohotels.com; Harry Thuku Rd; s/d US$281/337, ste US$361-557; ☒ ☐ ☒) Built in 1904, Nairobi's oldest hotel was *the* place to stay during colonial days, and still attracts plenty of guests who at least look like old-school settlers. The stylish Ibis Grill Restaurant (mains KSh1300 to KSh3500) is one of the best in Kenya.

Hilton Hotel (Map pp282-3; ☎ 250000; rm.nairobi@ hilton.com; Mama Ngina St; s/d from US$179/209; ☒ ☒ ☐ ☒) The Hilton dominates the city centre with its distinctive round tower, occupying virtually an entire block with its rooms, restaurants, shops and other facilities. Prices are exclusive of 26% tax and service charge.

Milimani & Nairobi Hill

BUDGET

Upper Hill Campsite (Map pp280-1; ☎ 2720290; www .upperhillcampsite.com; Menengai Rd, Nairobi Hill; camping KSh300, tents KSh450-1000, dm/r KSh400/1000; ☐) Off Hospital Rd near the Indonesian embassy, Upper Hill offers a range of accommodation in a pleasant and secure compound, plus a well-used little restaurant and bar. Facilities include hot showers and a cosy fireplace. There's a vehicle-maintenance bay and the owners can help you find a mechanic. It's a 15-minute walk from the city centre, or you can take bus or *matatu* 18 from Kenyatta Ave to the Kenyatta National Hospital, which is just around the corner.

Nairobi Youth Hostel (Map pp280-1; ☎ 2723012; kyha@africaonline.co.ke; Ralph Bunche Rd, Milimani; dm KSh600-700, d with shared bathroom KSh800, apt KSh2000; ☐) A well looked-after budget option, Nairobi's Hostelling International (HI) branch is still usually a good place to meet other travellers. A year's HI membership costs KSh400, or you can pay a KSh100 surcharge per day. Any *matatu* or bus going down either Valley or Ngong Rds will drop you off. Many people have been robbed returning to the youth hostel by foot after dark; always take a *matatu* or taxi at night.

MIDRANGE & TOP END

Heron Hotel (Map pp280-1; ☎ 2720740; www.heron hotel.com; Milimani Rd, Milimani; s/d/tr KSh3295/4490/5780; ☐ ☒) Management here is *very* keen to shake the reputation gleaned when the house bar was the most notorious whorehouse in Nairobi. Today it's a model of respectability, and the kitchenette doubles are a bargain.

High Point Hotel (Map pp280-1; ☎ 2724312; www.highpointcourt.com; Lower Hill Rd, Nairobi Hill; ste KSh4000-5000, apt KSh4000-7000; ☐ ☒) If you're looking for space and seclusion, this World Bank–affiliated suite and apartment complex is an excellent choice. The split-level rooms come with kitchenette and living room.

Palacina (☎ 2715517; www.palacina.com; Kitale Lane, Milimani; ste per person US$190, penthouses US$490; ☐ ☒) Possibly the first genuine boutique hotel in Kenya, this fabulous collection of impossibly stylish suites must be one of the country's top addresses for well-heeled sophisticates.

Fairview Hotel (Map pp280-1; ☎ 2711321; www .fairviewkenya.com; Bishops Rd, Milimani; s/d from KSh5900/8200; ☒ ☐ ☒ ☺) A good top-end

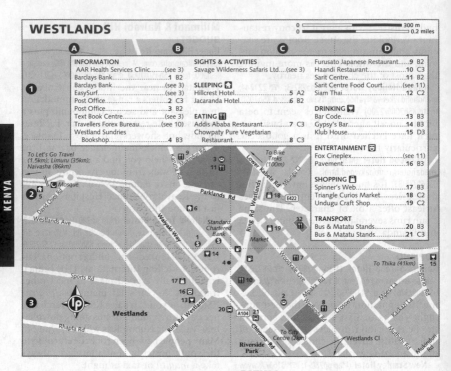

WESTLANDS

INFORMATION	
AAR Health Services Clinic........(see 3)	
Barclays Bank.....................................1 B2	
Barclays Bank.............................(see 3)	
EasySurf.....................................(see 3)	
Post Office.......................................2 C3	
Post Office.......................................3 B2	
Text Book Centre.......................(see 3)	
Travellers Forex Bureau............(see 10)	
Westland Sundries	
Bookshop..................................4 B3	

SIGHTS & ACTIVITIES
Savage Wilderness Safaris Ltd....(see 3)

SLEEPING
Hillcrest Hotel................................5 A2
Jacaranda Hotel..............................6 B2

EATING
Addis Ababa Restaurant..................7 C3
Chowpaty Pure Vegetarian
  Restaurant...................................8 C3

Furusato Japanese Restaurant......9 B2
Haandi Restaurant........................10 C3
Sarit Centre.................................11 B2
Sarit Centre Food Court...........(see 11)
Siam Thai....................................12 C2

DRINKING
Bar Code.....................................13 B3
Gypsy's Bar.................................14 B3
Klub House..................................15 D3

ENTERTAINMENT
Fox Cineplex...........................(see 11)
Pavement....................................16 B3

SHOPPING
Spinner's Web.............................17 B3
Triangle Curios Market...............18 C2
Undugu Craft Shop.....................19 C2

TRANSPORT
Bus & Matatu Stands..................20 B3
Bus & Matatu Stands..................21 C3

choice nicely removed from the central hubbub. It's near the scarily well-guarded Israeli Embassy.

Hotel Salama Annexe (Map pp280-1; ☎ 2729272; Milimani Rd, Milimani; s KSh1500, d KSh2500-3000) The Salama Annexe has a budget feel to it, even in the generously furnished 'deluxe' rooms, and it may be possible to camp here. Rates include breakfast in the popular but shabby *nyama choma* bar-restaurant.

Westlands

Hillcrest Hotel (Map p288; ☎ 4444883; hillcrest@ africaonline.co.ke; Waiyaki Way; s/d KSh1300/1700) The only mid-priced option this side of Museum Hill Rd, a short walk from the Sarit Centre. There's plenty of space, and the general atmosphere is pleasant and relaxed.

Jacaranda Hotel (Map p288; ☎ 4448713; jacaranda hotel@africaonline.co.ke; Westland Rd; s/d US$120/150; 🖥 🐾) Westlands' other convenient accommodation option is a smart former Block Hotels property, slightly worn around the edges but generally offering good standards. There are restaurants on site, and free shuttle buses run to the city three times daily.

EATING

Nairobi is well stocked with places to eat, particularly in the city centre, where you can choose anything from the cheap workers' canteens around River Rd to Chinese feasts and full-on splurges off Kenyatta Ave. For dinner it's also worth heading out to the suburbs, which offer dozens of choices of cuisine from all over the world; Westlands has the best range, and there are some good choices in Hurlingham. The posher places listed here accept credit cards, and most add 17% value added tax (VAT) to the bill.

There are Nakumatt and Uchumi supermarkets all over town, and all the big shopping centres have extensive food courts.

Kenyan & Swahili

Like the rest of the country, lunch is the main meal of the day, and city workers flock to the dozens of cheap canteens dishing up simple, classic dishes.

Chic Joint (Map pp280-1; ☎ 337119; Utalii House, Utalii St; mains KSh150-250) One of our favourite new bar-restaurant discoveries, chic might not be the first word that springs to mind, but grills, stews and *nyama* by the kilo should never go out of fashion.

Malindi Dishes (Map pp282-3; Gaberone Rd; mains KSh80-200) As the name suggests, this place serves great food from the coast. You'll get a grand feed, but it's a Muslim place, so it's closed for prayer at lunchtime on Friday.

FK Restaurant (Map pp280-1; ☎ 223448; Hazina Towers, Monrovia St; mains KSh120-200) This immaculate daytime cafétaria at the rear of an office block makes an appealing alternative to the surrounding grubbier canteens.

Beneve Coffee House (Map pp282-3; ☎ 217959; cnr Standard & Koinange Sts; dishes KSh20-140; ◷ Mon-Fri) A small self-service chop shop that has locals queuing outside in the mornings waiting for it to open.

Seasons Restaurant (Map pp282-3; ☎ 227697; Nairobi Cinema, Uchumi House, Aga Khan Walk; mains KSh240-280, buffets KSh280) Whatever the season, the cafeteria vats here always brim with cheap Kenyan and Western favourites.

NYAMA CHOMA

Kenyans tend to give short shrift to vegetarianism – *nyama choma* (p277) is the national dish and just about every pub-restaurant in town will throw a goat leg on the coals for you any time of day. For a more exotic take on things there are some amazing restaurants where you can sample game meats; the most famous is Carnivore in Langata (p298).

Nyama Choma Place (Map pp280-1; ☎ 2720933; Sagret Hotel, Milimani Rd; meals KSh400-600) This restaurant is highly rated by Kenyans. It's best to come in a group, as meat is sold in the form of whole goat legs or complete racks of ribs.

Nyama choma stalls (Map pp282-3; Haile Selassie Ave) A definite step down the scale, but worth it for the atmosphere, are the backstreet stalls near the Railway Museum, behind the Shell petrol station.

Indian

Haandi (Map p288; ☎ 4448294; The Mall Shopping Centre, Ring Rd Westlands, Westlands; mains KSh600-995; ◷ noon-2.30pm & 7-10.30pm; ❈) An international award-winner widely regarded as the best Indian restaurant in Kenya. The menu reads like a recipe book crossed with a guide to *mughlai* (North Indian) cuisine.

Chowpaty Pure Vegetarian Restaurant (Map p288; ☎ 3755050; Shimmers Plaza, Westlands Rd, Westlands; mains KSh200-350; ◷ 11am-11pm) A great place with lots

of South Indian dishes, such as *dhosa* (lentil pancakes stuffed with vegetable curry).

Supreme Restaurant (Map pp282-3; ☎ 331586; River Rd; meals KSh170-250) Near the junction with Tom Mboya St, this place offers excellent Punjabi vegetarian *thalis* (plate meals) and superb fruit juices.

Taj (Map pp282-3; Taveta Rd; dishes KSh20-100) Basic, ultracheap Indian soul food.

Ethiopian

Blue Nile Ethiopian Restaurant (Map pp280-1; ☎ 0722-898138; bluenile@yahoo.com; Argwings Kodhek Rd, Hurlingham; mains KSh300-450) Blue Nile's quirky painted lounge couldn't be mistaken for anywhere else. For the full communal African eating experience, order the seven-person *doro wat* (spicy traditional chicken stew, KSh3500).

Addis Ababa Restaurant (Map p288; ☎ 4447321; Woodvale Grove, Westlands; mains KSh400-500; ◷ noon-3pm Mon-Sat & from 6pm daily) Up some stairs in an unremarkable block, you'll find good authentic food and occasional live music here.

Chinese & Thai

Nairobi's Oriental restaurants offer 'large' (good for two people) and 'small' portions (enough for one), but add 16% VAT to the bill, so prices can soon mount up.

Panda Chinese Restaurant (Map pp282-3; ☎ 213018; Fedha Towers, Kaunda St; mains KSh380-1480; ◷ noon-2.30pm & 6-10pm) A spacious, very classy Asian restaurant hidden away on Kaunda St. The food is the best Chinese chow we found in Nairobi.

KENYA

Hong Kong Restaurant (Map pp280-1; ☎ 228612; rhk@wananchi.com; College House, Koinange St; mains KSh300-600; ☉ noon-2.30pm & 6-10pm) A bright-red restaurant with good food and not *too* much clichéd décor. It's the cheapest proper Chinese in town.

Tanager Bar & Restaurant (Map pp282-3; ☎ 221615; Rehema House, Kaunda St; mains KSh280-350; ☉ 11am-11pm Mon-Sat) A cheap and simple Chinese-African eatery right in the city centre.

Siam Thai (Map p288; ☎ 3751728; Unga House, Muthithi Rd, Westlands; mains KSh250-680) This attractive restaurant has an extensive menu of actual Thai food (gasp!).

Japanese

Restaurant Akasaka (Map pp282-3; ☎ 220299; Standard St; mains KSh450-800; ☉ noon-2.30pm & 6-10pm Mon-Sat) A wonderful restaurant next to the Sixeighty Hotel. It's always a little quiet, but this fits with the Japanese décor and the food is very authentic.

Furusato Japanese Restaurant (Map p288; ☎ 4442508; Karuna Rd, Westlands; set meals KSh700-1500) Behind the Sarit Centre, this is a very stylish place with seductive set Japanese meals, including sushi, *teppanyaki* and *tempura*. Reservations are recommended.

International

Fiesta Restaurant & Bar (Map pp282-3; ☎ 240326; Koinange St; mains KSh450-1800; ☉ 7am-midnight) Despite the Latin resonances, Fiesta concentrates on upmarket international dishes, such as *nasi goreng* and pork chops with a honey and mustard glaze. The popular bar area occasionally hosts low-key live crooners.

Alan Bobbé's Bistro (Map pp282-3; ☎ 226027; Cianda House, Koinange St; mains KSh987-1850) The talented M Bobbé established this superb French bistro in 1962, and Nairobi gourmets have been worshipping at his culinary altar ever since. Reservations and smart dress are encouraged, cigars and pipes are not.

Thorn Tree Café (Map pp282-3; ☎ 228030; New Stanley Hotel, Kimathi St; mains KSh350-1380) The Stanley's legendary café still serves as a popular meeting place for travellers of all persuasions, and caters to most tastes with a good mix of food.

Tamarind Restaurant (Map pp282-3; ☎ 251811; Aga Khan Walk; mains KSh900-1800; ☉ 2.30-4.30pm & 8.30pm-midnight) Nairobi's best seafood restaurant, laid out in a sumptuous modern Arabic-Moorish style. Smart dress is expected, and

you'll need to budget at least KSh2500 for the full works.

Trattoria (Map pp282-3; ☎ 340855; cnr Wabera & Kaunda Sts; mains KSh400-1800; ☉ 7.30am-midnight) A very popular central Italian swathed in trellises and plants, offering excellent pizza, pasta dishes, varied mains and a stack of desserts.

Quick Eats

Sarit Centre (Map p288; ☎ 3747408; www.saritcentre .com; Parklands Rd, Westlands) This huge food court on the 2nd floor has a variety of small restaurants and fast-food places, including Indian, Chinese, Italian and African food. The Hidden Agenda pub-restaurant (mains KSh360 to KSh800) comes recommended, with Western and Thai menus.

DRINKING
Cafés

Western café culture has hit Nairobi big time, seized on enthusiastically by local expats and residents pining for a decent cup of Kenyan coffee.

Nairobi Java House (Map pp282-3; ☎ 313565; www .nairobijava.com; Mama Ngina St; snacks KSh80-180; ☉ 7am-8.30pm Mon-Sat) This fantastic coffee house is rapidly turning itself into a major brand, and afficionados say the coffee's some of the best in Kenya.

Kahawa (Map pp282-3; ☎ 221900; zulmawani@ ispnbi.com; Fedha Towers, Kaunda St; mains KSh190-410) The dhow-themed Kahawa offers an ever-changing cavalcade of unexpected specials, from frittata to a 'Mexican breakfast'.

Dormans Café (Map pp282-3; ☎ 0724-238976; Mama Ngina St; coffee KSh100-190) This venerable firm only recently branched out into the café business, opening an outlet right opposite its main rival Nairobi Java House.

Bars

The cheap but rough bars around Latema and River Rds aren't recommended for female travellers, and even male drinkers should watch themselves. There are some friendlier watering holes around Tom Mboya St and Moi Ave, and many restaurants and hotels are fine places for a drink. You can also head to Westlands, where the drinking scene attracts in a lot more expats.

Even in cosmopolitan Nairobi, foreign women without a man in tow will draw attention virtually everywhere. To avoid this, head for the outer suburbs (see p298).

Casablanca (☎ 2723173; Lenana Rd, Hurlingham; ⊙ from 6pm) This hip new Moroccan-style lounge bar has been an instant hit with Nairobi's fastidious expat community, and you don't have to spend much time here to become a convert.

Zanze Bar (Map pp282-3; ☎ 222532; Kenya Cinema Plaza, Moi Ave) A lively and friendly top-floor bar with pool tables, a dance floor, cheap beer and reasonable food. During the week things are relatively quiet, but from Friday to Sunday it rocks until the early hours.

Gypsy's Bar (Map p288; ☎ 4440836; Woodvale Grove, Westlands) This long-running bar is made up of several parts, none of which are called Gypsy's! Identity crisis aside, it's probably the most popular bar in Westlands, pulling in Kenyans, expats and prostitutes. It's as close as you'll get to a gay-friendly venue in Kenya.

Taco Bell (Map pp282-3; Tumaini House, 15 Moi Ave) With an open balcony overlooking the street, this popular bar has DJs from Thursday to Sunday. We suspect the Taco Bell Corporation doesn't know they've borrowed the name…

Green Corner Restaurant & Cactus Pub (Map pp282-3; ☎ 335243; Tumaini House, Nkrumah Lane) This very popular after-work bar and restaurant has live bands on Thursday and Sunday and DJs the rest of the week.

Bar Code (Map p288; Westview Centre, Ring Rd Westlands, Westlands) It's nowhere near as cool as it thinks it is, but this very modern late-opening lounge bar does at least have a good range of drinks and semicompetent DJs.

Klub House (Map p288; ☎ 749870; Parklands Rd, Westlands) Further east, past the large Holiday Inn complex, the Klub House is an old favourite, with lots of pool tables.

ENTERTAINMENT

For information on all entertainment in Nairobi and for big music venues in the rest of the country, get hold of the *Saturday Nation*, which lists everything from cinema releases to live-music venues. There will also be plenty of suggestions run by the magazine *Going Out*.

Nightclubs

There's a good selection of dance clubs in the centre of Nairobi and there are no dress codes, although there's an unspoken assumption that males will at least wear a shirt and long trousers. Due to the high numbers of female prostitutes, men will generally get the bulk of the hassle in all these places, though even women in male company are by no means exempt.

Pavement (Map p288; ☎ 4441711; Waiyaki Way, Westlands; admission KSh500) Split between a relaxed ground-level bar and the big, modern basement club, Pavement is the dancefloor of choice for most resident expats. Weekends favour the kind of jump-up commercial dance music you might get on a night out in Europe.

Simmers (Map pp282-3; ☎ 217659; cnr Kenyatta Ave & Muindi Mbingu St; admission free) If you're tired of having your butt pinched in darkened discos, Simmers is the place to come to rediscover a bit of true African rhythm. The atmosphere at this open-air bar-restaurant is almost invariably amazing, with bands playing anything from Congolese rumba to Kenyan *benga*.

New Florida (Map pp282-3; ☎ 215014; Koinange St; men/women KSh200/100; ⊙ to 6am, later Sat & Sun) The 'Mad House' is a big, rowdy club housed in a bizarre blacked-out saucer building above a petrol station. Whichever night you choose, it's usually mayhem, crammed with bruisers, cruisers, hookers, hustlers and curious tourists. Entry is usually free before 9pm.

Florida 2000 (Map pp282-3; ☎ 229036; Moi Ave; men/women KSh200/100) The original blueprint for the New Florida, this big dancing den works to exactly the same formula.

Club Soundd (Map pp282-3; Kaunda St; admission free-KSh200; ⊙ from 3pm) Another central nightspot with a bit more to offer those who take their music seriously.

Toona Tree Bar & Restaurant (Map pp280-1; ☎ 3740802; toonatree@africaonline.co.ke; International Casino, Museum Hill Rd) Part of the massive International Casino complex, Toona Tree has live bands on Friday and Saturday, playing jazz, blues and 'classic hits'.

Cinemas

Nairobi is a good place to take in a few films at a substantially lower price than back home. The best deals are available on Tuesday.

Nu Metro Cinema (☎ 522128; numetro@swiftkenya .com; Village Market, Gigiri; tickets KSh350) The first entry in a chain of modern multiplexes springing up around Nairobi, showing new Western films fairly promptly after their international release.

KENYA

Fox Cineplex (Map p288; ☎ 227959; Sarit Centre, Westlands) A good modern cinema in the same price bracket as Nu Metro, located on the 2nd floor of the Sarit Centre.

20th Century Cinema (Map pp282-3; ☎ 210606; 20th Century Plaza, Mama Ngina St), **Kenya Cinema** (Map pp282-3; ☎ 227822; Kenya Cinema Plaza, Moi Ave) and **Nairobi Cinema** (Map pp282-3; ☎ 338058; Uchumi House, Aga Khan Walk) are all owned by the same chain. The first two show mainly Western movies, while the Nairobi Cinema often screens Christian 'message' films.

Theatre

Professional Centre (Map pp282-3; ☎ 225506; www .phoenixplayers.net; Parliament Rd) Local theatre troupe the Phoenix Players perform regularly here. Tickets cost KSh650, though strictly it should be US$20 for nonresidents.

Kenya National Theatre (Map pp280-1; ☎ 225174; Harry Thuku Rd; tickets from KSh200) This is the major theatre venue in Nairobi, staging contemporary and classic plays and special events.

For African theatre, the foreign cultural centres (p279) are often the places to head for.

SHOPPING

Nairobi is a good place to pick up souvenirs, but prices are typically higher than elsewhere in the country. Visit the 'Little India' area around Biashara St for fabric, textiles and those all-important souvenir Tusker T-shirts. If you're interested in buying local music, wander round the River and Latema Rds area and listen out for the blaring CD kiosks.

City Market (Map pp282-3; Muindi Mbingu St) The city's souvenir business is concentrated in this covered market, which has dozens of stalls selling woodcarvings, drums, spears, shields, soapstone, Maasai jewellery and clothing. It's an interesting place to wander round, though you generally need to be shopping to make the constant hassle worth the bother.

Gallery Watatu (Map pp282-3; ☎ 228737; Lonhro House, Standard St) If you want fine Kenyan art, check out what's happening here prior to investing your hard-earned cash. Be prepared to part with at least KSh20,000 just for something small.

Spinners Web (Map p288; ☎ 4440882; Viking House, Waiyaki Way, Westlands) Works with workshops and self-help groups around the country. It's a bit like a handicrafts version of Ikea,

with goods displayed the way they might look in Western living rooms, but there's some classy stuff on offer, including carpets, wall hangings, ceramics, wooden bowls, baskets and clothing.

Maasai Market (Map pp282-3; ☼ Tue) Busy, popular Maasai markets are held every Tuesday on the waste ground near Slip Rd in town.

Village Market (☎ 522488; Limuru Rd, Gigiri) This beautifully conceived shopping centre also has a selection of entertainment activities to while away an afternoon. You can get here with *matatu* 106 (KSh40) from near the train station.

GETTING THERE & AWAY

Air

The national carrier **Kenya Airways** (Map pp280-1; ☎ 32074100; Barclays Plaza, Loita St) operates international and domestic services out of Jomo Kenyatta International Airport. Fares come down rapidly if you can book more than a week in advance; if not, it's best to go through a travel agent.

Airkenya (☎ 501601; Wilson Airport, Langata Rd) and **Safarilink** (☎ 600777; Wilson Airport) offer domestic services to many smaller destinations at competitive prices.

One-way fares:

Destination	Fare	Frequency (daily)
Amboseli	US$85	2
Eldoret	KSh5700	1
Kisumu	from KSh5605	1
Lamu	from US$135	3
Malindi	from US$85	2
Masai Mara	US$105	3
Mombasa	from KSh6835	6
Nanyuki	US$60-80	2
Samburu	from US$115	3

The check-in time for all domestic flights is one hour before departure, and the baggage allowance is only 15kg. Make sure you reconfirm flights 72 hours before departure.

Bus

Most long-distance bus-company offices in Nairobi are in the River Rd area. Numerous companies do the run to Mombasa, leaving in the early morning or late in the evening; the trip takes eight to 10 hours. Buses leave from outside each company's office, and fares cost KSh400 to KSh700. **Coastline Safaris**

(Map pp282-3; ☎ 217592; cnr Latema & Lagos Rds) buses are the most comfortable.

Akamba (Map pp282-3; ☎ 340430; akamba_prs@skyweb.co.ke; Lagos Rd) is the biggest private bus company in the country, with an extensive, reliable network. Buses serve Eldoret, Kakamega, Kericho, Kisii, Kisumu, Kitale, Mombasa, Uganda and Tanzania, leaving from Lagos Rd; there's a **booking office** (Map pp282-3; ☎ 222027; Wabera St) near City Hall.

The government-owned **Kenya Bus Service** (KBS; ☎ 229707) is another large operator. It's cheaper than Akamba, but the buses are much slower. The main depot is on Uyoma St, and there's a **booking office** (Map pp282-3; ☎ 341250; cnr Muindi Mbingu & Monrovia Sts) in the city centre.

Easy Coach (Map pp282-3; ☎ 210711; easycoach@wananchi.com; Haile Selassie Ave) is a reliable new company serving western Kenyan destinations on the Kisumu/Kakamega route.

The **Country Bus Station** (Map pp280-1; Landhies Rd) is a disorganised place with buses running to Busia, Eldoret, Kakamega, Kisumu, Malaba, Meru, Nakuru, Nanyuki and Nyeri.

See p451 for details on other bus companies operating out of Nairobi. Typical fares:

Destination	Fare (KSh)	Duration (hr)
Eldoret	350-500	3
Kakamega	400-500	5
Kisii	350-550	4
Kisumu	400-550	4
Kitale	400-600	5
Malindi	800	9-10
Meru	250-350	3
Mombasa	500-1000	6-10
Naivasha	130	1-1½
Nakuru	200-300	2
Nanyuki	200	2
Nyeri	200	1½

Matatu

Most *matatus* leave from Latema, Accra, River and Cross Rds, and fares are similar to the buses. The biggest operator here is **Crossland Services** (Map pp282-3; ☎ 245377; Cross Rd), which serves destinations including Eldoret (KSh350, three hours), Kericho (KSh450, three hours), Kisii (KSh500, five hours), Kisumu (KSh550, four hours), Naivasha (KSh150, one hour), Nakuru (KSh250, two hours) and Nanyuki (KSh250, two hours).

Other companies are located on the surrounding streets. Head to the main bus and *matatu* station on Accra Rd (Map pp282-3) for *matatus* to Chogoria (KSh250, 2½ hours), Embu (KSh200, 1½ hours), Meru (KSh300 to KSh350, three hours) and Nanyuki (KSh200, 2½ hours). *Matatus* leave from Latema Rd for Nyahururu (KSh300, three hours) and Nyeri (KSh200, two hours). There are loads of *matatus* to Naivasha (KSh130, 1½ hours) and the Tanzanian border at Namanga (KSh250, three hours) from the corner of Ronald Ngala St and River Rd (Map pp282-3). For Thika (KSh70, 40 minutes), go to the Total petrol station on Racecourse Rd (Map pp280-1).

Train

Nairobi train station has a **booking office** (☎ 221211; Station Rd; ⏰ 9am-noon & 2-6.30pm). Only two useful passenger services currently run from Nairobi (see p456). For Mombasa (KSh3160/2275 in 1st/2nd class, 14 to 16 hours), trains leave Nairobi at 7pm on Monday, Wednesday and Friday. The return services depart at 7pm on Tuesday, Thursday and Sunday.

For Kisumu (KSh1415/720 in 1st/2nd class, 13 hours), trains depart at 6.30pm on the same days as the Mombasa services. It's advisable to book a few days in advance for either of these routes.

GETTING AROUND
To/From Jomo Kenyatta International Airport

Kenya's principal **international airport** (☎ 825400) is 15km out of the city centre. There's now a dedicated airport bus run by Metro Shuttle (part of KBS), which can drop you off at hotels in the city centre. Going the other way, the main departure point is across from the Hilton Hotel (Map pp282-3). The journey takes about 40 minutes and costs US$5 per person. Buses run every half-hour from 8am to 8.30pm daily and stop at both air terminals.

A cheaper way to get into Nairobi is city bus 34 (KSh30), but a lot of travellers get ripped off on this bus or when they step off in the city centre. Buses run from 5.45am to 9.30pm Monday to Friday, 6.20am to 9.30pm on Saturday and 7.15am to 9.30pm on Sunday. Heading to the airport, buses pass along Kenyatta Ave.

A much safer method (and your only option at night) is to take a taxi. The asking price is usually about KSh1200 in either direction, but you should be able to bargain down to KSh800 from the city centre, or even as little as KSh500 from the domestic terminal.

To/From Wilson Airport

To get to **Wilson Airport** (Map p296; ☎ 501941), for Airkenya and Safarilink services or charter flights, take bus or *matatu* 15, 31, 34, 125 or 126 from Moi Ave (KSh20). A taxi from the city centre will cost you KSh600 to KSh800 depending on the driver. In the other direction, you'll have to fight the driver down from KSh1000.

Bus

The ordinary city buses are run by **KBS** (☎ 229707), but hopefully you won't need to use them much. Most buses pass through central Nairobi, but the main KBS terminus is on Uyoma St, east of the centre.

Useful services include bus 46 from Kenyatta Ave for the Yaya Centre in Hurlingham (KSh10), and bus 23 from Jevanjee Gardens for Westlands (KSh10). There are services about every 20 minutes from 6am to 8pm Monday to Saturday. There's also a useful Metro Shuttle service from Moi Ave to Ngong Rd and Karen, passing the Karen Blixen Museum.

All these services cost KSh20 to KSh40, depending on where you get off.

Car

See p452 for information on car hire, road rules and conditions. If you are driving, beware of wheel-clampers: parking in the city centre is by permit only (KSh70 per day). If you park overnight in the street in front of your hotel, the guard will often keep an eye on your vehicle for a small consideration.

Matatu

Nairobi's horde of *matatus* follow the same routes as buses and display the same route numbers. For Westlands, you can pick up *matatu* 23 on Moi Ave or Latema Rd. *Matatu* 46 to the Yaya Centre stops in front of the main post office, and *matatus* 125 and 126 to Langata leave from in front of the train station. As usual, you should keep an eye on your valuables on all *matatus*.

Taxi

As people are compelled to use taxis due to Nairobi's endemic street crime, they are overpriced and undermaintained, but you've little choice, particularly at night. Taxis park on every other street corner in the city centre, and outside restaurants, bars and nightclubs at night.

Fares are negotiable but end up pretty standard. Any journey within the central Nairobi area costs KSh200, from the city centre to Milimani Rd costs KSh300, and for longer journeys, such as Westlands, fares cost KSh400 to KSh500.

AROUND NAIROBI

There are a number of interesting attractions within an hour's drive or *matatu* ride from Nairobi; Nairobi National Park starts right on the edge of town. Further afield are the Ngong Hills and the mysterious Lake Magadi, one of Kenya's many soda lakes.

NAIROBI'S SOUTHERN OUTSKIRTS
Sights
BOMAS OF KENYA

The **Bomas of Kenya** (Map p296; ☎ 891801; Langata Rd; nonresident adult/child KSh600/300, resident KSh100/25) is a cultural centre at Langata, near the main gate to Nairobi National Park. The talented resident artistes perform traditional dances and songs from the country's 16 tribal groups, including Swahili *taarab* music (combining African, Arabic and Indian influences), Kalenjin warrior dances, Embu drumming and Kikuyu circumcision ceremonies. It's touristy, of course, but it's still a spectacular afternoon out. Performances are held at 2.30pm Monday to Friday, and 3.30pm Saturday and Sunday. Bus or *matatu* 125 or 126 runs here from Nairobi train station (KSh30, 30 minutes).

NAIROBI NATIONAL PARK

This somewhat underrated **park** (Map p296; nonresident adult/child US$23/10, smartcard required) is the most accessible of all Kenya's wildlife parks, being only a few kilometres from the city centre. It's possible to visit as part of a tour or even by public transport, as the park runs its own wildlife bus (Sunday only).

Founded in 1946, the park's incongruous suburban location makes it virtually unique

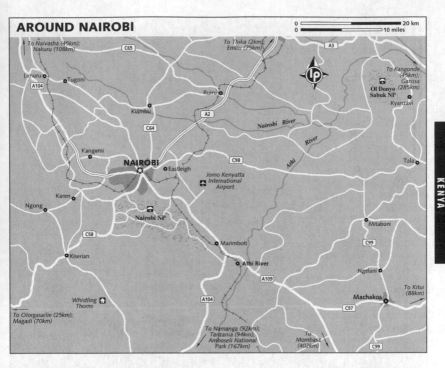

in Africa and adds an intriguing twist to the usual safari experience, pitting the plentiful wildlife against a backdrop of looming skyscrapers, speeding *matatus* and jets coming into land. As the animals seem utterly unperturbed by all the activity around them, you stand a good chance of seeing gazelles, warthogs, zebras, giraffes, ostriches, buffaloes, lions, cheetahs and leopards. The landscape is a mixture of savanna and swampland, and is home to the highest concentration of black rhinos in the world (over 50). The wetland areas sustain over 550 recorded species of bird, more than in the whole of the UK!

Nairobi National Park is not fenced and wildlife is still able to migrate along a narrow wildlife corridor to the Rift Valley. The concentrations of wildlife are higher in the dry season, as water is almost always available in the park.

The headquarters of the **KWS** (Map p296; ☎ 600800; www.kws.org) are at the main gate. Nearby is the **Nairobi Safari Walk** (Map p296; nonresident adult/child US$8/5, resident KSh500/100; ☷ 8.30am-5.30pm), a sort of zoo-meets-nature

boardwalk with lots of birds and other wildlife, including a pygmy hippo and a white rhino. The nearby **Animal Orphanage** (Map p296) charges the same rates, but it's basically a rather poor zoo.

The cheapest way to see the park is with the 'Park Shuttle,' a big KWS bus that leaves the main gate at 3pm Sunday for a 2½-hour tour of the park. The cost is US$20/5 per adult/child and you'll need to book in person at the main gate by 2.30pm. *Matatus* 125 and 126 pass the park entrance (KSh40, 45 minutes).

The main entrance to the park is on Langata Rd, but there are also public gates on Magadi Rd. The Cheetah Gate at the far (Athi River) end of the park is handy if you're continuing on to Mombasa, Amboseli or the Tanzanian border.

BUTTERFLY AFRICA

This **butterfly sanctuary** (Map p298; ☎ 884972; www.african-butterfly.org; 256 Dagoretti Rd; nonresident adult/child KSh400/200, resident KSh200/100; ☷ 9am-4.30pm) is housed in a large greenhouse full of tropical plants. There are around 1000

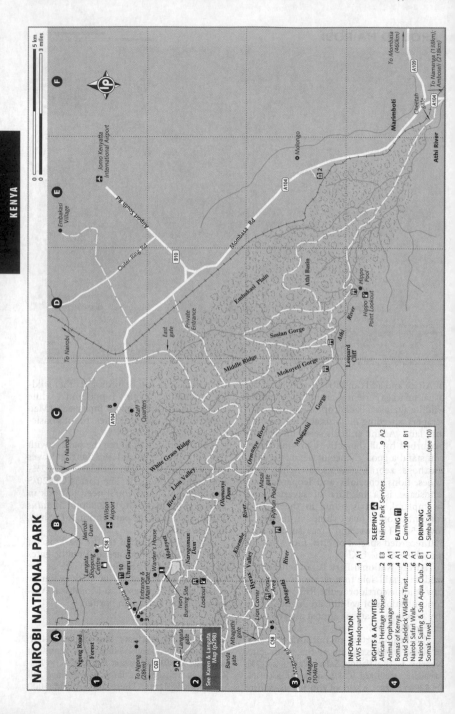

NAIROBI NATIONAL PARK

KENYA

INFORMATION
KWS Headquarters...................1 A1

SIGHTS & ACTIVITIES
African Heritage House.............2 E3
Animal Orphanage...................3 A1
Bomas of Kenya.....................4 A1
David Sheldrick Wildlife Trust.....5 A3
Nairobi Safari Walk................6 A1
Nairobi Sailing & Sub Aqua Club....7 B1
Somak Travel.......................8 C1

SLEEPING
Nairobi Park Services..............9 A2

EATING
Carnivore.........................10 B1

DRINKING
Simba Saloon...................(see 10)

See Karen & Langata Map (p298)

exotic butterflies fluttering around the place at any one time, with some interesting display boards to help identify them. It's out past the Karen roundabout on Dagoretti Rd; you can get here from Moi Ave on the 111 bus or *matatu*.

KAREN BLIXEN MUSEUM
This **museum** (Map p298; ☎ 882779; www.blixencoffee garden.co.ke; Karen Rd; nonresident adult/child KSh200/100, resident KSh50/20; ☒ 9.30am-6pm) is the farmhouse where Karen Blixen, author of *Out of Africa*, lived between 1914 and 1931. She left after a series of personal tragedies, but the lovely colonial house has been preserved as a museum. It was presented to the Kenyan government at independence by the Danish government along with the adjacent agricultural college. It's set in lovely gardens and is quite an interesting place to wander around, plus there's accommocation and a restaurant on site.

The museum is about 2km from Langata Rd. The easiest way to get here is via the Karen Metro Shuttle bus from City Hall Way (KSh20, 40 minutes). A taxi will cost about KSh900 one way. You can also come on an organised tour.

DAVID SHELDRICK WILDLIFE TRUST
Occupying a plot within Nairobi National Park, this nonprofit conservation **trust** (Map p296; ☎ 891996; www.sheldrickwildlifetrust.org) was established shortly after the death of David Sheldrick in 1977. David and his wife Daphne pioneered techniques of raising orphaned black rhinos and elephants and reintroducing them back into the wild. Rhinos and elephants are still reared on site and can be viewed between 11am and noon. There's no charge for visiting, but a donation of around KSh300 per person is appropriate. There's an information centre and usually someone around to answer questions.

From Moi Ave, take bus or *matatu* 125 or 126 and ask to be dropped off at the KWS central workshop, on Magadi Rd (KSh40, 50 minutes). It's about 1km from the workshop gate to the Sheldrick centre.

LANGATA GIRAFFE CENTRE
The **giraffe centre** (Map p298; ☎ 890952; Koitobos Rd; nonresident adult/child KSh500/250, resident 100/20; ☒ 9am-5.30pm), operated by the African Fund for Endangered Wildlife (AFEW), is about

18km from central Nairobi, reached by Langata South Rd. Here you can observe, handfeed or even kiss Rothschild's giraffes from a raised circular wooden structure, which is quite an experience, especially for children.

To get here from central Nairobi, take *matatu* 24 to the Hardy shops in Langata and walk from there, or take *matatu* 126 to Magadi Rd and walk from Mukoma Rd.

AFRICAN HERITAGE HOUSE
Designed by Alan Donovan, an African heritage expert and gallery owner, this stunning **exhibition house** (Map p296; ☎ 0721-518389; www.africanheritagebook.com) off Mombasa Rd, overlooking Nairobi National Park, can be visited by prior arrangement only. The mud architecture combines a range of traditional styles from across Africa, and the interior is furnished exclusively with tribal artefacts and artworks. For those with the money, it's possible to negotiate overnight stays (single/double US$125/250), meals (US$25 to US$30), and steam-train or even helicopter transfers.

NGONG HILLS
The green and fertile Ngong Hills were where many white settlers set up farms in the early colonial days. It's still something of an expat enclave, and here and there in the hills are perfect reproductions of English farmhouses with country gardens full of flowering trees – only the acacias remind you that you aren't rambling around the Home Counties of England.

Close to Point Lamwia, the summit of the range, is the grave of Denys George Finch-Hatton, the famous playboy and lover of Karen Blixen. A large obelisk east of the summit on the lower ridges marks his grave, inscribed with *The Rime of the Ancient Mariner*. The hills still contain plenty of wildlife, and there are legends about a lion and lioness standing guard at Finch-Hatton's graveside.

The hills provide some excellent walking, but robbery has been a risk in the past, so consult locals for the latest information. If you're worried, take an organised tour or pick up an escort from the Ngong police station or KWS office.

If you prefer a flutter to a stroll, join the Sunday crowds at the **Ngong Hills Racecourse** (Map p298; ☎ 573923; jck@karibunet.com; Ngong Rd), just east of Karen. The public enclosure is

KENYA

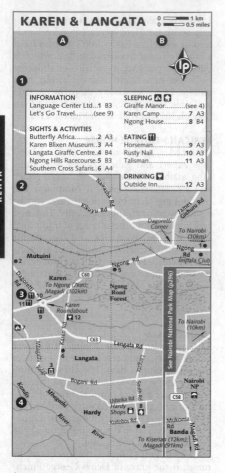

KAREN & LANGATA

INFORMATION	
Language Center Ltd...1	B3
Let's Go Travel.........(see 9)	

SIGHTS & ACTIVITIES	
Butterfly Africa...........2	A3
Karen Blixen Museum..3	A4
Langata Giraffe Centre.4	B4
Ngong Hills Racecourse.5	B3
Southern Cross Safaris..6	A4

SLEEPING 🛏 🏠	
Giraffe Manor..............(see 4)	
Karen Camp...............7	A3
Ngong House............8	B4

EATING 🍴	
Horseman...................9	A3
Rusty Nail.................10	A3
Talisman...................11	A3

DRINKING 🍷	
Outside Inn.............12	A3

free; entry to the grandstand is KSh100, or you can pay KSh250 for a platinum pass, which gives you access to the members' seating and the restaurant overlooking the course. There are usually three races every month during the racing season, which runs from October to July. You can get here on the Karen Metro Shuttle bus (KSh40, 30 minutes) and *matatus* 24 or 111 (KSh20) from Haile Selassie Ave.

Sleeping

As you might expect, Karen and Langata have some rather exclusive accommodation options tucked away amid their leafy lanes, and if you want to splash out for something special you're certainly better off here than

in Nairobi. Reservations are mandatory for most places here, as you're rarely permitted just to walk in off the street.

Giraffe Manor (Map p298; ☎ 891078; www.giraffe manor.com; Mukoma Rd; full board s/d US$385/595) Built in 1932 in the style of a typical English country manor, this elegant house is situated on 56 hectares next to the giraffe centre. You dine as the personal guests of the owners, and Rothschild's giraffes may peer through your window in the morning.

Ngong House (Map p298; ☎ 891856; ngonghouse@ form-net.com; Ndovo Rd; s/d US$450/600) Also a short walk from the giraffe centre, this is an altogether different sort of hotel. The four luxurious tree houses are set on stilts, with fine views out across the Ngong Hills. Rates include transfers, all meals and drinks, and a number of excursions are provided.

Karen Camp (Map p298; ☎ 883475; www.karencamp .com; Marula La; camping/dm/r US$3/5/20) A new venture aiming to draw the budget crowd out into the suburbs. The quiet location and smart facilities are already attracting travellers.

Nairobi Park Services (Map p296; ☎ 890325; nps@ swiftkenya.com; Magadi Rd; camping US$3, dm/d/tr US$6/ 15/18) You'll find this in a quiet residential area on the edge of Nairobi National Park, set in a garden with a great bar and restaurant. The vehicle work bays make it a good pit stop for overland trucks and self-drivers. To get here, take bus or *matatu* 125 or 126 from near the train station; the entrance is opposite the Langata Gate.

Whistling Thorns (☎ 072 721933; www.whistling thorns.com; Isinya/Kiserian Pipeline Rd; camping KSh250, with tent KSh450, d cottage per person KSh2500-3500; 🖳) Near Kiserian, this is an excellent place to stay in the Maasai foothills of the Ngong Hills. To get here, take bus or *matatu* 111 or 126 from Moi Ave to Kiserian (KSh50, one hour) and change to a Isinya/Kajiado *matatu*.

Eating & Drinking

Carnivore (Map p296; ☎ 605933; set meals KSh1325) Owned by the Tamarind chain, this is hands down the most famous *nyama choma* restaurant in Kenya, beloved of tourists, expats and wealthier locals alike for the last 25 years. Just to reinforce the point, it has twice been voted among the 50 best restaurants in the world. At the entrance is a huge barbecue pit laden with real swords of beef, pork, lamb, chicken and farmed game meats, such as camel, ostrich and crocodile. As long as the paper flag on your table is flying, waiters will keep bringing the meat, which is carved right at the table. Note that a hefty 26% tax and service charge is added to the bill. It's off Langata Rd.

Simba Saloon (Map p296; ☎ 501706; admission KSh200-300; ☒ Wed-Sun) This popular bar is right next door, usually rammed with wealthy Kenyans, expat teenagers, travellers and NGO workers, plus a fair sprinkling of prostitutes. At lunchtime, you can get here with *matatu* 126 from central Nairobi; the turn-off is signposted just past Wilson Airport. At night, you're best off hiring a taxi for the return trip. Including waiting the fare should be about KSh1200, or KSh650 one way.

Talisman (Map p298; ☎ 883213; 320 Ngong Rd; mains KSh500-900; ☒ from 9am Tue-Sun) This classy new café-bar-restaurant is incredibly fashionable right now, and rivals any of Kenya's top eateries for imaginative international food. The comfortable loungelike rooms mix modern African and European styles, and the courtyard provides some welcome air.

Rusty Nail (Map p298; ☎ 882461; rustynail@wananchi .com; Dagoretti Rd; mains KSh450-900) The Moroccan/ Turkish styling of this pavillion restaurant belies the range of food on offer; menus change weekly, offering anything from felafel and steak to coronation chicken.

Horseman (Map p298; ☎ 884560; Karen shopping centre, Langata Rd; mains KSh300-500; game meat KSh680-1000) Three restaurants in one, set in a leafy patio garden straight out of rural England, with a surprisingly authentic pub to match.

Outside Inn (Map p298; ☎ 882110; Plains House, Karen Rd) Perfect for a bit of rowdy drinkage, this semi-open barn of a bar is a firm favourite with residents for its relaxed, boozy atmosphere.

LAKE MAGADI

Lake Magadi is the most southerly of the Rift Valley lakes in Kenya, about 110km from Nairobi, and is rarely visited by tourists because of its perceived remoteness, although it actually makes an easy day trip from Nairobi if you have your own transport. The most mineral-rich of the soda lakes, it is almost entirely covered by a thick encrustation of soda that supports many flamingos and other water birds, and gives the landscape a weird lunar appearance.

A causeway leads across the most visually dramatic part of this strange landscape to a viewpoint on the western shore. It's worth a drive if you have a 4WD; otherwise you can head to the hot springs further south. They aren't particularly dramatic, but you can take a dip in the deeper pools, and there are large numbers of fish that have adapted to survive in the hot water.

The hot, dry climate and sparse scrubland make the area unsuitable for most human activity, and the only settlement of any size is Magadi town, built by the multinational ICI as a company town for staff working at the massive soda factory (now run by the Magadi Soda Co). Facilities are very limited, but you will find a couple of small bars, restaurants and shops.

Sights
A number of important archaeological finds were made at **Olorgasailie Prehistoric Site**, located 40km north of Magadi, in the 1940s, including hand axes and stone tools thought to have been made by *Homo erectus*. Fossils have also been discovered and some have been left in place. A guided tour (KSh200) is available.

Sleeping
Magadi is best visited from Nairobi or the Ngong Hills; Kiserian is convenient. Camping is probably the best option in Magadi itself. There's no shortage of space; ask at the roadblock for the best spot.

Camp site (camping KSh200, bandas s/d KSh500/800) This camp site at Olorgasailie is not a bad place to stay for the night. You'll need your own food, bedding and drinking water.

Getting There & Away
The C58 road from Nairobi is in good condition. Akamba no longer runs services here and there seems to be only one *matatu* a day to Nairobi (KSh200), leaving in the morning and returning to Magadi in the evening.

NAIROBI TO THE COAST

The main A109 road between Nairobi and Mombasa provides access to a variety of national parks and nature reserves, most importantly Tsavo National Park, Kenya's largest. There are also some interesting

KENYA

KENYA

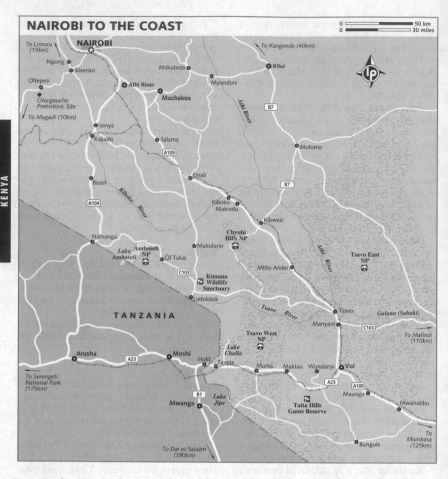

NAIROBI TO THE COAST

community-run nature projects in the area. The African townships of Voi and Wundanyi are worth a detour on your way down the coast.

AMBOSELI NATIONAL PARK

The most popular park in Kenya after the Masai Mara is **Amboseli** (☎ 045-622251; nonresident adult/child US$30/10, smartcard required), mainly because of the spectacular backdrop of Africa's highest peak, Mt Kilimanjaro, which broods over the southern boundary of the park. Cloud cover can render the mountain's massive bulk invisible for much of the day.

The park has been at the centre of some controversy since President Kibaki's 2005 decision to downgrade it from a national

park to a national reserve. Supporters claim that the move rightfully returns control of the land to the Maasai community, but many conservation bodies have argued that it's simply a political move aimed at securing the Maasai vote.

At 392 sq km, Amboseli is a small park and lacks the profusion of animal species found in the Masai Mara, but as the landscape provides limited cover you have a good chance of seeing some of the larger predators. The vegetation here used to be much denser, but rising salinisation, damage by elephants and irresponsible behaviour by safari vehicles has caused terrible erosion. Amboseli can turn into a real dust bowl in the dry season.

Buffaloes, lions, gazelles, cheetahs, wildebeests, hyenas, jackals, warthogs, zebras, Masai giraffes and baboons are all present, but the last few black rhinos were moved to Tsavo West in 1995 after a sustained period of poaching. In the permanent swamps of Enkongo Narok and Olokenya, large elephant herds can be seen grazing with Mt Kilimanjaro in the background, probably the definitive Kenyan wildlife shot.

Erosion and grass die-off is having a dramatic effect at Amboseli, and it's only a matter of years before the lack of food makes the animals move on. It's important for vehicles to stick to the defined tracks, so that the grasslands that drew all these animals here in the first place can be preserved.

Sleeping

Tortilis Camp (☎ 020-604053; www.chelipeacock.com; full board s/d low season US$340/520, high season US$400/640) This wonderfully conceived site is one of the most exclusive ecolodges in Kenya, commanding a superb spot with perfect Kilimanjaro vistas. Food is cooked without using firewood, solar power heats the water

and there's a huge organic vegetable garden. Prices include transfers, guided walks, cultural visits, laundry and most drinks, but not park fees or fancy wine.

Ol Tukai Lodge (☎ 020-4445514; oltukai@mit suminet.com; full board s/d low season US$114/143, high season US$176/220;) A splendid lodge with soaring *makuti* (thatched palm leaved) roofs and tranquil shaded gardens. The split-level bar has wonderful views, and the overall atmosphere is of peace and luxury. Two of the cottages have wheelchair access.

Amboseli Serena Lodge (☎ 020-2710511; www .serenahotels.com; full board s/d low season US$80/160, high season US$210/260;) A posh Serena hotel in junglelike gardens near the southern perimeter of the park. The low red adobe-style cottages make a change from the usual *makuti*, the very stylish lobby bar makes great use of hanging gourds, and the nearby Enkongo Narok swamp ensures constant bird and animal activity.

Amboseli Lodge (☎ 045-622440; low season s/d/tr US$70/90/122, full board high season s/d US$117/180;) This lodge consists of a number of comfortable wooden cabins dotted around an

KENYA

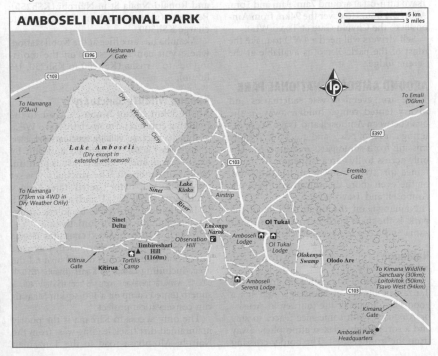

AMBOSELI NATIONAL PARK

0 — 5 km
0 — 3 miles

E396 — Meshanani Gate
C103
To Namanga (75km)
To Emali (90km)
E397
Dry Weather Only
Lake Amboseli (Dry except in extended wet season)
C103
Eremito Gate
To Namanga (71km via 4WD in Dry Weather Only)
Sinet
Lake Kioko
Airstrip
River
Sinet Delta
Enkongo Narok
Ol Tukai
Observation Hill
Amboseli Lodge
Ol Tukai Lodge
Iimbireshari Hill (1160m)
Olokenya Swamp
Olodo Are
Kitirua Gate
Kitirua
Tortilis Camp
To Kimana Wildlife Sanctuary (30km); Loitokitok (50km); Tsavo West (94km)
Amboseli Serena Lodge
C103
Kimana Gate
Amboseli Park Headquarters

expansive lawn and garden with sweeping Kili views. Quite a few tour groups drop in for lunch.

Getting There & Away

AIR

Airkenya has daily flights between Wilson Airport in Nairobi and Amboseli (US$88, one hour), departing from Nairobi at 7.30am. The return flight leaves Amboseli at 8.30am. Mombasa Air Safari flies here from Mombasa and Diani (US$220, one hour).

CAR & FOUR-WHEEL DRIVE

The usual approach to Amboseli is via Namanga. The road is sealed and in surprisingly good condition from Nairobi to Namanga; the 75km dirt road to the Meshanani Gate is pretty rough but passable (allow around four hours from Nairobi).

Some people also enter from the east via the Amboseli–Tsavo West road, although this track is in a bad way. During the 1990s there were bandit attacks in this area, so vehicles have to travel together, accompanied by armed guards. Convoys leave from the Tsavo turn-off at around 7am, 9am and 1pm. Allow 2½ hours to cover the 94km from Amboseli to the Chyulu Gate at Tsavo West.

Self-drivers will need a 4WD to make the most of the park. Petrol is available at the Serena lodge.

AROUND AMBOSELI NATIONAL PARK

There are several private sanctuaries and luxury tented camps hidden away in the bush between Amboseli and Tsavo West, offering a level of peace and quiet that is sadly missing from some parts of Amboseli. The only access to this area is the poorly maintained dirt track from Emali to Loitokitok, or the even more diabolical road between Amboseli and Tsavo West.

Namanga, on the opposite side of the park, is the main border crossing into Tanzania and has a few good places to stay.

Namanga

☎ 045

A large township has grown up around the Tanzanian border at Namanga, and it's a good place to break the journey to Arusha or Amboseli, with some nice places to stay and a surprisingly relaxed atmosphere away from the frontier itself. The border crossing

is open 24 hours and the two posts are close enough to walk across.

Numerous Maasai women come here to sell bead jewellery and other Maasai crafts, and seem to materialise like magic around tourist vehicles, especially at the petrol stations. There's great stuff on offer, but you'll have to haggle like a pro to get a bargain.

Namanga River Hotel (☎ 5132070; namangariver hotel@yahoo.com; camping KSh300, s/d KSh1550/2300) is a poshish affair with nice cottages, a good restaurant and bar, and a shady camping area. Half and full board are available.

Next door, **Namanga Safari Lodge** (☎ 0735-249527; camping KSh300, d/tw KSh600) offers cheap and cheerful accommodation and a garden full of stucco animals. Meals are available on request, and the staff are generally eager to please.

The Kobil petrol station marks the turnoff to Amboseli and is a good place to ask around for lifts. Fill up here if you're driving into Amboseli.

Buses between Nairobi and Arusha pass through daily (KSh250, two hours). *Matatus* also run here from the junction of River Rd and Ronald Ngala St in Nairobi (KSh250); Peugeots (shared taxis) on the same route charge KSh300.

Akamba has an office at the Kobil station, where you can book seats on the morning bus to Arusha (KSh200 to KSh250, 1½ hours).

Kimana Wildlife Sanctuary

About 30km east of Amboseli, close to the road that connects Amboseli to Tsavo West, is this 40-hectare **wildlife sanctuary** (admission US$10, vehicle KSh100). It's owned and run by local Maasai, and wildlife is just as plentiful here as in Amboseli. The sanctuary was set up with the help of the United States Agency for International Aid (Usaid) and the KWS in 1996 and has proved to be an encouraging template for similar initiatives.

As well as three guarded **camp sites** (camping KSh150) within the sanctuary itself, there are numerous luxury camps dotted around the area, including **Campi ya Kanzi** (Nairobi ☎ 020-605349; www.campiyakanzi.com; s/d from US$480/740), a superb tented camp on a 400-sq-km Maasai-run conservation project.

The only access to Kimana is the poorly maintained dirt track leading west from the Nairobi–Mombasa road to the Tanzanian border, or the even more diabolical road between Amboseli and Tsavo West. There's officially no need to join the Tsavo convoy if you're coming here from Amboseli, but the area south of the sanctuary has a reputation for banditry.

CHYULU HILLS NATIONAL PARK

Northwest of Tsavo West National Park are the dramatic **Chyulu Hills** (adult/child US$15/5), a collection of ancient volcanic cinder cones. The hills were gazetted as a national park in 1983, and have splendid views of Mt Kilimanjaro and populations of elands, giraffes, zebras and wildebeests, plus a small number of elephants, lions and buffaloes. Although there's loads to see, the park lacks even basic infrastructure, though there has been a serious drive to open it up for tourism lately.

Within the Chyulu Hills is Leviathan, the longest **lava tube** in the world, formed by hot lava flowing beneath a cooled crust. You'll need full caving equipment to explore it. Caving and trekking trips in the hills are possible with **Savage Wilderness Safaris Ltd** (Nairobi ☎ 020-2521590; www.whitewaterkenya.com; Sarit Centre, Westlands).

The **park headquarters** (PO Box 458, Kibwezi) are 1.3km inside the northwest gate, not far from Kibwezi on the Nairobi–Mombasa road. For the time being the best access is on the west side of the park, from the track between Amboseli and Tsavo West.

With no facilities inside the park, the most convenient accommodation option is **Ol Donyo Wuas** (Map p304; Nairobi ☎ 020-600457; www .richardbonhamsafaris.com; s/d from US$400/640; ☒), an innovative ecolodge. The cottages are built from local materials, and a US$20 conservation fee is charged to fund local community projects. Rates include wildlife drives and horse riding in the surrounding wildlife sanctuary.

Getting There & Away

Until the road from Kibwezi is brought up to standard, your best bet is the 4WD track that branches off the Amboseli–Tsavo West road about 10km west of Chyulu Gate. Ol Donyo Wuas can be reached via this track, although most guests fly in from Nairobi.

The park headquarters is signposted just outside Kibwezi, about 41km northwest of Mtito Andei on the main Nairobi–Mombasa road.

TSAVO NATIONAL PARK

At nearly 22,000 sq km, Tsavo is the largest national park in Kenya, divided administratively into Tsavo West National Park (9000 sq km) and Tsavo East National Park (11,747 sq km). Both parks feature some excellent scenery but the undergrowth is considerably higher than in Amboseli or Masai Mara, so it takes a little more effort to spot the wildlife. The compensation for this is that the landscapes are some of the most dramatic in Kenya, the animals are that bit wilder and the parks receive comparatively few visitors.

The northern half of Tsavo West is the most developed, with a number of excellent lodges. The landscape here is made of volcanic hills and sweeping expanses of savanna. The southern part of the park is rarely visited.

Tsavo East is more remote, but there are a number of lodges, and, refreshingly, a number of independent budget tented camps. Most of the action here is concentrated along the Galana River; the northern part of the park is bandit country and isn't really secure. The landscape is drier, with rolling plains hugging the edge of the Yatta Escarpment, a vast prehistoric lava flow.

During the dry season the landscape in both parks is dusty and parched, but it erupts into colour at the end of the wet season. Of course, that means there's more greenery to hide the wildlife.

Both parks were once the lands of the Orma, Watta, Maasai and Kamba people, but all the villagers were displaced when the park was gazetted. Some of these communities have now established wildlife sanctuaries and group ranches on the outskirts of the park.

Tsavo had terrible problems with poachers during the 1980s, when the elephant population dropped from 45,000 to just 5000 and rhinos were almost wiped out entirely. Populations are slowly recovering and there are now about 9000 elephants in the two parks, but still less than 100 rhinos. The last few years have once again seen a worrying upsurge in poaching.

Information

Entry is US$27/10 per adult/child per day, vehicles cost KSh200 and camping is US$10 per adult; as the two parks are administered

KENYA

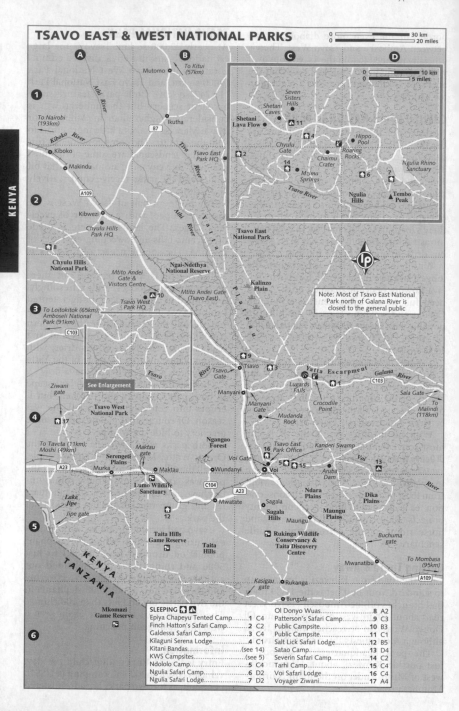

TSAVO EAST & WEST NATIONAL PARKS

SLEEPING		
Epiya Chapeyu Tented Camp	1	C4
Finch Hatton's Safari Camp	2	C2
Galdessa Safari Camp	3	C4
Kilaguni Serena Lodge	4	C1
Kitani Bandas	(see 14)	
KWS Campsites	(see 5)	
Ndololo Camp	5	C4
Ngulia Safari Camp	6	D2
Ngulia Safari Lodge	7	D2
Ol Donyo Wuas	8	A2
Patterson's Safari Camp	9	C3
Public Campsite	10	B3
Public Campsite	11	C1
Salt Lick Safari Lodge	12	B5
Satao Camp	13	D4
Severin Safari Camp	14	C2
Tarhi Camp	15	C4
Voi Safari Lodge	16	C4
Voyager Ziwani	17	A4

Note: Most of Tsavo East National Park north of Galana River is closed to the general public separately you have to pay separately for each. Both use the smartcard system; you'll need enough credit for your vehicle, entry fee and camping charges for as long as you're staying. Smartcards can be bought and re-charged at the Voi Gate to Tsavo East.

All track junctions in Tsavo East and Tsavo West have numbered and signposted cairns, but a map is helpful. Survey of Kenya publishes a *Tsavo East National Park* map (KSh500) and a newer *Tsavo West National Park* map (KSh700). Both are available from the main entrance gates and the visitor cen-tre at Tsavo West. Tourist Maps' *Tsavo Na-tional Parks* (KSh250) covers both parks.

Fuel is available at Kilaguni Serena and Ngulia Safari lodges in Tsavo West, and at Voi Safari Lodge in Tsavo East.

Tsavo West National Park

This fine national park covers a huge var-iety of landscapes, from swamps and natu-ral springs to rocky peaks, extinct volcanic cones to rolling plains and sharp reddish outcrops dusted with greenery. It's easily the more attractive of the two parks, but wildlife can be hard to spot because of the dense scrub. Birds are very common, and there are large populations of elephants, zebras, hippos and leopards. Lions are out there, but they tend to stay hidden.

The focus is **Mzima Springs**, which pro-duces an incredible 93 million gallons of fresh water a day. The springs are the source of the bulk of Mombasa's fresh water, and you can walk down to a large pool that is a favourite haunt of hippos and crocodiles. There's an underwater viewing chamber, which unfortunately just gives a view of thousands of primeval-looking fish. Be a little careful here – both hippos and crocs are potentially dangerous.

Chaimu Crater, just southeast of Kilaguni Serena Lodge and the **Roaring Rocks** view-point, can be climbed in about 15 minutes. The views from either spot are stunning, with falcons, eagles and buzzards whirling over the plains. While there is little danger walking these trails, be aware that the wild-life is still out there.

Another attraction is the **Ngulia Rhino Sanc-tuary**, at the base of Ngulia Hills, part of the Rhino Ark program. The 70-sq-km area is surrounded by a 1m-high electric fence and provides a measure of security for Tsavo West's 49 black rhinos. There are driving tracks and waterholes within the enclosed area, and there's a good chance of seeing one of these elusive creatures.

Some of the more unusual species to look out for in the park include the naked mole rat and the enigmatically named white-bellied go-away bird, which is often seen perched in dead trees. Red-beaked hornbills and bateleur eagles are also common.

It's possible to go **rock-climbing** at Tembo Peak and the Ngulia Hills, but you'll need to arrange this in advance with the **park warden** (☎ 043-622483).

Lake Jipe (*ji*-pay), at the southwest end of the park, is reached by a desperately dusty track from near Taveta. You can hire boats at the campsite to take you hippo- and crocodile-spotting on the lake (US$5). Huge herds of elephants come to the lake to drink and large flocks of migratory birds stop here from February to May.

SLEEPING

There is no real budget accommodation in Tsavo West. Campers can use the **public camp sites** (camping adult/child US$10/5) at Komboyo, near the Mtito Andei Gate, and Chyulu, just outside the Chyulu Gate, or a choice of **special camp sites** (camping adult/child US$15/5).

Ngulia Safari Camp (Voi ☎ 043-30050; tsavoh@ africaonline.co.ke; r KSh3500-6000) Formerly Ngulia Bandas, new management and a complete renovation have turned this hillside camp into Tsavo's best luxury bargain, offering thatched tent-fronted stone cottages right on the edge of the escarpment. Rooms come with or without kitchen, and there's a small bar-restaurant.

Severin Safari Camp (Mombasa ☎ 041-5485001; www.severin-kenya.com; s/d low season US$80/160, high season US$156/240) This is a fantastic complex of thatched luxury tents, with affable staff, Kilimanjaro views from the communal lounge area and nightly hippo visitations. The camp also has a simple but excellent self-catering annexe, Kitani Bandas (double/triple *bandas* US$50/65).

Kilaguni Serena Lodge (Namanga ☎ 045-340000; www.serenahotels.com; s/d low season US$80/160, high season US$210/260, ste US$565; 🖳 🖳) Kilaguni has recently been renovated and is as attractive a place as ever, with a splendid bar and restaurant overlooking a busy illuminated waterhole.

Finch Hatton's Safari Camp (Nairobi ☎ 020-553237; www.finchhattons.com; s/d/tr low season US$210/285/427, high season US$260/370/555; ⌨) An upmarket tented camp in fine old colonial style. It's situated among springs and hippo pools in the west of the park, with grounds so sprawling you have to take an escort at night.

Voyager Ziwani (Voi ☎ 043-30506; www.heritage-eastafrica.com; s/d low season US$130/180, high season US$220/295; ⌨) A luxury tented place by the Zimani Gate at the southwest end of the park, overlooking the Ziwa Dam.

Ngulia Safari Lodge (Voi ☎ 043-30000; nguliaIodge@kenya-safari.co.ke; full board s/d/tr low season US$80/160/228, s/d/tr high season US$150/200/280; ⌨) A curiously unattractive block in a spectacular location, constructed in the bad old days of emerging mass tourism. There's a waterhole right by the restaurant and sweeping views over the Ngulia Rhino Sanctuary.

GETTING THERE & AWAY

The main access to Tsavo West is through the Mtito Andei Gate on the Mombasa–Nairobi road in the north of the park, where you'll find the park headquarters and visitor centre. The main track cuts straight across to Kilaguni Serena Lodge and the Chyulu Gate. Security is a problem here, so vehicles going to Amboseli travel in armed convoys, leaving the Kilaguni Serena Lodge at 8am and 10am.

Another 48km southeast along the main road is the Tsavo Gate. It is handy for the Ngulia Hills lodges and the rhino sanctuary.

The tracks here are only really suitable for 4WDs, and roads in the south of the park are particularly challenging.

Tsavo East National Park

The landscape in Tsavo East is flatter and drier than in Tsavo West, despite the fact that one of Kenya's largest rivers cuts a green gash through the middle of the dusty orange plains. The main track through the park follows the Galana River from the Tsavo Gate to the Sala Gate. The park headquarters, where you can charge and buy smartcards, is at Voi Gate.

There are several places along the flat-topped escarpments lining the river where you can get out of your vehicle, with due caution, of course. Most scenic are **Lugards Falls**, a wonderful landscape of water-sculpted channels, and **Crocodile Point**, where you may

see hippos and crocs. There are usually armed guards around, but you shouldn't get too close to the water.

The bush is thinner than in Tsavo West, so wildlife is easier to spot, although it's not as plentiful. The rolling hills in the south of the park are home to large herds of elephants, usually covered in red dust. The action is concentrated around Voi Safari Lodge and the **Kanderi Swamp**, which is home to a profusion of wildlife. You can expect elephants to stroll through the campsite in the evenings.

The area north of the Galana River is dominated by the Yatta Escarpment, a vast prehistoric lava flow, but unfortunately much of this area is off limits because of the ongoing campaign against poachers. During the 1980s the rhino population here was decimated and there are worrying signs that poaching is once again on the increase.

Until their partial translocation to Tsavo East, the sole surviving population of hirola antelope was found near the Kenya–Somalia border. Intense poaching along with habitat destruction has reduced their numbers from an estimated 14,000 in 1976 to a pitiful 450 today, 100 of them being in Tsavo East. There are also around 48 black rhinos, moved here from Nairobi National Park, although how long they last in this hard-to-police sanctuary remains to be seen.

On the positive side, the recent translocation of 400 elephants from the Shimba Hills National Reserve (p321) has replenished the populations depleted by poaching, and should herald the start of efforts to rehabilitate the wild northern sector of the park.

SLEEPING

Ndololo Camp (☎ 043-30050; tsavoh@africaonline.co.ke; full board s/d/tr low season US$35/60/80, high season US$40/70/90) A great-value tented camp with knotted wooden furniture, mosquito nets, and canvas toilet and shower cubicles. Annoyingly, you have to pay the US$10 park camping fee on top of the room rates.

Tarhi Camp (Mombasa ☎ 041-5486378; kedev@africaonline.co.ke; half board s/d US$60/100) Owned by a German company, this is a reasonably priced camp on the edge of the Voi River. It's technically a special campsite, so an additional camping fee of US$15 is levied.

KWS camp sites (☎ 043-30049; tenp@africaonline.co.ke; camping adult/child US$10/5) There's a single camping ground with basic toilets near

KENYA

MAN-EATERS OF TSAVO

The lions of Tsavo National Park are unique in many ways. For a start the males lack the typical mane that usually distinguishes this species, a fact often attributed to the thorn-filled vegetation of their habitat, which makes long hair a real hindrance to free movement. As an Earthwatch study recently revealed, they are also the only lions known to move in social groups with just one single male – most normal prides have one or two younger hangers-on as well as the alpha male.

Remarkably, scientists now believe there may be a single cause for all these idiosyncracies: testosterone. When tested, Tsavo lions showed noticeably elevated levels of the male sex hormone, which could well be responsible for their hair loss and increased territorial behaviour.

This theory would also explain the famed aggression of the Tsavo lions, which has earned them a reputation as the fiercest predators in Africa. The best-known story concerns just two lions, who ate their way through 140 railway workers in a single year during the 19th century! The chief engineer, Colonel JH Patterson, eventually managed to trap and kill them, and subsequently wrote a best-selling book about the experience, *The Man-Eaters of Tsavo*, which was later filmed as *The Ghost and the Darkness*.

Although there's been nothing to compare to this since, quite a few local people have been attacked over the last decade, so be a little cautious when walking at Chaimu Crater, Mzima Springs or Lugards Falls. Hormonal or not, the Tsavo lions are not to be trifled with.

Kanderi Swamp. There are also a few special camp sites (adult/child US$15/5), which move from year to year.

Voi Safari Lodge (Mombasa ☎ 041-471861; voi lodge@kenya-safari.co.ke; s/d low season US$80/110, high season US$105/150; ⚑) Just 4km from Voi Gate, this is a long, low complex overlooking an incredible sweep of savanna, with a lovely rock-cut swimming pool and a natural waterhole.

Satao Camp (Mombasa ☎ 041-475074; www.satao camp.com; s/d low season US$80/120, high season US$160/200) On the Voi River, this popular upmarket camp is nicely laid out, with 20 canopied tents surrounding a waterhole.

Galdessa Safari Camp (Nairobi ☎ 020-7123156; www.galdessa.com; s/d low season US$336/512, high season US$446/684; ✹ closed May) On the Galana River, 15km west of Lugards Falls, this ecocamp is heavily involved in rhino conservation projects. Rates include wildlife drives.

Let's Go Travel (☎ 020-340331; www.lets-go-travel .net) in Nairobi handles bookings for **Epiya Chapeyu Tented Camp** (s/d US$72/144; ✹ closed Apr-Jul), by the Galana River, and **Patterson's Safari Camp** (s/d low season US$65/90, high season US$85/120), 9km from Tsavo Gate.

GETTING THERE & AWAY
Most tourist safaris enter Tsavo East via the Sala Gate, where a good dirt road runs east for 110km to Malindi. If you're coming from Nairobi, the Voi Gate (near the town of same name) and the Manyani Gate (on the Nairobi–Mombasa road) are just as accessible.

AROUND TSAVO NATIONAL PARK
There are a number of independent nature reserves in the bush on the edge of Tsavo West. The road between Voi and Taveta cuts through the lush hilly areas surrounding Voi, providing interesting detours for walkers and wildlife-spotters.

Taita Hills & Wundanyi
South of the dirt road from Voi to Taveta are the Taita Hills, a fertile area of verdant hills and scrub forest, a far cry from the semiarid landscape of Tsavo. Within the hills is the private **Taita Hills Game Reserve** (adult/child US$23/12), covering an area of 100 sq km. The landscape is extremely dramatic and all the plains wildlife is in abundance. If you stay at one of the lodges here, you can take a nocturnal wildlife drive, something that's not allowed in the national parks.

Wundanyi, the provincial capital, is an interesting little place high up in the hills. Trails crisscross the cultivated slopes around town, leading to dramatic gorges, waterfalls and cliffs. It's easy to find a guide, but stout walking boots and a head for heights are essential.

Other attractions include the butterflies of **Ngangao Forest** (6km northwest, near Werugha); the huge granite **Wesu Rock**; and the **Cave of Skulls**, where the Taita people once put the skulls of their ancestors.

SLEEPING
Salt Lick Safari Lodge (☎ 043-30270; saltlick@africa online.co.ke; s/d/tr high season US$185/226/286, low season US$132/161/195) This is the main accommodation for visitors in the Taita Hills reserve. Children under five are not admitted.

Taita Rocks (☎ 0735-651349; r KSh800-2000, per person with shared bathroom KSh400-500) The best of Wundanyi's very limited accommodation offerings, perched up a slope off the road into town.

GETTING THERE & AWAY
Frequent *matatu* services run between Wundanyi and Voi (KSh120, one hour). Leave Wundanyi by around 8.30am if you want to connect with the morning buses to Nairobi from Voi. There are also direct *matatus* to Mombasa (KSh300, four to five hours) and an irregular morning service to Nairobi (KSh600, seven hours).

Lake Challa
This deep, spooky crater lake is about 10km north of Taveta. There are grand views across the plains from the crater rim, with the mysterious waters shimmering hundreds of metres below. The lake gained notoriety in early 2002 when a gap-year student was killed by crocodiles here. You can walk around the crater rim and down to the water, but be very careful near the water's edge and under no circumstances consider swimming.

The road to Challa turns off the Voi–Taveta road on the outskirts of Taveta, by the second police post. On Taveta market days (Wednesday and Saturday) there are local buses to Challa village (KSh50), passing the turn-off to the crater rim.

VOI
☎ 043
Small but always busy, Voi is a key service town at the intersection of the Nairobi–Mombasa road and the road to Moshi in Tanzania. The Voi Gate to Tsavo East National Park is just east of the town, and Voi has plenty of cheap places to stay, which is great for travellers who can't afford the safari lodges inside the park. There's a lively market area and a general air of activity,

and there are some nice walks in the surrounding hills.

Information
Ashtec Computers (Fariji House) Email facilities.
Kenya Commercial Bank (☎ 30138; Nairobi–Mombasa road)
Post office (☎ 30253)
Telkom office (Nairobi–Mombasa road)

Sleeping & Eating
Tsavo Park Hotel (☎ 30050; info@tsavoparkhotel.com; s/d/tr incl breakfast KSh1200/1800/2500) The large rooms aren't bad value, with some satellite TVs, but ongoing building means the plumbing's a bit dodgy. There's a good-value restaurant.

Voi Town Lodge (☎ 30705; s with shared bathroom KSh400, s/d with private bathroom KSh650/1000) A friendly and economical alternative to the Tsavo Park Hotel, with a handful of odd windowless rooms. Some of the walls don't reach the ceilings, but it's comfortable enough.

Johari's Guest House (☎ 30489; s/d with shared bathroom KSh250/350) A cheap courtyard place behind a drycleaner, one block north of the main road through Voi.

Silent Guest Resort (☎ 30112; silentresort@yahoo.com; s/d incl breakfast KSh2200/3200) Technically this has a good claim to be the best hotel in town in terms of facilities, but there's not much justification for the exorbitant price tag.

Most of the guesthouses have reasonable restaurants, particularly the Tsavo Park Hotel, and there are a few small food *dukas* and cafés around the bus and *matatu* stand. As Voi is a transport hub, there's a low-key prostitution scene servicing the truck drivers, which can be a hassle in some bars.

Getting There & Away
Frequent buses and *matatus* run to Mombasa (KSh250, three hours), and buses to Nairobi (KSh500 to KSh800, six hours) pass through town at around 10.30am and midnight. There are daily *matatu* to Wundanyi (KSh100, one hour) and Taveta (KSh250, two hours), on the Tanzanian border.

The **train station** (☎ 30098), at the eastern end of town, has trains to Mombasa (KSh1410/1130 in 1st/2nd class) at around 4am on Tuesday, Thursday and Saturday, and to Nairobi (KSh2100/1475 in 1st/2nd class) at around 11pm on Tuesday, Thursday and Sunday.

THE COAST

It may seem at odds with the immediate mental image of safari Africa, but Kenya's Indian Ocean shoreline is one of its greatest assets, and the unique flavour of this steamy, sultry region never fails to weave a spell over its visitors. Even the most jaded beach bum can find something to delight in amid the palm-fringed white-sand stretches that run pretty much all the way from Tanzania to Somalia.

Don't be fooled into thinking it's all about the beaches, though. In fact, it's likely these will only play a minor part in your trip; for the adventurous independent traveller, the real draw of the coast is the Swahili culture that permeates every aspect of daily life here, from the bustling markets of Mombasa to the living history enshrined in Lamu's ever-captivating old town. Wandering narrow streets, exploring ancient ruins and setting sail in traditional dhows are the experiences that truly define a visit here, and you should take every opportunity to soak up the atmosphere that sets the region apart from the rest of Kenya.

For the active, the lure of coral reefs, remote islands and unlimited water sports is another hefty incentive to splash beneath the surface. Even away from the ocean, the region can muster up more than enough treats and surprises to enthrall its fans and convert its critics, with something unexpected at every turn. Sunbathing be damned – with coastal rainforest, tribal shrines, coral mosques, thumbless monkeys, elephants and elephant shrews, Kenya's coast should barely leave you time to relax.

HISTORY

The Swahili culture of the coast was a product of trade, initiated by Persian and Arab merchants, who used the monsoon winds to reach African shores and quickly established trading posts. By the 9th century a series of fully fledged city-states had spread out along the coast from Somalia to Mozambique, and the first African slaves began to appear in Arabia.

Intermarriage between Arabs and Africans gradually created the Swahili race, language and culture, and established some powerful dynasties. In the early 16th century the Portuguese swanned over the horizon, attracted by the wealth and determined to end the Arab trade monopoly.

It's fashionable to portray the Portuguese as the bad guys, but the sultans of Oman, who defeated them in 1698, were no more popular with the locals. Despite their shared faith, the Swahilis staged countless rebellions, even passing Mombasa into British hands from 1824 to 1826 to keep it from the sultans. Things only really quietened down after Sultan Seyyid Said moved his capital to Zanzibar in 1832.

Said's huge coastal clove plantations created a massive need for labour, and the slave caravans of the 19th century marked the peak of the trade in human cargo. News of massacres and human rights abuses soon reached Europe, galvanising the British public to demand an end to slavery. Through a mixture of political savvy and implied force, the British government was eventually able to pressure Said's son Barghash to ban the slave trade.

Of course, this 'reform' didn't hurt British interests: as part of the treaty, the British East Africa Company took over administration of the Kenyan interior. A 16km-wide coastal strip was recognised as the territory of the sultan and was leased by the British from 1887. Upon independence in 1963, the last sultan of Zanzibar gifted the land to the new Kenyan government.

Today the coast province remains culturally and socially distinct from the rest of the country, still heavily influenced by its Swahili past. Indians are the largest minority, descendants of railway labourers and engineers brought here by the British, and the population as a whole is predominantly Muslim.

MOMBASA
☎ 041 / pop 653,000

Mombasa is the largest city on the Kenyan coast and also the largest coastal port in East Africa. The city sprawls across a low-lying island at the mouth of a broad inlet, providing a fantastic natural anchorage for ships. Traders have been coming here since at least the 12th century, and goods from Uganda, Rwanda, Burundi and eastern Democratic Republic of the Congo (DR Congo) all still pass through here on their way overseas.

The city's population is overwhelmingly African, many of whom are Swahilis, but

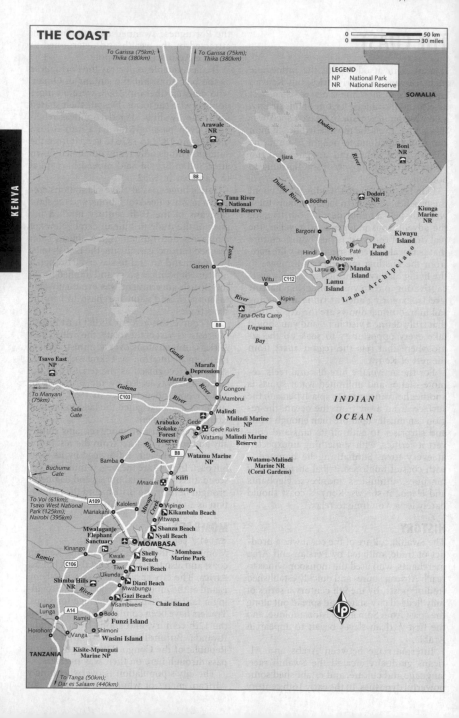

THE COAST

LEGEND
NP National Park
NR National Reserve

there are a remarkable range of races and cultures here, from Africans to British expats, Omanis, Indians and Chinese.

Most package tourists stay in the beach resorts north or south of town, but leaving Mombasa out of your itinerary completely would be a shame. The most interesting part is the characterful Old Town, with its narrow, winding alleyways, historic Swahili houses and the remains of the mighty Fort Jesus.

History

Mombasa has always been at the centre of the coast's key events, a crucial stronghold for local and invading powers ever since the Arab-Swahili Mazrui clan emerged as one of the most powerful families in 9th-century East Africa.

The first Portuguese forays into Arab territory took place here in 1505, when Dom Francisco de Almeida arrived with a huge armada and levelled the city in just 1½ days. The plundered remains were soon rebuilt, but in 1528 Lisbon struck again as Nuña da Cunha captured the city, first by diplomacy (offering to act as an ally in Mombasa's disputes with Malindi, Pemba and Zanzibar) and then by force. Once again Mombasa was burned to the ground while the invaders sailed on to India.

The Portuguese made a bid for permanency in 1593 with the construction of Fort Jesus, but the hefty structure quickly became a symbolic target for rebel leaders and was besieged incessantly. During the 17th and 18th centuries Mombasa changed hands dozens of times before the Portuguese finally gave up their claim to the coast in 1729.

Waiting to step into the power vacuum were the sultans of Oman, who had defeated the Europeans and occupied Fort Jesus after an incredible 33-month siege in 1698. The city remained in their control up until the 1870s, when British intervention ended the slave trade and gained for the Empire a foothold in East Africa.

Mombasa subsequently became the railhead for the Uganda railway and the most important city in British East Africa. In 1920, when Kenya became a fully fledged British colony, Mombasa was made capital of the separate British Coast Protectorate.

Today the cut and thrust of politics and power play largely passes Mombasa by, but it's still Kenya's second city and a crucial social barometer for the coast province as a whole.

Orientation

The main thoroughfare in Mombasa is Digo Rd and its southern extension Nyerere Ave, which run north–south through the city. The ferry to Likoni and the south coast leaves from the southern end of Nyerere Ave.

Running west from the junction between Nyerere Ave and Digo Rd is Moi Ave, where you'll find the tourist office and the famous sculpted 'tusks', two huge pairs of aluminium elephant tusks forming an M over the road, which were erected to mark a visit by British royal Princess Margaret in 1956. Heading east from the same junction, Nkrumah Rd provides the easiest access to the Old Town and Fort Jesus.

North of the city centre, Digo Rd becomes Abdel Nasser Rd, where you'll find many of the bus stands for Nairobi and destinations north along the coast. There's another big group of bus offices west of here at the intersection of Jomo Kenyatta Ave and Mwembe Tayari Rd. The train station is at the intersection of Mwembe Tayari and Haile Selassie Rds.

MAPS

Choices are limited but your best option is the 1:10,000 *Streets of Mombasa Island* map (KSh350), updated in 2004 and available from the tourist office. For more detailed coverage seek out the *Mombasa A to Z* (KSh300), which was fully revised in 2003 – it may be easier to find in Nairobi than in Mombasa itself.

Information

BOOKSHOPS

Bahati Book Centre (Map p314; ☎ 225010; Moi Ave)
Books First (Map p312; ☎ 313482; Nakumatt, Nyerere Ave; ▢) Well-stocked outlet with separate café.
City Bookshop (Map p314; ☎ 313149; Nkrumah Rd)

EMERGENCY

AAR Health Services (☎ 312409; ☾ 24hr)
Police (☎ 222121, 999)

INTERNET ACCESS

Blue Room (Map p314; ☎ 224021; www.blueroomonline.com; Haile Selassie Rd; per min KSh2; ☾ 9am-10pm)

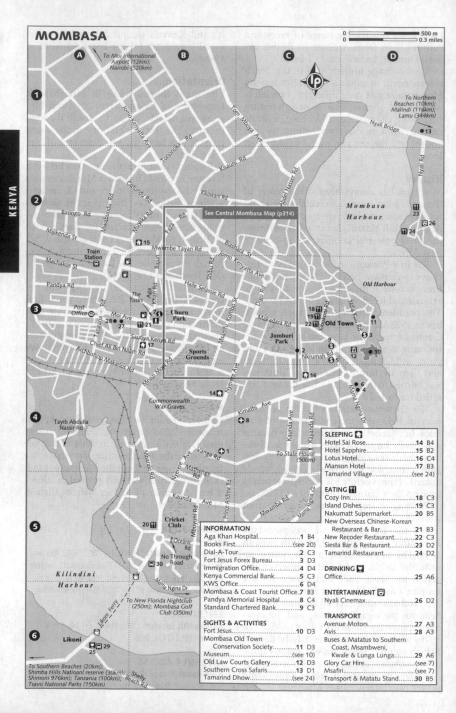

MOMBASA

0 — 500 m
0 — 0.3 miles

To Moi International Airport (12km); Nairobi (520km)

To Northern Beaches (10km); Malindi (116km); Lamu (344km)

Nyali Bridge

Mombasa Harbour

Old Harbour

Old Town

Uhuru Park

Jumhuri Park

Sports Grounds

Commonwealth War Graves

Tayib Abdulla Nassir Rd

The Tusks

Post Office

Train Station

Kilindini Harbour

To New Florida Nightclub (250m); Mombasa Golf Club (350m)

No Through Road

Oceanic Rd

Cricket Club

Likoni

Likoni Ferry

To State House (500m)

To Southern Beaches (20km); Shimba Hills National reserve (30km); Shimoni 976km); Tanzania (100km); Tsavo National Parks (150km)

See Central Mombasa Map (p314)

KENYA

INFORMATION

Aga Khan Hospital	1 B4
Books First	(see 20)
Dial-A-Tour	2 C3
Fort Jesus Forex Bureau	3 D3
Immigration Office	4 D4
Kenya Commercial Bank	5 C3
KWS Office	6 D4
Mombasa & Coast Tourist Office	7 B3
Pandya Memorial Hospital	8 C4
Standard Chartered Bank	9 C3

SIGHTS & ACTIVITIES

Fort Jesus	10 D3
Mombasa Old Town Conservation Society	11 D3
Museum	(see 10)
Old Law Courts Gallery	12 D3
Southern Cross Safaris	13 D1
Tamarind Dhow	(see 24)

SLEEPING

Hotel Sai Rose	14 B4
Hotel Sapphire	15 B2
Lotus Hotel	16 C4
Manson Hotel	17 B3
Tamarind Village	(see 24)

EATING

Cozy Inn	18 C3
Island Dishes	19 C3
Nakumatt Supermarket	20 B5
New Overseas Chinese-Korean Restaurant & Bar	21 B3
New Recoder Restaurant	22 C3
Siesta Bar & Restaurant	23 D2
Tamarind Restaurant	24 D2

DRINKING

Office	25 A6

ENTERTAINMENT

Nyali Cinemax	26 D2

TRANSPORT

Avenue Motors	27 A3
Avis	28 A3
Buses & Matatus to Southern Coast, Msambweni, Kwale & Lunga Lunga	29 A6
Glory Car Hire	(see 7)
Msafiri	(see 7)
Transport & Matatu Stand	30 B5

Info Café (Map p314; ☎ 227621; infomombasa@yahoo.com; Ambalal House, Nkrumah Rd; per min KSh1)
Wavetek (Map p314; ☎ 0735-295007; TSS Towers, Nkrumah Rd; per min KSh1) Also offers international calls from KSh15 per minute.

KENYA WILDLIFE SERVICE
KWS office (Map p312; ☎ 312744/5; Nguua Court, Mama Ngina Dr; ☯ 6am-6pm) Sells and charges smartcards.

MEDICAL SERVICES
All services and medication must be paid for upfront, so have travel insurance details handy.
Aga Khan Hospital (Map p312; ☎ 312953; akhm@mba.akhmkenya.org; Vanga Rd)
Pandya Memorial Hospital (Map p312; ☎ 229252; Kimathi Ave)

MONEY
Outside business hours you can exchange money at major hotels, although rates are usually quite poor. Exchange rates are generally slightly lower here than you'll find in Nairobi, especially for travellers cheques.
Barclays Bank Nkrumah Rd (Map p314; ☎ 224573); Digo Rd (Map p314; ☎ 311660)
Fort Jesus Forex Bureau (Map p312; ☎ 316717; Ndia Kuu Rd)
Kenya Commercial Bank Moi Ave (Map p314; ☎ 220978); Nkrumah Rd (Map p312; ☎ 312523)
Postbank (Map p314; ☎ 3434077; Moi Ave) Western Union money transfers.
Pwani Forex Bureau (Map p314; ☎ 221727; Digo Rd)
Standard Chartered Bank (Map p312; ☎ 224614; Treasury Sq, Nkrumah Rd)

POST
Post office (Map p314; ☎ 227705; Digo Rd)

TELEPHONE
Post Global Services (Map p314; ☎ 230581; inglobal@africaonline.co.ke; Maungano Rd; ☯ 7.30am-8pm; ☲) International calls are around KSh85 per minute. Owner Rashmi is re-establishing his travel agency, and can act as a capable and friendly 'fixer' for travellers.
Telkom Kenya (Map p314; ☎ 312811) Locations on Nkrumah Rd and Moi Ave.

TOURIST INFORMATION
Mombasa & Coast Tourist Office (Map p312; ☎ 225428; mcta@ikenya.com; Moi Ave; ☯ 8am- 4.30pm) Provides information and can organise accommodation, tours, guides and transport.

TRAVEL AGENCIES
Dial-A-Tour (Map p312; ☎ 221411; dialatour@ikenya.com; Oriental Bldg, Nkrumah Rd)
Express Travel (Map p314; ☎ 315405; PO Box 90631, Nkrumah Rd) AmEx agent. Mail can be held here for cardholders.
Fourways Travel (Map p314; ☎ 223344; Moi Ave)

VISA EXTENSIONS
Immigration office (Map p312; ☎ 311745; Uhuru ni Kari Bldg, Mama Ngina Dr)

Dangers & Annoyances
Mombasa is relatively safe compared to Nairobi, but the streets still clear pretty rapidly after dark so it's a good idea to take taxis rather than walk around alone at night. You need to be more careful on the beaches north and south of town. The Likoni ferry is a bag-snatching hot spot.

Visitors should also be aware of anti-Western sentiment among some Kenyan Muslims: hostile graffiti and Osama Bin Laden T-shirts abound, and demonstrations against Israel and America are increasingly common. Keep a low profile during any escalation of violence in the Middle East or terrorist activity in the West.

Malaria is a big risk on the coast, so remember to take your antimalarial drugs (see p643).

Sights & Activities
FORT JESUS
Mombasa's biggest tourist attraction dominates the harbour entrance at the end of Nkrumah Rd. The metre-thick coral walls make it an imposing edifice, despite being partially ruined. The fort was built by the Portuguese in 1593 to enforce their rule over the coastal Swahilis, but they rarely managed to hold onto it for long. It changed hands at least nine times in bloody sieges between 1631 and 1875, finally falling under British control.

The fort was the final project completed by Italian architect Joao Batista Cairato in his long career as Chief Architect for Portugal's eastern colonies. There are some ingenious elements in its design, especially the angular configuration of the west walls, which makes it impossible to attack one wall without being a sitting duck for soldiers on the opposite battlements.

These days the fort houses a **museum** (Map p312; ☎ 222425; nmkfortj@swiftmombasa.com; adult/child

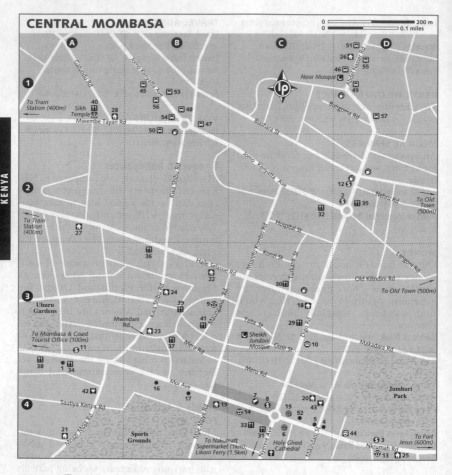

KSh200/100; 8am-6pm), built over the barracks. The exhibits are mostly ceramics, reflecting the variety of cultures that traded along the coast, but include other interesting odds and ends donated from private collections or dug up from sites along the coast. Also displayed are finds from the Portuguese frigate *Santo António de Tanná*, which sank near the fort during the siege in 1698, and the far end of the hall is devoted to the fascinating culture of the nine coastal Mijikenda tribes.

Exploring the battlements and ruined buildings within the compound is just as interesting, though the fort feels much smaller than it looks from the outside. The **Omani house** in the San Felipe bastion in the northwestern corner of the fort was built

in the late 18th century, and houses a small exhibition of Omani jewellery and artefacts. Nearby is a ruined church, a huge well and cistern, and an excavated grave complete with skeleton. The **eastern wall** of the fort includes an Omani audience hall and the **Passage of the Arches**, a passage cut through the coral to give access to the sea.

Coach tours arrive here late in the morning, so if you come early you may have the place to yourself. Many official and unofficial guides will offer their services, often for free, though a tip is expected. Alternatively, you can buy the 1981 *Fort Jesus* guide (KSh60) from the ticket desk and go it alone. At 7pm there's a daily 'sound and light show' illustrating the fort's history; tickets cost US$15.

INFORMATION			Glory Bed & Breakfast	22	B3	ENTERTAINMENT ⊟		
Bahati Book Centre	1	A4	Glory Guest House	23	B3	Kenya Cinema	44	D4
Barclays Bank	2	D2	Hotel Dorse	24	B3			
Barclays Bank	3	D4	New Palm Tree Hotel	25	D4	SHOPPING		
Blue Room	(see 30)		New People's Hotel	26	D1	Ketty Plaza	(see 16)	
City Bookshop	4	C4	Royal Court Hotel	27	A2			
Express Travel (Amex)	5	C4	Tana Guest House	28	A1	TRANSPORT		
Fourways Travel	(see 17)					Akamba	45	B1
Info Café	6	C4	EATING ⊞			Buses & Matatus to Malindi	46	D1
Italian Consulate	7	C4	Baron Restaurant & Pub	29	C3	Buses to Arusha & Moshi		
Kenya Commercial Bank	8	C4	Blue Room Restaurant	30	C3	(Mwembe Tayari		
Post Global Services	9	B3	China Town Restaurant	31	C4	Health Centre)	47	B1
Post Office	10	C3	Fayaz Baker & Confectioners	32	C2	Buses to Dar es Salaam &		
Postbank	11	A3	Fontanella Steakhouse &			Tanga	48	B1
Pwani Forex Bureau	12	D2	Beer Garden	33	C4	Busscar	(see 55)	
Telkom Kenya	13	D4	Little Chef Dinners Pub	34	A4	Busstar	49	D1
Telkom Kenya	14	C4	Main Market	35	D2	Coastline Safaris	50	B1
Wavetek	15	C4	New Chetna Restaurant	36	B3	Falcon	51	D1
			Pistacchio Café	37	B3	Falcon	(see 53)	
SIGHTS & ACTIVITIES			Rozina House Restaurant	38	A4	Kenya Airways	52	C4
Ketty Tours	16	B4	Shchnai Restaurant	39	B3	Kobil Petrol Station	(see 54)	
Safari Seekers	17	B4	Singh Restaurant	40	A1	Mash Express	53	B1
			Splendid View Restaurant	41	B3	Matatus to Voi &		
SLEEPING ⋒						Wundanyi	54	B1
Beracha Guest House	18	C3	DRINKING ⊟			Mombasa Raha	55	D1
Castle Royal Hotel	19	B4	Casablanca Restaurant &			Mombasa Raha	56	B1
Dancourt Hotel	20	C4	Club	42	A4	Oman Air	(see 7)	
Evening Guest House	21	A4	Toyz Disco	43	C4	TSS Express	57	D1

OLD TOWN

While Mombasa's Old Town doesn't quite have the medieval charm of Lamu or Zanzibar, it's still an interesting area to wander around. The houses here are characteristic of coastal East African architecture, with ornately carved doors and window frames and fretwork balconies, designed to protect the modesty of the female inhabitants. Sadly, many of these have been destroyed; there is now a preservation order on the remaining doors and balconies, so further losses should hopefully be prevented. The **Mombasa Old Town Conservation Society** (Map p312; ☎ 312246; Sir Mbarak Hinawy Rd) is encouraging the renovation of many dilapidated buildings.

From the outside there's little evidence of what any of these buildings were once used for. To flesh out their history, it's worth picking up a copy of the booklet *The Old Town Mombasa: A Historical Guide* (KSh200) from the tourist office or the Fort Jesus ticket office. This guide features old photos, a good map and building-by-building descriptions.

OLD LAW COURTS

The old law courts on Nkrumah Rd have been converted into an informal **gallery** (Map p312; Nkrumah Rd; admission free; ☙ 8am-6pm), with regularly changing displays of local art, Kenyan crafts, school competition pieces and votive objects from various tribal groups.

Tours

A number of tour companies have branches in Mombasa (see p94 for more details) and offer standard tours of the Old Town and Fort Jesus (from US$50 per person), plus safaris to Shimba Hills National Reserve and Tsavo East and Tsavo West National Parks. Most safaris are expensive lodge-based affairs, but there are a few camping safaris to Tsavo East and West.

Numerous activities are possible both north and south of Mombasa; most operators will pick you up from wherever you're staying for a small extra charge.

HARBOUR CRUISES

Luxury dhow cruises around the harbour are very popular in Mombasa and, notwithstanding the price, they are an excellent way to see the harbour, the Old Town and Fort Jesus, and get a slap-up meal at the end of it.

Topping the billing is the **Tamarind Dhow** (Map p312; ☎ 475074; www.tamarinddhow.com), run by the posh Tamarind restaurant chain of the same name. The cruise embarks from the jetty below the Tamarind restaurant in Nyali, and includes a harbour tour and a fantastic meal. The lunch cruises leave at 1pm and cost US$40/20 per adult/child, or US$80/40 when combined with a city tour. Longer and more splendid evening cruises leave at 6.30pm and cost US$70/35. There

KENYA

is a choice of seafood, steak and vegetarian dishes. Prices include a complimentary cocktail and transport to and from your hotel.

The other big operator is **Jahazi Marine** (☎ 5485001; www.severin-kenya.com), which offers evening trips for US$75. The price includes transfers, a sunset cruise, a walk through the Old Town and entry to Fort Jesus for the light show and a five-course meal; for an extra US$10 you can sample a casino and head on to the Bora Bora International Nightclub in Bamburi, in the northern beaches.

Festivals & Events

The **Mombasa Carnival** (zainab@africaonline.co.ke) is the city's major annual event, held every November. The festival sees Moi Ave come alive for the day with street parades, floats, and lots of music from the diverse cultural groups of the coastal region and the rest of Kenya.

Sleeping

There are plenty of budget choices in Mombasa, as well as some excellent midrange hotels, but there are few top-end options. Many people choose to skip Mombasa and head straight for the beaches to the north and south. All the places listed here have fans and mosquito nets as a minimum requirement, though their condition varies widely!

BUDGET

Most of the really cheap choices are in the busy, noisy area close to the bus stations on Abdel Nasser Rd and Jomo Kenyatta Ave. Women travelling alone might want to opt for something a little further up the price scale.

Tana Guest House (Map p314; ☎ 490550; cnr Mwembe Tayari & Gatundu Rds; s/d/tr KSh400/500/600) A simple but friendly place in the slightly seedy area close to the Jomo Kenyatta Ave bus stations. Rooms are clean, tidy and pretty much what you'd expect for the price.

New People's Hotel (Map p314; Abdel Nasser Rd; s/d with shared bathroom KSh200/350, with private bathroom KSh350/500) This basic dosshouse gets loads of noise from traffic and the Noor Mosque next door, but you can't argue with the prices. There's a good, cheap restaurant downstairs, and it's very convenient for buses to Lamu and Malindi.

Evening Guest House (Map p314; ☎ 221380; Mnazi Moja Rd; s/d with shared bathroom KSh600/800, s with private bathroom KSh700-800, d with private bathroom

KSh1000) Set in a thatched courtyard behind its own large restaurant area, the Evening does have something of the night about it, but is still mostly good value despite a few cramped singles.

Beracha Guest House (Map p314; ☎ 0722-673798; Haile Selassie Rd; s/d KSh500/750) This popular central choice has variable but clean rooms in a range of unusual shapes. There's a cheap restaurant, and ongoing building work should add a few more strange angles to the geometry.

Glory Bed & Breakfast (Map p314; ☎ 228282; Haile Selassie Rd; s/d/tr incl breakfast KSh700/1000/1400) Adequate, if a little cramped: rooms have fans but no mosquito nets. Taking a room with shared bathroom knocks KSh200 off the price. There have been no reports concerning security issues lately, but always be cautious when travelling.

MIDRANGE

Rates include breakfast for all of the following options.

Castle Royal Hotel (Map p314; ☎ 220373; info@680 hotel.co.ke; Moi Ave; s/d/tr KSh2300/3000/4200; 🍴 🖥) Quite simply the best hotel in town, and at these prices one of the best deals in the whole of Kenya. The newly renovated Castle Royal is a joy to stay in, with TV, phone, fridge, safe, iron-framed bed and stylish décor in every room, plus an excellent breakfast in the cool terrace restaurant at the front. A shop, travel agent and Chinese restaurant round out the amenities.

New Palm Tree Hotel (Map p314; ☎ 312623; Nkrumah Rd; s/d KSh1160/1740) The appealing New Palm Tree may be a step down from the competition in facilities, but it has character and charm in spades, with all the rooms set around a fantastic roof terrace. The mosquito nets are variable and hot water can be unreliable, but the rooms are big, the bar and restaurant are well priced, and it has the most sociable atmosphere in town.

Lotus Hotel (Map p312; ☎ 313207; lotus_hotel@ hotmail.com; Cathedral Rd; s/d/tr KSh1800/2500/3000; 🍴) A welcome change from dull everyday hotel design. The rooms don't quite live up to the delightful inner courtyard with its Muslim-style fountain, but they're quiet and well sized, with two bars and a restaurant catering amply for other needs.

Manson Hotel (Map p312; ☎ 222356; vnmulji@ africaonline.co.ke; Kisumu Rd; s KSh1050-1650, d KSh1650-2300; 🍴) This tall balconied block is hidden away in a quiet residential neighbourhood and is well looked after, with plain but spacious standard rooms. Security is very tight, and amenities include a restaurant, TV and pool room.

Hotel Dorse (Map p314; ☎ 222252; hoteldorse@africaonline.co.ke; Kwa Shibu Rd; s/d/tw KSh2500/3000/3500; ❀) Marketed at a conference clientele, this is a good low-lying building with balconies, big beds and showers designed for very tall people. As a minor downside, it's currently overlooked by shabby tenement blocks and a building site.

Hotel Sapphire (Map p312; ☎ 491657; hotelsapphire@africaonline.co.ke; Mwembe Tayari Rd; s/d/tr KSh2200/3300/4200; ❀ ⛲) The Sapphire offers passable rooms conveniently close to the train station, but the big multistorey building looks better from the outside than inside, and could do with a touch up in places. The swimming pool's often empty.

Dancourt Hotel (Map p314; ☎ 226278; swamboi2002@yahoo.com; Meru Rd; s/d KSh1500/2000) Only half built, the existing rooms show laudable ambition, with fancy carved doors and huge TVs, but the blocked views detract considerably. When the upstairs balcony rooms are finished they'll be much nicer and the charming pastel-orange patio café should come into its own.

Glory Guest House (Map p314; ☎ 228202; Kwa Shibu Rd; s/d/tr with shared bathroom KSh600/1000/1400, s with private bathroom KSh900-1500, d with private bathroom KSh1300-2000, tr with private bathroom KSh2100; ❀) This place shares a dodgy air with its fellow Glory properties, but most rooms are reasonable, especially the VIP rooms further up the scale. As the massive padlocks suggest, be conscious of the security of your belongings while travelling.

TOP END

Royal Court Hotel (Map p314; ☎ 223379; royalcourt@swiftmombasa; Haile Selassie Rd; s US$60-70, d US$75-95, ste US$130; ❀) The swish lobby is the highlight of this stylish business hotel – executive rooms are reasonably plush, but the standard rooms are beaten hands down by those at the Castle Royal, which cost half as much! Still, service and facilities are good, disabled access is a breeze, and you get great views and excellent food at the Tawa Terrace restaurant on the roof.

Tamarind Village (Map p312; ☎ 473161; www.tamarind.co.ke; Silos Rd, Nyali; apt KSh8000-16,000; ❀ ⛲)

The highly superior Tamarind restaurant chain now has its own highly superior accommodation complex, with a range of luxury serviced apartments for anyone too full, rich or highly superior to stagger back to town. Full kitchenettes give you the option of cooking, but really, with Tamarind and the resort's private Harbour restaurant next door, why on earth would you want to?

Hotel Sai Rose (Map p312; ☎ 222897; hotelsairose@iconnect.co.ke; Nyerere Ave; s US$30-40, d US$40-60, ste US$75; ❀) It has to be said that this is a bit of an oddity: a long narrow building with tight pastel corridors stuck between two patches of waste ground. For the price, though, rooms aren't bad at all, especially the Swahili-themed executive rooms and the blue honeymoon suite.

Eating

Eating on the coast can be a completely different experience from dining inland, with more variety, fresh seafood, and a whole new range of spices and flavours. There's a wide selection of restaurants in Mombasa, reflecting both Swahili tradition and the cosmopolitan ethnic make-up of the city itself.

RESTAURANTS
Kenyan & Swahili
Explore the Old Town for cheap, authentic Swahili cuisine; if in doubt, follow the locals to find the best deals. Most places are Muslim-run, so no alcoholic drinks are sold and they're closed until after sunset during Ramadan.

Island Dishes (Map p312; ☎ 0720-887311; Kibokoni Rd; mains KSh50-180) Once your eyes have managed to adjust to the dazzling strip lights, feast them on the tasty menu at this whiter-than-white Lamu-themed canteen. *Mishkaki* (kebabs), chicken tikka, fish, fresh juices and all the usual favourites are on offer to eat in or take away, though the biryani (curry and rice) is only available at lunchtime.

New Recoder Restaurant (Map p312; Kibokoni Rd; mains KSh50-180) A local favourite in a new location, slightly tattier than Island but with much the same coast cuisine.

Singh Restaurant (Map p314; ☎ 493283; Mwembe Tayari Rd; mains KSh50-150) The Sikh temple near the bus stands operates this small cafeteria restaurant, tipped by Mombasans in the know as one of the best places in town for

KENYA

vegetarians. KSh250 is more than enough to get you a massive feed.

Indian

Shehnai Restaurant (Map p314; ☎ 224801; Fatemi House, Maungano Rd; mains from KSh290; 🕑 noon-2pm & 7.30-10.30pm Tue-Sun) Mombasa's classiest curry house specialises in tandoori and *mughlai* (north Indian) cuisine, and has a huge menu, complimented by a tasteful line in drapery. It's very popular with well-heeled Indian families, and the food is authentic and very good.

Splendid View Restaurant (Map p314; ☎ 5487270; splendidrestaurants@yahoo.com; Maungano Rd; mains KSh100-300; 🕑 11.30am-2pm & 5.30-10.30pm) You'll be looking in vain if you expect magnificent vistas from the street seating here – the name merely refers to the Splendid Hotel opposite. Luckily the food compensates for this sly misnomer, covering styles from tandoori to Chinese-influenced *pili pili*, a kind of curry.

New Chetna Restaurant (Map p314; ☎ 224477; Haile Selassie Rd; mains KSh200-300) This is a very popular South Indian canteen restaurant with a long list of vegetarian goodies, including *masala dosa* (curried vegetables inside a lentil-flour pancake) and *idli* (rice dumpling). The various *thali* are great value.

Chinese

New Overseas Chinese-Korean Restaurant & Bar (Map p312; ☎ 230729; Moi Ave; mains KSh220-480) Despite the overblown name and the hilariously clichéd interior design, the New Overseas delivers on its Oriental promises and is particularly strong on seafood; a full Chinese or Korean feast will cost you up to KSh1000.

China Town Restaurant (Map p314; ☎ 315098; Nyerere Ave; mains KSh400-600) More incredibly chintzy décor, more great Korean and Chinese food. It's opposite the Holy Ghost Cathedral on Nyerere Ave.

International

Tamarind Restaurant (Map p312; ☎ 471747; Silos Rd, Nyali; lobster per 100g KSh330, mains KSh900-1800) Perhaps the finest of the various Tamarind ventures. Eating on the terrace of this grand Moorish building overlooking the water is a romantic splurge you can't afford to miss. Seafood is the focus, but meat eaters won't go hungry and vegetarians even get their own menu. The only bum note is the rather cheesy keyboard music, which takes a few *dawas* (vodka, lime and honey cocktails) to drown out.

Little Chef Dinners Pub (Map p314; ☎ 222740; Moi Ave; mains KSh100-210) Thankfully this funky green-hued pub-restaurant has nothing to do with the British motorway diners of the same name, dishing up big, tasty portions of Kenyan and international dishes from pilau to stroganoff. The 1st-floor bar has a pool table and a great breezy balcony, one of the most relaxed places in town for a beer. There are a couple more outlets in the area, but this is by far the nicest.

Baron Restaurant & Pub (Map p314; ☎ 314971; Digo Rd; mains KSh250-650) While it appears at first like a pretty average drinking hall, a glance at Baron's ambitious menu reveals a lot more than cold Tusker passing through the kitchen. Crocodile, ostrich, guinea fowl and lobster (KSh1750) all feature, and even the drinks list takes up a page or two.

Siesta Bar & Restaurant (Map p312; ☎ 474896; Nyali Rd, Nyali; mains KSh350-600; 🕑 from 5pm Tue-Sun) You say *mzungu* (white person), they say gringo...we just say *olé* – this is quite possibly the only Mexican restaurant in East Africa, set in a fine garden above the harbour by the Nyali Bridge. It's great for a sunset beer and the near-authentic food comes highly recommended.

Fontanella Steakhouse & Beer Garden (Map p314; ☎ 222740; City House, Moi Ave; mains KSh100-250) A popular open-air place in a courtyard off Moi Ave, with *nyama choma*, steaks and Western offerings, such as spag bol. There's a large birdcage for entertainment, though without many outside lights you can hardly see it (or the menus) at night.

Rozina House Restaurant (Map p314; ☎ 311107; Moi Ave; mains KSh500-1200) Walk along Moi Ave in the evening and you're bound to be approached by touts for this would-be upmarket eatery. The food is reputedly good, but if you've just been dragged in off the street the prices are distinctly off-putting. Cheaper meals are available at the café next door.

CAFÉS

Cozy Inn (Map p312; ☎ 0733-925707; Kibokoni Rd; mains KSh80-195; 🖳) A rare new addition to the Old Town scene, this friendly little café's classical music soothes the senses as you surf or snack. Lunch and dinner are planned weekly, with just four Italian-themed main dishes available each day.

Pistacchio Café (Map p314; ☎ 221989; cnr Meru Rd & Mwindani Rd; buffet lunch KSh450; ☒ Mon-Sat) A Swiss-run place, with excellent ice cream and popular lunchtime buffets, usually consisting of a mixture of Indian and Western dishes. À-la-carte staples such as spaghetti are also served.

QUICK EATS

There are dozens of inexpensive local cafés and restaurants serving quick meals and snacks. Street food is an even faster option: stalls around town sell snacks like cassava, samosas, bhajis and kebabs, while a few set up trestle tables to dish out stew and *ugali* (maize meal). For dessert, vendors can ply you with *haluwa* (an Omani version of Turkish delight), fried taro roots, sweet baobab seeds and sugared donuts.

Blue Room Restaurant (Map p314; ☎ 224021; Haile Selassie Rd; snacks KSh20-50, mains KSh110-325; ☐) The Blue Room is hugely popular for its fast food, from cakes and sandwiches to curries, steaks and pizza. Drinks are made with filtered water, and there are no fewer than two back-up generators in case of power cuts! There's also a highly recommended ice-cream parlour.

Fayaz Baker & Confectioners (Map p314; ☎ 220382; Jomo Kenyatta Ave) Mombasa's 'Master Baker' cooks up excellent cakes and muffins in several locations around town; great for breakfast on the run or a leisurely mid-morning snack.

SELF-CATERING

Nakumatt supermarket (Map p312; ☎ 228945; Nyerere Ave) Close to the Likoni ferry, with an astounding selection of provisions, drinks, consumer goods and hardware items, just in case you need a TV, bicycle or lawnmower to go with your groceries.

Main market (Map p314; Digo Rd) Mombasa's dilapidated 'covered' market building, formerly the Mackinnon Market, is packed with stalls selling fresh fruit and vegetables. Roaming produce carts also congregate in the surrounding streets, and dozens of *miraa* (bundles of leafy twigs and shoots that are chewed as a stimulant and appetite-suppressant) sellers join the fray when the regular deliveries come in.

Drinking

There are plenty of good drinking holes in Mombasa and many restaurants cater primarily to drinkers in the evening. Keep an eye out for flyers advertising reggae concerts and other events.

New Florida Nightclub (☎ 313127; Mama Ngina Dr; admission men/women KSh150/70; ☒ 24hr; ☒) This vast seafront complex houses Mombasa's liveliest nightclub, which boasts its own casino, restaurants and even an open-air swimming pool. It's owned by the same people as the infamous Florida clubs in Nairobi, and offers much the same atmosphere, clientele and Las Vegas–style floorshows. A taxi fare here is around KSh400.

Office (Map p312; ☎ 451700; Shelly Beach Rd, Likoni) Perched above the Likoni ferry jetty and *matatu* stand, the entirely unaptly named Office is a real locals' hang-out, with regular massive reggae and dub nights shaking the thatched rafters.

Casablanca Restaurant & Club (Map p314; Mnazi Moja Rd; admission KSh50-100) Amid the *makuti* and cartoon animals, this loud split-level bar-club pulls in plenty of Westerners, but also a *lot* of prostitutes – all-male groups will be mobbed mercilessly, especially on the dance floor.

Toyz Disco (Map p314; ☎ 313931; Baluchi St; admission KSh100) A loud and lively Kenyan nightspot just off Nkrumah Rd. The 'Be Casual' sign outside announces in graphic form that drugs, nudity, fighting and weapons are banned, which seems to work as it's perfectly friendly inside. Admission is free for women. Expect plenty of gangsta rap and jangly Congolese music.

Entertainment

Nyali Cinemax (Map p312; ☎ 470000; info@nyalicinemax.com; Nyali Centre, Nyali Rd, Nyali; tickets KSh250-350) A plush, modern cinema complex close to Tamarind, also incorporating a casino, sports bar, cybercafé, Indian deli and restaurant, plus a bowling alley.

Kenya Cinema (Map p314; ☎ 312355; Nkrumah Ave; tickets stalls/balcony KSh120/150) An appealing old cinema that screens Hindi movies regularly (usually with English subtitles) and Western blockbusters occasionally.

Getting There & Away

AIR

Flights are available with **Kenya Airways** (Map p314; ☎ 221251; www.kenya-airways.com; TSS Towers,

Nkrumah Rd) between Nairobi and Mombasa's **Moi International Airport** (☎ 433211) at least six times daily (KSh6835, one hour).

Mombasa Air Safari (☎ 433061; www.mombasaairsafari.com; Moi International Airport) flies to Malindi (US$21, 25 minutes), Lamu (US$90, 1¼ hours), and Amboseli (US$220, one hour), Tsavo (US$220, on request) and Maasai Mara (US$229) National Parks.

BUS & MATATU
Nairobi
There are dozens of daily departures in either direction (mostly in the early morning and late evening). Recommended companies:

Akamba (Map p314; ☎ 490269; Jomo Kenyatta Ave)
Busscar (Map p314; ☎ 222854; Abdel Nasser Rd)
Busstar (Map p314; Nairobi ☎ 02-219525; Abdel Nasser Rd)
Coastline Safaris (Map p314; ☎ 312083; Mwembe Tayari St)
Falcon (Map p314; Nairobi ☎ 02-229662) Offices on Abdel Nasser Rd and Jomo Kenyatta Ave.
Mash Express (Map p314; ☎ 491955; Jomo Kenyatta Ave)
Mombasa Raha (Map p314; ☎ 225716) Offices on Abdel Nasser Rd and Jomo Kenyatta Ave.
Msafiri (Map p312; ☎ 314691; Aga Khan Rd)

Daytime services take at least six hours, while the overnight trip takes anywhere from eight to 10 hours. Fares vary from KSh500 to KSh1000. Most companies have at least four departures daily.

All buses travel via Voi (KSh300), which is also served by frequent *matatus* from the Kobil petrol station on Jomo Kenyatta Ave (KSh200).

Heading North
Red Metro Mombasa city buses run north from the Likoni ferry, which lands roughly every 45 minutes, passing through town on Digo Rd and heading to Mtwapa (KSh30, 40 minutes) or Malindi (KSh120, two hours).

There are numerous daily *matatus* and small minibuses up the coast to Malindi, leaving from in front of the Noor Mosque on Abdel Nasser Rd. Buses take up to 2½ hours (KSh100), *matatus* about two hours (KSh120). You can also catch an 'express' *matatu* (KSh150), which takes longer to fill up, but is then supposedly nonstop all the way.

Tawakal, Falcon, Mombasa Raha and TSS Express have buses to Lamu, most leaving at around 7am (report 30 minutes early) from their offices on Abdel Nasser Rd. Buses take around seven hours to reach the Lamu ferry at Mokoke (KSh400 to 500), stopping in Malindi (KSh150, two hours).

Heading South
For buses and *matatus* to the beaches south of Mombasa you first need to get off the island via the Likoni ferry (see below). Very frequent buses and *matatus* leave from the mainland ferry terminal and travel down the southern coast.

TRAIN
The popular overnight train to/from Nairobi is a great place to meet other travellers and hook up for safaris or travel on the coast. Trains leave from Mombasa at 7pm on Tuesday, Thursday and Sunday, arriving the next day somewhere between 8.30am and 11am. The fares are KSh3160/2275 in 1st/2nd class with dinner, breakfast and bedding; reserve as far in advance as possible. The **booking office** (☎ 312220; ☽ 8am-5pm) is at the station in Mombasa.

Getting Around
TO/FROM THE AIRPORT
There is currently no public transport to/from the airport, so you're best taking a taxi; the fare to central Mombasa is around KSh650. Coming from the city centre, the usual fare is KSh800, but you'll have to bargain down from KSh1000.

BOAT
The two Likoni ferries connect Mombasa Island with the southern mainland, running at frequent intervals throughout the day and night. It's free to pedestrians and KSh35 for a car. To get to the jetty from the centre, take a Likoni *matatu* from Digo Rd (KSh10).

CAR & MOTORCYCLE
Recommended car-hire companies in Mombasa include the following:

Avenue Motors (Map p312; ☎ 225126; Moi Ave)
Avis (Map p312; ☎ 314950; Southern House, Moi Ave)
Budget (☎ 221281; budgetmba@budget-kenya.com; Moi International Airport)
Glory Car Hire (Map p312; ☎ 313561; Moi Ave) Insurance excess costs KSh150,000.
Hertz (☎ 4332405; mombasa@hertz.co.ke; Moi International Airport)

MATATU

Matatus charge KSh10 to KSh20 for short hops. For the Likoni ferry and Nakumatt supermarket, loads of *matatus* run south along Nyerere Ave to the transport stand by the ferry terminal.

TAXI

Mombasa taxis are just as expensive as those in Nairobi, only harder to find. Assume it'll cost KSh200 to KSh300 from the train station to the city centre.

SHIMBA HILLS NATIONAL RESERVE

This 320-sq-km **reserve** (adult/child US$23/10; 🕙 6am-6pm) lies directly inland from Diani Beach and covers a wonderful landscape of steep-sided valleys, rolling hills and lush pockets of tropical rainforest, rated one of the country's best surviving biodiversity zones. The hills are home to a healthy population of leopards and a vast abundance of birdlife, and you may also spot the reserve's most famous resident, the rare sable antelope. This tall, regal antelope has a striking black-and-white coat and long, curved horns, and is now protected after the population plummeted to less than 120 animals in the 1970s.

The other main attraction is the large community of elephants. In 2005 numbers reached an amazing 600, far too many for this tiny space; instead of culling the herds, KWS organised an unprecedented US$3.2 million translocation operation, capturing no fewer than 400 elephants and moving them to Tsavo East National Park.

Highly recommended guided forest walks are run by the **KWS** (☎ 040-4159; PO Box 30, Kwale) from the Sheldrick Falls ranger post at the southern end of the park down to scenic Sheldrick Falls on the Machenmwana River. Walks are free but a tip would be appropriate.

One more initiative that should be fully operational by the time you read this is the **Shimba Hills Triangular Forest** project, a community initiative run by the forest guides on the northeastern boundary of the reserve. This biologically rich area is being developed as an ecotourism attraction, with 90-minute tours taking in a replica *kaya* (sacred forest) shrine, troupes of resident Sykes monkeys and over 40 species of butterfly.

SAFETY ON THE COAST

Security along the coast has improved in recent years, but you still need to be careful around the popular resorts. Muggings are a risk on the minor roads that run between the main highway and the various beach hotels. Take a taxi or *matatu*, particularly at night.

All the resorts and cottages on the coast employ *askaris* (guards) to keep out undesirables, but once you're on the beach it's easy to become a target for 'snatch and run' crimes. Leave watches, wallets, jewellery and other items of value in your room.

Beach boys – young Kenyan men who walk up and down the beaches selling everything from woodcarvings to marijuana and sexual favours – are a fact of life at the big resorts and their dogged persistence can be wearing. All you can do is refuse politely; they should move on quickly.

Sleeping

Shimba Rainforest Lodge (☎ 040-4077; Kinango Rd; full board with shared bathroom per person US$120) A good Treetops-style affair built from indigenous woods, with a walkway through the rainforest and a viewing platform and bar. Children under seven years are not admitted. The floodlit waterhole here attracts quite a lot of wildlife, including leopards.

Mukurumuji Tented Camp (☎ 040-2412; www .dianihouse.com; full board per person US$94) Set on a forested hill, this place is perched above the Mukurumuji River on the southern boundary of the park. Guests can enjoy walking trips along the river and to Sheldrick Falls. Transfers from Diani cost US$10 each way.

The **public campsite** (per person US$8) and excellent round **bandas** (per person US$20) are superbly located on the edge of an escarpment close to the main gate, with stunning views down to Diani Beach. It's also possible to camp at Hunter's Camp, close to Sheldrick Falls.

Getting There & Away

You'll need a 4WD to enter the Shimba Hills National Reserve. From Likoni, small minibuses (number 34) to Kwale pass the main gate (KSh40). Most visitors come on overnight safari packages, but the Mukurumuji Tented Camp can organise transfers from Diani Beach.

MWALUGANJE ELEPHANT SANCTUARY

This **sanctuary** (☎ 040-41121; nonresident adult/child US$15/2, vehicles KSh150-500; ☷ 6am-6pm) is a good example of community-based conservation and most local people are stakeholders in the project. It was opened in October 1995 to create a corridor along an ancient elephant migration route between the Shimba Hills National Reserve and the Mwaluganje Forest Reserve, and comprises 2400 hectares of rugged, beautiful country along the valley of the Cha Shimba River.

More than 150 elephants live in the sanctuary and you're likely to see a large variety of other fauna and flora, including rare cycad forest. (This primitive, palmlike plant species is over 300 million years old.) There's a good information centre close to the main gate and a second ticket office on the outskirts of Kwale. Don't miss the chance to buy the unique postcards and paper goods as souvenirs for the folks back home – they're all made from recycled elephant dung!

The main entrance to the sanctuary is about 13km northeast of Shimba Hills National Reserve on the road to Kinango. A shorter route runs from Kwale to the Golini gate, passing the Mwaluganje ticket office. It's only 5km, but the track is 4WD only.

TIWI BEACH

☎ 040

This wonderfully undeveloped beach is reached by two dirt roads that wind their way through the coastal scrub about 20km south of Likoni. It's a world away from the bustle down the road at Diani Beach, and while the seclusion does mean you have to be a bit careful walking around, it's worth it for the real sense of peace and quiet on the beautiful white-sand beach.

Tiwi is a tranquil haven but it's still very popular with those in the know, so you should book well ahead if you intend to visit during the high season. Beach boys and souvenir sellers are fairly prevalent at the southern end of Tiwi, but are almost unheard of at the northern end of the strip.

Sleeping & Eating

Unlike the all-inclusive resorts at Diani, self-catering is the name of the game here. The options are divided into two groups, linked by a bumpy track just inland from the beach (walking is not recommended).

Sand Island Beach Cottages (☎ 3300043; www .sandislandtiwi.com; cottages low season KSh2750-5500, high season KSh3000-6050) A lively posse of dogs enhances the warm welcome you'll get at these lovely colonial-style cottages, set in a tidy garden at the northern end of the beach. Nearby Sand Island is a lovely place to relax and catch some sun.

Maweni Beach Cottages (☎ 3300012; www.maweni beach.com; cottages low season KSh2000-4700, high season KSh2500-5200) Owned by the Tiwi Beach Resort, this place consists of attractive *makuti*-roofed cottages overlooking a peaceful cove, with a choice of garden or sea views. There's no direct beach frontage, but facilities are good.

Moonlight Bay Cottages (☎ 3300040; cottages low season KSh3000-5400, high season KSh3400-6200) Just next door to Sand Island, this is a decent option, with well-equipped one- to three-bedroom cottages and a shady open-air bar-restaurant area.

Coral Cove Cottages (☎ 3205195; coralcove.tiwi beach.com; cottages KSh3500-5200) A fantastically friendly place, with a wide variety of comfy, nicely decorated cottages sleeping one to five people. The larger cottages have kitchens, and cooks/cleaners can be hired for KSh500 per day.

Twiga Lodge (☎ 3205126; camping KSh200, s/d KSh800/1500, cottages KSh1500) The only really backpacker-oriented place in Tiwi, Twiga is a good place to meet younger independent travellers. Accommodation runs from the beachfront camp site and basic four-bed cottages to the superior 'show rooms' (B&B KSh3000 to KSh4500). Local taxi drivers tout quite heavily for this place, and there always seems to be a crowd of hangers-on; you'd be sensible not to leave valuables lying around.

Tiwi Beach Resort (☎ 3202801; www.tiwibeach resort.com; half board s/d low season US$46/79, high season US$54/96; ☷ ☐ ☐) This vast package-holiday complex is the diametric opposite of the little family-run concerns here, with long whitewashed accommodation blocks, three restaurants, a nightclub and a rather snazzy pool design.

Nagina supermarket (A14 Hwy) Near the turn-off to the Tiwi Beach Hotel, self-caterers can pick up supplies here.

Getting There & Away

Any buses and *matatus* on the Likoni–Ukunda road can drop you at the start of

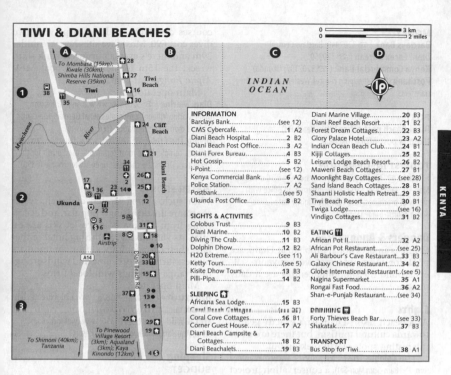

TIWI & DIANI BEACHES

INFORMATION	
Barclays Bank	(see 12)
CMS Cybercafé	1 A2
Diani Beach Hospital	2 B2
Diani Beach Post Office	3 A2
Diani Forex Bureau	4 B3
Hot Gossip	5 B2
i-Point	(see 12)
Kenya Commercial Bank	6 A2
Police Station	7 A2
Postbank	(see 5)
Ukunda Post Office	8 B2

SIGHTS & ACTIVITIES	
Colobus Trust	9 A3
Diani Marine	10 B2
Diving The Crab	11 B3
Dolphin Dhow	12 B2
H2O Extreme	(see 11)
Ketty Tours	(see 5)
Kisite Dhow Tours	13 B3
Pilli-Pipa	14 B2

SLEEPING	
Africana Sea Lodge	15 B3
Coral Beach Cottages	(see 26)
Coral Cove Cottages	16 B1
Corner Guest House	17 A2
Diani Beach Campsite & Cottages	18 B2
Diani Beachalets	19 B3

Diani Marine Village	20 B3
Diani Reef Beach Resort	21 B2
Forest Dream Cottages	22 B3
Glory Palace Hotel	23 A2
Indian Ocean Beach Club	24 B1
Kijiji Cottages	25 B2
Leisure Lodge Beach Resort	26 B2
Maweni Beach Cottages	27 B1
Moonlight Bay Cottages	(see 28)
Sand Island Beach Cottages	28 B1
Shaanti Holistic Health Retreat	29 B3
Tiwi Beach Resort	30 B1
Twiga Lodge	(see 16)
Vindigo Cottages	31 B2

EATING	
African Pot II	32 A2
African Pot Restaurant	(see 25)
Ali Barbour's Cave Restaurant	33 B3
Galaxy Chinese Restaurant	34 B2
Globe International Restaurant	(see 5)
Nagina Supermarket	35 A1
Rongai Fast Food	36 A2
Shan-e-Punjab Restaurant	(see 34)

DRINKING	
Forty Thieves Beach Bar	(see 33)
Shakatak	37 B3

TRANSPORT	
Bus Stop for Tiwi	38 A1

either track down to Tiwi (KSh30); keep an eye out for the sign to Tiwi Beach Resort. The southern turn-off by the supermarket, known locally as Tiwi 'spot', is much easier to find.

Although it's only 3.5km to the beach, both access roads are notorious for muggings, so be sure to take a taxi (KSh300) or hang around for a lift.

DIANI BEACH & UKANDA
☎ 040

As the principal package resort on the southern coast, Diani Beach tends to inspire mixed feelings among its various visitors. There's certainly not much Kenyan about the massive hotel complexes that line the long beach, but the setting as a whole is certainly more exotic than your average Mediterranean holiday strip; the inland parks and southern islands are within easy reach; and the number of activities on offer should be enough to keep even the most cynical tourist from grumbling. If you're just out for a drink, a laugh and a bit of time out between 'serious' travel, the atmosphere is as good as you'll find anywhere on the Kenyan coast.

Orientation
The town of Ukunda, which is on the main Mombasa–Tanzania road, is the turn-off point for Diani Beach. It has a post office, a bank, several shops, and a number of basic lodging houses and restaurants. From there, Palm Ave runs about 2.5km to a T-junction with the beach road, where you'll find everything Diani has to offer.

Information
EMERGENCY
Diani Beach Hospital (☎ 3202435; www.dianibeach hospital.com; ☾ 24hr)
Police (☎ 3202121, 3202229; Ukunda)

INTERNET ACCESS
CMS Cybercafé (Palm Ave, Ukunda; per min KSh1.50; ☾ 8am-8pm Mon-Sat, 10.30am-7pm Sun)
Hot Gossip (☎ 3203307; wellconnectednet@hotgossip .co.ke; Legend Casino Complex; per min KSh5; ☾ 9am-6pm Mon-Fri, 9am-2pm Sat) Also offers international phone and fax services.

KENYA

KENYA

MONEY

Barclays Bank (☎ 3202448; Barclays Centre)
Diani Forex Bureau (☎ 3203595)
Kenya Commercial Bank (☎ 3202197; Ukunda)
Postbank (Diani shopping centre) Western Union money transfers.

POST

Diani Beach post office (Diani Beach Rd)
Ukunda post office (Ukunda)

TOURIST INFORMATION

i-Point (☎ 3202234; Barclays Centre; 🕑 8.30am-6pm Mon-Fri, 9am-4pm Sat) Private information office with plenty of brochures. Also sells the slightly dated *Diani Beach Tourist-Guide* (KSh50).

Dangers & Annoyances

Crime is an occasional problem at Diani; see p321 for more information. Souvenir sellers around the shopping centres are a daily nuisance.

Sights

As a beach resort Diani isn't exactly geared towards cultural tourism, but there are a few interesting spots worth seeking out.

The **Colobus Trust** (☎ 3203519; www.colobustrust .org; 🕑 8am-5pm Mon-Sat), a conservation project aimed at protecting Diani's population of endangered colobus monkeys, offers informative guided walks (KSh500) from its research station off the southern part of Diani Beach Rd. They provide an excellent introduction to the coral rainforest habitat and a good chance of seeing other indigenous wildlife alongside the resident monkeys.

Inaugurated in 2001, **Kaya Kinondo** (☎ 0722-344426; kayakinondo@hotgossip.co.ke) is a superb grass-roots ecotourism project south of Diani. Guided walks take you through the *kaya* itself, a forest sacred to the Digo people, and include visits to a traditional village, a tribal medicine man and the main primary school. The local community is involved at every level, managing the conservation process, training guides, and producing crafts and other goods for sale to visitors.

Activities

DIVING

All the big resorts either have their own dive schools or work with a local operator. Rates are fairly standard: Professional Association of Diving Instructors (PADI) open-water

courses cost €490, and reef trips with two dives cost €90. Most dive sites here are under 29m and there's even a purposely sunk shipwreck, the 15m former fishing boat MFV *Alpha Funguo*, at 28m.

Main operators:
Diani Marine (☎ 3203450; www.dianimarine.com; Diani Marine Village) Very professional German-run centre with its own accommodation (see opposite).
Diving The Crab (☎ 3202003; www.divingthecrab.com; Nomads complex) The most commonly used outfit for the big hotels. Offers the cheapest open-water course (€350).

WATER SPORTS

With such a long stretch of beach, water sports are unsurprisingly popular, and everything from banana boats to jet skis are on offer. As with diving, all the big hotels either have their own equipment (for common activities, such as snorkelling and windsurfing) or arrange bookings with local firms.

Main operators:
H20 Extreme (☎ 0721-495876; www.h20-extreme.com; Nomads complex)
Wet & Wild (☎ 0722-705350; www.wetandwilddiani .com; Aqualand, Pinewood Village Resort)

Sleeping

BUDGET

Corner Guest House (☎ 3203355; Ukunda; s/d with shared bathroom KSh400/500) If you really need to sleep cheap, Ukunda's your only option. This is the best of a number of basic lodgings near the Diani junction; rooms are simple but clean, with fans and piped music until midnight. Add KSh50 from November to March. Breakfast is available for KSh200.

Diani Beach Campsite & Cottages (☎ 3203192; dianicampsite@yahoo.com; camping low/high season KSh300/400, cottages low season KSh1500-2500, high season KSh3000-6000) The only budget choice anywhere near the beach, although unless you're camping, even the low-season prices are steep. The tent space is a small, simple lawn site with toilets and an eating area. The compact cottages sleep up to four people.

Glory Palace Hotel (☎ 3203392; Palm Ave; low season s KSh800, d KSh1200-2000, tr 2000, high season s KSh1000, d KSh2000-3000, tr KSh2500; 🅿 🏊) Not exactly a bargain but the cheapest hotel option for solo travellers, and at least you get breakfast, security and use of the swimming pool for your money. With constant *matatus* passing by, it's easy to get to the beach strip or the Ukunda transport stage.

MIDRANGE

All of Diani's other accommodation is spread out along the beach road. Unless otherwise indicated, all places in this category are self-catering.

Kijiji Cottages (☎ 3300035; forbes@wananchi.com; cottages KSh5000-7000; ☒) These big, characterful cottages, sleeping up to five people, are set along winding paths in their own garden complex, giving them an exclusive feel. Even better, the secluded beach is often cut off from the beach boys by the tide. Rates drop by KSh1000 in May and June but almost double over Christmas and New Year.

Coral Beach Cottages (☎ 3202205; cottages low season KSh4000-5000, high season KSh7000-10,000) Just north of the junction, Coral Beach has large, well-appointed cottages set in a neat garden. The atmosphere is pleasant and relaxed, and the excellent African Pot Restaurant (p326) is right at the entrance gate.

Diani Marine Village (☎ 3202367; www.dianimarine .com; s/d low season €25/30, high season €30/35) Although primarily a dive resort, the huge guest rooms are appealing, with fans, stone floors and four-poster mosquito nets. Unlike most places in this class it's not self-catering.

Vindigo Cottages (☎ 3202192; vindigocottages@ kenyaweb.com; cottages low season KSh1500-3500, high season KSh2000-4000) A rather sweet collection of little orange cottages sloping down to the sea, each sleeping between two and eight people. There are no fans but the sea breeze keeps you cool, and all the cottages have mosquito nets.

Diani Beachalets (☎ 3202180; dianibeachalets@ wananchi.com; bandas per person KSh550, cottages low season KSh900-2500, high season KSh1300-3400) Towards the southern end of the strip, this place is a little old, but offers plenty of space. The accommodation options vary hugely, from two-person *bandas* to four-bedroom seafront cottages with kitchen.

TOP END

There are at least 13 flashy resort complexes spread out along the beach strip. Unless otherwise stated, prices listed are all-inclusive rates for standard rooms. Note that many of these places close for renovation between May and June.

Diani Reef Beach Resort (☎ 3202723; www.diani reef.com; half board s/d low season from US$100/160, high season from US$190/250; ☒ ☐ ☒ ☼) One of the sharpest resorts on the south coast, Diani Reef is well executed in every respect and boasts excellent facilities, including a health club, casino, water slide, six bars, three presidential suites and an open-air disco. The rooms themselves are nicely laid out, with spotless bathrooms and ethernet connections, and there's good disabled access.

Indian Ocean Beach Club (☎ 3203730; www .jacarandahotels.com; full board s/d low season US$96/150, high season US$130/200; ☒ ☒ ☐ ☒) A tasteful, low-key hotel in a Moorish style, near the mouth of the Mwachema River. It's one of the more sensitively designed places, consisting of 100 cottage-style rooms. Rooms have minibars and baths, and some are specially equipped for disabled guests.

Leisure Lodge Beach Resort (☎ 3203624; www .leisurelodgeresort.com; s/d low season from €64/100, high season from €110/144; ☒ ☐ ☒ ☼) Bring your sense of direction if you want to stay here: the complex is so vast it's practically a small town in its own right, and even the staff sometimes have to consult the handy pathside maps! The sports facilities are particularly good and include an 18-hole golf course. Offers some disabled access.

Shaanti Holistic Health Retreat (☎ 3202064; shaantihhr@yahoo.co.uk; low season s KSh7000-7900, d KSh12,200-13,700, high season s KSh11,500-13,300, d KSh19,400-22,300; ☒ ☒) This brand-new Ayurvedic sanctuary is the antithesis of the usual resort blocks, appealing to New Agers and pleasure seekers alike. There are just eight rooms, designed and decorated in a distinctly Indian-influenced sandstone style. Rates include the full-day's yoga spa program; other packages are available, and non-guests can also visit for the various classes and treatments.

Forest Dream Cottages (☎ 3203224; www.forest dreamcottages.com; cottages €124-290; ☒ ☒) If you're not bothered about the beach, Forest Dream is a fantastic luxury choice, set in an actual forest reserve. The six thatched houses are set up to an excellent standard; koi ponds, Jacuzzis and fully fitted kitchens are just some of the other treats on offer.

Pinewood Village Resort (☎ 3203720; www.pine wood-village.com; half board s/d US$79/112, ste US$164; ☒ ☐ ☒ ☼) On Galu Beach, down past the far end of the Diani strip, this tasteful, comprehensively equipped villa resort is run by Southern Cross Safaris. The Aqualand water-sports centre (☎ 3202719) is one of the best in the area.

Eating

African Pot Restaurant (☎ 3203890; Coral Beach Cottages; mains KSh200-220) Meals work to a simple formula: you order your meat (chicken, beef or goat), then choose from one of five or six ways to have it prepared and add any accompaniments you like. The house speciality, *karanga*, a tomato-based sauce with garlic, coriander and onions cooked in a real earthenware pot, is highly recommended. There's another branch (African Pot II) on Palm Ave.

Ali Barbour's Cave Restaurant (☎ 3202033; mains KSh550-900; ☯ from 7pm) A very sophisticated semi-open restaurant built into a cave near the Diani Sea Resort. Seafood is the main attraction, with lobster at KSh1800. Use the courtesy bus or take a taxi as people have been mugged walking down the track.

Galaxy Chinese Restaurant (☎ 3202529; Diani Complex; mains KSh305-615; ☯ noon-6.30pm) A smart Chinese restaurant with an outdoor 'island' pavilion bar and seating area. Courtesy bus available.

Shan-e-Punjab Restaurant (☎ 3202116; Diani Complex; mains KSh300-600) A very popular Indian restaurant opposite the Diani Reef Beach Resort. A wide range of curries are on offer, including some vegetarian options.

Globe International Restaurant (☎ 0733-740938; Diani Beach shopping centre; mains KSh380-850) As the name suggests, the Globe spans a number of far-flung cuisines, though much of the emphasis is on good old British cooking.

Rongai Fast Food (Palm Ave, Ukunda) Head for the painted flames to sample this local butchery restaurant, highly recommended for *nyama choma*. You can also buy fresh meat for beach barbecues here.

Self-caterers can stock up at the supermarkets in Diani's shopping centres, or at any of the shops, *dukas* and market stalls in Ukunda.

Drinking & Entertainment

Forty Thieves Beach Bar (☎ 3203419) Part of the Ali Barbour empire, this is easily the best bar on the strip, frequented on a daily basis by a crowd of expats and regulars known affectionately as the Reprobates. Food is served during the day, and it's open until the last guest leaves, ie pretty damn late.

Shakatak (☎ 3203124) Essentially the only full-on nightclub in Diani not attached to a hotel, Shakatak is quite hilariously seedy, but can be fun once you know what to expect. Like most big Kenyan clubs, food is served at all hours.

Getting There & Around

AIR

Mombasa Air Safari's routes to Lamu and the southern national parks originate in Diani, passing through Mombasa (see p319).

BUS & MATATU

Numerous *matatus* run south from the Likoni ferry directly to Ukunda (KSh50, 30 minutes) and further south. From the Diani junction in Ukunda, *matatus* run down to the beach all day for KSh20.

TAXI

Taxis hang around Ukunda junction and all the main shopping centres; most hotels and restaurants will also have a couple waiting at night. Fares should cost KSh150 to KSh650, depending on distance.

SHIMONI & WASINI ISLAND
☎ 040

The village of Shimoni sits at the tip of a small peninsula about 76km south of Likoni. Dhow tours to nearby Wasini Island and the coral reefs of Kisite Marine National Park have become a big industry here. They're well run, but you can easily organise your own trip directly with the boatmen.

Sights

Villagers have opened up the old **slave caves** (adult/child KSh100/25; ☯ 8.30-10.30am & 1.30-6pm) as a tourist attraction, with a custodian who'll take you around the dank caverns to illustrate this little-discussed part of East African history.

Wasini Island is at its most appealing in the peace of the evening. There are several worthwhile things to see, including some ancient **Swahili ruins** and the **coral gardens** (adult/child KSh100/20), a bizarre landscape of exposed coral reefs with a boardwalk for viewing.

KISITE MARINE NATIONAL PARK

Just off the south coast of Wasini Island, this **marine park** (adult/child US$5/2) is one of the best in Kenya, also incorporating the **Mpunguti Marine National Reserve**. The park covers 28 sq km of pristine coral reefs, and offers excellent diving and snorkelling. You have a reasonable chance of seeing dolphins in the Shimoni Channel, and humpback whales are sometimes spotted between August and October.

It's easy to organise your own boat trip with a local captain; the going rate is KSh1500 per person or KSh6000 per boat, including lunch and a walk in the coral gardens on Wasini Island. Masks and snorkels can be hired for KSh200. A good place to start looking for a boatman is the office of **KWS** (☎ 52027; ◷ 6am-6pm), about 200m south of the main pier.

The best time to dive and snorkel is between October and March. Avoid June, July and August because of rough seas, silt and poor visibility.

Tours

Various companies offer organised dhow tours for snorkelling, all leaving Shimoni by 9am. Transfers from north- and south-coast hotels are available (US$10 to US$20), and longer trips with overnight stays can also be arranged. Certified divers can take one/two scuba dives for an extra US$30/50 with any of these companies.

Main operators:

Dolphin Dhow (Map p323; ☎ 52255, office 3202144; www.dolphindhow.com; office Barclays Centre, Diani Beach; tours US$75)

Kisite Dhow Tours (☎ 3202331; www.wasini-island .com; office Jadini Beach Hotel, Diani Beach; tours US$55-75) Popular ecotourist trips.

Pilli-Pipa (☎ 3202401; www.pillipipa.com; office Colliers Centre, Diani Beach; tours US$80) Diving trips from US$130.

Sleeping & Eating

Mpunguti Lodge (☎ 52288; Wasini Island; camping KSh300, half board r with shared bathroom per person KSh1200) This is the only accommodation in Wasini village. The rooms are uncomplicated, with mosquito nets and small verandas; water comes from rain barrels. You'll need to bring towels, soap and any alcoholic drinks from the mainland.

Camp Eden (☎ 52027; KWS, Shimoni; camping adult/child US$8/5, bandas per person US$10) Behind KWS headquarters, this camping ground offers accommodation with 'birdsong and insect noise' in the tropical forest south of the main jetty. There's a camp site, a covered cooking area, pit toilets and showers.

Pemba Channel Fishing Club (☎ 0722-205020; www.pembachannel.com; Shimoni; full board per person low season US$85, high season US$150; ▣) A proper

slice of elegant colonial style, with a handful of airy cottages set around a swimming pool. Deep-sea fishing is almost mandatory here; boats cost from US$500 for nine hours (valid for up to four fishers).

Coral Reef Lodge (☎ 52015; www.oneearthsafaris .com; Shimoni; per person low season US$52/64, high season US$80/104; ▣) A pleasant resort-type place on a bluff overlooking the Shimoni Channel.

Getting There & Around

There are *matatus* every hour or so between Likoni and Shimoni (KSh100, one hour) until about 6pm. It's best to be at Likoni by 6.30am if you want to get to Shimoni in time to catch one of the dhow sailings.

The price of getting across the channel to Wasini Island depends to a degree on who you meet on arrival, how many are in your group and how affluent you look. Crossings should cost KSh300 to KSh500 each way, less if you negotiate return journeys.

MOMBASA TO KILIFI
☎ 041

Like the south coast, the coastline north of Mombasa has been extensively developed, although this trails off once you get north of Shanzu Beach. It's mostly set up for European package tourists on all-inclusive holidays, but there are some decent choices for independent travellers.

The northern beaches are also dogged by seaweed at certain times of the year. They are usually clear between December and April, but at other times the sand can vanish under piles of black seaweed. The expensive resort hotels employ people to burn or bury the troublesome weed on the beach.

Going north from Mombasa, the beaches are Nyali, Bamburi, Shanzu, Kikambala and Vipingo.

Sights & Activities
MAMBA VILLAGE CROCODILE FARM

A rather bizarre combination of commercial crocodile farm, animal park, sports bar and nightclub, **Mamba Village** (☎ 475184; mambavillage2001@hotmail.com; Links Rd, Nyali Beach; nonresident adult/child KSh450/250; ◷ 8am-6pm) has around 10,000 scaly inmates baring their teeth for the public. There's a feeding show at 5pm, which rouses the lethargic beasts quite dramatically.

KENYA

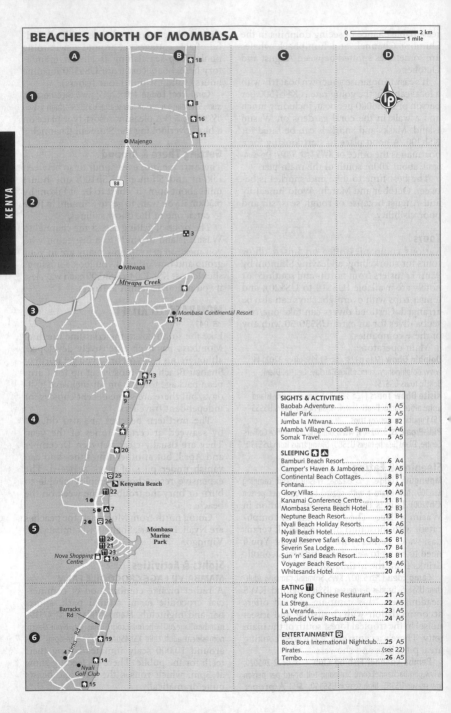

BEACHES NORTH OF MOMBASA

0 — 2 km
0 — 1 mile

Majengo

B8

Mtwapa

Mtwapa Creek

Mombasa Continental Resort

Kenyatta Beach

Mombasa
Marine
Park

Nova Shopping
Centre

Barracks
Rd

Links Rd

Nyali
Golf Club

SIGHTS & ACTIVITIES
Baobab Adventure	1	A5
Haller Park	2	A5
Jumba la Mtwana	3	B2
Mamba Village Crocodile Farm	4	A6
Somak Travel	5	A5

SLEEPING
Bamburi Beach Resort	6	A4
Camper's Haven & Jamboree	7	A5
Continental Beach Cottages	8	B1
Fontana	9	A4
Glory Villas	10	A5
Kanamai Conference Centre	11	B1
Mombasa Serena Beach Hotel	12	B3
Neptune Beach Resort	13	B4
Nyali Beach Holiday Resorts	14	A6
Nyali Beach Hotel	15	A6
Royal Reserve Safari & Beach Club	16	B1
Severin Sea Lodge	17	B4
Sun 'n' Sand Beach Resort	18	B1
Voyager Beach Resort	19	A5
Whitesands Hotel	20	A4

EATING
Hong Kong Chinese Restaurant	21	A5
La Strega	22	A5
La Veranda	23	A5
Splendid View Restaurant	24	A5

ENTERTAINMENT
Bora Bora International Nightclub	25	A5
Pirates	(see 22)	
Tembo	26	A5

BAOBAB ADVENTURE

The former Bamburi Cement Company plant was a derelict eyesore until the creation of **Baobab Adventure** (☎ 5485901; Malindi Rd, Bamburi Beach), an ingenious complex of nature trails and wildlife sanctuaries. The main attraction is **Haller Park** (nonresident adult/child KSh450/225; ⊙ 8am-5pm), which includes a wildlife sanctuary, crocodile farm, fish farm, reptile park and drive-through giraffe compound.

The various parts of the Baobab Adventure are well signposted from the highway north from Mombasa and have well-marked bus stops.

JUMBA LA MTWANA

Just north of Mtwapa Creek is this **national monument** (Mtwapa; adult/child KSh200/100; ⊙ 8am-6pm). The ruins are from a 15th-century Swahili settlement, and some interesting structures remain, of which the **Mosque by the Sea** stands out. A handy guidebook may be available from the ticket office for KSh20, or the custodian will happily give you the tour for a small gratuity. The site is a 3km walk down a dirt track, signposted from the highway about 1km north of Mtwapa bridge; a taxi there and back should cost KSh200.

Sleeping
BUDGET

Budget accommodation is in short supply along this strip, and if you want to be anywhere near the beach you'll need to find the extra cash to step up a price category.

Kanamai Conference Centre (☎ 32046, kanamai@ iconnect.co.ke; Kikambala Beach; dm/s/d KSh700/1800/3000, cottages KSh1800-2700) This is a quiet Christian conference centre with a tranquil, laidback atmosphere. Alcohol is prohibited, but there's a cafeteria serving breakfast and meals. All the rooms are simple but comfortable, and the self-catering cottages are particularly immaculate.

Glory Villas (☎ 474758; Nyali Beach; s KSh800, d KSh1200-2000, cottages KSh3000; 🅿 🍴) The only vaguely budget option for miles, this entry in the Glory empire is a complex of odd conical towers behind the Nova shopping centre. Nyali Beach is a 15-minute walk away.

MIDRANGE

Bamburi Beach Resort (☎ 0733-474482; www.bamburiresort.com; Bamburi Beach; r US$20-90; 🅿 🍴) This tidy little complex has direct access to the beach, and a choice of appealing bamboo-finished hotel rooms and self-catering rooms (outdoor kitchens).

Fontana (☎ 5487554; Malindi Rd, Bamburi Beach; d low/high season KSh2500/3000; 🅿 🍴) While the rooms are liveable, the highlight of this small place is the big thatched lobby restaurant (mains KSh420 to KSh700), which resembles a musty safari lodge stuffed with Africana. The beach is 100m beyond the compound.

Continental Beach Cottages (☎ 32190; manasseh@ wananchi.com; Kikambala Beach; B&B/full board per person KSh950/1450, cottages KSh1700-3850; 🅿 🍴) A quiet little place with a beach bar. The cottages are neat and well looked after, with kitchens and palm gardens facing onto the beach.

Camper's Haven & Jamboree (☎ 5486954; campers_haven@yahoo.com; Bamburi Beach; camping per tent KSh500, r low/high season KSh2500/5500) A large, slightly bumpy camping ground going right up to the beach. Four-person tents are available for KSh1500; room prices include breakfast in the low season and half board during the high season.

TOP END
Nyali Beach

Voyager Beach Resort (☎ 475114; www.heritage-eastafrica.com; Barracks Rd; s/d low season US$185/260, high season US$230/310; 🅿 🖥 🍴 🛗) The nautical theme is possibly stretched a bit far, but Voyager can happily cruise through life on its reputation as Nyali's best luxury resort. Facilities are comprehensive, prices are all-inclusive, staff are well drilled, the grounds are huge and the beach is right there.

Nyali Beach Hotel (☎ 471541; www.blockhotelske.com; Beach Rd; s/tw low season US$118/147, high season US$184/234; 🅿 🖥 🛗) At the southern end of the beach, this is Voyager's main competition, managing to take up even more space and offer even more facilities.

Nyali Beach Holiday Resorts (☎ 472325; nbhr@ wananchi.com; Beach Rd; s/d low season KSh3500/5800, high season KSh4500/6800, cottages from KSh5500; 🅿 🖥 🍴 🛗) A good option if you want the Kenyan beach experience without the European price tag. It's less luxurious than the other resorts, but you still get a restaurant, bar, games room and self-catering cottages.

Bamburi Beach

Whitesands Hotel (☎ 485926; www.sarovahotels.com; s/d low season from US$90/140, high season from US$140/180; 🅿 🖥 🍴 🛗) This multi-award-winning and

KENYA

almost invariably busy place could be justi-fied in dubbing itself the best resort hotel on the coast, offering consistently good service, thoughtful design, full luxury facilities and general high standards throughout. There are an amazing five pools and the grounds front directly onto the sand.

Severin Sea Lodge (☎ 5485001; www.severin-kenya .com; s/d low season US$54/108, high season US$165/206; ❄ � ✈) This place is so classy it actually has a Swiss consulate on the grounds. Ac-commodation is in appealing round cottages running down to the beach, and there are some nice bars and restaurants, including a funky restaurant in a converted dhow.

Neptune Beach Resort (☎ 5485701; www.neptune hotels.com; s/d/tr low season KSh2700/4400/6600, high sea-son KSh4300/7000/10,500; ❄ � ✈) Best described as an endearing eyesore, the haphazard col-our scheme and curiously panda-shaped pool do at least help Neptune stand out from the competition. High-season rates are all-inclusive.

Shanzu Beach
Mombasa Serena Beach Hotel (☎ 485721; www .serenahotels.com; half board s/d low season US$95/190, high season US$200/260; ❄ ▯ ➣ ✈) Serena's only Kenyan beach resort is so extensive that it's styled on a traditional Swahili village – the pathways around the tree-filled complex even have street names. The split-level rooms are equally impressive, and the design lends an incongruous intimacy.

Kikambala Beach
Royal Reserve Safari & Beach Club (☎ 32022; www .royalreserve.com; apt US$66-100; ❄ ➣ ✈) Possibly the best-value self-catering on the coast, with all-new fittings, including microwave and utensils, complemented by a full range of facilities and activities. It's heavily mar-keted for timeshares, so book early in the high season.

Sun'n'Sand Beach Resort (☎ 32621; www.sun nsand.co.ke; half board s/d low season US$45/90, high sea-son US$70/100; ❄ ▯ ➣ ✈) Despite its 900-head capacity there's a really nice feel to the pastel-orange Sun'n'Sand, and it's known as one of the best hotels on the north coast for kids.

Eating
La Veranda (☎ 5485482; Nyali Beach; mains KSh350-650) This is a reliable Italian restaurant behind the Nova shopping centre, with a big pizza oven, alfresco veranda dining and reasonable prices. It's closed between 3pm and 6pm on weekdays.

Hong Kong Chinese Restaurant (☎ 5485422; Ma-lindi Rd, Nyali Beach; mains KSh280-595) On the main road next to the shopping centre, the Chi-nese food dished up in this round pavilion-style building is a good example of its breed and will definitely fill a hole. Choose from small and large portions or set menus for up to six people (KSh1900 to KSh6850).

Splendid View Restaurant (☎ 5487270; Malindi Rd, Bamburi Beach; mains KSh100-500; ☽ noon-2pm & 7-10pm Tue-Sun) Sister to the original branch in Mombasa, this is definitely the more attrac-tive sibling aesthetically and also has a wider menu, serving up the customary Indian cui-sine plus a handful of Western dishes. It's right at the start of the strip, next to the Nova complex; ironically the views here aren't that much better than in town.

La Strega (☎ 5487431; stephanie@africaonline.co.ke; Pirates complex, Bamburi Beach; mains KSh350-1000) You wouldn't think so to look at it, but the thatched restaurant next to the Pirates night-club is a great Italian eatery in its own right, with a small but well-tempura'd Japanese menu to boot.

Entertainment
Mamba International Nightclub (☎ 475180; Mamba Crocodile Village, Links Rd; admission KSh100-200) Who knows what twisted genius thought it was a good idea to have a disco in a crocodile farm, but the result is one of the most popular in-dependent nightspots around Mombasa.

Bamburi is also known for its infamous nightclubs, which pull in a slightly wild crowd of locals, tourists, prostitutes and hus-tlers. Pirates, Bora Bora International and Tembo are the big players.

KILIFI
☎ 041

Like Mtwapa to its south, Kilifi is a gorgeous river estuary with effortlessly picture-perfect views from its massive road bridge. Many white Kenyans have yachts moored in the creek, and there are numerous beach houses belonging to artists, writers and adventurers from around the globe.

The main reasons that most come here are to stay at one of the pleasant beach resorts at the mouth of the creek or to visit the ruins of

Mnarani, high on a bluff on the south bank of the creek.

Information

Barclays Bank (Ronald Ngala St) ATM only.
Kenya Commercial Bank (☎ 522034; Ronald Ngala St)
Tourist police (Kilifi Shopping Arcade)

Sights

The **Mnarani ruins** (nonresident adult/child KSh100/50; ☺ /am-6pm) are high on a bluff just west of the old ferry landing stage on the southern bank of Kilifi Creek. Only partly excavated, the site was occupied from the end of the 14th century to around the first half of the 17th century, when it was abandoned following sieges by Galla tribespeople from Somalia and the failure of the water supply.

The best-preserved ruin is the **Great Mosque**, with its finely carved inscription around the *mihrab* (the niche showing the direction of Mecca). Also here are a group of **carved tombs** (including a restored pillar tomb), a small mosque dating back to the 16th century and parts of the town wall. Tucked away in the woods are all manner of other ruins and unexcavated structures. The path up to the ruins (about 300m long) is clearly signposted off the Tarmac road behind Mnarani village.

Sleeping

Dhows Inn (☎ 522028; dhowsinn_kilifi@yahoo.com; Malindi Rd; s/d KSh650/900) On the main road south of Kilifi Creek. It's a small but well-maintained hostelry, with simple but decent thatched blocks set around a garden. The Mnarani ruins are within easy walking distance, and there's a popular bar and restaurant.

Makuti Villas (☎ 522415; s/d incl breakfast KSh800/ 1000; ☻) Also known as Mkwajuni Motel or Dhows Inn Annex, this bungalow complex isn't nearly as grand as it sounds, but you're certainly not short on space in the big thatched buildings. Prices include breakfast at the bar-restaurant on site.

Tushauriane Bar & Lodge (☎ 522521; s/d with shared bathroom KSh150/300) This is a bright-yellow building behind the bus station. Unsurprisingly at this price, rooms are basic, with just beds, mosquito nets and plenty of market noise.

Mnarani Club (☎ 522318; mnarani@africaonline.com; s/d low season US$62/99, high season US$79/115; ☒ ☻) Atop the cliff on the southern side of Kilifi Creek, this very stylish resort complex has a choice of garden and creek views and an amazing trompe l'oeil pool, which seems to blend into the ocean. The hotel has an adults-only policy.

Eating & Drinking

Kilifi Members Club (☎ 525258; mains KSh100-260) A fantastic spot for sunset, perched on the northern cliff edge with a clear sight line to the creek bridge. There's a good menu with lots of *nyama choma* (up to KSh460 per kg) and the Tusker's very reasonable for these parts (KSh70). Despite the name you don't have to be a member.

Kilifi Boatyard (☎ 522552; mains KSh350) A very nice sand-floored café serving excellent seafood and cold beers to expat boating types. It's a long walk from town down a dirt road off the highway just south of Kilifi. A taxi will cost around KSh600 return.

New Kilifi Hotel (☎ 0733-793700; Biashara St; mains KSh80-140) Just past the bus station is this very popular local canteen with good pilau and biryanis, plus the usual stew and *ugali* options.

Getting There & Away

All buses and *matatus* travelling between Mombasa (up to 1½ hours) and Malindi (1¼ hours) stop at Kilifi; the fare to either destination is KSh70. Falcon, Busstar and Busscar all have offices here for their Nairobi–Malindi route; buses to Mombasa and on to Nairobi leave at around 7.45am and 7.45pm (KSh600).

WATAMU

☎ 042

About 24km south of Malindi, Watamu is popular beach village with sandy beaches and plenty of hotels, though the atmosphere is a lot more resortlike than in Kilifi. Offshore is the southern part of Malindi Marine Reserve, and the unspoilt forests of Arabuko Sokoke Forest Reserve and the Swahili ruins of Gede are both a short distance away.

The coast at Watamu is broken up into three separate coves divided by eroded rocky headlands. Each of the bays becomes a broad white strand at low tide, and many people walk across to the offshore islands to sunbathe and swim. Like the southern resorts, Watamu is inundated with seaweed at certain times of the year, but the sand is usually clear between December and April.

KENYA

Information

There are now no banks in Watamu, so your only options are the foreign exchange bureaus at the big hotels and Tunda Tours. If you need to use an ATM, your nearest choices are Kilifi and Malindi. Online information can be found at www.watamu.net.

Corner Connections (Watamu Supermarket) Internet access.

Post office (Gede road)

Telkom Kenya office (Beach Way Rd)

Tunda Tours (☎ 32079; Beach Way Rd; per minute KSh5) Heavily touted Internet access.

Sights

BIO KEN SNAKE FARM & LABORATORY

This excellent **snake farm** (☎ 32303; snakes@ africaonline.co.ke; adult/child KSh500/free; ☉ 10am-noon & 2-5pm) is by far the best of the snake parks along the coast. It was established by the late James Ashe, a reptile expert and former curator from the National Museums of Kenya. As well as touring the facilities, staff can take you on a day safari to look for snakes in their natural habitat (KSh4500).

The centre is just north of Watamu village on the main beach road.

WATAMU MARINE NATIONAL PARK

The southern part of Malindi Marine Reserve, this **marine park** (adult/child US$5/2) includes some magnificent coral reefs and abundant fish-life. It lies around 2km offshore from Watamu. To get to the park you'll need to hire a glass-bottomed boat, which is easy enough at the **KWS office** (☎ 32393), at the end of the coast road, where you pay the park fees. For marine park trips, boat operators ask anything from KSh1800 to KSh3500 per person, excluding park fees; it's all negotiable. All the big hotels offer 'goggling' (snorkelling) trips to nonguests for around KSh1500.

Activities

DIVING

With the marine park just offshore, diving is understandably popular. **Aqua Ventures** (☎ 32420; www.diveinkenya.com; Ocean Sports Hotel Turtle Bay) offers guided dives in the marine park for UK£18 and an open-water PADI dive course for UK£275. The best time to dive and snorkel is between October and March. Avoid diving from June to August because of rough seas and poor visibility. Also popular

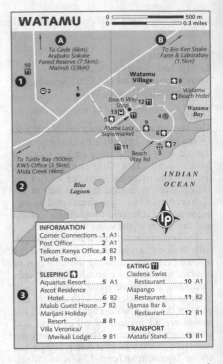

INFORMATION
Corner Connections....1	A1
Post Office................2	A1
Telkom Kenya Office.3	B2
Tunda Tours............4	B1

SLEEPING
Aquarius Resort........5	A1
Ascot Residence Hotel..................6	B2
Malob Guest House...7	B2
Marijani Holiday Resort................8	B1
Villa Veronica/ Mwikali Lodge......9	B1

EATING
Cladena Swiss Restaurant..........10	A1
Mapango Restaurant..........11	B2
Ujamaa Bar & Restaurant..........12	B1

TRANSPORT
Matatu Stand...........13	B1

are dive trips to the **Tewa Caves**, at the mouth of Mida Creek, where a group of giant rock cod loiter menacingly at the bottom.

DEEP-SEA FISHING

If you want to ape the fish-wrestling antics of Ernest Hemingway, deep-sea fishing is possible at Ocean Sports Hotel and Hemingway's Resort for around UK£540 per boat (high season, up to four anglers). People are a little more environmentally sensitive now than in old Ernie's day – tag and release is standard procedure (see the boxed text, opposite).

Sleeping

BUDGET

Malob Guest House (☎ 32260; Beach Way Rd; s KSh600) Opposite Ascot, Malob is a good small budget choice. Rooms are clean and well looked after, and are set around a peaceful courtyard.

Villa Veronika/Mwikali Lodge (☎ 0735-499836; Beach Way Rd; d KSh600) A friendly, secure family-run lodging. Rooms come with fans, mosquito nets and fridges; they're a bit scrappy and don't always have power, but you could do worse. In the high season breakfast is available for KSh100.

MIDRANGE
Marijani Holiday Resort (☎ 32448; marijani@swift malindi.com; s/d €18.50/20.50, cottages €38.50-52) Easily the best place to stay in the village: distinctive coral facing, traditional furnishings, comfy balcony sofas and local art set this very personal guesthouse a cut above any competition. To get here, take the path beside the Mama Lucy supermarket and turn left at the Beach Way Shop.

Ascot Residence Hotel (☎ 32326; info@ascot residence.com; Beach Way Rd; s/d KSh1600/2800, apt KSh3500-7000; ☒) This is a comfortable complex of tidy rooms and apartments set in a garden with a dolphin-shaped pool (no, really). Security is good and there's a fine pizza restaurant.

Scuba Diving Watamu (☎ 32099; www.scuba -diving-kenya.com; Turtle Bay; cottages €29-52; ☒) No prizes for figuring out what the main line of business is here – luckily for keen self-caterers the German owners also offer accommodation in five charming one- and two-bedroom cottages.

TOP END
Turtle Bay Beach Club (☎ 32003; www.turtlebay.co .ke; r per person low season €58-85; high season €93-122; ☒ ☐ ☒ ☝) At the far end of the cove, Turtle Bay is one of the best resorts of its kind in the area, with palm-planted gardens to disguise the size of the site. Facilities are excellent and it's particularly strong on kids' entertainment. Loads of excursions are on offer at the community-oriented Discovery Centre, most of which are open to non-guests. Prices quoted are all-inclusive.

Ocean Sports Hotel (☎ 32008; oceansps@africa online.co.ke; Turtle Bay; half board s/d low season US$82/111, high season US$100/160; ☒ ☝) A small, informal family-run resort with a deep-sea fishing slant. It's modest considering the prices, but the atmosphere's very relaxed. Good cheap snorkelling trips are available (KSh800).

Hemingways Resort (☎ 32624; www.hemingways .co.ke; Turtle Bay; half board s/d low season UK£57/82, high season UK£143/203; ☒ ☒) Next door to Ocean Sports, this very stately luxury lodge has snappy service and an exclusive ambience. Prices include transfers from Malindi airport, snorkelling in the marine park, and trips to Malindi and Gede.

Aquarius Resort (☎ 32069; www.aquariuswatamu .com; full board s/d low season €64.50/86, high season €78/104; ☒ ☒ ☝) A brand-new place set back from the water. The *makuti*-roofed buildings are set in a lovely garden and there are peaceful communal balconies overlooking the pool. The Mapango Restaurant, in a separate compound nearer the beach, is highly recommended.

Eating
As the better hotels cater more than amply for their clients, there's not much need for an independent restaurant scene in Watamu, and most places close relatively early.

Ujamaa Bar & Restaurant (mains KSh150-600; ☽ noon-2pm & 5-9pm) This central village eatery has some tourist standards, such as steak and spaghetti, thrown in to complement the local favourites (and up the prices).

Cladena Swiss Restaurant (☎ 32500; mains KSh200-600) It's not often you get a taste of the Alps in coastal Kenya, so if you have a hankering for fondue and sausage this is the place to come.

Getting There & Around

There are *matatus* between Malindi and Watamu throughout the day (KSh50, one hour). All *matatus* pass the turn-off to the Gede ruins (KSh10). For Mombasa, the easiest option is to take a *matatu* to the highway (KSh10) and flag down a bus or *matatu* from there.

Taxis charge KSh800 to the Gede ruins and KSh1800 to Malindi. There are also a handful of motorised rickshaws, which are cheaper and can be handy for the long beach road.

ARABUKO SOKOKE FOREST RESERVE

Close to the marine park at Watamu, **Arabuko Sokoke Forest Reserve** (adult/child US$10/5) is the largest tract of indigenous coastal forest remaining in East Africa, with four distinct vegetation zones. Gazetted in 2002 as an International Heritage Site, it's administered jointly by the Forestry Department and KWS, and contains an unusually high concentration of rare species, especially birds (240 species) and butterflies (260 species). A good deal of work has gone into involving the local community in the protection of the forest.

The most high-profile birds are: Clarke's weaver, found nowhere else in the world; the beautiful miniature Sokoke scops owl, only 15cm tall; the east coast akalat; the Sokoke pipit; the Amani sunbird; and the spotted ground thrush. The reserve's signature animal is the charming golden-rumped elephant-shrew.

The **Arabuko Sokoke Visitor Centre** (Malindi Rd; ☎ 042-32462; ☺ 8am-4pm) is very helpful; it's at Gede Forest Station, with displays on the various species here. The shop sells the excellent KWS/Forestry Department guide *Arabuko Sokoke Forest & Mida Creek* (KSh300) and Tansy Bliss' *Arabuko-Sokoke Forest – A Visitor's Guide* (KSh120). The noticeboard in the visitor centre shows the sites of recent wildlife sightings.

From the visitor centre, a series of nature trails, running tracks and 4WD paths cut through the forest. Trained bird and wildlife **guides** (☎ 0734-994931) can be hired at KSh600 for up to three hours, KSh1200 for a full day, and KSh800 for a half day or a highly recommended night walk (leaving the visitor centre at 6pm). They're very knowledgeable about the forest, and also offer walks in Mida Creek on the opposite side of the highway.

There are basic **camp sites** (per person US$8) close to the visitor centre and further south near Spinetail Way.

The forest is just off the main Malindi–Mombasa road. The main gate to the forest and visitor centre is about 1.5km west of the turn-off to Gede and Watamu, while the Mida entrance is about 3km further south. All buses and *matatus* between Mombasa and Malindi can drop you at either entrance. From Watamu, *matatus* to Malindi can drop you at the main junction.

GEDE RUINS

Some 4km from Watamu, just off the main Malindi–Mombasa road, are the famous **Gede ruins** (adult/child KSh200/100; ☺ 7am-6pm), one of the principal historical monuments on the coast. Hidden away in the forest is a vast complex of derelict houses, palaces and mosques, made all the more mysterious by the fact that there seem to be no records of Gede's existence in any historical texts.

Gede (or Gedi) was established and actively trading by at least the 13th century. Excavations have uncovered porcelain, glass and glazed earthenware, indicating not only trade links, but a taste for luxury among Gede's Swahili elite. Within the compound are ruins of ornate tombs and mosques, and the regal ruins of a Swahili palace, further evidence of Gede's prosperity.

When the city was abandoned in the 17th or 18th century, the forest took over and the site was lost to the world until the 1920s. Since then, there have been extensive excavations, revealing the remains of substantial Swahili houses and complex sanitation facilities, including toilets and cisterns for ritual washing. Most of the excavated buildings are concentrated in a dense cluster near the entrance gate, but there are dozens of other ruins scattered through the forest.

Walking Tour

The tree-shrouded ruins are very atmospheric and you'll often have the site to yourself if you visit early in the morning. Guides are available at the gate for KSh300; they definitely help bring the site to life, pointing out the various trees and plants as well as interesting features of the buildings, but

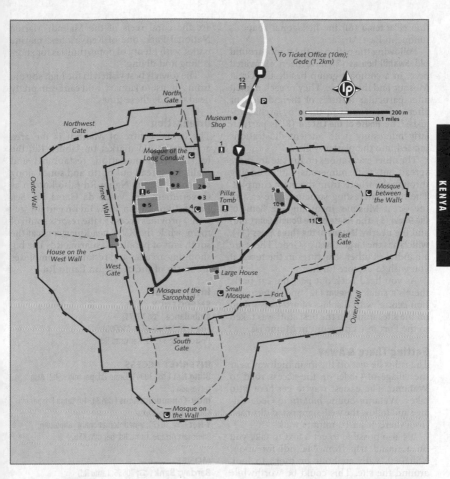

KENYA

will generally stick to a standard circuit of the most important ruins.

Gedi – Historical Monument (KSh50), a guidebook to the ruins containing a map and descriptions of many buildings, should be available at the ticket office or the museum shop.

On your right as you enter the compound is the **Dated Tomb** (1), so called because of the inscription on the wall, featuring the Muslim date corresponding to 1399. This tomb has provided a reference point for dating other buildings within the complex. Near it, inside the wall, is the **Tomb of the Fluted Pillar** (2), which is characteristic of such pillar designs found along the East African coast.

Past the tomb, next to the **House of the Long Court** (3), the **Great Mosque** (4) is one of Gede's most significant buildings. It originally dates from the mid-15th century, but was rebuilt a century later, possibly after damage sustained at the time of Gede's first abandonment. The mosque is of typical East African design with a *mihrab* or echo chamber facing Mecca.

Behind the mosque are the ruins of an extensive **palace** (5) spread out over a quarter of an acre and thought to have been owned by the former ruler of Gede. This regal structure is entered through a complete arched doorway and many interesting features have been preserved, including the great audience hall and a strongroom with no doors or windows. The palace also has a particularly fine **pillar tomb** (6); the hexagonal shape is unique in East Africa.

Following the path past the tomb, around old **Swahili houses** (7) have been excavated here, in a compact group beside the Great Mosque and the palace. They're each named after particular features of their design or after objects found in them by archaeologists. The **House of the Cistern** (8) is particularly interesting, with ancient illustrations incised into the plaster walls.

The other excavations on the site are more spread out, with numerous paths running through the woods from the main complex. The most interesting structures are east of the Great Mosque, including the **House of the Dhow** (9), the **House of the Double Court** (10) and the nearby **Mosque of the Three Aisles** (11), which has the largest well at Gede. There are a handful of other structures in the forest if you wish to explore further.

As you head back out past the car park, there's a small **museum** (12) and 'interpretation centre' with displays of artefacts found on the site, although the best stuff was taken to the Fort Jesus museum in Mombasa.

Getting There & Away

The ruins lie just off the main highway near the village of Gede, on the access road to Watamu. The easiest way to get here is to take a Watamu-bound *matatu* to Gede Village and follow the well-signposted dirt road from there; it's a 10-minute walk.

It's also possible to get a taxi to take you on a round trip from Malindi for about KSh1000, with an hour or more to look around the site. This could be worthwhile if your time is limited.

MALINDI & AROUND
☎ 042

Malindi is one of those holiday towns that inspire wildly opposite reactions in people. For many, especially Italians, this is their Kenyan beach paradise and even adopted home; for others it's a cynical tourist trap with few redeeming features. If you're new to Africa, the high-season hassle may well incline you towards the latter angle, but once you get under its skin you may well find there's more to the town than pizza and sunloungers.

From a tourist perspective, modern Malindi is all about the beaches, with little in the way of cultural attractions. Offshore

are the coral reefs of the Malindi Marine National Park, one of Kenya's best marine parks, with plenty of opportunities for snorkelling and diving.

The town is best visited in the high season, from August to January, and can seem pretty dead outside these times.

Orientation

The actual centre of Malindi is the area around the old market on Uhuru Rd; the tourist accommodation, restaurants and malls are spread out north and south along the coast. Mama Ngina Rd (also known as Government Rd, Vasco da Gama Rd, Sea Front Rd or Ocean View Rd on certain sections) provides access to the resorts south of town, while the KWS headquarters is at the south end of parallel Casuarina Rd. The big shopping arcades and restaurant complexes are north of the centre on Lamu Rd.

Information

EMERGENCY
Ambulance (☎ 30575)
Fire (☎ 31001, 0733-550990)
Police (☎ 31555; Kenyatta Rd)

INTERNET ACCESS
Bling Net (☎ 30041; Lamu Rd; per min KSh2) Also serves food.
Inter-Communications (☎ 31310; Lamu Rd; per min KSh1; ☉ 8am-11pm)
Y-Net (☎ 30171; y-netinternational@yahoo.com; Stanchart Arcade, Lamu Rd; per min KSh2)

MONEY
Barclays Bank (☎ 20656; Lamu Rd)
Dollar Forex Bureau (☎ 30602; Lamu Rd) Rates may be slightly better here than at the banks.
Kenya Commercial Bank (☎ 20148; Lamu Rd)
Postbank (Malindi Complex, Lamu Rd)
Standard Chartered Bank (Stanchart Arcade, Lamu Rd)

POST
Post office (Kenyatta Rd)

TOURIST INFORMATION
Tourist office (☎ 20689; Malindi Complex, Lamu Rd; ☉ 8am-12.30pm & 2-4.30pm Mon-Fri) Staff are friendly but really don't have much information to dispense.

VISA EXTENSIONS
Immigration office (☎ 30876; Mama Ngina Rd) Travellers seeking visa extensions are often referred to Mombasa.

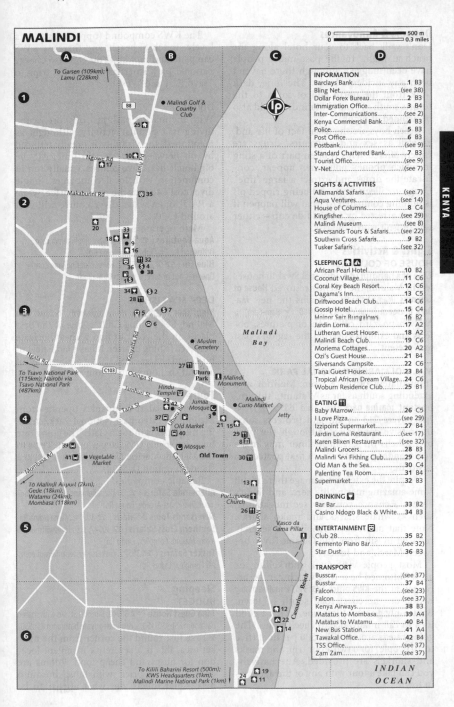

MALINDI

0 _____ 500 m
0 _____ 0.3 miles

INFORMATION
Barclays Bank...........................1 B3
Bling Net................................(see 38)
Dollar Forex Bureau...................2 B3
Immigration Office....................3 B4
Inter-Communications...............(see 2)
Kenya Commercial Bank.............4 B3
Police....................................5 B3
Post Office..............................6 B3
Postbank...............................(see 9)
Standard Chartered Bank...........7 B3
Tourist Office..........................(see 9)
Y-Net....................................(see 7)

SIGHTS & ACTIVITIES
Allamanda Safaris....................(see 7)
Aqua Ventures........................(see 14)
House of Columns.....................8 C4
Kingfisher..............................(see 29)
Malindi Museum.......................(see 8)
Silversands Tours & Safaris.........(see 22)
Southern Cross Safaris...............9 B2
Tusker Safaris.........................(see 32)

SLEEPING
African Pearl Hotel....................10 B2
Coconut Village.......................11 C6
Coral Key Beach Resort..............12 C6
Dagama's Inn..........................13 C5
Driftwood Beach Club................14 C6
Gossip Hotel...........................15 C4
Hninor Seiz Bungalows..............16 B2
Jardin Lorna...........................17 A2
Lutheran Guest House...............18 A2
Malindi Beach Club...................19 C6
Moriema Cottages....................20 A2
Ozi's Guest House.....................21 B4
Silversands Campsite.................22 C6
Tana Guest House....................23 B4
Tropical African Dream Village.....24 C6
Woburn Residence Club.............25 B1

EATING
Baby Marrow...........................26 C5
I Love Pizza............................(see 29)
Izzipoint Supermarket...............27 B4
Jardin Lorna Restaurant.............(see 17)
Karen Blixen Restaurant.............(see 32)
Malindi Grocers........................28 B3
Malindi Sea Fishing Club............29 C4
Old Man & the Sea....................30 C4
Palentine Tea Room..................31 B4
Supermarket...........................32 B3

DRINKING
Bar Bar.................................33 B2
Casino Ndogo Black & White.......34 B3

ENTERTAINMENT
Club 28.................................35 B2
Fermento Piano Bar..................(see 32)
Star Dust...............................36 B3

TRANSPORT
Busscar.................................(see 37)
Busstar.................................37 B4
Falcon..................................(see 23)
Falcon..................................(see 37)
Kenya Airways.........................38 B3
Matatus to Mombasa.................39 A4
Matatus to Watamu...................40 B4
New Bus Station.......................41 A4
Tawakal Office........................42 B4
TSS Office..............................(see 37)
Zam Zam...............................(see 37)

Malindi Bay

INDIAN OCEAN

Casuarina Beach

KENYA

Dangers & Annoyances

Don't walk back to your hotel along the beach at night. In the past many people have been mugged, although there haven't been any incidents lately. The long, dark walk from the north end of town to the resorts south of central Malindi should also be avoided at night.

Beach boys are the usual fact of life and, as well as sex and souvenirs, drugs are widely offered. This is often part of a sting in which phoney policemen appear, confiscate the drugs and extract a large 'fine'. Drugs *are* illegal here, and being ripped off is nothing compared to what will happen if you are arrested by a bona fide cop – either way, it isn't worth the risk.

Sights & Activities

HOUSE OF COLUMNS

One of a handful of traditional Swahili houses left in Malindi, the recently restored **House of Columns** (Mama Ngina Rd) contains the new **Malindi museum** (adult/child KSh200/100; 8am-6pm), a fairly haphazard collection of pictures, objects and exhibits covering the region's past and present.

MALINDI MARINE NATIONAL PARK

Immediately offshore from Malindi and extending south as far as Watamu, this important **marine park** (adult/child US$5/2; 7am-7pm) covers 213 sq km and protects impressive coral reefs, although the piles of seashells on sale in Malindi may make you wonder just how much that protection is worth.

Despite the extensive damage there is still some amazing marine life here, and there's always a chance you may see megafauna, such as whale sharks and mako sharks. Note that underwater visibility is severely reduced by silt from the Galana River between March and June.

Most people visit on a snorkelling or glass-bottomed boat trip, which can be arranged at the **KWS office** (31554; malindimnp@kws.org) on the coast road south of town. Boats only go out at low tide, so it's a good idea to call in advance to check times. The going rate is around KSh3500 per boat (five to 10 people) for a two-hour trip, and masks and snorkels are provided. Alternatively, you can take a tour with any of the agencies in town.

The KWS compound (opposite) sits on a lovely stretch of beach, and there's a KWS campsite and *bandas*. You can also charge national park smartcards here for trips to Tsavo East and West.

DIVING

With the marine park just offshore, scuba diving is a popular activity, although, as mentioned, the visibility is greatly reduced by silt between March and June. All the big hotels have dive centres, usually run in conjunction with local companies. Single dives cost €40 plus the park entry fee, while a PADI open-water diver course will cost around €330.

Main operators:

Aqua Ventures (32420; www.diveinkenya.com; Driftwood Beach Club, Mam Ngina Rd)

Blue Fin (0722-261242; www.bluefindiving.com) Operates out of several resorts in Malindi.

DEEP-SEA FISHING

Kingfisher (31275; Mama Ngina Rd), below the Malindi Sea Fishing Club, is one of the best places on the coast to find a cheap, private deep-sea fishing charter. It has a large fleet of boats and charges US$350 for a 'short day' of around six hours (up to four anglers).

Tours

Numerous safari companies operate from Malindi to Tsavo East National Park, entering the park via the Sala Gate. The going rate for a day trip is US$120 per person. Trips to the Malindi Marine National Park are also a standard option (US$20).

Reliable companies:

Allamanda Safaris (31272; allamanda@swiftmalindi .com; Stanchart Arcade, Lamu Rd)

Silversands Tours & Safaris (30014; Mama Ngina Rd)

Southern Cross Safaris (30547; sxsmld@swiftmalindi .com; Malindi Complex, Lamu Rd)

Tusker Safaris (30525; tuskersaf@swiftmalindi.com; AG Complex, Lamu Rd)

Sleeping

BUDGET

Tana Guest House (30940; Jamhuri St; s/d with shared bathroom KSh350/450, s/d/tr with private bathroom KSh550/550/650) Just round the corner from the market area, this is a severely convenient location for buses and cheap food. Rooms are decent for the price, with fans, mosquito nets, squat toilets and what appear to be changing rooms. You can buy day-old chicks at reception, if you so wish.

Lutheran Guest House (☎ 30098; tw/tr/q with shared bathroom KSh800/1200/1500, tw with private bathroom KSh1000, bungalows KSh1500) This Lutheran religious centre has simple rooms with fans, mosquito nets and little else; the bungalows have living rooms and kitchens. Alcohol is prohibited.

Dagama's Inn (☎ 31942; Mama Ngina Rd; s/d KSh600/800) Big, bare doubles and rather smaller singles in a modern block, now under new management, with a decent Indian restaurant downstairs (mains KSh190 to KSh495). Only one room has a fan, but there's plenty of breeze through the slatted walls.

KWS compound (☎ 31554; Casuarina Beach; camping adult/child US$8/5, bandas per person KSh600) KWS provides a shady camp site, with lights and a cooking area, and eight popular *bandas*. Water and bedding are provided and there's a kitchen and mess hall you can use for KSh300. Mountain bikes can be hired for KSh200 per day.

Silversands Campsite (☎ 20412; camping adult/child KSh200/100, bandas KSh500-600) On the southern beach strip, this is a much-loved site for travellers and there are good facilities, but limited shade. The simple tented *bandas* have recently been fully refurbished. Bicycles can be hired for KSh200 per day.

MIDRANGE

African Pearl Hotel (☎ 0733-966167; www.africanpearl .com; Lamu Rd; s/d from KSh1800/2200, cottages KSh2000-4500; ✗ ☎) Blessed with a real personal touch, this is the kind of pearl it's worth shuckin' a few shellfish for. Rooms are spacious and light, all with their own balconies, and foregoing a room with air-con to get an atmospheric wood-panelled fan room is no hardship.

Ozi's Guest House (☎ 20218; ozi@swiftmalindi.com; Mama Ngina Rd; s/d/tr with shared bathroom KSh600/1200/1800) Barely out of the budget category, this friendly hostelry is a travellers' favourite, though with the mosque next door light sleepers may want to start praying.

Jardin Lorna (☎ 30658; harry@swiftmalindi.com; Mtangani Rd; r KSh2500-3500; ✗ ☎) Don't be fooled by the French nom de plume – Lorna is as unpretentious as they come, providing accommodation mainly for students of the Hospitality Training & Management Institute. Rooms are endearingly quirky.

Heiner Seiz Bungalows (☎ 20978; Lamu Rd; s/d KSh1400/1600; ✗ ☎) These quiet German-run cottages are subdivided into unfancy but well-kept rooms with fridges. Some kitchens are also available to guests.

Moriema Cottages (☎ 31326; s/d KSh1400/2500) These large cottage-style rooms are a pretty good deal, but whoever thought of putting in carpets and dull green furnishings was way off the mark aesthetically. They're tucked away in a quaint garden behind the Sabaki shopping centre.

Gossip Hotel (☎ 0723-516602; Mama Ngina Rd; s/d KSh700/1200) Just down from Ozi's, the Gossip aims for much the same backpacker clientele. Rooms have four-poster mosquito nets, dark wood and plastic chairs, and the downstairs restaurant boasts an intriguing TV lounge/junk corner.

TOP END

Tropical African Dream Village (☎ 31673; www .planhotel.ch; Casuarina Rd; s/d/tr low season from €94/130/175, high season from €116/160/216; ✗ ☐ ☎ ☝) This place consists of three resorts around the intersection of Mama Ngina and Casuarina Rds. The Tropical African Dream Village section is a rather grand complex of *makuti*-roofed plantation-style houses. Around the corner, the fancy Malindi Beach Club section has accommodation in stylish Moorish cottages, while the cheaper Coconut Village is a more predictable collection of villas.

Kilili Baharini Resort (☎ 20169; www.kilili baharini.com; Casuarina Rd; half board s/d from US$153/182; ✗ ☎) This is a splendid Italian resort, with flamboyant décor and Swahili beds set all over the complex so you can read and catch the sea breeze. It fronts directly onto the sand, and the light, spacious rooms are clustered around attractive pools.

Coral Key Beach Resort (☎ 30717; www.coralkey malindi.com; Mama Ngina Rd; s/d low season from €23/31, high season from €44/58; ✗ ☎ ☝) A huge mass-tourism resort catering particularly for young Italians. It's very lively, with activities such as water-volleyball and a climbing wall. Rooms are divided into groups within five themed areas, each block with its own separate pool.

Driftwood Beach Club (☎ 20155; www.driftwood club.com; Mama Ngina Rd; s/d/tr KSh5300/7600/9120, cottages KSh16,500; ✗ ☎ ☝) One of the best-known resorts in Malindi, Driftwood prides itself on an informal atmosphere and attracts a more independent clientele than many of its peers. The restaurant, bar and other facilities are all open to nonguests for a temporary membership fee of KSh200 per day.

Woburn Residence Club (☎ 31085; www.woburn residencemalindi.com; s/d from €79.20/104, apt low season €152-232, high season €190-290; ✖ ☎) If you're not bothered about direct beach access, this swish complex offers modern rooms and apartments with giant marble bathrooms.

Eating

Palentine Tea Room (☎ 31412; Uhuru Rd; mains KSh60-140; 💻) A recommended all-hours Muslim canteen opposite the old market, serving stews, curries, pilau and soups in tiled surroundings. It's friendly and almost always busy.

Old Man & the Sea (☎ 31106; Mama Ngina Rd; mains KSh300-590, seafood KSh550-1100) Definitely the daddy of Malindi's restaurants, this old Moorish house on the seafront really has no competition. The food's superb, service is attentive and you can get decent wine by the glass (KSh110). A 16% VAT charge is added to the bill.

Jardin Lorna Restaurant (☎ 30658; Mtangani Rd; mains KSh150-550) Amid the trees and obsolete beer pumps, this peaceful garden restaurant serves a limited but unusual selection of French, Italian and African dishes.

Malindi Sea Fishing Club (☎ 30550; Mama Ngina Rd; mains KSh240-400; 💮 noon-8pm) A popular hang-out for the deep-sea fishing crowd. The walls feature some huge stuffed sharks and billfish in dramatic poses. The seafood is excellent. It's a great place for a sundown beer, but it closes early and you have to pay a KSh100 temporary membership fee.

I Love Pizza (☎ 20672; Mama Ngina Rd; nwright@ africaonline.co.ke; pizza KSh300-550, mains from KSh600) A very popular Italian restaurant on the seafront, full of diners pointedly ignoring the naff name. Luckily the pizza is excellent.

Baby Marrow (☎ 0733-542584; Mama Ngina Rd; mains KSh350-800) Everything about this place is quirkily stylish, from the thatched veranda and the plant-horse to the Italian-based menu and the tasty seafood (KSh1400 to KSh1800).

Karen Blixen Restaurant (☎ 0733-974756; celty3@ yahoo.it; Galana Centre, Lamu Rd; mains KSh600-950) A fine (wait for it) Italian terrace restaurant hinting at Art Deco style. The menu has all the usuals and an added dose of Chinese, seafood and grill dishes, plus crocodile and warthog (!) for KSh1000. It's also good for a morning cappuccino.

Useful outlets for self-caterers:

Izzipoint supermarket (☎ 30652; Uhuru Rd)
Malindi Grocers (☎ 20886; Lamu Rd)
Supermarket (Galana Centre, Lamu Rd)

Drinking & Entertainment

Bar Bar (Sabaki Centre, Lamu Rd) A perennially popular high-season courtyard bar, restaurant and ice-cream parlour with nonstop Italian cable TV in the background.

Fermento Piano Bar (☎ 31780; Galana Centre, Lamu Rd; admission KSh200; 💮 from 10pm Wed, Fri & Sat; ☎) Fermento has the town's hippest dance floor, apparently once frequented by Naomi Campbell. It's young, trendy and Italian, so wear your showiest outfit.

Casino Ndogo Black & White (☎ 0724-236476; Lamu Rd; admission KSh100; 💮 24hr) A typical semi-open *makuti* bar-club with regular live Congolese *lingala* bands.

The main nightclubs outside the resorts are **Star Dust** (Lamu Rd) and **Club 28** (Lamu Rd), which open erratically out of season but are generally crammed when they do.

Getting There & Away

AIR

There are daily afternoon/evening flights with **Airkenya** (☎ 30646; Malindi Airport) to Nairobi (US$85, 1¼ hours). **Kenya Airways** (☎ 20237; Lamu Rd) flies the same route at least once a day (from KSh4010).

Mombasa Air Safari (☎ 041-433061) has daily flights to Mombasa (US$21, 25 minutes) and Lamu (US$62, 30 minutes) in the high season; booking in Malindi is through Southern Cross Safaris.

BUS & MATATU

The new bus station just off Mombasa Rd is currently only used by Mombasa Raha, which has numerous daily buses to Mombasa (KSh150, two hours). Metro Mombasa buses and Mombasa *matatus* (KSh100 to KSh150) stop at the road stage near here.

Companies such as Busstar, Busscar, TSS and Falcon have offices opposite the old market in the centre of Malindi. All have daily departures to Nairobi at around 7am and/or 7pm (KSh800, 10 to 12 hours), going via Mombasa.

Thanks to improvements on the Malindi–Garissa road, taking a bus to Lamu is an easier and safer proposition than a few years ago, though buses are still accompanied by armed guards for some of the way. Among the various companies offering services, Tawakal buses leave at 8.30am, Falcon at 8.45am and Zam Zam at 10.30am; the fare is KSh300 to KSh400. The journey takes at least four hours between Malindi and the jetty at Mokowe. The ferry to Lamu from the mainland costs KSh50 and takes about 20 minutes.

Getting Around
Taxis are mainly concentrated along Lamu Rd and out the front of any of the big hotels south of town (the best place to start is Coral Key Beach Resort). From the southern resorts, it costs KSh200 to Malindi town, KSh300 to Lamu Rd and KSh500 to the airport.

Malindi also has Kenya's biggest fleet of Indonesian-style tuk-tuks, which are cheaper than taxis; a trip from town to the KWS office should cost around KSh100.

LAMU
☎ 042
Lamu town is the core of everything the Lamu archipelago stands for in the hearts and minds of inhabitants and visitors alike, a living throwback to the Swahili culture that once dominated the entire Indian Ocean coast. In 2001 it was added to Unesco's list of World Heritage Sites. The winding streets, carved woods and traditional houses are simply captivating, and few experiences can compare with wandering the narrow lanes, immersed in the everyday sights and sounds of another age. It's simply a different world, and one you'll be in no hurry to leave.

Orientation
Although there are several restaurants and places to stay along the waterfront (Harambee Ave), most of the guesthouses are tucked away in the confusing maze of alleys located behind. Lamu's main thoroughfare is Kenyatta Rd, a long winding alley known popularly as 'Main St', which runs from the northern end of town past the fort and then south to the Muslim cemetery and the inland track to Shela.

Information
INTERNET ACCESS
Lynx Infosystems (☎ 833134; per min KSh2; ⊗ 8am-10pm) Temperamental connections over a Safaricom line – worth a look when the post office is closed. To find it, head west down the street next to the Khadi Star office and turn left at the end.

MEDICAL SERVICES
King Fadh Lamu District Hospital (☎ 633012) One of the most modern and well-equipped hospitals on the coast. It's south of the town centre.
Lamu Medical Clinic (☎ 633438; Kenyatta Rd; ⊗ 8am-9pm)

MONEY
If you're stuck outside bank times, ask around: local shopkeepers may be able to help you out with changing money, sometimes at surprisingly reasonable rates.
Kenya Commercial Bank (☎ 633327; Harambee Ave) The only bank on Lamu. No ATM, Visa advances only. Beware of large commissions on cards and travellers cheques.

POST
Post office (Harambee Ave) Postal services, cardphones and the best Internet connections in town.

TOURIST INFORMATION
Tourist information office (☎ 633449; ⊗ 9am-1pm & 2-4pm) A commercial tour and accommodation agency that also provides tourist information. It's off Kenyatta Rd.

VISA EXTENSIONS
Immigration office (☎ 633032) There's an office off Kenyatta Rd near the fort where you should be able to get visa extensions, although travellers are sometimes referred to Mombasa.

Dangers & Annoyances
Beach boys are the primary nuisance in Lamu. Most loiter around the waterfront offering dhow trips, marijuana and other 'services'. Men can generally get away with a friendly chat, but single women and even groups of female travellers are likely to have constant company, which can get *very* wearing. There's not a lot you can do except be firm, stay polite and keep on walking.

Lamu has long been popular for its relaxed and tolerant atmosphere, but it's still a Muslim island, with all the associated views of acceptable behaviour. Keep public displays of affection to a minimum and respect local attitudes to modesty.

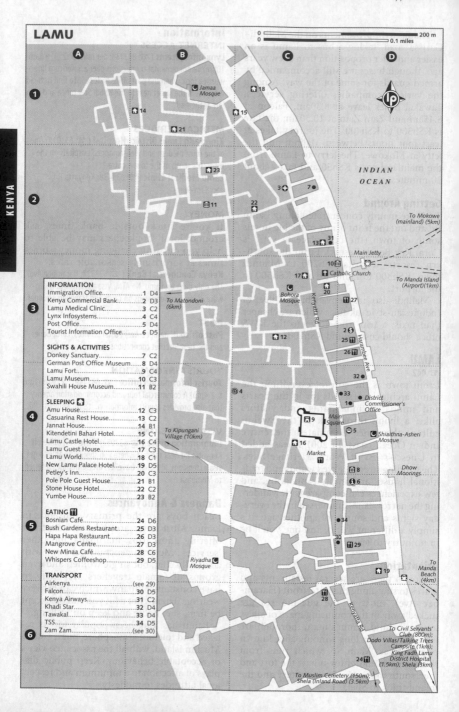

LAMU

KENYA

0   200 m
0   0.1 miles

INDIAN OCEAN

To Mokowe (mainland) (5km)

Main Jetty

To Manda Island (Airport)(1km)

To Matondoni (6km)

Bohora Mosque

To Kipungani Village (10km)

Main Square

District Commissioner's Office

Shiaithna-Asheri Mosque

Market

Dhow Moorings

Riyadha Mosque

To Manda Beach (4km)

To Civil Servants' Club (800m); Dodo Villas/Talking Trees Campsite (1km); King Fadh Lamu District Hospital (1.5km); Shela (3km)

To Muslim Cemetery (150m); Shela (Inland Road) (3.5km)

Jamaa Mosque

Catholic Church

INFORMATION
Immigration Office..................1 D4
Kenya Commercial Bank..........2 D3
Lamu Medical Clinic................3 C2
Lynx Infosystems...................4 C4
Post Office...........................5 D4
Tourist Information Office.........6 D5

SIGHTS & ACTIVITIES
Donkey Sanctuary...................7 C2
German Post Office Museum....8 D4
Lamu Fort............................9 C4
Lamu Museum.....................10 C3
Swahili House Museum..........11 B2

SLEEPING
Amu House.........................12 C3
Casuarina Rest House............13 C2
Jannat House......................14 B1
Kitendetini Bahari Hotel.........15 C1
Lamu Castle Hotel................16 C4
Lamu Guest House................17 C3
Lamu World.........................18 C1
New Lamu Palace Hotel.........19 D5
Petley's Inn.........................20 C3
Pole Pole Guest House...........21 B1
Stone House Hotel................22 C2
Yumbe House......................23 B2

EATING
Bosnian Café.......................24 D6
Bush Gardens Restaurant.......25 D3
Hapa Hapa Restaurant...........26 D3
Mangrove Centre..................27 D3
New Minaa Café...................28 C6
Whispers Coffeeshop.............29 D5

TRANSPORT
Airkenya.........................(see 29)
Falcon...............................30 D5
Kenya Airways.....................31 C2
Khadi Star..........................32 D4
Tawakal.............................33 D4
TSS..................................34 D5
Zam Zam.......................(see 30)

Sights

All of Lamu's museums are open from 8am to 6pm daily. Admission to each is KSh200/100 for a nonresident adult/child.

LAMU MUSEUM

Housed in a very grand Swahili warehouse on the waterfront, the Lamu Museum is an excellent introduction to the culture and history of Lamu Island. It's one of the most interesting small museums in Kenya, with displays on Swahili culture, the famous coastal carved doors, the Maulid Festival, Lamu's nautical history and the tribes who used to occupy this part of the coast in pre-Muslim days, including the Boni, who were legendary elephant-hunters.

The pride of the collection are the remarkable and ornate *siwa* (ceremonial horns) of Lamu and Paté, dating back to the 17th century. Lamu's *siwa* is made of engraved brass but it pales beside the glorious ivory *siwa* of Paté, carved from a single massive elephant tusk. Swahili relics from Takwa and other sites in the archipelago are displayed in the gallery downstairs.

SWAHILI HOUSE MUSEUM

If the Lamu Museum stokes your interest in Swahili culture, this beautifully restored traditional house tucked away off to the side of Yumbe House hotel will put you firmly back in the past. Inside you'll find a re-creation of a working Swahili home, with cookware, beds and other furniture. The attendant will give you a whistle-stop but informative tour in between small talk, including some fascinating descriptions of the regimented lives of Swahilis in the 18th and 19th centuries. The museum is well signposted from Kenyatta Rd.

LAMU FORT

The bulky, atmospheric Lamu Fort squats on Lamu's main square like a weary intruder among the airy Swahili roofs. The building of this massive structure was begun by the Sultan of Paté in 1810 and completed in 1823. From 1910 right up to 1984 it was used as a prison, and it now houses the island's library, and some lacklustre displays on natural history and the environment, which a guide will show you around. The highlight is scaling the ramparts for some sweeping town views.

GERMAN POST OFFICE MUSEUM

In the late 1800s, before the British decided to nip German expansion into Tanganyika in the bud, the Germans regarded Lamu as an ideal base from where they could successfully and safely exploit the interior. As part of their efforts the German East Africa Company set up a post office on Kenyatta Rd, and the old building is now a museum exhibiting photographs and memorabilia from that fleeting period of colonial history.

DONKEY SANCTUARY

With around 3000 donkeys active on Lamu, *Equus asinus* is still the main form of transport here, and this **sanctuary** (☎ 633303; Harambee Ave; admission free; ☒ 9am-1pm Mon-Fri) was established by the International Donkey Protection Trust of Sidmouth, UK, to improve the lot of the island's hard-working beasts of burden. The project provides free veterinary services to donkey owners and tends to injured, sick or worn-out animals.

Activities

Taking a **dhow trip** is almost obligatory and drifting through the mangroves is a wonderful way to experience the islands. Prices vary depending on where you want to go and how long you go for; with a bit of bargaining you should pay around KSh500 per person. Groups of more than five aren't recommended as the boats aren't very big.

Whatever you arrange, make sure you know exactly how much you'll be paying and what that will include, to avoid misunderstandings and overcharging. Don't hand over any money until the day of departure, except perhaps a small advance for food. On long trips, it's best to organise your own drinks. Make sure you take a hat and some sunscreen, as there is rarely any shade on the dhows.

Most day trips meander around the channel between Lamu and Manda Islands, and the price includes fishing and snorkelling. Lunch is usually served on a beach on Manda Island. Longer trips head for Manda Toto Island, which has better snorkelling. Multiday trips head out to the remote island of Kiwayu (p356).

Dhows without an outboard motor are entirely dependent on wind and tides, so it's probably unwise to go on a long trip if you have a flight or other appointment to meet.

KENYA

Walking Tour

The best, indeed only, way to see Lamu town
is on foot. This tour will take you past some
of the more noteworthy buildings in under
an hour, but don't feel bound to follow it too
rigidly. In fact, getting slightly lost is a vital
part of the process!

Most of Lamu's buildings date back to
the 18th century and are constructed out
of local materials, with cut coral-rag blocks
for the walls, wooden floors supported by
mangrove poles and intricately carved shut-
ters for windows. Lavish decorations were
created using carved plaster, and carpenters
were employed to produce ornately carved
window and door frames as a sign of the
financial status of the owners. There are
so many wonderful Swahili houses that it's
pointless to specify examples – keep your
eyes open and don't forget to look up.

Starting at the **main jetty (1)**, head north
past the **Lamu Museum (2**; p343) and along the
waterfront until you reach the **door carving
workshops (3)**. In recent years there has been
a real revival in woodcarving, and you can
once again see traditional carved lintels and
doors being made in workshops like these
all over Lamu.

From here head onto Kenyatta Rd, passing an original Swahili **well (4)**, and head
into the alleys towards the **Swahili House Museum (5**; p343). When you've had your fill
of domestic insights, take any route back
towards the main street.

Once you've hit the main square and the
fort (6; p343), take a right to see the crumbled
remains of the 14th-century **Pwani Mosque (7)**,
one of Lamu's oldest buildings; an Arabic
inscription is still visible on the wall. From
here you can head round and browse the
covered **market (8)**, then negotiate your way
towards the bright Saudi-funded **Riyadha
Mosque (9)**, the centre of Lamu's religious
scene, founded by the great scholar Habib
Swaleh in 1891.

From here head back to the waterfront,
then stroll back up along the promenade,
diverting for the **German Post Office Museum
(10**; p343) if you haven't already seen it – the
door is another amazing example of Swahili
carving. If you're feeling the pace, take a rest
and shoot the breeze on the **baraza ya wazee**
(Old Men's Bench; **11**) outside the appealing
stucco minarets of the **Shiaithna-Asheri Mosque
(12)**. Benches of this kind were a crucial fea-

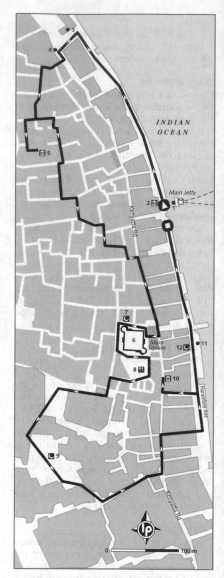

ture of any Swahili home, providing an informal social setting for men to discuss the
issues of the day.

Carrying on up Harambee Ave will bring
you back to the main jetty and the end of
our tour.

(Continued on page 353)

Elephant, Amboseli National Park (p300),
Kenya

White rhinoceros with lesser flamingo by the thousands, Lake Nakuru National Park (p364), Kenya

Zebras, Ngorongoro Conservation Area (p197), Tanzania

Lirhanda Hill Lookout, Kakamega Forest Reserve (p406), Kenya

ANDERS BLOM

Herd of wildebeest, Masai Mara National Reserve (p393), Kenya

GARY STEER

DAWN DELANEY

Heavily cultivated land at the base of the Bisoke volcano, Parc National des Volcans (p583), Rwanda

Moorland vegetation on the north face,
Mt Kilimanjaro (p175), Tanzania

Giraffe, Mt Meru (p190), Tanzania

Source of the Nile (p493), Lake Victoria, Uganda

ERIC L WHEATER

Musician (p39) at Kebirigo, near Kisii, Kenya

Makonde woodcarving (p40),
Dar es Salaam, Tanzania

DENNIS JOHNSON

TOM COCKREM

Colourful Maasai necklace (p40), Kenya

Maasai men dancing, Hell's Gate National Park (p360), Kenya

JANE SWE

Crowded dhow, Zanzibar (p130), Tanzania

Local woman, Democratic Republic of the Congo (p559)

Three-wheeler tuk-tuk on the streets of Nairobi (p278), Kenya

Stall holder, Kigali (p572), Rwanda

DOUG MCKINLAY

Zanzibar markets, Zanzibar (p130), Tanzania

WAYNE WALTON

Busy street, Kampala (p470), Uganda

DENNIS JO

Looking for a spot to fish, Lake Naivasha (p358), Kenya

MARK DAFFEY

JOHN BORTHWICK

Fishing dhow, Mangapwani
(p144), Zanzibar, Tanzania

Traditionally painted dhow, Lamu (p341), Kenya

ARIADNE VAN ZANDBERGEN

River safari, Rufiji River, Selous Game Reserve (p236), Tanzania

Hot-air balloon (p89), Rift Valley, Kenya

Hiker and local guide, Mbeya (p230), Tanzania

Safari van, Masai Mara National Reserve (p393), Kenya

(Continued from page 344)

Festivals & Events

The **Maulid Festival** celebrates the birth of the Prophet Mohammed. Its date shifts according to the Muslim calendar, and it will fall on 20 March 2007 and 20 March 2008. The festival has been celebrated on the island for over 100 years and much singing, dancing and general jollity takes place around this time. Organised events include swimming galas, poetry reading, calligraphy competitions, donkey races for young boys and dhow races for all the dhow captains.

The **Lamu Cultural Festival** is another colourful cultural event held in the last week of August, though it's actually a recent initiative, established in 2000 and aimed more at tourists than local people. Attractions include traditional dancing, displays of crafts, such as *kofia* embroidery (a *kofia* is a cap worn by Muslim men), and dhow races.

Sleeping

BUDGET

Lamu has been catering for budget travellers for several decades and still has loads of inexpensive guesthouses. Prices are remarkably consistent because of the competition for clientele, although you get what you pay for.

Rates rise by up to 50% from August to September and around Christmas and New Year. At other times there's plenty of scope for negotiation, especially if you plan to stay for more than a day or two. Touts will invariably try and accompany you from the jetty to get commission; the best way to avoid this is to book at least one night in advance, so you know ahead of time what you'll be paying.

Casuarina Rest House (☎ 633123; s/d/tr with shared bathroom KSh300/500/700, s/d with private bathroom KSh400/800) Exactly the kind of friendly personal vibe that gets people backpacking in the first place. The roof terrace acts as a social lounge, the staff are great fun and the breezy top-floor balcony double is fantastic. It's often full both in and out of season; ongoing expansion should create a few more berths.

Pole Pole Guest House (☎ 0722-652477; s/d KSh500/1000) Pole Pole is north of the centre of town and back from the waterfront. One of the tallest buildings in Lamu, it has bright doubles with fans and mosquito nets. There's a spacious *makuti*-roofed terrace area with great views and its own mini 'tower'.

Lamu Guest House (☎ 633338; Kenyatta Rd; s/d/tr with shared bathroom KSh400/800/900, s/d with private bathroom KSh500/1000,) Behind Petley's Inn, the basic rooms are very plain, but the upper-floor ones are better and catch the sea breeze. The 'official' rates posted in reception are a good KSh500 more than quoted here!

Lamu Castle Hotel (☎ 0722-355240; s/d with shared bathroom KSh300/400) A lick of fresh pink paint has left the Castle looking rather spruce, but inside it's just the basics, and even some of the walls seem to be left a little short.

MIDRANGE

Yumbe House (☎ 633101; lamuoldtown@africaonline.co .ke; s/d/tr low season KSh1100/2100/2900, high season KSh1290/2700/3860) Close to the Swahili House Museum, Yumbe is a tall, traditional house with a leafy courtyard. The pleasant rooms have fridges and are spotlessly clean, decked out with *kangas* (printed cotton wrap-around, incorporating a Swahili proverb), woven rugs and Lamu furniture. Go for the big, chic 'tower' room right under the thatch.

Jannat House (☎ 633414; www.jannathouse.com; s/d with shared bathroom KSh2175/3675, with private bathroom KSh2625/4500; 🏊) The architects clearly had a field day designing the Jannat House: it's essentially two houses spliced together around a courtyard, with several levels and multiple terraces. The lower rooms are disappointing but the upper levels are as nice as you'd hope for. Follow the signs from Kenyatta Rd; you'll need to keep looking up.

Stone House Hotel (☎ 633544; half board s/d US$45/ 66) Another wonderful old Swahili place with Escher-like stairways and a fine leafy courtyard. The hotel has its own superb rooftop restaurant (no alcohol) with views over the town and waterfront. Rooms can be booked with Kisiwani Ltd (☎ 020-4446384).

Amu House (☎ 633420; amuhouse@aol.com; s/d/tr KSh1700/2300/2700) Of all the restored Swahili hotels, this beautiful 16th-century house has received perhaps the greatest attention to detail. Rates include breakfast, transfers from Manda airstrip and a free water-skiing lesson at Shela Beach. Knock KSh500 or so off in the low season.

Kitendetini Bahari Hotel (☎ 633172; s/d incl breakfast KSh700/1200) A borderline budget option set around a neat rectangular courtyard. All rooms have fans, mosquito nets and fridges, though the toilets lack seats. Prices are usually negotiable.

TOP END

Lamu World (☎ 633491; www.lamuworld.com; Harambee Ave; s/d low season US$90/100, high season US$150/200, ste low/high season US$150/250; 🖳 🖳) It almost rankles to recommend something so new in such a traditional town, but the pale stone design of this luxury establishment is such a perfect modern interpretation of Swahili style that it frankly outshines even some of the authentic places. There are just 10 rooms shared between two houses, all with immaculate fittings.

Petley's Inn (☎ 633107; www.chaleislandparadise .com; Harambee Ave; s/d US$70/90; 🖳) Petley's has plenty of traditional touches, but is looking a bit worn these days. It's a fine place, though, especially the 'penthouse' room and rooftop bar. Rates include transfers to and from Manda Island airstrip.

New Lamu Palace Hotel (☎ 633164; Harambee Ave; s/d US$70/90) This modern hotel is not as sensitively designed as its peers, but rooms are smart and comfortable, and there's a good restaurant (mains KSh650 to KSh1200) and a bar. The problem, as with all the top-end options here, is that you could rent a whole Swahili house for these prices!

Eating

It's important to know that *all* the cheap places to eat and many of the more expensive restaurants are closed all day until after sunset during the month of Ramadan.

Bush Gardens Restaurant (☎ 633285; Harambee Ave; mains KSh180-800) The Bush Gardens is the template for a whole set of restaurants along the waterfront, offering breakfasts, seafood – excellent fish, top-value 'monster crab' (KSh400) and the inevitable lobster in Swahili sauce (KSh750) – and superb juices and shakes. Just about every traveller on Lamu ends up here at some point.

Hapa Hapa Restaurant (Harambee Ave; mains KSh150-750) Very much in the same vein as Bush Gardens, and advocated just as vehemently by its regulars, this waterfront eatery is a bit more informal and African under its low thatch.

New Minaa Café (meals under KSh120; 🕑 6.30am-midnight) On the road towards the Riyadha Mosque, this busy, clean rooftop café serves Swahili favourites, such as beef kebabs, *maharagwe* (beans in coconut milk), chicken tikka and *samaki* (fried fish). It's cheap and popular with both locals and travellers.

Mangrove Centre (Harambee Ave; mains KSh250-380) Facing the main jetty, the restaurant does a lively trade at lunchtime, and it's handy for a juice while you wait for a boat or find your feet on arrival. You'll find a video store and an informal cinema behind the eating area.

Whispers Coffeeshop (Kenyatta Rd; mains KSh240-550; 🕑 9am-9pm) In the same building as the posh Baraka Gallery, this is a great place for an upmarket meal, a freshly baked cake or a real cappuccino. There's a lovely palm-shaded courtyard and simple meals are available even during Ramadan, though it closes in the low season.

Bosnian Café (Kenyatta Rd) One of several dirt-cheap local canteens at the far end of the main street that set up takeaway stalls in the evening, selling samosas, chapatis, *mishkaki* (kebabs), chips and the like from 10 bob apiece.

Drinking & Entertainment

As a Muslim town, Lamu caters very poorly for drinkers; Petley's Inn (left) and New Lamu Palace Hotel (left) are about the only places you can sink a cold beer.

Civil Servants' Club (admission KSh100) Along the waterfront towards Shela village. Virtually the only reliable spot for a drink and a dance at weekends. It's small, loud, rowdy and great fun, though women travelling alone should run for cover.

Getting There & Away

AIR

Daily afternoon flights are available with **Airkenya** (☎ 633445; Baraka House, Kenyatta Rd) between Lamu and Wilson Airport in Nairobi (US$143, 1¾ hours). The inbound flights also continue to Kiwayu Island (US$65, 15 minutes). **Safarilink** (Nairobi ☎ 020-600777) runs virtually identical services (US$140).

Kenya Airways (☎ 633155; Casuarina House, Harambee Ave) has daily afternoon flights between Lamu and the domestic terminal at Nairobi's Kenyatta International Airport (KSh10,860, 2¼ hours).

Mombasa Air Safari (Mombasa ☎ 041-433061) flies to Mombasa (US$90, 1¼ hours) via Malindi (US$21, 30 minutes). Book through **Ndau Safaris** (☎ 633576).

The airport at Lamu is on Manda Island, and the ferry across the channel to Lamu costs KSh100.

BUS

The main bus companies operating between Mombasa, Malindi and Lamu are TSS, Falcon, Zam Zam, Khadi Star and Tawakal.

There are booking offices for all these companies on Kenyatta Rd, apart from Khadi Star, which has its office on the waterfront. The going rate to Mombasa is KSh400 to KSh500; most buses leave between 7am and 8am, so you'll need to be at the jetty at 6.30am for the boat to the mainland. Tawakal also has 10am and 1pm services. It takes at least four hours from Lamu to Malindi, plus another two hours to Mombasa. Book early as demand is heavy.

Getting Around

There are ferries (KSh40) between Lamu and the bus station on the mainland (near Mokowe). Boats leave when the buses arrive at Mokowe; in the reverse direction they leave at around 6.30am to meet the departing buses. Ferries between the airstrip on Manda Island and Lamu cost KSh100 and leave about half an hour before the flights leave.

SHELA

This ancient Swahili village, often spelled Shella, sits at the start of glorious Shela Beach on Lamu island. In some places it seems even more medieval than Lamu, with few signs of modernity along its mazelike alleyways. Although it's something of a European enclave, with almost unseemly amounts of building going on to cater for foreign demand, it's still an atmospheric place to wander around, and the mood is as languorous and laid-back as it's always been.

Most people come here for the **beach**: this spectacular dune-backed strip runs for 12km around the headland, so you're guaranteed a private stretch of sand, and it's a good place to comb the beach for shells. The Indian Ocean tsunami washed away a lot of sand here, revealing some sharp rocks, but it's expected to return to normal within a few seasons.

There's no surf at Shela village because it's still in the channel between Lamu and Manda Islands, which makes it a prime spot for **windsurfing**. For traditional surfing, there are real breakers at the mouth of the channel, although this is also the realm of some substantial sharks.

SLEEPING & EATING

Stopover Guest House (☎ 633459; mtendeni@ikenya .com; d incl breakfast KSh3000) This is the first place you come to on the waterfront, above the popular restaurant of the same name. The rooms are nice and light with big beds; prices should be thoroughly negotiable when it's not busy.

Shella Bahari Guest House (☎ 632046; bahari guest@swiftlamu.com; d low season KSh2000-3000, high season KSh2500-4000) Another waterfront place with a very similar setup to the Stopover. Again, you can often bargain down; aim for around KSh500 per person.

Dodo Villas/Talking Trees Campsite (☎ 633500; camping per tent KSh400, r KSh600-1200, apt per person KSh200) This is Lamu's only budget beach option, 50m back from the seafront on the Shela–Lamu track. The main building has large, unfussy rooms and several concrete blocks hold apartments for up to 10 people, with more being built.

Peponi Hotel (☎ 633421; www.peponi-lamu.com; s/d high season US$220/300; ✕ closed May & Jun; ⊠) At the east end of Shela is *the* top resort hotel on the island, right on the waterfront facing the Lamu Channel. It blends neatly into the surrounding Swahili buildings and offers just 24 individually styled rooms. The hotel has excellent facilities, plus a bar and up-market restaurant, all open to nonguests.

Kijani House Hotel (☎ 633235; www.kijani-lamu .com; d US$160-180; ✕ closed May & Jun; ⊠) Set in splendid gardens, Kijani was painstakingly rebuilt over 10 years from the remains of three separate Swahili houses. Like Peponi, all manner of activities and trips can be arranged.

Island Hotel (☎ 633290; half board s/d US$37/52) In the centre of Shela is a superb Lamu-style house with a romantic rooftop restaurant. It's only five minutes' walk from the waterfront, along the alley beside Kijani House, but you'll probably have to ask for directions.

Kisiwani Ltd (Nairobi ☎ 020-4446384; www.lamu homes.com) Rents out whole houses in Shela from US$180 to US$280 per day. Properties include Mnarani House, behind the Mnarani Mosque, and Mtakuja House and Jasmine House, behind the Kijani House Hotel. Book well in advance.

GETTING THERE & AWAY

To get to Shela, you can take a motorised dhow from the moorings in Lamu for

KSh100 per person (or KSh250 to KSh300 for a solo ride). Alternatively, you can walk it in about 40 minutes.

ISLANDS AROUND LAMU

The Lamu archipelago has plenty to offer outside Lamu itself. The easiest to get to is **Manda Island**, just across the channel, where most visitors go on dhow trips for snorkelling and to visit the Takwa ruins. The tiny Manda Toto Island, on the other side of Manda, has perhaps the best reefs on the coast.

Further northeast, **Paté Island** was the main power centre in the region before Lamu came to prominence, but is rarely visited now, preserving an uncomplicated traditional lifestyle as much by necessity as by choice. A regular motor launch shuttles between the towns of Mtangawanda, Siyu, Faza and Kizingitini.

Even further out, remote **Kiwayu Island** is part of the Kiunga Marine National Reserve, and gets most of its scant tourist traffic from extended dhow trips and visitors to the exclusive luxury resort on the mainland. Snorkelling here is highly recommended.

THE RIFT VALLEY

Around eight million years ago Mother Earth tried to rip Africa clear in two; Africa bent, Africa buckled, but Africa never gave in. The continent's battle scar, stretching thousands of kilometres from Ethiopia to Mozambique, forms a series of stunning landscapes.

Some of the most attractive wounds are found in Kenya's famed Rift Valley, where serrated escarpments and splintered volcanoes tower over ochre soils, grassy plains and shallow soda lakes. Perhaps it's Earth's anger over failing to crack Africa that still causes steam and boiling fluids to spurt from its surface at Lake Bogoria and Hell's Gate National Park…

Today the valley's fertile floor, dotted with several large freshwater and soda lakes, is alive with some of Kenya's most spectacular wildlife. Lake Nakuru's shores are often famously dyed pink with hundreds of thousands of wading fluorescent flamingos, while its forested slopes host significantly bigger treats, like rhinos, giraffes, buffaloes, antelopes and leopards. And if you under-

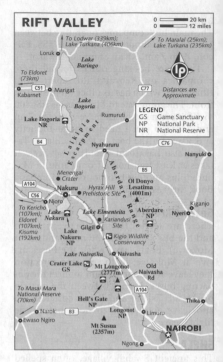

take the challenge to walk or cycle unguided through the dramatic gorges of Hell's Gate National Park, you'll never see a zebra or giraffe in the same way again – being on foot is the ultimate amplifier of observation.

Hikes up the valley's various dormant volcanoes are rewarding and offer tremendous views over the rift. Similar views are also available from the viewpoints on the Old Naivasha Rd as it drops into the valley from the town of Limuru.

Geography

Kenya's Rift Valley is part of the Afro-Arabian rift system, which stretches 6000km from the Dead Sea in the Middle East to Mozambique in southern Africa, passing through the Red Sea then Ethiopia, Kenya, Tanzania and Malawi. A western branch forms a string of lakes in the centre of the continent, including Albert and Edward on the Uganda–DR Congo border, Kivu on the DR Congo–Rwanda border, and Tanganyika on the Tanzania–DR Congo border, which joins the main system at the northern tip of Lake Malawi.

In Kenya the Rift Valley can be traced through Lake Turkana, the Cherangani Hills, and Lakes Baringo, Bogoria, Nakuru, Elmenteita, Naivasha and Magadi. A string of volcanic peaks and craters also lines the valley. While most are now extinct, 30 remain active, and according to local legend, Mt Longonot erupted as recently as 1860. This continuing activity supports a considerable number of hot springs and provides ideal conditions for geothermal power plants, which are increasingly important in Kenya's energy supply.

Besides providing fertile soil, the volcanic deposits have created alkaline waters in most Rift Valley lakes. These shallow soda lakes, formed by the valley's lack of decent drainage, experience high evaporation rates, which further concentrates the alkalinity. The strangely soapy and smelly waters are, however, the perfect environment for the growth of microscopic blue-green algae, which in turn feed lesser flamingos, tiny crustaceans (food for greater flamingos) and insect larvae (food for soda-resistant fish).

LONGONOT NATIONAL PARK

Few places offer better Rift Valley views than the serrated crater rim of Mt Longonot, rising 1000m above the baking valley floor. In dog years this dormant volcano is ancient, while in geological terms it's a wee pup at 400,000 years of age.

Since the best vistas in this park (adult/child US$15/5) are only reached with some effort on foot, peace and quiet accompany the panoramas. The steep climb to the rim takes just under an hour, while the rewarding jaunt to the summit (2777m) and around the crater takes another three hours. Despite the bounty of Rift Valley views, your eyes may just be drawn inward to the 2km-wide crater, a little lost world hosting an entirely different ecosystem. Calculating time for gawking, this 11km trek should take about six hours.

Although security has improved and the KWS no longer requires rangers to escort you, double-check the situation at the gate.

You can camp in the park, or there are plenty of hotels in nearby Naivasha.

Getting There & Away

If you're driving, the national park is 75km northwest of Nairobi on the Old Naivasha Rd. If you're without a vehicle, take a *matatu* from Naivasha to Longonot village, from

where there's a path to the park's access road (ask locals how to find it).

NAIVASHA

☎ 050

Bypassed by the new A104 Hwy to Nairobi, Naivasha has become an agricultural backwater. The streets have descended into cratered madness and services primarily focus on the area's blossoming flower industry. Although a convenient base for visits to Longonot National Park, staying at nearby Lake Naivasha (p358) is more enjoyable.

The only conceivable reason to stop is for supplies en route to the lake, as there are very limited stocks in the *dukas* further on.

Information

Barclays Bank (Moi Ave)
Cyber Cafe (Kenyatta Ave; per hr KSh120)
Kenya Commercial Bank (Moi Ave)
Medical Clinic (Biashara Rd; ☒ 9am-7pm Mon-Sat, 11am-4pm Sun)
Post office (Moi Ave)

Sleeping

La Belle Inn (☎ 2021007; Moi Ave; s/d incl breakfast KSh2500/2900) A classic colonial-style option, with rooms of various sizes and a level of cleanliness unseen anywhere else in town.

Ken-Vash Hotel (☎ 2030049; s/d/tw KSh1400/2000/2200) A large tourist-class place with TVs and thick shag carpets, but lacking La Belle's character. It's off Moi Ave.

Naivasha Silver Hotel (☎ 2020580; Kenyatta Ave; s/tw KSh600/1000) A slightly more pleasant option than other budget lodgings. Rooms and beds vary in size, so scope out a few. It has a decent restaurant and secure parking.

Kafico Lodge (☎ 2021344; Biashara Rd; s/tw KSh350/600) One of the odd places that 'seal' the rooms after cleaning, meaning that you can only see your accommodation after paying. The rooms are tattered, the toilets lack seats, but they're comfy enough, and security is good.

Sam's Holiday Inn (☎ 0721-474556; Mbaria Kaniu Rd; s/tw KSh250/400) It's a bit gloomy, but should do the trick. Rooms have mosquito nets.

Eating

La Belle Inn (Moi Ave; meals KSh180-400) Whether your stomach is rumbling for curry, steak, pork, fresh *tilapia* (Nile Perch) or even apple pie, this colonial veranda is for you. It's also a great place for drinks.

KENYA

Ming Yue Chinese Restaurant (Moi Ave; meals KSh300-700; ☺ Mon-Sat) With a menu boasting the likes of bean curd satay, fried *bok choi* and scrumptious spring rolls, it's safe to say that there's nothing else like this for miles.

Dancing Spoons (Biashara Rd; meals KSh60-130) Located below the Kafico Lodge, this is the restaurant of choice for simple Kenyan fare.

Jolly Cafe (Kenyatta Ave; meals KSh80-220) While Martha Stewart would gasp at the window treatments and fluorescent chairs, she wouldn't choke on the Kenyan and Western dishes here.

Getting There & Away

The main bus and *matatu* station is off Mbaria Kaniu Rd, close to the municipal market. Frequent buses and *matatus* leave for Nakuru (KSh120, 1¼ hours), Nairobi (KSh150, 1½ hours), Nyahururu (KSh200, 1¾ hours) and points west. Some Nairobi *matatus* and all those for Kongoni via Fisherman's Camp (KSh70, 45 minutes) leave from Kenyatta Ave.

LAKE NAIVASHA

☎ 0311

The area around Naivasha was one of the first settled by *wazungu* (whites) and was a favourite haunt of the decadent Happy Valley set in the 1930s. Along with Karen, near Nairobi, it is now probably the largest remaining settler and expat community in Kenya.

The lake level has ebbed and flowed over the years, as half-submerged fencing posts indicate. Early in the 1890s it dried up almost completely, but over the next 20 years it rose a phenomenal 15m and inundated a far larger area than it presently occupies. It currently covers about 170 sq km and is home to an incredible variety of bird species, including the fish eagle.

As a freshwater lake, Naivasha's ecology is quite different from that of the Rift Valley's soda lakes. Since the water can be used for irrigation, the surrounding countryside is a major agricultural production area; the flower market has become a major industry here.

Naivasha has been a focus of conservation efforts in Kenya, and in 1995 the Lake Naivasha Riparian Association was formed to educate the estimated 300,000 people dependent on the lake about the environmental issues involved. The results are promising, but so far improvement has

been slow, and further drops in the water level are predicted for the next 15 to 20 years.

Sights & Activities

On the western side of Lake Naivasha, north of the village of Kongoni, is the **Crater Lake Game Sanctuary** (admission KSh100), a small park set around a beautiful volcanic crater. Wildlife is plentiful, and the tiny jade-green crater lake is held in high regard by the local Maasai, who even believe its water helps soothe ailing cattle.

On the eastern side of the lake is **Crescent Island** (adult/child nonresident US$14/7), a wildlife sanctuary you can visit by boat or car.

A couple of kilometres past Fisherman's Camp on Moi South Lake Rd you'll find **Elsamere Conservation Centre** (☎ 2021055; elsa@africa online.co.ke; admission KSh500; ☺ 8am-6.30pm), the former home of the late Joy Adamson of *Born Free* fame. The site is now a public conservation centre; entry includes afternoon tea (with a chance to see the eastern black-and-white colobus monkeys), a visit to the memorial room and a showing of the weathered 40-minute *Joy Adamson Story*. The only way to visit outside of hours is to sleep here or to book in for a meal. All bookings should be made in advance.

Sleeping

BUDGET

Due to its popularity, Lake Naivasha has the Rift Valley's best range of budget

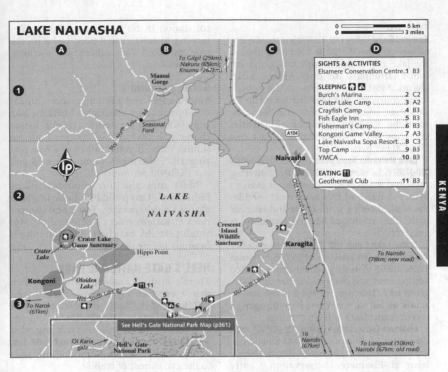

LAKE NAIVASHA

To Gilgil (25km);
Nakuru (65km);
Kisumu (267km)

Maasai Gorge

Seasonal Ford

Moi North Lake Rd

A104

Naivasha

LAKE NAIVASHA

Old Naivasha Rd

Crater Lake Game Sanctuary

Crater Lake

Hippo Point

Crescent Island Wildlife Sanctuary

Karagita

To Nairobi (78km; new road)

Kongoni

Oloiden Lake

Moi South Lake Rd

Moi South Lake Rd

To Narok (61km)

See Hell's Gate National Park Map (p361)

Ol Karia gate

Hell's Gate National Park

To Nairobi (67km)

To Longonot (10km); Nairobi (67km; old road)

SIGHTS & ACTIVITIES
Elsamere Conservation Centre...1 B3

SLEEPING
Burch's Marina 2 C2
Crater Lake Camp 3 A2
Crayfish Camp 4 B3
Fish Eagle Inn 5 B3
Fisherman's Camp.............6 B3
Kongoni Game Valley........7 A3
Lake Naivasha Sopa Resort...8 C3
Top Camp 9 B3
YMCA 10 B3

EATING
Geothermal Club 11 B3

KENYA

accommodation. All sites are located on or near Moi South Lake Rd unless otherwise specified.

Fisherman's Camp (☎ 2030088; camping KSh200, dm KSh500, s/tw with shared bathrooms from KSh800/1600) Spread along the grassy tree-laden southern shore, this is a perennial favourite of campers, overland companies and hungry hippos. The site is huge, enabling you to get away from the overlander crowds and the noise from the popular bar and restaurant. With overpriced simple rooms and basic *bandas*, camping is clearly the best option.

Top Camp (☎ 2030276; camping KSh200, s/tw bandas from KSh500/1000, 5-person cottages KSh5000) Although lacking Fisherman's lakeside location, Top Camp boasts crazy lake views from its hill-top perch. It's a quiet place with various tin-roofed, bamboo-walled *bandas* (almost all have bathrooms).

YMCA (camping KSh250, dm KSh250, bandas per person KSh300-450) For basic roofed accommodation, you'll do no better than the Y. There are two dorms and a number of spartan *bandas*; firewood and bedding can be provided for a small charge.

MIDRANGE
Crayfish Camp (☎ 2020239; craycamp@africaonline.co.ke; camping KSh250, s with shared bathroom KSh750, s/d with private bathroom KSh2500/3000; 🖳) Crayfish Camp can seem more like a beer garden than a campsite, but it's not a bad option. The pricey new rooms are a bit minimalist, but have some charm, while the petite rooms with shared facilities are very plain Jane. There's a restaurant and two bars, kitchen facilities, pool tables, and tent, bicycle and boat hire.

Burch's Marina (☎ 0733-660372; camping KSh200, 2-person rondavels KSh600, cottages d/tr/q KSh2200/ 2600/3000) A pleasant and well-shaded site, with hot showers, a communal cooking area and a well. It has a choice of basic twin-bed rondavels (circular buildings with conical roofs) or thatched four-bed family cottages. Advance booking is mandatory.

Fish Eagle Inn (☎ 2030306; fish@africaonline.co.ke; camping KSh220, dm KSh450, s KSh2110-2660, d KSh3550-4100; 🍺) If you have money to burn and find plywood charming, you'll love the overpriced DIY standard rooms. The 'Jumbo House' rooms are even more pricey, but have satellite TV and canopy beds.

TOP END

Kongoni Game Valley (☎ 2021070; www.kgvalley.com; full board per person US$150; ☑) Nothing around the lake can compare with this grand colonial farmhouse for utter African safari charm. Most rooms surround the house's lovely courtyard, and boast hardwood floors, rich rugs, comfortable beds and bear-claw bathtubs. Packages including all activities and trips to Hell's Gate National Park cost US$300 per person.

Lake Naivasha Sopa Resort (☎ 2050358, Nairobi 020-3750235; full board s/d US$188/250; ☑) Towering cacti and manicured gardens front massive luxury cottages at this new resort. Besides the pool, there's a gym, sauna and lakeside path. The arc-shaped bar and restaurant is gorgeous.

Crater Lake Camp (☎ 2020613; crater@africaonline .co.ke; low season full board s/d KSh4930/8925, high season KSh5880/10500) A luxury tented camp nestled among trees and overlooking the tiny jade-green lake. The food is good and the service excellent, but we're not sure how the owner's recent tragic death will affect things.

Elsamere Conservation Centre (☎ 2021055; elsa@ africaonline.co.ke; full board s/d US$85/140) Small bungalows with great lake views dot the lovely lawn at Elsamere Conservation Centre (p358). Although lacking the 'wow' factor of others, it's comfortable, friendly and a relative bargain.

Eating

Since food and drinks can be had at most of the places listed earlier, there's little in the way of independent wining and dining.

Geothermal Club (meals KSh140-270) Set in a beautiful spot above the lake about 45 minutes' walk from Fisherman's Camp, this relaxed restaurant caters for employees of the KenGen thermal power plant but will happily serve visitors.

Getting There & Away

Frequent *matatus* (KSh80, one hour) run along Moi South Lake Rd between Naivasha town and Kongoni on the lake's western side, passing the turn-offs to Hell's Gate National Park and Fisherman's Camp.

It's a 5km walk from Kongoni to Crater Lake, but don't do this alone due to recent muggings.

There's one daily *matatu* along Moi North Lake Rd, leaving from the Total petrol station in Naivasha around 3pm. Returning to town, you'll need to be on the road by about 7am, otherwise it's a long, dusty walk.

Getting Around

Most budget and midrange accommodation options hire reasonable boats for lake trips (KSh2500 per hour). Top-end lodges charge KSh3000 to KSh4000 per hour for similar rides. If you'd rather row row row yourself, Fisherman's Camp can help you out (KSh300 per hour).

Most sites also hire mountain bikes; Fisherman's Camp and Fish Eagle Inn both charge KSh500 per day. You'll find cheaper rides at various places signposted off Moi South Lake Rd, but check the contraptions carefully before paying.

HELL'S GATE NATIONAL PARK

There's visiting national parks and then there's experiencing national parks – and **Hell's Gate** (☎ 050-2020284; adult/child US$15/5) is an experience indeed. The park is truly unique, as it allows you to walk or cycle unguided across its breadth. Knowledge that cheetahs, lions and leopards may be lurking only adds to the excitement of it all!

Keep an eye out for the massive lammergeyers (bearded vultures), which are slowly being reintroduced. Their wingspans can reach almost 3m.

The scenery is dramatic, with rich ochre soils and savanna grasses squeezed between looming cliffs of rusty columnar basalt. Marking the eastern entrance to **Hell's Gate Gorge** is **Fischer's Tower**, a 25m-high volcanic column named after Gustav Fischer, a German explorer who reached here in 1882 only to have his party slaughtered by local Maasai. The tower is one of the park's many popular rock-climbing sites.

Rising from the gorge's southern end is the large **Central Tower** (climbing prohibited). A picnic site and ranger's post are close by, from where an excellent walk descends into the **Lower Gorge** (Ol Njorowa). This narrow sandstone ravine has been stunningly sculpted by water, and the incoming light casts marvellous shadows. It's a steep and very slippery descent, but some steps have been cut into the rock and whole school parties manage it on a regular basis. Flash floods are common, so check with rangers before proceeding.

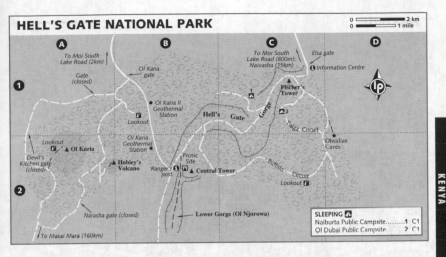

HELL'S GATE NATIONAL PARK

To Moi South Lake Road (2km)

Gate (closed)

Ol Karia gate

Ol Karia II Geothermal Station

Lookout

Hell's Gate

To Moi South Lake Road (800m); Naivasha (15km)

Elsa gate

Information Centre

Fischer's Tower

Gorge

2

Tuiga Circuit

Lookout

Ol Karia

Ol Karia Geothermal Station

Devil's Kitchen gate (closed)

Hobley's Volcano

Picnic Site

Ranger's post

Central Tower

Obsidian Caves

Buffalo Circuit

Lookout

Narasha gate (closed)

Lower Gorge (Ol Njorowa)

To Masai Mara (160km)

0 ——— 2 km
0 ——— 1 mile

SLEEPING
Naiburta Public Campsite..........1 C1
Ol Dubai Public Campsite 2 C1

KENYA

If you want to explore further, the **Buffalo Circuit** offers fine views over Hell's Gate Gorge, the surrounding countryside and the serrated profile of a distant Mt Longonot. This circuit has more soft sections of sand, which isn't conducive to cycling.

The park's western half is much less scenic and hosts the **Ol Karia Geothermal Station**. The plumes of rising steam can be seen from many of the park's viewpoints. It's usually possible to have a look around the site; ask the guards at Ol Karia II.

Camping here is highly recommended. Ol Dubai and Naiberta camp sites are probably the best. See p358 for details on other places to stay and opposite for information on how to get to the park.

NAKURU

☎ 051 / pop 163,000

Although Nakuru is Kenya's fourth-largest town, it still has a relaxed atmosphere and makes a pleasant base for a few days. It's on the doorstep of the delightful Lake Nakuru National Park and is only a few kilometres from the deep, dramatic Menengai Crater.

Information

Changing cash and travellers cheques in Nakuru is easy, with numerous banks and foreign exchange bureaus. Barclays ATMs are the most reliable. Plenty of cardphones are scattered around town.

Aga Khan Satellite Laboratory Lab services and malaria tests (KSh160). It's off Court Rd.

Crater Travel (☎ 2215019) One of the few reputable travel agencies in town. It's off Kenyatta Ave.

Dreams Cyber World (Kenyatta Lane; per hr KSh120; ☻ 8am-8pm, closed 1-2pm Fri) Fast connections and open Sunday.

Post office (Kenyatta Ave)

Sleeping

BUDGET

Mount Sinai Hotel (☎ 2211779; Bazaar Rd; s/tw/tr KSh350/500/650) A big, clean place with sound security (iron bars all over!). The rooms on the scenic roof terrace are the brightest of the bunch.

Joska Hotel (☎ 2212546; Pandhit Nehru Rd; s KSh400) Foam mattresses have shag-carpet covers in these basic rooms. Everything is rather clean, but you'll have to be a porcelain jockey – the toilets lack seats. Ask for an upstairs or inward-facing room, as they're more quiet.

Tropical Lodge (☎ 2216847; Moi Rd; s/tw with shared bathroom KSh250/350) While the bathrooms are shared, they do have toilet seats (a rarity in these parts). The rooms are simple, quiet and baby blue. It's run by a cheerful woman, which makes up for the odd cockroach.

Crater View Lodge (☎ 2216352; Mburu Gichua Rd; s/tw KSh300/350) All rooms face a bright inner courtyard, and noise is less than you'd suspect. The twin rooms are a bargain, even if the bathrooms are a bit rough. Secure parking is available.

Gituamba Lodge (Gusii Rd; s/tw with shared bathroom KSh260/345, with private bathroom KSh310/400) Rooms are all bare-bones basics, but they're rather

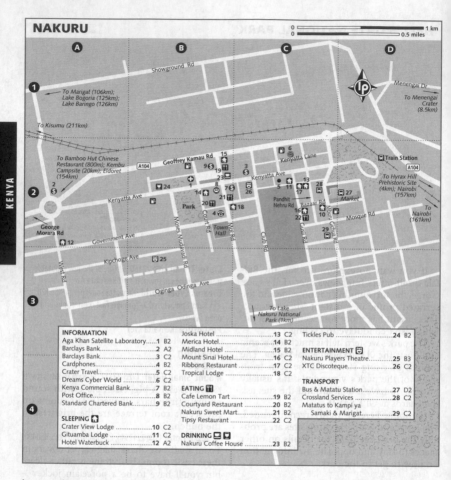

NAKURU

large and some have big bright windows. It can be noisy, so take a top-floor room.

There is no camp site in Nakuru itself, but you can camp in the national park or 20km west of town at **Kembu Campsite** (☎ 0722-361102; kembu@africaonline.co.ke; camping US$4, 1-/2-bedroom cottages KSh3000/6000). Kembu has a great atmosphere and it's particularly popular with overlanders; however, there's enough space for smaller parties not to be overwhelmed. The larger cottages have kitchens and are great for families. To get here, take a *matatu* heading to Molo (via Njoro; KSh80) and ask to be dropped at the metal gecko sign, about 6km northwest of Njoro on the C56. It's also signposted from the A104.

MIDRANGE
Hotel Waterbuck (☎ 2215672; West Rd; s/d/tw KSh2000/2500/2500; 🏊) Behind this boring exterior lurk large kitschy African-themed doubles. Although a bit brash, they're comfortable and more memorable than any other room in town. The singles and twins are small, dull and lack balconies.

Midland Hotel (☎ 2212125; Geoffrey Kamau Rd; s/d from KSh2300/3700) This popular place has a wide range of rooms with wall-to-wall carpets and varying levels of comfort. A third wing has recently been added.

TOP END
Merica Hotel (☎ 2216013; merica@kenyaweb.com; Kenyatta Ave; half board s/d US$65/110; 🍴 🏊) Opened

in 2003, this contemporary tower hosts Nakuru's only top-end rooms. Besides modern comfort, there's classic fun in Nakuru's best swimming pool (nonguests KSh200).

Eating

Bamboo Hut Chinese Restaurant (Giddo Plaza, George Morara Rd; meals KSh300-700) Highly recommended by Nakuru's expat community, this place serves great Chinese fare.

Courtyard Restaurant (meals KSh250-500) This place off Court Rd scratches a variety of itches, from Indian to Italian and beef stew to seafood. As the name suggests, it's got a nice courtyard.

Ribbons Restaurant (Gusii Rd; meals KSh50-200) One of the best restaurants for cheap Kenyan dishes. There's a balcony overlooking the street and the servers are pretty in pink.

Cafe Lemon Tart (Moi Rd; meals KSh100-200) A bright and popular café serving Kenyan fare. No alcohol is served, which guarantees a peaceful ambience.

Tipsy Restaurant (Gusii Rd; mains KSh100-250) A fast-food feel, complete with 1970s swivelling chairs. It's well liked by locals, and offers reasonable value for Indian and Western-style food, although dishes can be greasy.

Nakuru Sweet Mart (Gusii Rd) A perennial favourite, this bakery dishes out Indian sweets, puff pastries and tasty gingerbread men.

Drinking

Plenty of places in town serve idiot juice (beer), including the top-end hotels, and one wee shop even brews great coffee.

Nakuru Coffee House (Kenyatta Ave) For a straightforward caffeine fix, this café grinds out excellent fresh roasts.

Tickles Pub (Kenyatta Ave) This mellow pub is the friendliest choice and has several TVs for footy fans. Things pick up on weekends when it hosts local DJs.

Entertainment

Unusually for a rural town, there's actually a choice of evening options here.

Nakuru Players Theatre (Kipchoge Ave) Four evenings a month this theatre stages entertaining Kenyan plays.

XTC Discoteque (Kenyatta Ave) With strobe lights and a dark dance floor, it's the nearest you'll get to a proper nightclub in Nakuru. They were playing J-Lo when we visited – we'll try not to hold it against them.

Getting There & Away

Buses, *matatus* and occasional Peugeots leave the chaotic stands off Mburu Gichua Rd for Naivasha (KSh120, 1¼ hours), Nyahururu (KSh100, 1¼hours), Kericho (KSh200, two hours), Nyeri (KSh250, 2½ hours), Eldoret (KSh200, 2¾ hours), Nairobi (KSh200, three hours), Kitale (KSh350, 3½ hours), Kisumu (KSh350, 3½ hours) and Kisii (KSh375, 4½ hours).

Matatus for Molo (KSh100, one hour) leave from **Crossland Services** (Mburu Gichua Rd), while services to Kampi ya Samaki (for Lake Baringo) via Marigat (for Lake Bogoria) leave further south on Mburu Gichua Rd. Kampi ya Samaki (KSh200, 2½ hours) costs slightly more and takes 30 minutes longer to reach than Marigat.

Buses serve most of the same destinations at slightly cheaper rates.

AROUND NAKURU
Menengai Crater

The gentle slopes of this dormant volcano conceal a stunning hidden crater, where striking red cliffs radiate outward to encircle a cauldron of convoluted black lava flows. While lush vegetation now proliferates on the harsh crater floor, some 480m below, the violent and dramatic volcanic history is easily seen.

A grim local legend states that the plumes of steam rising from the bottom are the souls of Maasai warriors thrown into the crater after a territorial battle, trying to make their way to heaven.

While hiking to the viewpoint from town offers great views back over Lake Nakuru, it's rather isolated and tourists have been mugged. To be safe, the 9km walk from town should only be done in groups. Alternatively, you can take a taxi for KSh1000.

Hyrax Hill Prehistoric Site

This **archaeological site** (adult/child KSh100/50; ☻ 8.30am-6pm) is located just outside Nakuru on the Nairobi road. A small visitor's guide is available from the site's museum.

Archaeological excavations were conducted here from 1937 well into the 1980s, although the significance of the site was first mooted by Louis Leakey in 1926. Finds at the site indicate that three settlements were made here, the earliest possibly 3000 years ago, the most recent only 200 to 300 years ago.

KENYA

From the museum at the northern end you can take a short stroll around the site, starting with the Northeast Village where 13 enclosures, or pits, were excavated. On the other side of the hill, you come to the Iron Age settlement and, just north of it, a series of burial pits where 19 skeletons were found (unfortunately, souvenir seekers have stolen the bones). Two Neolithic burial mounds were also discovered here, along with more Iron Age pits. Finally, if you follow the path back to the museum, there's a *bau* board carved in a large rock. This popular game is still played throughout East Africa.

You're free to wander the site, but it's rather cryptic and a guide is useful – a tip of KSh100 is plenty.

Lake Elmenteita

Its bleached shoreline often fringed in pink thanks to thousands of brilliant flamingos, Elmenteita is another of the major Rift Valley soda lakes. It's not a national park, so there are no entry fees and you can walk around parts of the shoreline that aren't privately owned. For some water action, Flamingo Camp hires canoes for a paltry KSh100.

Surrounded by lovely gardens and overlooking Lake Elmenteita, **Lake Elmenteita Lodge** (☎ 051-8508630; high season full board s/d US70/100, low season US$120/155; 🏊) has bungalows with dated but well-maintained rooms. Horseback riding (KSh1500 per hour) and walks to the lake are offered.

Set right on shore, **Flamingo Camp** (☎ 0722-832001; camping KSh200, s/d KSh2000/4000) has small rooms spread between three stone rondavels. Although it's comfortable and the tiny terraces offer good views, it's overpriced. The camp site isn't bad but would be a more attractive option with some shade. A restaurant and bar are on site.

LAKE NAKURU NATIONAL PARK

With a pink sea of flamingos lapping at its shores, rich areas of grassland, euphorbia and acacia forests, and rocky cliffs supporting a myriad of animal and bird species, there's little doubt why **Lake Nakuru National Park** (☎ 051-2217151; adult/child US$30/10, smartcard required) is rivalling Amboseli as Kenya's second most visited park after the Masai Mara.

Sightings of grazing or lazing white rhinos at the lake's southern end now seem to be commonplace since the species was reintroduced several years ago. The shy black rhinos, browsers by nature, are more difficult to spot. If you're very very lucky, you'll catch a glimpse of a rare tree-climbing lion. Warthogs are common all over the park, providing light relief from the 'serious' animals with their amusing gait and upright tails (known to locals as Kenyan antennas). Along the shore you'll come across waterbucks and buffaloes, while Thomson's gazelles and reedbucks can be seen further into the bush, where there's also a good chance of seeing leopards. Around the cliffs you may catch sight of hyraxes and birds of prey amid the countless baboons. A small herd of hippos generally frequents the lake's northern shore.

There's no better view of the park than that seen from atop **Baboon Cliff** as the afternoon sun casts a warm glow over the lake.

Since the 180-sq-km park's creation in 1961, the population of lesser and greater flamingos has risen and fallen with the soda lake's erratic water levels. When the lake dried up in 1962 (happy first birthday!), the population plummeted as it later did in the 1970s, when heavy rainfall diluted the lake's salinity affecting the lesser flamingo's food source (blue-green algae). Over much of the last decade healthy water levels have seen flamingo numbers blossom again. If future droughts or flooding make them fly the coop again, you'll probably find them at Lake Bogoria.

Sadly, not all is picture perfect, as in recent years pressures on the lake have increased. Pollution from Nakuru town, pesticide run-off from surrounding farms and massive deforestation within the water catchment area have all caused concern. A World Wildlife Fund (WWF) project is making considerable progress in countering these problems, and the local afforestation program continues to plant thousands of indigenous tree seedlings.

Walking in the park isn't permitted, so you'll have to hire a taxi, go on a tour or be lucky enough to hitch a ride. You can get out of your vehicle on the lakeshore and at certain viewpoints, but don't drive too close to the water's edge, as the mud is very soft!

The main gate is 2km south of the centre of Nakuru. KWS smartcards and official guidebooks (KSh750) are available here.

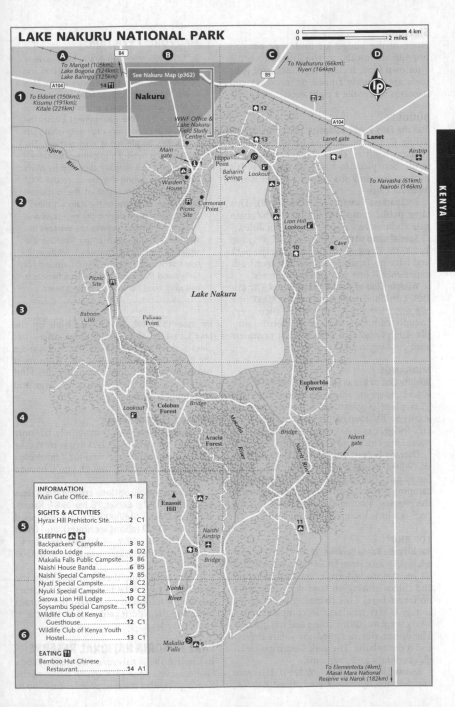

LAKE NAKURU NATIONAL PARK

0 ———————— 4 km
0 ———————— 2 miles

To Marigat (105km);
Lake Bogoria (124km);
Lake Baringo (125km)

To Eldoret (150km);
Kisumu (191km);
Kitale (221km)

To Nyahururu (66km);
Nyeri (164km)

Nakuru

See Nakuru Map (p362)

WWF Office &
Lake Nakuru
Field Study
Centre

Njoro River

Main gate

Warden's
House

Picnic
Site

Hippo
Point

Baharini
Springs

Cormorant
Point

Lookout

Lion Hill
Lookout

Cave

Lanet gate

Lanet

Airstrip

To Naivasha (61km);
Nairobi (146km)

KENYA

Picnic
Site

Baboon
Cliff

Pelican
Point

Lake Nakuru

Euphorbia
Forest

Lookout

Colobus Forest

Bridge

Acacia
Forest

Makalia
River

Bridge

Nderit
River

Bridge

Nderit
gate

Enasoit
Hill

Naishi
Airstrip

Bridge

Naishi
River

Makalia
Falls

To Elementeita (4km);
Masai Mara National
Reserve via Narok (182km)

INFORMATION	
Main Gate Office	1 B2

SIGHTS & ACTIVITIES	
Hyrax Hill Prehistoric Site	2 C1

SLEEPING	
Backpackers' Campsite	3 B2
Eldorado Lodge	4 D2
Makalia Falls Public Campsite	5 B6
Naishi House Banda	6 B5
Naishi Special Campsite	7 B5
Nyati Special Campsite	8 C2
Nyuki Special Campsite	9 C2
Sarova Lion Hill Lodge	10 C2
Soysambu Special Campsite	11 C5
Wildlife Club of Kenya Guesthouse	12 C1
Wildlife Club of Kenya Youth Hostel	13 C1

EATING	
Bamboo Hut Chinese Restaurant	14 A1

Sleeping

None of the budget or midrange options provide any meals, so you'll have to bring your own food. If camping, make sure your tents are securely zipped or monkeys and baboons will make a right mess.

BUDGET

Makalia Falls Public Campsite (adult/child US$10/5) While it may be hard to get to and have cruder facilities than Backpackers', this is the best place to camp in the park. It's picturesque and sits next to the seasonal Makalia Falls.

Backpackers' Campsite (adult/child US$10/5) This large public camp site sits inside the main gate and has very good camping facilities.

Special camp sites (adult/child US$15/5, plus set-up fee KSh5000) These are dotted all over the park and have no facilities, but offer a true bush experience – just you and the animals!

Wildlife Club of Kenya Youth Hostel (☎ 051-850929; dm KSh150; s with shared bathroom KSh300, s/tw with private bathroom KSh500/1000) A nice, very friendly camp site with clean dorms, simple singles and two-bed *bandas*, complete with cooking areas.

MIDRANGE

Wildlife Club of Kenya Guesthouse (☎ 051-851559; PO Box 33, Nakuru; s/tw with shared bathroom KSh800/1600) This place is great: facilities include hot showers, TV lounge, and use of the kitchen's fridge, gas cooker and microwave. The rooms are clean and comfortable.

Eldorado Lodge (☎ 051-851263; camping KSh300, s/d KSh1000/1500; ☒) Just outside the park's Lanet gate, this place is a viable option for camping if you roll up to closed park gates in the evening. Rooms are overpriced and the pool is a little too green for our liking.

TOP END

Naishi House Banda (bookings ☎ 051-2217151; 6-person cottage plus 2-person annexe Jan-Jun US$200, Jul-Dec US$250) Sit on the shady terrace and watch zebras and rhinos grazing on your very doorstep – no fences here! This charming self-catering cottage is very comfortable, complete with a lovely fireplace, sitting room and full kitchen. The annex was designed for safari drivers and is pretty basic. The park's main gate handles bookings and payments.

Sarova Lion Hill Lodge (☎ 020-2713333; www .sarovahotels.com; high season full board s/d from US$160/220,

low season US$80/140; ☒) Sitting high up the lake's eastern slopes, this lodge offers 1st-class service and comfort. The views from the open-air restaurant/bar and from most rooms are great. Rooms are understated but pretty, while the flashy suites are large and absolutely stunning.

Getting There & Away

If you don't have your own vehicle, the only way into the park from Nakuru is by taxi or on an organised tour. A taxi for a few hours should cost KSh2000, though you'll have to bargain hard.

More enjoyable options are **One World Tours & Safaris** (☎ 0733-621598; PO Box 13047, Nakuru), which charges KSh6000 for an open-topped eight-seat 4WD (about six hours), and **Crater Travel** (☎ 051-2215019; off Kenyatta Ave, Nakuru), which has three-seater jeeps for KSh4500 (also for six hours).

If you're driving, there's access from the main gate, just outside Nakuru; the Lanet gate, a few kilometres south on the Nairobi road; and the Nderit gate, near the southern end of the lake.

LAKE BOGORIA NATIONAL RESERVE

In the late 1990s this reserve's shallow soda lake achieved fame as 'the new home of the flamingo', with a migrant population of up to two million birds. In 2000 it was designated a Ramsar site, establishing it as a wetland of international importance. While lesser flamingo numbers have dropped significantly now that Lake Nakuru has recovered from earlier droughts, this **reserve** (☎ 0722-377252; PO Box 64, Marigat; adult/child KSh1500/200) is still a fascinating place to visit and a world away from any other Rift Valley lake.

Backed by the bleak Siracho Escarpment, moss-green waves roll down Lake Bogoria's rocky, barren shores, while **hot springs** and **geysers** spew boiling fluids (keep your distance!) from the earth's insides nearby. Amazingly this inhospitable alien environment is a haven for birdlife and at **Kesubo Swamp**, just to the north, more than 200 species have been recorded. One lucky soul spotted 96 species in one hour – a Kenyan record.

The lack of dense brush also makes this one of the best places in Kenya to see the greater kudu. The isolated wooded area at the lake's southern end is also home to leopards, klipspringers, gazelles, caracals and buffaloes. Oh, you'll also see your fair share of donkeys and cattle, too.

While the odd Kenyan tourist visits the springs, few people venture further south, meaning you may well have the place to yourself. You now have the bonus of being able to explore on foot or bicycle, though stay clear of the small buffalo population. If you'd like a guide (half-/full day KSh500/1000), enquire at Loboi gate.

Sleeping & Eating

Camping is the only sleeping option within the reserve. If you'd prefer a roof, there's a top-end hotel nearby and various dives near the Loboi gate.

Fig Tree Camp (camping KSh500) Nestled beneath a stand of massive fig trees is this fantastic site. The loos lack doors and baboons can be a nuisance, but there are brilliant views down the lake and the 2km drive (4WD only) or hike from the main park road is worth the trip alone.

Acacia Camp (camping KSh500) A pretty lakeside site shaded by acacias, with some soft grass for pitching tents. You'll have to bring your own water.

Lake Bogoria Hotel (☎ 051-2216441; lakebogoria@ wanachi.com; s/d incl breakfast US$70/90; ☒) Set in lovely grounds 2km before the Loboi gate, this is a quality option with two swimming

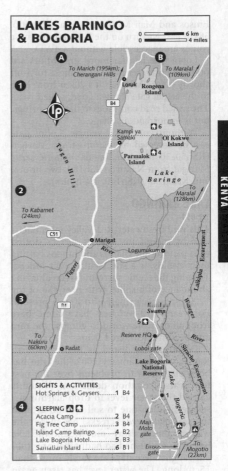

LAKES BARINGO & BOGORIA

pools. Rooms in the hotel are large and bright, while those in the new cottages (same price) are more modern and much more comfortable. The restaurant (lunch/dinner buffets KSh600/KSh700, mains KSh100 to KSh350) serves a variety of dishes, including several vegetarian options.

Some cheap accommodation is available in the nearby town of Marigat. This area is also a good place to buy locally produced *asali* (honey), which is sold from countless roadside kiosks for around KSh150 a bottle.

Getting There & Away

There are three entrance gates to Lake Bogoria – Emsos in the south, Maji Moto in the west and Loboi in the north. The turn-off for

Emsos and Maji Moto gates is at Mogotio, 38km past Nakuru on the B4, but both these routes are inaccessible without a 4WD.

Loboi gate is a far more straightforward point of entry, reached by taking a turn-off shortly before Marigat. It's 20km from here to the actual gate along a good, sealed road. The sealed road continues to the hot springs, but is in horrendous shape.

Without your own vehicle, Loboi gate can be accessed by *matatu* from Marigat (KSh50, 30 minutes). Regular *matatus* serve Marigat from Nakuru (KSh180, two hours) and Kabarnet (KSh140, 1¼ hours).

LAKE BARINGO
☎ 051

This rare freshwater Rift Valley lake, encircled by mountains and its surface dotted with picturesque islands and hippos batting their eyelids, is a spectacular sight indeed. Topping the scenic surrounds is an amazing abundance of birdlife, with over 450 of the 1200 bird species native to Kenya present. For years bird-watchers have come here from all over the world to glimpse the rare and beautiful feathered flyers.

Despite being listed as Kenya's fourth Ramsar site in January 2002, the lake has been plagued with problems over the past few years. Irrigation dams and droughts caused the water level to drop alarmingly; severe siltation due to soil erosion around the seasonal *luggas* (creeks) has meant the water is almost always muddy; and the lake has been overfished so badly that any *tilapia* caught these days are rarely more than 15cm long. The water level has risen again recently, but the situation is still very delicate, and with further droughts expected the ecosystem remains at risk.

Lake access is easiest from **Kampi ya Samaki** on the lake's western shore, some 15km north of Marigat. This small, quiet town used to be a fishing village, but now depends almost entirely on tourism. Sadly the recent problems have caused visitor numbers to drop, resulting in even tougher times for the community. It's still a lovely place to visit and locals would greatly appreciate the business.

Activities
The most popular activity around Lake Baringo and touted as competitively as the Masai Mara is in Nairobi are **boat rides** – there are

---

BARINGO WILDLIFE

Crocodiles and hippos apart, Lake Baringo's main attraction is the birdlife and the lake is the bird-watching centre of Kenya. Over 1200 different species of bird are native to the country, and more than 450 of them have been sighted here. People come from all over the world to try to catch a glimpse of something rare; Lake Baringo Club (opposite) even has a 'resident ornithologist' who leads bird-watching walks and gives advice to guests. A few years ago she set a world record for the number of species seen in one 24-hour period – over 300!

---

boat offices all over town, and literally everyone you talk to will claim to have access to a boat and be able to undercut anyone else's price. A speciality is a trip to see fish eagles feeding; the birds have learned to dive for fish at a whistle, making for great (if slightly contrived) photo opportunities.

There's a constant twittering, chirping and cooing of birds in the trees around the lake, and even if you're not an avid 'twitcher', it's hard to resist setting off on a dawn **bird walk**, when you have a good chance of seeing hornbills or a magnificent fish eagle in action. Lake Baringo Club (opposite) offers the most knowledgeable guides and charges KSh1100 per person for a 60- to 90-minute walk.

Cultural tours to Pokot, Tugen and Njemps villages close to the lake are also offered by the Lake Baringo Club (KSh 600); the Njemps are local cousins of the Maasai, mainly practising pastoralism and fishing. You'll usually be allowed to walk around freely and take photos, but in return you'll probably be hassled to buy handicrafts. There's an additional KSh500 charge for entering each village.

If nothing mentioned so far has floated your boat, there's even an uninhabited and uncharted **'Devil's Island'**, with a fearsome reputation among the normally prosaic locals. The rock forming the cliffs outside of town are also apparently suitable for **technical rock-climbing**.

Sleeping
BUDGET
Bahari Lodge & Hotel (☎ 851425; Kampi ya Samaki; s/tw with shared bathroom KSh200/400) Bahari is

popular with the drivers of safari vehicles, which is generally a good sign! The rooms are a little shabby but OK. The toilets are rather odoriferous.

Weavers Lodge (☎ 0721-556153; Kampi ya Samaki; s/tw KSh350/700) Down a rocky alley off the town's main drag, Weavers has good-sized rooms that come with fans, mosquito nets and comfortable beds; sadly toilet paper, soap and hot water are often lacking, and the constant loud music from the bar can be a pain.

MIDRANGE

Roberts' Camp (☎ 851879; camping KSh350, bandas s/ tw with shared bathroom KSh1000/2000, 4-person cottages KSh5000) Easily spotted off Kampi ya Samaki's main drag, this fantastic camp site is right on the lake, and offers great camping facilities, tents, comfortable cottages, cooking facilities and an open-air restaurant/bar. Campers need to exercise some common sense regarding the hippos, which may graze right outside your tent at night. Ideally you should stay at least 20m away from them when you can. No-one's been seriously hurt by a hippo in almost 15 years here, but some readers have had decidedly close calls!

TOP END

Lake Baringo Club (☎ 850880, Nairobi ☎ 020-650500; blockbaringo@africaonline.co.ke; Kampi ya Samaki; full board s/d low season US$120/150, high season US$150/180; ☒) Set in sprawling lakeside gardens, this is a grand old place. The rooms are pleasant if uninspired, with angled wooden ceilings, comfortable beds, wee terraces and linoleum floors. Facilities include a swimming pool, games room, badminton court and library, all open to nonguests for KSh200. There's a nightly slide show featuring beautiful birds sighted around Lake Baringo.

Island Camp Baringo (bookings ☎ 020-4447151; full board s/d US$220/295; ☒) This luxury tented lodge sits on Ol Kokwe Island's southern tip and makes a perfect hideaway. It's beautifully conceived with 23 double tents set among flowering trees, all overlooking the lake. Facilities include two bars and water-sports equipment. Price includes transfers from town.

Samatian Island (bookings ☎ 020-4447151; Kampi ya Samaki; full board s/d US$255/510) For a truly exclusive experience, this is the place to be. The three chalets on this tiny island are

rented as a unit, and the hefty price tag is worth it for the glorious isolation. Transfers from Kampi ya Samaki are included.

Eating & Drinking

Thirsty Goat (Roberts' Camp, Kampi ya Samaki; meals KSh300-450) This lovely open-air restaurant and bar serves a welcome variety of foreign fare. It's a bit pricey, but when your nose gets a whiff of the Moroccan meatballs, your taste buds will step on your whinging wallet's tongue.

Lake Baringo Club (Kampi ya Samaki; lunch/dinner buffets KSh1300/1460, mains KSh300-700) As you'd hope for this price, the food is mostly excellent. While you may shed a tear paying KSh120 for a large Tusker, one sip of it on the shady terrace or lakeside lawn and you'll soon be laughing again.

Self-caterers should remember that fresh vegetables and fruit are generally in short supply in Kampi ya Samaki. Bring much of what you need – Marigat usually has a good selection

Getting There & Away

A 25-seater bus leaves Kampi ya Samaki for Nakuru each morning between 6.30am and 9.30am (KSh 200, 2½ hours). Failing that, hop on one of the regular pick-up trucks to Marigat (KSh50, 30 minutes) and catch more frequent *matatus* from there to Nakuru (KSh160, two hours) or Kabarnet (KSh140, 1¼ hours).

A gravel track connects Loruk at the top end of the lake with the Nyahururu to Maralal road. If you have your own transport, it's a rough but bearable road; there's no public transport along it and hitching is extremely difficult. You can usually buy petrol at Lake Baringo Club; if you're heading northeast, it's worth noting that after Marigat, there's no reliable supply until Maralal.

CENTRAL HIGHLANDS

Forming the eastern wall of the Rift Valley and climbing from the heat of the northern plains are the Central Highlands, Kenya's undisputed heartland. What better monument to the region's importance than Mt Kenya, the country's highest mountain and Africa's second-highest peak.

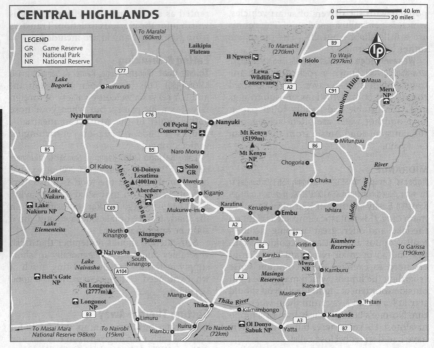

CENTRAL HIGHLANDS

LEGEND
GR   Game Reserve
NP   National Park
NR   National Reserve

Densely populated and intensively cultivated, the Central Highlands are home to the Kikuyu people, Kenya's largest and most politically favoured group. Squeezed gloriously into the mix are the national parks of Mt Kenya, Aberdare and Meru, which hold an array of landscapes, wildlife, flora and fauna unseen elsewhere, as well as some amazing trekking possibilities.

The Central Highlands' Laikipia Plateau, which stretches into northern Kenya from Nanyuki, is also home to a pioneering conservation project that has communities and ranches working together to protect and foster wildlife outside national parks. This effort can only bode well for the region's future.

That said, the Central Highlands does have its problems, most of which are tied back to the purchase, division and distribution of many white farmers' lands to the Kikuyu after independence. This subdivision, with its frequent encroachment on one of Kenya's few remaining large forested areas, has lead to frequent water crises and soil erosion. Although there's still a great

deal of forest remaining, demand for timber to be used as construction material and firewood (the most common form of fuel for cooking and heating) puts it at risk.

NYERI
☎ 061

A well-provisioned, lively place and one of the Central Highlands' largest towns, Nyeri is the administrative headquarters of Central Province and gateway to Aberdare National Park. In colonialism's early days Nyeri was a garrison town, but quickly became a trading and social centre for white cattle ranchers, coffee growers and wheat farmers. The verdant surrounds are intensively cultivated for vegetables, sugar cane, citrus fruits, bananas, tea, coffee and macadamia nuts.

On a clear morning you can see distant Mt Kenya in all its snowcapped glory. However, few travellers linger more than two nights.

Information
Barclays Bank (Kenyatta Rd)
Kenya Commercial Bank (Kenyatta Rd)
Standard Chartered Bank (Kenyatta Rd)

Sights & Activities

SOLIO GAME RESERVE

This private 17,500-acre **reserve** (☎ 55271; B5 Hwy; adult/child/vehicle KSh1600/free/500), 22km north of Nyeri, plays a major part in preserving and breeding black rhinos in Kenya. Most of the hook-lipped horned beasts wandering national parks were actually born here. Its current population of rhinos would make some sub-Saharan countries blush!

The reserve also hosts animals like oryxes, gazelles, hartebeests, giraffes and buffaloes. While visiting you'll probably see the beautiful crowned crane and several varieties of paradise birds.

Self-drive safaris are permitted, with free maps available at the front gate. Allmendinger's guesthouse (p372) offers half-day trips for US$60 per person (minimum two people, plus admission).

BADEN-POWELL MUSEUM

Sitting within the Outspan Hotel's beautiful grounds, this **museum** (admission KSh100; ⏲ 8am 6pm) was the former cottage of Lord Baden-Powell, founder of the international Scout Association. You'll find oodles of scouting paraphernalia and great mid-20th-century photos. The man himself is buried behind **St Peter's Church** (B5 Hwy).

OTHER ACTIVITIES

Wildlife drives into Aberdare National Park are available through Nyeri's three top-end hotels. Outspan Hotel is the most reasonable, charging KSh2500 per person (minimum two passengers) plus park fees for a two-hour drive.

If you fancy getting your head in the clouds, the **Gliding Club of Kenya** (Map p374; ☎ 0733-760331; gliding@africaonline.co.ke; PO Box 926, Nyeri), based 2km south of Mweiga, fits the bill. A 10-minute flight costs US$50.

Every Sunday and public holiday the **Green Hills Hotel** (Map p372; Bishop Gatimu Rd) hosts a day-long mini-festival of traditional dance, music and puppetry. It's free and great for kids. A dip in the swimming pool is KSh200.

Sleeping

BUDGET

Most of the cheap options will curl your toes, so here are some of the better picks.

Central Hotel (Map p372; ☎ 2030296; Kanisa Rd; s/tw incl breakfast KSh600/850) Central hosts bright, clean yet slightly cramped twins and more roomy singles, with many boasting balconies. Service is a step up from most.

Ibis Hotel (Map p372; ☎ 2034858; Kimathi Way; s/tw KSh500/800) Representing good value, Ibis has comfortable and clean rooms with brilliant power-showers.

Paresia Hotel (Map p372; ☎ 2032765; s/tw KSh300/500) With red cement floors and blue linoleum showers, Paresia is as colourful as it is cheap. Some rooms smell a bit musty, so sniff a few. It's off Gakere Rd.

Nyeri Star Restaurant & Board & Lodging (Map p372; ☎ 2031083; Gakere Rd; s/tw KSh300/500) Slightly

---

BEHIND THE BEANS

Kenya is a great place to buy coffee, and it is one thing you'll have no problem taking out of the country. However, next time you're sipping a frappuccino or demanding extra froth on your US$4 skinny latte, spare a thought for Kenyan coffee farmers, who number among the planet's worst-exploited commodity producers.

Coffee became something of a cause célèbre in 2002 when Oxfam International launched its Make Trade Fair campaign, highlighting the huge gulf between farmers' earnings and the massive profits enjoyed by multinational 'roasters'. According to Oxfam, coffee prices had slumped to a 30-year low, with farmers worldwide receiving around US$1 per kilogram, while the international industry, worth over US$2 billion annually, charged consumers almost US$15 per kilo.

The global market remains hugely oversupplied and buyers effectively force farmers to accept whatever price they offer. Kenyan growers receive as little as 4% of auction prices – a serious crisis for a country exporting up to 32,000 tonnes of coffee annually.

Thankfully the Make Trade Fair campaign has made gains and some major roasters now deal partially in Fair Trade Coffee, albeit an infinitesimal fraction of their business. The sooner you demand Fair Trade Coffee for your skinny latte, the sooner the unjust imbalance facing Kenyan farmers will be rectified. So get ordering – you can sleep later!

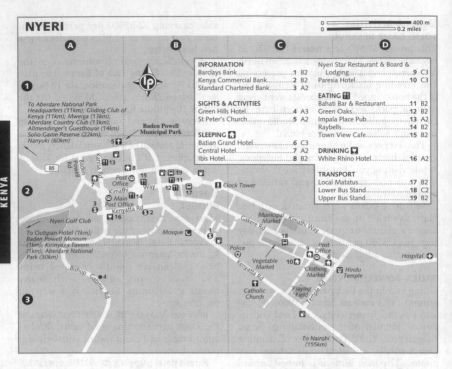

NYERI

INFORMATION	
Barclays Bank	1 B2
Kenya Commercial Bank	2 B2
Standard Chartered Bank	3 A2

SIGHTS & ACTIVITIES	
Green Hills Hotel	4 A3
St Peter's Church	5 A2

SLEEPING	
Batian Grand Hotel	6 C3
Central Hotel	7 A2
Ibis Hotel	8 B2

Nyeri Star Restaurant & Board &	
Lodging	9 C3
Paresia Hotel	10 C3

EATING	
Bahati Bar & Restaurant	11 B2
Green Oaks	12 B2
Impala Place Pub	13 A2
Raybells	14 B2
Town View Cafe	15 B2

DRINKING	
White Rhino Hotel	16 A2

TRANSPORT	
Local Matatus	17 B2
Lower Bus Stand	18 C2
Upper Bus Stand	19 B2

rougher around the edges than nearby Paresia, it still has hot showers and some sizable rooms. The upstairs outward-facing rooms are brightest and most quiet.

MIDRANGE
Batian Grand Hotel (Map p372; ☎ 2030743; batian hotel@wanachi.com; Gakere Rd; s/tw KSh700/1000) Front rooms face Mt Kenya at this well-appointed place with good facilities (when the boilers aren't leaking). The small inward-facing singles are darker than the larger carpeted twins and doubles. A coffee shop, restaurant and pub are downstairs.

TOP END
Outspan Hotel (Map p374; ☎ 2032424, Nairobi ☎ 020-4452103; www.aberdaresafarihotels.com; Apr–mid-Jul full board s/tw from US$98/130, mid-Jul–Mar US$130/160) Formerly part of Block Hotels, this lovely property has new owners, who are keen to up the standard while maintaining the historic character. The 'standard' rooms (15 to 21), with stone fireplace and doors opening onto beautiful gardens, have the most character.

Aberdare Country Club (Map p374; ☎ 2055620, Nairobi ☎ 020-216940; www.fairmont.com; low season full board s/tw US$87/172, high season US$162/230; ☒) Surrounded by its own 500-hectare sanctuary east of Mweiga, this club sits atop a hill and has glorious views. Its new owners, Fairmont, plan on pumping millions into the place. The view and character should remain, but the rooms and service will be truly 1st class.

Allmendinger's Guesthouse (Map p374; ☎ 0733-760331; gliding@africaonline.co.ke; PO Box 926, Nyeri; full board s/tw US$98/148) Just west of the Aberdare Country Club, Allmendinger's comes highly recommended, although the road here can be difficult during the rains. Prices include walking, hiking and bird-watching.

Eating & Drinking
Green Oaks (Map p372; Gakere Rd; meals KSh80-220) A local favourite, with tasty curries and stews, a lively bar and a great vantage point from the balcony.

Raybells (Map p372; Kimathi Way; meals KSh90-220) An excellent Western-style 'family' restaurant and takeaway, serving everything from samosas to pizza.

Town View Cafe (Map p372; Kimathi Way; meals KSh60-180) A small but welcoming option for traditional Kenyan fare.

Impala Place Pub (Map p372; Kanisa Rd; lunch buffets KSh200; ☯ 12.30-4pm Mon-Fri) While aiming to please the business-lunch crowd, it should put a smile on your face, too.

Bahati Bar & Restaurant (Map p372; Kimathi Way; chicken & chips from KSh150) When we asked to see the menu, staff stated, 'We do chicken and chips.' Need we say more?

Kirinyaga Tavern (Outspan Hotel; Map p374) While located behind the posh hotel's gates, it is actually reasonable and separate from the hotel's bar. It has a bonfire and traditional dancing on Saturday nights.

White Rhino Hotel (Map p372; Kenyatta Rd) The bar is the only reasonable remnant of this old hotel. Look out for its ever-popular reggae nights.

Getting There & Away

The upper bus stand deals with big buses and sporadic *matatus* to most places, while the lower stand houses local buses and multitudes of *matatus* heading in all directions. Some local *matatus* are also found on Kimathi Way.

Matatus run to Nanyuki (KSh100, one hour), Nyahururu (KSh130, 1¼ hours), Thika (KSh200, two hours), Nakuru (KSh250, 2½ hours), Nairobi (KSh250, 2½ hours) and Eldoret (KSh400, five hours). Buses duplicate most of these lines; you may occasionally have to change at Karatina for Nairobi.

ABERDARE NATIONAL PARK

Created in 1950, this **park** (☎ 061-2055024; adult/child US$30/10, smartcard required) essentially encloses two different environments: the striking 60km stretch of moorland, peaks and forest atop the western Kinangop Plateau, and the eastern outcrop of dense rainforest known as the Salient.

The park has varieties of fauna, flora and scenery not found elsewhere. Elephants and buffaloes dominate, but other species, including black rhinos, giant forest hogs, black servals and rare black leopards, can also be seen. Look out for the few remaining lions (most were removed to protect endangered bongo antelopes) from the viewing platforms next to the dramatic **Chania Falls** and **Karura Falls**. **Gura Falls**, which drops a full 300m down into thick forest, is less accessible.

Viewing wildlife here isn't like on the open savanna of Amboseli and Masai Mara. The dense rainforest of the Salient provides excellent cover for the animals, so take your time and stay a few nights.

Thanks to rough terrain and minor roads turning into mud traps during the rains, KWS restricts entry to all but 4WD vehicles. If you're prepared to hire a vehicle, join the lodges' tours, or hoof it on foot, your efforts will be rewarded.

If you want to enter through the Treetops or Ark gates, simply ask permission at the park headquarters, between Mweiga and Nyeri on the B5 Hwy, where you can buy smartcards and excellent 1:25,000 maps (KSh450). Map proceeds go directly to the Rhino Ark Charitable Trust, which is constructing an electric fence around the perimeter of the Aberdare National Park and greater Aberdare Conservation Area.

Activities

KWS currently advises against trekking in the Salient, as the dense cover makes walking dangerous for visitors, but the high moorland and four main peaks (all 3500m to 4000m) are excellent trekking locations. As on Mt Kenya, heavy rain can arrive at any time, so you must be prepared. Mud and reduced visibility are two good reasons not to trek during the heavy rains (March to May). You'll need advance permission from the warden, who'll provide an armed ranger (KSh1000 per day) to guide you. Lonely Planet's *Trekking in East Africa* has full details of the walks.

Trout fishing here is very popular, especially high up on the moors, but requires a permit from park headquarters (KSh100). Kiandongoro Fishing Lodge makes a good base and the Chania River is great for brown trout, but watch your back – there are tales of fishers being stalked by lions! Lions or not, best get an armed ranger to escort you.

Sleeping

BUDGET & MIDRANGE

Public camp sites and the following accommodation options must be booked through park headquarters.

Kiandongoro Fishing Lodge (Jan-Jun 7-person cottages US$200, Jul-Dec US$250) Sitting in an excellent spot on the high moor by the Gura River, these two large stone cottages offer

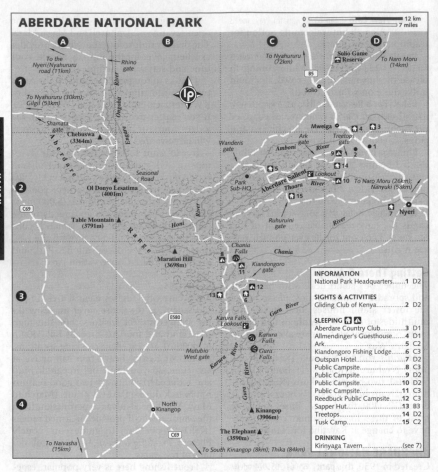

ABERDARE NATIONAL PARK

INFORMATION	
National Park Headquarters	1 D2

SIGHTS & ACTIVITIES	
Gliding Club of Kenya	2 D2

SLEEPING	
Aberdare Country Club	3 D1
Allmendinger's Guesthouse	4 D1
Ark	5 C2
Kiandongoro Fishing Lodge	6 C3
Outspan Hotel	7 D2
Public Campsite	8 C3
Public Campsite	9 D2
Public Campsite	10 D2
Public Campsite	11 C3
Reedbuck Public Campsite	12 C3
Sapper Hut	13 B3
Treetops	14 D2
Tusk Camp	15 C2

DRINKING	
Kirinyaga Tavern	(see 7)

bathrooms, gas-powered kitchens, dining rooms and fireplaces.

Sapper Hut (exclusive use per night KSh2000) A simple *banda*, with an open fire, two beds and a hot-water boiler, overlooking a waterfall on the Upper Magura River.

Tusk Camp (exclusive use per night KSh6000) Near Ruhuruini gate, these four wee cottages provide beds for eight to 10 people.

TOP END
The following prices include transfers (self-drive isn't permitted). Children under seven are prohibited at both lodges.

Treetops (☎ 020-4452095; www.aberdaresafari hotels.com; mid-Jul–mid-Dec full board s/tw with shared bathroom US$135/180, mid-Dec–mid-Jul US$198/250) It

was at this floodlit waterhole in 1952 that a sleeping princess became Queen Elizabeth II. After the Mau Mau guerrillas turned the original into ashes, a much larger rendition was built. Today Treetops' exterior quite resembles a weathered shipwreck, but despite its quirks, the place reeks of charm.

Ark (☎ 020-216940; www.fairmont.com; low season full board s/tw US$75/150, high season US$185/250) What this modern upscale version of Treetops lacks in history and charm, it makes up for in comfort and wildlife viewing. Sitting higher in the Aberdares, Ark's floodlit waterhole is surrounded by grasses and mountain forest, which attracts a wider array of animals than Treetops.

Getting There & Away

Access roads from B5 Hwy to the Wanderis, Ark, Treetops and Ruhuruini gates are in decent shape, while the road from Nyeri to Kiandongora gate is horrendous.

Regular Nyeri–Mweiga *matatus* (KSh50, 35 minutes) pass KWS headquarters and the main park gates. Since trekking the Salient is inadvisable, most trekkers use the Wanderis gate.

Nyeri's Outspan Hotel charges KSh2500 per person (minimum two people) for wildlife drives into the lower Salient, while the Aberdare Country Club charges US$160 per vehicle.

NYAHURURU & THOMSON'S FALLS
☎ 065

Set next to Thomson's Falls, one of Kenya's most impressive waterfalls and the town's former namesake, is the town of Nyahururu. At 2360m, it is Kenya's highest major town and has a cool, invigorating climate. Besides the falls and some nice forested walks, most travellers find little reason to linger more than a day or two.

One of the last white settlements to be established in the colonial era, Nyahururu didn't take off until the arrival of the Gilgil railway spur in 1929, but the trains now carry only freight, and the town is once again becoming an agricultural backwater. The surrounding plateau is intensively cultivated with maize, beans and sweet potatoes.

The best approach to town is the amazingly scenic road from Nakuru, which snakes up and down through the Sukukia Valley's undulating farmlands and dense forests.

Information

Barclays Bank (cnr Sulukia & Sharpe Rds)
Clicks Cyber Cafe (Mimi Centre, Kenyatta Rd; per hr KSh180)
Kenya Commercial Bank (Sulukia Rd)
Post office (Sulukia Rd)

Sights

Located on the town's outskirts and formed by the waters of the Ewaso Narok River, **Thomson's Falls** plummets over 72m into a ravine and the resulting spray bathes the dense forest below in a perpetual mist. Get down, get close and get wet, we say! A series of stone steps leads to the bottom of the ravine – don't attempt to go down any other way as the rocks on the side of the ravine are often very loose.

There are some fantastic **walks** downstream through the forested valley of the Ewaso Narok River and upstream a couple of kilometres to one of the highest hippo pools in Kenya. Take time to explore a little. Guides are fairly easy to find, especially around the souvenir shacks overlooking the falls, but you'll have to bargain hard.

The falls were named by Joseph Thomson, the first European to walk from Mombasa to Lake Victoria in the early 1880s.

Sleeping

Nyahururu has a couple of places with single rooms for KSh150, but that's really scraping the bottom of the barrel.

Safari Lodge (Go Down Rd; s/tw KSh300/500) This massive new place is clean, bright and very affordable. Hot water is on demand and there are even sockets to charge your mobile.

County Hostel (s KSh200) Off Sulukia Rd behind the Nyandarua County Council headquarters, this place has quiet rooms with bathrooms and even toilet seats. At this price that's saying something!

Nyaki Hotel (☎ 22313; s/tw KSh350/800) This relatively modern building hosts small but comfy singles and large clean twins that are essentially poor-man's suites. There are also hot-water showers and secure parking. It's off Kenyatta Rd.

Thomson's Falls Lodge (☎ 22006; tfalls@africaonline .co.ke; camping KSh300, s/tw incl breakfast KSh2200/2800) While the white planters are long gone, this nostalgic and cosy lodge overlooking the falls still has character to spare. The main building and cottages have rooms with log fireplaces and decent facilities. The grassy camping ground is a right bargain, with free firewood and hot showers. It's off B5 Hwy.

Eating

Thomson's Falls Lodge is the best (and only) place to go for a minor splurge. Stuff yourself at a buffet (KSh800), or delve into some Irish stew, mutton specialties and beef burgers (mains KSh150 to KSh500). The grounds are a great place for a picnic, though it will cost KSh50 per group.

Noni's Cafe (Mimi Centre, Kenyatta Rd; meals KSh60-150) Easily the cleanest and most welcoming of Nyahururu's local eateries. It's a great spot for breakfast.

KENYA

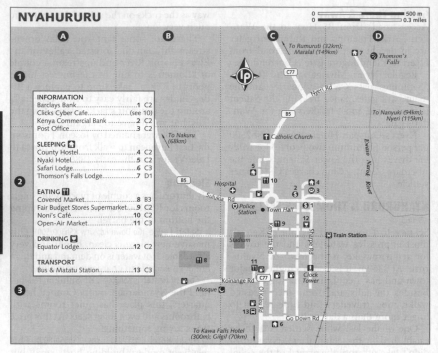

NYAHURURU

0 _____ 500 m
0 _____ 0.3 miles

INFORMATION
Barclays Bank...........................1 C2
Clicks Cyber Cafe..............(see 10)
Kenya Commercial Bank 2 C2
Post Office...............................3 C2

SLEEPING
County Hostel...........................4 C2
Nyaki Hotel..............................5 C2
Safari Lodge.............................6 C3
Thomson's Falls Lodge...............7 D1

EATING
Covered Market.........................8 B3
Fair Budget Stores Supermarket....9 C2
Noni's Café.............................10 C2
Open-Air Market......................11 C3

DRINKING
Equator Lodge........................12 C2

TRANSPORT
Bus & Matatu Station................13 C3

KENYA

For those who want to prepare their own meals, there are fruit and vegetables at the open-air market (off Koinange Rd). The brave can also find meat at the covered market (off Koinange Rd). The **Fair Budget Stores supermarket** (Kenyatta Rd) is fairly well stocked.

Drinking & Entertainment

Equator Lodge (Sharpe Rd) We'll give this local bar an 'A' for effort regarding its kitschy forested façade. Inside it gets a 'C' for late night carnage.

Kawa Falls Hotel (Ol Kalou Rd; admission KSh100; ☺ weekends) This popular hotel disco occasionally hosts well-known Kenyan DJs.

Getting There & Away

Numerous *matatus* run to Nakuru (KSh100, 1¼ hours) and Nyeri (KSh150, two hours) until late afternoon. Less plentiful are services to Naivasha (KSh200, 1½ hours), Nanyuki (KSh250, three hours) and Nairobi (KSh250, three hours). The odd morning *matatu* reaches Maralal (KSh300, three hours). Several early morning buses also serve Nairobi (KSh230 to KSh250, three hours).

MT KENYA NATIONAL PARK

Astoundingly, just 16km from the equator, 12 glaciers continue to shape the jagged roots of what was once Africa's tallest mountain. After seeing the 5199m worth of dramatic remnants that today comprise Mt Kenya (now Africa's second-highest mountain), it's easy to understand why the Kikuyu people deified it and still believe it's the seat of their supreme god Ngai.

Fortunately for the many travellers who try the ascent every year, Ngai doesn't seem to be concerned by trekkers. However, you'd be wise not to temp fate, so treat Mt Kenya with the utmost respect (see Responsible Trekking, p437). Besides being venerated by the Kikuyu, Mt Kenya has the rare honour of being both a Unesco World Heritage Site and a Unesco Biosphere Reserve.

Mt Kenya's highest peaks, Batian (5199m) and Nelion (5188m), can only be reached by mountaineers with technical skills. However, Point Lenana (4985m), the third-highest peak, can be reached by trekkers and is the usual goal for most mortals, offering a fantastic experience without the risks of technical climbing. As you might imagine, there are superb views over the surrounding country from Point Lenana, although the summit is often cloaked in mist from late morning until late afternoon. Above 3000m is mountain moorland, characterised by remarkable alpine flora.

As marvellous as the summit is, a common complaint from trekkers is that they didn't allow enough time to enjoy the entire mountain. Walks through the foothills, particularly those to the east and northeast of the main peaks, and the Summit Circuit around Batian and Nelion, are dramatic and tremendously rewarding. You won't regret setting aside a week or 10 days rather than just four days for a summit rush.

Information

The daily fees for the **national park** (☎ 061-55645; PO Box 253, Nyeri; adult/child US$15/8) are charged upon entry, so you must estimate the length of your stay. If you overstay, you must pay the difference when leaving. You'll have to pay an additional KSh50 per day for each guide and porter you take with you. Always ask for a receipt.

Before you leave Nairobi, buy a copy of *Mt Kenya 1:50,000 Map & Guide* (1993) by Mark Savage and Andrew Wielochowski. It has a detailed topographical map, and full descriptions of the routes, mountain medicine, flora and fauna, and accommodation.

Lonely Planet's *Trekking in East Africa* has more information, details on wilder routes and some of the more esoteric variations that are possible on Mt Kenya.

Technical climbers and mountaineers should get a copy of **Mountain Club of Kenya's** (MCK; Nairobi ☎ 020-602330; www.mck.or.ke) *Guide to Mt Kenya & Kilimanjaro*, edited by Iain Allan. MCK also has up-to-date mountain information posted on its website.

Safety

Mt Kenya's accessibility and the technical ease with which Point Lenana is reached create their own problems for enthusiastic trekkers. Many people ascend much too quickly and end up suffering from altitude sickness. By spending at least three nights on the ascent, you'll enjoy yourself much more; with proper clothes and equipment, you stand a much better chance of making it back down as well.

Another problem can be unpredictable, harsh, cold, wet and windy weather. The trek to Point Lenana isn't easy and people do die on the mountain every year. The best time to go is from mid-January to late February or from late August to September.

Unless you're a seasoned trekker with high altitude experience and a good knowledge of reading maps and using a compass, you'd be flirting with death by not taking a guide or qualified companion. Even those with ample experience should take a guide if attempting the Summit Circuit.

Equipment Hire

Well-maintained hire gear is available at the Naro Moru River Lodge (p383), although it can't be reserved and is relatively expensive (US$4 per day for a sleeping bag). Most guiding companies will have cheaper equipment for hire, although you'll have less choice and lower standards.

Guides, Cooks & Porters

Considerable effort has been made in recent years to regulate guides and porters operating on the mountain. The KWS now issues vouchers to all registered guides and porters, who should also hold identity cards; they won't be allowed into the park without them.

Female guides are becoming more common, and technical guides for climbing Batian and Nelion are widely available.

COSTS

Basic qualified guides and cooks will cost you KSh750 per day, while porters charge KSh650. More knowledgeable guides will set you back US$15 per day, cooks and porters US$12 per day. These fees don't include park entry fees and tips (budget around a day's wages per person as a tip, but make it clear it is only for good service).

If you ascend the mountain along one route and descend along a different one, you'll be responsible for arranging and paying to transport guides and porters back to your starting point. It is wise to sort this out before you start and agree on a price for return transport plus any additional costs.

Porters will carry up to 18kg for three-day trips or 16kg for longer trips, excluding the weight of their own food and equipment. If you want them to carry more, you'll have

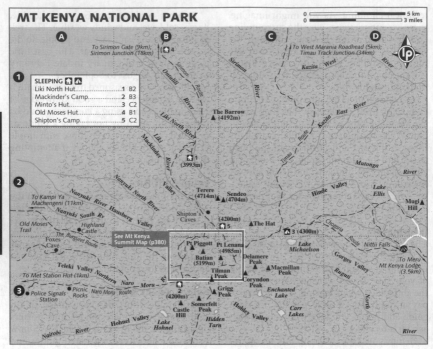

MT KENYA NATIONAL PARK

SLEEPING 🏠
Liki North Hut.....................1 B2
Mackinder's Camp................2 B3
Minto's Hut.........................3 C2
Old Moses Hut.....................4 B1
Shipton's Camp....................5 C2

to negotiate an added cost. A normal day's work is regarded as one stage of the journey; if you want to go further you'll have to pay two days' wages, even if porters don't do anything the following day.

Organised Treks

If time is limited or you'd prefer someone else to make all the trekking arrangements, there are plenty of possibilities. All-inclusive packages – which include park entry and camping fees, food, huts, a guide, cook and porters, and transfers to and from the mountain – can be a good deal, particularly if you don't have any equipment.

Picking the right company is even more important here than on a normal wildlife safari, as an unqualified or inexperienced guide could put you in real danger as well as spoil your trip.

Mountain Rock Safaris Resorts & Trekking Services (☎ 020-242133; www.mountainrockkenya.com; PO Box 15796-00100, Nairobi) is a real specialist at Mt Kenya climbs and runs the Mountain Rock Lodge (p383) near Naro Moru. Its day rates for all-inclusive trips start at US$135 per per-

son per day, but drop as low as US$80 for five or more people.

Naro Moru River Lodge (p383) also runs a range of all-inclusive trips. Its prices are more expensive than most (US$135 to US$220 per person per day), but it's the only company that can guarantee you beds in the Met Station Hut and Mackinder's Camp.

There are several safari companies in Nairobi that offer Mt Kenya treks, but many just sell other operators' treks. See p94 for listings. Local companies with their own treks:
KG Mountain Expeditions (☎ 062-62403; www .kenyaexpeditions.com; PO Box 199, Naro Moru) Offers all-inclusive packages from US$265 per day (depending on group size), as well as budget options for around US$80.
Mountain View Tours & Trekking Safaris (☎ 062-62088; PO Box 48, Naro Moru) Recommended by readers as being cheap and reliable. Prices are negotiable, but expect to pay around US$60 to US$70 per day.

Naro Moru Route

Although the least scenic, this is the most straightforward, popular route, and still a spectacular and very enjoyable trail. Allow a minimum of four days for the trek; it's possible in three if you arrange transport between Naro Moru and the Met Station, but doing it this quickly risks serious altitude sickness.

GUIDES & PORTERS

Apart from the Naro Moru River Lodge in Naro Moru itself, guides, porters and cooks can be booked through Mt Kenya Guides & Porters Safari Club (p383). Its office is 5km along the road towards the Naro Moru gate, but staff also scout for business at hotels in town.

Mountain Rock Lodge (Map p382; ☎ 062-62625; info@mountainrockkenya.com) also provides guides/porters for this route at US$15/12 per day.

THE TREK

Starting in Naro Moru town, the first part of the route takes you along a relatively good gravel road for some 13km to the start of the forest. Another 5km brings you to the park entry gate (2400m), from where it's 8km to the road head and the **Met Station Hut** (Map p382; 3000m), where you stay for the night.

On the second day set off up the Teleki Valley to the edge of the forest at about 3200m. From here you scale the so-called **Vertical Bog** onto a ridge, where the route divides into two. You can either take the higher path, which gives better views but is often wet, or the lower, which crosses the Naro Moru River and continues gently up to **Mackinder's Camp** (Map p378; 4160m). This part of the trek should take about 4½ hours. Here you can stay in the dormitories or camp.

On the third day you can either rest at Mackinder's Camp to acclimatise or aim for **Point Lenana** (4895m). This stretch takes four to five hours, so it is common to leave around 2am (you'll need a torch or flashlight) to reach the summit in time for sunrise. From the bunkhouse, continue up past the ranger station to a fork in the path. Keep right and go across a swampy area, followed by a moraine and then up a very long scree slope – this is a hard slog. **Austrian Hut** (Map p380; 4790m) is three to four hours from Mackinder's and about one hour below the summit of Lenana, so it's a good place to rest before the final push. Facilities are basic, although the hut has been recently refurbished.

The section of the trek from Austrian Hut up to Lenana takes you up a narrow rocky path that traverses the southwest ridge parallel to the Lewis Glacier, which has shrunk more than 100m since the 1960s. A final climb or scramble brings you up onto the peak. In good weather it's fairly straightforward, but in bad weather you shouldn't attempt to reach the summit unless you're experienced in mountain conditions or have a guide.

From Point Lenana most people return along the same route; assuming you summit early, you can reach the Met Station on the same day. Alternatively, you can return to Austrian Hut, then take the Summit Circuit around the base of the main peaks to reach the top of one of the other routes before descending.

Sirimon Route

A popular alternative to Naro Moru, this route has more spectacular scenery, greater flexibility and a gentler rate of ascent, although it is still easy to climb too fast, so allow at least five days for the trek. It's well worth considering combining it with the Chogoria route for a six- to seven-day traverse that will really bring out the best of Mt Kenya.

GUIDES & PORTERS

In Nanyuki guides operating out of **Mt Kenya Mountaineering Information Office** (Map p384; ☎ 0733-340849; Mt Kenya Paradise Hotel) are generally quite reliable, but ask to see their KWS registration and go over your planned route in detail. The people at **Montana Trek & Information Centre** (Map p384; ☎ 062-32731; Jambo House Hotel, Lumumba Rd, Nanyuki) seem to know their stuff.

Guides/porters are also available for hire from Mountain Rock Lodge for US$15/12 per day.

THE TREK

It is 15km from Nanyuki to the Sirimon Gate, and transport is included with prebooked packages. Otherwise take a *matatu* towards Timau or Meru, or arrange a lift from town. From the gate it's about 9km through the forest to **Old Moses Hut** (Map p378; 3300m), where you can spend the first night.

On the second day you could head straight through the moorland for Shipton's Camp, but it is worth taking an extra day to go via **Liki North Hut** (Map p378; 3993m), a tiny place on the floor of a classic glacial

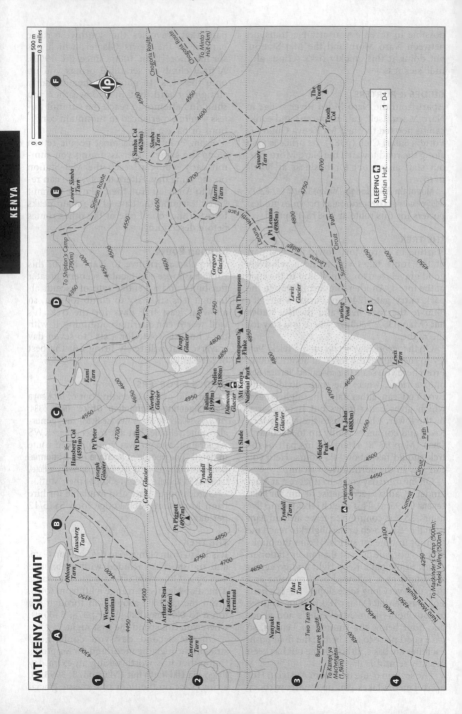

MT KENYA SUMMIT

SLEEPING 🏠	
Austrian Hut	1 D4

valley. The actual hut is a complete wreck and is only meant for porters, but it's a good camp site, with a toilet and stream nearby. You can also walk further up the valley to help acclimatise.

On the third day head straight up the western side of the Liki North Valley and over the ridge into Mackinder's Valley, joining the direct route about 1½ hours in. After crossing the Liki River, follow the path for another 30 minutes to reach the bunkhouse at **Shipton's Camp** (Map p378; 4200m), set in a fantastic location right below Batian and Nelion and within sight of two glaciers, which can often be heard cracking.

From Shipton's you can push straight for **Point Lenana** (4895m), a tough three- to four-hour slog via Harris Tarn and the tricky north face approach, or take the Summit Circuit in either direction around the peaks to reach **Austrian Hut** (Map p380; 4790m), about one hour below the summit. The left-hand (east) route past Simba Col is shorter but steeper, while the right-hand (west) option takes you on the Harris Tarn trail nearer the main peaks.

From Austrian Hut take the standard southwest traverse up to Point Lenana. If you're spending the night here, it's worth having a wander around to catch the views up to Batian and down the Lewis Glacier into Teleki Valley, as well as the spectacular **ice cave** by the Curling Pond.

Chogoria Route

This route is justly famous for crossing some of the most spectacular and varied scenery on Mt Kenya, and is often combined with the Sirimon route (usually as the descent). The only disadvantage is the long distance between Chogoria village and the park gate. Allow at least five days for a trek here.

GUIDES & PORTERS

The best place to organise guides and porters is the **Mt Kenya Chogoria Guides & Porters Association** (Map p382; ☎ 064-22096) at the Transit Motel (p389) near Chogoria village. Guides and porters aren't available beyond Chogoria Forest Station.

If you want porters to walk the whole stretch between Chogoria and the park gate, you may be charged two extra days' wages – make sure you negotiate everything before you leave.

THE TREK

The main reason this route is more popular as a descent is the 29km bottom stage. While it is not overly steep, climbing up for that distance is much harder than descending it. Either way, it's a beautiful walk through farmland, rainforest and bamboo zones. You can camp near the **Forest Station** (Map p382), 6km out of town, but you'll still have 23km to walk the next day. Transport is available from the village, but it'll cost you, and even a Land Rover may struggle in the wet.

Camping is possible at the gate, or you can stay nearby in **Meru Mt Kenya Lodge** (Map p382; 3000m); with transport to town available and a small shop selling beer, it's a favourite with people coming down.

On the second day head up through the forest to the trailhead (camping is possible here). From here it's another 7km over rolling foothills to the Hall Tarns area and **Minto's Hut** (Map p378; 4300m). Like Liki North, this nasty hut is only intended for porters, but the area makes a decent camp site. It has a stream for water and a long-drop loo, which, incidentally, finally has a door (though it won't close!). Don't use the tarns here to wash anything, as they have already been polluted by careless trekkers.

From here you follow the trail up alongside the stunning **Gorges Valley** (another possible descent route for the adventurous) and scramble up some steep ridges to meet the Summit Circuit, which can take you in either direction. It is possible to go straight for the north face or southwest ridge of Point Lenana, but stopping at Austrian Hut or detouring to Shipton's Camp is probably a better idea and gives you more time to enjoy the scenery.

Sleeping

You can **camp** (adult/child US$10/5) anywhere on the mountain; the nightly fee is payable to KWS at any gate. Most people camp near the huts or bunkhouses, as there are often toilets and water nearby.

There are several huts on the mountain owned by MCK, but the only one that's in reasonable shape nowadays sits 5188m up on Nelion's summit – not for the typical punter!

Accommodation along the major trekking routes, whether in huts or larger bunkhouses, is described under each route.

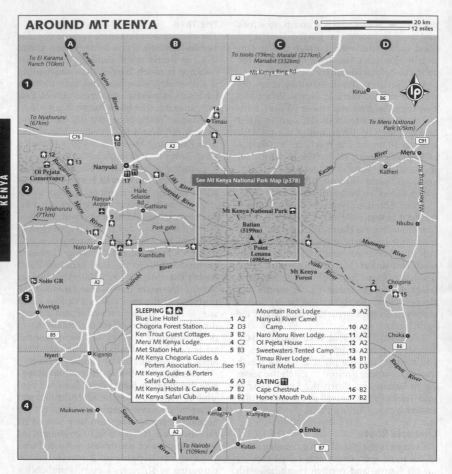

AROUND MT KENYA

SLEEPING		
Blue Line Hotel	1	A2
Chogoria Forest Station	2	D3
Ken Trout Guest Cottages	3	B2
Meru Mt Kenya Lodge	4	C2
Met Station Hut	5	B3
Mt Kenya Chogoria Guides &		
Porters Association	(see 15)	
Mt Kenya Guides & Porters		
Safari Club	6	A3
Mt Kenya Hostel & Campsite	7	B2
Mt Kenya Safari Club	8	B2
Mountain Rock Lodge	9	A2
Nanyuki River Camel		
Camp	10	A2
Naro Moru River Lodge	11	A2
Ol Pejeta House	12	A2
Sweetwaters Tented Camp	13	A2
Timau River Lodge	14	B1
Transit Motel	15	D3

EATING		
Cape Chestnut	16	B2
Horse's Mouth Pub	17	B2

Eating

The best range of food suitable for consumption on the mountain is to be found in Nairobi's supermarkets, especially Nakumatt and Uchumi. Elsewhere there's a good range in the towns around the mountain, but you'll find precious little at Naro Moru or Chogoria.

When you're buying dehydrated foods, get the precooked variety to cut down on cooking time – two-minute noodles are a good solution. It's a smart idea to bring these from home.

To avoid severe headaches caused by dehydration or altitude sickness, drink at least 3L of fluid per day and bring rehydration sachets.

NARO MORU

☎ 062

The village of Naro Moru, on the western side of the mountain, is little more than a dusty string of shops and houses, with a couple of very basic hotels and a market, but it's the most popular starting point for treks up Mt Kenya. There's a post office with Internet access, but no banks.

Sleeping & Eating

Although there are a number of basic hotels situated in Naro Moru town, the best options are to stay in the surrounding few kilometres. Eating options are incredibly slim, with only a very few hotels offering meals.

BUDGET

Note that the two top-end options both have great camp sites.

Mt Kenya Hostel & Campsite (Map p382; ☎ 62412; mtkenyahostel@wananchi.com; camping KSh250, dm KSh400) About 8.5km from town and 7.5km from the park gate, this place offers simple accommodation, a large camp site, kitchen facilities, and a restaurant and bar. It hires limited mountain gear as well as a 4WD vehicle. Mt Kenya treks can be arranged here, too.

Mountain View Hotel (☎ 62088; A2 Hwy; s KSh520) This is the best option in town and is very basic. Red cement floors host large single beds and the bathrooms have hot showers. Treks and equipment can be arranged here.

Blue Line Hotel (Map p382; ☎ 62420; camping KSh150, s/d KSh400/800) Similar to its sister hotel Mountain View, though hot showers are only available in the morning. Blue Line is 3km from town and 1.5km from the Mt Kenya Guides & Porters Safari Club office (convenient for organising guides), but 13km short of the park gate. The hotel is generally pleasant and quiet, and has a bar and restaurant (meals KSh180 to KSh280).

Mt Kenya Guides & Porters Safari Club (Map p382; ☎ 62015; camping KSh150) You may also camp here. The club can provide tents (two-person tent KSh600). The site is rather primitive and the loos are rather grim – showers come in buckets.

MIDRANGE & TOP END

Naro Moru River Lodge (Map p382; ☎ 62212, Nairobi ☎ 020-4443357; mt.kenya@africaonline.co.ke; camping US$10, dm US$8, low season half board s/tw from US$55/82, high season from US$90/120; ⚘) This relaxing lodge is about 1.5km north of town and is set on the sloping bank of the Naro Moru River in beautifully landscaped gardens. There's also a well-equipped camp site and a dormitory block. Campers can use all the hotel facilities, which include two bars and a restaurant (breakfast/dinner KSh500/KSh1000).

Mountain Rock Lodge (Map p382; ☎ 62625; info@ mountainrockkenya.com; camping US$5, standard s/tw US$24/32, superior s/tw or tr US$32/48) This place is 6km north of Naro Moru, tucked away in the woods less than 1km from the Nanyuki road. You can save a few dollars by renting a fixed tent (single/twin/triple US$15/20/24) or using the camp site. It is friendly and reliable, with a spacious dining room, two bars and a lounge.

Getting There & Away

There are plenty of buses and *matatus* heading to Nanyuki (KSh60, 30 minutes), Nyeri (KSh80, 45 minutes) and Nairobi (KSh300, three hours).

NANYUKI

☎ 062

Founded by white settlers in 1907, Nanyuki is a small but very energetic country town. It is a popular and friendly place to base Mt Kenya treks, especially if taking on the Sirimon and Burguret routes, though you'll probably experience some initial hassle from the slew of guides, touts, hawkers and cheeky street kids.

Besides lapping against Mt Kenya's slopes, Nanyuki also sits on the edge of the massive Laikipia Plateau, which is currently one of Africa's most important wildlife conservation sites. Here local communities and ranches are being encouraged to share their space with local fauna, allowing wildlife to flourish while at the same time decreasing potential human-animal conflict.

Information

Barclays Bank (Map p384; Kenyatta Ave)
Kenya Commercial Bank (Map p384; Kenyatta Ave)
Mt Kenya Cyberworld (Map p384; Kenyatta Ave; per hr KSh60)
Post office (Map p384; Kenyatta Ave)
Standard Chartered Bank (Map p384; Kenyatta Ave)

Sleeping

BUDGET

Nanyuki River Camel Camp (Map p382; ☎ 0722-361642; camellot@wananchi.com; camping US$6, half-board huts with shared bathroom US$22) The only camping near Nanyuki is at this fabulous place off C76 Hwy 4km out of town. Firewood is free and there are decent facilities. The woven huts are modelled on a traditional Somali nomadic village and are highly authentic – spending the night in one is an experience indeed. The food is excellent, and the 200 camels are available for hire.

Ibis Hotel (Map p384; ☎ 31536; Lumumba Rd; s/tw KSh500/900) Bright rooms and a brighter covered courtyard lurk behind the Ibis's fresh tiles and woodwork. Angle for a room with a Mt Kenya view.

Mt Kenya Paradise Hotel (Map p384; ☎ 0722-899950; s/tw KSh400/600) Formerly the Nanyuki Riverside Hotel, this place off Kenyatta Ave

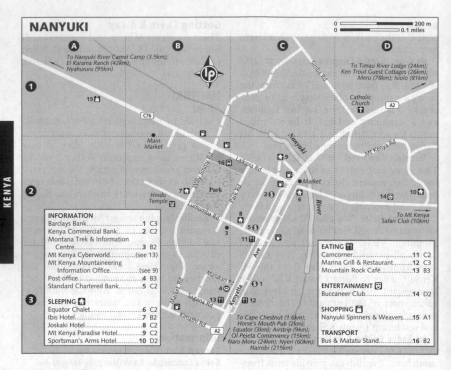

NANYUKI

0   200 m
0   0.1 miles

To Nanyuki River Camel Camp (3.5km);
El Karama Ranch (42km);
Nyahururu (95km)

To Timau River Lodge (24km);
Ken Trout Guest Cottages (26km);
Meru (78km); Isiolo (81km)

Catholic Church

Main Market

Hindu Temple

Park

Market

River

To Mt Kenya Safari Club (10km)

To Cape Chestnut (1.6km);
Horse's Mouth Pub (2km);
Equator (3km); Airstrip (9km);
Ol Pejeta Conservancy (15km);
Naro Moru (24km); Nyeri (60km);
Nairobi (215km)

INFORMATION
Barclays Bank...............................1 C3
Kenya Commercial Bank............2 C2
Montana Trek & Information
  Centre.......................................3 B2
Mt Kenya Cyberworld..........(see 13)
Mt Kenya Mountaineering
  Information Office.............(see 9)
Post office...................................4 B3
Standard Chartered Bank.........5 C2

SLEEPING
Equator Chalet............................6 C2
Ibis Hotel....................................7 B2
Joskaki Hotel...............................8 C2
Mt Kenya Paradise Hotel............9 C2
Sportsman's Arms Hotel...........10 D2

EATING
Camcorner.................................11 C2
Marina Grill & Restaurant.........12 C3
Mountain Rock Café..................13 B3

ENTERTAINMENT
Buccaneer Club.........................14 D2

SHOPPING
Nanyuki Spinners & Weavers.....15 A1

TRANSPORT
Bus & Matatu Stand..................16 B2

on the Nanyuki River is a little dog-eared but has large clean rooms and is a good place to meet other travellers. Relax on the terrace to the sound of birds and gurgling water, but avoid weekends (the disco is *loud*).

Joskaki Hotel (Map p384; ☎ 31473; Lumumba Rd; s/tw/d KSh300/400/450) This is the best of the budget establishments. If you wander, you may hit the Joskaki jackpot: a room with some sun and a toilet seat!

MIDRANGE
Equator Chalet (Map p384; ☎ 31480; Kenyatta Ave; s/tw/d incl breakfast KSh800/1200/1450) This newish place in the centre of town gives substantial comfort bang for minimal buck. Rooms surround a breezy internal courtyard that opens onto two balcony areas and a roof terrace.

TOP END
Sportsman's Arms Hotel (Map p384; ☎ 32348; www .sportsmansarms.com; s/d/tw incl breakfast KSh3000/4000/ 4600, 4-person cottages KSh7000; ☒) Set in land-scaped gardens off Laikipia Rd east of town, this was once the white settlers' main ren-

dezvous, and is still popular with tourists and soldiers. The complex boasts a sauna, gym, Jacuzzi, tennis, squash, a restaurant and three bars (with table football).

Mt Kenya Safari Club (Map p382; ☎ 30000, Nairobi ☎ 020-216940; www.fairmont.com; full board s/d US$270/390, 4-person cottages US$995; ☐ ☒) Originally the homestead of a white set-tler family, this club was founded in the 1950s by a group including the late actor William Holden. Already one of the flashi-est top-class resorts in Kenya, it's recently been bought by Fairmont, which has big posh plans. If golf, tennis, croquet, snooker, fishing, bowls, an art gallery and a private wildlife sanctuary with a herd of rare bongo antelopes tickle your fancy, sign right up (though most cost extra).

Eating
You'll find that Nanyuki's best restaurants are attached to the hotels, though there are some independent options.

Camcorner (Map p384; Kenyatta Ave; meals KSh60-260) A delightful oddity serving the usual stews and steaks, as well as fiery curries and a selection of camel products (including camel *biltong* – jerky).

Marina Grill & Restaurant (Map p384; Kenyatta Ave; meals KSh90-350) Sit on the rooftop and delve into a burger or steak. The pizza is tasty but very small.

Cape Chestnut (Map p382; off Kenyatta Ave; ☯ Mon-Sat) This is an excellent coffee garden and snack place catering mostly for white farmers, expats and tourists. It's off Kenyatta Ave, 1km south of town.

Horse's Mouth Pub (Map p382; Haile Selassie Rd; meals KSh150-400) This place near Cape Chestnut caters for a similar clientele.

Mountain Rock Café (Map p384; Kenyatta Ave; meals KSh60-200) Popular with locals, this is a good spot for cheap Kenyan fare.

Drinking & Entertainment

Cape Chestnut and the Horse's Mouth Pub are pleasant places to enjoy a daylight beer, while in the evening the rooftop of Marina Grill & Restaurant is a good choice.

Duccanoor Club (Map p384; Laikipia Rd; ☯ Wed & Sat evenings) May look like a UFO, but its disco is nothing out of this world.

Shopping

There are a number of souvenir stalls and shops around town.

Nanyuki Spinners & Weavers (Map p384; Laikipia Rd) For something less tacky. This is a women's craft cooperative that specialises in woven woollen goods. The product and pattern design is high quality and cheaper than the same work in Nairobi.

Getting There & Away

There are daily flights from Wilson Airport in Nairobi to Nanyuki with **Airkenya** (☎ 020-605745; www.airkenya.com) and **Safarilink** (☎ 020-600777; www.safarilink.co.ke). A return trip on Airkenya/Safarilink is US$130/149, while one-way fares for northbound and southbound flights are US$60/70 and US$80/90 respectively.

There are daily buses and *matatus* to Nyeri (KSh100, one hour), Isiolo (KSh150, 1½ hours), Meru (KSh120, 1½ hours) and Nairobi (KSh350, three hours).

AROUND NANYUKI

The tiny town of **Timau** is a convenient stop between Isiolo and Nanyuki, and has a couple of interesting accommodation options

offering a range of activities. **Timau River Lodge** (Map p382; ☎ 062-41230; timauriverlodge@hotmail.com; camping KSh300, cottages incl breakfast per person KSh1400) is a wonderfully offbeat place, consisting of several lovely thatched cottages and a well-equipped camp site off the A2 Hwy. Three kilometres south of town, off the A2 Hwy, **Ken Trout Guest Cottages** (Map p382; ☎ 0720-804751; camping KSh300, half-board cottages per person KSh2500) is a more mainstream establishment, with an excellent restaurant and some very good fishing. Any *matatu* running between Nanyuki and Isiolo or Meru will drop you in Timau or at the turn-off to either sleeping option.

About 42km to the northwest of Nanyuki, **El Karama Ranch** (☎ 062-32526, Nairobi ☎ 020-340331; info@letsgosafari.com; bandas per person KSh2500) is on the Ewaso Ngiro River. Although still a working ranch, wildlife conservation is paramount and the 5668-hectares play home to rare northern species, like Grevy's zebras and reticulated giraffes. Billed as a 'self-service camp', accommodation is in basic but comfortable riverside *bandas*. Activities include wildlife walks, horse riding and camel safaris (see www.horsebackin kenya.com). Let's Go Travel (p284) in Nairobi provides a map with directions. During the rainy seasons you'll need a 4WD to get here; however, as driving around the ranch is discouraged and there's little public transport, it's usually better to phone and arrange to be picked up from Nanyuki.

Ol Pejeta Conservancy

Formerly called the Sweetwaters Game Reserve, this impressive 97-sq-km (soon to be 300-sq-km) **wildlife conservancy** (Map p382; adult/child US$25/13) is home to a wide variety of plains wildlife, including the Big Five, massive eland antelopes and a plethora of birdlife. There's also an important **chimpanzee sanctuary** (☯ 9-10.30am & 3-4.30pm), operated by the Jane Goodall Institute.

There are two top-end accommodation options in the reserve, both recently purchased by Serena Hotels. **Sweetwaters Tented Camp** (Map p382; ☎ 062-32409, Nairobi ☎ 020-2710511; sweetwaters@serena.co.ke; low season full board s/d US$90/180, high season US$235/310) is a collection of 30 luxury tents straddling the equator, while **Ol Pejeta House** (Map p382; ☎ 062-32400, Nairobi ☎ 020-2710511; swtc@kenyaweb.com; low season full board s/d US$210/270, high season US$270/390) was once home to Lord Delamere and now-bankrupt international arms dealer Adnan Kashoggi.

The reserve can be visited independently if you have your own vehicle. Access is off the A2 Hwy south out of Nanyuki. Mt Kenya Safari Club runs half-day wildlife drives here for US$55 per person (minimum two passengers); guests staying two or more nights at the club are entitled to free entry to the conservancy and lunch at Sweetwaters Tented Camp.

MERU

☎ 064

Stretched out along the eastern side of the Mt Kenya ring road, Meru is more of a travel hub than a base for Mt Kenya or Meru National Park. If you end up having to spend the night here or just stop to stock up on various commodities, it's worth a look around.

As it's a regional service centre and not a tourist destination, you'll rarely be hassled on the streets, despite them being alive with activity. The colourful main market is worth a stroll and if you ever thought of chewing *miraa* (see opposite), Meru is the epicentre of Kenyan production.

It's quite a climb up to Meru from either Isiolo or Embu, and in the rainy season you'll find yourself lost in the clouds. However, when the weather is clear there are superb views for miles over the surrounding lowlands, and you may catch glimpses of Mt Kenya.

Information

Café Candy (opposite) has Internet access for KSh180 per hour.
Barclays Bank (Tom Mboya St)
Kenya Commercial Bank (Njiru Ncheke St)
Meru County Council (Kenyatta Hwy) Bookings for Meru Mt Kenya Lodge on the Chogoria route.
Post office (Kenyatta Hwy)
Standard Chartered Bank (Moi Ave)

Sights

The small **Meru National Museum** (☎ 20482; adult/child KSh200/100; 🕙 9.30am-6pm, 1-6pm public holidays) off Kenyatta Hwy is worth visiting. The usual displays are present, with an explanation of evolution, and copious stuffed and mounted wildlife, but there's also a small, informative section concerning the clothing, weapons, and agricultural and initiation practices (including clitoridectomies) of the Meru people.

Sleeping

Goodnight Lodge (☎ 30057; Mosque Hill Rd; s incl breakfast KSh350) Probably the best budget option. Rooms and bathrooms (hot-water showers but no toilet seats) are clean and the upstairs options take in some sun.

Brown Rock Hotel (☎ 20247; Njiru Ncheke St; s/tw KSh350/450) Although the brown and white floor tiles are failing one by one, this is still your best bet for cheap twin-bed rooms. Hot water is sketchy at times.

Pig & Whistle (☎ 31411; s/tw incl breakfast KSh1000/1200) This place off Kenyatta Hwy has a dis-

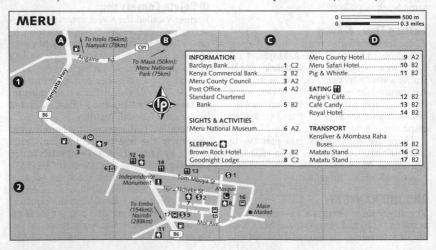

MERU

0   500 m
0   0.3 miles

INFORMATION	
Barclays Bank........................1	C2
Kenya Commercial Bank.........2	B2
Meru County Council..............3	A2
Post Office............................4	A2
Standard Chartered	
Bank................................5	B2

SIGHTS & ACTIVITIES	
Meru National Museum..........6	A2

SLEEPING	
Brown Rock Hotel..................7	B2
Goodnight Lodge..................8	C2

Meru County Hotel.................9	A2
Meru Safari Hotel.................10	B2
Pig & Whistle......................11	B2

EATING	
Angie's Café........................12	B2
Café Candy.........................13	B2
Royal Hotel.........................14	B2

TRANSPORT	
Kensilver & Mombasa Raha	
Buses..............................15	B2
Matatu Stand......................16	C2
Matatu Stand......................17	B2

To Isiolo (56km); Nanyuki (78km)
C91
Angaine Rd
To Maua (50km); Meru National Park (75km)
Kenyatta Hwy
B6
Independence Monument
To Embu (154km); Nairobi (288km)
Tom Mboya St
Njiru Ncheke St
Mosque
Main Market
Moi Ave
B6

MIRAA – MAKING MANY PLANS

The small twigs and leaves you'll see people chewing around Mt Kenya are *miraa*, also known as *khat*, the product of an evergreen tree native to East and southern Africa, Afghanistan and Yemen. Chewing *miraa* is an increasingly popular pastime in Kenya, but it's not nearly as important as in Somalia, where the drug is ingrained in the culture.

Some of the best *miraa* in the world is grown around Meru and it's a whopping US$250-million export industry. Of course much of the demand is from Somalia, and since *miraa*'s potency is diminished 48 hours after picking, massively overladen pick-ups race nightly to Wilson Airport in Nairobi for the morning flight to Mogadishu.

Miraa is a mild stimulant, usually chewed in company to encourage confidence, contentment and a flow of ideas. Locals selling the stuff are often heard saying 'when you chew *miraa* you'll make many plans…' Make plans is right, though getting around to doing anything about them is another thing entirely! The active ingredient, *cathinone,* is closely related to amphetamine, and the euphoric effects can last for up to 24 hours depending on how much is chewed.

Chewing too much can be habit-forming and has serious consequences, known medically as 'khat' syndrome'. Aggressive behaviour, nightmares and hallucinations are common mental side effects, while reduced appetite, constipation and brown teeth are common physical consequences. Even less pleasant are claims that *miraa* can cause spermatorrhoea (abnormal leakage of sperm – just delightful), leading to infertility.

Miraa is illegal in the USA, but is legally imported into several European countries. In Kenya it's sold in handfuls known as *kilos* or *gizas* for KSh100 to KSh300, depending on size. Meru is a good place for curious travellers to give it a go, but the taste is unlikely to prove enticing. The texture is rather unpleasant, too – funnily enough, it's just like chewing twigs.

---

tinctly ramshackle charm to it, with nice quiet grounds and a colonial-style bar/restaurant and lounge. Most cottages are uninspiring concrete blocks, but TV, phone and a dining area go some way towards compensating. More memorable stays are to be had in the 1934-vintage wooden cabins.

Meru County Hotel (☎ 20432; Kenyatta Hwy; s/tw incl breakfast from KSh1000/1500) This is the other midrange contender in town, with less style but a few more creature comforts. The 'studio' suites, with balconies and TV, are well worth the extra KSh100.

Meru Safari Hotel (☎ 31500; Kenyatta Hwy; s/tw KSh600/800) Considering hot water comes from the kitchen in buckets, this place is overpriced. The terrace bar is its greatest asset.

Eating & Drinking

The Pig & Whistle and Meru County Hotel have the best bar-restaurants in town.

Royal Hotel (Tom Mboya St; meals KSh80-150) Deep pots ensure it still has food late in the evenings when most places are coming up empty. The bar is packed on weekends.

Café Candy (Tom Mboya St; meals around KSh50-180) A very popular place with locals, this is a good place for cheap vegetarian curries, stews and fish during the day.

Angie's Café (Kenyatta Hwy; meals KSh50-150) Sedated goldfish patrol the aquarium and watch over some simple menus. Locals recommend the biryani.

Getting There & Away

There are 13 daily departures from 6.45am onwards with **Kensilver** (Mosque Hill Rd) to Embu (KSh250, two hours), Thika (KSh280, 3½ hours) and Nairobi (KSh300, 4½ hours). **Mombasa Raha** (Mosque Hill Rd) has a daily 5pm service to Mombasa (KSh900, 10 hours).

Regular *matatus* serve the same destinations for similar costs and leave from the main stand, near the main market, and from opposite the Shell petrol station. *Matatus* also serve Nanyuki (KSh120, 1½ hours) and Isiolo (KSh120, 1½ hours).

MERU NATIONAL PARK

This **park** (☎ 062-21320; adult/child US$27/10) is the cornerstone of the Meru Conservation Area, a 4000-sq-km expanse that also includes the adjacent Kora National Park, and Bisanadi, Mwingi and North Kitui National Reserves (which are closed), covering the lowland plains east of Meru town.

KWS has big plans for this park. In the 1970s the huge populations of elephants and

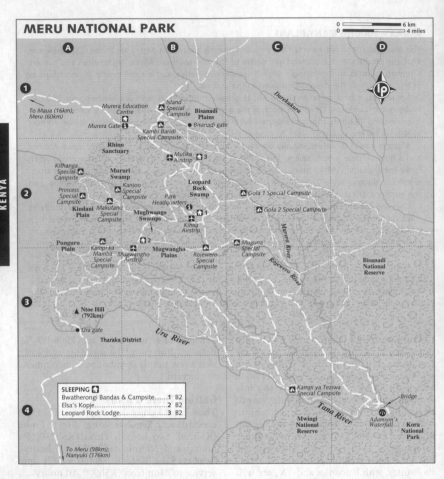

MERU NATIONAL PARK

0 ___ 6 km
0 ___ 4 miles

SLEEPING
Bwatherongi Bandas & Campsite........1 B2
Elsa's Kopje.................................2 B2
Leopard Rock Lodge......................3 B2

rhinos could pull in up to 40,000 visitors a year, but banditry and poaching during the 1980s effectively put paid to tourism here, wiping out the white rhinos and leaving the area almost abandoned until the late 1990s. Today substantial foreign investment has enabled a flurry of rehabilitation projects: a new rhino sanctuary opened in 2001 and now houses 25 rhinos (24 white), a new sealed access road is half completed and all the main park roads have been upgraded.

Now that security is settled, these improvements are starting to pay off and visitor numbers are steadily climbing from the meagre 1000 in 1997 to well over 10,000 in 2004. With two luxury lodges and some of the best budget options in any of Kenya's

national parks, Meru's fortunes should soon be on the up again.

This resurgence is definitely a good thing, as the park is a complete contrast to the nearby savanna reserves of Samburu, Buffalo Springs and Shaba. Abundant rainfall and numerous permanent watercourses support a luxuriant jungle of forest, bush, swamp and tall grasses, which, in turn, provide fodder to a wide variety of herbivores, and shelter to them and their predators. This is one of the most geographically diverse parks in Kenya and a favourite with the safari cognoscenti; you need to spend a few days here to fully appreciate what the park has to offer.

While on the rise, wildlife is still not as abundant here as in other parks. To make things more challenging, the limited elephant numbers have led to an increase in vegetation cover, making it difficult to spot those species that do exist. However, with a little patience you can see elephants, leopards, lions and cheetahs, along with lesser kudus, elands, waterbucks, gazelles and oryxes. Buffaloes, reticulated giraffes and Grevy's zebras are common, while monkeys, crocodiles and a plethora of bird species, including the palm nut vulture and Marshal eagle, can be found in the dense vegetation along the watercourses.

Sleeping

Elsa's Kopje (☎ 020-604053; safaris@chelipeacock.co.ke; full board low season s/d US$320/600, high season US$520/920; ☒) Wake to glorious panoramic views and sweet breezes in these gorgeous open-fronted thatched cottages that blend seamlessly into the upper reaches of Mughwango Hill. This place is the definition of sensitively designed luxury. Hefty prices include three wildlife drives (one at night), walking safaris, fishing and transfers.

Leopard Rock Lodge (☎ 020-600031; leopardmico@wananchi.com; Apr-Jun full board s/d from US$285/440, Jul-Mar US$340/515; ☒) With landscaped gardens, a stilted restaurant on the Murera River and comfortable cottages, this lodge would shine anywhere else in Kenya, but here it's entirely outmatched by Elsa's Kopje.

Bwatherongi Bandas & Campsite (adult/child US$10/5, bandas per person US$15; ☒) Perhaps the best KWS camp in Kenya, this site has great showers, toilets, barbecue pits, a swimming pool and an *askari* in attendance. There are also four excellent thatched *bandas*.

Special camp sites (adult/child US$15/5, plus set-up fee KSh5000) There are about a dozen of these seasonal bush camp sites (no facilities) located throughout the park.

Getting There & Away

Simply put, there's no point reaching the park without a vehicle. If you don't want to join a tour, your cheapest option is to acquire a 4WD (and driver) from a local in the village of Maua, 31km from the gate. Regular *matatus* service Maua from Meru town (KSh100, one hour).

On Wednesday, Friday and Sunday **Airkenya** (☎ 020-605745; www.airkenya.com) connects Meru to Nairobi (one way/return US$150/300) and Samburu (one way/return US$60/120).

A one-way ticket from Nairobi to Samburu with a stopover in Meru is US$190.

CHOGORIA
☎ 064

The only reason to come to this small town on the lower eastern slopes of Mt Kenya is to access one of the mountain's most scenic climbs – the Chogoria route (p381). Sadly Chogoria has quite a reputation for hassle, with every man and his dog offering to take you up the mountain. On arrival, it's much better to bypass the village altogether, get yourself sorted at the Transit Motel, then head back if you need basic supplies.

The well-signposted **Transit Motel** (Map p382; ☎ 22096; PO Box 190, Chogoria; camping per tent KSh500, s/tw incl breakfast KSh1000/1600) is as great for arranging Mt Kenya treks as it is for flaking out when the enjoyable slog is over. The rooms are clean, and sport hot-water showers, mosquito nets and balconies. There's also a decent bar and restaurant (meals KSh100 to KSh300). It is a 1.5km walk from the signposted turn-off just south of Chogoria. Don't believe rival touts claiming the motel has burnt down – it's a cement structure!

Regular buses and *matatus* ply the road heading north to Meru (KSh60, 30 minutes) and south to Embu (KSh150, 1½ hours) and Nairobi (KSh280, four hours).

EMBU
☎ 068

Surrounded by intensively cultivated hills on the fringes of Mt Kenya's southeastern slopes is Embu, the unlikely capital of the Eastern Province. Given that this agricultural backwater town barely sits in the province, our best guess is that it was chosen as capital because of its agreeable climate.

Despite its local significance, there's not a lot to detain travellers here, and it's a long way from the mountain. However, it can make a good stopover on the way to Thika.

Information
Barclays Bank (B6 Hwy)
Cyberlink (per hr KSh120) Off Kenyatta Hwy.
Embu Provincial Hospital (Kenyatta Hwy)
Post office (Kenyatta Hwy)

Sleeping
Kenya Scouts Training Centre (☎ 30459; Kenyatta Hwy; camping KSh100, dm KSh250) This spotless place

has great facilities and is a bargain. Four- or five-bed dorms are only rented to one group at a time, so if you're alone you'll get the room to yourself for only KSh250.

Embu Motel (☎ 0722-462277; s/d incl breakfast from KSh700/900) Quietly set back off the B6 Hwy, this is another great option. Cleanliness pervades throughout and the toilets even have seats. The motel has a comfy TV room, a spartan dining area and a safe spot to park your metal steed.

Highway Court Hotel (☎ 20046; Kenyatta Hwy; s/tw from KSh400/800) While the rooms are clean, they don't gleam like those at the Embu Motel. It's a comfortable place, with hot-water showers, mosquito nets and TVs (only in the large twins, KSh1200). The only drawback is noise from the lively bar and restaurant.

Izaak Walton Inn (☎ 20128; izaakwalton@winnet .co.ke; Kenyatta Hwy; s/d incl breakfast from US$32/50) About 1.5km north of town is this well-known place set in fantastic old colonial grounds. Some standard rooms have a cabin feel, with wood-lined walls, while others are more contemporary. All rooms have TV and there's a great cosy bar.

Prime Lodge (☎ 30692; s/tw KSh650/1050) Prices have jumped, but quality clearly hasn't. On the upside, it's clean and most rooms catch some sun. It's off the B6 Hwy.

Eating

If you want the full treatment, head for the restaurant at Izaak Walton Inn.

Eastern Inn (Mama Ngina St; meals KSh40-150) Fronted by a shady awning, this Christian restaurant serves sandwiches, samosas, fried chicken and fish.

Kamuketha Hotel (B6 Hwy; meals KSh80-200) It says that it fries up the best *tilapia* in town – many locals would agree.

Getting There & Away

Regular Kensilver buses to Meru (KSh250, two hours) and Nairobi (KSh250, three hours) leave from the BP petrol station in town. Mombasa Raha heads for Mombasa (KSh700, 10 hours) at 7.30am daily.

Numerous *matatus* serve Chogoria (KSh150, 1½ hours), Meru (KSh250, two hours), Thika (KSh200, two hours), Nyeri (KSh150, two hours), Nanyuki (KSh220, 2½ hours), Nyahururu (KSh300, three hours), Nairobi (KSh250, three hours) and Nakuru (KSh400, 4½ hours).

OL DONYO SABUK NATIONAL PARK

This tiny **park** (adult/child US$15/5) was gazetted in 1967 and covers an area of just 20.7 sq km. The focus of the park is the summit of **Ol Donyo Sabuk** (2146m), surrounded by an oasis of dense primeval forest that supports a huge variety of birds and numerous primates, including black and white colobus and blue monkeys. The Kikuyu call the mountain Kilimambongo (buffalo mountain) and buffaloes are indisputably the dominant animals here. Below the picnic site and communications tower on the summit is a salt lick that attracts regular herds.

It's possible to explore on foot if accompanied by a ranger (per half-/full day KSh500/KSh1000). It's a 9km hike (three or four hours) to an amazing 360-degree view at the summit.

There's a pretty **camp site** (adult/child US$10/5) just before the main gate, with soft grass and shady trees. Facilities include one long-drop toilet, a rusty tap and free firewood.

Getting There & Away

From Thika take a *matatu* to the village of Ol Donyo Sabuk (KSh70, 50 minutes), from where it's a 2km walk along a straight dirt road to the gate. You could also take a *matatu* heading to Kitui and hop off at Kilimambongo (KSh50, 45 minutes), which is 6km from Ol Donyo Sabuk village.

THIKA
☎ 067

Thika isn't much more than a busy little agricultural service town, and there aren't many of those famous flame trees to be seen. That said, it's a leafy place and quite pleasant for a stroll. The only true 'attractions' are **Chania Falls** and **Thika Falls**, about 1km to the north of town on the busy Nairobi–Nyeri road.

Information

Barclays Bank (Kenyatta Hwy)
Cyber Cafe (Uhuru St; per hr KSh60)
Post office (Commercial St)

Sleeping & Eating

December Hotel (☎ 22140; Commercial St; s/d KSh600/800) The best and brightest of the budget bunch. The large rooms and bathrooms are well kept. Some rooms see more sun than others.

Thika Inn (☎ 31590; Kenyatta Hwy; s/tw incl breakfast KSh650/1200) Just south of town, behind the Caltex petrol station, Thika Inn has reasonable rooms. While the bedding is fresh and clean, the bathrooms are slightly grungy. Thankfully the rooms are sheltered from their lively Vybestar Club restaurant (meals KSh150 to KSh350) and disco.

Blue Post Hotel (☎ 22241; blueposthotel@africa online.co.ke; s/d KSh1600/1900; 🖳) Set among lovely gardens and next to the Chania River 2km north of town, this pleasant place has very comfortable rooms with four-poster canopy beds, polished wooden floors and TV. Room numbers 101 to 106 offer shady balconies and glimpses of Chania Falls. It has a great bar and a decent restaurant (meals KShh120 to KShh240) serving Western selections.

Primos Hotel (Kame Nkrumah; meals KSh50-220) With comfy seats and views over the street, Primos prepares Kenyan dishes, burgers and basic sandwiches. It also takes a stab at beef stroganoff.

Getting There & Away

There are plenty of *matatus* heading to Nairobi (KSh70, 45 minutes), Embu (KSh200, two hours) and Nyeri (KSh200, 1¾ hours). The odd service reaches Naivasha (KSh200, 1½ hours).

WESTERN KENYA

Imagine western Kenya and you'd be forgiven for only thinking of Masai Mara's beloved savanna and plethora of exciting wildlife. After all, the Mara is astounding and the only part of this region most travellers ever see.

For those few who conjured up images of craggy 4000m peaks, thick rainforests crawling with birdlife and rare primates, rolling hills draped in aromatic tea plantations, and small fishing boats dotting Lake Victoria's endless horizon, well done! You've probably already experienced some of what this amazing region has to offer.

Western Kenya's highlands climb steeply out of the Rift Valley and sit atop the striking Elgeyo and Mau Escarpments. Incredibly verdant, the north is a heavily cultivated patchwork of family farms and the south an abode to countless tea plantations. Kakamega Forest Reserve and Saiwa

Swamp National Park are two bastions of pristine wilderness and wildlife amid this agricultural heartland. With massive Mt Elgon and the Cherangani Hills rising skyward from the highland's northern reaches, unique trekking possibilities are also on the menu.

Sitting in the long morning shadows of the highlands are Lake Victoria's captivating lowlands, home to the friendly city of Kisumu, Ruma National Park, Mfangano Island and numerous diminutive fishing villages.

The Luo, the third-largest tribe in Kenya, live around Lake Victoria, while the Luyha, Gusii and Kalenjin call the cool highlands home. With the exception of the Mara's Maasai, who've been inundated with tourists, western Kenya is your best opportunity to truly get to know the locals.

NAROK
☎ 050

Two hours west of Nairobi, this small, ramshackle provincial town is Masai Mara's main access point. It is not great for independent travellers, as prices reflect the heavy tourist traffic, and Narok is rife with transport touts and rip-off merchants – enjoy!

Kenya Commercial Bank is the town's only bank and has an unreliable ATM (Visa only). Cardphones are found at the post office (with Internet).

Sleeping & Eating

Kim's Dishes Hotel (☎ 22001; s/d/tw KSh500/800/1000) With secure parking, great bathrooms, 24-hour hot water and new mosquito nets, Kim's is Narok's best-value option. The restaurant (meals KSh80 to KSh200) downstairs serves tasty Kenyan dishes.

Spear Hotel (☎ 22035; s/tw with shared bathroom KSh250/500, with private bathroom KSh400/750) The rooms are spacious and have mosquito nets, but some mattresses are better than others. Hot water only flows in the morning. Locals love the restaurant (meals KSh100 to KSh200), and you may see traditionally dressed Maasai gathered to watch Oprah!

Chambai Hotel (☎ 22591; s KSh650, super s/tw KSh1000/1400) Simple standard rooms, plus new 'super' rooms with balconies, large TV and huge bathrooms. The bar and restaurant (meals KSh250, buffets KSh350) are civilised and worth trying.

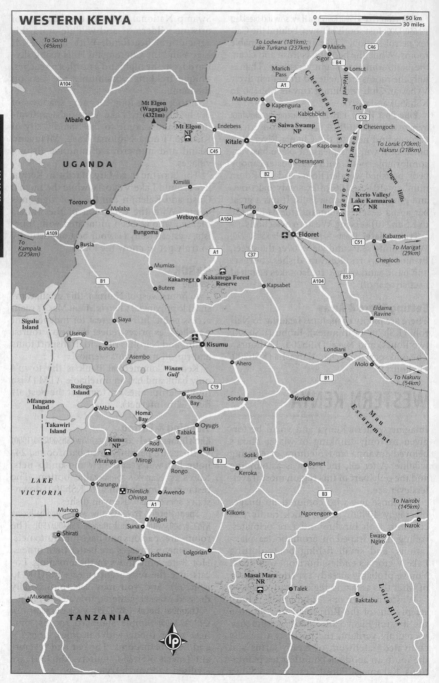

WESTERN KENYA

Getting There & Away

Frequent *matatus* run between Narok and Nairobi (KSh250, 2½ hours), with other departures to Naivasha (KSh200, three hours) and Kisii (KSh300, three hours). There is also usually daily transport to Sekenani and Talek gates for around KSh350.

Petrol is much cheaper here than in the reserve.

MASAI MARA NATIONAL RESERVE

Backed by the spectacular Esoit Oloololo (Siria) Escarpment, watered by the Mara River and littered with an astonishing amount of wildlife is this world-renowned reserve (adult/child US$30/10). Its 1510 sq km of open rolling grasslands, the northern extension of the equally famous Serengeti Plains, are actually the agglomeration of the Narok (managed by Narok County Council) and Transmara National Reserves (managed by Mara Conservancy).

Although concentrations of wildlife are typically highest in the swampy area around the reserve's western edge, superior roads draw most visitors to the eastern side. Of the big cats, lions are found in large prides everywhere and it is not uncommon to see them hunting. Cheetahs and leopards are less visible but still fairly common. Elephants, buffaloes, zebras and hippos also exist in large numbers.

Of the antelopes, the black-striped Thomson's gazelle and larger Grant's gazelle are most prevalent, although the numbers of impalas, topis, Coke's hartebeests and wildebeests aren't far behind. Other common animals include Masai giraffes, baboons, warthogs, jackals, bat-eared foxes and matriarchal clans of spotted hyenas. The few dozen black rhinos are rarely seen.

The ultimate attraction is undoubtedly the annual wildebeest migration in July and August, when millions of these ungainly beasts move north from the Serengeti seeking lusher grass before turning south again around October. While you're more likely to see endless columns grazing or trudging along rather than dramatic TV-style river fordings, it is nonetheless a staggering experience.

During the migration there seem to be as many minibuses as animals, and many tend to take off, making new tracks wherever they feel fit. This shouldn't be encouraged.

Wherever you enter, make sure you ask for a receipt: it is crucial for passage between the reserve's Narok and Transmara sections and your eventual exit.

Sights & Activities
WILDLIFE DRIVES & WALKS

Whether bouncing over the plains in pursuit of elusive elephant silhouettes or parked next to a pride of lions and listening to their bellowed breaths, wildlife drives are *the* highlight of a trip to the Mara.

All top-end places offer wildlife drives, which can usually be negotiated into the rate while booking. Guided walks and other activities, such as **horse riding** and **bush dinners**, are typically booked during your stay.

If you've arrived by *matatu*, you can organise drives with most lodges, as they're fairly friendly towards independent travellers. Basecamp Masai Mara (p395) is easiest because it is outside the park and only a 1.5km walk from Talek. Two-hour drives (day or night) typically cost US$35 per person plus park fees.

Alternatively, walk with a Maasai *moran* (warrior) outside the park, where there is still a large amount of wildlife. This can be a wonderful experience, but be aware that local Maasai groups may charge you a fee for crossing their land.

BALLOONING

If you can afford US$390, balloon safaris are superb and worlds away from the minibus circuit. Trips can be arranged through top-end lodges. See p435 for more details.

MAASAI VILLAGE

The Maasai village between Oloolaimutiek and Sekenani gates welcomes tourists, though negotiating admission can be fraught – prices start as high as US$20 per person! If you're willing to drop this kind of cash for free rein with the camera, go ahead, but don't expect a genuine cultural experience.

Sleeping
OLOOLAIMUTIEK & SEKANANI GATES

While outside the Oloolaimutiek gate, these camps are within the reserve and sleeping here will incur park fees.

Acacia Camp (☎ 020-210024; camping US$5, s/tw with shared bathroom US$35/40) Thatched roofs shelter

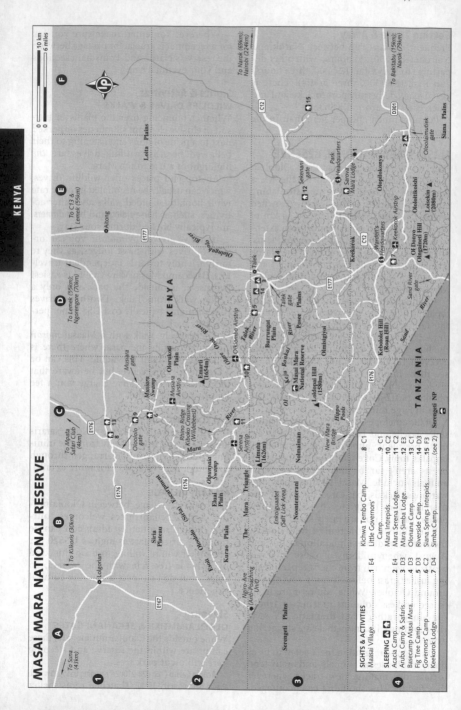

MASAI MARA NATIONAL RESERVE

SIGHTS & ACTIVITIES	
Masai Village	1 E4

SLEEPING	
Acacia Camp	2 E4
Aruba Camp & Safaris	3 D3
Basecamp Masai Mara	4 D3
Fig Tree Camp	5 D3
Governors' Camp	6 C2
Keekorok Lodge	7 D4
Kichwa Tembo Camp	8 C1
Little Governors' Camp	9 C1
Mara Intrepids	10 C2
Mara Serena Lodge	11 C2
Mara Simba Lodge	12 E3
Olonana Camp	13 C1
Riverside Camp	14 D3
Siana Springs Intrepids	15 F3
Simba Camp	(see 2)

THE HARD SELL

A common complaint among travellers, particularly in the Mara, is that Maasai can be incredibly hard-nosed in business, and 'cultural' visits to villages often become high-pressure sales ventures the moment you arrive.

While it would be unfair to generalise, it's certainly true that some Maasai, especially in high-density tourist areas, will treat you as a cash cow. Favourite techniques include dropping wares in your lap and refusing to take them back; coming into camp sites to offer dances at non-negotiable rates; and charging for absolutely everything, from camping to crossing their land. While this behaviour isn't limited to Maasai, their aggressive and unapologetic attitude upsets more travellers than day-to-day hassle elsewhere.

If you feel you're being taken for a ride, Maasai or otherwise, stand up for yourself. But ask yourself, if your people had been consistently dispossessed for over a century and were now subjected to streams of gawping foreigners with seemingly bottomless pockets, wouldn't you do the same?

---

closely spaced, spartan semipermanent tents in this quaint camp. They're slightly cheaper (single/twin US$30/35) without bedding. There are numerous cooking areas, a bar and a campfire pit, but no restaurant. Bathrooms are clean and hot water flows in the evening. The only downside for campers is the lack of shade.

Siana Springs Intrepids (☎ 020-4446651; siana@ africaonline.co.ke; low season full board s/d US$150/210, high season US$260/350; 🐾) This tented camp offers comfort without luxury intruding on the African bush experience. The best tents dot the edge of a beautiful clearing (bamboo group) or nestle in the forest (palm group); spacing is generous, so privacy is guaranteed.

Keekorok Lodge (bookings ☎ 020-4447151; low season full board s/d US$140/180, high season US$200/250; 🐾) This has always been a great option, with bungalows, cabins and cottages to choose from. After major renovations were completed in mid-2005, it's now better than ever. It has the usual top-end facilities, with the added attraction of a hippo pool.

Mara Simba Lodge (☎ 020-4343961; enquiries@ marasimba.com; low season full board s/d US$100/150, high season US$180/250; 🐾) Large log-sided cabins house comfortable rooms with plank floors, balconies and fans; ask for upstairs rooms as they boast better views.

Simba Camp (per tent KSh800) Next to Acacia Camp, this dishevelled camp site has tin-shack toilets and no running water. Dog-eared tents (some with beds, some without) are for rent at KSh900. Prices include a farcical security fee.

TALEK GATE

Basecamp Masai Mara (☎ 020-577490; www.base campexplorer.com; low season full board s/d US$90/140, Nov-Mar US$120/190, Jul-Oct US$140/200) Masai Mara's only ecolodge is an incredibly friendly place. Solar panels provide power, organic waste is composted and dirty water is reused to water the grounds. One of the superb observation towers has a small exhibition space where local conservationists give informal lectures. The 16 individually designed permanent tents have thatched roofs, beautiful outdoor showers and large verandas with day beds.

Aruba Camp & Safaris (☎ 0723-997524; gerdi .simon@web.de; camping KSh300) Just outside the reserve, on the Talek River's scenic north bank, is this up-and-coming option. Joining the bare-bones camp site will soon be Masai Mara's first midrange tented safari camp. For less than US$100 per person, you will get full-board accommodation and wildlife drives.

Riverside Camp (☎ 0720-218319; camping KSh350, bandas per person KSh2000) Run by Maasai, this camp site has good facilities, like running water, hot showers and a kitchen area. Trees provide shade for campers, while simple *bandas* provide shelter for the tentless.

Fig Tree Camp (☎ 020-605328; sales@madahotels .com; Jan-Jun full board s/d US$80/120, Jul-Dec US$165/220; 🐾) Vegetate on your tent's veranda, watching the Talek's waters gently flow by. Cabins with equally basic interiors cost the same but lack the river views. There's also a small but scenic pool and a trendy treetop bar.

Mara Intrepids (☎ 020-4446651; maraintrepids@ heritagehotels.co.ke; low season full board incl wildlife drives s/d US$245/370, high season US$450/615; 🐾) The 30 permanent tents offer comfort, four-poster canopy beds and stone bathrooms. A lovely pool, with diving board, sits riverside.

MUSIARA & OLOOLOLO GATES

Mara Serena Lodge (☎ 020-22059; mara@serena.co.ke; low season full board s/d US$80/160, high season US$210/260; ☒) Built to resemble a futuristic Maasai village, Serena is the most colourful lodge in the reserve. Hip rooms, with vibrant curved walls and Juliet balconies, line a ridge and overlook the grassy plains below. Blending beautifully with its surroundings and offering 1st-class service, it's justifiably popular.

Kichwa Tembo Camp (☎ 020-3740920; alice@cons corp.co.ke; low season full board s/d US$120/240, Mar & Nov–mid-Dec US$155/310, rest of year US$185/370; ☒) Just outside the northern boundary, Kichwa has permanent tents with grass-mat floors, stone bathrooms and tasteful furnishings. Hop in a hammock and take in spectacular savanna views. The food has an excellent reputation.

Olonana Camp (☎ 020-6950244; kenya@sanctuary lodges.com; low season full board per person US$225, Oct–mid-Dec US$340, rest of year US$450; ☒) Twelve tents with thatched shelters, large decks, wooden floors and beautiful stone bathrooms call this camp home.

Mpata Safari Club (☎ 020-310867; mpata4@africa online.co.ke; Mar-May s/d US$240/380, Jun-Feb US$340 /480; ☒) Up the Esoit Oloololo Escarpment, Mpata offers Mara's grandest views and most luxurious accommodations. With brave contemporary styling, spiralling roofs, circular skylights, glass walls and quirky furniture, you will be talking about more than just animals.

Governors' Camp (☎ 020-2734000; www.governors camp.com; low season full board s/d US$165/330, high season US$370/550; ☒) and **Little Governors' Camp** (low season full board s/d US$180/360, high season US$405/600; ☒) have tents similar to those at Kichwa, and offer great service, pleasing riverside locations and activities aplenty. The hefty rates include three wildlife drives.

Eating & Drinking

If you can't afford to sleep at the lodges, drop in for drinks or a meal. Lovely lunches/dinners will set you back US$15/25, but the views and ambience are free.

A tiny shop, eatery and lively Maasai market are in Talek village.

Getting There & Away

AIR

Daily flights are available with **Airkenya** (☎ 020-605745; www.airkenya.com) and **Safarilink** (☎ 020-600777; www.safarilink.co.ke) to Masai Mara.

Return flights on Airkenya/Safarilink are US$191/201.

You must state which Mara airstrip you require, and be early when leaving as the aeroplane doesn't wait for latecomers.

MATATU, CAR & FOUR-WHEEL DRIVE

Although it's possible to arrange wildlife drives independently, there are few savings in coming here without transport. That said, Talek and Sekenani gates are accessible from Narok by *matatu*. From Kisii a *matatu* will get you as far as Kilkoris or Suna on the main A1 Hwy, but you will have problems after this.

For those driving, the first 52km west of Narok on the B3 and C12 are smooth enough, but after the bitumen runs out it gets bumpy. The C13, which connects Oloololo gate with Lolgorian in the west, is very rough, rocky and poorly signposted – a highway it's not.

Expensive petrol is available at Mara Sarova, Mara Serena and Keekorok Lodges.

LAKE VICTORIA

Spread across 70,000 sq km and gracing the shores of Kenya, Tanzania and Uganda, Lake Victoria is East Africa's most important geographical feature. Amazingly, despite its massive girth, the lake is never more than 80m deep, compared to 1500m in smaller Rift Valley lakes.

The lake's 'evolving' ecosystem has proved to be both a boon and a bane for those living along its shores. For starters, its waters are a haven for mosquitos and snails, making malaria and bilharzia too common here. Then there are Nile perch (introduced 50 years ago to combat mosquitos), which eventually thrived, growing to over 200kg in size and becoming every small fishing boat's dream. Sadly, now it's only large commercial fishing vessels thriving. Horrifyingly, the ravenous perch have wiped out over 300 species of smaller tropical fish unique to the lake.

Last and not least is the ornamental water hyacinth. First reported in 1986, this 'exotic' pond plant had no natural predators here and quickly reached plague proportions, covering 17,230 hectares and confining many large ships to port. Millions of dollars have been ploughed into solving the problem; the investment seems to be paying off and the most recent satellite photos show hyacinth covering just 384 hectares.

Despite the ecological and economic turmoil, the lives of Kenyans living along the shore go on, and a peek into their world is as fascinating as ever.

KISUMU
☎ 057

Set on the sloping shore of Lake Victoria's Winam Gulf, Kisumu is the third-largest town in Kenya. Declared a city during its centenary celebrations in 2001, it still doesn't feel like one; its relaxed atmosphere is a world away from that of Nairobi and Mombasa. Amazingly, like much of western Kenya, Kisumu receives relatively few travellers.

Until 1977 the port here was one of the busiest in Kenya, but decline set in with the demise of the East African Community (Kenya, Tanzania and Uganda), and it sat virtually idle for two decades. Although increasing cooperation between these countries (now known as Comesa) has established Kisumu as an international shipment point for petroleum products, surprisingly the lake plays no part – raw fuel for processing is piped in from Mombasa and the end products are shipped out by truck. With Kisumu's fortunes again rising, it is hoped Lake Victoria will once more start contributing to the local economy.

If you've arrived from the higher country east, you will immediately notice the humidity. Kisumu is a few degrees hotter than the highland cities, and the steamy conditions add to the generally languid air.

Orientation
Kisumu is a fairly sprawling town, but everything you will need is within walking distance. Most shops, banks, cheap hotels and other facilities can be found around Oginga Odinga Rd, while the train station and ferry jetty are short walks from the end of New Station Rd.

Jomo Kenyatta Hwy is the major thoroughfare, connecting town with the main market and the noisy bus and *matatu* station.

The most pleasant access to the lake itself is at Dunga, a small village about 3km south of town along Nzola Rd.

Information
Pel Travels (p400) is the most helpful travel agent in town.

Abacus Cyber Cafe (Al-Imran Plaza, Oginga Odinga Rd; per hr KSh60; ✆ 8am-8pm)
Aga Khan Hospital (☎ 2020005; Otiena Oyoo St; ✆ 24hr) A large hospital with modern facilities and 24-hour emergency room.
Barclays Bank (Kampala St)
Crystal Communications (Mega Plaza, Oginga Odinga Rd; per hr KSh60; ✆ 8am-6pm) Internet access.
Immigration office (1st fl, Reinsurance Plaza, cnr Oginga Odinga Rd & Jomo Kenyatta Hwy) Visa extensions.
Kenya Commercial Bank (Jomo Kenyatta Hwy)
Police station (Uhuru Rd)
Post office (Oginga Odinga Rd)
Sanhedrin Cyber Joint (Swan Centre, Accra St; per hr KSh60; ✆ 8am-10pm)
Standard Chartered Bank (Oginga Odinga Rd)

Dangers & Annoyances
While open storm drains and steep curbs are probably your biggest worry when walking around at night, it's still best not to do it too often, as robberies do occur.

Sights & Activities
Unlike many local museums, **Kisumu Museum** (Nairobi Rd; admission KSh200; ✆ 8am-6pm) is an interesting and often informative place. There is a very good collection of traditional everyday items, including agricultural implements, bird and insect traps, food utensils, clothing, furniture, weapons and musical instruments. There is also a fairly motley array of stuffed birds and animals, including an amazing airborne lion mauling a wildebeest. Outside, a traditional Luo homestead has been constructed.

On the road to Dunga is the 1-sq-km KWS **Impala Sanctuary** (adult/child US$5/2; ✆ 6am-6pm). Besides being home to a small impala herd, it also provides important grazing grounds for local hippos. You will find a pleasant nature trail and a not so pleasant animal orphanage.

Covering a large area of swampland, **Kisumu Bird Sanctuary** (✆ 6am-6pm), off A1 Hwy, 8km southeast of town, is an important breeding ground for herons, storks, cormorants and egrets. The best time to visit is in April or May. Transport is easy along the A1, but you will have a 3km walk from the turn-off. Visitor fees may be implemented in the near future.

Gazetted in 1986, **Ndere Island National Park** (adult/child US$15/5) is a very beautiful forested 4.2-sq-km island housing a variety of bird

KENYA

KENYA

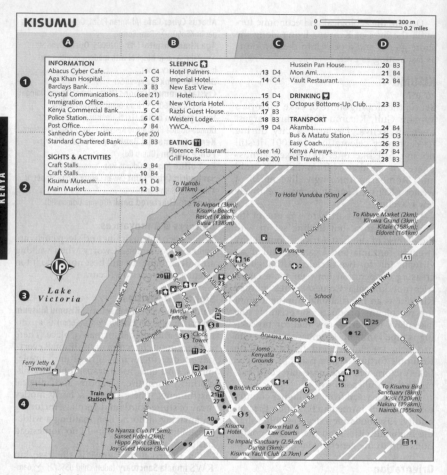

KISUMU

INFORMATION	
Abacus Cyber Cafe	1 C4
Aga Khan Hospital	2 C3
Barclays Bank	3 B3
Crystal Communications	(see 21)
Immigration Office	4 C4
Kenya Commercial Bank	5 C4
Police Station	6 C4
Post Office	7 B4
Sanhedrin Cyber Joint	(see 20)
Standard Chartered Bank	8 B3

SIGHTS & ACTIVITIES	
Craft Stalls	9 B4
Craft Stalls	10 B4
Kisumu Museum	11 D4
Main Market	12 D3

SLEEPING	
Hotel Palmers	13 D4
Imperial Hotel	14 C4
New East View Hotel	15 D4
New Victoria Hotel	16 C3
Razbi Guest House	17 B3
Western Lodge	18 B3
YWCA	19 B3

EATING	
Florence Restaurant	(see 14)
Grill House	(see 20)

Hussein Pan House	20 B3
Mon Ami	21 B4
Vault Restaurant	22 B4

DRINKING	
Octopus Bottoms-Up Club	23 B3

TRANSPORT	
Akamba	24 B4
Bus & Matatu Station	25 D3
Easy Coach	26 B3
Kenya Airways	27 B4
Pel Travels	28 B3

species, plus hippos, impalas (introduced) and spotted crocodile, a lesser-known cousin of the larger Nile crocodile. Tsetse flies can be problematic after the rains. Unfortunately tourism hasn't taken off here; there is nowhere to stay and chartered boats are your only transport option. Kisumu Beach Resort (opposite) charters 20 passenger boats for KSh3000 per hour, with typical return trips taking five hours.

Kisumu's **main market** (off Jomo Kenyatta Hwy) is one of Kenya's most animated, as is the huge **Kibuye Market** (Jomo Kenyatta Hwy), which draws people from all around the district each Sunday. Everything from second-hand clothes to furniture and food can be found. The various **craft stalls** near Kisumu

Hotel are among the best places in Kenya for soapstone carvings.

Sleeping

BUDGET

Western Lodge (☎ 2023707; Kendu Lane; s or d KSh500) This lodge has a number of smallish singles (or cosy doubles) with mosquito nets and bathroom. There is a nice common balcony with plants, tables and a slice of lake view.

Razbi Guest House (☎ 2025488; Kendu Lane; s/tw with shared bathroom KSh400/500, s with private bathroom KSh600) A secure place, with small, mosquito-net-clad rooms, some decidedly brighter than others. The shared toilets pass the nostril test and there is a private TV lounge/restaurant upstairs.

Kisumu Beach Resort (☎ 0733-749327; camping KSh300, s/tw KSh1250/1500) This scruffy lakeside 'resort' is set across the bay from town. With loads of space, wicker loungers, a pool table, volleyball, a decent restaurant and well-stocked bar, it's easy to see why it's popular with overlanders and campers. To get here, take a 'Pipeline' *matatu* (KSh20) from the main station to the airport, from where you can hire a *boda-boda* (bicycle taxi; KSh10) or walk the remaining 1.8km.

YWCA (☎ 0733-992982; dm KSh300, full board KSh500) Bare-bones bunks in airy rooms for bottom dollar here. The shared bathrooms look clean, but are rather pungent. It's off Anaawa Ave.

MIDRANGE

Hotel Palmers (☎ 2024867; Omolo Agar Rd; s/tw KSh1000/1400) An understated place with a perceptible warmth to its atmosphere. The rooms are on the small side, but they see some sun, have decent bathrooms and are home to breezy fans. The hotel also has a comfortable lounge, an outdoor restaurant and secure parking.

New Victoria Hotel (☎ 2021067; Gor Mahia Rd; s with shared bathroom KSh600, s/tw/tr with private bathroom KSh850/1050/1550) Bright on the outside and gleaming green on the inside, this hotel has some good options. Rooms have fans, mosquito nets and comfy foam mattresses, while a few boast balconies with lake views.

Hotel Vunduba (☎ 2020043; Mosque Rd; s/tw/ste KSh800/1300/2500) Rooms in this place surround a sunny courtyard and offer good value. The singles are small but squeaky clean, while the twins are more sizable and comfy. The suites are perfect for families, and the courtyard is an ideal spot for weary vehicles to snooze.

New East View Hotel (☎ 0722-556721; Omolo Agar Rd; s/tw KSh1200/1600) Although less atmospheric than its neighbour, Hotel Palmers, this hotel's rooms offer more character. The bathrooms are rather aged.

Joy Guest House (☎ 0720-272037; Dunga; tw with shared bathroom KSh800, with private bathroom KSh1000) Located 3km south of town near Hippo Point's turn-off, this welcoming place has a homey feel. Cooking facilities, solid-rock sofas (sit slowly or risk a broken arse) and cramped rug-clad rooms, with fans and the odd balcony, call Joy's home. Sadly, prices don't include breakfast.

TOP END

Imperial Hotel (☎ 2022211; www.imperialkisumu.com; Jomo Kenyatta Hwy; s/d incl breakfast from US$75/85, ste US$175; ⚟ ▢ ⚞) Offering friendly 1st-class service, this old dame is Kisumu's most luxurious hotel. Full-length windows afford grand views and, if opened, heavenly breezes. Weekend rates are a bargain, and the Florence Restaurant is rated the best in town.

Nyanza Club (☎ 2022433; s/tw incl breakfast KSh2500/3000; ⚞) While this blindingly white option off Jomo Kenyatta Hwy is slightly past its prime, its leafy and sporty surrounds make for an entertaining stay. The rooms are huge and those upstairs have lovely shaded balconies with lake views. There is a plethora of activities available, but since they're strictly for members, you will have to become a temporary member (per day KSh100).

Eating

If you want an authentic local fish fry there is no better place than the dozen tin-shack restaurants siting on the lake's shore at the end of Oginga Odinga Rd. Open flames, a lot of smoke and boisterous locals all add to the experience. Dive in from 11am to 6pm and a 1.5kg fish will set you back KSh150.

Florence Restaurant (☎ 2022211; Jomo Kenyatta Hwy; mains KSh200-450) Housed within the glam Imperial Hotel, the Florence is renowned as Kisumu's best restaurant. The poached Nile perch is lovely, as are the chicken Kiev and mutton masala.

Kisumu Yacht Club (☎ 2022050; Dunga; meals KSh200-300) Sitting on the lake's edge, just past the Impala Sanctuary, is this fine choice with a lovely patio and teak furnishings. The menu ranges from delicately stuffed fish to Indian selections, such as chicken biryani, butter chicken and *palak paneer*. A temporary membership is necessary to indulge (KSh200).

Grill House (Swan Centre, Accra St; meals KSh100-450; ☯ Tue-Sun) Wicker and shady umbrellas sit street-side at this German-owned eatery. The menu is a bit of a cultural hotchpotch – the spring rolls are quite nice.

Hussein Pan House (Swan Centre, Accra St; meals KSh150-300; ☯ 6-11pm) Smoky stoves grace the pavement here each evening and pump out amazing Asian selections, like chicken tikka and mutton pilau. The boneless chicken *mushkati* is divine.

KENYA

KENYA

Mon Ami (Mega Plaza, Oginga Odinga Rd; meals KSh150-350) A favourite expat pit stop, with Western standards, such as hamburgers, pasta and pizza.

Vault Restaurant (meals KSh300-600) Pizza (with real cheese), pasta and even veal grace this Italian restaurant's menu. Housed in a former bank off Oginga Odinga Rd, the massive vault still lurks in the shadows.

Follow the local crowds and descend into the subdued interior of the brightly coloured New Victoria Hotel (p399) for a filling feed in the morning (meals KSh150 to KSh300).

Drinking & Entertainment

Kisumu's nightlife has a reputation for being even livelier than Nairobi's, but thanks to many of the best parties and live Congolese bands cropping up at various venues, such as the **Kimwa Grand** (Jomo Kenyatta Hwy), along the roads out of town, it's harder to find; check flyers and ask locals who are plugged into the scene.

Easy to find and always good for a drink, Mon Ami (above) is a lively bar with a pool table, welcoming expat crowd and satellite TV, which blasts European footy in the evenings.

Octopus Bottoms-Up Club (Ogada St) A short stroll from Oginga Odinga Rd, this popular bar has two pool tables, a foosball table, its own disco (admission KSh100) and more Michael Jackson posters than we're comfortable with. Women travelling alone may not find it the most appealing of places.

Getting There & Away

AIR

There are daily morning flights with **Kenya Airways** (☎ 2020081; Alpha House, Oginga Odinga Rd) to Nairobi (KSH7500, one hour), and an extra evening flight on Friday and Sunday. Hopefully the fact that its model Kenya Airways plane has lost its starboard engine won't put you off!

BUS & MATATU

Most buses, *matatus* and Peugeots to destinations within Kenya leave from the large bus and *matatu* station just north of the main market.

Matatus offer the only direct services to both Kakamega (KSh120, one hour) and Eldoret (KSh250, 2½ hours). Plenty of other *matatus* serve Busia (KSh250, two

hours), Kericho (KSh200, two hours), Kisii (KSh200, two hours), Homa Bay (KSh250, three hours), Nakuru (KSh300, 3½ hours), Nairobi (KSh550, 5½ hours) and Isebania (KSh350, four hours), on the Tanzanian border.

There are very few direct services to Kitale (KSh300, four hours); head to Kakamega or Eldoret and change there.

Akamba (off New Station Rd) has its own depot in the town's centre. Besides four daily buses to Nairobi (KSh500, seven hours) via Nakuru (KSh300, 4½ hours), there are daily services to Busia (KSh200, three hours) and Kampala (KSh750, seven hours). Easy Coach (off Mosque Rd) serves similar destinations with some added comfort and cost.

TRAIN

After being shut down for years, the train service to Nairobi (KSh1415/720 in 1st/2nd class, 13 hours) is once again on the roll. Trains are scheduled to depart on Sunday, Tuesday and Thursday at 6.30pm, though they usually leave late.

Getting Around

TO/FROM THE AIRPORT

A taxi is probably the easiest way to get into town from the airport, and should cost KSh500. Pipeline *matatus* (KSh20) pick up and drop off passengers outside the airport gate.

CAR

Your only option for a hire car is with **Pel Travels** (☎ 2022780; travels@pel.co.ke; Oginga Odinga Rd), which charges KSh4000 per day, including insurance. Excess is set at KSh35,000.

MATATU

Matatus 7 and 9 (KSh20), which run north along Oginga Odinga Rd before turning up Anaawa Ave and continuing east down Jomo Kenyatta Hwy, are handy to reach the main *matatu* station, main market and Kibuye Market – you can just wave an arm to stop them and hop on anywhere you see one.

TAXI

A taxi around town costs KSh100 to KSh200, while trips to Dunga or Kisumu Beach Resort range from KSh200 to KSh300.

AROUND LAKE VICTORIA
Homa Bay
☎ 059

This section of lakeshore, blanketed with green and dotted with intriguing, conical volcanic plugs (the plumbing of ancient volcanos exposed through erosion) makes for an interesting visit and a handy base for nearby attractions.

Climb nearby Mt Homa (one hour) for a panoramic vista, take in the bustling harbour or just wander the dusty streets to the Caribbean beats radiating from various *dukas*. It is also a great place to find tapes of traditional Luo music.

INFORMATION
The Co-operative Bank of Kenya exchanges US dollars, while Post Bank offers Western Union. The new Kenya Commercial Bank should be open by the time you read this. The post office has Internet and telephone services. The **warden's office** (☎ 22544) for Ruma National Park is found up the hill in the district commissioner's compound.

SLEEPING & EATING
Bay Lodge (☎ 22568; s with shared bathroom KSh250, s/tw with private bathroom KSh300/450) An aquamarine sanctuary of simplicity nestled between the bus station and the post office. It is tidy, quiet, has secure parking, and the staff are lovely and helpful.

Little Nile Guest House (☎ 0720-997718; s/tw incl breakfast KSh800/1200) On the hill leading into town, this shiny new option is bright, comfortable and houses colourful murals.

Ruma Tourist Lodge (☎ 0734-590868; s/d KSh600/900) Lurking behind a messy entrance, Ruma's bungalows offer comfy rooms and great bathrooms. Unfortunately the town's best bar, with cold beers, decent tunes, pool table and restaurant (meals KSh150 to KSh230), also lives here, so noise can be problematic. It is signposted behind the Total petrol station.

GETTING THERE & AWAY
Akamba's office is just down the hill from the bus station. Its buses serve Nairobi (KSh550, 8½ hours, 7am and 7.30pm) via Kericho (KSh300, four hours) and Nakuru (KSh450, six hours). Several other companies and *matatus* (operating from the bus station) also ply these routes, as well as Mbita

(KSh150, 1½ hours) and Kisumu (KSh250, three hours).

Ruma National Park
Bordered by the dramatic **Kanyamaa Escarpment**, and home to Kenya's only population of roans (one of Africa's rarest and largest antelopes), is the surprisingly seldom-visited **Ruma National Park** (adult/child US$15/5). While hot and often wet, it's beautiful, and comprises 120 sq km of verdant riverine woodland and savanna grassland within the Lambwe Valley.

Besides roan, other rarities like Bohor's reedbuck, Rothschild's giraffe, Jackson's hartebeest and the tiny oribi antelope can be seen. Birdlife is prolific, with 145 different bird species present, including the mighty fish eagle and white egret. Tsetse flies can be a problem after the rains.

The park is set up for those with vehicles, but contact the **warden** (☎ 059-22544; PO Box 420, Homa Bay) in Homa Bay and you may be able to organise a hike, though you will have to pay a ranger to accompany you (KSh500/1000 per half-/full day).

There are two simple **camp sites** (adult/child US$8/5) near the main gate, and the guesthouse will soon be rebuilt.

To get here, head south from Homa Bay and turn right onto the Mbita road. About 12km west is the main access road and from there it's another 11km. The park's roads are in decent shape, but require a 4WD in the rainy season.

Rusinga & Mfangano Islands
Set on the sandy shoreline of Lake Victoria and marking Winam Gulf's entrance is Mbita, a lonely village with a palpably warm frontier feel. A short causeway connects it to **Rusinga Island**, which is a great place for a day's wander – the craggy hill makes an attractive viewpoint. On the island's north side is **Tom Mboya's mausoleum**. A child of Rusinga and former sanitary inspector in Nairobi, Mboya was one of the few Luos ever to achieve any kind of political success in the government of Kenya, and was widely tipped to become Kenya's second president before he was assassinated in 1969. He's still well remembered today.

Mfangano Island, to the southwest, is also well worth a day or two, accommodating monitor lizards, curious locals, intriguing

KENYA

rock paintings and the imposing but assailable Mt Kwitutu (1694m). Thanks to a refreshing absence of vehicles, only footpaths crisscross the island – a guide is invaluable (KSh500 per day is fair).

It is about a 1½- to two-hour climb from the Sena village jetty to the sublime vista atop Kwitutu, on the southeastern side of the island. The rock paintings, both revered and feared by locals, are found northwest of Kwitutu towards the village of Ukula.

SLEEPING & EATING

Lake Victoria's Safari Village (☎ 0721-912120; www .safarikenya.net; s/d incl breakfast US$35/55) A Lake Victoria beachfront haven if there ever was one. Lovely traditionally thatched roofs tower over comfy beds and impressive bathrooms in each of the pretty cottages.

Mbuta Campsite (☎ 0722-617953; per tent KSh100) Located 2.5km south of Mbita, this grassy camp site is set on a small section of beach and is a perfect place to laze away a day or two. Look for the small camping sign en route to the well-signposted Lake Victoria's Safari Village.

Elk Guest House (s/tw with shared toilet KSh300/400, tw KSh600) Backing the bus stand in Mbita, this place will do perfectly for a night's kip. Besides being clean, it has mosquito nets and private showers.

Rusinga Island Club (bookings ☎ 020-340331; info@ letsgosafari.com; full board incl all activities s/d US$410/700) This is an exclusive place on the northern side of Rusinga Island. Fishing is the dominant activity, but if you're not a keen worm-dangler there are various water sports available and the birdlife is prolific.

Mfangano Island Camp (bookings ☎ 020-2734000; governors@reservation.com; full board s/d US$370/550; ☷ Jun-Mar) The only formal accommodation on Mafangano island. Built in traditional Luo style (albeit with modern amenities), this is primarily a fishing resort.

GETTING THERE & AWAY

Four daily buses run from Mbita to Kisumu (KSh200, five hours) each morning between 6am and 11am. *Matatus* to Homa Bay are far more frequent (KSh100, 1½ hours). The odd *matatu* heads to Rusinga Island and past the mausoleum (KSh50).

Until the ferries get their act together, sporadic 10m canoes are the only transport to Mfangano Island (per person KSh150)

from Mbita. If you don't want to wait for passengers, you will have to fork out KSh4000 for the entire boat.

WESTERN HIGHLANDS

Benefiting from reliable rainfall and fertile soil, the Western Highlands make up the agricultural heartland of Kenya, separating Kisumu and Lake Victoria from the rest of the country. The south is cash-crop country, with vast patchworks of tea plantations covering the region around Kisii and Kericho, while further north, near Kitale and Eldoret, insanely dense cultivation takes over.

The settlements here are predominantly agricultural service towns, with little of interest unless you need a chainsaw or water barrel. For visitors, the real attractions lie outside these places: the rolling tea fields around Kericho, the tropical beauty of Kakamega Forest, trekking on Mt Elgon, the prolific birdlife in Saiwa Swamp National Park and exploring the dramatic Cherangani Hills.

KISII

☎ 058

Whether inspired by nearby soils (some of the most fertile in Kenya) or by the growing non Bantu–speaking tribes around them (Maasai to the south, Luo to the west and north, and Kipsigis to the east), the Bantu-speaking Gusii people of this region are producing offspring at one of the world's fastest rates. An amazing 50% of the 1.5 million Gusii are below the age of 15! With all those new mouths to feed, the rapidly expanding town of Kisii is bursting with activity.

Besides being the region's transport hub and hosting a variety of facilities, this hilly city has little to offer travellers besides muddy, rubbish-laden streets, noise and an entertaining nightlife (its saving grace).

While the fêted Kisii soapstone does obviously come from this area, it's not on sale here. Quarrying and carving go on in the village of **Tabaka**, 23km northwest of Kisii, where you can usually visit the workshops. Since most carvings are sold to dealers and shops in Nairobi at rock-bottom prices, they'll happily accept a fair price from you.

Information

Barclays Bank (Moi Hwy)
Cyber Cafe (Hospital Rd; per hr KSh90)

Postbank (Hospital Rd) Western Union services.
Post office (Moi Hwy)

Sleeping & Eating

Kisii Hotel (☎ 30254; off Moi Hwy; s/tw incl breakfast KSh750/950) Double the price, but triple the pleasure. This is a relaxed place with large gardens and sizable rooms, each with decent bathrooms. The restaurant (meals KSh150 to KSh300) is deservedly popular.

Mwalimu Hotel (Moi Hwy; d/ste KSh800/1500) Set in its own compound opposite the Mobile petrol station at the southeastern end of town, this hotel isn't atmospheric but provides good value and secure parking. The rooms are bright, average sized and have mosquito nets. The hotel has a popular bar and terrace, as well as a restaurant (meals KSh80 to KSh230) that serves a mix of Kenyan, Western and Indian dishes.

Sabrina Lodge (s/tw with shared bathroom KSh300/ 500) Just up from Postbank, Sabrina has clean, concrete Santa specials, with rooms boasting red floors and bright green walls. The toilets (missing seats) are clean enough, but there is no running water. Hot bucket showers are available in the morning. The beds aren't great, but they do have mosquito nets.

Zonic Hotel (☎ 30298; Hospital Rd; s/d US$25/40, ste from US$65; 🖳) Although bizarre, Zonic is home to the town's most comfortable rooms, each large, clean and sporting a balcony. There is a rooftop swimming pool and a cavernous restaurant (meals KSh250 to KSh350), which produces some tasty Asian curries and a good beef tenderloin.

Blues Restaurant (Hospital Rd; meals KSh150-250) Feeling more like a modern pub, this friendly restaurant cooks up some great Chinese stir-fries, complete with fresh ginger. The chicken stew isn't bad either.

Kawanji's Cafe (Ogemba Rd; meals KSh120-180) Lurking behind a wall of foliage, this pleasant restaurant serves the best Kenyan dishes in Kisii.

Drinking & Entertainment

To compensate for its other shortcomings, Kisii has plenty of evening venues and some of the cheapest beer around (KSh60 for a large Tusker).

Blues Restaurant (Hospital Rd) A good spot for a beer, with a balcony overlooking the market and proper cable TV to catch up on the world outside.

Jazz Pub (Hospital Rd) A similar crowd (Kenyan yuppies) to Blues, this place has a warm vibe and an odd absence of jazz music.

Pub dotCom (Ogemba Rd) Reggae cuts radiate through this tiny, welcoming bar.

Satellite Bar (Sansora Rd) Rain doesn't even seem to dampen the late night spirits at this rooftop bar. Thankfully there is a shelter over the pool table.

Club Backyard (Hospital Rd) The best nightclub in town, this place gets packed Friday and Saturday nights. It usually hosts well-known DJs; look for posters throughout town.

Getting There & Away

Matatus line the length of Moi Hwy; look for the destination placards on their roofs. Regular departures serve Homa Bay (KSh100, one hour), Kisumu (KSh200, two hours), Kericho (KSh180, two hours) and Isebania (KSh150, 1¾ hours) on the Tanzanian border.

Tabaka *matatus* leave from the Victoria Cafe, while local *matatus* (and additional Kericho services) leave from the stand at the end of Sansora Rd.

Akamba (Moi Hwy) has a daily bus to Nairobi (KSh550, eight hours) via Nakuru (KSh290, 5½ hours) departing at 7.30am; it's wise to book a day in advance. International bus departures for Mwanza in Tanzania also leave from here.

KERICHO

☎ 052
In comparison to Kisii, Kericho is a haven of tranquillity. Its surrounds are blanketed by an undulating patchwork of manicured tea plantations, each seemingly hemmed in by distant stands of evergreens. While there is little to do in Kericho, it's a pleasant place to wander among the shade cast by leafy trees.

There is little doubt why Kericho is the tea capital of western Kenya: the soil is perfect, the climate consistent and afternoon rain falls almost daily. Luckily these downpours are generally too brief to be a nuisance, and the atmosphere is cool enough to keep it fresh instead of humid.

Settlers attribute the town's name to John Kerich, a herbalist and early tea planter who lived here at the turn of the 20th century, while locals believe it's derived from the Maasai chief Ole Kericho, killed here by the Gusii during an 18th-century territorial battle. Who's right is anyone's guess.

KENYA

KERICHO

INFORMATION
Aga Khan Satellite Laboratory..1 D1
Barclays Bank........................2 C3
Kenya Commercial Bank..........3 C2
Post Office...........................4 C2
Standard Chartered Bank.........5 C3
Telecare Centre.....................6 C3

SIGHTS & ACTIVITIES
Gurudwara............................7 B3

SLEEPING
Mwalimu..............................8 C2
New Sunshine Hotel................9 B2
Tea Hotel.............................10 D1

EATING
Chai Supermarket...................11 B2
Ripples Pub & Restaurant.........12 D1
Sunshine Hotel......................13 B2

TRANSPORT
Bus & Matatu Stand................14 C1
Buses.................................15 C3
Buses to Kisumu, Kisii &
    Homa Bay........................16 C3
Caltex Petrol Station...........(see 15)

Information

The Tea Hotel has Internet access for KSh1200 per hour.

Aga Khan Satellite Laboratory (Moi Hwy) Malaria and other blood tests.

Barclays Bank (Moi Hwy)

Kenya Commercial Bank (Moi Hwy)

Post office (Moi Hwy)

Standard Chartered Bank (Moi Hwy)

Tea Hotel (Moi Hwy; per hr KSh1200) Internet access.

Sights & Activities

Organised **tea plantation tours** are surprisingly uncommon in Kericho, but if you ask at Kimugu River Lodge it can usually set something up. The Tea Hotel can do the same, although you will pay through the nose.

If you're only interested in seeing the fields up close, it's an easy walk to the nearest plantation, which sits behind the Tea Hotel. Head through the hotel grounds and follow the path out the back gate, which leads through the tea bushes to the hotel workers' huts. If you're lucky, there may be picking in progress. You can also arrange hikes through tea estates and **guided river walks** at Kimugu River Lodge.

Africa's largest **Gurudwara** (Sikh place of worship) is found on Hospital Rd.

Sleeping & Eating

New Sunshine Hotel (☎ 30037; Tengecha Rd; s/tw/d KSh600/900/1000) Boasting faux-wood paintwork that's almost funny enough to be charming, this place is worth a look. A bamboo roof and cheesy artificial waterfall grace the restaurant (meals KSh80 to KSh190), which serves Western snacks, sandwiches and burgers.

Mwalimu (☎ 30656; Moi Rd; s/tw KSh400/550) A secure place for a night's kip. The rooms are much brighter than the gloomy corridors and host soft foam mattresses. The bathrooms are dark and dreary, but hot water flows in the morning and evening.

Kimugu River Lodge (☎ 0733-504942; camping KSh150; s/d/tr from KSh1000/1500/2000) Set off Moi Hwy on the scenic bank of the Kimugi River, which runs behind the Tea Hotel, this lodge is a good option for campers (if you can handle cold showers). Unfortunately, the *bandas* are unreasonably expensive. Enjoy the bar and devour a spicy south Asian meal at the restaurant (meals KSh160 to KSh300).

Tea Hotel (☎ 30004; teahotel@africaonline.co.ke; Moi Hwy; camping KSh300, s/d US$60/84, ste US$102-108; ☒) Glorious gardens envelop this grand property, built in the 1950s by the Brooke Bond company. Ask for a room in the stone cottages – they've aged more gracefully than the hotel rooms and cost not a penny more. All rooms have TVs, fireplaces and dated bathrooms.

Ripples Pub & Restaurant (Moi Hwy; meals KSh130-350; ☒ Tue-Sun) Despite being part of the Kobil petrol station, it's definitely Kericho's most colourful restaurant. There is a good range of pizza, sandwiches and Indian dishes, like spicy chicken tikka.

Sunshine Hotel (Kenyatta Rd; meals KSh60-160) Locals pile in to devour fried *tilapia* (its specialty) and other Kenyan selections.

Chai Supermarket (Kenyatta Rd) Perfect for self-caterers to stock up.

Getting There & Away

While most buses and *matatus* use the main stand in the town's northwest corner, many also pick up passengers on the Moi Hwy near the Caltex petrol station. Buses to Nairobi (KSh450, 4½ hours) are frequent, as are *matatus* to Kisumu (KSh150, two hours), Kisii (KSh180, two hours), Eldoret (KSh250, 3½ hours) and Nakuru (KSh200, two hours).

KAKAMEGA
☎ 056

This small but busy town is spread out along the A1 Hwy north of Kisumu. There is no real reason to stay here, but if you arrive late in the day it can be convenient to sleep over and stock up with supplies before heading to nearby Kakamega Forest Reserve, one of western Kenya's star attractions. The region is part of the traditional Bungoma district (see the boxed text, below) and home to the Luyha people, who are quite Westernised and unobtrusive as a community.

Information
Barclays Bank (A1 Hwy)
Kenya Commercial Bank (Kenyatta Ave)
KWS Area Headquarters (☎ 30603; PO Box 88, Kakamega) Kakamega Forest information.
Post office (A1 Hwy)
Telkom Kenya (A1 Hwy) Calling cards and cardphones.

Sights & Activities

Perched on a ridge south of town is the **Crying Stone of Ilesi**, a local curiosity that has become a regional emblem. The formation, looking like a solemn head resting on weary shoulders, consists of a large boulder balanced atop an 8m column of rock. While legend has it that tears never stop flowing down its length, it was dry during our visit – perhaps it was just happy to see us! Still, stains from years of eerie weeping are evident and it's worth a look. Maybe it won't be so happy to see you...

THE KINDEST CUT

The Bungoma/Trans-Nzoia district goes wild in August with the sights and sounds of the **Bukusu Circumcision Festival**, an annual jamboree dedicated to the initiation of young boys into manhood.

The tradition was apparently passed to the Bukusu by the Sabaot tribe in the 1800s, when a young hunter cut the head off a troublesome serpent to earn the coveted operation (too symbolic to be true?). The evening before the ceremony is devoted to substance abuse and sex; in the morning the fortunate youngsters are trimmed with a traditional knife in front of their entire village.

Unsurprisingly, this practice has attracted a certain amount of controversy in recent years. Health concerns are prevalent, as the same knife can be used for up to 10 boys, posing a risk of AIDS and other infections. The associated debauchery also brings a seasonal rush of underage pregnancies and family rifts that seriously affect local communities.

Education and experience now mean that fewer boys undergo the old method, preferring to take the safe option at local hospitals. However, those wielding the knife are less likely to let go of their heritage. To quote a prominent circumciser: 'Every year at this time it's like a fever grips me, and I can't rest until I've cut a boy'. It seems that in Bukusuland some traditions die hard.

Sleeping & Eating

Bendera Hotel (Sudi Rd; d KSh350) Consistently the best budget hotel in town. It was closed for renovations during our visit, so it should be better than ever when you arrive.

Golf Hotel (☎ 30150; Khasakhala Rd; s/d incl breakfast US$60/75; ☒) While the large rooms, each with a balcony and garden view (some even glimpse Mt Elgon), are bright and pleasant, this hotel is seriously overpriced. On a positive note, readers rave about the swimming pool and fish dishes in the restaurant (meals KSh180 to KSh350).

Snack Stop Cafe (Cannon Awori Rd; meals KSh65-130) The restaurant of choice for most locals, offering simple Kenyan standards, including *ugali wimbi* (sorghum porridge, reputed to slow ageing).

Getting There & Around

Easy Coach (off Kenyatta Ave) serves Kisumu (KSh150, one hour), and has early morning and evening buses to Nairobi (KSh650, 7½ hours) via Nakuru (KSh450, five hours). Nearby, Akamba (off Kenyatta Ave) has one evening bus to Nairobi (KSh600, 8pm).

Behind the Total petrol station on the town's northern edge, *matatus* leave for Kisumu (KSh120, one hour), Kitale (KSh190, 2½ hours) and Eldoret (KSh180, 2½ hours).

KAKAMEGA FOREST RESERVE

☎ 056

This superb small slab of virgin tropical rainforest is the only Kenyan vestige of the unique and once mighty Guineo-Congolian forest ecosystem. It is so wild here trees actually kill each other – really! Parasitic fig trees grow on top of unsuspecting trees and actually strangle their hosts to death. Potential victims include the lovely Elgon teak.

Less murderous and more exciting is the forest's array of wildlife. An astounding 330 species of birds, including casqued hornbill, Ross's turaco and great blue turaco, have been spotted here. During darkness hammerheaded fruit bats and flying squirrels take to the air. The best viewing months are June, August and October, when many migrant species arrive. The wildflowers are also wonderful in October, supporting around 400 species of butterfly.

Dancing in the canopy are no less than seven different primate species, including the exceedingly rare De Brazza's monkey,

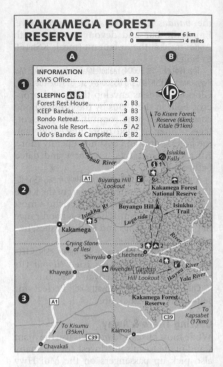

the red-tailed monkey, blue monkey, and thumbless black and white colobus.

The northern section of the forest around Buyangu is more accessible and comprises the **Kakamega Forest National Reserve** (adult/child US$10/5, vehicle KSh300). Maintained by the KWS, this area has a variety of habitats but is generally very dense, with considerable areas of primary forest and regenerating secondary forest; there is a total ban on grazing, wood collection and cultivation in this zone. Isolated a few kilometres north, but still part of this reserve, is the small **Kisere Forest Reserve**. An excellent guide to the forest is available at the KWS office (KSh300) and Rondo Retreat (KSh500).

The southern section, centred around Isecheno, forms the **Kakamega Forest Reserve** and is looked after by the Forest Department. This region supports several communities, and is under considerable pressure from farming and illegal logging.

Tribal practices in the forest persist: *mugumu* trees are considered sacred, circumcisions are sometimes performed in the forest, and bullfights are still held on Sunday in

Khayega and Shinyalu. Intervillage wrestling also used to be common, but was eventually banned, as the prize (the victor's pick of the young women present) tended to provoke more fights than the match itself.

Sights & Activities

The best way to appreciate the forest is to walk, and trails radiate from Buyangu and Isecheno areas. It is possible to drive, but the roads are pretty tough going, and the engine noise will scare off any wildlife nearby as well as annoying everyone else present.

Official **guides** (per person for short/long walk KSh200/600), trained by the Kakamega Biodiversity Conservation and Tour Operators Association, are well worth the money. Not only do they prevent you from getting lost (many of the trail signs are missing), but most are excellent naturalists who can recognise birds by call alone and provide information about numerous animals.

Rangers state that trails vary in length from 1km to 7km, but the enjoyable **Isiukhu Trail**, which connects Isecheno to **Isiukhu Falls**, seems much longer. Short walks to **Buyangu Hill** in the north or **Lirhanda Hill** in the south for sunrise or sunset are highly recommended. As ever the early morning and late afternoon are the best times to view birds, but night walks can also be a fantastic experience.

Sleeping & Eating

Udo's Bandas & Campsite (☎ 30603; PO Box 879, Kakamega; camping adult/child US$8/5, bandas per person US$10) Named after Udo Savalli, a well-known ornithologist, this place is run by KWS. It is a tidy, well-maintained camp site with seven simple thatched *bandas*; mosquito nets are provided, but you will need your own sleeping bag and other supplies. There are long-drop toilets, bucket showers, and a communal cooking and dining shelter.

KEEP Bandas (keeporg@yahoo.com; s/tw KSh500/1000) Opened in May 2005 by the Kakamega Environmental Education Programme, these *bandas* are a more comfortable option than the rest house and have more facilities, including a nice dining area.

Forest Rest House (☎ 30603; PO Box 88, Kakamega; camping KSh150, s/tw KSh350/700) Beds are housed in four rudimentary twin rooms, while bare-bones bathrooms (no hot water) are in a rickety stilted wooden building that looks directly out over the forest. You will need your own sleeping bag, food and preferably something to cook on. You can get basic supplies from the *dukas* about 2km back towards Shinyalu.

Rondo Retreat (☎ 30268; tfrondo@multitechweb.com; full board s/tw KSh9000/11,600) Originally built as a sawmiller's residence in the 1920s, this charming choice is about 3km east of Isecheno. Seven cottages, each with striking traditional fittings and large verandas, sit in gorgeous gardens through which plenty of wildlife passes. The main house oozes atmosphere (ask for Bob & Betty's room), though some of its rooms share a bathroom.

Savona Isle Resort (☎ 31095; d/tw/tr KSh1500/1500/5000; ☒) This resort is too far from the forest to make a walking base, but is a fine option if you have a car. Rooms are in slightly aged thatched *bandas*, each with a balcony backing onto the bamboo-lined river. Meals (KSh200 to KSh400) are available in the atmospheric restaurant.

Getting There & Away

Matatus heading north towards Kitale can drop you at the access road for the main Buyangu area of the reserve, about 18km north of Kakamega town (KSh50). It is a well signposted 2km walk from there to the park office and Udo's. Regular *matatus* link Kakamega with Shinyalu (KSh60), but few continue to Isecheno. Shinyalu is also accessed by rare *matatu* service from Khayega. Odd vehicles ferry between Shinyalu and Isecheno (KSh30 to KSh60).

The improved roads are still treacherous after rain and you may prefer to walk once you've seen the trouble vehicles have. To Shinyalu it's about 7km from Khayega and 10km from Kakamega. From Shinyalu it is 5km to Isecheno.

ELDORET

☎ 053

Mmmmm...cheese! While the pull of a fine Gouda, Gruyère, Stilton, Brie or Cheddar can vary depending on how long you've been on your African safari, a stop in Eldoret is a must for all cheese lovers.

Dairy haters and the lactose-intolerant will find little else in this large service town besides banking facilities and a good night's sleep before venturing into the nearby Kerio Valley and Kamnarok National Reserves.

EDUCATION FOR ALL!

After the 2002 elections the new government managed to create a long-awaited provision guaranteeing free primary education for all Kenyans, a move applauded by parents across the nation. One great-grandfather by the name of Kimani Nganga Maruge clapped a little louder than most.

On the first day of class this cane-wielding knobbly kneed 84-year-old, dressed in school uniform – shorts, knee socks and all – was right there with the kids, sitting in the front row (he is hard of hearing, after all). What ran through the teacher's mind is anyone's guess!

Mr Maruge was there to start collecting his long-overdue education, and wouldn't let anyone say otherwise. Besides basic maths, he was keen on learning to read. This would allow him to study the Bible and confirm his suspicions that his local preacher wasn't actually following it!

Not only does Mr Maruge continue to attend classes in the Eldoret area, but he's also been made prefect and his teacher is said to rave about his influence over the students. The venerable scholar is also a fast learner and has some of the top marks in his class. Perhaps he's being tutored by his grandchildren, who attend the same school.

President Moi hailed from the area, and during his presidency the city controversially received many beneficial developments, such as Moi University and the international airport. Simultaneous construction of a munitions factory next to the airport also raised many eyebrows – critics wondered what exports were intended.

Information

Barclays Bank (Uganda Rd)
Cyber Hawk Internet Café (Nandi Arcade, Nandi Rd; per hr KSh60)
Eldoret Hospital Off Uganda Rd. One of Kenya's best hospitals, with 24-hour emergency service.
Kenya Commercial Bank (Kenyatta St)
Post office (Uganda Rd)
Safari Forex Bureau (KVDA Plaza, Oloo Rd) Exchanges cash and travellers cheques (no commission). Western Union services.
Standard Chartered Bank (Uganda Rd)
Telkom Kenya (cnr Kenyatta & Elijaa Cheruhota Sts)

Sights

An odd but tasty attraction, the **Dorinyo Lessos Creameries Cheese Factory** (Kenyatta St; ☺ 8am-6pm) produces over 30 different types of cheese. You can taste most for free and the average price is KSh500 per kilogram, with a minimum purchase of 250g. The company also makes yummy ice cream (KSh23 for 100ml).

Sleeping

BUDGET

New Lincoln Hotel (☎ 0723-676699; Oloo Rd; s/d KSh600/800) The most comfortable of the budget options, this pleasant place has decent rooms spread around its courtyard. The bathrooms and hot-water plumbing are slightly disfigured but seem to do the job.

Mountain View Hotel (☎ 0720-486613; Uganda Rd; s/tw KSh450/550) While a little noisy and small, these bright clean rooms have mosquito nets, reasonable bathrooms and balconies, complete with potted plants. Taking a cell-like inside-facing single without a balcony only saves 50 bob. Security is distinctly prisonlike (you have to be let out as well as in). It also has a respectable terrace bar and restaurant.

Naiberi River Campsite (☎ 2063047; campsite@ africaonline.co.ke; camping KSh250, dm KSh500, cabins KSh1200; ☐) This place, 22km southeast of town on the C54 to Kaptagat, is your best option for camping, as it has tonnes of facilities, although it is very popular with overland companies. Phone for directions.

Aya Inn (Oginga Odinga St; s/tw incl breakfast KSh500/1000) With clean rooms, large beds (somewhat saggy), hot-water showers and a courtyard for vehicles, this place is a reasonable option. There are some cheaper singles (KSh400) with shared bathrooms.

MIDRANGE

Eldoret Wagon Hotel (☎ 2062270; Oloo Rd; s/d incl breakfast KSh1550/2250) This option has a certain amount of colonial charm. It is overpriced, but retains some suitably eccentric memorabilia, and there is a casino to make you feel like a high roller.

White Castle Motel (☎ 2033095; Uganda Rd; s/d KSh850/1550) Lonely beds sit strangely away from all the walls in these sizable austere rooms. Some rooms have decent views and all have aged but clean bathrooms. The expensive special singles are not worth the money.

ELDORET

```
0                    700 m
0                    0.4 miles
```

INFORMATION
Barclays Bank 1 C3
Cyber Hawk Internet Café.........2 B4
Eldoret Hospital 3 D3
Kenya Commercial Bank............4 C3
Post Office 5 A2
Safari Forex Bureau 6 C3
Standard Chartered Bank 7 C3
Telkom Kenya 8 C3

SIGHTS & ACTIVITIES
Dorinyo Lessos Creameries Cheese
  Factory...................................9 B4

SLEEPING
Asis Hotel 10 A3
Aya Inn 11 C4
Eldoret Wagon Hotel 12 C2
Mountain View Hotel 13 A2

New Lincoln Hotel 14 B4
Sirikwa Hotel..............................15 C2
White Castle Motel....................16 B3

EATING
Golden Dragon Restaurant 17 B4
Sizzlers Cafe 18 B4
Will's Pub & Restaurant............19 B3

DRINKING
Shakers.......................................20 C4
Will's Pub ....(see 19)

ENTERTAINMENT
Club Opera..................................21 B4

TRANSPORT
Bus & Matatu Stand...................22 B3
Eldoret Travel Agency 23 B4
Local Matatus.............................24 C4
Matatus to Iten & Kabarnet.....25 C3
Matatus to Malaba.....................26 B2

KENYA

Asis Hotel (☎ 2061807; Kimathi Ave; s/tw incl breakfast KSh750/1250) Alone on the west side of town, this conference-class place is very clean and comfortable. From some rooms farsighted guests will enjoy countryside views, while nearsighted guests will glare at the litter outside.

TOP END
Sirikwa Hotel (☎ 2063614; hotelsirikwa@multitechweb .com; Elgeyo Rd; s/tw incl breakfast KSh4000/5000, ste from KSh8500; 🏊) This is Eldoret's only top-end hotel and boasts a long list of facilities, including a lovely swimming pool and beautiful terrace. Hopefully planned renovations won't touch the suites, which scream '70s velvet chic.

Eating

Slide onto Sirikwa Hotel's grand terrace and sample some sumptuous selections. Local well-to-do's rave about the marinated lamb and chicken curry (KSh250 to KSh400).

Will's Pub & Restaurant (Uganda Rd; meals KSh200-450) The burgers and shoestring fries will leave you smiling. Thanks to the fried fish and lamb stew also being justifiably popular, tables come at a premium.

Golden Dragon Restaurant (Kenyatta St; meals KSh300-400; ☽ Wed-Mon) A tad pricey, but Chinese food will give your taste buds something new to sing about.

Sizzlers Cafe (Kenyatta St; meals KSh100-235) Grab a curry and get stuffed for minimal coinage at this undeniable favourite.

Drinking & Entertainment

Shakers (Oginga Odinga Rd) An atmospheric, albeit isolated (take a taxi) place just waiting for introductions... Arse, meet wicker. Eyes, meet European footy. Beer, meet throat.

Will's Pub (Uganda Rd) A tame but lively place for a cold drink or three. It is a friendly spot for female travellers.

Club Opera (Kenyatta St) Day-Glo paint, black lights and occasional live bands grace this raucous nightclub.

Getting There & Away

AIR
There are daily flights between Eldoret and Nairobi (KSh5700, one hour) with the little-known Aero Kenya. Bookings are handled by **Eldoret Travel Agency** (☎ 2062707; Kenyatta St).

BUS & MATATU
The main bus and *matatu* stand is in the centre of town, by the market. Regular *matatus/* Peugeots serve Kitale (KSh150/200, 1¼ hours), Kisumu (KSh250/300, 2½ hours), Kericho (KSh250/300, 3½ hours), Nakuru (KSh200/400, 2¾ hours) and Nairobi (KSh400/700, six hours). Buses duplicate these routes.

Local *matatus* and more Kericho services leave from Nandi Rd. Irregular *matatus* to Iten and Kabarnet leave opposite Paradise Bar on Uganda Rd. Further west on Uganda Rd, *matatus* leave for Malaba (KSh300, 2½ hours) on the Uganda border.

Akamba (Moi St) buses to Nairobi (KSh500, 10.30am and 9pm) via Nakuru (KSh250) leave from its depot. There is also a noon (KSh1000, six hours) and a midnight (KSh1150) service to Kampala.

Getting Around
A *matatu* from the airport costs KSh50, and a taxi will cost KSh1000. *Boda-bodas* are rare, though some linger near the bus stand.

LAKE KAMNAROK & KERIO VALLEY NATIONAL RESERVES

These two little-visited national reserves lie in the heart of the beautiful Kerio Valley, sandwiched between the **Cherangani Hills** and the **Tugen Hills**, and are divided by the Kerio River. Prolific birdlife, crocodiles, wonderful landscapes and the chance to get totally off the beaten track are the main attractions.

Lake Kamnarok, on the river's eastern side, is the most accessible of the two reserves,

although there are absolutely no facilities. Bush camping is possible by the lake and no park fees are currently being charged by the KWS. At present you can walk anywhere on foot, but it is best to ask rangers and locals if there have been any recent wild dog attacks in the area.

It is possible to cross into Kerio Valley National Reserve from Kamnarok during the dry season, but you will have to wade across the river north of the lake. To the south of the reserve is the beautiful **Cheploch Gorge**.

The rest of the Kerio Valley begs to be explored and there is still talk of two other national reserves being created: one around Kapkut (2799m), a beautiful mountain close to Eldama Ravine, and another in the Tugen Hills.

To reach Lake Kamnarok, head 25km north up the rough dirt track from the village of Cheploch, which sits just east of the Kerio River on the Kabarnet–Iten road. A 4WD is required in the dry season – don't even think about it during the rains.

CHERANGANI HILLS
Northeast of Kitale and forming the western wall of the spectacular **Elgeyo Escarpment** are the Cherangani Hills. This high plateau has a distinctly pastoral feel, with thatched huts, patchwork *shambas* (plots of land) and wide rolling meadows cut by babbling brooks. You could easily spend weeks exploring here and never come across a single tourist.

You won't be alone though, as the plateau is home to the interesting Marakwet people (part of the greater Kalenjin grouping), who migrated here from the north. They settled here because the area was secure, and the consistent rainfall and streams were ideal for agriculture.

There are a couple of great five-day **treks**, namely from Kabichbich to Chesengoch and Kapcherop to Sigor. These two treks are both detailed in Lonely Planet's *Trekking in East Africa*. Sirikwa Safaris (p412) and Marich Pass Field Studies Centre (p430) can both arrange rewarding day and multiday treks in the region.

Kabichbich is best accessed from Kapenguria on a *matatu* (KSh100, 1¼ hours), while Kapcherop is accessible from Kitale with some patience and a *matatu* change in Cherangani.

KITALE
☎ 054

Kitale is considerably smaller than its nearest neighbour Eldoret and has more of an agricultural feel, although there are more street kids than in most normal service towns. Although it has an interesting museum, Kitale's main function for travellers is as a base for explorations further afield – Mt Elgon and Saiwa Swamp National Parks – and a take-off point for a trip up to the western side of Lake Turkana. As such, Kitale is a pleasant enough town and can be an enjoyable place to pass through.

Information

Barclays Bank (Bank St)

Mt Elgon Northwest Ecotourism (Menowecto; ☎ 30996; Kitale Museum, A1 Hwy) Nonprofit organisation providing tourist information.

MultiTech (Askari Rd; per hr KSh60)

Post office (Post Office Rd)

Standard Chartered Bank (Bank St)

Telkom Kenya (Post Office Rd)

Western Union (Askari Rd) Money transfer services.

Sights & Activities

The **Kitale Museum** (☎ 30996; A1 Hwy; adult/child KSh200/20; ☉ 8am-6pm) was founded on the collection of butterflies, birds and ethnographic memorabilia left to the nation in 1967 by the late Lieutenant Colonel Stoneham. The more recent ethnographic displays of the Pokot, Akamba, Marakwet and Turkana peoples are a bit more interesting than the rows of dead things (although the stuffed cheetah is comical). The outdoor exhibits include some traditional tribal homesteads, as well as the inevitable snakes, crocodiles and tortoises, plus an interesting 'Hutchinson Biogas Unit'.

The best thing here is the small **nature trail** that leads through virgin rainforest at the back of the museum and links with the arboretum of the Olaf Palme Agroforestry Centre. The forest is teeming with birdlife, insects, and the odd colubus monkey.

Next to the museum along the highway is the **Olaf Palme Agroforestry Centre** (A1 Hwy; admission free; ☉ 8am-5pm), a Swedish-funded program aimed at educating local people about protection and rehabilitation of the environment by integrating trees into farming systems. The project includes a small demonstration farm and agroforestry plot,

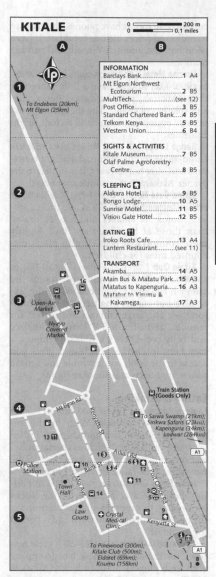

KITALE

0 — 200 m
0 — 0.1 miles

INFORMATION	
Barclays Bank	1 A4
Mt Elgon Northwest Ecotourism	2 B5
MultiTech	(see 12)
Post Office	3 B5
Standard Chartered Bank	4 B5
Telkom Kenya	5 B5
Western Union	6 B4

SIGHTS & ACTIVITIES	
Kitale Museum	7 B5
Olaf Palme Agroforestry Centre	8 B5

SLEEPING ⌂	
Alakara Hotel	9 B5
Bongo Lodge	10 A5
Sunrise Motel	11 B5
Vision Gate Hotel	12 B5

EATING 🍴	
Iroko Roots Cafe	13 A4
Lantern Restaurant	(see 11)

TRANSPORT	
Akamba	14 A5
Main Bus & Matatu Park	15 A3
Matatus to Kapenguria	16 A3
Matatur to Kisumu & Kakamega	17 A3

an information centre and an arboretum containing 46 rare species of indigenous trees; it's well worth a visit.

Sleeping

Alakara Hotel (☎ 31554; Kenyatta St; s with shared bathroom KSh500, s/tw/d with private bathroom KSh700/1000/1500) This is about the best value in town. The comfortable rooms have phones, the staff are friendly and prices include breakfast. It has a good bar, restaurant, TV room and parking facilities.

Sunrise Motel (☎ 31841; Kenyatta St; s KSh700-850, tw KSh900-1000) Rooms have a little more flair than Alakara's, with hardwood floors, rugs and splashes of colour. The slightly more expensive options are larger and include bright balconies.

Bongo Lodge (☎ 30972; Moi Ave; s/tw KSh500/600) Good-value rooms surround a bright courtyard and offer hot showers. It is similar to the pricier Alakara, but is a little more aged.

Vision Gate Hotel (☎ 0734-894177; Askari Rd; s/d incl breakfast from KSh1000/1250) While these spotless rooms are smaller and less decorated than those at Sunrise, they have slightly more comfortable beds. It also offers discounted rates for children.

Kitale Club (☎ 31330; A1 Hwy; s KSh1200-2700, tw KSh2000-3700; ⚑) The 'standard' rooms are rather bland and overpriced, while the 'executive' options are brighter and more comfortable. The large cottages are perfect for families, and offer a TV lounge, fireplace and baby cot. There's a KSh500 temporary membership charge, which also gives you access to the pool, sauna, tennis and squash courts, and darts and snooker rooms.

Eating & Drinking

Lantern Restaurant (Sunrise Motel, Kenyatta St; meals KSh190-300; ☽ 6pm-midnight) With meals ranging from English fish and chips to Indian specialties and some delicious vegetarian selections, this is *the* place to eat. The cocktail bar adds to the fantastic atmosphere.

Iroko Roots Cafe (Moi Ave; meals KSh50-110) Feeling more like a coffee shop in the Rocky Mountains, this spotless, unique place serves the best Kenyan dishes in town and is perfect for breakfast.

Pinewood (A1 Hwy; meals KSh180-480) A great new place for Indian or Chinese fare (complete with fresh ginger). Sit outside with views of Mt Elgon or head inside to the plethora of pine. The pub here is also great.

Getting There & Away

Matatus, buses and Peugeots are grouped by destination in and around the chaotic main bus and *matatu* park. Regular *matatus* run to Endebess (KSh70, 45 minutes), Kapenguria (KSh80, 45 minutes), Eldoret (KSh150,

1¼ hours) and Kakamega (KSh180, two hours). Less regular services reach Mt Elgon National Park (KSh80, one hour), Nakuru (KSh350, 3½ hours) and Kisumu (KSh300, four hours).

Most bus companies have offices around the bus station and serve Eldoret (KSh150, one hour), Nakuru (KSh350, 3½ hours) and Nairobi (KSh500, six hours). Akamba's buses leave for Nairobi at 9am (KSh550) and 9pm (KSh600) from its office on Moi Ave.

Several buses now run up to Lodwar (KSh700, 8½ hours) each day.

SAIWA SWAMP NATIONAL PARK

This **park** (adult/child US$15/5) northeast of Kitale is a delight. Originally set up to preserve the habitat of the *nzohe* (sitatunga antelope), the 3-sq-km reserve is home to blue, vervet and De Brazza's monkeys, and some 370 species of birds. The fluffy black and white colobus monkey and the impressive crowned crane are both present, and you may see the Cape clawless and spot-throated otters.

The best part is that this pint-sized park is only accessible on foot. Marked walking trails skirt the swamp, duckboards go right across it and there are some extremely rickety observation towers (number four is the best placed). For an eyeful, come first thing in the morning.

Thanks to a new and energetic warden Saiwa Swamp is seeing better days. A new perimeter fence is protecting the sought-after trees, and rangers are working to protect wild sage (sitatunga's typical food) from the suffocating growth of tall grasses that have blossomed thanks to fertilizers from nearby fields. Education programs are also having success encouraging local people to get involved in the protection of the park.

Sleeping

Sirikwa Safaris (☎ 0733-793524; camping KSh415, s/d tent KSh1240/1650, farmhouse with shared bathroom s/d KSh2750/3850) Owned and run by the family that started Saiwa, Sirikwa Safaris is a treasure-trove of information and activities. While camping costs are typical, the basic furnished tents and two cosy farmhouse rooms are pretty steep for what you get. Various excursions can be arranged from here, including ornithological tours of the Cherangani Hills and Saiwa Swamp (bird guides KSh825 per half-day).

Getting There & Away

The park is 18km northeast of Kitale; take a *matatu* towards Kapenguria (KSh60, 30 minutes) and get out at the signposted turn-off, from which it is a 5km walk.

MT ELGON NATIONAL PARK

With its deep volcanic crater straddling the Kenya–Uganda border and its forested flanks extending well into both countries, massive Mt Elgon is a sight indeed. With the dramatic 7km-wide caldera dotted with several peaks – including the basalt column of Koitoboss (4187m), Kenya's second-highest, and Wagagai (4321m) in Uganda – this extinct volcano offers some of the best treks in Kenya. The **national park** (adult/child US$15/5) extends from the lower slopes right up to the border.

Despite its lower altitude making conditions less extreme than Mt Kenya, it sees a fraction of its bigger cousin's visitors. This is due in part to its greater distance from Nairobi, its wetter weather and the fact that most visitors are more interested in claiming they've climbed Kenya's tallest mountain. While this lack of interest is a shame, it only means those not concerned about bragging rights will have far fewer people to share the mountain with.

Although rarely seen, the mountain's most famous attractions are the elephants known for their predilection for digging salt out of the lower eastern slopes' caves. The elephants are such keen excavators that some people have been fooled into believing they are totally responsible for the caves. Sadly, the number of these saline-loving creatures has declined over the years, mainly due to incursions by Ugandan poachers.

Four main lava tubes (caves) are open to visitors: **Kitum**, **Chepnyalil**, **Mackingeny** and **Rongai**. Mackingeny, with a waterfall cascading across the entrance, is the most spectacular. A good flashlight is essential and you should be wary of rock falls – the bones of a crushed elephant stand as evidence.

The mountain's fauna and flora are also great attractions. Starting with rainforest at the base, the vegetation changes as you ascend, to bamboo jungle and finally alpine moorland with the bizarre giant groundsel and giant lobelia plants. Commonly sighted animals include buffaloes, bushbucks, olive baboons, giant forest hogs and duikers; Defassa waterbucks are also present. The lower forests are the habitat of the black and white colobus, and the blue and De Brazza's monkeys (most likely seen near waterways).

There are more than 240 species of birds here, including red-fronted parrots, Ross's turacos and casqued hornbills. On the peaks you may even see a lammergeyer raptor gliding through the thin air. The **Elephant Platform** and **Endebess Bluff** viewpoints are good places to survey the scene on the way up.

Mt Elgon is wet much of the year, but driest between December and February. As well as bringing waterproof gear, you will need warm clothes, as it gets cold up here at night. Altitude may also be a problem for some people.

Access to the 169-sq-km national park is now permitted without a vehicle. Even if you have a 4WD, walking is the best way to get around as the roads are treacherous. Get a ranger to guide you (KSh500/1000 per half-/full day), wherever you walk. For the higher slopes you will need a tent and all your own camping gear.

Lonely Planet's *Trekking in East Africa* has more juicy details on the various trekking and walking routes, and Andy Wielochowski's *Mt Elgon Map & Guide* is an essential purchase.

Trekking

Trekkers are encouraged to stay within the park boundaries, as security has previously been a problem. Check the situation with **KWS headquarters** (☎ 020-600800; kws@kws.org; PO Box 40241, Nairobi) in Nairobi or **Mt Elgon National Park** (☎ 054-31456; PO Box 753, Kitale) before you plan anything. Crossing into Uganda isn't currently permitted, but ask for the latest at the gate.

Allow at least four days for any round trip and two or three days for any direct ascent of **Koitoboss** if you're walking from the Chorlim gate. It is best to arrange any guiding requirements at the park headquarters in advance.

The **Park Route** offers some interesting possibilities, and there is a well-worn route from Chorlim gate up to Koitoboss peak that requires one or two overnight camps. If you have a vehicle, you can drive up to

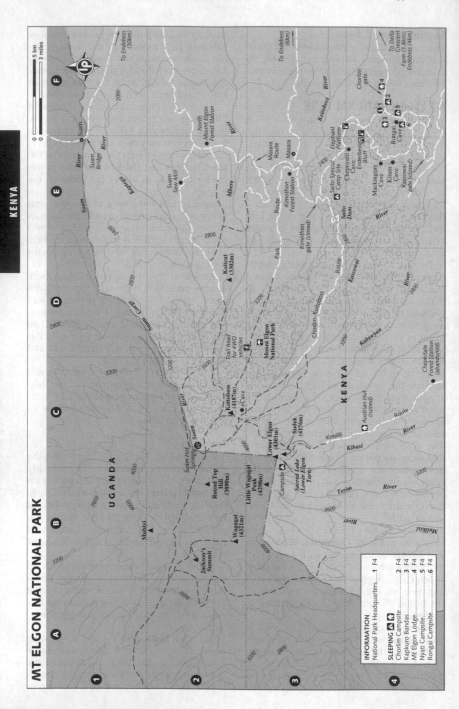

MT ELGON NATIONAL PARK

INFORMATION
National Park Headquarters.....1 F4

SLEEPING
Chorlim Campsite.....................2 F4
Kapkuro Bandas........................3 F4
Mt Elgon Lodge.........................4 F4
Nyati Campsite..........................5 F4
Rongai Campsite.......................6 F4

3500m, but the current state of the road means the 32km drive can take half a day, and then it's a two- to three-hour walk up to the peak.

Descending, you have a number of options. Firstly you can descend northwest into the crater to **Suam Hot Springs**. Alternatively, if the security situation improves, you could go east around the crater rim and descend the **Masara Route**, which leads to the small village of Masara on the eastern slopes of the mountain (a trek of about 25km) and then returns to Endebess. Lastly, you can head southwest around the rim of the crater (some very hard walking) to **Lower Elgon Tarn**, where you can camp before ascending **Lower Elgon Peak** (4301m). To return you simply head back the way you came.

Sleeping & Eating

If you're trekking your only option is to **camp** (adult/child US$8/5). This fee is the same wherever you pitch your tent. Chorlim Campsite has the park's best facilities but is less scenic than the other public sites, Nyati and Rongai.

Kapkuro Bandas (US$30) These excellent stone *bandas* can sleep three people in two beds, and have simple bathrooms and small kitchens. Hot water is provided by a wood stove, while solar panels provide electricity. Bring food, as there's only one small shop nearby.

Delta Crescent Farm (☎ 0722-2489317; camping KSh200, tw with shared bathroom incl breakfast KSh2000) Conveniently located between Endebess and Chorlim gate, this farm has three huge areas for campers along with three basic, clean *bandas*. Four-person and 12-person rental tents are also available for KSh800 and KSh2000 respectively (plus camping fees). Transfers to Chorlim Gate and Kitale are available (KSh1500 per vehicle), as are 4WD tours of the park.

Mt Elgon Lodge (☎ 0722-866480; PO Box 7, Endebess; s/tw incl breakfast KSh3500/5000) Despite the mountain views, huge fireplaces and some colonial charm, this tattered lodge is severely overpriced, though after a few days of trekking a meal in its restaurant (meals KSh350 to KSh450) is a godsend.

Getting There & Away

Sporadic *matatus* and Peugeots now reach the Chorlim gate from Kitale (KSh80, one hour). More regular services reach Endebess (KSh70, 45 minutes), a 9km walk from the gate. If you want to break up the walk, make for Delta Crescent Farm, spend the night there and then walk the remaining 5.5km to the gate the next morning (you'll need time to organise guides in any case). Locals will happily point you in the right direction.

If you're driving, the road up to the park is OK, but once inside a 4WD is essential.

NORTHERN KENYA

Northern Kenya is more an experience than a series of destinations. There's constantly something catching your eye, whether it's enthralling Gabbra tribespeople walking the desolate, shattered lava fields, extinct volcanos rising from desert seas or simply the road tracking across the plains. The complete and utter beauty of the 'Jade Sea' (Lake Turkana), the baking, barren shores of which stretch over the horizon to a distant Ethiopia some 250km away, can't be overstated.

The Turkana, Samburu, Rendille, Gabbra, Boran and El-Molo tribes of northern Kenya are some of the most fascinating people on earth – a respectful glimpse into their world is priceless. Many choose to have little contact with the modern world, preferring centuries-old traditional lifestyles that bind members of the tribe together.

Unique wildlife, like the reticulated giraffe and endangered Grevy's zebra, also call northern Kenya home, mixing with the likes of lions, elephants and oryxes in the varied landscapes of Samburu, Buffalo Springs and Shaba National Reserves.

For those with extra energy to burn, there's great hiking potential around Marich, Maralal and Marsabit. If walking isn't your thing, it's also the perfect place for a camel safari.

Where there's reward, there's usually some risk and northern Kenya is no exception; see p418. The heat will fry your brain and your 4WD will beg for mercy. Don't worry, you'll love every minute of it!

ISIOLO TO ETHIOPIA

Besides being a gateway to Ethiopia's riches, this route offers northern Kenya's best wildlife viewing along with some incredible culture and landscapes. New hiking possibilities in the Ndoto Mountains and several pioneering community wildlife-conservation projects only add to the region's appeal.

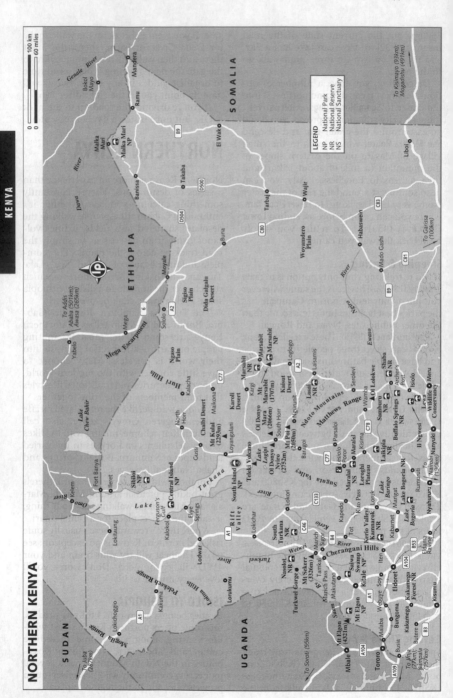

NORTHERN KENYA

LEGEND
NP   National Park
NR   National Reserve
NS   National Sanctuary

Isiolo
☎ 064

Isiolo is a vital pit stop on the long road north, as it's the last place with decent facilities until Maralal or Marsabit.

How you interpret this frontier town depends on which direction you're coming from. Arrive from the south and you'll get your first taste of the remote northeast (hopefully not a mouthful of dirt blown up by late-afternoon squalls!). Besides arid conditions, you'll undoubtedly notice the large Somali population (descendants of WWI veterans who settled here), and the striking faces of Boran, Samburu and Turkana people walking the streets. Pull in from the north and you'll notice little other than the verdant Central Highlands and omnipresent Mt Kenya towering in the distance. Your mind will wander to thoughts of crisp air and cool nights – heaven ahead indeed!

In respect of Isiolo's strong Muslim community, women should avoid wearing shorts or short skirts.

INFORMATION

Banks are scarce in the north, so plan ahead.

Consolidated Bank of Kenya (A2 Hwy) No ATM. Changes cash and AmEx travellers cheques.

District Hospital (Hospital Rd; ⏳ 24hr)

Isiolo Telephone Exchange (Hospital Rd) Calling cards and cardphones.

Post office (Hospital Rd)

SLEEPING

Mocharo Lodge (☎ 52385; s/tw KSh350/450) Sizable clean rooms proffer mosquito nets, comfy beds and hot water (morning only). Some toilets are seatless, so if you don't want to be a porcelain jockey check out a few rooms. There's also secure parking, a decent restaurant and TV room.

Range Land Hotel (☎ 0721-434353; A2 Hwy; camping KSh200, tw cottage per person KSh1000) About 6km south of town, this is a nice option for campers and families. Shade is rare, but there's now grass to plant your tent on and one of the stone cottages, with a nice bathroom, chairs and TV, is set aside for your use.

Jamhuri Guest House (s/tw with shared bathroom KSh120/200, s with private bathroom KSh250) Popular with budget travellers in the past, it's simple, clean enough and has secure parking.

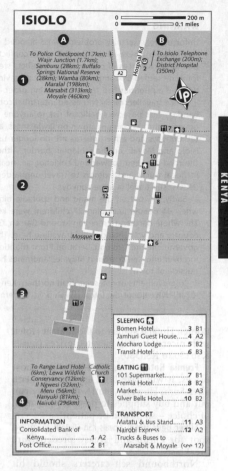

ISIOLO   0 ─── 200 m   0 ─── 0.1 miles

INFORMATION
Consolidated Bank of Kenya.....................1 A2
Post Office.....................2 B1

SLEEPING 🏠
Bomen Hotel.....................3 B1
Jamhuri Guest House.....................4 A2
Mocharo Lodge.....................5 B2
Transit Hotel.....................6 B3

EATING 🍴
101 Supermarket.....................7 B1
Fremia Hotel.....................8 B2
Market.....................9 A3
Silver Bells Hotel.....................10 B2

TRANSPORT
Matatu & Bus Stand......11 A3
Nairobi Express.....................12 A2
Trucks & Buses to
   Marsabit & Moyale (see 12)

To Police Checkpoint (1.7km); Wajir Junction (1.7km); Samburu (28km); Buffalo Springs National Reserve (28km); Wamba (80km); Maralal (198km); Marsabit (313km); Moyale (460km)

To Isiolo Telephone Exchange (200m); District Hospital (350m)

To Range Land Hotel (6km); Lewa Wildlife Conservancy (12km); Il Ngwesi (32km); Meru (56km); Nanyuki (81km); Nairobi (296km)

Catholic Church

Mosque

Transit Hotel (☎ 52083; s/tw KSh500/900) It's dropped its rates substantially, but rooms are still just more expensive versions of Mocharo Lodge's.

Bomen Hotel (☎ 52389; s/tw/ste KSh900/1500/2500) NGO's favourite home, the Bomen has the town's brightest (ask for one facing outward) and most comfortable rooms. Prices are steep, especially since some toilets are seatless, but some rooms have TV and shared terraces with views.

EATING

Transit Hotel is a rare place serving more than the local usuals, with fried *tilapia*, pepper steak, vegetable cutlets and curries up for grabs (meals KSh120 to KSh250). The

WARNING

Unfortunately, security problems have plagued northern Kenya for years. In the 1990s a massive influx of cheap guns from the many conflict zones just outside Kenya dramatically altered traditional balances of power. Minor conflicts stemming from grazing rights and cattle rustling, formerly settled by compensation rather than violence, quickly escalated into ongoing gun battles and authorities had trouble restoring order.

While travellers rarely witnessed intertribal conflict, the abundance of guns led to increases in banditry that posed a significant risk to anyone moving through the region. However, the new government has clamped down on lawlessness, and security in the north has turned for the better. Convoys and armed guards are no longer used between Marich and Lodwar and between Isiolo and Moyale on the Ethiopian border. Although the notoriously dangerous conditions on the road between Lodwar and Lokichoggio, near the Sudanese border, have improved enough for local trucks and *matatus* to travel unguarded, the UN and nongovernmental organisations (NGOs) still travel in large convoys.

Sadly, all isn't on the mend and sporadic bloody tribal conflicts still arise, like in July 2005 when 44 people (including 27 children) were killed in Marsabit district's remote Turbi region. The whole northeastern region around Garsen, Garissa, Wajir and Mandera is still *shifta* (bandit) country and you should avoid travelling here. Thanks to a 1999 conflict between the Ethiopian government and Oromo Liberation Front (fighting for independence in southern Ethiopia) spilling over into Kenya around Moyale, landmines have been reported – stick to well-marked paths outside of town.

Improvements or not, security in northern Kenya is a dynamic entity and travellers should seek local advice about the latest developments before travelling and never take unnecessary risks.

Bomen Hotel is similar to the Transit Hotel, with nicer seats and elevated prices (meals KSh130 to KSh380).

Fremia Hotel (meals KSh50-100) Like most places, it will have little left on the menu after 8pm. However, staff will actually run out and buy supplies to prepare your meal of choice – smile and be patient!

Silver Bells Hotel (meals KSh 60-150) A good spot for cheap and greasy predeparture breakfasts.

Northbound self-caterers should hit 101 Supermarket and the market near the mosque to purchase food and drink, as there's very little available beyond here.

GETTING THERE & AWAY

Although convoys are no longer being used north to Marsabit, check the security situation thoroughly with locals and the police checkpoint north of town before leaving.

Bus & Matatu

The best option to Nairobi is **Nairobi Express** (A2 Hwy), operating daily buses (KSh500, 4½ hours) at 6.45am. The bus north to Marsabit (KSh600, 8½ hours) and Moyale (KSh1200, 17 hours) picks up passengers at Nairobi Express between 11pm and midnight.

For Maralal take an early *matatu* to Wamba (KSh300, 2½ hours), and then the midday Maralal *matatu* (KSh300, 2½ hours). Regular *matatus* leave from a chaotic stand around the market, and also serve Archer's Post (KSh80, 45 minutes), Meru (KSh120, 1½ hours), Nanyuki (KSh150, two hours) and Nairobi (KSh450, five hours). Peugeots also service Meru (KSh150, 1¼ hours).

Four-Wheel Drive

Isiolo marks the Tarmac's northern terminus and the start of the corrugated dirt and gravel, which will shake the guts out of you and your vehicle. There are several petrol stations, so top up as prices climb and supply diminishes northward. If you're heading south, Central Highlands petrol is cheaper.

Hitching

Trucks are filthy and uncomfortable, but a viable option for the northbound adventurous. Although they pick up passengers at the police checkpoint north of town, better seats are available if you board when they stop near Nairobi Express. Drain your bladder, purchase enough food, water and sunscreen, and hop aboard.

Around Isiolo

LEWA WILDLIFE CONSERVANCY

While the massive 263-sq-km **Lewa Wildlife Conservancy** (LWC; ☎ 064-31405; www.lewa.org; admission incl in accommodation rates) could boast about its luxury lodges, stunning scenery, astounding wildlife activities and repeatedly hosting Prince William, staff would rather talk about their community and conservation projects. Founded in 1995, LWC now spends an amazing 30% of its budget on healthcare and education for surrounding villages, 40% towards community projects, with the rest funding conservation and security.

Their conservancy effort has been astounding and 20% of the world's Grevy's zebras, 8% of Kenya's black rhinos, a rare population of aquatic sitatunga antelopes, and sizable populations of white rhinos, elephants, buffaloes, leopards, lions and cheetahs now call this magical place home.

Wildlife drives in private vehicles aren't permitted and only guests of the LWC's lodges are allowed into the conservancy. A plethora of activities, ranging from drives and walks to camel rides and conservation outings, are available at most lodges.

Sleeping & Eating

Lewa House (☎ 064-31405; c.moller@lewa.org; exclusive use per night incl wildlife drives US$840; 🏊) Six sublime thatched-roof African chalets, comfortably sleeping 12 people, form Lewa House. Privacy is guaranteed since it's rented exclusively to one group at a time. For full board, add US$120 per person per night.

Lewa Safari Camp (☎ 064-31405; www.lewasafaricamp.com; full board s/d incl wildlife drives US$285/570; 🏊 closed Nov) Twelve luxurious octagonal tents hang beneath charming thatched roofs, offering privacy and a slice of the African safari dream. The lounge, dining room, food and service are all top-notch.

Getting There & Away

LWC is only 12km south of Isiolo and is well signposted on A2 Hwy. **Airkenya** (☎ 020-605745; www.airkenya.com) and **Safarilink** (☎ 020-600777; www.safarilink.co.ke) have daily 'request stop' flights to LWC from Nairobi. Return fares on Airkenya/Safarilink are US$199/222.

IL NGWESI

Il Ngwesi is a pioneering project linking wildlife conservation and community development. The Maasai of Il Ngwesi, with substantial help from their neighbour LWC, have transformed this undeveloped land, previously used for subsistence pastoralism, into a prime wildlife conservation area hosting the likes of white and black rhinos, waterbucks, giraffes and many other plains animals. It's truly fitting that Il Ngwesi translates to 'people of wildlife'.

The community now supplements its herding income with tourist dollars gained from its award-winning ecolodge, **Il Ngwesi Group Ranch** (☎ 020-340331; info@letsgosafari.com; full board s/d US$209/418; 🏊). Six open-fronted thatched cottages boast views from a dramatic escarpment that will have you smiling yourself to sleep and shaking your head when the sun rises (especially in cottages one and five, where the beds roll out beneath the stars). Natural materials are used throughout and you'll never be so in love with twisted, crooked wood – who likes straight lines anyway? The best part is that profits go straight to the Maasai community. Advance reservations are essential and getting here requires a serious 4WD.

SAMBURU, BUFFALO SPRINGS & SHABA NATIONAL RESERVES

These three **national reserves** (adult/child US$30/10), comprising some 300 sq km, straddle the Ewaso Ngiro River and include a breadth of wildlife, vegetation and landscapes. Shaba, with its great rocky *kopjes* (isolated hills), natural springs and doum palms, is the most physically beautiful, while open savannas, scrub desert and verdant river foliage in Samburu and Buffalo Springs virtually guarantee close encounters with elephants, reticulated giraffes, Grevy's zebras, Somali ostriches, Beisa oryxes and the elegant giraffe-necked gerenuks.

After brazen lodge hold-ups in Samburu several years ago, security has improved, with ranger and KWS lookouts at vantage points throughout the reserve. However, this didn't stop poachers killing 25 elephants in early 2002. Things have been quiet since, and visitor numbers are steadily increasing.

Information

Conveniently, admission for Buffalo Springs, Shaba and Samburu is transferable, so you only pay once, even if you're visiting all three in one day.

KENYA

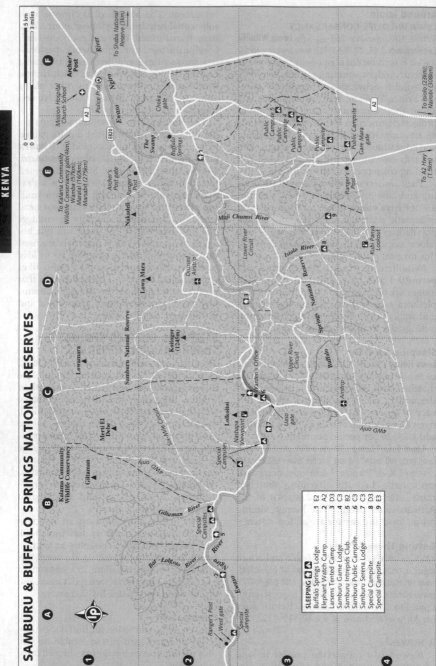

SAMBURU & BUFFALO SPRINGS NATIONAL RESERVES

SLEEPING 🛏️

Buffalo Springs Lodge	1	E2
Elephant Watch Camp	2	A2
Larsens Tented Camp	3	D3
Samburu Game Lodge	4	C3
Samburu Intrepids Club	5	B2
Samburu Public Campsite	6	C3
Samburu Serena Lodge	7	C3
Special Campsite	8	D3
Special Campsite	9	E3

0 ───── 5 km
0 ───── 3 miles

If you're driving, Survey of Kenya's map *Samburu & Buffalo Springs Game Reserves* (SK 85) is helpful, but hard to find. Getting around isn't difficult, but some minor roads are 4WD only and the maze of wayward minibus tracks can be confusing.

Petrol is available at Shaba Sarova Lodge and Samburu Game Lodge.

Sleeping & Eating

Each reserve is blessed with at least one luxury lodge and several camp sites. For campers and day visitors, all the luxury lodges have buffet meals (around KSh1825).

BUFFALO SPRINGS NATIONAL RESERVE

Samburu Serena Lodge (☎ 064-30800, Nairobi ☎ 020-2710511; cro@serena.co.ke; full board low season s/d US$80/160, high season US$200/260; ☒) Though not as extravagant as Shaba Sarova Lodge, it's still lovely and offers plenty of activities, like slide shows, bird walks, hikes up L'Olgotoi Hill and camel rides. Comfy cottages, with breezy verandas, reed-lined ceilings and canopy beds, line the riverbank.

Buffalo Springs Lodge (Box 71, Isiolo; s/tw KSh1000/2000) The state of the swimming pool speaks volumes – it's half-empty, or is it half-full? On the positive side, the wood, reed-lined cottages are rather charming and easily the best value around. On the negative side, there's no food available, the thatched cement cottages are dreary and have lumpy beds, and let's not forget the pool!

Special camp sites (camping KSh825) While scenically located by freshwater springs along the Isiolo and Maji ya Chumvi Rivers, there are no facilities.

SAMBURU NATIONAL RESERVE

Elephant Watch Camp (☎ 020-891112; www.elephant watchsafaris.com; full board incl guided walks s/d Apr & Nov US$320/640, rest of year US$360/720) Undoubtedly the most unique and memorable stay in the reserves. Massive thatched roofs cling to crooked acacia branches and tower over cosy, palatial eight-sided tents and large terraces. Natural materials pervade and the bathrooms are stunning.

Samburu Game Lodge (☎ 020-559529; wilderness@ mitsuminet.com; full board s/tw low season US$130/165, high season US$200/250; ☒) Several thatched log cottages and one large apartmentlike block sit riverside in this perennial favourite. The bright cottages are much better value, offer-

ing more privacy, tasteful décor, modern bathrooms and larger verandas.

Larsens Tented Camp (☎ 020-559529; wilderness@ mitsuminet.com; full board low season s/tw US$169/226, high season US$251/320) Sitting beneath acacias and spread along the riverbank are spacious and oh so very comfortable semipermanent tents. Each boasts scenic verandas, rugs, modern bathrooms and king-size beds, complete with headboards resembling colonial-style leather chests. Two tents are wheelchair accessible.

Samburu Intrepids Club (☎ 064-30453, Nairobi ☎ 020-446651; www.heritage-eastafricas.com; full board s/d US$300/450; ☒) Grab a G&T, sink into the bar's teak loungers and gaze over the Ewaso Ngiro. While thatched roofs and canopy beds in the luxurious tents scream Africa, the refined furniture unfortunately shrieks Fortune 500. The friendly service is unmatched.

Samburu Public Campsite (camping KSh440) Spread along the Ewaso Ngiro River's northern bank, this site is blessed with new bathroom blocks and some secluded spots for tents.

SHABA NATIONAL RESERVE

Shaba Sarova Lodge (☎ 020-713333; reservations@ sarova.co.ke; full board s/d Mar-Jun US$87/135, Jul-Feb

US$130/185; 🛌) This spectacular, almost over-the-top place nestles on the Ewaso Ngiro River. Next to the magnificent pool, natural springs flow through the gorgeous open-air bar and beneath the lofty 200-seat restaurant. The rooms? They're pretty lavish, too!

Special camp sites (camping KSh825) Of the several special camp sites (no facilities) here, Funan, set in Shaba's core, takes the cake. Shaded by acacias, it's next to a semipermanent spring, which provides water for visitors and wildlife alike. A ranger must accompany you to these camp sites; the cost is included in the fee but a tip is appropriate.

Getting There & Away

Daily flights from Nairobi to Samburu are available with **Airkenya** (☎ 020-605745; www.airkenya.com) and **Safarilink** (☎ 020-600777; www.safarilink.co.ke). Return fares on Airkenya/Safarilink are US$199/222. The vehicle-less can probably rustle up a 4WD and local driver for about KSh6000 per day.

MATTHEWS RANGE

West of the remarkable flat-topped mountain **Ol Lolokwe** and north of **Wamba** is the **Matthews Range**. Its thick evergreen forests support elephants, lions, buffaloes and Kenya's most important wild dog population. These dramatic mountains (highest peak 2285m) offer great opportunities to explore the depths of Kenya's wilds. With few roads, only those willing to go the extra mile on foot will be rewarded with the spoils.

In 1995 local Samburu communities collectively formed the **Namunyak Wildlife Conservation Trust**, now one of Kenya's most successful community conservation programs. The trust is unique because it's run by a democratically elected board, each community having one trustee. Now endorsed by KWS, it oversees 750 sq km and has substantially increased animal populations by successfully combating poaching.

To capitalise on its wildlife resources and fund community projects, the trust built **Sarara Tented Camp** (☎ 020-600457; info@bush-and-beyond.com; full board s/d incl conservancy fee US$490/780; 🌙 closed May & Nov; 🛌). With its grand, thatched open-fronted lounge, enveloping comfort, sublime surrounds and natural rock pool, guests benefit as much as the cause.

For budgeteers, the basic **El-Moran** (s with shared bathroom KSh150, with private bathroom KSh250)

in Wamba is the only option besides bush camping. If it's full, you could try the local mission (which incidentally has northern Kenya's best hospital, a fact worth remembering while in the bush).

While *matatus* from Isiolo and Maralal reach Wamba, there's no point in coming without a vehicle. Getting to Sarara Camp isn't easy, even with a 4WD – it's probably best to arrange a transfer or get detailed directions when booking.

NDOTO MOUNTAINS

Climbing from the Korante Plain's sands are the magnificent rusty bluffs and ridges of the Ndoto Mountains. Kept a virtual secret from the travelling world by their remote location, the Ndotos abound with hiking, climbing and bouldering potential. **Mt Poi** (2050m), which resembles the world's largest bread loaf from some angles, is a technical climber's dream, its sheer 800m north face begging to be bagged. If you're fit and have a whole day to spare, it's a great hike to the summit and the views are extraordinary.

The tiny village of Ngurunit is the best base for your adventures and is interesting in its own right, with captivating, traditionally dressed Samburu people living in simple, yet elegantly woven grass huts.

Ngurunit is best accessed from Loglogo, 47km south of Marsabit and 233km north of Archer's Post. It's a tricky 79km drive (1¾ hours), with many forks, through the Kaisut Desert.

MARSABIT
☎ 069

Approach Marsabit in fading light and you'll undoubtedly rub your weary eyes in disbelief. Scattered across the plains, surrounded by desert and strangely reminiscent of Egyptian pyramids (we did say weary eyes!) are fields of dramatic cinder cones (volcanic vents). Climbing towards town, the bleached yellows and browns turn to rich shades of green and the mercury takes a heavenly dip downward, adding pleasure to your continued feelings of astonishment.

The entire area surrounding Marsabit is actually a behemoth 6300-sq-km shield volcano, whose surface is peppered with no less than 180 amazing cinder cones and 22 volcanic craters (*gofs* or *maars*), many housing lakes. Mt Marsabit's highest peak,

Karantin (1707m), is a rewarding 5km hike from town through lush vegetation and moss-covered trees. The view from Karantin is astounding.

While the town is less attractive than its lush surrounds, which comprise the 1500-sq-km Marsabit National Reserve, it's interesting due to an intriguing migrant population and a (sometimes volatile) mixture of local tribes. The best place to take in the cornucopia of culture is the lively market.

Information

Kenya Commercial Bank Off Post Office Rd. No ATM. Changes cash and travellers cheques.

Medical clinic (Post Office Rd; ☺ 8am-7pm Mon-Sat, noon-7pm Sun)

Post office (Post Office Rd)

Sleeping

JeyJey Centre (☎ 2296; A2 Hwy; s/tw/tr with shared bathroom KSh250/400/600, s with private bathroom KSh400) Owned by government MP JJ Falana, this is the best lodge in town. Clean rooms with mosquito nets surround a colourful courtyard, and bathrooms (even shared ones) sport on-demand hot water. There's also a TV room, a decent restaurant and an unattractive camp site (per person KSh150). Spot the guard 50 bob and your vehicle will sleep safely.

Diku's Complex Lodge (☎ 2465; A2 Hwy; s/tw with shared bathroom KSh300/600) North of JeyJey and tucked behind a wholesale store is this simple and slightly overpriced place. The spartan rooms (four walls and a bed) are spacious, but lack mosquito nets. The shared showers are clean, while the cement-block squat toilets could use a wee wash.

Eating & Drinking

Five Steers Hotel (A2 Hwy; meals KSh70-130) It's easily the best local eatery. The half-Federation meal (a bulging pile of rice, spaghetti, beef, vegetables and chapati) is filling and surprisingly tasty.

Mamba Cafe (A2 Hwy; meals KSh50-100) This small shack next to JeyJey Centre is perfect for breakfast and its *chai* is spot on.

If you're short of food or supplies check out the market and **Nomads Shopping Store** (Post Office Rd; ☺ Mon-Sat).

Thanks to a strong Muslim influence, beer can be hard to find. The best spot for a cold one is **New Saku Bar** (Post Office Rd), which has a lively interior and relaxed outdoor section.

Getting There & Away

Although improved security meant convoys and armed guards weren't being used to Moyale or Isiolo during our research, it's still wise to get the latest security and Ethiopian border information from locals and the police station before leaving town.

BUS

With security on the mend, a bus now connects Marsabit to Moyale (KSh600, 8½ hours). There's no designated stop; simply flag it down on the A2 Hwy as it comes through town around 5pm each day (en route from Nairobi!). The same service heads south to Isiolo (KSh600, 8½ hours) at 9am.

FOUR-WHEEL DRIVE

You'll find the Moyale road less corrugated than that to Isiolo, but its sharp stones will devour your tyres and the deep ruts will give your undercarriage a good scrub. The only fuel north is in Moyale, so stock up here. As a rule, if buses and trucks travel in a convoy or take armed soldiers on board, you should too! For advice on travel to Loyangalani, see p428.

HITCHING

Trucks regularly ply the bus routes for about KSh100 less, but balancing your malnourished butt on a metal bar above discontented cows for eight hours, while simultaneously battling the sun, wind and dust, is one tricky, tiring act! On the flip side, you'll have a life time of memories. One or two trucks a week also leave Marsabit for Loyangalani (KSh700, seven hours) via Kargi. Most trucks pick up opposite JeyJey Centre.

MARSABIT NATIONAL PARK

This relatively small **park** (adult/child US$15/5), nestled on Mt Marsabit's upper slopes, hosts thick forests and a variety of wildlife, including lions, leopards, elephants and rhinos. During our visit we were lucky enough to see a large cobra at close range, with its neck spread into the infamous 'hood'. We say lucky because we were in our truck at the time!

You won't get to see much big wildlife on a quick drive-through of the park, so stick around and camp at **Lake Paradise**. This small lake, which occupies the Gof Sokorte Guda's crater floor, is lovely and the views

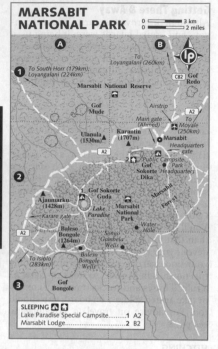

MARSABIT NATIONAL PARK

0 — 3 km
0 — 2 miles

SLEEPING
Lake Paradise Special Campsite..........1 A2
Marsabit Lodge................................2 B2

from the escarpment above are simply stunning.

Although there's nothing except lake water and firewood, the picturesque **Lake Paradise Special Campsite** (adult/child US$10/5, plus set-up fee KSh5000) is easily the best place to stay in the park. Thanks to roaming buffaloes and elephants, a ranger must be present when you camp here.

The **Marsabit Lodge** (☎ 0735-555747; s/tw/tr incl breakfast KSh5500/5900/6950) has long shingle-roofed bungalows around the Gof Sokorte Dika lake, and offers fine views. Even with the location, the spartan rooms are over-priced. With its gargantuan fireplace and comfy chairs, the lounge is the lodge's most redeeming feature.

Despite it being a short walk to the park gate from town, you need your own 4WD to explore. In the wet season you may find some park roads closed.

MOYALE

Let's be honest, nobody comes to Moyale to see Moyale; people come because it's the gateway to one of the world's most

fascinating countries, Ethiopia. The drive from Marsabit is long and hard (on you and your 4WD), with the Dida Galgalu Desert's seemingly endless black shattered lava fields stretching out before you, and the imposing Mega Escarpment seemingly climbing ever higher as you approach near Sololo.

In stark contrast to the solitary journey here, Moyale's small, sandy streets burst with activity. The town's Ethiopian half is more developed, complete with sealed roads, and there's a palpable difference in its atmosphere.

It's possible to enter Ethiopia for the day without a visa, but Ethiopian officials will hold your passport until you return. The border closes at 6pm – don't be late! The Commercial Bank of Ethiopia, 2km from the border, changes travellers cheques (0.5% commission), as well as US dollars and euros. While it doesn't exchange Kenyan Shillings, the Tourist Hotel will swap them for Ethiopian Birr (10KSh to Birr1).

There are a few simple places to stay and eat on both sides of the border: **Sherif Guest House** (s/tw with shared bathroom KSh150/200) and **Baghdad Hotel II** (meals KSh80-150) fly the Kenyan flag, while the **Tourist Hotel** (s with shared toilet Birr15) and **Ethio-Kenya** (breakfast Birr3-6) keep up the Ethiopian end.

A bus leaves daily for Marsabit (KSh600, 8½ hours) and Isiolo (KSh1200, 17 hours) at 9.30am. Trucks servicing the same destinations pick up passengers near the main intersection. Drivers should note that petrol on the Ethiopian side of Moyale is half the cost of that in Kenya.

MARALAL TO TURKANA'S EASTERN SHORE

With vibrant Samburu and Turkana tribes, treks along lush cliffs dropping from the Loroghi Plateau, desert camel safaris, mesmerising barren volcanic landscapes and the north's jade jewel, Lake Turkana, this region of northern Kenya has it all.

The 130km drive from Nyahururu to Maralal along the C77 is bumpy but straightforward, despite the tarmac running out at Rumuruti (we hope you said goodbye, because you won't see it any time soon!). Punctures on this route are common and the scenery is ummm…well, let's just say that once you've set eyes on the Jade Sea, you'll have forgotten all about it.

If you're not in a hurry, **Bobong Camp** (☎ 062-32718; olmaisor@africaonline.co.ke; PO Box 5, Rumuruti; camping KSh250, 4-person bandas KSh3000) offers some of Kenya's cheapest self-catered **camel safaris** (per camel per day KSh1000) and **cultural visits** (per group KSh5000) to Turkana and Samburu communities. Nyahururu–Maralal *matatus* (KSh60, 45 minutes) can drop you here, but may charge full fare (KSh300).

Maralal
☎ 065

Tin roofs poke from the forested Loroghi Hills overlooking Maralal's wide tree-lined boulevards below. Sounds pretty, but it's not. Where Maralal's charm lies is in its frontier rough-and-ready atmosphere, with colourful Samburu people wandering the dusty streets and weathered characters sitting beneath shabby street-side verandas. It all seems eerily reminiscent of the classic Wild West.

Maralal has gained an international reputation for its fantastically frenetic **International Camel Derby** (see p426) and a visit over its duration is truly unforgettable. Less

crazy but almost as memorable are the year-round camel safaris and trekking that are offered here.

Sadly, most self-drivers don't delve into Maralal, stopping only for a night en route to Lake Turkana. The opposite is true for independent travellers, who end up spending more time here than planned, simply because transport north is erratic at best. Let's face it though, there are worse places to get stuck!

People here are generally friendly, but you'll quickly encounter Maralal's own professional tout posse. You'll be offered everything from bangles to guiding services, friendly 'advice' and Samburu weddings, and their persistence can be truly astounding – use your best judgment and keep your wits about you.

INFORMATION
Yare Camel Club & Camp (p426) can exchange travellers cheques, but at low rates. Maralal Safari Lodge (p426) changes travellers cheques outside banking hours, also at low rates.

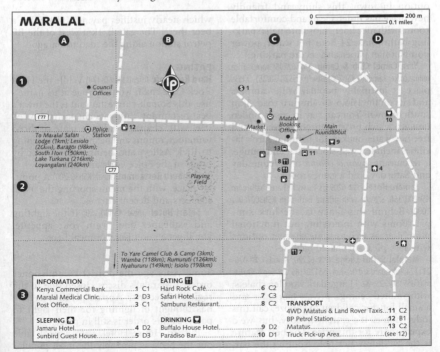

MARALAL

To Maralal Safari Lodge (1km); Lesiolo (2km), Baragoi (98km); South Ilori (150km); Lake Turkana (216km); Loyangalani (240km)

Council Offices

Police Station

Market

Matatu Booking Office

Main Roundabout

Playing Field

To Yare Camel Club & Camp (3km); Wamba (118km); Rumuruti (126km); Nyahururu (149km); Isiolo (198km)

0   200 m
0   0.1 miles

INFORMATION		
Kenya Commercial Bank	1	C1
Maralal Medical Clinic	2	D3
Post Office	3	C1

SLEEPING 🏠		
Jamaru Hotel	4	D2
Sunbird Guest House	5	D3

EATING 🍴		
Hard Rock Café	6	C2
Safari Hotel	7	C3
Samburu Restaurant	8	C2

DRINKING 🍷		
Buffalo House Hotel	9	D2
Paradiso Bar	10	D1

TRANSPORT		
4WD Matatus & Land Rover Taxis	11	C2
BP Petrol Station	12	B1
Matatus	13	C2
Truck Pick-up Area	(see 12)	

Kenya Commercial Bank Behind the market. Changes cash and travellers cheques. No ATM.
Maralal Medical Clinic (☺ Mon-Sat)
Post office Next to market.

SIGHTS & ACTIVITIES

Featuring some of Kenya's most astounding vistas, **trekking** the Loroghi Hills Circuit takes a rewarding five days and covers 78km. This trek is detailed in Lonely Planet's *Trekking in East Africa*.

Yare Camel Club & Camp organises guides and camels for independent **camel safaris** in the region. Self-catered day/overnight trips cost US$20/35 per person. Fully catered overnight trips are US$95.

Surrounding town is the **Maralal National Sanctuary**, home to zebras, impalas, hyenas, elephants, elands, buffaloes and other varieties of plains wildlife, which you can see for free from the road leading into Maralal from the south.

SLEEPING

Sunbird Guest House (☎ 62015; PO Box 74, Maralal; s/tw/d KSh350/450/600) Easily the best budget option in town, this shiny and friendly new place has quiet, clean and comfortable rooms with nice linen, mosquito nets, sparkling bathrooms, 24-hour hot water, power points, toilet paper and secure parking.

Yare Camel Club & Camp (☎ 62295; yare@africaonline.co.ke; camping KSh200, s/tw/tr US$20/28/35) This place is justifiably popular with campers and sits on the Isiolo–Nyahururu road, 3km south of town. You can stay in cosy wooden *bandas*, which boast bathrooms, towels and free hot-water buckets for bathing. Yare's facilities include a well-stocked bar and lounge, a restaurant, *nyama choma* on Wednesday and Saturday, and a games room.

Jamaru Hotel (☎ 62093; s/tw with shared bathroom KSh200/350, s/tw/tr with private bathroom KSh300/600/1000) Behind this fancy façade lurk simple rooms with interesting but functional plumbing, as well as some cheaper options with less-pleasant shared facilities.

Maralal Safari Lodge (☎ 62220, Nairobi ☎ 020-211124; full board s/d Oct-Jun US$120/185, Jul-Sep & Christmas US$150/225; ⌨) Large dark wooden chalets, with vaulted ceilings, private balconies and a small loft for children to snooze, call this lodge home. It's extremely cosy, but we'd expect more for this price. The best feature is the wildlife water hole fronting the bar,

> ### MARALAL INTERNATIONAL CAMEL DERBY
>
> Inaugurated by Yare Safaris in 1990, the annual Maralal International Camel Derby held in early August is one of the biggest events in Kenya, attracting riders and spectators from the world's four distant corners. The races are open to anyone and the extended after-parties at Yare Camel Club & Camp (left) are notorious – you're likely to bump into some genuine characters here!
>
> Not interested in parties and just want some fast-moving camel action? Then you'll be overjoyed that the derby's first race is an amateur event, open to all comers. Ante up KSh1500 for your entry and KSh2500 for your slobbering steed and get racing. It's a butt-jarring 11km journey. Don't even start complaining about your glowing cheeks – the professional riders cover 42km!
>
> For further information contact **Yare Safaris** (☎ 065-62295; yare@africaonline.co.ke; PO Box 63006, Nairobi) or Yare Camel Club & Camp in Maralal.

which nearly justifies paying KSh125 for a beer there. The gate is 1km west of the BP petrol station along the road to Baragoi.

EATING

Hard Rock Café (meals KSh60-170) While the Hard Rock Café chain would cringe at its name's use, this Somali-run restaurant is the town's best restaurant. Enjoy its chapo-fry (spiced beef with chapatti and side plate of diced tomatoes, onions and beans) while listening to Rick Astley, and being peered over by mugs of the Spice Girls and 2Pac.

Samburu Restaurant (meals KSh80-200) A popular place, with the menu sporting the usual suspects and decent curries.

Safari Hotel (meals KSh80-150) If the lighting and wallpaper don't ruin your appetite, you'll get a good Kenyan meal here.

DRINKING

Some years ago the district commissioner ordered Maralal's discos closed due to the region's insecurity. Apparently no-one here has thought of fighting for their right to party, as this order is still in place.

Buffalo House Hotel, with a pool table out the back, is probably the most popular boozer in town. Another place to shoot some stick and down a Tusker is Paradiso Bar. The bars at Yare Camel Club & Camp and Maralal Safari Lodge are much nicer, but transport back to town may pose a problem!

GETTING THERE & AWAY

Matatus serve Nyahururu (KSh300, three hours), Rumuruti (KSh250, 2½ hours) and Wamba (KSh350, 3½ hours) on a daily basis, usually in the mornings and early afternoons. Reaching Isiolo involves overnighting in Wamba to catch the early-morning southbound *matatu*. There are no direct services to Nairobi; take a *matatu* or bus (KSh300, three hours) to Nyahururu and transfer there.

During the dry season a few 4WD *matatus* and Land Rover taxis head north weekly to Baragoi (KSh300, three hours). If you're intending to head to Lake Turkana, you'll have to wait a few days to a week for a truck (KSh800 to KSh1000, nine to 12 hours). To shorten your wait, inquire around the town's petrol stations and its transport hub (the main roundabout) when you arrive instead of waiting until you want to leave. While breaking the truck journey in Baragoi or South Horr may seem like a good idea, remember that you may have to wait there for a week before another truck trundles through.

Most transport leaves from the main roundabout, while trucks usually pick up passengers at the **BP petrol station** (C77 Hwy).

The BP petrol station is the most reliable. Petrol is KSh10 more per litre here than in Nyahururu, but cheaper than you'll find it further north.

Baragoi

The long descent off the Loroghi Plateau towards Baragoi serves up some sweet vistas, but none can compare with the sheer magnitude of **Lesiolo** or World's View, which perches atop an escarpment at the plateau's dramatic end, offering an outrageous 120km panoramic view over the Rift Valley and serrated Tiati Hills. Lesiolo is part of the Malasso Ecotourism Project and a viewing fee (adult/child US$5/3) is now charged – pricey, but worth every penny!

When you reach the foot of the plateau, the road ahead is laid out before you; it meanders across the acacia-dotted plains before disappearing into jagged hills that seemingly erupt from the horizon. Reaching Baragoi itself is a bit of an anticlimax as the dusty, diminutive town is clearly outdone by its surroundings.

Treks through the Suguta Valley to Lake Turkana are possible from Baragoi, and there are several English-speaking guides here to remind you! Make sure you get a good appraisal of the security situation before attempting this trek.

Be careful not to take photographs in town, as it's supposedly forbidden and police are keen to enforce the rule.

The **Mt Ngiro General Shop** (C77 Hwy) sells pricey petrol from the barrel, and the **Morning Star Guest House** (C77 Hwy; s/tw with shared bathroom KSh200/400) provides a decent place for a night's kip. Just south of the post office, it offers secure parking, decent rooms and mosquito nets. Fine dining (spot blatant overstatement) is found at **Al-Mukaram Hotel** (C77 Hwy; meals KSh60).

Those with bulging wallets can stay at **Desert Rose** (☎ 0722-638774; www.desertrosekenya.com; full board incl activities low season s/d US$400/600, high season US$450/700; ⌂), a stunning ecolodge nestled on the southern slopes of Ol Donyo Nyiro. Each cottage is truly unique and blends into the stunning natural surrounds. The Desert Rose turn-off is 18km north of Baragoi, marked by a gas canister.

The dirt track from Maralal to Baragoi is much improved but still very rocky in places. The drive takes between 2½ and four hours.

Approaching the Lake

The road between Baragoi and South Horr, the next town along, is in reasonable shape and consists of compacted sand and bumpy rocky sections. Almost 23km north of South Horr, when the valley opens to the northern plains, you'll see massive Mt Kulal in the distance and Devil's Hand, a large rock outcrop resembling a fist, to your immediate right. Just north is the eastern turn-off to Marsabit via Kargi, so if you're heading for Turkana keep left. If you get mixed up, just remember that Mt Kulal on your right is good and that Mt Kulal on your left is very, very bad (unless, of course, you're heading to Marsabit!).

Further north, the scrub desert suddenly scatters and you'll be greeted by vast volcanic armies of shimmering bowling ball–size boulders, cinder cones and reddish-purple hues – if they could talk they'd welcome you to Mt Kulal's shattered lava fields. If this arresting and barren Martian landscape doesn't take your breath away, the first sight of the sparkling Jade Sea a few kilometres north certainly will.

As you descend to the lake, South Island stands proudly before you, while Teleki Volcano's geometrically perfect cone lurks on Turkana's southern shore. Before you jump in the water, remember that Turkana has a large crocodile population.

Loyangalani

An oasis of doum palms, natural springs and vivid Turkana tribespeople, Loyangalani is one of northern Kenya's most fascinating places. It overlooks Lake Turkana and is surrounded by small ridges of pillow lava (evidence that this area used to be underwater) peppered with Turkana families' traditional stick and palm dwellings. Other than the post office and the Catholic mission (which occasionally sells petrol at exorbitant prices), there's little in the way of services.

The El-Molo tribe, one of Africa's smallest, lives on the lakeshore just north of here in the villages of **Layeni** and **Komote**. Although outwardly similar to the Turkana, the El-Molo are linguistically linked to the Somali and Rendille. Unfortunately the last speaker of their traditional language died before the turn of the millennium.

As with the Maasai, tourism has wrought inevitable changes in the El-Molo and Turkana peoples' lifestyles and many travellers feel that the tribal issue has been overly commercialised. You'll certainly pay handsomely for taking any photographs.

SIGHTS & ACTIVITIES

Opened as a public reserve in 1983 and made a World Heritage Site by Unesco in 1997, the 39-sq-km volcanic island of **South Island National Park** (adult/child US$15/5) is completely barren and uninhabited apart from large populations of crocodiles, poisonous snakes and feral goats. Spending the night at a **special camp site** (adult/child US$8/5) makes for an even more eerie trip. All the sites lack water, firewood (there are no trees on the island) and toilets. The southern site is the most sheltered from the wind, so your tent is less likely to take flight here.

In calm weather a speedboat can reach the island in 30 minutes and circumnavigate it in another hour. If winds crop up, trip times can easily double. You can hire a boat from Oasis Lodge (per hour KSh2500) or from a local, but always check the vessel's seaworthiness and the impending weather.

Dominating Lake Turkana's eastern horizon, **Mt Kulal's** forested volcanic flanks offer some hiking possibilities. No matter what local guides tell you, trekking up to the summit (2293m) from Loyangalani in a day isn't feasible. Plan on several days for a return trip, or part with substantial sums of cash (KSh8000 to KSh12,000) for a lift up Mt Kulal to the villages of Arapal or Gatab. From there you can head for the summit and spend a long day (eight to 10 hours) hiking back down to Loyangalani. The volcano's view over Lake Turkana and Chalbi Desert are sublime.

SLEEPING & EATING

Palm Shade Camp (camping KSh350, s/tw rondavel with shared bathroom KSh500/1000) Drop your tent on some grass beneath acacias and doum palms or crash in the simple domed rondavels. The huts have simple wooden beds with foam mattresses, and unique walls with meshed cutouts that let light and heavenly evening breezes in. Throw in the town's best toilets and showers, a cooking shelter and electricity until 10pm, and your decision is easy.

Oasis Lodge (☎ 020-503267; willtravel@swiftkenya .com; full board s/tw US$150/200; ⚿) This overpriced lodge offers simple bungalows with dated bathrooms. The food, spring-fed swimming pools (KSh300 for nonguests) and view from the open-air bar are its best assets.

New Saalama Hotel (meals KSh50-110) Although it lacks any signage (ask a local to point it out), this little shack with wooden benches, crooked tables and candlelight is the best place for a local meal. It's usually out of food soon after sunset.

Cold Drink Hotel (meals KSh50-110) Run by a local Somali family, this hotel serves Kenyan dishes and a version of Ethiopian *injera* (a thin, spongy pancake). Its smoky *chai* is worth skipping.

GETTING THERE & AWAY

There are one or two trucks a week that stop in Loyangalani en route to Maralal

(KSh1000, 10 to 12 hours) from Marsabit. Trucks heading in any other direction are even more rare.

If you're travelling in your own vehicle, you have two options to reach Marsabit: continue northeast from Loyangalani across the dark stones of the Chalbi Desert towards North Horr, or head 67km south towards South Horr and take the eastern turn-off near Devil's Hand (see p427). The 270km Chalbi route (seven to eight hours) is OK in the dry season but can be treacherous after rain. Make sure you're carrying adequate food and water with your spare tyres, compass and fuel when you set out. It's also wise to ask for directions every chance you get, otherwise it's easy to take the wrong track and not realise until hours later. The 241km southern route (six to seven hours) via Devil's Hand, the Karoli Desert and Kargi is composed of compacted sands and is less difficult in the rainy season.

For those with money to burn, Oasis Lodge can arrange air transport and hires vehicles for KSh5000 per day plus KSh100 per kilometre.

Sibiloi National Park

A Unesco World Heritage Site and probably Kenya's most remote **national park** (www .sibiloi.com; adult/child US$15/5), Sibiloi is located far up the eastern shore of Lake Turkana and covers an area of 1570 sq km. It was here that Dr Richard Leakey discovered the skull of a *Homo habilis* believed to be 2½ million years old, and where others have unearthed evidence of *Homo erectus*. Despite the area's fascinating prehistory, fossil sites and wonderful arid ecosystem, the difficulties involved in getting this far north tend to discourage visitors, which is a real shame. It seems slightly ironic that the so-called 'Cradle of Mankind' is now almost entirely unpopulated.

Today it's possible to see fossils of a giant tortoise that lived three million years ago, an ancient species of crocodile *(Euthecodon brumpti)* that grew up to 15m long, and a big-tusked behemoth *(Elephas recki)*, a predecessor of today's elephant. The petrified forest south of these sites is evidence that the area was lush and densely forested seven million years ago. Every year the rains and the wind expose more fossils, so many that the most impressive are simply ringed with stones. When visiting these sites, never remove any fossils as future research may be compromised.

The National Museums of Kenya (NMK) maintains a small museum and **Koobi Fora** (www.kfrp.com), a research base that is often home to permanent researchers, visiting scientists and students. It's usually possible to sleep in one of the base's **bandas** (per person KSh1000) or to pitch a tent in the KWS **camp sites** (adult/child US$8/5).

It's best to come in July and August, when the ferocious temperatures break slightly and when activity increases at Koobi Fora. Contact both **KWS** (kws@kws.org; PO Box 219, Lodwar) and **NMK** (☎ 020-3742131; www.museums.or.ke; PO Box 40658, Nairobi) before venturing in this direction.

In the dry season it's a tricky seven-hour drive north from Loyangalani to Sibiloi. Make sure you get precise directions from locals in Loyangalani, as well as from the KWS and NMK, before heading north. In the wet season your only real option is to fly.

MARICH TO TURKANA'S WESTERN SHORE

Despite boasting some of northern Kenya's greatest attributes, like copious kilometres of Jade Sea shoreline, striking volcanic landscapes and vivid Turkana tribes, this remote corner of the country has seen relatively few visitors. With security on the mend there's now a unique opportunity for independent travellers to explore here, thanks to regular public transport currently covering the breadth of the region. The only downside is that you can't get your vehicle across the lake or into Sudan, which makes for a lot of backtracking.

Marich

The spectacular descent from Marich Pass through the lush, cultivated Cherangani Hills leads to arid surroundings, with saisol plants, cactus trees and acacias lining both the road and the chocolate-brown Morun River. Just north, the minuscule village of Marich, near the A1's junction with the B4 Kerio Valley road, marks your entrance into northern Kenya.

SIGHTS & ACTIVITIES

Although the northern plains may beckon, it's worth leashing the 4WD and heading into the hills for some eye-popping and leg-loving trekking action. **Mt Sekerr** (3326m) is a few kilometres northwest of Marich and can be climbed comfortably in a three-day round trip via the agricultural plots of the Pokot tribe, passing through forest and open moors. The views from the top are magnificent in clear weather.

The Marich Pass Field Studies Centre (below) offers English-speaking Pokot and Turkana guides for half-day (KSh450), full-day (KSh550) and overnight (KSh1000) treks. The guides can also help you explore the numerous small **caves** dotted around the hills, most of which have special significance for the local Pokot.

If you'd rather explore with your vehicle, you can head southeast from Marich past Sigor and check out the **Elgeyo Escarpment**, which rises above the Kerio Valley to more than 1830m in places, and offers spectacular views and waterfalls. At the foot of the escarpment (and accessible by *matatu*) is **Lomut** and its fascinating Saturday market, which brings together the pastoral Pokot from the northern plains and the farming Pokot from the southern hills.

About 15km north of Marich along the A1 Hwy to Lokichar is the turn-off for **Nasolot National Reserve** (admission adult/child US$15/5) and **Turkwel Gorge** (admission incl with Nasolot NR). Although the reserve is home to elephants, lesser kudus, lions and leopards, you'll likely only spot the diminutive dik-diks bounding by the roadside. The main attraction is the gorge itself, with towering rock walls and plenty of pretty precipices. The imposing hydroelectric dam sits about 23km from the reserve gate, which is 6km off the A1. Those without vehicles are allowed to hike in the park with an escort (free with reserve admission). With security back under control, the KWS is hoping to soon reopen the camp sites.

Just when you're getting to like the feel of the scrub desert en route to Lokichar, a sudden and all-too-brief burst of green and heavenly cool envelop the road and act as a stark reminder of the lushness you've left behind.

SLEEPING & EATING

Marich Pass Field Studies Centre (www.gg.rhul.ac.uk /MarichPass; PO Box 564, Kapenguria; camping KSh300, dm KSh350, s/tw/tr/q with shared bathroom KSh700/950/ 1425/1900, with private bathroom KSh1100/1500/2250/ 3000) The only reasonable accommodation between Marich and Lokichar is at this centre, which is well signposted just north of Marich and the A1's junction with the B4. Essentially a residential facility for visiting student groups, it's also a great place for independent travellers to base their adventures. The centre occupies a beautiful site alongside the Morun River, and is surrounded by dense bush and woodland. The birdlife here is prolific, monkeys and baboons have the run of the place, and warthogs, buffaloes, antelopes and elephants are all occasional visitors. Facilities include a secure camp site, with drinking water, toilets, showers and firewood, as well as dorm beds and simple, comfortable *bandas*. There's a restaurant (meals KSh220 to KSh350) with vegetarian options, but all meals should be ordered in advance. It also offers self-catering facilities, though there are few supplies in the area. Besides guides for trekking, it offers guided walks discussing ethnobotany (KSh500) and birds (KSh600) for groups of up to five people.

GETTING THERE & AWAY

The easiest way to get to Marich is from Kitale via Makutano and Marich Pass on the oh-so-scenic A1 Hwy, which is often described as Kenya's most spectacular Tarmac road. The buses plying the A1 between Kitale and Lodwar can drop you anywhere along the route, whether at Marich, the field studies centre or at the turn-off to Nasolot National Reserve. You may be asked to pay the full fare to Lodwar (KSh700), but a smile and some patient negotiating should reduce the cost.

The other route is extremely rough (4WD only), and approaches Marich along the B4 from Lake Baringo through the Kito Pass and across the Kerio Valley to Tot; it's tough going with little in the way of signs, but it allows you to visit the hot waterfalls at Kapedo. From Tot, the track skirts the northern face of the Cherangani Hills and may be impassable after heavy rain.

Between Marich and Lokichar the A1 is a bumpy mess of corrugated dirt and lonely islands of Tarmac. The first 40km north of Lokichar is better, but you'll still spend more time on the shoulder than on the road. The opposite is true for the remaining

60km to Lodwar, where patches outnumber potholes and driving is straightforward.

If security takes a turn for the worse, the police checkpoint just north of Marich may again start requiring vehicles to travel in convoy to Lodwar. Another thing to keep an eye out for on this stretch are the flash floods that periodically fill the odd dry river bed with churning chocolate milk – be patient and remember that the water can drop as quickly as it rose.

Lodwar
☎ 054

Besides Lokichoggio near the Sudan border, Lodwar is the only town of any size in the northwest (although that's not saying much). Barren volcanic hills skirted by traditional Turkana dwellings sit north of town and make for impressive early morning sunrise spots. Lodwar has outgrown its days as just an isolated administrative outpost of the Northern Frontier District, and has now become the major service centre and tourist hub for the whole region. If you're visiting Lake Turkana, you'll find it convenient to stay here for at least one night.

INFORMATION

The Kenya Commercial Bank (no ATM) changes cash and charges 1% commission (minimum KSh250) for travellers cheques. The post office has Lodwar's only Internet connection.

SIGHTS & ACTIVITIES

There's little to do in the town itself, but the atmosphere is not altogether unpleasant if you can stand the heat, and just listening to the garrulous locals is entertainment in itself. The small market is a good place to watch women weaving baskets, and there's an endless stream of Turkana hawkers who wander around town selling the usual souvenirs.

You're bound to be approached by several sharp young businessmen calling themselves the Lodwar Tour Guides Association. They'll offer to escort you to Lake Turkana, into the hills and local communities, or even to Central Island National Park. They try hard to please and are a useful source of information, although their prices are a bit steep for the services provided – KSh1500 just for a guide to the lake!

SLEEPING

Unless you're cold-blooded and thick-skinned, it's worth spending more for a room with a fan and mosquito net. The cheaper places are hellishly hot and the mosquitoes can be something fierce.

Nawoitorong Guest House (☎ 21208; camping KSh200, s/tw with shared bathroom KSh400/600, s/tw cottages from KSh700/900) Built entirely out of local materials and run by a local women's group, Nawoitorong is an excellent option, and the only one for campers. Thatched roofs alleviate the need for fans and all rooms have mosquito nets. There's a pleasant restaurant, and the shared-bathroom prices include breakfast. The one-bedroom Ekaato cottages are cheap, but not nearly as charming as the two-bedroom Nadoua cottage, which also has a cooking area. The Napekitoi cottage is perfect for families.

Hotel Splash (☎ 21099; PO Box 297, Lodwar; s KSh450) Well signposted and west of the main crossroads, Hotel Splash has great, smallish singles with fans, mosquito nets, sitting chairs, reading lamps and decent bathrooms. The foam mattresses are pleasantly firm and there's secure parking to boot.

Turkwel Lodge (☎ 21099; s/tw KSh350/700, cottages s/d KSh800/1350) Turkwel offers spacious rooms containing fans and mosquito nets, but lacks the crisp, clean feel of the Splash. Some beds are a bit of an Ikea experiment gone horribly wrong – not so comfy. There's secure parking, and quiet, roomy cottages at the rear.

EATING

Turkwel Hotel (meals KSh60-210) Its green lentil curry is particularly good, but get your order in about three hours early, and don't forget to order the chapatis at the same time! Its local dishes require less waiting and are some of the best in town.

Nawoitorong Guest House (meals KSh160-225) Burgers and toasted sandwiches join local curries and various meaty fries on its menu.

Africana Silent Lodge (meals KSh40-110) A popular eatery with locals for cheap Kenyan fare and fried fish.

If you're self-catering, there's a well-stocked Naipa Supermarket next to the Kobil petrol station.

GETTING THERE & AWAY

Several companies, including Kenya Witness, have daily buses to Kitale (KSh500, 8½ hours)

KENYA

each night at 7.30pm (most services pick up passengers near the New Salama Hotel), while erratic *matatus* serve Kalokol (KSh150, one hour) and Lokichoggio (KSh500, three hours).

While UN vehicles were still travelling in armed convoys along the sublimely sealed 210km stretch of Tarmac to Lokichoggio at the time of research, the security situation had improved enough that local trucks and *matatus* weren't feeling the need to travel in convoy or to take armed escorts. Always check with locals and police to ascertain the latest security situation before travelling on this road.

Drivers will find several petrol stations here, though it's almost KSh20 more per litre than in Kitale.

Eliye Springs

Spring water percolates out of crumbling bluffs and brings life to this remote sandy shore of Lake Turkana, some 66km northeast of Lodwar by road. Growing from the moist sloping sands are oodles of doum palms that give this usually barren environment a downright tropical feel, albeit incongruous. Down on the slippery shore children play in the lake's warm waters, while Central Island lurks magically on the distant horizon. These lake views are almost as spellbinding as the stars that occupy the dark night sky.

On arrival you'll encounter an instant small crowd of colourful Turkana women selling trinkets, ranging from bracelets and fish-backbone necklaces to fossilised hippo teeth. As only a few vehicles visit each week, it's a real buyer's market and prices are absurdly low. It's worth a look because the same items in Lodwar cost much more, despite most of them being made here!

Beneath the bluff the skeleton of an old beach resort sits half eaten by its surroundings and makes for an interesting place to drop your tent. Locals now manage the leftovers and charge KSh200 for camping and KSh250 for sleeping beneath one of the remaining thatched roofs. Besides the spring water there are no facilities, so you'll have to be entirely self-sufficient. Note that more than the odd scorpion and carpet viper also call this place home, so shoes are a good idea!

The turn-off for Eliye Springs is signposted about halfway along the Lodwar–Ka-

lokol road. The gravels are easy to follow until they suddenly peter out and you're faced with a fork in the road – stay left. The rest of the way is a mix of gravel, deep sand and dirt tracks (4WD only), which can turn into a muddy nightmare in the wet season.

If you don't have your own vehicle, you can usually arrange a 4WD in Lodwar to drop you off and pick you up at a predetermined time later for about KSh4500.

Ferguson's Gulf

While a more accessible part of Lake Turkana than Eliye Springs, Ferguson's Gulf has none of its southern neighbour's tropical charm. Fishing boats in various states of disrepair litter its grubby western beach and a definite feeling of bleakness pervades. The gulf's eastern shore (accessible by boat only) is just as desolate, but has an inexplicably attractive air about it.

Birdlife is prolific, particularly in March and April, when thousands of European migratory birds stop here on their way north. There are also hippos and crocodiles (and bilharzia, so seek local advice before diving in.

If you're planning on visiting Central Island National Park (opposite) or Sibiloi National Park (p429), this is the best place to arrange a boat.

Set on the eastern shore, **Lake Turkana Lodge** (☎ 0722-703666; turkana@hillbarrett.com; camping US$10, s/tw US$25/40) is the only official accommodation in the area. Sixteen large timber cabins, each with their own bathroom and scenic veranda, provide sleeping quarters, but lighting is limited at best – bring a torch! The skeleton staff can provide meals (with advance warning) or for a small fee you can use the kitchen. The bar is an excellent place to absorb the scenery, and is usually well stocked with beer, water and soft drink. Boat transfers across the gulf are an additional US$10.

Ferguson's Gulf is accessed from the village of Kalokol, which is reachable by *matatu* from Lodwar along a good 75km stretch of Tarmac. From Kalokol, follow the Tarmac north for a few kilometres before turning left onto the dirt road next to the fading Italian fishing project sign. This leads towards a substantial building before veering to the right and dropping you in the middle of the gulf's fishing fleet.

Central Island National Park

Rising from the depths of Lake Turkana and climbing 170m above its surface is the Central Island Volcano, which was last seen belching molten sulphur and steam just over three decades ago. Today the island is quiet, but its stormy volcanic history is told by the numerous craters scarring its weathered façade. Several craters have coalesced to form two sizeable lakes that are almost 1km wide and 80m deep.

Both a **national park** (adult/child US$15/5) and Unesco World Heritage Site, Central Island is an intriguing place to visit and the view atop the cinder cones is well worth the short scramble. But no matter how temping, stay clear of the lakes as the island is famous for its 14,000 or so Nile crocodiles, some of which are massive in proportion! Like Ferguson's Gulf, the island boasts countless numbers of migratory birds in March and April.

Camping (adult/child US$8/5) is possible and unlike South Island National Park, there are trees to tie your tent to. However, there's no water available or any other facilities, so come prepared.

Hiring a boat from Ferguson's Gulf is the only real option to get here. Depending on what you drive up in, locals can ask anywhere from KSh10,000 to KSh50,000 for the trip. A fair price is KSh6000 for a motorboat – don't even think about being cheap and taking a sailboat! The 10km trip and sudden squalls that terrorize the lake's waters aren't to be taken lightly, so ensure the craft is sound before boarding.

LOKICHOGGIO

Although the A1 Hwy from Lodwar to Lokichoggio via the UN refugee camps at Kakuma has been off limits to everyone but armed aid convoys for the last several years, improved security has meant that the odd intrepid traveller is now able to taste this remote northwest corner of Kenya. Remember that it's imperative to check with locals, NGOs and police in Lodwar before heading off.

The perfect Tarmac between Lodwar and Lokichoggio is almost a sight in itself – simply transcendent! As you head northwest from Lodwar, you'll wind through some rocky bluffs before dropping into a vast valley resembling a lush lawn in wet season and a white sea during drier periods. After passing through the Pelekech Range's stratified

slopes that mark the valley's western side, you'll see a dramatic and seemingly fictitious horizon of sharp mountainous peaks beyond the numerous refugee camps at Kakuma. In reality your eyes are making mountains out of mole hills, as the seemingly large peaks are only 100m- to 200m-high volcanic cinder cones.

Along the entire route you'll encounter rather marvellous Turkana people in striking tribal attire, either walking the roadside, selling sacks of charcoal or resting in the shade of lonely trees. Your steady gaze at these colourful souls will only be broken by the odd termite mound mystifyingly giving you the middle finger.

Despite being backed by the impressive Mogila Range, Lokichoggio itself is rather unattractive. However, what it lacks in looks it makes up for in aid activity, with the World Food Program (WFP), UN and other NGOs basing their Sudanese operations here.

Lokichoggio has a post office, but no banks. The need to house NGO workers has resulted in some pretty plush accommodation options being added to the mix; **Trackmark Camp** (☎ 054-32245; lokicamp@yahoo.com; full board tents s US$50, bandas s/d US$55/80; ⊠ ▢ ▣) is an absolute haven despite the junkie name, while **Makuti Bar** (☎ 0722-257262; A1 Hwy; d with shared bathroom KSh400-500) is the only reasonable budget option in town.

Petrol is readily available and costs KSh10 less per litre than in Lodwar. Road conditions and transport options between Lokichoggio and Lodwar are discussed on p431. The border with Sudan was closed at the time of writing – check for updates at Lodwar's military post.

KENYA DIRECTORY

ACCOMMODATION

Kenya has a good range of accommodation options, from basic cubicle hotels overlooking city bus stands to luxury tented camps hidden away in the national parks. There are also all kinds of camp sites, budget tented camps, simple *bandas* (often wooden huts) and cottages scattered around the parks and rural areas.

During the low season many companies offer excellent deals on accommodation on the coast and in the main wildlife parks,

KENYA

often working with airlines to create packages aimed at the local and expat market. The website of **Let's Go Travel** (www.lets-go-travel.net) displays almost all the major hotels and lodges in Kenya, giving price ranges and descriptions, while www.kenyalastminute.com is a good port of call for discounted bookings at some of the more expensive camps, lodges and hotels, particularly on the coast.

Where appropriate we have split accommodation options into budget, midrange and top-end categories for ease of reference. In general, a budget double room is defined as anything under KSh1000. Surprisingly, bedding, towels and soap are almost always provided however much you pay.

In most of the country, midrange accommodation falls between KSh1000 and KSh3500 for a double room; the major exception to this is Nairobi, where you can pay anything up to KSh6000 for the same standard. In this bracket you'd usually expect breakfast, private bathroom, telephone and good-size double beds with proper mattresses; the more you pay the more facilities you get.

Everything over KSh3500 (or US$80 in Nairobi) counts as top end, and what you get for your money varies enormously. Once you hit the US$100 mark you should certainly count on breakfast, TV, phone, air-con (on the coast), room service and toiletries as standard, and in the upper realms of the price range the extras can include anything from complimentary mini-bars to casinos, Jacuzzis and a range of free activities.

Although most midrange and top-end places quote prices in US dollars, payment can be in local currency. Note that most places have separate rates for residents, and these are often much less than the nonresident rates. All prices quoted in this book are nonresident rates.

Many midrange and (especially) top-end options also change their prices according to season, which can be confusing as very few places use exactly the same dates. In principal there are high, low and shoulder seasons, but some hotels can divide their year into five or more distinct pricing periods! For lodges in the national parks, the norm is to charge high-season prices from July to March, with low-season prices only

applicable from April to June. On the coast, where things are much more seasonal, peak times tend to be July to August and December to March.

In this book, 'high season' refers to rates quoted for the longest peak period and 'low season' refers to the lowest prices available out of season – any other variations should fall between these two guidelines.

African Safari Club

Although it's package tourism at its most developed, the UK-based **African Safari Club** (UK ☎ 020-8466 0014; www.africansafariclub.com) has some splendid properties on the coast and in several of the national parks. Rates are typical for upmarket resorts, but are quoted as part of holiday packages so few offers are for less than a week or so.

Bandas

Bandas are basic huts and cottages, usually with some kind of kitchen and bathroom, that offer excellent value for budget travellers. There are KWS *bandas* at Shimba Hills, Tsavo West, Meru and Mt Elgon, and near the marine reserves at Malindi and Shimoni. Some are wooden huts, some are thatched stone huts and some are small brick bungalows with solar-powered lights; facilities range from basic dorms and squat toilets to kitchens and hot water provided by wood-burning stoves. The cost varies from US$10 to US$20 per person. You'll need to bring all your own food, drinking water, bedding and firewood.

Camping

There are many opportunities for camping in Kenya and it is worth considering bringing a tent with you, although gear can also be hired in Nairobi and around Mt Kenya. There are KWS camp sites in just about every national park or reserve, though these are usually very basic. There will be a toilet block with a couple of pit toilets, and usually a water tap, but very little else.

As well as these permanent camp sites, KWS also runs so-called 'special' camp sites in most national parks; these temporary sites have even fewer facilities than the standard camps, but cost more because of their wilder locations and set-up costs. A reservation fee of KSh5000 per week is payable on top of the relevant camping fee.

Private sites are few and far between, but they do offer more facilities and may hire out tents if you don't have your own.

Hostels

The only youth hostel affiliated with Hostelling International (HI) is in Nairobi. It has good basic facilities and is a pleasant enough place to stay, but there are plenty of other cheaper choices that are just as good. Other places that call themselves 'youth hostels' are not members of HI and standards are very variable.

Hotels & Guesthouses

Real budget hotels (often known as 'board and lodgings' to distinguish them from '*hotelis*', which are often only restaurants) are widely used as brothels and tend to be very rundown. Security at these places is virtually nonexistent; the better ones are set around courtyards and are clean if not exactly comfortable.

Proper hotels and guesthouses come in as many different shapes and sizes as the people who stay in them. As well as the top-end Western companies, there are a number of small Kenyan chains offering reliable standards across a handful of properties in particular towns or regions, and also plenty of private family-run establishments. At the top end of the scale are the all-singing, all-dancing beach resorts along the coast.

Self-catering options are common on the coast, where they're often the only mid-priced alternative to the top-end resorts, but not so much in other parts of the country. A few fancier places offer fully fitted modern kitchens, but more often than not the so-called kitchenettes will be a side room with a small fridge and a rusty portable gas hob.

Terms you will come across frequently in Kenya include 'self-contained', which just means a room with its own private bathroom, and 'all-inclusive', which differs in exact meaning from place to place – generally all meals, certain drinks and possibly some activities should be included in the room rate.

Safari Lodges & Tented Camps

Hidden away inside or on the edges of national parks are some fantastic safari lodges. These are usually visited as part of organised safaris, and you'll pay much more if you just turn up and ask for a room. Some of the older places trade heavily on their more glorious past, but the best places feature five-star rooms, soaring *makuti*-roofed bars and restaurants overlooking waterholes full of wildlife. Staying in at least one good safari lodge is recommended, if only to see how the other half live! Rates tend to come down a lot in the low season.

As well as lodges, many parks contain some fantastic luxury tented camps. These places tend to occupy wonderfully remote settings, usually by rivers or other natural locations, and feature large, comfortable, semipermanent safari tents with beds, furniture and bathrooms. The really exclusive properties occupy locations so isolated that guests fly in and out on charter planes.

ACTIVITIES
Ballooning

Balloon trips in the wildlife parks are an absolutely superb way of seeing the savanna plains and, of course, the animals. The almost ghostly experience of floating silently above the plains with a 360-degree view of everything beneath you is incomparable, and it's definitely worth saving up your shillings.

The flights typically set off at dawn and go for about 1½ hours, after which you put down for a champagne breakfast. You'll then be taken on a wildlife drive in a support vehicle and returned to your lodge. Flights are currently available in the Masai Mara for around US$390.

Cycling

An increasing number of companies offer cycling and mountain-biking trips in Kenya. Popular locations include the edge of the Masai Mara, Hell's Gate National Park, the Central Highlands and the Kerio Valley. The best specialist operator is **Bike Treks** (☎ 020-446371; www.biketreks.co.ke).

Many local companies and places to stay around the country can arrange cheap bicycle hire, allowing you to cycle through places such as Arabuko Sokoke Forest Reserve and Hell's Gate National Park. Hire usually costs KSh300 to KSh500 per day. See p451 for more information on cycling in Kenya. For details of companies offering cycling safaris, see p94.

Diving & Snorkelling

There is a string of marine national parks spread out along the coast between Shimoni and Malindi (see p309 for further details), with plenty of opportunities for snorkelling and scuba diving. The better marine parks are those further away from Mombasa. The Lamu archipelago (p356) also has some fine reefs off the islands of Manda Toto and Kiwayu.

There are distinct seasons for diving in Kenya. October to March is the best time; during June, July and August it's often impossible to dive due to poor visibility caused by heavy silt flow from some of the rivers on the coast. This doesn't necessarily mean that no companies will take your money for trips during this period! In 1997 there was a huge coral die-off as part of a warming of the ocean attributable to El Niño and global warming. However, the coral is slowly recovering, and there are thousands of colourful fish species and even marine mammals.

If you aren't certified to dive, almost every hotel and resort on the coast can arrange an open-water diving course. By international standards, they aren't cheap – a five-day PADI certification course will cost US$330 to US$450. Trips for certified divers, including two dives, go for around US$90.

Nairobi Sailing & Sub Aqua Club (Map p296; ☎ 020-501250; Nairobi Dam, Langata Rd, Nairobi) offers British Sub Aqua Club diver training, and runs diving trips to the coast between September and April.

If you're going to scuba dive on the coast, note that the only decompression chamber in the region is in Mombasa and is run by the Kenyan navy.

Fishing

The **Kenya Fisheries Department** (Map pp280-1; ☎ 020-3742320; Museum Hill Rd, Nairobi), opposite National Museums of Kenya, operates a number of fishing camps in various parts of the country. However, they're difficult to reach without your own vehicle and directions from the Fisheries Department, from which you'll also need to get a fishing licence.

The deep-sea fishing on the coast is some of the best in the world, and various private companies and resorts in Shimoni, Diani Beach, Watamu and Malindi can arrange fishing trips. Boats cost US$250 to US$500 and can usually fit four or five anglers. You'll pay the same price if it's just you in the boat. The season runs from August to April.

For freshwater fishing, there are huge Nile perch as big as a person in Lakes Victoria and Turkana, and some of the trout fishing around the Aberdares and Mt Kenya is quite exceptional. Fishing licences for Mt Kenya, Mt Elgon and Aberdare National Parks cost KSh100 per day.

Gliding & Flying

The **Gliding Club of Kenya** (Map p374; ☎ 0733-760331; gliding@africaonline.co.ke; PO Box 926, Nyeri), near Nyeri in the Central Highlands, offers silent glides over the Aberdares.

Flying lessons are easily arranged in Nairobi, and are much cheaper than in Europe, the USA and Australasia. Contact the **Aero Club of East Africa** (☎ 020-608990) and **Ninety-Nines Flying Club** (☎ 020-500277), both at Wilson Airport.

Sailing

Kilifi, Mtwapa and Mombasa all have sailing clubs, and smaller freshwater clubs can also be found at Lake Naivasha and Lake Victoria, which both have excellent windsurfing and sailing. If you're experienced, you may pick up some crewing at the various yacht clubs, although you'll need to become a temporary member. While it isn't hands-on, a traditional dhow trip out of Lamu is an unforgettable experience.

Trekking & Climbing

For proper mountain trekking Mt Kenya (p376) is the obvious choice, but other promising and relatively unexplored walking territory includes Mt Elgon (p413) on the Ugandan border, the Cherangani Hills and Kerio Valley (p410) east of Kitale, the upper reaches of the Aberdares (p373) and even the Ngong Hills (p297), close to Nairobi.

For more trekking information refer to the relevant chapters in this book, get hold of a copy of Lonely Planet's *Trekking in East Africa* or contact the **Mountain Club of Kenya** (MCK; ☎ 020-602330; www.mck.or.ke). Its website has good advice on Mt Kenya, as well as on technical climbing and trekking throughout Kenya.

Savage Wilderness Safaris (☎ 020-521590; www .whitewaterkenya.com; Sarit Centre, PO Box 1000, Westlands, Nairobi) offers mountaineering trips to Mt Kenya and rock climbing at sites around the country, as well as some more unusual options, like caving.

Water Sports

Conditions on Kenya's coast are ideal ... windsurfing – offshore reefs protect the waters, and winds are usually reasonably strong and constant. Most resort hotels south and north of Mombasa have sailboards for hire; rates vary from KSh400 to KSh800 per hour, and instruction is also available. The sheltered channel between Lamu and Manda Islands (p355) is one of the best places to windsurf on the coast.

As well as the ubiquitous windsurfing, diving and snorkelling on offer, some of the larger resorts have water-sports centres giving visitors the opportunity to try out everything from jet skis and banana boats to bodyboarding and traditional surfing. Kite-surfing is the latest craze to catch on, with tuition available. Diani Beach (p323), south of Mombasa, is the best place to go for all these activities.

White-Water Rafting

The Athi/Galana River has substantial rapids, chutes and waterfalls, and there are also possibilities on the Tana River and Ewaso Ngiro River near Isiolo. The most exciting times for a white-water rafting trip are from late October to mid-January and from early April to late July, when water levels are highest.

The people to talk to are **Savage Wilderness Safaris** (☎ 020-521590; www.whitewaterkenya.com; Sarit Centre, PO Box 1000, Westlands, Nairobi), run by the charismatic Mark Savage. Depending on water levels, rafting trips of up to 450km

---

RESPONSIBLE TREKKING

Trekking can place great pressure on the environment in popular areas. You can help preserve the countryside by taking note of the following information.

- Carry out all your rubbish. Never ever bury it.

- Where there's no toilet, at lower elevations bury your faeces in a 15cm-deep hole (consider carrying a lightweight trowel for this purpose). At higher altitudes soil lacks the organisms needed to digest your faeces, so leave your waste in the open where UV rays will break it down – spreading it facilitates the process. Always carry out your toilet paper (Ziplock bags are best). With either option make sure your faeces is at least 50m from any path, 100m from any watercourse and 200m from any building.

- Don't use detergents or toothpaste within 50m of watercourses, even if they're biodegradable.

- Stick to existing tracks and avoid short cuts that bypass a switchback. If you blaze a new trail straight down a slope, it will erode the hillside with the next heavy rainfall.

- Avoid removing plant life, as it keeps topsoil in place.

and three weeks' duration can be arranged, although most trips last one to four days and cover up to 80km. The company also offers a wide range of other land- and water-based activities, including kayaking and sailing.

BUSINESS HOURS

Most government offices are open Monday to Friday from 8am or 8.30am to 1pm and from 2pm to 5pm. Post offices, shops and services open roughly from 8am to 5pm Monday to Friday and 9am to noon on Saturday. Internet cafés generally keep longer evening hours and may open on Sunday.

Banking hours are 9am to 3pm Monday to Friday and 9am to 11am Saturday; some smaller branches may only open on the first and last Saturday of the month. Barclays Bank at Nairobi's Jomo Kenyatta International Airport is open 24 hours and is the only bank in the country open on a Sunday.

Restaurant opening hours vary according to the type of establishment: as a rule cafés and cheap Kenyan canteens will open at around 6am or 7am and close in the early evening, while more expensive ethnic restaurants will be open from 11am to 10pm daily, sometimes with a break between lunch and dinner. Bars that don't serve food are open from around 6pm until late, while nightclubs open their doors around 9pm and can keep going until 6am or later on weekends!

In this book we have only given specific opening hours where they differ significantly from these broad guidelines.

CHILDREN

Many parents regard Africa as just too dangerous for travel with children, but it is possible if you're prepared to spend a little more and take comfort over adventure for the core of the trip. The coast is the best region to aim for, with most resorts offering European-standard kids' facilities and dedicated staff to take them off your hands once in a while.

Local attitudes towards children vary in Kenya just as they do in the West: screaming babies on *matatus* elicit all the usual sighs and tuttings, but usually kids will be welcomed anywhere that's not an exclusively male preserve, especially by women with families of their own.

For invaluable general advice on taking the family abroad, see Lonely Planet's *Travel with Children* by Cathy Lanigan.

CLIMATE

Kenya's diverse geography means that temperature, rainfall and humidity vary widely, but there are effectively four distinct zones.

The hot, rainy plateau of western Kenya has rainfall throughout the year, the heaviest usually during April when as much as 200mm may be recorded, and the lowest in January with an average of 40mm. Temperatures range from a minimum of 14°C to 18°C to a maximum of 30°C to 36°C throughout the year.

In the temperate Rift Valley and Central Highlands, average temperatures vary from a minimum of 10°C to 14°C to a maximum of 22°C to 28°C. Rainfall varies from a minimum of 20mm in July to 200mm in April, falling in essentially two seasons – March to the beginning of June (the 'long rains') and October to the end of November (the 'short rains'). Mt Kenya and the Aberdare mountains are the country's main water catchments, with falls of up to 3000mm per year.

In the semiarid bushlands of northern and eastern Kenya, temperatures vary from highs of up to 40°C during the day to less than 20°C at night. July is usually the driest month, and November the wettest. The average annual rainfall varies between 250mm and 500mm.

The consistently humid coast region has rainfall averages from 20mm in February to around 300mm in May. The average annual rainfall is between 1000mm and 1250mm (less in drought years). Average temperatures vary little during the year, ranging from 22°C to 30°C.

For the latest local weather forecasts online, visit the **Kenya Meteorological Office** (www.meteo .go.ke).

COURSES

If you intend to spend considerable time in Kenya, learning Swahili is an excellent idea. The best language school is run by the Anglican Church of Kenya (ACK). Taking a language course (or any course) also entitles you to a 'Pupils' Pass', an immigration permit allowing continuous stays of up to 12 months. The following language schools offer courses:

ACK Language & Orientation School (Map pp280-1; ☎ 020-2723200; www.ackenya.org; Bishops Rd, Upper Hill, PO Box 47429, Nairobi) Full-time courses (US$450) last 14 weeks and take up five hours a day. More flexible is private tuition, which costs US$4 per hour. Study materials will cost around US$40.

Language Center Ltd (Map p298; ☎ 020-570610; Ndemi Close, off Ngong Rd, PO Box 40661, Nairobi) This is a good cheaper option; classes cost KSh250 per hour in a group or KSh450 for one-on-one tuition, and you can study two, three or seven days a week.

CUSTOMS

There are strict laws about taking wildlife products out of Kenya. The export of products made from elephant, rhino and sea turtle are prohibited. The collection of coral is also not allowed. Ostrich eggs will also be confiscated unless you can prove you bought them from a certified ostrich farm. Always check to see what permits are required, especially for the export of any plants, insects and shells.

The usual regulations apply to items you can bring into the country: 50 cigars, 200 cigarettes, 250g of pipe tobacco, 1L of alcohol, 250ml of perfume and other personal items, such as cameras, laptop computers and binoculars. Obscene publications are banned, which may extend to some lads' magazines.

You are allowed to take up to KSh100,000 out of the country.

DANGERS & ANNOYANCES

While Kenya is a safe destination in African terms, there are still plenty of pitfalls for the unwary or inexperienced traveller, from everyday irritations to more serious threats. A little street sense goes a long way here, and getting the latest local information is essential wherever you intend to travel.

Banditry

Wars in Somalia, Sudan and Ethiopia have all had their effect on the stability and safety of northern and northeastern Kenya. AK-47s have been flowing into the country for many years, and the newspapers are filled with stories of hold-ups, shoot-outs, cattle rustling and general lawlessness. Bandits and poachers infiltrating from Somalia have made the northeast of the country particularly dangerous, and with the American 'War on Terror' shutting down the funding for many warring factions within Somalia, these problems are only going to get worse.

In the northwest, the main problem is armed tribal wars and cattle rustling across the Sudanese border. There are Kenyan *shifta*

too, of course, but cross-border problems seem to account for most of the trouble in the north of the country.

Despite all the headlines, tourists are rarely targeted, as much of the violence and robberies take place far from the main tourist routes. Security has also improved considerably in previously high-risk areas, such as the Isiolo–Marsabit, Marsabit–Moyale and Malindi–Lamu routes. However, you should check the situation locally before taking these roads, or travelling between Garsen and Garissa or Thika.

The areas along the Sudanese and Ethiopian borders are very risky, although most visitors are very unlikely to have any reason to go there in the first place.

Crime

Even the staunchest Kenyan patriot will readily admit that the country's biggest problem is crime. It ranges from petty snatch theft and mugging to violent armed robbery, carjacking and, of course, white-collar crime and corruption. As a visitor you needn't feel paranoid, but you should always keep your wits about you, particularly at night.

Perhaps the best advice for when you're walking around cities and towns is not to carry anything valuable with you. Most hotels provide a safe or secure place for valuables, although you should be cautious of the security at some budget places. Cheap digital watches and plastic sunglasses can be bought in Kenya for under KSh100 and you won't miss them if they get taken.

While pickpocketing and bag-snatching are the most common crimes, armed muggings do occur in Nairobi and on the coast. However, they usually happen at night or in remote areas, so always take taxis after dark or along lonely dirt roads. Conversely, snatch-and-run crimes happen more in crowds. If you suddenly feel there are too many people around you, or think you are being followed, dive straight into a shop and ask for help.

In the event of a crime, you should report it to the police, but this can be a real procedure. You'll need to get a police report if you intend to make an insurance claim. In the event of a snatch theft, think twice before yelling 'Thief!'. It's not unknown for people to administer summary justice on the spot, often with fatal results for the criminal.

STREET KIDS

Nairobi in particular has huge problems with street children, many of whom are AIDS orphans, who trail foreigners around asking for food or change. It's up to you whether you give, but if you do, the word will go around and you won't get a moment's peace. It's also debatable how much your donations will help, as the older boys operate like a minimafia, extorting money from the younger kids.

If you want to help out, money might be better donated to the charity **Homeless Children International** (☎ 020-573013; www .hcikenya.org), which works to improve conditions for these children.

Although crime is a fact of life in Kenya, it needn't spoil your trip. Above all, don't make the mistake of distrusting every Kenyan just because of a few bad apples – the honest souls you meet will far outweigh any crooks who cross your path.

Scams

At some point in Kenya you'll almost certainly come across people who play on the emotions and gullibility of foreigners. Nairobi is a particular hot spot, with 'friendly' approaches a daily if not hourly occurrence (see p285 for examples of favourite tricks). It's OK to talk to these people if they're not actively hassling you, but you should always ignore any requests for money.

Be sceptical of strangers who claim to recognise you in the street, especially if they're vague about exactly where they know you from – it's unlikely that any ordinary person is going to be *that* excited by seeing you twice. Anyone who makes a big show of inviting you into the hospitality of their home also probably has ulterior motives. The usual trick is to bestow some kind of gift upon the delighted traveller, who is then emotionally blackmailed into reciprocating to the order of several hundred shillings.

Tourists with cars also face a whole set of potential rip-offs. Don't trust people who gesticulate wildly to you as you are driving along, indicating your front wheels are wobbling; if you stop, chances are you'll be relieved of your valuables. Another trick is to splash oil on your wheels, then tell you the wheel bearings, differential or something else has failed, and direct you to a nearby garage where their friends will 'fix' the problem – for a substantial fee, of course.

DISABLED TRAVELLERS

Travelling in Kenya is not easy for physically disabled people, but it's not impossible. Very few tourist companies and facilities are geared for disabled travellers, and those that are tend to be restricted to the expensive hotels and lodges. However, if you're polite you're likely to get assistance from people wherever you need it. Visually or hearing-impaired travellers, however, will find it very hard to get by without an able-bodied companion.

In Nairobi, only the ex-London taxis are spacious enough to accommodate a wheelchair, but many safari companies do regularly take disabled people out on safari. The travel agency **Travel Scene Services** (☎ 020-215404; travelscene@insightkenya.com) has lots of experience with disabled travellers.

Many of the top-end beach resorts on the coast have facilities for the disabled, whether it's a few token ramps or fully equipped rooms with handrails and bathtubs. Many of the hotels owned by **Lonrho Hotels** (Nairobi ☎ 020-216940; www.lonrhohotels.com) can make provisions for disabled people – Mount Kenya Safari Club has its own wheelchair for guests' use. In Amboseli National Park, **Ol Tukai Lodge** (Nairobi ☎ 020-4445514; oltukai@mitsuminet.com) has two disabled-friendly cottages.

EMBASSIES & CONSULATES
Kenyan Embassies & Consulates
Australia (☎ 02-6247 4788; kenrep@dynamite.com.au; QBE Bldg, 33-35 Ainslie Ave, Canberra, ACT 2601)
Canada (☎ 613-563 1773; www.kenyahighcommission .ca; 415 Laurier Ave, East Ottawa, Ontario, KIN 6R4)
Ethiopia (☎ 01-610033; kenya.embassy@telecom.net.et; Fikre Miriam Rd, PO Box 3301, Addis Ababa)
France (☎ 01 56 62 25 25; kenparis@wanadoo.fr; 3 Rue Freycinet, 75116 Paris)
Germany (☎ 030-25922660; embassy-kenya.bn@ wwmail.de; Markgrafenstr 63, 10969 Berlin)
Israel (☎ 03-57546333; kenya04@ibm.net; 15 Rehov Abba Hillel Silver, Ramat Gan 52522, PO Box 52136, Tel Aviv)
Italy (☎ 396-8082714; www.embassyofkenya.it; Via Archmede 165, 00197 Rome)
Japan (☎ 03-3723 4006; www.embassy-avenue.jp/kenya; 3-24-3 Yakumo, Meguro-Ku, Tokyo 152)

Netherlands (☎ 070-350 42 15; kenre@dataweb.nl; Niewe Parklaan 21, 2597 The Hague)

South Africa (☎ 012-362 2249; kenp@pta.lia.net; 302 Brooks St, Menlo Park, 0081 Pretoria)

Sudan (☎ 011-460386; Street 3Amarat, PO Box 8242, Khartoum)

Tanzania (☎ 022-2112955; khc@raha.com; NIC Investment House, Samora Ave, PO Box 5231, Dar es Salaam)

Uganda (☎ 041-258235; Plot No 41, Nakasero Rd, PO Box 5220, Kampala)

UK (☎ 020-7636 2371; www.kenyahighcommission.com; 45 Portland Place, London W1N 4AS)

USA (☎ 202-387-6101; www.kenyaembassy.com; 2249 R Street NW, Washington DC 20008)

Embassies & Consulates in Kenya

A selection of countries that maintain diplomatic missions in Kenya are listed below.

Australia (Map pp280-1; ☎ 020-445034; www.embassy .gov.au/ke.html; ICIPE House, Riverside Dr, Nairobi)

Canada (☎ 020-3663000; www.nairobi.gc.ca; Limuru Rd, Nairobi)

Ethiopia (Map pp280-1; ☎ 020-2732050; State House Ave, Nairobi)

France (Map pp280-1; ☎ 020-316363; www.ambafrance -ke.org; Barclays Plaza, Loita St, Nairobi)

Germany (☎ 020-4262100; www.nairobi.diplo.de; 113 Riverside Dr, Nairobi)

Ireland (☎ 020-556647; irconsul@swiftkenya.com; Masai Rd, Nairobi)

Israel (Map pp280-1; ☎ 020-2722182; Bishops Rd, Nairobi)

Italy (Mombasa (Map p314; ☎ 041-314705; Jubilee Bldg, Moi Ave, Mombasa); Nairobi (Map pp282-3; ☎ 020-319198; cooperazione@utlnairobi.org; International Life House, Mama Ngina St, Nairobi)

Japan (Map pp282-3; ☎ 020-315850; embjap@wananchi .com; ICEA Bldg, Kenyatta Ave, Nairobi)

Netherlands (☎ 020-4447412; Riverside Lane, Nairobi)

South Africa (Nairobi (☎ 020-2827100; Roshanmaer Pl, Lenana Rd, Nairobi)

Spain (Map pp282-3; ☎ 020-246009; embespke@mail .mae.es; International House, Mama Ngina St, Nairobi)

Sudan (Map pp280-1; ☎ 020-2720883; sudanemb@ wananchi.com; AON-Minet Bldg, Mamlaka Rd, Nairobi) At the time of research, this embassy did not issue visas.

Tanzania (Map pp282-3; ☎ 020-311948; Reinsurance Plaza, Aga Khan Walk, Nairobi)

Uganda (Kenyatta Ave, Nairobi (Map pp282-3; ☎ 020-311814; Uganda House, Kenyatta Ave, Nairobi); Riverside Paddocks, Nairobi (☎ 020-4445420; www.ugandahigh commission.co.ke; Riverside Paddocks, Nairobi)

UK (Map pp280-1; ☎ 020-2844000; www.britishhigh commission.gov.uk/kenya; Upper Hill Rd, Nairobi)

USA (☎ 020-3636000; http://nairobi.usembassy.gov; United Nations Ave, Nairobi)

FESTIVALS & EVENTS

Major events around Kenya include the following:

Maulid Festival Falling in March or April for the next few years, this annual celebration of the prophet Mohammed's birthday is a huge event in Lamu town, drawing hundreds of visitors (see p353).

Tusker Safari Sevens (www.safarisevens.com) International rugby tournament held every June near Nairobi (see p286).

Kenya Music Festival (☎ 020-2712964) The country's longest-running music festival, held over 10 days in August (p286).

Mombasa Carnival (zainab@africaonline.co.ke) November street festival, with music, dance and other events (see p316).

East Africa Safari Rally (www.eastafricansafarirally.com) Classic car rally now in its 50th year, covering Kenya, Tanzania and Uganda using only pre-1971 vehicles. Held in December.

FOOD

You can eat well in Kenya, though outside the major towns variety isn't always a priority; see p277 for a full rundown of the restaurant scene. In general you should be able to snack for KSh10 to KSh100 on the street and fill up for under KSh200 in any cheap Kenyan cafeteria; an Indian or standard Western meal will cost around KSh500, a Chinese meal anything up to KSh1000, and a top-flight meal in a classy restaurant with wine and all the trimmings can easily exceed KSh2000 per person.

In this book we have organised restaurants by type of food where appropriate, for ease of reference.

GAY & LESBIAN TRAVELLERS

Even today there is still a widespread perception across Africa that homosexuality is somehow an un-African phenomenon, introduced to the continent by degenerate European colonials. It goes on covertly, of course, but under Kenyan law homosexuality is still punishable by up to 14 years in prison. There are very few prosecutions under this law, but it's certainly better to be discreet; some local conmen do a good line in blackmail, picking up foreigners then threatening to expose them to the police!

Although there are probably more gays and lesbians in Nairobi, the coast is more tolerant of gay relationships, at least privately.

The closest Kenya has to a 'scene' is the tolerant Gypsy's Bar (p291) in Westlands,

Nairobi, though as of September 2005 the organisation **Gay Kenya** (www.gaykenya.com) has introduced an official bimonthly gay night, also in Westlands; call ☎ 020-4452691 for details.

The **Purple Roofs travel directory** (www.purple roofs.com/africa/kenyata.html) lists a number of gay or gay-friendly tour companies in Kenya and around the world who may be able to help you plan your trip. For luxury all-inclusive packages, the travel agents **Atlantis Events** (www .atlantisevents.com) and **David Tours** (www.davidtours .com) can arrange anything from balloon safaris to luxurious coastal hideaways, all with a gay focus. For information, **Behind the Mask** (www.mask.org.za) is an excellent website covering gay issues and news from across Africa.

HOLIDAYS

All government offices and banks close on public holidays, and most shops and businesses will either close or run according to their usual Sunday opening hours. Popular events can cause a run on accommodation at the lower end of the budget scale, and transport may run less frequently or be more crowded than usual.

Muslim festivals are significant events along the coast. Many places to eat in the region close until after sundown during the Muslim fasting month of Ramadan, which will run from 24 September 2006, 13 September 2007 and 2 September 2008. The Maulid Festival (p353), marking the birth of the Prophet Mohammed, is also widely celebrated, especially on Lamu. This will take place on 20 March 2007 and 20 March 2008.

Public Holidays

New Year's Day 1 January
Easter (Good Friday and Easter Monday) March/April
Labour Day 1 May
Madaraka (Self-Rule) Day 1 June
Moi Day 10 October
Kenyatta Day 20 October
Independence Day 12 December
Christmas Day 25 December
Boxing Day 26 December

INTERNET ACCESS

Email is firmly established in Kenya, although connection speeds fluctuate wildly, even in Nairobi. Most towns have at least one Internet café where you can surf freely and access webmail accounts or instant messenger programs. In Nairobi or Mombasa you can pay as little as KSh1 per minute for access, but in rural areas and top-end hotels the rate can be as high as KSh20 per minute.

With the increasing popularity of Internet cafés, the national Posta network has stepped in and virtually revolutionised the industry by offering Internet access at almost every main post office in the country. The real beauty of this is that every branch charges the same fixed rate of KSh1.16 per minute (KSh1 plus VAT). It's run on a prepay system: you pay KSh100 for a card with a PIN code, which you can then use to log in at any branch as often as you like until the money runs out. While the service can't often compete with the flashier private offices in big cities like Nairobi and Mombasa, it's well worth investigating if you're further afield.

LEGAL MATTERS

All drugs except *miraa* are illegal in Kenya. Marijuana (commonly known as *bhang*) is widely available but highly illegal, and possession carries a penalty of up to 10 years in prison. Dealers are common on the beaches north and south of Mombasa, and frequently set up travellers for real or phoney cops to extort money. African prisons are unbelievably harsh places; don't take the risk.

Note that *miraa* is illegal in Tanzania, so if you do develop a taste for the stuff in Kenya you should leave it behind when heading south.

MAPS

Bookshops, especially the larger ones in Nairobi, are the best places to look for maps in Kenya. The *Tourist Map of Kenya* gives good detail, as does the *Kenya Route Map*; both cost around KSh250. Marco Polo's 1:1,000,000 *Shell Euro Karte Kenya* and Geocenter's *Kenya* (1:1,000,000) are useful overview maps that are widely available in Europe. For those planning a longer trip in southern and East Africa, Michelin's 1:4,000,000 map 955 (Africa Central and South) is very useful.

Macmillan publishes a series of maps to the wildlife parks and these are not bad value at around KSh250 each (three are available in Europe – *Amboseli*, *Masai Mara* and *Tsavo East & West*). Tourist Maps also publishes a national park series for roughly the same price. They might look a bit flimsy

LEGAL AGE

- Age of majority: 18 years
- Voting age: 18 years
- Age of consent (heterosexual): 16 years
- Age of criminal responsibility: 8 years
- Drinking age: 18 years

on detail, but they include the numbered junctions in the national parks.

The most detailed and thorough maps are published by the Survey of Kenya, but the majority are out of date and many are out of print. Better bookshops in Nairobi usually have copies of the most important maps, including *Amboseli National Park* (SK 87), *Masai Mara Game Reserve* (SK 86), *Meru National Park* (SK 65), *Tsavo East National Park* (SK 82) and *Tsavo West National Park* (SK 78).

MONEY

The unit of currency is the Kenyan shilling (KSh), which is made up of 100 cents. Notes in circulation are KSh1000, 500, 200, 100, 50 and 20, and there are also new coins of KSh40, 20, 10, 5 and 1 in circulation. Old coins are much bigger and heavier, and come in denominations of KSh5 (seven-sided) and KSh1. The old 50¢, 10¢ and 5¢ coins are now pretty rare, as most prices are whole-shilling amounts. Note that most public telephones accept only new coins. Locally the shilling is commonly known as a 'bob', after the old English term for a 1-shilling coin.

The shilling has been relatively stable over the last few years, maintaining fairly constant rates against a falling US dollar and a strong British pound. Both these currencies are easy to change throughout the country, as is the euro, which is rapidly replacing the US dollar as the standard currency quoted for hotel prices on the coast. Cash is easy and quick to exchange at banks and foreign exchange bureaus, but carries a higher risk of theft, while travellers cheques are replaceable, but not as widely accepted and often carry high commission charges. Carrying a combination of these and a Visa ATM card will ensure you're never stuck for cash.

ATMs

Virtually all banks in Kenya now have ATMs at most branches, but their usefulness to travellers varies widely. Barclays Bank has easily the most reliable ATMs for international withdrawals, with a large network of ATMs covering most major Kenyan towns. They support MasterCard, Visa, Plus and Cirrus international networks.

Standard Chartered and Kenya Commercial Bank ATMs also accept Visa but not the other major providers, and are more likely to decline transactions. Whichever bank you use, the international data link still goes down occasionally, so don't rely on being able to withdraw money whenever you need it.

Cash

While most major currencies are accepted in Nairobi and Mombasa, once away from these two centres you'll run into problems with currencies other than US dollars, British pounds and euros. Away from the coast, you may even struggle to change euros. Play it safe and carry US dollars – it makes life much simpler.

Credit Cards

Credit cards are becoming increasingly popular, with old fraud-friendly, fully manual swipe machines slowly being replaced by electronic systems that dial up for every transaction. While there's less chance of someone making extra copies of chits this way, the connections fail with tedious regularity. Visa and MasterCard are now widely accepted, but it would be prudent to stick to upmarket hotels, restaurants and shopping centres to use them.

Be aware that credit-card companies will not post cards to Kenya, so you'll have to arrange a courier.

Moneychangers

The best places to change money are foreign exchange or 'forex' bureaus, which can be found everywhere and usually don't charge commission. Watch out for differing small bill (US$10) and large bill (US$100) rates; the larger bills usually get the better rates.

Banks also change money, but they charge large commissions and there's a fee per travellers cheque, so you're better off carrying larger denominations. Travellers cheque rates may be better than at the bureaus, and you'll have the added bonus of being able to put your money away in the secure setting of the bank foyer. AmEx has offices in Mombasa and Nairobi, where you can buy and sell AmEx travellers cheques.

INTERNATIONAL TRANSFERS

Postbank, a branch of the Kenyan Post Office, is the regional agent for Western Union, the global money-transfer company. Using its service is an easy way (if the phones are working) of receiving money in Kenya. Handily, the sender pays all the charges and there's a Postbank in most towns, often within the post office itself or close by. Senders should contact **Western Union** (www .westernunion.com; Australia ☎ 1800-501500; New Zealand ☎ 0800-270000; UK ☎ 0800-833833; USA ☎ 1800-3256000) to find out the location of their nearest agent.

Tipping

Tipping is not common practice among Kenyans, but there's no harm in rounding up the bill by a few shillings if you're pleased with the service in a cheap restaurant. In tourist-oriented businesses a service charge of 10% is often added to the bill, along with the 16% VAT and 2% catering levy. Most tourist guides and all safari drivers and cooks will expect some kind of gratuity at the end of your tour or trip. As fares are negotiated in advance, taxi drivers do not need to be tipped unless they provide exceptional service.

PHOTOGRAPHY & VIDEO

Photographing people remains a sensitive issue in Kenya. Some tribal groups request money for you to take their photo.

You should never get your camera out at border crossings or near government or army buildings; even bridges can sometimes be classed as sensitive areas.

Film & Equipment

You'll find Kodak and Fuji 100, 200 and 400 ASA (ISO) print and slide film widely available in Nairobi, but even 100 ISO slide film is hard to find in Mombasa. If you plan to use 64 or 800 ASA film, bring it from home. As an indication of price, 36-exposure slide film in Nairobi costs about KSh400; 36-exposure colour print film is

cheaper at KSh250 to KSh350. Watch out for out-of-date batches.

Both VHS and Hi-8 video film is available in Nairobi and Mombasa, but it's relatively expensive. You may also be able to find memory cards and other accessories for digital and DV cameras, but again prices are high and quality is not guaranteed.

Film Processing

Shops and booths offering film processing are popping up in small towns and villages all over Kenya. In addition, there are plenty of one-hour film-processing labs in Nairobi, and at least one in all other major towns. They can handle any film speeds, but results can vary. Depending on the print size, processing and printing costs about KSh480 to KSh650 for a 36-exposure film. E6 slide processing can only be done in Nairobi and costs around KSh450 for a 36-exposure film.

POST

The Kenyan postal system is run by the government Postal Corporation of Kenya, now rebranded as the dynamic-sounding Posta. Letters sent from Kenya rarely go astray, but can take up to two weeks to reach Australia or the USA. Incoming letters to Kenya take anywhere from four days to a week to reach the poste-restante service in Nairobi.

The following table lists airmail rates (in KSh) for items posted from Kenya:

Item	East Africa	Europe	USA & Australia
letter	55	75	95
small postcard	30	40	55
large postcard	55	75	95
aerogram	35	45	45

Note that there are different prices for large and small postcards – if in doubt, go with the large postcard price.

Parcels

If sent by surface mail, parcels take three to six months to reach Europe, while airmail parcels take around a week. As a rough guide, a 1kg parcel sent by air/surface mail would cost KSh1160/940 to East Africa, KSh1270/1030 to Europe and KSh1330/1070 to the rest of the world.

Most things arrive eventually, although there is still a problem with theft within the system. Curios, clothes and textiles will be OK, but if your parcel contains anything of obvious value, send it by courier. Posta has its own courier service, EMS, which is considerably cheaper than the big international courier companies.

Receiving Mail
Letters can be sent care of poste restante in any town. Make sure your correspondents write your name in block capitals and also underline the surname.

Some travellers use the **American Express Clients Mail Service** Mombasa (Map p314; ☎ 041-315405; Nairobi Express Kenya Ltd, PO Box 90631, Nkrumah Rd); Nairobi (Map pp282-3; ☎ 020-222906; Express Kenya Ltd, PO Box 40433, Hilton Hotel, Mama Ngina St) and this can be a useful, and more reliable, alternative. You'll need to have an AmEx card or be using its travellers cheques to avail yourself of this service.

TELEPHONE
The Kenyan fixed-line phone system, run by **Telkom Kenya** (www.telkom.co.ke), is more or less functional, but has been overtaken by the massive popularity of prepaid mobile phones.

International call rates from Kenya have come down recently, but are still relatively expensive, charged at a flat rate of US$0.90 per minute during peak periods and US$0.64 per minute off-peak to any destination. Operator-assisted calls are charged at the standard peak rate but are subject to a three-minute minimum. You can always dial direct using a phonecard. All phones should be able to receive incoming calls (the number is usually scrawled in the booth somewhere).

Reverse-charge (collect) calls are possible, but only to countries that have set up free direct-dial numbers allowing you to reach the international operator in the country you are calling. Currently these include: the **UK** (☎ 0800-220441), the **USA** (☎ 0800-111, 0800-1112), **Canada** (☎ 0800-220114, 0800-220115), **New Zealand** (☎ 0800-220641) and **Switzerland** (☎ 0800-220411).

The minimum charge for a local call from a payphone is KSh5 for 97 seconds, while long-distance rates vary depending on the distance. When making a local call from a public phone, make sure you put a

coin into the slot first. Calls to Tanzania and Uganda are priced as long-distance calls, not international.

For the international dialling code, see Quick Reference inside the front cover of this book.

Mobile Phones
An estimated 80% of all calls here are now made on mobile phones, and coverage is good in all but the furthest rural areas. Kenya uses the GSM 900 system, which is compatible with Europe and Australia but not with the North American GSM 1900 system. If you have a GSM phone, check with your service provider about using it in Kenya, and beware of high roaming charges. Remember that you will generally be charged for receiving calls abroad as well as for making them.

If your phone isn't locked into a network, you can pick up a prepaid starter pack from one of the Kenyan mobile-phone companies; the main players are **Safaricom** (www.safaricom.co.ke) and **Celtel** (www.ke.celtel.com). A SIM card will cost about KSh100, and you can then buy top-up 'scratchcards' from shops and booths across the country. An international SMS costs around KSh10, and voice charges vary according to tariff, time and destination of call.

You can easily buy a handset anywhere in Kenya, generally unlocked and with SIM card. Prices start around KSh2500 for a very basic model.

Mobile-phone numbers have a four-digit prefix beginning with 07.

Phonecards
With the new Telkom Kenya phonecards, any phone can now be used for prepaid calls – you just have to dial the **access number** (☎ 0844), and enter in the number and passcode on the card. There are booths selling the cards all over the country. Cards come in denominations of KSh200, KSh500, KSh1000 and KSh2000, and call charges are slightly more expensive than for standard lines (peak/off-peak US$1/70¢).

TIME
Time in Kenya is GMT/UTC plus three hours year-round. You should also be aware of the concept of 'Swahili time', which perversely is six hours out of kilter with the rest of the world. Noon and midnight are

6 o'clock *(saa sitta)* Swahili time, and 7am and 7pm are 1 o'clock *(saa moja)*. Just add or subtract six hours from whatever time you are told; Swahili doesn't distinguish between am and pm. You don't come across this often unless you speak Swahili, but you still need to be prepared for it.

TOURIST INFORMATION
Local Tourist Offices
Considering the extent to which the country relies on tourism, it's incredible to think that, at the time of writing, there was still no tourist office in Nairobi. There are a handful of information offices elsewhere in the country, ranging from helpful private concerns to underfunded government offices; most can at least provide basic maps of the town, and brochures on local businesses and attractions.

i-Point Diani Beach (Map p323; ☎ 040-3202234; Barclays Centre)
Lamu (Map p342; ☎ 042-633449) Off Kenyatta Rd.
Malindi (Map p337; ☎ 042-20689; Malindi Complex, Lamu Rd)
Mombasa (Map p312; ☎ 041-225428; mcta@ikenya.com; Moi Ave)

Tourist Offices Abroad
The Ministry of Tourism maintains a number of overseas offices.
Canada (☎ 905-891 3909; www.kcocanada.org; 1599 Hurontario St, Ste 100, Mississauga, Ontario L5G 4S1)
Germany (☎ 089-23662194; think@magnum.de; c/o The Magnum Group, Herzogspitalstrade 5, D-80331 Munich)
Italy (☎ 02-481 02 361; kenya@adams.it; c/o Adam & Partner Italia, Via Salaino 12, 20144 Milano)
Netherlands (☎ 020-421 26 68; kenia@travelmc.com; Leliegracht 20, 1015 DG Amersterdam)
Spain (☎ 93-292 06 55; kenya@ketal.com; c/o Tuset 10, 3o4a, 08006 Barcelona)
UK (☎ 020-7836 7738; kenya@iiuk.co.uk; 69 Monmouth St, London WC2H 9JW)
USA (☎ 1-866-44-53692; infousa@magicalkenya.com; Carlson Destination Marketing Services, PO Box 59159 Minneapolis, MN 55459-8257)

VISAS
Visas are now required by almost all visitors to Kenya, including Europeans, Australians, New Zealanders, Americans and Canadians, although citizens from a few smaller Commonwealth countries are exempt. Visas are valid for three months from the date of entry and can be obtained on arrival at Jomo Kenyatta International Airport in Nairobi. The visa fee is UK£35 or US$50 for a single-entry visa, and UK£70 or US$100 for multiple entries. If you have any other currencies, you'll have to change them into Kenyan shillings. Tourist visas can be extended for a further three-month period, but seven-day transit visas (US$20) cannot.

It's also possible to get visas from Kenyan diplomatic missions overseas, but you should apply well in advance, especially if you're doing it by mail. Visas are usually valid for entry within three months of the date of issue. Applications for Kenyan visas are simple and straightforward in Tanzania and Uganda, and payment is accepted in local currency. Visas can also be issued on arrival at the land borders with Uganda and Tanzania.

Visa Extensions
Visas can be renewed at immigration offices during normal office hours, and extensions are usually issued on a same-day basis. Staff at the immigration offices are generally friendly and helpful, but the process takes a while. You'll need two passport photos and KSh2200 for a three-month extension. You also need to fill out a form registering as an alien if you're going to be staying more than 90 days. Immigration offices are only open Monday to Friday; note that the smaller offices may sometimes refer travellers back to Nairobi or Mombasa for visa extensions.

Local immigration offices:
Kisumu (Map p398; 1st fl, Reinsurance Plaza, cnr Jomo Kenyatta Hwy & Oginga Odinga Rd)
Lamu (Map p342; ☎ 042-633032) Off Kenyatta Rd.
Malindi (Map p337; ☎ 042-30876; Mama Ngina Rd)
Mombasa (Map p312; ☎ 041-311745; Uhuru ni Kari Bldg, Mama Ngina Dr)
Nairobi (Map pp282-3; ☎ 020-222022; Nyayo House, cnr Kenyatta Ave & Uhuru Hwy)

Visas for Onward Travel
Since Nairobi is a common gateway city to East Africa and the city centre is easy to get around, many travellers spend some time here picking up visas for other countries that they intend to visit. If you are going to do this, you need to plan ahead of time and call the embassy to confirm the hours that visa applications are received (these change

frequently in Nairobi). Most embassies will want you to pay visa fees in US dollars (see p441 for contact details).

Just because a country has an embassy or consulate here, it doesn't necessarily mean you can get that country's visa. The borders with Somalia and Sudan are both closed, so you'll have to go to Addis Ababa in Ethiopia if you want a Sudanese visa, and Somali visas are unlikely to be available for the foreseeable future.

For Ethiopia, Tanzania and Uganda, three-month visas are readily available in Nairobi and cost US$50 for most nationalities. Two passport photos are required for applications and visas can usually be issued the same day.

WOMEN TRAVELLERS

Within Kenyan society, women are poorly represented in positions of power, and the few high-profile women in politics run the same risks of violence as their male counterparts. However, in their day to day lives, Kenyans are generally respectful towards women, although white women in bars will attract a lot of interest from would-be suitors. Most are just having a go and will give up if you tell them you aren't interested. The only place you are likely to have problems is at the beach resorts on the coast, where women may be approached by male prostitutes as well as local romeos. It's always best to cover your legs and shoulders when away from the beach so as not to offend local sensibilities.

With the upsurge in crime in Nairobi and along the coast, women should avoid walking around at night. The ugly fact is that while men are likely just to be robbed without violence, rape is a real risk for women. Lone night walks along the beach or through quiet city streets are a recipe for disaster, and criminals usually work in gangs, so take a taxi, even if you're in a group.

Regrettably, black women in the company of white men are often assumed to be prostitutes, and can face all kinds of discrimination from hotels and security guards, as well as approaches from Kenyan hustlers offering to help rip off the white 'customer'. Again, the worst of this can be avoided by taking taxis between hotels and restaurants etc.

WORK

It's difficult, although by no means impossible, for foreigners to find jobs. Apart from voluntary and conservation work, which you usually pay to participate in, the most likely areas for gainful employment are the safari business, teaching, advertising and journalism. As in most countries, the rule is that if an African can be found to do the job, there's no need to hire a foreigner.

Work permits and resident visas are not easy to arrange. A prospective employer may be able to sort out the necessary paperwork for you, but otherwise you'll find yourself spending a lot of time and money at the **immigration office** (Map pp282-3; ☎ 020-222022; Nyayo House, cnr Kenyatta Ave & Uhuru Hwy) in Nairobi.

TRANSPORT IN KENYA

GETTING THERE & AWAY

Unless you are travelling overland from southern Africa or Egypt, flying is by far the most convenient way to get to Kenya. Nairobi is a major African hub, and flights between Kenya and the rest of Africa are easy to come by and relatively cheap. Most overland routes pass through several war zones and should only be considered after some serious planning and preparation.

For information on getting to Kenya from outside East Africa, see the Transport in East Africa chapter (p631).

Entering Kenya

Entering Kenya is generally straightforward, particularly at the international airports, which are no different from most Western terminals. Visas are typically available on arrival for most nationalities (passport photos required), but you should contact your nearest Kenyan diplomatic office to get the most up-to-date information. Exchange offices or moneychangers are always present, and visa fees can be paid in local currency or US dollars. If you enter Nairobi with no onward or return ticket, you may run foul of immigration and be forced to buy one on the spot – an expensive exercise.

Passport

There are no restrictions on which nationalities can enter Kenya. Citizens of Tanzania, Uganda, the Republic of Ireland, Rwanda,

Scandinavia, Sudan and certain Commonwealth countries did not require visas at the time of writing; see p446 and check the latest situation before travelling.

Air

Most international flights to and from Nairobi are handled by **Jomo Kenyatta International Airport** (NBO; ☎ 020-825400; www.kenyaairports.co.ke), 15km southeast of the city. By African standards it's a pretty well-organised place, with two international terminals, a smaller domestic terminal, and an incredible number of shops offering duty-free and expensive souvenirs, snacks and Internet access.

Some flights between Nairobi and Kilimanjaro International Airport or Mwanza in Tanzania, as well as many domestic flights, use **Wilson Airport** (WIL; ☎ 020-501941), which is 6km south of the city on Langata Rd. The other arrival point in the country is **Moi International Airport** (MBA; ☎ 041-433211) in Mombasa, 9km west of the city centre, but apart from flights to Zanzibar this is mainly used by charter airlines and domestic flights.

Kenya Airways is the main national and regional carrier, and has a generally good safety record. There are good connections from Nairobi to most regions of Africa: Kenya Airways and the relevant national airlines serve everywhere from Abidjan to Yaoundé at least a few times a week.

Airlines flying to and from Kenya, with offices in Nairobi except where otherwise indicated:

Air India (airline code AI; Map pp282-3; ☎ 020-340925; www.airindia.com) Hub: Mumbai.

Air Malawi (airline code QM; ☎ 020-240965; www.airmalawi.net) Hub: Lilongwe.

Air Zimbabwe (airline code UM; ☎ 020-339522; www.airzim.co.zw) Hub: Harare.

Airkenya (airline code QP; ☎ 020-605745; www.airkenya.com) Hub: Wilson Airport, Nairobi. Kilimanjaro only.

British Airways (airline code BA; Map pp282-3; ☎ 020-244430; www.british-airways.com) Hub: Heathrow Airport, London.

Daallo Airlines (airline code D3; ☎ 020-317318; www.daallo.com) Hub: Hargeisa.

Egypt Air (airline code MS; Map pp282-3; ☎ 020-226821; www.egyptair.com.eg) Hub: Cairo.

Emirates (airline code EK; Map pp282-3; ☎ 020-211187; www.emirates.com) Hub: Dubai.

Ethiopian Airlines (airline code ET; Map pp282-3; ☎ 020-330837; www.ethiopianairlines.com) Hub: Addis Ababa.

Gulf Air (airline code GF; ☎ 020-241123; www.gulfairco.com) Hub: Abu Dhabi.

Kenya Airways (airline code KQ; Map pp280-1; ☎ 020-32074100; www.kenya-airways.com) Hub: Jomo Kenyatta International Airport, Nairobi.

KLM (airline code KL; Map pp280-1; ☎ 020-32074100; www.klm.com) Hub: Amsterdam.

Oman Air (airline code WY; Map p314; ☎ 041-221444; www.oman-air.com) Hub: Muscat. Office in Mombasa.

Precision Air (airline code PW; ☎ 020-602561; www.precisionairtz.com) Hub: Dar es Salaam.

Rwandair (airline code WB; ☎ 0733-740703; www.rwandair.com) Hub: Kigali.

Safarilink Aviation (☎ 020-600777; www.safarilink.co.ke) Hub: Wilson Airport, Nairobi. Kilimanjaro only.

SN Brussels Airlines (airline code SN; ☎ 020-4443070; www.flysn.com) Hub: Brussels.

South African Airways (airline code SA; ☎ 020-229663; www.saakenya.com) Hub: Johannesburg.

Swiss International Airlines (airline code SR; ☎ 020-3744045; www.swiss.com) Hub: Zurich.

Land

BUS

Entering Kenya by bus is possible on several major routes, and it's generally a breeze: while you need to get off the bus to sort out any necessary visa formalities, you'll rarely be held up for too long at the border. That said, arranging your visa in advance can save you time and a few angry glares from your fellow passengers.

CAR & MOTORCYCLE

Crossing land borders with your own vehicle is straightforward as long as you have the necessary paperwork; see p452 for details on requirements and general road rules. Petrol, spare parts and repair shops are readily available at all border towns, though if you're coming from Ethiopia you should plan your supplies carefully, as stops are few and far between on the rough northern roads.

If you're planning to ship your vehicle to Kenya, be aware that port charges in Kenya are very high. There are numerous shipping agents in Nairobi and Mombasa willing to arrange everything for you, but check all the costs in advance.

TO/FROM ETHIOPIA
Border Crossings

With the ongoing problems in Sudan and Somalia, Ethiopia offers the only viable overland route into Kenya from the north.

The security situation around the main entry point at Moyale is changeable, and although the border is usually open, security problems have forced its closure several times. Cattle- and goat-rustling are rife in the area, triggering frequent cross-border tribal wars, so check the security situation carefully before attempting this crossing.

From immigration on the Ethiopian side of town it's a 2km walk to the customs posts. Be aware that a yellow-fever vaccination is required to cross either border at Moyale. Unless you fancy being vaccinated at the border, get your jabs in advance and keep the yellow-fever certificate with your passport. A cholera vaccination may also be required. If you're travelling in the other direction, through Ethiopia to Sudan, you'll have to go to Addis Ababa to get your Sudanese visa.

Those coming to Kenya with their own vehicle could also enter at Fort Banya, on the northeastern tip of Lake Turkana (just a point on the map). However, it's a risky route and fuel stops are few and far between. There is no border post, so you must already possess a Kenyan visa and get it stamped on arrival in Nairobi; immigration officials are quite used to this, although not having an Ethiopian exit stamp can be a problem if you want to re-enter Ethiopia.

Addis Ababa
If you don't have your own transport to Moyale, lifts can be arranged with the trucks from Isiolo for around KSh1000.

On the Ethiopian side of the border, a bus leaves for Addis Ababa (Birr78.6) each morning around 5.30am. The two-day journey is broken with a night's sleep at Awasa or Shashemene.

TO/FROM SUDAN
Recent progress in the Sudanese peace process has raised many people's hopes for the future, but Kenya's neighbour to the north is still far from untroubled. If things continue to improve, the Kenya–Sudan border may reopen, but at time of writing it was still only possible to travel between the two countries by air or via Ethiopia.

TO/FROM TANZANIA
Border Crossings
The main land borders between Kenya and Tanzania are at Namanga, Taveta, Isebania

and Lunga Lunga, and can be reached by public transport. There is also a crossing from the Serengeti to the Masai Mara, which can only be undertaken with your own vehicle, and one at Loitokitok, which is closed to tourists.

Main bus companies serving Tanzania:
Akamba (Map pp282-3; ☎ 020-340430; akamba_prs@skyweb.co.ke; Nairobi)
Davanu Shuttle (☎ 057-8142; Arusha) Arusha/Moshi shuttle buses.
Easy Coach (Map pp282-3; ☎ 020-210711; easycoach@wananchi.com; Nairobi)
Riverside Shuttle Nairobi (Map pp282-3; ☎ 020-229618); Arusha (☎ 057-2639) Arusha/Moshi shuttle buses.
Scandinavia Express (Map pp282-3; ☎ 020-247131; Nairobi)

Arusha & Moshi
From Nairobi, there are frequent services to Moshi, travelling via Arusha in Tanzania. Most leave from the hectic River Rd area in Nairobi; thefts are common there so watch your baggage. Easy Coach is a good option, as services leave from its office compound near Nairobi railway station. Buses from Nairobi to Dar es Salaam (see p450) also travel via Arusha, and small local buses leave from Accra Rd every morning. The average cost of these services is KSh700 to KSh1000 to Arusha and KSh1000 to KSh1200 to Moshi, more for the real luxury liners.

It's also easy, though less convenient, to do this journey in stages, since the Kenyan and Tanzanian border posts at Namanga are right next to each other and regularly served by public transport.

If you're coming from Mombasa, there are a number of rickety local buses to Arusha and Moshi that leave every evening from in front of the Mwembe Tayari Health Centre on Jomo Kenyatta Ave (Map p314). Fares are around KSh500 to Moshi (six hours) and KSh800 to Arusha (7½ hours). These buses cross the border at Taveta, which can also be reached by *matatu* from Voi (see p308).

Mwanza
A sealed road runs all the way from Kisumu to just short of Mwanza in Tanzania, offering a convenient route to the Tanzanian shore of Lake Victoria. From Nairobi, probably the most comfortable way to go is with Scandinavia Express or Akamba; prices cost

around KSh1000 to KSh2000, and the journey should take roughly 12 hours.

From Kisumu, regular *matatus* serve the Tanzanian border at Isebania/Sirari (KSh350, four hours); local services head to Mwanza from the Tanzanian side. Buses going direct to Mwanza (KSh500, four hours) leave frequently from Kisii.

Tanga & Dar es Salaam

Several Kenyan companies have buses from Nairobi to Dar es Salaam. Scandinavia Express and Akamba both have reliable daily services from their offices in the River Rd area, with prices ranging from KSh1600 to real luxury coaches at KSh3000. Journey time is around 16 to 18 hours with stops.

Numerous buses run along the coast road from Mombasa to Tanga and Dar, crossing the border at Lunga Lunga/Horohoro. Most people travel on through buses from Mombasa, but it's easy enough to do the journey in stages by local bus or *matatu* if you'd rather make a few stops along the way.

In Mombasa, buses to Dar es Salaam leave from around Jomo Kenyatta Ave, near the junction with Mwembe Tayari Rd (Map p314). The average cost is around KSh1000 to Dar (eight hours) and KSh500 to Tanga (two hours), depending on the company you travel with and the standard of the buses.

In Dar es Salaam, buses leave from the Mnazi Mmoja bus stand on Bibi Titi Mohamed Rd, near Uhuru and Lindi Sts, along the southeast side of Mnazi Mmoja Park.

If you want to do the journey in stages, there are frequent *matatus* to Lunga Lunga from the Mombasa ferry jetty at Likoni. A *matatu* can then take you the 6.5km between the two border posts. On the Tanzanian side, there are regular *matatus* from Horohoro to Tanga (TSh200).

TO/FROM UGANDA
Border Crossings

The main border post for overland travellers is Malaba, with Busia an alternative if you are travelling via Kisumu. Numerous bus companies run between Nairobi and Kampala, or you can do the journey in stages via either of the border towns.

Main bus companies serving Uganda:
Akamba (Map pp282-3; ☎ 020-340430; akamba_prs@skyweb.co.ke)

Falcon (Map p314; ☎ 020-229692)
Scandinavia Express (Map pp282-3; ☎ 020-247131)

Kampala

Various companies cover the Nairobi to Kampala route. From Nairobi, and at the top end of the market, Scandinavia Express and Akamba have buses at least once daily, ranging from ordinary buses at around KSh1000 to full-blown luxury services with drinks and movies, hovering around the KSh2000 mark. All buses take about 10 to 12 hours and prices include a meal at the halfway point. Akamba also has a service to Mbale in Uganda (KSh800, 10 hours).

Various other companies have cheaper basic services leaving from the Accra Rd area in Nairobi. Prices start at around KSh800 and journey times are more or less the same as the bigger companies, with a few extra allowances for delays and general tardiness.

If you want to do the journey in stages, Akamba has morning and evening buses from Nairobi to Malaba, and a daily direct bus from here to Kampala (KSh450, 4½ hours). There are also regular *matatus* to Malaba (KSh650) from Cross Rd, Nairobi.

The Ugandan and Kenyan border posts at Malaba are about 1km apart, so you can walk or take a *boda-boda*. Once you get across the border, there are frequent *matatus* until the late afternoon to Kampala, Jinja and Tororo.

Buses and *matatus* also run from Nairobi or Kisumu to Busia, from where there are regular connections to Kampala (KSh500, four hours) and Jinga.

Tours

It's possible to get to Kenya as part of an overland truck tour originating in Europe or other parts of Africa (many also start in Nairobi bound for other places in Africa). See p83 for more details on tours and safaris.

Most companies are based in the UK or South Africa, but Flight Centres is a good local operator, with offices in Nairobi, Cape Town and Victoria Falls, Zimbabwe. Trips can last from just a few days to epic grand tours of up to 13 weeks.

Acacia Expeditions (UK ☎ 020-7706 4700; www.acacia-africa.com)
African Routes (South Africa ☎ 031-569 3911; www.africanroutes.co.za)

Dragoman (UK ☎ 01728-861133; www.dragoman.co.uk)

Explore Worldwide (UK ☎ 01252-760000; www.explore worldwide.com)

Flight Centres Cape Town (☎ 021-385 1530; cpt@africa travelco.com); Nairobi (Map pp282-3; ☎ 020-210024; www.flightcentres-kenya.com); Victoria Falls (☎ 013-40172; vfa@africatravelco.com)

Gametrackers Ltd (Map pp282-3; ☎ 020-338927; www.gametrackersafaris.com)

Guerba Expeditions (UK ☎ 01373-826611; www.guerba .co.uk)

GETTING AROUND
Air

Four domestic operators of varying sizes, including the national carrier Kenya Airways, now run scheduled flights within Kenya. All appear to have a clean slate safetywise. Destinations served are predominantly around the coast and the popular southern national parks, where the highest density of tourist activity takes place.

Book well in advance (essential during the tourist high season) with all these airlines. You should also remember to reconfirm return flights 72 hours before departure, especially when connecting with an international flight.

Airlines flying domestically:

Airkenya (☎ 020-605745; www.airkenya.com) Amboseli, Kiwayu, Lamu, Lewa Downs, Masai Mara, Malindi, Meru, Nanyuki, Samburu.

Kenya Airways (Map pp280-1; ☎ 020-3274100; www .kenya-airways.com) Kisumu, Lamu, Malindi, Mombasa.

Mombasa Air Safari (☎ 041-433061; www.mombasa airsafari.com) Amboseli, Lamu, Malindi, Masai Mara, Mombasa, Tsavo, Ukunda.

Safarilink (☎ 020-600777; www.safarilink.co.ke) Amboseli, Chyulu Hills, Kiwayu, Lamu, Lewa Downs, Masai Mara, Naivasha, Nanyuki, Samburu, Tsavo West.

Bicycle

Loads of Kenyans get around by bicycle, and while it can be tough for those not used to the roads or the climate, plenty of hardy visiting cyclists do tour the country every year. If you intend to cycle here, do as the locals do and get off the road whenever you hear a car coming. No matter how experienced you are, it would be suicidal to attempt the road from Nairobi to Mombasa on a bicycle.

The hills of Kenya are not particularly steep but can be long and hard. You can expect to cover around 80km per day in the hills of the Western Highlands, somewhat more where the country is flatter. Hell's Gate National Park, near Naivasha, is particularly popular for mountain biking.

It's possible to hire road and mountain bikes in an increasing number of places, usually for less than KSh500 per day. Few places require a deposit, unless their machines are particularly new or sophisticated. Several tour operators now offer cycling safaris (see p88 for details).

Boat
DHOW

Sailing on a traditional Swahili dhow along the East African coast is one of Kenya's most memorable experiences, and unlike Lake Victoria certain traditional routes are very much still in use.

Dhows are commonly used to get around the islands in the Lamu archipelago (p356) and the mangrove islands south of Mombasa (p326). For the most part, these operate more like dhow safaris than public transport. Although some trips are luxurious, the trips out of Lamu are more basic.

Most of the smaller boats rely on the wind to get around, so it's quite common to end up becalmed until the wind picks up again. The more commercial boats, however, have been fitted with outboard motors so that progress can be made even when there's no wind. Larger dhows are all motorised and some of them don't even have sails.

LAKE VICTORIA

There has been speculation for years that ferry transport will start again on Lake Victoria, but for the foreseeable future the only regular services operating are motorised canoes going to Mfangano Island from Mbita Point, near Homa Bay. An occasional ferry service runs between Kisumu and Homa Bay.

Bus

Kenya has an extensive network of long- and short-haul bus routes, with particularly good coverage of the areas around Nairobi, the coast and the western regions. Services thin out the further away from the capital you get, particularly in the north, and there are still plenty of places where you'll be reliant on *matatus*.

Fares start around KSh80 for an hour-long journey between nearby towns. At the other end of the scale, you'll seldom pay more

KENYA

than KSh500 for a standard journey, but so-called 'executive' services on the overnight Nairobi–Mombasa route can command prices of up to KSh1500, almost as much as the equivalent international services.

Buses are operated by a variety of private and state-owned companies that offer varying levels of comfort, convenience and roadworthiness. They're considerably cheaper than taking the train or flying, and as a rule services are frequent, fast and often quite comfortable. However, many travellers are put off taking buses altogether by the diabolical state of Kenyan roads.

In general, if you travel during daylight hours, buses are a fairly safe way to get around, and you'll certainly be safer in a bus than in a *matatu*, simply due to its size. The best coaches are saved for long-haul and international routes, and offer DVD movies, drinks, toilets and reclining airline-style seats. On the shortest local routes, however, you may find yourself on something resembling a burnt-out prison bus.

Whatever kind of conveyance you find yourself in, don't sit at the back (you'll be thrown around like a rag doll), or right at the front (you'll be the first to die in a head-on collision, plus you'll be able to see the oncoming traffic, which is usually terrifying).

KBS, the government bus line, runs the local buses in Nairobi and also offers long-haul services to most major towns around the country. Its buses tend to be slower than those of the private companies, but are probably safer for this reason. Of the private companies, Akamba has the most comprehensive network, and has a good, but not perfect, safety record. Easy Coach is another private firm quickly establishing a solid reputation for efficiency and comfort.

There are a few security considerations to think about when taking a bus in Kenya. Some routes, most notably from Malindi to Lamu and Isiolo to Marsabit, have been prone to attacks by *shiftas* in the past; check things out locally before you travel. Another possible risk is drugged food and drink: if you want to reach your destination with all your belongings, politely refuse any offers of drinks or snacks from strangers.

Main bus companies operating in Kenya:
Akamba (Map pp282-3; ☎ 020-340430; akamba_prs@skyweb.co.ke) Eldoret, Kakamega, Kericho, Kisii, Kisumu, Kitale, Machakos, Mombasa, Nairobi, Namanga.

Busscar (☎ 020-227650) Kilifi, Kisumu, Malindi, Mombasa, Nairobi.
Coastline Safaris (Map pp282-3; ☎ 020-217592; coastpekee@ikenya.com) Kakamega, Kisumu, Mombasa, Nairobi, Nakuru, Voi.
Easy Coach (Map pp282-3; ☎ 020-210711; easycoach@wananchi.com) Eldoret, Kakamega, Kisumu, Kitale, Nairobi.
Eldoret Express (☎ 020-6766886) Busia, Eldoret, Kakamega, Kisii, Kisumu, Kitale, Malaba, Nairobi.
Falcon (Map p314; ☎ 020-229662) Kilifi, Lamu, Malindi, Mombasa, Nairobi.
KBS (Map pp282-3; ☎ 020-229707) Busia, Eldoret, Kakamega, Kisii, Kisumu, Kitale, Malaba, Mombasa, Nairobi.
Mombasa Metropolitan Bus Services (Metro Mombasa; ☎ 041-2496008) Kilifi, Kwale, Malindi, Mombasa, Mtwapa.

Car & Motorcycle

Many travellers bring their own vehicles into Kenya as part of overland trips and, expense notwithstanding, it's a great way to see the country at your own pace. Otherwise, there are numerous car-hire companies who can hire you anything from a small hatchback to Toyota Land Cruiser 4WDs, although hire rates are some of the highest in the world.

A few expats have off-road (trail) motorcycles, but they aren't seen as a serious means of transport, which is a blessing considering the lethal nature of the roads.

DRIVING LICENCE

An International Driving Permit (IDP) is not necessary in Kenya, but can be useful. If you have a British photocard licence, be sure to bring the counterfoil, as the date you passed your driving test – something car-hire companies here may want to know – isn't printed on the card itself.

FUEL & SPARE PARTS

At the time of research in Nairobi regular petrol was KSh70 per litre, super KSh75 and diesel KSh65. Rates are generally lower outside the capital, but can creep up in remote areas, where petrol stations are often scarce and you may end up buying supplies out of barrels from roadside vendors.

Anyone who is planning to take their own vehicle with them needs to check in advance what spare parts are likely to be available. Even if it's an older model, local suppliers in Kenya are very unlikely to have every little part you might need.

HIRE

Hiring a vehicle to tour Kenya (or at least the national parks) is an expensive way of seeing the country, but it does give you freedom of movement and is sometimes the only way of getting to the more remote parts of the country. However, unless you're sharing with a sufficient number of people it's likely to cost more than you'd pay for an organised camping safari with all meals included.

Unless you're just planning on travelling on the main routes between towns, you'll need a 4WD vehicle. None of the car-hire companies will let you drive 2WD vehicles on dirt roads, including those in the national parks, and if you ignore this proscription and have an accident you will be personally liable for any damage to the vehicle.

A minimum age of between 23 and 25 years usually applies for hirers. Some companies prefer a licence with no endorsements or criminal convictions, and most require you to have been driving for at least two years. You will also need acceptable ID, such as a passport.

It's generally true to say the more you pay for a vehicle, the better condition it will be in. The larger companies are usually in a stronger financial position to keep their fleet in good order. Whoever you hire from, be sure to check the brakes, tyres (including the spare), windscreen wipers and lights before you set off.

The other factor to consider is what the company will do for you (if anything) if you have a serious breakdown. The major hire companies *may* deliver a replacement vehicle and make arrangements for recovery of the other vehicle at their expense, but with most companies you'll have to get the vehicle fixed and back on the road yourself, and then try and claim a refund.

Costs

Starting rates for hire almost always sound very reasonable, but once you factor in mileage and the various types of insurance you'll be lucky to pay less than KSh6000 per day for a saloon car or KSh8000 per day for a small 4WD. As elsewhere in the world, rates come down rapidly if you take the car for more than a few days.

Vehicles are usually hired with either an allowance of 100km to 200km per day (in which case you'll pay an extra fee for every kilometre you go over), or with unlimited kilometres, which is often the best way to go. Rates are usually quoted without insurance, and you'll be given the option of paying around KSh900 to KSh1500 per day for insurance against collision damage and theft. It would be financial suicide to hire a car in Kenya without both kinds of insurance. Otherwise, you'll be responsible for the full value of the vehicle if it's stolen or damaged.

Even if you have collision and theft insurance, you'll still be liable for an excess of KSh2000 to KSh150,000 (depending on the company) if something happens to the vehicle. Always check this before signing. You can usually reduce the excess to zero by paying another KSh900 per day for an Excess Loss Waiver. Note that tyres, damaged windscreens and loss of the tool kit are always the hirer's responsibility.

Most companies can provide drivers for around KSh1000 per day; the big advantage of this is that the car is then covered by the company's own insurance, so you don't have to pay any of the various waivers and will not be liable for any excess in the case of an accident. In addition, having someone in the car who speaks Swahili, knows the roads and is used to Kenyan driving conditions can be absolutely priceless, especially in remote areas.

The deposit required on hired vehicles can vary significantly. It can be as much as the total estimated hire charges plus whatever the excess is on the Collision Damage Waiver (CDW). You can cover this with cash, signed travellers cheques (returnable) or credit card.

If you want to hire a vehicle in one place and drop it off in another there will be additional charges. These vary depending on the vehicle, the company, and the pick-up and drop-off locations. In most cases, count on paying KSh10,000 between Nairobi and Mombasa and about KSh5000 between Mombasa and Malindi.

As a final sting in the tail, you'll be charged 16% VAT on top of the total cost of hiring the vehicle. Any repairs that you end up paying for will also have VAT on top, and if you don't return the vehicle with a full tank of petrol, the company will charge you twice the going rate to fill up.

Hire Agencies

At the top end of the market are some international companies. All have airport and/or town offices in Nairobi and Mombasa. Of these, Budget is the best value, though it's well worth paying for the Excess Loss Waiver.

Central Rent-a-Car is probably the best of the local firms, with a well-maintained fleet of fairly new vehicles and a good backup service. Its excess liability is also the lowest (KSh2000), but vehicles are self-drive only, with no drivers available. Apart from Central, all of these companies have steep excesses.

Most safari companies will also hire out their vehicles, though you would have few of the guarantees that you would have with the companies listed here. **Let's Go Travel** (☎ 020-340331; www.letsgosafari.com) organises reliable car hire at favourable rates through partner firms.

On the coast, it is possible to hire motorcycles, scooters and quads at Diani Beach and Bamburi Beach.

Local and international hire companies:

Avenue Car Hire (Map pp282-3; ☎ 020-313207; www.avenuecarhire.com)

Avis (Map pp280-1; ☎ 020-316061; www.avis.co.ke)

Budget (Map pp282-3; ☎ 020-223581; www.budget-kenya.com)

Central Rent-a-Car (Map pp282-3; ☎ 020-222888; www.carhirekenya.com)

Glory Car Hire (Map pp282-3; ☎ 020-225024; www.glorycarhire.com)

Hertz (☎ 020-248777; www.hertz.co.ke)

PARKING

In small towns and villages parking is usually free, but there's a pay-parking system in Nairobi, Mombasa and other main towns. Attendants issue one-day parking permits for around KSh70, valid anywhere in town. If you don't get a permit you're liable to be wheel-clamped, and getting your vehicle back will cost you at least KSh2000. It's always worth staying in a hotel with secure parking if possible.

ROAD CONDITIONS

Road conditions vary widely in Kenya, from flat smooth highways to dirt tracks and steep rocky pathways. Many roads are severely eroded at the edges, reducing the carriageway to a single lane, which is usually occupied by whichever vehicle is bigger in any given situation. The roads in the north and east of the country are particularly poor. The main Mombasa–Nairobi–Malaba road (A104) is badly worn due to the constant flow of traffic.

Roads in national parks are all *murram* (dirt) and have been eroded into boneshaking corrugations through overuse by safari vehicles. Keep your speed down and be careful when driving after rain. Although some dirt roads can be negotiated in a 2WD vehicle, you'll be much safer in a 4WD.

ROAD HAZARDS

The biggest hazard on Kenyan roads is quite simply the other vehicles on them, and driving defensively is essential. Ironically, the most dangerous roads in Kenya are probably the well-maintained ones, which allow drivers to pick up enough speed to do really serious damage in a crash. On the worse roads, potholes are a dual problem: driving into them can damage your vehicle or cause you to lose control, and sudden erratic avoidance manoeuvres from other vehicles are a constant threat.

On all roads, be very careful of pedestrians and cyclists – you don't want to contribute any more to the death toll on Kenya's roads. Animals are another major hazard in rural areas.

If you're driving in remote areas, acacia thorns are a common problem, as they'll pierce even the toughest tyres. The slightest breakdown can leave you stranded for hours in the bush, so always carry drinking water, emergency food and, if possible, spare fuel.

Certain routes have a reputation for banditry, particularly the Garsen–Garissa–Thika road, which is still essentially off limits to travellers, and the dirt track from Amboseli National Park to Tsavo West National Park, where you're usually required to join a convoy. The roads from Isiolo to Marsabit and Moyale and from Malindi to Lamu have improved considerably securitywise in the last few years, but you're still advised to seek local advice before using any of these routes.

ROAD RULES

You'll need your wits about you if you're going to tackle driving in Kenya. Driving practices here are some of the worst in the world and all are carried out at breakneck speed. Indicators, lights, horns and hand signals can mean absolutely anything, and should never be taken at face value.

Kenyans habitually drive on the wrong side of the road whenever they see a pothole, an animal or simply a break in the traffic – flashing your lights at the vehicle hurtling towards you should be enough to persuade the driver to get back into their own lane. Never drive at night unless you absolutely have to, as few cars have adequate headlights and the roads are full of pedestrians and cyclists. Drunk driving is also very common.

Note that foreign-registered vehicles with a seating capacity of more than six people are not allowed into Kenyan national parks and reserves. Jeeps should be fine, but camper vans may have problems.

Hitching

Hitchhiking is never entirely safe in any country in the world, and we don't recommend it. Travellers who decide to hitch should understand that they are taking a small but potentially serious risk; it's safer to travel in pairs and let someone know where you are planning to go. Also, beware of drunken drivers.

On the other side of the wheel, foreign drivers will be approached all the time by Kenyan hitchers demanding free rides, and giving a lift to a carload of Maasai is certainly a memorable cultural experience.

Local Transport

BOAT

The only local boat service in regular use is the Likoni ferry between the mainland and Mombasa island, which runs throughout the day and night, and is free for foot passengers (vehicles pay a small toll).

BODA-BODA

Boda-bodas are common in areas where standard taxis are harder to find, and also operate in smaller towns and cities, such as Kisumu. There is a particular proliferation on the coast, where the bicycle boys also double as touts, guides and drug dealers in tourist areas. A short ride should never cost more than KSh20.

BUS

Nairobi is the only city with an effective municipal bus service, run by KBS. Routes cover all the suburbs and outlying areas during daylight hours, and generally cost no more than KSh40.

MATATU

Local *matatus* are the main means of getting around for local people, and any reasonably sized city or town will have plenty of services covering every major road and suburb. Fares start at KSh10 and may reach KSh40 for longer routes in Nairobi.

Minibus transport is not unique to Kenya, but the *matatu* has raised it into a cultural phenomenon, and most Kenyans use them regularly for both local and intercity journeys. The vehicles themselves can be anything from dilapidated Peugeot 504 pick-ups with a taxi on the back to big 20-seater minibuses. The most common are white Nissan minibuses (many local people prefer the name 'Nissans' to *matatus*).

In the bad old days *matatus* were notorious for dangerous driving, overcrowding and general shady business, but in 2003 then Transport Minister John Michuki banned all *matatus* from the roads until they complied with a new set of laws, ensuring amazingly speedy results. *Matatus* must now be fitted with seatbelts and 80kph speed governors, conductors and drivers must wear clearly identifiable red shirts, route numbers must be clearly displayed and a 14-person capacity applies to vehicles that used to cram in as many as 30 people. Frequent police checks have also been brought in to enforce the rules.

The changes are immediately noticeable and represent an improvement of sorts, but it hasn't taken operators long to find loopholes. Many drivers still also chew *miraa* leaves to stay awake beyond what is a reasonable or safe time.

Apart from in the remote northern areas, where you'll rely on occasional buses or paid lifts on trucks, you can almost always find a *matatu* going to the next town or further afield, so long as it's not too late in the day. Simply ask around among the drivers at the local *matatu* stand or 'stage'. *Matatus* leave when full and the fares are fixed.

Wherever you're going, remember that most *matatu* crashes are head-on collisions – under no circumstances should you sit in the 'death seat' next to the *matatu* driver. Play it safe and sit in the middle seats away from the window.

KENYA

SHARED TAXI (PEUGEOT)

Shared Peugeot taxis are less common but make a good alternative to *matatus*, though they're not subject to the same regulations. The vehicles are usually Peugeot 505 station wagons (hence the local name) that take seven to nine passengers and leave when full.

Peugeots take less time to reach their destinations than *matatus* as they fill quicker and go from point to point without stopping, and so are slightly more expensive. Many companies have offices around the Accra, Cross and River Rds area in Nairobi, and serve destinations mostly in the north and west of the country.

TAXI

Even the smallest Kenyan towns generally have at least one banged-up old taxi for easy access to outlying areas or even remoter villages, and you'll find taxis on virtually every corner in the larger cities, especially in Nairobi and Mombasa, where taking a taxi at night is virtually mandatory. Fares are invariably negotiable and start at around KSh200 for short journeys.

Train

The Uganda Railway was once the main artery of trade in East Africa, but these days the network has dwindled to two main routes, Nairobi–Kisumu and Nairobi–Mombasa. Both are night services of around 13 hours, much slower and less frequent than going by air or road but considerably more comfortable and significantly safer. The trip between Nairobi and Mombasa is still considered one of the great rail journeys in Africa.

CLASSES

There are three classes on Kenyan trains, but only 1st and 2nd class can be recommended. Note that passengers are divided up by gender.

First class consists of two-berth compartments with a washbasin, wardrobe, drinking water and a drinks service. Second class consists of plainer, four-berth compartments with a washbasin and drinking water. No

compartment can be locked from the outside, so remember not to leave any valuables lying around if you leave it for any reason. You might want to padlock your rucksack to something during dinner and breakfast. Always lock your compartment from the inside before you go to sleep. Third class is seats only and security can be a real problem.

Passengers in 1st and 2nd class on the Mombasa line are treated to the full colonial experience, including a silver-service dinner in an old-fashioned dining car. Meals typically consist of stews, curries or roast chicken served with rice and vegetables, all dished up by uniformed waiters. There's always a vegetarian option. Tea and coffee is included; sodas (soft drinks), bottled water and alcoholic drinks are not, so ask the price before accepting that KSh1500 bottle of wine! Cold beer is available at all times in the dining car and can be delivered to your compartment.

COSTS

The only downside to the train is the price of tickets, over KSh3000 for 1st class on the Nairobi–Mombasa route, including meals (dinner and breakfast) and bedding. You can reduce this considerably by just paying for the seat, though you're missing out on the fun half of the experience that way. The Kisumu route is much less fancy, and 1st-class tickets cost around KSh1500. Reduced rates apply for children aged three to 11.

RESERVATIONS

You must book in advance for both 1st and 2nd class, otherwise you'll probably find there are no berths available; two to three days is usually sufficient. Visa credit cards are accepted for railway bookings. If you book by phone, you'll need to arrive early to pay for your ticket and make sure you're actually on the passenger list. Compartment and berth numbers are posted up about 30 minutes prior to departure.

There are **booking offices** (Mombasa ☎ 041-312220; Nairobi ☎ 020-221211) in major cities and at Kisumu railway station.

Uganda

Uganda is Africa condensed, with the best of everything the continent has to offer packed into one small but stunning destination. Uganda is home to the highest mountain range in Africa, the Rwenzoris or Mountains of the Moon. It is the source of the mighty River Nile, the world's longest river, offering the best white-water rafting in the world. It has the highest concentration of primates in the world, including the majestic mountain gorillas, one of the rarest animals on earth.

On top of all this, the scenery is so striking that it looks like a watercolour, the beautiful national parks see far fewer visitors than in neighbouring Kenya and Tanzania, and the capital Kampala is safer and friendlier than most in Africa. Winston Churchill called it the 'Pearl of Africa'. He was right.

However, Idi Amin's antics and Uganda's long string of tragedies in the 1970s and '80s is etched into the Western consciousness to such an extent that some people, wrongfully, still regard the country as dangerously unstable. The reality is vastly different. Stability has returned to most parts of the country and tourists are welcomed with open arms.

Despite the trials and tribulations of the past, Ugandans have weathered the storm remarkably well. You won't meet a sullen, bitter or cowed people. Rather they are smiling and friendly, with an openness absent in other places – truly some of the finest folk in Africa.

Uganda is a captivating country with a great deal to offer, and sooner or later the mainstream masses will 'discover' its delights – make sure you get here before they do.

FAST FACTS

- **Area** 236,580 sq km
- **Capital** Kampala
- **Country code** 256
- **Famous for** Idi Amin; source of the River Nile; white-water rafting
- **Languages** English, Luganda, Swahili
- **Money** Ugandan Shilling (USh); US$1 = USh1807; €1 = USh2189
- **Population** 27.6 million

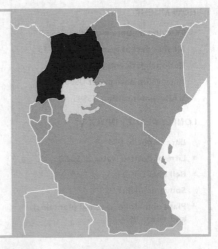

HIGHLIGHTS

- **Bwindi Impenetrable National Park** (p523) Penetrate the Impenetrable Forest to marvel at the mountain gorillas in the wild.
- **White-water Rafting** (p495) Take on the wild waters at the source of the Nile, quite simply the best rafting in the world.
- **Murchison Falls** (p541) Check out the world's most powerful waterfall on a wildlife-watching bonanza on a boat up the Victoria Nile.
- **Kampala Nightlife** (p483) Party on with the Kampala crew, a vibrant capital brimming with bars, clubs and live music.
- **Lake Bunyoni** (p528) Chill out at the most beautiful lake in Uganda, a mythical landscape of terraced hillsides and hidden bays.

CLIMATE & WHEN TO GO

As most of Uganda is at a fairly constant altitude, with mountains only in the extreme east (Mt Elgon), extreme west (the Rwenzori Mountains) and close to the Rwandan border, the bulk of the country enjoys the same tropical climate, with temperatures averaging about 26°C during the day and about 16°C at night. The hottest months are from December to February, when the daytime range is 27° to 29°C. It can get considerably cooler at night in the highland areas.

The rainy seasons in the south are from April to May and October to November,

the wettest month being April. In the north the wet season is from April to October and the dry season is from November to March. During the wet seasons the average rainfall is 175mm per month. Humidity is generally low outside the wet seasons.

The best times for a visit to Uganda are January and February, and June to September, as the weather during these months is generally dry. However, travel during the wet seasons to most destinations is also possible, just a bit slower. For more details, see p622.

HISTORY

For the story on Uganda's history in the years before independence, see p28.

Independence

Unlike Kenya and, to a lesser extent, Tanzania, Uganda never experienced a large influx of European colonisers and the associated expropriation of land. Instead, farmers were encouraged to grow cash crops for export through their own cooperative groups. Consequently, Ugandan nationalist organisations sprouted much later than those in neighbouring countries, and when they did, it happened along tribal lines. So exclusive were some of these that when Ugandan independence was eventually discussed, the Buganda people even considered secession.

By the mid-1950s, however, a Lango schoolteacher Dr Milton Obote managed to put together a loose coalition headed by the Uganda People's Congress (UPC), which led Uganda to independence in 1962 on the promise that the Buganda would have autonomy. The *kabaka* (king) became the new nation's president, Edward Mutesa II, and Milton Obote became Uganda's first prime minister.

It wasn't a particularly favourable time for Uganda to come to grips with independence. Civil wars were raging in neighbouring southern Sudan, Democratic Republic of the Congo (DR Congo) and Rwanda, and refugees streamed into Uganda, adding to its problems. Also, it soon became obvious that Obote had no intention of sharing power with the *kabaka*. A confrontation loomed.

Obote moved in 1966, arresting several cabinet ministers and ordering his army

---

HOW MUCH?

- **Tracking mountain gorillas** US$360
- **Meal at decent restaurant** US$5-15
- **National park entry** US$20
- **New Vision newspaper** US$0.50
- **White-water rafting** US$95

LONELY PLANET INDEX

- **Litre of petrol** US$1
- **Litre of bottled water** US$0.50
- **Bell beer** US$1
- **Souvenir T-shirt** US$10
- **Plate of matoke (mashed plantains) and beans** US$0.40

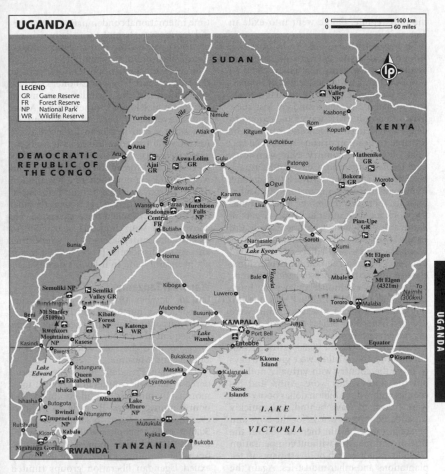

UGANDA

LEGEND
GR Game Reserve
FR Forest Reserve
NP National Park
WR Wildlife Reserve

chief of staff, Idi Amin, to storm the *kaba-ka*'s palace. The raid resulted in the flight of the *kabaka* and his exile in London, where he died in 1969. Following this coup, Obote proclaimed himself president, and the Bugandan monarchy was abolished, along with those of the kingdoms of Bunyoro, Ankole, Toro and Busoga. Meanwhile, Idi Amin's star was on the rise.

The Amin Years

Under Obote's watch, events began to spiral out of control. Obote ordered his attorney general, Godfrey Binaisa, to rewrite the constitution to consolidate virtually all powers in the presidency and then moved to nationalise foreign assets.

In 1969 a scandal broke out over US$5 million in funds and weapons allocated to the Ministry of Defence that couldn't be accounted for. An explanation was demanded of Amin. When it wasn't forthcoming, his deputy, Colonel Okoya, and some junior officers demanded his resignation. Shortly afterwards Okoya and his wife were shot dead in their Gulu home, and rumours began to circulate about Amin's imminent arrest. It never came. Instead, when Obote left for Singapore in January 1971 to attend the Commonwealth Heads of Government Meeting (CHOGM), Amin staged a coup. The British, who had probably suffered most from Obote's nationalisation program, were among the first to recognise the new regime. Obote went into exile in Tanzania.

So began Uganda's first reign of terror. All political activities were quickly suspended and the army was empowered to shoot on sight anyone suspected of opposition to the regime. Over the next eight years an estimated 300,000 Ugandans lost their lives, often in horrific ways: bludgeoned to death with sledgehammers and iron bars, or tortured to death in prisons and police stations all over the country. Nile Mansions, next to the Conference Centre in Kampala, became particularly notorious; the screams of those who were being tortured or beaten to death there could often be heard around the clock for days on end. Prime targets of Amin's death squads were the Acholi and Lango tribes, who were decimated in waves of massacres; whole villages were wiped out. Next Amin turned on the professional classes; university professors and lecturers, doctors, cabinet ministers, lawyers, businesspeople and even military officers who might have posed a threat to Amin were dragged from their offices and shot or simply never seen again.

Also targeted was the 70,000-strong Asian community. In 1972 they were given 90 days to leave the country with virtually nothing but the clothes they wore. Amin and his cronies grabbed the billion dollar booty they were forced to leave behind, and quickly squandered it on new toys for the boys and personal excess. Amin then turned on the British, nationalising without compensation US$500 million worth of investments in tea plantations and other industries. Again the booty was squandered.

Meanwhile the economy collapsed, industrial activity ground to a halt, hospitals and rural health clinics closed, roads cracked and became riddled with potholes, cities became garbage dumps and utilities fell apart. The prolific wildlife was machine-gunned by soldiers for meat, ivory and skins, and the tourism industry evaporated. The stream of refugees across the border became a flood.

Faced with chaos and an inflation rate that hit 1000%, Amin was forced to delegate more and more powers to the provincial governors, who became virtual warlords in their areas. Towards the end of the Amin era, the treasury was so bereft of funds that it was unable to pay the soldiers. At the same

time international condemnation of the sordid regime was strengthening daily, as news of massacres, torture and summary executions leaked out of the country.

One of the few supporters of Amin at the end of the 1970s was Colonel Gaddafi, who bailed out the Ugandan economy in the name of Islamic brotherhood – Amin had conveniently become a Muslim by this stage – and began an intensive drive to equip the Ugandan forces with sophisticated weapons.

The rot had spread too far, however, and was beyond the point where a few million dollars in Libyan largesse could help. Faced with a restless army beset with intertribal fighting, Amin looked for a diversion. He chose a war with Tanzania, ostensibly to teach that country a lesson for supporting anti-Amin dissidents. It was his last major act of insanity and in it lay his downfall.

War with Tanzania

On 30 October 1978 the Ugandan army rolled across northwestern Tanzania virtually unopposed and annexed more than 1200 sq km of territory. Meanwhile, the air force bombed the Lake Victoria ports of Bukoba and Musoma.

Tanzanian President Julius Nyerere ordered a full-scale counterattack, but it took months to mobilise his ill-equipped and poorly trained forces. By early 1979, however, he had managed to scrape together a 50,000-strong people's militia composed mainly of illiterate youngsters from the bush. This militia joined with the many exiled Ugandan liberation groups (united only in their determination to rid Uganda of Amin). The two armies met. East Africa's supposedly best-equipped and best-trained army threw down its weapons and fled, and the Tanzanians pushed on into the heart of Uganda. Kampala fell without a fight, and by the end of April 1979 organised resistance had effectively ceased.

Idi Amin fled to Libya, where he remained until Gaddafi threw him out following a shoot-out with Libyan soldiers. Amin died in exile in Saudi Arabia in 2003.

Post-Amin Chaos

The Tanzanian action was criticised, somewhat half-heartedly, by the Organisation for African Unity (OAU), but most African countries breathed a sigh of relief to see the madman finally brought to heel. All the same Tanzania was forced to foot the entire bill for the war, estimated at US$500 million, a crushing blow for an already desperately poor country.

The rejoicing in Uganda was short-lived. The Tanzanian soldiers who remained in the country, supposedly to assist with reconstruction and to maintain law and order, turned on the Ugandans when their pay did not arrive. They took what they wanted from shops at gunpoint, hijacked trucks arriving from Kenya with international relief aid and slaughtered more wildlife.

Once again the country slid into chaos and gangs of armed bandits roamed the cities, killing and looting. Food supplies ran out and hospitals could no longer function. Nevertheless, thousands of exiled Ugandans began to answer the new president's call to return home and help with reconstruction.

Yusuf Lule, a modest and unambitious man, was installed as president with Nyerere's blessing, but when he began speaking out against Nyerere, he was replaced by Godfrey Binaisa, sparking riots supporting Lule in Kampala. Meanwhile, Obote bided his time in Dar es Salaam.

Binaisa quickly came under pressure to set a date for a general election and a return to civilian rule. Obote eventually returned from exile to an enthusiastic welcome in many parts of the country and swept to victory in a blatantly rigged vote. Binaisa went into exile in the USA.

It was 1981 and the honeymoon with Obote proved to be relatively short. Like Amin, Obote favoured certain tribes. Large numbers of civil servants and army and police commanders belonging to the tribes of the south were replaced with Obote supporters belonging to the tribes of the north. The State Research Bureau, a euphemism for the secret police, was re-established and the prisons began to fill once more. Obote was on course to complete the destruction that Amin had begun. More and more reports of atrocities and killings leaked out of the country. Mass graves unrelated to the Amin era were unearthed. The press was muzzled and Western journalists were expelled. It was obvious that Obote was once again attempting to achieve absolute power. Intertribal tension was on the rise, and in mid-1985 Obote was overthrown in a coup staged by the army under the command of Tito Okello.

The NRA Takeover

Okello was not the only opponent of Obote. Shortly after Obote became president for the second time, a guerrilla army opposed to his tribally biased government was formed in western Uganda under the leadership of Yoweri Museveni, who had lived in exile in Tanzania during Amin's reign.

A group of 27 soon swelled to a guerrilla force of about 20,000, many of them orphaned teenagers. In the early days few gave the guerrillas, known as the National Resistance Army (NRA), much of a chance. Few people outside Uganda even knew of the existence of the NRA, due to Obote's success in muzzling the press and expelling journalists.

The NRA was not a bunch of drunken thugs like the armies of both Amin and Obote had been. New recruits were indoctrinated in the bush by political commissars and taught that they had to be the servants of the people, not their oppressors. Discipline was tough. Anyone who got badly out of line was executed. Museveni was determined that the army would never again disgrace Uganda. Also, a central thrust of the NRA was to win the hearts and minds of the people, who learnt to identify totally with the persecuted Bugandans in the infamous Luwero Triangle.

By the time Obote was ousted and Okello had taken over, the NRA controlled a large slice of western Uganda and was a power to be reckoned with. Museveni wanted a clean sweep of the administration, the army and the police. He wanted corruption stamped out and those who had been involved in atrocities during the Amin and Obote regimes brought to trial. These demands were, of course, anathema to Okello, who was up to his neck in corruption and responsible for many atrocities.

The fighting continued in earnest, and by late January 1986 it was obvious that Okello's days were numbered. The surrender of 1600 government soldiers holed up in their barracks in the southern town of Mbarara, which was controlled by the NRA, brought the NRA to the outskirts of Kampala itself. With the morale of the government troops at a low ebb, the NRA launched an

UGANDA

all-out offensive to take the capital. Okello's troops fled, almost without a fight, though not before looting whatever remained and carting it away in commandeered buses. It was a typical parting gesture, as was the gratuitous shooting-up of many Kampala high-rise offices.

During the following weeks Okello's rabble were pursued and finally pushed north over the border into Sudan. The civil war was over, apart from a few mopping-up operations in the extreme north. The long nightmare was finally over.

Rebuilding

Despite Museveni's Marxist leanings dating back to his political science studies in Dar es Salaam in the early 1970s, he has proved to be a pragmatist since taking control. Despite the radical stand of many of his officers on certain issues, he appointed several arch-conservatives to his cabinet and made an effort to reassure the country's influential Catholic community.

In the late 1980s peace agreements were negotiated with most of the guerrilla factions who had fought for Okello or Obote and were still active in the north and northeast. Under an amnesty offered to the rebels, as many as 40,000 had surrendered by 1988, and many were given jobs in the NRA. In the northwest of the country, almost 300,000 Ugandans returned home from Sudan.

With peace came optimism – services were restored, factories that had lain idle for years were again productive, agriculture was back online, the main roads were resurfaced, and the national parks' infrastructure was restored and revitalised. On the political front, all political parties were banned.

There was, however, still one thorn in Museveni's side: the refugee problem from neighbouring Rwanda. Western Uganda was saddled with some 250,000 refugees who had fled Rwanda's intermittent tribal conflicts, and feeding and housing them was a severe drain on Ugandan resources. On several occasions Museveni tried hard to persuade Rwanda's President Habyarimana to set up a repatriation scheme, but to no avail. It seems Museveni's patience finally snapped, and in late 1990 Rwanda was invaded by a 5000-strong guerrilla force from western Uganda, which included NRA units and weaponry.

Evidence supports the contention that Museveni knew of preparations for the invasion, though he denies it. In any event, the rebels were thrown back across the border by the Rwandan army, assisted by troops from Belgium, France and DR Congo, and the ensuing witch-hunt of Tutsi inside Rwanda added to the number of refugees inside western Uganda. But the rebels were back in force shortly afterwards and by early 1993 were in control of around one-third of Rwanda, and finally came to power following the blood bath of 1994.

The 1990s

The stability and rebuilding that came with President Museveni's coming to power in 1986 were followed in the 1990s with economic prosperity and unprecedented growth. For much of the decade Uganda was the fastest-growing economy in Africa, becoming a favourite among investors.

One of the keys to the success of the last few years was the bold decision to invite back the Asians who had been so unceremoniously evicted under Amin. As in Kenya, the Asians had a virtual monopoly on business and commerce. Without these people the economy was going nowhere fast, and it was clear to Museveni that Uganda needed them. Not surprisingly, they were very hesitant about returning, but assurances were given and kept, and property was and is still being given back to returned Asians or their descendants.

In 1993 a new draft constitution was adopted by the National Resistance Council (NRC). One surprising recommendation in the draft was that the country should adopt a system of 'no-party' politics for at least another five years, basically extending Museveni's National Resistance Movement (NRM) mandate for that period. However, given the potential for intertribal rivalry within a pluralist system, as history had shown, it was a sensible policy. Under the draft constitution, a Constituent Assembly was formed, and in 1994 elections for the assembly showed overwhelming support for the government.

Also in 1993 the Bugandan monarchy was restored, but with no political power. This gave rise to concern among the Buganda that the existence of their tribal kingdom in the future would be threatened. In protest against the NRM government, they joined

THE MOVEMENT FOR THE RESTORATION OF THE 10 COMMANDMENTS OF GOD

On 17 March 2000 the small village of Kanunga near Rukungiri hit the headlines in what appeared to be the most serious case of mass suicide since Jonestown, when a church burned to the ground packed full of followers of the Movement for the Restoration of the 10 Commandments of God. However, as police probed deeper, it became apparent that this was no mass suicide, but mass murder. Mass graves were turned up at cult sites throughout the southwest, and a Ugandan Human Rights Commission report released in 2002 put the final death toll at around 800, including at least 340 killed in the church fire.

The movement was founded by former prostitute Cledonia Mwerinde in 1994; she and her lover Joseph Kibwetere built up a popular cult that demanded followers give up their earthly possessions and await the end of the world on 31 December 1999. Just as the 'millennium' bug came to nothing, so the cult's prediction never happened, and many followers became sceptical, demanding the return of property and money.

Former followers of the cult who fled before the fire believed Mwerinde killed Kibwetere in 1999, fearing he had AIDS. She went one step further in 2000, systematically ordering the mass killing of cult followers in subdistricts before unleashing the final apocalypse at a small church in Kanunga. Investigators believe Mwerinde perished in the fire, taking her cult with her into the history books.

Something about the Ten Commandments seems to inspire particularly deranged fervour in remote Uganda; Joseph Kony and his Lord's Resistance Army (LRA) have been battling for a government based on the Ten Commandments since 1986. Believing they are immune to bullets, kidnapping young children as fighters and sex slaves, and mutilating victims suggests that their grip on theology is tenuous to say the least.

forces with the two main opposition groupings, former president Obote's UPC and the Democratic Party (DP), led by Foreign Affairs minister Dr Paulo Ssemogerere. In 1994 the Constituent Assembly voted to limit the *kabaka's* role to a purely ceremonial and traditional one.

Democratic 'no-party' elections were called for May 1996. Despite strong opposition from supporters of political parties, the elections went ahead. The main candidates were Museveni and Ssemogerere, who had resigned as foreign minister in order to campaign. For all intents, it was still a party-political election, between Museveni's NRM (officially a 'movement' and not a political party), and Ssemogerere, being supported by the former DP in alliance with the immensely unpopular (among the Buganda) UPC. Museveni won a resounding victory, capturing almost 75% of the vote. The only area where Ssemogerere had any real support was in the anti-NRM north.

Museveni's election carried with it great hope for the future, as many believed Uganda's success story could only continue with a genuine endorsement at the ballot box. However, Museveni's period as a democratically elected leader has been far less comfortable than his leadership period prior to the elections. The reasons for this are related to events both within Uganda and beyond its borders, in the civil wars of its neighbours. At home, one corruption scandal after another has blighted the administration, and while Museveni has maintained a clean pair of hands, some big heads have rolled. Abroad, Uganda found itself mired in Africa's first great war to control the destiny of the DR Congo and managed to fall out with its long time ally, Rwanda. Despite these concerns, Museveni remained popular for the stability he brought to the lives of average Ugandans and he was re-elected head of state in 2001.

Uganda Today

The debate about the formation of political parties has dominated the agenda in the current parliament. Museveni recently shifted his position on a return to multi-party politics, and in July 2005 a referendum was held that overwhelmingly endorsed democracy. The fact that voter turnout was tiny seemed to suggest no-one was really that interested in the issue.

An issue they definitely were interested in was Museveni's move to scrap constitutional limits on presidential terms. Museveni himself put in place the two-term limit and promptly changed his mind as the end of his tenure drew closer. MPs were bullied and bribed into voting for the change, and the way is now open for Museveni to run again in 2006. However, this has not gone down well with donors, old friends and regional leaders. Museveni's international stock is falling faster than a dot.com crash right now, as Laura Bush and Cherie Blair snubbed him on an HIV/AIDS awareness visit to the region, Bob Geldof called for him to go and fellow East African politicians voiced their concerns about his ambitions. The latter is particularly worrying for Museveni, as traditionally African leaders are cagey about criticising each other and this could have implications for moves towards an integrated East African Community. In Uganda some people are worried he is setting himself to be president for life and draw unflattering comparisons with Robert Mugabe. But maybe everyone is underestimating President Museveni, who has, after all, pulled off many surprises in the past. Inviting the Asians back was a bold move that kickstarted the Ugandan economy – perhaps he has one more trick up his sleeve?

The other dominant domestic concern has been the ongoing war against insurgents within the country. The Lord's Resistance Army (LRA) has been fighting a war in northern Uganda for two decades now and the mindless violence shows few signs of coming to an end despite peace efforts. The LRA was supported by the Sudanese government in Khartoum until 2002, while Uganda for its part supported southern Sudanese rebels fighting against the Islamic north. The peace agreement between Sudan and Uganda was meant to end the wars, which it largely has in southern Sudan, but in northern Uganda the LRA stepped up attacks, killing villagers and brutalising children. The LRA's original aim was to establish a state based on the 10 Commandments, but given they have broken every commandment in the book, they seemed to have lost touch with their goal a long time ago. They are one of the most vicious insurgent movements on the planet, kidnapping children to use as soldiers and sex slaves, slicing off lips, noses and ears to subdue the population, and generally laying waste to vast tracts of

the north. Museveni has continually staked his reputation on ending the war through any means necessary, but this has proven beyond his reach. Peace talks have been on and off again, but peace and the LRA seem a contradiction in terms.

It is not only the LRA that has destabilised Uganda's drive for development. The threat of the Interahamwe, the remnants of the Rwandan Hutu militia responsible for the 1994 genocide (see p567 for more information), has remained very real, and exploded onto world headlines in 1999 when eight tourists were murdered in Bwindi Impenetrable National Park. Uganda and Rwanda invaded DR Congo in 1996 and helped Laurent Kabila drive then President Mobutu from power. Kabila soon failed to deliver on his part of the deal, which was to shore up security in Eastern Congo, and Rwanda and Uganda launched a second war to remove him from power. This turned into Africa's first cross-continental war, as neighbours piled in to pick off the country's unrivalled natural resources. Old friends Rwanda and Uganda soon became enemies and backed rival factions in the bloody civil war. Both countries were accused of shamelessly plundering DR Congo's mineral wealth and their international reputations took a tumble. Uganda finally pulled its troops out in 2002, but has yet to rebuild its former friendship with Rwanda.

Uganda is a country with much promise, but there are a number of tricky hurdles for it to overcome before it can fulfil its true potential. Firstly it needs to address the rampant corruption that continues to plague government, as this is rattling confidence among donors and the electorate, as well as choking development as earmarked funds disappear into deep pockets.

Secondly, when pluralism does return to Uganda, it is to be hoped that a new generation of politicians brought up on the no-party system will form their parties based on policy not pedigree, although the sad truth is that lines are already being drawn among tribes once again.

But real political stability is only possible if the government can bring the war with the LRA to an end within its own borders, and avoid costly and unnecessary involvement in events beyond its borders. Peace will bring the biggest dividend of all – further development, and not just development for Kampala and the elite, but a genuine development in fields such as education and healthcare that takes the whole country forward together.

THE CULTURE
The National Psyche

Despite the years of terror and bloodshed, Ugandans are a remarkably positive and spirited people, and no-one comes away from the country without a measure of admiration and affection for the people. Education levels have traditionally been high by African standards and most Ugandans are keen debaters, discussing politics and personality in equal measure. They are opinionated and eloquent during disagreements, yet unfailingly polite and engagingly warm. The national personality, if a country can be said to have one, is in stark contrast to the brutality and bloodshed of the past.

Idi Amin, 'Big Daddy', the Last King of Scotland – call him what you will – casts a long shadow over Uganda both at home and abroad. Mention Uganda to the average person in the west and it's still sadly Idi Amin that is namechecked first. His character has become the country's caricature, although for the majority of Ugandans it is a past they would rather forget. But the tendency to favour one tribe above another was not confined to his rule and many leaders contributed to Uganda's descent into darkness. It only ended with Museveni's accession to power in 1986, when party politics were banned. A successful formula for almost two decades, it remains to be seen what the future holds now that the country has embraced full democracy once more.

The 'Big Man' school of African politics is better known to Ugandans than most, having experienced the ultimate big man in the giant shape of Idi Amin. However, there are fears in some quarters that President Museveni is venturing down that road. In July 2005 the constitution was amended to allow unlimited presidential terms and it looks like Museveni will run again in 2006. Uganda waits with baited breath, but many of the population still supports Museveni for the progress he has brought to the country and the lack of any obvious alternative.

Despite the evident progress in Uganda, it remains a country divided. Kampala and the south have experienced peace and prosperity for two decades, but Gulu and points north have been mired in an intractable cycle of violence as the government fights against the brutal insurgency of the LRA. This has destroyed thousands of lives and livelihoods, and is holding back development throughout the country. Kampala may have found peace, but Uganda has not, and the tribal partisan politics of the past cannot be laid to rest until the north and south experience peace and prosperity together.

Daily Life

Ugandans are a very polite and friendly people, and will often greet strangers on public transport or in rural areas. This is not just a simple 'hello' but also 'How are you?' or 'How is your family?', and the interest is genuine. Hence, in social situations it is always best to ask after the wellbeing of whomever you are introduced to, rather than just a simple hello.

Life in Uganda has been one long series of upheavals for the older generations, while the younger generations have benefited from the newfound stability. Society has changed completely in urban areas in the past couple of decades, but in the countryside it is often business as usual. Until recently polygamy was common, even among non-Muslim Ugandans, but with the relative emancipation of women in the last decade, few in urban areas would now tolerate it.

This may be in no small part due to the impact of HIV/AIDS on sexual patterns in Uganda. One of the first countries to be struck by an HIV/AIDS outbreak of epidemic proportions, Uganda acted swiftly in promoting AIDS awareness nationwide and safe sex in society. This was very effective in radically reducing infection rates throughout the country, and Uganda went from experiencing an infection rate of around 25% in the late 1980s to an infection rate of as low as 6% today. However, there seems to be a change in the air today, with abstinence taking precedence over protection and young people being encouraged to wait until they are married. All good and well in principle, but teenagers will be teenagers and anything that dilutes the message of safe sex is dabbling with danger.

And all this ties into religion. Uganda is a spiritual society, and Catholicism and

Protestantism have always been popular among the population. However, evangelical Christianity has been making inroads in recent years and many of the groups have their roots in the US, where the Christian right has flourished under the Bush presidency. Abstinence is in, abortion out and in President Museveni's wife Janet, Bush may have found a fellow traveller.

Education has been a real priority in Uganda and President Museveni has been keen to promote free primary education for all. It's a noble goal, but Uganda may lack the resources to realise it. Sure, more pupils are attending class, but often the classes are hopelessly overcrowded in the countryside and many teachers lack experience.

Beyond the upwardly mobile urban areas, agriculture remains the single most important component of the Ugandan economy. It accounts for 70% of its gross domestic product (GDP) and employs 90% of the workforce. Coffee, sugar, cotton and tea are the main export crops. Crops grown for local consumption include maize, millet, cassava, sweet potato, beans and cereals.

Population
Uganda's estimated population of 27.6 million people is increasing at the rapid rate of close to 2.5% per annum. It is made up of a complex and diverse range of tribes. Lake Kyoga forms the northern boundary for the Bantu-speaking peoples, who dominate much of East, central and southern Africa and, in Uganda, include the Buganda (17%) and several other tribes, like the Bugosa (8%) and Bagisu. In the north are the Lango (near Lake Kyoga) and the Acholi (towards the Sudanese border), who speak Nilotic languages. To the east are the Iteso (8%) and Karamojong, who are related to the Maasai and who also speak Nilotic languages. Small numbers of pygmies live in the forests of the west.

There is a sizeable community of Asians in Uganda, who first settled here generations ago during the days of the British Empire. Expelled by Idi Amin in 1971, President Museveni invited them to return and reclaim their property, and this has driven the Ugandan economy forward.

SPORT
The most popular sport in Uganda, as in most of Africa, is football (soccer) and it is possible to watch occasional international games at the Nelson Mandela Stadium on the outskirts of Kampala on the road to Jinja. There is also a domestic league, with matches held most weekends at the smaller Nakivubo Stadium opposite the New Taxi Park in the centre of Kampala.

Boxing is very popular in Uganda, and Kassim Ouma is the current IBF light middleweight champion. His is an amazing story of rags to riches, as he was once a child soldier forced to fight for the LRA. Nicknamed 'The Dream', he now lives in the US. Other famous boxers from the past include John 'The Beast' Mugabi and one Idi Amin.

Long distance running has never been as big as in Kenya and Ethiopia, but that may all be set to change with the success of Docus Inzikuru in the 3000m steeplechase at the 2005 World Championships. Inzi struck gold and the nation went wild, suggesting more youngsters will take up running in the coming years.

RELIGION
While about two-thirds of the population is Christian, a large number of rural people still practise animism (a belief in the spirits of the natural world), and there's a small percentage who follow Islam. There were large numbers of Sikhs and Hindus in the country until Asians were expelled in 1972, and many have returned following the presidential invitation.

ARTS
Cinema
A Hollywood film crew was in town during our last visit to shoot a big screen version of The Last King of Scotland (see Literature, below). Starring Forrest Whitaker as the 'Big Daddy', this should help to put Uganda on the movie-making map, as all the locations are right here in the 'pearl of Africa'.

Literature
The Last King of Scotland by Giles Foden (1998) is a must for every visitor planning a trip to Uganda. This bestseller chronicles the experience of Idi Amin's personal doctor, as he slowly finds himself becoming confidant to the dictator. It is based on a true story and affords the reader a number of quirkyinsights into life in Uganda under Idi Amin.

The *Abyssinian Chronicles* by Moses Isegawa (2001) tells the story of a young Ugandan coming of age during the turbulent years of Idi Amin and the civil war. It offers some fascinating insights into life in Uganda and the transition from a rural existence to life in the city. More than a touch autobiographical, the main character, like the author, ends up living in the Netherlands. More recently, another of his works, *Snakepit*, has been translated from Dutch to English, a piece of political intrigue telling the fictional story of the extreme ups and downs of a high-flying civil servant during the Amin years.

Music & Dance
Uganda has a lively music scene, and travelling around by bus you will soon be familiar with all the latest local sounds. Chameleon is one of the most popular local artists, combining rap and traditional chanting in a cutting-edge combination. Several Ugandan artists have made a name for themselves on the international scene, including Geoffrey Oryema, based in Paris, who sings in English and his native language Acholi. His influences include tribal and traditional, as well as Western pop, making for an eclectic mix. For more on music in Ugandan, check out www.musicuganda.com.

Kampala is the best place to experience live music and several local bands play at nightclubs each weekend. Best of all is the jam session at the National Theatre every Monday – see p483 for more details

The most famous dancers in the country are the Ndere Troupe. Made up from a kaleidoscope of tribes in Uganda, they perform traditional dances from every region of the country. For more on where to catch a performance of the Ndere Troup, see p484.

ENVIRONMENT
The Land
Uganda is a blizzard of greens, a lush landscape of rolling hills blanketed with fertile fields. Uganda has an area of 236,580 sq km, small by African standards, but a similar area to Britain. Lake Victoria and the Victoria Nile River, which flows through much of the country, combine to create one of the most fecund areas in Africa. The highest peak is Mt Stanley (5109m) in the Rwenzori Mountains on the border with DR Congo.

The land varies from semidesert in the northeast to the lush and fertile shores of Lake Victoria, hemmed in by the Rwenzori Mountains in the west and the beautiful, mountainous southwest.

The tropical heat is tempered by the altitude, which averages more than 1000m in much of the country.

Wildlife
Uganda is home to more than half the world's mountain gorilla population, and viewing them in their natural environment is one of the main attractions for visitors to this country. For more information on these gentle creatures, their habitat, where to consider tracking them, and the dos and don'ts once there, see p97. Uganda is also a hotspot for other primates and has some of the cheapest chimp viewing on the continent, as well as huge troops of colobus monkeys.

Uganda is a fantastic country for bird life, with more than 1000 species recorded. It is one of the best bird-watching destinations in Africa (if not the world), and it is quite possible to see several hundred species during a two-week visit; with a keen eye, some binoculars and a field guide, of course. For bird-watchers coming to Uganda, the shoebill stork is one of the most sought-after birds, but there are many other rare and interesting species to be seen throughout the country.

National Parks & Reserves
Uganda has an excellent collection of national parks and reserves. While they may not be bursting with wildlife like in Kenya or Tanzania, they are also not bursting with visitors, which makes them an altogether more relaxing place to be. They also offer quite different experiences to those in neighbouring countries: viewing the mountain gorillas in Bwindi Impenetrable National Park, the chimps in Kibale Forest National Park or Budongo Central Forest Reserve, and the Nile's Murchison Falls are all highlights not to be missed. Uganda's community reserves are protected areas run by and for the benefit of local communities, a form of community-based ecotourism. Wildlife numbers may have declined dramatically during the years of turmoil, but the parks are in good shape and animal numbers are on the rise (see p543).

UGANDA

STALKING THE SHOEBILL

For anyone with a keen interest in birds, there is no more important bird to see in Uganda than the unique shoebill stork. Also known as the whale-head stork, this peculiar-looking bird has a gigantic, broad bill that aids it in catching prey in the water. Its favoured diet is the lungfish, but it also eats amphibians and small reptiles, including baby crocodiles (assuming mum and dad aren't around!) and snakes. Shoebills are not all that common in Uganda. However, if you visit an area where they're found, there is a good chance of a sighting, as they hunt by waiting motionless around papyrus swamps and marshes.

The best places to see the shoebill stork in Uganda include: the Nabajjuzzi swamp just out of Masaka on the way to Mbarara; the banks of the Victoria Nile River in Murchison Falls National Park; the shores of Lake Albert in Semliki Valley Game Reserve; and around Lake Kikorongo in Queen Elizabeth National Park. Should all else fail, try the Ugandan Wildlife Education Centre in Entebbe for a guaranteed sighting.

While the low number of visitors is a great bonus, it's also a disadvantage that the infrastructure of the parks is less developed than elsewhere in the region – the luxury lodges and tented camps common in the parks of Kenya and Tanzania are few and far between here. Also, the organised safari options, especially for budget travellers, are much more limited. Despite this many of the parks are relatively easy to visit, and the rewards are ample for those who make the effort.

Uganda Wildlife Authority (Map p471; UWA; ☎ 041-346287; www.uwa.or.ug; 7 Kira Rd; ☼ 8am-1pm & 2-5pm Mon-Fri, 9am-noon Sat), with its headquarters based near the Uganda Museum in Kampala, administers the national parks. It covers all of Uganda's protected areas. This is the place to make bookings to see the gorillas in Bwindi Impenetrable and Mgahinga Gorilla National Parks. In addition to information on the gorillas, the office also has useful free leaflets on each of the national parks.

The UWA has its own version of the general guidelines listed on p75, these should be observed by all visitors to the country's national parks:

- Do not camp or make campfires, except at official sites.
- Do not drive off the tracks.
- Do not disturb wildlife by sounding the car horn.
- Do not drive in the parks between 7.15pm and 6.30am.
- Do not bring dogs or other pets into the parks.
- Do not discard litter, burning cigarette ends or matches.
- Do not bring firearms or ammunition into the parks.
- Do not pick flowers or cut or destroy any vegetation.
- Do not exceed the parks' speed limit of 40km/h.

Uganda's park entry fees are fairly reasonable compared with those of its bigger neighbours. However, it is the hidden extras that quickly add up and make visiting the national parks an expensive experience. See the boxed text (opposite) for fees that apply to all national parks; for more details on specific costs in individual national parks, including for climbing and trekking, see the relevant sections in this chapter. All prices are lower for Ugandan residents and much lower again for Ugandan citizens.

Entry fees are reasonable and decrease by the day; a stay of a week or more costs as little as US$50. For vehicles, a one-off entry payment is required. Transport hire within the parks is USh2500 per kilometre for 4WDs. In the larger parks, rangers are available for wildlife drives and the charge is US$5 per vehicle for a half-day trip and US$10 for a full day.

Also available are launch trips to Murchison Falls (US$15) and along the Kazinga Channel in Queen Elizabeth National Park (US$10).

ACCESS

Access is the big headache when it comes to visiting many of Uganda's protected areas. In order to visit many of the larger parks, it really helps to have your own vehicle, both for entry into the park and then exploring the park once inside. Even the smaller parks are not always easy to reach, as transport to these remote, sparsely inhabited areas is

NATIONAL PARK FEES

Park	Per day (US$)	Per two days (US$)	Per three or more days (US$)
Bwindi Impenetrable	20	30	50
Kibale Forest	20	30	50
Kidepo Valley	20	30	50
Lake Mburo	15	25	30
Mgahinga Gorilla	20	30	50
Mt Elgon	15	25	30
Murchison Falls	20	30	50
Queen Elizabeth	20	30	50
Rwenzori Mountains	20	30	50
Semuliki	15	25	30

Vehicle	Foreign-registered (US$)	Ugandan-registered (USh)
motorcycle	15	5
car	20	6
minibus	50	15
4WD & pick-up	40	15
tour-company vehicle	100	10
bus & truck	200	100

Entry fees are per person and include overnight and until 6pm the following day. ISIC card holders receive a 25% discount. Group discounts are offered for 10 or more people. For details of fees for reserves, see the relevant sections in this chapter.

irregular to say the least. However, a number of the parks are simple to get to without your own transport and are easily manageable on foot once there, including Kibale Forest, Mgahinga Gorilla and Mt Elgon National Parks. Murchison Falls National Park is also now much easier to reach, as there are budget safaris available through the hostels in Kampala. Queen Elizabeth and Lake Mburo National Parks are hard to travel to and explore without transport, although with patience or good timing it can be done. Kidepo Valley and Bwindi Impenetrable National Parks are also tough to reach without transport, but once you're there, exploration is straightforward – Bwindi due to its size, and Kidepo Valley because much of the wildlife is concentrated around the Apoka headquarters.

In the long term it is to be hoped that the UWA wakes up to the fact that it is losing revenue by not providing transport between park headquarters and nearby towns. It would not be that difficult to operate a daily shuttle between places like Masindi and Paraa (for Murchison Falls) and Katunguru and Mweya (for Queen Elizabeth).

Environmental Issues

With its relatively low population density and scarcity of wildlife, the latter courtesy of the decimation that occurred during the bad old days, Uganda lacks many of the environmental pressures faced by others in the region. The absence of any notable numbers of tourists in the last 20 years means that the national parks and wilderness areas are generally in good shape, and conditions are ideal for the native wildlife to re-establish itself.

Uganda is therefore ideally placed to ensure that the environment remains in good condition. Programs are already in place for the responsible management of the national parks and reserves and community tourism projects around the country are bringing the local population onboard.

One of the main environmental issues in Uganda centres on electricity supply, and on construction of the dams required to fulfil demand. The most contentious of them all is the proposed Bujagali Falls Dam, which will wipe out many of the rapids that makes Uganda one of the world's leading whitewater rafting destinations.

FOOD & DRINK

Local food is much the same as elsewhere in the region, except that in Uganda *ugali* (food staple made from maize or cassava flour) is called *posho*, and is far less popular than *matoke* (mashed plantains). Beyond cosmopolitan Kampala, you'll only have the choice of cheap local food, or more expensive Western food from the upmarket hotels and lodges. Indian food is pretty common throughout Uganda, but other international cuisines are only really found in the capital.

Most local dishes are meat-based, so vegetarians will have little else other than *posho*, *matoke* and the occasional Indian dish to choose from. For more info on local cuisine, see p41.

Soft drinks (sodas) are everywhere, the most popular being the international giants, plus regional favourites, Krest (lemon soda) and Stoney (ginger beer). Like all East Africans, Ugandans love their beer, and, mercifully, they don't have a fetish for drinking the stuff warm – if a town has electricity you can be sure it will have a fridge, and this will have beer in it!

Uganda Breweries and Nile Breweries are the two local companies, and they produce some drinkable lagers. Bell is a light beer renowned for its 'Great night, good morning' advertising campaign. Nile Special, with an alcohol content of 5.6%, is substantially stronger. For the brave (or stupid), there is also Chairman's ESB, a potent brew with an alcohol content of 7.2%. You'll also find locally brewed South African Castle beer and Tusker Malt, plus local brews Pilsner and Club. Bottled beer costs USh1500 to USh2500 a bottle, depending on where you're drinking.

Waragi is the local millet-based alcohol and is relatively safe, although it can knock you around and give you a horrible hangover. It is a little like gin and goes down well with a splash of tonic. In its undistilled form, it is known as *kasezi bong* and would probably send you blind if you drank enough of it.

Imported wines are quite expensive and not that common beyond Kampala or the top-end accommodation options in national parks and towns around the country. Imported spirits are relatively cheaper, although, like wine, availability is somewhat restricted.

KAMPALA

☎ 041 / pop 1.2 million

Kampala is a dynamic and engaging city, the centre of political intrigue, commercial activity and intellectual excellence in Uganda. Today's forward-looking capital is vastly different from the battered city to which it was reduced to in the 1980s. In the period since Museveni's victory, Kampala has been transformed from a looted shell to a thriving, modern place befitting the capital of the pearl of Africa – the infrastructure is rehabilitated, mobile phones are *de rigueur*, and the shops and markets are once again well stocked.

Modern buildings have sprung up all over the city and old, dilapidated ones are steadily being renovated. And it is not only the buildings that are in better shape; there is a confidence about Kampala residents today that is infectious, and the nightlife in the city is something to savour. Kampala has some excellent international restaurants, including some of the best Indian eateries on the African continent.

One of the best aspects about Kampala, though, is that it's pretty safe to walk around during the day in virtually any part of the capital. The city is green and verdant, and the people are very friendly, all adding up to a great place to spend some time.

The worst thing about Kampala is the traffic. Near gridlock descends on the city during rush hour and it can take more than an hour to break out. The valleys fill up with the belching fumes of the minibuses and some days you can chew the air.

HISTORY

The capital suffered a great deal during the years of civil strife following Idi Amin's defeat at the hands of the Tanzanian army in 1979. The turmoil only ended with the victory of Yoweri Museveni's NRA in early 1986.

Unless you've had previous experience of upheavals like these, it's hard to believe the amount of gratuitous destruction and looting that went on: office blocks and government offices had the bulk of their windows shattered; the buildings were riddled with bullets; plumbing, electrical fittings and telephone receivers were ripped from walls; buses were shot up and abandoned; and shops were looted of everything.

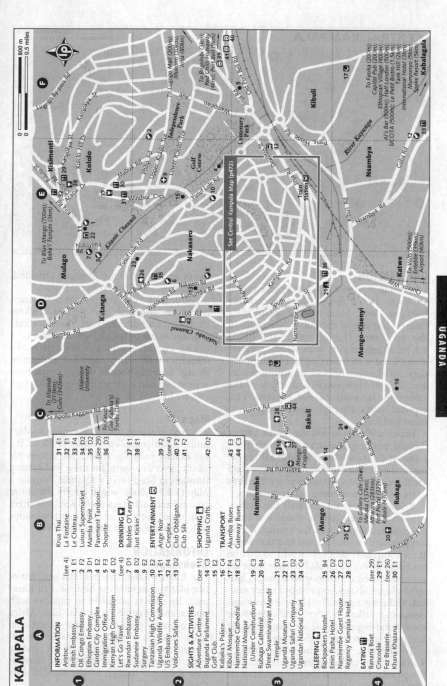

KAMPALA

INFORMATION
Aristoc....................................(see 4)
British Embassy.............................1 E1
DR Congo Embassy..........................2 F2
Ethiopian Embassy..........................3 D1
Garden City Complex.......................4 E2
Immigration Office...........................5 F3
Kenyan High Commission..................6 D2
Let's Go Travel............................(see 4)
Rwandan Embassy...........................7 D1
Sudanese Embassy...........................8 D2
Surgery...9 E2
Tanzanian High Commission.............10 E2
Uganda Wildlife Authority.................11 E1
US Embassy..................................12 F4
Volcanoes Safaris...........................13 D2

SIGHTS & ACTIVITIES
Adventure Centre.........................(see 11)
Buganda Parliament.......................14 C3
Golf Club....................................15 E2
Kabaka's Palace.............................16 C4
Kibuli Mosque...............................17 F4
Namirembe Cathedral.....................18 C3
National Mosque
  (Under Construction)...................19 C3
Rubaga Cathedral..........................20 B4
Shree Swaminarayan Mandir
  Temple.....................................21 D3
Uganda Museum............................22 E1
Uganda Safari Company...................23 D2
Ugandan National Court...................24 C4

SLEEPING
Backpackers Hostel.........................25 B4
Emin Pasha Hotel...........................26 D2
Namirembe Guest House..................27 C3
Regency Kampala Hotel...................28 C3

EATING
Banana Boat...............................(see 29)
Crocodile....................................29 E1
Fez Brasserie..............................(see 26)
Khana Khazana.............................30 E1

Krua Thai....................................31 E1
La Fontaine..................................32 E1
Le Chateau..................................33 F4
Luisun Supermarket........................34 D2
Mamba Point................................35 D2
Pavement Tandoor.....................(see 29)
Shoprite......................................36 D3

DRINKING
Bubbles O'Leary's..........................37 E1
Just Kickin'..................................38 E1

ENTERTAINMENT
Ange Noir....................................39 F2
Cineplex..................................(see 4)
Club Obbligato.............................40 F2
Club Silk.....................................41 F2

SHOPPING
Uganda Crafts..............................42 D2

TRANSPORT
Akamba Buses..............................43 E3
Gateway Buses.............................44 C3

UGANDA

Map directional notes and labels:
To Blue Mango (700m); Bahá'í Temple (3km)
To Masindi (213km); Gulu (342km)
Makerere University
Sir Apollo Kaggwa Rd
To Kasubi (Sse Kabaka's) Tombs (1km)
Mulago
Nakayima Rd
K-tanga
Bombo Rd
Hoima Rd
Namirembe
Mengo
To Gallery Cafe (2km); Masaka (137km); Mbarara (283km); Fort Portal (322km); Kabale (430km)
Rubaga
Bakuli
Mengo Hospital
Mengo-Kisenyi
Nakasero
Kisementi
Koldio
Kololo Hill Dr
Independence Park
Golf Course
Centenary Park
Nsambya
Kibuli
Katwe
Kabalagala
Train Station
River Kayunga
Press House Rd
Old Port Bell Rd
To Bugolobi (3km); Red Chilli Hideaway (4km); Port Bell (10km)
To Lugogo Mall (200m); Mukono (20km); Jinja (80km)
To Fasika (200m); Capital Pub (200m); Ethiopian Village (400m); Half London (500m); Le Petit Bistro (1.5km); International Hotel (3km); Tank Hill (3km); Speke Resort (5km)
To AV's Bar (500m); UCOTA (500m); Nakumatt (3km)
To Volt (900m); Entebbe (35km); Airport (40km)
See Central Kampala Map (p472)

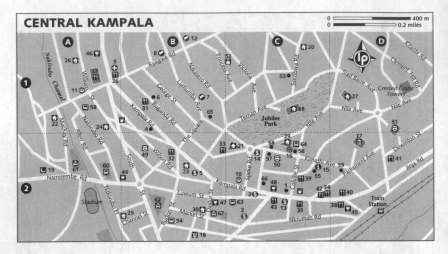

ORIENTATION

Like Rome, Kampala is built on seven hills, although that is where the comparisons begin and end. Most visitors spend their time on just one of the hills – Nakasero, in the city centre. The top half of this hill is a type of garden city, with wide, quiet avenues lined with flowering trees, and large, detached houses behind imposing fences and hedges. Here you'll find many of the embassies, international aid organisations, top-end hotels, the high court and government buildings.

Between Nakasero and the lower part of the city is Kampala's main thoroughfare – Kampala Rd (which turns into Jinja Rd to the east and Bombo Rd to the west). On this road are the main banks, the main post office, lots of shops, and a few hotels and restaurants.

Below Kampala Rd, towards the bottom of the valley, are heaps of shops and small businesses, budget hotels, the market, Hindu temples, and the bus station and taxi parks. It's a completely different world to that on the upper side of Kampala Rd. Here there are congested streets thronging with people, battered old minibuses, impromptu street markets and pavement stalls. There are hawkers, newspaper sellers, hustlers, and one of the most mind-boggling and seemingly chaotic taxi parks you're ever likely to see.

To the east, across the golf course, is Kololo, a fairly exclusive residential area, and the popular Cooper Rd area with its restaurants and bars. To the west is Namirembe, on top of which stands the Anglican cathedral, and nearby is the Backpackers Hostel.

South of the city centre, across the train tracks, lie Kabalagala and Tank Hill, where there are some midrange hotels, good restaurants and some of the city's wildest bars.

The biggest orientation obstacle is the frequency with which street names seem to change. Several streets in the city centre have at least two names depending on which sign you are looking at.

Maps

The best available map of Kampala is Macmillan's *Kampala Tourist Map* (1:8500). It's not exactly bang up to date, but covers the whole city. Also useful for those just passing through is Macmillan's *Uganda Traveller's Map* (1:1,350,000), which covers the entire country and includes a useful Kampala street map inset. Both are available in bookshops in Kampala and cost about USh8000.

INFORMATION
Bookshops

For English-language publications **Aristoc** (Map p472; Kampala Rd) is the best place in Kampala. Its shelves are filled to capacity with books and maps on Uganda, East Africa and beyond, plus novels and educational texts. Prices are pretty reasonable for imported books, so stock up here for reading material before a long road trip. There is also a second branch in the Garden City Complex.

Emergency

Police or ambulance (☎ 999)

Internet Access

It's hard to walk far in Kampala without tripping over an Internet café. Prices cost USh20 to USh40 per minute and many places offer discounts on weekends. Red Chilli Hideaway offers free Internet access to guests, which is popular. Also recommended:

Chipper's (Map p472; Kampala Rd) One of the cheapest places in the city, enjoy an ice cream at the same time.

Web City Café (Map p472; Kimathi Ave) The biggest operation in the city with 30 terminals and a fast connection.

Medical Services

There are two well-known surgeries for medical treatment in Kampala.

International Medical Centre (Map p472; ☎ 041-341291, emergency ☎ 077-741291; iclark@infocom.co.ug; ☼ 24hr) Housed in the Kampala Pentecostal Church building opposite Hotel Equatoria, this clinic is run by Dr Ian Clarke. It offers professional medical services, including dependable malaria smears. It operates an ambulance service in an emergency.

Surgery (Map p471; ☎ /fax 041-256003, emergency ☎ 075-756003; stockley@imul.com; 2 Acacia Dr; ☼ 8am 6pm Mon-Fri, 9am-1pm Sat, 10am-noon Sun) Run by Dr Dick Stockley, resident medical expert in The Eye magazine, this well-respected clinic stocks self-test malaria kits for those heading into remote areas for long periods.

Money

Kampala Rd is where most of the banks and many foreign exchange bureaus are located. The foreign exchange bureaus generally stay open longer than the banks, and offer competitive rates with no commission. Rates at the main bureaus are listed in the daily *New Vision* newspaper. Other than the foreign exchange bureaus, the best exchange rates are generally offered by **Crane Bank** (Map p472), which has a branch at Speke Hotel that is open daily until at least 8.30pm. However, for small bills, Barclays Bank offers the same rates as for large bills, which makes it the best place to change US$20 and smaller notes.

Amex travellers cheques can be changed at **Standard Chartered Bank** (Map p472) branches in the city. The head office is opposite the

UGANDA

Grand Imperial Hotel. Other banks are not that keen on changing cheques, but Barclays and Crane can usually deal with smaller sums and Thomas Cook travellers cheques.

Barclays Bank (Map p472; Kampala Rd) For US-dollar or Ugandan-shilling credit-card cash advances, head here. It offers the equivalent of US$700 per day, but at a hefty commission of US$15 or USh30,000.

Centenary Rural Development Bank (Map p472; 7 Entebbe Rd) Western Union money transfers are available.

Express Uganda (Map p472; ☎ 041-236767) At the Sheraton Hotel, this is the Amex agent.

Standard Chartered Bank (Map p472) Another main bank offering credit-card compatible ATMs, with a maximum daily withdrawal of USh400,000. The ATMs aren't always reliable, so it is best to use them during business hours in case of a problem.

National Parks Office

Uganda Wildlife Authority (Map p472; UWA; ☎ 041-346287; www.uwa.or.ug; 7 Kira Rd; ☯ 8am-1pm & 2-5pm Mon-Fri, 9am-noon Sat) Looks after the country's national parks and protected areas. It recently moved into a flagship headquarters near the Uganda Museum.

Post

Main post office (Map p471; cnr Kampala & Speke Rds; ☯ 8am-6pm Mon-Fri, 8am-2pm Sat) Offers postal and telecom services. The poste restante service is well organised and as the volume of mail here is low, things don't go astray.

Telephone & Fax

The main post office also houses the international telephone exchange, and there are public phones where you can ring and fax overseas.

Phonecards are sold in booths throughout the city, and there are MTN and UTL (mobile-phone companies that also operate card phones) cardphones all over town. Connection is pretty straightforward to most countries. There are also Simu4u booths in the city where you pay cash for calls at pretty reasonable rates.

Tourist Information

For up-to-the-minute information on Kampala, pick up the free listings magazine *The Eye: The In & Out Guide to Uganda* from selected hotels and restaurants.

Uganda Community Tourism Association (Map p471; Ucota; ☎ 041-501866; ucota@africaonline.co.ug; Kabalagala) Heavily geared towards independent travellers, it can advise on travel arrangements to its countrywide projects. Ucota operates a number of community camping grounds on the periphery of Uganda's national parks. The office is quite a way out of the centre of the city up the Gaba Rd.

Uganda Tourist Board (Map p472; UTB; ☎ 041-342196; www.visituganda.com; 15 Kimathi Ave; ☯ 8am-1pm & 2-5pm Mon-Fri, 8.30am-12.30pm Sat) The nerve centre of tourism promotion in Uganda. Staff are quite well informed, although there's not a whole lot of printed information to take away.

Travel Agencies

For information on tour operators offering tours and safaris in Uganda, see p95.

Let's Go Travel (Map p471; ☎ 041-346667; www.letsgo safari.com; Uganda@letsgosafari.com; 1st fl, Garden City Complex) Part of a global empire.

Speedwing Travel Bureau (Map p472; ☎ 041-231052; rcm@infocom.co.ug; 1 Kimathi Ave) For airline tickets, this is a reliable stop for fair prices.

Uganda Travel Bureau (Map p472; UTB; ☎ 041-232555; www.utb.co.ug; Kimathi Ave) Not to be confused with the nearby tourist office, this is a private agent offering worldwide ticketing services.

DANGERS & ANNOYANCES

Kampala is a fairly safe city as far as Africa's capitals go. Incidents can and sometimes do happen, like anywhere else in the world, so it pays not to have all your valuables on you in poorly lit areas at night. Take care late at night around the taxi parks, as pickpockets and thieves operate here. Still, there is no need to be paranoid when out and about.

Due to low-level terrorist campaigns in Kampala in the late 1990s, and current worldwide jitters about international terrorists, security at government buildings, embassies, bars and nightclubs is extremely tight. However, you get used to the searches pretty quickly and, remember, it is for your own safety.

Uganda doesn't have much of a social-security system, so begging is quite common, especially in central Kampala.

One recurrent annoyance in Kampala is that taxi drivers have a tendency to run out of petrol at the most inconvenient times. Drivers often have the bare minimum of fuel in their tank, so that if the car gets stolen it won't get far. Daft though it sounds, it is no joke, and often they miscalculate how much they have left and don't make it to the nearest garage – make sure you get into a taxi at the top of a hill!

SCAMS

It is quite common to meet children around the city asking for sponsorship for schooling, often claiming to be refugees from Sudan or Somalia. While some cases may be genuine, locals say that many are bogus and begging on behalf of their parents. Worse still, others say that waving the paper in your face is simply a diversion for a spot of sneak theft, so keep your eyes open.

SIGHTS & ACTIVITIES

Low key is the phrase to remember here. What is on offer in Kampala is fairly limited when compared with the amazing attractions elsewhere in the country. Unless, of course, you consider a night on the town an activity, then Kampala competes with the best of them!

Kasubi Tombs

The **Kasubi Tombs** (Sse kabaka's Tombs; Kasubi Hill; admission USh3000; ☉ 8am-6pm), just off Masiro Rd, were first built in 1881 and are worth a look for a dose of traditional culture. There are several huge traditional reed and bark cloth buildings of the *kabakas* of the Buganda people. The group of buildings contains the tombs of Muteesa I, his son Mwanga (Sir Daudi Chwa II) and his son Edward Muteesa II, father of the current *kabaka*, Ronald Mutebi II (known also by his Bugandan name, Muwenda). Edward Muteesa II died in London in 1969, three years after being deposed by Obote. The tombs are taken care of by the Ganda clans.

The Kasubi Tombs are open year-round, including holidays. Remove your shoes before entering the main building. You can get to the tombs by minibus, either from the old taxi park in the city centre (ask for Hoima Rd) or from the junction of Bombo and Makerere Hill Rds. The minibuses to get are the ones that terminate at the market at the junction of Hoima and Masiro Rds. The tombs are a few hundred metres walk up the hill from here and are signposted.

Uganda Museum

The **Uganda Museum** (Map p471; Kira Rd; adult/child USh3000/1500; ☉ 10am-6pm Mon-Sat, noon-6pm Sun) is quite run-down given that it is meant to be the showcase for the nation. It has a few good ethnological exhibits covering hunting, agriculture, war and religion, as well as

> ### THE NAKED TRUTH ABOUT CRIME IN KAMPALA
>
> Some of Africa's capitals are notorious for muggings and robberies, but Kampala has never been one of them. At last the reasons have been exposed and they are pretty revealing. In many African cities, thieves are dealt with through mob justice, and lynchings are not uncommon throughout the continent. However, Ugandans have opted for something a little less final and a little more humiliating – stripping thieves down to their 'Adam suits' or ripping all their clothes off in public.
>
> Several cases of these mob strips are reported each day in Kampala's newspapers and even a few women have fallen victim to this brand of instant justice. Officially the police are trying to discourage this practice, as they feel that mob justice often fails to discriminate between the guilty and innocent.
>
> There is a prevalent view held by most Kampala citizens that it is not only the mob who have difficulty discriminating between the guilty and innocent. Police corruption is a subject of concern for the Ugandan government. However, police chiefs downplay corruption in the force; one officer is on the record as saying that the 'police are like your buttocks, you only notice their importance when you have a boil on them'.

archaeological and natural history displays. Perhaps its most interesting feature is a collection of traditional musical instruments, but even these are falling apart. Basically, the museum is crying out for some tender, loving care. More recently some photo exhibitions have been held here and this could be a good way to reinvigorate the place. There is an USh5000 fee for cameras and an USh20,000 fee for video cameras, money down the drain given the paucity of exhibits.

To get here, catch a Kamjokya shared taxi from the old taxi park (USh300).

Buildings of the Buganda Kingdom

Kampala has always been the heartland of the Buganda kingdom, and within the capital are a number of its impressive administrative centres and royal buildings. Most of these are located in and around Mengo and include the **kabaka's palace** (Map p471), inside a vast walled enclosure, the **Buganda parliament** (Map p471; Kabakanjagala Rd), located at the end of a ceremonial driveway leading from the palace and the **Buganda Court of Justice** (Map p471), now the location for Uganda's National Court. However, none of these are open to the public.

The **kabaka's Trail** (☎ 041-501866; www.cultural heritagetrails.com; Ucota office, Kabalagala) is a community tourism project to introduce visitors to the secret history of the Buganda people. See p487 for more details.

Religious Buildings

There are several prominent religious buildings in Kampala that might interest some spiritually inclined travellers, including the gleaming white **Kibuli Mosque** (Map p471) dominating Kibuli Hill on the other side of the train station from Nakasero Hill; the huge, domed Roman Catholic **Rubaga Cathedral** (Map p471) on Rubaga Hill; the twin towers of the Anglican **Namirembe Cathedral** (Map p471), where the congregation is called to worship by the beating of drums; the enormous **Hindu temples** (Map p472) in the city centre; and the beautiful **Baha'í temple** way out towards Kira.

There is also a **national mosque** (Map p471) under construction in old Kampala, originally begun under Idi Amin and now being funded by Colonel Gadaffi. Idi Amin had planned a towering minaret to be visible all over the city, but the unfinished pillar had begun to lean precariously in recent years and has been rebuilt on a smaller scale.

Other Activities

Kampala is a good base for activities beyond the city. By far the most popular is whitewater rafting at the source of the Nile, near Jinja. See p495 for more details. Other popular activities on and around Lake Victoria include boating, fishing and horse riding – see p489 for more details.

KAMPALA FOR CHILDREN

Kampala isn't exactly bursting with activities for children, but with a bit of time and effort it is possible to keep the young-uns entertained. Swimming pools are always a winner and the Speke Resort (p490) at Munyono has one of the best in the city. The Blue Mango

(opposite) is another good option, as parents can while away some time at its excellent restaurant and bar. Otherwise, Entebbe is worth a visit, as the Uganda Wildlife Education Centre (p487) provides a comfortable home for such diverse animals as chimpanzees, rhinos and the peculiar looking shoebill stork. There are also the Entebbe Botanical Gardens (p487), with plenty of space to roam about.

Otherwise, head east to Jinja where there are the enticing options of a family float rafting trip on the Nile or quad biking for kids (see p498).

SLEEPING

Accommodation in Kampala doesn't offer particularly impressive value for money, particularly if you want anything with a modicum of comfort and a bathroom.

Budget

Most travellers choose to stay at Backpackers Hostel, Red Chilli Hideaway or the Blue Mango – all excellent places – as the cheap hotels are mostly near the noisy bus station and taxi parks, an area which is pretty noisy at all times of day and night.

HOSTELS

There are a couple of great hostels in Kampala, but both fill up fast during peak season, so be sure to book ahead.

Backpackers Hostel (Map p471; ☎ 077-430587; www.backpackers.co.ug; Natete Rd, Lunguja; camping USh5000, dm USh7000-10,000 s/d USh14,000/25,000, d with bathroom USh35,000-45,000; 🖳) The first budget hostel to open its doors in Kampala and still going strong. Set in lush gardens, it is an escape from the bustle of the city and local staff ensure a warm welcome. As well as dorm beds in various shapes and sizes, there are also attractive *bandas* (thatch-roofed huts) and some more sophisticated self-contained doubles with hot-water bathrooms. Cooking facilities are available for campers, but tasty, inexpensive set meals and snacks are readily available, including nightly specials. The bar draws a mix of travellers and expats, includes a pool table and stays open late. Broadband Internet access is available. This is also the place for reliable information on tracking the mountain gorillas in DR Congo, as this is the representative in Uganda. This popular hostel is a 10-minute minibus ride out of the city centre, not far from the landmark Namirembe Cathedral. Take a Natete shared taxi from the new taxi park (USh500 uphill, but only USh300 return!) – just ask for 'Backpackers'. The team also runs a new beach resort on Bussi Island in Lake Victoria (see p490).

Red Chilli Hideaway (☎ 041-223903; www.redchilli hideaway.com; camping USh6000, dm USh9000, tw from USh22,000, d with bathroom from USh35,000; 🖳) An oasis in the city, Red Chilli is the hub of a growing empire that includes budget camps at Murchison Falls and Mgahinga Gorilla National Parks. It is very popular with long-term guests for its wide range of rooms and it gets most of the overland truck business. It has several doubles – named after chilli varieties – and some rooms include bathroom. There are also sweet two-bedroom cottages (USh85,000) with lounge, bathroom and kitchen facilities, which are great for families. Guests can use the swimming pool at the nearby Silver Springs Hotel for USh3000. There is decent food available throughout the day and a lively bar. Equally popular is the free Internet access on offer. Check out the reliable travel information here before moving on and take a look at its bargain budget three-day Murchison Falls trips. This great spot is up in Bugolobi district, about 6km out of the city centre, off the road to Port Bell. Take a minibus from the eastern end of Kampala Rd to Bugolobi for USh500, get off opposite the Silver Springs Hotel and take the road opposite up the hill, following signs from there.

The excellent Blue Mango (right) also offers dorm beds, which include access to the swimming pool.

HOTELS

The budget hotels are all in the busy part of the city centre near the taxi parks and domestic bus station. Some people find this part of Kampala quite intimidating, so with the great hostels around the city there are few foreigners staying here. There's a large choice these days, but all offer the same standard – choosing where to stay is more a question of a thousand shillings or a bathroom here and there.

L'Hotel Fiancée (Map p472; ☎ 041-236144; Channel St; s/d with bathroom USh16,000/20,000) Promising a 'concentration of elegancy', this is the smartest place in this not-so-smart part of the city.

> ### THE AUTHOR'S CHOICE
>
> **Blue Mango** (☎ 041-543481; bluemango@info com.co.ug; Old Kira Rd; dm US$8, s/d US$25/35, with bathroom US$35/45, cottages US$55/70; 🖳) Looking for the atmosphere of a lodge in the city? Look no further, as this place has lush gardens, soft lighting and a swimming pool. All rooms are attractively decorated, although the cheapest have shared bathroom. The larger cottages are perfect for families or small groups, with a lounge and kitchen facilities. Budget travellers can take advantage of the dorms, as the price includes access to the swimming pool. Book ahead, as it is pretty popular. There is also a lively restaurant and bar here, plus a sophisticated craft shop.

Rooms are bright and clean, plus free tea is available on request.

Midland Guesthouse (Map p472; ☎ 041-340264; 7 Nakivubo Rd; s/d USh12,000/17,000) Looming large over the bustling bus station, this place is perhaps noisier than most, but does offer good-value rooms. It promises service with a personal touch, but there is an element of wishful thinking here – a lethargic touch is more the reality.

Hotel Sun City (Map p472; ☎ 041-345542; William St; s USh12,000, s/d with bathroom USh18,000/25,000) Moving closer to the city centre, but still in the chaotic part of Kampala, the Sun City is a good compromise between the bustle of the taxi parks and the higher prices of Kampala Rd. Staff are friendly, the rooms are a reasonable size and the bathrooms have hot water.

Midrange

Tourist Hotel (Map p472; ☎ 041-251471; www.tourist hotel.net; Dastur St; s US$25-30, d US$35-40) This stands head and shoulders above the city-centre competition, as it offers high standards at midrange prices, making it exceptional value. It overlooks the lively Nakasero Market and has executive style rooms, with key card, safety deposit box, spotless bathroom, TV and telephone. Breakfast is an extra US$5. This is definitely the best place in the city for those who want a little more comfort, but don't want to break the bank.

Namirembe Guest House (Map p471; ☎ 041-273778; www.namirembe-guesthouse.com; Willis Rd; s USh35,000-55,000, d USh60,000-75,000) This place is church run and promises 'a million dollar view', and does indeed offer some of the best city scapes in Kampala. Set in spacious grounds in a quiet suburb, there are several buildings housing a variety of meticulously clean rooms. Breakfast is included.

Regency Kampala Hotel (Map p471; ☎ 041-272095; Namirembe Rd; s/d USh95,000/125,000) This large business hotel offers top-end comfort at midrange prices. It is a touch sterile, but that might appeal after a stint in the bush.

New Gloria Hotel (Map p472; ☎ 041-257790; fax 041-269616; William St; s/d/tr USh25,000/40,000/50,000) A small place with an intimate atmosphere, the self-contained rooms are reasonably good value for the city centre.

Hotel City Square (Map p472; ☎ 041-256257; fax 041-251440; 42 Kampala Rd; s/d USh35,000/45,000) Sitting in a strategic position on Kampala Rd, the hotel looks pretty drab from the exterior, but the rooms aren't bad, with a bathroom, TV and telephone. Rates include breakfast.

Havana Hotel (Map p472; ☎ 041-343532; hotel havana@hotmail.com; 28 Mackay St; s/d US$40/45, with air-con US$50/55; ⚡) Catering primarily to local business travellers, this offers a slice of real Kampala, overlooking the busy new taxi park. Rooms include all the obvious trimmings, although the furnishings are clearly from another era. Rates include breakfast.

Fang Fang Hotel (Map p472; ☎ 041-235828; fang fang@africaonline.co.ug; Ssezibwa Rd; s/d with breakfast US$55/75) Just below the Sheraton Hotel, this place is good value when compared with certain top-end hotels, where prices double for the same type of room. Rooms are modern, clean and well appointed. There is also a good Chinese restaurant here, part of the Fang Fang chain.

Hotel Diplomate (☎ 041-510343; s/d US$50/65, cottages US$65/75, ste US$75/90) If it's views that you're after, this place offers them from its imperious location on the summit of Tank Hill. The hotel has a fair choice of rooms, and the suites are a worthwhile investment for the huge sunken baths and smarter trimmings. Rates include breakfast and taxes. Forget about staying here unless you have your own transport, as it's a fair distance from minibus routes.

Hotel International (☎ 041-510200; Tank Hill Rd; s/d USh90,000/100,000; ⚡) Located in the Tank Hill area, this modern business hotel offers some of the largest standard rooms in the city. Like the Diplomate, there are some seriously big

views from the back of this hotel, and facilities include a swimming pool.

Top End

Although most of the accommodation in this price bracket is quoted in hard currency (US dollars), payment in local currency is always possible. Most of the prices quoted exclude value-added tax (VAT) of 17%, unless otherwise stated.

Speke Hotel (Map p471; ☎ 041-259221; www.speke hotel.com; Nile Ave; s/d US$95/100; ⚡) One of Kampala's oldest hotels, this characterful address was recently given a major facelift to add creature comforts to age and grace. All rooms now have air-con, wooden floors, satellite TV and minibar. With a central location, this is definitely the hotel of choice for those looking to spend a hundred bucks. The terrace bar is a popular meeting place, there's a good Italian restaurant (Mama Mia) and heaving On the Rocks bar is right next door. The luxurious Speke Resort is run by the same owners – see page p490.

Emin Pasha Hotel (Map p471; ☎ 041-236977; www .eminpasha.net; 27 Aki Bua Rd; s/d from US$220/250; ⚡ ⚡ ⚡) Kampala's first boutique hotel is beautifully housed in an elegant old colonial property that has been thoughtfully restored. The 20 rooms are the best in the city, blending atmosphere and luxury, and more expensive suites feature such touches as claw-foot bathtubs. The expansive grounds include a swimming pool, and attached is the respected Fez Brasserie.

Sheraton Kampala Hotel (Map p472; ☎ 041-420000; www.sheraton.com; Ternan Ave; s/d US$265/290; ⚡ ⚡) Looming large over the capital, this concrete behemoth was long considered the best hotel in Kampala. Rooms were undergoing much needed renovations at the time of writing, as they were ageing badly, but the prices still seem absurdly high compared to Sheratons in other parts of the world. Facilities include tennis and squash courts, several restaurants and bars, and a shopping precinct. Rates include breakfast and service, but not tax – that adds up to US$300 or more, ouch!

Grand Imperial Hotel (Map p472; ☎ 041-250681; imperialhotels@utlonline.co.ug; 6 Nile Ave; s/d US$140/160; ⚡ ⚡) One of the extended family of Imperial hotels in and around Kampala, this is smaller and more intimate than the Sheraton, and has good facilities, including a small swimming pool, bars, a café and restaurants.

Nile Hotel (Map p472; Nile Ave) One of the best-known properties in Kampala, this hotel is currently undergoing a massive renovation by the Soneva chain and will open its five-star doors during the lifetime of this book.

EATING

Kampala is packed with quality restaurants, ensuring no-one goes hungry. Some of the cheapest places to eat in Kampala are the ubiquitous takeaways that dot the city centre. It is impossible to recommend any in particular as they are fairly standard outfits, offering dishes such as chicken, meat, sausages, fish and chips, as well as samosas and chapatis. Prices are the same whether you eat in or takeaway, and cost about USh1000 to USh3000 for a meal. Look out for the takeaway signs sticking out of buildings all over the city, but be aware that grease is a consistent ingredient at every establishment.

Many of the markets around the city have local food stalls that are even cheaper than takeaways. For USh1000, they usually offer a heaped plate of *matoke*, potatoes, groundnut sauce, beans, greens, and meat or fish.

It is worth noting that quite a lot of the better restaurants in Kampala are closed on Sunday or Monday, so check in advance to avoid disappointment.

Ugandan

Canaan Restaurant (Map p472; Kampala Rd; mains USh4000-8000) Just off Kampala Rd, the outdoor terrace here is popular for people-watching during the busy lunch hour in the city centre. Local businessmen and officials fill the tables, and drinking is just as popular as dining. The menu is limited, but if you need a quick steak or a roast chicken, it can deliver.

Half London (Gaba Rd; meals USh5000-15,000) A Kampala institution that now houses a small branch of the famous Carnivore from Nairobi. Both the space and menu are tiny when compared to those in Kenya, but this is the place to try bush meat if you must. Service is slow to the point of non-existent, however. The outdoor bar is one of *the* places to check out in the evening. For more details, see p483.

Kampala Casino (Map p472; Kimathi Ave) Head here on Thursday evening to sample the Ugandan

buffet, which is pretty good value for such a fancy place. There's live music while you eat, but you need to be reasonably smartly dressed to get in here.

Chinese & Thai

Chinese restaurants are surprisingly prolific in Kampala, but some are better than others. All are open daily.

Fang Fang (Map p472; ☎ 041-344806; Colville St; mains USh5000-10,000) The consensus in the city is that this is the best Chinese restaurant and the sheer numbers that pack the place each night attest to the quality of the food. Located in an anonymous office block, the interior is typical of a Chinese restaurant anywhere, but there's a large outdoor terrace for breezy nights. There's a full selection of Chinese classics, and specialities include fried crispy prawns with ginger and garlic.

Chopsticks (Map p472; ☎ 041-250781; Hotel Equatoria, William St; mains around USh7000) It's more of a multinational menu here with Chinese dishes the main star, ably supported by a cast of Thai and Vietnamese favourites for good measure. Look out for promotional menus at lunchtime, including four courses for USh10,000.

Krua Thai (Map p471; ☎ 041-234852; Windsor Cres; meals USh10,000) If you are after the taste of Thailand, Krua Thai is an authentic family-run restaurant up in the popular Kololo area of the city. The menu includes all the familiar greatest hits, including *pad Thai*, *laab* and *tôm yam kung*, as well as some regional specialities. Those used to dining in Thailand might want to ask staff to up the chilli count, as they tone down the spices on most dishes.

Continental

Blue Mango (Kira Rd; meals USh6000-15,000) For a good selection of grub from all over the globe, head to the suburban sanctuary that is the Blue Mango. Big bush furniture, cushions to sink in and flowing African drapes provide the backdrop for a very relaxed meal. The menu includes cheaper bar meals, such as pies with mash and crisp salads, and a more sophisticated range of meat, poultry and fish with a regional accent. On Friday it fills up with the post-work crowd.

Fez Brasserie (Map p471; ☎ 041-236977; mains USh10,000-20,000) Set in the grounds of Kampala's first boutique hotel, the Emin Pasha,

UGANDA

this restaurant has quickly won over the discerning local crowd thanks to a fusion menu that includes flavours from five continents. Highlights from the ever-evolving menu include the signature aubergine tower with goats cheese, roast peppers and pesto, Moroccan lamb and Cuban spatchcock poussin… impressive stuff! Vegetarians are also well represented.

Crocodile (Map p471; ☎ 041-254593; Cooper Rd; ☺ Tue-Sun) A very popular café-bar up in the lively Kisimenti district, the Crocodile has a tempting range of salads, pasta dishes and sophisticated snacks. It gets very busy on Sunday, as the healthy flavours are good for a hangover.

La Fontaine (Map p471; ☎ 077-4061976; Bukoto St; mains USh6000-12,000) La Fontaine is a popular café-restaurant in this area. There is a filling lunchtime buffet for USh8000, a great range of salads, including spicy Thai or blue cheese, and a good juice selection.

Le Petit Bistro (Gaba Rd; steaks from USh8000) Like much of Africa, steak is very popular in Uganda and this simple little restaurant cooks up some of the best meat in the city. Prices are pretty low and a selection of sauces is available. That's the good news. The bad news is that it can take as long as two hours for food to arrive, so be patient and let the drinks flow.

Le Chateau (Map p471; Gaba Rd; meals around USh20,000) Popular for serious steaks, Le Chateau is home to the Quality Cuts butchery, guaranteeing top meat. This place is absurdly fashionable among well-to-do Ugandans. The extensive menu favours French cuisine, and includes frogs' legs and snails, so if you are looking to indulge, this is a good place to do it.

Ethiopian

Fasika (☎ 041-268571; Gaba Rd; dishes USh5000-7000) Right opposite the crazy Capital Pub in Kabalagala, Fasika is the leading Ethiopian restaurant in Kampala. The menu is a good introduction to Ethiopian eats and includes a tasty Ethiopian answer to a thali (mixed curry selection, including rice and pappadams), with a little bit of everything served on *injera* (unleavened bread).

Ethiopian Village (Muyenga Rd; mains USh7000) An Ethiopian eatery in the same part of town as Fasika, there is a large, lush garden here for al fresco dining.

Indian

Masala Chaat House (Map p472; ☎ 041-255710; 3 Dewinton Rd; mains USh3000-7000) The sheer number of Indians eating here should tell you something about the authentic flavours and affordable prices at this local institution. Located opposite the National Theatre, it serves cheap vegetarian thalis and has stacks more to keep vegetarians smiling for the night. Meat and fish dishes are also available, as well as a wide selection of tasty *masala dosas* (a large savoury crepe stuffed with a delicious filling of potatoes cooked with onions and curry leaves) and other southern Indian delights.

City Bar & Grill (Kampala Rd; dishes USh5000-10,000) Housed in a classic Art Deco building, this is a popular stop for lunch, serving excellent tandoori dishes. A small subcontinental selection is available, as well as Western meals, such as steaks. Check out the full-sized snooker table, which sorts out the men from the boys.

Pavement Tandoori (Map p471; ☎ 041-344994; Cooper Rd; mains USh5000-10,000) This place is right in the middle of the action on the popular Cooper Rd strip. The Indian food here is delicious and elegantly presented. Try the vegetarian sizzler for an introduction to Indian starters.

Khana Khazana (Map p471; ☎ 041-233049; 20 Acacia Dr; mains USh10,000-20,000) Regarded by some expat residents as the classiest Indian restaurant in Kampala, this is housed in a residential villa near the golf course. It is the most expensive option in the city, but this doesn't dissuade the discerning crowd. It has recently spread its wings to Kigali, Rwanda.

Italian

Mamba Point (Map p471; ☎ 077-243225; www.mamba -point.com; 22 Aki Bua Rd; mains USh15,000-30,000; ☺ Mon-Sat) For the best in Italian dining, make for Mamba Point, where the pasta is home-made and the menu as close to the homeland as you might hope to find in Africa. Save space for the exquisite desserts, which include lime syllabub and chocolate truffle torte.

Caffé Roma (☎ 077-501847; Tank Hill Parade; pizzas USh10,000, pasta from USh8000; ☺ Tue-Sun) If you are thinking of a night in Kabalagala, why not kick off with an affordable Italian meal at this place up on Tank Hill. Pizza comes with all the favourite toppings and there is a good choice of popular pasta dishes.

There is also a long-running Italian restaurant in the Speke Hotel called Mama Mia and the small pizzas (from USh8000) are just about enough for a meal. There is also a genuine gelato bar here for ice-cream lovers.

Quick Eats

Fast food is popular among Kampalans and several regional chains have set up shop in the past few years.

Antonio's (Map p472; Kampala Rd; mains USh3000) This is a pretty good greasy spoon café, serving Indian, Mexican and Ugandan favourites at lightning speed. Curries and burritos are cheap, and portions are large.

Domino's Pizza (Map p472; ☎ 041-251513; 2 Kampala Rd) Believe it or not, this isn't actually part of the vast international empire, but a local place that has managed to hang on to the name. Still the pizza is just as good as its internationally famous namesake.

Nando's (Map p472; Kampala Rd) and **Chicken Inn** (Map p472; Kampala Rd), both in the same building, turn out chicken in every size and shape at reasonable prices (USh4000 to USh8000) – Nando's offers the slightly more flavoursome spicy option.

Further west on Kampala Rd, **Steers** (Map p472; Kampala Rd) is a South African burger joint that does pretty much the same sort of things as chain burger joints the world over. Plus there is a branch of **Debonair's** (Map p472; Kampala Rd; pizza from USh6000) in the same complex.

Cafés

As Kampala continues to develop, something of a café culture is emerging.

1000 Cups Coffee House (Map p472; 18 Buganda Rd; ☺ 8am-9pm) For a coffee kick from Brazil to Vietnam and everything in between, caffeine cravers should head here. 'A cup for every nation' is its motto and it doesn't neglect the homebrews from Uganda. There is also a menu of light bites, such as salads and sandwiches, and sweet pastries. It's a good place to hang out and catch up with the rest of the world, as there is a large selection of international newspapers and magazines.

Café Pap (Map p472; 13 Parliament Ave) A stylish café on bustling Parliament Ave, this might be the place to meet some movers and shakers. Uganda coffees are promoted here from the slopes of Elgon, the Rwenzoris and the Virungas, but there is also an excellent menu of sandwiches, paninis and full breakfasts.

Vasili's Bakery (Map p472; Kampala Rd) This is a bakery to remember, serving perhaps the best range of pies and cakes in the city, a top spot for breakfast or afternoon tea. Chelsea buns, apple crumble and other old-world favourites are plentiful here.

Tricia's Terrace (Map p472; Daisy's Arcade, Buganda Rd; light meals USh3500-7500) A combination of a café and restaurant, this popular little lunch spot specialises in delicious, inexpensive sandwiches. Fillings include chicken, bacon and avocado. The hot toasties are also a hit.

Bancafé (Map p472; Grand Imperial Hotel Arcade) An old favourite that remains popular thanks to a good selection of freshly ground coffee, fresh juices and fruit shakes, and some tasty cakes. Sandwiches and salads cost about USh5000, making it a popular stop for a light lunch.

Gallery Cafe (Masaka Rd; dishes from USh5000) A tranquil bolthole from the hustle and bustle of the city centre. It is 2km along Masaka Rd, not far from Natete. The gallery itself is well worth a look (p484); sit back on the front veranda and enjoy a tasty lunch from the small eclectic menu.

Ice-Cream Parlours

Ice cream is very popular in Kampala and there are several parlours spread across the city. The best ice cream in Kampala is found at **Le Chateau** (Map p471; Gaba Rd), but the location is inconvenient for a casual treat.

In the city centre, Mama Mia at Speke Hotel has very good gelato, with some deliciously rich flavours from amaretto to zabaglione.

UGANDA

Chipper's is very popular, and it has a couple of branches, one on Kampala Rd and another in Kabalagala. It has scoop and whip ice cream, and sundaes.

Self-Catering

Luisun Supermarket (Map p471; 11 Bombo Rd) This Italian delicatessen is stuffed to the ceiling with cheeses, salamis, and home-made cakes and biscuits. It also has a range of wines and some little luxuries, like stuffed olives. It now operates a small deli-café in the middle of the shop, including full meals like lasagne and grilled chicken, as well as the obvious antipasto treats.

Shoprite (Map p471; clock tower roundabout) A sort of South African Tesco, this huge supermarket is overflowing with products. There is a fresh bakery, as well as the best range of imports in the city. There is a second branch in the new Lugogo Mall on Jinja Rd.

DRINKING

Nightlife in Kampala is something to relish these days, with a host of decent bars and clubs throughout the city. There is generally something happening in the city on most nights of the week, although Friday and Saturday are definitely the big nights out. However, Kampalans are a trendy, fickle bunch and places that are in today are gone tomorrow – it pays to ask around on arrival.

Kampala's bars are up there with the best in the region. Most places are open at least from 7pm until midnight and many of the popular places are open much later. Usually only nightclubs have cover charges.

All of the most popular places to stay have bars: Red Chilli is pretty busy and attracts a few regular expats, as well as travellers; the lively Backpackers has a leafy garden and a popular pool table; and Blue Mango is the place to be on weekends, when the bar steps it up a gear. The Speke Hotel has a popular terrace bar out the front, and some punters like the pub feel of the Lion Bar at the Sheraton Hotel.

The following places are listed starting in the city centre and fanning out into the suburbs.

Midland Guesthouse (2 Nakivubo Rd) Overlooking the bus station, trek all the way to the rooftop bar for some incredible views of the madness below during evening rush hour. Cheap beers and huge crowds during televised Premiership matches.

Slow Boat Pub (Map p472; ☎ 041-255647; Kampala Rd) At the heart of the city, this is much more of a local drinkers' bar than the location might suggest. It's a good place to hang out for an afternoon session with a few beers and watch Kampala life go by.

Sax Pub (Map p472; Luwum St) Forget the name, there is no jazz here, but plenty of action. It started out pretty sane with a good mix of African and Western tunes, but lately things have become pretty wild with working girls and an 'anything goes' atmosphere.

On the Rocks (Map p472; Speke Hotel) One of the definitive stops on the Kampala nightshift, this cool place has a covered bar and a huge outdoor area, absolutely heaving with people from about 9pm. The complex includes a couple of small dance floors and drinks are a fair deal, given it is part of the Speke Hotel. Prostitutes hang out here in numbers and pickpocketing is not unheard of on a busy night.

Rouge (Map p472; 2 Kampala Rd; ☿ Tue-Sat) Kampala's first lounge club, the über-hip Rouge wouldn't be out of place in a Euro-capital. Cocktail hour continues into the evening and sooner or later dancing takes over from drinking. Tuesday is jazz, Wednesday is salsa and Friday hip hop.

Just Kickin' (Map p471; Cooper Rd) This is the top sports bar in Kampala that helped make Kisimenti the kickin' place it is today. Big rugby and football matches draw the faithful, but it's a busy bar any time. A sign above the front door reads: 'No hookers. Props and locks welcome.' Well, that's the idea, anyway. Good bar food in case you get the munchies.

Bubbles O'Learys (Map p471; ☎ 031-263815; 30 Windsor Cres) Kampala's contribution to the growing legion of Irish pubs, this is one of the more authentic. The bar and all the furnishings were shipped in from an old Irish pub back home on the emerald isle. This is now the 'in' place to be on Friday, for the next five minutes at least, and draws a fun crowd. Live music on Wednesday, DJs on weekends, but there is a cheeky cover charge of USh5000 on big nights.

Al's Bar (Gaba Rd) A legend in Kampala, this is the most famous bar in Uganda, although notorious might be a better word! This is the one place in Kampala that you can be guaranteed to find some people propping up the bar into the wee hours of the morning. It gets very busy on weekends, and attracts a regular crowd of expats, Ugandans and a fair number of prostitutes, meaning half the customers or more. There are two pool tables, but you might need to stay all night to get a game. Drinks are reasonable, and it is not uncommon for this bar to be open 24 hours. It's just down the road from the Half London (right). Special-hire taxis between here and the city centre cost anything from USh4000 to USh8000, depending on your negotiating skills and how drunk you are by the time you leave.

Capital Pub (☎ 041-269676; Muyenga Rd) An infamous imbibing institution in Kabalagala, this is cut from the same cloth as Al's. Check out the elaborate eaved roof at the back, with nearly a dozen pool tables, making getting a game that much easier. This place is always busy and has more than its fair share of pushy prostitutes from all over the region, but most of them troop off to Al's by the early hours.

ENTERTAINMENT

Nightlife in Uganda may be fairly low-key, but Kampala, the rocking capital, is thankfully the exception to the rule. Here there are nightclubs and discos, some of which have live music. Many of them rage on well into the night and one or two are open virtually 24/7.

Nightclubs

Several of the bars have a nightclub feel to them in the early hours of the morning and on weekends there is pretty much guaranteed to be dancing at Just Kickin', On the Rocks and Al's Bar (opposite).

There are a couple of discos out in the industrial area of the city, just off Jinja Rd, east of the two main roundabouts. Both play a lot of swing and house, and locals dance until late into the night. Charges rise as the weekend comes around and both places have more-expensive VIP areas upstairs, but there is not a whole lot of point upgrading.

Ange Noir (Map p471; admission USh2000-10,000; ☾ 9pm-5am) The 'black angel' is pronounced locally as 'Angenoa', a pretty fair rendition of the French, and is the most popular club for dancing. Everyone knows it, but it's not signposted on the main road.

Club Silk (Map p471; admission USh2000-10,000; ☾ 9pm-5am) In the same street as Ange Noir, this is an identikit club that is also heaving with locals. The floor décor is luminous and hideous, so try not to be feeling nauseous heading in here.

Volts (Entebbe Rd; admission various) Located a little way out of the city on the Entebbe Rd, this is a major league club with a serious sound system. Themed nights include Caribbean tunes and '60s flashbacks. Look out for the searching spotlights scoping the sky.

Live Music

To be sure of catching live music while in Kampala, check out Friday's listings page in the *New Vision* newspaper, as there is usually something going down over the weekend.

Musicians Club 1989 (Map p472; admission free; ☾ 7-10pm Mon) Kampala musicians get together every Monday at the National Theatre for informal jam sessions and live performances. This is a must if you are in the city, as the place fills up with Ugandans letting off steam after a Monday back at work and the drinks flow. On the second and last Monday of the month, the whole event shifts outside the theatre and becomes a mini-festival, complete with beer tents and a serious sound system. A great night out.

Half London (Gaba Rd) A landmark on the popular Gaba Rd strip, this is one of the most famous addresses in Kampala for live music from Thursday to Saturday. The music is a great introduction to the best the region has to offer and this place is always heaving at the hinges. It's partially open-air at the back, the crowd is mixed, the bar is friendly and boisterous, and everyone drinks until they dance. Get here early on the weekend if you want a table. Minibuses run here (USh500) until about 10.30pm from the old taxi park (just ask for the Half London or Kabalagala); later in the evening, find a special-hire taxi.

Club Obbligato (Old Port Bell Rd) A top local joint for Ugandan music, the popular Afrigo Band plays here every weekend and is well worth catching. Warm up here to some live music before hitting one of the nearby nightclubs.

Sabrina's Pub (Map p472; Bombo Rd) Though little more than a local bar from the front, peek through the double doors at the back and it transforms into a huge gig venue. Live bands perform on the large stage out the back most weekends, including the famous

UGANDA

Stone Band on Friday, whipping the crowd into a dancing frenzy.

Traditional Dance

If you're interested in traditional dance and music, try to catch a performance of the Ndere Troupe. It's composed of members of the many ethnic groups in Uganda and has gained international acclaim on world tours. The troupe has a new base in Ntinda, the **Ndere Centre** (☎ 041-288123; www.ndere.com; Kisaasi Rd), out beyond the Blue Mango, which includes an auditorium, a restaurant-bar and even some accommodation. Performances take place every Sunday at 6pm and cost just USh3000. It also promotes a comedy night (USh2000) every Friday at 7pm. Those with a serious interest in African dance could stay here. 'You stay in this guesthouse, you are sure to become a philosopher', it promises.

Cinemas

The leading cinema group in Uganda is **Cineplex** (Map p472; Wilsons Rd), with two locations, the original on Wilson Rd and a new one in the Garden City Complex (right). The newer one screens new Hollywood releases and charges USh11,000 evenings and weekends, while the original screens slightly more dated features.

Casinos

Kampala Casino (Map p472; Kimathi Ave; ⊙ 2pm-late) In addition to the usual range of gaming tables, the casino has a good buffet (p479), live music, and free beer if you're playing the tables. No shorts or scruffy gear are allowed here. It is pretty busy most nights, and minimum stakes are low by international standards.

SHOPPING

While Uganda lacks the shop 'till you drop' opportunities found in other African countries, such as Kenya and South Africa, it does have a few interesting crafts to look out for and a lot of pieces imported from DR Congo. The best items produced in Uganda include woven baskets and bags, bark-cloth paintings and batik, plus some woodcarvings and soapstone figures. Kampala has the best selection of things to buy in Uganda, although with a fledgling tourism industry, there isn't a huge range of shops selling crafts.

Uganda Arts & Crafts Village (Map p472; ⊙ 9am-7pm Mon-Sat, 10am-4pm Sun) Hidden away behind the National Theatre, this 'village' has a number of stalls selling handicrafts, such as caneware, woodcarvings and small trinkets from around the country, all at quite reasonable prices if you bargain.

Exposure Africa (Map p472; 13 Buganda Rd) Next door to Daisy's Arcade, this is the biggest craft market in Kampala, with about 30 stalls offering crafts from Uganda and beyond. Prices vary wildly between stalls, so shop around and don't forget your bargaining hat. Much of the merchandise comes from neighbouring Kenya, despite what the sellers claim.

Uganda Crafts (Map p471; Bombo Rd) A nonprofit shop selling a wide variety of crafts, including goods made from leather, wood and cane, plus there's a likeable little open-air café.

Gallery Cafe (Masaka Rd) Out of the city along the Masaka Rd near Natete, this is a good source of contemporary crafts (ceramics, fabrics, sculpture) and paintings. To get here by public transport, take a Natete shared taxi from the old taxi park, and get off just after it passes the large Uganda Railways locomotives workshop on the left; the gallery is on the right.

Banana Boat (Map p471; Cooper Rd) An expanding empire, this sophisticated craft shop now has three branches. The original has a few local items, but many of the smart pieces come from all over Africa, including cards, batik, jewellery, clothing and carvings. There is a similar branch in the Garden City Complex, plus a branch with an emphasis on homes and interiors in the newer Lugogo Mall.

Nommo Gallery (Map p472; 4 Victoria Ave) When it comes to aesthetic art of the collectable sort, this gallery, higher on the hill above the Sheraton Hotel, is the best-known place in Kampala and doubles as a free museum for browsers.

There are gift shops at many of the guesthouses and hotels around Kampala, and the prices rise incrementally with the room rates! Blue Mango has something similar to Banana Boat, stocking items mostly from further south in Africa.

Apart from the lively local markets (opposite), the best places for shopping are the two big shopping centres in the city. **Garden City Complex** (Map p471; Yusuf Lule Rd) has several floors of shops, including a supermarket, bookshop and department store, plus a cinema, bowling alley and food court. The newer **Lugogo Mall** (Jinja Rd) includes a Barclays Bank, a large Shoprite supermarket and Game, a huge DIY and household shop from South Africa.

Markets

The busiest market in Kampala is Owino Market, which sprawls around the Nakivubo Stadium, near the taxi parks. Here you can find all sorts of goods for sale, but it is most popular with travellers for its wide range of second-hand clothes from Europe, Asia and the USA. Bargain hard, as they tend to raise the prices when *mzungus* (white people) are sniffing around.

Nakasero Market is Kampala's most famous market and is just below Kampala Rd. It is divided into two areas, one partially covered, where produce is sold, and another located in an attractive old building, where hardware, clothes and even a few tourist items are on sale.

GETTING THERE & AWAY
Air

For contact details of the international airlines flying in and out of Entebbe International Airport, see p554.

There are two small domestic airlines in Uganda that mainly cater to government officials and NGOs, as they don't really serve any obvious tourist destinations:
Eagle Uganda (Map p472; ☎ 041-344292; 11 Portal Ave) Flights to Arua, Gulu, Kitgum, Kotido, Moroto and Moyo.
United Airlines (Map p472; ☎ 041-344292; 11 Portal Ave) Not to be confused with the famous American airline, this local outfit has flights to Adjumani, Arua and Gulu.

Boat

There used to be ferries to the Ssese Islands twice a week from Kampala's Port Bell, but these have been suspended. However, there is talk of a new ferry early in the lifetime of this book. The best way to the islands now is from Masaka, although you can still catch fishing boats from Kasenyi (near Entebbe). Unfortunately, these are small, leave in the afternoon (so travel in the dark) and are none too safe. For more details, see p538.

MWANZA (TANZANIA)

There are no longer passenger ferries connecting Tanzania and Uganda, but it is possible to board a Tanzania or Uganda Railways cargo ferry with a little planning. Shared taxis to Port Bell leave from the old taxi park in Kampala. See p556 for more details.

Bus

For buses within Uganda, the **main bus station** (Map p472; cnr Allen Rd & Luwum St) is below Kampala Rd. It's a busy place, with daily buses to every main town in the country. Most leave very early in the morning, so make inquiries the day before and get there early for a decent seat. There are lots of different companies operating different routes, but all are well marked. It's usually necessary to bargain the fare down a bit on the popular tourist routes, as there is some overcharging.

To Butogota (for Bwindi Impenetrable National Park), there is one departure at 6.30am daily with Silverline (USh18,000, 10 hours). There are daily buses to Kabale (many bus lines; USh12,000 to USh15,000, six hours) via Masaka and Mbarara; to Kasese (USh12,000, eight hours); to Masindi (USh9000, three hours); and to Fort Portal (USh10,000, four hours). For further details, see the Getting There & Away entries under each town.

EMS POST BUS

These buses depart at 8am daily, except Sunday, from the **main post office** (Map p472; ☎ 041-236436; 35 Kampala Rd) for Kabale (USh11,000) via Mbarara; Fort Portal (USh10,000, 10 hours); Kasese (USh11,000, eight hours); Hoima (USh8000, five hours) via Masindi; and Soroti (USh10,000, seven hours) via Tororo and Mbale.

These buses are a safe way to travel. Bookings are not possible, so rock up in Kampala between 7am and 7.30am to be sure of a seat. From originating provincial towns to Kampala, they depart from the post offices a little earlier (about 6.30am).

INTERNATIONAL BUSES

There are daily buses to Nairobi in Kenya with the following lines: **Akamba** (Map p471; ☎ 041-250412; 28 Dewinton St), located on the eastern edge of the city centre; **Busscar** (Map p472; ☎ 041-233030; 8 Burton St), which is just on the hill above the new taxi park; **Scandinavian Express** (Map p472; ☎ 078-260409; 8 Colville St); just below the Speke Hotel; and **Regional Coach**

(Map p472; ☎ 041-256862; 4 Luwum St), just below Kampala Rd. Akamba and Scandinavian Express buses also continue to Arusha and Dar es Salaam.

For Kigali (Rwanda), there are daily services with the following companies: **Jaguar Executive Coaches** (Map p472; ☎ 041-251855; 26 Nakivubo Rd), near the main bus station; **Gaso Bus** (☎ 041-572917; Bus Park, Kampala), in the bus station; and Regional Coach.

See p554 for details and prices of international services.

Minibus & Taxi

Kampala has two taxi parks for minibuses. Although at first appearance these places seem chaotic, and at second appearance absolutely anarchic, there is in fact a significant degree of organisation, and minibuses for a particular destination always leave from the same place within each park. Both parks serve destinations within Kampala and around the country. The old taxi park (Map p472), on the triangle formed by Burton, Luwum and South Sts, is the bigger of the two and serves all parts of the city and country to the east; the new taxi park (Map p472) services destinations west and north.

As with buses, there are shared taxis travelling to all major parts of the country, including Jinja (USh4000, one hour), Mbale (USh10,000, three hours), Malaba (USh9000, two hours), Masindi (USh9000, three hours), Fort Portal (USh12,000, six hours), Kabale (USh15,000, six hours), Masaka (USh5000, two hours) and Mbarara (USh9000, four hours). However, for all but the shortest journeys, you are better off taking a bus, as they stop less frequently and are safer due to their size.

Train

All passenger trains ceased operating about a decade ago, which is probably a blessing in disguise, as they were painfully slow and very uncomfortable.

GETTING AROUND

Traffic jams are now a major headache in Kampala, so no matter where you are going in the city, plan ahead if you need to get somewhere at an appointed time. Rush hour is particularly bad, usually from 7.30am to 9.30am and about 5pm to 7pm. The easiest

way to avoid the traffic troubles is to use a *boda-boda* (motorbike taxis), although some of the drivers can be quite reckless.

To/From the Airport

The international airport is at Entebbe, 41km from Kampala. A special-hire taxi from Kampala to Entebbe airport costs about USh35,000 or US$20. A cheaper option is to take a minibus between Kampala (from the old taxi park) and Entebbe town (USh1500), then catch another shared taxi from there to the airport (USh1000 per person or USh5000 for the vehicle, 3km). Several of the upmarket hotels offer an airport pick-up service.

Boda-bodas

These motorbike taxis are now the fastest way to get around Kampala, as they can weave in and out of the traffic jams. It's not necessarily the safest way to travel and best avoided at night, but during the day two wheels can save a lot of time.

Minibus

The ubiquitous white minibus taxis leave from the two taxi parks and fan out all over the city. They are cheap and leave every few minutes to most destinations in the city. To find the minibus taxi you want, simply ask around at the taxi parks – people are generally very helpful. However, with Kampala's traffic problems, it can be quicker to flag one down on Kampala Rd, as they don't need to navigate the nightmare tailbacks around the taxi parks.

Special-Hire Taxi

Actually in Kampala itself, there are plenty of 'special-hire' taxis, mostly marked with black-and-white checks. Good places to find them in the city centre are outside the taxi parks, around Nakasero Market and at the upper end of Colville St. At night though, they will usually find you, as they wait in great numbers outside popular bars and clubs.

A standard short-distance fare is around USh3000 to USh5000. Negotiate a price for longer distances, including waiting time if that's what you want. Charges are a little higher at night, although what you end up paying depends on how much you have drunk.

AROUND KAMPALA

KABAKA'S TRAIL

The **Kabaka's Trail** (☎ 041-501866; www.cultural heritagetrails.com; Ucota office, Kabalagala) is a community tourism project to introduce visitors to the secret history of the Buganda people. Six **sites** (admission each USh3000) around Kampala make up the trail, including several tombs, a prison and a waterfall.

The **Naggalabi Buddo Coronation Site**, a short distance off the road to Masaka, is where the Buganda kings are crowned, including the current *kabaka* Ronald Mutebi II. There are several huts similar to those at Kasubi Tombs, as well as a natural throne from a tree root. This is the most accessible of all the sites, as minibuses (USh1500) run here from the new taxi park in Kampala – ask for Naggalabi Buddo stage.

Ssezibwa Falls is a popular beauty spot with locals, just off the road to Jinja. Take a Lugazi-bound minibus from either taxi park in Kampala as far as Kayanja (USh2000, 45 minutes) and then negotiate for a *boda-boda* to the falls (about USh1000).

Other sites on the trail include **Katereke Prison**, a prison ditch where royal prisoners were starved during the upheavals of 1888–89; the **Wamala Tombs**, which are the resting place of early Bugandan kings and predate the more famous Kasubi Tombs; the nearby **Tomb of Nnamasole Kanyange**; and the **Tomb of Nnamasole Baagalayaze**, where there is a local cultural centre with traditional performances.

ENTEBBE

☎ 041

Located on the shores of Lake Victoria, Entebbe is an attractive, verdant town that was once the capital of Uganda during the early years of the British protectorate. With the traffic troubles and overcrowding now dogging Kampala, there might be a case for once again moving the political capital back to its lakeside origins. It is home to the Botanical Gardens, which offer a nice escape from the hustle and bustle of life in Kampala, and the Uganda Wildlife Education Centre, which provides a home for rare animals rescued from traffickers and poachers. It is also the location of Uganda's international airport, making Entebbe a convenient place to spend a night when arriving late or departing early by plane.

Information

There are several kiosks to exchange cash at Entebbe airport, but rates are a little lower than in Kampala. The major hotels can also change cash, but usually at poor rates.

The post office has international telephone and fax services, and there are also cardphones and a small post office at the airport.

Stanbic Bank (Kampala Rd) Best bank in town, it can change cash and travellers cheques.

Surfing Corner (Kampala Rd; per hr USh2000) Offers sluggish Internet access.

Sights & Activities

UGANDA WILDLIFE EDUCATION CENTRE

The **Uganda Wildlife Education Centre** (☎ 041-320520; www.ugandawildlifecentre.com; Lugard Ave; adult/child USh10,000/5000; ☀ 9am-6.30pm), just below the Imperial Botanical Beach Hotel, is a world-class animal refuge, which has benefited from much international assistance in recent years. This is not a zoo and none of the animals here are exhibits: all are recovered from poachers and traffickers. Star attractions include the first rhinos in Uganda since the war, lions, chimpanzees and shoebill storks. This is probably the easiest place to get good photos of wildlife in Uganda, especially the often elusive shoebill stork. A visit is a must if you are in Entebbe.

ENTEBBE BOTANICAL GARDENS

Worth a wander if you have some time to spare are the **Entebbe Botanical Gardens** (admission per person USh1000, per car/camera/video camera USh1000/2000/5000; ☀ 9am-7pm). Laid out in 1898 by A Whyte, the first curator, they're along the lake shore between the sailing club and the centre of Entebbe. Locals claim that some of the Johnny Weismuller *Tarzan* films were made here, although there aren't any chimps like Cheetah today. Even if you're not particularly enthusiastic about botany, there are some interesting, unusual trees and shrubs, and the gardens are fairly well maintained. There is quite a variety of bird species found in the gardens, some monkeys and, for arachnophiles, there is a spider walk, with plenty of big spiders clinging to their webs.

UGANDA

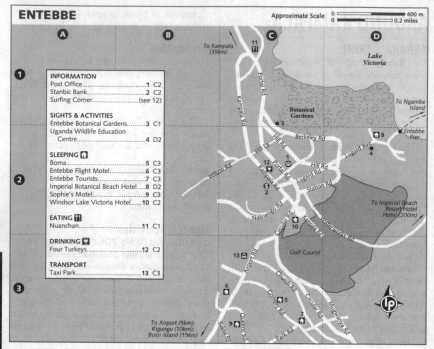

ENTEBBE

Approximate Scale

UGANDA

Sleeping

Several flights leave Entebbe ludicrously early and it can save an hour or two in the morning if you stay out here.

Entebbe Tourists (☎ 041-320432; frankstourists@ hotmail.com; Gomers Rd; camping USh5000, dm USh8000, s/d USh13,000/15,000, with bathroom USh25,000) Bringing budget accommodation to central Entebbe, this friendly place is signposted from the airport road just after the Windsor Lake Victoria Hotel. Rooms are spacious, shared facilities are kept clean and the helpful owners can suggest things to do around town.

Entebbe Flight Motel (☎ 041-320812; flimotel@ utlonline.co.ug; Airport Rd; s/d USh40,000/50,000) Pretty much the closest hotel to the airport, this is the best all-round deal among the midrange places in town, as rooms include satellite TV and bathroom. It is just beyond the Windsor Lake Victoria Hotel, and rates include breakfast.

Sophie's Motel (☎ 041-320885; Queens Rd; smotel@ africaonline.co.ug; s/d with bathroom USh60,000/80,000, cottages USh100,000/120,000) Signposted from the road to the airport, all the rooms are named after African countries. The cottages are

virtual suites complete with TV and fridge. Readers say the owners are very friendly, making the stay more akin to a sojourn with family. Rates include a free airport shuttle.

Boma (☎ 077-467929; thebomaentebbe@infocom.co .ug; Gomers Rd; s/d US$75/100) Entebbe's answer to the upmarket B&B, this little luxurious guesthouse has just six rooms. Prices are on the high side, but the atmosphere is intimate. Breakfast is included and meals are also served.

Imperial Botanical Beach Hotel (☎ 041-320800; reservations@ibbhotel.com; s/d US$153/177, incl tax; 🏊) Sitting on the shores of Lake Victoria, this hotel hosted President Bill Clinton back in 1998. If you are feeling flush, you can check into his presidential suite for just US$413. Facilities include a swimming pool and several restaurants. Rates include breakfast.

Imperial Resort Beach Hotel (☎ 041-320244; www.imperialhotels.co.ug; Mpigi Close; s/d from US$150/ 180; 🏊 🖥 🏊) Under the same ownership as the Imperial Botanical Beach Hotel, you'll find this offers the smartest rooms in town, but what's with the crazy blue colour? Ugly and there's an ugly 17% tax on top.

Windsor Lake Victoria Hotel (☎ 041-320645; windsor@imul.com; s/d from US$133/170; 🏊) This hotel has long played on history as a selling point, but history is catching up with it every day. Atmospheric enough, but it needs a major facelift to justify these prices, as the décor is from another era. The bar and restaurants are popular with nonguests, who can also use the pool for USh5000.

Eating & Drinking

When it comes to food in Entebbe, quite a few people end up eating at their hotel. The Windsor Lake Victoria Hotel has a massive selection of menus, encompassing Chinese, Indian, Italian and fast food. Most dishes cost USh6000 to USh10,000, and they can be ordered poolside.

Take a deep breath… there's a Lao restaurant in Entebbe. No, not Thai, but Lao.

Nuanchan (☎ 071-980018; 2 Kintu Rd; dishes USh5000-8000) Run by two sisters from Laos living in Entebbe, the small menu is very authentic and includes some spicy salads, tôm yam soup and fried pork. Sadly, no Beer Lao, though.

Four Turkeys (Kampala Rd) The leading bar in town, although don't expect the nightlife to rock like Kampala in this small town. There's good bar food, and always a few local expats propping up the bar.

Just behind Four Turkeys is Legends, a local nightclub where the action continues towards the weekend.

Getting There & Away

Minibuses run between Entebbe and Kampala (USh1500) throughout the day from the new taxi park in Kampala or the Entebbe roundabout.

Getting Around

To get to the airport from Entebbe, either take a shared taxi (USh1000 per person) or charter the entire car for USh5000.

LAKE VICTORIA

Ngamba Island Chimpanzee Sanctuary

There is a chimpanzee sanctuary located on Ngamba Island in Lake Victoria, nicknamed 'Chimp Island', which is now a popular day trip for tourists staying in Kampala. Relocated here in 1998, the original group of 19 has swelled to around 40 chimps. They can be viewed at very close range during feeding times (11am and 2.30pm). The chimps are free to wander about their forested home, and visitor fees are ploughed back into this and other chimpanzee conservation projects.

There is also now a **luxury tented camp** on the island, which allows for a more intimate chimp encounter for those with the time

UGANDA

HIJACKING ENTEBBE'S REPUTATION

Entebbe would probably be one of the world's more obscure airports were it not for an infamous hijack that took place in June 1976. A planeload of Israelis was hijacked in a combined operation involving Palestinian and German terrorists, and the pilot was forced to land at Entebbe. After releasing all non-Israeli hostages, the terrorists demanded the release of prisoners held in Israeli jails, and money, in return for the remaining captives.

Idi Amin offered his services as mediator between the hijackers and the Israeli government, but was manipulating things behind the scenes. His sympathies for the Arab cause were widely publicised and he had already expelled Israeli military advisers from the country some years earlier. This made him a less-than-ideal mediator and the Israelis decided to apply their own solution to the problem.

They launched a surprise raid, with help from German and Kenyan authorities. Israeli paratroopers landed a plane on the runway, pulling out of the hold in a presidential Mercedes to dupe the hijackers into believing it was Idi Amin returning from negotiations. Almost all the hostages were freed and the hijackers shot dead in a clinical operation. This caused much embarrassment to Idi Amin, as he had been flouncing about attempting to engineer his own peculiar settlement. In retaliation, he broke off relations with Kenya, signalling the death knell of the already weakened East African Community. One of the Israeli hostages, Dora Bloch, who had been taken to hospital after choking on her food, was never seen again, presumably killed in retaliation for Amin's humiliation.

The old airport building is no longer used, as a newer airport has since been built.

and money. It costs US$280 per person per night, including boat transfers, accommodation, meals and experiencing two chimp feedings.

The island is 23km from Entebbe. Trips out to visit the chimpanzees have to be arranged in advance with tour companies in Kampala (see p95). **Wild Frontiers** (☎ 041-321479, 077-502155; www.wildfrontiers.co.ug), based in Entebbe, is the official booking agent and offers transfers by speedboat. It costs US$260 for the boat for up to four people and US$65 per person for additional passengers, and takes about one hour. These prices include admission to the chimp sanctuary.

Fishing Trips

Several safari companies offer fishing trips on Lake Victoria, including The **Uganda Safari Company** (☎ 041-251182; www.safariuganda.com) and Wild Frontiers. The quarry is the gigantic Nile perch, specimens of which often come in at more than 100kg. Prices for an all-day trip, including lunch, start at about US$100 per person for a small group and rise as numbers drop.

Speke Resort & Country Club

The huge **Speke Resort** (☎ 078-227111; www.speke resort.com; admission Sat & Sun USh2000; s/d from US$120/140) at Munyonyo marina, beyond Kabalagala, offers something for everyone, including tennis courts, an Olympic-size swimming pool (admission USh10,000), a modern gym, and a restaurant and bar complex.

The **Speke Equestrian Centre** offers horse riding around Lake Victoria and has a variety of rides from just one hour (USh22,500) to the whole day (USh60,000, minimum five).

Bussi Island

Backpackers Hostel (☎ 077-430587; www.backpackers .co.ug; camping USh6000, dm USh10,000 bandas USh25,000-50,000) has developed a new island retreat out on Bussi, about 10km from Entebbe in Lake Victoria. The lush camping ground includes a private beach, and it is a short walk to the equator for those who like to have a foot in both hemispheres. It costs USh4000 by boat from Kigungu, a short minibus ride from Entebbe (USh1000). Contact Backpackers for more information and keep an eye out for future full-moon parties.

MABIRA FOREST RESERVE

This large, attractive **forest reserve** (admission 1/2 days USh6000/10,000) is one of the more convenient places to see some of Uganda's myriad birds – it is home to more than 300 species. Monkeys are also easily spotted, but the bigger animals that may be present, such as leopards, are rarely seen. There is a well-established trail system here that offers access to pristine forest and bird life.

There is an attractive community **camp site** (camping USh3000, s/d bandas USh10,000/15,000, bandas for 3 or more people USh20,000) here and bandas have been tarted up recently. The staff can also prepare food (from USh3000). It is a great place to escape the traffic and noise of Kampala, and mountain bikes are available for hire (USh8000).

To get here just jump on a minibus travelling between Kampala and Jinja and get off when you see the signpost for the reserve. It lies about 20km west of Jinja.

MPANGA FOREST RESERVE

About 37km southwest of Kampala on the road to Masaka, **Mpanga Forest Reserve** (admission USh3000) is another little getaway if the rigours, or nightlife, of the capital become too much. This is a young forest, little more than 50 years old, as it was used as a tropical research institute, but the sheer size of the trees attest to the progress that can be made with well-managed reforestation programs.

This reserve is well known for its many butterflies (181 species) and birds (141 species), and a number of clearly marked paths have been cut out of the thick undergrowth to enable closer viewing. There are also red-tailed monkeys around.

There is a small inexpensive **camp site** (camping per night USh3000, bandas per night USh10,000) here. Food is usually available, but take some supplies just in case.

To get here, take a minibus from the new taxi park in Kampala to Mpigi for USh3000 and then a *boda-boda* on to Mpanga for USh1000. Alternatively, take a bus or minibus heading to Masaka (USh5000) and ask to get off at Mpanga.

THE EQUATOR

Uganda is one of only 10 countries in the world through which the equator passes, and this has led to the usual monument and souvenir shops that spring up in destinations from Ecuador to Indonesia. The equator crosses the Kampala to Masaka road at a point 78km south of the capital. There are two cement circles marking the line and it isn't such a bad spot for a photo opportunity, although it is altogether more convenient for those with transport.

One place that makes the equator a more worthwhile stop is the excellent **Equation Café** (www.aidchild.org), a great little café-restaurant that also sells high-quality handicrafts. Run by Aidchild to fund its activities to assist HIV/AIDS orphans, the art gallery here is 1st class, 'possibly the best shop on the planet' according to actress Emma Thompson. Iced coffee and a muffin sets you up for the journey southwest.

To get here from Kampala, jump on a Masaka bus and minibus and hope to pay USh3500, although it is likely you will be charged the full Masaka fare (USh5000).

EASTERN UGANDA

Eastern Uganda is as good as a must on any visit to the 'Pearl of Africa' thanks to an intoxicating blend of adrenaline adventures. White-water rafting at the source of the Nile River leads the way, but quad biking, kayaking and bungy jumping are a pretty popular second around Jinja, East Africa's answer to Vic Falls. Further east is the massif of Mt Elgon, an extinct volcano that offers some of the most affordable trekking in the region, while nearby Sipi Falls is stunning, a beautiful spot to soak up the scenery and a great place to recover from the rigours of a trek.

Jinja is the largest town in the east, where the mighty Nile begins its epic journey north. As well as the daring diversions here, there are also more sedate activities, such as a round of golf or chilling out on a river island resort. Other towns in the region pale in comparison, but Mbale has a certain charm and fine views of Mt Elgon, while Moroto is a must for those attempting an overland assault on Kidepo Valley National Park.

For those with a taste for wild Africa, the overland journey to Kidepo is textbook rough, passing right through the heartland of the Karamojong people, a tough tribe of cattle herders who have managed to resist control from outsiders, black and white, for

centuries now. However, this is not a journey that should be undertaken lightly – see the boxed text, p507, for more details.

The roads in eastern Uganda are generally pretty good, but the main road from Jinja to the Kenyan border had more holes than a Swiss cheese at the time of writing. Most towns are well connected by regular buses and minibuses, but heading north of Moroto pickings are slim and the roads deteriorate rapidly.

JINJA
☎ 043

Jinja has some of the world's best white-water rafting on the doorstep, and is emerging as the adrenaline centre of East Africa, picking up punters as fast as Zimbabwe is losing them.

The town has a lush location on the shores of Lake Victoria and is the major market centre for eastern Uganda. It is a buzzing little place with much Indian-influenced architecture, reflecting the days when the town had a huge Asian community. Many Asians have returned to reclaim their businesses and properties, having been forced to leave during the Amin years, and with their return the town is once again flourishing. Check out the spacious mansions overlooking the lake along Nile Cres, opposite the town's golf course, for an insight into how wealthy this town once must have been. Jinja didn't suffer as badly as many other centres during the last civil war and does not wear the same cloak of dereliction. According to local residents, Okello's retreating troops were told in no uncertain terms that they weren't welcome.

The town itself may be short on big hitters, but nearby Bujagali Falls has them in abundance, and visitors can chose from white-water rafting, kayaking, quad biking or bungee jumping. The source of the Nile is also a sight to behold if you consider how far the water has to travel on its huge journey to the Mediterranean through Sudan and Egypt.

Coming from Kampala, the Owen Falls Dam forms a spectacular gateway to the town: as you coast across the top, look down on the raging river below. The dam supplies Uganda with the bulk of its electricity, or doesn't supply it with much electricity, depending on which way you look at it.

UGANDA

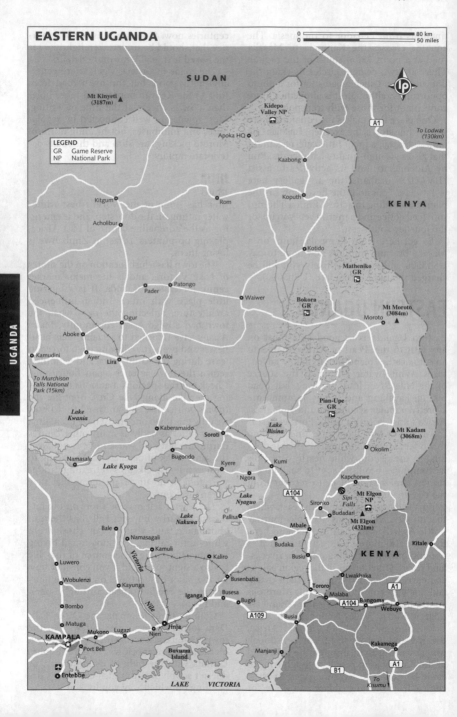

EASTERN UGANDA

0   80 km
0   50 miles

SUDAN

Mt Kinyeti
(3187m)

Kidepo
Valley NP

Apoka HQ

Kaabong

LEGEND
GR   Game Reserve
NP   National Park

A1

To Lodwar
(130km)

Kitgum   Rom   Koputh

Acholibur

KENYA

Kotido

Matheniko
GR

Pader   Patongo

Waiwer

Bokora
GR

Mt Moroto
(3084m)

Ogur   Moroto

Aboke

Kamudini

Ayer   Lira   Aloi

To Murchison
Falls National
Park (15km)

Lake
Kwania

Pian-Upe
GR

Lake
Bisina

Mt Kadam
(3068m)

Kaberamaido

Soroti

Namasale

Bugondo

Lake Kyoga

Kyere

Ngora

Kumi

Okolim

Kapchorwe

Mt Elgon
NP

Sironko

Sipi
Falls

Budadari

Mt Elgon
(4321m)

Lake
Nyaguo

Pallisa

Lake
Nakuwa

Mbale

Bale

Namasagali

Budaka

Kitale

Luwero

Kamuli

Kaliro

Busiu

KENYA

Wobulenzi

Kayunga

Busenbatia

Lwakhaka

Bombo

Iganga   Busesa

Bugiri

Tororo

A1

Malaba

Bungoma

Matuga   Lugazi

A109

Busia

A104

Webuye

KAMPALA   Mukono

Njeri

Jinja

Nile

Victoria

Port Bell

Buvuma
Island

Manjanji

Kakamega

Entebbe

LAKE   VICTORIA

B1

A1

To
Kisumu

UGANDA

Orientation

Jinja is seriously spread out, so getting your bearings away from the centre can take time. The centre of town is built on a simple grid, with Main St at its heart, home to the post office, plus most of the banks, shops and cafés. All roads that cross Main St have an east and west side, like in New York, indicated in this section as 'E' and 'W'. The taxi park and bus station are a few blocks east of the northern end of Main St. The town centre is easily negotiable on foot, but use a *boda-boda* if venturing to the riverfront area of town.

Information

INTERNET ACCESS

Email and Internet services are available in Jinja at several places along Main St.

Indigo (61 Main St; per min USh40) Cheap online access and one of the fastest connections in town.

Source Café (20 Main St; per min USh50) A popular place to get online, the Source is also a cracking little coffee shop (p496).

MONEY

There are several banks that change cash and travellers cheques, plus a few foreign exchange bureaus along Main St that stay open later than the banks. Note that the whitewater rafting companies accept credit cards, but charge a commission (US$5 or 7%).

Crane Bank (☎ 043-122060; 40 Lubas Rd) This place can deal with small amounts of travellers cheques and cash.

Standard Chartered Bank (☎ 043-122661; Main St) Probably the most useful bank, it offers currency exchange, travellers-cheque encashment and has an ATM for international credit cards.

POST

Main post office (cnr Main St & Bell Ave)

TOURIST INFORMATION

There is no government-run tourist office in Jinja, so the best place to pick up tourist information is through **Nile River Explorers Backpackers** (☎ 043-120236; rafting@starcom.co.ug; 41 Wilson Ave) or the adventure companies out at Bujagali Falls. The handy noticeboards are packed with flyers and information covering Jinja and Uganda beyond.

Sights & Activities

SOURCE OF THE NILE

The **source of the Nile** (admission per person/car/motorcycle USh2000/1200/500) is promoted as one of Jinja's premier drawcards and tourists are bussed in from Kampala to marvel at the start of this mighty river. In reality there is not a whole lot to see. Before the building of the Owen Falls Dam, this was the site of the Ripon Falls, where the Nile, known locally as Omugga Kiyara, thundered out of Lake Victoria on its long journey to the Mediterranean. The falls were blown away to ensure a steady flow of water for the dam, but it's just about possible to make out where they were from the turbulence in the river.

Bell Breweries now sponsors the area, so everything has been painted yellow and red in keeping with the corporate image. It is pretty garish, but at least you can get a cold drink under the shade of some trees. There is a large plaque covering the 'discovery' of the source by John Speke, although many Africans contend that their ancestors knew this was the Nile's source long before the white man found out about it. For more on the story of the search for the source of the Nile and the contending claims in Burundi and Rwanda, see the boxed text 'The Search for the Source' (p613).

It is possible to organise boat rides on the river from here. Locals will charge around USh10,000 or contact Rumours bar for something more organised (p497).

GANDHI'S SHRINE

Near the source of the Nile plaque is a small **memorial garden** commemorating Mahatma Gandhi, the centrepiece of which is a bronze bust donated by the Indian Government. This area is becoming quite a pilgrimage site for Ugandan Indians, as this is one of the places where Gandhi's ashes were scattered. So Gandhi was rafting the Nile long before the Adrift team came to town.

NILE BREWERY

For those consuming copious amounts of Nile Special in Kampala, this alternative 'source of the Nile' makes a lively day out, and includes the obligatory complimentary beer. Free guided tours can sometimes be arranged in advance by calling ☎ 033-210009. There is a small souvenir shop where you can buy T-shirts, bottle openers and the like. It is certainly a more original brewery visit than the one to the Heineken brewery in Amsterdam.

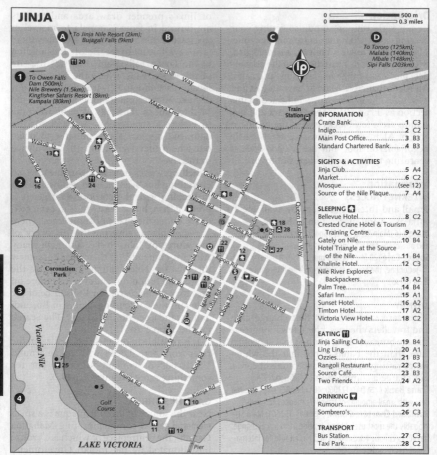

JINJA

INFORMATION
Crane Bank...........................1 C3
Indigo..................................2 C2
Main Post Office..................3 B3
Standard Chartered Bank.....4 B3

SIGHTS & ACTIVITIES
Jinja Club............................5 A4
Market.................................6 C2
Mosque..........................(see 12)
Source of the Nile Plaque........7 A4

SLEEPING
Bellevue Hotel.....................8 C2
Crested Crane Hotel & Tourism
  Training Centre.................9 A2
Gately on Nile.....................10 B4
Hotel Triangle at the Source
  of the Nile.......................11 B4
Khalinie Hotel....................12 C3
Nile River Explorers
  Backpackers.....................13 A2
Palm Tree..........................14 B4
Safari Inn..........................15 A1
Sunset Hotel......................16 A2
Timton Hotel......................17 A2
Victoria View Hotel..............18 C2

EATING
Jinja Sailing Club................19 B4
Ling Ling...........................20 A1
Ozzies...............................21 B3
Rangoli Restaurant.............22 C3
Source Café.......................23 B3
Two Friends.......................24 A2

DRINKING
Rumours............................25 A4
Sombrero's.........................26 C3

TRANSPORT
Bus Station.........................27 C3
Taxi Park...........................28 C2

JINJA CLUB

Part of **Jinja Golf Club**, the club offers the only public swimming pool (USh5000 a day) in Jinja, tennis and squash (USh3000), and a nine-hole golf course (USh10,000 per round). There is also a bar and a small restaurant with reasonably priced meals. Golfers need to pay an extra USh15,000 for the clubs, unless you are crazy enough to be lugging your own around Uganda!

Sleeping
BUDGET

For campers or those wanting a peaceful spot with breathtaking scenery, there are some great options out at Bujagali Falls (p498).

Nile River Explorers Backpackers (☎ 043-120236; rafting@starcom.co.ug; 41 Wilson Ave; camping US$3, dm/d US$5/20) Jinja's original budget crash pad and is still going strong. The most popular place in town, it has a buzzing bar, free pool and satellite TV, as well as wholesome information on attractions across Uganda. Things can really kick off if a truck or two pass through, but that's nothing compared to the sister camping ground out at Bujagali. Credit cards are accepted for raft bookings, so you can lump your accommodation in with this if you are short of cash. It also has some successful community projects up and running – see p498. Next door is Kilombera, producing handwoven Ugandan cotton throws and wraps

Victoria View Hotel (☎ 043-122319; 36 Kutch Rd E; r USh10,000) Dix points when it comes to imagination on the name, as it's miles from the lake. Still, it's a good budget option, as the 25 self-contained rooms are a fair deal. It is conveniently located near the taxi park for an early escape.

Khalinie Hotel (☎ 071-865874; 46 Lubas Rd; s/d with bathroom USh10,000/15,000) If hot water is a must but cash a concern, this hotel is reasonably good value, although lacking anything in the way of soul. Still, it's not as if Jinja is the home of soul after all. It's also not the nicest part of town.

Bellevue Hotel (☎ 043-120328; 4 Kutch Rd W; s USh10,000-25,000, d USh15,000-30,000) Long popular with NGOs, thanks to a combination of clean rooms and value for money, the cheaper rooms involve sharing a bathroom with neighbours, but hot water is available throughout.

There are plenty more cheapies spread across Jinja, but many of these cater solely for students studying here.

MIDRANGE

Timton Hotel (☎ 043-120278; 15 Jackson Cres; camping USh3000; s/d/ste USh20,000/30,000/50,000) The long-running Timton is a friendly little family house set in spacious and well-tended grounds. Its motto is 'a home away from home', the suites include a TV and all rates include breakfast. It also has a verdant garden, where tents can be pitched cheaply.

Safari Inn (3 Nalufenya Rd) This is the Annesworth Hotel reborn. It was under renovation

---

WHITE-WATER RAFTING AT THE SOURCE OF THE NILE

The source of the Nile is one of the most spectacular white-water rafting destinations in the world and for many visitors to Uganda a rafting trip is the highlight of their visit. There are now four companies offering exhilaration without compromise. The two most popular players are the pioneers **Adrift** (the Adventure Centre; ☎ 041-252720, 077-454206; www.surfthesource.com; 7 Kira Rd) based in Kampala (in the Uganda Wildlife Authority compound) and popular **Nile River Explorers** (NRE; ☎ 041-120236; www.raftafrica.com), with an office at Explorers Backpackers in Jinja and its campsite at Bujagali Falls. The other two operators include **Equator Rafts** (☎ 041-123712; rafting@utonline.co.ug), based at Speke Camp, Bujagali Falls, and the newcomer **Nalubale Rafting** (☎ 078-638938; www.nalubalerafting.com). Depending on who you talk to, you might hear good or bad stories about any of them, but ultimately, you'll have a blast with all the operators. Prices for a full day on the water currently cost US$95, but competition sometimes drives them a little lower.

All the companies take on the Big Four, all monster Grade Five rapids, including **Itanda** (The Bad Place), but there is always a safety boat on hand if you decide the rapids are just too big for you. All of them also include a host of incentives to lure you over, including meals and beers. They also offer DVDs and videos of your big day out if you think that no-one will believe you were brave enough back home. All operators accept credit cards, and you can also book trips through guesthouses and hotels in Kampala. They can all pick up punters from the popular hostels and hotels in Kampala, and drop off in the evening for those not staying in Jinja.

Adrift also offers a popular family float trip over two days, which gives younger children a taste of river action and gives the adults a chance to try their hand at river boarding (below). It also offers two- or three-day combinations for the full Nile experience and a rafting-bungee combo if you really want to push your buttons.

NRE offers the longest day ride (30km) on the river, as it puts in further upstream than the competition. The team also offers a second day of rafting at just US$40 for repeat offenders. NRE also operates the most popular camping ground in town above Bujagali Falls; see later in this section for details.

Other river activities are also growing in popularity, including river boarding for the brave-hearted – taking on the mighty waters of the Nile armed only with a boogie board, and kayaking courses to learn how to tame the raging river with a paddle. Check out **Kayak the Nile** (www .kayakthenile.com) for more on professional kayaking courses from three to five days, as well as tandem kayaking trips and sunset paddles. All in all, the Nile looks set to compete with the Zambezi for the title of Africa's favourite river for frolics in the coming years.

UGANDA

GANDHI IN UGANDA?

It comes as something of a surprise to find a statue commemorating Mahatma Gandhi (or more precisely, the scattering of his ashes) at a Hindu temple near Jinja.

It seems that on Gandhi's death in 1948, his ashes were divided up and sent to many locations around the world to be scattered, and some ended up in the Nile River in Uganda. There were also some that ended up in a bank vault in India and were only released in 1997 following a lengthy custody dispute.

when we were in town, but things looked very promising, with fully renovated rooms, spacious grounds and a restaurant-bar.

Two Friends (☎ 077-984821; 6 Jackson Cres; r USh40,000-80,000) Jinja's popular pizzeria has added some rooms in an adjoining house. The new pad boasts some plush décor, but the cheaper rooms with shared bathroom are a little on the expensive side given you might have to wander the corridors at night.

Crested Crane Hotel & Tourism Training Centre (☎ 043-121954; htti@source.co.ug; 4 Hannington Sq; s/d/executive ste USh45,000/50,000/100,000) A Ministry of Tourism property, as the name suggests, the government uses it to train staff in the tourism industry. Before you start cringing, fear not; trainees are not let loose in the hotel itself. Rooms are well appointed and executive suites are large; breakfast is included.

Sunset Hotel (☎ 043-120115; www.sunsethotel uganda.com; Kira Rd; r USh75,000-150,000; 🖵) Rooms come in various shapes and sizes, the price increasing with the number of gadgets thrown in. Shelling out on the top-whack rooms brings a Jacuzzi, not necessarily something you'd expect in Jinja. Rates include breakfast. It overlooks the Nile, making its bar a top spot for a sundowner.

Hotel Triangle at the Source of the Nile (☎ 043-122099; s/d/ste USh50,000/60,000/70,000) Occupying a commanding ridge above Lake Victoria, it has a great location, but unfortunately the building itself is pretty unattractive, with no thought given to traditional design. When it comes to the smart rooms, in practice, ground-floor rooms are USh50,000, while those upstairs with a better view cost USh60,000.

TOP END

Gately on Nile (☎ 043-122400; www.gately-on-nile.com; 34 Kisinja Rd; s/d US$60/86) Set in a grand old colonial house with sumptuous grounds, this is the leading choice in Jinja. It offers a selection of thoughtfully decorated rooms, some with fine views, and boasts communal areas that have a great atmosphere for relaxing. New bungalows have been added in the garden and include Balinese-style open bathrooms. Rates include breakfast, and its restaurant (opposite) is one of the best in town.

Palm Tree (☎ 077-500400; palmtreejinja@yahoo.com; 24 Kisinja Rd; s/d USh95,000/100,000) Just down the road from Gately in a former presidential lodge that may have housed Amin, Obote and Museveni over the years, Palm Tree offers a small selection of smart rooms with panoramas across the gardens. There is also a restaurant and bar downstairs, and breakfast is included.

Jinja Nile Resort (☎ 043-122190; www.madahotels .com; s/d/tr from US$80/100/120; 🖵 🖵) The biggest resort in the Jinja area, this popular conference venue has a swimming pool, gym and tennis courts. Located a short way off the road to Bujagali Falls, it offers fine views of the Nile for those willing to pay an extra US$20. Look out for weekend specials when there is no conference business in town.

Kingfisher Safaris Resort (☎ 077-510197; www .kingfishersafaris.com; s/d from €35/50, f from €60; 🖵 🖵) Clearly visible from the source of the Nile, this traditionally designed resort is about a 9km drive from Jinja. The thatched *bandas* are comfortably kitted out and there is an impressive swimming pool set among the green gardens.

Eating

The cuisine scene in Jinja has really started to move in the last few years, with some fine restaurants at the top-end hotels and a great new option out at Bujagali Falls (p498).

Source Café (☎ 043-120911; 20 Main St; mains USh1500-4500) Hit the Source for a fair selection of light bites, salads, brownies and pastries. This is the place for a coffee fix, as it has several speciality varieties.

Rangoli Restaurant (42 Main St; mains USh2000-5000) Still probably the most popular Indian restaurant in town, although there's not a whole lot of competition. There is a pretty good selection of subcontinental standards, including large thalis at USh5000 with meat or USh4000 for vegetarian. Guaranteed to keep the hunger at bay.

Ozzies (Main St; mains USh2500-6000) A deservedly popular hole-in-the-wall type of place that turns out an impressive range of Western favourites, like full English breakfasts and burgers, pizza and pasta dishes, all at reasonable prices.

Gately on Nile (☎ 043-122400; 34 Kisinja Rd; mains USh5000-15,000) The restaurant at Jinja's popular boutique hotel is a must for lovers of fine food. The fusion menu blends the best of local produce and international flair, and includes memorable moments like chunky pork chops in a sherry and garlic marinade.

Two Friends (☎ 077-984821; 6 Jackson Cres; pizza USh7500-12,000) Tucked away on the quiet crescent between Explorers Backpackers and the Crested Crane, this is the number one name for Italian food in Jinja. Higher prices than Kampala don't deter the regulars, and the menu also includes some steaks and Indian dishes. A lovely garden setting rounds things off.

Ling Ling (Kampala Roundabout; mains USh5000-10,000) Formerly Fang Fang, this place has one of the weirdest locations for any Chinese restaurant – in the forecourt of a petrol station – but don't let that distract from the food. The best Chinese beyond Kampala, tuck into a good spread with drinks for around USh15,000.

Jinja Sailing Club (Nile Cres) This was long one of the best spots in town to sip a cold drink and watch the sun go down across the lake. However, it was closed at the time of writing, although it seems inevitable that an institution will rise from the ashes one day soon.

Drinking & Entertainment

There is not a lot of entertainment in Jinja, but for those arriving from Nairobi, it might be considered entertaining enough just being able to walk the streets at night without the fear of being mugged.

Explorers Backpackers is always a popular drinking hole thanks to the travellers and overland trucks regularly passing through, although the real action seems to go on out at Bujagali Falls these days.

The best thing about bars in Jinja is that most of them are very close together. For those who like a beer or two, Main St offers a suitable strip for a bar crawl, as every other shopfront seems to be a bar by night.

Sombrero's (Spire Rd) If you are already tanked up and feeling cheesy, head to the leading club in town, although if you have seen the places it is leading, that isn't quite the commendation it sounds. Local expats hit it once in a while and it's a more Ugandan experience than life at the camping grounds.

Rumours (☎ 077-984821; source of the Nile) A popular local spot for a beer, but a little out the way for most tourists. It has perhaps the best location of any bar in Jinja and is prime sunset territory. It is built entirely from wood and has a series of walkways running along the edge of the river. To get here take a *boda-boda* to the source of the Nile plaque and head upriver a short way. It is quite a descent to the riverbank from the side of the road, so watch out on a dark, wet night after a few ales.

Getting There & Away
BOAT
Uganda Railways ferries operate between Jinja and Mwanza in Tanzania, but they don't take passengers. If you want to get to Mwanza by ferry, it is necessary to take a Uganda or Tanzania Railways cargo ferry from Port Bell. See p556 for details.

BUS
The road between Jinja and Kampala is 80km of solid tarmac, so the trip takes anything from one to two hours by minibus or bus, depending on the traffic in or out of the capital. Minibuses from Kampala (USh4000) leave from the new taxi park. Coasters (small buses) are slightly cheaper at USh3500 and possibly slightly safer because of their size, but take longer to fill up with passengers.

There are minibuses from Jinja to the Kenyan border at either Malaba (USh7000, two hours) or Busia (USh6000, 1½ hours). Those heading to Mbale (two hours) for Sipi Falls or Mt Elgon need USh6000 handy.

Getting Around
The centre of Jinja is compact enough to wander about on foot. However, if you are heading to the source of the Nile, the Owen Falls Dam or the Nile Brewery, you might be advised to take a *boda-boda*. These cost USh500 to USh1500, depending on your negotiating skills.

AROUND JINJA
Bujagali Falls

More than a series of large rapids than a conventional waterfall, **Bujagali Falls** (admission USh2000) remains one of Uganda's outstanding natural beauty spots, and is very popular with locals on weekends. This is one of East Africa's more laid-back locations and it is well worth setting some time aside to chill for a few days. A lot of travellers end up staying out here before or after a rafting trip, as there are two popular camping grounds here. During our last visit, a deal was signed for a multi-million dollar resort to be built here, so things may change very fast and don't be too disappointed if there is some serious construction going on in the area. There is also the chance that the controversial Bujagali Falls Dam will finally go ahead, having been suspended several times due to corruption. One way or the other, change is coming, but there will still be adrenaline and adventure in large doses.

Ugandans take a peculiar delight in watching local men throw themselves into the top of the falls with nothing more than a plastic jerry can, sealed with an avocado, to keep them alive. Each to their own and all that, but this is a seriously dangerous practice. Should they lose their grip, they are dead. Surely this is taking risking one's life to make a living to extremes, and it should not be encouraged by tourists. Save your USh5000 for something else, or give the guys USh5000 not to chuck themselves in, as they likely have families to look after. However, a couple of guys are real pros at this art and have formed the **Bujagali Swimmers**, mastering a safe route through the turbulent waters.

ACTIVITIES
Quad Biking

Quad biking along the beautiful banks of the Victoria Nile is a real blast thanks to **All Terrain Adventures** (☎ 077-377185; www.travel uganda.co.ug/ata; Bujagali Falls). It now has more than a dozen quads and after a little spin on the practice circuit, it is time to explore the paths and trails that criss-cross the nearby countryside. This is huge fun if you've never tried this sort of thing before, and those with experience will love some of the longer trips. There are several spins available, starting with a one-hour short-haul safari at USh60,000, right up to a trailblazer that

takes half a day (USh120,000). Another popular option includes the twilight cruiser with a meal in a local home, and plans are afoot to develop quad-biking safaris through Lake Mburo National Park. Rafting and quad-biking specials are also available. Contributions are made to local communities in the area, ensuring a wild welcome on the way.

Bungee Jumping

Nile High Bungee is Uganda's only bungee jump, a 44m plunge into the Nile River. Set close to the riverbank, it looks scary from above but is very safe. Look at the arrow on the roof and pull out your finest swan dive. Contact the **Adventure Centre** (☎ 041 252720; www.surfthesource.com; Kira Rd, Kampala) for bookings and information, or drop in on the Nile High Camp (see opposite), Adrift's base near the Jinja Nile Resort.

Nile Flyer

Under development during our visit, the Nile Flyer is your chance to fly across the River Nile supported by a steel wire. Sort of like hang gliding with a guaranteed safe landing, this will be another way to get up close and personal with the mighty Nile. Ask around in Bujagali, Jinja or Kampala for more details.

Community Projects

There are plenty of projects to support the local communities around Bujagali Falls. **Soft Power Education** (www.softpowereducation.com) has a popular volunteer program to assist local schools in the area and people can sign up for a few days or a few months. The results are evident for all to see, with school buildings in better shape and education standards improving. NRE also offers **community walks** to help fund community activities, costing US$5 per person. These sort of initiatives are a great thing to get involved in for travellers, particularly when you bear in mind that the cost of rafting is equivalent to about three or four months' salary for the average Ugandan.

SLEEPING & EATING

Nile River Explorers Campsite (☎ 043-120236; camping US$3, dm US$5, bandas US$15) The most popular place to stay in the Jinja area, always packed to the gunnels with overland trucks and backpackers. Thoughtful terracing means some brilliant views for those in *bandas* and tents, while the showers look out over the river, which can make a scrub up a whole lot more interesting than usual. The restaurant and bar are packed to the rafters come the evening, so pitch your tent far enough away if you plan a quiet one. If not, just join the party.

Nile Porch (☎ 043-120236; www.nileporch.com; s/d/tr US$54/84/108) Under the same ownership as NRE Campsite, but a world away in style and standards, the Nile Porch brings the lodge experience to Bujagali. The luxurious tents are superbly set on a cliff above the river, and include hot-water bathrooms and elegant furnishings. There is a swimming pool for guests and some family units available for those travelling in numbers. A great place, and great value when compared with what's on offer in the national parks around East Africa.

Black Lantern (☎ 078-321541; www.nileporch.com; mains USh5000-15,000) Bujagali's premier dining destination, this is the restaurant at the Nile Porch. Set under a traditional thatched roof, the extensive menu includes several stops around the world, including Western, Indian, Chinese and Italian. Spare ribs are a speciality and the portions are enormous. Vegetarians, quiver not at the mention of ribs; there are several non-meat options as well.

Speke Camp Site (☎ 077-379566; camping US$2, banda dm US$5, d bandas US$15) Boasting the best location of any camping ground in Uganda, Speke is right next to the falls themselves. The site offers camping and *bandas*, but may not be around much longer if the planned mega-resort goes ahead. There is also a popular restaurant and bar here, a good spot to take in a beer at the end of the day.

Eden Rock Resort (☎ 077-501222; www.edenrocknile.com; camping US$3, r USh27,000) Eden Rock Resort played host to Prince William when he came rafting in Uganda a few years ago, although it's unlikely his grandmother would have approved of the rooms. It offers basic *bandas* with bathrooms, set amid impressive gardens. It is a good choice for campers who are turned off by the sight of too many trucks at NRE Campsite. There is a nice central bar and restaurant, with the only satellite TV link in the area, plus there is a weird right-angle pool table to confuse the hustlers.

ATA Café (☎ 077-377185) Drop in on this friendly little café, part of the quad-biking set up, for good company and cheap eats.

The menu is small, but includes plenty of Western favourites and the best-value all-day breakfast in Uganda.

Nile High Camp (☎ 077-237438; nilehigh@surfthesource.com; Kimaka Rd; camping US$2, dm US$5; r per person from US$20) Not exactly Bujagali but just off the road back towards Jinja, Nile High is Adrift's base for rafting and bungy jumping. The pretty camp includes solid dorms, large open camping grounds and a couple of new bungalows with big river views. Best of all will be the new restaurant and bar under construction with a bird's-eye view of the bungy.

GETTING THERE & AWAY

Bujagali Falls is about 9km from Jinja. To get here, head northwest out of town and go straight ahead at the Kampala roundabout. Follow this sometimes smooth, sometimes bumpy road and turn left at the large signpost pointing to the falls. Minibuses head out this way (USh500, 20 minutes) on weekends, while by *boda-boda* it costs about USh3000 and to charter a special taxi USh8000 or so.

Hairy Lemon

Yes, it's kind of unique to give a camp its own entry, but then **Hairy Lemon** (☎ 075-893086; lemonthenile@yahoo.com; dm USh30,000, s/d furnished tents USh60,000/80,000, all full board) is a unique kind of place and pretty much in the middle of nowhere. But that's the idea, it's a getaway, a retreat, an isolated island for relaxation and reflection. Facilities include hot showers, and three hearty meals are served a day, including veggie options. Volleyball, swimming and bird-watching are all possible, and just down the river is Nile Special, a world-class hole for those with their own kayak and plenty of experience. As space is limited, it's absolutely essential to book ahead, and telephoning is more reliable than email. To get here, take a minibus from Njeru taxi stand opposite the Nile Brewery in Jinja to Nazigo (USh1500). From Nazigo, take a *boda-boda* (USh2000) to the Hairy Lemon. Bang on the wheel hub and a boat will come across to welcome you.

TORORO
☎ 045

There's not a lot to lure visitors to Tororo and most travellers prefer to base themselves in Jinja or Mbale. Located in the far east of Uganda, not far from the border with Kenya, the town has not aged particularly well during the long years of trouble. Two large Hindu temples suggest it had a substantial Asian community in the years before Amin, and Asian interests are once again controlling its celebrated cement factory. Today the only redeeming feature is the intriguing, forest-covered volcanic plug that rises up abruptly from the plain at the back of the town. The views from the top are definitely worth the climb up should you happen to find yourself stuck in the area.

Information

Stanbic Bank (cnr Busia Rd & Uhuru Dr) is the best bet for exchanging cash or travellers cheques. The post office offers international telephone and fax services.

Sleeping & Eating

There is no shortage of fleapits in Tororo, but cutting to the chase, the following option is better than the rest.

Deluxe Guesthouse (☎ 045-44986; 10 Market St; s/d USh8000/15,000) The doubles come with their own bathroom and are a better bet than the pokey singles downstairs.

Crystal Hotel (☎ 045-45180; 22 Bazaar St; s/d USh20,000/25,000) Moving up a gear, this is the most comfortable hotel in the centre of town. It has clean enough twin-bedded rooms with mosquito net and hot-water bathrooms. There's a restaurant downstairs that is popular with locals for its hearty fare, as well as a bar.

Rock Classic Hotel (☎ 045-45069; info@rockclassic hotel.com; 70 Malaba Rd; s/d USh45,000/50,000; ☑) A venerable hangover from the British era in Uganda, this hotel was recently given a full facelift and is now pretty plush for this part of Uganda. Located on the outskirts of town on the road to Malaba, rooms have TV and hot-water bathrooms. Camping is also available for just USh5000, a top deal if you happen to get stuck here and want to cool off in the pool.

Getting There & Away

Minibuses run to Kampala (USh10,000, three to four hours), Jinja (USh6000, two hours), Mbale (USh3000, one hour) and Malaba on the Kenyan border (USh1500, 30 minutes).

MBALE
☎ 045

When it comes to location, Mbale has a striking setting at the base of Mt Elgon and the city is the logical base for an assault on the mountain from the Ugandan side. A bustling provincial city, it is one of the nicer places in which to spend some time. It's also a good starting point for a trip to Sipi Falls, the country's most beautiful waterfall, 55km to the northeast.

Information

There are several banks along Republic St, including Stanbik Bank and Centenary Rural Development Bank. The post office has international telephone and fax services, but it has some competition from MTN, which has phone booths across the city.

Serve Supermarket (5 Cathedral Ave; per min USh50) A reliable Internet connection located upstairs in a local supermarket.

Standard Chartered Bank (☎ 045-35141; 37 Republic St) The best bank for travellers, as it changes major currencies, travellers cheques and has an ATM for credit-card withdrawals.

Uganda Wildlife Authority office (UWA; ☎ 045-33720; www.uwa.or.ug; 19 Masaba Rd; ☑ 8am-5pm) For information on climbing Mt Elgon, visit this office on the way to the Mt Elgon Hotel (not to be confused with the Mt Elgon View Hotel!). The staff can help organise a trek. For details on climbing Mt Elgon, see p503.

Sleeping
BUDGET

Budget options below the USh10,000 mark are eminently missable, but there are a couple of good places for those prepared to spend USh15,000 or so.

Mt Elgon View Hotel (☎ 045-34668; 1 Cathedral Ave; s/d USh12,000/15,000, d with bathroom USh25,000) This hotel has been around for an eternity, but remains the most popular place at this price. Not to be confused with the more expensive Mt Elgon Hotel, on a clear day you might just get a view of the base of the looming mountain. Double rooms are better value than the cubicles that pass as singles, but all are well looked after. There is a lively little bar and pool table on the 1st floor, while downstairs is the excellent Nurali's Café (p502).

Mbale Tower Lodge (☎ 045-34620; 1 Pallisa Rd; s/d USh6000/10,000) When it comes to the cheapest of the cheap, this pad has a good location

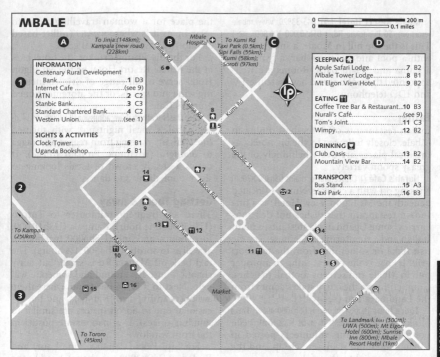

MBALE

INFORMATION
Centenary Rural Development Bank	1 D3
Internet Cafe	(see 9)
MTN	2 C2
Stanbic Bank	3 C3
Standard Chartered Bank	4 C2
Western Union	(see 1)

SIGHTS & ACTIVITIES
Clock Tower	5 B1
Uganda Bookshop	6 B1

SLEEPING
Apule Safari Lodge	7 B2
Mbale Tower Lodge	8 B1
Mt Elgon View Hotel	9 B2

EATING
Coffee Tree Bar & Restaurant	10 B3
Nurali's Café	(see 9)
Tom's Joint	11 C3
Wimpy	12 B2

DRINKING
Club Oasis	13 B2
Mountain View Bar	14 B2

TRANSPORT
Bus Stand	15 A3
Taxi Park	16 B3

overlooking the central clock tower. Rates vary depending on the bed size and access to hot water. Check out the philosophical musings on the wall behind reception.

Apule Safari Lodge (☎ 077-502421; 5 Naboa Rd; s USh8000, s/d with bathroom USh12,000/14,000) This little courtyard lodge offers what it claims is 'executive accommodation', although it is doubtful that many corporations would rate it as such. Each room is named after one of Uganda's many lakes.

Salem Mbale (☎ 077-505595; camping USh2000, dm USh4000, r USh15,000-25,000) Those with their own wheels might like to make for Salem Mbale. It is some distance out of town, but all proceeds from the guesthouse go towards local projects, such as childcare and a health centre in Nakaloke district. Rooms are set in attractive *banda*s, and meals and refreshments are available. To get here, take a minibus to Nakaloke (USh500) and then a *boda-boda* to the guesthouse for about USh500.

MIDRANGE

Mt Elgon Hotel (☎ 045-33454; 30 Masaba Rd; s USh45,000-75,000, d 55,000-85,000; 🏊) Recently given a much

needed makeover, this colonial-era stalwart is once again one of the better addresses in Mbale. The rooms are large and spacious with satellite TV, and more expensive options include air-con. It's in a quiet part of the city, surrounded by its own verdant grounds, and now includes a little crazy golf course out the front. The bar is a lively gathering place for guests, local aid workers and government officials. Rates include breakfast and tax.

Sunrise Inn (☎ 045-33090; r USh40,000-60,000) Even further out of the city than the Mt Elgon Hotel, off Masaba Rd, this place is perennially full thanks to its good reputation. Rooms are very well kept and include satellite TV and a telephone. Bookings advised.

Landmark Inn (☎ 045-33880; r USh30,000) Set in a grand old house with expansive gardens, this is Mbale's answer to the budget boutique hotel. The huge rooms have high ceilings and large bathrooms that might pass as a single room in some Kampala crash pads. There is an excellent Indian restaurant downstairs, which competes with Nurali's Café for the title of best food in the city.

Mbale Resort Hotel (☎ 045-33920; www.mbale resort.org; 50 Bungokho Rd; r USh50,000-100,000; 🖭) This is the top bill in Mbale, a smart resort, with a pool and swim-up bar, a gym, and a sauna and steam bath. Rooms are well-appointed throughout and have satellite TV and IDD telephone.

Eating
Indian restaurants offer the best dining in Mbale, closely followed by the big hotels, as the local places are overwhelmingly of the greasy spoon variety.

Nurali's Café (1 Cathedral Ave; mains USh3000-7000) Kicking off with a cracker, Nurali's (located beneath the Mt Elgon View Hotel) is a fine Indian restaurant that dishes out delicious curries, some Ugandan greatest hits, a bit of Italian and a smattering of Chinese. Try the fish tikka or something from the tandoori grill. Its bar is the closest thing to a proper pub in Mbale and screens football matches. Competition in the curry stakes comes from the Landmark Inn (see p501).

Tom's Joint (Naboa Rd; mains USh1000-4000) This blink-and-you'll-miss-it spot has long been popular with young volunteers posted in Mbale. Food and drink are cheap, and the owners are mighty cheerful.

Wimpy (Cathedral Ave; mains USh2000-4000) Check out the kitsch advertising posters from decades gone by for a flashback to English burger bars of old. The menu is not exactly authentic Wimpy cuisine, but most consider this a blessing in disguise. Bargain burgers, plus omelettes and Ugandan staples.

Coffee Tree Bar & Restaurant (Manafa Rd; meals from USh2000) This local canteen is a busy spot for breakfast and lunch The open-air terrace bar overlooking the street is a potential place for a cold beer or two on a quiet afternoon.

For something more international in accent, consider the restaurants at Mt Elgon Hotel, Sunrise Inn and Mbale Resort Hotel. The menus won't set the pulse racing, but they have a lot more to offer than local eateries in town. Plan to spend USh5000 to USh10,000 for a filling feed.

Drinking & Entertainment
There are a few lively local bars around town, including the upstairs **Mountain View Bar** (Kumi Rd), but it can get a bit too lively some nights with local drunks hassling you left, right and centre. Definitely not the place for a woman travelling alone to relax in, as it is where *waragi* (millet-based alcohol) rules with the local guys.

For the discerning drinker, the hotel bars at the Mbale Resort Hotel or the Mt Elgon Hotel serve a full range of drinks, including wine and spirits, or the aforementioned Nurali's Café.

Club Oasis (Cathedral Ave; admission USh1000; 🕑 Wed-Sun) Mbale's local nightspot, with themed music nights ranging from reggae and ragga to *bhangra* (rhythmic Punjabi music). It draws a steady crowd of locals looking to shoot pool, drink and dance.

Getting There & Away
There are frequent minibuses to Tororo (USh3000, one hour), Kampala (USh10,000, three hours) and Jinja (USh6000, two hours), as well as to Soroti (USh4500, 1½ hours). The taxi park off Manafa Rd is small, but fairly chaotic – just ask around and someone will help. Next to it is the bus stand, where there are buses to Jinja and Kampala, and the occasional one to Soroti (prices are similar to minibus prices). Destinations are posted in the front window.

For Sipi Falls (USh4000, one hour) and Budadari (USh3000, one hour), head to the Kumi Rd taxi park. Services are less frequent to these smaller places.

Getting Around
For travel around Mbale, there are plenty of bicycle *boda-bodas*. The fare to the Mt Elgon Hotel or the Uganda Wildlife Authority office should be USh300, but USh500 is more likely *mzungu* price.

MT ELGON NATIONAL PARK
Mt Elgon has become a popular destination for budget trekking, at least budget when compared with the cost of climbing the Rwenzori Mountains or Mt Kilimanjaro in Tanzania. Established in 1993, it is one of the most recently created of Uganda's national parks and encompasses the upper regions of Mt Elgon to the Kenyan border (see p413 for information on trekking Mt Elgon from across the border).

The mountain is said to have one of the largest surface areas of any extinct volcano in the world, and is peppered with cliffs, caves, gorges and waterfalls. Wagagai is the highest peak (4321m). The views from the higher reaches across the wide plains are among the most spectacular in Uganda. The upper slopes are clothed in tropical montane forest, while above this a vast tract of alpine moorland extends over the caldera, a collapsed crater covering some 40 sq km at the top of the mountain.

Trekking on Mt Elgon

Tourism on Mt Elgon remains relatively underdeveloped, so visitors need to be resourceful, patient, self-sufficient and not expect well-worn paths, such as those found on Mt Kenya and Mt Kilimanjaro. However, it is also possible to hike for days without seeing another tourist, an impossible dream on Mt Kilimanjaro.

Bring camping and cooking equipment, food, appropriate clothing and a guide. For indulgences, such as chocolate or biscuits, Mbale is best for shopping, but for simple staples it is best to buy from locals at Budadari with assistance from the guides. For those without a tent or sleeping bag, they can be rented from the Forest Exploration Centre near Sipi. Don't attempt to trek without a guide, as it is illegal and could end in tears – Elgon is a big mountain. One more thing to bear in mind is that not everyone has the same level of fitness, so groups of travellers getting together for a trek might want to do a short walk around Sipi Falls to see if they are running at the same speed. It's not much fun to be halfway up the mountain and realise that everyone wants to go at a different pace.

Some readers have complained about the amount of rubbish left at each camp site. Please take all rubbish with you in order to leave this mountain in its natural state for future visitors.

The best time to climb the mountain is from June to August or December to March, but the seasons are unpredictable and it can rain at any time.

Trekking on Mt Elgon costs US$30 per person per day (half this price for those under 18 years of age). The cost includes park entry fees, camping and ranger-guide fees. It does not include porters, who charge USh8000 per day. These prices cover food for the guide and porters as well, but not tips, which are very welcome.

The **Uganda Wildlife Authority office** (Mt Elgon National Park Office; ☎ 045-33170; www.uwa.or.ug; 19

Masaba Rd; ☒ 8am-5pm) in Mbale can help with information about trekking on the mountain, as can the visitor centres at Budadari, Kapkwata and the Forest Exploration Centre, all open in theory from 9am to 5pm daily. It is possible to pay park fees at these offices, as well as arrange guides and porters, and find information on accommodation and routes. Mt Elgon Guides and Porters Association has been organising training for both guides and porters.

ROUTES
Sasa Trail

So far, there are three established camp sites along the Sasa trail, the most popular and fastest route to the summit. It requires a minimum of three days to do this trek, and five in order to reach Jackson's Summit, Wagagai and Suam Gorge.

From Budadari, which is considered the trail head, a road leads to Bugitimwa, then it's about three hours' walk to the forest. Almost as soon as you enter the forest, you reach Mudangi Cliffs, which are scaled via 'ladders' (piles of branches). From the top, the trail is well defined and less steep. About a 30-minute walk up this path is bamboo forest and a further 30 minutes across the other side of the Sasa River brings you to the first camp site. Getting across the river involves boulder-hopping or wading knee-deep through fast-flowing water, depending on the season.

The camp site is marked by a well-used fireplace, and there are enclosed toilets and a rubbish pit. If it's still early in the day when you get here, you have the option of continuing another two hours further up the trail to stay at the next camp site, some 300m to the left of the trail near the Environmental Task Force Hut.

The next part of the trail goes up to the top of the forest and into the heath land, where there's another possible camp site close to a small cave (about three hours' walk beyond the first camp site). The moorland is studded with giant senecio (groundsel) and you'll often see duikers bounding through the long grass and lammergeier vultures overhead.

A further three hours' walk brings you to a split in the path just before the caldera. The left fork leads directly into the caldera and the hot springs at the head of the Suam Gorge. The right fork leads to Jackson's Summit via Jackson's Pool. The latter path crosses a permanent stream, and there is a possible camp site if you wish to stay up here.

Jackson's Summit and Wagagai can be reached in a minimum of 14½ hours, allowing for a comfortable return to the second camp site in good light. The return journey from the second camp site back to the road can be done in five to six hours.

For those planning to continue into Kenya without backtracking to Malaba or Busia, UWA offers cross-border treks in collaboration with the Kenya Wildlife Service, with a handover at the hot springs. Check with UWA for more details.

Other Trails

As well as the popular Sasa trail, there are two more trails up to the caldera. The **Piswa trail** runs from Kapkwata in the north, while the newer **Sipi trail** runs from near Sipi Falls and is growing in popularity. It is possible to combine two different routes going up and down for maximum variety. Ascending via the Sasa trail and descending on the Sipi trail makes sense, as you could chill out at Sipi for a day or two.

Day Hikes

There are three short trails for hiking around the Forest Exploration Centre near Sipi, all offering an insight into Mt Elgon's flora for those that cannot spare the time for a full trek. The **Bamboo Loop** takes in some huge bamboo, as well as offering a view of Elgon's summits on a clear day, few and far between, unfortunately. The **Chebonet Falls Loop** passes a scenic waterfall, while the **Ridge Loop** offers some good views above and below. There is also a longer 11km walk to the huge **Tutum Cave**. Day walks currently cost US$30.

Sleeping & Eating

Rose's Last Chance (camping per tent USh5000, r USh7000) Located near the trail head in Budadari, this is a popular place to stay before or after scaling the heights. It is a fun and friendly place that brings guests closer to the local scene – testing local brews is a favourite activity. Watch out for the graphic photos of male circumcision ceremonies on the walls. It also serves tasty, filling meals and rates include a local breakfast.

Forest Exploration Centre (camping USh7500, dm USh11,000, cottage s/d USh20,000/30,000) Those using the Sipi trail have the choice of staying at Sipi Falls without a park fee, or being right at the trail head at this centre in Kapkwai, located about 1½ hours from Sipi on foot. The cottages here are really tasteful and food and drink is available here. Contact the UWA office in Mbale for bookings.

Kapkwata Guesthouse (r USh11,000) Not many people opt for the Piswa trail, but there is some basic accommodation here before or after a trek.

Getting There & Away

There are regular, if infrequent, taxis to Budadari from Mbale (USh3000, one hour). There is no regular transport to the Forest Exploration Centre (p504), but minibuses between Sipi and Kapchorwe pass the signposted turn-off, from where it is a 6km walk to the centre. See the Sipi Falls entry following for details on getting from Mbale to Sipi. Between Mbale and Kampala there are frequent minibuses (USh10,000, three hours).

SIPI FALLS

Sipi Falls is a stunner, arguably the most beautiful waterfall in all of Uganda, and it is now much more accessible thanks to one of the best roads in the country linking it to Mbale. The falls are about 55km north of Mbale, in the foothills of Mt Elgon and not far from the town of Kapchorwe. Not only are the falls spectacular, so too are the views of Mt Elgon above them, and the wide plains of eastern and northern Uganda disappearing into the distance below. There are three levels of falls, but the two upper levels are fairly small compared with the main drop. It is well worth spending a night or two in this peaceful and pretty place.

Activities

There are some excellent walks on a network of well-maintained local trails, and beautiful scenery in every direction. It is easy enough just to ramble off on your own, but all the lodges and camp sites in the area offer guided walks from US$2 to US$4 per person or the local equivalent. These include short walks around the falls area and longer walks up to the tree line at the base of Mt Elgon. There are also forest walking trails from the nearby Forest Exploration Centre (opposite).

Rob's Rolling Rock (☎ 077-800705) is a local outfit offering climbing and abseiling around Sipi Falls, with a variety of climbs for beginners and the experienced. The falls provide an outstanding backdrop for abseiling. It is possible to abseil all three falls in one day, but the iconic final drop is the real deal.

Sleeping & Eating

There is a good range of tasteful camp sites to suit all budgets in Sipi, including two small camp sites catering to independent travellers, as well a couple of more upmarket lodges.

Crow's Nest (☎ 077-800705; thecrowsnets@yahoo .com; camping USh6000, dm USh12,000, cabins USh30,000) Sitting in splendid isolation on a cliff opposite Sipi Falls, this camp site offers breathtaking views of the main drop. It was set up by Peace Corps volunteers and the cabins are Scandinavian in style, including doubles with expansive terrace views. There is a small restaurant and bar with inexpensive food (mains USh2000 to USh5000), including pancakes and French toast for breakfast, chunky sandwiches for lunch, and pasta dishes or curries for dinner. Yes, someone really did make a mess of the email address: crowsnets, not nest!

Moses' Camp Site (camping USh4000, bandas per person USh10,000) A smaller operation, this has a spectacular location to the side of the falls and offers unhindered views of the lowlands below. The *bandas* are very basic, but the staff are always friendly and the children from the nearby primary school will treat you like an Oscar winner every time you walk by. Drinks are available, but meals need to be ordered in advance.

Lacam Lodge (☎ 075-292554; www.lacamlodge.co .uk; camping USh25,000, rooms per person USh20,000-35,000) This new lodge is now the closest to Sipi Falls, with a great view of the main drop. Accommodation is full board, including breakfast, lunch and a slap-up dinner. The more expensive options are large *bandas*, and there are several smaller rooms with shared bathroom.

Sipi Falls Rest Camp (☎ 041-346464; www.volcanoes safaris.com; s/d US$135/200) Run by Volcanoes Safaris and set very close to the falls, this is an upscale resort offering accommodation in well-appointed *bandas* with private bathroom. The old house here was used as a residence by the last British governor of Uganda, and it certainly has an authentic colonial feel to it. Prices cover full board, including a three-course dinner. Nonguests can eat here for USh10,000 for set meals and the bar is open to all.

Getting There & Away

Minibuses run between Mbale and Sipi Falls daily (USh4000, one hour). Arrive at Mbale's Kumi Rd taxi park early or it may take some time for the minibus to fill up. Minibuses returning to Mbale from Kapchorwe often come through Sipi Falls, so it may be necessary to do a two-stage journey to get out, first by truck to Kamu for USh500 and then by minibus to Mbale for USh3000, sneakily saving USh500 in the process. Those travelling in a group should consider hiring a taxi if it is late in the day. The road is one of the best in Uganda, constructed by a Bosnian company with experience of Balkan mountain roads, so it comes complete with safety railings and drainage channels.

SOROTI

Grotty Soroti! It has such a ring to it, but it's actually not that grotty, just rather dull. Few travellers make it here, unless they get stuck on the overland route to Kidepo Valley

National Park. Like Tororo to the southeast, it has a curious volcanic plug poking skywards on the edge of town, from which there are probably fine views of the surrounding countryside, but climbing it is prohibited due to a military presence in the area.

Most of the cheaper places are on the same strip on Solot Ave in the centre of town. The best of the bunch is currently the **Silent Night Inn** (☎ 077-610205; small/large tw with bathroom USh15,000/25,000), with clean enough rooms and water that actually works in the private bathroom, not a dead cert in the other cheapies.

For something a bit more sophisticated, try the **Soroti Hotel** (☎ 077-301154; s/d with bathroom USh40,000/60,000), an attractive place set among verdant gardens, with considerably smarter rooms than the central establishments. Rates include breakfast.

When it comes to eating, Soroti doesn't inspire, but there are a few cheap local joints on the main strip, Solot Ave.

Getting There & Away

Minibuses run between Mbale and Soroti (USh5000, two hours) on a good, sealed road. From Kampala, there are direct buses departing daily (after 7am) for USh12,000. The EMS Post Bus also makes a daily run from the capital, but stops at a whole host of places along the way; see p485 for details.

For those feeling adventurous or with their own transport, there is also a dirt road west to Lira and beyond to Murchison Falls National Park, but this route is definitely not recommended at the time of writing due to security problems in the north.

Buses also travel the dirt road northeast to Moroto (USh8000, four hours), but check the latest security situation before setting off, as ambushes can and do happen.

MOROTO

The final frontier in many ways, Moroto is a small district capital and the gateway to the wilds of Karamojaland to the north. Many of the inhabitants of the town are Karamojong, but this is not obvious as they have forsaken traditional tribal dress, or rather lack of it, and now dress as other Ugandans.

Be aware that the town suffers from chronic water shortages and electricity is available only between the hours of 7pm and 11pm. If you are heading north on the overland route to Kidepo Valley National Park, this is the last real centre for supplies, so stock up.

When it comes to accommodation, the choice is between the cheap and basic **Guluna Lodge** (r USh5000), with plain rooms that have a fan and mosquito net, or the more expensive **Moroto Hotel** (r USh30,000), a relic from the days of the British protectorate. Rates would be understandable if things like water and electricity were reliable, but it may get a facelift during the lifetime of this book. The restaurant is arguably the best place to eat in town, however.

Getting There & Away

Flights to Moroto are available with **Eagle Air** (☎ 078-810499 in Moroto), but at US$110 one way they are more likely to appeal to government workers and NGOs than tourists.

Most locals advise that travelling by bus is safest and that private vehicles run the remote risk of being ambushed. The most convenient way to get to Moroto from Kampala is by direct bus, but many prefer to break the journey in somewhere like Mbale. Gateway runs daily services from the bus station in Kampala (USh18,000, 11 hours) departing at about 6am.

The direct road between Mbale and Moroto is beautiful, but is considered unsafe due to infrequent ambushes – always go via Soroti, as it is both safer and faster (see the boxed text, opposite).

MOROTO TO KIDEPO VALLEY NATIONAL PARK

For those hardy souls heading overland to Kidepo Valley National Park, the next stop on the journey north from Moroto is **Kotido**, a 'wild east' town, where the Karamojong dress in traditional clothes, and AK-47s are as common as walking sticks and blankets. A daily bus leaves Moroto for Kotido at 5pm (1½ hours). This bus starts out in Kampala at about 6am, so gluttons for punishing bus rides could actually go straight through to Kotido in one day to save time. In Kotido, **Airport Lodge** (r USh7000) is basic, but a secure place to stay.

The next leg of the journey sees you bidding goodbye to civilisation, although some would say that happened on leaving Kampala. From Kotido, there are daily pick-ups leaving early in the morning for **Kaabong** (USh5000, 1½ hours) along a pretty bad road. There is also a daily bus – the one that serves Kampala to Kotido continues to Kaabong in the morning. Should you get stuck in Kaabong you could stay at Karamojong Lodge.

The final leg of the journey involves chartering a vehicle from Kaabong to the Kidepo Valley National Park headquarters at **Apoka**, or jumping on an irregular pick-up to **Karenga** and getting off at the Apoka fork, just 2km from the headquarters. Chartering a vehicle is expensive, probably around USh40,000 or so depending on your bargaining skills, so if you have the time (which you obviously do if you have come this far by public transport already!), catch the pick-up to Karenga.

Doing the journey in reverse is a little easier, as the rangers at Kidepo know when the pick-ups between Karenga and Kaabong are passing by.

However, it must once again be stressed that this is not a journey to be undertaken lightly and it is of paramount importance to check security every step of the way. For those with the budget, renting a 4WD and a local driver would be the way to go.

KIDEPO VALLEY NATIONAL PARK

This lost valley in the extreme northeast of the country, along the border with Sudan, is considered by many to offer the most stunning scenery of any protected area in Uganda. Surrounded by mountains, the **Kidepo Valley National Park** (entry per one/two/three or more days US$20/35/50) covers 1440 sq km and is notable for a number of animals that are found nowhere else in Uganda, including cheetahs, ostriches and bat-eared foxes. There are also large concentrations of elephants, zebras, buffaloes and bushbucks, and a healthy number of predators, including lions, leopards and hyenas.

It is also a good bird-watching destination, with a number of endemic birds of prey, including the pygmy falcon and secretary bird. Game drives are available here using a park vehicle, but it costs a hefty USh2500 per kilometre, expensive if you have come overland on a budget.

A place worth looking out for, although you'll have no chance of finding a bed these days, is Grand Katurum Lodge, constructed during Idi Amin's regime. It never really saw any guests, as his domestic policies

---

WARNING: SECURITY AROUND KARAMOJALAND

Pay attention to developments in Karamojaland in the northeast, as groups of local cattle herders, the Karamojong, have been known to ambush highway travellers. There is often fighting among the Karamojong themselves, and to make matters more complicated, large numbers of Turkana tribesmen from Kenya often cross the border looking to steal cattle – this attracts the attention of the Ugandan army. Sometimes it becomes too dangerous to travel to Moroto by road from Soroti because of fighting between the Karamojong, the Turkana and the Ugandan army. Check the latest security conditions with reliable sources in Kampala before setting out, and check local security conditions at every town or village along the way, because trouble is often not far away in Karamojaland.

---

were not exactly consistent with tourism growth. However, it occupies a fantastic location, built into a huge rock bluff that overlooks the Narus Valley and Mt Lotuke in Sudan.

Apoka Headquarters (s/d USh15,000/25,000) offers basic *bandas* with shared bathrooms, which are the only option for independent travellers. The old Apoka Rest Camp is undergoing rebirth as a luxury lodge owned by **The Uganda Safari Company** (TUSC; ☎ 041-251182; www .safariuganda.com), and if Semliki Lodge is anything to go by, it will be a fantastic place to stay for those with the budget. Once open, likely by the time you are reading this, it will be promoted as part of a package, including flights and other safari destinations around Uganda. It will also offer a full restaurant and bar, the only place to eat in the park. Overland travellers should come with their own provisions, but park staff can help with the cooking.

This is an unstable region and caution should be taken when travelling overland here – see the boxed text, above. For those short on time and with money to spend, it is possible to fly by charter plane from Kampala. TUSC will offer its own flights once the lodge opens or try **KAFTC** (☎ 077-706105; barnsey@ imul.com), which has charter services out of Entebbe.

SOUTHWESTERN UGANDA

If Uganda is the 'pearl of Africa', then south-western Uganda is the mother of pearl, a hauntingly beautiful region of fecund land-scapes and towering mountains. The major-ity of Uganda's big hitters are found in the southwest, home to the most striking scen-ery in the country, almost half the world's remaining population of mountain gorillas, the greatest variety of primates found in one location, and Africa's highest mountain range, the Rwenzoris.

Not enough? Don't worry, it also has sev-eral of the country's most celebrated national parks, including Kibale Forest, Queen Eliza-beth and Lake Mburo, Uganda's chill-out capitals in the shape of Lake Bunyoni and the Ssese Islands, and the breathtaking Virunga volcanoes that form the border with Rwanda and DR Congo.

Plan on spending the lion's share of your time here, as even though the only lions you will see are in the Queen Elizabeth National Park or Semliki Valley Game Reserve, the chimpanzees, gorillas, elephants, leopards, antelopes, hippos, zebras and other large mammals should keep things ticking along in the meantime. To say nothing of the bird life, which combines the best of Uganda with a host of Albertine rift endemics.

Transport and infrastructure are in pretty good shape, with good roads linking the major towns of the region and decent enough dirt roads away from the trail. Buses and minibuses link most destinations, but start to dry up around some of the national parks, such as Bwindi Impenetrable, Lake Mburo and Queen Elizabeth. However, Kibale Forest and Semuliki National Parks are pretty straightforward. For those with their own wheels, life's a breeze.

FORT PORTAL

☎ 0493

There may be no fort, but it is definitely a portal to places that offer sublime scenery, abundant nature and genuine adventures. Explore the beautiful crater lakes in the area, track the chimps in Kibale Forest National Park and drop into the Semliki Valley, with its wildlife, hot springs and Pygmy villages.

The town of Fort Portal is lush and live-able, and one of the nicer urban centres in Uganda. Located at the northeastern end of the Rwenzori Mountains, it is the heartland of a verdant tea-growing area and the pro-vincial headquarters for Kabarole District. With so much to experience in the sur-rounding areas, the town is little more than a base from which to explore; this area of Uganda is well worth an indulgence, so set aside a week to make the most of it.

Information

The post office has international cardphone services, but more central is the MTN booth, which has several cardphones.

Centenary Rural Development Bank (Rukidi III St) Represents Western Union if you need money in a hurry.

Kabarole Tours (☎ 0493-22183; ktours@infocom.co.ug; ⏰ 8am-6pm) Signposted behind the Esso petrol station, this is a reliable local tour agency and information bureau covering all of the area's places of interest. The staff are friendly and helpful, although tour prices are high for just one or two people, so gather a group to share the cost. It offers departures to the Semuliki, Kibale Forest and Queen Elizabeth National Parks, plus affordable mini-treks into the foothills of the Rwenzoris.

Rafrisa Info-Services (Kyebambe Rd; per min USh50) The best Internet connection in town.

Stanbic Bank (Lugard Rd) This is the place to exchange cash; exchanging travellers cheques was being trialled during our visit.

Sleeping

Most people are only passing through Fort Portal for one night, heading to the crater lakes or nearby national parks where there is a more interesting range of accommodation.

Rwenzori Travellers Inn (☎ 077-500273; Kyebambe Rd; s/d with bathroom USh25,000/35,000) A modern hotel in the centre of town, business has been so brisk that it is already expanding. Rooms are clean and include hot-water bathrooms, plus some fancier options may be unveiled in the new wing. Downstairs is one of the best restaurants in town and a lively local bar. Everything you need under one roof...

Ruwenzori View Guest House (☎ 0493-22102; ruwview@africaonline.co.ug; s/d with bathroom USh42,000/ 55,000) A blissful little guesthouse on the outskirts of town, this is the most atmos-pheric place to stay in town. Run by an Anglo-Dutch couple, it feels refreshingly rural and offers great views of the moun-

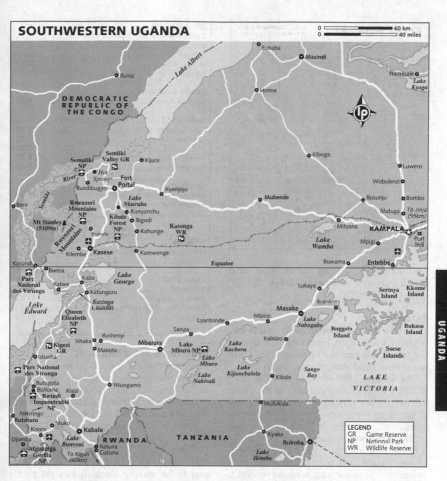

SOUTHWESTERN UGANDA

LEGEND
GR   Game Reserve
NP   National Park
WR   Wildlife Reserve

tains. There are also some cheaper rooms available with shared bathroom, costing USh30,000/40,000 a single/double. Rates include a hearty breakfast, and home-cooked meals are served around the family table. As homey as it gets!

Continental Hotel (☎ 077-484842; Lugard Rd; s/d USh8000/10,000, d with bathroom USh20,000) It is not ageing as gracefully as some, but it remains the best choice among the cheaper places. It offers clean rooms around a courtyard and has a small restaurant downstairs, where films are shown nightly.

Wooden Hotel (☎ 0493-22034; 4 Kyebambe Rd; s/d USh7000/12,000, with bathroom USh10,000/15,000) Opposite the string of cheapies, this place must be as old as the town. The rooms are pretty scruffy, but that is to be expected at these prices. Downstairs is a bar and restaurant with décor that could have been inspired by a visit to a New Orleans brothel. Light sleepers should steer clear, as it has a bangin' all-night disco from Wednesday to Saturday.

Mountains of the Moon Hotel (☎ 077-801383) Around for many a year, this hotel was undergoing a much-needed renovation during our visit, so could be the best in town once it reopens.

If money is more important than comfort, there's a whole string of cheapies along Balya Rd. They are all much of a muchness, with few redeeming features but their price. Places include the **Economic Lodge**

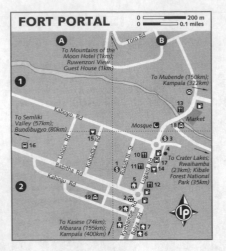

(s/d USh3000/6000), stating the obvious, and the slightly smarter **New Linda Lodge** (☎ 0493-22937; s/d USh5500/8000).

Eating

As well as the good homecooked food at Ruwenzori View Guest House and the tempting menu at Rwenzori Travellers Inn, there are several good local restaurants in town.

The Gardens (☎ 0493-22925; Lugard Rd; meals USh3000-6000) Hidden away next to the Pepsi factory on the way to the post office, this deserves its reputation as one of the better restaurants in town. It has a lively menu with some good Indian staples, including a filling vegetable curry, and all of the *mochomo* (barbecued meat) you could ever imagine, and some you perhaps couldn't. There is also an African buffet at lunchtime, which is a good introduction to Ugandan food if you haven't tried it, but probably best avoided if you are already *matoked* out!

African Village Bar & Restaurant (Lugard Rd) A bit of a local hole-in-the-wall, this is the place to try some African staples, such as meat or fish with all the usual sides of *matoke*, Irish potatoes or rice.

For those needing to buy their own provisions for some serious trekking, there are a couple of supermarkets in town, both on Lugard St. Andrew Brothers Stores is the best, with a good range of products for a provincial place, while Midtown Supermarket is also worth a peek.

Drinking & Entertainment

There are not many places to go for a drink in Fort Portal, when compared with life out at the lakes. The liveliest local bar is **Don's Plaza** (8 Lugard Rd), which draws a drinking crowd into the night and screens big football matches.

Otherwise it is disco fever all the way. The Wooden Hotel has a basement disco (Wednesday to Saturday nights) that rocks until dawn, literally. Bad news if you happen to be staying there. It can get pretty raucous, what with all the local drunks and prostitutes. Try not to think about fire safety while you are there or you could get very paranoid.

Heartbeat (Kuhadika Rd; entry USh2500) Kicking off with 'ladies night' (best pronounced 'leddies' in a sultry voice) on Wednesday, this is the main 'club' in town. Friday and Saturday are the other nights, and you can't miss the place thanks to its monstrous strobes lighting up the sky above town.

Getting There & Away

There are daily EMS Post Bus services connecting Fort Portal and Kampala; one direct and the other via Kasese and Mbarara. For details of these services, see p485.

Kalita Transport (☎ 077-590067; 14 Lugard Rd) runs buses to Kampala (USh10,000, four hours). It offers seven services a day between 7am and 3pm, with pick-ups at the bus stand or the office.

From the bus stand at the western end of Babitha Rd, there's also a daily bus to Kabale (USh13,000, via Kasese, six hours) at about 6am.

The **taxi park** (Kahinju Rd) is near the junction with Lugard Rd. As elsewhere, there's no schedule, so just hang around until the taxis are full, but there are regular-ish departures to Hoima (USh12,000, five hours), Kasese (USh5000, two hours) and Kampala (USh12,000, five hours).

Local minibuses or shared taxis (pick-ups) to Kamwenge (for Kibale Forest National Park; USh2000, 45 minutes) and Rwaihamba (for Lake Nkuruba; USh2000, 45 minutes) leave from the intersection near where the main road crosses the river. There's not a lot of traffic, but usually a few shared taxis daily. Monday and Thursday are market days in Rwaihamba, so there are plenty then.

AROUND FORT PORTAL
Kibale Forest National Park
Kibale is a lush tropical forest, believed to have the highest density of primates in the world, including an estimated 600 chimpanzees. Set at an altitude of 1200m, this 560-sq-km **national park** (admission 1/2/3 or more days US$20/30/50), 35km southeast of Fort Portal, is home to several species of colobus monkeys, such as the rare red and the Angolan; larger mammals, such as bushbucks, sitatungas, duikers, civets and buffaloes; and Uganda's largest concentration of forest elephants.

The stars of the show, however, are the **chimpanzees**, five groups of which have been habituated to human contact. Nevertheless, there is only an 85% chance of seeing them on any particular day, though you'll almost certainly hear them as they scamper off into the bush on your approach. If you want to be sure of sighting them, plan on spending a couple of days here. However, with yet another hike in price for the chimp visit, it is now considerably cheaper to view chimps in and around Murchison Falls National Park, see p545 for more details. US$50 here and less than US$7 there, do the maths!

The park visitor centre is at Kanyanchu, signposted on the left from Fort Portal about 6km before the village of Bigodi. Reception closes daily at 6pm sharp.

ACTIVITIES
At the visitor centre, it is possible to arrange guided walks along well-marked tracks (3km to 5km return) in search of the chimps. There are daily walks from 8am to 11am (the best time to go) and from 3pm to 6pm, costing US$50 per person on top of park entry fees. The price includes a guide, but a tip is generally expected. The group size is limited to six people but any number of groups can set off, as long as they go in different directions. Even if you don't see the chimps, you will see colobus monkeys and the incredible number of butterflies and birds that live in this lush forest. For the ultimate primate encounter, the park also offers the chimpanzee habituation experience, which allows visitors to spend from de-nesting in the morning through to bedtime with the chimps – US$220 for one day, US$700 for four days.

Other walks through the forest are also offered daily. Forest hikes cost just US$5/10 for a half/full day, while hikes geared towards those with a particular interest in the more than 300 species of birds in the park cost the same. Night hikes (US$10) are also possible, to view the species of nocturnal primates that live in the forest. Longer walks of several days can be arranged on demand.

SLEEPING & EATING
Safari Lodge (camping USh6000, bandas USh8000 per person) This popular budget digs is located in Nkingo village, about 6km from Kanyanchu towards Bigodi village. Facilities are basic, but the welcome is warm, and all rates include breakfast. However, take care of valuables, as the rooms aren't all that secure. Host Charles cooks excellent, tasty meals with a bit of notice – look out for chicken in red wine sauce, followed by his famous pineapple pie.

John Tinka's Homestay (☎ 077-886865; USh30,000) Homestays are a new community tourism activity in Uganda and John Tinka knows more about community tourism than most, having established the Kabaka's Trail around Kampala (see p487). Stay with his family in Bigodi village for the genuine Uganda experience. Rates include all meals.

Mantana Safaris (☎ 041-321552; mantana@africaonline.co.ug; s/d with full board US$137/220) A luxury tented camp near Kibale Forest National

Park, signposted about 1km beyond Bigodi village. Service is exemplary, the welcome is friendly and it is a very comfortable place to stay for those with the budget. There are always plenty of colobus monkeys cavorting in the trees around the camp.

There are more accommodation options nearby in the crater lakes region (see right).

There is a good choice of accommodation at Kanyanchu, including camping for USh10,000 per person; single/double *bandas* for USh20,000/30,000; a sort of studio *banda* at USh60,000; and a sky tree house for USh40,000. The downside is you have to pay the national park fee as long as you stay here. The *bandas* are some of the smartest to be found in Uganda's national parks and are well looked after, although running water can be a problem. The elevated studio *banda* is a different option for families or small groups, while the sky house is very basic, but makes up for it with great views over an elephant drinking hole. However, be warned, the sky house is about 500m from the other accommodation down a forested track – not that simple at night. The popular canteen here is run by a Bigodi women's group and tasty, cheap meals are available daily, although it is best to give some notice. All proceeds go to the local community. There is also a small shop with some basic supplies.

Over at the newer Sebitoli area, camping costs USh5000 per person and *bandas* are available for USh10,000/15,000 per single/double.

GETTING THERE & AWAY
The dirt road between Fort Portal and Kibale Forest National Park is in good condition, apart from a couple of rough patches. Minibuses to Kamwenge from Fort Portal pass the park visitor centre (USh3000, 45 minutes) and continue to Bigodi (USh4000, one hour). However, drivers may try to charge USh1000 for a backpack if it takes up a lot of space, as they like to play sardines on this route. Alternatively, charter a special-hire taxi, although this is going to take some negotiation to get a good price; think around USh15,000 or so.

Bigodi Wetland Sanctuary
The **Bigodi Wetland Sanctuary** (☎ 077-886865), established to protect the **Magombe Swamp**, is a haven for birds, with 137 species, plus butterflies and a number of primates. The guided walks through this sanctuary have been developed with the aim of assisting community-development projects in the Kibale area, so the project deserves support. Many of the guides have a good knowledge of bird life in the sanctuary, and are also adept at spotting colobus monkeys and the beautiful blue touraco from a distance. It is often easier to spot colobus monkeys here than in Kibale Forest National Park, as the vegetation is more open. Three-hour guided walks (USh10,000) depart from the visitor centre on demand. The best time to go is early morning or late afternoon.

Bigodi Wetland Sanctuary is just off the road between Fort Portal and Kamwenge, about 6km southeast of Kanyanchu. For transport details, see left.

The Crater Lakes
The landscape south of Fort Portal is dotted with picturesque crater lakes, all of which offer great **walking** and exploration opportunities. There are several accommodation options throughout the area, although further south they dry up fast. Most of the lodges and guesthouses can help out with suggestions for walks and activities in the area, and it is increasingly popular for visitors to stay in the lakes area before continuing on foot to Kibale Forest National Park and Bigodi Wetland Sanctuary.

Walking is not the only activity available. **Cycling** is also a rewarding option, as the roads wind their way around these beautiful lakes. The lakes are believed to be bilharzia-free, but that doesn't mean they're hippo- and crocodile-free – check with locals before plunging into the waters.

Also in this area is **Mahoma Waterfall**, small but attractive and a great spot for a natural power-shower.

LAKE NKURUBA
Probably the winner among the many contenders for title of most beautiful crater lake, this is one of the only lakes still surrounded entirely by dense tropical forest. Located about 20km south of Fort Portal, there are good **walking** opportunities from the camp site here, including a one-hour trek to Lake Nyabikere, from where you can continue to Rweteera and Kibale Forest National Park or Bigodi.

One of the best-known community projects in Uganda, everyone who stays at **Lake Nkuruba Community Camp Site** (☎ 077-814327; camping USh5000, dm USh10,000, lakeside cottage USh25,000; meals USh3000-6000) loves the place. Facilities are basic, but the team here is very friendly and the setting is perfect for a few days of relaxation. There are two areas in which to camp, one at the lake shore, with the other higher up the hillside with views of the surrounding landscape. The *bandas* are clean and comfortable, but function as dorms unless you pay for all the beds. There is also a more sophisticated lakeside cottage that offers more privacy. Bicycles are available for hire to explore the area at USh5000 per day. Filling meals are available (order in advance) and bread is also baked here. Limited supplies are also available in the village of Rwaihamba, a short distance away.

Shared taxis from Fort Portal to Kasenda or Rwaihamba pass Lake Nkuruba (USh2000), which is signposted on the left just before Rwaihamba. At least three vehicles a day do the trip, and on Monday and Thursday (market days in Rwaihamba) there's plenty of traffic.

LAKE NYINAMBUGA

This lake is located south of Lake Nkuruba and is another beautiful body of water ringed by forest. The luxurious **Ndali Lodge** (☎ 077-221309; www.ndali.co.uk; s/d US$180/250) is stunningly situated on a ridge above the lake, and offers accommodation in elegant cottages set around an attractive central restaurant. The views are breathtaking, with the Mountains of the Moon looming on the horizon, making it a great place for incurable romantics. Rates include full board and discounts are sometimes available in the low season.

LAKE NYABIKERE

Yet another beautiful and tranquil spot, this lake lies just off the road to Kibale Forest National Park, about 15km northwest of Kanyanchu visitor centre or 21km from Fort Portal. Dugout canoes are available from CVK Resort for exploring the lake.

A long running resort, **CVK Resort** (☎ 077-792274; ruyooka@forest.mak.ac.ug; camping US$3, s/d bandas US$15/30, s/d US$25/50) offers a bewildering choice of sleeping options at various prices depending on facilities. *Bandas* include the cheaper partly furnished option for US$6.

The rooms are a little ambitiously priced compared with what is on offer in Fort Portal, but they do have a better view. Like the other crater lake resorts, it is a good base for walking in the area, and community-related activities are also promoted here. There is also a restaurant (mains USh2000 to USh15,000) that serves tasty meals.

Semliki Valley

The Semliki Valley is a cracking natural corridor forming a link between the heights of East Africa and the vast steaming jungles of central Africa. The views on the descent into the valley from Fort Portal are breathtaking, sweeping across the rainforest and savanna of the Semliki Valley and into DR Congo.

The main attractions located in the valley are **Semuliki National Park** (admission 1/2/3 or more days US$15/25/30), with its hot springs, near Sempaya, and the **Batwa Pygmy villages** near Ntandi, a few kilometres before Bundibugyo. Semuliki National Park is a continuation of the huge Ituri Forest in DR Congo and includes some excellent bird-watching for central African species at their eastern limits, such as the Congo serpent eagle, although sightings are harder than in other parks due to the dense vegetation. There are also several primate species and some small mammals that are found nowhere else in East Africa. Another attraction at the park is the **hot springs**, although this is not Bogoria National Park (Kenya), and it's worlds away from the geysers of Rotorua (New Zealand) and Iceland. There is a walking trail around the springs and other trails through the forest.

The Pygmy villagers are seriously commercialised – their culture for sale – and all in all many find it a depressing proposition. Much of a visit will be spent with the villagers trying to find ways to help you part with your shillings. That said, they have been dispossessed of their ancestral lands by a government that generally views them with disdain, so they have little choice but to cash in on their culture. In some ways it is only this commercialisation process that ensures the survival of the pygmies as a distinct ethnic group within Uganda. The Batwa have always been at the bottom of the social pile and with much of their natural territory already turned over to forested national parks, such as Bwindi Impenetrable and

Mgahinga Gorilla, they have found it very hard to adapt to modern life. Ironically, it is tourism that has allowed them a way to be proud of their identity and culture, and make a bit of money from it at the same time. Either way, visits can end up taking on a 'human safari' feel, which is pretty unfortunate for everyone involved.

SLEEPING & EATING
Semuliki National Park headquarters (camping USh10,000) At Ntandi, this has a basic camp site for those with tents, but you need to be fairly self-sufficient.

Mpora Rural Family (☎ 0493-22636; mmorence@ yahoo.com; banda per person US$10) It is also possible to stay with this family near the Kichwamba Technical College, on the road to Bundibugyo. Morence Mpora has long been offering accommodation in an effort to help finance the orphanage he runs. The rate for the *banda,* including three meals a day, is very good value. Minibus drivers can drop you off at the technical college.

GETTING THERE & AWAY
There are regular shared taxis and pick-ups between Fort Portal and Bundibugyo, which are a cheap way to go if you don't mind staying a night or two out of town. To get to the park headquarters from Fort Portal costs an USh3500 and to Bundibugyo USh5000. Hitching isn't easy, as there is not all that much traffic. If you are travelling in a small group, it might be best to charter a special-hire taxi or minibus, although don't forget to bargain.

Semliki Valley Game Reserve
Often referred to on older maps as Toro Game Reserve, the **Semliki Valley Game Reserve** (admission per person one/two/three days US$15/25/30) was once one of the best-stocked wildlife parks in Africa. It was the first gazetted game reserve in Uganda and by the 1960s was one of the most popular parks in East Africa. However, the years of civil war took their toll and after the war with Tanzania, the Tanzanian soldiers went home with truckloads of dead bush-meat. Now wildlife is slowly starting to recover and there are plans to reintroduce some lost species. Currently you can expect to encounter kobs, bushbucks, buffaloes, elephants and colobus monkeys. A number of lions have also recently returned

to the reserve, most likely refugees from the conflict in the DR Congo, and leopards are sighted quite regularly. For bird-watchers, there is a range of species found within the park, including the elusive shoebill stork on the shores of Lake Albert. A **chimpanzee habituation project** has been under way in the reserve for almost a decade now, offering yet another activity for visitors.

Wildlife drives, chimp tracking and boat excursions on Lake Albert can be arranged through Semliki Safari Lodge. The wildlife drives include the daunting option of a foot safari through a dense forest of bamboo, where you may encounter buffaloes or elephants. Visibility is no more than about five metres, so the chances of a charge or stand-off are very real.

SLEEPING & EATING
Semliki Safari Lodge (The Uganda Safari Company; ☎ 041-251182; www.safariuganda.com; s/d with full board US$198/298; ▨) A decade on from its birth, this luxurious lodge is still one of the finest properties in Uganda. Luxury tents are set under thatched *bandas,* and have Persian carpets, four-poster beds and bathrooms with reliable hot water. The lounge and dining room feature a huge eaved roof, with plush furnishings, Congolese crafts and plenty of room to relax. There is also a small swimming pool for cooling off.

Campsite (per person USh10,000) There is now a small UWA campsite near Ntoroko on the shores of Lake Albert, but bring your own supplies.

GETTING THERE & AWAY
Most visitors arrive at Semliki Safari Lodge by light aircraft from Kampala as part of an all-inclusive package. However, it is possible to get here by road from Fort Portal, a bumpy journey taking about two hours. First take the road for Bundibugyo and then fork right at Karagutu, 30km down the valley. Another 25km of rough track brings you to the lodge. It can just about be done in a regular car, but not in the wet season. Independent travellers will have a hard time getting here and are probably best off chartering a vehicle from Fort Portal.

Katonga Wildlife Reserve
This small **wildlife reserve** (admission US$10) is home to the very elusive Sitatunga antelope,

which is known for its curious webbed feet. Few visitors make it here, as it isn't particularly close to other major attractions. Much of the park is swampland and a canoe trip (USh15,000) is possible for exploring the wetlands. There is a very basic **camp site** (per person USh5000), but no *bandas*. Getting here involves taking a bus as far as Kyegegwa on the road between Fort Portal and Kampala, and then picking up a minibus heading south on the reasonable gravel road to Katonga.

KASESE
☎ 0483

Kasese is a boom-and-bust town that tasted glory during the copper years and more recently had a short-lived renaissance thanks to cobalt, but generally seems to have passed its use-by-date. It is the base from which to organise an assault on the Rwenzori Mountains, but there's absolutely no other reason to visit – it's a small, hot, dusty, quiet town in a relatively infertile and lightly populated area, and it wears an air of permanent torpor. However, it was once crucial to the economy because of the nearby copper mines at Kilembe, though these are long closed. As if that wasn't bad enough, even the train line to Kampala is no longer operating. Thankfully for the town, the Rwenzori Mountains have reopened, otherwise tourism would go the way of the minerals here – into history.

Information

There are several cardphones around town for international calls, but for faxes try the post office.

Centenary Rural Development Bank (Portal Rd) Represents Western Union for those that suddenly decide they must conquer the mountains but lack the hefty US$567 required.

Reroc Internet (Rwenzori Rd; per min USh100) Offer slow Internet connection.

Rwenzori Mountaineering Services (RMS; ☎ 0483-44936/078-325431; rwenzorims@yahoo.co.uk; PO Box 33, Kasese) Has an information and booking office (open daily) located beneath the Saad Hotel. This is the place to make arrangements for trekking or climbing the Rwenzori Mountains (p516).

Rwenzori Mountains National Park Office (Rwenzori Rd) Offers information on climbing the mountains. Most punters pay their fees in advance at the UWA headquarters in Kampala, but it is possible to pay here for those making the decision at short notice.

Stanbic Bank (Rwenzori Rd) The best place to change cash and travellers cheques, if it still changes the latter.

Sleeping & Eating

Mariana Hotel (☎ 077-493414; 17 Stanley St; s/d with bathroom USh17,500/35,000) When it comes to clean and comfortable midrange hotels, the Mariana is the pick of the pack. Set on a popular hotel strip, the well-tended rooms include a bathroom and a balcony. Downstairs is a lively little bar and basic restaurant.

Saad Hotel (☎ 0483-44139; Rwenzori Rd; r in old/new wing USh17,000/27,000; 🏊) Once the most popular place to stay in town, the rooms are in need of a little tender loving care these days. Still, they remain pretty good value, as the old doubles come with bathroom, and the 'newer' ones with carpets and air-con for good measure. Downstairs is a reasonable restaurant, but no alcohol is served, shocking if you have just spent seven days in the mountains.

Ataco Holiday Inn (Stanley St; s/d USh7000/11,000) No, don't get excited, it's definitely not part of the famous international chain, though it does have the smartest of the cheap rooms in town for those on a budget.

Margherita Hotel (☎ 0483-44015; reco@swift uganda.com; s/d from US$40/50) This is the fanciest hotel in town, the only problem being that it is not really in town, but 3km out on the road up to Kilembe. All the rooms are now very smart, making it a popular choice with those who have already shelled out a lot for their trek. The hotel has a delightful setting looking out towards the Rwenzoris on one side and the golf course on the other, surrounded by flowering trees. The restaurant (mains around USh7000) serves decent grub, and rates include breakfast.

Good Times Restaurant (Stanley St; meals USh1000-2000) Pretty much opposite the Saad Hotel, this local joint knocks together huge portions of cheap Ugandan standards and is great value for a filling feed.

Titi's Supermarket (Rwenzori Rd) Currently the best-stocked supermarket in Kasese, this is a useful port of call for those heading up the Rwenzori Mountains, although it's hardly up to Shoprite's standards in Kampala.

Drinking & Entertainment

If you are bored to tears by day, impressions change by night. Kasese draws people in from surrounding villages as far away as

UGANDA

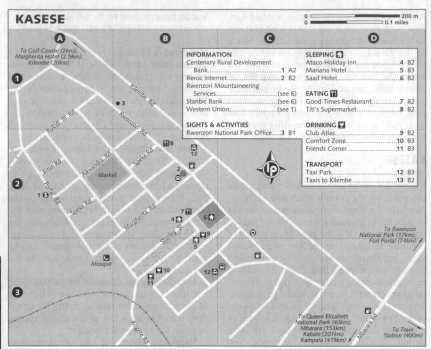

KASESE

0   200 m
0   0.1 miles

INFORMATION			SLEEPING		
Centenary Rural Development			Ataco Holiday Inn	4	B2
Bank	1	A2	Mariana Hotel	5	B3
Reroc Internet	2	B2	Saad Hotel	6	B2
Rwenzori Mountaineering					
Services	(see 6)		EATING		
Stanbic Bank	(see 6)		Good Times Restaurant	7	B2
Western Union	(see 1)		Titi's Supermarket	8	B2

SIGHTS & ACTIVITIES			DRINKING		
Rwenzori National Park Office	3	B1	Club Atlas	9	B2
			Comfort Zone	10	B3
			Friends Corner	11	B3

			TRANSPORT		
			Taxi Park	12	B3
			Taxis to Kilembe	13	B2

To Golf Course (2km);
Margherita Hotel (2.5km);
Kilembe (20km)

To Rwenzori
National Park (17km);
Fort Portal (74km)

To Queen Elizabeth
National Park (40km);
Mbarara (153km);
Kabale (201km);
Kampala (419km)

To Train
Station (400km)

the DR Congo. Wednesday night is ladies' night in town, while it really gets going on the weekend.

The best bars in town are on Stanley St. Always busy Comfort Zone has some pool tables, although you might get hustled. Next door, Friends Corner screens big football games and has a lively crowd.

Club Atlas (Stanley St; admission USh2000; ☺ Wed & Fri) The most happening place in town – perhaps a bit too happening if you happen to be staying in the nearby Saad Hotel. Entry is free for women on Wednesday and it rocks on until dawn.

Getting There & Away

The EMS Post Bus runs from Kampala to Kasese daily, via Mbarara. For more information, see p485.

There are daily buses in both directions between Kasese and Kampala via Mbarara (USh12,000, about seven hours).

There's also a daily bus in both directions between Fort Portal and Kabale via Kasese and Mbarara. It starts from Fort Portal at 6am, arriving in Kasese at about 8am. It then continues on to Kabale (about five hours). The fare from Kasese to Kabale is USh10,000.

There are frequent minibuses to Fort Portal (USh3000, one hour) and Mbarara (USh6000, two hours).

Getting to Queen Elizabeth National Park is straightforward. Catch a Mbarara minibus and ask for the national park entrance, which is signposted on the left just before the village of Katunguru. From here hitch into the park, although you may have to wait a while for a lift.

RWENZORI MOUNTAINS NATIONAL PARK

The legendary, mist-covered Rwenzori Mountains on Uganda's western border with the DR Congo were once as popular with travellers as Mt Kilimanjaro and Mt Kenya, but they are definitely a more demanding climb. Closed during much of the 1990s, they have been open since 2001 and are again luring trekkers to the challenge. They have a well-deserved reputation for being very wet at times. This was best summed up by a comment on the wall of Bujuku hut: 'Jesus came here to learn how to walk on water. After five days, anyone could do it'. Take warm, waterproof clothing.

The mountain range, which is not volcanic, stretches for about 100km. At its centre are several mountains that are permanently snow- and glacier-covered: Mt Speke (Vittorio Emmanuele is its highest peak at 4890m); Mt Baker (Edward is its highest peak at 4843m); Mt Gessi (Iolanda, 4715m); Mt Emin (4791m); and Mt Luigi di Savoia (4627m). The three highest peaks in the range are Margherita (5109m), Alexandria (5083m) and Albert (5087m), all on Mt Stanley.

Information

Seven days is the standard for a trek through the range, but climbers need to add a day or two to reach the peaks. It can be done in six days at a push. The best times to trek are from late December to the end of February, and from mid June to mid August, when there's less rain. Even at these times, the higher reaches are often enveloped in mist, though this generally clears for a short time each day. October is considered the wettest month.

Walking trails and huts are in pretty good shape thanks to significant USAID help in the 1990s. The huts have essentials, such as kitchens, walls and roofs, and there's a wooden pathway over the bog and bridges over the larger rivers. All this has been done to lessen the impact of walkers on the fragile environment.

Some mountaineering experience is really required to reach one of the main summits. The routes to the peaks on Mts Stanley and Baker all cross snow and glaciers, and require the use of ice-axes, ropes and crampons, plus a competent guide. In the right conditions, the summit of Mt Speke is an easier proposition, but it still requires some mountain experience.

Be aware of the dangers of Acute Mountain Sickness (AMS). In extreme cases it can be fatal. See p647 for more information.

BOOKS & MAPS

Before attempting a trek in the Rwenzori Mountains, it is strongly recommended that you seek out a copy of *Rwenzori – Map & Guide* by Andrew Wielochowski. This is an excellent large-scale contour map of the mountains, with all the main trails, huts and camp sites marked (as well as other features).

On the reverse side of the map are detailed descriptions of the various possible treks, as well as sections on history, flora and fauna, weather and climate, necessary equipment and advice in the event of an accident. However, do bear in mind that the practical information is very dated.

Lonely Planet's *Trekking in East Africa* is useful for those requiring detailed practical information on trekking in the Rwenzori Mountains.

For a sublime souvenir once you have conquered the peaks, check out the coffee-table book, *Uganda Rwenzori* by David Pluth, also available in recommended Kampala bookshops.

FOOD & EQUIPMENT

Prepare for the Rwenzori Mountains trek in Kasese, where there is a reasonable selection of food, as well as equipment for rent from **Rwenzori Mountaineering Services** (RMS; ☎ 0483-44936/078-325431; rwenzorims@yahoo .co.uk). The RMS office organises guides and porters, hires equipment (see the table, p518) and arranges transport to the trail head at Ibanda/Nyakalengija, off the Kasese–Fort Portal road. RMS also controls all the facilities on the mountain, as guides and porters are compulsory for anything other than a short day walk. However, bookings should be made through the **UWA head office** (☎ 0483-346287; www.uwa.or.ug) in Kampala.

As far as food supplies are concerned, be warned that the variety of food available in Kasese is limited. If there's anything you particularly want to eat on the trek or you have any special requirements, bring these items with you; don't assume they can be bought in Kasese. Bring a camp cooker of some description, as fires are banned in the park. Kerosene and methylated spirits are readily available in Kasese.

No special equipment is required for a trek if you don't go onto the ice or snow, but bring clothing that is warm and waterproof, and a decent pair of walking boots. Sneakers or trainers are definitely not recommended – your feet will get soaked walking through the bogs, making you cold and miserable all day.

UGANDA

A waterproof jacket is an essential item, as it's almost impossible to stay dry in these mountains. Waterproof trousers (or at least a waterproof covering) are also advisable. Your extra clothing, sleeping bag and perishable food should be wrapped in strong plastic bags to protect them from the elements. A small day pack is useful if porters are going to be carrying the bulk of your equipment.

Since night temperatures often drop below zero, you'll need a good sleeping bag, an insulating sleeping mat and suitable warm clothing. This should include a warm hat (up to 30% of body heat is lost through your head).

Don't forget insect repellent, maximum-protection sunscreen, sunglasses, a torch (flashlight), water bottle, first-aid kit, cutlery and a cup.

EQUIPMENT HIRE

The RMS has the following equipment for hire in Kasese:

Item	Cost per trek (USh)
climbing boots	15,000
closed-cell mat	5000
crampons	15,000
gaiters	5000
harness	20,000
ice-axe	15,000
raincoat	5000
rope	20,000
rubber boots	5000
sleeping bag	20,000

GUIDES, PORTERS & FEES

Since the park reopened, fees just keep on rising, surprising given visitor numbers haven't returned to their old levels yet. It now costs US$567 for a seven-day trek, including park entrance, rescue fees, guides, porters, accommodation, heating fuel and VAT. Extra days for climbing the peaks attract extra charges as follows: US$20 for park entrance per day, US$5 per porter per stage, US$7 per guide per stage and US$15 for accommodation per night. The US$567 fee includes two porters per person, who can carry a total of 25kg, additional porters cost US$35. This price does not include transport to/from the trail head (USh10,000 return).

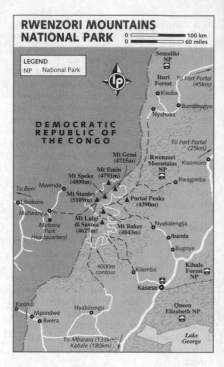

RWENZORI MOUNTAINS NATIONAL PARK

LEGEND
NP   National Park

Ascending the peaks costs extra and assumes an additional two days in the mountains. Charges cost US$692 for Margherita to US$656 for Speke.

Those extending their trip for extra days should also note that guides' and porters' fees are per *stage* not per day. The stages are: Ibanda/Nyakalengija to Nyabitaba; Nyabitaba to John Mate; John Mate to Bujuku; Bujuku to Kitandara (or to Irene Lakes, Speke Peak or Margherita); Elena Hut to Margherita; Kitandara to Guy Yeoman (or to Baker or Lugigi); Guy Yeoman to Nyabitaba; and Nyabitaba to Ibanda/Nyakalengija. Walk two stages in the day, pay for two stages that day.

Remember that to have a good trip, it is best to befriend the guides and porters. These people are drawn from the Bakonjo, a hardy but friendly mountain people, most of whom have Biblical names. They'll be staying in rock shelters overnight while you stay in the huts, so be generous with small handouts and give a decent tip at the end of the journey. See the Kilimanjaro entry (p176) for tipping suggestions.

Routes

Ibanda or Nyakalengija is the starting point for a trek in the Rwenzori Mountains. There are two basic trails up the mountain starting from here that pass between the peaks of Mt Baker and Mt Stanley. They both have the same approach as far as Nyabitaba Hut on the first day. After that you can go either clockwise or anticlockwise between the peaks. There are quite a few other minor trails, both up the mountain and across the top to Mutwanga in the DR Congo – the border essentially crosses the peaks, although crossing the frontier this way is illegal.

The following description applies to the clockwise route (the anticlockwise route is the reverse).

STAGE 1

Nyakalengija to Nyabitaba Hut (2650m), the first stage, is a fairly easy walk taking four to five hours.

STAGE 2

From Nyabitaba Hut, take either the old route to Guy Yeoman Hut (3450m, five to six hours) or the new safer route (seven hours). Along the new route, there is also the choice of staying at Kuruguta Hut/camp site (2940m). The route passes through tropical vegetation, over two minor streams, across the Mahoma River and finally up the side of a steep valley to the ridge on which the hut is situated.

STAGE 3

From Guy Yeoman Hut, the route passes through a bog to the Kabamba rock shelter (3450m) and waterfall, then via the Bujongolo rock shelter and the Freshfield Pass (4215m) to the Kitandara Hut (3990m). This takes about seven hours. The hut is picturesquely situated on the shore of the lake of the same name.

STAGE 4

This is the most interesting part of the trek. After leaving the twin Kitandara lakes, the trail climbs over boulders at the foot of Mt Baker on the one side and the glaciers of Savoia and Elena on the other. From here it crosses Scott Elliot Pass (4372m) and continues down to Bujuku Hut (3900m). The walk takes about four hours. If you are scaling the heights of Mt Stanley, on the other

hand, you will continue climbing to Elena Hut (4547m), in which case both you and your guide and porters will need appropriate equipment to deal with ice and snow.

STAGE 5

Assuming you don't scale Mt Stanley, the trek from Bujuku Hut to John Mate Hut (3350m) is all downhill. The walk takes about five hours. En route you pass Bigo Hut (3400m), where you have the option of taking a difficult track north leading to Mt Gessi, Mt Emin and Lac de la Lune via a series of bogs. There are also three bogs between Bujuku Hut and John Mate Hut, but it's here you'll come across stands of giant heather, groundsel and bamboo. Should you decide to spend the night at Bigo Hut, it sleeps up to 12 people and there is room for tents.

STAGE 6

From John Mate Hut, it's downhill again along a rough track to Nyabitaba (about five hours).

STAGE 7

The final stage is the return to Nyakalengija (about four to five hours) and onward travel to Kasese.

Organised Treks

If it's time rather than money that is limited, safari companies in Kampala can make all the bookings in advance of your arrival. **Adrift**

(The Adventure Centre; ☎ 041-252720, 077-454206; www
.surfthesource.com; Kira Rd) is now organising climbing trips in the Rwenzoris to add mountaineering to its stable of adrenaline activities.

Sleeping

Ruboni Community Campsite (camping USh10,000,
cottages USh30,000) For a cheaper taste of the
Rwenzoris, this community-run place near
the Nyakalengija park entrance offers a couple of comfortable cottages and camping facilities. It has an attractive setting outside
the park boundary, so there are no park
fees to pay. There is also now a restaurant
(mains USh2000 to USh5000) here serving
local food and international snacks. Contact
Ucota (☎ 041-501866; www.ucota.or.ug) in Kampala
for more details.

Tour Holiday Inn Ibanda (☎ 0483-44068; s/d
USh15,000/25,000) The only accommodation in
central Ibanda, this little lodge has basic but
comfortable rooms, plus meals are available.

Getting There & Away

The easiest way to access the Rwenzoris is to
catch a minibus (USh1500) from Kasese to
the park headquarters at Ibanda. From here
you can walk to the park entrance or take a
boda-boda (USh1500) to Ruboni Community
Campsite. It is possible to charter a special-
hire taxi from Kasese (about USh20,000) or
organise a vehicle with RMS.

QUEEN ELIZABETH NATIONAL PARK

Covering almost 2000 sq km, and bordered
to the north by the Rwenzori Mountains and
to the west by Lake Edward, this **national
park** (admission per person per 1/2/3 or more days US$20/
30/50, local/foreign cars USh10,000/US$20, local/foreign
4WDs USh20,000/US$40) is one of the most popular
in Uganda.

Queen Elizabeth National Park was once
a magnificent place to visit, with its great
herds of elephants, buffaloes, kobs, waterbucks, hippos and topis. However, like
Murchison Falls National Park, most of
the wildlife was wiped out by the retreating troops of Amin and Okello and by
the Tanzanian army, which occupied the
country after Amin's demise. They all did
their ivory-grabbing, trophy-hunting best.
Thankfully, the animal numbers are recovering, although there is still far less wildlife
in the park compared with parks in Tanzania and Kenya. The park has the highest

number of mammal species in Uganda and
various antelopes are here in large numbers,
as well as buffaloes, hippos, elephants, leopards and lions. It is also popular with bird-
watchers, as it provides a habitat for more
than 600 species. The park is well worth
a visit to take the boat trip on the Kazinga
Channel, with its huge numbers of hippos.
In the east, Kyambura (Chambura) Gorge
is a beautiful scar of green running through
the savanna, a little Eden brimming with
chimpanzees and other primates.

Information

The main Katunguru gate is on the Mbarara
to Kasese road near the small village of Katunguru, where the road crosses the Kazinga
Channel. From here it's 24km along a track
that follows the channel to Mweya in the
northwest of the park, where most of the
tourism activity, including a luxury lodge
and other budget accommodation, is based.
A much less visited area is that around Ishasha, in the southern part of the park on the
border with the DR Congo. The lions in this
area are famous for their habit of climbing
trees, and the setting is superb, although
check on the latest security before visiting,
due to its proximity to an unstable region
of the DR Congo. Some of the tracks in this
more remote section of the park can become
impassable during the wet season. However,
in the dry season it offers a convenient way
to combine a visit to Bwindi Impenetrable
National Park with Queen Elizabeth National Park. The Maramagambo Forest in
the southeastern section of the park includes a small tourism centre, camp site and
upmarket lodge.

Activities

KAZINGA CHANNEL LAUNCH TRIP

Almost every visitor takes a launch trip up
the Kazinga Channel to see the thousands of
hippos and the pelicans. With a little luck, it
is also possible to catch sight of one of the
elephant herds and very occasionally see a
lion or a leopard. The two-hour trip costs
US$10 per person or US$150 minimum for
the whole boat if numbers are low. There
are trips at 9am (the best time), 11am, 3pm
and 5pm. The 3pm trip is US$10 per person
even if numbers are low. Bookings can be
made at Mweya Safari Lodge (p522), and
the trips leave from just below the lodge.

QUEEN ELIZABETH NATIONAL PARK

KYAMBURA (CHAMBURA) GORGE WALKING SAFARI

In the eastern corner of the park is the beautiful Kyambura (Chambura) Gorge, and walking safaris can be arranged at the small ranger post here. The gorge is home to a variety of primates, including chimpanzees, and these are often visible on the walking safaris, which last from three to five hours and cost US$30 per person; children under 15 years are not permitted. Bookings can be made at Mweya Safari Lodge or you can just show up.

WILDLIFE DRIVES

There is a small network of trails around Mweya Safari Lodge and Katunguru gate that usually reveal waterbucks, kobs, elephants

and occasional leopards. North of the road to Katwe there are some stunning craters within the park. **Baboon Cliffs** is a viewpoint that gives excellent views over the surrounding area. Kasenyi, in the northeast of the park, offers the best chance of spotting lions, although for the tree-climbers, it's a long haul south to Ishasha. Over in **Kyambura (Chambura) Game Reserve** there are some salt lakes, which attract flamingos in huge numbers. Vehicle hire is USh2500 per kilometre and ranger-guides cost US$5/10 per half/full day – money well spent, as predators can be hard to find.

FOREST WALKS

In the southeastern section of the park, guided forest walks are available in the

Maramagambo Forest – great if you enjoy bird-watching – for US$5/10 per half/full day.

Walks can also be arranged in **Kalinzu Forest**, which is a cheaper option as it lies outside the national park boundary. It contains numerous bird species (381 at the last count), several types of primates, including the rare L'Hoest monkey, and many varieties of butterfly. Guided walks here cost USh5000/6000 during the day/night.

Sleeping & Eating
MWEYA
The majority of places to stay are on the Mweya Peninsula close to Mweya Safari Lodge.

Mweya Safari Lodge (lodge ☎ 0483-44266, bookings ☎ 039 260260; www.mweyalodge.com; s/d with full board US$99/180; ☒) This sophisticated safari lodge has a stunning setting on the raised peninsula of Mweya, with excellent views over Lake Edward to the west and along the Kazinga Channel to the east. It is something of a lodge and hotel combined, making it perfect for a break from bush showers in the middle of a safari, as all rooms have full bathrooms and extras, such as TV and minibar. Sitting on the terrace with a cold drink at sunset is perfect and the swimming pool has an enviable setting. For a memorable meal, à la carte dining is available at the classy restaurant here (meals USh8000 to USh15,000). Even for non-guests, it's a must for a sundowner and a full spread one night. Book ahead during peak season and weekends, as the lodge gets very busy. Watch out for the mongooses that scamper around; at night hippos linger on the lawns, so watch where you're walking!

Students' Camp (dm USh10,000, camping USh10,000) The cheapest beds are here, but it is very basic and the chances are that it will be full of Ugandan schoolchildren on educational visits. Campers should be vigilant at night, as hippos wander through here.

Ecology Institute (dm USh15,000, r per person USh20,000) This is the more reliable option for actually finding a cheap bed. The rooms are spartan but cleanly kept and include access to shared bathrooms. Said shared bathrooms are sometimes subject to insect infestation at night, however, so take sandals on a toilet run.

Tembo Canteen (meals USh2500-5000) Located at the Students' Camp, this is where the safari drivers hang out. It serves decent meals, but it is best to order in advance as service can be slow. There are also basic food supplies available in the nearby shop.

ISHASHA
Ishasha Camp (camping USh10,000, banda s/d USh10,000/15,000) In the remote southern area of the park there are basic *bandas* here, as well as camp sites. Access is pretty tough without your own wheels.

MARAMAGAMBO FOREST
Camp site (camping USh10,000) Set right at the foot of the Kichwamba Escarpment, but is a bit out of the way to draw independent travellers.

Jacana Camp (s/d with full board US$87/150; ☒) A furnished tented camp, quite luxurious if a little rustic, offering striking views over Lake Nyamusingiri. Facilities include a swimming pool and sauna. This is a charming spot to stay for those on an upmarket safari. It's operated by **Inns of Uganda** (☎ 041-258273; www.innsofuganda.com).

KALINZU FOREST
Kalinzu Forest Reserve (admission for 1/2 days USh6000/9000; camping per night USh2500, 2 nights USh4000) Camping is possible here. The entry fee is a lot cheaper than the charge for Queen Elizabeth National Park; and community projects in villages around the reserve receive 40% of the entry fees. To get here, turn off the Kasese road at Butare village and after 10km you come to the Kalinzu ecotourism site. In the wet season you will need a 4WD to get here.

Getting There & Away
Any vehicle travelling between Mbarara and Kasese passes through Katunguru. There are regular minibuses from Katunguru to Kasese (USh3000, one hour) and Mbarara (USh5000, two hours). Hitching out of the park from Mweya is easy – just stand by the barrier at Mweya Safari Lodge. Better still, try to make arrangements the night before at the lodge. Hitching into the park can be much harder, although weekends are not too bad. If traffic is thin, it may be necessary to charter a vehicle from Katunguru for about USh20,000 plus the vehicle entry fee.

For Maramagambo Forest, get off the bus or shared taxi at the village of Ndekye, south of Katunguru, from where a 10km path leads through small villages to Mara-magambo (also known locally as Nyamus-ingiri, after the lake here). Ask locals for directions.

The road from Katunguru to the village of Ishasha cuts through the park and passes Ishasha gate. Although it is not necessary to pay any park entry fees to travel this road, you'll be fined USh100,000 if you're caught venturing off it and into the park. From Ishasha, you can head south for Butogota and Bwindi Impenetrable National Park; it takes around five hours to drive from Bwindi to Mweya in the dry season.

Both Mweya Safari Lodge and Jacana Camp offer inclusive three-day safaris with transport, accommodation and meals, which work out to be good value.

BWINDI IMPENETRABLE NATIONAL PARK

Also known as the Impenetrable Forest, **Bwindi** (admission per 1/2/3 or more days US$20/30/50) is one of Uganda's most recently created national parks. It is in the southwest of the country, very close to the DR Congo border. The park, which covers 331 sq km, encompasses one of the last remaining habitats of the mountain gorilla, and is where almost half – an estimated 330 individuals – of the surviving mountain gorillas in the world live. However, more recently experts have decided the Bwindi gorillas may be a distinct subspecies, different from the mountain gorillas of the Virungas. Bwindi was the main place in East Africa for seeing the mountain gorillas during Rwanda's troubled years, but these days Parc National des Volcans, and even Parc National des Virungas in DR Congo, are also drawing visitors in numbers again.

Bwindi hit the headlines in March 1999 when the kidnap and subsequent murder of eight tourists tarnished Uganda's image. In light of this dreadful incident, gorilla bookings nose dived and security was upgraded significantly. There is now a large, invisible army presence down here and it is considered safe to visit. However, given what once took place here, it doesn't hurt to check in Kampala for the latest security situation at Bwindi.

A major conservation effort has been going on here for a number of years to protect the gorillas' habitat. As a result, encroachment on the montane forest by cultivators has been stopped, poaching has ceased and the gorilla families have been gradually habituated to human contact.

Gorillas are not the only animals to have benefited from this project. The park contains about 20 forest elephants, at least 10 species of primate (including chimpanzees, colobus monkeys and baboons), duikers, bushbucks and the rare giant forest hog, as well as a host of bird and insect species. It is one of the richest areas in Africa for flora and fauna.

For bird-watchers it is one of the most exciting destinations in the country, with more than 300 species of bird. These include 23 of the 24 Albertine rift endemics and several endangered species, including the African green broadbill, but it might not be easy to spot many birds because of the density of their habitat.

The park headquarters is at Buhoma on the northern edge of the park. The gorilla visits start from here and this is where all the accommodation is located. There is also a new sector at Nkuringo in the south of the park. Be aware that this area is rainforest, and not surprisingly it rains a hell of a lot – be prepared.

There are no vehicle charges here, as vehicles are not allowed to proceed beyond park headquarters.

For more on Bwindi, pick up a copy of *Mgahinga Gorilla National Park & Bwindi Impenetrable National Park*, available from UWA headquarters in Kampala.

Activities
GORILLA TRACKING

There are now four habituated groups of gorillas in Bwindi Impenetrable National Park: three groups are located within walking distance of Buhoma, while the newest Nkuringo group are located in the south of the park, accessible only from Kisoro. At the time of research, the Mubare group has 10 individuals, the Habinyanja group 18 individuals and the Rushegura group 10 individuals. Eight tourists per day can visit each family, which adds up to a total of 24 permits per day available at Bwindi. The Nkuringo group numbers 19 individuals and a further eight permits are available here. However, the chances are an upmarket lodge will be opening at Nkuringo early in the lifetime of this book and it will be given the bulk of the permits, leaving only standby permits for independent travellers.

The bad news is that demand generally far exceeds supply for most of the year. The big safari companies often book blocks of permits months in advance, meaning that for the individual visitor it can be difficult to get a confirmed place. All bookings must be made through the **UWA office** (☎ 041-346287; www.uwa.or.ug; 7 Kira Rd) in Kampala, although staff will often tell you that there are no vacancies for days at a time. Be persistent, call around at backpacker places in Kampala and Jinja, where cancellations are often advertised, or, if necessary, turn up at the park and see if there are any no-shows.

Gorilla-trekking permits cost US$360, including the park entry fee, payable in US dollars cash only. The trips leave at 8.30am daily, but aim to report to park headquarters by 8am. Note that children under 15 years old are not permitted to trek to the gorillas, and anyone with a cold or other illness is likewise excluded. Do not try to feign good health if you are unwell, as you could be endangering these rare creatures' lives. A full refund is given to anyone who withdraws due to ill health.

Once you finally join a tracking group, the chances of finding the gorillas are excellent. The terrain in Bwindi Impenetrable National Park is mountainous and heavily forested; if the gorillas are a fair distance from Buhoma, it can be quite a challenge reaching them. On a lucky day it might be less than one hour to reach them, but if you are unlucky, it could take four hours or more. Make sure you are in good enough shape. The time you actually spend with the gorillas once you find them is limited to one hour, and not a minute more. It is pretty dark in the forest of Bwindi, so photo opportunities are limited without fast film.

For more information on the mountain gorillas, their habitat, where to see them and responsible tracking, see p100. It is essential to check out this section for a compare and contrast, and where to track the gorillas... Uganda, Rwanda or the DR Congo.

FOREST WALKS

The park headquarters at Buhoma is in a beautiful setting, and there are several walks in the area that are well worth the time. Most take pretty much half a day, but there is a short loop just outside the park for those who want a taste but don't have much time. For the walks inside the park, the cost is US$5/10 for a half/full day (in addition to the park entry fee) and a ranger accompanies all walkers.

The **Waterfall trail** includes, surprise, surprise, a 33m waterfall on the Munyaga River. It's a fairly strenuous walk that takes about three hours return.

The **Muzabijiro Loop trail** gives excellent views south to the Virunga volcanoes and the western Rift Valley in the DR Congo, weather permitting. It also takes about three hours.

The **Buhoma village tourist walk** is very popular, and includes a section of relic forest and a look at the local lifestyle. Proceeds from this walk are ploughed back into the community to improve lives. There are also several community handicraft projects already underway in the village – check out the small shops for a souvenir wooden gorilla.

Sleeping & Eating
BUHOMA

Given that there are only 24 gorilla permits per day available, there are a whole lot of lodges competing for business. Most of the upmarket lodges cater to guests on safari and several almost exclusively work with their own clients. There are a couple of tiny hotels scattered throughout Buhoma village, but these are primarily catering for local drivers on safari with their clients.

Buhoma Community Rest Camp (camping US$3, bandas per person US$10) Enjoying a beautiful setting right next to park headquarters, this is by far the most popular budget deal at Bwindi. All profits go towards funding community-development projects. Bandas come in a variety of shapes and sizes, and represent good value. Hot water is available by the bucket – good news on a cool day. There is also a small canteen and bar here.

Gorilla View Rest Camp (camping USh5000, dm USh10,000, banda s/d USh12,000/15,000) Quite literally opposite the community camp, this banda operation is pretty much the same sort of deal, but without the feelgood factor of channelling the proceeds into community development.

Buhoma Homestead (s/d with full board US$100/170) Another spot located inside the park boundary, this private set-up has recently been taken over by **Wild Frontiers** (www.wild frontiers.co.ug) in Kampala. Being brutally honest, these prices are pretty poor value compared with what is on offer elsewhere in Uganda, but then this is Bwindi and the gorilla permits aren't cheap either. Upgrade to the next level if you can afford it.

Volcanoes Safaris (☎ 041-346464; www.volcanoes safaris.com; s/d with full board US$240/360) For a dramatic setting this camp is hard to beat, situated opposite the wall of green that is the Impenetrable Forest. The old tents have been replaced by luxury *bandas*, although not necessarily luxurious enough to justify the hefty price tag. The restaurant has a good menu and the staff are very welcoming.

Mantana African Safaris (☎ 041-321552; mantana@ africaonline.co.ug; s/d with full board US$110/180) A little way out from the main concentration of camps, Mantana runs a small, luxury tented camp. The tents are about as good as it gets for camping, including hot water and electricity, and very atmospheric at night with the soundtrack of the forest nearby.

Gorilla Forest Camp (☎ 041-340290; gfcamp@ africaonline.co.ug; s/d with full board US$260/416) Run by the bespoke travel company Abercrombie & Kent, this is the ultimate jungle camp, offering opulent tents complete with grand beds, luxury bathrooms and forest views. It really is spectacular, but at these prices most of us will be taking a peek rather than enjoying the sleep.

Most visitors at Bwindi tend to eat meals where they are staying. Most of the fancier places are with full board, so this is no surprise. At the budget end, there are a couple of local spots knocking together cheap food, but they are nothing special.

BUTOGOTA

This is where the direct bus from Kampala terminates, so some travellers get stuck in Butogota on the way to Bwindi, although there is absolutely no reason to stay here if it can be avoided.

Butogota Travellers Inn (s/d USh20,000/30,000) The prices are a little ambitious for what is essentially a spit and sawdust kind of show… perhaps it has been inspired by some of the places at Bwindi.

Pineapple Lodge (s/d USh6000/8000) Although it's more basic, at least it has a basic understanding of room pricing.

Getting There & Away

Butogota is the nearest village to Buhoma and is the closest place to the park with public transport links. Without transport it's too far from the park to use as a base for gorilla trekking, but some travellers spend a night here en route from Kabale or Kampala before walking or hitching the 17km to Buhoma the next day, and visiting the gorillas the day after. It's a lot of time to squander given that pick-ups (USh20,000) or motorcycles (USh10,000) can be chartered to Bwindi.

There is a direct Silverline bus daily in each direction between Kampala and Butogota, which goes via Kisizi. It leaves Kampala pretty early (6.30am), arriving in Butogota around dark; the fare is USh18,000. Slightly faster, but slightly more complicated is to take a bus to Kihihi (USh16,000) and change there for a pick-up to Butogota (USh2000).

The other alternative is the irregular pick-ups and shared taxis that connect Kabale and Butogota (USh9000), but this is hardly straightforward. There are plenty available on Tuesday and Friday, but other days are a nightmare. If there is nothing from Kabale to Butogota, take a Kihihi shared taxi as far as Kanyantorogo, through which the bus from Kampala passes. If all else fails or you are in a group, charter a vehicle from Kabale – USh100,000 is quoted by locals in the know, but they are unlikely to take tourists for much under US$70, as they know how much a gorilla permit costs!

By private vehicle the better route is via Kabale, as you stay on the bitumen a lot longer. The turn-off to Bwindi/Buhoma is signposted off the road to Kisoro, and the trip from Kabale takes three to four hours. It's a very scenic road through mountainous rainforest.

KABALE
☎ 0486

Kabale is the biggest town in Kigezi district, dubbed the 'Switzerland of Africa' by tourist brochures and travellers alike, although there weren't many volcanoes in the Alps at last count. The 'New Zealand of Africa' could be closer to the mark. Whatever the comparisons, this southwestern corner of Uganda is undeniably beautiful, with its intensively cultivated and terraced hills, forests and lakes. There are breathtaking views of the Virunga chain of volcanoes from the

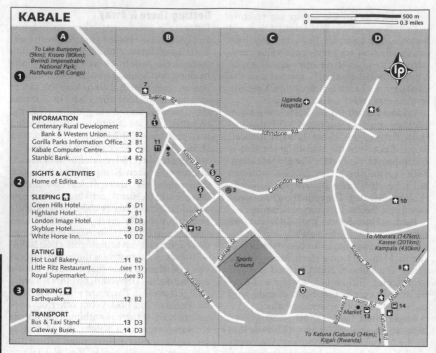

KABALE

0 ———— 500 m
0 ———— 0.3 miles

To Lake Bunyonyi
(9km); Kisoro (80km);
Bwindi Impenetrable
National Park;
Rutshuru (DR Congo)

Bugongi Rd

Uganda
Hospital

Johnstone Rd

Kisoro Rd

Corryndon Rd

Nyererere Dr

Garage St

Sports
Ground

Mutambuka Rd

Suspect Rd

Mbarara Rd

Kisoro Rd

Katuna Rd

Buteckwara St

Market

To Mbarara (147km);
Kasese (201km);
Kampala (430km)

To Katuna (Gatuna) (24km);
Kigali (Rwanda)

INFORMATION		
Centenary Rural Development		
Bank & Western Union	1	B2
Gorilla Parks Information Office	2	B1
Kabale Computer Centre	3	C2
Stanbic Bank	4	B2

SIGHTS & ACTIVITIES		
Home of Edirisa	5	B2

SLEEPING		
Green Hills Hotel	6	D1
Highland Hotel	7	B1
London Image Hotel	8	D3
Skyblue Hotel	9	D3
White Horse Inn	10	D2

EATING		
Hot Loaf Bakery	11	B2
Little Ritz Restaurant	(see 11)	
Royal Supermarket	(see 3)	

DRINKING		
Earthquake	12	B2

TRANSPORT		
Bus & Taxi Stand	13	D3
Gateway Buses	14	D3

summits of precarious passes, such as the Kanaba Gap, about 60km from Kabale on the road to Kisoro. There are also tea-growing estates all the way from Kabale to the Rwandan border at Katuna (Gatuna).

While Kabale itself is nothing to write home about, it is a handy base from which to explore some superb hiking country, as the area is honeycombed with tracks and paths, trading centres and farms. It is also the gateway to Lake Bunyoni, the number one spot for serious rest and relaxation in southwest Uganda. It's a good staging post for trips to the gorillas at Bwindi Impenetrable and, possibly, Mgahinga Gorilla National Parks.

Kabale is Uganda's highest town at about 2000m and can get pretty cool at night, so keep some warm clothes handy. Water pressure in town is intermittent at best, so you may want to check that water is likely to come out of the pipes before you strip off under a shower on a cold evening!

Information

For the fuller flavour of Kabale, pick up a copy of the *Lake Bunyoni & Kabale In Your Pocket* guide (USh1000), available at the Home of Edirisa (opposite).

Getting cash in Kabale has traditionally been a bit of a mess. Most foreign exchange bureaus and banks offer terrible rates compared with Kampala, about 15% or so lower. The best place to change travellers cheques is currently **Royal Supermarket** (Kisoro Rd), but coming with cash from Kampala is the safest bet.

The post office has international phone and fax services, and connections are reasonably reliable. There are also MTN cardphones spread throughout town.

Centenary Rural Development Bank (Kisoro Rd) The place to arrange a Western Union transfer.

Global Internet Café (Kisoro Rd; per min USh50) The leading local spot for Internet access.

Gorilla Parks Information Office (Kisoro Rd) The UWA maintains this office in Kabale, but as the staff cannot actually book gorilla trips here and are not in direct contact with either Bwindi Impenetrable or Mgahinga Gorilla National Parks, there's very little they can do. They are, however, in contact with the UWA head office in Kampala and know how many permits are already booked for each day, and are usually informed about cancellations.

Stanbic Bank (Kisoro Rd) Check here to see if decent exchange rates are available for travellers cheques now… it was going live during our visit.

Sights

Home of Edirisa (☎ 077-558558; www.edirisa.org; admission USh3000; ☉ 9am-11pm) Kabale's first and only museum, the main attraction here is a replica traditional homestead of the Bakiga tribe. Displays introduce visitors to the life and times of the Bakiga people, as museum founder Festo Karwemera is a Bakiga elder. There is also accommodation, food, a gift shop and Internet access, making it a lively little centre in Kabale.

Sleeping

BUDGET

There is a good range of budget accommodation in Kabale and several of the best places are slap-bang on top of each other near the taxi park.

Skyblue Hotel (☎ 0486-22154; Mbarara Rd; s/d USh8000/12,000) Part of a growing nationwide chain, service is slick here. All the rooms are named after the planets – if you are suffering with bad guts you might need to think about Uranus. Rooms are super clean with towel and soap provided and bucket hot water on request. There are also a few self-contained doubles available at USh20,000.

Home of Edirisa (☎ 077-558558; www.edirisa.org; dm USh3000, s/d USh5000/15,000) Experience the novelty of staying in a museum, plus it's free entry for guests! The dorms are cheaper than camping anywhere else in Uganda, while the bigger rooms are a good investment, as they include a bathroom. Facilities include a book exchange, and great shakes and coffees in the little café. Book ahead to avoid disappointment.

MIDRANGE

Highland Hotel (☎ 0486-22175; highland@imul.com; Kisoro Rd; s/d USh15,000/30,000) It's the perfect name given the rugged hills that surround the town, but they are no longer the perfect rooms, as they are showing their age these days. However, rates sort of reflect this and include breakfast. The staff are also pretty helpful, and the attached restaurant is one of the more reliable in town.

London Image Hotel (☎ 078-320488; 31 Mbarara Rd; s/d USh15,000/20,000, with bathroom USh25,000/30,000) Not the London image that is the

Dorchester or the Savoy, but then you'd hardly expect that in little old Kabale. But the rooms are a good size and the price is right. The friendly old matriarch runs a tight ship.

TOP END

White Horse Inn (☎ 0486-26010; fax 23717; Corryndon Rd; s/d/ste USh68,000/85,000/140,000) Tucked away near the golf course on the hill overlooking the town, this is Kabale's most famous address. It's an attractive place with verdant gardens, but its design definitely owes something to another era, including the furnishings, which could come straight out of a '70s porn flick. The hotel has a popular bar and restaurant, and rates include breakfast.

Green Hills Hotel (☎ 0486-24442; fax 24443; Suspect Rd; s/d 40,000/60,000; ☒) Across the other side of the golf course, Green Hills is clearly better value than the White Horse, thanks to its modern rooms, swimming pool, and new sauna and steam bath. Book ahead, as it often fills up with conference guests.

Eating

Among the aforementioned sleeping options, the Home of Edirisa has a good menu of Western-style snacks at exceedingly low prices, while the Skyblue Hotel does filling breakfasts and has a pretty good choice of meals for the provinces. The restaurant at the Highland Hotel has an open fire that could prove tempting on a cold night.

Hot Loaf Bakery (cakes from USh500) Kabale's main bakery, the Hot Loaf has great cakes, and also offers fresh bread, pizza and tasty samosas. Definitely a useful place to pick up some snacks for a long road journey to Bwindi or Kisoro.

Little Ritz Restaurant (meals USh3000-6000) Located directly above the Hot Loaf Bakery, this is the leading restaurant in town, offering an eclectic menu of Western, Indian and African dishes. Start the day with its 'BEST' breakfast – baked beans, egg, sausages and tomatoes. The attached bar screens major football matches.

Royal Supermarket (Kisoro Rd) Anyone planning to do a bit of self-catering at Bwindi or Lake Bunyoni should hit the Royal, the best-stocked supermarket in town.

Drinking & Entertainment

Kabale and bars don't exactly go together and most visitors drink at one of the hotels.

UGANDA

Earthquake (Nyerere Dr) Kabale isn't the dance capital of Africa, but it is home to the local disco that could just make the earth move under your feet. It only really rocks on the weekend, when it goes on into the small hours, and attracts a healthy provincial crowd of drunkards and hookers.

Getting There & Away

The EMS Post Bus operates daily, except Sunday, between Kabale and Kampala. For details, see p485.

There are numerous daily buses to Kampala, which take about six hours and cost USh12,000 to USh15,000 depending on the company. For Fort Portal, there's a daily bus via Mbarara and Kasese (USh12,000, about eight hours), but it leaves at the alarming hour of 4am.

Minibuses travel regularly between Kabale and Kisoro (USh7000, up to three hours). There are scheduled departures to Kisoro at 10am and 4pm. Otherwise, they go when full, and 'full' means exactly that! Most of them are dangerously overloaded, but the ride, over a very dusty road, is absolutely magnificent, offering superb views.

For all the difficult details on getting from Kabale to Bwindi, see p525.

For details about travel to Lake Bunyoni, see opposite.

There are also direct minibuses (USh1000, 30 minutes) and shared taxis (USh15,000) to the Rwandan border at Katuna (Gatuna) from near the Shell petrol station on the Katuna road. See p555 for details on getting to Kigali from Kabale or Kampala.

AROUND KABALE
Lake Bunyoni

A magical place, Lake Bunyoni's beguiling beauty defies description. Undoubtedly the most lovely lake in the country, Bunyoni has caught up with the Ssese Islands as *the* place for travellers to chill out on a long trip through Uganda, although chill might be the operative word, as the water temperature is quite cool. It is a large and irregularly shaped lake dotted with islands, and the surrounding hillsides are intensively cultivated like parts of Nepal. The area is ideal for activities, such as canoeing, cycling or hiking. Mark Bunyoni down as a must if you are travelling through southwest Uganda.

SIGHTS & ACTIVITIES

There are endless opportunities for activities in the Lake Bunyoni region. Many of the villagers, and several of the guesthouses and camp sites, have boats and it isn't difficult to arrange a trip on the lake. **Canoeing** is a popular activity and dugouts can be rented from most of the camps. Charges are pretty reasonable, but practise for a while before heading off on an ambitious trip around the islands, as many tourists end up going round and round in circles, doing what's known locally as the *mzungu* corkscrew.

There are endless walking opportunities in the area and for those who want a challenge, you can boat across the lake before trekking down to Kisoro. **Guided walks** are also popular and these can usually be arranged through camps here. However, if you want an easygoing amble along the shores of the lake, it is straightforward enough to find your own way.

Mountain bikes (per day USh10,000) can be hired from Bunyoni Overland Camp and are a great way to get along the lake shore, although getting to Kabale would require a king of the mountains, Tour de France style effort.

Kyevu market is held every Wednesday and Saturday, drawing villagers from all over the region. It is a long way from all the camps around the lake, and involves a three-hour trip by dugout. However, most of the camps should be able to arrange an oarsman to help out, or secure a motorboat for rent. The people out here are pretty shy, so be sensitive with a camera. There are also a number of Batwa villages in this part of the region and if you can link up with a friendly guide at the market, you might be able to arrange a visit to a Batwa community.

Nearer to the camps is **Punishment Island**, located midway between Bushara and Njuyera Islands; so named because it was once the place where unmarried pregnant women were dumped to die. Tragically, most of them did die trying to swim for shore, because they usually didn't have the stamina to make it. It is easy to spot – it has just one small tree in the centre.

SLEEPING & EATING

Lake Bunyoni is one of Uganda's most popular destinations for whiling away the days, and there is a good choice of resorts and camps, both on land or the nearby islands. Most places also have restaurants and bars offering food and drink.

Mainland

Bunyonyi Overland Camp (☎ 0486-23741; highland@ imul.com; camping USh6000, furnished tent s/d USh20,000/ 30,000, s/d USh25,000/35,000, s/d cottage USh30,000/ 50,000) One of the most attractive camps in Uganda, the wide range of accommodation, sculpted gardens and lakeside setting ensure this place is extremely popular with travellers and overland companies. Wannabe campers with no tent can rent one for USh8000, while the fixed double tents come fully furnished. Stepping up the style, there are some homey little cottages with attached bathroom. For those relying on shared facilities, the camp boasts some of the best toilets in Uganda and regular hot water. There is a small swimming pier, and kayaks and mountain bikes are available for rent to explore the area. There is a lively restaurant and bar, too, although meals often take more than one hour to arrive if it is busy… order well in advance!

Crater Bay Cottages (☎ 0486-22801; camping USh2000, banda USh30,000) Located just around a small bay from Bunyonyi Overland Camp, this place looks set to soar in popularity thanks to bargain camping and smart self-contained *bandas*. Built on a series of terraces, the *bandas* have lake views and there are several garden pavilions for relaxing, as well as a swimming pier on the lake shore.

Bamboo House (☎ 0486-26255; bandas USh5000) If cash is more important than comfort, the cheapest rooms around the lake are found here. Choose from small circular *bandas* or rather dingy singles. It's away from the water's edge, however.

Karibuni Camp (camping USh3000, r USh15,000) When it comes to gardens, this little camp is up there with the best of them, but unfortunately the facilities lack the same flourish. New rooms were under construction, but there is currently no restaurant. Could be good for campers who want to get away from it all.

Islands

Byoona Amagara (☎ 075-652788; www.lakebunyoni .net; all rates per person, camping USh3000, dm USh6000, r USh8000, geodome USh11,000, cabin USh14,000) Billing itself a backpacker's paradise, it is hard to disagree given its blissful hillside setting on

Itambira island. There is a unique choice of rooms, all at very reasonable prices, and all proceeds go towards supporting community projects in the fields of education and agriculture. Everyone has access to solar-powered showers and a good selection of inexpensive meals are available. To get here, take the Lake Bunyoni secondary school boat (USh7500, 12 minutes) or a dugout (USh2500, 50 minutes) from the Rutinda market pier.

Bushara Island Camp (☎ 077-464585; bushara island@africaonline.co.ug; camping USh2500, furnished tents US$13-20, cottages US$20-36) This private island camp is run by the Church of Uganda and offers the choice of secluded safari tents or comfortable cottages with bathrooms. Self-sufficient campers can hang out here for less than US$2 a night. There is a well-regarded restaurant serving pizza, crayfish dishes and tasty desserts, like cara-melised bananas and crepes. There's also a snack bar, picnic area, outdoor barbe-cue and volleyball court, plus sailing and windsurfing. A motorboat transfer from Rutinda costs USh10,000 or just USh2000 by dugout.

Nature's Prime Island (☎ 077-423215; natures primeisland@yahoo.co.uk; cabins per person US$37, tents per person US$32, both full board) Formerly Far Out Camp, Nature's Prime occupies a lovely little island just across the bay from Bunyonyi Overland Camp. The cabins are Scandinavian-style and have lakeviews, while the tents are set on raised platforms. The bar-restaurant is a fine place to relax over a beer with great views across the lake.

GETTING THERE & AWAY

To get to Lake Bunyoni, there are minibuses (USh1000, 30 minutes) travelling on Monday and Friday only when there is a market at Rutinda. Otherwise, there is the choice of chartering a special hire (USh10,000) or taking a *boda-boda* (USh4000). Finally, for those on a really tight budget, there is the option of hitching or walking the 9km from Kabale.

Coming from Kabale, take the access road for Bunyoni about 1km out of town on the Kisoro road, signposted on the left. If you're walking, you can take a shortcut by heading straight uphill alongside the stream just past the small dams, but it is a long way with a backpack.

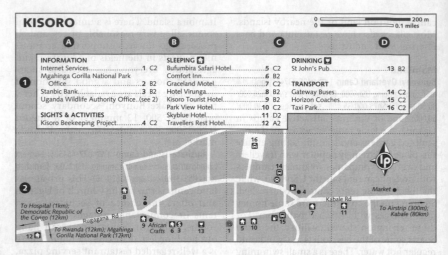

KISORO

INFORMATION		SLEEPING 🏠		DRINKING 🍺	
Internet Services.............................1 C2		Bufumbira Safari Hotel....................5 C2		St John's Pub.................................13 B2	
Mgahinga Gorilla National Park		Comfort Inn....................................6 B2			
Office....................................2 B2		Graceland Motel............................7 C2		TRANSPORT	
Stanbic Bank...............................3 B2		Hotel Virunga................................8 B2		Gateway Buses.............................14 C2	
Uganda Wildlife Authority Office..(see 2)		Kisoro Tourist Hotel.......................9 B2		Horizon Coaches...........................15 C2	
		Park View Hotel...........................10 C2		Taxi Park......................................16 C2	
SIGHTS & ACTIVITIES		Skyblue Hotel...............................11 D2			
Kisoro Beekeeping Project...........4 C2		Travellers Rest Hotel....................12 A2			

KISORO

Kisoro, the gateway to Mgahinga Gorilla National Park, is at the extreme southwestern tip of the country on the Ugandan side of the Virungas. As a town it has absolutely nothing to recommend it; the main draw for travellers is as a base from which to visit the gorillas of Mgahinga to the south or the gorillas at Djomba in Parc National des Virungas just over the border in DR Congo, now things are up and running there again. However, on a clear day, the views of the Virunga chain of volcanoes from this dusty little town are fantastic.

Information

Try **Stanbic Bank** (Rugagana Rd) if you need to exchange cash or travellers cheques, but there is no guarantee these services will be available. Call Stanbic in Kampala to double-check rather than take the risk. Anyone crossing into DR Congo to view the mountain gorillas at Djomba or Bukima should bear in mind that the Congolese will only accept cash payment in US dollars.

The post office offers limited telephone services, but MTN has cardphones here for reliable international connections.

Internet Services (Rugagana Rd; per min USh100) The only Internet connection in town.

Mgahinga Gorilla National Park office (☎ 0486-30098; ⏰ 8am-12.30pm & 2-5pm) On the main road in the centre of town, inquire here about the possibility of a gorilla visit at Mgahinga. Staff can also arrange transport out to the park. However, it is important to pay for the

gorilla permit in advance in Kampala, that is assuming the gorillas ever return to the Ugandan side.

Sights & Activities

As well as seeing the nearby gorillas, there is a good range of activities available in the Kisoro area, including **trekking** the volcanoes in Mgahinga Gorilla National Park and **cave exploration** near the park (p532).

Another interesting option is to take a **snake safari** to Lake Mutanda. Trips to see the large pythons at the lake cost about US$20, including transport. Other activities include **bird watching, canoeing** and a visit to a **pygmy village**. Local guide **Joseph Kwiha** (☎ 078-497730; kwihaj@yahoo.co.uk) has a whole range of cheap local tours available. Track him down at his little shop **African Crafts** (Rugagana Rd).

Those with a sweet tooth might like to call in at the **Kisoro Beekeeping Project**, a local cooperative producing natural honey with the love and care of a whisky distiller or vineyard owner. There are several types of honey on sale and the staff can demonstrate the process of preparing the honey.

Sleeping

Travellers Rest Hotel (☎ 0486-30123; postmaster@ gorillatours.com; s/d with bathroom US$35/45) This is a hotel with a history. Originally set up by the so-called father of gorilla tourism, Walter Baumgartel, Dian Fossey stayed here as her home away from home. As well as smart little standard rooms with elegant décor and hot water on tap, there are a couple of suites

(US$50) with room to spread out. The restaurant has the best food in town, and rates include breakfast.

Kisoro Tourist Hotel (☎ 0486-30135; s/d with bathroom USh60,000/90,000) Lacking the charm and history of Travellers Rest, this modern hotel is more about function than form. The smart rooms include satellite TV and the bathrooms have hot water. There is a restaurant and bar downstairs, complete with open fire. Rates include breakfast.

Hotel Virunga (☎ 0486-30109; camping US$3, s/d USh8000/15,000, d with bathroom USh30,000) This place has really taken off with overland trucks now that DR Congo is open for gorilla tracking once more. The camping area is organised and attractive and the simple rooms are sensibly priced. Out front is a buzzing little restaurant that rocks on as a bar on busy nights and movies play nightly in a side room.

Graceland Motel (☎ 077-837963; s/d USh20,000/ 25,000) There are no signs of Elvis at this graceland, but for those busting for a bathroom they are the best value in town. It also has larger doubles at USh35,000, and all rates include breakfast.

Skyblue Hotel (☎ 0486-30076; s/d USh8000/12,000) Anyone that has seen the sister hotel in Kabale knows what to expect. Clean rooms, exemplary service and shared facilities are the main ingredients. Speaking of ingredients, the restaurant has range of meals.

On the cheap, cheap, cheap front, Bufumbira Safari Hotel, Comfort Inn and Park View Hotel are all on the same stretch, and all offer identikit singles/doubles at USh3000/6000. These are no-frills set-ups, with just a couple of beds in each room and shared bathrooms.

For two places at Mgahinga Gorilla National Park that offer superb views of the volcanoes, check out p532.

Eating & Drinking

There is not a great deal of choice in town, so most visitors usually end up eating at the hotel or guesthouse in which they are staying. The best menu is found at **Travellers Rest** (meals USh4000-6000), which also has a well-stocked bar and fireplace, while Hotel Virunga and Skyblue Hotel offer an enticing combination of discount dining with some international touches.

If you are looking for nightlife in Kisoro, you might well be looking a long time. How-

ever, **St John's Pub** (Rugagana Rd) is a reasonable little spot in the middle of town, with a pool table, darts and a selection of cheap drinks, or check out the aforementioned Hotel Virunga if you see some overland trucks in town. This will be the place to get the lowdown on DR Congo over a couple of cold beers.

Getting There & Away

Horizon Coaches and Gateway have several buses a day to Kampala (USh18,000, nine hours) departing between about 4.30am and 9am.

Between Kabale and Kisoro there are frequent daily minibuses, which depart when full and cost USh7000 (see p528 for more details). These take from two to three hours depending on the season. There are also two scheduled departures at 7am and 1pm. Coming from Kabale, these minibuses continue on a further 12km to the DR Congo border at Bunagana (USh1000).

For details on how to get to Mgahinga Gorilla National Park, see p533.

The Rwandan border south of Kisoro at Cyanika is open, but the road is in poor shape on the Ugandan side. Minibuses (USh1500, 30 minutes) make the run infrequently. On the Rwandan side, it is in excellent condition, so takes about 1½ hours, including paperwork, to travel between Kisoro and Ruhengeri. See p555 for the full story on the routes into Rwanda.

LAKE MUTANDA

This is a beautiful lake set against the towering backdrop of the Virunga volcanoes. It lies 14km north of Kisoro and is a nice area for walking. Large pythons nest in the lake region and you can observe them at close quarters if you wish, although bearing in mind their girth, you may want to keep a sensible distance (see opposite for more details).

MGAHINGA GORILLA NATIONAL PARK

Although it may be the smallest of Uganda's national parks at just 34 sq km, **Mgahinga Gorilla National Park** (admission per 1/2/3 or more days US$20/30/50) punches above its weight and is perhaps the most visually stunning of all the protected areas. Tucked away in the far southwestern corner of the country, the tropical rainforest cloaking the volcanoes

MOUNTAIN GORILLAS IN THE DR CONGO

For the inside story on visiting the mountain gorillas in DR Congo, sometimes the only place where it is possible to pick up a permit in the region, see p563.

provides a refuge for the rare mountain gorilla. The park is contiguous with the Parc National des Volcans in Rwanda, and the Parc National des Virungas in DR Congo. Together, the three parks form the Virunga Conservation Area, which covers 420 sq km, and is home to an estimated half of the world's mountain gorilla population of about 700 animals – or all of them if you go along with the classification of those in Bwindi Impenetrable National Park as a new subspecies.

As in Bwindi Impenetrable National Park, it is possible to track gorillas here, but it is less convenient as the gorillas have a tendency to duck across the mountains into Rwanda or DR Congo. At the time of writing the gorillas had been absent for the best part of a year, raising questions as to whether or not they will ever return. If not, perhaps Mgahinga Gorilla National Park will need to consider a name change. Even if the gorillas eventually return, fewer people visit the gorillas here, instead opting for the more reliable choices of Bwindi, Parc National des Volcans in Rwanda or Parc National des Virungas in DR Congo.

At Mgahinga, there was just one group of gorillas habituated to visitors, with 11 individuals, including two silverbacks. It takes longer to find the gorillas here than at Bwindi, but the going is not as hard as in the Impenetrable Forest.

Three volcanoes loom large over the park headquarters: Muhavura, Gahinga and Sabinyo. Muhavura has a crater lake at its summit and is the highest point in the park, at 4127m.

The park headquarters is about 12km from Kisoro at Ntebeko Camp.

Activities

GORILLA TRACKING

When the gorillas are based on the Uganda side, eight people can visit per day, departing from park headquarters at 8am. Reservations for the trips must be made at the **UWA head office** (☎ 041-346287; www.uwa.or.ug) in Kampala and the cost is US$360, including park fees, a ranger-guide and armed guards (all of whom will expect a tip of around USh5000 to USh10,000). Try to check in at the booking office in Kisoro (near Hotel Virunga) by 5pm on the day before your trip just to confirm your arrival. It is generally much easier to get a confirmed booking at Mgahinga than at Bwindi, as tour companies don't book blocks of permits here. For more information on the mountain gorillas and a summary of the various tracking options in Uganda, Rwanda and DR Congo, see p100.

GOLDEN MONKEY TRACKING

If the gorillas continue to hang out in Rwanda, then golden monkeys will have to take up the challenge to lure tourists to Mgahinga. These are beautiful creatures and are quite playful. It costs US$20 to track golden monkeys here, but don't forget to throw in the US$20 park fee on top.

TREKKING

Any one of the volcanoes in the park (Mt Muhavura at 4127m, Mt Sabinyo at 3669m or Mt Gahinga at 3474m) can be climbed for US$40 per person, including a ranger-guide; the climbs take between four and six hours each. You'll see stunning vistas across to the neighbouring volcanoes. There is also the popular option of a border walk, which takes trekkers to the frontier with Rwanda and DR Congo for that experience of jumping back and forth between three countries. There's also a 13km nature trail (US$5/10 per half/full day), which offers the chance to spot some of the more than 100 species of birds found in the park, including the Rwenzori touraco and the scarlet-tufted malachite sunbird.

CAVING

Garama Cave is about 2km from park headquarters (outside the park boundary) and visits have been whacked up to a rather offputting US$25 per person. The cave is approximately 3km long and takes about four hours to explore. Bring a torch (flashlight).

Sleeping & Eating

Red Chilli Gorilla Camp (camping USh3000, dm USh6000, bandas USh20,000) Formerly the Mgahinga Community Camp, this excellent place is now part of the great little Red Chilli empire. With choice views of the Virunga volcanoes, this camp is right next to the main park gate. Cheap camping is available for those with their own tents and beds in the *bandas* are good value given the views. Food and drink are also available, following the Red Chilli recipe from Kampala.

Mt Gahinga Rest Camp (s/d US$240/360) This upmarket camp has upped its standards and prices in the last few years, in line with its improved camp in Bwindi and the stunning new property near Ruhengeri in Rwanda. Accommodation is in smart stone *bandas*, but it may struggle to find business given the gorilla action is all in Bwindi or Rwanda right now. The camp, located just outside the park, is operated by **Volcanoes Safaris** (☎ 041-346464; www.volcanoessafaris.com).

The only other options are 12km away in Kisoro (see p530 for details).

Getting There & Away

There is no scheduled transport along the rough 12km track between Kisoro and park headquarters; without your own vehicle you can walk (about three hours) or try and hitch, although traffic is light. The most straightforward way to get out to the park is to arrange a local pick-up from Kisoro, costing USh20,000 (USh30,000 in the wet season), or ask at the UWA office about occasional lifts with national parks' vehicles for around USh10,000.

MBARARA
☎ 0485
Mbarara, the main town between Masaka and Kabale, is really a transit town and few tourists end up spending more than one night here. Mbarara suffered a great deal during the war to oust Idi Amin but now bears few scars of those times. It's a very spread-out place, but pleasant enough, with a good range of hotels and eateries.

Information
The post office has international telephone and fax services.
Centenary Rural Development Bank (High St) Western Union money transfers are available here.
Source Internet Café (High St; per min USh100) Linked to the Source Café in Jinja, this is a reliable place to check email.

Standard Chartered Bank (☎ 0485-20088; 24 High St) The most useful one-stop shop for all money needs; has a credit card-compatible ATM, and can change cash and travellers cheques in most major currencies.

Sleeping
BUDGET
There isn't quite the range of cheap, basic guesthouses you find in other provincial towns, although this may be good news for some people.

Mayoba Inn (☎ 0485-21161; 1 High St; s/d USh7500/ 9000, with bathroom USh12,000/14,000) Sporting a central location, this friendly hotel might just about merit half a star for effort. Downstairs, the hotel has its own bar and restaurant.

Hotel Plaza (☎ 077-482159; 35 Mbaguta St; s/d USh5000/8000) Current holder of the cheapest hotel in town trophy, the Plaza offers eight simple (read bare bones) rooms with shared bathroom, but is a little rough around the edges.

MIDRANGE
Pelikan Hotel (☎ 0485-21100; fax 21704; Bananuka Dr; r USh10,000, s/d with bathroom USh15,000/25,000, ste USh60,000) The long-running Pelikan is a quiet place on a back street near the centre of town. Room prices rise and fall depending on little extras, like TV, but the expensive rooms are unimpressive value compared with top-end places in town. Credit cards are accepted, however, which might be handy in a fix.

Oxford Inn (☎ 077-683097; Bananuka Dr; s/tw USh35,000/45,000) Just along from the Pelikan, this is a more sophisticated little hostelry, where all rooms have satellite TV and bathrooms with hot water. There is a small restaurant and bar downstairs.

TOP END
Lake View Hotel (☎ 0485-21398; lvh@infocom.co.ug; s/d USh60,000/75,000, ste USh130,000; ≋) Long the place to be in Mbarara, it has had to wake up to the reality of competition in the past few years. Located on the outskirts of town off the road to Kasese, this modern hotel sits in front of a tiny lake and has 70 bedrooms, all with bathroom, hot water, satellite TV and telephone. Flash facilities include a swimming pool, sauna, bar and restaurant.

Speaking of the competition, it comes from three directions.

Classic Hotel (☎ /fax 0485-20609; 57 High St; s/d USh40,000/50,000) For those wanting to be right

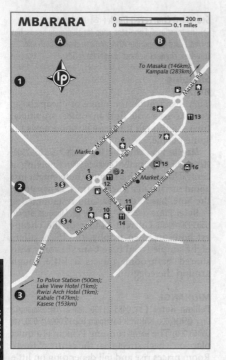

MBARARA

0 —————— 200 m
0 —————— 0.1 miles

To Masaka (146km);
Kampala (283km)

Market

To Police Station (500m);
Lake View Hotel (1km);
Rwizi Arch Hotel (1km);
Kabale (147km);
Kasese (153km)

INFORMATION

Centenary Rural Development Bank	1	A2
Source Internet Café	2	B2
Stanbic Bank	3	A2
Standard Chartered Bank	4	A2
Western Union	(see 1)	

SLEEPING

Agip Motel	5	B1
Classic Hotel	6	B2
Hotel Plaza	7	B2
Mayoba Inn	8	B1
Oxford Inn	9	A2
Pelikan Hotel	10	A2

EATING

Friends Corner	11	B2
Mbarara Coffee Shop	12	A2
Metro/Kwiksave	13	B1
Western Hotel	14	B2

TRANSPORT

Bus Park	15	B2
Taxi Park	16	B2

in the thick of the action, if Mbarara has such a thing, then this is in the middle of town. Smart business-like rooms come with TV, telephone and bathroom.

Agip Motel (☎ 0485-21615; Masaka Rd; s/d/ste USh60,000/70,000/95,000) Sort of sounds like a petrol-station hotel, and it sort of is, but that doesn't mean it should be sneered at. The smart executive-style rooms are popular with travelling businessmen.

Rwizi Arch Hotel (☎ 0485-20821; rwizi-arch@ africaonline.co.ug; s/tw USh64,000/70,000, ste USh125,000; ☒) This could be the smartest hotel in town, but the judges would require a photo finish. The rooms are fully equipped with all the trimmings, and facilities include a health club and swimming pool. The hotel also boasts the best restaurant in town.

Eating

Mbarara Coffee Shop (High St; dishes USh3000-5000) Head here to sample from an excellent menu of pasta, curries and African standards, plus for inveterate snackers there are inexpensive sandwiches and cakes. It is very popular with locals and offers efficient service for

those in a hurry to move on to other parts of Uganda.

Up in price somewhat, all the midrange and top-end hotels have restaurants that serve fine food.

Rwizi Arch Hotel (dishes USh5000-8000) Leading the pack, this hotel has one of the most varied menus to be found in provincial Uganda, including pasta, meat and fish, and unexpected treats, like creme caramel and banana fritters.

For good, cheap, steaming mountains of local food, try the following options, both in the centre of town:

Friends Corner (Bremba Rd; meals USh1500)

Western Hotel (Bremba Rd; meals USh1500)

Metro/Kwiksave (Mbaguta St) Self-caterers who are heading into Lake Mburo National Park should call in here for a good selection of supplies. In fact it wouldn't hurt anyone to pop in to pick up something from its range of imported snacks.

Getting There & Away

There are frequent buses and shared taxis from Mbarara to Kampala (USh9000, four hours), Masaka (USh6000, at least two hours), Kabale (USh6000, two hours) and Kasese (USh8000, 2½ hours). There are also EMS Post Buses running this route (see p485 for more information).

To get to Queen Elizabeth National Park, catch a Kasese-bound shared taxi and ask to be let off at Katunguru (USh6000, 1½ hours), from where you'll need to hitch into the park.

LAKE MBURO NATIONAL PARK

This is the premier spot in the country for spotting zebras. Located between Mbarara and Masaka and covering an area of 260 sq km, **Lake Mburo National Park** (admission per 1/2/3 or more days US$15/25/30) is mainly savanna with scattered acacia trees. There are five lakes here, the largest of which is Lake Mburo. Created in 1982, the park features some of the rarer animals in Uganda, such as impalas, elands, roan antelopes, reedbucks, klipspringers and topis, as well as buffaloes and hippos. Adjacent to the park are the ranches of people of the Bahima tribe, who herd the famed long-horned Ankole cattle that are a common sight here, but there is a certain amount of friction between conservationists and herders over access to land in and around the park.

This is one of the parks in which visitors can walk (accompanied by a ranger), as well as take one of the usual wildlife drives. Boat trips (US$5 per person, USh30,000 minimum) are available on Lake Mburo for something a bit more up close and personal with the hippos.

Sleeping

There are several **camp sites** (camping USh10,000) in the park, but most people stay at either the pleasant lakeside site or Rwonyo.

Rwonyo Rest Camp (banda s/d/tr USh10,000/15,000/20,000) Located at park headquarters, the rest camp has rustic *bandas* with bedding, mosquito nets and shared bathroom facilities. Good meals are available here and at the atmospheric lakeside restaurant. Fishermen often sell fresh fish from the lake each morning, which is great for campers on the lakeside site. There's no electricity or refrigeration at either place, but kerosene lanterns, pit toilets and warm bucket showers are available.

Mantana African Safaris (☎ 041-321552; mantana@ africaonline.co.ug; s/d with full board US$144/232) This company runs a luxury tented camp on a hill with commanding views of Lake Mburo. Sunrises and sunsets across the lake are striking. Service is sophisticated; meals are taken under the roof of a central bar and restaurant.

Getting There & Away

There are three possible ways into the park from the main Masaka–Mbarara road, but if you are hoping to hitch into the park or arrange a special-hire taxi or *boda-boda*, it is best to use the route from the Sanga gate. Trips to Sanga cost about USh2000 from Mbarara and USh4000 from Masaka. It's possible to hitch lifts with the irregular but accommodating park vehicles from the main road. If you're taking your own vehicle, a 4WD is recommended, but the trip is possible in a 2WD car during the dry season.

Coming from Kampala, the first turn-off for the park is 13km after Lyantonde. If you have your own vehicle, it is easier to take this first turn-off. The second turn-off is at Sanga, 24km after Lyantonde, and 50km before Mbarara.

MASAKA

☎ 0481

Despite the best efforts of the Masaka tourism promotion board, Masaka is not a place to hang around. In 1979 it was trashed by the Tanzanian army in the closing stages of the war that ousted Idi Amin and has taken longer than most towns to recover. It is a sprawling place and blends into nearby Nyendo, from where direct buses to Kalangala on the Ssese Islands leave each day. There's very little to do in Masaka, and for most visitors it is just an overnight stop en route to the Ssese Islands in Lake Victoria or south into Tanzania.

Information

The best bank in town is Stanbic Bank, which should be able to deal with cash and travellers cheques by the time you read this. Western Union money transfers are available through **Centenary Rural Development Bank** (Hobert Ave).

The post office offers international telephone and fax services. Internet access is available through **Masaka Internet Services** (Kampala Rd; per min USh50).

Sights & Activities

Birders on the hunt for the elusive shoebill stork should venture to the Nabajjuzzi swamp just out of Masaka on the way to Mbarara. It also provides a habitat for the web-footed antelope, better known as the sitatunga. There is a large bird-watching

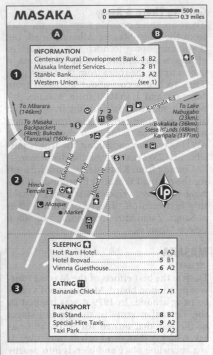

MASAKA

0 ——————— 500 m
0 ——————— 0.3 miles

INFORMATION
Centenary Rural Development Bank..1 B2
Masaka Internet Services....................2 B1
Stanbic Bank.....................................3 A2
Western Union.............................(see 1)

To Mbarara
(146km)

To Masaka
Backpackers
(4km); Bukoba
(Tanzania) (160km)

Kampala Rd

To Lake
Nabugabo
(23km);
Bukakata (36km);
Ssese Islands (48km);
Kampala (137km)

Edward Rd
Elgin Rd
Hobert Ave

Hindu
Temple
Mosque
Market

SLEEPING
Hot Ram Hotel...............................4 A2
Hotel Brovad.................................5 B1
Vienna Guesthouse........................6 A2

EATING
Bananah Chick...............................7 A1

TRANSPORT
Bus Stand....................................8 B2
Special-Hire Taxis..........................9 A2
Taxi Park...................................10 A2

UGANDA

tower next to the highway, which costs
USh2000 to climb, and a shoebill sighting is
almost guaranteed. Early morning to about
noon is the best time to see the shoebill.

Sleeping & Eating
The most atmospheric place to stay in town
is ironically 4km out of town.

Masaka Backpackers (☎ 077-619389; camping
USh3500, dm/bandas USh5000/15,000) Has a nice rural
feel, the owners are friendly and helpful, and
meals are available. To get here from Masaka, take a Kirimya shared taxi for USh500,
get off at Kasanvu and follow the signs.

There are a cluster of budget guesthouses
in the south of the town.

Vienna Guesthouse (55 Hobert Ave; s/d/tw
USh10,000/15,000/20,000) The best all round deal
among the identikit bunch. The cheapest
rooms involve a shared bathroom.

Hot Ram Hotel (☎ 0481-20906; Elgin Rd; s/d
USh25,000/40,000) Ignoring the name, which
clearly conjures up images of a dodgy
brothel, this new hotel has a smart selection
of rooms with satellite TV and hot water.
Rates include breakfast.

Hotel Brovad (☎ 0481-21455; www.hotelbrovad.com;
s/d/tr USh40,000/65,000/80,000) The smartest
rooms in town have their home here. All
rooms have satellite TV, fridge and phone,
and are super clean. The restaurant and bar
are pretty busy by night, thanks to a large à
la carte menu and a cheaper snack menu.

Bananah Chick (Kampala Rd; meals USh2000-5000)
Masaka's answer to fast food; drop in for
fried chicken, steaks or curries.

Getting There & Away
Buses and minibuses run frequently to Kampala (USh5000, two hours) and Mbarara
(USh6000, two hours), and less frequently
direct to Kabale (four hours).

Bukakata (from where ferries leave for the
Ssese Islands) is 36km east of Masaka along
a dirt road, which is in reasonable shape,
except for a couple of rough stretches. Kalangala Express has two big buses a day
(departing at 10am and 2pm) from the turn-
off at Nyendo (3km from Masaka) straight
through to Kalangala (USh6000, three to
four hours).

Getting to Bukakata with your own transport can be an exercise in frustration, as
there are no signposts whatsoever and the
only people who seem to know the way are
are other drivers. Basically, head downhill
back towards Kampala from Masaka centre,
cross over the river bridge and then turn
right (where there's a sign for the Church
of Uganda Holiday & Conference Centre).
From here go straight across the first junction and turn left at the next T-junction by
the petrol station. Continue on this road
for about 30km and take the left fork at the
major junction – the right fork goes to a
fishing village. The car ferry departs from
Bukakata just three times a day at 8am,
noon and 4pm, and from Liku at 9am, 1pm
and 5pm. On Sunday, there are only two
crossings, at 1pm and 4pm, returning one
hour later. However, the schedule is not set
in stone, due to breakdowns and waiting for
the bus from Nyendo (Masaka).

Masaka is also the starting point for crossing into Tanzania via the Kagera salient and
Bukoba. See p556 for details.

AROUND MASAKA
Lake Nabugabo
Lake Nabugabo is a small, attractive lake,
separated from its much bigger sister,

Victoria, by a small strip of forest. The advantage it holds over Lake Victoria is that the water is cleaner and apparently free of bilharzia.

Church of Uganda Holiday & Conference Centre (camping USh5000, dm USh6000, d/family bandas USh20,000/30,000) is located on the lake shore. The large family *bandas* have their own lounge and bathroom. Good meals cost about USh4000, but alcohol is not available.

Getting here is not so straightforward, as it is 4km off the road between Masaka and Bukakata. If you don't mind walking the last 4km, just get on a minibus to Bukakata and ask to get off when you see the sign, about 15km from Masaka. If you don't like the idea of walking, negotiate with a special-hire taxi in Masaka, which you might be able to get for USh15,000 if you bargain well.

SSESE ISLANDS

While not exactly the Bahamas of Lake Victoria, this lush group of islands does boast the best beaches in Uganda and the largest, Buggala Island, is a popular resting spot for time out from life on the road. This group of 84 islands lies off the north-western shore of Lake Victoria, east of Masaka and south of Entebbe. The islands are connected to the mainland by ferries from Bukakata to Liku, and fishing boats from Kasenyi to Kalangala.

The islands offer an insight into an alternative Uganda that is worth exploring, but don't come here looking for 'action' – this is R&R time. Unlike the mainland, these islands escaped the ravages of the civil wars and so remain largely unspoiled. The people, known as the Basese, form a distinct tribal group with their own language, culture and folklore. They are primarily fishermen, and farmers of coffee, sweet potatoes, cassavas, yams and bananas. As you might expect, fish forms a major part of their diet.

Most islanders are members of one of the various Christian sects. A minority are Muslims. Communities are tightly knit and wandering around the islands on foot is considered safe. In fact, this is the best way to see them. The main islands of Buggala, Bufumira, Bukasa, Bubeke and Kkome are hilly and, where not cultivated, forested with a wide variety of trees. Animals include various species of monkey, hippos, crocodiles and many different types of birds,

but there are no large predators, other than crocodiles.

Many spots afford beautiful views over the lake and across to other islands. You'll have no problems persuading the fishermen to take you out on their boats. Swimming is also possible off most of the islands, as long as you observe the usual precaution about avoiding reedy areas (where the snails that carry the bilharzia parasite potentially live).

All up, you're looking at a very mellow and peaceful time on these islands. There is a plentiful variety of food and, although they remain popular, the islands are far from overrun with visitors.

Information
The main town on the islands is Kalangala on Buggala Island. It's the administrative centre, with a post office that has telephone connections to the rest of the world, and a branch of Stanbic Bank, which should be able to handle cash and travellers cheques' exchange. However, the safest move is to bring all the cash you need, as getting money changed is generally very difficult on the Ssese Islands.

Sleeping & Eating
Most of the accommodation is centred on Buggala Island, on the attractive Lutoboka Bay beneath Kalangala village. There are a couple of very basic places in Liku as well, but they are best avoided given the choices around Kalangala.

Hornbill Camp (☎ 077-729478; www.hornbillcamp .com; camping USh4500, dm/bandas USh7500/20,000) The most popular budget camp on Buggala, Hornbill has its own secluded beach. Located about a 15-minute (500m) walk below Kalangala, the Dutch owner and his team are very friendly, making it a fun place to stay. The *bandas* are basic, but the camping ground runs down to the lakeshore. Kayaks are available for hire for just USh3000 per hour. There is also a selection of filling meals from the restaurant-bar (meals USh3000 to USh5000).

PTA Andronico's Lodge (☎ 0481-255646; camping USh3000, tw per person USh5000, d USh8000) Anyone who rocks up in Kalangala late can crash here, but crash is the operative word, as things are basic with a capital B. Beds are in tiny rooms and camping is possible, although space is tight. Cheap meals are

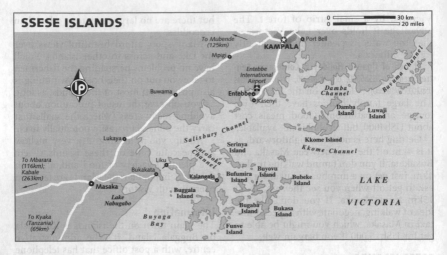

SSESE ISLANDS

available with the family, as well as beers and soft drinks. There is a second branch of this landmark just above Liku where the ferry docks from Bukakata.

Panorama Camping Safaris (☎ 077-406371; camping USh3000, bandas with/without bathroom USh30,000/ 20,000) A step up from the standards at Hornbill, the camping here is very atmospheric, as it is set in the rainforest. The *bandas* are spacious and some include bathroom. Hot showers can be arranged on request. To find the place, walk down to the lake opposite the post office and look for the red-roofed stone huts.

There are also a couple of upmarket resorts around Lutoboka.

Ssese Palm Beach (☎ 077-623984; bandas US$25-65) Boasting the best location of any of the resorts here, it is on a headland with its own private beach. There are two types of *banda* available, and packages range from bed only to full board. Some *bandas* are detached, some paired up in a single unit, but all include bathroom. The restaurant has a prime location for a sunset drink and is open to allcomers.

Ssese Islands Beach Hotel (☎ 077-505098; www .sseseislandsbeachhotel.com; s USh30,000-60,000, d USh50,000-100,000; set meals USh10,000) Sitting in a wooded glade near Bugwanya Beach, this smart hotel has a selection of cottages and the top rates include full board. The hotel has hot water on demand and a generator for lighting at night. The restaurant is open to nonguests, and offers a pricey menu

of European dishes for lunch and dinner. Nice, but not as charming as Palm Beach.

Scorpion Lodge (camping USh3000, s/d USh4000/8000) If you are unlucky enough to get stuck in Liku, this 'lodge' is located above the Bukakata ferry docks. Bare-bones rooms only, but bikes are available for hire should you want to escape.

Getting There & Away

A ferry links Buggala Island with the mainland at Bukakata (35km east of Masaka), while small wooden boats run from Kasenyi (a 35-minute minibus ride from Kampala), but these aren't the safest way to go. There is a direct bus from Kampala to Kalangala (USh12,000), which leaves the new taxi park in Kampala daily at 8.30am and arrives about 4pm in Kalangala.

See p536 for details of buses to Bukakata and Kalangala. If you use the ferry between Bukakata and Liku with your own vehicle, you will have to pay USh5000 to USh10,000 for the crossing, depending on the size of the vehicle.

NORTHWESTERN UGANDA

Much of northwestern Uganda remains effectively off limits to travellers due to the ongoing war in the north, but Murchison Falls National Park remains the region's saving grace, the best all-round protected area in the country for wildlife and attractions. The largest park in Uganda, Murchison not only has increasing concentrations of lions, leopards, elephants, giraffes and hippos, but is named in honour of one of the most dramatic falls in the region. Murchison Falls sees the Nile River surge through a narrow gorge, and the boat trip up the river to the base of the falls is a relaxed and rewarding way to view wildlife.

For all practical purposes the rest of the northern part of Uganda is a separate country from the southern part. Politically it is very isolated from the south and the continuing war effort is a drain on national resources, creating huge numbers of refugees and wiping out large tracts of agricultural land. While tourism has taken off in Kampala, Jinja and all points south, the north has seen little or no tourism due to the very real dangers in the region.

When it comes to road conditions in the north (at least the roads tourists can safely use), most are in pretty good shape. The roads in Murchison are some of the best in Uganda, as they also form crucial transport links to parts of the north. Public transport is fine to towns like Masindi and Hoima, but nonexistent in Murchison Falls itself. Public transport to points north of Murchison Falls and towns, such as Gulu and Arua, is inadvisable due to possible rebel ambushes.

MASINDI
☎ 0465

Masindi is a quiet provincial headquarters, the last town of any substance on the road to Murchison Falls National Park. It's a good place to stock up on provisions, but there is little of intrinsic interest in the town itself.

Information

Try Stanbic Bank for exchanging money and, possibly, travellers cheques. The post office has international telephone and fax services, and there are plenty of cardphones scattered about the town.

The UWA office may be able to assist with transport into and around the park.

Sleeping & Eating

Executive Lodge (s/d USh3000/6000) There is nothing executive about this cheap place, but it is the pick of the budget options and is

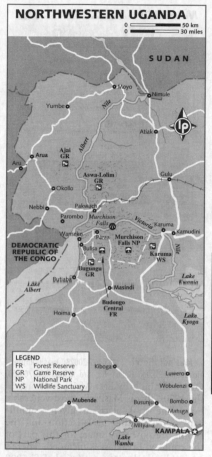

NORTHWESTERN UGANDA

conveniently near the taxi park. Large rooms include soap and towels, but bathrooms are shared.

Karibuni Guesthouse (☎ 0465-20443; s/d USh7000/10,000, d with bathroom USh20,000) 'Probably the best in town' is the claim here. Probably not, but the self-contained doubles are larger than most of the budget places and also include breakfast, which is taken in a large open-air bar area.

Alinda Guesthouse (☎ 0465-20482; 86 Masindi Port Rd; s/d USh10,000/18,000, d with bathroom USh20,000) Located on the main road from Kampala, this friendly guesthouse is the most popular with NGOs among the cheaper places to stay in Masindi. All rooms are clean, and rates include breakfast.

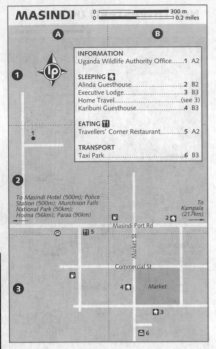

Masindi Hotel (☎ 0465-20023; masindihotel@africaonline.co.ug; Hoima Rd; s/d USh55,000/70,000) Originally built by East Africa Railways in the 1920s, this is Masindi's most venerable hotel. The whole place was given a significant overhaul after privatisation and the rooms are now very smart for this part of the country. Breakfast is included. There's a good bar and restaurant (meals USh5000 to USh7000), which makes a convenient lunch-time stop on the way to/from Murchison Falls, as it is right next to the park turn-off.

Travellers' Corner Restaurant (Masindi Port Rd; mains USh3000-5000) In the middle of town near the post office, this is a popular gathering spot for locals and tourists alike. It caters to *mzungu* tastes, making it a good lunch and dinner haunt. It has some of the best sausages found outside Kampala.

Getting There & Away

The road between Masindi and Kampala is in pretty good condition, particularly once it merges with the road from Gulu. Minibuses between Kampala and Masindi (USh9000,

three hours) travel throughout the day. There are also irregular departures to Hoima (USh4000, one hour), Bulisa (USh7000, two hours) and Wanseko (USh8000 2½ hours). **Home Travel** (☎ 0465-20459) has a daily bus to Kampala (USh8000, four hours) at 7am, which leaves from near Executive Lodge.

For details of getting to Paraa, see p544.

HOIMA

Hoima is not a town with a great deal to offer the casual visitor, but some travellers do end up spending a night here when taking the dirt road between Fort Portal and Murchison Falls National Park. Hoima is also a useful starting point for a back route into the national park via Lake Albert. Bring cash to this town, as there are no banks or foreign exchange bureaus.

The best budget choice in the centre of town is **Classic Inn** (s/d USh6000/10,000), offering basic rooms with mosquito nets and shared facilities. There is also an inexpensive restaurant and bar out the front where locals gather to quaff an ale or two in the evening. There is a sign saying 'no idlers allowed', which is probably aimed more at Ugandans than backpackers.

More interesting is **Africa Village Guest Farm** (www.traveluganda.co.ug/africanvillageguestfarm; camping USh4000, cottages USh30,000), which has great little *bandas* with balconies spaced around its large grounds. There is a well-regarded restaurant, which is popular with locals, plus the possibility of camel rides in the near future.

Getting There & Away

The road from Fort Portal is reasonable, if dusty in the dry season, but is hard work in the wet season. Direct minibuses cost USh12,000, if available, and the trip takes about five hours. More likely, it will require a change in Kyenjojo on the main Fort Portal to Kampala road. The road from Masindi is a short stretch by minibus (USh4000, one hour).

Minibuses run to Butiaba (USh5000, two hours), an atmospheric fishing port on Lake Albert. The last leg of the journey is spectacular (see p545).

MURCHISON FALLS NATIONAL PARK

This **park** (admission per 1/2/3 or more days US$20/30 /50) is the best all-rounder in Uganda, with animals in plentiful supply and the raging Murchison Falls easily accessible by boat. Sir Samuel Baker named the Murchison Falls in honour of a president of the Royal Geographic Society, and the largest park in the country was subsequently named after the falls. The Victoria Nile River flows through the park on its way to Lake Albert.

This used to be one of Africa's best national parks; during the 1960s as many as 12 launches filled with eager tourists would buzz up the river to the falls each day. The park also used to contain some of the largest concentrations of wildlife in Africa, including as many as 15,000 elephants. Unfortunately, poachers and troops, both armed with automatic weapons, wiped out practically all wildlife, except the more numerous (or less sought-after) herd species (see the boxed text, p543). There are now no rhinos and only a few groups of lions, but other wildlife is recovering fast and you can see good numbers of elephants, giraffes, Ugandan kobs (antelopes), buffaloes, hippos and crocodiles.

Wildlife drives usually take place on the north bank of the Victoria Nile, in the area between Paraa and Lake Albert. There is very little wildlife south of the river, and driving in from Masindi you could be forgiven for thinking you were on a vegetarian safari.

If you want to take your vehicle into the park it incurs a one-off fee of US$6/20 for local/foreign-registered cars and US$15/40 for 4WDs.

While the Paraa area of the park is considered safe these days, several embassies still warn against visiting, so it is worth checking the latest security situation in Kampala before setting off.

For more information on the park, pick up a copy of *A Guide to Murchison Falls National Park* by Shaun Mann. Although dated, it is still the best guide to the park and its attractions.

Murchison Falls

Despite there being less wildlife in the park than in Kenyan or Tanzanian parks, it is well worth visiting to see the falls, which involves a superb ride up the Victoria Nile River to their base. En route there are crocodiles and hippos, thousands of birds and, usually, elephants and giraffes. If you are very lucky, you may also catch a glimpse of the rare shoebill stork, as there are several pairs in the park.

The falls are awesome when viewed up close, they were once described as the most spectacular thing to happen to the Nile along its 6700km length. The gorge through which the Nile passes is just 6m wide, making this possibly the most powerful natural surge of water to be found anywhere in the world.

There is a beautiful walking trail linking the base of the falls with the top, and this offers some stunning views of the raging water and sections of the waterfall that those on the boat trip or at the viewing point never get to see.

There's an old ranger station at the top of the falls, which is staffed by local people who sell soft drinks and will guide you around for a small fee. There's also a picnic area with shaded *bandas* and a basic camp site with pit toilets. Hopefully, a more sophisticated camping ground will be developed here with *bandas*, as it is a great place to spend the night (although not for sleepwalkers perhaps).

You can also visit the falls by vehicle. A rough track leads off from the main access track 24km south of Paraa, and from here it's about a 30-minute drive; 2WD is OK, but take care.

UGANDA

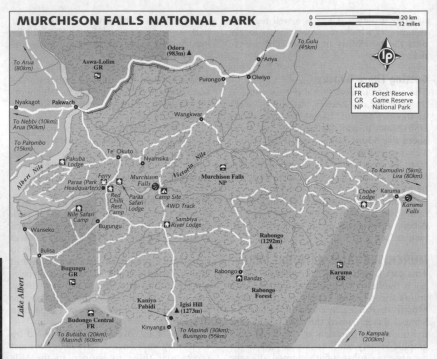

MURCHISON FALLS NATIONAL PARK

0 ─── 20 km
0 ─── 12 miles

LEGEND
FR	Forest Reserve
GR	Game Reserve
NP	National Park

Activities

LAUNCH TRIP

The three-hour launch trip from Paraa up to the base of the falls operates daily at 9am and 2pm if there's enough demand. The cost is US$15 per person if there are eight or more people, with a minimum charge of USh300,000 for the whole boat. On the weekend, there's a good chance of finding other people to share the cost with; on weekdays you may have to cough up the full whack.

If you take the morning launch up the river, it is possible to ask the captain to let you off at a trail head for the recommended walk up to the top of the falls. He can then pick you up later if there is an afternoon launch. This is also a good way for backpackers to get to the camping ground at the top of the falls, where you can camp overnight before returning to Paraa the next day.

WILDLIFE DRIVES

There are several circuits on the north bank of the Victoria Nile River (see p545 for details of ferry times and prices). The best routes for wildlife viewing are the Queen and Albert Nile tracks, which lie just to the west of the Pakwach road, bordered by the Albert and Victoria Niles. This area is the best for spotting some of the park's healthy giraffe population. It is also possible to see lions, leopards and hyenas in this part of the park, as well as the more numerous herd species, such as buffaloes and elephants.

SECURITY AT MURCHISON FALLS

Murchison Falls National Park has also witnessed its share of troubles, although these incidents have all been north of the Nile in more isolated parts of the park. Long-term resident Steve WIllis was tragically shot dead by LRA gunmen in a remote part of the park in November 2005, but as a promoter and operator in the park, he would hate to think that his death caused visitors to desert the park he so loved. The Paraa section of the park is still considered safe, although many embassies currently warn against visiting Murchison.

UGANDA

Those with their own vehicles should definitely take a ranger-guide (US$5/10 per half/full day) – they are adept at spotting elusive predators. Red Chilli Rest Camp offers four-hour wildlife drives costing USh25,000 per person (minimum USh100,000), including guide and ferry crossing, which is pretty handy for independent travellers.

CHIMPANZEE TRACKING

Run by the Forestry Department rather than the UWA, the chimp visits are very affordable in Murchison when compared with the prices in Kibale Forest and Queen Elizabeth National Parks. It costs just USh12,000 at either Busingiro or Kaniyo Pabidi Forest, but bear in mind that the latter is inside the national park boundaries, meaning you pay the US$20 park fee on top. See p545 for all the details.

SPORT FISHING

It is possible to fish for the gargantuan Nile perch in the national park. A permit costs US$50 per day, US$100 for four days and US$300 per year. You will also need a boat; these are available for US$150/300 per half/full day. There is now an annual fishing competition on the river here if you fancy yourself as a serious angler. For the full story on fishing opportunities at Murchison Falls, check out **Sport Fishing Murchison Falls Uganda** (www.fishingmurchison.com), which is packed with useful information. Fishing gear is available for hire from Red Chilli Rest Camp.

Sleeping & Eating

PARAA

The park headquarters at Paraa is on the southern bank of the Victoria Nile. There's a small village for park workers and their families.

Red Chilli Rest Camp (☎ 077-709510; www.redchillihideaway.com; camping USh10,000, safari tent USh25,000, banda tw USh30,000, with bathroom USh45,000) The popular Red Chilli team from Kampala has been running this rest camp for several years, bringing a budget option to backpackers in Murchison. Camping is on a grassy site with some views of the river. The *bandas* are comfortable, and some have their own bathroom if you don't fancy wandering the camp at night. The restaurant and bar area is set under a huge thatched roof and is popular on weekends. The international

menu includes the signature hippo breakfast so popular in Kampala.

Paraa Safari Lodge (bookings ☎ 078-260260; www.paraalodge.com; s/d with full board US$99/150; ☒) On the northern bank of the river, this hotel-style lodge has a striking location with expansive views upriver towards the falls, and excellent facilities, including a swim-up bar overlooking the Victoria Nile. The rooms are pretty much four-star standard, so don't be put off by the exterior, which looks rather like a Japanese POW camp.

ELSEWHERE IN THE PARK

Camp Site (camping USh10,000) At the head of the falls this camp site has a very nice position right on the river, although you'll definitely need a 4WD to get to the best sites near the river's edge. You'll also need to be self-sufficient, as there are no supplies of any sort, and the only facilities are a pit toilet.

For information on the camp site at Kaniyo Pabidi, see p545.

Bandas (dm USh7500, bandas s/d USh10,000/15,000, with bathroom USh20,000/30,000) There are national

UGANDA

park *bandas* in Rabongo Forest, in the remote southern part of the park. Few visitors make it to this part of the park, however, due to its remoteness and lack of good trails.

Sambiya River Lodge (bandas s/d USh65,000/110,000, with bathroom USh80,000/140,000, cottages US$50/100) Just off the main track beside the turn-off to the falls, this is a modern, comfortable lodge in a secluded spot with a tempting mix of *bandas* and cottages. Full board rates are available at an extra USh20,000 per day. Campers are also welcome for USh10,000, which includes access to the swimming pool. There is also a large bar and restaurant. Unlike Paraa, this area is pretty much free of mosquitoes. It's run by **Afri Tours & Travel** (☎ 041-233596; www.afritourstravel.com).

North of the river are two old lodges: Pakuba Lodge, which is very close to the Albert Nile in the western part of the park, and Chobe Lodge on the Victoria Nile River in the far east of the park. Pakuba Lodge is a massive, empty old place put up by Idi Amin during the 1970s. The location, overlooking the Albert Nile, is fantastic, but the building is pretty much beyond repair these days.

OUTSIDE THE PARK

Arguably the nicest place to stay actually lies outside the park's western boundary, between Bugungu gate and Lake Albert.

Nile Safari Camp (s/d with bathroom & full board US$135/180; ⛲) This camp site has an unrivalled position, high up on the south bank of the Victoria Nile River, with sweeping views over the water. Accommodation is in comfortable permanent tents, each with a balcony with river views. There's also an atmospheric bar and dining area, as well as a lovely swimming pool with a view. The well-signposted turn-off to the camp is 15km from Bulisa (on Lake Albert) and 4.5km from Bugungu gate; the camp is then a further 11.5km along a rough track. It's operated by **Inns of Uganda** (☎ 041-258273; www.innsofuganda.com).

Getting There & Away

AIR

Several of the top-notch safari companies include charter flights to Murchison, using the Pakuba airstrip on the northern bank of the Nile. Landing fees are USh5000 per person.

ROAD

From Masindi there is the choice of the direct northern route or the longer but more scenic route, which heads west to Lake Albert and then enters the park via the western Bugungu gate. A return trip might be best for those with a vehicle, entering via one route and leaving by the other. Both routes go through Budongo Central Forest Reserve, a recommended stopover.

Getting from Masindi directly to Paraa by public transport is not possible. With a bit of bargaining, however, you can charter a minibus (USh75,000) or special-hire taxi (USh60,000) to take you all the way.

From Masindi the only scheduled public transport are the buses and taxis to Wanseko on Lake Albert. These run daily, and are popular because local people from the Arua region in the northwest often prefer to travel to Kampala via the lake rather than via Gulu, because of security problems along the Arua–Gulu road. Either go as far as Bulisa for USh7000, from where you can negotiate for a *boda-boda* to take you to Paraa for around USh10,000, or go to Wanseko for USh8000 and then negotiate with the minibus driver to continue to Paraa for about USh40,000. Bulisa is the obvious option for solo travellers, but groups should carry on to Wanseko.

The best chance of hitching a lift is with the park vehicles that come from Masindi a few times a week. On the weekend there's a good chance of getting a lift with other tourists from Masindi – hang out at Travellers' Corner Restaurant and Masindi Hotel for hitching opportunities, as these are popular rest stops. Getting out of the park is much easier in this respect, as you can find out where vehicles are heading to and book yourself a ride.

The other option is to go on an organised safari from Kampala. The most popular options are the budget safaris offered through Red Chilli Hideaway and Backpackers Hostel, both in Kampala (see p476 for details). These leave at least twice weekly in the high season, and include park entrance, accommodation, meals, chimp tracking, a launch trip, wildlife drive and transport, making them one of the best deals in East Africa.

More upmarket safari companies also offer trips to Murchison Falls (see p95 for contact details). Paraa Safari Lodge, Nile

Safari Camp and Sambiya River Lodge offer three-day safaris, including transport, accommodation and meals, that are good value, particularly those of Sambiya, which sometimes advertises prices under US$200 per person for groups of six.

Getting Around

BOAT

A vehicle ferry crosses the river at Paraa. It operates to a schedule but breakdowns are not uncommon and you may have to wait a few hours. The crossings take just a few minutes, and are scheduled pretty much hourly from 7am until 7pm. The fare is USh1500 one way for passengers, USh20,000 each way for passenger vehicles and USh60,000 for overland trucks. Unscheduled crossings cost USh100,000 minimum. Guests staying overnight in the park pay only once and can cross back and forth throughout the day.

You can take a small speedboat across the river at any time for USh6000 per person return. All ferry and speedboat fees are payable at a small booth near the ferry landing.

CAR

Tracks within the park are generally well maintained, and a 2WD vehicle with good ground clearance should have little trouble. However, the tracks can be treacherous in the wet season. There are also some nasty bumps where drainage channels have been built, so look out for concrete culverts on the side of the road and slow down.

Fuel is available on the northern side of the Victoria Nile River at Paraa, but it's much more expensive (about an extra 20%) than in Masindi.

BUDONGO CENTRAL FOREST RESERVE

The main attractions of Budongo Forest are the numerous primates and affordable chimp visits, the prolific bird life and the huge mahogany trees that dominate this area. The forest is right on the road to Murchison Falls, just to the south of the park, and is a great place to stop and have a guided walk through the dense virgin tropical forest.

The forest's **'Royal Mile'** is thought by many to offer the best bird-watching in the whole of Uganda. There are more than 350 species found here, including several types of kingfisher, hornbill and eagle. At dusk it is possible to view bat hawks.

Two areas have been developed for chimpanzee habituation and viewing, **Kaniyo Pabidi** (admission USh12,000; camping USh10,000, bandas per person USh15,000) and **Busingiro** (admission USh12,000; camping USh10,000, bandas per person USh15,000). Both offer combination packages for guided walks and accommodation, effectively halving the cost of your stay. Kaniyo Pabidi is on the main Masindi–Paraa road, 29km north of Masindi and actually inside the southern boundary of Murchison Falls National Park – you will have to pay the US$20 park entry fee for the park on top of the chimp fee. Busingiro is 40km west of Masindi on the road that connects Masindi with the national park via Lake Albert, and is outside the park, making it by far the cheapest place in Uganda to track chimpanzees. Both are part of the Budongo Forest Ecotourism Project, which aims to protect the forest in cooperation with local communities.

At both places guided walks (with a guide and an armed ranger) take place daily at 7am (8am at Kaniyo Pabidi) and 3pm, although they can basically be arranged on demand, as there are no minimum numbers. Walks last anything from one to three hours. Kaniyo Pabidi is one of the few sites in Uganda to employ a female ranger-guide, a breakthrough some travellers might like to encourage. The forest is also more dramatic at Pabidi.

The camp sites are liveable enough, with pit toilets and hot showers. The *bandas* are simple, with shared facilities. There are information centres at both of these places, but no food or cooking utensils – come with everything you might need. Beers and drinks are available, however.

Kaniyo Pabidi is not served by regular public transport, but it is possible to arrange a charter from Masindi for about USh30,000. Busingiro is on the route used by buses and minibuses heading for Bulisa or Wanseko (see opposite). The trip should cost about USh4000. Access to the Royal Mile is pretty limited without transport – the turn-off is 32km from Masindi, marked by the Nyabyeya Forestry College signpost.

LAKE ALBERT

Lake Albert is part of the Rift Valley system that extends from the Middle East to Mozambique, and since 1894 has formed part of the border between Uganda and DR

Congo. The first European to spot the lake was the British explorer Sir Samuel Baker in 1864, who named it after Albert, prince consort of Queen Victoria.

The people who live by the lake make their living from fishing its waters, and a visit to one of these fishing villages along the eastern shore makes an interesting diversion. The approach for the turn-off to the fishing village of **Butiaba** on the eastern shore is spectacular as you wind down the Albertine Escarpment, with sweeping views of the lake and the Blue Mountains of DR Congo in the distance. The village itself is small, but judging by some of the old buildings had its share of Asian traders. It was from here that the East Africa Railways Corporation used to run river steamers up to Fajao at the base of Murchison Falls. The majestic old boats were slowly decaying in the lake's waters for many years, but, sadly, were hacked apart for scrap.

The best time to visit is late morning when the fishing catch is brought ashore from the small fishing boats – huge Nile perch weighing in excess of 50kg are quite common.

While there is no formal accommodation in the village, you could probably find someone willing to put you up for a day or two, but be sure to agree on a fair price for them. There are some excellent sandy beaches near Butiaba, for that Costa del Congo experience.

GULU

Gulu, the largest town in the north of the country, is heavily militarised – it is the supply centre for the government's war against the LRA. As long as the war continues, there is absolutely no reason for tourists to come here and plenty of reasons to stay away. About 30km north of Gulu at Patiko is Baker's Fort, built by the British in the 1870s as a base from which to suppress the slave trade.

Diana Gardens Guesthouse (r with/without bathroom USh12,000/6000) is considered the best of the cheaper hotels in town, while **Hotel Roma** (s/d with bathroom USh25,000/35,000) is currently the smartest option.

There are a huge number of local restaurants around town, catering to the many government personnel and soldiers who pass through this town.

Getting There & Away

Buses and minibuses go between Kampala and Gulu (USh12,000). The road has good bitumen most of the way and the buses absolutely fly along here, doing the trip in around four hours.

Gulu is on the railway line that connects Pakwach with Tororo in the southeast, but passenger services were suspended some years ago because of security problems.

ARUA

Arua is the largest town in the far northwest, with a large population of aid workers, as it is the distribution centre for relief efforts in southern Sudan and DR Congo. This means there is also a large number of Sudanese and Congolese refugees living in tented camps on the outskirts of town, which is a pretty sorry sight if you have never seen this sort of suffering before.

Few travellers make it up here, due to dangerous stretches of road between here and Kampala. However, the market is very lively, as it attracts people from all over the region.

It is possible to change cash at **Centenary Rural Development Bank** (Adumi Rd), which also represents Western Union for money transfers. The post office is the place to make phone calls, and there are cardphones nearby.

Hotel Pacific (Adumi Rd; s/d with bathroom USh10,000/15,000) is reasonably comfortable, but is often full of aid workers. There is also a small restaurant and bar here.

Rhino Inn (s/d with bathroom USh25,000/35,000), also popular with aid workers, is the smartest place in town. Rooms are clean and the restaurant is a good bet at night.

Nile Coach runs daily buses between Kampala and Arua (USh22,000) that leave at 6am, but it is a long direct journey of about nine or 10 hours. Check the security situation extremely carefully before travelling, as buses have been attacked along this route.

If you want to visit friends up here or travel for work, **Eagle Air** (☎ 041-344292; www .flyeagleuganda.com) flies here daily, charging US$95/180 one way/return.

UGANDA DIRECTORY

This section covers information specific to Uganda. For general information applicable to the region, see p617.

ACCOMMODATION
Camping
Almost every destination in Uganda offers some sort of camping, so it's worth carrying a tent if you're on a budget. Kampala has several options, as do most other popular towns and all the national parks. The cost of camping is usually USh3000 to USh10,000 per person per day, plus the entry fee if you're staying at a national park (US$10 to US$20 per person per day). When it comes to camping at some of the smaller national parks, it is possible to use camping grounds just outside the park boundaries, thus saving on the park entry fee. Facilities are generally basic (pit toilets, cold water) at the national parks.

Hotels
Hotels range from fleapits to five-star, although at the moment the former far outnumber the latter in most towns. Places are not exceptional value when compared with some other parts of Africa. As tourism and commerce continue to pick up, so does the construction of new hotels and lodges. Currently, genuine upmarket hotels are limited to Kampala; elsewhere the best you'll find are no more than about three-star quality.

The same applies to the lodges in the national parks. Again, things are gradually improving, and a number of sophisticated operations have opened their doors (or tent flaps) for business.

At the other end of the scale, you can count on all small towns having at least one basic lodge. Some of these are pretty miserable places to stay, but as the towns get bigger, so does the choice of hotels.

Budget single/double rooms are available from about USh5000/8000, rooms with bathroom start at USh10,000/15,000, and comfortable rooms with TV and hot water can be found from USh40,000/60,000. Top-end hotels and lodges start at around US$100 and can go a lot higher.

National Parks & Reserves
There is a wide range of accommodation available within Uganda's national parks, from simple camp sites with pit toilets and campfires, to *bandas* (thatch-roofed huts) with camp canteens, to luxury tented camps and lodges with prices to match the facilities.

Camping in most national parks costs USh10,000 per person per night and tents are usually available for hire for an additional USh10,000. *Bandas* usually cost about USh10,000/15,000 a single/double with shared facilities and USh20,000/30,000 with bathroom. As for the luxury tented camps and lodges around Uganda, they charge anything from US$65 to US$200 per person per night with full board, depending on the facilities and the time of year.

Accommodation charges do not include park entry fees, so many independent travellers opt to stay outside the national parks in nearby towns, guesthouses or camping grounds. Uganda Community Tourism Association (Ucota) has a number of excellent community camping grounds around the country, including on the edges of Bwindi Impenetrable, Mgahinga Gorilla and Rwenzori Mountains National Parks, and around the Kibale Forest area. See p474 in the Kampala section for more details. For more on Uganda's national parks, see p467.

ACTIVITIES
Bird-Watching
Uganda is one of the world's best birding destinations, a twitcher's fantasy offering

more than 1000 species in this compact country of contrasting terrain and climatic diversity. Bird-watching legends, such as the shoebill stork, are found in the west, while the country's unique geographical position allows visitors to view Albertine rift endemics in Semuliki National Park (p513) on the same trip as dry-season eastern specials in Kidepo Valley National Park (p507). Even amateurs will be enthralled by the diversity of beauty among Uganda's bird life.

Boating

There are two famous launch trips on offer in Uganda: the journey up the Victoria Nile River to the base of Murchison Falls, and the cruise along the Kazinga Channel in Queen Elizabeth National Park. Both trips offer the opportunity of viewing hundreds of hippos, buffaloes and often a few elephants. Although it is often more common to see predators, such as lions and leopards, along the banks of the Kazinga Channel, the Murchison Falls trip is ultimately more spectacular – the falls themselves are awesome, and there is a reasonable chance that bird-watchers will spot the elusive shoebill stork (see the boxed text, p468).

Caving

For information on caving near Mgahinga Gorilla National Park, see p532.

Chimpanzee Tracking

Primate tracking is a very popular activity in Uganda and there are several places where viewing chimpanzees is possible. Most popular of these are Budongo Central Forest Reserve (p545, part of Murchison Falls National Park) and Kibale Forest National Park (p511). The chance of seeing chimps at both of these parks is very high – as good as 85%. It is best to set aside two days for chimpanzee walks, so if you draw a blank on the first day, you can try a second time. As Budongo Central Forest Reserve is run by the forestry department, chimp viewing here (USh12,000) is far cheaper than in Kibale Forest National Park (US$50). Budget Murchison Falls trips operating out of Kampala include chimp tracking in Budongo.

Kyambura (Chambura) Gorge, part of Queen Elizabeth National Park (p521), is a truly stunning setting in which to track chimps (US$30) Sightings here are not as certain as in Budongo and Kibale, but the walk itself is enchanting. Semliki Valley Game Reserve (p514) also has a chimp habituation project well under way.

For guaranteed chimp sighting, the sanctuary on Ngamba Island in Lake Victoria (near Entebbe) is the place to go – the chimps live in a semi-tame, protected environment here. For details, see p489.

Fishing

The Victoria Nile River is a favoured habitat of the massive Nile perch, some weighing more than 100kg. Sport-fishing permits are available for US$50 per day in Murchison Falls National Park. Some companies also offer fishing trips on Lake Victoria – see p490 for more details.

Gorilla Tracking

Gorilla tracking is one of the major draws for travellers in Uganda. It's possible to track the mountain gorillas in Bwindi Impenetrable National Park (p523; US$360 per person) throughout the year. It is also sometimes possible to see them at Mgahinga Gorilla National Park near Kisoro, but they had not set foot in Uganda for several months during our last visit. Bookings should be made with the UWA office (p474) in Kampala. For more information on the mountain gorillas, see p97.

Guided Walks

Guided walks are offered in many of the forested national parks and a number of smaller forest reserves throughout Uganda. The most popular are the chimpanzee-viewing walks; however, there is also a variety of other types of forest walks available at Bwindi Impenetrable, Kibale Forest and Mgahinga Gorilla National Parks, offering an opportunity to view some of Uganda's many birds and monkeys.

Beyond the national parks, there are some excellent trails in smaller community reserves around the country, particularly at the Bigodi Wetland Sanctuary (p512), near Fort Portal, as well as at Mabira (p490) and Mpanga (p490) Forest Reserves, which are both found around Kampala and are easy day trips from the capital. Sipi Falls (p504), in the foothills of Mt Elgon, also offers some splendid walking country and local guides know the terrain well.

At Lake Mburo National Park (p535) it's possible to undertake a walking safari with an armed ranger and have close encounters with hippos, buffaloes and herds of zebras, particularly around water holes in the dry seasons.

Most guided walks now cost US$5/10 per person per half day/full day in national parks, often less in community forest reserves.

Hiking & Trekking

Uganda has always had a strong attraction among the dedicated trekking fraternity, mainly for the opportunities presented by the Rwenzori Mountains and Mt Elgon. Both Rwenzori Mountains and Mt Elgon National Parks are in pristine condition, and serious trekkers consider the Rwenzori Mountains one of the best ranges in Africa, if not the world. The Rwenzoris or 'Mountains of the Moon' present one of the most challenging mountain experiences in Africa and offer the chance for genuine climbing if you attempt one of the peaks. However, Mt Elgon is the more affordable option for the casual climber. See p519 and p503 for more.

It is also possible to climb the three volcanoes at Mgahinga Gorilla National Park (p532) – Mt Muhavura, Mt Sabinyo and Mt Gahinga. These are day climbs and each costs US$40 per person. The views towards Rwanda and DR Congo are spectacular.

White-Water Rafting & Kayaking

Only in Uganda is it possible to raft the source of the mighty Nile River, and the water here is big, oh so very big, with four Grade Five rapids waiting for the uninitiated.

The trips are operated by four companies – Adrift, Equator, Nabulale and Nile River Explorers – and can be booked in Kampala or Jinja. For details, see the boxed text, p495.

The Nile offers world-class kayaking and a couple of the white-water-rafting companies offers kayaking classes. Check out **Kayak the Nile** (www.kayakthenile.com) for more on one-, three- and five-day classes and an introduction to tandem kayaking, taking on the wild waters without the responsibility. For more details, see p495.

Wildlife Watching

There are four national parks in Uganda that offer the opportunity for wildlife drives:

Murchison Falls, Queen Elizabeth, Kidepo Valley and Lake Mburo.

The greatest variety of wildlife is to be seen on a drive through Queen Elizabeth National Park, as it has the highest number of species of any park in Uganda; however, Murchison Falls, north of the Nile, offers the larger mammals in greater concentration and fast-recovering populations of giraffes not seen in Queen Elizabeth National Park. At both parks you should see elephants, buffaloes, bushbucks and kobs; and, although it's not so easy to spot predators, with a bit of luck you might also see lions and leopards. Taking a ranger-guide will increase the chances significantly.

In Kidepo Valley National Park, much of the wildlife is within a short walking distance of the Apoka rest camp, so organised wildlife drives aren't so necessary. However, to have an opportunity to spot cheetahs or giraffes, you may need to venture further afield.

As Lake Mburo National Park is the only savanna environment in Uganda where you can undertake guided walks with an armed ranger, many people don't bother with wildlife drives. It's also usually possible to see the large herds of zebras, for which it is famous, as you drive into the park.

BOOKS

There are not a whole lot of books that relate specifically to Uganda, but several excellent works of fiction dealing with Uganda's turbulent past have come out in the past few years. For more on these titles, see p466.

Guidebooks

The Uganda Tourist Board (UTB) has published several informative books covering wildlife and national parks in the country. For keen bird-watchers, *Where to Watch Birds in Uganda* by Jonathan Rossouw and Marco Sacchi is an absolute must; it covers every major bird-watching area in the country, with a rundown on what to look out for and where. The book has some excellent photographs of some of Uganda's more than 1000 bird species and some good maps of the country's national parks. UTB has also produced guides to several other national parks, including Murchison Falls, Bwindi and Mgahinga, and Kibale Forest.

If you want a guidebook for the coffee table once the trip is over, *Eye of the Storm –*

A Photographic Journey Across Uganda by David Pluth is worth picking up.

For some more information on field guides to the wildlife and bird life of East Africa, see p73.

History & Politics

Uganda – From the Pages of Drum is a lively compilation of articles that originally appeared in the now-defunct *Drum* magazine. These chronicle the rise of Idi Amin, the atrocities he committed, as well as Museveni's bush war and his coming to power. It includes photos and forms a powerful record of what the country experienced.

For a better understanding of the man who has controlled Uganda for almost two decades, try *Sowing the Mustard Seed*, President Yoweri Museveni's autobiography.

Fong & the Indians by Paul Theroux is set in a fictional East African country that bears a remarkable likeness to Uganda. It is set in pre-civil war days, and is at times both funny and bizarre as it details the life of a Chinese immigrant and his dealings with the Asians who control commerce in the country.

The Man with the Key has Gone! by Dr Ian Clarke is an autobiographical account of the time spent in Uganda's Luwero Triangle district by a British doctor and his family. It is a lively read and the title refers to a problem that many a traveller may encounter in provincial Uganda.

BUSINESS HOURS

Government offices and businesses in Uganda are generally open between 8.30am and 4.30pm or 5.30pm, with a short break for lunch some time between noon and 2pm. Most shops and banks do not break for lunch, but some banks close early at 3.30pm.

Local restaurant hours are 7am to 9pm, and international-type restaurants are open 11.30am to 2.30pm and 5.30pm to 10.30pm.

CHILDREN

Uganda can be a lot of fun for children, with some great national parks, lots of water-based activities and lots of attention from the Ugandan people. That said, the prevalence of dangerous diseases makes it a place to travel cautiously. As elsewhere in the region, make them cover up and apply repellent religiously, as malaria is an ever-present threat. Baby products are widely available in Kampala and other major centres, but soon dry up elsewhere. Cots are available in major hotels in the capital, but not elsewhere, and child seats are hard to come by in restaurants or for hired cars. That said, hundreds of expats bring their children up happily in Kampala, it's just upcountry where a little more care and caution needs to be applied.

DANGERS & ANNOYANCES

Even today, two decades on from Museveni's rise to power, Uganda still has a lingering image as a dangerous and unstable country to visit. This is a great shame, as for the most part it is one of the more stable countries in the region – at least the parts that most tourists visit – and also one of the safer, as mugging and petty theft are still relatively rare in Kampala.

That said, there are still some places where your safety cannot be guaranteed. The north has long had a reputation for instability and, at the time of writing, remains the most dangerous part of the country. The rebels of the LRA have been running amok since they were dispersed from their bases in southern Sudan, and it is unwise to travel to Gulu, Lira and all points north. Even Murchison Falls National Park has been affected and remote areas of the park are considered unsafe. The LRA doesn't usually operate in the northeast, but this doesn't make it that much safer – there is cattle rustling and banditry there. It is imperative to check local security conditions before attempting to make an overland trip to Kidepo Valley National Park.

As for the southwest, it has been very stable since the murder of eight tourists in Bwindi Impenetrable National Park in March 1999. Bwindi now has a large military presence to ensure that visitors are kept safe; Mgahinga Gorilla National Park also has some military presence, although less than at Bwindi. It is still wise to check the latest conditions if you are planning on visiting remote border regions, such as Ishasha in Queen Elizabeth National Park, though, as it would be easy for Congolese rebels to infiltrate these porous border areas.

The most important thing to remember about security is that there is absolutely no substitute for researching current conditions when you enter the country. Read newspapers, ask other travellers and hotel staff for the latest, and check locally once you are in the provincial areas. Things can change – for the better and worse – very quickly in East Africa, and it pays to be well informed.

DISCOUNT CARDS

It is worth carrying an ISIC card when travelling to Uganda, as student visas are available for just US$20. There is also a 25% discount for entry into national parks, which can save a lot of cash during a long safari.

EMBASSIES & CONSULATES
Ugandan Embassies

For Ugandan embassies in Kenya, Rwanda or Tanzania, see the relevant section in those chapters. Ugandan embassies worldwide:

Belgium (☎ 02-762 5825; Ave de Tervuren 317, 1150 Brussels)
Canada (☎ 613-613 7797; 231 Cobourg St, Ottawa, Ontario KIN 8J2)
Denmark (☎ 31 62066; Sofievej 15, DK 2900, Hellerup)
Ethiopia (☎ 01-513531; Africa Ave H-18, K-36, Addis Ababa)
France (☎ 01 53 70 62 70; 13 Ave Raymond Poincare, 75116 Paris)
Italy (☎ /fax 06-322 5220; Via Ennio Quirino Visconti 8, 00193 Rome)
Japan (☎ 03-3465 4552; 39-15 Oyama-chi, Shibuya-ku, Tokyo 151)
South Africa (☎ 012-344 4100; Trafalgar Ct, Apt 35B, 634 Park St, Arcadia 0083, Pretoria)
UK (☎ 020-7839 5783; Uganda House, 58/59 Trafalgar Sq, London WC2N 5DX) Represents Australia and New Zealand also.
USA (☎ 202-726 0416; 5909 16th St NW, Washington DC 20011-2896)

Embassies in Uganda

Foreign embassies in Kampala:

Belgium (☎ 041-349559; Rwenzori House, Lumumba Ave)
Burundi (☎ 041-235850; Hannington Rd; 🕑 9am-1pm & 2-5pm Mon-Fri) A one-month single-entry visa costs US$40, requires two passport photos and can usually be issued the next day. Visas are available at land borders and the airport, however.
Denmark (☎ 041-350938; 3 Lumumba Ave)
DR Congo (☎ 041-230610; 20 Philip Rd, Kololo) Anyone planning to visit DR Congo can obtain an eight-day visa (US$35) at the border.
Ethiopia (☎ 041-341885; Nakayima Rd; 🕑 8.30am-12.30pm & 2-5.30pm Mon-Fri) Visas cost US$50 for most nationalities and require two passport photos. Visas take at least 24 hours to process – often longer, depending on your nationality.

France (☎ 041-342120; 16 Lumumba Ave)
Italy (☎ 041-250450; 11 Lourdel Rd, Nakasero)
Kenya (☎ 041-258235; 41 Nakasero Rd; 🕑 8.30am-12.30pm & 2-4.30pm Mon-Fri) A visa costs US$50 and two passport photos are required. If you apply before noon, the visa can usually be issued the same day. It's easier to get it on arrival.
Netherlands (☎ 041-346000; Rwenzori House, Lumumba Ave)
Rwanda (☎ 041-344045; 2 Nakayima Rd; 🕑 8.30am-12.30pm & 2.30-5pm) Next door to the Uganda Museum. Visas cost US$60 (the same for all nationalities), require two passport photos and are issued the same day if you apply in the morning. They are also available on arrival.
South Africa (☎ 041-230001; 15A Nakasero Rd)
Sudan (☎ 041-243518; 21 Nakasero Rd; 🕑 10am-3pm Tue & Thu) A visa costs US$30 for single entry and can take up to one week to process.
Tanzania (☎ 041-256272; 6 Kagera Rd; 🕑 9am-4pm Mon-Fri) Visas are valid for three months, require two passport photos and take 24 hours to issue. Costs vary according to your country of origin.
UK (☎ 078-312000; Kira Rd)
USA (☎ 041-259791; Gaba Rd)

HOLIDAYS

New Year's Day 1 January
NRM Anniversary Day 26 January
International Women's Day 8 March
Easter (Good Friday, Holy Saturday and Easter Monday) March/April
Labour Day 1 May
Martyrs' Day 3 June
Heroes' Day 9 June
Independence Day 9 October
Christmas Day 25 December
Boxing Day 26 December

INTERNET ACCESS

Internet access is easy in Kampala and there are places all over town, charging USh25 to USh50 per minute. Access has spread beyond the capital, but it is more expensive – from USh100 to USh300 per minute. Access is currently possible in popular places like Jinja, Mbale, Fort Portal, Mbarara and Kabale.

INTERNET RESOURCES

There isn't exactly an abundance of useful material on the Internet about Uganda, but the **Uganda Travel Planner** (www.traveluganda.co.ug) is the best place to start looking. It's a comprehensive online travel guide to Uganda and has plenty of links to other Uganda websites.

MAPS

The best available map of Uganda is Macmillan's *Uganda Traveller's Map* (1:1,350,000), which is available in bookshops in Kampala (USh8000). It includes insets of the Murchison Falls, Queen Elizabeth and Rwenzori Mountains National Parks, and a street map of Kampala.

MONEY

The Ugandan shilling (USh) is a relatively stable, if rather weak, currency that floats freely against the US dollar.

Notes in circulation are USh1000, USh5000, USh10,000, USh20,000 and USh50,000, and coins are USh50, USh100, USh200 and USh500.

ATMs

The only banks in Uganda with ATMs that accept international credit cards are Standard Chartered Bank and Barclays Bank. Standard Chartered has a network of ATMs at branches and Shell petrol stations in Kampala, and at branches in Jinja, Mbale and Mbarara. Stanbic Bank has a comprehensive network of local ATMs nationwide and was talking about upgrading them to accept international credit cards; check on progress at the main branch in Kampala.

Cash

The Ugandan shilling trades at whatever it's worth against other major currencies and there's usually little fluctuation from day to day. However, it has been on a slow downwards path over the last decade. Small-denomination US-dollar notes attract a much lower rate of exchange than US$50 and US$100 notes, so unless you don't mind losing as much as 20% of your money in a transaction, come with large notes. Barclays Bank is the one bank that exchanges at the same rate for all notes. Notes issued before 2000 are also deemed unacceptable, so come with newer bills. Barclays Bank in Kampala will change notes issued from 1996–99, but at a 1% commission with a minimum charge of US$10.

Credit Cards

For credit-card cash advances, the only realistic option is Barclays Bank in Kampala, although in a fix you might be able to persuade an upmarket hotel to give you a cash advance against your card. Barclays Bank offers advances in US dollars or Ugandan shillings, but charges a hefty commission.

International Transfers

Money transfers are actually more straightforward than one would imagine, even in provincial areas, but they are an expensive way to secure some cash. Western Union is quite well represented in major towns throughout the country, as it has a partnership with Centenary Rural Development Bank.

Moneychangers

There is no black market. As a result, it doesn't really matter too much where you change your money, though the foreign exchange bureaus generally offer a slightly better rate than the banks. The trouble is that not every town has a foreign exchange bureau and, where one doesn't exist, the banks take advantage of this by offering poor rates. Likewise, hotels give bad rates. The best bank rates are available at Crane Bank, which is represented in Kampala and Jinja. Standard Chartered Bank is another option in Mbale and Mbarara. The best all-rounder these days is Stanbic Bank, as it covers all major towns in Uganda.

Tipping & Bargaining

Tipping is not always expected in Uganda, but as wages are very low by Western standards, a tip will always be appreciated. The size of a given tip is up to the individual, but as a guideline 10% is probably fair in restaurants, while USh5000 to USh10,000 is reasonable for ranger-guides or escorts in national parks.

For bargaining tips while shopping, see p626. It's a good idea to bargain when looking for transport, for example, on minibuses beyond Kampala, *boda-bodas* and special hires.

Travellers Cheques

Thanks to a major scam a few years ago, travellers cheques are now rarely accepted by banks or foreign exchange bureaus outside of Kampala. Where they can be changed in the capital, rates offered are generally slightly lower than those advertised for cash. Standard Chartered Bank can change Amex travellers cheques in Kampala, Jinja, Mbale and Mbarara at just 1%.

Elsewhere it can be very difficult, attracting dire rates even if it is possible. Stanbic Bank was in the process of trialling the exchange of travellers cheques at the time of writing and this will be a welcome development if it lasts, as it's the most widespread local network.

PHOTOGRAPHY & VIDEO
Film & Equipment
Colour print film and APS film are widely available in Kampala, but harder to come by elsewhere. Expect to pay around USh6000 for a 36-exposure colour print film. Slide film is much harder to find, so it's safer to bring your own. For a wide selection of film, including one slide option (100 ASA/ISO) and B&W, try **Colour Chrome** (54 Kampala Rd). This is also a reliable place to get your films developed. Think twice before developing any shots in the provinces, as the washed-out look seems to be fashionable these days! For cheap film there are lots of shops along Wilson Rd, and these places can also do passport photos in about an hour. There are also quite a number of instant photo booths around town for those in a hurry. Most Internet cafés and some photo shops can burn digital pictures to CD if the memory card is filling up fast.

POST
The cost of sending a postcard is USh1100 to Europe and USh1200 to the US or Australia. There is an efficient poste restante service at the main post office in Kampala.

Provincial post offices are reasonably reliable, and with the EMS Post Bus servicing a number of provincial capitals, postage often only takes a day or two more than from Kampala.

TELEPHONE
Telephone connections, both domestic and international, are pretty good, although not always so reliable in the provincial areas. The two big operators are Uganda Telecom (UTL) and MTN. Both have cardphones in towns throughout the country – try outside the post office if they aren't obvious elsewhere. UTL and MTN rates are pretty similar. Calls can also be made from privately operated booths in major towns across the country. This can be useful for short calls if you don't have the cash for a phonecard handy.

From public phone boxes international calls are charged at the rate of USh1000 to USh3000 per minute.

The country code for Uganda is ☎ 256. To make an international call from Uganda, dial ☎ 000. The number for directory inquiries is ☎ 901.

Mobile Phones
Mobile (cell) phones are very popular: mobile codes include ☎ 071 (UTL), ☎ 075 (Celtel), and ☎ 077 and ☎ 078 (MTN). All mobile-phone companies sell prepaid starter packs with SIM cards and airtime vouchers for topping up credit. For those on roaming, MTN probably has the best coverage across the country.

TOURIST INFORMATION
There isn't an abundance of tourist information in Uganda. UWA has the best information, but it only covers the national parks. Most travellers get their information from the most popular backpacker places in Kampala and Jinja.

Uganda Community Tourism Association (Map p471; Ucota; ☎ 041-501866; www.ucota.or.ug; Kabalagala) Promotes community tourism in Uganda.

Uganda Tourist Board (Map p472; UTB; ☎ 041-342196; www.visituganda.com; 15 Kimathi Ave, Kampala; ⏱ 8am-1pm & 2-5pm Mon-Fri, 8.30am- 12.30pm Sat) Responsible for tourism promotion in Uganda.

Uganda Wildlife Authority (Map p471; UWA; ☎ 041-346287; www.uwa.or.ug; 7 Kira Rd) Promotes the country's national parks and protected areas.

VISAS
Most non-African passport holders visiting Uganda require visas. One-month single-entry tourist visas cost US$30. If you are a student, this visa costs US$20, so it is worth having some ID handy for the embassy or border guards. It is easiest just to rock up at the airport or border and arrange one there, as no photo is required. For those who like to organise things in advance, two passport photos are required and the visa is issued within 24 hours, possibly the same day if you plead.

VISA EXTENSIONS
For visa extensions, pay a visit to the **immigration office** (Map p471; Jinja Rd, Kampala), which is 300m northeast of the roundabout after Centenary Park. Kampala is a good place

for picking up visas to other countries, as there are usually few queues at the various embassies. For visas to neighbouring countries, see p551

VOLUNTEERING

Uganda has more volunteering opportunities than many African countries thanks to a number of good grassroots organisations operating around the country. One of the most popular places to volunteer is at Bujagali Falls through **Soft Power Education** (www .softpowereducation.com), which has a number of projects to upgrade schools and improve education in the area. Also consider the local cultural organisation **Edirisa** (www.edirisa .org), which may be able to use volunteers to help with some of its education projects around Lake Bunyoni and Kabale.

Another good group to link up with is the **Uganda Community Tourism Association** (Map p471; Ucota; ☎ 041-501866; www.ucota.or.ug; Kabalagala) based in Kampala. It works with tourism-related projects across the country and should be able to advise on volunteer opportunities.

TRANSPORT IN UGANDA

GETTING THERE & AWAY

For information on getting to Uganda from outside East Africa, see p632.

Air

Located on the shores of Lake Victoria about 41km south of the capital, **Entebbe International Airport** (EBB) is the international gateway to Kampala and Uganda. Few budget travellers enter Uganda by air because most of the discounted air fares available in Europe and North America use Nairobi (Kenya) as the gateway to East Africa. However, for tourists on a short trip, there are some pretty good airlines offering smooth worldwide connections, including British Airways, Emirates and KLM.

AIRLINES IN UGANDA

Air Burundi (airline code 8Y; ☎ 041-256137) Hub: Bujumbura.

Air Tanzania (airline code TC; ☎ 041-345773; www.air tanzania.com) Hub: Dar es Salaam.

British Airways (airline code BA; ☎ 041-257414; www .britishairways.com) Hub: London.

EgyptAir (airline code MS; ☎ 041-233960; www.egypt air.com.eg) Hub: Cairo.

Emirates (airline code EK; ☎ 041-349941; www.emirates .com) Hub: Dubai.

Ethiopian Airlines (airline code ET; ☎ 041-254796; www .flyethiopian.com) Hub: Addis Ababa.

Gulf Air (airline code GF; ☎ 041-230524; www.gulfairco .com) Hub: Abu Dhabi.

Kenya Airways (airline code KQ; ☎ 041-344304; www .kenya-airways.com) Hub: Nairobi.

KLM (airline code KL; ☎ 041-344304; www.klm.com) Hub: Amsterdam.

Rwandair Express (airline code WB; ☎ 041-232555; www.rwandair.com) Hub: Kigali.

SN Brussels Airline (airline code SN; ☎ 041-234200; www.brusselsairlines.com) Hub: Brussels.

South African Airways (airline code SA; ☎ 041-345772; www.flysaa.com) Hub: Johannesburg.

Sudan Airways (airline code SD; ☎ 041-230438; www .sudanair.com) Hub: Khartoum.

TO/FROM BURUNDI

Air Burundi is currently the only airline offering flights between Bujumbura and Entebbe. There are, however, more expensive indirect tickets available with Kenya Airways.

TO/FROM KENYA

Kenya Airways is the only consistent option connecting Entebbe and Nairobi.

TO/FROM RWANDA

Rwandair Express offers reliable connections between Entebbe and Kigali, while Air Burundi also touch down in Kigali on flights to Burundi.

TO/FROM TANZANIA

Air Tanzania offers the only connections between Dar es Salaam and Entebbe.

Land

Uganda shares popular land border crossings with Kenya, Rwanda and Tanzania. Bus services connect the major cities in each country or local transport is available for those wanting to break their journey along the way. There are also land border crossings with DR Congo and the Sudan, but with the exception of the Bunagana border post between Uganda and DR Congo for mountain gorilla visits, it is currently not advisable to travel overland to these countries due to civil instability (see p556).

TO/FROM KENYA

The two main border crossings that most overland travellers use are Malaba and Busia, with Malaba being by far the most popular.

The Ugandan and Kenyan border crossings are about 1km from each other at Malaba and you can walk or take a *boda-boda*. Taking a vehicle through this border crossing is fairly straightforward and doesn't take more than an hour or so.

The other crossing is via Busia, which is further south. Busia only appeals to those travelling direct from Jinja or Kampala to Kisumu. There are frequent minibuses between Jinja and Busia (USh6000), and *matatus* (shared minibuses) between Busia and Kisumu.

Doing the journey in stages, there are frequent minibuses between Malaba and Kampala (USh9000, three hours) or Jinja (USh6000, two hours) until late afternoon. There are also frequent minibuses between Tororo and Malaba (USh1500, approximately 30 minutes).

On the Kenyan side there are daily buses between Malaba and Nairobi with various companies, departing at about 7.30pm and arriving at about 5.30am the next day. If you prefer to travel by day there are plenty of *matatus* between Malaba and Bungoma, which take about 45 minutes. If you need to stay in Bungoma overnight there are plenty of cheap hotels to choose from. From Bungoma there are several buses daily to Nairobi, which leave at about 8am and arrive about 5pm the same day.

Most travellers avoid local transport altogether and opt for the direct buses running between Kampala and Nairobi, which range from basic to luxurious. Some of the overnight services arrive in Nairobi in the early hours of the morning – take care, as Nairobi is a more dangerous city than Kampala.

Scandinavian Express (☎ 041-348895; 8 Colville St, Kampala) operates a luxury coach to Nairobi (USh50,000, 12 hours, departing at 1pm) that includes drinks and movies, making it possibly the company of choice, although the arrival time is a bit of a nightmare.

Akamba (☎ 041-250412; 28 Dewinton Rd, Kampala) operates two classes daily. The 'executive'-class buses cost USh23,000, take about 12 hours, and depart at 7am and 3pm. The daily 'royal' service is more comfortable, with larger seats similar to business class in an

aircraft; there are only three seats per row! Tickets cost USh38,000 and the route goes via Kisumu (approximately 12 hours, 7am departure).

Regional Coach (☎ 041-256862; 4 Luwum St, Kampala) has modern buses and has a daily service to Nairobi (USh23,000, approximately 12 hours, departing at 4pm).

Busscar (☎ 041-233030; 8 Burton St, Kampala) also operates a service to Nairobi (USh22,000, departing at 3pm), but the buses aren't quite as comfortable as the other options.

RWANDA

There are two main border crossing points: between Kabale and Kigali via Katuna (Gatuna on the Rwandan side), and between Kisoro and Ruhengeri via Cyanika.

Between Kabale and Kigali there are lots of minibuses, but these involve a change of vehicle at the border. There are minibuses (USh1000) and special-hire taxis (USh15,000 for the whole car) travelling back and forth between Kabale and Katuna. It takes up to one hour to get through the two border crossings. On the Rwandan side there are minibuses travelling to Kigali (RFr1500, 1½ hours) throughout the day, but they can take time to fill up. There are several military checkpoints between the border and Kigali where all baggage is searched.

From Kisoro to Ruhengeri via Cyanika the road is in reasonable condition on the Ugandan side and in excellent shape on the Rwandan side. Infrequent minibuses link both sides of the border with Kisoro (USh1000, 12km) and Ruhengeri (RFr500, 25km). If transport is thin on the ground consider taking a motorbike.

There is also the option of taking a direct bus between Kampala and Kigali. **Jaguar Executive Coaches** (☎ 041-251855; 26 Nakivubo Rd, Kampala) offers a 'VIP' bus (USh20,000, departing at 7am and 9am) and a standard service (USh15,000, departing at 5am and 6am) taking anything from eight to 10 hours, including a slow border crossing. The

VIP bus is worth the extra cost and includes movies.

Regional Coach (☎ 041-256862; 4 Luwum St, Kampala) has one bus a day to Kigali (USh23,000), approximately nine hours, departing at about 9am).

Gaso Bus (☎ 041-572917; Bus Park, Kampala) has one bus a day to Kigali (USh20,000) leaving at the rather ridiculous hour of 2am. Hit the town first for some beers and save a night's accommodation perhaps? This service continues to Bujumbura (USh40,000) in Burundi, arriving at 4pm.

TANZANIA

The most commonly used direct route between Uganda and Tanzania is on the west side of Lake Victoria between Bukoba and Masaka, and goes via the border crossing at Mutukula. Road conditions have improved dramatically over the last few years, and it's possible to do the journey from Kampala to Bukoba in just half a day. See p634 for more information.

There's another border crossing at Nkurungu, to the west of Mutukula, but the road is bad and little transport passes this way.

For information on Scandinavian Express connections between Kampala and Dar es Salaam via Nairobi and Arusha, see p555. Akamba also has a service to Dar es Salaam (USh53,000, departing at 7am and 3pm) passing through Arusha (USh38,000). See p555 for contact details of both these companies.

Lake

There used to be passenger services on Lake Victoria between Port Bell (near Kampala) and Mwanza (Tanzania) via Bukoba (Tanzania), but they were discontinued several years ago.

Some travellers have managed to book passage to Mwanza on cargo ferries run by **Tanzania Railways** (☎ 041-233384). Permission for this can be arranged at the railway station in Kampala and should cost about USh20,000. The trip takes 16 hours and it is usually possible to make a deal with one of the crew members for their bunk once on board.

Tours

For all the juicy details on safaris and tours in Uganda, see the comprehensive Safaris section (p95); for more on international

---

> ### CROSSING INTO DR CONGO OR SUDAN?
>
> #### DR Congo
> It is now possible to cross the border into DR Congo to visit the mountain gorillas at either Djomba or Bukima in Parc National des Virungas – see p561 for more details. However, much of DR Congo has been embroiled in a messy civil war for many years, and even with the advent of peace there are still several rival rebel factions roaming the countryside. For this reason, we cannot currently recommend crossing at any border, except the Bunagana crossing, and even in this case, check, check and check again in Kampala and Kisoro so you are not heading into the unknown.
>
> #### Sudan
> The civil wars in northern Uganda and southern Sudan effectively wiped overland travel between the two countries off the map. Peace has come to southern Sudan and there is talk of regular land borders opening once again. However, even if the situation in southern Sudan is now considered stable, travelling this way still involves extensive travel through northern Uganda, the most dangerous region of the country due to the brutal activities of the LRA. Do not undertake such a journey without checking the security situation every step of the way.

operators organising tours to Uganda and elsewhere in East Africa, see p635.

GETTING AROUND
Air
AIRLINES IN UGANDA

Domestic flights are few and far between in Uganda. There are some smaller airlines offering both scheduled and charter flights from Kampala. **Eagle Uganda** (☎ 041-344292; 11 Portal Ave) and **United Airlines** (☎ 041-349841; Kimathi Ave) offer connections to remote towns in the north, but these aren't really destinations of interest to the average tourist.

Other private operators, such as **KAFTC** (☎ 077-706106; barnsey@imul.com), offer charter services to destinations like Kidepo Valley and Murchison Falls National Parks.

Boat

Given the immense size of Lake Victoria, there are very limited opportunities for travel by boat, the only options being the short ferry to the Ssese Islands from Bukakata (east of Masaka) and the small boats operating from Kasenyi (a 30-minute taxi ride from Kampala). See p538 for details.

Bus

Standard buses connect the major towns on a daily basis. They're usually slightly cheaper than minibuses, but travel just as fast; too fast in fact – some drivers seem reckless to the point of being nutters. Standard buses usually stop far less frequently than minibuses, which saves time on longer journeys. From Kampala, standard buses rarely have fixed departure times, as they leave only when full, but there will be at least one bus per day to most towns, the first one leaving as early as 4.30am. However, returning from provincial destinations, they tend to have scheduled departure times.

In addition to the normal private buses, there are EMS Post Buses. These travel from Kampala to all the major centres daily. They cost about the same as a normal bus, but they are safer and stop less frequently than minibuses.

See p485 for details of routes, schedules and prices.

MATATUS

Uganda is the land of shared minibuses (known as taxis or *matatus*), and there's never any shortage of them. Fares are fixed and vehicles leave when full. Travel on the major routes out of Kampala is relatively civilised, even though many drivers are speed maniacs who go much too fast to leave any leeway for emergencies. However, overcrowding is a big problem as soon as you are a fair distance away from urban centres and stuffing as many as 30 people into a 14-seat minibus is common.

Car & Motorcycle

There's a pretty good system of sealed roads between most major population centres in the southern part of the country. It is somewhat pointless to talk of which particular roads are good and which are bad, as this changes rapidly from year to year. Uganda has two wet seasons, which means the roads

take a serious pounding from the elements, and surfaces deteriorate rapidly. Roads that are good this year are bad the next and, if repaired, good again the following year. When travelling on sealed roads, it is necessary to have your wits about you – large potholes often appear from nowhere.

The quality of dirt roads varies widely depending on whether it is the wet or dry season. In the dry season dirt roads are very, very dusty and you'll end up choking behind trucks and taxis, while covering the local population in a fine layer of orange dust. In the wet season a number of the dirt roads become muddy mires, almost carrot soup, and may be passable only in a 4WD vehicle. If you are travelling around Uganda in the wet seasons, always ask about the latest road conditions before setting off on a journey.

Road signs are totally absent in Uganda. There are hardly any, even outside major towns. Unless you know where you're going, it's possible to get hopelessly lost.

Carrying a map is one solution, but you'll also need a compass, since there are no decent large scale maps. Getting out of the vehicle and talking to local people is obviously the best idea, but sometimes they don't know the way either! A GPS is handy for a serious adventure.

Another problem in Uganda is road safety. Bus and minibus drivers seem to be hellbent on overtaking everything on the road, even if it is quite clearly travelling faster! Horrific crashes are fairly common, which means the utmost vigilance is required when driving on Ugandan roads. Thankfully, the further you travel from Kampala the lighter the traffic becomes.

DRIVING LICENCE

If you have an International Driving Permit, you should bring it (although you really only need your local driving licence from home).

FUEL & SPARE PARTS

Fuel is expensive by regional standards. Petrol costs about USh2000 per litre; diesel is about USh1600 per litre. In provincial areas, fuel is a little more expensive the further you get away from major towns.

HIRE

Uganda's vehicle-hire industry is small scale and that means prices are very high compared to other parts of the world. Many independent travellers find it cheaper to negotiate directly with 'special-hire' taxi drivers or local minibus touts.

Hertz (Map p472; ☎ 077-450460; Colville St, Kampala) is a trusted if expensive option, charging around US$65 for a small car with insurance and US$130 and up for 4WDs. This doesn't include excess kilometres above the paltry 100km allowance, which are charged at US$0.30 for a small car and US$0.50 for a 4WD.

It works out considerably cheaper to deal with one of the local travel companies hiring cars. **City Cars** (☎ 077-412001; www.driveuganda .com) is one of the leading local car-hire companies. It charges US$35 per day for a small car, with 150km and US$0.20 per kilometre thereafter. A Land Rover will cost US$70 per day, also with 150 free kilometres per day (US$0.30 each excess kilometre). Drivers are available for an extra US$20 per day, and more luxurious vehicles include the Land Rover Discovery or Toyota Landcruiser.

Wemtec (☎ 043-121314; engineering@wemtec.biz), based in Jinja, has reasonably priced Land Rovers for hire with drivers. A 109 soft top costs USh130,000 per day and a 110 hard top is USh170,000.

There are also saloon-car taxis throughout the country, known commonly as 'specials' or 'special-hire' taxis. These can be chartered around the capital, between cities and into national parks, but are more expensive than minibuses. However, they can be a cheap alternative to hiring a car if you are prepared to bargain hard, and cover the driver's food and accommodation as you go. You may be able to negotiate something

around USh35,000 a day, excluding fuel and the driver's accommodation and food.

Hitching

Without your own transport, hitching is virtually obligatory in some situations, such as getting into national parks, to which there's no public transport. Most of the lifts will be on trucks, usually on top of the load at the back, which can be a very pleasant way to travel, though sun protection is a must. Free lifts on trucks are the exception rather than the rule, so ask before you board.

Other sources for lifts are rangers and staff who work in the parks, international aid workers, missionaries, businesspeople and the occasional diplomat, but you may have to wait a long time in some places before anyone comes along. See p638 for more on hitching in the region, including safety.

Local Transport

Kampala has a local minibus network, as well as 'special-hire' taxis for private trips. Elsewhere you'll have to rely on bicycle taxis (known locally as *boda-bodas*, as they originally shuttled people between border posts) or, in places like Kampala, Jinja and Fort Portal, motorbike taxis.

Train

There are two main railway lines in Uganda. The first starts at Tororo and runs west all the way to Kasese via Jinja and Kampala. The other line runs from Tororo northwest to Pakwach via Mbale, Soroti, Lira and Gulu. However, at the time of research all passenger services had been suspended indefinitely and they are unlikely to resume.

Detour: Democratic Republic of the Congo

A country so vast it spans the African continent from Angola to Uganda and Sudan to Zambia, the Democratic Republic of the Congo (DR Congo) is the size of western Europe. Home to some of the last unexplored wildernesses on earth and one of the mightiest rivers, DR Congo is perhaps our planet's last great adventure. The long civil war is drawing to a close and for travellers in East Africa it is once again possible to cross into DR Congo to view mountain gorillas in the Parc National des Virungas and climb the towering volcano of Nyiragongo.

However, the peace is young and fragile and security in DR Congo is tenuous at best. Check the latest in Kampala or Kisoro (Uganza), Kigali or Gisenyi (Rwanda), before crossing into DR Congo and do not attempt an overland journey to Kinshasa. Things can change very fast in Africa, and it pays to be well informed.

Most of DR Congo falls outside East Africa, but the areas near the borders of Uganda and Rwanda covered here are beginning to draw a trickle of travellers thirsting for adventure. The lure of mountain gorillas and active volcanoes seems too much to resist – at least it was for us!

FAST FACTS

- **Area** 2,345,410 sq km
- **Birthplace of** Mobutu Sese Seko, Claude Makalele (France, Real Madrid, now Chelsea)
- **Capital** Kinshasa
- **Country code** 243
- **Famous for** gorillas, Congo River, *Heart of Darkness*
- **Languages** French and Kingwana
- **Money** Congo francs (CFr); US$1 = CFr440; €1 = CFr515
- **Population** 60 million

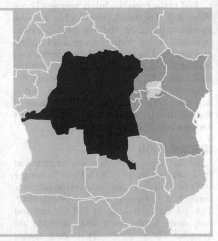

HISTORY

DR Congo is the original heart of darkness, raped and pillaged first by King Leopold of Belgium, who ran it is a personal colony, and later President Mobutu (his official title was President Mobutu Sese Seko Kuku Ngbendu Waza Banga, which meant 'the fearless warrior who will go from strength to strength leaving fire in his wake'), who used state coffers to fund essential Concorde charters to Disney World and the like. He took plunder to a new level, creating a new form of government along the way: kleptocracy, governance by theft. But the black hole that followed became Africa's first great war, sucking in as many as nine countries at its height and leading to the deaths of more than 3 million Congolese. After Rwanda, they said 'never again'. In Africa, that means 'à la prochaine' or 'till the next time'.

Even Mugabe found an angle, sending his airforce north to bomb Ugandan and Rwandan positions around Kinshasa as the capital was about to fall for a second time back in 1998. The sweetener? He was given control of state mining company Gecamines, running the richest vein of minerals in central Africa. Mobutu was famed for his extravagant shopping trips to Paris and before departure he would call up the beleaguered boss of Gecamines and demand US$150 million pocket money. Just imagine what Robert Mugabe made in three years. Look at the map, it is not far from Lubumbashi down to Harare.

Add to the mess the Interahamwe (Those Who Kill Together), responsible for the Rwandan genocide; the Mai Mai, who believe holy water protects them from bullets and wear sink plugs around their necks; and Mobutu's old henchmen still living off the land, and DR Congo has been through the mixer. Peace is slowly breaking out, but it will take time to overcome the trauma of the last 10 years. It's not that democratic, it's barely a republic, but it is Congo.

INFORMATION

Eight-day Congolese visas are available at the Goma border for US$35. Visas for longer stays of 30 days are also available in advance through a Congolese embassy for US$80. The US dollar is king in DR Congo and only notes issued from 2000 onwards are accepted. The local currency is Congo francs and during the time of our visit, the rate was similar to that of the Rwandan franc. There are moneychangers at the border post. Everyone in Goma seems to have two mobile phones, one for the Congolese network and one for the Rwandan network.

GOMA

Goma is a modern-day Pompeii, swallowed by the lava of Nyiragongo when the volcano erupted on 17 January 2002. Whole streets were smothered and the centre of the city buried under 2m of molten mess. The death toll remained low, as the lava moved slowly enough to allow residents to be evacuated. Today Goma is getting back to normal, although the centre looks more like a moonscape than a modern city. It is the capital of North Kivu province, a bustling commercial centre and a base to climb Nyiragongo volcano or visit the mountain gorillas at Bukima in Parc National des Virungas.

Sleeping & Eating

Surprisingly, there are lots of good hotels and restaurants in Goma. Most of the popular places are located on or just off the main road to Rwanda. There are plenty of good local restaurants in the city centre turning out brochettes (kebabs), fresh fish and lashings of Primus beer. International restaurants are incredibly expensive.

Stella Matutina Lodge (☎ 085 87616; Himbi; r US$80-100) This lodge has the most comfortable rooms in town, set in the spacious grounds of a grand villa to the west of the centre in Himbi district. Plush bathrooms, fine furnishings and an expensive restaurant make this the choice for high-flyers in town.

Ihusi Hotel (☎ 081 3532300; Blvd Kanyamuhanga; r incl breakfast US$55-75) Popular with UN staff and aid workers, this large hotel has 44 smart rooms. There is a nice garden and a popular lakeside bar and restaurant. This is a good place to catch up on events in DR Congo.

Bird Hotel (☎ 088 86367; Ave Bougainvillier; r US$35) For something a little bit cheaper, Bird Hotel has small rooms with bathroom and satellite TV.

Shu Shu Guesthouse (☎ 97286221; Ave Grevilleas; r US$10) Home to the cheapest rooms in town, it costs US$10 for a big bed in a room with a shared bathroom. It feels slightly out the way up a back street for those worried about security.

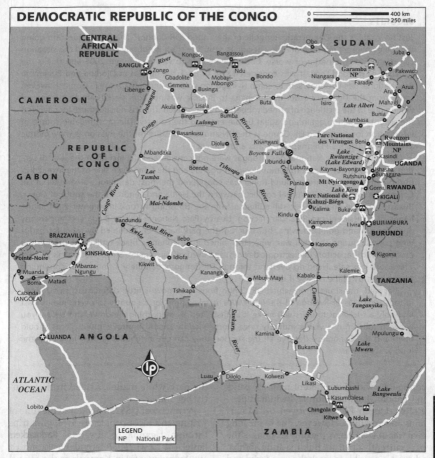

DEMOCRATIC REPUBLIC OF THE CONGO

LEGEND
NP   National Park

Hotel des Grands Lacs (☎ 98899943; Blvd Kanyamuhanga; s/d US$20/30) Once Goma's grandest hotel, this colonial relic still proudly displays its four stars in the lobby, but it would struggle to earn just one star these days. The cavernous rooms include a bathroom, but it really needs a face-lift.

Restaurant Le Chalet (☎ 088 18725; Himbi; mains US$13-25) Lavishly decorated with Congolese crafts and with a beautiful lakeside setting, this is Goma's leading restaurant. The food is French and includes juicy grills and imported duck.

Entertainment
Congolese nightlife is legendary and Goma is no exception. There are lots of good local nightclubs on Blvd Kanyamuhanga, including Cap Sud and Coco Jambo, where the locals are dancing before they have hit the entrance. Super Club Dallas conjures up images of JR and Sue Ellen, but it is a backstreet club with good local tunes.

Chez Doga (Blvd Kanyamuhanga) One of the most popular places in town, this bar-restaurant really picks up at night. UN workers, smart locals and plenty of prostitutes make for a messy mix and the party goes on into the night.

PARC NATIONAL DES VIRUNGAS
Befitting such a vast country as DR Congo, Parc National des Virungas is quite simply enormous. To put it in perspective, it is

SECURITY

Just how safe is the Democratic Republic of the Congo (DR Congo)? That is the question going though everyone's mind before they decide to visit. The truth is nobody knows and the situation can change for the better or worse, but we were able to visit in summer 2005 and this is the situation as it stood then. It was considered safe to track the gorillas at Djomba and Bukima in Parc National des Virungas, safe to climb Nyiragongo volcano and safe to stay in Goma. However, travel from the Uganda border at Bunagana to Bukima was not considered safe at the time of writing due to the incidence of armed robberies on this stretch. There is no substitute for checking the security situation again and again before entering the country. The most reliable source of information for security in DR Congo is the UN and their website for the mission is www.monuc .org, which includes PDF maps of Goma and Bukavu.

Other parts of Parc National des Virungas were not considered safe, including the Rwindi section opposite Queen Elizabeth National Park in Uganda and the Congolese side of the Rwenzoris. Ituri province and the area around Bunia was considered the most dangerous area in all of DR Congo due to the ongoing tribal conflict between the Hema and Lendu. To the south of Goma, Bukavu was safe enough, but still suffering from the thrashing it took in summer 2004 at the hands of a dissident pro-Rwandan faction. Nearby Parc National Kahuzi-Biéga was apparently open for lowland gorilla viewing, but much of the park had been occupied by rebel forces for long periods during the civil war, who strip-mined it for coltan (a black tarlike ore used in the production of capacitors in electronic devices) and lived off bush meat. Steer clear unless you are 110% sure it is safe. Heading overland through DR Congo is definitely a no-no, but continuing to Kinshasa by plane is easy if expensive.

That said, the situation in which DR Congo finds itself now is little different to say Uganda in the late 1980s or Rwanda in the mid-1990s. It takes time for a country to overcome its past and only a trickle of tourists will make it at first. Step by step, things improve and before you know it, tourism is a viable industry once more. Security should improve, more places should open and the Congolese deserve all the support they can get in rebuilding their lives after the long years of war.

contiguous with five different national parks in Uganda: Mgahinga Gorilla, Bwindi Impenetrable, Queen Elizabeth, Rwenzori Mountains and Semuliki. However, due to the long civil war in DR Congo, the only sections of the park currently open are Bukima and Djomba, where it is possible to track the wonderful and rare mountain gorillas, one of the most magical experiences in Africa.

Information

There are currently 36 permits per day available to track the mountain gorillas in Parc National des Virungas: 28 permits at Bukima and eight permits at Djomba. There is currently almost no wait time to visit the gorillas in DR Congo, as there is no long-term booking system and tour companies are still steering clear for the time being. Security is provided by the Congolese army and rangers and equipped with walkie talkies and GPS units. The rangers speak both English and French and deserve a healthy tip, as they struggled to protect the park while madness ruled in the country beyond.

Permits cost US$250 per day at the time of writing and most people are arranging trips through Uganda or Rwanda. **Backpackers Hostel** (☎ 256-41-274767; backpackers@infocom.co.ug; www.backpackers.co.ug) in Kampala is the official Uganda representative for gorilla visits in DR Congo and **Alex Mujyambere** (☎ 256-71-626194; mujaalex@yahoo.co.uk) makes the journeys up and down to DR Congo every week. **Jambo Safaris** (fax 250-543030) are the Congolese agents selling permits on behalf of the Institut Congolais pour la Conservation de Nature (ICCN), the Congolese national parks authority. They have a representative office on the Congolese side of the Bunagana border with Uganda. Arranging trips from Uganda is the easiest option as it includes transport, which is pretty scarce on the Congo side.

Dangers & Annoyances

In August 1998 four tourists were kidnapped at Djomba while attempting to visit the gorillas; one was released, but three were never found, presumed dead.

Gorilla Tracking

The four gorilla families at Bukima include Kabirizi with 30 members, Humba with 12, Rugendo with nine and Munaga with seven. Kabirizi is popular due to the large number of gorillas, but the small Munaga group includes three silverbacks. Gorilla families of less than 10 are only allowed six visitors per day. All these families are usually located between 30 minutes and three hours from the Bukima ranger post.

The habituated family at Djomba is called Mapuwa and has 11 members. The Rugendo family from Bukima sometimes strays towards Djomba meaning another eight permits available here, but it all depends on their movements. Djomba is currently the most popular place to track in DR Congo, as some visitors don't want to spend too long in the country and it is less than one hour from the Ugandan border.

Sleeping

There is a small hut at Bukima ranger post, which was derelict at the time of our visit, but the United Nations Development Programme (UNDP) are looking to redevelop it for overnight stays.

Beds are available at the small resthouse in Djomba, which has a stunning setting on a ridge below Sabyino volcano. It costs US$30 for a bed with full board, and camping is possible for US$5 per person. There is also an upmarket lodge under construction on hilltop above Djomba.

Getting There & Away

Bukima is about 40km from Goma. The main road is in reasonable condition, but the 15km access road is appalling and only passable by 4WD. It takes about two hours to get here from Goma, three hours from the Ugandan border at Bunagana, but the latter option was considered unsafe at the time of writing.

Djomba is only about 7km from Bunagana as the crow flies, but a little further by road. The road is in poor condition and best undertaken by 4WD. It is possible to walk to Djomba from the Ugandan border if you take a local as a guide.

NYIRAGONGO VOLCANO

Beautiful and brooding, locals in Goma know only too well the power of Nyiragongo. This active volcano last erupted in 2002, swallowing half of Goma in the process. It is possible to climb the volcano and camp overnight at the summit, rising early to stare down into the bubbling crater. It costs US$100 to climb, but you need your own tent, as there are no facilities at the summit. It takes about five hours to climb, about half that to descend, but it is more atmospheric to spend the night here. Bring warm clothing as it is chilly at the top. Porters are available for US$12 to carry water, food and bags to the summit. Buy all the provisions you need in Goma, as nothing is available here. The small ranger post here is about 15km from Goma on the road north to Bunagana and Uganda.

TRANSPORT

For the full lowdown on crossing into DR Congo from Uganda, Rwanda or Burundi, see the Transport sections of those individual chapters. The most commonly used crossings to enter or exit DR Congo are the Bunagana border with Uganda near Kisoro and the Goma border with Rwanda at Gisenyi. Visitors wanting to carry on to Kinshasa to link up with West Africa should only fly at the time of writing. Flights are expensive at around US$350 one way, but it saves more than a month of overland travel by road and river, and, quite possibly, your life.

Rwanda

Welcome to 'Le Pays des Milles Collines' or the Land of a Thousand Hills: Rwanda is a lush country of endless mountains and stunning scenery. Nowhere are the mountains more majestic than the peaks of the Virunga volcanoes in the far northwest of the country, forming a natural frontier with Democratic Republic of the Congo (DR Congo) and Uganda. Hidden among the bamboo and dense jungle of the volcanoes' forbidding slopes are some of the world's last remaining mountain gorillas, and it is the opportunity to encounter these contemplative creatures at close quarters that continues to draw visitors to Rwanda.

A beautiful yet brutalised country, Rwanda is all too often associated with the horrific events that unfolded here in 1994. It has been etched into the world's consciousness as one of the most savage genocides in the history of mankind. What happened here is beyond belief, but the country has taken giant strides towards recovery in the years since.

Rwanda has more than the magical mountain gorillas. The shores and bays of Lake Kivu conceal some of the best inland beaches on the African continent, pretty handy given how far it is to the sea. Deep in the southwest, Parc National Nyungwe Forest is the most extensive montane rainforest in the region and provides a home for many primates. But it's not all monkey business in Rwanda, as the capital Kigali is safe and sophisticated.

Many visitors are unsure about travelling to Rwanda given its history. However, as long as security and stability persist, Rwanda is a refreshing country in which to travel, where tourists remain a relative novelty and the rewards of the present outweigh the risks of the past.

FAST FACTS

- **Area** 26,338 sq km
- **Birthplace of** Paul Kagame
- **Capital** Kigali
- **Country code** 250
- **Famous for** Mountain gorillas
- **Languages** Kinyarwanda, French and English
- **Money** Rwandan franc (RFr); US$1 = RFr554; €1 = RFr668
- **Population** 8.6 million

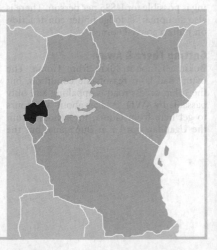

RWANDA

HIGHLIGHTS

- **Parc National des Volcans** (p583) Experience the ultimate animal encounter with the rare mountain gorillas on the slopes of the Virunga volcanoes.
- **Kigali Memorial Centre** (p576) Learn more about the horrors of the past at this haunting genocide memorial in the capital city.
- **Gisenyi** (p586) Chill out on the country's best beaches on Rwanda's very own Costa del Kivu.
- **National Museum** (p589) Check out one of Africa's best ethnographical museums in Butare, Rwanda's intellectual capital.
- **Parc National Nyungwe Forest** (p591) Get down to some monkey business in this towering forest, with a visit to the huge troops of colobus.

CLIMATE & WHEN TO GO

The average daytime temperature is around 24°C with a possible maximum of 30°C, except in the higher mountains, which take up a lot of the country, where the daytime range is 10° to 15°C. There are four discernible seasons: the long rains from mid March to mid-May, the long dry from mid-May to September, the short rains from October to mid-December and the short dry from mid-December to mid-March.

It rains more frequently and heavily in the northeast, where volcanoes are covered by rainforest. The summit of Karisimbi (4507m), the highest of these volcanoes and the highest peak in Rwanda, is often covered with sleet or snow.

For details about planning your trip, and what to bring, see the boxed text, p16.

With the infrastructure in such reasonable shape, Rwanda can be visited at any time of year. However, if you don't like rain, avoid the long rains of mid-March to mid-May. The dry season from mid-May to September is easier for tracking mountain gorillas, but the endless hills can look quite dry and barren, a contrast to the verdant greens of the wet season. See Climate Charts p621. Peak season for gorilla tracking is July and August; travelling outside this time means it is easier to arrange a permit.

HISTORY

For the background on Rwanda's history prior to independence in 1962, see p28.

HOW MUCH?

- **Tracking the mountain gorillas** US$375
- **Fresh fish at a decent restaurant** US$5 to US$10
- **Internet access per hour** US$1 to US$2
- **New Times newspaper** US$0.50
- **100km bus ride** US$2

LONELY PLANET INDEX

- **Litre of petrol** US$0.90
- **Litre of bottled water** US$0.50
- **Primus Beer 720ml** US$1.50
- **Souvenir T-shirt** US$10
- **Street snack (beef brochettes)** US$0.50

Independence Time

Rwanda, like Burundi, was colonised first by Germany and later Belgium, and like their southern neighbour, the Europeans played on ethnic differences to divide and conquer the population. Power was traditionally concentrated in the hands of the minority Tutsi, with the Tutsi *mwami* (king) playing the central role.

However, in 1956, Mwami Rudahigwa called for independence from Belgium and the Belgians began to switch allegiance to the Hutu majority. The Tutsi favoured fast-track independence, while the Hutus wanted the introduction of democracy followed later by independence. Following the death of the *mwami* in 1959, armed clashes began between groups of Hutu and Tutsi, marking the start of an ethnic conflict that was to culminate in the 1994 genocide. Tutsi fled the country in numbers, resettling in neighbouring Uganda, Kenya and Tanzania.

Following independence in 1962, the Hutu majority came to power under Prime Minister Gregoire Kayibanda. The new government introduced quotas for Tutsis, limiting opportunities for education and work, and small groups of Tutsi exiles began to launch guerrilla raids from across the border in Uganda. In the fresh round of bloodshed that followed, thousands more

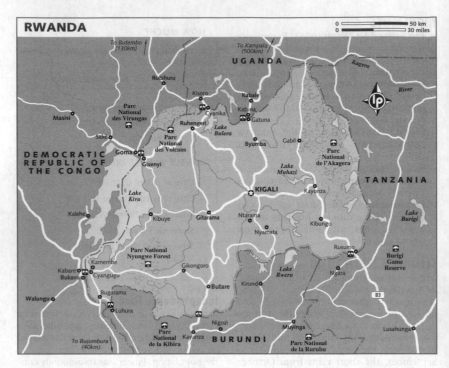

Tutsis were killed and tens of thousands fled to neighbouring countries.

Intertribal tensions continued to simmer under the surface and erupted once again in 1972, when tens of thousands of Hutu tribespeople were massacred in neighbouring Burundi by the Tutsi-dominated government in reprisal for a coup attempt. The slaughter reignited the old hatreds in Rwanda and prompted army commander Major General Juvenal Habyarimana to oust Kayibanda in 1973. He made some progress towards healing the ethnic divisions during the early years of his regime, but before long it was business as usual. However, events unfolding in Uganda in the 1980s were to have a profound impact on the future of Rwanda. Yoweri Museveni came to power there in 1986 after fighting a five-year bush war and some of his key lieutenants were Rwandan exiles, including current president Paul Kagame.

The Civil War Erupts

On 1st October 1990 the whole intertribal issue was savagely reopened. Rwanda was invaded by 5000 well-armed rebels of the Rwandan Patriotic Front (RPF), a Tutsi-dominated military organisation led by Paul Kagame, a former security chief of the Ugandan army. All hell broke loose. Two days later, at Habyarimana's request, France, Belgium and DR Congo flew in troops to help the Rwandan army repulse the rebels.

With this support assured, the Rwandan army went on a rampage against the Tutsi and any Hutu 'suspected' of having collaborated with the rebels. Thousands were shot or hacked to death and countless others indiscriminately arrested, herded into football stadiums or police stations and left there without food or water for days. Many died. Congolese troops joined in the carnage. Thousands of refugees fled to Uganda.

President Yoweri Museveni of Uganda was accused of encouraging the rebels and supplying them with equipment. The accusations were denied but it seems inconceivable that Museveni was totally unaware of the preparations that were going on, and it was also common knowledge that Uganda was keen to see the repatriation of the 250,000 Tutsi refugees based in western Uganda.

The initial setback for the RPF was only temporary, however. It invaded again in 1991, this time better armed and prepared. The government forces were thrown back over a large area of northern Rwanda, and by early 1993, the RPF was within 25km of Kigali. At this point a ceasefire was cobbled together and the warring parties were brought to the negotiating table in Arusha (Tanzania).

Negotiations stalled several weeks later and hostilities were renewed. French troops were flown in, ostensibly to protect foreign nationals in Kigali, but they were accused by the RPF of assisting the Rwandan army. The accusations were denied but TV footage of their activities didn't quite confirm their denials. Meanwhile, with morale in the Rwandan army at a low ebb, the RPF launched an all-out offensive. Habyarimana attempted to contain this by calling a conference of regional presidents to which the RPF was invited. Power sharing was on the agenda.

Habyarimana came away from this conference in April 1994 with somewhat less than he would have liked, but just as his light jet was about to land at Kigali airport, it was shot down by a surface-to-air missile. Both he and President Cyprien Ntaryamira of Burundi died in the crash. It will probably never be known who fired the missile, but most observers believe it was Hutu extremists who had been espousing ethnic cleansing over the airwaves of Radio TV Libre de Milles Collines. Whoever was responsible, this event unleashed one of the 20th century's worst explosions of blood-letting.

The Genocide

Extremists among Habyarimana's Hutu political and military supporters decided at this point to activate a well-planned 'final solution' to the Tutsi 'problem' by exterminating them. The principal player among those in favour of this course of action was the cabinet chief of the Ministry of Defence, Colonel Theoneste Bagosora, who had been in charge of training the Hutu Interahamwe militia, an extremist group, for more than a year. (For more information on the Interahamwe, see the boxed text, p570.) One of his first acts was to direct the army to kill the 'moderate' Hutu prime minister,

Agathe Uwilingiyimana, and 10 Belgian UN peacekeepers. The killing of the UN peacekeepers prompted Belgium to withdraw all of its troops – precisely what Bagosora had calculated – and the way was then open for the genocide to begin in earnest.

Rwandan army and Interahamwe death squads ranged at will over the countryside killing, looting and burning, and roadblocks were set up in every town and city. Every day thousands of Tutsi and any Hutu suspected of sympathising with them or their plight were butchered on the spot. The streets of Kigali were littered with dismembered corpses and the stench of rotting flesh was everywhere. Those who attempted to take refuge in religious missions or churches did so in vain and, in some cases, it was the nuns and priests themselves who betrayed the fugitives to the death squads. Any mission that refused the death squads access was simply blown apart. But perhaps the most shocking part of the tragedy was the enthusiasm with which ordinary Hutu – men, women and even children as young as 10 years old – joined in the carnage.

It's probably true to say that a large number of Hutu who took part in the massacre were caught up in a tide of blind hatred, fear and peer pressure, but there's no doubt whatsoever that it was inspired, controlled and promoted by the Rwandan army and Interahamwe under the direction of their political and military leaders. Yet the carnage also proved to be their nemesis. While up to one million people were being butchered – mainly Tutsi but also many so-called 'moderate' Hutu – the RPF pressed on with its campaign and with increasing speed pushed the Rwandan army and the Interahamwe militia out of the country into DR Congo and Burundi. The massacre finally ended with the RPF in firm control of the country but with two million of the country's population huddled in refugee camps in neighbouring countries.

The UN Assistance Mission for Rwanda (Unamir) was in Rwanda throughout the genocide, but was powerless to prevent the killing due to an ineffective mandate. Although UN Force Commander Lt General Romeo Dallaire had been warning senior UN staff and diplomats about the coming bloodshed, his warnings went unheeded. The international community left

Rwanda to face its fate. Unamir was finally reinforced in July, but it was in the words of Dallaire, 'too much, too late'. The genocide was already over, as the RPF had taken power in Kigali.

The Aftermath

That, of course, is far from the end of the story. Within a year of the RPF victory, a legal commission was set up in Arusha to try those accused of involvement in the genocide; Rwandan prisons are still overflowing with suspects (including women and youths). However, many of the main perpetrators of the genocide – the Interahamwe and former senior army officers – fled into exile out of the reach of the RPF.

Some went to Kenya where they enjoyed the protection of President Moi who long refused to hand them over, which led to the breaking of diplomatic relations. Others – including Colonel Theoneste Bagosora, the alleged architect of the genocide, and Ferdinand Nahimana, the director of the notorious Radio TV Libre de Milles Collines, which actively encouraged Hutu to butcher Tutsi – fled to Cameroon where they enjoyed the protection of that country's security boss, John Fochive. However when Fochive was sacked by the newly elected president of Cameroon, Paul Biya, the Rwandan exiles were arrested.

Of more importance though were the activities of the Interahamwe and former army personnel in the refugee camps of DR Congo and Tanzania. Determined to continue their fight against the RPF, they manipulated the situation in the camps to their advantage by spreading the fear among the refugees that if they returned to Rwanda they would be killed. When Rwanda began to demand the repatriation of the refugees, the grip of the Interahamwe on the camps was so complete that few dared move.

What was of most concern to the RPF was that the Interahamwe used the refugee camps as staging posts for raids into Rwanda, with the complicity of the Congolese army. By 1996 Rwanda was openly warning DR Congo that if these raids did not stop, the consequences would be dire. The raids continued and the RPF mounted a lightning two-day campaign into DR Congo and targeted one of the main refugee camps north of Goma. Tens of thousands fled further west into the bush along with the Interahamwe, but hundreds of thousands more took the opportunity to return home to Rwanda.

Several months after this, events in eastern DR Congo totally changed the picture. In October 1996 a new guerrilla movement known as the Alliance of Democratic Forces for the Liberation of Congo/Zaïre, led by Laurent Kabila, emerged with the secret support of Rwanda and Uganda. The rebels, ably supported by Rwandan and Ugandan regulars, swept through eastern DR Congo and, by December, were in control of every town and city in the region.

The Congolese army retreated west in disarray towards Kisangani, looting and pillaging as they went. They were joined by their allies, the Interahamwe and former Rwandan army personnel.

The grip the Interahamwe had on the refugee camps was broken. Hundreds of thousands of refugees began streaming back into Rwanda, not only from DR Congo but also from Tanzania. The government was faced with a huge refugee resettlement task and began to build new villages throughout the country. Much of Parc National de l'Akagera was given over to this 'villagisation' program and much of the northwest, a former battle zone, has been steadily resettled.

Rwanda Today

Rwanda has done a remarkable job of getting back onto its feet and has achieved an astonishing level of safety and security in a remarkably short space of time, albeit with considerable help from a guilty international community that ignored the country in its darkest hour. Visiting Kigali today, it is hard to believe the horror that visited this land in 1994, although the scars are much more visible in the impoverished countryside.

Things have been rather less remarkable on the international front, as Rwanda has been embroiled in the conflict in DR Congo, which has cost somewhere between three and four million lives. Rwanda and Uganda joined forces to oust Mobutu in 1996 and then tried to use the same tactics two years later to force out their former ally Laurent Kabila. What ensued was Africa's first great war, sucking in as many as nine neighbours at its height. Rwanda and Uganda soon fell out, squabbling over the rich resources that were there for the plunder in DR Congo. Rwanda backed the Rally for Congolese Democracy and Uganda the Movement for the Liberation of Congo and the two countries fought out a proxy war. Peace negotiations began in 2002 and DR Congo continues to edge towards peace. Rwanda withdrew its forces, but if and when an international inquiry is launched into the war in DR Congo, Rwanda may find itself in the dock. Rwanda's motives for entering the fray were just, namely to wipe out remnants of the Interahamwe militia and former soldiers responsible for the genocide, but somewhere along the line, elements in the army may have lost sight of the mission.

Back on the domestic front, Paul Kagame assumed the presidency in 2000 and was overwhelmingly endorsed at the ballot box in presidential elections in 2003 that saw him take 95% of the vote. Parliamentary elections followed in October, but EU observers say the poll was marred by irregularities and fraud. Meanwhile, the search for justice continues at home and abroad; for more on this, see the boxed text, p570.

Looking at the bigger picture, Rwanda is home to two tribes, the Hutu and the Tutsi, and the former Belgian colonialists encouraged a hostile division of the two. The Hutu outnumber the Tutsi by more than four to one and while the RPF government is one of national unity with a number of Hutu representatives, it's viewed in some quarters as a Tutsi government ruling over a predominantly Hutu population. However, the RPF government has done an impressive job of promoting reconciliation and restoring trust between the two communities. This is no small achievement after the horrors that were inflicted on the Tutsi community during the genocide of 1994. It would have been all too easy for the RPF to embark on a campaign of revenge and reprisal, but instead the government is attempting to build a society with a place for everyone, regardless of tribe. There are no more Tutsis, no more Hutus, only Rwandans. Idealistic perhaps, but it is also realistically the only hope for the future.

THE CULTURE
The National Psyche
Tribal conflict has torn Rwanda apart during much of the independence period, culminating in the horrific genocide which unfolded in 1994. There are basically two schools of thought when it comes to looking at Rwandan identity.

The colonial approach of the Belgians was to divide and rule, issuing ID cards that divvied up the population along strict ethnic lines. They tapped up the Tutsis as leaders to help control the Hutu majority, building on the foundations of precolonial society in which the Tutsi were considered more dominant. Later, as independence approached, they switched sides, pitting Hutu against Tutsi in a new conflict which simmered on and off until the 1990s when it exploded onto the world stage.

In the new Rwanda, the opposite is true. Ethnic identities are out and everyone is now a Rwandan. The new government is at pains to present a Rwandan identity and blames the Belgians for categorising the country along tribal lines that set the stage for the savagery that followed. Rwanda was a peaceful place before. Hutu and Tutsi lived side by side for generations and intermarriage was common, or so the story goes.

The truth, as always, is probably somewhere in between. Rwanda was no oasis before the colonial powers arrived, but it was a sophisticated state compared to many others in Africa at this time. However, Tutsis probably had a better time of it than Hutus, something that the Belgians were able to exploit as they sought control. However, it is true to say that there was no history of major bloodshed between the two peoples before 1959 and the foundations of this violence were laid by the Belgian insistence on ethnic identity and their cynical political manipulation. The leaders of the genocide merely took this policy to its extreme, first promoting ethnic differences and then playing on them to manipulate a malleable population to kill, all because they were driven by hate and fear and a desire to protect their political power.

Paul Kagame is trying to put the past behind and create a new Rwanda for Rwandans. Forget the past? No, but learn from it and move on to create a new spirit of national unity. It will take time, maybe a generation or more, but what has been achieved in just over a decade is astonishing. Rwandans are taking pride in their country once more, investment is on the

THE SLOW HAND OF JUSTICE

Following a slow and shaky start, the **International Criminal Tribunal for Rwanda** (www.ictr.org) has managed to net most of the major suspects wanted for involvement in the 1994 genocide.

The tribunal was established in Arusha in 1995, but was initially impeded in its quest for justice by the willingness of several African countries to protect suspects. Countries such as Cameroon and Kenya long harboured Kigali's most wanted, frustrating the Rwandan authorities in their attempts to seek justice. However, due to changes in attitude or government, some big fish have been netted in the last decade. Most important was Prime Minister Jean Kambanda, one of the first to be tried in 1998, who filed a guilty plea and provided the trial with much inside information on other architects of the genocide. His was the first-ever conviction of a head of state for the crime of genocide.

Many of the former ministers of the interim cabinet that presided over the country during the genocide have been located. Since the 1996 change of government in Cameroon, the authorities there have arrested many suspects including the most senior military figures who oversaw the killing. One such suspect is Colonel Theoneste Bagosora. Colonel Bagosora was essentially army commander during the genocide. Other suspects were tracked down all over Africa and beyond, in Belgium and the UK.

In April 2002 former chief of staff General Augustin Bizimungu was handed over by the Angolan authorities. Even more encouraging was the arrest of Colonel Tharcisse Renzaho, prefect of Kigali-ville during the genocide, the first time DR Congo had actually cooperated with the tribunal. Many of the Interahamwe militia leaders involved in the genocide had managed to evade justice by fighting with the Kinshasa government against forces from Rwanda and Uganda. With the Congolese on board in the quest for justice, there are now very few places left for the genocidaires to hide.

It is not just Congolese cooperation that is important, but the US 'Rewards for Justice' campaign that offers significant cash for a list of nine key suspects. This may have played its part in the Angolan arrest and most of the suspects are now in custody. Of the 88 individuals indicted, 15 have been sentenced, five released, seven are appealing verdicts, 26 are on trial, 17 are awaiting trial and 17 are at large. Of the 17 at large, some may already be dead, as one suspect has died of natural causes during detention. The tribunal hopes to complete its work by 2008.

The prisons in Rwanda are still overflowing with genocide suspects. Prison numbers are thought to be around 120,000, and many of these prisoners are seen all over the country in their pink uniforms, helping on civil works programs. Security may look lax, but that is because the prisoners have little motivation to escape.

There are three categories of prisoner: category-one suspects are those who planned and orchestrated the genocide; category-two prisoners are those who oversaw massacres and failed to prevent them when in a position to do so; and category three are those who killed or looted during the genocide. Most prisoners are category three, but evidence against them is mainly hearsay, hence the government has revived the *gacaca*, a traditional tribunal headed by village elders, to speed up the process. However, the quest for justice in Rwanda looks set to be a long one and will cast a long shadow over the country's attempts to make a new start. Justice is a necessary part of reconciliation, but remains a principle rather than priority as the country simply has too many cases to deal with and too many other problems to worry about.

boil and people are once again optimistic about their future. The real challenge is to make sure the countryside comes along for the ride, as many of the investors in Kigali are overseas Tutsi finally returning home, and many of the poorest farmers are Hutus who have always tilled the land. To avoid the divisions of the past once again surfacing in the new Rwanda, democratic development is required that favours all, urban and rural, rich and poor, and is blind to tribe.

As East Africa moves towards greater integration once more, it is to be hoped that Rwanda and Burundi are invited along for the ride. This way, the ethnic divide between Hutu and Tutsi may become submerged in a wider mosaic of regional peoples.

Daily Life

Urban Rwanda is a sophisticated place and people follow a Mediterranean pattern of starting early before breaking off for a siesta or long boozy lunch. The rhythm of rural life is very different and follows the sun. People work long hours from dawn until dusk, but also take a break during the hottest part of the day. However, it is a hard life for women in the countryside, who seem burdened with the lion's share of the work while many menfolk sit around drinking and discussing.

Faith is an important rock in the lives of many Rwandan people and Christianity remains the dominant religion. The church in Rwanda was tainted by its association with the genocide in 1994, but that doesn't seem to have dampened people's devotion to the word of God.

Rwanda's economy was decimated during the genocide, as production ground to a halt and foreign investors were scared away. However, the current government has done an amazing job of turning things around and the economy is now fairly stable with steady growth, low inflation and investors once again prepared to do business in Kigali.

Agriculture is the main employer and export earner, contributing about half of GDP, with coffee by far the largest export, accounting for about 75% of export income. Tea and pyrethrum (a natural insecticide) are also important. The majority of farmers are subsistence and grow plantain, sweet potato, beans, cassava, sorghum and maize.

Like many countries in Africa, the government is keen to promote universal primary education. However, the education system suffered badly during the genocide, with many teachers killed and a number of schools and colleges destroyed. Only about half the current teachers are actually qualified, although a number of international organisations are involved in programs to train teachers. There are only about 2000 primary schools, 300 secondary schools and two universities in the whole country. Illiteracy runs as high as 50%.

Population

The population is moving towards nine million, which gives Rwanda one of the highest population densities of any country in Africa. The population is believed to be about 85% Hutu, 14% Tutsi and 1% Twa pygmy.

One of Rwanda's largest 'exports' during the long years of conflict and instability was refugees, but most of these returned home in the second half of the 1990s; virtually the only ones who haven't are those who had some involvement in the genocide of 1994 and are roaming the jungles of DR Congo, terrorising local populations.

SPORT

Like all of Africa, football is Rwanda's national obsession and the 'Wasps', as the national team are known, are a growing force in the sport. In 2004 they qualified for the African Nations Cup for the first time.

RELIGION

About 65% of the population are Christians of various sects, although Catholicism is predominant, a further 25% follow tribal religions, often with a dash of Christianity, and the remaining 10% are Muslim.

ARTS

Dance

Rwanda's most famous dancers are the *Intore* troupe. Their warriorlike displays are accompanied by a trancelike drumbeat similar to that of the famous Tambourinaires in Burundi.

Cinema

Hotel Rwanda has put Rwanda back on the map for moviegoers. Although it was shot in South Africa, it tells the story of Hotel des Milles Collines manager Paul Rusesabagina, played by Don Cheadle, turning this luxury hotel into a temporary haven for thousands fleeing the erupting genocide. *100 Days* and the HBO miniseries *Sometimes in April* also convey the story of the Rwandan genocide in a powerful way.

Gorillas in the Mist is based on the autobiography of Dian Fossey and her work with the rare mountain gorillas in Parc National des Volcans. Essential viewing for anyone visiting the gorillas.

ENVIRONMENT

The Land

Known as the 'Land of a Thousand Hills', it is hardly surprising to find that Rwanda's endless mountains stretch into the infinite horizon. Rwanda's 26,338 sq km of land is one of the most densely populated places on earth, and to feed the people, almost every available piece of land is under cultivation, except the national parks. Since most of the country is mountainous, this involves a good deal of terracing and the banded hillsides are similar to those in Nepal or the High Atlas of Morocco. Coffee and tea plantations take up considerable areas of land.

Wildlife

Rwanda shares much of the flora and fauna of its larger neighbours in the region. For more information on the rare mountain gorillas of Parc National des Volcans, see p101.

National Parks & Reserves

Due to its small size, Rwanda only has a small network of national parks. The most popular protected area and the focus of most visits to Rwanda is Parc National des Volcans, a string of brooding volcanoes that provides a home for the rare mountain gorillas. It costs US$375 to track the gorillas here and other volcano treks are available.

Nyungwe Forest is the newest national park, a tropical montane forest that is one of the richest primate destinations in the region. Entry is US$20 per day and chimp tracking is possible at US$50. See p591 for more information.

Parc National de l'Akagera is the third of Rwanda's parks, but is sadly a shadow of its former self, as many animals fled across the border into Tanzania during the civil war of the early 1990s.

Environmental Issues

Soil erosion resulting from overuse of the land is the most serious problem confronting Rwanda today. The terracing system in the country is fairly anarchic, unlike in Bali or the Philippines, and the lack of coordinated water management has wiped out much of the topsoil on the slopes. This is potentially catastrophic for a country with too many people in too small a space, as it points to a food-scarcity problem in the future.

Population density has also had a detrimental effect on the country's national park system, reducing Parc National des Volcans by half in 1969 and Parc National de l'Akagera by two-thirds in 1998.

When travelling through the countryside by bus, you will see children chasing the vehicle shouting 'agachupa', which means 'little bottle'. They want your water bottle to carry water to school or to sell to recyclers, so this is an easy way to get involved in helping the environment.

FOOD & DRINK

African fare in Rwanda is very similar to that in Kenya (see p277) and prices are reasonable in local restaurants. Popular dishes include tilapia (Nile perch), goat meat and beef brochettes (kebabs). There's also a wide variety of continental food available; some of it is excellently prepared and presented, but it is more expensive than local fare.

It is important not to drink tap water in Rwanda. Bottled water is generally RFr250 a bottle in shops, a little more in restaurants. Soft drinks (sodas) and the local beers, Primus (720ml) and Mulzig (330ml and 660ml), are available everywhere, as is the local firewater, konyagi, but wines (both South African and European) are generally only available in the more expensive restaurants and hotels.

KIGALI

pop 600,000

Rwanda was known once the 'Land of Eternal Spring' and its capital Kigali still fits the bill. Sprawled over ridges, hills and valleys, it is a small, attractive city with superb views over the intensively cultivated and terraced countryside beyond. The mountains and hills seem to stretch forever and the abundant rainfall keeps them a lush green.

The city took a pounding during the genocide in 1994 (see opposite), but a massive amount of rehabilitation work has been undertaken in recent years and there is a major construction boom in the city centre today. This is a city on the move, looking ahead to development rather than looking back at its destruction.

There aren't a huge number of sights in the city, but the Kigali Memorial Centre, documenting the Rwandan genocide, is a must for all visitors to Rwanda. The city has a reasonable range of hotels and restaurants to suit most budgets, and while nightlife is not quite as pumping as Kampala or Nairobi, it is worth a whiff at the weekend. Many of the most popular restaurants and nightspots are spread across the extensive suburbs that surround the city centre.

HISTORY

Walking the streets of Kigali today it is hard to imagine the horrors that unfolded here during those 100 days of madness in 1994. Roadblocks were set up at strategic points throughout the city, manned by Interahamwe militia, and thousands upon thousands of innocent Rwandans were bludgeoned or hacked to death. People swarmed to the churches for sanctuary, but the killers soon followed them there.

Unamir stood by and watched, shackled by the shortsightedness and cynicism of bureaucrats and politicians who failed to grasp the magnitude of what was unfolding. After 10 Belgian peacekeepers were murdered at the start of the genocide, the Belgian government withdrew its contingent, leaving Unamir to fend for itself with a minimal mandate and no muscle. There was little the 250 troops that remained could do but watch and rescue or protect the few they could.

Unbelievably, a contingent of the RPF was holed up in the parliamentary compound throughout this period, a legacy of the Arusha 'peace' process. Like the Unamir troops, there was little they could do to stop such widespread killing, but they did mount some spectacular rescue missions from churches and civic buildings around the city.

Hotel des Milles Collines became a refuge for those fleeing the violence and thousands of people were holed up there living in the most dire conditions. *Hotel Rwanda* (see p571) tells this heroic story. Meanwhile Unamir was protecting thousands more civilians holed up at its base in the Amahoro Stadium near the airport.

When the dust finally settled and the RPF swept the genocidaires from power in early July 1994, Kigali was wrecked. What little of the population remained were traumatised; dead and decaying bodies littered the streets; and buildings lay in ruin. Dogs had to be shot en masse, as they had developed a taste for human flesh. As the Kigali Memorial Centre so aptly puts it, Rwanda was dead.

And it's all the more remarkable that there are few signs of this carnage today. Kigali is now a dynamic and forward-looking city, the local economy is booming, investment is the buzz word and buildings are going up like mushrooms. There are few outward signs of the damage, although the parliament building still bears scars of mortar shells and bullets. The inner damage? That's another story, but Kigali, and Rwanda beyond, have recrossed the Rubicon and deserve all the support they can get.

ORIENTATION

It is not that easy to get to grips with Kigali when you first arrive, as it is spread across several hills and valleys. The centre fans out above Place de l'Unité Nationale, the busy commercial heartland along Ave de la Paix and the side streets heading west. Heading north down the valley from the centre of town is Blvd de Nyabugogo, which leads to the Nyabugogo bus terminal and all roads upcountry.

South of the centre along Blvd de la Revolution and surrounding streets is where many of the embassies are found, and to the southwest is the plush suburb of Kiyovu, with several popular restaurants. Across the valley to the east of the centre is Kacyiru, a sophisticated suburb that includes government buildings, embassies, hotels and restaurants. Further out towards the airport is Remera, with several hotels for those wanting a quick getaway.

Maps

It is hard to get hold of good maps of Kigali. The best one is the pullout map that comes with the free *What's on Rwanda* guide, but this isn't that well distributed at the moment. There is also an older *Map of Kigali* produced in association with MTN Rwandacell which costs RFr2000, but is also hard to track down.

INFORMATION
Bookshops

There are a few bookshops in Kigali, selling mainly French-language publications.

Librairie Caritas (Ave du Commerce) A central bookshop for French titles.

Librairie Ikirezi (☎ 571314; Ave de la Paix; ✆ 9am-12.30pm & 2-6pm Mon-Fri, 9am-12.30pm Sat & Sun) The best bookshop in town, it stocks a wide range of French- and English-language books on Rwanda and the world beyond. No, the name doesn't mean crazy bookshop.

KIGALI

0 ——————————— 500 m
0 ——————————— 0.3 miles

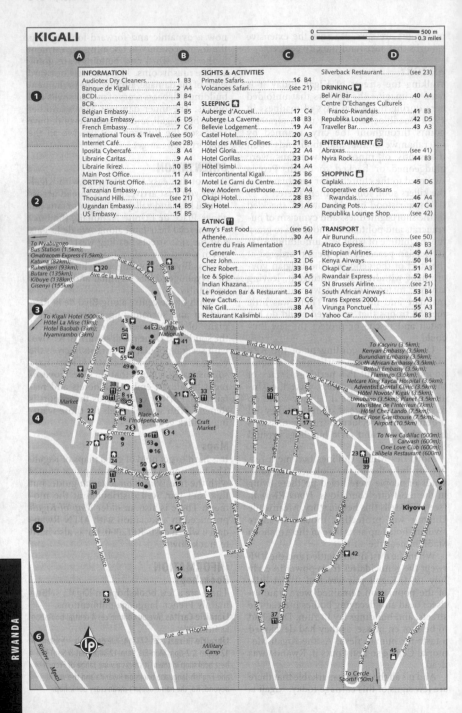

INFORMATION
Audiotex Dry Cleaners...................1 B3
Banque de Kigali...........................2 A4
BCDI..3 B4
BCR...4 B4
Belgian Embassy............................5 B5
Canadian Embassy.........................6 D5
French Embassy..............................7 C6
International Tours & Travel.....(see 50)
Internet Café...........................(see 28)
Iposita Cybercafé..........................8 A4
Librairie Caritas.............................9 A4
Librairie Ikirezi...........................10 B5
Main Post Office..........................11 B4
ORTPN Tourist Office...................12 B4
Tanzanian Embassy......................13 B4
Thousand Hills.......................(see 21)
Ugandan Embassy.........................14 B5
US Embassy....................................15 B5

SIGHTS & ACTIVITIES
Primate Safaris...............................16 B4
Volcanoes Safari.....................(see 21)

SLEEPING
Auberge d'Accueil..........................17 C4
Auberge La Caverne.......................18 B3
Bellevie Lodgement.......................19 A4
Castel Hotel.....................................20 A3
Hôtel des Milles Collines...............21 B4
Hôtel Gloria....................................22 A4
Hotel Gorillas.................................23 B4
Hôtel Isimbi....................................24 A4
Intercontinental Kigali..................25 B6
Motel Le Garni du Centre..............26 B4
New Modern Guesthouse...............27 A4
Okapi Hotel.....................................28 B3
Sky Hotel...29 A6

EATING
Amy's Fast Food.....................(see 56)
Athenée...30 A4
Centre du Frais Alimentation
  Generale.......................................31 A5
Chez John.......................................32 D6
Chez Robert....................................33 B4
Ice & Spice.....................................34 A5
Indian Khazana..............................35 C4
Le Poseidon Bar & Restaurant......36 B4
New Cactus.....................................37 C4
Nile Grill...38 A4
Restaurant Kalisimbi......................39 D4

Silverback Restaurant.............(see 23)

DRINKING
Bel Air Bar......................................40 A4
Centre D'Echanges Culturels
  Franco-Rwandais.........................41 B3
Republika Lounge..........................42 D5
Traveller Bar...................................43 A3

ENTERTAINMENT
Abraxas....................................(see 41)
Nyira Rock......................................44 B3

SHOPPING
Caplaki..45 D6
Cooperative des Artisans
  Rwandais.......................................46 A4
Dancing Pots..................................47 C4
Republika Lounge Shop...........(see 42)

TRANSPORT
Air Burundi.............................(see 50)
Atraco Express................................48 B3
Ethiopian Airlines..........................49 A4
Kenya Airways................................50 B4
Okapi Car..51 A3
Rwandair Express...........................52 B4
SN Brussels Airline..................(see 21)
South African Airways...................53 B4
Trans Express 2000........................54 A3
Virunga Ponctuel...........................55 A3
Yahoo Car.......................................56 B3

To Nyabugogo
Bus Station (1.5km);
Onatracom Express (1.5km);
Katuna (82km);
Ruhengeri (93km);
Butare (135km);
Kibuye (138km);
Gisenyi (155km)

Rue du Lac Ihasho

Ave de la Justice

Blvd de Nyabugogo

Place
de l'Unité
Nationale

To Kigali Hotel (500m);
Hôtel La Mise (1km);
Hotel Baobab (3km);
Nyamirambo (3km)

Blvd de l'OUA

Rue de la Concorde

To Kacyiru (3.5km);
Kenyan Embassy (3.5km);
Burundian Embassy (3.5km);
South African Embassy (3.5km);
British Embassy (3.5km);
Flaminyca (3.5km);
Netcare King Fayçal Hospital (3.5km);
Adventist Dental Clinic (3.5km);
Hôtel Novotel Kigali (3.5km);
Umubano (3.5km); Planet (3.5km);
Ministère de l'Intérieur (7km);
Hôtel Chez Lando (7.5km);
Chez Rose Guesthouse (7.5km);
Airport (10.5km)

Rue du Lac Nasho

Ave du Commerce

Ave du Travail

Market

Rue de Kalisimbi

Place de
l'Independance

Craft
Market

Ave du Commerce

Ave des Milles Collines

Blvd de la Revolution

Ave de la Paix

Ave de l'Armée

Blvd de la Revolution

Rue Paul VI

Rue de Nianza

Ave du Lababduque

Ave de Rusumo

Rue Depute Kamuzinzi

Mont Juru

Ave des Grands Lacs

Rue Depute Kayuku

Rue de l'Akagera

Rue Depute Kayuku

Rue des Parcs

Ave de la Jeunesse

Rue de Bigogwe

To New Cadillac (500m);
Carwash (600m);
One Love Club (600m);
Lalibela Restaurant (600m)

Kiyovu

Ave de Kyovu

Ave de Masaka

Rue de l'Akagera

Ave de Kyovu

Ave de la Justice

Rue Paul VI

Rue de Nyarugunga

Rue Depute Kayuku

Rue de l'Hôpital

Military
Camp

Rue de la Culture

To Cercle
Sportif (50m)

Rivière Mpazi

RWANDA

Cultural Centres
Centre D'Echanges Culturels Franco-Rwandais (Ave de la République) Overlooking Place de l'Unité Nationale, this place has live music at the weekend (see p580).

Emergency
Police (☎ 083 11170) A 24-hour emergency number.

Internet Access
Internet access is widespread and very cheap in Kigali. There are plenty more places throughout the centre, meaning no online junkie need go without their fix.
Iposita Cybercafé (per hr RFr400) Part of the post office complex.
Internet Café (Blvd de Nyabugogo; per hr RFr500) There is a handy Internet café in the lobby of this popular hotel.

Laundry
Most hotels seem to have an aversion to standard laundry and offer only more expensive dry-cleaning. This means for those at the budget end, DIY might be the way to go.
Audiotex Dry Cleaners (Ave de la Justice) Those in midrange hotels could try this place.

Medical Services
Some embassies also have medical attachés who offer services through private practices.
Adventist Dental Clinic (☎ 582431) Located near the Novotel in Kacyiru district, this place is run by an international dentist based in Kigali.
Netcare King Faycal Hospital (☎ 582421) Also near the Novotel, this South African–operated hospital is the best in Kigali. Prices are high but so are standards.

Money
For cash transactions banks are best avoided, as the bureaucracy and paperwork is a pain. Street rates are generally better, but it may be safer to use of the many foreign exchange (forex) bureaus in Kigali, mainly located around the post office.
Banque de Kigali (Ave du Commerce) When it comes to travellers cheques or credit-card cash advances Banque de Kigali is the only option at the time of writing. Both involve hefty commissions of about US$15 minimum!

There were plenty of ATMs in Kigali, but none were accepting international credit cards. In case they do:
Banque Commerciale de Rwanda (BCR; Blvd de la Revolution)
Banque de Commerce, de Developement et de l'Industriel (BCDI; Ave de la Paix)

Post
Main post office (Ave de la Paix; ☯ 8am-5pm Mon-Fri, to noon Sat) Poste restante services available.

Telephone
There are quite a few telecommunications kiosks opposite the post office that are open throughout the day and into the night. There are also MTN kiosks and public payphones throughout the city. One of the funniest sights in Kigali are all the 'mobile' telephones you see around the city. These are full-sized desktop telephones, but they are somehow looped into the mobile network and young boys run around with them offering cheap calls. They are definitely not trying to sell the telephones, as we first suspected.

Tourist Information
ORTPN (☎ 576514; www.rwandatourism.com; BP 905, 1 Blvd de la Revolution; ☯ 7am-5pm Mon-Fri, 8am-2pm Sat & Sun) The national tourism office, right in the centre of town. The office has a glossy brochure *Rwanda – Home of the Mountain Gorilla*, a few leaflets (in French and English) about the mountain gorillas and some maps, but not a whole lot more. Staff here speak French and English and are pretty helpful in assisting with enquiries. This is also the place for independent travellers to make reservations to track the mountain gorillas in Parc National des Volcans, as they keep a computerised record of all bookings. See p585 for more details.

Travel Agencies
There are quite a few travel agencies around town these days, most of which sell international air tickets and local tour packages.
International Tours & Travels (☎ 574057; www.itt .co.rw; Ave des Milles Collines) A reliable place for air tickets, it also represents Air Burundi.
Thousand Hills (☎ 501151; www.thousandhills.rw; Ave de la République) The helpful team here have years of experience in the travel business.

ACTIVITIES
If you're feeling energetic or need a workout, try the **Cercle Sportif** (Ave du Rugunga), where there are facilities for swimming, tennis and golf. However, be warned, they sometimes don't allow outsiders in for no apparent reason.

TOURS
ORTPN (above) offers a Kigali city tour (US$20, three hours) departing at 8am or 2pm daily. The tour includes the Kigali Memorial Centre and some other prominent

THE GENOCIDE REMEMBERED...

More than a memorial for Kigali, more than a memorial for Rwanda and its tragedy, this is a memorial for all of us, marking the Rwandan genocide and many more around the world that never should have come to pass. The **Kigali Memorial Centre** (www.kigalimemorialcentre.org; admission free, donations welcome, ☺ 10am-5pm) is a must for all visitors in Rwanda wanting to learn more about how it was that the world watched as a genocide unfolded in this tiny landlocked country.

Downstairs is dedicated to the Rwandan genocide and the informative tour includes background on the divisive colonial experience in Rwanda and the steady build-up to the genocide. Exhibits are professionally presented and include short video clips. As the visit progresses, it becomes steadily more powerful, as you are confronted with the crimes that took place here. The sections on the cold and calculated planning of the genocide and its bloody execution are particularly disturbing and include moving video testimony from survivors. The story continues with sections on the refugee crisis in the aftermath of the genocide and the search for justice through the international tribunal in Arusha and the local *gacaca* courts (traditional tribunals headed by village elders) around the country. Finally you are confronted with a room full of photographs of Rwandan victims of the genocide. The effect is very similar to Tuol Sleng, the Khmer Rouge prison in Phnom Penh, Cambodia. You feel yourself suffocating under the weight of sadness and despair, the wasted lives and loves of the nameless people surrounding you. Quotes stand out from the faces and Apollon Katahizi's words are particularly resonant as killings continue across the world today: "When they said 'never again' after the holocaust, was it meant for some people and not for others?"

Upstairs is a moving section dedicated to informing visitors about other genocides that have taken place around the world to set Rwanda's nightmare in a historical context. Armenians, Jews, Cambodians, all have been victims of the mass slaughter we now know as genocide. Finally there is a section on Rwandan children who fell victim to the killers' machetes. Young and innocent, if you have remained impassionate until this point, the horror of it all catches up with you here. Life-size photos are accompanied by intimate details about their favourite toys. Why? Why? Why? The Kigali Memorial Centre explains it as best it can, but no one can answer the fundamental question of what it takes to turn man into beast.

Buried in the memorial gardens here are the remains of more than 250,000 victims of the genocide, gathered here as a final resting place.

Set up with assistance from the **Aegis Trust** (www.aegistrust.org), the Kigali Memorial Centre is located in the Kisozi district of town. It can be visited as part of the Kigali city tour promoted by ORTPN (p575) or you can come independently by taxi or taxi-motor.

buildings around town. It's not amazing value given the memorial currently has no entry charge, but the guides are very knowledgeable and take you closer to the capital.

KIGALI FOR CHILDREN

This definitely isn't the world's most exciting city for children. The best bet is to check into a hotel with a swimming pool and take it from there. Otherwise, head out of town to Parc National Nyungwe Forest (p591) for some monkey business or across to Gisenyi (p586) or Kibuye (p593) for some 'beach' time on Lake Kivu.

SLEEPING

Finding accommodation is not a great problem, but advance reservations at more expensive places are recommended. Accommodation is spread across town, but those without their own transport should head for the city centre. There are slim pickings at the budget end, making this a worthwhile city in which to splash some extra cash.

Budget

Auberge La Caverne (☎ 574549; Blvd de Nyabugogo; r RFr5000-15,000) Clearly a cut above the competition at the cheaper end of the scale, this little *auberge* is tucked away beneath the main road. The cheapest rooms are pretty small, but the more francs you spend the more they begin to expand. RFr10,000 gets a huge room and the top rate tier is a suite with TV and raised bathtub. Book ahead as there are only 15 rooms.

One Love Club (☎ 575412; Ave des Poids Lourds; camping RFr5000, r RFr15,000) 'Let's get together and feel alright, altogether now'…if it's the spirit of peace and harmony you are after, then this little retreat is the place for you. Expensive camping is available, but then it is currently the only place to camp in Kigali. The large rooms are fairly basic, but include a bathroom and space to spread out. The lush gardens include an Ethiopian restaurant, Lalibela Restaurant. Most importantly, it's all for a good cause, as profits are ploughed back into a local nongovernmental organisation (NGO) to help the disabled community in Rwanda.

Hôtel Gloria (☎ 571957; fax 576623; cnr Rue du Travail & Ave du Commerce; s/d RFr6000/8000) Possibly the longest running budget digs in town, Hôtel Gloria's location is great, as it is right in the heart of the city. It's clean enough, although there is an undeniable air of neglect about the place and the attached bathrooms are cold water only.

Kigali Hotel (☎ /fax 571384; s/d RFr5000/7000) On a bang-for-your-buck basis, this is probably the best value in town, but the big drawback is that it is quite a long way from the action, tucked away behind the mosque on the road to Nyamirambo. Oh, and that mosque – don't forget the early morning wake-up calls. The large, clean rooms come with TV, telephone and bathroom.

Also central are a couple of local dives down a small alley off Ave du Commerce. **Bellevie Logement** (☎ 557158; s/d RFr4000/5000) and **New Modern Guesthouse** (☎ 574708; s/d RFr4000/5000) are right opposite each other, but both are big-time basic and the shared facilities aren't ideal. Bellevie is the slightly better of the two, but better still, upgrade to somewhere else.

Midrange

Okapi Hotel (☎ 576765; www.okapi.co.rw; Blvd de Nyabugogo; s/d US$40/50; 🖳) The most popular choice in this range, Okapi has a reasonable location just below the city centre. The area looks a bit rough-and-ready with the unsurfaced road, but security is fine. It offers smart rooms with TV, hot-water bathtub and a balcony at reasonable rates. There are also some cheaper rooms in an extension below the main building with just a hot shower and these go for US$20/26. All rates include a buffet breakfast. There is

an excellent restaurant here with a healthy selection of dishes from around the world, plus a reliable Internet café.

Castel Hotel (☎ 576377; castelhotel@rwanda1.com; Ave de la Justice; s/d RFr16,000/18,000) Another excellent establishment, this place offers prime views across the valley to Kacyiru. A modern business hotel, the clean rooms here include satellite TV, telephone and hot-water showers. Make sure you ask for one at the back with the big views.

Hôtel Isimbi (☎ 575109; isimbi@hotmail.com; Rue de Kalisimbi; s/d incl breakfast RFr15,000/18,000) The most central of the midrange hotels, this place offers functional rooms with TV and bathroom, and rates include breakfast. It's a good option for those who don't fancy walking up and down the endless hills near the centre. There's a restaurant with a good menu, as well as a TV lounge downstairs, but both are lacking atmosphere.

Sky Hotel (☎ 516693; sky hotel1@yahoo.fr; Ave de la Justice; s/d RFr14,000/18,000) Perched on the edge of the valley on the road to Nyamirambo, this is another place with first-class views. Rooms are smart and well equipped, and there is a great little terrace bar below the hotel with big breezes blowing up from the valley below.

Auberge d'Accueil (☎ 578915; 2 Rue Député Kayuku; s/d RFr11,800/14,200) Housed in the Église Presbytérienne au Rwanda, the rooms here aren't fantastic value when compared with facilities at the leading hotels in this range. That said, the bathrooms have reliable hot water, the staff are friendly and there is a restaurant with a small menu. Visa accepted.

Chez Rose Guesthouse (☎ 08505545; s/d RFr13,000/18,000) The Remera suburb of town is popular with expats, thanks to its proximity to the airport, and Chez Rose is a friendly little guesthouse up here. The large rooms are well lit and include attached bathrooms with hot water.

Top End

Hôtel Chez Lando (☎ 584328; www.hotelchezlando.com; s/d from US$50/60) A Kigali institution out in the suburb of Remera, the rooms here are in single-storey units set around a lush garden. It's a pretty good deal, although it's a long way out of town for those without transport. The restaurant and bar here are often packed and at the weekend DJs crank up the tunes as bar becomes club.

RWANDA

THE AUTHOR'S CHOICE

Hotel Gorillas (☎ 501717; www.hotelgorillas
.com; Rue des Parcs; s/d US$50/70, large s/d with
bathtub US$60/80) A slick little hotel in the
upmarket Kiyovu area of the city, this place
is winning over a lot of customers thanks
to its spacious rooms with a touch of deco-
rative flair. One of the best deals in town,
it is also home to the popular Silverback
Restaurant.

Motel Le Garni du Centre (☎ 572654; garni@
rwanda1.com; Ave de la République; s/d incl breakfast
US$75/90; ☒) Kigali's answer to the boutique
guesthouse, this atmospheric little *auberge*
is tucked away on a side road below Hôtel
des Milles Collines. The well-equipped
rooms come with TV, fridge and telephone,
and there's a buffet breakfast. All rooms
are built around the swimming pool, which
doesn't draw the crazy crowds like the big
hotel pools.

Hôtel des Milles Collines (☎ 576530; www.milles
collines.net; Ave de la République; r US$88/103; ☐ ☒)
Welcome to the Hotel Rwanda. With the
international success of the movie, this
hotel looks set to see a surge in bookings.
The hotel used in the movie was actually
down in South Africa, but the original hotel
where horror and hope collided was right
here, the Milles Collines. Rooms here are a
four-star standard and rates are pretty flexible so don't be surprised if you are quoted
different prices. Rumours of a renovation
abound, probably to cash in on the hotel's
new-found fame. Use of the hotel swimming pool costs RFr3000 for nonguests,
and is a popular place to relax at weekends.
There is also a poolside bar, a tennis court
and business centre.

Intercontinental Kigali (☎ 597100; adminich@
rwanda1.com; Blvd de la Revolution; s/d US$180/192;
☒ ☐ ☒) Kigali's first and currently only
five-star hotel, the Intercontinental is certainly the smartest address in town. Formerly the Diplomates, it is just a short walk
from the city centre. Rooms are the up to the
usual Intercon standards and the bar and
restaurants here are popular with Kigali's
high-flyers.

Hôtel Novotel Kigali (☎ 585816; umubano@
rwanda1.com; s/d US$135/150; ☒ ☐ ☒) Long con-
sidered the best in town, the Novotel has

lost that title to the Intercontinental. A
long way out in the suburb of Kacyiru, this
is another place for those with transport.
Francophones will no doubt stay loyal to
the brand and the rooms are exactly what
you would expect from the Accor family.

EATING

The dining scene in Kigali is getting more
sophisticated and the current crop of restaurants includes Rwandan, Ethiopian, Indian, Chinese, Italian and French.

Chez Robert (☎ 501305; Ave de la République; meals
RFr2000-5000) Formerly home to the extravagant Aux Caprices du Palais, it now plays
host to a Brussels exile, Chez Robert. The
menu is French and Belgian and is great
value for money for those that want a sophisticated meal without the sophisticated
bill at the end. The steaks are particularly
good and the blue-cheese sauce the perfect
complement.

Chez John (Rue de Masaka; meals RFr2000-4000) For
a more local experience, head to Chez John,
a Rwandan restaurant specialising in meat
and maize. The surroundings may have gone
upmarket, but everyone still gets stuck into
their grills and it is a good place to sink some
beers.

Restaurant Kalisimbi (☎ 575128; Rue de l'Akanyaru;
mains RFr2000-5000) Just down the road from
Hotel Gorillas, this continental restaurant
has one of the best Italian selections in town,
including reliable pizzas. Service comes with
a personal touch making it a popular place
with local residents.

Silverback Restaurant (☎ 501717; Rue des Parcs;
mains RFr4000-10,000) One of the best restaurants
in Kigali, the accent here is most definitely
French. Foie gras, duck à l'orange and even
rabbit are available for the discerning diner.
The wine list is impressive, but so are the
prices at around US$40 a bottle.

Indian Khazana (Rue Député Kajangwe; full meal
RFr7500) Kampala's most celebrated Indian
restaurant comes south to Kigali. Khana
Khazana has been spicing up people's lives
for years in the Ugandan capital and now
Rwanda can enjoy the subtle flavours of the
subcontinent. One of the hottest places in
town right now.

Ice & Spice (Rue du Travail; curries RFr3000) Another
Indian restaurant near the city centre, this
place is popular for reasonable prices and
big portions. All the old favourites are here,

like chicken tikka masala, and you can cool off with an ice cream for dessert, made on the premises.

Lalibela Restaurant (☎ 575412; Ave des Poids Lourds; mains RFr3000) Set in the grounds of the One Love Club, this is Kigali's only Ethiopian restaurant following the demise of the Addis. It has a laid-back atmosphere in keeping with the Rasta owner and serves big portions of spicy chicken and the like on *injera* (unleavened bread). It rocks on as a bar later in the evening.

Flamingo (☎ 586589; 6th fl, Telecom House, Blvd de l'Umuganda; mains RFr3000-7500) Like the famous Fang Fang in Kampala, the Flamingo has moved into an anonymous office block in Kacyiru, but it doesn't seem to be affecting its pulling power. The sizzling platters are quite a sight, plus there is a serious selection for vegetarians, not often the case in Kigali. That said, someone should probably tell them that bean curd with beef doesn't count!

Nile Grill (Rue de Kalisimbi; ⏰ 7.30am-8pm) There are several local joints in the city centre doing a roaring trade in lunchtime buffets and cheap eats. Nile is one of the best known and has a vegetarian buffet for RFr1500 or a meaty choice for RFr2000.

Le Poseidon Bar & Restaurant (Blvd de la République; mains RFr1500-3000) This is Kigali's very own fast-food spot, with a lively bar and local restaurant offering sandwiches, burgers, pizzas and pastas. It draws a healthy work crowd at lunchtime and can fill up with stragglers leaving the office on Fridays.

Amy's Fast Food (Ave de la Paix; snacks RFr1500) A popular spot in town for snacks and light bites like sandwiches, burgers and pizzas. Check out the little terrace for people-watching on a sunny day.

Hotel Baobab (☎ 575633; dishes from RFr2000) It is worth venturing into the wilds of Nyamirambo to this popular garden restaurant. It is also a good place to go for a meal if you want some privacy or are catching up with people you haven't seen for a while, as dining is in private pavilions. The menu is extensive, including steaks, fish and some pretty good pizzas.

Athenée (Rue de Kalisimbi) Travellers who want to do a spot of self-catering or who are planning some time in Parcs National Nyungwe Forest or de l'Akagera will find a small selection of things here, a sort of alimentation-style store near the main post office.

Centre du Frais Alimentation Generale (Ave des Milles Collines) Probably the best stocked of the central supermarkets, including a good range of far-flung imports. There is also a bakery on the premises.

DRINKING

The good folk of Kigali take their drinking and partying pretty seriously and there are some good bars around town, some of which turn into clubs as the night wears on. Ask around to be sure all the following places are open and to see what's hot and what's not.

Republika Lounge (Rue de l'Akanyaru) The rebirth of cool! Once Zanzibar was the place to be, now the former owner has bounced back with Republika, definitely the place to be in Kigali. In the fancy Kiyovu area, there are huge views from the large terrace here. Lush furnishings, a well-stocked bar and a small menu for the midnight munchies keep the crowds happy.

Carwash (Ave des Poids Lourds) Quite literally a carwash, but don't worry we are not going mad. There is also a brilliant garden bar here with stacks of space. You may not always get a seat, but you won't be elbow to elbow either. Rwandans drop their cars off for a wash and give their tonsils a bit of a tickle with beer. It's cheaper to drink here than in New Cadillac, so drop by on the way.

Traveller Bar (Ave du Commerce) This local used to pull the crowds thanks to its strategic location opposite the local bus park. With the closure of said park, the crowds have quietened down, but the beer and brochettes are cheap.

Bel Air Bar (Ave du Commerce) Another popular local haunt with some great views over the centre of town. The beer is cheap and the atmosphere lively. 'Pass through the corridor and go upstairs' it says outside. Yes, they have finally got rid of the stairs of certain death.

The swimming pool at Hôtel des Milles Collines ends up serving as the city's most popular daytime bar at weekends, as half the expats in the city come here to relax by the water. There is a happy hour here from 5pm to 7pm every day.

Hôtel Chez Lando is another popular hotel bar and draws a local crowd almost every night, whether for drinking, dining or dancing, as it also has DJs at the weekend.

ENTERTAINMENT

Cranking it up a gear, the following places double up as nightclubs and often have live music.

New Cadillac (admission RFr2000; ☺ Wed-Sun) This long-running club is still just about holding off all-comers to remain the most popular place in town. Located in the Kimikurure district not far from the centre of Kigali, this is a large, partly open-air venue that plays a mixture of East African pop, Congolese *soukous* (dance music) and Western hits most nights. Drinks are pricey (RFr1500 for Primus) but you are paying to be seen. It doesn't really pick up until after midnight, but once it does, it really rocks.

Nyira Rock (Ave du Commerce; admission RFr1000) A local nightclub in the city centre, there is usually a friendly crowd here. Don't be put off if it looks closed from the main road, as the entrance is up the alley to the right. DJs, cheap beers and plenty of action towards the weekend.

Abraxas (Ave de la République; admission RFr2000) On Fridays and Saturdays, the Centre D'Echanges Culturels Franco-Rwandais plays host to leading local bands. The music is an eclectic mix of Rwandan, reggae and international covers, and after a few beers everyone finds their rhythm. Very popular.

Planet (Kigali Business Centre, Ave du Lac Muhazi; admission RFr3000) This trendy nightclub is often called KBC by locals due to its location. The most popular place in town with the beautiful people, it really goes off at weekends.

SHOPPING

Rwanda produces some attractive handicrafts, but the lack of tourists in the country has kept development of souvenir shops to a

minimum. Look for basketry, batik, drums, woodcarvings and the famous cow-dung art of symmetrical symbols. There are also a lot of Congolese handicrafts, including the ever-popular masks.

Kigali isn't exactly the shopping capital of Africa, but there are a few good places to have a sniff around. There are some good craft shops selling locally produced carvings, cards and paintings, mostly located near the main post office in the centre of town.

Caplaki (Ave de Kiyovu) The old street market of crafts along Ave de l'Armée next to the Milles Collines has been moved to a new home funded by the French. Sellers are now organised in fixed stalls and popular items include a range of carvings and masks from across the border in DR Congo. Prices start high, as they are, of course, 'antiques' but as most are modern replicas, bargain down to something sensible.

Cooperative des Artisans Rwandais (Rue de Kalisimbi) This is one of the best craft shops about. Prices are generally fixed, but small discounts may be offered.

Republika Lounge Shop (Rue de l'Akanyaru) For something more sophisticated, check out the handicraft shop beneath this bar. There are some nice pieces of art and the best quality souvenir T-shirts you are likely to find in Rwanda.

Dancing Pots (Rue Député Kamuzinzi) This is a fair-trade project established to assist the Batwa pygmies. The Forest Peoples' Project has been training potters to produce terracotta pieces which can be bought here.

GETTING THERE & AWAY
Air

For contact details of the international airlines flying in and out of Gregoire Kayibanda International Airport, see p599.

Rwandair Express (☎ 503687; www.rwandair.com; Ave de la Paix) is the national airline and is planning domestic flights to Gisenyi.

Bus & Minibus

Several bus companies operate services to major towns, which are less crowded and safer than local minibuses. Okapi Car runs to Butare, Gisenyi, Kibuye and Ruhengeri; Atraco Express to Butare, Ruhengeri and Gisenyi, including a through service to Goma; Trans Express 2000 to Butare; and Virunga Ponctuel to Ruhengeri. See the individual town entries for more details on journey times and road conditions. All buses depart from company bus offices in the city centre. Onatracom Express have larger 45-seat buses, which could be considered safer, and these run to Ruhengeri and Gisenyi (three daily), plus Butare and Cyangugu (two daily). These services depart from the Nyabugogo bus terminal.

Local minibuses depart from the Nyabugogo bus terminal for towns all around Rwanda, including Butare (RFr1200, two hours), Katuna (RFr1500, 1½ hours), Kibuye (RFr1300), Ruhengeri (RFr1100, two hours) and Gisenyi (RFr1600, four hours). These minibuses leave when full throughout the day, except at weekends when they tend to dry up after 3pm. Just turn up and tell someone where you're going. See the respective town entries for further details.

Nyabugogo is about 2km north of the city centre in the valley and minibuses (RFr200) are available from the city centre, although there is no longer a local bus station in the centre.

GETTING AROUND
To/From the Airport
Gregoire Kayibanda International Airport is at Kanombe, 10km east of the city centre. A taxi costs about RFr5000, but a direct minibus from the city centre is cheaper (RFr300).

Minibus
There is no longer a local bus station in the city centre, so minibuses cruise the streets looking for passengers. All advertise their destination in the front window and run to districts throughout the city. Costs are very cheap, from RFr100 to RFr300.

Taxi
There are no metered taxis, but a fare within the city centre costs, on average, RFr1500 to RFr2000, double that out to the suburbs or later at night.

Taxi-Motor
These small Japanese trail bikes can be a swift way to get around Kigali, although it can be quite scary travelling out to the suburbs as the drivers really hit the throttle. Short hops are just RFr200 to RFr500, while out to the suburbs is RFr700 to RFr1000.

AROUND KIGALI

NYAMATA & NTARAMA GENOCIDE MEMORIALS
During the genocide, many horrific massacres took place in churches around the country, to which victims had fled in the hope of refuge. Nyatama, about 30km south of Kigali, is a deeply disturbing memorial where skulls and bones of the many victims are on display. The church at Ntarama is more understated but no less powerful. The church has not been touched since the bodies were removed more than a decade ago and there are many bits of clothing on the floor. This church is about 25km from Kigali and both these memorials can be visited in one day trip.

NORTHWESTERN RWANDA

The northwest of Rwanda is where the country really earns its nickname as the Land of a Thousand Hills. It's a beautiful region and the peaks culminate in the stunning Virunga volcanoes, forming a formidable natural border between Rwanda, Uganda and DR Congo.

RUHENGERI
For most travellers, Ruhengeri is a staging post on their way to magnificent Parc National des Volcans, the best place in Africa to track rare mountain gorillas.

It's a small, insignificant town, but the views make up for it, with the mighty Virunga volcanoes looming over town to the north and west – Karisimbi, Bisoke, Mikeno, Muside, Sabinyo, Gahinga and Muhabura.

Forget any ideas about climbing the hill (Nyamagumba) near the post office – it's a military area and access is prohibited.

Information
Banks in Ruhengeri aren't that helpful as they can only change cash and cannot deal with travellers cheques or credit cards.

Banque de Kigali (Ave de 5 Juillet)
BCDI (Ave de la Nutrition) Represents Moneygram.
BCDR (Rue Muhabura) Represents Western Union.
ORTPN office (Ave du 5 Juillet) In the prefecture headquarters (local government headquarters), where it is

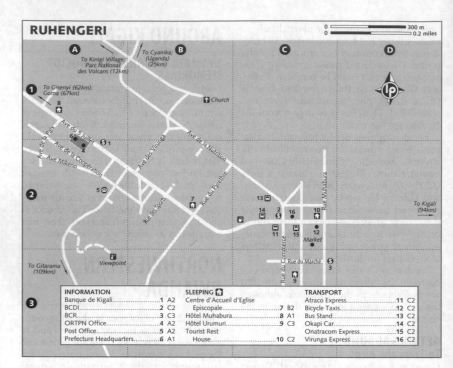

RUHENGERI

0 300 m
0 0.2 miles

INFORMATION		SLEEPING		TRANSPORT	
Banque de Kigali	1 A2	Centre d'Accueil d'Eglise		Atraco Express	11 C2
BCDI	2 C2	Episcopale	7 B2	Bicycle Taxis	12 C2
BCR	3 C3	Hôtel Muhabura	8 A1	Bus Stand	13 C2
ORTPN Office	4 A2	Hôtel Urumuri	9 C3	Okapi Car	14 C2
Post Office	5 A2	Tourist Rest		Onatracom Express	15 C2
Prefecture Headquarters	6 A1	House	10 C2	Virunga Express	16 C2

necessary to meet at 7am for departure on gorilla visits. For details about visiting the mountain gorillas, see opposite.

Post office (☷ 8am-noon & 2-4pm Mon-Fri) Offers basic telephone and postal services.

Sleeping

Arguably the best places to stay in Ruhengeri are not in Ruhengeri itself, but on the edge of Parc National des Volcans around Kinigi. See p586 for more details. But a few places in Ruhengeri are worth checking out.

Tourist Rest House (☎ 546635; Rue Muhabura; s/tw RFr3000/5000) Part of the same group as the popular Skyblue hotels in Uganda, this is a well-run little establishment for budget travellers. Rooms are small but clean and there is hot water in the shared showers, making it good value.

Hôtel Urumuri (☎ 546820; r RFr3500) For those wanting a bathroom on tap, so to speak, this local hotel is the best deal in town. Tucked away on a side street off Rue du Marché, it is a friendly spot and bathrooms have hot water.

Hôtel Muhabura (☎ 546296; Ave du 5 Juillet; r/apt RFr15000/20,000) Ruhengeri's leading hotel,

the lack of competition in town has seen prices double here in the last few years. Close to the ORTPN office, the Muhabura offers large, clean, airy rooms with bathroom and hot water, and several apartments that are verging on minisuites. Definitely book ahead here, as it is often full with tour groups and NGOs.

Centre d'Accueil d'Eglise Episcopale (☎ 546857; cnr Rue du Pyrethre & Ave du 5 Juillet; r RFr5000-30,000; ☷) This church-run establishment has moved into the hotel stakes in recent years, with the widest range of rooms in town. Cheap rooms are in a small block with shared bathrooms, but as you start spending more, facilities improve, including, at the top of the scale, TV and a bathtub. There is a small swimming pool here, which is also open to nonguests for RFr1000.

Eating & Drinking

Dining options are pretty limited in Ruhengeri given the number of foreigners passing through these days. The best restaurant in town is at the Hôtel Muhabura, which has a continental menu of brochettes,

RWANDA

steaks, *tilapia* and some well-dressed salads. Meals run from RFr2000 to RFr4000. Although Ruhengeri is a quiet place in the evenings, the bar here is the place to meet international movers and shakers, and big European football games are screened here at weekends.

Hôtel Urumuri has an outdoor courtyard restaurant with a good value menu, including brochettes, pastas and salads, with most meals in the RFr1000 to RFr1500 range. It also has very cold beers and draws locals for a drink.

Getting There & Away

Numerous bus companies offer scheduled hourly services between Ruhengeri and Kigali, including **Okapi Car** (Ave du 5 Juillet), **Virunga Express** (Ave du 5 Juillet) and **Atraco Express** (Ave du 5 Juillet), all charging RFr1300. These buses are less crowded than normal minibuses. **Onatracom Express** (Ave du 5 Juillet) has three large buses per day passing through, connecting Kigali and Gisenyi; tickets are available at the petrol station.

There are normal minibuses from Ruhengeri to Kigali (RFr1100, two hours), on a breathtaking mountain road, as well as to Cyanika (RFr400, 45 minutes), on the Rwanda–Uganda border, and to Gisenyi (RFr800, 1½ hours).

Getting Around

There are few taxis in Ruhengeri, but plenty of *boda-bodas* (bicycle taxis) for those needing a rest. A typical fare from the centre to the Hôtel Muhabura is RFr200. Taxi-motors are also available, but they are pretty optimistic with their prices.

PARC NATIONAL DES VOLCANS

This is the definitive location to track the rare and captivating mountain gorilla *(Gorilla gorilla beringei)* in Africa. This area along the border with DR Congo and Uganda also happens to be one of the most beautiful sights in Africa. There is a chain of no less than seven volcanoes, the highest, Karisimbi, more than 4500m.

On the bamboo- and rainforest-covered slopes of the volcanoes are some of the last remaining sanctuaries of the mountain gorilla, which was studied in depth first by George Schaller and, more recently, by Dian Fossey.

Fossey spent the best part of 13 years living at a remote camp high up on the slopes of Bisoke in order to study the gorillas and to habituate them to human contact. She'd probably still be there now had she not been murdered in December 1985, most likely by poachers with whom she had made herself very unpopular. Without her tenacious efforts to have poaching stamped out and the work of committed locals since her death, there possibly wouldn't be any mountain gorillas remaining in Rwanda.

Fossey's account of her years with the gorillas and her battle with the poachers and government officials, *Gorillas in the Mist*, makes fascinating reading (see p75). Pick up a copy before coming here. Her story has also been made into a film of the same name (p571), and following its success, the tourism industry in the country boomed for a while, until fighting between the government and the RPF put the area out of bounds to tourists. Things were on and off until 1999, when the park fully reopened, and it is now receiving visitors daily.

During the early part of the last civil war, these mountains were the focus of intense fighting that included artillery duels. This was hardly conducive to good gorilla-human relations and it was reported that at least seven of the gorillas had met their end. Poaching continues to threaten their existence today and in 2002 two females of the remote Susa group were killed to capture their infants for sale on the international market.

It isn't just poaching or soldiers, however, that threaten the gorillas. Also clawing away at their existence is local pressure for grazing and agricultural land, and the European Community's pyrethrum project – daisylike flowers processed into a natural insecticide. In 1969 this project was responsible for reducing the size of the park by more than 8900 hectares – almost half its area! The park now covers just 0.5% of the total land area of Rwanda.

Activities

VISITING THE GORILLAS

An encounter with these beautiful creatures is the highlight of a trip to Africa for many visitors. An encounter with a silverback male gorilla at close quarters can be a hair-raising experience if you've only ever seen

RWANDA

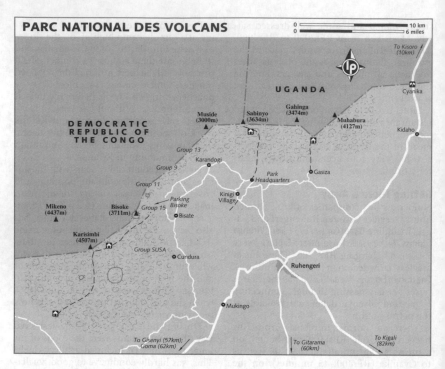

PARC NATIONAL DES VOLCANS

large wild animals behind the bars of a cage or from the safety of a car. Despite their size, however, they're remarkably nonaggressive animals, entirely vegetarian, and are usually quite safe to be around. For most people, it's a magical encounter.

It is no joy ride, however. The guides can generally find the gorillas within one to four hours of starting out, but this often involves a lot of strenuous effort scrambling through dense vegetation up steep, muddy hillsides, sometimes to more than 3000m. There are many stinging plants at higher altitudes and they can make it through light clothing such as trekking trousers. It also rains a lot in this area, so without the right footwear, clothing and a pair of gloves to avoid the stingers, it can be tough going.

There are five habituated gorilla groups in Parc National des Volcans, including the Susa group, which has 35 members. The Susa group is the largest but hardest to reach of all the groups, as much as three to four hours up the slopes of Karisimbi, and, at an altitude of more than 3000m, the going is tough if you are not fit. The other groups –

Sabinyo with 13 members, Amahura with 16 and Group 13 with just six – are all easier to reach as roads go right up to the forest line near Bisoke and Sabinyo volcanoes. Numbers of people allowed to visit each group are limited to a maximum of eight people per day, limiting the total number of daily permits to an absolute maximum of 40.

Visits to the gorillas are restricted to one hour and flash photography and video cameras are banned unless you are prepared to pay a huge sum for a filming permit! Children under 15 are not allowed to visit the gorillas.

For a compare and contrast look at the competing mountain gorilla experiences in Rwanda, Uganda and DR Congo, see p97.

Reservations

Bookings for gorilla permits can be made through the ORTPN tourist office (see p575) in Kigali or a Rwandan tour company (see p96). Those visiting on a tour package will have everything arranged for them, but independent travellers are also encouraged to make advance reservations where possible. It is not always that easy to deal with ORTPN by phone or email from overseas, so it might be easier to book a permit through a Rwandan tour operator to be twice as sure the booking is confirmed. With tourism in Rwanda now on the up and up, it is getting more difficult to secure permits during the peak seasons of December/January and July/August so book well in advance if there is no room for flexibility with the date. Bookings are secured with a US$50 deposit and full payment must be made 30 days prior to the visit. Independent travellers who have only decided to visit the gorillas in Rwanda once in the East Africa region can turn up at the ORTPN offices in Kigali or Ruhengeri and try to secure a booking at the earliest available date. During the high season, waits of several days are not uncommon. If bookings are really solid, consider tracking the mountain gorillas in DR Congo, if the security situation remains stable (p563).

Having made a booking and paid the fees, head to the ORTPN office in Ruhengeri ready for the experience of a lifetime. Ideally get there the afternoon before just to double check everything is OK, but it is also no problem to turn up at 7am on the day of the visit. It is also necessary to arrange a vehicle through the ORTPN office to take you to the point at which you start climbing up to where the gorillas are situated, which costs about US$50 shared between however many there are in the group. In practice, however, it should be possible to hitch a ride with other tourists or expats who have their own vehicles. If the only option available is to charter a vehicle and you are alone, it will be cheaper to arrange a taxi-motor for the 13km ride.

Permit Fees

Fees are now a hefty US$375 per person for a gorilla visit (including park entry, compulsory guides and guards), payable in hard currency. However, there are reliable rumours that this could rise again to US$500 during the lifetime of this book. Resident foreigners pay just US$200 and Rwandan nationals RFr10,000. Porters are also available but you pay extra for this service (US$2). The guides, guards and any porters will expect a tip (around US$5 each depending on the quality of the service) at the end, plus it is

a good idea to tip the driver for those who get a free ride up to the park.

GOLDEN MONKEY TRACKING

Golden monkey tracking is a relative newcomer on the wildlife scene of East Africa, but is rapidly rising in popularity both in Parc National des Volcans and across the border at Mgahinga in Uganda. More like chimp viewing than a gorilla encounter, these beautiful active monkeys bound about the branches of bigger trees. Currently classified as an endangered species, hopefully this new activity will ensure their future. It costs US$75 to track the golden monkeys, although it may be worth noting that the fee is just US$20 across the other side of the Virungas at Mgahinga in Uganda. Factoring in the park fees, that adds up to US$100 in Rwanda, only US$40 in Uganda.

TREKKING THE VOLCANOES

The stunning volcanoes are an evocative backdrop for a guided trek. There are several possibilities for trekking up to the summits of one or more of the volcanoes in the park. The treks range from several hours to two days. A guide is compulsory but porters are optional. Overnight treks are currently suspended, but should they resume you'll need to bring your own sleeping gear, but not tents as there are huts on the mountain.

The ascents pass through some remarkable changes of vegetation, ranging from thick forests of bamboo, giant lobelia or hagenia on to alpine meadows. If the weather is favourable, the reward is some spectacular views over the mountain chain. It is forbidden to cut down trees or otherwise damage vegetation in the park and you are only allowed to make fires in the designated camping areas.

The two-day climb up Karisimbi costs US$150, including park fees and a guide. The Bisoke crater climb or a visit to the grave of Dian Fossey and the gorilla graveyard cost US$50.

The following treks are among the more popular.

Bisoke

The return trip to Bisoke (3711m) takes six to seven hours from Parking Bisoke. The ascent takes you up the steep southwestern flanks of the volcano to the summit, where you can see the crater lake. The descent follows a track on the northwestern side, from where there are magnificent views over the Parc National des Virungas and Lake Ngezi.

There is also another trek to visit the grave of Dian Fossey, who did so much research on the slopes of Bisoke, part of the gorilla graveyard where many of her subjects were buried, including the famous Digit.

Karisimbi

Climbing Karisimbi (4507m) takes two days. The track follows the saddle between Bisoke and Karisimbi and then ascends the northwestern flank of the latter. Some five hours after beginning the trek, there is a metal hut in which to spend the night (the hut keys are available at Parking Bisoke). The rocky and sometimes snow-covered summit is a further two to four hours walk through alpine vegetation. To do this trek, take plenty of warm clothing and a very good sleeping bag. It gets very cold, especially at the metal hut, which is on a bleak shoulder of the mountain at 3660m. The wind whips through, frequently with fog, so there is little warmth from the sun. This trek was not available at the time of writing, but should be reinstated some time during the lifetime of this book.

Other Treks

Before the genocide, there were several other treks available that have not yet been reinstated, but we describe them here, as they may be reintroduced soon.

- The return walk to Lake Ngezi (about 3000m) takes three to four hours from Parking Bisoke. This is one of the easiest of the treks, and at the right time of the day it is possible to see a variety of animals coming to drink.
- Climbing Sabinyo (3634m) takes five to six hours from the park headquarters near Kinigi. The track ascends the southeastern face of the volcano, ending up with a rough scramble over steep lava beds along a very narrow path.
- Climbing Gahinga (3474m) and Muhabura (4127m) is a two-day trip from Gasiza. The summit of the first volcano is reached after a climb of about four hours along a track that passes through a swampy saddle between the two mountains. The trip to the summit of Muhabura takes about four hours from the saddle.

Sleeping

Kinigi Guesthouse (☎ 546984; www.rwanda-gorillas .com; s/d incl breakfast US$20/25) This is the best-value option in the vicinity of the national park and the good news is that is run for a cause. Located very close to park headquarters in Kinigi village, all profits from this local lodge are ploughed back into the Association de Solidarité des Femmes Rwandaises, which assists vulnerable Rwandan women of all backgrounds and ages. Set in lush gardens, the wooden bungalows are good value and the staff friendly.

Gorilla's Nest Camp (☎ 546331; gorillanest@yahoo .fr; s/d incl breakfast US$80/100) Also in the Kinigi area is this midrange lodge, with wonderful views up to the volcanoes. Rooms are smart and include hot-water showers. The breakfast is hearty and other meals are available.

Virunga Lodge (☎ 502452; www.volcanoessafaris .com; s/d US$265/400) One of the most stunningly situated camps in the region, the new Volcanoes-run Virunga Lodge is nestled on a ridge above Lake Burera and offers incredible views across to the Virunga volcanoes. Accommodation is in individual stone chalets, but the price is definitely more about atmosphere than absolute luxury. There is a striking bar and restaurant with a 360-degree view of the lakes and volcanoes beyond.

Getting There & Away

The access point for the national park is Ruhengeri. To get to the park from Ruhengeri, you can arrange a vehicle through the ORTPN office in Ruhengeri (about US$50), or try hitching a ride with fellow trekkers. There are usually enough vehicles around, especially at weekends.

GISENYI

Welcome to the Costa del Kivu! Gisenyi is a resort town for rich Rwandans, expat escapees and, increasingly, tourists. Landscaped villas, plush hotels and private clubs occupy much of the Lake Kivu frontage and are quite a contrast to the African township on the hillside above.

For those with the money, there's a variety of water sports available, plus plush hotels and restaurants. For those without, there are magnificent views over Lake Kivu and, looking northwest, the 3470m-high volcano of Nyiragongo, which blew its top and swallowed much of Goma in neighbouring DR

Congo in early 2002. Swimming and sunbathing on the sandy beaches are also free.

Information

BCR (Rue de Ruhengeri), representing Western Union, and **BCDI** (Rue des Poissons), representing Moneygram, both have branches near the market, while **Banque de Kigali** (Ave de Fleures) is near the lakefront in the lower part of town. Currently these banks can only deal with cash exchanges. **Modern Internet** (Rue de Ruhengeri) offers the best Internet connection in town, sometimes the only connection.

There is no DR Congo consulate here, but visas (US$35) are available on the border if crossing to Goma to trek Nyiragongo volcano or visit the mountain gorillas in Parc National des Virungas (see p560).

Sights & Activities

Gisenyi is home to the **Primus Brewery**, the factory responsible for churning out all those blessed bottles of lager found up and down Rwanda. We were able to arrange a tour of the brewery, located about 7km out of town along a lovely lakeshore road. The tour is free and may include a beer, but keep cameras well out of sight, as they are very sensitive about photographs.

Sleeping

The cheaper places are all found around the upper part of town, but it is better to spend a little more and stay down near the lakeside.

Centre d'Accueil de l'Église Presbytérienne (☎ 540397; Ave du Marché; dm RFr1000-1500, d RFr4800) This church-run hostel has the cheapest beds in town. Dorms come with varying numbers of beds and the more expensive ones have just four people per room. The double rooms are clean and include a bathroom. Basic meals are served in a small restaurant and there is a craft shop selling banana-leaf cards and stuffed toys to raise money for local women's groups.

Auberge de Gisenyi (☎ 540385; Ave de l'Umuganda; s/d RFr5000/6000) The pick of the pack among the cheaper guesthouses in the upper part of town, the rooms here face onto an attractive courtyard garden. The doubles are almost suites, making them a good deal, and the restaurant is popular at night for both food and beer.

Hôtel Palm Beach (☎ 085 59551; uwinya@yahoo .fr; Ave de la Coopération; r RFr15,000-30,000) Housed

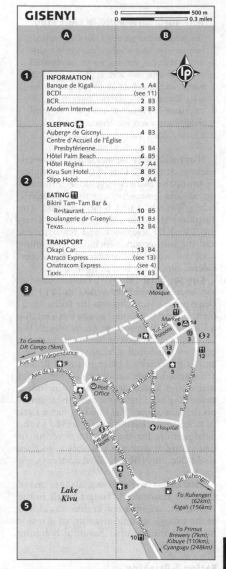

in a rambling old colonial-era house, the rooms here are spacious and comfortable. The cheaper rooms include a bathroom with hot water, while the most expensive options have a lake view and satellite TV. It has its own stretch of private beachfront, a beachside bar and a popular restaurant-bar downstairs.

RWANDA

WARNING: SWIMMING IN LAKE KIVU

There are certain parts of Lake Kivu, particularly around Gisenyi, where it is very dangerous to swim, as volcanic gases are released from the lake bed and, in the absence of wind, tend to collect on the surface of the lake. Quite a few people have been asphyxiated as a result. Watch where the local people swim and you should be safe.

Stipp Hotel (☎ 540540; www.stippag.co.rw; Ave de la Révolution; s/d US$60/70) One of the newest hotels in town, the owners have done a number on an old property, creating Gisenyi's, surely Rwanda's, first boutique hotel. The 10 rooms are packed with extras like satellite TV, IDD telephone and big bathtubs and the lush grounds include a swimming pool and sauna. The restaurant here is considered one of the best in town.

Kivu Sun Hotel (☎ 541111; kivusun@southernsun.com; Ave de la Coopération; s/d from US$85/95;) Once upon a time this was the Izuba Meridien, a resort hotel that used to feel a bit like a Club Med that got lost on its way to the Seychelles. However, it has risen from the ashes as the South African–run Kivu Sun and is the smartest place in town. Rooms are packed with creature comforts and many offer a lake view. Facilities include a swimming pool and some prime beachfront on the lake shore. The building has a dark past, however, having briefly served as the headquarters for the interim government that presided over the genocide – so they could flee into DR Congo when things got too hot.

Hôtel Régina (Ave de la Coopération) Once one of the most atmospheric budget hotels in the region, the colonial-era Regina was closed at the time of writing, awaiting an investor to turn it into another beautiful boutique hotel.

Eating & Drinking

Most visitors end up eating at the bigger hotels, as there isn't a great selection of restaurants in town. There are several simple restaurants on the main road in the upper part of town serving cheap meals, but the standard isn't up to much.

Among the hotels, the Palm Beach has a popular restaurant, which includes a beachfront bar for a meal at sunset. The menu is predominantly French and it draws a local crowd most nights. The bar has a pool table and hustlers come from as far afield as Goma to show their skills.

The restaurants at Stipp Hotel and Kivu Sun Hotel are both highly regarded, serving continental cuisine. Meals run from about RFr2000 to RFr10,000 and service at either place is swift.

Texas (Rue de Ruhengeri; snacks RFr1000-3000) For something completely different, head to this sophisticated coffee shop in the upper part of town. The décor is definitely more international than most in Gisenyi and the menu includes fresh breads, pastries and even pizzas, plus creative coffees and juices.

Bikini Tam-Tam Bar & Restaurant (Ave de la Production; mains RFr1500-3000) In a great location on the beach in the south of town, the menu here is limited but the setting more than makes up for it. Who knows where they came up with the name, but it's easy to remember. It gets busier at the weekends when the drinking crowd rolls in.

For self-caterers, there's a wide variety of fruit and vegetables available at the main market. For cheese, meats, yogurts and fresh bread try **Boulangerie de Gisenyi** (Rue des Poissons).

Getting There & Away
BOAT
All passenger ferries across Lake Kivu to other Rwandan ports are currently suspended. However, there are fast boats between Goma and Bukavu, taking just two hours, although this would require a DR Congo visa and there are potentially serious security question marks over this route.

BUS & MINIBUS
It is a beautiful journey from Ruhengeri through rural farms and villages and there are panoramic views of Lake Kivu as the road descends into Gisenyi. **Okapi Car** (Ave du Marché) and **Atraco Express** (Ave du Marché) operate minibuses between Gisenyi and Kigali (RFr1800, three hours) and the advantage with this service is that it does not stop all the time for people getting on and off. There are also regular minibuses between Gisenyi and Ruhengeri (RFr700, two hours). **Onatracom Express** (Ave de l'Umuganda) runs big buses and has three services a day to Ki-

gali (RFr1600) passing through Ruhengeri (RFr800). All the buses terminate on Ave de l'Umuganda.

There are only infrequent minibuses running between Gisenyi and Kibuye, but one bus (RFr1200, six hours) a day heads in each direction around 8am.

For the lowdown on crossing the border into DR Congo, see p600. It is easy enough to reach the border by taxi-motor for RFr200 or taxi for RFr1000.

Getting Around

If you need wheels, taxi-motors do the run between the market and lakeside areas of town for RFr200.

SOUTHWESTERN RWANDA

The endless mountains don't stop as you head south towards Burundi. Highlights here include the intellectual centre of Butare and the magnificent forest of Parc National Nyungwe Forest, not forgetting of course the stunningly beautiful blue waters of Lake Kivu.

BUTARE

Butare is the intellectual centre of Rwanda, home to the National University, the National Institute of Scientific Research and the excellent National Museum. The town itself is a step down in size after bustling Kigali, but all the same, it offers a good range of hotels and many of the locals speak English or French.

Information

There are branches of BCR, BCDI, and Banque de Kigali on the main Rue de Kigali, but they can only deal with cash.

Computer Link @ Butare (Rue de Kigali; per hr RFr500) The place for Internet access in town.

Expo Vente (Rue de Kigali) A large handicrafts shop exhibiting local products made by cooperatives in villages around Butare. One of the best-value places to buy crafts in the country.

Librairie Caritas (Rue de la Prefecture) A good bookshop frequented by students from the university.

Post office (Rue de Kigali) Has postal services, but no telephones. For domestic and international calls try the shops opposite Hôtel Ibis.

Sights

The excellent **National Museum** (☎ 530586; Rue de Kigali; admission RFr1000; ⏰ 8-5pm) opened in 1989 and is one of the best museums in East Africa. It's certainly the most amazing building in the country. A gift from Belgium to commemorate 25 years of independence, it's well worth a visit for its ethnological and archaeological displays. The museum is about 2km north of the centre, past the minibus stand. It is probably best to take a *boda-boda* for RFr200 or try a short hitch.

Those interested in Africa flora might like to check out the **Arboretum de Ruhande** near the university.

Sleeping

Hôtel Faucon (☎ 086 17657; Rue de Kigali; s/apt RFr5000/ 10,000) Not so many years ago, this place provided serious competition for the Ibis, but standards have slipped. However, this is great news for budget travellers, as it offers huge rooms at rockbottom prices. Apartments come with a bathroom, satellite TV and seating area, and breakfast is included, making for enticing value.

Hôtel Ibis (☎ 530335; campionibis@hotmail.com; Rue de Kigali; s/d RFr15,000/18,000, apt RFr20,000-23,000) Probably the best hotel in town thanks to a central location and comfortable rooms. The normal rooms are fine, but for a touch more class, take an apartment with space to spread your stuff around. There is an excellent terrace bar-restaurant here that serves drinks and snacks.

Hôtel des Beaux-Arts (☎ 530032; Ave du Commerce; r RFr4000-6000) Set a little way back from Ave du Commerce, this hotel has character for a cheapie. The hotel is attractively decorated with local products and there's a handicraft shop selling a selection of what is displayed on the walls. All rooms include hot-water bathrooms making them the real deal.

Motel Dusabane (☎ 085 59220; Rue Rwamamba; s/d RFr2500/3500) The basic rooms found here are nothing to write home about, but you'd have to be pretty sad to be writing home about hotel rooms anyway. No room for complaints at these prices.

Motel Gratia (☎ 530278; Rue Rwamamba; r RFr5000) This small hotel is mildly more inviting than the other budget options thanks to all the rooms facing on to a small garden. The simple rooms are clean and furnished and hot water is available on request.

RWANDA

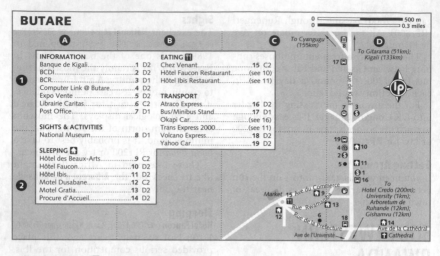

BUTARE

INFORMATION		
Banque de Kigali	1	D2
BCDI	2	D2
BCR	3	D1
Computer Link @ Butare	4	D2
Expo Vente	5	D2
Librairie Caritas	6	C2
Post Office	7	D1
SIGHTS & ACTIVITIES		
National Museum	8	D1
SLEEPING		
Hôtel des Beaux-Arts	9	C2
Hôtel Faucon	10	D2
Hôtel Ibis	11	D2
Motel Dusabane	12	C2
Motel Gratia	13	D2
Procure d'Accueil	14	D2

EATING		
Chez Venant	15	C2
Hôtel Faucon Restaurant	(see 10)	
Hôtel Ibis Restaurant	(see 11)	
TRANSPORT		
Atraco Express	16	D2
Bus/Minibus Stand	17	D1
Okapi Car	(see 16)	
Trans Express 2000	(see 11)	
Volcano Express	18	D2
Yahoo Car	19	D2

Hotel Credo (☎ 530505; Ave de l'Université; s RFr10,000-23,000, d RFr13,000-26,000) A modern hotel on the road to the university, this place draws well-to-do Rwandans visiting their kids at college, as well as business folk travelling between Rwanda and Burundi. Rooms are smart and come with a varying degree of gadgets at a variety of prices.

Procure d'Accueil (Ave de la Cathédral) Church-run, this place with very pretty gardens was undergoing a thorough renovation during our last visit, so should be in slick shape.

Eating & Drinking

Like many towns in Rwanda, this is another place where most visitors tend to eat at the guesthouses and hotels. Budget hotels can turn out basic food such as brochettes and rice, while the fancier hotels have pretty impressive menus at attractive prices.

Chez Venant (☎ 085 04115; Rue Rwamamba; mains RFr1000-5000) One of the few restaurants in town, this place brings the taste of China to Butare. All the usual suspects turn up on the menu, including spring rolls and beef in black bean sauce, but there are also a few local dishes for good measure.

Hôtel Ibis restaurant (☎ 530335; campionibis@ hotmail.com; Rue de Kigali; meals RFr2000-3000) This hotel restaurant serves delicious food including a selection of meats, fish and pastas, and a wholesome range of salads for around RFr1000. This terrace here is also a popular drinking stop, whether at lunchtime or dinner.

Hôtel Faucon restaurant (☎ 086 17657; Rue de Kigali) The restaurant here seems to have taken a dive and is now pretty dead. However, the bar is still a lively place to be in the evening and has cheap Primus.

Entertainment

There is a traditional Rwandan dance troupe based near Butare and their show is spectacular. The *Intore* dance originated in Burundi and involves elaborate costumes and superb drumming routines. Performances can be organised through the National Museum and cost RFr10,000 for up to five people and then rises by RFr2000 for each additional five people. This is pretty good value for a group as photography is allowed, although not video. At weekends, prices rise by 25% and an evening performance is 50% more.

Contact the **museum** (☎ 532136) to book and confirm the dancers are in town, as they are sometimes on tour.

Shopping

In the surrounding area are several craft centres, such as Gihindamuyaga (10km) and Gishamvu (12km). Anyone thinking of buying anything at these places should look first at the quality and prices of what's for sale at the National Museum shop and Expo Vente opposite the Hôtel Ibis.

Getting There & Away

There are several bus companies operating between Butare and Kigali (two hours) found on Rue de Kigali: Atraco Express, Okapi Car, Trans Express 2000 and Volcano Express have almost hourly services in both directions, costing RFr1300. Atraco Express (8am and 2pm) and Onatracom Express (9.15am and 3.30pm) have daily departures to Cyangugu (RFr1700).

Yahoo Car and New Yahoo Coach operate minibuses between Kigali and Bujumbura (Burundi) that stop in Butare at 9.30am daily. Butare to Bujumbura costs RFr3000. However, check security conditions very carefully before crossing this way. There are also local minibuses to the Burundi border at Kayanza Haut.

The minibus stand is just a patch of dirt about 1km north of the town centre, by the stadium. Arriving minibuses often drop passengers in the centre of town, but when leaving, you must go to the bus stand. *Boda-bodas* abound, so this is no problem.

Minibuses run between Butare and Kigali (RFr1100, two hours) and Kamembe (for Cyangugu, RFr1600, three hours) on a spectacular road in places, passing through the Nyungwe Forest, which contains some amazing virgin rainforest between Uwinka and Kiutabe.

GIKONGORO

Gikongoro would be a fairly forgettable town, but for the unforgettable horrors that took place here during the genocide. The location of a well-known technical college before the war, during the genocide many flocked here to seek protection from the killers. Then the Interahamwe came and in a matter of days thousands were dead. This is one of the most graphic of the many genocide memorials, as hundreds of bodies have been preserved with powdered lime, left exactly as they looked when the killers struck. Wandering through the rooms at this former institute of learning, the scene becomes more and more macabre, beginning with the contorted corpses of adults and finishing with a room full of toddlers and babies, slashes from the machetes still visible on the shrivelled bodies. This is horrific and not everyone can stomach it. It is, however, another poignant reminder to all of us of what came to pass here and why it must never be allowed to happen again.

Gikongoro is 28km west of Butare and there are regular minibuses running between the two, costing RFr500. The memorial is 2km beyond the town and taxi-motors can run you there.

PARC NATIONAL NYUNGWE FOREST

Nyungwe Forest is the newest of Rwanda's parks to receive national park status, but the protected area covers one of the oldest rainforests in Africa. It is one of the leading attractions in Rwanda, easily the equal of Kibale Forest in Uganda. One of the largest protected montane rainforests in Africa, it covers 970 sq km and offers superb scenery overlooking the forest and Lake Kivu, as well as views to the north of the distant volcanoes of the Parc National des Virungas.

The project to protect the forest began in 1988 and has been sponsored by the Peace Corps, the World Conservation Society and the Rwandan government. The project aims to promote tourism in an ecologically sound way while also studying the forest and educating local people about its value.

The main attraction is the guided tours to view large groups of black-and-white Angolan colobus monkeys (up to 400 in each troop) or the chimpanzees. The lush, green valleys also offer outstanding hiking across 20km of well-maintained trails, passing through enormous stands of hardwoods, under waterfalls and through a large marsh. There are about 270 species of tree, 70 or more species of mammal, 275 species of bird and an astonishing variety of orchids and butterflies.

The park headquarters is at Uwinka, where there is an information centre. It costs US$20 per day to visit Nyungwe Forest, but this includes unguided walks on any of the colour-coded forest trails. Chimpanzee walks leave from Uwinka at 6am and cost US$50, while other primate walks, such as colobus walks, leave between 9am and 3pm, and cost US$30. There are now seven hiking trails in the forest, ranging from 1km to 10km, all of which offer the chance of primate sightings. There is no law against spotting primates on a normal walk, but there is certainly the likelihood of more sightings on a specific primate walk. The short Blue Trail passes through colobus territory, while the longest Red Trail may offer a chimpanzee sighting and you are guaranteed some waterfalls. For a different scene, the Kamiranzovu Trail leads to a marshy area, where elephants used to be seen. For those staying at the ORTPN Resthouse or those with wheels, there is a waterfall trail with good birding and the chance to view a group of fairly easy-going Angolan colobus in a small section of forest near the local tea estate. Whatever the colour of your walks, good footwear, binoculars and rain gear are advisable.

Sleeping

Those with their own transport usually opt to stay in Cyangugu or Butare, but there are a couple of options in and around Nyungwe Forest.

There is a camp site at the Uwinka headquarters, occupying a ridge (2500m) overlooking the forest that offers impressive views in all directions, but the camping fee has been whacked up to a prohibitive US$20. Campers should bring pretty much everything they need – tent, sleeping bag, cooking equipment, food and warm clothes – as only drinks are available. The nearest towns for provisions are Cyangugu, Gikongoro and Butare. There is little here other than toilets, charcoal and wood.

ORTPN Resthouse (r per person $15-20) A more sophisticated option for those without a tent but with transport (it's 18km west of Uwinka). It offers wholesome meals with a bit of notice for RFr2500. The big problem is location, location, location, as it is a long haul to Uwinka for those with no transport.

Getting There & Away

The Nyungwe Forest lies between Butare and Cyangugu. Minibuses travel between Butare (90km, two hours) and Kamembe (for Cyangugu, 54km, one hour) throughout the day. The Uwinka headquarters is well marked with a picture of a colobus monkey. The trip between Uwinka and Kigali takes between four and five hours.

CYANGUGU

Clinging to the southern tip of Lake Kivu and looking across to Bukavu in DR Congo, Cyangugu is an attractively situated town on the lakeshore. Kamembe, a few kilometres above the lake, is the main town and transport centre and an important location for the processing of tea and cotton, while most of the better hotels are down below in Cyangugu proper, right next to the border. It is also the nearest major town to Parc National Nyungwe Forest, one of the richest primate destinations in Africa.

Information

There is a branch of BCR in Kamembe that changes cash, but for Congolese transactions, it is better to change near the border post in Cyangugu. Anyone planning to travel on to DR Congo can obtain an eight-day visa on the border for US$35, but as Bukavu has experienced more unrest than most eastern towns, check carefully before crossing; see p562 for more details.

Sleeping & Eating

Hotel du Lac (☎ 537172; s RFr5000-8000, d RFr12,000-15,000; ☒) So close to the border it's almost in DR Congo, this popular hotel has a good mix of rooms, although some of them are showing signs of age, so don't be shy about asking to see more than one. Smaller doubles come with bathroom and balcony, while there are also a couple of larger doubles with a bathtub. The swimming pool here is open to nonguests for RFr1000 per day. The lively terrace bar and restaurant is the place to be at night, with an inexpensive selection of snacks, while the 2nd-floor restaurant offers à la carte, but sans atmosphere.

Hotel des Chutes (☎ 537405; r RFr8000-10,000) Set back on the hill just above the lake, this hotel offers fine views. All the bathrooms have hot water, but it is worth spending a little extra for satellite TV and balconies overlooking the action below. There is also a great little restaurant here with a range of European cuisine available (mains from RFr2000), including steaks, lake fish and crisp salads. The bar here includes a pool table, which is popular with locals, and an outdoor terrace overlooking the lake.

Hôme St François (☎ 537915; s/d/tr RFr1500/2500/3700) Very close to the DR Congo border, this is a cheap and convenient stop for those heading east. It's friendly, spotlessly clean and offers excellent value for money, but couples may be separated unless obviously married. The meals, at around RFr1500, are also good value.

Muli Peace Guesthouse (☎ 537799; s/d RFr3000/5000) Kind of in the middle of nowhere, this is another religion, another guesthouse, with well-tended rooms, clean shared bathrooms and hot water. There are pretty impressive views from here across the lake to Bukavu. Only really for those with their own transport.

Ten to Ten Paradise Hotel (☎ 537818; deluxe/lake view/ste RFr10,000/12,000/14,000) Up in more rough-and-ready Kamembe, this is the most modern hotel in town with some pretty smart rooms with satellite TV and bathroom. However, putting charm above comfort, you are better off down in Cyangugu.

There are also several hole-in-the-wall local restaurants up in Kamembe, which can provide a quick snack before or after a bus journey.

Getting There & Away
BOAT
All passenger ferries across Lake Kivu to other Rwandan ports are currently suspended. However, there are some fast boats between Bukavu and Goma, taking just two hours, although this would require a DR Congo visa and there are potentially serious security question marks over this route.

MINIBUS
Minibuses for the short hop between Cyangugu and Kamembe cost RFr100. Atraco Express and Onatracom Express have four daily departures between them to Butare (RFr1700). From Kamembe to Butare local minibuses cost RFr1600 and take about three hours. This road is incredibly spectacular in parts and passes through the superb Nyungwe rainforest, where it is possible to see troops of Angolan colobus playing by the roadside.

See p594 for details on the daily bus service connecting Cyangugu and Kibuye.

KIBUYE
Kibuye has a stunning location, spread across a series of tongues jutting into Lake Kivu. With good road connections to Kigali, it rivals Gisenyi as beach and water-sports capital of Rwanda, but sandy beaches are less common on this part of the lake. It's a pleasant place to relax for a few days and it is safe to swim here, unlike Gisenyi where there are sometimes dangerous volcanic gases.

Information
There is a post office near Guest House Kibuye with international services, plus plenty of MTN phones in the centre of town.

Bethanie Guesthouse (☎ 568509; bethanie@epr.org .rw; per hr RFr500) For Internet access.

Sights & Activities
To help ensure no one forgets the horrors that were perpetrated here in 1994, there is a **genocide memorial** in the church near Hôme St Jean – Kibuye was hardest hit of all prefectures during the killings, with about 90% of the Tutsi population murdered.

Before it was closed down by the government, Kibuye Guesthouse was offering **water-skiing** and **boat trips** to the surrounding islands, and these may restart once new investors are found.

There is a busy **market** on the lakeshore on Friday and this attracts traders from as far afield as DR Congo.

When returning on the road to Kigali, keep an eye out for the 100m-high waterfall **Les Chutes de Ndaba** after about 20km – buses usually slow down and helpful locals point it out.

Sleeping & Eating
Hôme St Jean (☎ 568526; dm RFr1500, s/d RFr2500/ 4000) Sitting on an isolated hillside to the west of town, this church-run pad has great views and the rooms are the cheapest in town, but for those without transport it means a lot of walking.

Bethanie Guesthouse (☎ 568509; bethanie@epr.org .rw; dm from RFr2000, r RFr7000-12,000; 🖳) Run by the Presbyterian Church, this popular guesthouse occupies a peaceful location on a wooded peninsula jutting into the lake. There are plenty of dorm beds and the price depends on how many beds are in the room. The private rooms are smart, but it's wise to book ahead as this is Kibuye's leading conference venue. There is a basic restaurant, as well as Internet access.

Eden Golfe Rock Hotel (☎ 568524; r RFr10,000-14,000) This big hotel is open to the public once more, having housed the Chinese road-construction crew working on the Kigali road for many years. The location is not as nice as Bethanie, but the rooms are the smartest in town. The most expensive rooms include a balcony with views over Lake Kivu.

Guest House Kibuye (☎ 568554) Long the most popular place in town, offering cottages on the lakeside, water sports and fine dining, the government decided to close it, as

RWANDA

apparently the owners had failed to upgrade it. Not that the guests seemed to notice. No doubt other investors will step in and it should be up and running again some time during the lifetime of this book.

Restaurant Nouveauté (meals RFr1000) This place, in the centre of town near Okapi Car, has a basic menu of goat stew or brochettes, beans, rice, potatoes and so on. It also offers cold beers and soft drinks.

Getting There & Away

The Chinese-built road linking Kibuye with Kigali is endlessly winding but in excellent shape, making it very accessible from the capital. Okapi Car runs buses between Kigali (2½ hours, departing 8am, noon and 2pm) and Kibuye (departing 7am, noon and 2pm), costing RFr1400. Local minibuses also run this way for RFr1200, but are more crowded. Getting between Kibuye and either Cyangugu or Gisenyi is more difficult without your own vehicle as shared taxis and buses are very infrequent. There is a daily bus at 7.30am in either direction between Kibuye and Cyangugu (RFr1200, six hours) which involves one of the most spectacular roads in the country, complete with hairpin bends and plunging drops. There are infrequent minibuses to Gisenyi charging RFr1200. Friday is generally the easiest day for heading north or south, due to the market.

There are no ferry services currently in operation on Lake Kivu.

EASTERN RWANDA

The landscape changes in Eastern Rwanda, as the hills drop away to the plains of Tanzania. Sights are light and most people only pass through if visiting Akagera or taking the road less travelled to Tanzania.

PARC NATIONAL DE L'AKAGERA

Created in 1934 and covering an area of 2500 sq km, **Parc National de l'Akagera** (admission US$10, wildlife viewing 1/2/3 days US$20/30/50, car/minibus/jeep/truck US$10/15/20/50) used to be one of the least visited but most interesting wildlife parks in Africa. However, with the massive numbers of refugees who returned to Rwanda in the late 1990s, as much as two-thirds of the park was degazetted and resettled with new

villages. This human presence led many of the animals in the remaining sector to take a holiday in Tanzania and a visit to this park became something of a vegetarian safari in recent years. However, the government is once again committed to promoting the park and the old Akagera Game Lodge has been rehabilitated by South African investors, offering genuine comfort.

There are three distinct environments in the park: standard savanna as seen in much of the region; an immense swampy area along the border with Tanzania that contains six lakes and numerous islands, some of which are covered with forest; and a chain of low mountains on the flanks of the park with variable vegetation, ranging from short grasses on the summits to wooded savanna and dense thickets of forest.

The best time to visit is during the dry season (mid-May to September). November and April are the wettest months. Tsetse flies can be bad in the north and east, so bring a fly swat and/or a good insect repellent.

Hiring a guide is a good idea, as the trails aren't that well marked, plus it will help give the rangers some encouragement as they really don't get many visitors. It doesn't necessarily mean more animals with a guide, however. The park's animals include hippos, buffaloes, zebras, topis, giraffes and elephants. The lion population is extremely small, but the park is a good destination for birders with the possibility of more than 500 species. Rather dated park maps, for sale at the tourist office in Kigali, are reasonably accurate for the remaining sector of the park and these are not on sale at the park. A wildlife handbook is also a useful thing to have, plus the obligatory pair of binoculars. Also fill up on fuel, as nothing is available once in the park.

Double-check on the entry charges with ORTPN in Kigali (p575), as is seems like a double whammy right now: an entry charge, plus a wildlife-viewing charge. There are discounts for students and children.

Sleeping

Akagera Game Lodge (☎ 567805; agl@rwanda1.com; s/d US$100/144; ▣) Great news for those on an upmarket safari in the region, the Akagera Lodge has finally been rehabilitated and now offers four-star comfort for park visitors. Fully renovated by a South African hotel group, this is really more a hotel than a lodge and the rooms are very well equipped with satellite TV, deluxe bathroom and IDD telephone. Full-board deals are available, a wise choice given there are no other restaurants in the park. Day-trippers should head here for lunch.

Camping (adult/child US$10/5) is possible at the park headquarters on the shores of Lake Ihema, but more attractive is the second, basic camp site at Lake Shakani, a few kilometres north. However, at either place facilities are so minimal as to be verging on nonexistent!

Getting There & Away

The problem with Akagera is that it is only really accessible for those with their own transport. Safari and tour companies in Kigali can arrange a vehicle, but charges are rather expensive. It might be cheaper to negotiate with private taxis around Kigali. Alternatively save the park experience for Uganda, Kenya or Tanzania and concentrate on primates in Rwanda.

RWANDA DIRECTORY

ACCOMMODATION
Camping

The only fully functioning camp sites in the country are at Parcs National Nyungwe Forest and de l'Akagera, but it may be possible to camp at some of the missions around the country on request.

Hostels

Dorm accommodation at the mission hostels costs RFr1000 to RFr2500 per night without food. A private double room at the hostels costs from RFr2500 to RFr15,000 per night depending on facilities.

Mission hostels are places run by churches or missionaries; these differ from ordinary places in that few foreigners stay at them and the hostels usually enforce a curfew – the door is usually closed at 10pm (or earlier). They seem to attract an exceptionally conscientious type of manager who takes the old adage 'cleanliness is next to godliness' fairly seriously. There might not be hot water but the bed and room will be spotless. It's a possibility that couples may be separated unless obviously married.

PRACTICALITIES

- Rwanda uses the metric system and distances are in kilometres.

- Electricity in Rwanda is 240V, 50 cycles, and plugs are mainly two-pin.

- The English-language *New Times* is published several times a week, plus the *New Vision* and *Monitor* are available from Uganda. French magazines and international titles are available in Kigali.

- Radio Rwanda is the government-controlled station, broadcasting in Kinyarwanda, French, Swahili and English.

- Television Rwandaise (TVR) is the state-owned broadcaster.

Hotels

Compared with mission hostels, hotels are generally more expensive and, at the rock-bottom budget end, not always worth the extra amount, especially where they are often none too clean. More expensive budget hotels and midrange places usually offer satellite TV and hot showers, but rates are sometimes higher than elsewhere in the region.

Top-end hotels, mostly found in Kigali, are much the same as their counterparts elsewhere in Africa. Some of the newer, smaller places offer better value for money and more character than the international chains. There are also now a couple of up-market camps located near Ruhengeri on the edge of Parc National des Volcans.

ACTIVITIES
Bird-Watching

Bird-watching in Rwanda may not be in the same league as Uganda, but there are some good opportunities for ornithologists in Parc National Nyungwe Forest (p591), where a host of Albertine Rift endemics can be seen, as well as Parc National de l'Akagera (opposite), in the east of the country, which offers an alternative range of savanna birds.

Gorilla & Chimpanzee Tracking

Without a doubt the number-one attraction for all visitors to Rwanda, an encounter with the enigmatic mountain gorillas is simply magical. It's possible to track the mountain gorillas in Parc National des Volcans (p583) throughout the year. Bookings should be made with the ORTPN office (p575) in Kigali. For more information on the mountain gorillas, see p97.

Primate tracking is also beginning to take off at Parc National Nyungwe Forest (p591), but sightings are not as common as in Uganda, as habituation is still ongoing. However, there are also huge troops of colobus monkeys in Nyungwe and these are easy to spot from the well-marked walking trails that cut through the forest.

Hiking & Trekking

Trekking is beginning to take off again in Rwanda. As the waiting list for gorilla permits grows longer in peak season, more travellers are taking the opportunity to trek on the volcanoes or track the golden monkeys at Parc National des Volcans (p583). There is also an excellent network of colour-coded walking trails at Parc National Nyungwe Forest (p591), the largest tropical montane forest in the East Africa region.

Wildlife Watching

The only opportunity for wildlife-watching drives in Rwanda is in Parc National de l'Akagera (p594), but with wildlife numbers still recovering, it is not quite the Kenya or Tanzania experience yet.

BOOKS

Many of the most powerful books written about Rwanda cover the tragedy of the 1994 genocide. For an in-depth insight into the Rwandan genocide, read *The Rwanda Crisis – History of a Genocide* by French historian Gerard Prunier.

One of the most hard-hitting books on the genocide is *We Wish to Inform You That Tomorrow We Will Be Killed with Our Families* by Phillip Gourevitch; see p37 for more.

Another journalist who bore witness to much of the killing was BBC correspondent Fergal Keane, who returned to write *Season of Blood*. Full of first-hand accounts of unbelievable horrors, this is hard reading.

Shake Hands With the Devil by Lt Gen Romeo Dallaire tells the inside story of the UN mission in Rwanda; see p32 for more.

Leave None to Tell the Story, published by African Rights Watch, is a meticulous record of the genocide through the eyes of victims who survived and government records which attest to the clinical planning of it all.

A Sunday by the Pool in Kigali by Gil Courtemanche is a fictional account of a relationship between a French reporter and a beautiful Tutsi woman during the genocide. No doubt based on very real events, this is an ill-fated love story that perfectly captures the horrors of the time.

Gorillas in the Mist by Dian Fossey is another classic; see p75 for a review.

BUSINESS HOURS

Government offices and businesses are generally open between 8.30am and 4.30pm or 5.30pm, with a short break for lunch sometime between noon and 2pm. Most shops and banks do not break for lunch, but some banks close early at 3.30pm.

Local restaurant hours are 7am to 9pm, and international-type restaurants are open 11.30am to 2.30pm and 5.30pm to 10.30pm.

DANGERS & ANNOYANCES

Mention Rwanda to most people and they think of it as a highly dangerous place. In fact the reality today is very different and security has returned to all parts of the country. That said, it is still worth checking security conditions before entering the country as it is in a very unstable area of the world. There is always the remote possibility of Interahamwe rebels re-entering the country or problems spilling over from DR Congo. The most important thing to remember about security is that there is absolutely no substitute for researching current conditions before arrival and again once in the country. Read newspapers, ask other travellers and hostels for the latest and check again locally once in the provinces. Things can change very fast in Africa, for the better or worse, and it pays to be well informed.

Urban Rwanda is undoubtedly one of the safer places to be in this region of Africa, and Kigali is a genuine contender for the safest capital in Africa, but like in any big city take care around unlit areas at night.

Out in the countryside, do not walk along anything other than a well-used track; there may still be land mines in some remote areas, although most have now been cleared by international organisations.

Never take photographs of anything connected with the government or the military (post offices, banks, bridges, border crossings, barracks, prisons, dams). Film, and maybe the equipment, will be confiscated. In fact take care of where you point your camera anywhere in the country, as most Rwandans are very sensitive to who and what you are snapping.

The most common annoyance is the roadblocks on all of the main roads around Rwanda, particularly close to the capital Kigali. Vehicles must stop at these and passengers and their baggage may be searched. On roads near borders, the soldiers will also want to check passports and travel documents.

EMBASSIES & CONSULATES
Rwandan Embassies
For Rwandan embassies in Burundi, Kenya, Tanzania or Uganda, see the relevant section in those chapters. Useful Rwandan embassies worldwide:

Belgium (☎ 02-771 2127; 1 Ave de Fleurs, Brussels)
South Africa (☎ 012-460 0709; 35 Marais St, Pretoria)
UK (☎ 020-7224 9832; 120-122 Seymour Place, London)
USA (☎ 202-232 2882; 1724 New Hampshire Ave, Washington DC)

Embassies in Rwanda
Quite a number of embassies are now located on Blvd de l'Umuganda, across the valley in the Kacyiru suburb of Kigali.

Belgium (☎ 575551; Rue de Nyarugenge)
Burundi (☎ 517529; Kacyiru)
Canada (☎ 571762; Rue de l'Akaqera)
France (☎ 575206; 40 Ave Paul VI)
Kenya (☎ 583332; Blvd de l'Umuganda)
South Africa (☎ 583185; Blvd de l'Umuganda)
Tanzania (☎ 505400; Ave de la Paix)
Uganda (☎ 572117; Ave de la Paix)
UK (☎ 585280; Blvd de l'Umuganda)
USA (☎ 505601; Blvd de la Revolution)

HOLIDAYS
New Year's Day 1 January
Democracy Day 8 January
Easter (Good Friday, Holy Saturday and Easter Monday) March/April
Labour Day 1 May
Ascension Thursday May
Whit Monday May
National Day 1 July
Peace & National Unity Day 5 July

Harvest Festival 1 August
Assumption 15 August
Culture Day 8 September
Kamarampaka Day 25 September
Armed Forces Day 26 October
All Saints' Day 1 November
Christmas Day 25 December

INTERNET ACCESS
Internet access in Rwanda is reasonable by regional standards and is now widely available in Kigali, as well as on a more limited basis in Butare, Cyangugu, Kibuye and Ruhengeri. It is cheap at around RFr500 per hour.

INTERNET RESOURCES
Rwanda doesn't have a huge presence in cyberspace, but there are a few useful websites to keep an eye out for.
International Criminal Tribunal for Rwanda (www.ictr.org) The official website for the genocide trials taking place in Arusha.
New Times (www.newtimes.co.rw) For the latest news on Rwanda in English.
Tourism in Rwanda (www.rwandatourism.com) The official tourist website on Rwanda, with information on national parks and local culture.

MAPS
It's difficult to get hold of decent maps of Rwanda before getting to the country. The best map currently is *Rwanda Burundi – International Travel Map* by ITMB Publishing at a scale of 1:400,000. Once in Kigali, it may be possible to buy older maps of some of the national parks from the ORTPN office or from local bookshops.

MONEY
The unit of currency is the Rwandan franc (RFr). It is divided into 100 centimes, but these are no longer in circulation. Notes come in RFr100, RFr500, RFr1000, RFr5000 and RFr10,000 denominations. Coins come in RFr1, RFr5, RFr10, RFr20 and RFr50.

ATMs
Banks in Kigali have a network of ATMs, but they are not yet wired up for international transactions, despite the Visa signs at some. Ask locals on arrival for the latest rather than wander the city from ATM to ATM experiencing disappointment as happened to us.

RWANDA

Black Market

There is still a bit of a black market in Rwanda, but there is not much difference in the rate offered on the street and in banks and forex places. Moneychangers gather around the main post office in Kigali, but count your cash very carefully if you change on the street.

Cash

It is definitely best to come with US dollars or euros cash to Rwanda, as travellers cheques and credit-card withdrawals attract a hefty commission, and rates against other currencies are poor. There are a number of banks open in Kigali, but some can be very slow at dealing with currency exchange. There are branches of Banque Commerciale de Rwanda (BCR), Banque de Commerce, de Developement et de l'Industrie (BCDI) and Banque de Kigali in Butare, Cyangugu, Gisenyi, Gitarama and Ruhengeri, but they usually only deal with either US dollars or euros cash.

Another option is to change cash on the street or in shops, usually attracting a slightly higher rate than elsewhere, particularly for non-US currencies.

Credit Cards

Credit cards are generally only accepted in relatively expensive hotels and restaurants in Kigali. It is possible to make cash withdrawals against credit cards at Banque de Kigali in the capital, but minus a commission of around US$15 and a lot of time, plus a bill in euros.

Tipping

Tipping is common in the cities these days due to the large international presence. As in many parts of the developing world, Rwandan salaries are low and a tip of about 10% will be appreciated.

Travellers Cheques

Travellers cheques attract a hefty combination of commissions adding up to about US$16 per transaction, so it is well worth changing all the money you'll need in one go. Irritatingly enough, Banque de Kigali is the only place that can exchange travellers cheques and only in Kigali. Yes, that's right, your travellers cheques are useless beyond the capital.

PHOTOGRAPHY & VIDEO

Bring plenty of film to Rwanda, as it is very expensive here and the choice is extremely limited. Slide film is pretty much impossible to obtain. If you do buy film, check the expiry dates.

Be extremely careful wherever you take photos in Rwanda; see p596.

To take photos of the gorillas in the Parc National des Volcans, bring higher-speed film. Depending on where you encounter them, it is often very dark in their dense forest habitat, so normal film can produce very disappointing results when developed. Carry 200 ISO (ASA) and 400 ISO (ASA) and consider pushing it one stop when developing it if conditions are particularly dark.

POST

Postal rates for postcards going overseas are RFr200 for Africa, RFr250 for Europe and North America and RFr300 elsewhere. There is a poste restante facility at the post office in Kigali. See p575 for details.

TELEPHONE

There are two main operators in Rwanda, MTN and Rwandatel. International calls are relatively expensive at RFr500 to RFr1000 per minute to most countries including Europe, North America and Australia. There are currently no area codes in Rwanda. The international code for Rwanda is ☎ 250. Mobile telephone numbers start with the prefixes ☎ 083, ☎ 085 and ☎ 086. Visit www .rwandaphonebook.com when looking for telephone numbers in Rwanda.

TOURIST INFORMATION

The tourist office, ORTPN, is in Kigali; see p575 for more on contact details and its services. With no network of hostels or camps around the country, there is very little travel information available in Rwanda and it is easier to pick up information in Kampala (Uganda) before coming here.

VISAS

Visas are required by everyone except nationals of Canada, Germany, South Africa, Sweden, the UK, the USA and other East African countries. For other passport-holders visas cost US$60 in most countries, require two photos, and allow up to a three-month stay if requested. When applying, there is no need to show an onward ticket or 'sufficient funds'.

When applying for a visa, you should request a multiple-entry visa if you intend to re-enter Rwanda from Uganda, DR Congo or Burundi. There's no extra cost and it offers flexibility.

Most of the travellers visiting Rwanda, however, get their visa on arrival at the border. The 15-day visa also costs a whopping US$60, but is issued instantly.

Those driving their own vehicles are required to buy an entry permit at the border for RFr5000 and insurance is compulsory, available from **Sonarwa** (in Kigali ☎ 573350) for about RFr4000 per day.

VISA EXTENSIONS

Both tourist and transit visas can be extended in Kigali at **Ministère de l'Intérieur** (MININTER; ☎ 585856) in the Kacyiru district, about 7km northeast of the city centre. Extensions take a week or more to issue and cost RFr15,000 per month.

VISAS FOR ONWARD TRAVEL

Anyone wanting visas for neighbouring countries while in Rwanda should take note of the following (see p597 for the addresses):

Burundi Visas cost US$40 for one month single entry, although check on the security situation very carefully before visiting. Also available on the border.

DR Congo At the time of research, visas were not being issued for travel to Kinshasa as the embassy had not yet reopened. However, for land crossings to eastern DR Congo eight-day visas are available at Bukavu or Goma for US$35.

Kenya Visas cost US$50 or the equivalent in local currency, require two photographs and are issued the same day if you apply before 11.30am. However, visas are also available on arrival.

Tanzania Visas require two photos and generally take 24 hours to issue. The cost depends on nationality.

Uganda Visas cost US$30, require two photos and are issued in 24 hours. However, it is far easier to get them at the border on arrival.

WOMEN TRAVELLERS

Although Rwanda is a safe place in which to travel, it is sensible not to venture too far off the beaten track alone and to avoid wandering down darks streets in larger towns. In general, women will find that they encounter far fewer hassles from men than on the coast of Kenya.

WORK

With all the international money sloshing around Rwanda, one might be forgiven for thinking it would be easy to pick up some work here; however, most international organisations tend to recruit professionals from home. Anyone considering looking for work must secure a work permit from a Rwandan embassy before entering the country. The permit costs more than US$300.

TRANSPORT IN RWANDA

GETTING THERE & AWAY

For information on getting to Rwanda from outside East Africa, see p631.

Entering Rwanda

Yellow-fever vaccination certificates are in theory compulsory for entry or exit, but are rarely requested in reality.

Air

Gregoire Kayibanda International Airport (KGL) is located at Kanombe, 10km east of Kigali centre. Few budget travellers enter Rwanda by air because most of the discounted air fares available in Europe and North America use Nairobi as the gateway to East Africa. Most high-end tourists also enter by land as part of a two-country safari including Uganda. Air tickets bought in Rwanda for international flights are expensive and compare poorly with what is on offer in Nairobi or Kampala. It is possible to pay in local currency.

AIRLINES IN RWANDA

Air Burundi (airline code 8Y; ☎ 572113; Ave des Milles Collines) Hub: Bujumbura.

Ethiopian Airlines (airline code ET; ☎ 575045; www .flyethiopian.com) Hub: Addis Ababa.

Kenya Airways (airline code KQ; ☎ 577972; www.kenya -airways.com; Ave des Milles Collines) Hub: Nairobi.

Rwandair Express (airline code WB; ☎ 503687; www .rwandair.com) Hub: Kigali.

SN Brussels Airline (airline code SN; ☎ 575290; www .brusselsairlines.com) Hub: Brussels.

South African Airways (airline code SA; ☎ 577777; www.flysaa.com; Blvd de la Revolution) Hub: Johannesburg.

RWANDA

TO/FROM BURUNDI

Rwandair Express, Air Burundi and Ethiopian Airlines all connect Kigali and Bujumbura.

TO/FROM KENYA

Rwandair Express and Kenya Airways offer daily services between Kigali and Nairobi.

TO/FROM TANZANIA

Rwandair Express has direct flights between Kigali and Kilimanjaro, which offer a great way to combine ascending Mt Kili and tracking the mountain gorillas. Visit their website for more details.

TO/FROM UGANDA

Rwandair Express and Ethiopian Airlines connect Kigali with Entebbe International Airport for Kampala.

Land

Rwanda shares land borders with Burundi, DR Congo, Tanzania and Uganda. However, most travellers only tend to use the crossings with Uganda. The main crossing with Tanzania is considered safe, but passes through some pretty remote country. There are also land border crossings with DR Congo, but with the exception of the Gisenyi border post for visiting Goma and the mountain gorillas, it is currently not advisable to cross. Finally the land border with Burundi has to be considered risky as long as rebels remain active there. We crossed here, but check the security situation in Burundi before travelling this way.

TO/FROM BURUNDI

The main border crossing between Rwanda and Burundi is via Butare and Kayanza, on the Kigali to Bujumbura road, which is sealed pretty much all the way. The border post is called Kayanza Haut and Burundian visas are available on arrival for US$40. Bus companies Yahoo Car, New Yahoo Coach and Gaso Bus all run daily buses between Kigali and Bujumbura (RFr4000 small bus, RFr5000 big bus, about six hours), departing at about 7am.

There is also a direct road from Bujumbura to Cyangugu, but this is not in such good condition and should be considered unsafe as long as one Burundian rebel faction remains at large.

TO/FROM DR CONGO

There are two main crossings between Rwanda and DR Congo, both on the shores of Lake Kivu. To the north is the crossing between Gisenyi and Goma and this is considered safe to cross at the time of writing, although only for day trips to Goma, climbing Nyiragongo volcano or visiting the mountain gorillas. Longer trips into DR Congo or overland trips through the country are inadvisable at the time of writing. The southern border between Cyangugu and Bukavu is also open for crossing, but the security situation around Bukavu is a little more volatile than Goma. Check carefully in Cyangugu before venturing across and be very wary of visiting Parc National Kahuzi-Biega, as there have been security problems there. For more on visiting DR Congo, see p562.

TO/FROM TANZANIA

Travelling between Rwanda and Tanzania is slow going due to a lack of reliable transport on the Tanzania side. Hitching lifts with trucks or chartering a car is sometimes the only way to make progress further into Tanzania. Don't forget that Rwanda is tiny and getting to either Mwanza or Kigoma is pretty much double the distance of the longest journey in Rwanda. It is arguably faster to backtrack through Uganda.

From Kigali, take a minibus to Rusumo, the last Rwandan town before the border (RFr1500, three hours), and then a pick-up truck from there across the border to Ngara. From Ngara, there are some buses direct to Mwanza. Otherwise, you'll need to do the trip in stages via Benako and Lusahunga. Once in Lusahunga, you can catch onward transport to Biharamulo, Geita and Mwanza, or take the longer and slightly pricier but smoother southern route via Kahama and Shinyanga. Both routes are expeditions in themselves, and can easily take two days.

From the border at Rusumo, take a shared taxi to Benako (about TSh3000). At Benako there are several basic guesthouses, if you need a room. From Benako, there are minibuses to Lusahunga and Nyakanazi (about 25km further south) for about TSh5000. From Lusahunga, there are buses three times weekly on to Kasulu and Kigoma, although they're often full when they reach Lusahunga. Otherwise, you'll need to do the trip in stages via Kibondo and Kasulu. Many aid workers travel this route, so hitching is also possible. From Lusahunga to Kigoma on the Tanzanian side is rough going, and you should get an update on security here before setting off.

TO/FROM UGANDA

There are two main crossing points for foreigners: between Kigali and Kabale via Gatuna (Katuna), and between Ruhengeri and Kisoro via Cyanika.

The border is called Gatuna on the Rwandan side, Katuna on the Ugandan side. There are lots of minibuses between Kigali and the border at Gatuna (RFr1500, 1½ hours) throughout the day. There are also plenty of minibuses (USh1000) and special hire taxis (USh15,000 for the whole car) travelling back and forth between Katuna and Kabale.

From Ruhengeri to Kisoro via Cyanika the road is in excellent shape on the Rwandan side and poor condition on the Ugandan side. With Parç National des Volcans increasingly popular, the Rwandan military have prioritised security on this stretch. Minibuses link either side of the border with Ruhengeri (RFr500, 25km) and Kisoro (USh1000, 12km).

Those travelling direct between Kigali and Kampala can travel with **Jaguar Executive Coaches** (☎ 086 14838), which offers an executive bus (RFr7000) and a standard service (RFr5000), both departing at 5.45/6.15/9am from the Nyabugogo Bus Station and taking eight to nine hours, including a long border crossing. **Regional Coach** (☎ 575963) also offers a bus to Kampala (RFr6500, 6.30am), which continues to Nairobi (RFr14,000).

Tours

For more info on a few companies running organised tours, see p96.

GETTING AROUND
Air

There are currently no domestic flights in Rwanda, but distances are so short that it hardly matters. Rwandair Express may introduce flights from Kigali to Gisenyi early in the lifetime of this book.

Bus

Rwanda has a reasonable road system, for the most part due to its small size and a large

---

> **CROSSING TO BURUNDI?**
>
> Don't cross into Burundi by land without carefully checking the current security situation in the north of the country. At the time of research, we were able to safely travel by bus from Bujumbura to Kigali, but there is no substitute for double checking the latest story. At the time of writing, one rebel group is still fighting the new government and that means ambushes are a remote possibility.

dose of foreign assistance. The only major unsealed roads are those running alongside the shore of Lake Kivu and some smaller stretches around the country.

The best buses are privately run, scheduled services operated by Okapi Car, Trans Express 2000, Atraco Express and Virunga Ponctuel. Destinations covered include Butare, Gisenyi, Kibuye and Ruhengeri and departures are guaranteed to leave, hourly in many cases. They are less crowded and drive more carefully than the normal minibuses, but cost a little more. Onatracom operate bigger buses on longer routes, including Cyangugu and Gisenyi. See p580 for more details.

You will find there are plenty of well-maintained, modern minibuses serving all the main routes. Head to the bus stand in any town between dawn and about 3pm, and it is quite easy to find one heading to Kigali and nearby towns. Destinations are displayed in the front window and the fares are fixed (you can ask other passengers to be sure). However, anyone who gets stuck somewhere late in the afternoon is going to have to pay top price for the privilege of getting out.

Minibuses leave when full, and this means when all the seats are occupied (unlike in Kenya and Tanzania, where most of the time they won't leave until you can't breathe for the people sitting on your lap and jamming the aisle). They are, however, still quite cramped. There is no extra charge for baggage. Many minibuses have decent sound systems, so there might be some good African tunes that aren't ear-splitting.

Whichever form of transport you end up taking, you should be prepared to be

---

CROSSING INTO DR CONGO?

Think twice, maybe twice again, before crossing into DR Congo. At the time of research, we were able to safely cross into Goma and visit both Bukima and Djomba before crossing back into Uganda at Bunagana. However, things have been very volatile in DR Congo over the terrible years of civil war, so it is extremely important to do your own homework before visiting. Should things stay stable, a DR Congo loop between Rwanda and Uganda is an enticing prospect, but check, check and check again before you sign up.

---

stopped at military checkpoints. These vary in number depending on the route, but at each it is necessary to get out and allow the soldiers to examine all luggage. Other than the time it takes, there's no hassle at all, plus it is to ensure your security.

Car & Motorcycle

Cars are suitable for most of the country's main roads, but those planning to explore Parc National de l'Akagera or follow the shores of Lake Kivu might be better off with a 4WD.

Car hire isn't well established in Rwanda, but most travel agents and tour operators in Kigali can organise something from RFr25,000 per day for a small car and up.

Ferry

Before the latest civil war, there were ferries on Lake Kivu that connected the Rwandan ports of Cyangugu, Kibuye and Gisenyi but these are suspended at present. Speedboat charters are currently the only option between these ports, but they are expensive.

Hitching

Hitching around Rwanda can be relatively easy because of the prodigious number of NGO vehicles on the roads. Drivers will rarely ask for payment for a lift. Women who decide to hitch should realise that accepting a lift from long-distance truck drivers is unwise, but the NGOs should otherwise be OK. Remember, travellers who decide to hitch should understand that they are taking a small but potentially serious risk.

Local Transport

TAXI

These are only really necessary in Kigali. See p581 for details. It is also possible to find the odd taxi in most other major towns.

TAXI-MOTOR

Most towns are compact enough to get around on foot, but where you need transport, the taxi-motor is a good bet. It's just a motorcycle, but the driver can usually sling a pack across the petrol tank. They generally drive safely, if a little fast – there's no helmet for the passenger.

Burundi

Beautiful Burundi has been blighted by a generation of ethnic conflict, but with the advent of peace, this charming country may at long last be able to put its dark past to rest. A tiny little nation of soaring mountains and languid lakeside communities, Burundi is sandwiched between the African giants of Democratic Republic of the Congo (DR Congo) and Tanzania. The scenery is stunning and the welcome warm and it may once again begin to receive a trickle of travellers as the word gets out that the war is over.

The steamy capital Bujumbura has a lovely location on the shores of Lake Tanganyika and just outside the city are some of the finest inland beaches on the continent. Burundians have an irrepressible *joie de vivre* and this has carried them through the crises of the last decade. They know how to party like there is no tomorrow and a weekend in Bujumbura is a lesson on life in the fast lane.

The tourist industry died a quick death with the outbreak of civil war in 1993 and many of the upcountry attractions have been off limits for more than a decade. Choose from the southernmost source of the Nile, the ancient forest of Parc National de la Kibira or the spot where Stanley was reputed to have uttered those timeless words 'Dr Livingstone I presume?' Yes, you've guessed it, there's not a lot to see, but the stunning scenery and warmth of the Burundians more than compensates.

Intertribal tensions have devastated the country since independence in 1962 and there is always a chance things could kick off again. It is a young peace, so make sure you check before embarking on an adventure in Burundi.

FAST FACTS

- **Area** 27,835 sq km
- **Capital** Bujumbura
- **Country code** 257
- **Famous for** Les Tambourinaires
- **Languages** Kirundi, French and Swahili
- **Money** Burundi franc (BFr); US$1 = BFr924; €1 = BFr1118
- **Population** 7.3 million

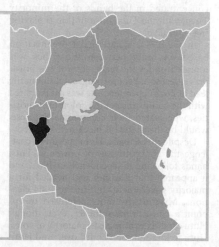

HIGHLIGHTS

- **Bujumbura** (p607) Dine out in style before dancing the night away in this city where people love to live it up.
- **Saga Beach** (p612) Hit the best inland beaches in Africa for some fun in the sun.
- **Source Du Nil** (p612) Journey to Burundi's very own pyramid, marking the south-ernmost source of the Nile at Kasumo.
- **Being in Burundi** (p607) Enjoy the novelty of being pretty much the only tourist in the country.

CLIMATE & WHEN TO GO

The climate in Burundi varies widely depending on whether you are in the hot and steamy lowlands around Lake Tanganyika, where temperatures average 30°C, or the more mountainous north, where the usual temperature is a much milder 20°C. The rainy season in Burundi lasts from around October to May, with a brief dry spell in December and January. See Climate Charts p621.

HISTORY

For information on Burundian and East African history prior to independence, see p28.

Independence Days

Burundi, like Rwanda, was colonised first by Germany and later by Belgium, and like the northern neighbour, the Europeans played on ethnic differences to divide and conquer the population. Power was traditionally concentrated in the hands of the minority Tutsi, with the Tutsi *mwami* (king) playing the central role.

In the 1950s a nationalist organisation based on unity between the tribes was founded under the leadership of the *mwami's* eldest son, Prince Rwagasore. But in the lead up to independence he was assassinated with the connivance of the colonial authorities, who feared their commercial interests would be threatened if he came to power.

Despite this setback, Hutus began to challenge the concentration of power in Tutsi hands following independence in 1962, and it appeared that Burundi was headed for a majority government. But in the 1964 elections, Mwami Mwambutsa refused to appoint a Hutu prime minister, even though Hutu candidates attracted a majority of votes. Hutu frustration soon boiled over, and Hutu

---

HOW MUCH?

- **Cheaper hotel room with bathroom** US$20 to US$40
- **Plate of garnished brochettes** US$2
- **Internet access per hour** US$1 to US$2
- **Local newspaper** US$0.50
- **100km bus ride** US$2

LONELY PLANET INDEX

- **Litre of petrol** US$1
- **Litre of bottled water** US$0.50
- **Primus beer** US$1
- **Souvenir T-shirt** There aren't any!
- **Street snack (grilled goat brochettes)** US$0.50

---

military officers and political figures staged an attempted coup. Although it failed, the coup led to the flight of Mwambutsa into exile in Switzerland, and he was soon replaced by a Tutsi military junta.

A wholesale purge of Hutu from the army and bureaucracy followed, and in 1972 another large-scale Hutu revolt resulted in more than 1000 Tutsi being killed. The Tutsi military junta responded with selective genocide: any Hutu with wealth, a formal education or a government job was rooted out and murdered, often in the most horrifying way. After three months 200,000 Hutu had been killed and another 100,000 had fled into neighbouring countries.

The Bagaza Years

In 1976 Jean-Baptiste Bagaza came to power in a bloodless coup, and three years later he formed the Union Pour le Progrès National (Uprona). As part of a so-called democratisation program, candidates (for the most part Tutsi and all approved by Uprona) were voted into the National Assembly during the elections of 1982. The elections gave the Hutu a modicum of power in the National Assembly, but it was very limited. During the Bagaza years, there were some half-hearted attempts by the Tutsi government to remove some of the main causes of intertribal conflict, but these were mostly only cosmetic.

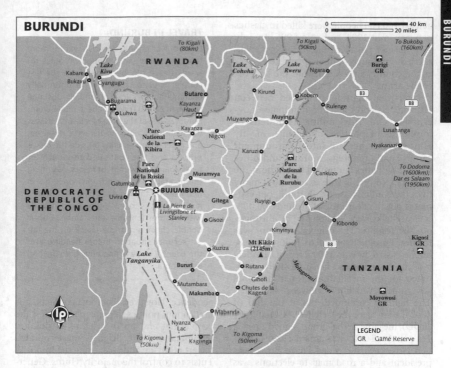

In 1985 the government tried to lessen the influence of the Catholic Church, which it believed was sympathetic to the Hutu majority. Its fears of a church-organised Hutu revolt were heightened by the fact that Hutus were in power in Rwanda and were discriminating against Tutsis. Priests were put on trial and some missionaries were expelled from the country.

Bagaza was toppled in 1987 in a coup led by his cousin Major Pierre Buyoya. The new regime improved relations between the government, the Catholic Church and international aid agencies. It also attempted to address the causes of intertribal tensions yet again by gradually bringing Hutu representatives back into positions of power in the government. However, there was a renewed outbreak of intertribal violence in northern Burundi in summer 1988; thousands were massacred and many more fled into neighbouring Rwanda.

A Bloody Civil War

Buyoya finally bowed to international pressure, and multiparty elections were held in June 1993. These brought a Hutu-dominated government to power, led by Melchior Ndadaye, himself a Hutu. However, a dissident army faction, led by a Tutsi, Colonel Sylvestre Ningaba, staged a bloody coup in late October the same year, and assassinated president Ndadaye. The coup eventually failed when army generals disowned the plotters, but in the chaos that followed the assassination, thousands were massacred in intertribal fighting and almost half a million refugees fled across the border into Rwanda. Several days after the assassination, surviving members of the government, who had holed up in the French embassy in the capital, Bujumbura, were able to reassert some degree of control with the help of loyal troops.

In April 1994 Cyprien Ntaryamira, the new Hutu president, was killed in the same plane crash that killed Rwanda's president Juvenal Habyarimana and sparked the planned genocide there. Sylvestre Ntibantunganya was immediately appointed interim president. Nevertheless, both Hutu militias and the Tutsi-dominated army went on the offensive. No war was actually declared, but at least 100,000 people were killed in clashes between mid-1994 and mid-1996. In July 1996 former president Pierre Buyoya again carried out a successful coup and took over as the country's president with the support of the army.

Intertribal fighting continued between Hutu rebels and the Tutsi-dominated government and Tutsi militia. Hundreds of thousands of political opponents, mostly Hutus, were herded into 'regroupment camps', and bombings, murders and other horrific activities continued throughout the country. No-one is sure exactly how many lives the conflict has cost Burundi, but estimates put the death toll at around 300,000.

Peace talks were held on and off throughout the conflict. The original mediator was former Tanzanian president Julius Nyerere but he passed away in 1999. Nelson Mandela took up the reins and he successfully negotiated for the installation of a transitional government, which took power in late 2001. The fighting continued, but at the end of 2002 the Force for the Defence of Democracy (FDD), the largest rebel group, signed a peace deal. In April 2003 prominent Hutu Domitien Ndayizeye succeeded Pierre Buyoya as president and a road map to elections was hammered out.

Burundi Today
In 2004 the UN began operations in Burundi, sending more than 5000 troops to enforce the peace. Parliamentary elections were successfully held in June 2005 and the former rebels, the FDD, emerged victorious. Pierre Nkurunziza, leader of the FDD, was sworn in as president in August. One rebel group, the Forces for National Liberation (FNL) remains active in the country, but it remains to be seen how long they will hold out, as they are now fighting their former allies and a Hutu majority government. Burundi is finally on the road to stability and all sides need to embrace the spirit of national unity to bring Burundi back from the brink.

THE CULTURE
The National Psyche
Like Rwanda to the north, Burundi has been torn apart by tribal animosities, and the conflict between Hutus and Tutsis has claimed hundreds of thousands of lives since inde-

pendence. However, like most conflicts, it is more about politics than people, and it is the people that end up the victims of political manipulation. The Belgians masterminded the art of divide and rule, using the minority Tutsis to control the majority Hutus. Generations of intermarriage and cooperation went out the window, as the population was forced into choosing sides, Hutu or Tutsi. The pattern continued into independence as the minority Tutsis clung to power to protect their privileges, and only with the advent of peaceful elections in the summer of 2005 does it look like this cycle may come to an end.

Unlike Rwanda, Burundi debates its divisions. In Rwanda, there are only Rwandans, and the history is being reinterpreted in the spirit of unity. In Burundi, there are Hutu and Tutsis and they work together in political parties and drink together in bars and are happy to discuss their differences. Two very different approaches to the same problem of ethnic division, both countries could probably learn a little from each other. For now, Burundi and its people deserve all the support they can get as they try to forge a Burundian identity that transcends the tribalism of the past.

Daily Life
Like the other countries of East Africa, there is a huge difference between urban and real

life. Burundi is more Francophone than any other country in the region, and as a result the city dwellers take their siesta very seriously. Shops and businesses shut down from noon to 3pm and consequently it is hard to get anything done. Do as the locals do and save some energy for the evening.

Out in the countryside, most people are engaged in farming, at least when they have not been fleeing the civil war as refugees in neighbouring countries. Coffee and tea are popular crops, but most people are growing to survive and subsistence crops include cassava, bananas, sweet potatoes, maize and sorghum.

Population

The population is around 7 million, of which approximately 84% is Hutu, 15% is Tutsi and 1% is Twa Pygmy.

ARTS

Burundi is famous for its athletic and acrobatic forms of dance. Les Tambourinaires du Burundi is the country's most famous troupe; it has performed in cities such as Berlin and New York. Its performances are a high-adrenaline mix of drumming and dancing that drowns the audience in waves of sound and movement.

ENVIRONMENT
The Land

Like Rwanda to the north, Burundi may be a minnow of a country by African standards, but it is incredibly beautiful. Taking up a mere 27,835 sq km, most of the country is made up of mountains that vanish into the horizon. Mt Kikizi, in the southeast of the country near the border with Tanzania, is the highest peak at 2145m. Lake Tanganyika dominates the west of the country and here the landscape is flat and fertile. The capital, Bujumbura, is on the northeastern tip of this great lake.

National Parks

Burundi's tourist infrastructure is in tatters after the long war, and most of the national parks have been closed for more than a decade.

Assuming the situation improves with the coming of peace, it may be possible to visit Parc National de la Kibira, essentially a continuation of Parc National Nyungwe Forest in southwestern Rwanda and the largest rainforest in Burundi, home to colobus monkeys and chimpanzees, and Parc National de la Rurubu, the largest protected area in the country, with wonderful hiking and views.

The most accessible national park – and the only one currently open – is Parc National de la Rusizi, just 15km from Bujumbura. It's a wetland environment and provides a habitat for hippos, sitatungas (antelopes) and a wide variety of birds.

FOOD & DRINK

Bujumbura is a contender for gastronomic capital of East Africa, as locals take their food very seriously. Brochettes (kebabs) and frites are a legacy of the Belgian colonial period, but there is also succulent fish from Lake Tanganyika and serious steaks. The local diet in the countryside is much the same as elsewhere in the region. When it comes to drink, Burundi is blessed with a national brewery churning out huge bottles of Primus and a very drinkable version of Amstel. Wine and spirits are widely available in the capital but are much more expensive than beer.

BUJUMBURA

Long considered the land of the lotus eaters before the intractable civil war, Bujumbura may be on the verge of a rebirth. 'Buj', as many foreign residents refer to it, has a striking location on the shores of Lake Tanganyika and many of its suburbs sprawl up the looming mountains that ring the city to the north and east.

Frozen in time thanks to the war, there has been almost no development here since the 1980s, a stark contrast to the changes in Kigali and Kampala to the north. The Burundian capital is a mixture of grandiose colonial town planning, with its wide boulevards and imposing public buildings, and the sort of dusty, crowded streets found in many African cities. It is also one of the most important ports on Lake Tanganyika.

Bujumbura has a freewheelin' reputation and the dining, drinking and dancing scene can compete with the best in the region. Despite the official midnight curfew, people usually manage to party on long into the night. That said, it's not the safest city in the region by night, so it is important to take taxis after dark. Security has improved with the influx of UN peacekeepers, but robberies are still common.

A short way out of the city are some of Africa's best inland beaches. White sand, turquoise waters and beachside bars. Pinch yourself, this is Burundi, not the Caribbean? Sipping a cold beer on the shores of the lake, Ethiopian peacekeepers to your left, local surfers to your right, maybe Burundi is not so bad after all.

ORIENTATION

Bujumbura is a fairly small city and most of the action takes place on Chaussée Prince Rwagasore and the streets nearby. Blvd de l'Uprona, Blvd de la Liberté and Chaussée du Peuple Burundi are the main roads in and out of the city and house some government buildings, embassies and hotels and restaurants. To the west of the centre is Lake Tanganyika and some popular restaurants and residences, but there are also some edgy areas near the port. North of town along the lakeshore are beautiful white-sand beaches, which draw huge crowds at the weekend.

INFORMATION
Emergency

The official emergency number for police is ☎ 17, but most expats and locals alike say that the police aren't much help. Try and make contact with your embassy in the event of an emergency.

Internet Access

There are Internet cafés throughout the city centre.

Cyberposte (cnr Blvd Lumumba & Ave du Commerce; ☼ 8am-10pm) Cheap and fast Internet access in the city centre.

Face à Face (Blvd de l'Uprona; ☼ 8am-10pm) A stylish Internet café with a fast connection and tasty snacks.

Tropicana Net Café (Chaussée Prince Rwagasore; ☼ 8am-10pm) Under the same ownership as Face à Face, another sophisticated spot to surf.

Medical Services

In the event of a medical emergency, it is best to get out of the country to somewhere with first-class medical facilities like Nairobi.

Money

Banque du Crédit de Bujumbura (Rue Science) and **Interbank Burundi** (Blvd de la Liberté) both offer credit-card cash advances but commissions are high. Both charge 2.5% plus a flat fee of €10. Interbank Burundi has several branches around town and represents Western Union if you need an urgent transfer. For more information on getting your hands on money in Bujumbura, see p614.

Post

Main post office (cnr Blvd Lumumba & Ave du Commerce; ☼ 8am-noon & 2-4pm Mon-Fri, 8-11am Sat) Postal and telecommunication services.

Tourist Information

Office National du Tourisme (☎ 222202; Ave des Euphorbes; ☼ 7.30am-noon & 2-4.30pm Mon-Fri) Not many tourists in Burundi equals not much information in the tourist office. It's just off Blvd de la Liberté near the cathedral. The more centrally located 'tourist office' on Blvd de l'Uprona is actually just a government craft shop with no info available.

DANGERS & ANNOYANCES

Bujumbura is a more dangerous city than Kampala or Kigali, but is not quite in the league of Nairobi. It is generally safe to wander about on foot during the day, although it is best to avoid the rough-and-ready port area. The character of the city changes around 8pm, as the streets empty and 'les petits bandits' move in. These gangs of youths are not averse to robbing people daft enough to be walking the streets at night, so take a taxi. Take particular care around popular nightspots, as you never know who is lurking in the dark.

SIGHTS & ACTIVITIES

The so-called sights of Bujumbura aren't really up to much. There was a world-famous chimpanzee sanctuary here before the war, but the chimps were relocated to safety more than a decade ago. The biggest drawcard are the beaches (see p612) on Lake Tanganyika, by far the best in the region and comparable with those in Malawi to the southeast.

None of the so-called museums are really worth the time to visit, as they have been long neglected. Opening times are as erratic as the collections. The **Musée Vivant** (Ave du 13 Octobre; admission BFr2000) is a reconstructed traditional Burundian village with some exhibits about baskets, pottery and drums, but it's also a part-time zoo and the animals aren't kept in very impressive conditions.

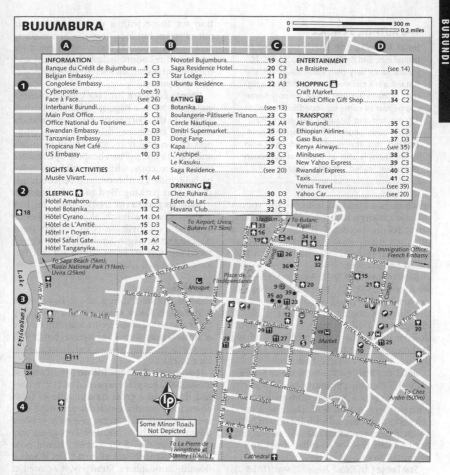

BUJUMBURA

0 ———— 300 m
0 ———— 0.2 miles

INFORMATION
Banque du Crédit de Bujumbura ...**1**	C3
Belgian Embassy..........................**2**	C3
Congolese Embassy.....................**3**	D3
Cyberposte...............................(see 5)	
Face à Face............................(see 26)	
Interbank Burundi.......................**4**	C3
Main Post Office........................**5**	C3
Office National du Tourisme........**6**	C4
Rwandan Embassy.......................**7**	D3
Tanzanian Embassy.....................**8**	D3
Tropicana Net Café.....................**9**	C3
US Embassy..............................**10**	D3

SIGHTS & ACTIVITIES
Musée Vivant.............................**11**	A4

SLEEPING
Hotel Amahoro..........................**12**	C3
Hotel Botanika..........................**13**	C2
Hôtel Cyrano............................**14**	D4
Hôtel de L'Amitié.......................**15**	D3
Hôtel Le Doyen.........................**16**	C2
Hôtel Safari Gate.......................**17**	A4
Hôtel Tanganyika.......................**18**	A2

Novotel Bujumbura....................**19**	C2
Saga Residence Hotel.................**20**	C3
Star Lodge..............................**21**	D3
Ubuntu Residence......................**22**	A3

EATING
Botanika................................(see 13)	
Boulangerie-Pâtisserie Trianon....**23**	C3
Cercle Nautique.......................**24**	A4
Dmitri Supermarket....................**25**	D3
Dong Fang..............................**26**	C3
Kapa.....................................**27**	C3
L'Archipel...............................**28**	C3
Le Kasuku..............................**29**	C3
Saga Residence.......................(see 20)	

DRINKING
Chez Ruhara...........................**30**	D3
Eden du Lac............................**31**	A3
Havana Club............................**32**	C3

ENTERTAINMENT
Le Braisière...........................(see 14)	

SHOPPING
Craft Market............................**33**	C2
Tourist Office Gift Shop.............**34**	C2

TRANSPORT
Air Burundi..............................**35**	C3
Ethiopian Airlines......................**36**	C3
Gaso Bus................................**37**	D3
Kenya Airways.......................(see 35)	
Minibuses..............................**38**	C3
New Yahoo Express...................**39**	C3
Rwandair Express......................**40**	C3
Taxis....................................**41**	C3
Venus Travel.........................(see 39)	
Yahoo Car............................(see 20)	

SLEEPING

Hotel prices in Bujumbura have shot up with the arrival of the UN in town. This is a good city to splash out on something a bit nicer. There are also a couple of options out at the beaches on Lake Tanganyika (see p612) for those with no pressing need to be in the city centre. There are a few cheaper hotels dotted about the centre, which are a good option for those trying to stick to a budget.

Hotel Amahoro (☎ 247550; Rue de l'Industrie; r US$30-70; 🌀) One of the newer hotels in town, the Amahoro has rapidly established a name for itself as a comfortable, centrally located place to stay with a good range of amenities. More expensive rooms include

air-con, but all have satellite TV, fridge and hot water in the bathroom.

Saga Residence Hotel (☎ 242225; Chaussée Prince Rwagasore; r US$35-49) Under the same ownership as the popular Saga Beach complex on Lake Tanganyika, this is the most atmospheric of the cheaper hotels. The friendly owners extend a warm welcome to all guests and the decoration is a cut above the competition in town. There are also some budget rooms available at US$26. The restaurant, Saga Residence, is a good venue for dinner.

Hôtel Cyrano (☎ 223886; Blvd de l'Indépendance; d/apt US$40/50) Formerly the Nikamor Hotel, this apartment-style place is popular with long-term residents in Bujumbura. It is also a good option for those wanting a bit more

THE AUTHOR'S CHOICE

Hotel Botanika (☎ 226792; hotelbotanika@
hotmail.com; Blvd de l'Uprona; s/d US$60/70; ⊠)
Bujumbura's very own boutique hotel, the
Botanika is a charming retreat from the rigours of life in Burundi. There are only seven
rooms and all come equipped with satellite
TV, minibar and beautiful bathroom. Four-
poster beds round off the atmosphere,
making this the residence of choice in
town. There is also an excellent European
restaurant, called Botanika, here.

space than a standard hotel, as the rooms
include a lounge, bathroom and fridge, and
are tastefully decorated. It may be ageing a
little, but it still smacks of character. There
is a popular restaurant here and a lively bar,
called Le Braisière.

Hôtel Le Doyen (☎ 224378; Ave du Stade; r BFr20,000;
with air-con BFr35,000; ⊠) This rambling colonial-
era building, set amid verdant grounds, has
the cheapest rooms in town, as it is still
charging in local currency rather than US
dollars. Rooms have high ceilings and big
bathrooms at the top end, but the cheaper
options involve a shared bathroom.

Hôtel de l'Amitié (☎ 226195; Rue de l'Amitié; r
US$20-45) Once the cheapest place in the city
centre, the new US dollar rates make it less
alluring than it was. Still, there is a good
selection of rooms, all with their own bathroom. Bigger rooms include a little balcony,
but be aware that the so-called 'satellite TV'
is limited to one channel.

Star Lodge (☎ 226868; Ave du RD Congo; r US$20-35)
One block east of l'Amitié, the Star is one
of the best budget deals, with large, clean
rooms, including TV, fridge and hot water.

Novotel Bujumbura (☎ 222600; novobuja@cbinf
.com; Chaussée du Peuple Burundi; s/d US$120/135; ⊠
🖥 🍽) The only international chain hotel
in town, the Novotel has all the four-star
facilities you would expect from this sort of
place. The only problem is that said facilities haven't been upgraded for years due to
the long civil war, making it not such good
value as it might first appear. Great cakes in
the patisserie, however, and the best pool
in town.

Hôtel Safari Gate (☎ 214779; r US$30-40) A colo-
nial building with character near the shores
of Lake Tanganyika, Safari Gate is an op-

tion for those with a vehicle. It's not far
out of town, but locals say the surrounding
area can be unsafe at night. Set in extensive
grounds, the rooms include bathrooms and
the rooftop restaurant and bar here are popular come sunset.

Ubuntu Residence (☎ 244064; ubuntu.residence@
usan-bu.net; Ave de la Plage; apt US$80-120) Tucked
away on the corner of Rue des Swahilis
near the lakeshore, this apartment complex comes highly recommended by locals
and expats alike. The cheapest options are
lacking a balcony, while the more expensive
pads include a bathroom and bedroom upstairs, plus parking. Best to book ahead.

Hotel Tanganyika (☎ 224433; Ave de la Plage) Just
a short distance north along the lakeside
is Hotel Tanganyika, a beautiful Art Deco
building set in elegant grounds. It was closed
for a long summer break during our visit, but
looks to be well worth considering.

EATING

One of the best things about Bujumbura
is the food. There are great bakeries, lively
cafés and some of the best restaurants in the
region. It may sound surprising, but it's all
down to the fine folk of Bujumbura, who
love to eat out.

Boulangerie-Pâtisserie Trianon (Ave du Commerce;
BFr500-2000) This place is packed out for breakfast thanks to a great combination of fresh
croissants, healthy omelettes and local coffee. The ham and cheese croissant washed
down with a hot chocolate is a good way
to start the day. Solo women should note
that the clientele was all male, but it was a
friendly atmosphere. Strangely, it's closed at
lunchtime.

Kapa (Rue Science; BFr 500-2000) Another colos-
sus on the café scene, this little bakery turns
out pastries, sandwiches and some of the
best coffee in town. Again it is popular in
the morning and afternoons, but closed for
lunch. Alright, siestas and all that, but one
of the bakeries is missing a market.

Le Kasuku (☎ 243575; Rue de l'Industrie; mains
BFr4000-10,000) A little garden oasis in the
heart of the city, Kasuku has a hearty range
of European dishes, including tender steaks
with pepper, red-wine or blue-cheese sauce.
The pizzas here are also some of the best
in the city.

L'Archipel (Blvd de la Liberté; mains BFr3000-7000;
🕑 closed Mon) This huge restaurant is a popular

THE AUTHOR'S CHOICE

Cercle Nautique (☎ 222056; Ave de la Plage; mains BFr 3000-10,000) Probably the most famous spot in Bujumbura, the Cercle is one of those colonial-era clubs that remains resolutely popular with expats and locals alike. Set on the shores of Lake Tanganyika, this is a great place to sip a cold beer and watch the sun go down. There is also a good restaurant here serving fresh lake fish and other continental classics. A must when passing through Buj.

stop with locals on the hunt for good-value food with good company. Partly set outdoors, at weekends they bring in the DJs, crank up the music and it rocks on all night.

Chez André (Chaussée Prince Rwagasore; mains BFr5000-15,000) Housed in a huge villa on the eastern extreme of Chaussée Prince Rwagasore, this is one of many contenders for the best restaurant in the city, with a flamboyant menu that wouldn't look out of place in Brussels or Paris. The wine list and desserts are well worth a closer look. There is also a popular health club here if you feel the belt busting after a major meal.

Botanika (☎ 226792; Blvd de l'Uprona, mains BFr4000-12,000) Located in the Hotel Botanika, this excellent restaurant has an intimate courtyard setting and some of the most expressive French cuisine in the city.

Saga Residence (☎ 242225; Chaussée Prince Rwagasore; mains BFr4000-7000) Also a hotel restaurant, this impressive place has a large menu of steaks and fresh lake fish and is exquisitely decorated with Congolese crafts and local textiles.

Dong Fang (☎ 241529; meals BFr3000-8000) Proving the theory that every capital city in the world has a Chinese restaurant, Dong Fang brings the reasonably authentic flavours of the Far East to Bujumbura. Crispy fried duck, *mapo tofu* (marinated pork, mashed black beans and bean curd) and cheap noodles make it a bolt hole for the brochetted out.

Dmitri Supermarket (Chaussée Prince Rwagasore; ⏱ 8am-12.30pm & 2.30-7.30pm Mon-Fri, 8am-12.30pm Sat & Sun) Another of Bujmumbura's unexpected treats, this supermarket is the best stocked in town, selling Swiss chocolate, superb salami, European cheeses and wines from around the world.

DRINKING & ENTERTAINMENT

Nightlife in Bujumbura is legendary and despite the curfew and long civil war, the party goes on. At the time of research, there was still a midnight curfew (*couvret feu* in French) in place, but most expats say this is only an issue in the suburbs. In the centre you should be alright moving about, although given the suspect security situation at night, use a taxi or private vehicle. Otherwise, it's a case of 'go hard or go home', as several clubs and restaurants have 'lock-ins' at the weekend.

Eden du Lac (Ave de la Plage) A little way north of the Cercle Nautique, this garden bar is a local institution and is namechecked by most young Burundians when you ask them where to go. Drinking with a view and discerning dining.

Havana Club (Blvd de l'Uprona) Back in town, Havana Club is a popular nightspot throughout the week, but do take care in the surrounding area, as 'les petits bandits' are lurking.

Chez Ruhara (Ave France) The ultimate club in Buj, Chez Ruhara is a cross between an underground rave in Africa and a scene straight out of Mad Max. Set in the basement of an unfinished tenement block on the back streets, there are steel poles sticking out and leaks on the stairs. But once inside, it really rocks and has deservedly earned the nickname 'Jazz Club'. African and international tunes, a steady flow of drinks and the option to go all night – welcome to the alternative Burundi.

Le Braisière (Blvd de l'Indépendance) For a bit of live music, try Le Braisiere at Hôtel Cyrano, which usually has a local band playing on Saturday night from 7pm.

SHOPPING

Burundi is hardly famous for its handicrafts, but a lot of excellent work makes its way across the border from DR Congo and is cheaper than in Rwanda or Uganda.

The best place to browse for souvenirs is the small craft market near Hôtel le Doyen on Ave du Stade. You'll need to haggle hard to get a good price, but there are bargains to be had.

The tourist office gift shop has a few basic pieces for browsers, but is noteworthy for having some of the only Burundian postcards around town. That's something your friends don't receive every day!

GETTING THERE & AWAY

For contact details of the international airlines serving Burundi, see p615.

Minibuses ply the major routes around the country, and leave from the minibus station near the market area. They usually dry up around lunchtime due to the security situation upcountry.

GETTING AROUND

To get to central Bujumbura from the airport costs about US$10 or the local equivalent. It may be possible to negotiate a cheaper fare on the return or you could take a taxi-motor, essentially a motorbike that doubles as a two-wheeled taxi, for about BFr2500. You might get some strange looks from airport security, however.

The centre of Bujumbura is small and negotiable on foot by day. After 8pm, always take a taxi in the city, no matter how short the distance, as robberies are common. Taxi fares range from BFr1000 for short hops in the centre to BFr5000 to Saga Beach. Taxi-motors are another good option.

AROUND BUJUMBURA

It is all about the beaches around Bujumbura. Just a short distance along the lakeshore are some strips of sand that are more Bahamas than Burundi.

BEACHES

Bujumbura's beaches are some of the best found in any landlocked country in Africa. The sand is white and powdery, and the waves should keep the bilharzia at bay. The stretch of beach that lies about 5km northwest of the capital is the most beautiful and used to be known as Plage des Cocotiers (Coconut Beach). However, a number of resorts are located along the road and most locals now call it **Saga Beach** (pronounced Sagga), in honour of the most popular restaurant and bar here.

Saga Beach Resort (☎ 241540) has a couple of large restaurants and a brilliant beachfront bar turning out cold Primus at bargain prices. It draws huge crowds at the weekends and the whole complex rocks on as a club by night. Rooms were under construction during our visit. Another definitive stop on a visit to Bujumbura.

Next door is **Karera Beach** (☎ 246818; r US$40-60), a smaller bar-restaurant complex that offers some attractive *banda*-apartments in its garden. They are almost small houses, complete with a kitchen, lounge and raised bedroom. Oh for someone to build something similar in Rwanda or Uganda. For those with transport, this could be the best accommodation in Bujumbura.

Minibuses to Gatumba can drop you off at the beach and charge about BFr200. A taxi-motor will cost more like BFr1000 and a normal taxi is about BFr5000.

LA PIERRE DE LIVINGSTONE ET STANLEY

This large rock is alleged to mark the spot where the infamous 'Dr Livingstone, I presume?' encounter between Livingstone and Stanley took place. Ujiji, across Lake Tanganyika in Tanzania, makes the same claim to fame. Come on Tanzania, play fair, you have Kilimanjaro, Ngorogoro and Zanzibar, can't you let Burundi bank this one? Some graffiti, along the lines of 'Livingstone and Stanley woz 'ere' records the date as 25 November 1871. The rock is at Mugere, about 10km south of the capital.

SOURCE DU NIL

Burundi lays claim to the source of the Nile (see the boxed text, opposite). It is not quite as obvious and impressive as Jinja in Uganda, but this insignificant-looking little spring at Kasumo, southeast of Bujumbura, may well be the southernmost source of the Nile. In a nice touch, it is marked by a stone pyramid, but unless you have your own transport it is almost impossible to reach. There are also some security question marks until peace is fully established in the country.

GITEGA

Gitega is the second-largest town in Burundi. It is home to the **National Museum**, which, although small, is educational and worth a visit.

A good day trip from Gitega is to the **Chutes de la Kagera**, near Rutana. These waterfalls are spectacular in the wet season (especially from October to January), but there's no public transport there, so you'll have to charter a vehicle.

Minibuses from Bujumbura make the run to Gitega throughout the day (BFr2000,

THE SEARCH FOR THE SOURCE

The mighty Nile River is the world's longest river, snaking from the heart of East Africa for 6650km through Uganda, Sudan and Egypt before spilling into the Mediterranean Sea. It is the river that gave birth to one of humanity's earliest civilisations in ancient Egypt, and the quest to find its source was an obsession for a generation of explorers in the 19th century.

John Hanning Speke is widely credited with having 'discovered' the source of the Nile on 28 July 1863, when he set eyes on the Ripon Falls near what is today Jinja in Uganda. 'Discovered' because local tribes assert they knew the importance of this river long before white explorers came to town. Earlier generations of explorers had tried and failed to find the source, including the Romans, who sent an expedition south but became bogged down in the marshes of the Sudd, today part of southern Sudan.

However, Speke's discovery was not the end of the story. Several explorers were drawn to the murky brown currents that flow through Lake Victoria from the Kagera River in Tanzania. Following its waters upstream in 1898, German doctor Richard Kandt located the source of the Nile in the remote Nyungwe Forest in southwest Rwanda. Four decades later in 1937, another German explorer, Burkhart Waldecker, followed the same waters to a remote mountain-top spring known as Kasumo, near the equator in Burundi.

This leaves us with three contesting claims to the source of the Nile and in the spirit of East African unity, there is room for everyone. Burundi boasts the southernmost source of the Nile, Rwanda can claim the longest source of the Nile and Uganda has the major source of the Nile. That said, you'd have trouble rafting the source of the Nile in Burundi and Rwanda, so for marketing purposes Uganda takes the trophy.

---

one hour). As with all road journeys in Burundi, it is imperative to check the security situation before travelling, as ambushes are still a possibility as long as one rebel group remains at large.

BURUNDI DIRECTORY

ACCOMMODATION

The choice of accommodation is reasonable in Bujumbura but fairly limited elsewhere in the country. The arrival of the UN in Burundi has, as it always does, inflated the prices. Rooms in the capital range from cheapies around US$20 to a couple of places of international standard charging around US$100.

BUSINESS HOURS

They value their siestas in Burundi, so ministries, banks and the like tend to close for a couple of hours at lunch. Most eateries are open from 7am to about 9pm.

DANGERS & ANNOYANCES

At long last Burundi's civil war appears to be nearing an end. With the new government in power, the last rebel group has few reasons to continue its fight. As long as

they remain at large, then it is well worth approaching a visit to Burundi with caution. Travel overland as little as possible and consider restricting your visit to the capital. Should a full peace prevail in Burundi, overland travel should rapidly become no more dangerous than anywhere else in the region…down to the driver of course! Bujumbura is safe by day due to a massive UN and military presence, though the mood changes at night, as 'les petits bandits' take to the streets and robbery is a real possibility.

Kigali (Rwanda) and Kigoma (Tanzania) are probably the best places to pick up reliable information about current events in Burundi.

EMBASSIES & CONSULATES
Burundian Embassies & Consulates

For Burundian embassies in Kenya, Rwanda, Tanzania or Uganda, see the relevant section in those chapters. Useful Burundian embassies worldwide:

Belgium (☎ 02-23 045 35; 46 Place Marie-Louise, Brussels)
France (☎ 01 45 20 60 61; 24 Rue Raynouard, Paris)
UK (☎ 020-8381 4092; 26 Armitage Rd, London)
USA (☎ 202-342 2574; 2233 Wisconsin Ave, Washington DC)

Embassies & Consulates in Burundi

Foreign embassies in Bujumbura include the following:

Belgium (☎ 233641; Blvd de la Liberté)
DR Congo (Ave du RD Congo)
France (☎ 251484; 60 Blvd de l'Uprona)
Rwanda (☎ 226865; Ave du RD Congo)
Tanzania (☎ 248636; 4 United Nations Rd)
USA (☎ 223454; Chaussée Prince Rwagasore)

HOLIDAYS

Some of these holidays may change with the formation of a new government of national unity.

New Year's Day 1 January
Unity Day 5 February
Easter (Good Friday, Holy Saturday and Easter Monday) March/April
Labour Day 1 May
Independence Day 1 July
Assumption 15 August
Victory of Uprona Day 18 September
Anniversary of Rwagasore's Assassination 13 October
Anniversary of Ndadaye's Assassination 21 October
All Saints' Day 1 November
Christmas Day 25 December

INTERNET ACCESS

Internet access is widespread and inexpensive in Bujumbura; see p608.

INTERNET RESOURCES

The official UN website covering the Burundi mission is www.un.org/Depts/dpko/missions/onub/.

MAPS

It is hard to get hold of decent maps of Burundi. Currently the best map of Rwanda is *Rwanda Burundi – International Travel Map* published by ITMB Publishing at a scale of 1:400,000.

MONEY

The unit of currency is the Burundi franc (BFr). This is a cash economy and the US dollar is king. Unless you like giving up lots of money in commissions to banks, carry cash with you.

There's an open black market in Bujumbura. Dealers hang around the market and along Chaussée Prince Rwagasore. Rates vary according to the official exchange rates and the amount to be changed (large bills are preferred). At the time of research, the

street rate was perhaps 10% better than at banks.

The commission for changing travellers cheques is bad news at most banks – most charge around 7%. Travellers cheques can also be changed at the large hotels in Bujumbura.

There are no ATMs in Burundi at the time of writing. For banks in Bujumbura, see p608.

POST

The postal service is reasonably efficient and things take about one week to get to Europe or North America. Postcards to worldwide destinations cost BFr650.

TELEPHONE

Rates for international telephone calls are quite reasonable, working out at about US$1 per minute. Phonecards are available from the telecommunications office behind the post office.

There are no telephone area codes within the country. The country code for Burundi is ☎ 257.

VISAS

One-month tourist visas cost US$40 and are now available on arrival at both the international airport and international land border crossings. Visas can also be arranged from a Burundian embassy or consulate before arrival, requiring two photographs.

Visas for Onward Travel

There are slim pickings for other visas in Burundi, and visas for neighbouring countries – DR Congo, Rwanda and Tanzania – are all available on the borders.

TRANSPORT IN BURUNDI

GETTING THERE & AWAY

Air

Bujumbura International Airport (BJM) is located about 12km north of the city centre. There are very few international airlines still serving Burundi, as flights were severely disrupted during the long civil war.

AIRLINES IN BURUNDI

Air Burundi (airline code 8Y; ☎ 223460; airbdi@cbinf .com; Ave du Commerce) Hub: Bujumbura.
Ethiopian Airlines (airline code ET; ☎ 226820; www .flyethiopian.com, Ave Victoire) Hub: Addis Adaba.
Kenya Airways (airline code KQ; ☎ 223542; www.kenya -airways.com) Hub: Nairobi, sold through Air Burundi.
Rwandair Express (airline code WB; ☎ 251850; www .rwandair.com; Ave du Commerce) Hub: Kigali.

TO/FROM KENYA

Kenya Airways offers daily services between Bujumbura and Nairobi.

TO/FROM RWANDA

Air Burundi and Rwandair Express both connect Kigali and Bujumbura.

Lake

TO/FROM TANZANIA & ZAMBIA

Typical, isn't it? Just as things start to finally settle down in Burundi, the popular lake ferries linking Bujumbura with Kigoma in Tanzania and Mpulungu in Zambia stop calling here. Ask around in Bujumbura, as this service may resume with the advent of peace. In the meantime, it could be worth visiting Bujumbura's busy docks to see if there is any space on a cargo boat. Crew members might be willing to give up a cabin if you can negotiate a deal.

Land

Burundi shares land borders with DR Congo, Rwanda and Tanzania. However, due to the long-running civil war, very few travellers have crossed this way in the last decade or more. Before deciding to cross by land into Burundi, read the boxed text, right.

TO/FROM DR CONGO

The main crossing between Burundi and DR Congo is at Gatumba on the road between Bujumbura and Uvira, about 15km west of

---

CROSSING BY LAND INTO BURUNDI?

Burundi was long wiped off the overland map due to the intractable civil war in the country. That war looks to be drawing to a close at the time of writing, but one rebel group is still active. This means ambushes remain a remote possibility and you should check the security situation very carefully from the safety of Rwanda before venturing down here. That said, we were able to travel safely by land between Bujumbura and Kigali during research on this book. Day crossings to Uvira in DR Congo should be fine, although it would be unwise to venture further into the country unless you are 100% certain things have stabilised over there. Crossing into Tanzania should be fine as and when the last rebel group join the peace process. In the meantime, the safest bet is to follow the road south along the Tanganyika lakeshore, as the flat landscape and lack of forest cover isn't suitable for staging ambushes. Assuming security stabilises, travelling overland through Uganda and Rwanda, down into Burundi and along the lakeshore to Gombe Stream National Park and Kigoma in Tanzania will be a great way to avoid backtracking.

---

the capital. Almost no travellers have crossed this way in recent years due to the long civil wars in both Burundi and DR Congo. However, if peace settles in both countries, it could be an option for linking Bujumbura and Bukavu (Rwanda). UN staff and NGOs cross this way every day. For more on visiting DR Congo see p559.

TO/FROM RWANDA

The main crossing point is between Kayanza (Burundi) and Butare (Rwanda) on the main road linking Bujumbura and Kigali. The border is at Kayanza Haut and both Burundian (US$40) and Rwandan (US$60) visas are available on arrival here. We were able to use this crossing during research on this title, but as long as one rebel group remains at large it would be prudent to check the security situation on the road from the safety of Bujumbura or Kigali.

The safest and quickest option for travel between Bujumbura and Kigali is to use one of the scheduled bus services that

CROSSING INTO THE DEMOCRATIC REPUBLIC OF THE CONGO?

Think twice, maybe even three times, before crossing into DR Congo. Things have been very volatile in DR Congo during the terrible years of civil war, so it is extremely important to do your own homework before visiting this country.

depart daily. Yahoo Car, New Yahoo Express, Venus Travel and Gaso Bus all run buses in both directions. Most companies have the choice between a big bus and a minibus, the latter costing less as it is more crowded and considered less secure. Prices range from BFr9000 to BFr12,000 and departures are all around 8am. It is also possible to get off in Butare in southern Rwanda, handy for visiting Parc National Nyungwe Forest, and this costs BFr8000.

There is also a direct road from Bujumbura to Cyangugu at the southern tip of Lake Kivu in Rwanda, but this is not in such good condition and should be considered unsafe as long as one rebel faction remains at large.

TO/FROM TANZANIA

There are several border crossings between Burundi and Tanzania, including one near Kobero in the north of the country and one near Nyanza Lac in the south of the country, which connects with Gombe Stream National Park and Kigoma in western Tanzania (see p211). However, due to the uncertain security situation in the east of the country during research, we were unable to travel to these areas. Ask around in Bujumbura for more details.

GETTING AROUND

Air

Air Burundi, the national airline, does not operate regular internal flights.

Road

As in Rwanda, most major roads in Burundi are sealed. Public transport mostly consists of modern Japanese minibuses, which are cheaper than shared taxis and not overcrowded. Destinations are displayed in the front window, and minibuses depart when full. You can usually find a minibus or shared taxi heading your direction any day between early morning and early afternoon at the gare routière (bus station) in any town.

However, travelling around the countryside should be considered highly risky as long as rebels remain at large in the countryside. Ambushes are common, so ask around before heading out of Bujumbura, even to the second city of Gitega. Assuming the war finally comes to an end, road travel should be safe as locals are very friendly.

East Africa Directory

CONTENTS

This East Africa directory gives an overview of the nuts-and-bolts information that you'll need for travel in the region. For country-specific details, see the Directory sections at the end of each country chapter.

ACCOMMODATION

East Africa boasts a wide range of accommodation, ranging from humble cinder-block rooms with a communal bucket bath to some of Africa's most luxurious safari lodges. Expect to pay high-season prices in July and August and again around the Christmas/New Year holiday; in much of the region it's often possible to negotiate significant discounts during the low-season travel months between March and early June.

Sleeping listings in this book are divided into three categories: budget (approximately

US$10 to US$25 per double room), midrange (US$30 to US$100) and top-end (US$100 and up).

Camping

Most national parks have established camp sites. Elsewhere you can almost always find something in or near major towns, and in some rural tourist areas local villagers maintain camping grounds. Facilities vary from none at all to well-established full-service camping grounds with hot showers and cooking areas, and prices average US$3 to US$5 per person per night. Camping away from established sites is not advisable; in rural areas, ask permission from the village head or elders before pitching your tent. Camping prices in this book are per person unless otherwise noted. The exceptions to all this are Rwanda and Burundi, where camping possibilities range from limited to nonexistent.

In coastal areas, you'll sometimes find bungalows or *bandas* – basic wooden or thatched huts, often with only a mattress and mosquito net – that offer a good alternative to camping for those on a tight budget.

Hostels, Guesthouses & Budget Hotels

Kenya has a limited selection of hostels, and you'll also find hostels in many of Tanzania's northern parks (where student groups have priority). In some areas, especially Rwanda, there are mission hostels and guesthouses, which are invariably clean, safe and spartan but good value. While most are primarily for missionaries and aid-organisation staff, they're generally happy to accommodate travellers if space is available.

In budget guesthouses and hotels, you generally get what you pay for, though there's the occasional good deal. The cheapest ones – and every town will have one – are usually poorly ventilated cement-block rooms with reasonably clean sheets, shared toilets, cold showers or a bucket bath, sometimes a fan and mosquito net and often only a token lock on the door. Rates for this type of place average from US$2 to US$5 per room per night. A few dollars more will get you a somewhat more comfortable room, often with a bathroom (although not always with running or hot water).

Many budget places double as brothels, and at many of the cheapest ones, you are likely to feel uncomfortable if you're a woman travelling alone. If peace and quiet is what you're after, guesthouses without bars are the best choice.

Backpackers and dormitory-style places aren't as common as they are in southern Africa, but there are a few scattered around the region. Prices per bed are generally the same or slightly higher than you'd pay for a room in a basic guesthouse.

Hotels, Lodges & Luxury Safari Camps

All larger towns have one or several mid-range hotels, most with private bathroom, hot water and a fan or an air-conditioner. Facilities range from faded to good value, and prices range from US$15 to US$50 per person. Capital cities and major tourist areas, especially in Kenya and Tanzania, also have a good selection of top-end accommodation with all the amenities you would expect for the price you will pay – from about US$80 to US$200 or more per person per night. Hotel prices in this book include

private bathroom and continental breakfast, except as noted.

On the safari circuits, there are some wonderful and very luxurious lodges costing from US$100 to US$500 per person per night; at the upper end of this spectrum prices are usually all-inclusive.

At many national parks, you'll find 'permanent tented camps' or 'luxury tented camps'. These offer comfortable beds in canvas tents – usually en suite – with screened windows and most of the comforts of a hotel room, but with a wilderness feel. 'Mobile' or 'fly' camps are temporary camps set up for several nights, or perhaps just for one season, and often used for walking safaris away from the main tented camp, or to give you the chance for an intimate bush experience.

Unless otherwise noted, listings in this book for lodges or camps in and near parks and wildlife reserves quote accommodation-and-breakfast-only prices.

ACTIVITIES
Bird-Watching

The East African skies are filled with the chirping and twittering of over 1000 bird species, and the region is an excellent destination for ornithologists, with Uganda a particular highlight. Most bird-watching is done in connection with safaris to the national parks. See Activities in the country chapter Directories for more information.

DIVE OPERATORS

When choosing a dive operator, quality rather than cost should be the priority. Consider the operator's experience and qualifications; knowledgeability and competence of staff; and the condition of equipment and frequency of maintenance. Assess whether the overall attitude is serious and professional, and ask about safety precautions: radios, oxygen, boat reliability and back-up engines, emergency evacuation procedures, first-aid kits, safety flares and life jackets. On longer dives, do you get an energising meal, or just tea and biscuits? One advantage of operators offering PADI courses is that you'll have the flexibility to go elsewhere in the world and have what you've already done recognised at other PADI dive centres.

Boating

Local dhow trips can be arranged from various places along the coast; for more, also on the realities of dhow travel, see p637. It is better to contact one of the coastal or island hotels, most of which can help you charter a reliable dhow for a cruise. For boat safaris, see p250 and p548.

Cycling & Mountain Biking

Touring East Africa by bicycle is gaining in popularity, and while it has its hazards (such as speeding buses and no shoulders on main roads), it's one of the best ways to get to know the region. See p636 for more information and p92 for operators that organise cycling trips.

Diving & Snorkelling

Slide beneath the Indian Ocean's turquoise surface and a whole new world opens up, as shadowy manta rays float by in the depths, barracuda swim slowly past brightly coloured coral and dolphins cavort in the swells.

If you've ever thought about learning to dive, or want to brush up on your skills, East Africa is a rewarding if somewhat pricey place to do this. The main areas are the Zanzibar Archipelago in Tanzania and around Malindi in Kenya, both of which have a good array of operators and courses. See Activities in the relevant country Directories for more.

Be sure to allow a sufficient surface interval between the conclusion of your final dive and any onward/homeward flights. The Professional Association of Dive Instructors (PADI) recommends at least 12 hours, or more if you have been doing daily multiple dives for several days. Another consideration is insurance, which you should arrange before coming to East Africa. Many policies exclude diving, so you'll likely need to pay a bit extra, but it's well worth it in comparison to the bills you will need to foot should something go wrong. There are decompression centres in Kenya and South Africa.

Fishing

Among the best places are around Mafia Island and in the Pemba Channel (Tanzania), and along the Kenyan coastline from Mombasa to Malindi. For lake and river fishing, good areas include Lake Victoria,

---

RESPONSIBLE DIVING

Wherever you dive in East Africa, consider the following tips, and help preserve the ecology and beauty of the reefs:

- Never use anchors on a reef, and take care not to ground boats on coral.

- Avoid touching or standing on living marine organisms or dragging equipment across a reef. Polyps can be damaged by even the gentlest contact. If you must hold on to a reef, only touch exposed rock or dead coral.

- Be conscious of your fins. Even without contact, the surge from fin strokes near a reef can damage delicate organisms. Take care not to kick up clouds of sand, which can smother organisms.

- Practise and maintain proper buoyancy control. Major damage can be done by divers descending too fast and colliding with a reef.

- Take great care in underwater caves. Spend as little time within them as possible, as your air bubbles may be caught within the roof and thereby leave organisms high and dry. Take turns inspecting the interior of a small cave.

- Resist the temptation to collect or buy corals or shells, or to loot marine archaeological sites (mainly shipwrecks).

- Ensure that you take home all your rubbish and any litter you may find as well. Plastics in particular are a serious threat to marine life.

- Do not feed fish.

- Minimise your disturbance of marine animals, and never ride on the backs of turtles or attempt to touch dolphins.

Lake Turkana (Kenya), and the Aberdares area (Kenya). See the country Directories for more information.

Gorilla & Chimpanzee Tracking

Most gorilla activity focuses on Uganda's Bwindi Impenetrable National Park, Rwanda's Parc National des Volcans and, increasingly now, Parc National des Virungas in the Democratic Republic of the Congo (DR Congo).

RESPONSIBLE TREKKING

Following are some tips for helping to preserve the ecology and beauty of East Africa's wilderness areas:

- Carry out all your rubbish, and make an effort to carry out rubbish left by others. Sanitary napkins, tampons, condoms and toilet paper should be carried out despite the inconvenience. They burn and decompose poorly.

- Minimise waste by taking minimal packaging and no more food than you will need. Take reusable containers or stuff sacks.

- Contamination of water sources by human faeces can lead to the transmission of all sorts of nasties. Where there is a toilet, use it. Where there is none, bury your waste. Dig a small hole 15cm (6in) deep and at least 100m (320ft) from any watercourse. Cover the waste with soil and a rock. In snow, dig down to the soil. Also ensure that these guidelines are applied to a portable toilet tent if one is being used by a large trekking party.

- Don't use detergents or toothpaste in or near watercourses, even if they are biodegradable. For personal washing, use biodegradable soap and a water container at least 50m (160ft) away from the watercourse. Disperse the waste water widely to allow the soil to filter it fully. Wash cooking utensils 50m (160ft) from watercourses using a scourer, sand or snow instead of detergent.

- Hillsides and mountain slopes, especially at high altitudes, are prone to erosion. Stick to existing trails, and avoid short cuts. If a well-used trail passes through a mud patch, walk through the mud so as not to increase the size of the patch. Avoid removing the plant life that keeps topsoils in place.

- Don't depend on open fires for cooking. The cutting of wood for fires in popular trekking areas such as Kilimanjaro can cause rapid deforestation. Cook on a light-weight kerosene, alcohol or Shellite (white gas) stove and avoid those powered by disposable butane gas canisters.

- If you are trekking with a guide and porters, supply stoves for the whole team. In cold conditions, ensure that all members are outfitted with enough clothing so that fires are not a necessity for warmth. If you patronise local accommodation, try to select places that don't use wood fires to heat water or cook food.

- Fires may be acceptable below the tree line in areas that get very few visitors. If you light a fire, use an existing fireplace. Don't surround fires with rocks. Use only dead, fallen wood, and only what you need for cooking. Remember the adage 'the bigger the fool, the bigger the fire'.

- Ensure that you fully extinguish a fire after use. Spread the embers and flood them with water.

See the relevant country chapters and p97 for more information, and check with your embassy about the current security situations before setting your plans.

For chimpanzee tracking, see the Activities sections of the Uganda, Tanzania and Rwanda chapters.

Hiking & Trekking

Popular destinations include Mt Kilimanjaro, Mt Meru and the Usambara Mountains in Tanzania; Mt Kenya and Mt Elgon in Kenya (Elgon can also be approached from Uganda), and – security permitting – the Rwenzori Mountains on the western Ugandan border with DR Congo.

Most hikes and climbs require local guides, and many require a full range of clothing, from lightweight for the semitropical conditions at lower altitudes to full winter gear for the high summits. Waterproof clothing and equipment is also important at any altitude, no matter what the season.

Lonely Planet's *Trekking in East Africa* is a worthwhile investment if you're considering hiking in the region.

White-Water Rafting

Depending on water levels, you can arrange rafting trips of several hours to several days on some of East Africa's waterways. The main bases are Nairobi (for the Tana and

Galana Rivers) and Jinja and Kampala in Uganda (for the Victoria Nile). See the relevant country Directories for more.

Wildlife Watching

East Africa is one of the best places on earth for observing large animals in their natural environment. Tanzania and Kenya – each with a stellar collection of national parks and protected areas – are the main bases, followed by Uganda in a distant but nevertheless rewarding third place. For more on safaris, see p83 and on wildlife, p57, plus national parks coverage in the country chapters.

BUSINESS HOURS

Usual business hours are listed inside the front cover, with exceptions noted in individual listings. In addition to regular banking hours, many forex bureaus remain open until 5pm Monday through Friday, and until noon on Saturday. Throughout the region, shops and offices often close for one to two hours between noon and 2pm, and, especially in coastal areas, on Friday afternoons for mosque services.

CHILDREN

Most East Africans are very friendly and helpful towards children, and while there are few attractions specifically targeted at children, travelling in the region with young ones in tow is unlikely to present any major problems.

The main concerns are likely to be the presence of malaria; the scarcity of decent medical facilities outside major towns; the length, discomfort and safety risks involved in many road journeys; and the difficulty of finding clean, decent bathrooms outside of midrange and top-end hotels.

Some wildlife lodges have restrictions on accommodating children under 12; otherwise, most hotels are family friendly. Many places – including most national parks – offer significant discounts for children on entry fees and accommodation or camping rates, although you'll generally need to specifically ask about these, especially if you're booking through a tour operator. In hotels, children under two or three years of age often stay free, and those up to 12 years old sharing their parents' room pay about 50% of the adult rate. In hotels without special rates,

triple rooms are commonly available for not too much more than a double room. Many midrange and top-end places have pools or grassy areas where children can play.

It's a good idea to travel with a blanket to spread out and use as a makeshift nappy-changing area. Though expensive, processed baby foods, powdered infant milk, disposable nappies and similar items are available in major towns, but carry your own wipes and food (and avoid feeding your children street food). Informal childcare is easy to arrange; the best bet is to ask at your hotel. Child seats for hire cars and safari vehicles are generally not available unless arranged in advance.

For protection against malaria, bring nets along for your children to sleep under, and check with your doctor regarding the use of prophylactics. Also bring long-sleeved shirts and trousers for dawn and dusk. In beach areas, keep in mind the risks of hookworm infestation in populated areas, and bilharzia infection in lakes. Other things to watch out for are sea urchins at the beach, and thorns and the like in the brush.

Wildlife watching is suitable for older children who have the patience to sit for long periods in a car, but less suitable for younger ones. Coastal destinations are a good bet for all ages.

Lonely Planet's *Travel with Children* by Cathy Lanigan is full of tips for keeping children and parents happy while on the road.

CLIMATE CHARTS

East Africa's climate varies tremendously, thanks to the region's diverse topography. Along the coast, the weather tends to be hot and humid, with temperatures averaging between 25°C and 29°C. Inland, altitude tempers the climate, with temperatures ranging from a minimum of about 14°C in highland areas to a maximum of about 34°C. One of the few places where you're likely to encounter extremely high temperatures is in the desert areas of northeastern Kenya, where the mercury can climb to 40°C. Throughout East Africa, the coolest months are from June to September, and the warmest from December to March.

In much of the region, there are two rainy seasons. The 'long' rains fall from mid-March through May, during which time it rains virtually every day, although

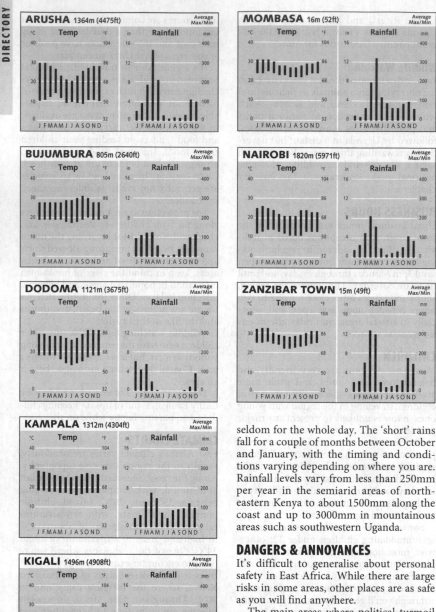

seldom for the whole day. The 'short' rains fall for a couple of months between October and January, with the timing and conditions varying depending on where you are. Rainfall levels vary from less than 250mm per year in the semiarid areas of northeastern Kenya to about 1500mm along the coast and up to 3000mm in mountainous areas such as southwestern Uganda.

DANGERS & ANNOYANCES

It's difficult to generalise about personal safety in East Africa. While there are large risks in some areas, other places are as safe as you will find anywhere.

The main areas where political turmoil and banditry pose security risks are in parts of Rwanda, Burundi, DR Congo and Uganda, as well as some sections of western Tanzania, and in northern and northeastern Kenya; see the country chapters for details, and check with your embassy and knowledgeable locals for security updates and advice if you're planning to head to any of these destinations.

Petty theft is a risk primarily in capital cities and tourist areas, particularly crowded setting, such as markets, public transport, and bus and train stations. Nairobi is notorious for muggings and more serious crimes; see p284. Throughout the region, however, most tourist-related crimes occur in isolated settings, in urban or tourist areas at night, or as part of confidence tricks or ruses playing on the emotions and gullibility of foreigners. By following a few simple precautions you'll minimise your risks and hopefully ensure that your journey will be trouble free.

- Avoid isolated areas – including beaches – at any time of day, whether you're alone or in a group. In cities, especially Nairobi, be alert for hustlers who will try any ploy to get you into a back alley and away from the watching eyes of onlookers so they can fleece you.
- Don't tempt people by flaunting your wealth. Avoid external money pouches, dangling backpacks and camera bags, and leave jewellery, fancy watches, portable stereos and the like at home. Daypacks instantly mark you as a tourist.
- Especially in crowded areas such as bus and train stations and markets, be wary of pickpocketing. If you don't have a reliable hotel safe, carry your passport, money and other documents in an inside pocket or pouch. When out walking, keep a small amount of cash separate from your other money and handy, so that you don't pull out large wads of bills for paying taxi fares or making purchases. If you should happen to get robbed, this may also be useful as a decoy to give to your assailant, while the remainder of your valuables remain safely hidden.
- It isn't safe to paddle or swim in lakes or slow-moving water anywhere in East Africa because of Bilharzia (see p645).
- Try not to look lost, even if you are. Walk purposefully and confidently, and don't refer to this guidebook or a map on the street – duck into a shop if you need to get your bearings.
- Arriving for the first time at bus stations in places such as Nairobi and Arusha can be a fairly traumatic experience, as you're likely to be besieged by touts as you get off the bus, all reaching to help with your pack and trying to sell you a safari. Have your luggage as consolidated as possible, with your valuables well hidden under your clothes. Try to spot the taxi area before disembarking, and make a beeline for it. It's well worth a few extra dollars for the fare, rather than attempting to walk to your hotel with your luggage.
- Don't leave your possessions scattered around your hotel room. If you have valuables, store them in a hotel safe, if there's a reliable one, ideally inside a pouch with a lockable zip to prevent tampering.
- Be wary of anyone who approaches you on the street saying 'Remember me?' or claiming to be an employee of the hotel where you're staying, and take requests for donations from 'refugees', 'students' or others with a grain of salt. Contributions to humanitarian causes are best done through an established agency or project.
- Keep the windows up in vehicles when stopped in traffic, and keep your bags out of sight, eg on the floor behind your legs.
- When bargaining or discussing prices, don't do so with your money or wallet in your hand.

DISABLED TRAVELLERS

While there are few facilities for the disabled, East Africans are generally quite accommodating, and willing to offer whatever assistance they can as long as they understand what you need. Disabled travel is becoming increasingly common on the Kenyan and Tanzanian safari circuits, and several tour operators listed in the Safaris chapter (p83) cater to disabled travellers. Some considerations are listed following:

- While the newer lodges have wheelchair-accessible rooms (noted in individual listings), few hotels have lifts, many have narrow stairwells and there are generally no grips or rails in bathrooms.
- Many park lodges and camps are built on ground level. However, access paths – in an attempt to maintain a natural environment – are sometimes rough or rocky, and rooms or tents raised, so it's best to inquire about access before booking.
- As far as we know, there are no Braille signboards at any parks or museums, nor any facilities for deaf travellers.

TRAVEL ADVISORIES

Government country-specific travel advisories are good sources of updated security information, and should be read before travel to East Africa:

- Australia – www.dfat.gov.au
- Canada – www.voyage.gc.ca/dest/ctry /reportpage-en.asp
- UK – www.fco.gov.uk
- US – http://travel.state.gov

- In most places taxis are small sedans, with the exception of Nairobi where you'll find some old London cabs that are spacious enough to take a wheelchair. Minibuses are widely available in Kenya, Tanzania and Uganda, and can be chartered for transport and customised safaris. Large or wide-door vehicles can also be arranged through car-hire agencies in major cities, and often with safari operators as well.

In general, Kenya is probably the easiest destination, and many safari companies there have experience taking disabled people on safari. Organisations that disseminate information on travel for the mobility impaired include the following:

Accessible Journeys (www.disabilitytravel.com)
Access-Able Travel Source (www.access-able.com)
Holiday Care (www.holidaycare.org.uk)
Mobility International (www.miusa.org)
National Information Communication Awareness Network (www.nican.com.au)

DISCOUNT CARDS

An International Student Identity Card (ISIC) or the graduate equivalent is useful for discounts on train fares, airline tickets and entry charges to museums and archaeological sites.

EMBASSIES & CONSULATES

As a tourist, it's important to realise what your embassy – the embassy of the country of which you are a citizen – can and can't do.

Generally speaking, it won't be much help in emergencies if the trouble you're in is remotely your own fault, as you're bound by the laws of the country you are in. Your embassy will not be sympathetic if you end up in jail after committing a crime locally, even if such actions are legal in your own country.

In genuine emergencies you might get some assistance but only if other channels have been exhausted. For example, if you need to get home urgently, a free ticket is exceedingly unlikely – the embassy would expect you to have insurance. If you have all your money and documents stolen, it might assist with getting a new passport, but a loan for onward travel is out of the question.

For lists of diplomatic representations, see the country Directory sections.

GAY & LESBIAN TRAVELLERS

Although there are quite likely more gays and lesbians in Nairobi and the other capital cities, the coast – notably Lamu (Kenya) and Zanzibar (Tanzania) – tends to be more tolerant of gay relationships, at least privately.

Officially, male homosexuality is illegal in Tanzania and Kenya. While prosecutions rarely occur, discretion is advised as gay sexual relationships are culturally taboo, and public displays of affection, whether between people of the same or opposite sex, are frowned upon. That said, it is unlikely that gay travellers will experience any particular difficulties.

The website www.purpleroofs.com/africa /kenyata lists a number of gay or gay-friendly tour companies in the region which may be able to help you plan your trip. Try **Atlantis Events** (www.atlantisevents.com) or **David Tours** (www .davidtours.com) for all-inclusive packages.

HOLIDAYS

For listings of national holidays see the country Directory sections.

Public Holidays

In Tanzania and in parts of Kenya, especially along the coast, major Islamic holidays are also celebrated as public holidays. The dates depend on the moon and fall about 11 days earlier each year. The most important ones:

Eid al-Moulid (Maulid) The birthday of the Prophet Mohammed.

Ramadan The annual 30-day fast when adherents do not eat or drink from sunrise to sunset.

Eid al-Fitr The end of Ramadan, and East Africa's most important Islamic celebration; celebrated as a two-day holiday in many areas.

Eid al-Kebir (Eid al-Haji) Commemorates the moment when Abraham was about to sacrifice his son in obedience to God's command, only to have God intercede at the last moment and substitute a ram instead. It coincides with the end of the pilgrimage (haj) to Mecca.

Estimated dates for these events are shown following. Although Ramadan is not a public holiday, restaurants are often closed during this time in coastal areas.

Event	2006	2007	2008	2009
Eid al-Moulid (Maulid)	11 Apr	31 Mar	20 Mar	9 Mar
Ramadan begins	24 Sep	13 Sep	2 Sep	23 Aug
Eid al-Fitr (end of Ramadan)	24 Oct	13 Oct	2 Oct	21 Sep
Eid al-Kebir (Eid al-Haji)	31 Dec	20 Dec	9 Dec	29 Nov

INSURANCE

Taking out travel insurance covering theft, loss and medical problems is highly recommended. Before choosing a policy spend time shopping around, as those designed for short package tours in Europe may not be suitable for East Africa. Be sure to read the fine print, as some policies specifically exclude 'dangerous activities', which can mean scuba diving, motorcycling and even trekking. A locally acquired motorcycle licence isn't valid under some policies. Some policies pay doctors or hospitals directly, while others require you to pay on the spot and claim later. If you have to claim later, keep all documentation. Most importantly, check that the policy covers an emergency flight home.

Before heading to East Africa, it's also well worth taking out a membership with the **African Medical & Research Foundation** (Amref; www.amref.org; Nairobi emergency lines ☎ 254-20-315454, 602492, satellite ☎ 873 762315580; Nairobi head office ☎ 254-20-699 3000). This membership entitles you to emergency regional evacuation by the Flying Doctors' Society of Africa, which operates a 24-hour air-ambulance service based out of Wilson airport in Nairobi (Kenya). A two-month membership costs US$25/50 for evacuations within a 500km/1000km radius of Nairobi. The 1000km membership encompasses the entire East African region, except for southernmost Tanzania around Songea, Tunduru and Mtwara.

INTERNET ACCESS

Urban East Africa is online, with numerous Internet cafés in all capitals and major towns. In rural areas, however, connections are few and far between. Prices range from less than US$1 per hour in capital cities to up to US$5 per hour in outlying areas. Most upscale hotels also have Internet access, though don't expect to be able to connect while on safari.

If you're travelling with a laptop, you'll be able to hook up at top-end hotels and the occasional midrange hotel (with a universal adaptor for the modem). Wireless Internet has yet to hit the region in a big way, although a handful of upscale hotels now have connection points.

LEGAL MATTERS

Apart from traffic offences such as speeding and driving without a seatbelt (mandatory in many areas for driver and front-seat passengers), the main area to watch out for is drug use and possession. Marijuana (*bangi* or *ganja*) is widely available in places like Nairobi, Dar es Salaam and Zanzibar, and is frequently offered to tourists – invariably part of a setup involving the police or fake police. If you're caught, expect to pay a large bribe to avoid arrest or imprisonment.

If you're arrested for whatever reason, you can request to call to your embassy, although the help they will be able to give you will generally be limited, see opposite.

If you get robbed, most insurance companies require a police report before they'll reimburse you. You can get these at the nearest police station, though it's usually a time-consuming process.

MAPS

Regional maps include Nelles' *Tanzania, Rwanda, Burundi, Kenya* and *Uganda* maps, Bartholomew's *Kenya & Tanzania,* and Hallwag's *Kenya & Tanzania,* which also includes Uganda, Rwanda and Burundi. Michelin's *Africa – Central & South* covers most of the region on a smaller scale.

MONEY

The best strategy with money is to bring a mix of cash (large and small denominations), travellers cheques (ideally a mixture of American Express and Thomas Cook, in a variety of denominations) and a credit card (Visa is most widely accepted) for withdrawing money from ATMs.

ATMs

With the exception of Rwanda and Burundi, there are ATMs in capital cities and many major towns. They take either Visa or MasterCard, occasionally both. Some banks in Kenya and Tanzania also have machines linked to the Plus and Cirrus networks. However, throughout the region, despite their growing use, ATMs are out of order with enough frequency that it's best not to rely on them as your only source of funds. There are very few ATMs away from major routes.

Black Market

Except for in Burundi, there is essentially no black market for foreign currency. Nevertheless, you'll still get shady characters sidling up beside you in Nairobi, Dar es Salaam and major tourist areas, trying to get you to change money and promising enticing rates. It's invariably a setup and changing on the street should be avoided.

Cash

Throughout the region, US dollars are the most convenient foreign currency and get the best rates. Euros, British pounds and other major currencies are readily accepted in major cities, but often not elsewhere, or at less favourable rates. You'll usually get higher rates for larger denomination bills (US$50 and US$100 notes), but you should carry a supply of US$10, US$5 and US$1 notes as well, as change can be difficult to find.

Credit Cards

Visa and MasterCard can be used for most top-end hotels, a few tour operators and the occasional midrange place, especially in major towns and especially in Kenya. However, like ATMs, they're best viewed as a stand-by unless you've confirmed things in advance with the establishment. In Rwanda and Burundi, they're not much help at all. Many places, notably in Tanzania, attach a commission – usually about 5% to 10% – to credit card payments.

You can also use Visa or MasterCard for cash withdrawals at some banks, generally with a hefty commission.

Exchanging Money

You can change cash, and sometimes travellers cheques as well, with a minimum of hassle at banks or foreign exchange (forex) bureaus in major towns and cities; rates and commissions vary, so it pays to shop around. In addition to regular banking hours, most forex bureaus are also open on Saturday mornings. If you get stuck for money outside banking hours and away from an ATM, ask shop owners if they can help you out, rather than changing with someone on the street (which should always be avoided). It's better to say something like 'The banks are closed; do you know someone who could help me out?' rather than directly asking if they will change money.

Tipping & Bargaining

Tipping generally isn't practised in small, local establishments. But in major towns, upmarket places and anywhere frequented by tourists, tips are expected. If a service charge hasn't been included, either round out the bill, or calculate about 10%.

Bargaining is expected by vendors in tourist areas, except in a limited number of fixed-price shops. However, away from tourist areas and for nontourist items, the price quoted will often be the 'real' price, so don't automatically assume that the quote you've been given is too high.

Where bargaining is appropriate, if you pay the first price asked – whether due to ignorance or guilt about how much you have compared with locals – you'll probably be considered naive. You'll also be doing fellow travellers a disservice by creating the impression that all foreigners are willing to pay any named price. Paying consistently above the curve can also contribute to goods being priced out of the reach of locals.

While there are no set rules for bargaining, it should be conducted in a friendly and spirited manner; losing your temper or becoming aggressive or frustrated will be counterproductive. In any transaction, the vendor's aim is to identify the highest price you will pay, while your aim is to find the lowest price at which the vendor will sell. Before starting, shop around to get a feel for the 'value' of the item you want, and ask others what they paid. Once you start negotiating, if things seem like a waste of time, politely take your leave. Sometimes sellers will call you back if they think their stubbornness is counterproductive. Few will pass up a sale, however thin the profit. If the vendor won't come down to a price you feel is fair, it means that they aren't making a profit, or that too many high-rolling foreigners have passed through already.

Travellers Cheques

Travellers cheques are easily exchanged in major towns and cities in Kenya and somewhat less readily in Tanzania (where you *must* have your purchase receipt). In Uganda, Rwanda and Burundi, it's less straightforward (capital cities only, with high commissions), and throughout the region it's generally not possible at all at bank branches in smaller towns and rural areas. Rates are generally slightly lower than for cash. American Express and Thomas Cook are the most widely recognised; it's best to get your cheques in US dollars, followed by pounds or euros. Bring a range of denominations so you don't get stuck at the end of your trip changing large cheques for final expenses, and because some banks charge a per cheque levy. Also, carry the original purchase receipt with you (and separately from the cheques), as many banks and forex bureaus ask to see it, and don't rely on travellers cheques as your only source of funds.

Direct payment with travellers cheques for accommodation and services is usually not accepted, and those places that do accept cheques for payment often charge an extra commission.

If your cheques are stolen, getting replacements while still in the region ranges from very time-consuming to impossible.

PHOTOGRAPHY & VIDEO
Film & Equipment

Nairobi has the best selection of film, equipment and spares, including both Kodak and Fuji slide and print film up to at least 400 ISO/ASA. The selections in Dar es Salaam and Kampala are more limited, although for nonspecialist items you should have no trouble finding what you need. For any remotely specialist requirements (including slide or high-speed film), it's best to bring what you'll need with you.

For processing, most serious photographers get their film developed in Nairobi (where you can also get slides processed) or

bring it home. There are photo shops in all major towns, although outside capital cities quality is unreliable.

Due to the intensity of the African sunlight, most people find 100 ISO more than adequate, with perhaps a few rolls of 200 ISO or 400 ISO for long-lens shots. If you're going to be in forested areas, consider bringing some high-speed film along, especially if you'll be gorilla-trekking or chimp-tracking, as flashes generally aren't permitted near the primates.

For wildlife photography, a single lens reflex (SLR) camera with a lens between 210mm and 300mm should do the trick.

Whatever accessories you carry, be sure to keep them well wrapped in a good bag to protect them from the inevitable dust. Sunlight, humidity and heat can also spoil your camera and film, so take precautions. Lonely Planet's *Travel Photography: A Guide to Taking Better Pictures* by Richard I'Anson is full of helpful tips for taking photographs while on the road.

Photographing People

Always ask permission before photographing people, and always respect their wishes. In many tourist areas, locals will ask for a fee before allowing you to photograph them, which is fair enough, though rates can be high. If you promise to send someone a photo, get their address and follow through with it, as your promise will be taken seriously.

Restrictions

Avoid taking pictures of anything connected with the government or the military, including army barracks, land or people anywhere close to army barracks, government offices, post offices, banks, ports, train stations and airports.

Some locals may object if you take pictures of their place of worship – this includes natural features with traditional religious significance – so always ask first. It usually helps if you're appropriately dressed. In mosques, for instance, wearing a long skirt or trousers and removing your shoes may make it less likely that your hosts will object.

SENIOR TRAVELLERS

East Africa is an excellent destination for travellers of all ages. Places such as Nairobi, Mombasa, Dar es Salaam, Arusha, Zanzibar and Kampala have the widest selection of accommodation and dining options, as well as direct international air access, and many luxury tour and safari operators cater extensively to senior travellers.

Some things to think about, whatever your age:

Food If you are particular about what you eat or prefer Western-style cuisine, stick to larger towns with better tourism facilities.

Luggage Unless you're on an organised tour or will be met at your destinations by friends with vehicles, backpacks are the most practical option.

Transport Road journeys can be long and taxing even for the most fit travellers. To minimise rigours here, consider hiring a vehicle or flying, though both of these options can be expensive.

Weather Those who find hot and humid weather a drain on energy should plan their travels for the cooler period from June to August, or concentrate on mountainous or elevated areas away from the coast.

SOLO TRAVELLERS

While you may be a minor curiosity in rural areas, especially solo women travellers, there are no particular problems with travelling solo in East Africa, whether you're male or female. Times when it is advantageous to join a group are for safaris and treks – when going in a group can be a significant cost saver – and when going out at night. If you go out alone at night, take taxis and use extra caution, especially in urban and tourist areas. Whatever the time of day, avoid isolating situations, including isolated stretches of beach. For more information see opposite.

TELEPHONE

You can make domestic and international calls from telecom offices in all major towns (usually located near the post office), from cardphones or from private communications shops. Occasionally you'll find Internet dialling for about half of official telecom prices. The mobile network covers major towns throughout the region, plus many rural areas as well; for more see the country Directories.

Country codes are given inside the front cover of this book. In all countries in the region, except Rwanda and Burundi, area codes must be used whenever you dial long-distance; see individual town listings for codes.

ON TIME?

While the discussion of time (see below) makes everything sound quite official and precise, when all is said and done, time is a very different concept in East Africa than in many parts of the West. Buses that are going 'now' rarely leave until they're full, regardless of how much engine revving takes place in the meantime. Agreed-upon times for appointments are treated as very approximate concepts. A meeting set for 9am today could just as likely happen at 11am, or that afternoon, or even the next day. Getting upset when things don't go like clockwork is often counterproductive. The best way to get things done efficiently is to stay relaxed, treat the person you're dealing with as a person, inquire how their family is going or how their children are doing at school, and take the time to listen to the answer. Then, sit back, wait and be patient – you'll usually get where you're going or what you're hoping for, but on East Africa's time rather than yours.

TIME

Time in Kenya, Uganda and Tanzania is GMT/UTC plus three hours year-round; in Rwanda and Burundi it's GMT/UTC plus two hours.

In Swahili-speaking areas, locals use the Swahili system of telling time, in which the first hour is *saa moja (asubuhi)*, corresponding with 7am. Counting begins again with *saa moja (jioni)*, the first hour in the evening, corresponding with 7pm. Although most will switch to the international clock when speaking English with foreigners, confusion sometimes occurs, so ask people to confirm whether they are using *saa za kizungu* (international time) or *saa za kiswahili* (Swahili time). Signboards with opening hours are often posted in Swahili time.

TOILETS

Toilets vary from standard long drops to full-flush luxury conveniences that can spring up in the most unlikely places. Almost all midrange and top-end hotels sport flushable sit-down types, although at the lower end of the price range, toilet seats are a rare commodity. Budget guesthouses often have squat toilets – sometimes equipped with a flush mechanism, otherwise with a bucket and scoop.

Cleanliness levels vary; if you go in expecting the worst, you'll often be surprised that they're not all that bad. Toilets with running water are a rarity outside major hotels. If you see a bucket with water nearby, use it for flushing. Paper (you'll invariably need to supply your own) should be deposited in the can that's usually in the corner.

Many of the upmarket bush camps have 'dry' toilets – just a fancy version of the long drop with a Western-style seat perched on the top – though it is all generally quite hygienic.

TOURIST INFORMATION

Kenya, Tanzania, Uganda and Rwanda all have tourist agency websites, and maintain tourist offices of varying degrees of helpfulness in major cities; see Tourist Information in the country Directories for more. General background information is also available from East African embassies.

VISAS

Your passport should have plenty of blank pages for entry and exit stamps, and be valid for at least six months after the conclusion of your planned travels.

It's best to arrange visas in advance, although currently all countries in the region are issuing visas at the airport and at most land borders. Regulations change frequently, so call the relevant embassy for an update. Many international airlines require you to have a visa before boarding the plane to East Africa.

Once in East Africa, a single-entry visa for Kenya, Tanzania or Uganda allows you to visit either of the other two countries (assuming you've met their visa requirements and have been issued a visa) and then return to the original country without having to apply for second visa for the original country. Thus, if you're in Tanzania on a single-entry visa, you can go to Kenya (assuming you also have a Kenyan visa), and then return to Tanzania without needing a new Tanzanian visa. This doesn't apply to Rwanda and Burundi, so if you will be including visits to these or other African countries in your regional itinerary, it will save you money to get a multiple-entry visa at the outset. Note that visas issued at land borders are usually for single entry

only. Also, at most borders (including the popular Namanga border crossing between Kenya and Tanzania) and at airport immigration, visa fees must be paid in US dollars cash. Carry extra passport-sized photos for visa applications.

Proof of an onward ticket or sufficient funds is rarely required if you apply for a visa at land borders. It's occasionally requested at airports in the region, but generally only if you give immigration officials reason to doubt that you'll leave.

WOMEN TRAVELLERS

East Africa (especially in Kenya, Tanzania and Uganda) is a relatively easy region to travel in, either solo or with other women, especially when compared with parts of North Africa, South America and certain Western countries. You're not likely to encounter any more specifically gender-related problems than you would elsewhere in the world and, more often than not, you'll meet only warmth, hospitality and sisterly regard, and find that you receive kindness and special treatment that you probably wouldn't be shown if you were a male traveller. That said, you'll inevitably attract some attention, especially if you're travelling alone, and there are some areas where caution is essential. Following are a few tips:

- Dressing modestly is the single most successful strategy for minimising unwanted attention. Wear trousers or a long skirt, and a conservative top with sleeves. Tucking your hair under a cap or scarf, or tying it back, also helps.
- Use common sense, trust your instincts and take the usual precautions when out and about. Try to avoid walking alone at night. Avoid isolated areas at all times, and be particularly cautious on beaches, many of which can become isolated very quickly. Hassling tends to be worse in tourist areas along the Kenyan coast than elsewhere in the region. While most of it is limited to verbal hassles, and many travellers – female and male – travel in this area without incident, take extra care here about where you go alone.
- If you find yourself with an unwanted suitor, creative approaches are usually fairly effective. For example, explain that your husband (whether real or fictitious) or a large group of friends will be arriving

imminently at that very place. Creative approaches are also usually effective in dealing with the inevitable curiosity that you'll meet as to why you might not have children and a husband, or if you do have them, why they are not with you. The easiest response to the question of why you aren't married is to explain that you are still young (*bado kijana* in Swahili), which, whether you are or not, will at least have some humour value. Just saying '*bado*' ('not yet') to questions about marriage or children should also do the trick. As for why your family isn't with you, you can always explain that you will be meeting them later.

- Seek out local women, as this can enrich your trip tremendously. Good places to try include tourist offices, government departments or even your hotel, where at least some of the staff are likely to be formally educated young to middle-aged women. In rural areas, starting points include women teachers at a local school, or staff at a health centre.
- In mixed-race situations in some areas of the region – specifically if you're a black woman with a white male – some East Africans may assume that you're a prostitute. Taking taxis if you go out at night and ignoring any comments are among the tactics that may help minimise problems here.

In Rwanda and Burundi, verbal hassles, hisses and the like tend to be more common than elsewhere in the region, although things rarely go further than this. The best strategy – in addition to following the preceding tips – is to ignore hissing and catcalls; don't worry about being rude, and don't feel the need to explain yourself. Due to the overall unstable security situation, especially in Burundi, you'll need to take particular care in more remote areas, but this applies to travellers of whatever gender.

A limited selection of tampons is available at pharmacies or large supermarkets in major towns throughout the region. Elsewhere, the choice is usually limited to pads.

WORK

The most likely areas for employment are the safari industry, tourism, scuba diving and teaching. For safari, diving and tourism-related positions, competition is stiff and the best way to land something is to get to know someone already working in the business.

Work and residency permits generally must be arranged through the employer or sponsoring organisation; residency permits normally should be applied for before arriving in the region. Be prepared for lots of bureaucracy.

Most teaching positions are voluntary, and best arranged through voluntary agencies or mission organisations at home. Also start your search from home for international staff positions with the many aid agencies operating in East Africa. There are numerous opportunities available, especially in Kenya (dealing with the crises in Somalia and Sudan), Uganda and Burundi. However, most organisations require applicants to go through their head office.

A number of foreign organisations can assist with arranging volunteer work. Some to try:

Voluntary Service Overseas (VSO; www.vso.org.uk) Helps with placements for young professionals.

Volunteer Abroad (www.volunteerabroad.com) Has a good selection of volunteer listings for East Africa.

Transport in East Africa

GETTING THERE & AWAY

This section tells you how to reach East Africa from elsewhere in the world. For details on travel between and around the individual countries, and for border crossing information, see under Transport in the individual country chapters.

AIR
Airports & Airlines
Nairobi (Kenya) is East Africa's major air hub, and the best destination for finding special airfares. Other major airports include Dar es Salaam and Kilimanjaro in Tanzania, and Entebbe in Uganda. There are also international airports in Kigali (Rwanda), Bujumbura (Burundi) and Zanzibar (Tanzania), and it's worth checking out cheap charter flights to Mombasa (Kenya) from Europe.

Tickets
Airfares from Europe and North America to East Africa are highest in December and January, and again from June through August. They're lowest from March through May, except around the Easter holidays. London is the main discount airfare hub, and a good place to look for special deals into Nairobi. When planning your trip, consider buying an open-jaw ticket, which enables you to fly into one country and out of another. This often works out cheaper than booking a standard return in and out of one city, plus a connecting regional flight. Charter flights are generally cheaper than scheduled flights, and are also worth considering. Some come as part of a package that includes accommodation, but most charter companies sell 'flight only' tickets.

Online ticket sellers:

Cheapflights (www.cheap-flights.co.uk)
Cheap Tickets (www.cheaptickets.com)
Expedia (www.expedia.com, www.expedia.ca)
Flight Centre (www.flightcentre.com)
Flights.com (www.eltexpress.com)
LowestFare.com (www.lowestfare.com)
Microsoft Expedia (www.expedia.co.uk, www.expedia.ca)
OneTravel.com (www.onetravel.com)
Orbitz (www.orbitz.com)
STA Travel (www.statravel.com)
Travel.com.au (www.travel.com.au) For travel out of and around Australia.
Travelocity (www.travelocity.com, www.travelocity.ca)

COURIER FLIGHTS
Courier fares can be a bargain, although you may be allowed carry-on luggage only, and have limited flexibility with flight dates and times. The **International Association of Air Travel Couriers** (www.aircourier.co.uk) and the **Air Courier Association** (www.aircourier.org) are good places to start looking; for both you'll need to pay a modest membership fee to access their fares. Note that many advertised courier fares are one-way only.

INTERCONTINENTAL (RTW) TICKETS
Intercontinental (round-the-world) tickets give you a limited period (usually a year) to circumnavigate the globe. You can go anywhere that the carrying airline and its partners go, as long as you stay within the set mileage or number of stops, and don't backtrack. However, as East African destinations generally aren't part of standard RTW packages, you'll probably need to pay extra to include them.

> **THINGS CHANGE...**
>
> The information in this chapter is particularly vulnerable to change. Check directly with the airline or a travel agent to make sure you understand how a fare (and ticket you may buy) works and be aware of the security requirements for international travel. Shop carefully. The details given in this chapter should be regarded as pointers and are not a substitute for your own careful, up-to-date research.

Travel agents can put together 'alternative' RTW tickets, which are more expensive, but more flexible, than standard RTW itineraries. For a multiple-stop itinerary without the cost of a RTW ticket, consider combining tickets from two low-cost airlines.

Online RTW ticket sellers:

Airbrokers (www.airbrokers.com) For travel originating in North America.

Airtreks (www.airtreks.com) For travel originating in North America.

Oneworld (www.oneworld.com) An airline alliance offering RTW packages.

Roundtheworldflights.com (www.roundtheworld flights.com) For travel originating in the UK.

Star Alliance (www.staralliance.com) An airline alliance offering RTW packages.

Africa & the Middle East

Following is a list of useful airlines and their connections:

Air Burundi (airbdi@cbinf.com) Connections from Bujumbura to Kigali, and (soon) Bujumbura to Kigoma (Tanzania).

Air Madagascar (www.airmadagascar.mg) Connections from Antananarivo (Madagascar) to Nairobi.

Air Tanzania (www.airtanzania.com) Connections between Moroni (Comoros), Johannesburg, Nairobi, Harare, Entebbe, Lusaka, and Dar es Salaam or Zanzibar.

Cameroon Airlines (www.iccnet.cm/camair) Connections from Douala to Addis Ababa (Ethiopia), from where you can connect on Kenya Airways or Ethiopian Airlines to Nairobi and Dar es Salaam.

EgyptAir (www.egyptair.com.eg) Connections from Cairo to Nairobi via Entebbe.

Emirates (www.emirates.com) Connections from Cairo to Nairobi, Dar es Salaam or Entebbe via Dubai.

Ethiopian Airlines (www.flyethiopian.com) Connections from Abidjan, Lagos and Cairo to Addis Ababa, and then onward connections to major East African airports.

Kenya Airways (www.kenya-airways.com) Connections from Abidjan, Cairo, Douala, Harare, Johannesburg,

Khartoum, Lilongwe and other cities to Nairobi, with onward connections to all East African capitals.

Linhas Aéreas de Moçambique (www.lam.co.mz) Connections from Maputo to Dar es Salaam via Pemba (Mozambique).

Precision Air (www.precisionairtz.com) Connections from Dubai, Blantyre and Lilongwe to Dar es Salaam, all in partnership with Air Malawi; and Kigoma to Bujumbura (in partnership with Air Burundi).

Rwandair Express (www.rwandair.com) Connections from Kigali to Nairobi, Kilimanjaro, Entebbe, Bujumbura and Johannesburg.

South African Airways (www.flysaa.com) Connections from Johannesburg to Dar es Salaam, Nairobi, Entebbe and Kigali.

SN Brussels Airline (www.flysn.com) Connections from Brussels to Entebbe, Nairobi and Kigali.

Always ask about return excursion fares (fares that have certain restrictions or prerequisites, such as advance purchase, limited lifespan or specified travel windows) for intra-African flights, as they are frequently significantly cheaper than standard return fares.

Rennies Travel (www.renniestravel.com) and **STA Travel** (www.statravel.co.za) have offices throughout southern Africa. In the Middle East, try **Al-Rais Travels** (www.alrais.com) in Dubai; **Egypt Panorama Tours** (☎ 2-359 0200; www.eptours.com) in Cairo; the **Israel Student Travel Association** (ISTA; ☎ 02-625 7257) in Jerusalem; or **Orion-Tour** (www .oriontour.com) in Istanbul.

Asia

Popular connections from Asia are via Singapore and the United Arab Emirates, or via Mumbai (Bombay), from where there are connections to Dar es Salaam and Nairobi on **Kenya Airways** (www.kenya-airways.com) and **Air India** (www.airindia.com). **Ethiopian Airlines** (www .flyethiopian.com) also flies this route, via Addis Ababa, and **Oman Air** (www.oman-air.com) is worth checking for flights to Zanzibar (Tanzania) from Mumbai or Madras via Muscat.

STA Travel (www.statravel.com) is ubiquitous in Asia, with branches in **Thailand** (☎ 02-236 0262; www.statravel.co.th), **Singapore** (☎ 6737 7188; www.statravel.sg), **Hong Kong** (☎ 2736 1618; www .statravel.com.hk) and **Japan** (☎ 03-5391 2922; www .statravel.co.jp). Another resource in Japan is **No 1 Travel** (☎ 03-3205 6073; www.no1-travel.com). In Hong Kong try **Four Seas Tours** (☎ 2200 7760; www.fourseastravel.com/english). **STIC Travels** (www .stictravel.com) has offices in dozens of Indian cities, including **Delhi** (☎ 11-233 57 468) and **Mumbai** (☎ 22-221 81 431).

Australia & New Zealand

There are no direct flights from Australia or New Zealand to anywhere in East Africa. However, from Australia, **Qantas** (www.qantas .com.au) flies from Sydney and Perth to Johannesburg, and **South African Airways** (www .flysaa.com) flies from Perth to Johannesburg – both several times weekly – from where you can connect to Nairobi, Dar es Salaam and Entebbe. Other options include **Emirates** (www.emirates.com) via Dubai to Dar es Salaam or Nairobi; Qantas or **Air India** (www .airindia.com) via Mumbai to Dar es Salaam or Nairobi; and **Air Mauritius** (www.airmauritius.com) to Nairobi via Mauritius. A RTW ticket is another possibility (see p631). Ticket discounters include **Flight Centre** (☎ 131 600; www .flightcentre.com.au) and **STA Travel** (☎ 1300-733 035; www.statravel.com.au), both with branches around the country.

To travel from New Zealand to Nairobi, with onward connections to elsewhere in the region, try Emirates via Dubai, or Qantas and South African Airways via Sydney and Johannesburg. **Flight Centre** (☎ 0800-243 544; www.flightcentre.co.nz) and **STA Travel** (☎ 0508-782 872; www.statravel.co.nz) both have branches throughout the country. The website www .travel.co.nz is recommended for online bookings. Also check with some of the operators listed on p635.

UK & Continental Europe

There are flights from many European capitals directly to East Africa. The best deals, both on commercial and charter flights, are on the London–Nairobi route. Airlines to check include **Swiss** (www.swiss.com) to Nairobi and Dar es Salaam; **KLM Royal Dutch Airlines** (www.klm.com) to Nairobi, Dar es Salaam and Entebbe; **British Airways** (www .britishairways.com) to Nairobi, Dar es Salaam and Entebbe; and **SN Brussels Airline** (www .flysn.com) to Entebbe, Kigali and Nairobi. Non-European carriers – including **Kenya Airways** (www.kenya-airways.com), **Egypt Air** (www .egyptair.com.eg) via Cairo, **Ethiopian Airlines** (www .flyethiopian.com) via Addis Ababa, and **Emirates** (www.emirates.com) via Dubai – service various European cities as well as East African destinations, and also offer good deals. **Oman Air** (www.oman-air.com) flies between London and Zanzibar via Muscat, and **Yemenia Yemen Airways** (www.yemenia.com.ye) flies between London and Dar es Salaam. Whichever route you travel, flights from Europe are heavily booked between late June and late August, so reserve well in advance. The lowest fares are usually for travel between January and May, apart from the Easter season.

In the UK advertisements for many travel agencies appear in the travel pages of the weekend broadsheet newspapers, as well as in *Time Out*, the *Evening Standard* and in the free magazine *TNT* (www.tntmagazine.com). Recommended travel agencies:

Bridge the World (☎ 0870 444 7474; www.b-t-w.co.uk)
Flightbookers (☎ 0870 814 4001; www.ebookers.com)
Flight Centre (☎ 0870 890 8099; www.flightcentre.co.uk)
North-South Travel (☎ 01245 608 291; www.north southtravel.co.uk) North-South Travel donates part of its profit to projects in the developing world.
Quest Travel (☎ 0870 442 3542; www.questtravel.com)
STA Travel (☎ 0870 160 0599; www.statravel.co.uk) For travellers under the age of 26.
Trailfinders (www.trailfinders.co.uk)
Travel Bag (☎ 0870 890 1456; www.travelbag.co.uk)

Agencies to try for discounted fares from continental Europe:

Airfair (☎ 0206-20 51 21; www.airfair.nl) Netherlands.
Anyway (☎ 08 92 89 38 92; www.anyway.fr) France.
Barcelo Viajes (☎ 902 11 62 26; www.barceloviajes.com) Spain.
CTS Viaggi (☎ 064 62 04 31; www.cts.it) Italy; specialising in student and youth travel.
Just Travel (☎ 089-747 3330; www.justtravel.de) Germany.
Lastminute France (www.lastminute.fr); Germany (www .lastminute.de)
Nouvelles Frontières France (www.nouvelles-frontieres .fr); Spain (www.nouvelles-frontieres.es)
OTU Voyages (www.otu.fr) France.
STA Travel (☎ 01805-456 422; www.statravel.de) Germany; for travellers under the age of 26.
Voyageurs du Monde (☎ 01 40 15 11 15; www.vdm .com) France.

USA & Canada

Most flights from North America are via Europe, and there are few bargain deals. Fares offered by Canadian discounters are generally about 10% higher than those sold in the USA.

Generally the cheapest way is to get to London on a discounted transatlantic ticket, then purchase a separate ticket on to

Nairobi or elsewhere in East Africa. Most of the airlines mentioned under UK & Continental Europe (p633) also offer through-fares from North America.

A roundabout – but sometimes cheaper – alternative is **South African Airways** (www.flysn .com), which flies from New York or Atlanta to Johannesburg, where you can connect to East Africa. Other options include flying with **Egypt Air** (www.egyptair.com.eg) between New York and East Africa via Cairo; **Ethiopian Airways** (www.flyethiopian.com) between New York and East Africa via Rome and Addis Ababa; and **Kenya Airways** (www.kenya-airways.com) together with **Virgin Atlantic** (www.virgin-atlantic .com) from New York into the region via London.

Discount travel agents in the USA are known as consolidators (although you will not see a sign on the door saying 'Consolidator'). San Francisco is the ticket consolidator capital of America, but some good deals can also be found in Los Angeles, New York and other big cities. See p631 for recommended online booking agencies. Other recommended discounters:

Flight Centre (☎ 888-967 5355; www.flightcentre.ca) Canada.
STA Travel (☎ 800-781 4040; www.statravel.com) USA; for travellers under 26.
Travel Cuts (☎ 800-667 2887; www.travelcuts.com) Canada.

Some of the operators listed opposite also sell flight-only packages.

LAKE

The main lake ferry connections to/from East Africa are between Malawi and Tanzania on Lake Nyasa (see p261), and between Zambia and Tanzania on Lake Tanganyika (see p260).

LAND

A few of the more popular possibilities for combining East Africa travels with overland travel in other parts of the continent are outlined here. Detailing how to drive your own vehicle to the region from elsewhere in Africa is beyond the scope of this book, although information on the required *carnet de passage* is included on p638. Other sources of information include the *Adventure Motorcycling Handbook*, by Chris Scott et al, with lots of useful information, especially if you're com-

bining the Sahara and West Africa with your East Africa travels; and *Africa by Road* by Bob Swain and Paula Snyder – very useful if you're exploring Africa in your own vehicle, with details on everything from paperwork and logistics to driving techniques.

North & West Africa

For information on trans-Saharan routes, see Lonely Planet's *West Africa*, and check the website of **Chris Scott** (www.sahara-overland .com). Once through West Africa, most travellers fly from Douala (Cameroon) over the Central African Republic and Democratic Republic of the Congo (DR Congo) to Nairobi, from where you can continue overland within East Africa. It's also possible, but difficult, to go overland via Chad and Sudan to Addis Ababa and from there on to Nairobi.

Northeast Africa

The Nile route through northeast Africa goes from Egypt into Sudan (via Lake Nasser, or the Red Sea from Suez to Port Sudan) to Khartoum. From there, most people fly to Nairobi, or go overland (security situation permitting) from northern Sudan through Eritrea and Ethiopia into Kenya.

Southern Africa

If you have the time, a combined southern Africa–East Africa overland itinerary is an excellent way to experience the continent.

The main gateways between them are Zambia and Malawi, both of which are straightforward to reach from elsewhere in southern Africa. Once in Zambia, head to Kapiri Mposhi where you can get the Tanzania–Zambia Railway (Tazara) northeast to Mbeya (Tanzania). From Mbeya continue by road or rail towards Dar es Salaam, and then by road towards Mombasa and Nairobi. Another route from Zambia goes to Mpulungu on the Zambian shore of Lake Tanganyika, from where you can travel by steamer to Kigoma. From Kigoma head by rail east to Dar es Salaam, or northeast towards Lake Victoria, Uganda and western Kenya.

From Malawi, after entering East Africa at Songwe River Bridge (at the Tanzanian border), head by bus to Mbeya and continue as outlined above.

Burundi's security situation permitting, other possibilities include following the route outlined earlier from Mpulungu to

Kigoma, from where you can continue by ferry (when it's running) or overland to Bujumbura, travel through Burundi, Rwanda and Uganda, and on into Kenya or Tanzania. Overland travel into East Africa from Mozambique is possible when the sporadically functioning vehicle ferry across the Ruvuma River is running (see p258). Once in Mtwara (Tanzania), it's straight – albeit somewhat bumpy – going on the currently-being-rehabilitated road to Dar es Salaam.

SEA

To reach East Africa by sea, the main option is trying to hitch a lift on a private yacht sailing along the coast. Durban (South Africa) is one of the better places to start looking. Several cargo shipping companies sailing from Europe to East Africa also have passenger cabins. Expect to pay from about UK£1350 one way for a 23-day journey from Felixstowe (UK) to Dar es Salaam via the Suez Canal.

Some useful contacts:

Freighter World Cruises Inc (☎ 800-531 7774, 626-449 3106; www.freighterworld.com) Based in the USA.

Strand Voyages (☎ 020-7836 6363; www.strandtravel .co.uk) Based in the UK.

TOURS

If you're short on time or new to travel in the region, an organised tour can be a good choice, although these are usually more expensive than organising things locally, in East Africa. They're normally booked in advance in your home country, either directly with the operating company or through an agent. Some packages include international flights, while with others these need to be arranged separately. Tours average two to three weeks, with shorter and much longer options also possible.

Organised tours can be low-budget affairs, where you travel in an 'overland truck' with 15 to 30 other people and some drivers/leaders, carrying tents and other equipment, buying food along the way, and cooking and eating as a group. At the other end of the spectrum are individually tailored tours, ranging in price from reasonable to very expensive. In between are the midrange tours, where you keep to a set itinerary and travel in a small group, usually either in a minibus or a Land Rover–style 4WD, staying at hotels and sometimes camping.

Some companies offer an option between all-inclusive tours and travelling completely independently, by providing you with pre-booked flights, vehicle hire and accommodation as required, but letting you decide exactly where and when you want to go.

There are dozens of tour companies operating through East Africa and the following list is just a sample; for additional listings, including locally based companies, see p83. If you have specialist interests, look in specialist magazines (such as nature magazines for wildlife tours, outdoor magazines for hiking tours etc).

Australia

Africa Travel Centre (☎ 02-9267 3048; Level 11, 456 Kent St, Sydney, NSW 2000) General travel arrangements, air tickets and tours.

African Wildlife Safaris (☎ 03-9696 2899, 1300-363302; www.africanwildlifesafaris.com.au) Discount airfares and safaris.

Peregrine Travel (☎ 03-9663 8611; www.peregrine.net .au) Everything from overland truck tours to upscale wildlife safaris and chimpanzee tracking.

New Zealand

Africa Travel Centre (☎ 09-520 2000; 21 Remuera Rd, Newmarket, Auckland) General travel arrangements, airfares and tours.

South Africa

Wild Frontiers (☎ 11-702 2035; www.wildfrontiers.com) Safaris, chimpanzee tracking and more.

UK

Abercrombie & Kent (☎ 0845-070 0610; www.aber crombiekent.co.uk) Upscale tours and safaris, including chimpanzee tracking.

Dragoman (☎ 0870-499 4475; www.dragoman.co.uk) Overland tours.

Explore Worldwide (☎ 01252-760000; www.explore worldwide.com) Small group tours, treks and safaris.

Footprint Adventures (☎ 01522-804929; www.foot print-adventures.co.uk) Treks and safaris.

Gane & Marshall (☎ 020-8441 9592; www.ganeand marshall.co.uk) Upscale tours and safaris.

Guerba (☎ 01373-826611; www.guerba.com) Overland tours, including visits to the gorillas and chimpanzees.

USA & Canada

Born Free Safaris (☎ 800-372 3274, 818-981 7185; www.bornfreesafaris.com) Safaris and tours.

Fresh Tracks (☎ 800-267 3347, 416-922 7584; www .freshtracks.com) Safaris, tours and gorilla tracking.

International Expeditions (☎ 800-633 4734, 205-428 1700; www.ietravel.com) Upscale safaris.
Thomson Family Adventures (☎ 800-262 6255, 617-923 2004; www.familyadventures.com) Family-friendly safaris and tours.

GETTING AROUND

This section summarises the ways to travel around East Africa. For specifics, see the individual country chapters.

AIR

Because of East Africa's size and the less-than-optimal condition of many roads, it's worth considering regional and domestic flights, especially if your time is limited. While international connections into the region are good, and air service within East Africa is relatively reliable, cancellations and delays should still be expected at any time of year. Always reconfirm your ticket several times, and allow extra time between regional and intercontinental flights.

Airlines in East Africa

For details of airlines flying within East Africa, see the country chapters.

BICYCLE

Cycling is an excellent way to explore East Africa if you have time, a sense of adventure and don't mind roughing things. Main sealed roads are best avoided (as traffic moves dangerously fast) but secondary roads can be ideal. Because of the distances involved, you'll need to plan your food and water needs in advance, and to pay attention to choosing a route. Throughout much of the region, cycling is best well away from urban areas, in the early morning and late afternoon hours, and in the cooler, dry season between June and August. When calculating daily distances, plan on taking a break from the midday heat, and don't count on covering as much territory each day as you might in a northern European climate.

Mountain bikes are best for flexibility and local terrain, and should be brought from home. While single-speed bicycles, and occasionally mountain bikes, can be rented in many towns (ask hotel staff or inquire at the local bicycle repair stand), they're only suitable for short rides.

Other things to consider when planning are water (carry at least 4L), rampaging motorists (a small rear-view mirror is a worthwhile investment), sleeping (bring a tent) and punctures (thorn trees are a problem in some areas). Bring sufficient spares (including at least four spare inner tubes, a spare tyre and plenty of tube patches), and be proficient at repairs. Cycling isn't permitted in national parks or wildlife reserves.

Bicycles can be transported on minibuses and buses (though for express or luxury buses, you may need to make advance arrangements with the driver to stow your bike in the hold). There's also no problem and no additional cost to bring your bicycle on any of the region's lake or coastal ferries.

As elsewhere in the world, don't leave your bike unattended unless it's locked, and secure all removable pieces. Taking your bike into a hotel room is generally no problem (and is a good idea). A highly recommended contact is the US-based **International Bicycle Fund** (www.ibike.org/bikeafrica), a socially conscious, low-budget organisation that arranges tours in East Africa and provides information. Several hotels and tour operators also offer bike hire and arrange shorter cycling or mountain-biking day trips; see the country chapters for specifics.

BOAT

On the Tanzanian section of Lake Victoria, there are passenger boats connecting Mwanza (Tanzania) with Bukoba, Ukerewe Island and various lakeside villages. In the Kenyan section of the lake, small boats connect the mainland around Mbita Point with Mfangano, Rusinga and the Takawiri Islands. In Uganda small boats connect mainland villages with the Ssese Islands; there are also regular cargo boats from Kampala to Mwanza that accept passengers.

On Lake Tanganyika, a passenger ferry connects Kigoma (Tanzania) with Mpulungu (Zambia). On Lake Nyasa, the main route is between Mbamba Bay and Itungi (both in Tanzania), via numerous lakeside villages. There's also a boat between Mbamba Bay and Nkhata Bay (Malawi).

The main coastal routes are between Dar es Salaam, Zanzibar and Pemba (covered in the Tanzania chapter), and the short run between the coast and the Lamu Archipelago (Kenya). Other routes with more sporadic

---

DHOW TRAVEL

With their billowing sails, graceful forms and long histories, these ancient sailing vessels have become a symbol of East Africa for adventurous travellers. Even the name has a certain allure, evoking images of nights spent under the stars sailing through distant archipelagos. Yet, despite their romantic reputation, the realities of dhow travel can be quite different.

If the wind is with you and the water calm, a dhow trip can be enjoyable, and will give you a better sense of the centuries of trade that shaped East Africa's coastal communities during the days when dhows reigned supreme. However, if you're becalmed miles from your destination, if seas turn rough, if the boat is leaking or overloaded, if it's raining, or if the sun is very strong, the experience will be much less pleasant.

Places to arrange dhow trips include Msimbati (p247), Mikindani (p247), Kilwa Kivinje (p242) and Bagamoyo (p158), all in Tanzania; and Lamu (p341) in Kenya. To experience dhow travel with a bit more comfort and fewer risks, many coastal hotels have their own boats or can help you arrange a local boat for a short sail.

The following are some things to keep in mind if you do decide to give a local dhow a try:

- Be prepared for rough conditions. There are no facilities on board, except possibly a toilet hanging off the stern. As sailings are wind and tide dependent, departures are often during the pre-dawn hours.

- Journeys often take longer than anticipated; bring plenty of extra water and sufficient food.

- Sunblock, a hat and a covering are essential, as is waterproofing for your luggage.

- Avoid overloaded boats and don't set sail in bad weather as capsizing is a concern.

- Travel with the winds, which blow from south to north from approximately July to September and north to south from approximately November to late February.

Note that what Westerners refer to as dhows are called either *jahazi* or *mashua* by most Swahili speakers. *Jahazi* are large, lateen-sailed boats. *Mashua* are similar in design, although smaller, and often with proportionately wider hulls and a motor. The *dau* has a sloped stem and stern. On lakes and inland waterways, the *mtumbwi* (dugout canoe) is in common use. Coastal areas, especially Zanzibar's east-coast beaches, are good places to see the *ngalawa* (outrigger canoe).

---

services include those between Dar es Salaam and Mtwara, and between Tanga and Pemba (all in Tanzania).

BUS

Buses are the most useful type of public transport. They're usually faster than trains or trucks, and safer and more comfortable than minibuses. In Kenya and Tanzania you often have the choice of going by 'luxury' or 'ordinary' bus. Luxury buses are more comfortable and more expensive, though not always quicker than ordinary buses. Some also boast the dubious advantage of a video system, usually playing bad movies at full volume for the entire trip. Uganda has ordinary buses only, except on the Kampala–Nairobi run. There are a few full-size buses in Rwanda and Burundi, although, especially in Burundi, minibuses are the rule.

For details of major bus companies, routes and schedules, see the Transport sections in the country chapters.

CAR & MOTORCYCLE

It's quite feasible to make your way around much of East Africa by car or motorcycle, though it's generally only an option used by those already living in the region with access to their own vehicle (as rentals can be very expensive) and local driving knowledge.

Throughout East Africa, main roads are sealed and in reasonable states of repair. In rural areas, however, they range from decent to terrible, especially in the wet season when many secondary routes become impassable. Most trips outside major towns require 4WD; motorcycles generally aren't permitted in national parks.

Whether you drive your own or a rental vehicle, expect stops at checkpoints where police and border officials will ask to see your driving licence, insurance paperwork and vehicle papers.

Bring Your Own Vehicle

To bring your own vehicle into East Africa you'll need to arrange a *carnet de passage*. This document allows you to take a vehicle duty-free into a country where duties would normally be payable. It guarantees that if a vehicle is taken into a country but not exported, the organisation that issued the carnet will accept responsibility for payment of import duties (generally between 100% and 150% of the new value of the vehicle). The carnet should also specify any expensive spare parts that you'll be carrying.

To get a carnet, contact your national motoring organisation at home, which will give you an indemnity form for completion by either a bank or an insurance company. Once you have deposited a bond with a bank or paid an insurance premium, the motoring organisation will issue the carnet. The cost of the carnet itself is minimal; allow at least a week to complete the process.

For longer trips, in addition to a carnet and mechanical knowledge, bring along a good collection of spares.

Driving Licence

If you're taking your own vehicle or are considering hiring one in East Africa, arrange an International Driving Permit (IDP) before leaving home. They're available at minimal cost through your national motoring organisation.

Fuel & Spare Parts

Fuel costs in the region average US$1/US$0.80 per litre of petrol/diesel. Filling and repair stations are readily available in major towns, but scarce elsewhere. In many areas, diesel is often easier to find than petrol. Top your tank up whenever you get the opportunity and carry basic spares. For travel in remote areas and in national parks, also carry jerry cans with extra fuel. Petrol sold on the roadside is unreliable, as it's often diluted with water or kerosene.

Hire

Car, 4WD and motorcycle hire is expensive throughout the region, averaging US$100 to US$150 per day for 4WD. Few agencies offer unlimited kilometres, and many require that you take a chauffeur (which is a good idea anyway). For self-drive rentals you'll need a driving licence and often an International Driving Permit as well. If you'll be crossing any borders, you'll need to arrange the necessary paperwork with the hire agency in advance.

Insurance

Throughout the region, liability insurance must generally be bought at the border upon entry. While cost and quality vary, in many cases you may find that you are effectively travelling uninsured, as there's often no way to collect on the insurance. With vehicle rentals – even if you're covered from other sources – it's a good idea to take the full coverage offered by hire companies.

Road Rules

Tanzania, Kenya and Uganda follow the British keep-left traffic system. In Rwanda and Burundi, driving is on the right-hand side. At roundabouts throughout the region, traffic already in the roundabout has the right of way.

Night-time road travel isn't recommended anywhere; if you must drive at night, be alert for stopped vehicles in the roadway without lights or hazard warnings. If you're not used to driving in Africa, watch out for pedestrians, children and animals, as well as for oncoming vehicles on the wrong side of the road. Especially in rural areas, remember that many people have never driven themselves and are not aware of necessary braking distances and similar concepts; moderate your speed accordingly. Tree branches placed in the roadway are used to signal a stopped vehicle or other problem ahead, and indicate that speed should be reduced. Passing (including on curves or other areas with poor visibility) is common practice and a cause of frequent accidents.

HITCHING

Hitching may be your only option in remote areas, although it's rare that you'll get a free ride unless you're lucky enough to be offered a lift by resident expats, well-off locals or aid workers – even then, at least offer to make a contribution for petrol on longer journeys, or to pick up a meal tab. To flag down a vehicle, hold out your hand at about waist level and wave it up and down, with the palm to the ground; the common Western gesture of holding out your thumb isn't used.

A word of warning about taking lifts in private cars: smuggling across borders is common practice, and if whatever is being smuggled is found, you may be arrested even though you knew nothing about it. Most travellers manage to convince police that they were merely hitching a ride (passport stamps are a good indication of this), but the convincing can take a long time.

As in other parts of the world, hitching is never entirely safe, and we don't recommend it. Those travellers who decide to hitch should understand that they are taking a potentially serious risk. If you do hitch, you'll be safer doing so in pairs and letting someone know of your plans.

LOCAL TRANSPORT
Minibus
Most East Africans rely heavily on mini-buses for transport. They're called *matatus* in Kenya, *daladalas* in Tanzania, and taxis or *matatus* in Uganda. Except in Rwanda and Burundi, minibuses are invariably packed to bursting point, and this – combined with excessive speed, poor maintenance and driver recklessness – means that they're not the safest way of getting around. In fact, they can be downright dangerous, and newspaper reports of *matatu* and *daladala* crashes are a regular feature. In Rwanda and Burundi travelling in minibuses is generally safer. If you have a large backpack, think twice about boarding, especially at rush hour, when it will make the already crowded conditions even more uncomfortable for others.

Taxi
In Kenya, Tanzania and Uganda you'll find shared taxis on some routes. These officially take between five and nine passengers, de-pending on size, leave when full and are usu-ally faster, though more expensive, than bus travel. They're marginally more comfortable than minibuses, but have their share of acci-dents. Private taxis are useful for short trips within a town, or – if you have the funds – for half- or full-day charters.

Truck
In remote areas trucks may be the only form of transport, and they're invariably the cheapest. For most regular runs there will be a 'fare', which is more or less fixed and is what the locals pay. It's usually equivalent to, or a bit less than, the bus fare for the same route. For a place in the cab, expect to pay about twice what it costs to travel on top of the load.

Many truck lifts are arranged the night before departure at the 'truck park' – a com-pound or dust patch that you'll find in most towns. Ask around for a truck that's going your way, and be prepared to wait, especially on remote routes where there may be trucks leaving only once or twice a week. For longer trips, ask what to do about food and drink, and bring plenty of extra drinking water – enough for yourself and to share.

TOURS
For safari and trekking operators, see p83. Many of the companies listed here can also organise local itineraries in addition to your safari or trek. For local tour operators, see listings in individual town sections of the country chapters.

TRAIN
The main passenger lines are the Nairobi–Mombasa route (Kenya), the Tazara 'express' line from Dar es Salaam to Mbeya (Tanza-nia), and the meandering Central line con-necting Dar es Salaam with Mwanza and Kigoma (Tanzania).

First class costs about double what the bus would cost, but is well worth it for the additional comfort. Second class is reason-ably comfortable, but the savings over 1st class are marginal. Economy-class travel is cheap, crowded and uncomfortable. There are no assigned seats, and for long trips you'll probably wind up sitting and sleeping on the floor. Reservations for 1st class are generally best made as early as possible.

In all classes, keep an eye on your lug-gage, especially at stops. Particularly in 1st and 2nd class, make sure the window is jammed shut at night to avoid the possibil-ity of someone entering when the train stops (there's usually a piece of wood provided for this), and keep your cabin door shut.

Food and drink (mainly soft drinks) are available on trains and from station ven-dors, although it's a good idea to bring sandwiches and extra water. Have plenty of small change handy.

Health
Dr Caroline Evans

CONTENTS

As long as you stay up to date with your vaccinations and take some basic preventive measures, you'd have to be pretty unlucky to succumb to most of the health hazards covered in this chapter. While East Africa has an impressive selection of tropical diseases on offer, you're much more likely to get a bout of diarrhoea, a cold or an infected mosquito bite than an exotic disease such as sleeping sickness. When it comes to injuries (as opposed to illness), the most likely reason for needing medical help in the region is as a result of road accidents – vehicles are rarely well maintained, the roads are potholed and poorly lit, and drink driving is common.

BEFORE YOU GO

A little planning before departure, particularly for pre-existing illnesses, will save you a lot of trouble later. Before a long trip get a check-up from your dentist and from your doctor if you take any regular medication or have a chronic illness, such as high blood pressure or asthma. You should also organise spare contact lenses and glasses (and take your optical prescription with you), get a first aid and medical kit together and arrange necessary vaccinations.

It's tempting to leave it all to the last minute – don't! Many vaccines don't take effect until two weeks after you've been immunised, so visit a doctor four to eight weeks before departure. Ask your doctor for an International Certificate of Vaccination (otherwise known as the yellow booklet), which will list all the vaccinations you've received. This is mandatory for many African countries, including some in East Africa, that require proof of yellow fever vaccination upon entry, but it's a good idea to carry it anyway, wherever you travel.

Travellers can register with the **International Association for Medical Advice to Travellers** (IMAT; www.iamat.org). Its website can help travellers to find a doctor who has recognised training. Those heading off to very remote areas might like to do a first aid course (contact the Red Cross or St John Ambulance) or attend a remote medicine first aid course, such as that offered by the **Royal Geographical Society** (www.wildernessmedical training.co.uk; prices vary according to courses chosen).

If you are bringing medications with you, carry them in their original containers, clearly labelled. A signed and dated letter from your physician describing all medical conditions and medications, including generic names, is also a good idea. If carrying syringes or needles be sure to have a physician's letter documenting their medical necessity.

How do you go about getting the best possible medical help? It's difficult to say – it really depends on the severity of your illness or injury and the availability of local help. If malaria is suspected, seek medical help as soon as possible or begin self-medicating if you are off the beaten track (see p643).

INSURANCE

Find out in advance whether your insurance plan will make payments directly to providers or will reimburse you later for overseas health expenditures (in many countries doctors expect payment in cash). It's vital to ensure that your travel insurance will cover the emergency transport required to get you to a hospital in a major city, to better medical facilities elsewhere in the region, or all the way home, by air and with a medical attendant if necessary. Not all insurance covers this, so check the contract carefully. If you need medical help, your insurance company might be able to help locate the nearest hospital or clinic, or you can ask at your hotel. In an emergency, contact your embassy or consulate.

Membership of the **African Medical and Research Foundation** (Amref; www.amref.org) provides an air evacuation service in medical emergencies that covers most of East Africa, as well as air ambulance transfers between medical facilities. Money paid by members for this service goes into providing grassroots medical assistance for local people (see p625 for more information).

RECOMMENDED VACCINATIONS

The **World Health Organization** (www.who.int/en/) recommends that all travellers be covered for diphtheria, tetanus, measles, mumps, rubella and polio, as well as for hepatitis B, regardless of their destination. The planning stage before travel is a great time to ensure that all routine vaccination cover is complete. The consequences of these diseases can be severe, and outbreaks of them do occur.

According to the **Centers for Disease Control and Prevention** (www.cdc.gov), the following vaccinations are recommended for all parts of Africa, including East Africa: hepatitis A, hepatitis B, meningococcal meningitis, rabies and typhoid, and boosters for tetanus, diphtheria and measles. Yellow fever is required for Rwanda and recommended for elsewhere in the region, and the certificate is an entry requirement for many other countries (see p646).

MEDICAL CHECKLIST

It is a very good idea to carry a medical and first aid kit with you, to help yourself in the case of minor illness or injury. The following is a list of items you should consider packing.

- Acetaminophen (paracetamol) or aspirin
- Acetazolamide (Diamox) for altitude sickness (prescription only)
- Adhesive or paper tape
- Antibiotics (prescription only), eg ciprofloxacin (Ciproxin) or norfloxacin (Utinor)
- Antibacterial ointment (eg Bactroban) for cuts and abrasions (prescription only)
- Antidiarrhoeal drugs (eg loperamide)
- Antihistamines (for hayfever and allergic reactions)
- Anti-inflammatory drugs (eg ibuprofen)
- Antimalaria pills
- Bandages, gauze, gauze rolls
- DEET-containing insect repellent for the skin
- Permethrin-containing insect spray for clothing, tents, and bed nets
- Pocket knife
- Rehydration salts (oral)
- Steroid cream or hydrocortisone cream (for allergic rashes)
- Scissors, safety pins, tweezers
- Sterile needles, syringes and fluids if travelling to remote areas
- Sun block
- Thermometer
- Water purification tablets (iodine)

If you are travelling through a malarial area, particularly an area where falciparum malaria predominates (see p643), consider taking a self-diagnostic kit that can identify malaria in the blood from a finger prick.

INTERNET RESOURCES

There is a wealth of travel health advice on the Internet. For further information, the **Lonely Planet website** (www.lonelyplanet.com) is a good place to start. The World Health Organization publishes a superb book, also available online for free, called **International Travel and Health** (www.who.int/ith/), which is revised annually. Other websites of interest are **MD Travel Health** (www.mdtravelhealth.com), which provides complete travel health recommendations for every country, and is updated daily, also at no cost; the **Centers for Disease Control and Prevention** (www.cdc.gov); and **Fit for Travel** (www.fitfortravel.scot.nhs.uk), which has up-to-date information and is user-friendly.

It's also a good idea to consult your government's travel health website before departure, if one is available:
Australia www.dfat.gov.au/travel/
Canada http://www.hc-sc.gc.ca/english/index.html
UK www.dh.gov.uk/PolicyAndGuidance/HealthAdvice ForTravellers/fs/en
USA www.cdc.gov/travel/

FURTHER READING

- *A Comprehensive Guide to Wilderness and Travel Medicine* by Eric A Weiss (1998)

- *Healthy Travel* by Jane Wilson-Howarth (1999)
- *Healthy Travel Africa* by Isabelle Young (2000)
- *How to Stay Healthy Abroad* by Richard Dawood (2002)
- *Travel in Health* by Graham Fry (1994)
- *Travel with Children* by Cathy Lanigan (2004)

IN TRANSIT

DEEP VEIN THROMBOSIS (DVT)

Blood clots can form in the legs during flights, chiefly because of prolonged immobility. This formation of clots is known as deep vein thrombosis (DVT), and the longer the flight, the greater the risk. Although most blood clots are reabsorbed uneventfully, some might break off and travel through the blood vessels to the lungs, where they could cause life-threatening complications.

The chief symptom of DVT is swelling or pain of the foot, ankle or calf, usually – but not always – on just one side. When a blood clot travels to the lungs, it can cause chest pain and breathing difficulty. Travellers with any of these symptoms should immediately seek medical attention.

To prevent the development of DVT on long flights you should walk around the cabin, perform isometric compressions of the leg muscles (ie contract the leg muscles while sitting), drink plenty of fluids, and avoid alcohol.

JET LAG & MOTION SICKNESS

If you're crossing more than five time zones you could suffer jet lag, resulting in insomnia, fatigue, malaise or nausea. To avoid jet lag try drinking plenty of fluids (nonalcoholic) and eating light meals. Upon arrival, get exposure to natural sunlight and readjust your schedule (for meals, sleep, etc) as soon as possible.

Antihistamines such as dimenhydrinate (Dramamine) and meclizine (Antivert, Bonine) are usually the first port of call for treating motion sickness. The main side effect of these drugs is some drowsiness. A herbal alternative is ginger (in the form of ginger tea, biscuits or crystallized ginger), which works like a charm for some people.

IN EAST AFRICA

AVAILABILITY & COST OF HEALTH CARE

Good, Western-style medical care is available in Nairobi (which is the main medical hub for the region and the main regional destination for medical evacuations), and to a lesser extent in Dar es Salaam, Kampala and other major cities. Elsewhere, reasonable to good care is available in larger towns, and in some mission stations, though availability is extremely patchy once off the beaten track. In general, private or mission-run clinics and hospitals are better equipped than government ones. If you fall ill in an unfamiliar area, ask staff at a top-end hotel or resident expatriates where the best nearby medical facilities are, and in an emergency contact your embassy. Most towns in the region have at least one clinic where you can get an inexpensive malaria test and, if necessary, treatment. With dental treatment, be aware that there is often an increased risk of hepatitis B and HIV transmission via poorly sterilised equipment.

Most drugs can be purchased over the counter in East Africa, without a prescription. However, there are often problems with ineffectiveness, if the drugs are counterfeit, for example, or if they have not been stored under the right conditions. The most common examples of counterfeit drugs are malaria tablets and expensive antibiotics, such as ciprofloxacin. Most drugs are available in capital cities, but remote villages will be lucky to have a couple of paracetamol tablets. It is strongly recommended that all drugs for chronic diseases be brought from home.

There is a high risk of contracting HIV from infected blood if you receive a blood transfusion in Africa. The **BloodCare Foundation** (www.bloodcare.org.uk) is a useful source of safe, screened blood, which can be transported to any part of the world within 24 hours.

INFECTIOUS DISEASES

It's a formidable list, but a few precautions go a long way…

Cholera

Cholera is usually only a problem during natural or artificial disasters – such as war, floods or earthquakes – although small outbreaks also occur at other times. Travellers are rarely affected. It is caused by a bacteria and spread via contaminated drinking water. The main symptom is profuse watery diarrhoea, which causes debilitation if fluids are not replaced quickly. An oral cholera vaccine is available in the USA, but it is not particularly effective. Most cases of cholera could be avoided by close attention to good drinking water and by avoiding potentially contaminated food. Treatment is by fluid replacement (orally or via a drip), but sometimes antibiotics are needed. Self-treatment is not advised.

Diphtheria

Found in all of East Africa, diphtheria is spread through close respiratory contact. It usually causes a temperature and a severe sore throat. Sometimes a membrane forms across the throat, and a tracheostomy is needed to prevent suffocation. Vaccination is recommended for those likely to be in close contact with the local population in infected areas and is more important for long stays than for short-term trips. The vaccine is given as an injection, alone or with tetanus, and lasts 10 years.

Filariasis

Tiny worms migrating in the lymphatic system cause filariasis. The bite from an infected mosquito spreads the infection. Symptoms include localised itching and swelling of the legs and/or genitalia. Treatment is available.

Hepatitis A

Hepatitis A is spread through contaminated food (particularly shellfish) and water. It causes jaundice and, although it is rarely fatal, it can cause prolonged lethargy and delayed recovery. If you've had hepatitis A, you shouldn't drink alcohol for up to six months afterwards, but once you've recovered, there won't be any long-term problems. The first symptoms include dark urine and a yellow colour to the whites of the eyes. Sometimes a fever and abdominal pain might be present. Hepatitis A vaccine (Avaxim, VAQTA, Havrix) is given as an injection: a single dose will give protection for up to a year, and a booster after a year gives 10-year protection. Hepatitis A and typhoid vaccines can also be given as a single dose vaccine, hepatyrix or viatim.

Hepatitis B

Hepatitis B is spread through infected blood, contaminated needles and sexual intercourse. It can also be spread from an infected mother to the baby during childbirth. It affects the liver, causing jaundice and occasionally liver failure. Most people recover completely, but some people might be chronic carriers of the virus, which could lead eventually to cirrhosis or liver cancer. Those visiting high-risk areas for long periods or those with increased social or occupational risk should be immunised. Many countries now routinely give hepatitis B as part of their routine childhood vaccination program. It is given singly or can be given at the same time as hepatitis A (hepatyrix).

A course will give protection for at least five years. It can be given over four weeks or six months.

HIV

Human immunodeficiency virus (HIV), the virus that causes acquired immune deficiency syndrome (AIDS), is an enormous problem throughout East Africa. The virus is spread through infected blood and blood products, by sexual intercourse with an infected partner and from an infected mother to her baby during childbirth and breastfeeding. It can be spread through 'blood to blood' contacts, such as with contaminated instruments during medical, dental, acupuncture and other body-piercing procedures, and through sharing used intravenous needles. At present there is no cure; medication that might keep the disease under control is available, but these drugs are too expensive for the overwhelming majority of East Africans, and are not readily available for travellers either. If you think you might have been infected with HIV, a blood test is necessary; a three-month gap after exposure and before testing is required to allow antibodies to appear in the blood.

Malaria

One million children die annually from malaria in Africa. The risk of malarial transmission at altitudes higher than 2000m is rare. The disease is caused by a parasite in the bloodstream spread via the bite of the female Anopheles mosquito. There are several types of malaria, with falciparum malaria the most dangerous type and the predominant form in

Africa. Infection rates vary with season and climate, so check out the situation before departure. Unlike most other diseases regularly encountered by travellers, there is no vaccination against malaria (yet). However, several different drugs are used to prevent malaria, and new ones are in the pipeline. Up-to-date advice from a travel health clinic is essential as some medication is more suitable for some travellers than others. The pattern of drug-resistant malaria is changing rapidly, so what was advised several years ago might no longer be the case.

Malaria can present in several ways. The early stages include headaches, fevers, generalized aches and pains, and malaise, which could be mistaken for flu. Other symptoms can include abdominal pain, diarrhoea and a cough. Anyone who develops a fever in a malarial area should assume malarial infection until a blood test proves negative, even if you have been taking antimalarial medication. If not treated, the next stage could develop within 24 hours, particularly if falciparum malaria is the parasite: jaundice, then reduced consciousness and coma (also known as cerebral malaria) followed by death. Treatment in hospital is essential, and the death rate might still be as high as 10% even in the best intensive-care facilities.

Many travellers are under the impression that malaria is a mild illness, that treatment is always easy and successful, and that taking antimalarial drugs causes more illness through side effects than actually getting malaria. In Africa, this is unfortunately not true. Side effects of the medication depend on the drug being taken. Doxycycline can cause heartburn and indigestion; mefloquine (Larium) can cause anxiety attacks, insomnia and nightmares, and (rarely) severe psychiatric disorders; chloroquine can cause nausea and hair loss; and proguanil can cause mouth ulcers. These side effects are not universal, and can be minimized by taking medication correctly, eg with food. Also, some people should not take a particular antimalarial drug, eg people with epilepsy should avoid mefloquine, and doxycycline should not be taken by pregnant women or children younger than 12.

If you decide that you really do not wish to take antimalarial drugs, you must understand the risks, and be obsessive about avoiding mosquito bites. Use nets and insect

---

THE ANTIMALARIAL A TO D

A Awareness of the risk – no medication is totally effective, but protection of up to 95% is achievable with most drugs, as long as other measures have been taken.

B Bites – avoid them at all costs. Sleep in a screened room, use a mosquito spray or coils, sleep under a permethrin-impregnated net at night. Cover up at night with long trousers and long sleeves, preferably with permethrin-treated clothing. Apply appropriate repellent to all areas of exposed skin in the evenings.

C Chemical prevention – antimalarial drugs are usually needed in malarial areas. Expert advice is required, as resistance patterns can change and new drugs are always in development. Not all antimalarial drugs are suitable for everyone. Most antimalarial drugs need to be started at least a week in advance and continued for four weeks after the last possible exposure to malaria.

D Diagnosis – if you have a fever or flu-like illness within a year of travel to a malarial area, malaria is a possibility, and immediate medical attention is necessary.

---

repellent, and report any fever or flu-like symptoms to a doctor as soon as possible. Some people advocate homeopathic preparations against malaria, such as Demal200, but as yet there is no conclusive evidence that this is effective, and many homeopaths do not recommend their use.

People of all ages can contract malaria, and falciparum causes the most severe illness. Repeated infections may result eventually in a less serious illness. Malaria in pregnancy frequently results in miscarriage or premature labour. Adults who have survived childhood malaria have developed immunity and usually only develop mild cases of malaria; most Western travellers have no immunity at all. Immunity wanes after 18 months of non-exposure, so even if you have had malaria in the past and used to live in a malaria-prone area, you might no longer be immune.

If you are planning a journey through a malarial area such as much of East Africa, and particularly where falciparum malaria predominates, consider taking standby treatment. Emergency standby treatment should be seen as emergency treatment aimed at saving the patient's life, and not as routine self-medication. It should be used only if you will be far from medical facilities (more than 24 hours away from medical help) and have been advised about the symptoms of malaria and how to use the medication. Medical advice should be sought as soon as possible to confirm whether the treatment has been successful. The type of standby treatment used will depend on local conditions, such as drug resistance, and on what antimalarial drugs were being used before standby treatment. The goal is to avoid contracting cerebral malaria, which affects the brain and central nervous system and can be fatal in 24 hours. As mentioned on p641, self-diagnostic kits, which can identify malaria in the blood from a finger prick, are also available in the West.

The risks from malaria to both mother and foetus during pregnancy are considerable. Unless good medical care can be guaranteed, travel throughout Africa when pregnant – particularly to malarial areas – should be discouraged unless essential.

Meningococcal Meningitis

Meningococcal infection is spread through close respiratory contact and is more likely in crowded situations, such as dormitories, buses and clubs. Infection is uncommon in travellers. Vaccination is particularly recommended for long stays and is especially important towards the end of the dry season (see p621). Symptoms include a fever, severe headache, neck stiffness and a red rash. Immediate medical treatment is necessary.

The ACWY vaccine is recommended for all travellers in sub-Saharan Africa. This vaccine is different from the meningococcal meningitis C vaccine given to children and adolescents in some countries; it is safe to be given both types of vaccine.

Onchocerciasis (River Blindness)

This is caused by the larvae of a tiny worm, which is spread by the bite of a small fly. The earliest sign of infection is intensely itchy, red, sore eyes. Travellers are rarely severely affected. Treatment in a specialised clinic is curative.

Poliomyelitis (Polio)

Generally spread through contaminated food and water. Vaccination is usually given in childhood and should be boosted every 10 years, either orally (a drop on the tongue) or

as an injection. Polio can be carried asymptomatically (ie showing no symptoms) and can cause a transient fever. In rare cases it causes weakness or paralysis of one or more muscles, which may be permanent.

Rabies

Rabies is spread by receiving the bites or licks of an infected animal on broken skin. It is always fatal once the clinical symptoms start (which might be months after an infected bite), so post-bite vaccination should be given as soon as possible. Post-bite vaccination (whether or not you've been vaccinated before the bite) prevents the virus from spreading to the central nervous system. Animal handlers should be vaccinated, as should those travelling to remote areas where a reliable source of post-bite vaccine is not available. Three preventive injections are needed over a month. If you haven't been vaccinated you will need a course of five injections starting 24 hours or as soon as possible after the injury. If you have been vaccinated, you will need fewer post-bite injections, and have more time to seek medical help.

Rift Valley Fever

This fever is spread occasionally via mosquito bites. The symptoms are of a fever and flu-like illness; and the good news is, it's rarely fatal.

Schistosomiasis (Bilharzia)

This disease is spread by flukes (minute worms) that are carried by a species of freshwater snail. The flukes are carried inside the snail, which then sheds them into slow-moving or still water. The parasites penetrate human skin during swimming, and then migrate to the bladder or bowel. They are passed out via stool or urine and can contaminate fresh water, where the cycle starts again. Do not paddle or swim in any freshwater lakes or slow-running rivers anywhere in East Africa. There might be no symptoms. There might be a transient fever and rash, and advanced cases might have blood in the stool or in the urine. A blood test can detect antibodies if you might have been exposed, and treatment is then possible in specialist travel or infectious disease clinics. If not treated the infection can cause kidney failure or permanent bowel damage. It is not possible for you to infect others.

HEALTH

Trypanosomiasis (Sleeping Sickness)

Spread via the bite of the tsetse fly. It causes a headache, fever and eventually coma. There is an effective treatment.

Tuberculosis (TB)

TB is spread through close respiratory contact and occasionally through infected milk or milk products. BCG vaccination is recommended for those likely to be mixing closely with the local population, although it gives only moderate protection against TB. It is more important for long stays than for short-term visits. Inoculation with the BCG vaccine is not available in all countries, but it is given routinely to many children in developing nations. The vaccination causes a small permanent scar at the site of injection, and is usually given in a specialised chest clinic. It is a live vaccine and should not be given to pregnant women or immunocompromised individuals.

TB can be asymptomatic, only being picked up on a routine chest X-ray. Alternatively, it can cause a cough, weight loss or fever, months or even years after exposure.

Typhoid

This is spread through food or water contaminated by infected human faeces. The first symptom is usually a fever or a pink rash on the abdomen. Sometimes septicaemia (blood poisoning) can occur. A typhoid vaccine (typhim Vi, typherix) will give protection for three years. In some countries, the oral vaccine Vivotif is also available. Antibiotics are usually given as treatment, and death is rare unless septicaemia occurs.

Yellow Fever

Tanzania, Kenya, Uganda and Burundi no longer officially require you to carry a certificate of yellow fever vaccination unless you're arriving from an infected area (which includes from anywhere in East Africa). However, it's still sometimes asked for at some borders, and is a requirement in some neighbouring countries, including Rwanda. When trying to decide whether to get jabbed or not, it's also worth considering that the vaccine is recommended for most visitors to Africa by the Centers for Disease Control and prevention (www.cdc.gov). Also, there is always the possibility that a traveller without a legally required, up-to-date certificate will be vaccinated and detained in isolation at the port of arrival for up to 10 days, or possibly even repatriated.

Yellow fever is spread by infected mosquitoes. Symptoms range from a flu-like illness to severe hepatitis (liver inflammation) jaundice and death. The yellow fever vaccination must be given at a designated clinic and is valid for 10 years. It is a live vaccine and must not be given to immunocompromised or pregnant travellers.

TRAVELLERS' DIARRHOEA

Although it's not inevitable that you will get diarrhoea while travelling in East Africa, it's certainly very likely. Diarrhoea is the most common travel-related illness – figures suggest that at least half of all travellers to Africa will get diarrhoea at some stage. Sometimes dietary changes, such as increased spices or oils, are the cause. To help prevent diarrhoea, avoid tap water unless you're sure it's safe to drink (see p648). You should also only eat fresh fruits or vegetables if cooked or peeled, and be wary of dairy products that might contain unpasteurised milk. Although freshly cooked food can often be a safe option, plates or serving utensils might be dirty, so you should be highly selective when eating food from street vendors (make sure that cooked food is piping hot all the way through). If you develop diarrhoea, be sure to drink plenty of fluids – preferably lots of an oral rehydration solution containing water, and some salt and sugar. A few loose stools don't require treatment but, if you start having more than four or five stools a day, you should start taking an antibiotic (usually a quinoline drug, such as ciprofloxacin or norfloxacin) and an antidiarrhoeal agent (such as loperamide) if you are not within easy reach of a toilet. If diarrhoea is bloody, persists for more than 72 hours or is accompanied by fever, shaking chills or severe abdominal pain, you should seek medical attention.

Amoebic Dysentery

Contracted by consuming contaminated food and water, amoebic dysentery causes blood and mucus in the faeces. It can be relatively mild and tends to come on gradually, but seek medical advice if you think you have the illness, as it won't clear up without treatment (which is with specific antibiotics).

Giardiasis

This, like amoebic dysentery, is also caused by ingesting contaminated food or water. The illness usually appears a week or more after you have been exposed to the offending parasite. Giardiasis might cause only a short-lived bout of typical travellers' diarrhoea, but it can also cause persistent diarrhoea. Ideally, seek medical advice if you suspect you have giardiasis, but if you are in a remote area you could start a course of antibiotics.

ENVIRONMENTAL HAZARDS
Altitude Sickness

The lack of oxygen at high altitudes (over 2500m) affects most people to some extent. Symptoms of Acute Mountain Sickness (AMS) usually develop in the first 24 hours at altitude but may be delayed up to three weeks. Mild symptoms are headache, lethargy, dizziness, difficulty sleeping and loss of appetite. Severe symptoms are breathlessness, a dry, irritative cough (followed by the production of pink, frothy sputum), severe headache, lack of coordination, confusion, vomiting, irrational behaviour, drowsiness and unconsciousness. There's no rule as to what is too high: AMS can be fatal at 3000m, but 3500m to 4500m is the usual range.

Treat mild symptoms by resting at the same altitude until recovered, usually a day or two. Paracetamol or aspirin can be taken for headaches. If symptoms persist or grow worse, however, immediate descent is necessary; even 500m can help. Drug treatments should never be used to avoid descent or to enable further ascent. Diamox (acetazolamide) reduces the headache of AMS and helps the body acclimatise to the lack of oxygen. It is only available on prescription.

To prevent acute mountain sickness:
- Ascend slowly – have frequent rest days, spending two to three nights at each rise of 1000m. Acclimatisation takes place gradually.
- Sleep at a lower altitude than the greatest height reached during the day if possible. Also, once above 3000m, care should be taken not to increase the sleeping altitude by more than 300m per day.
- Drink extra fluids. Monitor hydration by ensuring that urine is clear and plentiful.
- Eat light, high-carbohydrate meals for more energy.
- Avoid alcohol, sedatives and tobacco.

Heat Exhaustion

This condition occurs following heavy sweating and excessive fluid loss with inadequate replacement of fluids and salt, and is particularly common in hot climates when taking unaccustomed exercise before full acclimatisation. Symptoms include headache, dizziness and tiredness. Dehydration is already happening by the time you feel thirsty – aim to drink sufficient water to produce pale, diluted urine. Self-treatment requires fluid replacement with water and/or fruit juice, and cooling by cold water and fans. Treatment of the salt-loss component consists of consuming salty fluids, as in soup, and adding a little more table salt to foods than usual.

Heatstroke

Heat exhaustion is a precursor to the much more serious condition of heatstroke. In this case there is damage to the sweating mechanism, with an excessive rise in body temperature; irrational and hyperactive behaviour; and eventually loss of consciousness and death. Rapid cooling by spraying the body with water and fanning is ideal. Emergency fluid and electrolyte replacement is usually also required by intravenous drip.

Insect Bites & Stings

Mosquitoes might not always carry malaria or dengue fever, but they (and other insects) can cause irritation and infected bites. To avoid these, take the same precautions as you would for avoiding malaria (see p643). Use DEET based insect repellents. Excellent clothing treatments are also available, and mosquitos that land on the treated clothing will die.

Bee and wasp stings cause real problems only to those who have a severe allergy to the stings (anaphylaxis.) If you are one of these people, carry an 'epipen' – an adrenaline (epinephrine) injection, which you can give yourself. This could save your life.

Scorpions are frequently found in arid or dry climates. They can cause a painful bite that is sometimes life-threatening. If bitten by a scorpion, take a painkiller. Medical treatment should be sought if collapse occurs.

Bed bugs are often found in hostels and cheap hotels. They lead to very itchy, lumpy bites. Spraying the mattress with crawling insect killer after changing bedding will get rid of them.

HEALTH

Scabies is also frequently found in cheap accommodation. These tiny mites live in the skin, particularly between the fingers. They cause an intensely itchy rash. The itch is easily treated with malathion and permethrin lotion from a pharmacy; other members of the household also need treatment to avoid spreading scabies, even if they do not show any symptoms.

Snake Bites

Avoid getting bitten! Do not walk barefoot, or stick your hand into holes or cracks. However, 50% of those bitten by venomous snakes are not actually injected with poison (envenomed). If you are bitten by a snake, do not panic. Immobilise the bitten limb with a splint (such as a stick) and apply a bandage over the site, with firm pressure – similar to bandaging a sprain. Do not apply a tourniquet, or cut or suck the bite. Get medical help as soon as possible so antivenom can be given if needed.

Water

Never drink tap water unless it has been boiled, filtered or chemically disinfected (such as with iodine tablets). Never drink from streams, rivers and lakes. It's also best to avoid drinking from pumps and wells – some do bring pure water to the surface, but the presence of animals can still contaminate supplies. When buying bottled water, check to be sure the bottles are properly sealed, and haven't just been refilled with ordinary tap water.

TRADITIONAL MEDICINE

According to some estimates, over 70% of East Africans rely in part or in whole on traditional medicine, and close to two-thirds of the population have traditional healers as their first point of contact in the case of illness. The traditional healer holds a revered position in many communities throughout the region, and traditional medicinal products are widely available in local markets.

In part, the heavy reliance on traditional medicine is because of the high costs of conventional Western-style medicine, because of prevailing cultural attitudes and beliefs, or simply because it sometimes works. Often, though, it's because there is no other choice. In some parts of Tanzania, it is estimated that while there is only one medical doctor to 33,000 people, there is a traditional healer for approximately every 150 people. While the ratio is better in some parts of the region (and worse in others), hospitals and health clinics are concentrated in urban centres, and many are limited in their effectiveness by insufficient resources, and chronic shortages of equipment and medicine.

Although some traditional remedies seem to work on malaria, sickle cell anaemia, high blood pressure and some AIDS symptoms, most healers learn their art by apprenticeship, so education (and consequently application of knowledge) is inconsistent and unregulated.

Rather than attempting to stamp out traditional practices, or simply pretend they aren't happening, a positive first step taken by some East African countries is the regulation of traditional medicine by creating healers' associations and offering courses on such topics as sanitary practices. On a broader scale, the Organisation of African Unity has declared 2001 to 2010 the 'Decade of Traditional Medicine' across the continent.

Under any scenario, it remains unlikely in the short term that even a basic level of conventional Western-style medicine will be made available to all the people of East Africa, even though the cost of doing so is less than the annual military budget of some Western countries. Traditional medicine, on the other hand, will almost certainly continue to be widely practised throughout the region.

Language

CONTENTS

WHO SPEAKS WHAT WHERE?

In polyglot East Africa you'll find people speaking languages belonging to all four major African ethno-linguistic families. The largest of these is the Niger-Congo family, which encompasses Swahili and other Bantu languages. Others are the Nilo-Saharan family (which includes Nilotic and Nilo-Hamitic languages such as Maasai), and the Afro-Asiatic (or Hamito-Semitic) family, whose Cushitic branch includes Iraqw and Somali. The smallest family is Khoisan, which consists of only a few dozen languages, characterised by their distinctive 'clicks' (where clicking sounds are made by the tongue). The main click languages found in East Africa are Sandawe and, more distantly, Hadza (Hadzabe), both spoken by small, somewhat scattered populations in north-central Tanzania who still follow traditional hunter-gatherer lifestyles.

Throughout the region, attempting to speak even just a few words of Swahili – or whatever the local African language is – will enrich your travels and be greatly appreciated by the people you meet, no matter how rudimentary your attempts. Good luck and *Safari njema!* (happy travels).

Burundi

The official languages are Kirundi and French, although Swahili is also useful. Hardly anyone speaks English, except in Bujumbura.

Kenya

English and Swahili are the official languages and are taught in schools throughout Kenya, but Hindi and Urdu are still spoken by south Asian residents.

Most urban Kenyans and even tribal people involved in the tourist industry speak English, and many speak some German or Italian, especially around the coast.

There are many other major tribal languages, including Kikuyu, Luo, Kikamba, Maasai and Samburu, as well as a plethora of minor tribal languages. You may also come across Sheng, a mixture of Swahili and English along with a fair sprinkling of other languages – Sheng is favoured by younger Kenyans.

Rwanda

The national language is Kinyarwanda. The official languages are Kinyarwanda, French and English. Kinyarwanda is the medium of school instruction at primary level, and French is used at secondary level (only 10% of the population reach secondary level). Little English is spoken beyond Kigali, but Swahili can be useful in some areas.

Tanzania

Swahili and English are the official languages. English is widely spoken in major towns, but in rural areas it helps to know at least a few Swahili phrases. Outside cities and towns, far fewer people speak English than in comparable areas of Kenya.

The predominant Swahili dialect on the Tanzanian mainland is Kiunguja (the Swahili of Zanzibar Island), from which 'standard' Swahili has developed. Over 100 other African languages are spoken, including Sukuma, Makonde, Haya, Ha, Gogo and Yao, all of which belong to the Bantu group, and Maasai, which belongs to the Nilotic ethno-linguistic group.

Uganda

The official language is English, which most people can speak well – at least in urban areas. The other major languages are Luganda and Swahili, though the latter isn't spoken much east of Kampala or in the capital, as most Ugandans associate it with the bad old days when Idi Amin sought to make it the national language.

SWAHILI

Standard Swahili is based on the variety of the language spoken in Zanzibar Town, although several other dialects can be found throughout East Africa. Written Swahili – the language of newspapers, textbooks and literature – usually conforms to the coastal standards. This language guide uses the standard variety, as it should be more universally understood.

Although Swahili may initially seem a bit daunting, its structure is fairly regular and pronunciation uncomplicated. You'll soon discover that just a handful of basic words will rapidly break down barriers between you and the many people you meet on your travels in East Africa.

If your time is limited, concentrate first on the greetings and then on numbers (very useful when negotiating with market vendors, taxi drivers etc). The words and phrases included in this chapter will help get you started. For a more comprehensive guide to the language, get hold of Lonely Planet's *Swahili Phrasebook*.

PRONUNCIATION

Perhaps the easiest part of learning Swahili is the pronunciation. Every letter is pronounced, unless it's part of the consonant combinations discussed in the 'Consonants' section below. If a letter is written twice, it is pronounced twice – *mzee* (respected elder) has three syllables: *m-ZE-e*. Note that the 'm' is a separate syllable, and that the double 'e' indicates a lengthened vowel sound.

Word stress in Swahili almost always falls on the second-to-last syllable.

Vowels

Correct pronunciation of vowels is the key to making yourself understood in Swahili. If the following guidelines don't work for you, listen closely to Swahili speakers and spend some time practising. There's also a useful audio pronunciation guide available on the website: www.yale.edu/swahili/.

Remember that if two vowels appear next to each other, each must be pronounced in turn. For example, *kawaida* (usual) is pronounced *ka-wa-EE-da*.

a	as in 'calm'
e	as the 'ey' in 'they'
i	as the 'ee' in 'keep'
o	as in 'go'
u	as the 'oo' in 'moon'

Consonants

Most consonants in Swahili have equivalents in English. The only one that might be a bit unusual for an English speaker is the sound **ng**, but with a little practice it should come easily – say 'sing along' a few times and then drop the 'si', and that's how it sounds at the beginning of a word. The sounds **th** and **dh** occur only in words borrowed from Arabic.

r	Swahili speakers make only a slight distinction between **r** and **l**; use a light 'd' for 'r' and you'll be pretty close.
dh	as 'th' in 'this'
th	as 'th' in 'thing'
ny	as the 'ni' in 'onion'
ng	as in 'singer'
gh	like the 'ch' in Scottish *loch*
g	as in 'get'
ch	as in 'church'

ACCOMMODATION

Where's a ...?   ... iko wapi?
  camping ground   Uwanja wa kambi
  guesthouse   Gesti
  hotel   Hoteli
  youth hostel   Hosteli ya vijana

Can you recommend cheap lodging?
Unaweza kunipendekezea malazi rahisi?
What's the address?
Anwani ni nini?

Do you have   Kuna chumba kwa ...?
a ... room?
  single   mtu mmoja
  double   watu wawili, kitanda kimoja
  twin   watu wawili, vitanda viwili
  triple   watu watatu

How much is it per day/person?
Ni bei gani kwa siku/mtu?
Can I see the room?
Naomba nione chumba?
Where's the bathroom?
Choo iko wapi?
Where are the toilets?
Vyoo viko wapi?
I'll take it.
Nataka.
I'm leaving now.
Naondoka sasa.

CONVERSATION & ESSENTIALS

Greetings are probably the most important vocabulary for a traveller to East Africa. It's worth taking the time to familiarise yourself with the few we include here.

Jambo is a pidgin Swahili word, used to greet tourists who are presumed not to understand the language. There are two possible responses: *Jambo* (meaning 'Hello, now please speak to me in English'), and *Sijambo* (or 'Things aren't bad with me, and I'm willing to try a little Swahili').

If people assume you can speak a little Swahili, greetings may involve one or a number of the following exchanges:

How are you?   *Hujambo?*
I'm fine.   *Sijambo.*
How are you all?   *Hamjambo?*
We're fine.   *Hatujambo.*

The word *habari* (meaning 'news') can also be used for general greetings. You may hear the word *salama* substituted for *habari*, or the *habari* may be dropped altogether.

How are you?   *Habari?*
How are you all?   *Habari zenu?*
What's the news?   *Habari gani?*
What's happening?   *Habari yako?*
Good morning.   *Habari za asubuhi?*
Good day.   *Habari za leo?*
Good afternoon.   *Habari za mchana?*
Good evening/night.   *Habari za jioni?*

By memorising these three simple words, you can reply to almost anything:

Good.   *Nzuri.*
Fine.   *Salama.*
Clean.   *Safi.*

There is also a respectful greeting for elders:

Greetings.   *Shikamoo.*
Greetings. (response)   *Marahaba.*

Once you've dealt with all the appropriate greetings, you can move onto other topics:

What's your name?   *Jina lako nani?*
My name is ...   *Jina langu ni ...*
Where are you from? *Unatoka wapi?*
I'm from ...   *Natoka ...*
I like ...   *Ninapenda ...*
I don't like ...   *Sipendi ...*

Farewells are generally short and sweet:

Goodbye.   *Kwa heri.*
Until tomorrow. *Kesho.*
Later on.   *Baadaye.*
Good night.   *Usiku mwema.*

And a few basics never hurt ...

Yes.   *Ndiyo.*
No.   *Hapana.*
Please.   *Tafadhali.*
Thank you (very much). *Asante (sana).*
You're welcome.   *Karibu.*
Excuse me.   *Samahani.*
Sorry.   *Pole.*

SIGNS

Mahali Pa Kuingia	Entrance
Mahali Pa Kutoka	Exit
Maelezo	Information
Imefunguliwa	Open
Imefungwa	Closed
Ni Marufuku	Prohibited
Polisi	Police
Choo/Msalani	Toilets/WC
Wanaume	Men
Wanawake	Women

DIRECTIONS

Where's ...?   *... iko wapi?*
It's straight ahead. *Iko moja kwa moja.*

Turn ...   *Geuza ...*
  at the corner   *kwenye kona*
  at the traffic lights *kwenye taa za barabarani*
  left/right   *kushoto/kulia*

behind	nyuma ya
in front of	mbele ya
near	karibu na
next to	jirani ya
opposite	ng'ambo ya

EMERGENCIES

Help!	Saidia!
There's been an accident!	Ajali imetokea!
Call the police!	Waite polisi!
Call a doctor!	Mwite daktari!
I'm lost.	Nimejipotea.
Leave me alone!	Niache!

HEALTH

I'm sick.	Mimi ni mgonjwa.
It hurts here.	Inauma hapa.

I'm allergic to ...	Nina mzio wa ...
antibiotics	viuavijasumu
aspirin	aspirini
bees	nyuki
nuts	kokwa
peanuts	karanga

antiseptic	dawa ya kusafisha jeraha
condoms	kondom
contraceptives	kingamimba
insect repellent	dawa la kufukuza wadudu
iodine	iodini
painkillers	viondoa maumivu
thermometer	pimajoto
water purification tablets	vidonge vya kusafisha maji

LANGUAGE DIFFICULTIES

Do you speak (English)?
Unasema (Kiingereza)?
Does anyone speak (English)?
Kuna mtu yeyote kusema (Kiingereza)?
What does (asante) mean?
Neno (asante) lina maana gani?
Do you understand?
Unaelewa?
Yes, I understand.
Ndiyo, naelewa.
No, I don't understand.
Hapana, sielewi.
Could you please write ... down?
Tafadhali ... andika?
Can you show me (on the map)?
Unaweza kunionyesha (katika ramani)?

NUMBERS

0	sifuri
1	moja
2	mbili
3	tatu
4	nne
5	tano
6	sita
7	saba
8	nane
9	tisa
10	kumi
11	kumi na moja
12	kumi na mbili
13	kumi na tatu
14	kumi na nne
15	kumi na tano
16	kumi na sita
17	kumi na saba
18	kumi na nane
19	kumi na tisa
20	ishirini
21	ishirini na moja
22	ishirini na mbili
30	thelathini
40	arobaini
50	hamsini
60	sitini
70	sabini
80	themanini
90	tisini
100	mia moja
1000	elfu
100,000	laki

PAPERWORK

name	jina
nationality	raia
date of birth	tarehe ya kuzaliwa
place of birth	mahali pa kuzaliwa
sex/gender	jinsia
passport	pasipoti
visa	viza

QUESTION WORDS

Who?	Nani?
What?	Nini?
When?	Lini?
Where?	Wapi?
Which?	Gani?
Why?	Kwa nini?
How?	Namna?

SHOPPING & SERVICES

Where's a ...?	... iko wapi?
department store	Duka lenye vitu vingi
general store	Duka lenye vitu mbalimbali

I'd like to buy ...	Nataka kununua ...
I'm just looking.	Naangalia tu.
How much is it?	Ni bei gani?
Can you write down the price?	Andika bei.
Can I look at it?	Naomba nione.
I don't like it.	Sipendi.
Do you have others?	Kuna nyingine?
That's too expensive.	Ni ghali mno.
Please lower the price.	Punguza bei, tafadhali.
I'll take it.	Nataka.

Do you accept ...?	Mnakubali ...?
credit cards	kadi ya benki
travellers cheques	hundi ya msafiri

Enough.	Bas.
A bit more.	Ongeza kidogo.
Less.	Punguza.

Where's (a/the) ...?	... iko wapi?
bank	Benki
market	Soko
tourist office	Maarifa kwa watalii
... embassy	Ubalozi ...
hospital	Hospitali
post office	Posta
public phone	Simu ya mtaani
public toilet	Choo cha hadhara
telecom centre	Telekom

TIME & DATES

What time is it?	Ni saa ngapi?
It's (ten) o'clock.	Ni saa (nne).
morning	asubuhi
afternoon	mchana
evening	jioni
today	leo
tomorrow	kesho
yesterday	jana

Monday	Jumatatu
Tuesday	Jumanne
Wednesday	Jumatano
Thursday	Alhamisi
Friday	Ijumaa
Saturday	Jumamosi
Sunday	Jumapili

January	mwezi wa kwanza
February	mwezi wa pili
March	mwezi wa tatu
April	mwezi wa nne
May	mwezi wa tano
June	mwezi wa sita
July	mwezi wa saba
August	mwezi wa nane
September	mwezi wa tisa
October	mwezi wa kumi
November	mwezi wa kumi na moja
December	mwezi wa kumi na mbili

TRANSPORT
Public Transport

What time is the ... leaving?	
... inaondoka saa ngapi?	
Which ... goes to (Mbeya)?	
... ipi huenda (Mbeya)?	
bus	Basi
minibus	Daladala
plane	Ndege
train	Treni

When's the ... (bus)?	
(Basi) ... itaondoka lini?	
first	ya kwanza
last	ya mwisho
next	ijayo

A ... ticket to (Iringa).	
Tiketi moja ya ... kwenda (Iringa).	
1st-class	daraja la kwanza
2nd-class	daraja la pili
one-way	kwenda tu
return	kwenda na kurudi

cancelled	imefutwa
delayed	imeche leweshwa
platform	stendi
ticket window	dirisha la tiketi
timetable	ratiba

Private Transport

I'd like to hire a/an ...	Nataka kukodi ...
bicycle	baisikeli
car	gari
4WD	forbaifor
motorbike	pikipiki

Are you willing to hire out your car/motorbike?
Unaweza kunikodisha gari/pikipiki yako?
(How long) Can I park here?
Naweza kuegesha hapa (kwa muda gani)?

LANGUAGE

Is this the road to (Embu)?
Hii ni barabara kwenda (Embu)?
Where's a petrol station?
Kituo cha mafuta kiko wapi?
Please fill it up.
Jaza tangi/tanki.
I'd like ... litres.
Nataka lita ...

diesel	*dizeli*
leaded	*risasi*
unleaded	*isiyo na risasi*

I need a mechanic.	*Nahitaji fundi.*
I've had an accident.	*Nimepata ajali.*
I have a flat tyre.	*Nina pancha.*
I've run out of petrol.	*Mafuta yamekwisha.*

The car/motorbike has broken down (at Chalinze).
Gari/Pikipiki ime haribika (Chalinze).
The car/motorbike won't start.
Gari/Pikipiki haiwaki.

Could I pay for a ride in your truck?
Naweza kulipa kwa lifti katika lori lako?
Could I contribute to the petrol cost?
Naweza kuchangia sehemu ya bei ya mafuta?
Thanks for the ride.
Asante kwa lifti.

TRAVEL WITH CHILDREN

I need a/an ...	*Nahitaji ...*
Is there a/an ...?	*Kuna ...?*
baby change room	*chumba cha kuvalia mtoto*
baby seat	*kiti cha kitoto*
child-minding service	*anayeweza kumlea mtoto*
children's menu	*menyu kwa watoto*
disposable nappies/ diapers	*nepi*
(English-speaking) babysitter	*yaya (anayesema Kiingereza)*
highchair	*kiti juu cha mtoto*
potty	*choo cha mtoto*
stroller	*kigari cha mtoto*

Also available from Lonely Planet:
Swahili Phrasebook

Glossary

The following is a list of words and acronyms from Burundi (B), the Democratic Republic of the Congo (C), Kenya (K), Rwanda (R), Tanzania (T) and Uganda (U) you are likely to come across in this book. For a glossary of food and drink terms, see p43.

AMKO – Association of Mount Kenya Operators (tour guide association) (K)
askari – security guard, watchman
ASP – Afro-Shirazi Party on Zanzibar Archipelago (T)

banda – thatched-roof hut with wooden or earthen walls; simple wooden and stone-built accommodation
bangi – marijuana; also *ganja*
benga – musical style originating among the Luo in western Kenya, and characterised by its electric guitar licks and bounding bass rhythms (K)
Big Five, the – the five archetypal large African mammals: lion, buffalo, elephant, leopard and rhino
boda-boda – bicycle taxi
boma – living compound or camp; in colonial times, government administrative office or fort
bui-bui – black cover-all garment worn by some Islamic women outside the home

CCM – Chama Cha Mapinduzi (Party of the Revolution); Tanzania's governing political party (T)
chai – tea; bribe
chakula – food
chang'a – dangerous homemade alcoholic brew containing methyl alcohol
choo – toilet; pronounced cho
Cites – Convention on International Trade in Endangered Species
CUF – Civic United Front; Tanzania's main opposition party (T)

daladala – minibus or pick-up truck (T)
dhow – traditional Arabic sailing vessel, still common along the coast
dudu – small insect or bug; creepy-crawly
duka – small shop or kiosk (K)

forex – foreign exchange bureau
fundi – repairer of clothing, buildings, cars etc; expert

gacaca – traditional tribunal headed by village elders (R)
ganja – see *bangi*
gof – volcanic crater

hakuna matata – no problem
hatari – danger
hoteli – small informal restaurant

injera – unleavened bread
Interahamwe – Hutu militia (R)

jamaa – clan, community
jua kali – literally 'hot sun'; usually an outdoor vehicle-repair shop or market

kabaka – king (U)
kanga – printed cotton wraparound, incorporating a Swahili proverb, worn by women
karibu – Swahili for welcome
kikoi – printed cotton wraparound traditionally worn by men in coastal areas
kitenge – similar to a *kanga*, but usually a larger, heavier piece of cloth with no Swahili proverb
kitu kidogo – literally 'a little something'; bribe
KWS – Kenya Wildlife Service (K)

lingala – Congolese dance music; also *soukous* (C)
lugga – dry river bed, mainly in northern Kenya (K)

makuti – thatched roof made of palm leaves, mainly on the coast
malaya – prostitute
manamba – *matatu* tout, often a veritable style guru and all-round dude (K)
manyatta – Maasai or Samburu livestock camp often surrounded by a circle of thorn bushes (K)
marimba – musical instrument played with the thumb
matatu – minibus (K)
Maulid – birth of the prophet Mohammed and Muslim feast day, celebrated in many areas of East Africa
mihrab – prayer niche in a mosque showing the direction of Mecca
miraa – bundles of leafy twigs and shoots that are chewed as a stimulant and appetite-suppressant
moran – Maasai or Samburu warrior (K)
mpingo – African blackwood
msenge – homosexual
murram – dirt or partly gravelled road
mwalimu – Swahili for teacher; used to refer to Julius Nyerere (T)
mwami – king (B, R)
mwizi – thief
mzee – elderly person; respected elder
mzungu – white person (plural *wazungu*)

NCA – Ngorongoro Conservation Area (T)
Ngai – Kikuyu god
NRA – National Resistance Army (U)
NRM – National Resistance Movement (U)
nyatiti – traditional folk lyre

panga – machete, carried by many people in the east African countryside and often by thieves in the cities
papasi – literally 'tick'; used on the Zanzibar Archipelago to refer to street touts (T)
parking boys – unemployed youths who will help park a vehicle and guard it while the owner is absent
pesa – money

RMS – Rwenzori Mountaineering Services (U)
RPF – Rwandan Patriotic Front (R)

safari – Swahili for journey
shamba – small farm or plot of land
shetani – style of figurative art embodying images from the spirit world
shifta – bandit
shilingi – shilling; money

shuka – tie-dyed sarong
soukous – see *lingala*

taarab – Zanzibari music combining African, Arabic and Indian influences (T)
taka – rubbish
Tanapa – Tanzania National Parks Authority (T)
TANU – Tanganyika African National Union (T)
taxi – minibus (U)
taxi-motor – motorcycle taxi
tilapia – Nile perch
TTB – Tanzania Tourist Board (T)

uhuru – freedom or independence
ujamaa – Swahili for familyhood or togetherness (T)
Unguja – Swahili name for Zanzibar Island (T)
UWA – Uganda Wildlife Authority (U)

vibuyu – carved gourds

wazungu – see *mzungu*

ZIFF – Zanzibar International Film Festival (T)

Behind the Scenes

THIS BOOK

The 1st edition of *East Africa* was written by Geoff Crowther, who then teamed up with Hugh Finlay to write the next three editions. Hugh, Matt Fletcher, Mary Fitzpatrick and Nick Ray wrote the 5th edition. Mary coordinated the 6th edition with Tom Parkinson and Nick Ray. For this 7th edition this tried and tested team stayed on, with Mary at the helm and updating the Tanzania chapter, Tom revisiting Kenya and Nick updating Uganda, Rwanda and Burundi, as well as swooping into the Democratic Republic of the Congo to get the latest.

This book was commissioned in Lonely Planet's Melbourne office, and produced by the following:

Commissioning Editors Will Gourlay, Marg Toohey
Coordinating Editor Katie Lynch
Coordinating Cartographer Jacqueline Nguyen
Coordinating Layout Designer Steven Cann
Managing Cartographer Shahara Ahmed
Assisting Editors Helen Christinis, Pat Kinsella, Kristin Odijk, Charlotte Orr, Jeanette Wall, Simon Williamson
Assisting Cartographers Barbara Benson, Diana Duggan, Tony Fankhauser, Valentina Kremenchutskaya, Emma McNicol
Assisting Layout Designers Jessica Rose, Wibowo Rusli
Cover Designer Nic Lehman
Colour Designer Laura Jane
Project Managers Nancy Ianni, Ray Thomson
Language Content Coordinator Branislava Vladisavljevic

Thanks to Imogen Bannister, Sally Darmody, Adriana Mammarella, Raphael Richards, Jacqui Saunders, Suzannah Shwer, Kate Whitfield, Celia Wood

THANKS
NICK RAY

First and foremost a massive thanks to the good people of Uganda, Rwanda, Burundi and the DR Congo. Despite horrendous suffering during the long years of turmoil, most have managed to come out the other side with a warm welcoming smile for strangers from afar. A huge thank you to my wife Kulikar who indulged my wanderings to look after our young son Mr J and I promise to let you know next time before I wander into DR Congo for a few days. In Uganda many thanks to the staff at Uganda Wildlife Authority and Ucota. Thanks to the owners and staff at Backpackers Hostel and Red Chilli Hideaway, which both provide a home away from home in Kampala. Thanks to Bingo and John at Nile River Explorers and to Cam at Adrift. In Rwanda, a big hello to my good friend Patrice Shema. Thanks to Manzi and Jacqui at Thousand Hills and John Kayihura at Primate Safaris for updates on the travel scene. In Burundi, thanks to Adrien Nihorimbere for info and Tapani for chasing down some bits and pieces. Finally a big thanks to Alex Mujyambere for accompanying me into DR Congo and to Jambo Safaris in Goma for making it all possible. A huge collective thanks to everyone else I ran into along the way. It was a lot fun, as Africa should be.

TOM PARKINSON

A traditional *asanteni sana* to everyone who helped out and made this trip more pleasure than chore: Nicholas; Helen, Chelsea, Dex, Ian and Steve; everyone at New Florida; Line and Sara; Judy, Milan, Bree,

---

Nadia, David, Monique, Penny, Crystal and Barry; Steven the dancing man; Debbi, Lionel and friends; Rachel and the Muffin Man, Paul (thanks for driving and black tie!), James, Daryl, Phil, Adele, Tessa and Carlos Rock Spider; Pop and Grev; Linzi, Boris and the Twits; Chris and Rowena; Daniel and Natasha; the Colobus volunteers; Ben at KMC; Erik, Kate, Sam, Caleb, Rachid, Patrick and all at Casuarina; Isa, Djemba and the Shela boys; Magnus Malaria Boy and Blondie; Peter, Wouter, Yvonne, Bantu and everyone at ZIFF. At LP, thanks to Will G and Mary F for running everything smoothly, and to Matt P for providing his half of the text. Finally, special thanks, *beröm* and *vill ha dig nu* to my official biographer Cecilia Ohlsson, for scholarly appreciation and the lowdown on Lamu.

OUR READERS

Many thanks to the hundreds of travellers who used the last edition and wrote to us with helpful hints, useful advice and interesting anecdotes:

A Raf Aerts, Simon Akam, Lindy Alexander, Lola Reid Allin, Suhas Apte **B** Harinder Bachus, Richard Barber, Levi J Barclay, Rob Barclay, Fabio Barros, Rosanna Batista, Jeff Bell, R U Beynen, Nahida Bhegani, Haralampos Bizas, Erika Bloom, Tom Blunden, Karin Boekelberger, Luca Boero, Saskia Boesjes, Leah Bohle, Laura Brason, Shirley Brenda, Tim Briggs, Marius Brülhart **C** Christina Cacioppo, Sean Casey, Dennis Chiles, Jonas Christensen, Dagmar Christiansen, Karolina Claesson, Ruth Cohen, Tom Craven, Sarah Cunard Chaney **D** Lasse Danvar, Marc Dauma, Toby Davis, Madri de Jager, Anthony de Lannoy, Sharon Dennis, J M A Desmond, Arne Doornebal, Bram Duffhues **E** Sean Earle, Nils Edely **F** Dan Fahey, Lise Farquhar, Hannah Finholt, Grahame Finnigan, Jonathan Foschini, D Foster, Malcolm Fox, Christl Fuchslechner **G** Paul Gevers, Laurie Gold, Charmaine Grainger **H** Annelis Haesevoets, Taija Hämäläinen, James Hancock, Birte Happersberger, Sean Hartley, Shereen Harvey, Pieter Hemsley, Peter & Koen Hendrix, Tom Herbert, Matt Higgins, Michiel Hillenius, Paul Holdworth, Ruth Hughes, Izmir Husein **I** Doutsje Idzenga **J** Stipo Jurcevic **K** Hann Kaergaard, Lisette Kaptein, Raviv Karauk, Lucy Knowles, Rosemarie Kullik, Basar Kurtbayram **L** Deanna Lambert, Howard Lambert, Mark Lawford, Jérome Le Roy, Kim Lehmkuhl, Ashley Leigh, Yvette Lievens, Grant Lilford, Gernot Lucawiecki, Diderik Lund, Martin Lutsyk **M** Geralyn Macfadyen, Petra Maria Manske, Ussino Mara, Alexis Marchand, Perry Martin, Jen McDavid, Philip Mitchell, Sally Moate, Annette Mollel, Angela Moore, Sandra Mos, Sonja Munnix, Ingrid Mutima **N** Charlie & Kathy Nelson, Matthew Nelson, Fabrizio Nicoletti, Nienke Nijhoff **O** Andy Omotherley,

SEND US YOUR FEEDBACK

We love to hear from travellers – your comments keep us on our toes and help make our books better. Our well-travelled team reads every word on what you loved or loathed about this book. Although we cannot reply individually to postal submissions, we always guarantee that your feedback goes straight to the appropriate authors, in time for the next edition. Each person who sends us information is thanked in the next edition – and the most useful submissions are rewarded with a free book.

To send us your updates – and find out about Lonely Planet events, newsletters and travel news – visit our award-winning website: **www.lonelyplanet.com/feedback**.

Note: We may edit, reproduce and incorporate your comments in Lonely Planet products such as guidebooks, websites and digital products, so let us know if you don't want your comments reproduced or your name acknowledged. For a copy of our privacy policy visit www.lonelyplanet.com/privacy.

Heather Osborn **P** Sue Palin, David Parrish, Jonathan Parsons, Ed Patrick, Ari Paul, Laure Perrier, James Phillips, H Pieterse, Tanya Platt, Stephen Pratt **Q** Mark Quandt **R** Katharina Reinecke, Anton Rijsdijk, Pamela Riley, Greg Roberts, Deborah Rogerson, Mandy Romanowski, Dave Roscoe, Julian Rouse, Martin Ryan **S** Glen Sandve, Takuji Sasaki, Gail Sasse, Beth Schaeffer, Andrew C Scott, Frederik Seelig, Anna Seligman, Xia Shen, Stephen Simblet, Josie Simpson, Heidi Smith, Stephan Smout, James Smyth, Roger Smyth, Neil Somers, Manuela Stahl, Johannes Starostzik, Alistair Staton, Benjamin Sternthal, Kristine K Stevens, Simon Stevens, Joey Stewart **T** Kimberley Taylor, Sally Thompson, Moniqu Toubia **U** Rob Underhill, Shaun Unger **V** Roel Verhaak, Morten Vesterager, Michi Vojta, Detlev Vreeken **W** Laszlo Wagner, Brenda Walters, Heidi Wassersleben, Leann Webb, Savini Wijesingha, Ian Wikarski, Ruth Willmott, Katherine Wolf, Jessica Wood, Rebecca Wright **Y** J Young **Z** Andreas Zahner

ACKNOWLEDGMENTS

Many thanks to the following for the use of their content:

Globe on back cover ©Mountain High Maps 1993 Digital Wisdom, Inc.

Index

000 Map pages
000 Photograph pages

INDEX

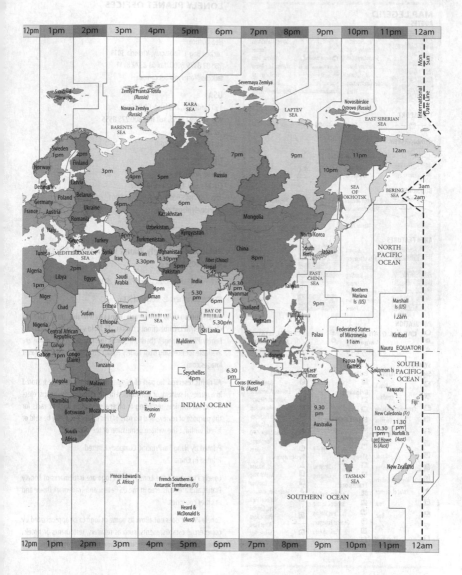

672

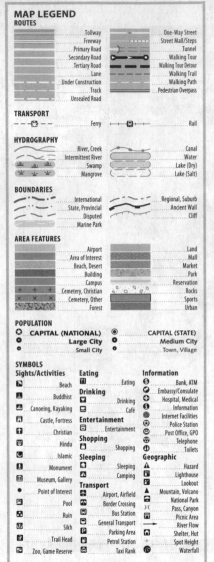

MAP LEGEND

ROUTES

Tollway	One-Way Street
Freeway	Street Mall/Steps
Primary Road	Tunnel
Secondary Road	Walking Tour
Tertiary Road	Walking Tour Detour
Lane	Walking Trail
Under Construction	Walking Path
Track	Pedestrian Overpass
Unsealed Road	

TRANSPORT

Ferry	Rail

HYDROGRAPHY

River, Creek	Canal
Intermittent River	Water
Swamp	Lake (Dry)
Mangrove	Lake (Salt)

BOUNDARIES

International	Regional, Suburb
State, Provincial	Ancient Wall
Disputed	Cliff
Marine Park	

AREA FEATURES

Airport	Land
Area of Interest	Mall
Beach, Desert	Market
Building	Park
Campus	Reservation
Cemetery, Christian	Rocks
Cemetery, Other	Sports
Forest	Urban

POPULATION

CAPITAL (NATIONAL)	CAPITAL (STATE)
Large City	Medium City
Small City	Town, Village

SYMBOLS

Sights/Activities
- Beach
- Buddhist
- Canoeing, Kayaking
- Castle, Fortress
- Christian
- Hindu
- Islamic
- Monument
- Museum, Gallery
- Point of Interest
- Pool
- Ruin
- Sikh
- Trail Head
- Zoo, Game Reserve

Eating
- Eating

Drinking
- Drinking
- Café

Entertainment
- Entertainment

Shopping
- Shopping

Sleeping
- Sleeping
- Camping

Transport
- Airport, Airfield
- Border Crossing
- Bus Station
- General Transport
- Parking Area
- Petrol Station
- Taxi Rank

Information
- Bank, ATM
- Embassy/Consulate
- Hospital, Medical
- Information
- Internet Facilities
- Police Station
- Post Office, GPO
- Telephone
- Toilets

Geographic
- Hazard
- Lighthouse
- Lookout
- Mountain, Volcano
- National Park
- Pass, Canyon
- Picnic Area
- River Flow
- Shelter, Hut
- Spot Height
- Waterfall

LONELY PLANET OFFICES

Australia
Head Office
Locked Bag 1, Footscray, Victoria 3011
☎ 03 8379 8000, fax 03 8379 8111
talk2us@lonelyplanet.com.au

USA
150 Linden St, Oakland, CA 94607
☎ 510 893 8555, toll free 800 275 8555
fax 510 893 8572
info@lonelyplanet.com

UK
72–82 Rosebery Ave,
Clerkenwell, London EC1R 4RW
☎ 020 7841 9000, fax 020 7841 9001
go@lonelyplanet.co.uk

Published by Lonely Planet Publications Pty Ltd
ABN 36 005 607 983

© Lonely Planet Publications Pty Ltd 2006

© photographers as indicated 2006

Cover photographs: black male rhinoceros in the grass, Ralph A Clevenger/APL/Corbis (front); dancers, El-Molo village, Tom Cockrem/ Lonely Planet Images (back). Many of the images in this guide are available for licensing from Lonely Planet Images: www.lonelyplanet images.com.

All rights reserved. No part of this publication may be copied, stored in a retrieval system, or transmitted in any form by any means, electronic, mechanical, recording or otherwise, except brief extracts for the purpose of review, and no part of this publication may be sold or hired, without the written permission of the publisher.

Printed by Hang Tai Printing Company Limited
Printed in China

Lonely Planet and the Lonely Planet logo are trademarks of Lonely Planet and are registered in the US Patent and Trademark Office and in other countries.

Lonely Planet does not allow its name or logo to be appropriated by commercial establishments, such as retailers, restaurants or hotels. Please let us know of any misuses: www.lonelyplanet.com/ip.

Although the authors and Lonely Planet have taken all reasonable care in preparing this book, we make no warranty about the accuracy or completeness of its content and, to the maximum extent permitted, disclaim all liability arising from its use.